The Salmon P. Chase Papers

Salmon Portland Chase
Courtesy of the Cincinnati Historical Society
(B-93-230, reversed).

The Salmon P. Chase Papers

VOLUME 1

Journals, 1829–1872

JOHN NIVEN, EDITOR

JAMES P. MCCLURE, SENIOR ASSOCIATE EDITOR

LEIGH JOHNSEN, ASSOCIATE EDITOR

WILLIAM M. FERRARO, ASSISTANT EDITOR

STEVE LEIKIN, ASSISTANT EDITOR

The Kent State University Press

KENT, OHIO, AND LONDON, ENGLAND

© 1993 by The Kent State University Press, Kent, Ohio 44242
ALL RIGHTS RESERVED
Library of Congress Catalog Card Number 93-16217
ISBN 0-87338-472-5
Manufactured in the United States of America

Library of Congress Cataloging-in-Publication Data

Chase, Salmon P. (Salmon Portland), 1808–1873
The Salmon P. Chase papers / John Niven, editor ; James P.
McClure, senior associate editor ; Leigh Johnsen, associate editor ;
William M. Ferraro, Steve Leikin, assistant editor[s].
p.   cm.
Includes bibliographical references and index.
Contents: v. 1 Journals, 1829–1872
ISBN 0-87338-472-5 (cloth : alk. paper) ∞
1. Chase, Salmon P. (Salmon Portland), 1808–1873—Archives.
2. United States—Politics and government—1849–1877—Sources.
3. Legislators—United States—Archives. 4. Judges—United States—
Archives. 5. United States. Congress. Senate—Archives.
6. Governors—Ohio—Archives. I. Niven, John. II. Title.
E415.6.C48 1993
977.1′03′092—dc20   93-16217
CIP

British Library Cataloging-in-Publication data are available.

Editorial Advisory Board

LaWanda Cox
Richard Nelson Current
David Herbert Donald
Don E. Fehrenbacher
John Hope Franklin
Harold M. Hyman
Robert W. Johannsen
Leonard W. Levy
Charles A. Lofgren
James M. McPherson
James A. Rawley
Robert V. Remini
Kenneth M. Stampp
Hans L. Trefousse

Contents

Acknowledgments ix

Introduction by John Niven xi

The Journals li

    General Description of the Edition   li
    Chase's Journals   lii
    Provenance   liii
    Description   lvi
    Arrangement   lxix

Editorial Procedures lxxiii

    Editorial Method   lxxiii
    Annotation   lxxvi

The Journals of Salmon P. Chase, 1829–1872 3

Bibliography 711

Index 729

Acknowledgments

PREPARATION of this volume was supported by the Claremont Graduate School, the National Historical Publications and Records Commission, the National Endowment for the Humanities, the L. J. Skaggs and Mary C. Skaggs Foundation, Theodore Ferraro, Johnson & Johnson (through its program of matching employees' gifts), and the Chase Manhattan Bank. For their assistance to the Chase project during the research and publication phases of this volume we wish to thank Gerald George, Frank Burke, and Richard Jacobs, current and former executive directors of the NHPRC; Nancy Sahli, Roger Bruns, Mary Giunta, Timothy Connelly, and Richard Sheldon of the NHPRC staff; and Douglas Arnold, Alice Hudgins, Guinevere Griest, Richard Ekman, Gordon McKinney, and David Nichols of the NEH. Project support at the Claremont Graduate School has been assisted by Murray Schwartz, vice president for academic affairs and dean of faculty; Daniel Mazmanian, former acting dean; Carol Gamble, director of budget and business affairs; Michael Groener, vice president for business and finance and treasurer of Claremont University Center; and Christopher Oberg, former vice president for operations.

Mary Bellamy, Stephen Sobieck, EuGene Taylor, and Dana Whaley all transcribed portions of Chase's journals. They and Maria Baglien, Scott Birrell, John Lloyd, and Charles Mitchell also did research or performed other essential tasks. Susan Leidy of Concord, New Hampshire, made initial transcriptions of journals located at the New Hampshire Historical Society. Mary Town and Betsy McClure assisted with proofreading. Charles Young, Richard McKirihan, and David Danielson advised us on Chase's rendering of Greek.

The reference and government publications sections of the libraries of the Claremont Colleges, as well as Ruth Palmer, Paula-Teresa Wiens, Jody Burke, and their assistants in interlibrary loan, helped us in our research. The project's staff also relied heavily on the resources of the Henry E. Huntington Library in San Marino and the Upland (California) Family History Center of the Church of Jesus Christ of Latter-day Saints. Knowledgeable professionals at the Historical Society of Pennsylvania, the Library of Congress, and the New Hampshire Historical Society were most supportive. Among those institutions' present and former staff members who assisted us were Linda Stanley, Louise Jones, Ellen Slack, and Anne-Marie Schaaf in Philadelphia; John McDonough, Oliver Orr, Mary Wolfskill, and the staff of the Manuscript Division reading room at the Library of Congress; and Stephen Cox, William Copeley, and Elizabeth Hamlin-Morin in Concord. We are grateful also to Edwin C. Hoyt, Chase's great-grandson, who shared historical materials and his knowledge of the Chase and Hoyt families. Finally, we appreciate the efforts of John Hubbell, Julia Morton, and their associates at the Kent State University Press in the last stages of preparation of this volume.

Introduction by John Niven

THE PAPERS of Salmon P. Chase form an interesting and significant commentary on American political and cultural history that spans the years from the presidency of John Quincy Adams to that of Ulysses S. Grant. The debate over slavery which eventually consolidated all the major political and cultural cross-currents during this chaotic period of change and growth permeates and dominates these papers. Chase was an early and earnest advocate of slavery restriction but unlike orthodox abolitionists, he blended a devotion to the Constitution and to lawful procedures with a determination to halt slavery where possible under the powers of a Congress that was increasingly shifting to a free-soil majority.

Chase's arguments were developed over many years of observation and participation in the antislavery cause—first in defense of fugitive slaves as a young lawyer in Cincinnati, Ohio, and then as an organizer of the Liberty party, the Free-Soil campaign, and the independent Democratic movement that culminated in the Republican party coalition of the 1850s.[1]

As a leading member of the Liberty party, the first political protest against slavery that claimed national attention, Chase reconciled the conservatism of many Northerners and their fear that abolitionism threatened property rights with their sense of moral commitment. Chase thus opened the antislavery movement to a much broader constituency. He was, at the same time, not unmindful of the political benefits that might accrue to him personally. Few politicians of the nineteenth century sought the presidency with more

---

1. See for example *Speech of Salmon P. Chase, in the Case of the Colored Woman, Matilda* (Cincinnati, 1837), and S. P. Chase, *Reclamation of Fugitives from Service. An Argument . . . Submitted to the Supreme Court of the United States . . . in the Case of Wharton Jones vs. John Vanzandt* (Cincinnati, 1847). There have been four biographies of Chase: Robert B. Warden, *An Account of the Private Life and Public Services of Salmon Portland Chase* (Cincinnati, 1874); Jacob W. Schuckers, *The Life and Public Services of Salmon Portland Chase* (New York, 1874); Albert Bushnell Hart, *Salmon Portland Chase* (Boston, 1899; reprint, New York, 1980); and Frederick J. Blue, *Salmon P. Chase: A Life in Politics* (Kent, Ohio, 1987).

dedication than Chase, and in this group we include such incessantly ambitious men as Stephen A. Douglas, Henry Clay, Daniel Webster, and John C. Calhoun. All of these claimants disguised their objectives behind a modest garb of disinterestedness. Yet none denied his desire for the presidency as frequently or as vehemently as Chase. Of course, this was the style in the early years of the Republic, but as his diaries clearly show, Chase seemed unaware that his devious and often clumsy efforts might alienate rather than secure potential supporters.

Salmon Portland Chase was born on January 13, 1808, in Cornish, New Hampshire, a town settled by his forebears in the mid-eighteenth century. With its many branches the Chase family was a formidable New England clan. Ithamar Chase, Salmon's father, had been a prosperous farmer, a justice of the peace, and a state senator. Ithamar's brothers, six of whom graduated from Dartmouth, were respected members of New England's educated elite. Philander, the youngest, was an Episcopal priest destined to become the Bishop of Ohio. Dudley was a United States senator from Vermont. Salmon and Baruch were successful lawyers, Heber and Corbett were physicians. Chase's mother, Jannette Ralston, was of Scottish origin and came from a well-to-do family herself.[2]

In Cornish the young Salmon shared with his siblings the work of the farm. He seemed, however, to have led a rather protected and indulged childhood. His father was no disciplinarian. "He kept me pretty straight, by the mildest means," Chase recalled. "He ruled by kind words & kind looks."[3] This would stand in stark contrast to his later experience with his Uncle Philander.

In the fall of 1815 Ithamar Chase moved the family to Keene, New Hampshire. They lived in the largest, most imposing house in town and the elder Chase managed a glass factory as well as his father-in-law's distillery and tavern.[4] But with Ithamar's bankruptcy and death in 1817, the family's comfort and security was rudely shattered. Jannette Ralston Chase had to move her family from the

---

2. Simon Goodell Griffin, *A History of the Town of Keene* (Keene, N.H., 1904), 282, 296, 301, 383–84, 638; William H. Child, *History of the Town of Cornish, New Hampshire, with Genealogical Record, 1864–1910* (Concord, N.H., 1911), 1:263, 2:58–59.

3. Chase to John T. Trowbridge, Dec. 27, 1863, Jan. 19, [1864] (Chase Papers, Hist. Soc. of Pa.). Some two dozen autobiographical letters from Chase to Trowbridge date from Dec. 27, 1863, to Mar. 22, 1864. The originals are in Chase's papers at the Library of Congress, the Historical Society of Pennsylvania, and the Cincinnati Historical Society. There are multiple drafts or copies of some of the letters. Trowbridge used the letters to produce a book for youths, *The Ferry-Boy and the Financier* (Boston, 1864). Apparently he had intended to create a campaign biography as well but never did. Trowbridge to Chase, Apr. 21, 1864 (Chase Papers, Hist. Soc. of Pa.).

4. Griffin, *Keene*, 363–64.

center of town to a small farm on its outskirts. This small holding was virtually all that remained of her husband's hard-earned competence and her share of her father's legacy.[5]

Despite her diminished resources, the harried widow continued the education of her younger children. At first young Salmon was sent to various schools in Keene where he studied Latin and ancient history. Yet soon he would be shuttled from place to place, first to Windsor, Vermont, for a year where he attended boarding school, then back home again for a short period of time until he was shipped off to Worthington, Ohio, to live under the tutelage of Philander Chase.[6]

In an unusually ambitious family even for status-conscious New England, Philander Chase was the most aggressive of his siblings. He was also the youngest and the largest in physical size. He stood well over six feet in height and was sturdy of build. A massive head and widely spaced, clear blue eyes completed his imposing appearance. Nearsighted, a genetic flaw he shared with his nephew Salmon, Philander fixed a penetrating view on the world around him. He was a compelling yet at the same time frightening figure to a sensitive boy.

The bishop was a rigid disciplinarian who was convinced of his own moral rectitude. It was quite in character, therefore, that the domineering uncle would seek to have the nephew who was committed to his care become an Episcopal priest, particularly since young Salmon had given evidence of precocity in the classes Philander supervised. With that in mind, Bishop Chase laid down a strict regimen of study. In addition to the long hours of reading Latin and Greek and religious tracts, Philander expected Salmon to help support the family with farm chores.[7]

Throughout his stay in Ohio, young Chase was restless and unhappy and his uncle's domination had instilled in the boy a lack of confidence. But probably of greater significance for Chase's later development, Philander imparted a confusing message to his charge. If one's ends were Christian, Philander believed, then one could

---

5. Chase to Trowbridge, Jan. 19, [1864] (Chase Papers, Hist. Soc. of Pa.).
6. Chase to John P. Bigelow, Sept. 23, 1854 (Houghton Lib., Harvard Univ.); Chase to Trowbridge, Jan. 21, 1864 (Chase Papers, Hist. Soc. of Pa.). During 1853 and 1854 Chase wrote two unusually long and detailed memoirs of his early life. One of these, an incomplete letter he perhaps never sent, was intended for an unnamed recipient. See Chase to ———, July 10, 1853 (Chase Papers, L.C.). He wrote the other to Bigelow, a Massachusetts Republican politician of some consequence and former Whig mayor of Boston.
7. Chase discussed life with the bishop at length in two letters to Trowbridge: Jan. 25, 1864 (Chase Papers, Cinc. Hist. Soc.), and Jan. 27, 1864 (Chase Papers, Hist. Soc. of Pa.).

employ any means necessary to achieve those ends. His uncle's self-assurance, dogmatic religiosity, and insistence on hard work confused means and ends in Chase's young mind in a way that would influence his behavior throughout his political career.

Not long after Chase's arrival in Worthington, his uncle accepted the presidency of Cincinnati College and moved his family to the bustling new city from which the school received its name. Although only thirteen years of age, young Chase was accepted as a first-year student at the college. After a two-year stint as president, chief fund-raiser, professor of theology, and chief executive of the diocese of Ohio, the indomitable Philander Chase decided to go to the fount of Episcopalianism, Great Britain, in the hopes of raising funds for a new seminary he had in mind. Fifteen-year-old Salmon accompanied his uncle as far as the home of an aunt in Kingston, New York, a town about halfway between Albany and New York City. Here they parted company, the bishop heading south and the nephew north to Albany for the journey across the Green Mountains to Keene.[8]

Upon his return home, Chase followed the pattern of other semi-educated New England boys who had to earn a living by teaching in several rural schools. His early efforts as a pedagogue, however, were unsuccessful. His letters reveal how certain character traits, such as a coldness that masked his bashfulness, a temper that was not always under control, and an excessive moralizing strain, combined to alienate his pupils, country boys and girls his own age and older.[9] These traits would translate in later life as driving ambition and the sometimes reprehensible acts he committed for political ends.

During these years his mother somehow managed to do without Salmon's income and supplied whatever additional funds were necessary for the completion of his education. He had been accepted in the junior class at Dartmouth after a perfunctory examination and graduated with distinction in 1826.[10] A considerable correspondence with family, friends, and classmates reveals a typical, industrious, rather sober student of the period. He did, however, have a penchant for romantic novels and interspersed with his study of Virgil, Cicero, Euclid, and the Greek New Testament were volumes of Scott and the Gothic tales of Horace Walpole, Anne Radcliffe, and William Beckford.

---

8. Chase to Trowbridge, Jan. 29, 31, 1864 (Chase Papers, Cinc. Hist. Soc.); same to same, Feb. 1, 1864, (Chase Papers, Hist. Soc. of Pa.).

9. See for instance Chase to Joseph A. Denison, Jr., July 17, Aug. 3, 1824 (Chase Papers, L.C.).

10. Chase to Bigelow, Sept. 23, 1854 (Houghton Lib., Harvard Univ.).

Chase's early training, his retentive memory, and his ingrained habits of self-discipline made it possible for him to achieve high scholastic standing without undue stress. He had a rather contemptuous view of the Dartmouth faculty and curriculum. The only singular occurrence of his two years at Dartmouth was his renewed interest in religion which his imperious uncle had dampened during the years at Worthington and Cincinnati. He attended the Episcopalian church to which his family belonged, but when revivals swept New England in the winter of 1826, he was at first unaffected. He wrote a classmate that he had not been "taught to believe much in the efficacy of such things but I do not . . . know enough concerning their effects to oppose them."[11] His latent interest quickened, however, and he was caught up in the spirit of the revival. Soon after his graduation from Dartmouth in the summer of 1826 he became a member of the Episcopal church at Hopkinton, New Hampshire, the home of one of his sisters.[12] In fact, he became a zealous practitioner of the forms of worship and a close student of both scripture and commentary. These habits of prayer and study would continue for the remainder of his life.

Chase had done well enough in his studies at Dartmouth to be elected to Phi Beta Kappa. His ideas about a career, however, were vague. He had ruled out the ministry despite his newfound religious fervor. His early experience as schoolmaster had left a strong distaste for an academic career, though he had a gift for languages, ancient and modern, and a liking for study and reading.

After conferring with his uncle, who had recently returned from his successful fund-raising venture in England, Chase chose teaching as a suitable if temporary means of support. Armed with letters of introduction from Philander and a family friend, Salmon headed for New Jersey and Maryland. He soon found that the prospects for establishing schools in these localities were poor and he decided to complete his journey in Washington where another of the redoubtable Chase clan, his uncle Dudley, was a United States senator from Vermont.

Chase hoped his uncle's influence would secure for him a government clerkship, but no assistance was forthcoming. Said Dudley Chase: "I once obtained an office for a nephew of mine and he was

11. Chase to Thomas Sparhawk, Mar. 16, 1826 (Chase Papers, Ohio Hist. Soc.). Chase's early letters to his friend Sparhawk were printed in Arthur Meier Schlesinger, "Salmon Portland Chase: Undergraduate and Pedagogue," *Ohio Archaeological and Historical Quarterly* 28 (Apr. 1919): 119–61.
12. He had been confirmed while living with his uncle in Ohio. Chase to Trowbridge, Jan. 29, Feb. 8, 1864 (Chase Papers, Cinc. Hist. Soc.); Chase to Bigelow, Sept. 23, 1854 (Houghton Lib., Harvard Univ.).

ruined by it. I then determined never to ask one for another." Adding a note of finality to his refusal, Senator Chase said, "I will give you fifty cents to buy a spade with but I will not help to put you in a clerkship."[13]

Family connections counted as far as establishing a school in the District, however. Salmon Chase's first effort at recruiting students in Washington was a failure, but Alexander R. Plumley, who directed a well-established school in Washington, offered Chase some of his students. Dudley Chase may well have been the instrument of Plumley's rescue mission. In any event, Chase accepted and for the next two years conducted a successful school for boys. He counted among his pupils sons of members of Adams's cabinet and of other leading Washington personalities.[14]

Two of Chase's students were sons of William Wirt, Adams's attorney general, the most prominent lawyer in the District and an admired man of letters. Through the boys Chase became acquainted with Wirt and his family. The attorney general had published a series of popular prose sketches and essays in the style of Addison and Steele's *Spectator,* and a biography of Patrick Henry. Largely self-taught in composition and in the law, Wirt was accounted a local celebrity. He was, moreover, a genial individual whose appealing wife and large family made the Wirt home an attraction for the younger set of Washington society as well as politicians and senior government officials.[15]

Lonely and uncertain about his future, Chase not only found a refuge in the hospitable Wirt home, but also a role model in the elder Wirt. He resolved to become a lawyer. Wirt accepted him as a student but mostly left him to his own devices as far as formal study was concerned. The Wirt daughters flirted with the tall, thin, ungainly Yankee and with a little more encouragement young Chase would have quite willingly fallen in love with any one of them. As it was he plied them with poetry that he composed and with what he thought was engaging conversation. His advances never got beyond friendship, yet—as illustrated by the diary he began to keep consistently in January 1829—Chase spent his happiest hours in Washington at the Wirt home.

Chase was also a frequent guest at the receptions and balls that marked the social season in the rustic little capital city. Taking his cue from Wirt, he alternated his legal study with composition, poetry to amuse and ingratiate himself with women, and a journal to

---

13. Chase to Trowbridge, Feb. 10, 1864 (Chase Papers, Hist. Soc. of Pa.).
14. Ibid.
15. John P. Kennedy, *Memoirs of the Life of William Wirt, Attorney General of the United States* (Philadelphia, 1849), 1:275–332, 2:35–65.

record the events and description of the local scene as a source for future literary endeavors.

From January 1, 1829, until December 1835, Chase kept a continuous and full account not just of his daily life and his business affairs, but frequently of descriptions of places and events that interested him. He also provided a series of vignettes and anecdotes of famous individuals he observed, retailed gossip on occasion, and indulged in political speculation. In the quiet of his bedroom after a full day of teaching, study, or attending an early evening social affair—perhaps a visit to the Wirts and other friends—he set down his impressions of the Washington scene. Often there was mention of prayer before bed or the reading of chapters of the Bible before his breakfast. Frequently, Chase interspersed his commentary with titles of books he was reading, quotations of phrases that took his fancy, and poems that he had composed for his female friends.[16]

Despite his extensive social life and his teaching responsibilities Chase managed to learn a good deal of law. Wirt proved an indifferent teacher and what jurisprudence Chase learned he got on his own. Nevertheless, he convinced William Cranch, chief judge of the circuit court of the District of Columbia, that he had sufficient legal knowledge to be admitted to the bar.[17] Here again, Chase had connections: Cranch was a New Englander, a relative of the Adams family, and a friend of Chase's Uncle Dudley.

Unfortunately, Chase had few friends in the new Jackson administration. The Wirts had left town to settle in Baltimore. Henry Clay had retired for the time being to his home in Kentucky. With his social circle broken up and his influence among the minor officeholders in Washington virtually nonexistent because of Jackson's removal policy, Chase decided Washington was not the place for him to begin a law practice. He thought of Baltimore where the Wirts now lived. But Maryland law required a three-year residence before a lawyer could begin his practice.[18] Nor did New Hampshire and Vermont seem particularly inviting.

The Northwest was said to be the land of opportunity and Ohio in particular was booming. Chase, of course, remembered Worthington and the Cincinnati of his boyhood with no particular pleasure. But Cincinnati had prospered mightily in the nine years that had passed since he was a student at his uncle's struggling college. Ever prudent, Chase consulted several individuals well acquainted with the prospects for a young lawyer in Cincinnati before making

16. See for example the poem in the journal entry for Jan. 10, 1829, below.
17. Chase to Bigelow, Sept. 23, 1854 (Houghton Lib., Harvard Univ.).
18. Chase to Hamilton Smith, May 29, 1833 (Smith MSS, Indiana Univ.).

a decision. Among these were Associate Justice John McLean of the U.S. Supreme Court and one of Ohio's senators, Jacob Burnet. Both men encouraged Chase to make the move. He took their advice and on March 4, 1830, embarked on his ten-day journey west.

Chase secured lodgings at one of Cincinnati's many boarding houses and surveyed the opportunities for setting up a practice. Like other young lawyers Chase found it difficult at first to develop enough business to support himself. He had had little experience in public speaking and was further afflicted with a lisp. His early tutelage with his domineering uncle, the bishop, had reinforced a habit of diffidence which he sought to overcome. At first he dreaded appearing in court, and when he did act as an advocate his performance was halting and his presentation uneven.

For almost two years Chase struggled to improve his courtroom presence as well as his financial status. He formed a partnership with two other attorneys only to be forced to relinquish his share after six months. When he tried again a short while later he found the lucrative practice he had been looking for and from that time forward his income was more than sufficient to meet his needs, pay off his debts, and provide an increasing surplus for investment. In this practice he acted as counsel for the Bank of the United States in Cincinnati and the Lafayette Bank, a prosperous institution that enjoyed increasing revenues as the city grew in the mid-thirties.

The diaries from these years shed considerable light on the development of Chase's career, political personality, religious convictions, family life, and health. From the beginning of his residence in Cincinnati, Chase led an active social life among the important and wealthy citizens of the town. He was an indefatigable self-improver as he actively promoted a variety of cultural and literary endeavors. With an eye to improving his status in the community, but also with a genuine interest in intellectual activities and in writing, Chase was a prime mover in establishing a lyceum where he and others gave weekly lectures on various subjects. In this social milieu Chase would meet both anti-abolitionist "gentlemen of property and standing" as well as future leaders of the antislavery movement.[19] He would also form views on political issues that reflected his then Whiggish biases.

At this time Chase began work on gathering and organizing the laws of the territory and the state of Ohio, a tedious job, but one that promised financial reward and prestige in his profession. He

---

19. Leonard L. Richards, *"Gentlemen of Property and Standing": Anti-Abolition Mobs in Jacksonian America* (New York, 1970). Richards explores the antislavery and anti-abolitionist milieu of Cincinnati in the 1830s.

also became interested in the Northwest Ordinance which, among other things, forbade slavery in the territory that became the states of Ohio, Indiana, Illinois, Michigan, and Wisconsin. His study of the ordinance led to the authorship of a history of Ohio, which became the introduction to his three-volume *Statutes of Ohio*. Chase got favorable notices for his work from such distinguished lawyers as Chancellor James Kent of New York and Joseph Story, an associate justice of the Supreme Court and a notable constitutional scholar.[20] The *Statutes* provided Chase with some essential income. But more importantly, the work made his name well known in legal circles throughout the Northwest and among local politicians. As a device for self-promotion, the year or so of tiresome labor resulted in a handsome payoff.[21]

Although he seemed physically vigorous, Chase suffered bouts of ill health, some of which were serious. He was plagued with headaches and what he called rheumatism—probably malaria, from which most inhabitants of the Ohio Valley suffered from time to time. His diary notes his ailments and when he was very sick, he gives full details written down while he was convalescing. His brother-in-law, Dr. Isaac Colby, who had followed Chase to Cincinnati, acted as his personal physician.[22]

Busy with his growing practice, his involvement with community and church-related affairs, his constant regimen of study and of writing, Chase also recounts, in a guarded way, his interest in various young women. He became acquainted with the Garniss family, fellow boarders at the Pearl Street House (considered the best hotel in Cincinnati). Though he did not form any fast friendships with the elder Garnisses—in fact he was rather critical of them—he was attracted to their daughter, Catharine. This relationship, which developed slowly, eventually led to their marriage on March 4, 1834.

On November 16, 1835, Catharine gave birth to a daughter (who was eventually named Catharine Jane after her mother). Chase left town on business as he believed that his wife was recovering from her confinement. Upon his return to Cincinnati he found she had died. The sorrowing Chase recorded the particulars of her death. He also read every medical text he could find on complications following childbirth.[23] He came to the conclusion that the physicians had erred in their insistence on excessive bleeding, and he

20. Blue, *Chase*, 19.
21. Journal entry for Jan. 18, 1833.
22. See for example the entry for Jan. 18, 1833.
23. Journal II, below, and entries for Dec. 28–29, 1835, and Jan. 2, 1836.

blamed his in-laws for permitting it to happen. As an anodyne from his grief he found refuge in religion, legal work, and cultural activities at lyceum meetings.

In politics Chase had affiliated himself with the National Republican and then the Whig party. He wrote editorials for the *Cincinnati American* supporting such Whig policies as protective tariffs, central banking, and federally funded internal improvements.[24] As a Whig he served on the Cincinnati city council, his first elective office. But more significantly he gained a reputation throughout the Northwest and even in eastern circles as a defender of fugitive slaves.

Cincinnati was an ideal place for this activity because only the Ohio River separated it from Covington, Kentucky, where slavery was legal. Thus the city received more fugitives than any other free state and more slave catchers for that matter. Moreover, a number of Cincinnati's leading citizens were from New England and other free states. They did not form a majority of the city's inhabitants, nor were most of them opposed to slavery in the South. Many business leaders of the city were in fact hostile to abolitionism. Yet these transplanted New Englanders formed enough of a presence that they could and did on occasion restrain proslavery mobs.

In such an atmosphere, James G. Birney, a former slave owner, established an abolitionist weekly newspaper, the *Philanthropist*, in nearby New Richmond. Chase had been introduced to Birney by his brother-in-law, Dr. Colby.[25] Birney and Chase shared deep religious convictions, literary aspirations, and opposition to slavery. Birney, however, a person of independent means, devoted himself entirely to the antislavery cause while Chase continued with his law practice and his interest in local cultural affairs.

Another individual Chase met at the lyceum meetings was Gamaliel Bailey, a Cincinnati physician who—like Birney—was fully committed to the abolitionist cause. When a fugitive named Matilda sought refuge with Birney and both were arrested and brought to trial—the former facing a return to slavery under federal law, the latter a fine under state law for harboring her—Chase was asked to defend them. He agreed and though he lost both cases, he carried Birney's conviction on appeal to the supreme court of Ohio, which

---

24. Robert B. Warden, an early biographer and associate of Chase, attributed some unsigned editorials in the *Cincinnati American* to Chase. Warden made this attribution on the basis of an association Chase had with the paper at the time and the presence of the editorials in a scrapbook of miscellaneous clippings in Chase's papers. Warden, *Chase*, 216–17, 250–51; "Party Violence," *Cincinnati American*, Dec. 13, 1830; "Mr. Calhoun," ibid., June 11, 1830.

25. Blue, *Chase*, 29.

overturned it. Chase gained considerable standing not just in the community but throughout the North for the arguments he presented.

Thereafter, Chase accepted numerous fugitive slave cases, the most notable being that of John Van Zandt who had been charged with assisting nine fugitives. In this case, William H. Seward acted as cocounsel, but Chase did most of the research. He made a three-hour argument before the United States Circuit Court and submitted a printed argument to the U.S. Supreme Court. Chase lost the case in both courts. But he made a telling, though not original, argument that when an individual left a state or locality where the law made him a slave and entered a free state or territory, he left behind him the artificial condition that made him a slave and became free as human beings were under natural law.

Chase's increasing involvement with the plight of fugitive slaves reinforced a long-held opinion that slavery was an immoral and inhuman institution. He had considered it as such from personal acquaintance during his three-year residence in Washington, yet during a long career of antislavery activism he rarely concerned himself with the problem of race relations. Servitude at the nation's capital was lawful and in fact the city housed a leading slave mart. Despite his repugnance to slavery, Chase did not publicly associate himself with abolitionists. In politics he remained a Whig, casting his vote for the Harrison-Tyler ticket in 1840. He sensed, however, the beginning of a popular mood in the state, especially among his fellow Yankees of the Western Reserve after his friend Birney ran for president in the 1840 campaign on the ticket of the newly formed Liberty party. He also realized that the city of Cincinnati had a Democratic majority which would provide an essential base for any aspiring politician.

After the election Chase's fortunes with the Whig party began to collapse. In April, just after President Harrison's death, he and his fellow Whigs on the Cincinnati city council were defeated for reelection. Chase then sought the Whig nomination for state senator from Hamilton County but was rejected by a very large margin in the county convention, primarily on the grounds that he was considered to be an abolitionist.[26] Mainline Whigs were not ready to accept any of Chase's antislavery ideas.

At this time Chase's share of a partnership he had formed on most favorable terms with a brilliant young trial lawyer, Samuel Eells, was producing a very substantial income, and it provided Chase with more leisure time that he could devote to politics. After the election

26. Hart, *Chase*, 88.

of 1840, he turned his attention to the new Liberty party. Careful not to overstep the limits of legality, Chase focused his attention on those Democrats and Whigs who were restive about their respective party's straddling of the slavery issue and concerned about the possible extension of slavery into the territories, all of which except Florida were north of the Missouri Compromise line.

Chase was also hopeful that Congress would eventually abolish the institution in the District of Columbia. As a conservative first step, however, he favored action to prohibit the slave trade in the nation's capital. In fact, Chase's public position on slavery was conservative in that he sought to broaden the appeal of the Liberty party on issues other than slavery.

If the diaries are not as informative as his letters on political matters, they offer abundant material on his personality. Chase was obsessed with order and regularity in his personal life. Time and again there are laments about wasted days when he did not complete the tasks he had set forth for himself or fulfill obligations of self-improvement that he felt were essential to reach personal goals he had set. Among these were continuous education towards a better understanding of himself and of his place in society, and always an underlying ambition to succeed in whatever area he chose for himself, whether it be memorizing biblical quotes that took his fancy, studying French, or persuading an acquaintance that slavery was a moral abomination. There is no question that this daily routine sharpened his powers of analysis and helped perfect his organizational techniques. Both of these qualities he exerted to the utmost in bringing order and discipline and a sense of practical, realizable goals to the antislavery movement.

Chase was now deeply involved in the organization of the Liberty party. At the same time he gravitated towards the party of Jefferson and Jackson. In his diary Chase makes plain that Jefferson's ideas on liberty and on natural rights, still the dominant ideology of the Democratic party, were much closer to the goal he wished to achieve than those of the Whigs. He would, if he could have his way, strengthen the antislavery cause and make the Liberty party the means to achieve a purified Democracy. His strategy was to line up the Liberty party in Ohio behind certain revered Democratic planks: free trade, hard money, and Van Buren's subtreasury system. He managed to convince Birney, Bailey, and other leaders of the party that this was a practical route to follow.

Accordingly, Chase drafted the call for a state convention to be held in Columbus on December 29, 1841. The convention was well attended. Chase managed to commit a majority of the delegates to his broadened platform. The convention then named Leicester

King, a prominent antislavery Whig, for governor, but made no further nominations.

Certain Liberty party leaders outside of the state, such as Gerrit Smith, roundly condemned Chase and the Ohio party for deviating from single-issue abolitionism. But Chase was convinced and rightly so that the only practical route to follow was with one of the major parties in Ohio. A third party might, in a close election, hold the balance between the two major parties and secure concessions that could further his own political ambitions and the antislavery cause. He now found his own career and the political objective of free soil indistinguishable. He considered the Democratic party to be more receptive than the Whigs on the human rights issue and equality of opportunity, provided, of course, that the Liberty party espoused other hallowed Democratic policy measures. The Democracy had broader appeal especially among the increasing foreign-born population of the state and of Chase's home base, Cincinnati. It seemed preferable to ally the Liberty party men with that organization than with the more aristocratic and ethnocentric Whigs.

Considering the state of the economy which was still struggling in the aftermath of the 1837 depression, and considering also the confused state of the Whig party, Chase's long-term strategy was a shrewd appraisal for the future of the antislavery cause in Ohio where the Democratic party, though a majority, was undergoing a bitter dispute between the hard- and the soft-money factions. Such an affiliation, however, left much to be questioned about the future of the Liberty party as a distinct organization. Proof that Chase was on the right track came when King, the Liberty party candidate for governor, polled over 5,400 votes, far more than Birney had received in Ohio when he ran for president.[27]

In 1839, while pondering his political future, Chase had married the eighteen-year-old Eliza Ann Smith, and shortly thereafter suffered the loss of his first child, Catharine, a victim of a scarlet fever epidemic. The journals and memoranda from 1840 through 1846 contain references to his family life as well as professional and political affairs. They reveal a congealing of his religious convictions, constant reexamination of his moral attitudes, and an overarching sense of guilt and self-reproach. His second wife gave birth to two daughters, only one of whom survived. Eliza herself died on September 29, 1845, leaving him with a five-year-old daughter, also named Catharine Jane, who was called Kate.[28]

---

27. Vernon L. Volpe, *Forlorn Hope of Freedom: The Liberty Party in the Old Northwest, 1838–1848* (Kent, Ohio, 1990), 47, 86.

28. The names of Chase's first wife and two daughters called Catharine are

Chase's family tragedies reinforced his sense of personal unworthiness but at the same time intensified his interest in political organization as he sought relief from his grief and remorse. He had thrown his energies and organizing skills into making the Liberty party a significant factor in Ohio politics. He also made several trips east during the 1840s. He visited leading Liberty party figures like Gerrit Smith, Joshua Leavitt, and Henry B. Stanton, though he seems to have kept the more radical abolitionists of the Boston area, William Lloyd Garrison and Wendell Phillips, at a distance.

Chase attended many of the Liberty party conventions in New York and Ohio, which were held in both states several times a year. For many of these county or state conventions he drafted the calls and wrote the addresses. He also placed himself in the antislavery vanguard by defending fugitive slaves and those who harbored them. But he was careful to avoid the stigma of abolition, a most unpopular, even blasphemous, word among the voters whatever their party affiliation. Rather, he repeatedly defined and refined a free-soil theme, and posed as an ardent antislavery man, though always within the limits of the federal Constitution.[29]

In 1844, Chase voted for Birney, the presidential candidate of the Liberty party. He was well satisfied that Birney's vote cost the Whigs New York and Ohio and thus the election. But after differences surfaced in the New York Democratic party during the early months of the Polk administration, Chase became less devoted to his initial idea of forming a broader Liberty party as a distinct, cohesive organization. When the Wilmot Proviso set off a furious debate in Congress over the issue of slavery in the territories, Chase saw an opportunity of utilizing the Liberty party at least in Ohio to bring about a merger with the Van Buren Democrats on the slavery issue and the important local issue of hard money.

There are frequent references in Chase's diaries from 1846 through 1848 to the political advantages to be gained for the free-soil position from an alliance between the Liberty party and the Van Buren Democrats. Chase followed up his political ideas with action when he attended the first Free-Soil convention at

---

spelled here, and their middle names given, as Chase wrote them in his "Family Memoranda" in a memorandum book (Chase Papers, L.C.). Kate Chase sometimes signed her name as Katharine.

29. For the differences between Chase's antislavery and other forms of abolitionism see: James Brewer Stewart, *Holy Warriors: The Abolitionists and American Slavery* (New York, 1976); Louis S. Gerteis, *Morality and Utility in American Antislavery Reform* (Chapel Hill, N.C., 1987); and Ronald G. Walters, *The Antislavery Appeal: American Abolitionism after 1830* (Baltimore, 1976). For a good appraisal of Chase's antislavery position see Eric Foner, *Free Soil, Free Labor, Free Men: The Ideology of the Republican Party before the Civil War* (New York, 1970).

Buffalo in the fall of 1848. There he played a prominent role in framing the platform that demanded a halt to the extension of slavery in the territories and called for the abolition of the institution in the District of Columbia. He also worked hard and successfully to bring the reluctant Liberty party leadership behind the nomination of Martin Van Buren on the Free-Soil ticket. It is quite clear from his correspondence and from his diary that he saw no future in a third party organized on the single issue of the abolition of slavery.

The two major parties denounced free soil as an unwarranted assumption of congressional power. Skirting the slavery issue in their platform, the Whigs nominated Zachary Taylor, Mexican-American War hero, a Southerner, and a slaveholder. Democrats named Lewis Cass, a New England-born Westerner and a veteran Jacksonian. Cass articulated the Democratic policy on slavery in the territories. In what was termed "squatter" or "popular" sovereignty, Cass would have given the residents of a territory the authority to accept or reject slavery.

The Free-Soil campaign was a spirited one. Chase and John Van Buren, the ex-president's son, made most of the stump speeches in the Northwest. By now Chase had pretty well conquered his lisp and his shyness about appearing before public audiences. His speeches lacked the spirit, the emotion, the broad humor, and the extravagant rhetoric that marked successful campaign oratory in the mid-nineteenth century. But he impressed his audiences with his careful delivery, his concise organization, and his powers of analysis which reduced complex issues to basics that everyone could understand. His six-foot, two-inch frame had filled out and, though balding and afflicted with a drooping eyelid, his was a magnificent physical presence.

The Free-Soil ticket went down to defeat but accomplished many things. Its 10 percent of the popular vote, concentrated primarily in Ohio, New York, and New England, cost Cass the election, but more than that it energized antislavery sentiment throughout the North, and no more so than in Ohio where organization Democrats who had voted reluctantly for Cass were involved in a factious dispute over local concerns. Chase reaped considerable advantages from the campaign. He had increased his political visibility outside of his home state, and in Ohio he emerged as the leader of the antislavery forces. Publicly in favor of orthodox Democratic party policy except on the extension of slavery, he was an appealing figure to the hard-money Van Buren Democrats. At the same time he had formed the Free-Soilers into a cohesive organization that drew from both of the major parties.

Under Chase's leadership, the Ohio Free-Soilers had made nominations for the legislature and elected twelve members to the lower house, two of whom, Dr. Norton Townshend and John F. Morse, considered themselves to be Free-Soil Democrats. The remainder were Free-Soil or Conscience Whigs. So close was the margin that separated the major parties in the legislature that the twelve Free-Soil members held the balance of power.[30]

Well before the legislature met, Chase worked actively behind the scenes to use the bargaining power now at his disposal and to make a deal with the Democratic party. With his usual mixture of idealism and opportunism, he guaranteed the Democrats at least two Free-Soil votes which would give them a majority in joint session if the ten Whig-leaning Free-Soilers went over to their opponents as expected. The Democrats would then receive all the benefits of majority rule in return for two favors to the Free-Soil cause: the elimination of the state's so-called Black Laws that discriminated against free blacks and the election of Salmon P. Chase to the United States Senate.

For the Democratic leadership, scrapping the Black Laws was a small price to pay for retaining their control in the legislature. If at some time in the future public or party opinion demanded the laws' reinstatement, it could always be done. For Chase and the Free-Soilers, the repeal demonstrated their dedication to human rights and above all their ability to use their strength shrewdly and adroitly. For Chase himself, the arrangement promised a great reward—the United States Senate. For an Ohio lawyer whose only public office had been as a member of the Cincinnati city council, election to the Senate was a dazzling prize. If the plan succeeded, it would propel him to a position of national leadership in the free-soil movement, paving the way, he hoped, to convert the Democratic party into an antislavery organization while it still retained its Jefferson-Jackson identity on other public issues. Like the Liberty party before it, the Free-Soil party as a separate political organization would be sacrificed in the interest of a national party. All of this was in the future, of course, but Chase's correspondence and his all too brief diary entries demonstrate he was thinking along these lines as early as the fall of 1848.

When the legislature met in January 1849, the fate of Chase's plans and his ambitions rested on two obscure members of the Ohio legislature, Townshend and Morse. Most Free-Soilers were, of

---

30. For Chase's role in the politics of Ohio at this time, see Stephen E. Maizlish, *The Triumph of Sectionalism: The Transformation of Ohio Politics, 1844–1856* (Kent, Ohio, 1983).

course, unaware of Chase's deal with elements of the Democratic leadership and all, whether leaning towards the Democrats or the Whigs, voted as a unit to repeal the Black Laws. But as Chase's deal became evident the Free-Soil Whigs became restive.

The Conscience Whigs, opposed to the Democrats and eager to maintain the integrity of their third party, fought against Chase's handiwork. However, the two-vote majority provided by Townshend and Morse was insurmountable. The legislature elected all Democratic nominees for state offices and awarded patronage to the Democratic faithful. And to conclude the deal, Chase was elected to the United States Senate for a six-year term. The ten Free-Soil Whigs balked and voted for Joshua Giddings, the antislavery congressman from Ohio's Western Reserve, but the same two Democratic free-soilers gave Chase a plurality.[31]

The first five years of Chase's term in the Senate were frustrating ones for him. As a Free-Soiler, even though he claimed to be a Democrat, he was not accepted by the party caucus in Congress. He was assigned the insignificant post of membership on the committee dealing with Revolutionary War claims. He was seldom scheduled for speeches and limited in his time for debate. His isolation was primarily due to the effective opposition of Southern members.

Chase's role in the debates that led to the Compromise of 1850 was minimal, though he was active in attempting to block the compromise measures.[32] His journal entries and memoranda for the early 1850s consist largely of brief records of his own letters; brief conversations with colleagues, friends, and acquaintances; and occasional notes on legal business and investments.

In contrast, Chase's role in opposing the Kansas-Nebraska Act is well documented. His participation with Giddings, Sumner, Gerrit Smith, Edward Wade (an Ohio Free-Soiler), and Alexander De Witt of Massachusetts in the famous "Appeal of the Independent Democrats in Congress to the People of the United States" is covered in his correspondence for January 1854. At this time Chase's party ties were loosening and he was soon to be replaced in the Senate by George Pugh, a fellow townsman and an orthodox Pierce Democrat.

Chase had been unsuccessful in organizing what he hoped would be a free-soil or "independent" Democratic party but the Kansas-Nebraska bill with its explicit repeal of the Missouri Compromise

---

31. A. G. Riddle, "Recollections of the Forty-Seventh General Assembly of Ohio, 1847–48," *Magazine of Western History* 6 (Aug. 1887): 341–51.
32. His most notable effort in the debates was a speech on the floor of the Senate on Mar. 26–27, 1850, given the title "Union and Freedom, Without Compromise," and issued as a pamphlet.

provided him with an excellent opportunity to purge the northern Democracy of its pro-Southern adherents. The draft of the "Appeal" which Chase edited was a brilliant piece of antislavery propaganda and it provided the impetus for the organization of a new party on free-soil principles. Chase's efforts since 1843 to build a free-soil structure on a Jeffersonian foundation would finally bear fruit in the formation of the Republican party.

Chase benefited politically from the anti-Nebraska mood that gripped the free states. A Republican/Know-Nothing fusion convention in July 1855 nominated him for governor of Ohio on a free-soil platform. In Chase's correspondence and his journal memoranda written between August 1854 and March 1855 there are references to the political deals he made to secure his gubernatorial election. Indeed, his involvement with the Know-Nothings was essential to the success of his campaign. He came in for considerable criticism, however. His Democratic principles were scorned as a pretext for his ambition, and many former Free-Soil Whigs and Democrats, especially those outside Ohio, charged him with opportunism.

As his papers indicate, Chase was well aware of the perils the Know-Nothing or American party held for the new Republican organization. The Know-Nothing party, which was the political expression of American nativism, attracted politicians of all hues and persuasions. It seemed quite possible at the time that the newly formed Republican party would be absorbed into the Know-Nothing organization.[33]

Chase was clever enough to develop a strategy that would gain a substantial immigrant vote in Ohio but at the same time receive the support of those Free-Soil Whigs and Democrats who had joined the American party. His new political policy which he enunciated whenever he was accused of being a Know-Nothing was to deny the charge, but at the same time discriminate among the new immigrants. Those who were Catholics, a minority among the foreigners who were settling in Ohio, he denounced as responsive to the dictates of an alien power, the papacy. Protestant immigrants, mainly German and British, he welcomed.

Chase's strategy permitted the Republican party in Ohio and in other Northern states to escape the odium of intolerance while creating a bridge to Protestant Americans. Horace Greeley may have railed against Chase's stand as blatant opportunism, but the tactic

---

33. On the role of nativism in politics see Maizlish, *Triumph of Sectionalism;* William E. Gienapp, *The Origins of the Republican Party, 1852–1856* (New York, 1987); and William E. Gienapp, "Salmon P. Chase, Nativism, and the Formation of the Republican Party in Ohio," *Ohio History* 93 (1984): 5–39.

paid off in Ohio.[34] It would also work in the delicate negotiations that led to fusion of the American party with the Republicans in the presidential campaign of 1856.

Chase actively promoted a preliminary organization meeting for the national Republican party to be held during the winter of 1856.[35] By the time a site had been found for the meeting he had created a sizable organization and he sought the nomination of the new party on the basis of his free-soil record, his service as United States senator, and his election to the governorship of Ohio in 1855. Indeed, his hopes were raised by the apparent groundswell of support he received. At the convention, however, no nominations were made. Unfortunately his journals do not address these events, although his correspondence fully covers his own role in promoting the convention and directing the activities of his political lieutenants at Pittsburgh.

Though Chase was the first political leader in the free states to push for a national organization and to propose a realistic approach to the nativist problem, he could not then command the united support of the Ohio delegates at the Republican convention held in Philadelphia during mid-June 1856. The national organization he had developed was co-opted by veteran politicians like Thurlow Weed, the former Whig boss of New York, and Francis Preston Blair, the old Jacksonian Democrat from Maryland, both of whom had recently joined the Republican ranks. Weed, Blair, and other conservative free-soil politicians found Chase too radical on the slavery issue to carry important free states. Similarly he was held to have been too outspoken on the tariff, currency, and other public policy issues that affected important factions in the North.

The result was that the Republican party nominated John C. Frémont, the popular western explorer, for president. Frémont was known to hold a moderate free-soil position; his preferences on other issues were unknown. The platform, however, was quite explicit on the containment of slavery in the territories. Chase's formula for building a bridge between the nativists and the immigrants influenced the convention's stance on this difficult and delicate problem. The carefully worded statement was phrased in such a way that both nativists and immigrants, especially Protestant Germans— a big factor in the voting population of the Middle West—could support the ticket.

Disappointed, Chase nonetheless loyally supported the Frémont ticket and waited expectantly for the nomination in 1860. There

34. Greeley to Chase, Apr. 16, 1852 (Chase Papers, Hist. Soc. of Pa.).
35. Gienapp, *Origins of the Republican Party*, 253–54.

were many obstacles ahead for him beyond developing and strengthening a national organization, however. Thus far he had utilized his position as governor of Ohio to enhance his national reputation and strengthen his constituency at home. Whenever possible he employed state patronage and his influence with the legislature to place allies in strategic places. He also sought, with some success, to hold together the fragile and frequently querulous coalition of Free-Soil Whigs, Democrats, and Know-Nothings. His task was made much more difficult by a political scandal in his administration that surfaced in 1857 and by the economic depression that fell with crushing effect on all of the industrializing Northern states. Its impact on Ohio where banking problems had been more or less endemic for the past ten years was particularly severe.

In June 1857, two months before the Republican state nominating convention, William H. Gibson, the state treasurer, was forced to admit a shortage of approximately a half million dollars in the Ohio treasury. The arrears were primarily the responsibility of his predecessor, John G. Breslin, a Democrat and one of the key figures in Chase's election to the United States Senate in 1849. Chase, horrified at the revelation, forced Gibson's resignation and moved as rapidly as possible to assure the solvency of the state. He also sought an indictment against Breslin, who fled to Canada and escaped prosecution.

The Breslin embezzlement cast a shadow over Chase's administration, which in most respects had been successful. The state constitution sharply circumscribed the powers of the governor, but it did provide the office with a forum for initiating and promoting legislation. Governors' messages were always the subject of wide newspaper coverage, not just in Ohio but in other states if they addressed topics of national interest. And by now Chase was well attuned to the mood of the free states, though more as a leader than a follower of public opinion. He spoke out for women's rights to property, and he attacked the Fugitive Slave Law, though he counseled citizens to obey it while it remained a law of the land. He also proposed a ceiling on railroad rates, a recommendation that the legislature ignored.

In the spring of 1857, Chase excoriated with vivid language the Dred Scott decision which, he declared, made the territories "one great slave pen."[36] Chase also used the pardon power freely. But his term as governor was open to severe criticism from the Democrats for the Breslin embezzlement. In addition he was blamed for the

---

36. Blue, *Chase*, 116.

depression not just by Democrats but by former Whigs within his own party because of his well-known hard-money views.

Chase was understandably reluctant to risk his political reputation on a campaign for reelection that had so many negative aspects. But he realized that if he refused to run, he would be accused of admitting responsibility for the Breslin fraud. Even if he were defeated, he would still gain favorable publicity that would certainly not hurt his presidential bid in 1860. If he won, he could claim that he had upheld free-soil principles against heavy odds and thus deserved the presidential nomination on his record of competence and party loyalty.

After much soul-searching, Chase agreed to be the Republican candidate for governor. Once nominated he worked as he had never worked before. He increased his already heavy political correspondence, but more than that he crisscrossed the state making stump speeches in virtually every population center. All of this took a heavy toll on his otherwise robust physique. Much of the time on the campaign trail he was plagued with headaches, diarrhea, and other physical complaints.[37] Despite his hard work, had it not been for the Know-Nothing candidate Philadelph Van Trump, Chase would have been defeated. Van Trump received 9,200 votes while Chase triumphed over the Democratic candidate, Henry B. Payne, by a mere 1,500 votes. The Democrats won control of the legislature.[38]

As he had in his first term, Chase used the governorship as a means of fostering his campaign for the Republican presidential nomination. Though he had no veto power, he denounced for the national press the legislature's repeal of laws designed to frustrate the operation of the Fugitive Slave Law. And he grasped whatever opportunity arose to keep the Kansas issue before the public.

For Chase personally the next two years were filled with strenuous activity as he again sought the presidential nomination and again failed. As in 1856, he was unable to develop an effective political organization, and unable to secure a united Ohio delegation behind his candidacy. He was never a serious threat to the nomination of Abraham Lincoln. Republican leaders, sensing victory in November after the Democrats broke into sectional factions, moved their party closer to the center of the antislavery movement. Both Chase and Seward, Lincoln's principal opponents, were deemed too radical on this issue. Chase's hard-money and free trade positions

37. Chase recounts his travels in a memorandum he entitled "Canvass of 1857." See Journal IV, Aug. 1857 (below).
38. Blue, *Chase*, 117.

were additional handicaps in Pennsylvania, a state crucial to the Republican cause. Industrialists of that state by now pretty well controlled its political destiny. Anything smacking of free trade was anathema to them. Chase felt betrayed by the party he had done so much to create, though there was some solace in his election to the Senate for a second term.

Chase was a man torn between a driving ambition and a sincere belief in advancing the cause of human rights, particularly the eventual abolition of slavery. He was singularly blind to his own shortcomings and could not understand why he was unpopular, while at the same time he presented an aloof, imperious attitude toward other politicians and even close friends and associates. That Chase was a man of intense feeling is abundantly evident in the diary entries devoted to his family life. The passages dealing with the death of his sister Alice in February 1859 are especially moving. One has the sense of deep personal loss, almost as profound as the grief he had described in his diaries on the death of his first wife many years earlier. The discussions in his journals of the final illnesses and deaths of his older brother Alexander, his brother-in-law Edmund Curtis Smith, and his close friend, Dr. Noah Worcester, say much about his own and his culture's attitudes toward death.

Chase's journals from the period before the Civil War show the depth and direction of his religiosity, his passionate efforts to improve himself in foreign languages, and his incessant reading of history, biography, and philosophical works. The diaries also graphically display a person whose private life was devoted to his family. As the most prominent and successful member of a large family, Chase was looked to for financial and other assistance. His papers also reveal the care and attention he lavished on his two daughters who lived beyond early childhood, Kate and Janet (known in the family circle as "Nettie"). In 1846, Chase had married for a third time. His new wife, Sarah Bella Dunlop Ludlow, was a member of one of the founding families of Cincinnati. She bore him three daughters, of whom only Nettie survived. Until her death in 1852, "Belle" sought to act as head of the little family when Chase was out of town. But she herself fell ill with tuberculosis and for the last years of her life was confined to her room or in treatment at various sanatoriums in a vain effort to prolong her life. Alice Chase assisted her brother in the upbringing of his children until her own death in 1859.

Chase was an indulgent but strict parent. The diaries reveal a pattern of religious training for both daughters, family prayers, regular attendance at church, sometimes three services on Sunday besides Sunday school. Chase also prescribed regular lessons in French and in English literature at home to supplement his daughters' formal schooling. He made strenuous efforts to mold the characters of his daughters and at the same time provide them with parental support.

When Chase established a home in Washington in 1861 both daughters made up the family household. Though overworked as secretary of the Treasury, Chase still managed to act as a protective parent, and he watched over Kate, who by now was the belle of Washington society, with an indulgent eye. To his dismay, however, Kate was quite careless about her personal expenses and he found it difficult to maintain the kind of lavish living standard she required.[39] Yet if Chase seemed to indulge Kate, he was also solicitous of Nettie's well-being and wrote her long and interesting letters on those infrequent occasions he was absent from Washington.

Chase did not keep a journal during the first months of the Civil War. For much of the period from December 1861 through mid-1866, however, he kept a series of diaries, some in his own hand and others in the neat handwriting of two secretaries, Homer Plantz and Jacob Schuckers.

The Civil War diaries are excellent, indeed unique, insights into the Lincoln administration by one who, as secretary of the Treasury, was directing the financial policies that supported the Union war effort. But they are more than that. They detail the course of military affairs in which Chase not only took an abiding interest, but until late 1862 was, along with Secretary of War Edwin M. Stanton, Lincoln's major advisor in the choice of top military leaders and the development of military strategy.

Included among Chase's journal for 1862 are four long, unusually graphic accounts of a trip Lincoln, Stanton, and Chase took to visit Fort Monroe and George B. McClellan's army as it made its laborious way up the peninsula between the York and James Rivers. This commentary takes the form of a "Narrative of Operations" and three lengthy letters Chase wrote to his younger daughter Nettie during May 1862. We get a close view of both Lincoln and Stanton, their seasickness on the revenue cutter *Miami* as she steamed through rough waters of Chesapeake Bay, and Lincoln's informality and keen interest in the naval and military operations under way.

One immediate and positive result of McClellan's ill-fated campaign was the capture of Norfolk, Virginia. Lincoln, Chase, and Stanton, for the only time during the war, actually directed the

---

39. Ibid., 208.

Union troops that surrounded the city. Chase describes these scenes with fresh, compelling narrative.

The journals amply chronicle Chase's ambivalent feeling towards Lincoln. It is worthy of note that as Chase began to seek the Republican presidential nomination of 1864, his private judgments about Lincoln and his policies are decidedly negative. Yet the diaries must also be understood within the context of the often bitter disputes among the men who made up the cabinet. As the war ground on, Chase and William H. Seward, the secretary of state, came to represent opposite poles in the cabinet on how the war should be conducted. Stanton generally sided with Chase. Postmaster General Montgomery Blair took a conservative stand on issues dealing with emancipation, while Gideon Welles, secretary of the navy, veered towards the Blair position. Lincoln was neither conservative enough for Blair nor radical enough to suit Chase and Stanton.[40]

Chase was preoccupied with issues of military strategy and emancipation. His influence with Lincoln contributed to the first dismissal of McClellan and his replacement by General John Pope. Pope's disastrous defeat at the Second Battle of Bull Run shook Lincoln's faith in Chase's judgment in military affairs. And against the opinion of Chase and most members of the cabinet, Lincoln reinstated McClellan to overall command.

Chase gave wholehearted support to the policy of emancipation Lincoln had been considering since the summer of 1862. When Lincoln broached the matter to Seward and Welles and brought it up at a cabinet meeting not long after, the cabinet was in the main favorable. Seward, however, objected to the timing and convinced Lincoln that emancipation be postponed until the Union forces won a military victory. The Battle of Antietam provided this victory and on September 22, 1862, Lincoln read his preliminary Emancipation Proclamation to the cabinet. Chase, who left us a full account of this famous meeting in his diary, was not completely satisfied with the proclamation but supported the president without hesitation.[41]

The struggle for power and influence within the cabinet and between the president and Congress intensified as the Republicans lost heavily in the congressional elections of 1862 and as the military suffered reversals during the late fall. With congressional confidence in the Lincoln administration in decline, Chase searched for the

---

40. John Niven, "Lincoln and Chase, a Reappraisal," *Journal of the Abraham Lincoln Association* 12 (1991): 1–15.
41. Gideon Welles and Chase left the only full accounts of this famous meeting in their diaries. Stanton made a brief memorandum of the discussion. Howard K. Beale, ed., *Diary of Gideon Welles: Secretary of the Navy Under Lincoln and Johnson* (New York, 1960), 1:142–43; Stanton memorandum (Stanton Papers, L.C.).

locus of power, uncertain with what entity to cast his political lot. He was, unfortunately, unable to conceal his frustration with Lincoln's policies. Suspecting Seward to be their architect, he made the mistake of offering his surmises in the garb of fact to Republican leadership in the Congress.

The result of this intrigue is well known. Lincoln headed off the congressional attack as well as Chase's underhanded role in it through meetings he conducted first with the congressional group, then the cabinet, and finally with the Republican congressional leadership and the cabinet present. Chase was in attendance at the meeting, Seward absent, when Lincoln demonstrated cabinet solidarity behind his measures and satisfied the congressmen that Seward was not the author of administration policies. Lincoln had Seward's resignation in hand and after this embarrassing episode Chase proffered his resignation also. The president rejected both and thereafter continued his conduct of the war without overt congressional challenge.[42]

Along with his participation in policy measures like emancipation and military affairs, and his more or less constant effort to capture the Republican presidential nomination in 1864, Chase's primary obligation was financing the Union war effort. He comments quite fully both in his diary and letters on the problems and the vexations of meeting unprecedented expenditures while maintaining the public credit of the Union. A hard-money man who long accepted the traditional Democratic view of currency and credit, Chase found it most difficult to abandon his fixed concepts and embark on a policy that featured a circulating medium, known as greenbacks, that was not backed by specie but simply the full faith and credit of the national government.[43]

Chase's financial policies have been sharply criticized over the years. Some contemporaries believed that his insistence early in the war on maintaining a specie basis for the circulating medium, as government expenditures far outstripped the nation's hard-money supply, was shortsighted and essentially harmful to the economy as a whole.[44] His initial reliance on borrowing through the issuance of bonds and Treasury notes, and his insistence that banks providing loans must purchase government equities with specie, drained the

---

42. Beale, *Diary of Welles*, 1:194–205.
43. For more on Civil War finances see Bray Hammond, *Sovereignty and an Empty Purse: Banks and Politics in the Civil War* (Princeton, 1970).
44. George S. Boutwell, *Reminiscences of Sixty Years in Public Affairs* (New York, 1902), 1:305, 2:209; Hugh McCulloch, *Men and Measures of Half a Century* (New York, 1888), 185–86.

banks' hard-money reserves and resulted in their suspension of specie payments in the late fall of 1861.

Chase was forced to look to other sources for the funds required to sustain the war effort. Slowly and reluctantly, working with the House Committee on Ways and Means, he raised excise rates on various consumer products and increased impost revenues from the higher tariff imposed by the Morrill Act. Congress also imposed a conservative income tax and, as the Constitution provided, levied a modest direct tax on the states.

But these areas of potential revenue were slight compared to the ever-mounting costs of the war. Like most political leaders and, indeed, most of the Northern public, Chase had counted on a short war. And even after the first Battle of Bull Run, optimism regarding a speedy end to the conflict persisted. Despite this error in judgment, shared by the cabinet and the president himself, Chase could have insisted that Congress enact a comprehensive plan for financing a long war. But a drastic increase in taxes would have been politically unwise at the end of 1861, and politically perilous a year later.

Thus Chase, with the assistance and support of unusually capable congressional finance committees led by Thaddeus Stevens in the House and John Sherman in the Senate, devised a program that featured borrowing to cover wartime expenditures. The government floated bond issues: the famed 5–20 bonds (redeemable after five years and maturing in twenty years, carrying 6 percent interest in coin); the 7.30s (Treasury notes carrying 7.3 percent interest); and finally in 1864 the 10–40s (redeemable after ten years, maturing in forty). That these financial instruments alone were inadequate to fund the war effort became evident by late 1862. Chase and the congressional finance committees were forced to rely on fiat currency to help make up the difference. Under several acts almost a half billion dollars worth of fiat currency backed only by the faith and credit of the government were issued. This currency, or greenbacks as they were commonly called, contributed mightily to inflation that reached a high point in the summer of 1864. As such they must be considered a regressive tax on consumers.

Chase sponsored and Congress approved a central banking system, a nationwide network of banks operating under government charter that were required to purchase and retain government bonds at a certain ratio to their note issue. The notes of these banks would circulate as a currency medium. Such an arrangement, known as the National Bank System, was established primarily to act as a market for government bonds. But for the first time since

Jackson's removal of government deposits from the Second Bank of the United States in 1833, the Union had an institution that offered a stable circulating medium other than specie.

Chase always believed that the National Banking System was his greatest achievement as secretary of the Treasury. Despite its many faults, the system would manage the currency of the nation for the next fifty years. Banks were slow to enter the system, however, and as purchasers of government bonds during the war, their impact was relatively slight.

Much more significant was the sale of government bonds directly to the public through mass merchandizing efforts. Desperate for funds, Chase finally came to the conclusion that the sale of bonds could best be accomplished by a sole agent who would deal directly with the public. He chose a Philadelphian and old Ohio associate, Jay Cooke, to undertake the task. Though Cooke made a fortune from the deal, he accomplished the task set for him. He developed a network of agents that covered the Union and advertised freely in the hundreds of local newspapers. Heretofore, government bonds had been taken by bankers, usually at a discount and rarely appeared in the hands of the average citizen. Now individuals all over the nation could subscribe to bonds in small or large denominations.

The debt the Union incurred during the war amounted to more than 2.6 billion dollars in 1865 terms. Considering the size and composition of the Union economy, this was a staggering sum, and as a percentage of gross national product it remained unequaled until World War II.[45]

Apart from the public policy measures that he initiated as secretary of the Treasury, Chase utilized his position to advance his political fortunes. Since Jackson's day, Treasury secretaries had employed their very considerable patronage for partisan purposes, but Chase broke new ground in using Treasury appointments for his own personal political advantage. In addition to long-standing political plums that came under the Treasury, like the customhouses and the mints, Congress enlarged Treasury patronage significantly by establishing a new class of agents to collect revenue produced by wartime taxes and especially to regulate internal trade as Confederate territory came under Union control.

There were major opportunities for graft in these positions, particularly as cotton became available for sale to Northern and

---

45. Irwin Unger, *The Greenback Era: A Social History of American Finance, 1865–1879* (Princeton, 1964), 16; U.S. Department of Commerce, *Historical Statistics of the United States: Colonial Times to 1970. Bicentennial Edition*, 2 vols. (Washington, D.C., 1975), 1:224, 2:1117, 1118.

European textile factories starved for lack of the staple. Chase never became involved in any of these transactions. His agents did, however, though few were ever prosecuted and those were primarily officials employed at the New York Custom House.

But the political activity of the Treasury network was another matter. Chase utilized Hiram Barney, his appointee as customs collector in New York, to push his presidential campaign and enlisted Treasury agents in his political cause. Although he always denied that he had any ulterior motives in his patronage policy, his capacity for rationalizing his actions in terms of public interest as opposed to his own ambitions was almost limitless.

To Republican dissidents, Chase seemed a logical candidate for president in 1864. His name had been kept before the public eye as a master of the mysterious ways of finance and his portrait had been broadcast throughout the land on the greenback notes which everyone was using as a common currency. Among many of the radicals in Congress, he was considered to have the best record of any public figure on emancipation and Reconstruction.

There were, of course, radical leaders in Congress like Benjamin Wade, a political rival in Ohio, who detested Chase. But despite a record of opportunism in politics and devious political conduct within the Lincoln administration, Chase was on good terms with most of the congressional radicals like Thaddeus Stevens in the House and Charles Sumner in the Senate. He could claim support from some moderates, too, men like John Sherman, his successor in the Senate and a working partner on financial measures.

Accordingly in late fall of 1863 Chase let it be known that he would not refuse the Republican nomination for the presidency. Even before he discreetly announced his intentions, Chase had been in touch with John T. Trowbridge about a campaign biography. As the New Year came around an informal committee of important congressmen, angered at Lincoln's proclamation on Reconstruction, the so-called ten percent plan, set up a Chase organization in the Senate. This committee—headed by Samuel C. Pomeroy, a patronage-hungry senator from Kansas, and John Sherman—engaged a New York journalist to write a long public letter entitled "The Next Presidential Election." This piece of anti-Lincoln pro-Chase propaganda was carried in most of the major newspapers. It also appeared as a pamphlet to be franked out by Chase supporters in Congress.

Shortly after the release of this campaign document, the committee issued another public letter signed by Pomeroy, Sherman, and a number of other radical congressmen that denounced Lincoln as an incompetent who, if nominated, would lose in November.

Chase was the only candidate whose views on national policy, especially Reconstruction, and on the conduct of the war, made him the appropriate choice for the nomination.[46]

The letter, which came to be known as the Pomeroy Circular, together with the anti-Lincoln pamphlet hurt rather than helped Chase's chances for the nomination. It became immediately clear that the Northern public may have been war-weary, but on the issue of Reconstruction and race relations they were decidedly supportive of Lincoln's moderate policies. Although the Pomeroy Circular indicated that Chase knew about the committee's activities, he denied any complicity. The president, certain politically astute members of his cabinet, and loyal state party leaders had long foreseen a Chase move for the nomination. Through an adroit application of patronage where it counted in New York, Connecticut, Ohio, Pennsylvania, and New Hampshire, the president claimed a majority of public opinion. By contrast the intemperate language of the two pro-Chase documents produced an almost instant reaction against his candidacy. Whatever chances Chase may have had for the nomination soon disappeared.

Chase's relationships with Lincoln and his cabinet colleagues, never especially warm, were scarcely improved. Lincoln, however, refused Chase's offer to resign (his third such offer) and dismissed the episode, seemingly accepting Chase's rather lame explanation that he did not know about the activities of his political friends. Chase's diaries are silent about this embarrassing demonstration of his driving ambition coupled with his political ineptitude.

Although Chase withdrew his candidacy his organization continued intact and he remained the conspicuous radical in the administration. Lincoln may have retained Chase after the Pomeroy Circular as much for his party connections as for his conduct of the Treasury Department. But the situation within the administration was rapidly becoming impossible.

Montgomery Blair, the conservative champion, was not even civil to Chase and avoided contact with Stanton. Blair's younger brother, Francis Preston Blair, Jr., or Frank as he was called, though a corps commander in Sherman's army, had run for Congress in Missouri and won his election in 1863. During his campaign the younger Blair had openly accused Chase of disloyalty to the administration. In the wake of the Pomeroy Circular, he bitterly attacked Chase on the floor of the House. Chase's partisans responded and for several months the conservative and radical factions deepened the gulf of bitterness that separated the two groups.

---

46. Blue, *Chase*, 222–23.

Grant's campaign against Lee seemed to be floundering in the wilderness of northern Virginia. Confederate General Joseph E. Johnston was holding Sherman's forces at bay before the approaches to Atlanta. A restive Republican coalition, renamed the Union party, nominated Lincoln for president and Andrew Johnson, a Union Democrat from Tennessee, for vice president in the summer of 1864. The Democrats named George B. McClellan to head their ticket.

On June 30, 1864, Lincoln accepted Chase's resignation as secretary of the Treasury. The president had finally decided that Chase's continued presence in the cabinet had become a liability. Chase's loyalty to the administration was questionable, and his inability to work with the members of the cabinet was a factor. But it was his stubborn stand on the rich Treasury patronage in New York City that precipitated the break. Chase had refused to accept any compromise solution to the appointments of the important posts of assistant treasurer and collector of customs in New York City.

Since the beginning of the Lincoln administration, Chase had jealously guarded these two positions as much for the service the incumbents rendered to the implementation of his policies as for their political support. In this effort, he came into conflict with the powerful Seward-Weed machine. The resignation of Assistant Treasurer John J. Cisco for health reasons brought the conflict to a head. When Chase refused to accept any interference in the appointment of a replacement, and offered his resignation, the president accepted it. Lincoln's action came as a surprise to Chase as his journal entry for that day indicates.

During the summer of 1864, while the military stalemate generated enormous casualties in Virginia and Georgia, the simmering feud between the radicals and the more moderate groups within the new Union party boiled up again. This time it posed a more serious danger to the administration than any previous move. Earlier, at a well-publicized meeting in Cleveland, Ohio, an unusual assemblage of individuals opposed to the Lincoln administration—ranging from abolitionists like Wendell Phillips and inveterate foes of executive power like Henry Winter Davis, the radical Maryland congressman, to a scattering of war Democrats and disaffected Republican politicians—nominated John C. Frémont on what was called a Radical Democrat ticket.

With Frémont as a third-party candidate, a small group of Republicans, primarily drawn from the radical ranks, began applying pressure within the Union party to force Lincoln's withdrawal as a candidate. But in late August the military situation suddenly and dramatically improved for the Union cause and for the Lincoln administration. The possibility of victory and peace in the not distant future headed off any radical insurgency, prompted Frémont's withdrawal as a candidate, and virtually guaranteed Lincoln's election. The president, however, in search of balance, decided to conciliate the radicals. He accepted Montgomery Blair's resignation. The removal of the two most contentious members of his cabinet, the one radical, the other conservative, made for a more harmonious administration and a more unified party.

While he was still in the cabinet, though increasingly involved in politics and patronage, Chase continued to devote most of his waking hours to the overwhelming problem of the Union's finances. By early 1864 greenback currency had depreciated significantly in terms of gold and speculation in precious metals was rampant. Chase saw clearly that the precipitous decline in value of greenback dollars was due to uncertainties in the financial communities about the fate of the Union and consequently its public credit. Something approaching parity between the fiat currency and gold could be achieved only through Union victories that made peace certain and an adequate program of taxation to meet the costs of the war. Despite his own accurate appraisal, however, Chase intervened in the gold market during early 1864 to curb speculation and stabilize greenback currency. He was unable to achieve either goal and in effect lost some credibility for the government in the money markets here and abroad. At the time of his resignation in late June 1864, greenbacks had fallen to a new low and two weeks after he left office greenbacks fell to their lowest point of $35.09 for a hundred dollars in gold. Chase's resignation had been a factor, but more importantly Grant's bloody repulses at Spotsylvania and Cold Harbor had drastically undermined the confidence of the financial community in the Union cause.

After his resignation, Chase left Washington for a much needed vacation in New York City and New England. Chase's journal has quite consistent entries for the period but is cryptic about his political activities. He notes that he talked with individuals who were known to be leaders in the movement to drop Lincoln, but he does not mention the substance of their conversations. His correspondence is likewise veiled on this particular subject. When Chase returned to Washington on September 14, Montgomery Blair had left the cabinet, the military picture had improved significantly, and most of Lincoln's critics were now reluctantly backing him. Chase followed suit and stumped Ohio for Lincoln and Johnson.

Chief Justice Roger B. Taney, who was eighty-seven years old and who for some time had been unable to carry on his judicial duties, died on October 12, 1864. Chase's friends in Congress, particularly Samuel Hooper of Boston and Charles Sumner, urged Lincoln to appoint Chase. The president knew Chase had been angling for the post since his resignation as secretary of the Treasury. It was politically prudent of Lincoln, however, to await the outcome of the election in November considering the state of the Union party. Radicals increasingly pitted themselves against the conservatives on matters of the conduct of the war and Reconstruction. Moreover, there were other candidates for the judicial post, some of whom represented considerable political strength within the party. Lincoln could not alienate those individuals before the election.

Chase's first reference to the judicial post came the day after Lincoln accepted his resignation from the Treasury Department. He relates a conversation with his friend Congressman Hooper who had just seen the president. According to Hooper, Lincoln said that he would nominate Chase to the Supreme Court when a vacancy existed. The next direct allusion to the court came on November 26, 1864, when Chase noted the efforts being made on his behalf by his supporters in Washington. But Chase's correspondence amplifies his anxiety about Lincoln's decision. Finally, on December 6, the day after the second session of the 38th Congress commenced, Lincoln nominated Chase to be chief justice. In a rare display of nonpartisanship, the Senate confirmed the nomination unanimously.

A shrewd judge of individuals, Lincoln probably did not expect Chase to confine himself exclusively to his judicial duties. His motives in appointing Chase had more to do with the condition of the party and his judgment of Chase's real abilities than with any pressing concern about his political behavior. The president had already eliminated Chase's political beachhead in New York with the removal of Hiram Barney as customs collector and the appointment of a Seward associate, Simeon Draper, to that important post. Seward and Weed now had control of the Custom House and the assistant treasurer's office in New York City.

Chase made few comments in his diary about these changes in his political fortunes, though his correspondence is much more revealing. Following his appointment to the bench he began to record again a relatively full and consistent account of his daily life in his journal. Far from apolitical or neutral on the policy issues of the day, Chase actively and forcefully backed the Thirteenth Amendment to the Constitution, which would abolish slavery throughout the country. He also favored expanded civil rights for the freed blacks, including suffrage for all black males who met age and residence requirements. He applauded Lincoln's views on limited suffrage for the freedmen, but in the longer term he advocated a policy considerably more radical than the one the administration had proposed thus far.[47] It is clear that he also recognized the importance of education in the process. He urged the freedmen to educate themselves and by work and sober, thrifty habits to prepare themselves for the vote.

Chase's record of Lincoln's assassination is one of the most interesting accounts of that tragic time. He learned of the assassination attempts on Lincoln and Seward soon after they occurred, but as he could not be of any service and might probably be in the way of those who could, he decided to wait until morning for further intelligence. Very early on April 15, while walking to Seward's home, he was informed that the president had died. He continued on to Seward's where he learned that the secretary was in critical condition. Then he proceeded to the Kirkwood House, Vice President Johnson's residence. He had a brief conversation with Johnson and then, accompanied by Secretary of the Treasury Hugh McCulloch and Attorney General James Speed, he went to Speed's office to consult precedents that covered the administration of the oaths of office to Vice Presidents Tyler and Fillmore on their succession to the presidency. Returning to the Kirkwood House, where other members of the cabinet had assembled, Chase administered the oath of office to Johnson.[48]

Chase had pressed Lincoln during the last days of his life to adopt a more radical view of Reconstruction and of civil rights for blacks after the Thirteenth Amendment's abolition of slavery, then before the states, was adopted. In fact, Lincoln had made reference to Chase's position in his last public address on April 11, 1865. Three days after the assassination, Chase had a long conversation with the new president and again put forward his ideas on Reconstruction and civil rights. Johnson seemed to agree with Chase, who saw the president frequently during the next ten days. At some point they discussed a trip Chase planned to take through the former Confederate States, where almost all resistance to the authority of the Union government had ceased.

With Johnson's encouragement and warm support from Secretary of War Stanton, Chase left Washington on May 1, 1865. The Treasury Department had made available the revenue cutter *Wayanda*, which Chase and his party boarded at Norfolk, Virginia. Accompanying Chase were his daughter Nettie, Treasury official

---

47. Chase to Lincoln, Apr. 11, 12, 1865 (Lincoln Papers, L.C.).
48. Beale, *Diary of Welles*, 2:283–90.

William Mellen, and young Cincinnati journalist Whitelaw Reid, who was one of a small group of influential reporters Chase had cultivated before and during the war.

During the trip that lasted almost two months, Chase wrote seven lengthy letters to Johnson on conditions as he saw them in the former Confederate states. A constant theme in these letters and in his diary entries was his firm belief that the former slaves were, for the most part, eager to improve their station in life and that they deserved every assistance the national government could provide to help them in this worthwhile effort. In particular he urged the president to use the powers of his office for the benefit of the freedmen, especially in compelling the Southern states to extend suffrage to them.

Chase admitted to Johnson that a majority of white Southerners opposed equal rights for the freedmen, though he apparently skewed the attitudes of prominent Southerners and omitted any adverse comments from Union military officers he met. Nevertheless, he felt that the majority of the people in the South wanted peace and law and order so desperately that they would accept, however reluctantly, any policy on Reconstruction that the president determined.[49]

Chase made it plain that he considered black suffrage not only the right and proper approach to Reconstruction but the all important first step in protecting the freedmen from their former masters. After Johnson outlined his Reconstruction policy, however, Chase realized that his advice had been rejected.[50]

Chase was accused of utilizing his southern journey as an electioneering device to secure the Republican nomination for the presidency in 1868. His diary entries demonstrate that he reinforced his ties with Treasury agents and other federal officeholders including sympathetic military men, whom he had placed while secretary of the Treasury and who still retained positions of authority in the South. His letters to Sumner and to Stanton during the trip also confirm his political position. Given the eminently political person that he was, given his inordinate ambition and his sense of political organization, Chase certainly saw the benefit of black suffrage to combat the masses of white Southerners whom he knew were over-

---

49. Chase to Johnson, May 12, 17, 1865 (Johnson Papers, L.C.).
50. Brooks D. Simpson et al., eds. *Advice After Appomattox: Letters to Andrew Johnson, 1865–1866: Special Volume No. 1 of the Papers of Andrew Johnson* (Knoxville, 1987), 16. For a discussion of the letters, see James E. Sefton, ed., "Chief Justice Chase as an Advisor on Presidential Reconstruction," *Civil War History* 13 (Sept. 1967): 242–64.

whelmingly supportive of the Democratic party and especially its orthodox peace wing.

Chase had seen firsthand the destruction of the Southern economy, the disruption of communication, and the collapse of civil authority in much of the region. Poverty and near poverty were evident in the cities and towns except in those population centers like New Orleans which had largely escaped the direct impact of the fighting and had been under Federal control for the past three years. The Union army was all that kept a semblance of order in the Southern states and it was stretched painfully thin. Yet Chase was supremely confident that a combination of black suffrage and the minority of loyal Unionists could provide the basis for a permanent settlement. With the temporary assistance of the military to maintain order these two groups could build a permanent base for a peaceful South reconstructed on the principles of equal rights for all.

Chase carried these cherished ideas to Washington when he returned to his home for the December term of the court. Johnson's Reconstruction program had been in force since midsummer and since then the chief justice had become highly critical of the president's policy which omitted black suffrage and undercut the minority of loyal whites in the Southern states.

At the same time Southern intransigence and the president's willingness to accommodate the former rebels led to a dramatic and unprecedented confrontation between the legislative branch, dominated by moderate and radical Republicans, and the executive. Congress was willing to impose on the South a much more stringent plan of Reconstruction than the president desired and the Supreme Court would inevitably be called upon to take an important part in this struggle. Chase at first relished this role, though in the long run his actions would result in a loss of political stature and criticism from his friends in Congress.

During these tumultuous times Chase found the business of the court a tedious exercise that required the review of hundreds of pages of trial transcripts and the search for precedents in civil cases involving fine distinctions in law. For many years he had devoted himself to politics and to administration and had largely abandoned his law practice. Moreover, he quickly discovered that as chief justice, he was only the first among equals and even in this capacity his only significant perquisite was in the assignment of cases for opinion. Used to getting his own way and immensely self-assured when he had made up his mind on any given point, Chase found himself politely but firmly thwarted by his brethren on the court, even by those who agreed with his opinions in general but found room for making distinctions of their own.[51]

Chase's years on the Supreme Court were significant ones for the future of the Union. With the Civil War over the court would play an integral role in national Reconstruction as it ruled on issues ranging from the nature of federalism to the constitutionality of greenbacks. As chief justice, however, Chase was far more interested in political affairs and in the shaping of public policy than he was in the technical aspects of jurisprudence. Yet he did find certain juridical issues of particular interest. With his background as Treasury secretary where one of his major responsibilities was enforcing the wartime naval blockade, Chase enthusiastically wrote the opinions in several important admiralty cases. He reversed a long-held American argument invoked during the Napoleonic Wars that neutral ships carried neutral goods wherever bound and approved the continuous voyage doctrine known as the Rule of 1756.

But the admiralty cases in which Chase took a personal interest were of far lesser importance than cases arising out of wartime infringement of civil rights and of postwar Reconstruction. In these cases Chase had not only an abiding interest but his own deeply felt position. He had long held with a tenacity akin to reverence the inviolability of habeas corpus. On the other hand, he was anxious to protect the civil rights of Southern blacks. Events would show that these two positions were at odds with each other. For in order to secure some measure of personal freedom from a community that held the blacks in complete contempt, adjudication in Southern courts by Southern judges of acts against former slaves had to be circumvented. Congress recognized this problem and created the Freedmen's Bureau which, among other things, set up tribunals that decided upon cases of infringement of civil rights.

The first of the civil rights cases, *Ex parte Milligan*, concerned a citizen of Indiana who had been tried and convicted of offenses against army officers by a military court-martial in 1864. The arrest of Milligan and other peace Democrats in Indiana and their subsequent trial was held under the auspices of Lincoln's suspension of the writ of habeas corpus for persons who were obstructing the war effort. The case that came to the Supreme Court involved the constitutionality of judicial procedures that were determined by agencies other than the courts. Thus, it brought into question the jurisdiction of the agents of the Freedmen's Bureau in determining questions of

---

51. Journal entries for Mar. 26, 31, 1870. Chase's tenure on the Supreme Court is discussed in detail in Charles Fairman, *Reconstruction and Reunion: 1864–88, Part One*, v. 6 of Paul A. Freund, gen. ed., *The Oliver Wendell Holmes Devise History of the Supreme Court of the United States* (New York, 1971).

black or white citizens' rights. Although the case seemed to threaten congressional Reconstruction, Chase sided with the majority in throwing out Milligan's conviction. His concurring opinion did not advance his political popularity with his congressional friends.

Recoiling from the adverse criticism of his radical associates in Congress and from some of the influential metropolitan newspapers, Chase became more circumspect about his belief in the sanctity of habeas corpus. He was in the minority on the test oath cases which the court declared unconstitutional because of their retroactive features. In these cases the court denied Congress and the states the power to withhold from their citizens the right to perform a variety of functions, including voting, serving as a juror, and teaching, on the basis of a loyalty oath. He joined his colleagues in a unanimous opinion in *Ex parte McCardle* that dismissed a clear case of infringement of speech by a military court. In this instance Congress passed an act removing appellate jurisdictions from all cases arising from military Reconstruction. Chase and the court prudently decided not to challenge Congress on this issue.

In *Texas v. White*, a case decided at the same session of the court, Chase wrote a majority opinion that proclaimed the United States "an indestructible Union, composed of indestructible States."[52] This decision protected states' rights within a federal union which rejected the concept of secession. Because the decision held that secession was illegal, it defined Reconstruction as a political process, leaving to the federal authorities the constitutional obligation to secure a republican form of government for the states.

In the Texas case the court also ruled that the new state constitutions had to conform to the conditions of emancipation and incorporate the freedmen as part of the people. At this point Chase was absolutely convinced that the black citizens in the South could protect their civil rights through universal suffrage and that the equal privileges and immunities clause of the Fourteenth Amendment would assist mightily in achieving this end. He was profoundly disappointed when a majority of his colleagues argued in the so-called Slaughter House cases that this clause did not overturn or circumvent the police powers of the states. As a consequence whites in the South, under various pretexts, could deprive black citizens of their vote.[53]

As chief justice, Chase also had to rule on a number of wartime financial measures he had instituted as secretary of the Treasury. In the case dealing with the legitimacy of greenbacks, *Hepburn v.*

---

52. *Texas v. White*, 7 Wall. 700 (1869), quotation p. 725.
53. Fairman, *Reconstruction and Reunion*, 1360; Blue, *Chase*, 306.

Griswold, Chase was able to reassert his underlying belief in a sound currency with a solid specie base. The Legal Tender Act of 1862, under which greenback notes were issued and which he had reluctantly supported during the war, he now ruled could not be used for the monetary settlement of contracts entered into prior to the passage of the act. Chase wrote the majority opinion for five of the eight justices who agreed with him. His reassertion of Jacksonian monetary theory, however, ignored the currency and credit demands of the emerging industrial state.[54]

The Hepburn decision in the long run would not stand. Two new Grant appointees to the court voted with the majority against Chase to hear appeals on the decision. Chase initially won what became a bitter fight when the appellants withdrew their appeals; but he would ultimately lose when on January 15, 1872, the court reversed the *Hepburn* ruling in the *Legal Tender Cases.* "It is I think a sad day," he wrote in his diary, "for the [country] & for the cause of constitutional government. . . . The only thing I regret in connexion with my administration of the Finances is that I ever expressed even a qualified opinion that the making the United States notes a legal tender was necessary."[55]

If Chase regretted his support of a paper currency, he held a more moderate view on the establishment of the national banking system. In *Veazie Bank v. Fenno,* he wrote the majority opinion sustaining a confiscatory tax on state banknotes, thus protecting the National Banking system from state bank competition in the areas of currency and discount rates.

Far from being cowed by Congress, the Chase court in the space of eight years took a very positive stand on its interpretation of the Constitution. In eight cases it invalidated acts of Congress.[56] Previously, since the establishment of the government in 1789, only two acts of Congress had been overturned by judicial review. This was no craven court. Unfortunately the diaries do not reflect in any depth Chase's judicial career. But his correspondence is quite full and illuminating on certain important cases, on his interaction with his colleagues on the court, and on his approach to Reconstruction.

Throughout his tenure on the court, Chase continued to aspire to the presidency. His chances in 1868 were scuttled, however, when

---

54. "Substance of remarks of the Chief Justice and Mr. Justice Nelson," [Apr. 1870], and copy of dissenting opinion to order for hearing Legal Tender cases, filed Apr. 19, 1870 (Chase Papers, Hist. Soc. of Pa.).

55. Entry for Jan. 15, 1872.

56. This is the figure used by Fairman. Another student of the subject, David F. Hughes, argues that the Chase court overturned congressional action in as many as eleven cases. Fairman, *Reconstruction and Reunion,* 1426–36; David F. Hughes, "Salmon P. Chase: Chief Justice," *Vanderbilt Law Review* 18 (Mar. 1965): 596-97.

he acted as presiding officer in the impeachment trial of President Johnson. In seeking to make the trial a judicial proceeding rather than a political event, Chase clashed frequently with the House managers over evidence and over the nature of his own powers. It became clear during the course of the trial that he disapproved of the proceedings and was deeply concerned not only over the future of the Constitutional distribution of powers, but also at the prospect of his political enemy Ben Wade, president pro tem of the Senate, becoming president should Johnson be removed. Chase came under heavy criticism from congressional radicals, many of whom had been close friends and supporters.

The immense popularity of Ulysses S. Grant well before the party's convention also frustrated Chase's hopes for the Republican nomination in 1868. But his overriding ambition for the presidency—that "maggot in the brain," as Lincoln had characterized it—led Chase to seek the Democratic nomination.[57] His correspondence during the summer of 1868 gives a wealth of interesting information about his campaign for the support of the Democrats. This desperate gamble left Chase open to the charge of hypocrisy and blatant opportunism by embracing political foes who stood for almost everything Chase had opposed during his political life.

The diaries that Chase kept after he suffered a stroke in the summer of 1870 are quite explicit in describing his decline in health and the various remedies he sought to improve his physical condition. As such they chart the rapid decay of a once vigorous mind and body. In keeping with his lifelong habit of self-delusion he refused to admit even to himself that his vital powers were becoming impaired. Almost to the very end of his life, with his considerable loss of weight and other ominous signs of critical disease, Chase continued to function on the court and to calculate his chances for a presidential nomination. He died from a final, fatal stroke in May 1873.

The diaries of Salmon P. Chase contained in this volume, and his correspondence to be published in subsequent volumes, provide unique insight into the life and times of an extraordinary figure in American history. His life embodied the ethos of moral reform in antebellum America as he thrust himself into the center of politics. Indeed, no one exemplifies better than he the coming together of altruism and pragmatic politics that marked his generation's struggles over slavery and its aftermath. Together, they transformed the nation.

57. John Bigelow, *Retrospections of an Active Life* (New York, 1909), 2:110.

The Journals

GENERAL DESCRIPTION OF THE EDITION

*P*APERS associated with Salmon P. Chase are located in over eighty libraries, historical societies, and document repositories in the United States. Two major collections predominate, the Chase Papers in the Manuscript Division of the Library of Congress, with an estimated 12,500 items, and the somewhat smaller but comparable collection at the Historical Society of Pennsylvania. Between them, those two groups of papers contain most of Chase's surviving private papers, including incoming and outgoing correspondence, letterbooks and letterpress copies, journals, memorandum books, scrapbooks, legal and financial papers, some speeches and pamphlets, and miscellaneous other items. If one were to draw together from their various record groups all of the documents in the National Archives associated with Chase as a U.S. senator, as chief justice of the U.S. Supreme Court, and especially as secretary of the Treasury, that collection would also include thousands of items. Other institutions' holdings are of a considerably more modest scale, but Chase's papers may be found in many of the important collections of manuscripts relating to America in the middle nineteenth century.

Those papers which the editors considered to be of greatest interest and use to researchers, approximately 14,500 items, appear in facsimile form in a selective microfilm edition of Chase's papers (University Publications of America, Inc., 1987). The present edition is intended to make an even more select group of the papers widely available in book form, clearly transcribed and supported by annotation. The first volume of the edition contains all of Chase's journals, including memoranda that took the form of journal entries but were not full diaries. Subsequent volumes will contain selected letters and other papers in chronological order.

The Journals

CHASE'S JOURNALS

Chase's surviving journals span, with gaps, the period 1829–72, from a time when he was not quite twenty-one until less than five months before his death. He was, in many respects, an imperfect diarist. Although a careful and methodical person, he did not create one seamless progression of entries day after day, year after year through his adult life. There are lapses within and between his journals. For Chase, the keeping of a diary could not always take precedence over other affairs. "I have neglected to write not because I have had nothing to record," he noted after one lapse of several months, "but because I thought I could not spare the time required."[1]

Through the years his journals took various forms. Some are notebooks about eight by ten inches in size. At least four times Chase purchased small pocket diaries, which assigned a fixed amount of space on a page for each day's entry. During the Civil War, he kept rough journals in his own hand but had his clerks recopy them in elegant copperplate handwriting. At times he made journal entries on sheets of paper folded into little makeshift pocket notebooks. He did not always make a strict distinction between journals and general memorandum books: volumes primarily devoted to diary entries might also have cash accounts, addresses, or miscellaneous notes at the front or rear, while an entry resembling those in his journals can be found in what would otherwise be considered a memorandum book.[2]

Chase did not place equal value on every record that took the general form of a daily journal. In the earliest of his surviving journals, which the editors call Journal I, he left off after the entry for July 3, 1843, and did not resume until April 22, 1849. He did make journal entries elsewhere covering part of the gap, most notably in the volume reproduced here as Journal IV, but when he returned to the first journal in 1849 he wrote: "Near six years have passed since I last wrote in this book—six eventful years— Some mema. of events &c have been written in another volume but they are few and imperfect."[3] For him there was a difference between what he did in the one volume and what he did in the other.

In a few instances Chase made different entries, in separate journals, describing the same day. In what we have labeled Journals XV

---

1. Entry for Mar. 1, 1831.
2. As in the case of the entry for Mar. 6, 1849.
3. Entry for Apr. 22, 1849.

and XVI, for example, he left two descriptions of April 14, 1865. The briefer entry in Journal XV, a pocket diary, includes prosaic notations of seeds sent to various people and breaks off at the point where Chase learned that Abraham Lincoln had been shot at Ford's Theatre. It is likely the earlier of the two entries. In Journal XVI, where he could devote unlimited space to an entry, Chase gave a descriptive account that carried the narrative beyond the night of the fourteenth.

As the entries for April 14, 1865, demonstrate, it is not always clear just when Chase composed a given entry. Sometimes he seems to have kept up his journals during the evenings of the days they described, in the classic manner of a methodical diarist. On occasion, however, he mentioned bringing his journal up to date, or used a single entry to describe several days' activities. He made some entries well after the events they describe. In some cases he had memoranda to assist his memory. He may have written other entries long after the fact without leaving any clues.

For all his idiosyncracies as a diarist, Chase persisted, relentless in his own way, coming back after lapses and never quitting for good. "I have again renewed my former practice," he wrote upon resuming his journal after a lapse, "because I think it so useful as to warrant the abstraction of a few moments from other occupations, to be devoted to this."[4] After the death of his first wife he noted that "I have now no wife to whom I can narrate any incident that concerns or interests me."[5] His journal may have provided one means for such a narration of events, but Chase rarely confided his innermost feelings to his diary. Taken as a whole, his journals were less his confidant than a workaday record of events to which he might refer. It is perhaps significant in that regard that he almost always used the term "journal" to characterize his entries. Twice he used the dry expression "memoranda" ("mema."). Only once did he call his own daily record a "diary."[6]

PROVENANCE OF THE JOURNALS

Chase was a systematic individual who saved a great many of what he considered to be his most important papers. At least once, during the winter of 1868–69, he made "a careful overhauling of all his

---

4. Entry for Mar. 1, 1831.
5. Entry for Dec. 25, 1835.
6. Entries for Apr. 22, 1849, May 25, 1857, Jan. 3, 1872.

letters and papers," destroying "many." There is no evidence, however, that he destroyed any of his journals.[7]

Not long before Chase's death in May 1873, a separation occurred within his papers that ultimately led to the existence of the two major collections at the Library of Congress and the Historical Society of Pennsylvania. Early in 1873, Chase agreed to have Robert B. Warden, an old associate, begin a biography and turned some papers over to him. Following Chase's death, his daughter Kate attempted unsuccessfully to block publication of Warden's book and sponsored Chase's friend and former secretary, Jacob W. Schuckers, to begin work on another biography. She and Schuckers attempted to regain possession of the papers in Warden's hands and to locate letters that Chase had written to some of his associates. Both biographies were published in 1874.[8]

Each party had control of some of Chase's journals. Warden claimed that Schuckers gained unauthorized access to a trunk of Chase's papers placed by Warden in a Washington, D.C., vault. Warned in advance of Schuckers's intentions, Warden removed from the trunk what he called "the most important diaries and letterbooks."[9] In the 1890s, historian Albert Bushnell Hart recovered much of Warden's collection of Chase journals from the daughter of Edward Stowe Hamlin, an old friend of Chase who had acquired seventeen manuscript volumes, including journals, letterbooks, and memorandum books. From the son of Chase's nephew James Ralston Skinner, Hart got another item from Warden's batch, a journal covering part of 1862 (called here Journal X). By paying accrued storage fees, Hart and fellow historian James Ford Rhodes also secured the trunks of Chase's papers which Warden had never reclaimed at the safe deposit company in Washington.[10]

Hart's collection of Chase papers went to the Massachusetts Historical Society in 1899, then was transferred to the Library of Congress in 1902, where it became the nucleus of the Chase collection in the Division of Manuscripts. In 1900 the collection contained, in

---

7. David Demarest Lloyd, "The Home-Life of Salmon Portland Chase," *The Atlantic Monthly* 32 (Nov. 1873): 528; Jacob W. Schuckers to John H. Oberly, June 10, 1882, portions quoted in "Garfield and Rosecrans," *New York Times*, June 12, 1882.

8. See Frederick Blue, "Kate's Paper Chase: The Race to Publish the First Biography of Salmon P. Chase," *The Old Northwest* 8 (1982–83): 353–63, and the sources cited there.

9. Warden, *Chase*, 401–2.

10. Remarks by Albert Bushnell Hart, in *Proceedings of the Massachusetts Historical Society*, 2nd ser., 13 (1899–1900): 375–78; research materials and correspondence related to Hart's preparation of his biography of Chase, Harvard University Archives. Warden's references mention one trunk of papers in the vault; Hart indicated that two trunks were recovered.

addition to thousands of other manuscripts, five volumes of diaries, eight volumes of miscellaneous memoranda, and eight letterbooks.[11] The five diaries were probably what are called here Journals I, IV, VIII, X, XIII, and XIV. (Journals VIII and XIII are treated here as separate journals, though they are in the same manuscript volume and were surely counted as one diary in 1900). Journal XVIII, covering 1870, must have been a later acquisition by the Library of Congress, as the description in 1900 mentioned five journals, none from later than 1864. Journals V, VI, and XI are now also at the Library of Congress, but if they were in the collection in 1900 they would have been described as memoranda, not diaries. Their exact provenance—whether they were in the trunks, among the items Hart acquired from Hamlin's daughter, or later additions to the L.C. collection—is unknown.

For his biography, Jacob Schuckers had access to papers which Chase had not turned over to Warden, anything he may have removed from Warden's trunk, and items which he and Kate Chase Sprague solicited from her father's old associates. Schuckers seems to have retained these papers after completion of his biography. He transferred some portion of them, probably quite substantial in quantity since it became the core of the Pennsylvania collection, to Brinton Coxe of Philadelphia. Before 1909 those papers came into the possession of the Historical Society of Pennsylvania, of which Coxe had been president.[12] Specific information about the collection at the time of its acquisition by the historical society is lacking, but it seems likely that the journals presently in that collection— designated here Journals III, XII, XVI, XVII, and XIX—came from Schuckers by way of Coxe.

Ironically, another part of the Schuckers collection later joined the papers at the Library of Congress—thus undoing in small part the splitting of Chase's manuscripts at the time of his death. In 1922 the L.C. purchased a lot of about five hundred items, including some of Chase's papers and some of Schuckers's own. It is unclear whether the lot included any of the journals now in the Library of Congress but not necessarily in the collection in 1900 (Journals V, VI, XI, and XVIII).[13]

---

11. "Fifth Annual Report of the Historical Manuscripts Commission," *Annual Report of the American Historical Association for the Year 1900* (Washington, D.C., 1901), 1:590–93; *Proceedings of the Massachusetts Historical Society*, 2nd ser., 18 (1903–4): 336.

12. Ellis Paxton Oberholtzer, "A Midnight Conference: And Other Passages from the Papers of Secretary Salmon P. Chase," *Scribner's Magazine* 45 (Feb. 1909): 144–50; proceedings in memory of Brinton Coxe, *Pennsylvania Magazine of History and Biography* 16 (1892): v–xxvii.

13. Collection description, Nov. 22, 1922, Chase Papers case file, Division of Manuscripts, L.C.; *American Historical Review* 28 (1923): 399, 622.

Two Chase journals from 1857 and 1865 (Journals VII and XV) are in the collections of the New Hampshire Historical Society. They were purchased from one F. J. Wilder in 1923. Their history prior to that year is unknown.[14] Schuckers and Warden did not refer to either of these diaries in their biographies of Chase.

Two other journals included in this volume, one of them primarily a memoir devoted to Chase's first wife, are now known only through extracts published in 1874 (see descriptions of Journals II and IX, below).

DESCRIPTION OF THE JOURNALS

Chase's journals are printed in this volume in chronological order. In several cases this means that text from one journal must be split, with text from another journal intervening. Chase had no uniform system for organizing or identifying all the documents printed here, some of which he considered to be memoranda or notes. To provide a uniform means of identifying each journal, the editors have assigned them roman numerals, I through XIX. A description of each journal appears below. Elsewhere in this volume the journals are all identified simply by their roman-numeral labels.

Each journal's description notes the repository where the original document may be found, as well as the location of a facsimile in the microfilm edition of the *Chase Papers*. For example, "*micro* 40:0021" means reel 40, frame 21, of the microfilm edition.

In general terms, the editors have included in this volume all entries which describe Chase's activities at particular times. Miscellaneous memoranda sometimes found in the same manuscript volumes as the journals, such as lists of addresses, cash accounts, or general notes, have been omitted. The description of each journal indicates whether any such general memoranda have been excluded from the transcription of a journal in this volume. Footnotes point out spots where entries within a journal have been rearranged for chronological order, and discuss editorial details not covered by the descriptions of the journals.

Journal I

1829–54 (with gaps), in Chase's hand (Chase Papers, L.C.; *micro* 40:0021). In this journal, especially in its earlier portions, Chase made some marginal headings to point out subjects mentioned within

14. Manuscript catalogue, New Hampshire Historical Society.

the entries. In the transcription of the journal below, Chase's marginal headings are reported in footnotes to avoid interruption of the text. Other marginalia on the journal's early pages, including check marks and references to page numbers in Robert B. Warden's 1874 biography of Chase, were probably left by Albert Bushnell Hart during a "word for word" comparison of the journal with Warden's book during the 1890s.[15] The note "W 146," for example, is in the margin alongside the journal's first entry, part of which is printed on page 146 of Warden's biography. These checkmarks and other marginalia originating after Chase's death have not been included in the transcription of the journal or reported in the notes.

What Chase probably considered the last "journal" entry in the manuscript volume describes May 20, 1850. Beginning with the next page, Chase assigned one page to each of the years 1830–55. Most of those pages are blank except for the year, written at the top in Chase's hand. Chase probably thought of the text in this section as general memoranda. What information he did record there is, however, similar in form to his journal entries, and the editors have treated them as part of the journal. Each of those entries is printed in this volume in its appropriate chronological spot. Within the actual body of the journal, a few entries seem more like Chase's memorandum-book entries (recording correspondence, for example) than journal entries. Since these entries are few in number, and since Chase himself incorporated them into the body of his journal rather than segregating them to another location, the editors have included them here as part of Journal I.

Journal II

[1835], printed in Warden, *Chase*, 238–41, 252, 256–63 (*micro* 40:0353). So far as the editors can determine, this "journal" survives only in the form of extracts included in Warden's biography. The original was among papers which Chase lent Warden, and was in Warden's possession at the time of Chase's death. "It is in appearance," Warden noted, "a mere memorandum-book, leather covered. The entries are partly in pencil and partly in ink."[16]

---

15. *Proceedings of the Massachusetts Historical Society*, 2nd ser., 13 (1899–1900): 377.
16. Warden, *Chase*, 237. Warden's references to Chase's different journals are so vague that without Journal I at hand it is difficult to distinguish Warden's Journal II extracts from those he made from Journal I. Warden's handling of the entries confused Thomas Graham Belden and Marva Robins Belden on this point, and led them to conclude also that Journal II was the "locked diary" to which Warden attached great importance. In fact the "locked diary" was Journal X. Belden and Belden, *So Fell the Angels* (Boston, 1956), 270–71.

Warden interspersed the extracts with other text. Apparently the manuscript volume was a compilation of information centering on the death of Chase's first wife, Catharine Garniss Chase ("Kitty"), in 1835. Only a small part of what Warden published consists of true journal entries. The first extracts contain Chase's recollection of his acquaintance with Catharine Garniss in the early 1830s and the beginning of their courtship. This memoir was probably written after her death. If it included any information about the couple's engagement or wedding, Warden silently omitted it, for the extracts jump from approximately April 1833 to November 14, 1835, two days before Catharine gave birth to Chase's first child (a daughter who died in 1840).

Beginning at that point, the extracts comprise an account of Catharine Chase's last days and her death on December 1, 1835. Chase was only present for part of this time, for on November 21, believing that his wife's condition was less serious than it proved to be, he departed on a business trip to Philadelphia. The extracts from mid-November until his departure, although they have the form of dated entries in Warden's book, appear to be Chase's recollection of events rather than contemporaneous records made on a daily basis. His description of his boat journey on November 21–22, however, very likely came from journal entries actually made on those days. Warden noted that one of the travel entries "was made before the entries rehearsing the story of the wife's illness and the birth of the child," but he gave no other explanation.[17] From November 22 through December 1, the extracts contain detailed daily entries recounting Catharine's condition and medical treatments. Since Chase was gone during that period, he must have made this record after his return, basing it on information gathered from others. The last of Warden's extracts describe Chase's return to Cincinnati shortly after Catharine's death.

Most of this "journal," then, consists not of diary entries but of Chase's reconstructions and recollections of past events. The two entries describing his boat trip were likely written first, since he probably composed them on November 21–22. The journal's final paragraph and the detail of the entries describing Catharine's final days imply that Chase wrote that portion of the document relatively soon after Catharine's death. His recollections of their courtship may date from that period also, or possibly from some later time.

Warden did not distinguish clearly between these different categories of text, nor did he describe how they were arranged within the original manuscript volume. His arrangement of the extracts in

---

17. Warden, *Chase*, 259.

his book, in chronological order according to the events they describe, probably does not reflect their order in the original. He did make it clear that he was printing only extracts of the original, although he did not indicate how much he omitted. In three places he stated that he was leaving text out for reasons of "delicacy."[18] In other places Warden used ellipsis points without explanation, apparently to show omissions. He probably omitted other text without noting the exclusion. It is unlikely, for example, that the original, recounting as it did the early phase of Chase's courtship of Catharine Garniss, contained nothing about their engagement and marriage.

Whether one calls it a diary or a memoir, Warden's use of this document—and those portions of Journal I recording Chase's grief after Catharine's death—was a sensitive issue. Critics of Warden's biography, including in particular Kate Chase Sprague, were unhappy with his extensive use of extracts from Chase's journals and letters, especially those relating to Chase's private life. Warden referred to his treatment of Chase's first marriage as "the most delicate and difficult undertaking" of his biography.[19]

Although not all of the extracts take the form of journal entries, and although Chase obviously wrote much of the document after the events it depicts, the editors' transcription of Journal II includes all of Warden's extracts that appear to have come from the now-lost manuscript volume. In the absence of the original, one cannot say with confidence what portions of it qualify as a "journal" in a strict sense. After all, in other journals Chase wrote entries sometime after the events they describe. The fact that Chase put recollections of his first wife into a manuscript volume which already contained journal entries is itself significant.

The text from Journal II is transcribed here in the order in which Warden's extracts appear, although, as noted above, that arrangement (chronological by events) is probably not the order in which Chase wrote the text. The memoir of Chase's courtship of Catharine Garniss actually includes part of the early 1830s, a period encompassed by Journal I. Due to the special nature of the document, however, Journal II is presented here as a single unbroken block

---

18. Ibid., 252, 257, 260. In our transcription of Journal II in this volume, omissions noted by Warden are identified by footnotes.

19. Ibid., 237. Warden's defense against his critics was published as *An Appeal by the Author of the "Best Abused Book of the Period"* (Washington, 1876). Blue, "Kate's Paper Chase," 356–57, speculates that Kate was jealous of the depth of Chase's feeling for Catharine Garniss and feared that Chase loved his first wife more than he did Kate's mother (his second wife). It seems as likely that Kate's sensitivity over Warden's biography stemmed from a general reluctance to have the emotional, private side of her father's life revealed (which correlates with Warden's statements).

of text. The transcription does not include Warden's commentary between extracts, nor indicate the breaks between his extracts unless Warden's notice of an omission or some other point requires an explanatory note. The double quotation marks used in Warden's book to set off the extracts, and at the beginning of each paragraph within them, are not reproduced here. Warden's version used single quotation marks to set off direct quotations within the extracts; these have been rendered here as double quotation marks. When an extract includes the date of the entry, the date is transcribed as it appears in Warden's book. If Warden indicated the date of an entry in his text, but did not include it in the extract itself, we have enclosed the date in square brackets.

There are apparent errors in Warden's rendition of Chase's entries: for example, a repetition of the word *the* at one spot; a misspelling of *proceed;* and instances in which Warden gave an entry either the wrong day of the week or the wrong calendar date. Although these mistakes are most likely a result of the haste in which Warden's biography was written and printed, they could reflect errors in the original. The text is given here as it appears in Warden's book, and any discrepancies within entries' dates are pointed out in the notes.

Journal III

December 1843–January 1844, September–December 1863, July–November 1864, in Chase's hand, portions in a clerk's hand with additions and changes by Chase (Chase Papers, Hist. Soc. of Pa.; *micro* 42:0358). A holograph title page reads: "Miscellaneous Journal / being Memoranda of incidents at / irregular dates—taken from / Note books or Memory." The first two pages of the manuscript contain memoranda which are not printed in this volume. On the first page is a list, in a clerk's hand, of "Members of Virginia Constitutional Convention. Alexandria, Feb. Mar. and Apr. 1864," with some notations by Chase. The second page has estimates, from the commissioner of internal revenue, of revenues for the fiscal year ending June 30, 1865. This page is also in a clerk's hand, with a few words of the title supplied by Chase. The first page of the journal proper, containing entries for 1863, has Chase's heading, "Irregular Dates—copied from Small Memm Book." It is not certain whether this title pertains only to the entries on that page, or to subsequent pages as well.

The entries are not in chronological order in the manuscript, although some sequences of entries are in order. All but a few of the journal's entries relate to 1863 and 1864. Following the entries for those years there are twenty-five blank pages, then a page containing four brief entries relating to late 1843 and the beginning of 1844. Chase gave no explanation for the presence of these four entries. It seems likely that he wrote them during the 1860s, the period to which everything else in the manuscript volume relates. Perhaps old clippings from the Cincinnati *Morning Herald,* which he cited in two of the entries, reminded him of his activities in December 1843 and January 1844.

Following the entries for the 1840s are over 150 more blank pages. Scattered among the blank pages are miscellaneous memoranda of 1863–66, including notes on the "Nature & consequences of Rebellion, 1866." These memoranda are in Chase's handwriting. They do not include journal entries and so have not been included in the transcription of Journal III.

The entries for August 10 through September 20, 1864, are in the hand of an unidentified clerk. From appearances the amanuensis was copying Chase's memoranda and was not adept at reading Chase's handwriting. Chase edited the copyist's work, filling in the many blank spaces (apparently left when the clerk could not decipher Chase's writing), making other insertions, and correcting the clerk's spellings. Chase's emendations of the clerk's text are so numerous, including sometimes writing over just part of a word, that the editors have not attempted to describe them in footnotes. The text as transcribed here is in its final form after Chase's corrections and changes. Readers wishing to see the details of what the clerk wrote and how it was altered by Chase should consult the original or a microfilm copy.

It is impossible to establish how many distinct sources—memorandum books, loose notes, memory—Chase drew on for the entries in this manuscript volume. For example, there are two entries, in different parts of the journal, for each of the dates September 16, 17, 18, and October 5, 1863, and four separate entries pertaining to October 1, 1863. There are clues that many of the entries were recorded long after the events they describe, although they may have been written from notes made at the time. In three instances, an entry or sequence of entries jumps to a page farther along in the manuscript. Presuming that in each of those cases the text on the intervening pages was already in place (thus forcing the jump to a new page), internal evidence suggests that the 1863–64 entries may have been recorded in the journal in the following order: *first,* entries for September 14–October 5, 1863, in scrambled order (p. 3 of the original); *second,* entries for October 1–5, 1863 (p. 4); *third,* entries for July 13–September 20, 1864 (pp. 5–24); *fourth,* an addition to the entry for August 23, 1864 (p. 25); *fifth,* the entry for September 23, 1863 (pp. 4, 26–29); *sixth*, entries for November 26–28, 1864 (p. 30); *seventh*, entries for September 21–November 11, 1864 (pp. 31–33); *eighth*, entries for September–December 1863 (pp. 29, 37). This ordering of entries indicates that much of the text pertaining to Chase's activities in 1863 was almost certainly put into the journal during, or even after, 1864. Placement of the 1864 entries, along with the clerk's apparent copying from Chase's notes for part of that year, shows that at least some of the entries for 1864, too, were entered in the journal sometime after the events they described. Almost certainly, none of the elements making up Journal III was a contemporaneous "diary." All of the entries are probably at least one step removed from any written records which Chase made on or near the dates he described.

Journal III contains entries for seven days in September 1863 for which there are also entries in Journal XIII, a polished journal in the handwriting of one of Chase's clerks. A few of Journal III's entries from October 1863 were printed in David Herbert Donald, ed., *Inside Lincoln's Cabinet: The Civil War Diaries of Salmon P. Chase* (New York, 1954), but others from that year were not. Donald included most of the journal's entries for 1864, but omitted some entries and parts of entries, showing the omissions with ellipses.

Journal IV

1845–59 (with gaps), in Chase's hand (Chase Papers, L.C.; *micro* 40:0542). This manuscript displays considerable mixing of journal entries and other material within a single set of covers. It contains miscellaneous memoranda written as late as March 1860, but the latest journal entries are from September 1859. Following the entry for March 25, 1856, are copies of nine letters, not in chronological order, from 1856–59. Chase placed explanatory notes before or after some of the letters. One letter is not in Chase's handwriting, and it is the only text in the manuscript volume not in his script. The editors have omitted all of these copies of letters from the journal text reproduced in this volume. In the same section of the original text, however, is an account of Chase's travels through Ohio in the election campaign of 1857. It is included here as part of Journal IV. Following the copies of letters in the original volume, one finds entries pertaining to the death of Chase's sister Alice in February 1859 and his campaign stumping in September of that year. Those entries are included in the transcription of the journal. Following the September 1859 entries are a number of miscellaneous entries from 1853–60. Some of these are records one would expect to find in a memorandum or commonplace book, not a diary, and they are not included in this volume. Entries from this miscellaneous group which describe Chase's activities on specific dates, on the other hand, are printed here (in their proper chronological places) as part of Journal IV.

Journal V

March 6, 1849, in Chase's hand (Chase Papers, L.C.; *micro* 41:0014). This "journal" consists of a single entry, describing Chase's admission to the Senate, within a memorandum book. The remainder of the manuscript volume contains miscellaneous information, not in the form of diary entries. Only the one entry is printed here as Journal V.

Journal VI

April–June 1853, in Chase's hand (Chase Papers, L.C.; *micro* 41:0466). These entries from the spring of 1853 are not from a bound journal. Instead, they are on sheets which Chase labeled "Personal Memoranda," and which also included Chase's recollections of his admission to the bar in Washington and anecdotal information about John Randolph. The leaves on which all of these memoranda appear were made by folding a long sheet of writing paper. Only the dated entries describing Chase's activities in 1853 are printed here as Journal VI.

Journal VII

January–October 1857, in Chase's hand (New Hamp. Hist. Soc.; *micro* 41:0819). Chase kept this journal in a small "Daily Pocket Diary." He made some travel notes, lists of dates and places which have not been transcribed in this volume, in the margins of printed almanac and calendar pages at the front of the diary. He also used memorandum pages at the end of the journal for lists of names, quotations from Spenser's *Faerie Queene,* and miscellaneous notes. He recorded some financial data on pages ruled for cash accounts and bills payable. Those notes, memoranda, and accounts, like the travel notes, are not printed in this volume.

The diary has printed date headings, three to a page, intended for daily entries. The heading for each entry has the day of the week and the date within the month; a running head on each page identifies the month and year. For clarity, the date headings for Journal VII in the present volume have been regularized to include day of week, month, and date, except for a few instances (identified by footnotes) in which Chase altered the printed form.

The Journals

Journal VIII

December 1861–May 1862, in the handwriting of Homer G. Plantz, a Treasury clerk (Chase Papers, L.C.; *micro* 42:0001). This journal is within the same manuscript volume as Journal XIII, but since there is a chronological gap between them and they were recorded by different clerks, they are treated here as separate journals. Journal VIII occupies pp. 1–69 of the manuscript. Following the entry for May 1, 1862, this journal includes copies of a May 16 letter from Chase to Abraham Lincoln, three letters to his daughter Janet (Nettie) Chase of May 7, 8, and 11, and a "Narrative of Operations" dictated in June. These items are all in Plantz's hand.

Chase seems to have intended the letters and "Narrative" to stand in the place of a journal for part of the spring of 1862, and they are included here with Journal VIII. Chase's letters to his daughter Nettie, as recorded in this journal, are not in all details exact reproductions of other extant versions of those letters. Rather than use footnotes to describe all such differences, the editors will print the other versions of the letters to Nettie in a later volume with other correspondence from the period. Footnotes accompanying the transcription of Journal VIII do, however, indicate the general relationship between the versions of the letters found there and those found elsewhere. The three letters were printed in Jacob W. Schuckers, *Life and Public Services of Salmon Portland Chase*, 366–74.

Plantz put marginal headings alongside the entries for December 1861. These notations serve as finding aids, pointing out subjects discussed in the entries. It is not known whether Chase had anything to do with these marginal notes, which Plantz may have written on his own initiative. In the transcription of the journal, the marginal notations have been reported in footnotes.

Journal VIII, including the letters and the June "Narrative," is in Donald, ed., *Inside Lincoln's Cabinet*.

Journal IX

January 12, 1862, printed in Maunsell B. Field, *Memories of Many Men and of Some Women: Being Personal Recollections* . . . (New York, 1874), 267–69. Like Journal II, this single day's entry is known only in printed form. Maunsell B. Field, who was an assistant secretary of the Treasury beginning in 1863, did not explain in his *Memories* how he came by a pocket diary containing Chase's pencilled entries. Robert B. Warden implied that the diary quoted by Field was among papers which Chase had entrusted to Warden and was pilfered from a trunk Warden had placed in a bank vault. It is not clear from Warden's statement, however, whether he knew for certain that the specific journal used by Field had indeed been taken from the trunk.[20]

Field printed the entry for January 12, 1862, as an "extract," and did not indicate how much other text was in the journal. He did state at the end of the extract that "there is more upon the same subject in the book, but, unfortunately, it can not be deciphered with any certainty." It is not clear whether the extract even includes all of the January 12 entry as Field found it in the original. According to Field, "much of the writing" in the original "is wholly or partly obliterated," and he noted that he transcribed the extract "not without a great deal of difficulty."[21] Journal VIII, the only extant original journal from early 1862, has no entry for January 12, skipping from the eleventh to the thirteenth with no extra space between. In the absence of the original seen by Field, it is impossible to determine what relationship existed between it and Journal VIII.

The small capitals used to highlight all surnames in Field's book are not reproduced in the transcription. Double quotation marks are used in place of the single quotation marks which appear within Field's extract. Donald, ed., *Inside Lincoln's Cabinet,* printed this entry from Field's book.

Journal X

July–October 1862, in Homer G. Plantz's hand (Chase Papers, L.C.; *micro* 42:0176). Plantz apparently copied much or all of this journal from Chase's notes or drafts of entries. The entry for September 12, 1862, for example, refers to Chase's temporary loss of "the first draft of my Journal" covering the two previous days. Journal XI, which contains entries in Chase's hand corresponding to the latter portions of Journal X, is an example of the kind of draft from which Plantz probably worked. Chase may have given Plantz sections of his draft journal out of chronological sequence, for several entries in this diary were recorded out of order. Plantz made cross-reference notes giving the locations of the entries copied out of sequence. The entries have all been transcribed below in correct order by date, and footnotes identify those sections located out of sequence in the original. Plantz's cross-reference notes have not been reproduced. In the original, there are several hundred blank pages following the last page containing a journal entry.

---

20. Warden, *Chase,* 401–2.
21. Maunsell B. Field, *Memories of Many Men and of Some Women: Being Personal Recollections* . . . (New York, 1874), 267, 269.

The Journals

According to Robert B. Warden, this journal was the "locked diary" that showed him the "revelations" to be found in Chase's diaries.[22] This journal was printed in Donald, ed., *Inside Lincoln's Cabinet,* and also in the Sixth Report of the Historical Manuscripts Commission, v. 2 of the *Annual Report of the American Historical Association for the Year 1902* (Washington, D.C., 1903).

Journal XI

September–November 1862, in Chase's hand (Chase Papers, L.C.; *micro* 42:0257). These entries are on leaves, now loose, which may have been part of a pocket notebook. The manuscript includes some memoranda and notes which do not take the form of journal entries and have not been transcribed. The first page of the original contains illegible text, possibly including a couple of journal entries but too faint to be read. In the manuscript, entries for November 8–9 are out of chronological order and may have been written before some of the entries for October. The entry for October 5, judging from later entries which intervene between two sections of its text, may have been completed after the day which it describes. The journal has been transcribed below in correct chronological order.

From September 26 to October 12 this journal overlaps with Journal X (a polished journal in Homer Plantz's hand). For this period, Chase's handwritten entries in Journal XI evidently served as the basis for the entries in Journal X. Two notations which Plantz made in Chase's rough journal provide a direct connection between the two manuscripts (see Sept. 30 and Oct. 6, 1862, Journal XI, below).

Journal XII

January, July 1863, in Chase's hand (Chase Papers, Hist. Soc. of Pa.; *micro* 42:0391). These entries, describing two days in January and one in July, were made on loose sheets. The January entries are on a single large sheet folded to make four leaves for writing. The July entry is on a single leaf that may at one time have been part of a similar arrangement made by folding a large sheet. This is the only "journal" found by the editors for the period between the autumn of 1862 and the beginning of Journal XIII (a polished journal in a clerk's hand) in August 1863.

22. Warden, *Chase,* 772. For confirmation of Journal X as the "locked diary," see ibid., 437, 752. Journal X has the remnants of a lock.

The Journals   { lxvii }

Journal XIII

August–September 1863, in the handwriting of Jacob W. Schuckers, who during the Civil War was a clerk in the Treasury Department (Chase Papers, L.C.; *micro* 42:0038). This journal occupies pp. 70–115 of the same manuscript volume in which Journal VIII is found. Schuckers used marginal notations, similar to those used by Homer Plantz in Journal VIII, to point out subjects discussed in some of the entries in the early part of this journal. The editors have reported these marginal headings, as in the similar cases of Journals I and VIII, in footnotes. There are seven days in September 1863 for which entries exist both in this journal and in Journal III, which is in Chase's hand. Journal XIII is printed in Donald, ed., *Inside Lincoln's Cabinet.*

Journal XIV

June–July 1864, in Chase's hand (Chase Papers, L.C.; *micro* 42:0638). The flyleaf of this manuscript volume bears the notation, "Nettie R. Chase. Washington. D.C.," with the date March 7, 1862. There is no indication that Chase's younger daughter actually used the book. The first page, which has not been included in the transcription of this journal, has a list of names in Chase's hand from March 1864, apparently an invitation list. Also not printed here in Journal XIV are Chase's draft beginning of an opinion in the Supreme Court case *Ex parte Milligan,* which follows the journal entries, and memoranda from three pages at the end of the manuscript volume, separated from the journal entries by a number of blank pages. In the manuscript, an added blue pencil line runs in the margin alongside some of the journal's entries.

In the original, the entries for June 26 through July 6 come first. Then follows the entry for June 24 with Chase's note, "copied from a loose sheet." In the transcription of Journal XIV below, the June 24 entry appears in its correct chronological place.

This journal is included in Donald, ed., *Inside Lincoln's Cabinet.*

Journal XV

1865, in Chase's hand (New Hamp. Hist. Soc.; *micro* 42:0827). Chase kept this journal in a small pocket diary. In the original volume, printed date headings appear at the tops of the pages intended for diary entries, one date per page. These headings give the name of the month, the day of the week, the date, and the year. The editors have regularized the components of the date headings to the form:

The Journals

day of week, month and date. Footnotes identify any alteration by Chase of the printed date headings.

In the original volume, on pages with printed headings for memoranda and accounts, Chase put various reminders, some cash accounts, miscellaneous memoranda, and addresses. Those notations have been omitted from the transcription of Journal XV. For ten days covered by this journal there are also entries in Journal XVI or Journal XVII.

Journal XVI

April 1865–October 1868 (with gaps), in Chase's hand (Chase Papers, Hist. Soc. of Pa.; *micro* 42:0802). In the original of this journal, the entry for December 18, 1865, precedes the entries for December 10–12; and a continuation of the entry for July 21, 1866, jumps over the entry for July 22. In the transcription below, the December 18, 1865, entry has been placed in its correct chronological position and the July 21, 1866, entry is consolidated. The journal contains no entries for 1867. There are entries for two days in February 1868 (pertaining to Andrew Johnson's impeachment trial), then after many blank pages the journal resumes with entries from August and October 1868. For those months and also September, Chase assigned one page to each month and numbered the days of the month down the left side of the page. He made brief entries alongside the appropriate dates, but entered information for only thirteen days of August and October (none for September).

This journal overlaps with Journal XV for six days in April and May 1865. Donald, ed., *Inside Lincoln's Cabinet*, printed Journal XVI's entries through May 1, 1865, only.

Journal XVII

May–June 1865, in Chase's hand (Chase Papers, Hist. Soc. of Pa.; *micro* 42:0913). These entries are in a homemade notebook created by folding a large sheet. The manuscript also includes some addresses and notes of letters sent and received which have not been transcribed here. Entries in this journal describe events which are also discussed in Journal XV.

Journal XVIII

1870 (portions), in Chase's hand (Chase Papers, L.C.; *micro* 43:0319). Chase made his entries for 1870 in a pocket journal, the "Patent Self Closing Diary for 1870." The diary's pages have printed date headings, giving the day of the week, month and date, and year. This form has been followed in the transcription of the journal, with the omission of the year. Miscellaneous memoranda by Chase, some appearing inside the front cover and on the flyleaf, others on memorandum pages at the end of the pocket diary, are not transcribed here. However, on loose sheets placed in the back of the original there are journal entries for several days in July and December. In the case of two days during December, Chase used these entries on loose sheets as the basis for entries which he later made in the little volume. These entries from sheets now found at the end of the original are included in the transcription of Journal XVIII and are identified by footnotes. There is other text also, much of it illegible, on the folded sheets bearing the July and December entries at the back of the journal. Of the legible text on those sheets, only that taking the form of journal entries has been included here as part of Journal XVIII.

Journal XIX

1872, in Chase's hand (Chase Papers, Hist. Soc. of Pa.; *micro* 43:0621). This journal is in a pocket diary with printed date headings, one per page. The headings are in the form: day of week, month and date, year. The transcription's headings take the same form, omitting the year. Footnotes point out any alteration of the printed datelines by Chase. In this, as in other printed diaries used by Chase, there are pages intended for memoranda and cash accounts. Miscellaneous memoranda which Chase wrote on those pages include business accounts, addresses, biblical references, and quotations in English and French on temperance and moderation. These memoranda are not included in the transcription of Journal XIX.

A separate manuscript volume contains "Farm Notes" from the spring of 1872 which touch on some activities mentioned also in Journal XIX. Rough notes by Chase provided the basis for some, but apparently not all, of the "Farm Notes" entries. These memoranda were probably made by a foreman or manager at Edgewood (Chase's home in the District of Columbia). The "Farm Notes" are all concerned with crops planted in the garden and chores performed by workers around Edgewood. Although arranged by date, they are not really a journal of Chase's activity, and are not included in this volume.

ARRANGEMENT OF THE JOURNALS

The list below outlines the chronological sequence of Chase's journals as they appear in this volume. For simplicity, gaps within chronological segments are not shown. Journal IV, for example, has no entries for the last eight months of 1847, and none for any months of 1848 except January and November, but the segment is listed as February 1847–November 1848.

When two journals are listed on the same line (such as at September–October 1862), it means that some dates within the segment are covered by both journals.

Journal No.	
I	Jan. 1829–June 1835
II	Nov.–Dec. 1835
I	Dec. 1835–July 1843
III	Dec. 1843–Jan. 1844
IV	Mar. 1845
I	Aug. 1845
IV	Nov. 1845–Apr. 1846
I	Sept. 1846
IV	Feb. 1847–Nov. 1848
I	late 1848
IV	Jan. 1849
V	Mar. 1849
I	Apr. 1849–May 1850
IV	Aug.–Sept. 1851
I	Nov. 1851
IV	Dec. 1852–Jan. 1853
VI	Apr.–June 1853
IV	Aug. 1853
I	fall 1853–Mar. 1854
IV	Aug. 1854–Mar. 1855
VII	Jan.–Aug. 1857
IV	Aug. 1857
VII	Sept.–Oct. 1857
IV	Oct. 1857–Sept. 1859
VIII	Dec. 1861–Jan. 1862
IX	Jan. 1862
VIII	Mar.–May 1862
X	July–Aug. 1862
X, XI	Sept.–Oct. 1862
XI	Nov. 1862
XII	Jan., July 1863
XIII	Aug. 1863
III, XIII	Sept 1863
III	Oct.–Dec. 1863
XIV	June–July 1864
III	July–Nov. 1864
XV	Jan.–Mar. 1865
XV, XVI	Apr.–May 1865

The Journals

Journal No.	
XV, XVII	May–June 1865
XV	July–Dec. 1865
XVI	Dec. 1865–Oct. 1868
XVIII	1870
XIX	1872

Editorial Procedures

EDITORIAL METHOD

As CHASE himself recognized, his handwriting can present formidable challenges. "I hope you will not find it too hard work to decipher my hieroglyphics," he wrote to one correspondent, and he sent a manuscript to a collector with the warning: "I think it will puzzle anybody to decipher it, unless he has been trained . . . to the business." Historians have dubbed his writing "horrendous" and "ungodly."[1] At its best, Chase's penmanship does not deserve such condemnation. At its worst, as when he wrote very hurriedly or in a tiny script, perhaps no epithet is strong enough. The renderings of Chase's journals in this volume represent the editors' best effort to present the complete text of the original entries. This is not to say that words shown here as illegible will never be deciphered. They have simply defied the attempts of the present team of editors to read them. Other words which the editors have confidently rendered in these pages may turn out to be in error. At times reading Chase's hand is more an act of interpretation than a mechanical copying process.

The transcription of Chase's journals in this volume reports all spelling, capitalization, and punctuation as they appear in the original. Canceled text is omitted. Insertions are incorporated silently into the text and are not indicated by any symbol or special typeface. Readers interested in the details of alterations to the manuscripts will want to consult the original documents or microfilm copies. If a cancellation or insertion merits comment—such as an insertion apparently added sometime after the other text in an entry was written—a footnote conveys the necessary information. The full text of anything construed as a "journal" is transcribed. Any ellipsis

---

1. Chase to Thomas W. Conway, Aug. 28, 1865 (Chase Papers, Hist. Soc. of Pa.); Chase to Gordon L. Ford, Jan. 21, 1864 (Rare Books and Manuscripts Division, New York Public Lib.); Blue, *Chase*, x; G. S. Boritt, introduction to reprint edition of Hart, *Chase*, xix, xxii, 416.

points within the journals' text are from the original and do not represent an omission of text by this volume's editors.

Underlined words in the original are shown in italic type. Double underlining is shown by small capitals. If the editors are uncertain about a reading, they have enclosed the uncertain text or punctuation within square brackets ([ ]). Where a few letters could be made out but no plausible word could be found to fit, the word is indicated as illegible. Editors' messages within the text are in italic type enclosed in square brackets, such as [*illeg.*] to indicate an illegible word and [*two words? illeg.*] to indicate what appears to be (with some uncertainty) two illegible words. To avoid confusion with the editors' square brackets, any square brackets found in the original are shown as { }. Scrolled brackets in the original are shown as { }.

Chase did not always form every letter of a word clearly. Moreover, he often corrected himself not by striking through a word and writing it anew, but by making the change directly on the original word. Almost as compensation, however, he was in general a good speller. In cases of ambiguity, if one cannot be certain which combination of letters Chase intended within a word, the editors have followed the modern correct spelling. Unambiguous misspellings are rendered as they appear in the original, even if the error seems merely a product of haste or inattention on the writer's part. Nor have we corrected other inadvertent errors by Chase or his clerks, such as omission or repetition of words in a sentence. Special textual circumstances which require explanation are addressed in footnotes. The advisory notice *sic* does not appear in this volume.

Chase's capitalization presents an interesting problem. He did not use capital letters as capriciously as a quick survey of his handwriting might suggest. His way of forming certain letters at the beginning of words can give the impression that he capitalized more than he actually did. In terms of meaning, there are two forms of a letter, a "lower case" or "small" version and an "upper case" or "capital." Chase, however, had more than two ways of making an *S* in the initial position, and a variant that should, according to his usage with other letters, be lower case may actually resemble a capital in size and shape. His *C* has fewer variants, but the problem is similar, with an overgrown lower case *C* sometimes standing taller than adjoining letters. The same problem arises, less often, with some other letters. The *E* presents its own difficulties. Chase seems frequently to have used what looks like a capital form of the letter in the initial position, particularly but not exclusively in the combinations *ex, en,* and *ev.* Unless he followed one rule of capitalization for *E* and another rule for everything else, what looks like a capital *E* must in fact be a variant lowercase form.

When confronting one of Chase's ambiguous forms of an initial letter, the editors have tended to show it as lower case unless Chase's usage, as demonstrated by the many letters of the alphabet for which there is no uncertainty, as well as by his earlier writing, where variant forms occur less frequently, indicates that he probably intended the word to be capitalized. This system is imperfect, of course, in that it relies on judgment and requires difficult decisions with such words as "state" and "constitution," but it avoids the imposition of errant capitalization which Chase never intended.

Missing punctuation has not been added. If punctuation appears within square brackets it means that the reading is uncertain, not that the editors have supplied missing punctuation. One special symbol has been used to substitute, in a sense, for punctuation. From time to time Chase did not bother to insert a period or dash at the end of a line. Instead, he allowed the right edge of his page to indicate a stop. In some such cases the reading is ambiguous and confusing without an indication of the line break. In those instances the end of the line in the original is shown by a / symbol.

Dashes are the dominant form of punctuation within some sections of the diaries. If, in the editors' judgment, Chase meant a dash to serve as terminal punctuation of a sentence, or left more space after one of a succession of dashes, then sentence spacing follows that dash just as it would a period. The editors have also used their best judgment and experience with Chase's handwriting to distinguish short dashes from periods.

Accents and diacritical marks on foreign words have been shown just as they appear in the original. The editors have not supplied missing quotation marks. Punctuation marks are shown within or outside quotation marks according to their placement in the original, which does not always match modern usage. If the position of the punctuation is ambiguous in the original, as when a period or comma appears directly below a quotation mark, the editors follow the appropriate rule in *The Chicago Manual of Style*. If a quoted passage in the original has quotation marks at the beginning of each line, the transcription omits the extraneous quotation marks, showing only those at the beginning of each paragraph and at the end of the passage. (An exception is made in the entry for Dec. 7, 1831, where we have retained all of the quotation marks in Chase's verses.)

Superscript characters have been brought down to the line. Any mark under a superscript character in the original is represented in the transcription by a period following the character. Chase, like many of his contemporaries, used superscript characters most frequently at the end of abbreviations, which he often formed by writing the first few letters of the word, then the final letter above the line. The editors have not expanded his abbreviations in the text, but have provided explanatory footnotes for any which may not be understood. Sometimes Chase's handwriting makes it difficult to distinguish between a word such as "morning" or "evening" and its abbreviation ("morng." or "eveng."). The editors have relied on their experience with Chase's hand in transcribing such cases.

Whenever in a single journal entry Chase made an obvious change from one color ink to another, changed from pencil to ink or vice versa, or made an insertion in a different color or medium from that used for the body of the entry, the change could be evidence that Chase composed the entry at more than one sitting. Such changes are footnoted. Where a new entry begins in a new ink color or with a different writing instrument, that change is not noted. Footnotes describe any rearrangement of entries within a journal's text for chronological order.

In general, the dates at the beginning of entries are transcribed as they appear in the original journals. Chase occasionally underlined a date heading to set it off from the body of the entry. For uniformity, that underlining has not been reproduced within date headings in this volume. In the case of diaries with printed date headings, the editors may have rearranged elements of the dates for clarity, and the year is omitted (see descriptions of Journals VII, XV, XVIII, and XIX above). If Chase or his clerk repeated the date at the start of a new page, the repetition is not shown in the transcription of the entry. When a journal includes marginal headings, repetition of a marginal note at the start of a new page is not reported. On occasion Chase wrote the month or year at the top of the page in a form of running head; these are not reproduced here.

Whenever the text shifts from one diary to another, a heading such as "Journal III" introduces the entries from the new journal. (For identification of the journals by roman numeral, see the journal descriptions, above.) Each new year is also introduced by a heading. These are the editors' headings, not a feature of the original journals.

ANNOTATION

Biographical information about a person mentioned in the journals usually appears in a footnote at the first mention. Such notes are intended to identify the person, especially with reference to Chase, and are not necessarily full biographies. No note appears if the editors were unable to identify a person or other reference in the text.

Sources of quotations and allusions are noted whenever possible. Many printed works were available in multiple editions in Chase's day. In most cases it is impossible to know exactly which version Chase used, so we generally cite the earliest editions known to us. Quotations from the Bible appearing in notes are from the King James version. All references to acts, scenes, and line numbers of Shakespeare's plays are from G. Blakemore Evans et al., eds., *The Riverside Shakespeare* (Boston, 1974).

Citations to "Family Memoranda" in the Chase Papers at the Library of Congress refer to a record of family events such as births, deaths, and marriages which Chase kept on pp. 13–14 and 93–96 of an undated memorandum book (*micro* 43:0882). The volume's annotation does not explain events of the Civil War which can be easily found in E. B. Long, *The Civil War Day by Day: An Almanac, 1861–1865* (Garden City, N.Y., 1971). Generally, Chase's words are not defined in the notes if they may be found in a modern unabridged dictionary. Foreign words are translated unless they appear in *Webster's Ninth New Collegiate Dictionary*, either in the Foreign Words and Phrases section or among the standard definitions.

After the first appearance of a printed work in a footnote it is identified by a short citation. The bibliography at the end of the volume contains full citations of works for which short citations have been used. Certain frequently cited reference works and nineteenth-century city directories are identified by abbreviations throughout the volume. Those abbreviations are expanded in lists at the beginning of the bibliography. Citations to manuscript repositories employ common or obvious abbreviations which are not expanded at the end of the volume. These include "Hist. Soc." for Historical Society, "Lib." for Library, "Univ." for University, "Collec." for Collection, "MSS" for Manuscripts, "Cinc." for Cincinnati, "L.C." for Library of Congress, "Nat. Arch." for National Archives, and standard abbreviations for state names ("Hist. Soc. of Pa.," for example).

The Salmon P. Chase Papers

The Journals of Salmon P. Chase, 1829–1872

1829

JOURNAL 1

JAN. 1   This Levee differed in nothing from the one which I described elsewhere, excepting that I was somewhat more conspicuous in the crowd.[1] The lady who leaned upon my arm was one of the most brilliant in the room and I shone a little by reflected light. She was elegantly attired in a Scottish dress of the most tasteful description and well did her accomplished manner become her graceful array. The time however passed rather heavily off as I was in charge of one who attracted too many to allow me opportunity for conversation. After leaving the President's we called upon Mrs. Porter, the lady of the Secretary of War.[2] She is a very uncommon woman. To the utmost ease she unites the most dignified propriety of manner. She has the art of setting all who approach her perfectly at their ease while she never permits them to forget even for a moment that respect which was due to her. All who had once been within her magical sphere felt the influence of her spells and none were ever heard to breathe a wish for disenchantment. If ever I should be joined "for better or worse" I would desire to be united to one like Mrs. Porter and having the added and more precious ornament of pure religion.

---

1. In margin: "President's Levee." At this time John Quincy Adams (1767–1848), sixth president of the U.S., occupied the White House. The existence of an earlier diary, which remains unlocated, is also implied below in the entry for Jan. 10, 1829. *DAB*, 1:84–93.
2. In margin: "Mrs. Porter." Letitia Breckenridge Porter, a Washington socialite and the wife of New York politician Peter Buell Porter (1773–1844). *DAB*, 15:99–100; Margaret Bayard Smith, *The First Forty Years of Washington Society* . . . (New York, 1906), 260–62.

Among the most popular of the preacher's at Washington is Mr. Campbell.[3] In the pulpit he has a mild and subdued expression which insensibly prepossess the hearer in his favour. This favourable impression however is usually neutralized when he begins to speak. The tones of his voice are not agreeable to the unused ear and the variety of intonation excites a suspicion of affectation. After a while however you forget all this and then his graceful and emphatic elocution never fails of it's full effect. I never knew a pulpit orator whose action was so entirely free from fault. He knows well how to impart to every gesture a meaning not less obvious and affecting than that conveyed in spoken language. He is not eloquent at least not eloquent in the truest sense of that word. But he is a perfect master of Rhetoric and very few people know the difference. Profound thought clothed in language which has a meaning of association, if I may so speak, deeper than the import of it's letter, is essential to an eloquent man and this Mr. C. has not. High reaching imagination and copious expression are his gifts and upon a skilful management of them his reputation is built.

JANY. 10   I called this evening upon Capt Lenox and found him and his family at home.[4] Capt. L. is one of a class of men always to be found in such a place as Washington, mechanics who have suddenly grown rich. But at W. instead of being elevated into notice among the fashionables by their wealth they must still be content to remain as they were. One of his daughters is a pedant the not—. I did not stay long but made my escape despite of requests from Miss Lucy to prolong my visit and went to Mr. Wirt's[5]

---

3. In margin: "Mr. Campbell." John Nicholson Campbell (1798–1864), a former chaplain to Congress, presided at the New York Avenue Presbyterian Church. *Appletons'*, 1:514.

4. In margin: "Capt. Lenox." Peter Lenox (1771–1832), commissioned a captain in the U.S. Army during the War of 1812, had previously served as foreman and clerk of works at the White House. In 1829 Lenox was clerk of works at the Capitol and a member of the Washington, D.C., Board of Aldermen. Allen C. Clark, "Walter Lenox, the Thirteenth Mayor of the City of Washington," *Records of the Columbia Historical Society* 20 (1917): 167–68.

5. William Wirt (1772–1834), the attorney general of the United States, under whom Chase had studied law since late 1827. Chase had also taught Wirt's three living sons, William C., Henry G. (1818–50), and Dabney Carr, and developed an interest in Wirt's unmarried daughters, Elizabeth Gamble (who married Louis Malesherbes Goldsborough), Catharine G., Rosa E. (d. 1849), Ellen Tazewell (who married Charles McCormick), and Agnes C. (1815–31). Biographical information on Wirt's children is fragmentary and often unreliable. *DAB*, 20:418–21; John B. Boles, ed., *A Guide to the Microfilm Edition of the William Wirt Papers* (Baltimore, 1971), 18; Chase to Joseph A. Denison, Jr., Nov. 10, 1827 (Chase Papers, L.C.); Chase to Thomas Sparhawk, Jan. 2, 1828 (Chase Papers, Ohio Hist. Soc.); Chase to William C. Wirt, Sept. 30, 1828 (Wirt Papers, Md. Hist. Soc.); William Wirt to Chase, Oct. 28, 1828, Ellen Wirt McCormick to Chase, Apr. 10, 1848 (Chase Papers, Hist. Soc. of Pa.).

January 1829 {5}

What a change to pass from the purseproud, vulgar and affected Lenoxes into the midst of a pure and gentle and refined and cultivated circle![6] It was enough to compensate me for facing a biting Northwest thro the intervening mile. Of Mr. Wirt I have spoken before and it is needless to repeat my observations here. Mrs. W[7] is a lady of graceful manners, tho' at times a little tincture of aristocratic feeling makes a stranger somewhat uneasy in her society. She has a cultivated taste and has displayed it in forming a Dictionary of the Floral language which she intends yet to give to the world.[8] Her person is good, rising to about the common height but not exceeding it. She has been religiously educated and is herself, I believe, in communion with the Presbyterian Church. As might be expected, she is not fond of the mixed society at Washington and seldom goes abroad except when the courtesies of society require of her the sacrifice. Her favourite spot is her own sweet home and her chosen employment the education of her daughters. Under such a teacher they could not but improve. As well might the rose refuse its beauty and fragrance to the wooing breath of Spring Elizabeth the elder is a noble creature

>   She is not very beautiful and yet
>   There is that in her dark bright joyous eyes
>   And in the expression of her speaking face
>   Where mid the graces dwell perpetual smiles
>   As sunshine dwells upon the summer wave
>   Changing forever yet forever bright
>   With the sweet frankness of confiding youth
>   And the pure light that evermore pours forth
>   From the mind's fountain that demanded more
>   Than the cold name of Beauty which may be
>   The attribute of being's whom no ray
>   Of Intellect illumines and no charm
>   Of Loveliness invests

She has bright raven locks and a fine frank open brunette countenance. She moves like a wind-borne thing over the earth. Her step

---

6. In margin: "Mr Wirt and his family."
7. Wirt's second wife, Elizabeth Washington Gamble Wirt (1784–1857). *Appletons'*, 6:579.
8. The book, first published as *Flora's Dictionary. By a Lady.* (Baltimore, 1829), suggested symbolic meanings for a selection of flowers and illustrated each definition with poetry. The entry below for Apr. 10, 1830, indicates that Chase helped transcribe early versions of the book. He also wrote at least a dozen poems which appeared in some editions (for example, the 1835 Baltimore edition). Elizabeth Wirt Goldsborough to Jacob W. Schuckers, June 20, 1873 (Schuckers Papers, L.C.).

is almost a dance so much is she borne up by the excitement of her joyous spirits. I would not trust her with a secret. If her lips did not speak of it her eyes would. Her sister is a more spirituelle being. There is more softness and more bland suavity in her manner. Her cheek is something paler and her has a mourful meaning. Perhaps she thinks of her lover who is away oer the sea. Perhaps she is only meditating upon the fleeting nature of all sublunary enjoyments. Wherever ye go pure Sisters, the friend who writes these words shall send his prayers for your unbroken felicity here and in a purer world[9]—

JAN 13   My birthday—and I have now no guardian save him whose wards we are thro life. I am twenty-one. "Tomorrow and tomorrow and tomorrow creeps in this petty pace from day to day;"[10] yet at length the most distant imaginable point of time will be reached. How precious a treasure is time and how have I lavishly squandered it! Oh that I could recall some of it from the abyss. Vain is the wish. Time lost can never be recalled or redeemed. Yet even now there is time if I will but resolve and resolutely act to do much. Knowledge may yet be gained and golden reputation. I may yet enjoy the consciousness of having lived not in vain. Future scenes of triumph may yet be mine. Let me awaken then to a just sense of my great deficiencies / Let me struggle earnestly for the prize of welldoing and leave the Event to the great Arbiter of all Destinies.

JAN 20   Read Mr Madison's letters to J: H: Cabell on the subject of the tariff.[11] They are characterized by his usual clearness and vigour and place the principle of protection on impregnable grounds. Yet the violent opposition of the Tariff will not I think be allayed by it. It has it's source not in a sense of actual grievance but in a narrow sectional jealousy and the high-reaching ambition of

---

9. An expanded version of Chase's tribute to Elizabeth Gamble Wirt and Catharine G. Wirt was published as "The Sisters," in William Turner Coggeshall, *The Poets and Poetry of the West: With Biographical and Critical Notices* (Columbus, 1861), 170–71.
10. *Macbeth*, act 5, scene 5, lines 19–21.
11. In 1827–28, former president James Madison (1751–1836) addressed several letters on the tariff question to Joseph Carrington Cabell (1778–1856), Virginia politician, planter, canal promoter, and official of the University of Virginia. Two of Madison's letters were published as *Two Letters (Addressed to Joseph C. Cabell, Esq.) on the Constitutionality of the Power in Congress to Impose a Tariff for the Encouragement of Manufacturers . . .* (Washington, D.C., 1829). *DAB*, 3:287–88, 12:184–93; James Madison, *Letters and Other Writings of James Madison*, 4 vols. (New York, 1884), 3:571–74, 636–60.

some sectional leaders / Assertion will I think be just as clamourous and dogmatical as before and Pride will be as loud and as obstinate.

JAN 28. As Mr. Adams was soon to go out of office his last Drawingroom was numerously attended. I had engaged to go with Miss Wirt and Miss Cabell and Mrs. Pleasonton was to matronize them.[12] At the proper hour I called for the ladies. They were not ready. I sat patiently down to await their pleasure. Mrs. P. came soon and evinced no little dissatisfaction at the delay tho' she endeavoured to conceal her displeasure under a mask of affected ease and gaiety. At length, however we were all in the carriage and "round went went the wheels" until we arrived at the President's gate. The whole avenue to the palace-door was filled with carriages of those who had arrived before us and we had only the meager satisfaction of not being the last of the train. Nearly fifteen minutes elapsed before we were able to reach the door. At length we were set at liberty and entered the house. An immense crowd was present. Three rooms were full of guests. Music was heard in the great and yet unfurnished East-Room inviting the dancers to engage in the cotillion. Many accepted the invitation and soon many light feet were tripping over the floor. At ten o'clock the dance broke off and the supper-room was thrown open. Long tables were spread in a spacious apartment covered with everything that could please the eye or gratify the taste. They were soon surrounded by a crowd by no means reluctant to disburden them of their load. As each company was satisfied and departed others filled the vacant places and the banquet did not end until after eleven o'clock. Then the dance was resumed for a little while until one by one the gay group diminished when the music played home sweet home as a finale and the pleasures of the evening were ended.

JAN 29. This evening I attended a concert with Miss E. W and Miss E. C.[13] The music was fine—the songs especially one by Mr. Pearman, was sufficient to take the [prisoned] soul and lap it in Elysium. It was full of deep and touching pathos and voice and manner were admirably adapted to the sentiment. Me. Feron who assisted Mr & Mrs. Pearman sung several solos but there was too

---

12. Probably Elizabeth Gamble Wirt; Elizabeth Cabell, William Wirt's niece and the daughter of former Virginia Governor William H. Cabell; and Mary Hopkins Pleasonton, wife of Treasury official Stephen Pleasonton. Alexander Brown, *The Cabells and Their Kin* . . . (Boston, 1895), 257–58; *DAB*, 3:390, 15:8.

13. Elizabeth Gamble Wirt and Elizabeth Cabell.

much art and too little nature in her manner.[14] I can see no reason why we should resort to a foreign land for singing when we have those at home who can vie with the best of the foreign vocalists. Music is an universal language and all men have been taught it's alphabet: so it may be well that we shd. adopt foreign airs but let us sing such words as our own poets furnish and with the organs which nature has given us. When we returned Mr. Swann occupied the vacant seat in the carriage.[15]

JAN 30. This evening I went again with the same ladies to see the Papyrotomia, a gallery of cuttings from Paper.[16] The young proprietor, a youth of sixteen years, received us and exhibited the results of his ingenuity. There were scenes of mountain and glen and secluded lake so ingeniously executed as to have the effect of the finest engraving. There were proud temples and palaces and scenes by the domestic fireside. There was a fair form bending gracefully to the harp and an admiring circle gathered round. The scissors of the boy had done the whole. He asked if he should take our profiles. Miss C—— assented and it was done with surprising rapidity. He took mine also, barely glancing at my face and presto! the work was done. Of course in his haste he was not always accurate but his speed was applauded and he was satisfied.

JAN 31. This day I rode to the Papyrotomia with the younger girls and returned rich in half a dozen black profiles. Mr. W—— was indisposed and I sat some time in his chamber conversing on various topics but principally upon the future course that it became me to pursue and upon the choice of a place of residence. In the evening the young ladies claimed precedence over their father and demanded my attention to the song and the Piano

14. William Pearman (b. 1792) was an English tenor who debuted in 1817 at the English Opera House. Mme. Feron (b. 1797), an English soprano and student of Rossini, appeared with Pearman and his wife in a "Grand Vocal Concert" of music by Mozart, Rossini, and others in Carusi's Assembly Room. *DNB*, 15:600–601; *Daily National Intelligencer*, Jan. 28, 1829; *Who Was Who in American History—Arts and Letters* . . . (Chicago, 1975), 152.

15. Thomas Swann (c. 1765–1840), United States district attorney for Washington, D.C., or his son, Thomas Swann, Jr. (c. 1806–83), director and president of the Baltimore and Ohio Railroad, 1847–53; elected mayor of Baltimore, 1856, 1858; Union Party governor of Maryland, 1865–69; and Democratic congressman, 1869–79. *Appletons'*, 6:4–5; *DAB*, 18:237–38; *Tyler's Quarterly Historical and Genealogical Magazine* 10 (Jan. 1929): 153.

16. This was opening night for the Papyrotomia, "a numerous collection of Cuttings in Paper, executed in a style which has astonished the first artists in Europe, and attracted admiring crowds in Great Britain and America." For fifty cents, each visitor could view the cuttings and "obtain a correct likeness in bust," created by the proprietor, "Master Hankes." *Daily National Intelligencer*, Jan. 29, 1829.

February 1829

FEBY 4. Mr. Clay gave a party this evening and I attended as I had neglected several previous evenings.[17] When I arrived I found that the company had not yet assembled and after paying my respects to Mr. & Mrs. Clay I took my station near the door to observe the various manners of the entering visitants. I soon tired of this employment and went into the next room and looked at the clock and the company alternately until half an hour had elapsed when I took my leave glad to escape from the scene of ceremonious frivolity.

FEBY 5. I have for some time lived in a dream from which I was partially awakened today[18]—

FEB. 9. Recd. thro the Wirts and invitation to Mrs. Porter's. They cd. not go and I did not wish to do so but they wished a discription of the party and so I went. Not a great many persons had been invited but there were enough. Mrs. P. kindly chid me for not bringing the Wirts but I assured that the fault was not mine and she pardoned me. A laughable incident occurred. Mr. Webster[19] was standing engaged in conversation with some ladies near the centre of the room when a servant presented to him what seemed to be wine. He took a glass and drank it off not without some involuntary grimaces which attracted the notice of Mrs. Porter who enquired the cause: when she discovered to her mortification as well as amusement that the servant thro mistake had brought us in some bottles of fine old whiskey. As soon as propriety allowed I took my leave and returned to Mr Wirt's where I spent a pleasant hour before "twal' o'clock" summoned me unwilling to my home.

17. During the time that Chase knew him, Kentucky politician Henry Clay (1777–1852) served as U.S. secretary of state, 1825–29, and as a U.S. senator, 1831–42, 1849–52. He had married Lucretia Hart in 1799. Chase had met Clay through an introduction provided by Bishop Philander Chase soon after Chase's arrival in Washington in Dec. 1826. Clay subsequently sent at least one of his sons to the "Select Classical School" which Chase opened early the next year. By Jan. 1828, Chase also instructed the offspring of several other members of John Quincy Adams's cabinet. Chase to Adeline M. Hitchcock et al., Dec. 19, 1826 (Chase Papers, Hist. Soc. of Pa.); Chase to Thomas Sparhawk, Jan. 2, 1828 (Chase Papers, Ohio Hist. Soc.); *DAB*, 4:173–79; *Daily National Intelligencer,* Dec. 23, 1826.
18. Possibly an allusion to a romantic interest. Chase had recently received a profession of love from an unidentified young woman, and was described by his landlady soon after as being "in love." Another possible allusion to this incident appears below at Mar. 30, 1829. Chase to Thomas Sparhawk, Feb. 23, 1829 (Special Collec., Dartmouth College Lib.).
19. Daniel Webster (1782–1852), congressman from New Hampshire and Massachusetts, 1813–17, 1823–27; U.S. senator from Massachusetts, 1827–41, 1845–50; and U.S. secretary of state, 1841–43, 1850–52. *Bio. Dir. U.S. Cong.,* 2021; *DAB*, 19:585–92.

FEB. 12 I read Dr. C——'s review of Napoleon's Life to day for the first time.[20] It is written with much power and in a most captivating style. He is characterized more than almost any writer of the day by a tone of elevated moral sentiment running thro' every sentence. Undazzled by the blaze of military and civil glory which surrounded the Hero, he has deeply penetrated and faithfully exhibited his real character. I cannot go with him wholly and do think that he has sacrificed a little, (unconsciously I am sure) of the truth of character to the desire of exhibiting a systematic character—of tracing every action to the influence of one mighty and oermastering passion but I admire the deep-sense of the rights—the forgotten rights of human nature which breathes thro' and animates the whole.

FEB 14 I heard Mr. Webster today for the first time in the Supreme Court.[21] It was a cause originally unimportant but time and the progress of improvement had augmented greatly the value of the property in controversy. Years ago the land was a waste, uninhabited and unimproved. A few dollars bought it and were applied to the payment of the debts of an intestate. Recently the heirs have discovered a flaw in the chain of title and have claimed the land. It is now covered by factories and dwellings and exhibits the busy scenes of a prosperous manufacturing town. Mr. Webster argued the cause for the heirs and with great power. He states his case with great clearness and draws his inferences with exceeding sagacity. His language is rich and copious; his manner dignified and impressive; his voice deep and sonorous; and his sentiments high and often sublime. He argues generally from general principles, seldom descending into minute analysis where intricacy is apt to embarrass and analogy, to mislead. He is remarkable for strength rather than dexterity and would easier rend an oak than untie a knot. If I could carry my faith in the possibility of all things to labour so far as to suppose that any degree of industry would enable me to reach his height, day and night should testify of my toils.

MAR. 4. Today the "People's president" was inaugurated.[22] Prodigious numbers assembled to witness the ceremony. Huge masses

---

20. In margin: "Channing Napoleon." William Ellery Channing, *Remarks on the Character of Napoleon Bonaparte, Occasioned by the Publication of Scott's Life of Napoleon. From the Christian Examiner. Vol. IV. No. V* (Boston, 1827); and *A Continuation of Remarks on the Character of Napoleon Bonaparte, Occasioned by the Publication of Scott's Life of Napoleon. From the Christian Examiner, Vol. V. No. II* (Boston, 1828).

21. In margin: "Mr. Webster." The case was *David Wilkinson v. Thomas Leland et al. Daily National Intelligencer*, Feb. 16, 1829.

22. In margin: "Inauguration." This was the inauguration of Andrew Jackson (1767–1845), seventh president of the U.S. *DAB*, 9:526–34.

of men covered all the area of the capitol in the portico of wh: the Genl. stood. The mob listened in breathless expectation while the Inaugural address was delivered but not a word reached their eager ears. The members of the last Cabinet were invited and seats were prepared for them but they did not choose to attend to hear themselves abused by insinuation. When the address was over the President mounted a horse and rode towards the President's House. The multitude followed, shouting, some on horseback and some on foot. The tide rolled on to the House. Mr. Adams had left it a few days before and retired to Meridian Hill,[23] calm and serene without and within / He had performed his duty and was content with that consciousness. The misled people could take from him his office but they could not deprive him of that. Every thing in the House had been left in the neatest arrangement. But half an hour threw every thing into confusion. The people rushed into the building. They swarmed in every room. They pried into every corner. Those who entered first were obliged to find their way out thro the windows for to return thro' the doors was almost an impossibility. At length curiosity was sated; and all had offered their congratulations. The Genl. gave the last shake of the hand with more pleasure than any before and retired again to the Hotel that the ravages of the mob might be repaired and the building prepared once more for his residence. Far more I would prefer to fall with the fallen than rise with the rising.

MAR 6. When we see uncommon talent connected with uncommon weakness;[24] when we see great genius subjugated by vicious appetite we are apt to accuse Nature of injustice and blame the unequal apportionment of her favours. Why, we are apt to inquire, are not the mighty in mind, strong in principle? Why are not the emancipated from ignorance secured from the worse thraldom of vice. These reflections naturally arose in my mind when I saw Mr. T—— displaying in the Supreme Court an acuteness and profundity of discernment and a comprehensiveness of grasp wonderful in any man but especially wonderful in one so young, and reflected that he was a slave to drink and that in a few hours those astonishing powers would be lost in intoxication.[25] Here is a mounful proof that

---

23. Previously the residence of Commodore David Porter, a mile north of the White House. *Daily National Intelligencer*, Jan. 28, 1829; *DAB*, 15:84; Smith, *First Forty Years*, 258.
24. In margin: "Mr. Talcott."
25. At this time, New York Attorney General Samuel Austin Talcott (1789–1836) was arguing against Daniel Webster in *John Inglis v. Trustees of Sailors Snug Harbor*. Talcott's talents were well known, but continuing difficulties with alcoholism led to his

talent and learning are ineffectual guards against vice; that it is not enough that the light of reason beam brightly upon the path, unless her decisions be carried into execution by strong moral principle. Reason indeed may show us the right but conscience and conscience alone can impel us to walk in it. Mr. T—— is about 35 years of age; of a slender form; and expressive countenance. It is darkened indeed by the influence of his vice but all its original glory is not yet lost. His mind still acts powerfully—the demon has not yet obtained the mastery over *that*—and, I suppose, when he is sober that he is still alive to a sense of reputation. He exerted all his strength today. Displaying a copious learning, an accurate research, a rich and harmonious diction, a deep and minute analysis he treated the most abstruse subjects as schoolboy themes and passed thro the darkest fields of discussion as if they had been familiar and accustomed walks. Every body was astonished by the unexpected display. As I went home from the Court with the Attorney General he remarked that for twenty years he had heard nothing equal to it. But his reputation, will fade away. He might incorporate his fame with Time and build for himself an indestructible monument—he might but will not. And in a few years when he himself has sunk into the final slumber, his name and his remembrance will pass away forever. Would that for his sake the opiate which then shall have power over him might master him forever.

MARCH 20   Wrote a sketch of an imaginary meeting of the Society in doggrell and sent it to E. G. W.[26]

MARCH 30   Almost awakened from my dream.

APRIL 2   Mr. Trist wished me to call with him at Mr. Wirts; we did so but finding no one at home we left our cards and returned to our boarding house.[27] I invited Mr. T—— into my room where we sat conversing a long time, principally upon the extent of human

---

dismissal in 1830. *Daily National Intelligencer,* Mar. 7, 1829; Charles Elliot Fitch et al., *Encyclopedia of Biography of New York . . . ,* 4 vols. (Boston, 1916), 1:129–32; John C. Fitzpatrick, ed., *The Autobiography of Martin Van Buren* (Washington, D.C., 1920), 173–76.

26. Chase and Elizabeth Washington Wirt seem to have been considering the possibility of forming a temperance society. The letter to Mrs. Wirt's daughter Elizabeth Gamble Wirt has not been found. Chase to Elizabeth Washington Wirt, Jan. 28, 1830, Elizabeth Washington Wirt to Chase, Jan. 25, 30, 1830 (Chase Papers, Hist. Soc. of Pa.).

27. Nicholas Philip Trist (1800–1874) had recently started his diplomatic career by securing an appointment as clerk in the U.S. Department of State. *DAB,* 18:645–46; Louis Martin Sears, "Nicholas P. Trist: A Diplomat With Ideals," *Mississippi Valley Historical Review* 11 (June 1924): 90; Smith, *First Forty Years,* 242.

knowledge. Mr. T—— has imbibed many of the notions of Wright and Owen;[28] and misled by an ignis fatuus which he believes to be a conductor to rational freedom he plunges headlong into bottomless abyss of infidel inconsistency. He read many extracts from the Free Inquirer,[29] with the hope of convincing me of the solidity of his opinion; but I was either to strongly wedded to my own sentiments or too thoroughly persuaded of the fallacy of his to be much affected by them.

[AP'L] 7. "You must write a few lines in my album to remind me of you when far aw'a" said Elizabeth Cabell to me this evening. Elizabeth is a pretty young lady of eighteen. She was born and educated I believe in the city of Richmond but one would suppose that such a bloom could be bestowed only by the breath of the mountain breeze. She is singularly sensible and intelligent; but timi[d] as a fawn. "My lyre is broken Miss Elizabeth" I replied. "Repair it then" said she "for you shall contribute something to my treasury of friendship's offerings." "Well, I will try" and went home and before going to bed wrote a few lines. The following are near the conclusion

> "Fain wd. I bind my memory" to all
> The glorious things of Heaven the beautiful
> Creations of the earth and teach the breeze
> To whisper of my name that I might be
> Tho' absent unforgotten.

APRIL 8. Today the loveliest part of Mr. Wirt's family left Washington for Richmond.[30] They had constituted almost the whole of my society and their absence was sensibly felt. For the cheerful and agreeable evenings I had been accustomed to spend in their society I could hope for no equivalent substitute. To regularly recurring

---

28. Scottish-American free thinkers Frances Wright (1795–1852) and Robert Dale Owen (1801–77) had acquired reputations as advocates of liberal divorce laws, socialism, and emancipation. Owen later served as a Democratic congressman from Indiana, 1843–47, as a U.S. diplomat in Sicily, 1853–58, and as an agent commissioned by the governor of Indiana to purchase arms in Europe, 1861–63. *DAB*, 14:118–20, 20:549–50.

29. Owen and Wright had started publishing the *Free Enquirer*, a weekly "devoted without fear, without reserves, without pledge to men, parties, sects, or systems, to free, unbiassed and universal enquiry," in 1828. *Free Enquirer*, Oct. 28, 1828; Frank L. Mott, *A History of American Magazines 1841–1850* (New York, 1930), 1:536–38.

30. Wirt had lost his position as attorney general after Andrew Jackson's election victory, and the Wirt family was moving to Baltimore. John P. Kennedy, *Memoirs of the Life of William Wirt, Attorney General of the United States* (Philadelphia, 1849), 2:260–62.

delight I can only look that general gloom shall succeed. For in solitude who can be cheerful and in society the recollection of past enjoyment weakens the pleasure of the present.

APRIL 13 Called at Mr. Wirt's who read to me a letter from the young ladies in which I was pleased to find that I was affectionately remembered.[31]

APRIL 14 The remainder of Mr. Wirt's family left Washington today / I rode to the steamboat and staid with them until 10. when I took a sorrowful leave and returned to the city. Mr. Clay's family had gone before and Genl. Porter's. Few were left in whom I felt any interest. Strangers will succeed. A new cabinet will fill or rather occupy the places of the old; but the society which has existed here cannot be renewed. A more savage spirit breathes in the administration and as a natural consequence distrust has come in place of confidence and reserve instead of frankness. Men do not now speak their sentiments freely. The spirit of cautious jealousy finds it away into the family circle and restraint is visible even in the intercourse of the fireside. How long will these things be?

APRIL 16. I found a melancholy pleasure in reading passages which I used to admire with my absent friends. Thus sorrow can beguile itself by recalling the image of the past to an association with the present.

APL. 20 Today a large quantity of furniture which Mr. Wirt left behind was exposed to public sale. I attended less to purchase some articles that had belonged to him than to pass once more thro the house. I went into the rooms where Elizabeth had performed the duties of the toilet—where she had spent many a moment elaborating her French Puffs while I was impatiently awaiting her appearance below. I passed into Mr. Wirts study which had often witnessed his midnight vigil; where he had invoked Fame and she had come at his call; where he had disciplined himself for the strife and made sure the triumph of the Forum. Could these walls have spoken what an instructive lesson they might have told! I passed into the garden and stole a few flowers. This was the favourite spot of Mrs. W——. She delighted to tend the flowers—to watch their blooming—and guard them against all nocent influences. But her step was no more among them. She was far away.... I went home.

---

31. In the original, the entry for April 13 follows that for April 14.

MAY 25 I attended this evening a public meeting to consider upon the establishment of an infant school in this city.[32] The meeting was very respectably attended and some addresses were delivered of considerable interest. It is wonderful to reflect upon the progress and excitement of society. Carried on by that progress and participating in that excitement it is not always perceptible to us. The stream rushes on but as we are borne upon its bosom we are insensible of its motion the atmosphere is hot and inflamed but a fever rages in our own viens and we are not aware that the temperature is at all changed. But if we, remove ourselves, in idea,—if we take a high and commanding elevation—if we get above this dim spot into the regions of pure and serene air, we obtain a view of the most extraordinary character. Man is seen rousing himself from the slumber of ages and shaking off the bondage of ignorance and indolence. Governments are seen remodelling—the old tottering to their fall and the new springing up in beautiful proportions and resting upon broad and stable foundations. Knowledge is diffusing her influences among the nations. The wilderness is receding before the advance of civilization. Cities are springing up where the forest recently stood and states are born and grow up to mature strength in less than half the time allotted to man upon earth. Space is almost annihalted. Human invention is approximating the remote and facilitating the difficult. The life of man embraces a far greater variety of incidents and may be made of far greater importance to himself and to others than it ever could before. And as if to meet the new demands made upon human intellect new methods of instruction are devised and the work is commenced earlier. Infant-schools begin with the earliest dawn. They train the mind of the babe to activity and observation. They store it with the thoughts of others and teach it to think for itself. The world is no longer a dull mass of matter of which the child knows nothing & cares to know nothing. It is full of wonders, and the very child now learns to send a delighted and intilligent eye over them. Young creatures whose fathers at their age had but learned to lisp nursery nonsense, have made larger attainments in really useful knowledge—knowledge likely to make them better, happier and more respectable. Yet the world is but half awake. The wonderful capabilities of humanity are known but to few. Colleges, schools, yet contain but a small portion of the population. Physical labour yet bears heavily upon the great multitude and their nobler faculties are almost unknown even to the possessors. Yet this state of things cannot last. The signs of the time indicate

---

32. In margin: "Infant School." The meeting was held in the First Presbyterian Church. *Daily National Intelligencer,* May 22, 1829.

the going on of a mighty revolution and oppressed human nature shall yet be redeemed from the thraldom of sin and ignorance and the serpent's head be effectually crushed.[33]

MAY 30. Was appointed orator for the 4th. of July.

JUNE 16. Received notice of my appointment to deliver one of two orations given to Candidates for the second degree in Dartmouth College.[34]

JUNE 24. My uncle from Ohio called.[35] An unexpected pleasure as I knew not that he was East of the Alleghanies.

JULY 4. My oration, which was hastily prepared, the leisure moments of less than ten days being devoted to it's composition, was not delivered in consequence of a heavy rain which confined almost all people at home.[36]

JULY 7. Wrote to President Lord accepting my appointment to deliver the Master's Oration at the coming commencement.[37]

JULY 12. SUNY. I went with the Revd. Mr. Johns to a dilapidated building about four miles from the city which goes by the name of Rock Creek church.[38] As we went out the clouds accumulated in heavy masses over our heads and rolled heavily but rapidly along. I felt that secret and sublime sensation which, I suppose, every body is impressed with at such moments—a [free] of deep reverential awe as if in the immediate presence of awful Omnipotence. Drops of rain had begun to fall when we arrived at the church. It was a very old building, having stood there since the earliest settlement of the district. It was never completed. The walls stood in their nakedness.

33. An allusion to the final defeat of Satan, foretold in Gen. 3:15.
34. Nathan Lord to Chase, June 9, 1829 (Chase Papers, L.C.).
35. Philander Chase (1775–1852), Dartmouth class of 1796, the Protestant Episcopal bishop of Ohio. *DAB*, 4:26–27.
36. Chase's oration, "The Dangers of American Liberty," was printed in the *Washington City Chronicle and Literary Repository*, July 4, 1829.
37. Congregational minister Nathan Lord (1792–1870) served as president of Dartmouth College, 1828–63. *DAB*, 11:409.
38. Technically, St. Paul's Episcopal Church, constructed in 1719. Chase's companion was evidently Henry Van Dyke Johns (1803–59), an Episcopal priest and the founder of Trinity Church in Washington, D.C., who later served as pastor of St. Paul's Church in Cincinnati. DeB. Randolph Keim, *Keim's Illustrated Hand-Book: Washington and Its Environs . . .* , 4th ed. (Washington, D.C., 1874), 223; *Nat. Cyc.*, 5:253; *Cinc. Dir. (1840)*, 236.

The roof was unconcealed by a ceiling. Bare rafters stretched their enormous length from side to side. It was almost an uncomfortable sensation to look up and see them impending above you. The congregation as might be expected in such a place, was very small. At length the clergyman began, saying, The Lord is in his holy Temple, let all the Earth keep silence before him:[39] and the old fabric gave back the echoed words as if conscious that even that rude place might be a fitting Temple for the most High, if humble hearts and contrite Spirits were met to worship there. The service proceeded but soon the rain fell in torrents and the Thunder mingled its dread tones with the rush of winds and the fall of waters. The tones of the Preachers voice were lost in the elemental roar and he was compelled to dismiss the congregation. They formed themselves in groups around the building and awaited the abating of the storm. Night was approaching when the rain partially ceased and we all seized the opportunity thus offered to return into the city: where however we did not arrive before the storm raged anew. Yet we kept on thro the midst of it and in a short time, tho wet and weary reached home.

JULY 31. I left Washington to day, with a view of taking a long journey Northward.[40] I travelled in the stage which afforded me many opportunities for observation while it subjected me to some inconveniencies. He who travels in a stage for a considerable distance, with the same companions, may see a miniature of this world. Selfishness is constantly ready to appropriate the most comfortable seats; and politeness is ready to sacrifice its own ease to the enjoyment of another. Physical strength gives it's possessor a superiority envied by the vulgar and wisdom, an unusual inmate, sometimes vindicates her claim to a deeper homage. I confess that I saw little of what I describe and shall here describe little of what I saw. It would no purpose to delineate scenes daily presented. It is enough to say that after nine hours riding thro a broiling sun we were set down at the door of one of the principal Hotels in Baltimore. I desired to be shewn to my room and to be furnished with a dinner. The room I found to be far from neat and resolved upon a change, in which resolution I was confirmed by Mr. Barrell, who

39. Hab. 2:20
40. Chase timed his trip to include commencement at Dartmouth, where he intended to visit with former classmates and deliver his master's oration. Chase to Charles Dexter Cleveland, July 11, 1829 (Chase Papers, L.C.); Chase to Hamilton Smith, July 14, 1829 (Smith MSS, Indiana Univ.).

had stopped at the same Hotel and had changed it for Barnum's.[41] After dinner I followed his example and soon found myself very comfortably situated. After conversing awhile with Mr. B—— I called upon my old friends the Wirts. I found them preparing to go into the country and at the request of the ladies I joined the party. We rode to Mrs. Pattersons; who has a lovely countryseat about two miles from the town.[42] A fine garden lies in the rear of the building furnished with numberless varieties of plants and flowers. A declivity, to north, descended by a winding path, brings you to a perennial spring of water, which gushes out of ground and wanders away to mingle its pure waters with those of the Chesapeake. The bay is seen from the Eastern windows and the dim outline of the Eastern Shore of Maryland, is traced in a deeper blue. We took tea with Mrs. P—— and returned to the city. Mrs. W—— asked how long I was to remain in town. I told her a day or two she said she expected to have been consulted in my arrangements, and that she intended to demand of me a week of my time at least. We found Mr. Wirt standing at the door who had just returned from the Court at Annapolis. The girls threw themselves upon his neck and seemed transported with joy. They seemed to forget that they were in the most public street of the city until their mother reminded them of it and drew them into the house. I left them to their enjoyment and returned to the Hotel. The next day it rained and the next I went early to the House but Mr. W—— had gone. The clouds still threatened rain but like many other menacers performed nothing. In the evening I walked with Elizabeth and the younger girls into Howard Park where the Monument stands.[43] I thought little of the Monument however or of any thing but the noble creature at my side. We had much interesting conversation which was continued till we returned to the house. Then the younger members of the family surrounded me. Rosa and Ellen had chairs before me, Catharine sat by my side and little Agnes, a lovely girl of fourteen threw herself

41. Probably Samuel Brown Barrell (1790–1858), a Washington, D.C., attorney and future U.S. diplomat. David Barnum operated Barnum's City Hotel at the corner of Calvert and Fayette Streets. Franklin Bowditch Dexter, *Biographical Sketches of the Graduates of Yale College with Annals of the College History* (New York, 1885–1912), 6:241–42; *Wash. Dir. (1830)*, 7; Writers' Program, Maryland, *Maryland: A Guide to the Old Line State* (New York, 1940), 226.

42. Possibly Springfield Estate, the country home of Baltimore merchant William Patterson (1752–1835), which stood on the outskirts of the city. Patterson was a widower, but the Mrs. Patterson whom Chase met could have been a daughter-in-law. *DAB*, 14:309–10; *Nat. Cyc.*, 18:20–21.

43. Construction of Baltimore's Washington Monument, a 160-foot marble column, had started in 1815. It was nearing completion at the time of Chase's visit and was finished in Nov. 1829. J. Thomas Scharf, *History of Baltimore City and County . . .* (Philadelphia, 1881), 265–66.

carelessly on the floor. To be in the midst of such a circle and to be conscious that I shared in the affections of that circle was an exquisite delight. The time however soon came that I must return to the Hotel and I parted from them with regret. The next day I was again with them. And again I passed some happy moments. E—— showed me some rings she had received from her friends at West River.[44] The motto on one was "Pensez à moi, on another ζοη μου σασ αγαπω.[45] I dined with them today and after dinner departed having prolonged my stay to the last moment possible. "Give my love to your Mother & sisters" said Catharine as I left the room.[46] "And mine" added Elizabeth but I did not [hear]. I reached the Boat just before she started. I found my friend Elliott from Washington with his Mother and a pretty young lady from Washington on board.[47] We had not got out of the Patapsco upon the Chesapeake before the shades of evening gathered round us. And a glorious evening it was. The dark blue waters beneath and the magnificent arch above and between the vessel moving like a living thing breathing smoke and fire. I sat upon the deck along time admiring the beauty of the scene and conversing with my friend. I was still there gazing with unsated admiration upon the heavens and the water when a cry thro' the vessel roused the sleepers to exchange their berths in the cabin for seats in the stage. We had

---

44. West River, Md., about six miles southwest of Annapolis. Jedediah Morse and Richard C. Morse, *A New Universal Gazetteer, or Geographical Dictionary*, 4th ed. (New Haven, Conn., 1823), 811.

45. The first motto means "think of me." The Greek inscription is from Byron's poem, "Maid of Athens, Ere We Part," and means "my life, I love you."

46. By this time, three of Chase's five sisters had married: Hannah Ralston Chase Whipple (1792–1850), Abigail Corbet Chase Colby (1799–1838), and Janette (Jane) Logan Chase Skinner (1803–56?), wives of John Whipple (d. 1857), Isaac Colby, and Josiah K. Skinner, respectively. The fourth, Alice Jones Chase (1805–59), remained single throughout her life, while the youngest, Helen Maria Chase (1815–64), later married Henry B. Walbridge. In 1829, Chase's widowed mother, Jannette Ralston Chase (1773–1832), and his two youngest sisters lived with Abigail in Hopkinton, N.H., where Hannah also resided. Janette Chase Skinner lived in Lockport, N.Y. Chase spelled his mother's name *Janet* in his "Family Memoranda," but she signed herself *Jannette*. William H. Child, *History of the Town of Cornish New Hampshire with Genealogical Record 1763–1910* (Concord, N.H., [1911?]), 2:64–65; Jannette Ralston Chase to Chase, [Aug. 1825], Abigail Colby to Chase, May 18, 1829, Apr. 7, 1830, Apr. 10, 1832, J. K. Skinner to Chase, July 21, 1829, Eliza C. Whipple to Chase, Aug. 31, 1857 (Chase Papers, Hist. Soc. of Pa.); Chase to Sarah Bella Chase, Jan. 29, 1850, Chase to E. S. Hamlin, June 12, 1856, and "Family Memoranda" (Chase Papers, L.C.); William Pool, ed., *Landmarks of Niagara County* (Syracuse, N.Y., 1897), 386; Washington *Evening Star*, Jan. 3, 1865.

47. Thomas Dawes Eliot (1808–70), an 1825 graduate of Columbian University (the predecessor to George Washington University), had spent the last four years studying law in Washington, D.C., and New Bedford, Mass. Later, he served as a Whig and Republican congressman, 1854–55, 1859–69, and was involved in the formation of the Republican party in Massachusetts. *Appletons'*, 2:325; Eliot to Chase, Jan. 31, 1851 (Chase Papers, L.C.).

arrived at French Town.[48] Scarcely were we in the stages when it began to rain and continued without intermission when we had reached the other boat until we arrived at Philadelphia. Here I immediately took a hack and rode to my cousin Geo: Ralston's to transact some business for my mother.[49] He was not at home but Mrs. R—— supplied his place as far as she could and I returned to the Boat. I found my baggage, transferred by the kind attention of Elliott to the New York Boat which was just ready to depart. In a few moments we were rapidly ascending the Delaware and in a few miles we were set ashore at a place a few miles below Trenton to cross the land to New Brunswick. Our stage was small and ill made; our horses were mere skeletons—and the road was horribly conditioned. The Jersey roads are certainly the worst in the United States. We arrived at New Brunswick as might be expected after the rest (who had taken the other route and found that all the best rooms in the Tavern had been engaged. We procured beds however and early on the following morning we left N.B for N.Y. where we arrived before noon. I called upon Mrs. Barrell who was to proceed to Boston under my charge and informed her of my intention to leave in the afternoon in the Fulton.[50] She promised to be at the wharf in season and I left her to perambulate Broadway and make some trifling purchases. Having completed them to my satisfaction I went on Board. Mrs. B. came soon and we left the city of Gotham. As we passed along I observed a wreck and enquired the cause.[51] I was informed that it was a vessel loaded with lime which had sprung a leak. The water came in contact with the lime and spontaneous combustion was the result. The vessel was burnt to the water's edge. There was a pair of runaway lovers on board who had been to New York to be married and were returning to Providence. He seemed to be a rake and she seemed to be an idiot and so I took little notice of them. It was three o'clock P.M. when we left New York. Night overtook when we had gone about forty miles; and I sought my cabin. The next morning we were at anchor. A thick fog

---

48. A landing in Cecil County, Md., at the northern end of the Chesapeake Bay. Morse and Morse, *New Universal Gazetteer*, 271.

49. George Ralston, a Philadelphia merchant, was probably the nephew of Chase's mother. The nature of Chase's business with him is not known. George Ralston to Chase, Aug. 17, 1832 (Chase Papers, Hist. Soc. of Pa.); *Phila. Dir. (1829)*, 156.

50. Catherine Maria Ward Barrell (1791–1877) was the wife of Samuel Brown Barrell. In Aug. 1829, the paddle-wheel steamer *Fulton,* the last passenger ship designed by American inventor Robert Fulton, served the New York City–Providence route under the direction of Capt. Charles Tomlinson. Charles Martyn, *The William Ward Genealogy . . .* (New York, 1925), 158; Cadwallader D. Colden, *The Life of Robert Fulton . . .* (New York, 1817), 275; *New York Evening Post,* Aug. 5, 1829.

51. The schooner *John and Nancy Haskell* had struck a ledge of rocks on the afternoon of July 20. *New York Evening Post,* July 21, 1829.

enveloped every thing and the Captain was afraid to proceed lest he might run upon rocks which are frequent in this part of the sound / In this pleasant situation we remained some hours when the fog lifted itself a little and the Captain gave orders to move. We had a political meeting in the fog and nominated Henry Clay for President with great unanimity. Towards evening we met the Ben Franklin from Providence.[52] She passed us as if borne on wings. The next morning we arrived at Providence and took carriages for Boston. I had been indisposed all the preceding day and was now so ill that I could hardly sit. However I patiently endured until we reached the Northern Athens where I left my charge with her father Judge Ward[53] and hastened myself to the Hotel and to my room. Here I sent for a physician who came and prescribed medicine which I did not take and gave me some advice which I did not follow. On the contrary debilitated as I was I took the Stage and on the evening of the same day arrived at Concord N.H. Here my friend Sparhawk called to see me and staid with me all night.[54] The next morning I rode with him to Hopkinton where my mother resides. Here I remained sick nearly a fortnight and of course did not deliver my Master's oration. As soon as I was able to travel I set out on my return, going down to Concord in the evening and spending the night with my friend Sparhawk, and proceeding to Andover the next day. My old classmate Ward was my Stage companion and we had a pleasant ride together, talking much of the persons and scenes of bygone times.[55] When arrived at Andover I walked with him to the Theological Institution where I saw one or two of my old classmates & friends. One of them, was going to Salem and I agreed to accompany him.[56] I found a most cordial reception in his family,

52. The steam packet *Benjamin Franklin* ran between New York City and Providence. Ibid., Aug. 5, 1829.

53. Artemas Ward (1762–1847), Massachusetts politician and chief justice of the commonwealth's Court of Common Pleas, 1820–39. *Bio. Dir. U.S. Cong.*, 2005–6; Martyn, *Ward Genealogy*, 157–58.

54. Thomas Sparhawk (1806–74), a college friend who graduated from Dartmouth in 1828, had interrupted medical studies at Harvard to attend his ill father in Concord. Charles Franklin Emerson, ed., *General Catalogue of Dartmouth College* . . . (Hanover, N.H., 1910–11), 242; Sparhawk to Chase, Aug. 6, 1829 (Chase Papers, Hist. Soc. of Pa.).

55. Teacher and Congregational minister James Wilson Ward (1803–73), Dartmouth class of 1826, studied for a year at the Andover Theological Seminary. George Thomas Chapman, *Sketches of the Alumni of Dartmouth College* . . . (Cambridge, Mass., 1867), 233.

56. George W. Punchard (1806–80), another member of Chase's class at Dartmouth, had recently received his A.M. from Andover Theological Seminary. He later served as a Congregational minister and as editor of the *Boston Traveller*, 1845–57, 1867–71. *Appletons'*, 5:136; Chase to Thomas Sparhawk, Sept. 30, 1829 (Chase Papers, Ohio Hist. Soc.).

some of whom were personally known to me before, and spent a day with them going out however in the meantime to Ipswich to see my Sister, there at school.[57] Thence I went to Boston, having written to Mrs. Wirt that I should be in Baltimore on Thursday evening. To fulfil that promise I left Boston on Monday morning—arrived at New York the following morning—took the steamboat immediately—reached Philadelphia in the evening of the same—called at G. Ralston's and finished my business with him—took the steamboat next morning, passed along the line of the Delaware and Chesapeake Canal and across the deep cut a vast excavation, sixty feet deep and some miles long,[58] and surprised the Wirts by sitting down in their parlour at Baltimore on Wednesday evening. The next day I made some calls with the girls. The next when I came after dinner E—— received me alone. We talked upon various but common topics for an hour when we were joined by the rest of the family. The next morning I quitted Balte. most unwillingly for Washington where I arrived about noon and found all my friends well and apparently very glad to see me once more among them.

SEPT. 5. A singular chain of occurrences had commenced in my absence. Mr. Campbell a Presbyterian clergyman in Washington had stated in confidence to Dr. Ely of Philadelphia with a view to prevent the appointment of Maj. Eaton to the Cabinet that Mrs. E. had been delivered of a child when she was Mrs. Timberlake, supposed to be by Maj. E—— and that various other reports, greatly prejudicial to the character of both had been for some time in circulation.[59] Dr. Ely made no use of this information then but some time afterwards wrote to the President informing him of the circumstances and giving Mr. Campbells name as the author of the report. The President immediately sent for Mr. C. who confessed that he had made the statement to Dr. E——, explained his motives and shewed his authority. The President was apparently contented. But the next day he had changed his mind and called upon Mr. C—— to deny his belief in the charge. Mr. C. replied that he could not—when the President became angry and talked of a suit for slander. Mr. C. now thought it expedient to prepare for the worst and with that view

---

57. Probably Chase's youngest sister, Helen.
58. The new fourteen-mile canal had opened on July 4, 1829. Its "deep cut," an excavation which actually measured eighty feet in places, was widely considered a technological marvel. Ralph D. Gray, *National Waterway: Chesapeake and Delaware Canal, 1767–1965* (Urbana, Ill., 1967), 51, 64.
59. As seen below, John Nicholson Campbell and Ezra Stiles Ely (1786–1861), pastor of Philadelphia's Pine Street Presbyterian Church, were central figures in the Peggy Eaton affair. *Appletons'*, 2:339–40.

requested me to call with him at Mrs. Williams today.[60] I went and the old lady told us that she was a neighbour to Mrs. Timberlake and that Mrs. O'Neale, the Mother of Mrs. T. had told her that she had had twins in the absence of Mr. T—— This was the amt. of her statement but from other sources Mr. C. collected a mass of evidence sufficient & more than sufficient to establish every allegation, he had before made not as of his own knowledge but as resting upon the credit of a particular individual and upon the strength of common report. A few days afterwards a conclave was held at the Palace for the extraordinary purpose of taking this affair into consideration.[61] Nearly the whole Cabinet was present and some extra councillors summoned for the special occasion. These last were Dr. Ely and Mr. Auditor Lewis.[62] Mr. C—— was summond to appear and answer for himself. I cannot state the particulars as they transpired. I have now no notes of the transaction and the minutiæ have glided from my memory. However the President became highly exasperated and attributed the whole affair to the agency of Mr. Clay and Mr C—— left the room indignant at the treatment he had received and determined to publish the whole affair to the world. Dr. Ely followed him and entreated him to change his resolution. At last he consented. Many other incidents grew out of this. The ladies of Washington excluded Mrs. E—— from their society and so the matter still rests. Eaton has threatened personal violence to Mr. C. but will not probably execute his threat and Mrs. E—— called herself on Mr C—— and after alternate abuse and entreaty, screaming and fainting finding the whole ineffectual declared that his blood shd. be spilt for his audacity.[63]

19 SEPT Called on Farley at G.T. who showed me some very fine engravings[64]—among others one of Cæsar sitting in a chair of state.

---

60. Probably Elizabeth Williams, a Washington, D.C., widow and Peggy Eaton's milliner. Charles Francis Adams, ed., *Memoirs of John Quincy Adams, Comprising Portions of His Diary from 1795 to 1848* (Philadelphia, 1876), 8:185; *Wash. Dir. (1830)*, 82.
61. In margin: "Sept. 10."
62. William Berkeley Lewis (1784–1866), an auditor at the U.S. Treasury and close personal friend of the president. *Appletons'*, 3:707; *DAB*, 11:226.
63. Chase's fascination with scandal in the Jackson cabinet appears to have continued until Dec., when William Wirt sent him a veiled warning about the possibility of a libel suit by Eaton and her husband. Edward I. Chase to Chase, Sept. 20, 1829 (Chase Papers, L.C.); Chase to Thomas Sparhawk, Sept. 30, 1829 (Chase Papers, Ohio Hist. Soc.); William Wirt to Chase, Dec. 21, 1829 (Wirt Papers, Md. Hist. Soc.).
64. John Farley (d. 1874), a resident of Georgetown, was a second lieutenant in the U.S. Army and the future fiancé of Catharine Wirt. Chase to C. D. Cleveland, June 2, 1830 (Chase Papers, L.C.); George Washington Cullum, *Biographical Register of the Officers and Graduates of the U.S. Military Academy . . .* , 3rd ed. (Boston, 1891), 1:246; Francis Bernard Heitman, *Historical Register and Dictionary of the United States Army . . .* (Washington, D.C., 1903), 1:413.

This is the finest engraving I have ever seen. The attitude is one of perfect dignity. The arm is extended as in the act of command. The very fingers seem to indicate authority and to be worthy of Cæsar. The face is full of haughty determination daring genius and lofty ambition. The tout ensemble is a worthy representation of him whose nod did awe the world. I spent a very pleasant hour with Mr. Farley conversing with him upon foreign scenes and men. He had been in Italy and shewed me a representation of the Forum as it was and as it is. The orator in former times spoke in the midst of the most glorious mementos. The trophies of conquest were every where around him. The temples of religion were on the right hand and on the left. The Senate House was near. One would think that in such a place and before such an audience stones might be eloquent. The scene is much changed now. The trophies have mouldered into dust—temples and triumphal arches have been broken down and but a few solitary columns or here and there naked and dilapidated walls are alone standing. It is melancholy to think of the change: Still more melancholy to reflect that the change which has passed upon the Eternal City may be but a prophecy of what is coming upon us when virtue has decayed and licentiouness and anarchy have struck upon the harp of time the discordant prelude to despotism & ruin.

SEPT 22. Read today the new novel Devereux.[65] It is like the preceding works of the same author full of gorgeous and exaggerated Description. It makes human nature assume a new aspect. It gives to crime a sublimity of terror which attracts even while it terrifies. It excites a feeling like that which one feels when gazing from an overhanging precipice into a yawning gulf—a strange propensity to plunge in reckless of consequences. I deem them most pernicious works—works which do more to taint the morality of society than almost all others. The author is doubtless a gifted being—but he has prostituted God's noblest gifts to the vilest purposes. He might be great in the noblest sense; he is only great in evil.

SEPT 26. Called at Mrs. Elgar's this evening and recd. thro Miss Margarette a rather unexpected message from Miss [E G W].[66]

---

65. Edward George Earle Lytton Bulwer-Lytton, *Devereaux. A Tale. By the Author of "Pelham" and "The Disowned"* ... (London, 1829).

66. Elizabeth Gamble Wirt. Mrs. Elgar and Margarette (or Margaret) were more than likely members of the family of Joseph Elgar, commissioner of public buildings for Washington, D.C. Charles Lanman, *Biographical Annals of the Civil Government of the United States* ... (Washington, D.C., 1876), 135; entry for Oct. 14, 1829, below.

SEPT. 29. "Music, heavenly maid,"[67] occasioned us a little trouble today. One of the boarders was so fond of his instruments that he greatly annoyed a neighbour who was disposed to study.[68] Neither wd. yield, and as most of the boarders (the Goths!) took part with the student the votary of Haydn was compelled to take his flute, french horn, flageolet, violin and violincello and find other quarters.

OCT 1. Called today on the banished Orpheus: and found him very comfortably situated in the third story whence he had a very fine prospect of the windings of the Potomac. His table was covered with musical instruments and papers and he was himself studying a mathematical theory of musical sounds.

OCT 9. Rose early and went to Baltimore with Dr. Collins in his gig.[69] Stopped at Mr. Wirt's and took the family by surprise. Elizabeth and Catharine had gone to bid farewell to Mrs. Ouseley who was about to embark for Europe.[70] They soon returned and I conversed with them for some time. I then went to my Hotel and spent the night. The next morning when I called E—— entrusted me with a token leaf for a friend at Washington and bidding them farewell we came away. As we were coming home we passed a man whose tattered rags seemed to plead eloquently tho silently for relief. I proposed to the Doctor to stop till he came up and offer him some money. To our surprise he refused it but requested clothes. These we had not to spare. He threw back his miserable cloak exhibiting the epitomized history of suffering under it and exclaimed "Twenty years ago I was master of thirty thousand Dollars and now I have not one picaune. Edward Livingston has brought me to this.["][71] I now wonder that I did not stop to hear some explanation of this strange charge against a man who stands high in in general esteem and at the present moment occupies a seat in the National Senate.

---

67. William Collins, *The Passions, an Ode . . . Set to Musick by Doctor Hayes* (Oxford, 1750), line 1.

68. Chase was living at Mr. Handy's Boarding House, near the intersection of Pennsylvania Avenue and I Street. Chase to Hamilton Smith, Sept. 9, 1829 (Smith MSS, Indiana Univ.); Perry M. Goldman and James S. Young, *The United States Congressional Directories 1789–1840* (New York, 1973), 207.

69. Probably Dr. S. Collins of Washington, D.C. *Wash. Dir.* (1830), 9, 21.

70. Maria Van Ness Ouseley (d. 1881), the wife of British diplomat Sir William Gore Ouseley. Chase to Hamilton Smith, Mar. 31, 1828 (Smith MSS, Indiana Univ.); *DNB*, 14:1258.

71. Lawyer and politician Edward Livingston (1764–1836), a member of New York's Livingston family, served at this time as U.S. senator from Louisiana. In 1803 he had become part owner of the Batture Sainte Marie, a valuable piece of New Orleans real estate whose title was in dispute. The object of Chase's interest was probably one of many squatters evicted from this land over the course of more than thirty years' litigation. *DAB*, 11:309–12; William B. Hatcher, *Edward Livingston: Jeffersonian Republican and Jacksonian Democrat* (University, La., 1940), 139–89.

When we arrived at our lodgings I was pleased to find my friend Smith awaiting my arrival.[72] With him I had a long conversation on subjects of great interest to me and asked his advice and finally obeyed the suggestion of my own fancy.

OCT 12 Called this evening with Smith at Mr. Pleasonton's.[73] Miss Matilda played for us and talked with us and laughed at us and was rewarded by Smith with the denomination of "a peice of statuary" when we returned home. Whereat Dr. Collins was offended because he said it was indelicate to compare ladies to statues; the latter being generally naked. Whereupon a learned discussion followed the particulars of which I do not remember and if I did should not probably deem them worthy of relation

OCT. 14 I went on the evening of this day to introduce my friend Smith to Mr. Elgars family. M. E.[74] the youngest of the ladies is a lively and intelligent girl with sparkling eyes and a speaking countenance. Her form is a very little embonpoint. The tones of her voice are like those of the sky lark. She sings well and plays admirably. Better than all she is disposed to exert her talents for the entertainment of her friends. Her sister is a couple of years older but strange to say age while it is a great recommendation to wine and poetry is seldom a recommendation to ladies. Eliza Elgar is decidedly more intelligent than her sister and has much more character. Yet everybody likes her sister best. They would confide in Eliza, but they would prefer the society of Margaret. The one inspires respect and esteem the other communicates pleasure and delight. In prosperity I would sail under Margaret's flag but when storms awake and dangers thicken I should resort to the prudence, the constancy and the devotion of Eliza.

OCT 16 This evening I introduced Smith to the family of Mr. Ringgold[75] and spent a few hours very pleasantly.

---

72. Hamilton Smith (1804–75), a friend from Dartmouth who came to Washington to take over Chase's school. Smith became a Louisville attorney, then from 1851 to 1873 was president of the American Cannel Coal Company and Indiana Cotton Mill of Cannelton, Ind. He and Chase were partners in a number of business dealings. Chapman, *Sketches of the Alumni*, 250; Emerson, *General Catalogue*, 243; Chase to Smith, May 10, July 14, Sept. 9, 1829 (Smith MSS, Indiana Univ.); Robert M. Taylor, Jr., et al., *Indiana: A New Historical Guide* (Indianapolis, 1989), 225.

73. Stephen Pleasonton (or Pleasanton; d. 1855), fifth auditor of the U.S. Treasury, 1817–55. Lanman, *Biographical Annals*, 338; Leonard D. White, *The Jeffersonians: A Study in Administrative History, 1801–1829* (New York, 1951), 180–81.

74. Margarette Elgar.

75. Tench Ringgold, the marshal of Washington, D.C. *Wash. Dir. (1830)*, 65.

OCT. 30 I read today the Life of Sir Isaac Newton as published by the Society for the Diffusion of useful Knowledge.[76] How do the persevering exertions of such great minds to acquire Knowledge and extend the borders of Science put to shame my feeble efforts. Yet I think to reach the Pinnacle of Learning. Alas that I should foolishly dream of extensive attainments when I suffer so much of my time to glide away in reverie—when I devote a still larger proportion to idle visiting: under such circumstances who could do anything worth the doing?

NOV. 5. The impressions mentioned on the preceeding page were confirmed powerfully by an article I read today upon Dwights travels in Germany.[77] Here I read of boys of eighteen whose attainments in Literature were far very far beyond mine and whose knowledge of the abstract sciences could hardly be compared to mine. It would be as 10 to 0. I consoled myself in some degree by imputing my ignorance to a defective education. But this is but miserable comfort; had I possessed energy, resolution[,] industry I might have made attainments large as theirs. But because I could not be suited as to the mode of study; because I could not surround myself with every thing that could assist labour or facilitate research I became tired and idle. Until these things can be shall I refuse to labour / Thus away with the fond expectations I have long indulged. They will never be gratified. Had the great men, had the German scholars—deferred the labour of the labour of application until placed in circumstances [precisely] according with their most extravagant imagination would their names ever have been committed to Time as a trust of which he might be proud. No. Let me no longer deceive myself—these miserable pretences are nothing more than apologies for laziness or cloaks for incapacity.

NOV. 14 Calling on Mrs. Elgar today she shewed me a letter she had just recd. from C. G. Wirt in which she reproached me with neglect of writing to them. I might say in the words of one mentioned in the old Testament, "Is there not a cause.[78]

---

76. Jean Baptiste Biot, *Life of Sir Isaac Newton* . . . (London, 1829).
77. See the review of Henry Dwight, *Travels in the North of Germany, in the Years 1825 and 1826* (New York, 1829) in the *American Quarterly Review* 6 (Sept. 1829): 189–216.
78. Shortly before slaying Goliath, David was accused by his oldest brother, Eliab, of arriving at Israelite headquarters in search of glory. David's response, quoted by Chase, explained his presence as the result of his father's instructions. 1 Sam. 17:29.

Nov 15 Went to hear Mr Hewitt preach on the subject of Temperance.[79] He exhibited an array of startling and terrible facts and upon them founded a most impressive discourse. Sometimes he rose into grandeur but he did not seem ambitious of display. His soul was in the cause. He felt that a great question was to be decided, and he struggled to impress his own thought deeply on other minds. He cared not a rush for the glitter of oratory. He forgot altogether his own reputation. He saw in vision a great nation likely to be destroyed by Intemperance. He knew that their fathers had left them freedom—a freedom purchased with blood. He knew that Intemperance might wrest this invaluable legacy from them. He felt as a man as a patriot, as a christian—as a man the degradation of our nature—as a patriot the impending dangers of freedom—as a christian the ruin of immortal hopes. And so feeling he spoke as a man so feeling always will speak with pathos, with energy, with irresistible power. The largest audience I had ever seen gathered in a Washington Church listened with profound and departed to their homes, all instructed and some doubtless reformed[80]

Nov. 16. I read today the speech of Benjamin Watkins Leigh in the Convention of Virginia.[81] It is an able and ingenious defence of the ancient order of things covering nearly eleven closely printed columns of the Richmond Enquirer. A portion of the speech contained sentiments in which I heartily concur—particularly in a vivid and striking delineation, of the degrading acts practised by office seekers. To other sentiments expressed in it I could by no means assent. The strange idea that the free labouring population of non slaveholding states was on the same level in the point of intelligence and should be on the same level in point of political privilege was unworthy of Mr. Leigh and utterly abhorrent to every principle of equal rights.

---

79. Nathaniel Hewit (1788–1867), a Presbyterian clergyman and general agent for the American Temperence Society, spoke at Washington's First Presbyterian Church. *Appletons'*, 3:191–92; *Daily National Intelligencer*, Nov. 14, 1829.
80. In his entry for Sept. 30, 1830 (below), Chase stated that he had written "about forty pages of this book" during the preceding month. In the original manuscript, those forty pages would begin at about this entry for Nov. 15, 1829. Chase may have relied on memoranda which have not survived in writing his journal entries between this spot and Sept. 1830.
81. Virginia politician Benjamin Watkins Leigh (1781–1849), a future U.S. senator, represented Chesterfield County in the commonwealth's constitutional convention of 1829–30. The speech, which was given on Nov. 3 and 4, appeared in the *Richmond Enquirer*, Nov. 10 and 12, 1829. *DAB*, 11:152–53.

NOV 17. Dr. Huntt was married this evening to the youngest daughter of Mr. Ringgold.[82] The evening was extremely unpropitious, yet a great crowd was present. I went as a looker on. I saw Mr. Van Buren moving about, paying compliments and hunting for good opinions.[83] Many beaux promenaded the rooms and many belles seemed dying for their attentions. Mr. R—— was bustling around like an [a man] determined that if his guests were not pleased it should be thro' no fault of his. The Doctor was as happy as old bachelor just [escaped] from the barren confines of single blessedness is apt to be on such an occasion and the bride was a very pretty bride. At 10 large folding doors were thrown open displaying to the gourmands of the company a most inviting spectacle. An instant rush was made towards the tables; yet the gallantry of the gentlemen them to desist until the fairer half of creation had retired / Then however hams, rounds of beef, chickens were not spared. Pyramids of ice were demolished in less time than is required to record their fate. Wine flowed in rivers— and rivers [were] drank dry. At length however the appetite of the most eager was sated and as there was nothing more to be seen I returned home.

NOV 18. I was introduced this evening to Mrs Randolph a daughter of Jefferson at Mrs. Smith's.[84] She is a dignified woman. It is said that she inherits much of her fathers intellect. I had no opportunity this evening to judge the truth of the opinion but was willing to take it on trust. A weak mind never inhabited a form so commanding or imparted so much expression to a countenance. Some of her daughters were also present but unfortunately in our country talent seems to go according to the Statute of distribution as well as estates. Very little of the ances-[85] possession ever reaches an individual of the third generation.

82. In margin: "Dr. Huntt's Wedding." Dr. Henry Huntt, a Washington, D.C., physician, married Anna Maria Ringgold, the daughter of Tench Ringgold. *Daily National Intelligencer,* Nov. 20, 1829; *Wash. Dir. (1830),* 42.
83. Martin Van Buren (1782–1862) held, among other offices, those of U.S. senator, 1821–28, secretary of state, 1829–31, vice president, 1833–37, and president of the United States, 1837–41. *DAB,* 19:152–57.
84. In margin: "Mrs Randolph." Martha Jefferson Randolph (1772–1836) was the oldest daughter of Thomas Jefferson and the widow of Thomas Mann Randolph. Margaret Bayard Smith (1778–1844) achieved prominence as a Washington author and hostess. Her husband was Washington editor and banker Samuel Harrison Smith. *DAB,* 15:370–71, 17:318–19; Henry S. Randall, *The Life of Thomas Jefferson,* 3 vols. (New York, 1858), 3:564; Julian Boyd, ed., *The Papers of Thomas Jefferson, Vol. 2, 1777 to 18 June 1779* (Princeton, 1950), 252; Smith, *First Forty Years,* vi.
85. Chase evidently intended to write *ancestor's,* but hyphenated at a page turn and failed to complete the word.

DEC. 1–2 &c   I was now engaged in reading large quantities of law daily. I read 30 pages in Espinasses Nisi Prius and 30 pages in Stephen on Pleading[86] besides attending to numerous and urgent duties. Of course I read superficially but my object was rather to finish a certain number of books before I applied for admission to the bar than to acquire legal knowledge. I effected my object but at a great sacrifice. I have given strength to a habit of superficial reading which was strong before. It will not now be easy to eradicate it and substitute for it a habit of close attention and patient reflection. Yet this must be done or my admission to the bar will do me little good.

DEC 7.   Went to Court to be admitted but were not examined. The Court assigned Tuesday for our examination

DEC 9.   Attended again and the Court again put off our examination till the 14th.

DEC 14   Attended the court and with several others was examined for admission to the bar. One was rejected two were deferred—three of whom I was one were admitted. So I am now an Attorney at Law. I have a profession. Let me not dishonour it.[87]

DECR. 24.   I went to Baltimore with Mr. King.[88] I had expected my friend Swann to accompany me on this visit but on the evening before I started I recd. a letter from him stating that inevitable duties detained him in the country and would detain him there until after Christmas. In Mr. K. however I had a very agreeable companion. He is a painter of great merit. His representations of still life are said by competent judges to equal the productions of the European masters. Unfortunately however he is not allowed to indulge his own taste or to apply his industry to that department in which his genius eminently qualifies to excel. Artists must live and there is not taste enough in our country or to speak more truly not

---

86. Isaac Espinasse, *A Digest of the Law of Actions at Nisi Prius* (London, 1789); Henry John Stephen, *A Treatise on the Principles of Pleading in Civil Actions; Comprising a Summary View of the Whole Proceedings in a Suit at Law* (Philadelphia, 1824).

87. According to the court's minutes, Chase was examined and admitted to the bar of the U.S. Circuit Court for the District of Columbia on Dec. 21, 1829, not Dec. 14. His formal application for examination was on Dec. 11. Chase later wrote recollections of his admission to the bar. Minute Books, U.S. Circuit Court for the District of Columbia (Recs. of U.S. District Courts, Nat. Arch.); [1853?] memorandum, part of the same group of memoranda as Journal VI, and Chase to ———, July 10, 1853 (Chase Papers, L.C.).

88. Washington, D.C., portraitist Charles Bird King (1785–1862) had studied art in London under Charles Robert Leslie and Washington Allston. *Appletons'*, 3:538.

wealth enough to enable any one to be a munificent patron of the arts. Multitudes however have enough to gratify vanity and an artist speedily finds that upon gratified vanity his principal dependance must be placed. In order to live he must paint the living and therefore is that almost all our distinguished painters have been portrait-painters— When we arrived in Baltimore I took lodgings at the Hotel. Mr. King had relations with whom he found quarters. The same evening I called at Mr. Wirt's but having business in the city did not remain long. At night I returned again and spent some hours in conversation with the family. The next day was Christmas and we were all to dine together at Mr. W's. In the morning[89] I went to church. The Revd. Mr. Johns of Baltimore preached. It is the habit of this clergyman to deliver his sermons memoriter. This gives him a great advantage over readers and over most extempore preachers also. His discourses are beautifully written and very impressively delivered. They seem to come fresh from the heart of the speaker and reach I doubt not the hearts of many of his auditory. After church I went to Mr. Wirt's where most of the other guests were already assembled. Our party was a very pleasant one and we sat at the table until dark. We then adjourned to the drawing-room where we spent the evening in social chat or innocent amusement.

26. DECR. The next evening as I was going home late I observed a bright red colour upon the Southern Sky; which soon showed me that there must be a prodigious conflagration in that quarter of the city[.] Every thing was perfectly still. No alarm was heard in the streets and scarcely a soul was stirring. The alarm as I found afterwards had been already given and the people had assembled in great numbers at the scene of action. Curious to witness the spectacle I bent my steps in the direction of the light. I soon found that the fire was more distant than I anticipated but unwilling to return until I had accomplished my object I still held on and my perseverance was fully rewarded. A large sugar-refining establishment was in flames. Large quantities of combustible liquids were stowed away in the edifice which as fast as the devouring element reached them flashed out into fearful effulgence. Thousands were gazing on the sight. Young children, old men, even women were out. The engines sent upon the burning pile rivers of water, but it was turned to vapour and supplied aliment to the flame. One side of the building soon fell in with a tremendous crash and the fiery element leaped madly up as if triumphing over its fall. Hundreds were seen

---

89. In margin: "25"; and at turn of page just after this line in the original, "25 Decr."

in the lurid moving upon the roofs of the adjacent buildings, pouring water spreading blankets and used every precaution to save them. Their generous and spirited exertions were successful. Only one building was consumed beside that in which the fire originally commenced.[90]

DEC. 27. I went out today to see the finished portion of the Baltimore & Ohio Rail Road.[91] Only two miles have been as yet completed but this distance suffices for experiments. The cars are very long and about as wide as ordinary road-waggons—containing without inconvenience from twenty to thirty people. They weigh as I was informed about 1500 pounds apiece. Yet I could set one of them in motion and draw it along with my little finger. Friction is reduced almost to nothing. I saw a horse draw a loaded car at the rate of ten miles an hour and apparently with ease. A small car manned by a single sailor was rigged with a mast and sails. He admitted two or three passed and the little vehicle shot off before the wind to the great amusement and delight of the surrounding spectators. This rail-road must be completed. It is a project of too great consequence to the country to be suffered to remain unexecuted. Many find fault with the proceedings of the Directors and accuse them of a needless waste of the funds of the company. I am not able to judge of the justice of this imputation but am willing to presume it to be without foundation. I know how easy it is to discover imperfections and I know how impossible it is to be perfect. Mr. Niles who is a man of great practical intelligence and generally fair & impartial speaks well of them, saying that "the concern could not be placed in abler or better hands. The board of directors is composed of an unusual number of deeply thinking, closely calculating and indefatigably industrious gentlemen."[92] I am willing to trust his judgement. The road is of incalculable importance. It removes the Allghanies. Annihilates them as an obstacle, to the intercourse between the East and the West while it leaves them still to answer the great ends for which Providence destined them. It makes Cincinnati and Baltimore neighbouring cities and renders every kind of communication be-

90. A description of the fire, which destroyed the steam sugar refinery of D. L. Thomas, also appeared in the Washington *National Journal,* Jan. 1, 1830.
91. The Baltimore & Ohio, which opened for service in Jan. 1830, was a pioneer in American railroad technology. Its innovations included the ball bearing "friction wheel," developed by inventor Ross Winans, and several experiments in locomotion. The sail car which Chase saw was probably the "Æolus," one such experiment that soon proved its impracticality. *DAB,* 20:371–72; Edward Hungerford, *The Story of the Baltimore & Ohio Railroad, 1827–1929* ... (New York, 1928), 1:76–83.
92. *Niles' Weekly Register,* Dec. 26, 1829. Hezekiah Niles (1777–1839) edited and published the paper. *DAB,* 13:521–22.

tween them as easy as it is now between Baltimore and New York. It will open to the West a market for their Produce and facilitate the introduction of the manufactures of the East. But it is useless to attempt an enumeration, of the benefits to be derived from the completion of this great work. Time alone can make out the catalogue and Time I am sure will make out a longer and more splendid list than it's most sanguine advocates now anticipate

29. DEC. Returned to Washington leaving Mr. King behind but enjoying the company of some friends from W—— We arrivd about 12 o'clock M. I will here relate an anecdote of Mr. Van Buren which exhibits in a striking manner the character of this intriguing politician this american Talleyrand. When Mr. Van Buren first came to Washington Mr. Swann was among the very first citizens who opened his house to him and extended to him the courtesies of hospitality. Mr. Van Buren was then merely a Senator with no apparent prospect of ever being any thing more. Of course Mr. Swann's attentions could be prompted by no spirit of selfishness / Indeed at that time no one thought it necessary to conciliate the favour of men in power in order to retain the stations they might hold. Fidelity was a surer guard than favour. Mr. Van Buren expressed and seemed to feel gratitude for Mr. Swann's attentions. He visited frequently in the family and continued to do so from winter to winter until the last when he was elected Govr. of New York. He had held this station but a short time when he was appointed Secretary of State by Genl. Jackson. Rumour had been busy in spreading the report of an anticipated proscription and Duff Green had announced the intention of the Executive "to reward his friends and punish his enemies."[93] Many gentlemen friendly to the administration of Mr. Adams, who had held offices under the Genl. Government became alarmed. Mr. Swann was of the number. When Mr. Van Buren came to the Seat of Government Mr. S—— and his son-in-law Maj. Mercer called upon him.[94] He did not reciprocate this civility. His intentions were unknown. It was thought and rumoured that he was against the policy of proscription. It was surmised that he intended to pursue a generous, magnanimous and liberal course and thus draw upon himself the regards of all parties. The thing

93. Duff Green (1791–1875), a member of Andrew Jackson's "Kitchen Cabinet," owned and edited the Washington, D.C., *United States' Telegraph*. His comment appeared in his newspaper on Nov. 3, 1828. *DAB*, 7:540–42.
94. John Francis Mercer (d. 1848), a militia officer and the son of a Maryland governor of the same name, had married Mary Scott Swann, daughter of Thomas Swann, Sr. Charles Winslow Elliott, *Winfield Scott: The Soldier and the Man* (New York, 1937), 195; James Mercer Garnett, "John Francis Mercer, Governor of Maryland, 1801–1803," *Maryland Historical Magazine* 2 (Sept. 1907): 213.

seemed feasible and likely and many expected that such would be his course: when the sudden dismissals of six clerks from his office shewed the fallacy of all these suppositions and evinced his determination to go far as the farthest. A friend of Mr. Swann, desirous to learn what wd. be his fate, now called upon Mr. Van Buren. He found sitting in his office and entered into a conversation with him upon general topics. At length he carelessly asked "What will be done with old Swann? We must not let him go until at least we have had some more of his old Madeira." Van Buren evaded the question but Hamilton who was acting Secretary and was then present writing at a table in the room raised his head from his paper and gruffly remarked "He must go with the rest."[95] Sometime after this it was ascertained that it was not the intention of Genl. J—— to remove Mr. Swann & Mr. Van Buren had no sooner ascertained this fact than he hastened to return the calls of Maj. Mercer and Mr. Swann and appropriate to himself and to his kind interference the whole merit of the service. But the artifice was too shallow. The contemptible intriguer was detected and his renewal of civilities was looked upon with disgust and contempt. Such is, the character of Martin Van Buren, cold, selfish, intriguiging base and faithless. May he never reach the golden round to which he so ardently aspires.

An acquaintance of mine called lately on Genl. Jackson to request public employment of him. He said that the Genel. told him that his claims should be considered whenever a vacancy occurred but that he could not remove any one to make a place for him. "You see" said he "What a fuss the people make about the removals which have been made already.

DEC 31. The last day of the year has arrived—a year that to me has been fruitful of events: some of them of a not unpleasing character. My vanity has been flattered by many proofs of the estimation in which I am held by my acquaintance—tho' my conscience tells me I am far from deserving it,—even in its lowest degree. During the last year I have made some attainments in Literature and Science not altogether valueless yet when I compare what I have done with what I might have done—when I place the reality by the side of the possibility and percieve into what insignificance it instantly shrinks, I feel humbled and mortified by the conviction that the Creator has gifted me with intelligence almost in vain. I am almost twenty two and have as yet attained but the threshold of knowledge.

---

95. James Alexander Hamilton (1788–1878), the son of Alexander Hamilton and longtime advisor to politicians of all parties, was serving on Andrew Jackson's Appointing Council. *DAB*, 8:188–89.

I have formed few settled opinions and have examined but few subjects. The night has seldom found me much advanced beyond the station I occupied in the morning and the end of the year has at length come round and finds me almost in the very spot I was in at it's commencement. I have learned little & have forgotten much and ready to conclude of the future from the past I almost despair of ever making any figure in the world. Yet let me consider that I have not reached that age when improvement is hopeless and that many obstacles have hither to surrounded me and impeded my progress. Let me console myself by this reflection and take courage. Let me once more resolve to struggle earnestly for the prize of well-doing[96] and looking in humble confidence to Him who is glorifiied in all the attainments of all his creatures press on again in the race of virtue, of learning and Science, to the gaol of virtuous and holy reputation.

1830

JAN 1. While all the world went today to pay their respects to Genl. Jackson, I remained at home or went abroad only to see a few friends. Among other places I called at Mr. Smith's the President of the bank of the United States[97] / This family has long been on the list of my visiting acquaintance but it is recently comparatively that I have begun to esteem them as friends. Mrs. Smith has written several little works; one of which was translated into French and republished in Paris.[98] She was here when the Federal City was in it's infancy and knew all the great men who have at different times adorned the councils of our republic or who have from foreign lands come to look upon our rising greatness. In consequence of such association she can tell much of bygone days & men. One evening she related to me the following anecdote of Jefferson.[99] A report had prevailed that J. had written a letter to Chas. Thompson, in which he professed a conversion to the Christian religion and

---

96. "I press toward the mark for the prize of the high calling of God in Christ Jesus." Phil. 3:14.

97. In margin: "Mr. Smith." Samuel Harrison Smith (1772–1845), former editor of the *National Intelligencer*, president of the Washington branch of the Bank of the United States, and husband of Margaret Bayard Smith. *DAB*, 17:343–44.

98. Margaret Bayard Smith's most notable works to date included *A Winter in Washington; or Memoirs of the Seymour Family* . . . , 2 vols. (New York, 1824), and *What is Gentility? A Moral Tale* . . . (Washington, D.C., 1828), reprinted under the pseudonym of L. P. E. A. Sédillot as *Les Mac-Carty, ou Qu'est-ce Queles Gens Comme Faut?* . . . (Paris, 1829).

99. In margin: "Jefferson." The anecdote refers to Thomas Jefferson (1743–1826), third president of the U.S. *DAB*, 10:17–35.

renounced the infidel opinions which he had formerly held.[1] Mrs. S—— delighted to hear this wrote to Mr. J. to enquire if such were the fact. He replied that he had written no such letter to Mr. Thompson and that his religious sentiments ought to be and were known only to himself and God.[2]   At Mrs. Smith's I became acquainted with Mrs. Randolph the daughter of Jefferson.[3] She is a very dignified lady, converses extremely well but sparingly. She repeated to me, in his own words, a description of John Adams by Doct. Franklin, "Always an honest man often a great man and sometimes a madman.[4]

JANUARY 7   This evening I went with my friend Swann to the President's Drawing Room.[5] The East-room now furnished splendidly but not gorgeously, was open for the reception of guests. Near the South centre stood Genl. Jackson with whom I now shook hands for the first time in my life. He is rather above the ordinary stature and has a graceful figure. His countenance would not inspire a disciple of Lavater, with an opinion of lofty talent or vigourous intellect.[6] True it is that age and hardship have done their work upon him; but the characters of mind are not to be effaced by causes whose influence reaches not beyond this diurnal sphere. Genl. J. is not a man of mind. In his manners he is graceful and agreeable and much excels his predecessor in the art of winning golden opinions from all sorts of men. Genl. J——'s career should be attentively observed by the political student who is endeavouring from the book of human affairs to glean the lessons of political experience. If his popularity continues it will be strange; for I have read of no instance in the history of nations where popular favour has for a long time followed an unworthy object. At the drawing-room this evening I saw little to interest me. The usual motley crowd was present. The high and low, the ins and the outs, the wise and the foolish, the learned and the ignorant, the old and the young, the black and

---

1. Charles Thomson (1729–1824), known also as a biblical scholar, served as secretary of the Continental Congress, 1774–89. *DAB*, 18:481–82.
2. Jefferson's reply to Smith, dated Aug. 6–16, 1816, has been reproduced in H. A. Washington, ed., *The Writings of Thomas Jefferson* . . . , 9 vols. (Washington, D.C., 1853–54), 7:27–28.
3. Martha Jefferson Randolph.
4. In margin: "J. Adams." Franklin's description is taken from a letter to Robert R. Livingston, July 22, 1783. Albert Henry Smyth, ed., *The Writings of Benjamin Franklin* . . . , 10 vols. (New York, 1906), 9:62.
5. In margin: "President's Drawing-Room."
6. Jean-Gaspard Lavater (1741–1801) a Swiss Protestant pastor and writer, was the founder of physiognomics, the art of reading personal characteristics by observing facial features. *Nouvelle Biographie Générale depuis les Temps les Plus Reculés jusqu'a Nos Jours* . . . (Paris, 1853–66), 29:995–1005.

the white and every intermediate hue were congregated for various purposes. Some came to see the President for the first time; some to bow and prattle to the ladies, some to exhibit their own important selves to announce to the world that they were yet alive and some to prosecute schemes of political ambition. It were a curious speculation to follow to a quiet chambers these several characters and trace their emotions of gratified hope or disappointed expectation. We might see the belle exulting as she numbered oer her conquests and the politician reconstructing the intricate web of policy which that night's occurrences had sadly disordered. But it is idle to dwell upon such fancies

This day I called at Mr. Ingham's to see my friend M. G. M.[7] This young lady has the most perfect skill in all the arts of pleasing or to speak more truly of her she has from nature the rare ability to please without art. Her face is not one which a sculptor would choose for a model; yet is it beautiful in feature and still more beautiful in expression. Even her looks of anger and scorn have a pretty gracefulness which half disarms them. Her form is slight and frail but exquisitely moulded. Her motion is free as the summer breeze; and like it soft & gentle or animated and unreserved. And she has a way of saying such sweet things with her voice of melody. Every word and tone of hers is a sweet music; sweeter because like the tones of the windharp, they are unsubjected to the rules of art. I was very near falling in Love with this lady—nay I should certainly have done so had not our tastes been in one particular wholly dissimilar. She is fond of the gay world—I have no desire to partake in it's vanities. She is disinclined to religion and it's duties; I value them more than any earthly possession. One evening I was in a gay company with her. She took my arm and asked me what it was that Miss S—— had been telling me about her. I replied that she had told me that I was her (M's) favourite. She drew back a step with the affectation of surprise. I told her not to be alarmed for I did not believe a word of it. I was far humbler in my pretensions. Upon this she made some flattering observation which induced me to ask if I might believe it. She answered that S. was her most intimate friend and knew her thoughts much better than she herself did. This was a strong temptation but I withstood it. I expect

7. In margin: "M. G. M." Mary Galloway Maxcy was a daughter of Virgil Maxcy, solicitor to the U.S. Treasury. Samuel Delucenna Ingham (1779–1860) was secretary of the Treasury and a former congressman from Pennsylvania. Judging from Chase's running head in the original journal, this paragraph relates to Feb. 1830. Chase to Elizabeth Washington Wirt, Jan. 28, 1830 (Chase Papers, Hist. Soc. of Pa.); *DAB*, 9:473–74, 12:434–35; John Martin Hammond, *Colonial Mansions of Maryland and Delaware* (Philadelphia, 1914), 141–42; Charles M. Wiltse et al., eds., *The Papers of Daniel Webster* (Hanover, N.H., 1974–86), Corres., 4:387–88.

now soon to see her united to a young friend of mine, of a disposition more congenial to her own and in every respect worthy of so much loveliness.

In the latter part of February my friend Swann proposed an excursion to Morven, his residence near Leesburgh[8] / I agreed and having made the necessary preparations on Monday morning we started in the stage. Our companions were a young officer in the army and his beautiful bride. She was formerly an admired belle but she loved and she married contrary to the wish of her father. It was a stolen match and the old gentleman has not yet forgiven from the heart. I could help pitying her as I saw a shade of sadness stealing over her cheek and a starting tear dimming her bright eye. There was besides in the stage a man with singular vision. He could see wit where others could discern nothing but folly and sense where others only perceived stupidity. He filled evidently a high place in his own esteem and doubtless should he hereafter publish a spelling-book he will like his immortal prototype dedicate it to the Universe / After riding some miles we stopped at a little house by the roadside,[9] much like those which a New England farmer would construct for the accommodation of his horses and pigs. Here we were to breakfast. The house did not wear a very inviting aspect but as I make it a rule not to judge by the outward appearance I went in. The breakfast was spead in the first room I entered. The table was covered with poultry and bacon and beef and vegetables. The bar was in convenient proximity and the kitchen at no great remove. But I must hurry to the end of the Journey. At night we arrived at Leesburgh and had a comfortable supper at Col. Osborn's Hotel. Here we passed the night / Early next morning we rose and mounting the horses which our friends had provided for us rode out to Morven a distance of about 3 miles. Our arrival was quite unexpected and we were obliged to go to the kitchen until a fire could be kindled in the parlour of the mansion. Very soon however every thing was in readiness. A cheerful fire was blazing on the hearth and an excellent breakfast spread upon the table. We were not disposed to keep Lent and the good things disappeared before us like the chance snowfall in April. After breakfast I took a more leisurely survey of the mansion and its appurtenances. It is situated upon the side of one of catoctin mountains; by which it is protected from the Northwest winds. A beautiful valley extends below far to the southeast where cultivated fields and extensive woodlands form a variety

---

8. In margin: "Excursion to Leesburgh February." The Swanns had owned "Morven Park" for about five years. Harrison Williams, *Legends of Loudoun: An Account of the History and Homes of a Border County* (Richmond, 1938), 177.

9. In margin: "Breakfast."

delightful to the eye.[10] At a small distance in front of the house is a garden; a lovely spot, in the season of flowers, as Swann told me, tho' there was little there now to attract the eye. The mansion itself is composed of a centre building, and two wings, which united by a narrow structure with a colonnade in front / There is also a colonnade or rather a portico in front of the central edifice. In the rear of the whole are two stoutbuildings for the overseer and house servants. Such is the house and such are the grounds according to the impressions I now retain of a visit made last month. After breakfast we rode to Col. Tutt's to see the country ladies.[11] Here I saw a very pretty and agreeable girl and a plain but kindhearted old lady. We chatted about an hour and went home for dinner. After dinner we rode to Raspberry Plain the residence of Mr. Hoffman.[12] Here I saw two originals in the shape of young ladies. Two agreeable, intelligent girls who had read much, thought much and (perhaps) talked more. They made subtle distinctions with a skill worthy of old Aristotle, and syllogized as if they been educated in the school of Duns Scotus or Thomas Aquinas. But I don't like argumentative ladies. They have no right to encroach upon our privileges. And is it not settled by grayheaded prescription that the masculine is the more worthy gender and that we are entitled to an exclusive monopoly of all the wit, sense & learning in the world. I thought I had two more pages but must break off abruptly.[13]

FEBY 21   I have witnessed this evening a scene unlike anything I ever saw, imagined or heard of.[14] There being no service at the other churches on account of the weather I attended the Methodist chapel.[15] I was in a degree for the sermon by the prayer. It was highly figurative and impassioned and earnest. The congregation was much excited and united audibly with the minister. Their utterance however was not articulate language but consisted of exlamations and groans and at times shouts of triumph. When the sermon commenced my attention was irresistibly drawn to the

---

10. In margin: "Morven."
11. Col. Charles Pendleton Tutt, the master of "Locust Hill." *William and Mary Quarterly*, 1st ser., 3 (Jan. 1895): 241.
12. "Raspberry Plain," previously the home of U.S. Senator Stevens Thomson Mason, had recently been acquired by George, John, Peter, and Samuel Hoffman of Baltimore. *DAB*, 12:374–75; Williams, *Legends of Loudoun*, 170.
13. Chase evidently wrote his description of the trip to Morven sometime after he wrote the entry for Feb. 21, which follows on the next page in the original journal. He did not allow sufficient space and had to end the Morven entry abruptly, squeezing the last portion in at the bottom of the page.
14. In margin: "Methodist Meeting."
15. The Ebenezer Methodist Church, led by Rev. William Ryland, was located near the Washington Navy Yard. *Wash. Dir. (1830)*, 66, 107.

preacher. He began in a low tone of voice and proceeded for some time in a simple didactic strain. By degrees however he became more and more animated until at length he forgot every thing around him and gave free utterance to his crowding thoughts. "What a paradoxical creed" said he "do these Christians recieve! Say the people of the world. "God in him and he in God? how can that be? In yonder blacksmith's shop you see the iron in the fire and the fire in the iron and the more the fire is infused into it, the more nearly does it assimilate itself to the nature of that element. If this can be in material things why not in spiritual?" Much similiar illustration was used throughout the sermon. He described the nature of the Christian hope and described the evidence of acceptance with God. The internal peace which constitutes much of this evidence might indeed he said be sometimes marred by an unhappy physical constitution. "The spirits of the believer may be depressed. He may faint in his march Zionward; and the tempter may thus obtain power over him; and his hope of glory may be obscured; and he may hang his harp upon the willows and sing no more the song of Zion:[16] but in a little while the clouds will break away and the light of God's countenance will shine upon him and he will take down his harp from the willows and tune it to a sweeter strain and strike the notes with a bolder hand till every chord resound Glory to God." He spoke of the delusive phantoms of pleasure which mock the pursuit of the ungodly. He dwelt upon the divine declaration "there is no peace to the wicked."[17] He described the transition from this state to "the peace of God". "At length" he said "the angel of deliverance approaches; and the prison-walls are shaken and the fetters fall off and the soul emerges from it's bondage into glorious liberty.[18] I tell you, a new song is put into his mouth and he shall sing it forever and ever."[19] I am conscious that I but feebly imitate his language. It was plain plainer than that I have attributed to him, but more expressive. There was besides a suddenness of transition from darkness to light and from deep horror to lofty rapture and a manner of delivery and a peculiarity of intonation which must be seen and heard to be understood. The whole was intended for present effect. And that end was answered. I never conceived it possible that declamation cd. so affect even so ignorant an audience. Some shouted aloud in anticipation of Heaven. Some shrieked in dread of hell. Sobs and groans resounded thro' the house mingled

16. Ps. 137:1–3.
17. Jer. 48:22.
18. Refers to the release of Paul and Silas from the prison in Philippi. Acts 16:25–26.
19. Rev. 5:9–13.

with the loud gratulations and thanksgivings of those who appropriated to themselves the rich promises of the preacher. Some started wildly from their seats as if to rush to joy or escape from woe; while many gazed with an earnestness of astonishment which demonstrated that such a scene was not common even in a Methodist Meeting.

FEB 22   The conversation this evening turned upon the Turks.[20] Commodore Crane stated that Mahmoud the present Sultan was a wise & sagacious, but unscrupulous prince.[21] He saw how far in the rear of other European nations they were. He undermined and finally destroyed the formidable power of the Janissaries / He commanded a change of dress which removed the impediments to active motion. He has introduced the European tactics. Comm. C. saw a negro man drilling a battalion. It is even said that he has permitted the women to go unveiled. The Turks deem a woman beautiful in proportion to her corpulency.[22] One was asked if his daughter was not soon to be married. "Yes" was the reply. "How soon?" As soon as she gets fat. I am fatting her now" And then he mentioned the quantity of nutriment she consumed daily. . . . The Turks are generally very honest in their dealings. Mr. Offely our consul at Smyna[23] had a large quantity of coffee on hand which he sold to a Turk at a certain price. The Turk took away a part for which he paid and promised to return for the rest in a few weeks. Months passed and he was not heard of. In the meantime large quantities of coffee came into the market and the price fell one half. At length when a year had expired a man presented himself to Mr. O. and asked "Did you not sell a certain quantity of Coffee last year at a certain price to such a one?" "Yes" Well he took the plague at Aleppo and died. I am his brother & have come to fulfil his contract". "But coffee is worth less now?" "No matter: I must fulfil the agreement as it was made." And he took the coffee and paid the money. . . .[24] Their notions of trade are limited.[25] The Comm. wished to buy a number of pipes and asked the price of one. "So much": of ten? "twenty times so much." They pretend that Champaign is not wine and they

---

20. In margin: "The Turks / Mahmoud."
21. William Montgomery Crane (1776–1846), commander of the U.S. Mediterranean squadron; Mahmud II ruled the Ottoman Empire from 1808 to 1839. *Appletons'*, 2:2; Frederick B. Artz, *Reaction and Revolution, 1814–1832* (New York, 1934), 248.
22. In margin: "Beauty."
23. In margin: "Honesty." David Offley (d. 1838), a merchant from Philadelphia, was the unofficial U.S. consul at Smyrna. *DAB*, 13:634–35.
24. Chase wrote a period followed by five more dots.
25. In margin: "Notions about Trade & Wine."

therefore drink it without scruple. Rum also & ardent spirits generally are exempted out of the prohibition against wine.

Judge Burnett of the Senate is a small man, of a not unpleasing countenance.[26] The indications of intellect are slight but by untiring industry he has acquired a high professional reputation. He converses with some appearance of effort and has been as yet a silent member of the Senate.[27] I held this morning some conversation with him respecting Cincinnati.[28] He said that the bar there was crowded as it is every where. That there were many young men of fine talents and acquirements without business but that this was imputable chiefly to their modesty. Still he said Cincinnati is growing rapidly. Population and wealth are increasing. Living is cheap. And on the whole it offers to you stronger inducements than any other place in the West.

Today I wrote for a young friend the foll. verses

To M. G. M.[29]

When Mary bids, once more, the lyre
    Long hushed, I wake again
Nor ask the *Nine* to aid my lay
    For *Mary* wills the strain.

Dull lyre! why trembleth every string
    With emulous desire
To tell, with sweetest tones, the flame
    That Mary's charms inspire?

To tell of all her witching graces,
    Her winning smile, her beaming eye,
Her radiant, mind-illumined face,
    Her voice of melody?

Not now the time—not thine the power
    Such notes as these to swell
Ah no: for Sadness claims the hour—
    Thou can'st but breath, Farewell!

---

26. In margin: "Judge Burnett." Jacob Burnet (1770–1853), a Cincinnati attorney and former member of Ohio's Supreme Court, had filled the position in the U.S. Senate left vacant in 1828 by the resignation of William Henry Harrison. *DAB*, 3:294–95.

27. In margin: "Feb. 23."

28. In margin: "Cincinnati."

29. In margin: "Verses to M. G. M." Chase wrote the poem to Mary Galloway Maxcy. See Jan. 7, 1830, above.

And on another page the following

A Wish—To M. G. M.[30]

> His love be thine, who is all truth
>   All nobleness, all mind,
> The ardours of whose generous Youth
>   By virtue are refined.
>
> Be, of the noblest and the best
>   The best and noblest, he;
> And, summing in one word, the rest
>   May he be worthy thee.

On expressing[31] to a lady this evening the pleasure I had enjoyed during a visit of a few days to the country, she remarked "It is not wonderful. *There you* would be of some consequence." I rejoined "And there is at least *one place,* not in the country, where *even I* am of some consequence". Alluding to the house of the lady addressed, where I then was.

May you, fair lady,[32] be like this flower, excepting it's evanescence. May you bloom like the rose but may you not fade like it.

Sweets to the sweet says the Arch-Poet; the great High Priest of the mysteries of Nature;[33]

Transient joys are the most exquisite: the rose that soonest fades breathes out most fragrance. While in artificial flowers like artificial mirth you observe a perpetual bloom but easily detect the cheat by the absence of perfume—

Pity it is that the beautiful should so soon pass away / The stars set and we scarcely notice their departure because we know that they will rise again to adorn the same scenes with their familiar beams—but when beauty passes it is to return hither no more.

One evening I staid at a tavern in Virginia where a Jury was (technically) hung.[34] The case under consideration was a matter of life or death. A man had been tried for the murder of his wife & they were to pass sentence upon him. They were not however disposed to do it after a common fashion. They obtained punch in profusion and soon were *plenissimi Bacchi.*[35] They danced, they

---

30. In margin: "A wish / M. G. M."
31. In margin: "Retort."
32. In margin: "Sentences for Conversation."
33. *Hamlet,* act 5, scene 1, line 243.
34. In margin: "A Virginia Jury."
35. "Thoroughly drunk."

turned somersets, they romped. The room was a scene of indescribable confusion and the uproar might be heard at the distance of half a mile. There was no prospect of a decision that night and the Sheriffs wished to leave one of their number in charge of the Jury while the rest of them should retire to their homes. This however the Jury were not inclined to permit. They were unable to see the reason why a Sheriff might go while a Juror was ditained. And now ensued a contest between the Sheriffs and Jury, which were the Genius of McFingal mine, I might paint in proper colours.[36] As it is I can only say that one Sheriff made his escape from the room; and came out shrugging his shoulders and rubbing his sides as if he had been running the gauntlet. Another was not so fortunate for the enemy caught him and reversed the order of Nature completely, suspending his feet high in air and compelling him to dance a hornpipe upon his hands. After awhile however the noise abated. The Spirit of alcohol exhausted itself at length and "Sleep covered them all over like a cloak."[37]

29 This evening I attended a party at Mrs. Inghams.[38] It was large and brilliant. Miss Livingston was there in all her splendour[39] & M. G. M. in all her attractive loveliness. Many other ladies were there but nearly all of them are strangers to me. I was dull and the hue of my feelings cast a shade all around me.

On the next day I went to Baltimore and, having made some other calls, visited Mrs. Wirt.[40] It was as it was wont to be. Some of the family were sick, others did not appear, and they who did seemed changed. Perhaps it was but the picturing of my fancy but I fear not. The next day, coming out of church I met one of the young ladies. I had not seen her on the preceding day and perhaps my own manner was somewhat affected by the reception I had

---

36. M'Fingal was a fictitious Tory squire created during the American Revolution by Connecticut novelist and poet John Trumbull (1750–1831). M'Fingal supposedly possessed the prophetic ability to foresee future greatness for the Patriot cause in spite of his own royalist convictions. *DAB*, 19:10–11; John Trumbull, *M'Fingal: A Modern Epic Poem* . . . (Philadelphia, 1776); Moses Coit Tyler, *The Literary History of the American Revolution* (New York, 1898), 1:430–43.

37. Miguel de Cervantes Saavedra, *The Visionary Gentleman Don Quixote de la Mancha*, trans. Robinson Smith, 3rd ed. (New York, 1932), 566.

38. In margin: "Mrs. Ingham's." Deborah Kay Hall Ingham was the wife of Treasury Secretary Samuel D. Ingham. *DAB*, 9:473–74.

39. Coralie Livingston Barton (1806–73), the daughter of Sen. Edward Livingston and, after 1833, the wife of Thomas Pennant Barton. *Appletons'*, 1:188; Louise Livingston Hunt, *Memoir of Mrs. Edward Livingston With Letters Hitherto Unpublished* (New York, 1886), 41; Virginia Tatnall Peacock, *Famous American Belles of the Nineteenth Century* (Philadelphia, 1901), 80–88.

40. In margin: "The Wirts."

met. She accused me of coldness. I defended myself as well as I could and went home with her. I called again the next day and bade them farewell

I spent the evening of the day I arrivd in Baltimore at Mr. Schroeders.[41] I had become acqua[inte] with this family in Washington and wished to continue the acquaintance. The evening passed pleasantly. Conversation and music mingled their charms.— The conversation was interesting and the music sweet—very sweet. Miss S. plays and sings delightfully. Her favourite instrument is the guitar—and it is mine too; for it is associated with many pleasant remembrances. I left at a late hour intending & promising to call again but from circumstances was obliged to leave Baltimore without doing so.

MARCH 1   The few days, after my return to Washington before I began my journey to this place,[42] were employed in arranging my affairs and bidding farewell to my friends and acquaintance. All this was at length over and on Thursday the 4th. of March I finally left Washington[43] which had now been my home for more than three years and where I had found much kindness and many friends. It was not without regret that I looked for the last time perhaps, on those familiar scenes. But we soon lost sight of them all and my mind turned from the contemplation of the past to the consideration of the future.

It was not with dismay or dread that I looked forward.[44] True there was little to invite in the foreground of the picture. I was fully aware that I must pass thro' a long period of probation. That day and night must be witnesses to the assiduity of my labours. That my mind must be disciplined to habits of deep reflection and patient toil. That many obstacles were to be overcome, many difficulties to be surmounted ere I could hope to reach the steep where Fame's proud temple shines. All this I knew. But in the background were deserved honour, eminent usefulness and "a crown of glory":[45] and pain, & toil & labour vanished from the sight which was directed over and beyond them.

I will not describe our stage company further[46] than to say that

41. In margin: "Miss S. S."
42. Cincinnati. Chase's statement at Sept. 30, 1830 (below) indicates that he wrote this portion of the journal during Sept.
43. In margin: "March 4."
44. In margin: "A Glance at Futurity."
45. 1 Pet. 5:4.
46. In margin: "Stage Company."

it consisted of a woman, whose occupation I could not divine, a young yankee, who was *wise* in his own eyes,[47] a female convict just discharged from the Penitentiary of Virginia; a young gentleman of the name of Brown from Washington[48] & myself.

The roads were in a miserable condition.[49] A frost had just hardened the surface enough to render it difficult for the horses to extricate their feet which went thro at every step. The upset once but nobody was injured. When I pass this road again I hope to travel on a railway. Nothing less will tempt me on it again for some time at least.

In the course of time we arrived at Hagerstown.[50] This is a small place with a mixed population of Germans and English, in number about 3,000. Our host was a German who perceiving that an Indian boy who was with us spoke English but imperfectly addressed him in Dutch; but strange to tell the boy still remained silent. I came very near losing all my money here by over-carefulness. I am in the habit of leaving all the cash I have with me in my pocket when I retire to rest. But this evg. lest by possibility I might lose it I took it out and placed it with my watch under my pillow. About midnight we were called to take the stage but my friend Brown was too unwell to go on and it went without us. Had we then taken the stage I should infallibly have left my money. As it was when I rose in the morng. I took my watch without once think that there was anything else. But Brown after I had left the room looked under my pillow and saw it and restored it to me. I remained here two days one of which was Sunday.

I left Hagerstown on Monday morning and after two & a half of hard riding night and day, arrived in Wheeling.[51] This is a pleasant little place on the banks of the Ohio. I visited their manufactory of cut glass and was astonished and delighted by the elegance & delicacy of their work.[52] I remained in W—— but a single day when I took the boat for Cincinnati. She was by some unfortunate mis-

---

47. Prov. 3:7.
48. Thomas Brown, son of the Rev. O. B. Brown, a chief clerk in the Post Office Department. Chase to ———, July 10, 1853 (Chase Papers, L.C.); *Wash. Dir. (1830)*, 8.
49. In margin: "Roads."
50. In margin: "Hagerstown."
51. In margin: "Wheeling."
52. Glass had been manufactured in Wheeling since 1821. Chase probably visited a flint glass works on the corner of Zane and Sixth Streets whose output, he claimed, rivaled "more costly productions of English skill." Chase to Hamilton Smith, Mar. 22, 1830 (Smith MSS, Indiana Univ.); Gibson Lamb Cranmer, ed., *History of Wheeling City and Ohio County, W. Virginia, and Representative Citizens* . . . (Chicago, 1902), 156, 318.

nomer called the Paragon;[53] an appellation to which She had good claim, if *parvitude* of size, meanness of accommodation & slowness of motion constitute one. On board this boat I became acquainted with Genl. Tipton from Indiana[54]

This gentleman was born I think in North Carolina or Tennessee. His parents were indigent and he consequently did not enjoy the advantages of a scholastic education. But he recd. one equally valuable. The difficulties with which he had to contend were rough but efficient teachers to a mind like his. Besides *he thought* and his mind became stronger by exercise. He is remarkable for his energy and strength and sagacity. He now strives to acquire knowledge by every means and I have heard him say that a consciousness of his want of it has frequently forced tears from his eyes.

On Saturday morning early we arrived at the landing of which at some future time I may give a description.[55] After breakfast we went to the Hotel, where I obtained a room much larger than I needed indeed, for I am but six feet by one or two & the chambre was at least 10 by six. After taking a survey of the premises I called upon Mr. Caswell[56] for whom I had a letter from Mr. Wirt. This gentleman ranks among the first at the bar of Cincinnati; but as I shall have occasion to say more of him hereafter I shall make no farther mention of him here

At Cincinnati I parted from my friend Brown who, together with my acquaintances from Indiana went round up the Wabash.

{7}[57] I dined this day at Mr. Caswell's with a small company, consisting for the most part of Kentuckians. The entertaiment was not in the profuse style of Virginian hospitality but, I confess, in a style much better suited to my taste. The repast was simple but ample. It was a little singular that the day was warm enough to make it expedient to ice the water and wine. Every thing passed

---

53. A 355-ton sidewheel steamer constructed in 1819. William Lytle, *Merchant Vessels of the United States, 1807–1868* (Mystic, Conn., 1952), 148.

54. In margin: "Genl. Tipton." John Tipton (1786–1839), a native of Tennessee and future U.S. senator, was brigadier general in the Indiana militia. *Appletons'*, 6:123; *DAB*, 18:563–64.

55. In margin: "Arrival." Chase may have written a description of Cincinnati and its river landing, at the foot of Front Street, which appeared in the *Cincinnati American*, Jan. 3, 1831. Robert Bruce Warden, *An Account of the Private Life and Public Services of Salmon Portland Chase* . . . (Cincinnati, 1874), 185–87; Chase to Thomas Sparhawk, June 12, 1830 (Chase Papers, Ohio Hist. Soc.); Chase to Charles D. Cleveland, Dec. 21, 1831 (Chase Papers, Hist. Soc. of Pa.).

56. Cincinnati attorney Daniel J. Caswell, who later became Chase's law partner, 1832–34. *Cinc. Dir. (1831)*, 31; entry for Nov. 1, 1832 (below).

57. April, according to Chase's page heading. In margin: "Dinner at Mr. Caswell's."

off pleasantly tho' as usual at our American dinners there was little conversation until we left the table. In the evg. there was a small party

Mr. Benham related to me an anecdote of Col. Davis who fell in the battle of Tippecanoe.[58] A poor woman in Kentucky had been robbed of two or three hogs and brought a civil action for damages against the thief. Mr. Davis was employed for the plaintiff and the cause came on for trial / Mr. Davis began and in a short time obtained complete possession of the feelings of the Jury. He described the poverty of the plaintiff and painted her poor and miserable cabin. He depicted her struggling for existence alone & unaided and spoke of the baseness and atrocity of that nature which cd. steal from such penury. When he concluded the jury returned hastily and after a very short absence brought in a verdict for 500 dollars damages. It was thought unreasonable & a second trial was granted in another county. When the day came Davis travelled to the court on foot; the same scene was again exhibited and he obtained a verdict for 600 dollars.

(10) On this day I united with the church of the Revd. Mr. Johnston in commemorating the Lord's passion.[59] It was in a small schoolroom in the city that the holy rite was celebrated: for an unhappy division has taken place in the Episcopal church here and the greater part of the communicants have withdrawn from the original society.[60] I trust I was actuated by proper motives in the act of participation and that it will be blessed to my spiritual welfare. By conviction I am a Christian. My reason is fully convinced and my understanding perfectly satisfied. My heart also, I think, cordially and gratefully assents to plan of salvation thro free grace in Christ Jesus. May he who endowed me with intellect enlighten my understanding. May He who has given me affections draw them supremely to Himself.

---

58. In margin: "Col. Davis." Joseph S. Benham (c. 1797–1840) was a Cincinnati attorney. Joseph Hamilton Daveiss (1774–1811), a Kentucky lawyer and militia officer, had gained fame as the federal district attorney who prosecuted Aaron Burr for conspiracy in 1806. *Cinc. Dir. (1831)*, 17; *Cincinnati Daily Gazette*, July 16, 1840; *DAB*, 5:80.

59. Samuel Johnston, the rector of St. Paul's Episcopal Church. In margin: "Personal." *Cinc. Dir. (1831)*, 85, 203.

60. The division centered on disputes over Johnston's salary and his resignation in Aug. 1827 from Christ Church, Cincinnati's original Protestant Episcopal congregation. William Henry Venable, *A Centennial History of Christ Church, Cincinnati 1817–1917* (Cincinnati, 1918), 18–24.

Wirt the Attorney General, when young, wrote a play in which the most eminent practitioners at the Virginia bar are introduced.[61] Among others James Barbour the late Minister to England who was then remarkable for large, swelling & brunonian[62] expression is represented as engaged in the conduct of a cause in the county Court. He has occasion to request the clerk to call some one into court and thus addresses him—"Mr. Jones, Have the benignity to vociferate Peter Jolley into court" Upon which the clerk bawls out, "Vociferate P. Jolley come into court." The court is convulsed with laughter but one kindly informs the clerk that he has misapprehended Mr. Barbour's meaning & the error is corrected. One the same occasion he is represented as examining a loquacious female witness. At last he loses all patience and exclaims "This woman ought to be deposited into Taciturnity." The woman in a violent rage retorts You may go to Tass Eternity yourself but I reckon you'll have none of my company Mr. Barbour."

I mentioned this story to Wirt & asked him if he plead guilty / He replied "I plead youth to it."

An honourable member of Congress[63] remarking upon a certain measure to a company of which I was one observed "That it was a bad measure, a fatal measure and that our ancestors wd. find it out at some future day to their cost.

An orator, the other day, said in a public discourse "they see it, *as it were,* invisibly["64]

This distingushed statesman[65] is an unfortunate politician yet a very great man. Few men in our country are gifted with more splendid abilities. He thinks with rapidity yet with correctness. The powerful impulse under wh—— his intellect acts seldom forces it out of the right line of reason. All that he does and utters and imagines is marked by his grand characteristic impetuous energy. It is said

---

61. In margin: "J. Barbour." James Barbour (1775–1842), a former governor of Virginia and U.S. senator, had served as minister to England, 1828–29. William Wirt wrote "The Path of Pleasure," which was never produced on stage, in the period 1811–13. *Appletons'*, 1:162; Kennedy, *Memoirs of Wirt*, 1:343–48; Joseph C. Robert, "William Wirt, Virginian," *Virginia Magazine of History and Biography* 80 (1972): 428–29.

62. Evidently a reference to the prose of Sir Thomas Browne (1605–82), an English physician who wrote on a variety of subjects. In Dec. 1829, William Wirt wrote to Chase that the use of the word *addiction* in a particular context "struck me as out of the way, erudite, Sir Thomas Brunonian and all that." Wirt to Chase, Dec. 11, 1829 (Chase Papers, Hist. Soc. of Pa.); *DNB*, 3:64–72.

63. In margin: "Mr. Vance." Joseph Vance (1786–1852) of Urbana, Ohio, served in Congress from 1822 to 1835. *Appletons'*, 6:235.

64. In margin: "An Orator."

65. In margin: "Mr Calhoun." At this time, South Carolinian John Caldwell Calhoun (1782–1850), a former U.S. congressman and secretary of war and future U.S. senator and secretary of state, served as vice president of the U.S. *DAB*, 3:411–19.

that he was desirous of supporting the administration of Mr. Adams but was overruled in his native state. "He proposed," a gentleman who had ample means of knowing the truth recently remarked to me "to support the administration in a Caucus of South Carolinians" The proposition was recieved with disgust and Gov. Taylor rose and exclaimed *"Crucify him"*.[66] So decided disapprobation alarmed and discouraged him. He fell in with the prevailing sentiment and went for Jackson; yet Jackson still remembers his original preference and there is no love between them. Calhoun afterwards composed the celebrated protest of the South Carolina Legislature against the Tariff.

It may be said of him not inappropriately

> On each glance of thought
> Decision follows as the thunderbolt
> Pursues the flash.

Walking in the garden with E. P.[67] I remarked to her that she ought to give me a bouquet as a reward for aiding her in transcribing Flora's Dictionary. She replied "I will. I will gather the flowers now and when we return to the house I will select such of them as have an appropriate meaning." "I should prefer to be the selector myself Miss E. Perhaps you might not choose such flowers as I should like" "Oh there is no fear of that," she observed smiling "You would not want any flowers which I should not be willing to give". "You must not be too confident" I answered "for you may be certain I shall choose the most expressive." We left the garden with our party and I escorted a part to their residence in a distant part of the city and in the evening returned to Mr. L[68] where E. was staying. She told me that her flowers had been taken away by some one but she had a geranium left which she gave me. "I will look for it's meaning" said I. It was "Preference" I shewed it to her. "May I have it now?" "Yes" "May I construe the gift as I think proper?" "Yes" And I took it and construed it as the artifice of a

---

66. Calhoun's purported antagonist was John Taylor (1770–1832), governor of South Carolina, 1826–28. Evidence to substantiate Chase's story has not been found. It is unlikely that Calhoun ever expressed such support, since his opposition to Adams is known to have existed since the beginning of the administration. *Appletons'*, 6:45; Calhoun to Joseph G. Swift, Mar. 10, 1825, in Clyde N. Wilson and W. Edwin Hemphill, eds., *The Papers of John C. Calhoun, Vol. X, 1825–1829* (Columbia, S.C., 1977), 10.

67. In margin: "E. P." Possibly Elizabeth Pearson (later Patterson). See Jan. 1, 1872, below.

68. Probably Nicholas Longworth (1782–1863), attorney, horticulturist, and Cincinnati real estate magnate. *DAB*, 11:393–94.

beautiful and admired coquette to gain another admirer and win another heart.

MAY[69] I was one of a party to Genl. Taylor's.[70] The mansion is pleasantly situated and is surrounded by many pleasant appurtenances. I shall remember the garden because I there learned a secret which surprised me not a little. I was conversing with Miss ——[71] and in the course of our dialogue I had occasion to ask; why she smiled. "Oh I was merely reflecting your good humour." I should be most happy if you would reflect me at all times for then you must become the image of me—another self." That I can't do" she said. Let me hear the reason if it be not locked in the chambers of your secresy. "Won't you tell?" "No" "Never?" "Never" "To no one in the world?" "To no one in the wide world". "Well then" said she pulling off her glove and exhibiting her pretty white hand and directing my attention to a ring upon one of her delicate fingers. "See there!" "The ring you know is binding." "Is there a name upon it" said I. "No" "May I ask the name of the favoured one?" "H"[72] "And what letters of the alphabet compose the rest of the precious word?" And she told me. I was thunder-struck. I could not believe her for I had heard her and seen her expressing feelings of repugnance towards him by word and look which I thought then and think still had too much nature in them to be feigned and besides there was a disparity of fifteen or twenty years between their ages. "Is it possible?" I exclaimed "Aye; even so" Just then we were called; for our party was about to return to the city.

(12) I recd. today from E. P.[73] a promised bouquet consisting of Rose Geranium, Periwinkle, Holly, White Rose-bud and a common rose.
"Don't you think that Mr. Grimké and I are somewhat alike" said Mr. G—— to Mr. C——[74] "Yes" replied the latter "You do resemble

69. In margin: "S. A."
70. James Taylor (1769–1848), the founder of Covington, Ky., and a brigadier general in the state militia. *Appletons'*, 6:44; Holman Hamilton, *Zachary Taylor*, 2 vols. (Indianapolis, 1941–51), 1:29.
71. Sarah Ann McLean, the youngest daughter of U.S. Supreme Court Justice John McLean. Chase to Hamilton Smith, May 26, 1830 (Smith MSS, Indiana Univ.); Francis Phelps Weisenburger, *The Life of John McLean: A Politician on the United States Supreme Court* (Columbus, 1937; reprint, New York, 1971), 218.
72. Joseph H. Hayward, an artist from Boston. Hayward and Sarah Ann McLean were married soon after her conversation with Chase. Weisenburger, *McLean*, 218, 219.
73. In margin: "E. P."
74. In margin: "Wm. G." Frederick Grimké (1791–1863) was a resident of Columbus and a judge in the state's court of common pleas. Chase's marginal note identifies "G" as William Greene (1797–1881), a Cincinnati attorney, Whig, and anti-

him in the tones of your voice and mode of delivery" "Oh it was not that I alluded to. I referred to his force of mind and rapidity of thought. Indeed I think he is the greatest man in the state."

Mr. B[75] another of our western lawyers was one evening asking a young lady to dance with him. She declining our hero fell upon one knee and drawing a dagger exclaimed "Dance with me or ———" "Pray Sir" said she "allow me to conduct you to the hearth lest your blood might stain the floor."

A watchmaker, of the name of Jeremiah Fugate, dwelt in bygone times in Norfolk.[76] A clock had been sent him for repairs, having upon its dial-plate the motto "Tempus fugit." A silly fellow coming into the shop one day enquired did you make that clock Fugate. "Yes to be sure." "I see your name upon it, but what is the meaning of Tempus. I did not know you had such a name." "Oh" said the other Tempus is the Latin for Timothy."

> Tis an old saying[77]—Idleness
> Is the world's curse and I have heard a story
> Out of old time instructive—
> King Matthew once, half tipsy, put three fellows—
> Three idle fellows—in a house to fatten
> And fate or forethought set the house on fire
> 'Ah! see, the house is burning!' cried the first
> 'If the King wants us' said the second Knave
> 'Why, he will send and save us'. In a rage
> 'Your tongue is very glib' exclaimed the third;
> and the house went on burning and—they perished.
> Oh there are many dogs like these
> Many who open wide their lazy mouths
> And think that roasted ortolons will enter. Paper.

There is an anecdote of Fred. offering a purse to the laziest of three soldiers wh. seems to have given the hint to the above.[78]

---

abolitionist. In 1862, Greene returned to his native state of Rhode Island, where he was elected lieutenant governor as a Republican in 1866 and 1867. "C" may have been either Daniel J. Caswell or Cincinnati attorney James F. Conover. *Appletons'*, 2:768; *Nat. Cyc.*, 8:193; *Cinc. Dir. (1831)*, 209; *Liberty Hall and Cincinnati Gazette*, Jan. 28, 1836.

75. In margin: "Mr. B———," repeated as "Mr. B———h" after page turn.

76. In margin: "Anecdote from the Nat. Intr." The source of the story, supposedly taken from the *National Intelligencer*, has not been found.

77. In margin: "Idleness. Three Idlers of King Mat: Corvinus." Matthias I (1443–90), also known as Matthias Corvinus, was king of Hungary, 1458–90. J. O. Thorne, ed., *Chambers's Biographical Dictionary*, rev. ed. (New York, 1969), 866.

78. In margin: "King Fred of Prussia." Either Frederick I (1657–1713) or Frederick II, "the Great" (1712–86). Ibid., 494–95.

MAY 22 I spoke this day in the moot court upon a case in wh. I was counsel for the plff. and failed completely. My voice was affected by a severe cold and my self possession nearly destroyed by the presence of several of the faculty

JUNE I was in the beginning of this month admitted to the courts of Ohio as a practitioner of Law.[79]

JULY 4 I went with my friends the Longworth's to hear an oration from a young gentleman of the Bar by the name of Peters.[80] It was a sensible and well written composition, displaying very considerable power of mind and giving tokens of more in reserve.

AUGUST This month passed without any incidents worthy of notice. I was somewhat embarrassed in my pecuniary concerns by a failure of expected remittances but was relieved by the kindness of a friend whose pecuniary assistance can easily be repaid but whose prompt aid entitles him to the regard always due to tried friendship.[81]

SEPT. 1. Commencing the practice of the law and assuming for the first time the responsible duties of my profession I feel as I did when I entered Washington more than three years ago a stranger and adventurer. I entered asking the favour and protection of the God of the fatherless and that which I desired was signally bestowed. I trust that I feel now the same confidence and I believe that my confidence will not be disappointed.

SEPT. 5 I am in my own office now.[82] Let this be the commencement of a new æra in my existence—an æra marked by devoted application, strenous exertion, unremitting industry & much thought!

---

79. The precise date of Chase's admission is unknown. It probably occurred sometime during the first twelve days of the month. Chase to C. D. Cleveland, June 2, 1830 (Chase Papers, L.C.); Chase to Thomas Sparhawk, June 12, 1830 (Chase Papers, Ohio Hist. Soc.).

80. Hugh Peters (1807–31), a Yale alumnus, poet, and Cincinnati attorney. *Appletons'*, 4:743.

81. Chase received financial assistance in the middle of 1830 from Josiah K. Skinner and from Hamilton Smith. Chase to Smith, May 26, June 15, 1830 (Smith MSS, Indiana Univ.); Skinner to Chase, July 10, 1830 (Chase Papers, Hist. Soc. of Pa.).

82. Chase established his first practice near the corner of Main and Third Streets in Cincinnati. His earliest known advertisement promised "prompt attention ... to professional business." *Daily Cincinnati Gazette*, Sept. 27, 1830.

SEPT 30   The month is ended. It's days have not gone without leaving a mark behind. My business has been very small yet exceeding my expectations. I have earned about fifteen dollars and perhaps shall be paid. In history I have read Pitkins United States, a work abounding in valuable information, conveyed in a dry but perspicuous style[83] / In the Newspapers I have read the account of the New French Revolution—the most wonderful event in the political history of man.[84] A great nation rending off the fetters rashly placed upon it by its rulers—overturning the old government without confusion tho' in the midst of carnage—depriving it's governors of power unworthily and establishing a new and better rule—and then quietly returning to it's accustomed employments—and all this in one week is a spectacle of moral sublimity which cannot be paralleled.

I have been endeavouring to get a distinct and full knowledge of Aristotle's life, character and writings and have made some progress, tho' the work is not ha[lf] done yet.[85] I have read, in Law, about eight hundred pages in Starkie's Evidence, of which the first volume pleases me best.[86] The second cannot of course be so methodical as the first—a different arrangement being adopted; but I do think that it is not so methodical as it might have been. It seems to me that the author, aware that this division of his subject was not so susceptible of luminous arrangement as the first, threw his matter carelessly together, without design of method or ambition of precision. I have, of course, read other books upon cases I have had.

In general literature I have done little—almost nothing / when I say I have read a few pages of Lucretius in course and a few pages in other authors without order I have completed the account.[87]

---

83. Timothy Pitkin, *A Political and Civil History of the United States of America, From the Year 1763 to the Close of the Administration of President Washington, in March 1797* . . . (New Haven, 1828).

84. The July Revolution of 1830 had forced the abdication of France's last Bourbon ruler, Charles X, and led to the establishment of a constitutional monarchy under Orleanist Louis-Philippe. David H. Pinkney, *The French Revolution of 1830* (Princeton, N.J., 1972).

85. Earlier in the month, Chase had written to Charles Dexter Cleveland (1802–69), a Dartmouth classmate, for advice about purchasing a copy of Aristotle's *Works*. Cleveland later taught Latin and Greek, promoted the antislavery cause, and was appointed U.S. consul at Cardiff, Wales, in 1861. Chase to Cleveland, Sept. 14, 1830 (Chase Papers, Hist. Soc. of Pa.); *Appletons'*, 1:650; Salmon Portland Chase and Charles Dexter Cleveland, *Anti-slavery Addresses of 1844 and 1845* (London and Philadelphia, 1867).

86. Thomas Starkie, *A Practical Treatise on the Law of Evidence, and Digest of Proofs, in Civil and Criminal Proceedings* . . . , 3 vols. (London, 1824).

87. Titus Lucretius Carus (c. 99–55 B.C.), Roman poet best known as the author of *De Natura Rerum*, available in various editions and translations. Thorne, *Chambers's Biographical Dictionary*, 815.

October 1830 { 55 }

In the Bible I have read almost the whole book of Psalms, finding new beauties and new glories at every perusal.

In composition, I have done little with regularity.[88] I have, brought up my journal, by writing about forty pages of this book and have commenced several pieces which are yet unfinished besides bringing up long arrears of an extensive correspondence.[89]

OCT 19. I have this day assisted in the mournful duty of paying the last tribute to a deceased acquaintance. His name was Appleton a son of the late President Appleton of Bowdoin College in Maine.[90] He came here a few months ago—In August—bringing with him an enviable reputation. His openness of heart and gentleness of manner gained for him the regard of many. He commenced the study of the Law in the office of Messrs Fales & Pendleton:[91] but Providence had decreed that his blossoming hopes should be blighted even in their blossom. His progress in study was arrested by a violent attack of typhus fever, which, in three weeks, in spite of the efforts of his physicians and the kindness of his friends, brought him down to the grave. He is buried in a strange land. There are none to weep over his grave. A mother's and a sister's

---

88. According to biographer Robert Warden, Chase served at this time as editor *pro tempore* of the *Cincinnati American* and wrote columns entitled "Party Violence," Dec. 13, 1830; "Our City," Jan. 3, 1831; "Mr. Calhoun," June 11, 1831; and "Mr. McDuffie's Speech," June 25, 1831. Chase's by-line or last initial may also be found on "A Lyceum," c. 1830 (Chase Papers, L.C.); and "Speech of Mr. Wirt in the Cherokee Case," July 2, 1831. In his journal for Mar. 1, 1831 (below), Chase mentioned "writing a column." In Jan. 1830, he denied being editor of the *American*, but acknowledged a "pecuniary interest" and admitted to contributing "regularly to its columns." His involvement appears to have continued until Apr. 1831, when growing responsibilities elsewhere persuaded him to sever ties with the paper. Warden, *Chase*, 185–87, 216–17, 250–51; Chase to Hamilton Smith, Jan. 26, Apr. 1, 1831 (Smith MSS, Indiana Univ.); Isaiah Thomas to Chase, July 18, 1831, and May 1832 (Chase Papers, L.C.).

89. The entry for Nov. 15, 1829, appears about forty pages earlier in the manuscript volume. In addition to the Sept. 14 letter to C. D. Cleveland, two of Chase's letters from Sept. 1830 have survived, both concerning the prospects for his legal practice in Cincinnati. During the month, Chase probably also replied to social letters which he received from two friends. Chase to Hamilton Smith, Sept. 22, 1830 (Smith MSS, Indiana Univ.); Chase to Edward I. Chase, Sept. 17, 1830, in Jacob W. Schuckers, *The Life and Public Services of Salmon Portland Chase* (New York, 1874), 32–33; Thomas Swann, Jr., to Chase, Aug. 29, 1830, Edward P. Cranch to Chase, Sept. 3, 1830 (Chase Papers, Hist. Soc. of Pa.).

90. William Appleton (1808–30) had gone to Cincinnati to continue legal studies begun in New Hampshire. His father, theologian Jesse Appleton (1772–1819), was president of Bowdoin College from 1807 until his death. Nehemiah Cleaveland, *History of Bowdoin College. With Biographical Sketches of its Graduates, from 1806 to 1879, Inclusive*, ed. and completed by Alpheus Spring Packard (Boston, 1882), 331–33; *DAB*, 1:328; *Cincinnati Daily Gazette*, Oct. 20, 1830.

91. The Cincinnati law firm of Nathaniel G. Pendleton and Stephen Fales. *Cinc. Dir. (1831)*, 54, 123, 208.

tears will be poured out for him but they will not water his silent resting-place. He sleeps in the great valley of the West where he fondly hoped to rear the fabric of his fame—and we trust that "he sleeps well".[92]

This evening I wrote the following verses and when I went to tea presented them to Miss L. C. L.

> The autumn wind sings mournfully
>   The death song of the year
> And, yielding to Time's stern decree
>   All bright things disappear.
> The pleasant birds have flown away
>   To sing in climes more blest
> Where fields and skies in robes of May
>   Perennially are drest.
> The Zephyr, that, with purfumed wing,
>   Played erewhile round our path,
> Hath flown away with gentle Spring
>   From winter's wakening wrath.
> The beautiful and fragrant flowers
>   Fair nature's crown and pride
> From rustic walks and garden bowers
>   Have faded all and died.
> And I with sad, presageful heart,
>   Contemplate the decay,
> Till summoned in my turn to part
>   I too shall pass away.

1831

MAR. 1. Today I resume my long neglected journal. I have neglected to write not because I have had nothing to record, but because I thought I could not spare the time required. I have again renewed my former practice because I think it so useful as to warrant the abstraction of a few moments from other occupations, to be devoted to this. This day has not been a remarkable one. I have jogged on in my old path. In the morning I read the second case in the Ohio Reports. The principles involved were obvious and the merits of the case clear. In the afternoon and evening, besides writing a column, I read two books of Akinside's pleasures of the

---

92. "Duncan is in his grave; After life's fitful fever he sleeps well." *Macbeth*, act 3, scene 2, lines 22–23.

Imagination.[93] I once admired this poem but I now begin to lose my relish for it. It is stiff and artificial. It wants life and feeling. In the evening Mr Peters called and I went with him to Mr. L's where we found Miss C. L. and Miss M——s just starting to go to the lecture.[94] We joined the party. I offered my arm to Miss C. L: Peters, his, to Miss M——s. The walk was pleasant & the lecture, very good, but somewhat tiresome. When we came out, I had forgotten my overcoat and returned to obtain it: Miss C L. having said she would await my return in the Hall, with Mr. P——. When I came back I found them gone. I followed in the way I supposed they had taken. But not finding after walking, half a square, I gave up the pursuit and returned to my office.

MAR. 2. I was a tardy riser this morning. The sun anticipated me by more than an hour. When up I read the Scriptures, finished Akinside's Poem, perused an Article in the Ed. Rev. on the effects of Machinery and accumulation, and about 50 pages of the Wealth of Nations and about a dozen pages of Say.[95] I went with Miss [illeg. initial] L. to hear Mr. Durbin but was disappointed.[96] Returning walked with Miss E. L. the other lady having taken the arm of her cousin. Mr. Young called and conversed half an hour.[97] Neither of us in very good Spirits.

APL. 29. I made this resolution today. I will try to excel in all things yet if I am excelled, without fault of mine, I will not be mortified. I will not withhold from any one the praise which I think

---

93. Mark Akenside, *The Pleasures of Imagination. A Poem. In Three Books* . . . (London, 1744).

94. Catherine Longworth, a daughter of Nicholas Longworth, later married Larz Anderson. Clara Longworth deChambrun, *The Making of Nicholas Longworth* . . . (New York, 1933), 40; Charles Frederic Goss, *Cincinnati, the Queen City* (Chicago, 1912), 4:214.

95. "The Opinions of Messrs Say, Sismondi, and Malthus, on the Effects of Machinery and Accumulation, Stated and Examined, London, 1821," *Edinburgh Review* 35 (Mar. 1821): 102–23; Adam Smith, *An Inquiry Into the Nature and Causes of the Wealth of Nations* (London, 1776); Jean Baptiste Say, *Traité d'Économie Politique* . . . (Paris, 1803). On Mar. 31, 1831, Chase presented a lecture to the Cincinnati Lyceum entitled "Influence of Machinery on the Condition and Prospects of Society." An edited version later appeared as "Effects of Machinery," *North American Review* 34 (Jan. 1832): 220–46. Chase to Hamilton Smith, Mar. 16, 1831 (Smith MSS, Indiana Univ.); manuscript lecture (Chase Papers, Hist. Soc. of Pa.).

96. John Price Durbin (1800–1876), a Methodist clergyman and professor of languages at Augusta College, Ky. *DAB*, 5:544–45.

97. Eliza Longworth was a daughter of Nicholas Longworth. Chase did legal work for John Young, a partner in the Cincinnati wholesale grocery firm of Barr, Young, and Vanhorne. DeChambrun, *Nicholas Longworth*, 40; *Cinc. Dir. (1831)*, 15, 173; John Young et al., power of attorney, Aug. 16, 1832 (Chase Papers, L.C.).

his due; nor will I allow myself to envy another's praise or to feel jealousy when I hear him praised. May God help me to keep it.

The modes of speech in the rustic parts of New England are so peculiar that I have determined to set down some of the odd phrases which I every day meet with.[98] Here they are.

"Sharp as the *little end of nothing whittled down.*" "You don't now, do you?" "I haint another another stick to save my gizzard." This is equivalent to a Mussalmans oath by his beard. "Gumption." "Never saw anything like this growing among corn"; which is an exclamation of astonishment. "A plaguey neat kind of a chap" which is an expression of commendation. "Curious varmint" which signifies "singular creature". "Make yourself scarce" an intimation that your company is not wanted. "Understood the whole squinting of the business as slick as a whistle," knew all about it. "I conclude its best to cut stick" a resolution to depart.

JULY 1831 This subject has acquired much interest in consequence of having been introduced into the Debate in the Senate between Messrs Webster and Hayne.[99] In an appendix to his Digest of American Law, Mr. Dane has taken the trouble to put the merits of the case in a clear point of view. He states, that the ordinance was not copied from the resolve of Mr. Jefferson as Mr. Benton asserted—that the plan of 84 (Mr. J.'s resolve) consisted of 2½ pages while his ordinance consisted of 8.—that the first page of the plan is entirely omitted in the ordinance.— That these provisions are transferred from the plan to the ordinance in substance. 1st. that the territory and states formed in it shall remain forever part of the confederacy subject to the articles of confederation. 2. That they be subject to the laws of Congress. 3. That they bear their part of the public debt / 4. That the primary disposal of the soil remain entirely with the U.S. 5. That the U.S. Property be untaxed. 6 Non resident proprietors to be taxed as residents— So much of the ordinance as goes to prohibit laws to impair contracts—to secure to the Indians their rights and property—to divest titles of feudal marks, is original— So much as relates to Titles to property—to the fundamental articles of compact save that securing religious liberty and that declaring the duty of government to encourage schools was taken from the constitution and laws of Massachusetts. (See the

98. In margin: "Yankee Phraseology."
99. In margin: "Mr. Dane & The Ordinance of '87." In 1830, Robert Young Hayne (1791–1839), U.S. senator from South Carolina, 1822–32, engaged Daniel Webster in a memorable Senate debate over tariffs, public lands, nullification, and other issues. *DAB*, 8:456–59; Wiltse et al., *Papers of Daniel Webster,* Speeches and Formal Writings, 1:285–393.

July 1831 {59}

quote itself.)¹ On this note, in a letter I have seen today addressed to Mr. Farnhame of Indiana,² Mr. Danes remarks in substance as follows.— As to the slave-article to the ordinance, which, or something like it was a part of the plan also, it may be that Mr. Howell of R.I.³ who was on the Committee that reported it may have been the first person who thought of it / At any rate it was defective and was rejected by Congress in '84— The next year Mr. King of Mass.⁴ moved to add a better but still imperfect article on that subject. Mr. Dane does not mention the fate of this article save that it was committed. When the ordinance of 87 was reported it occurred to Mr. D. *from what he heard* that a slave article might be added. He moved one therefore, and the motion was carried *unanimously* much to the honour of the Southern States. That Mr Dane made this motion is certain inasmuch as Mr. Otis in 1820 obtained from Mr. Brent⁵ an old printed copy of the ordinance with a manuscript draft of the 6th. Article in the handwriting of Mr. Dane. Mr. D—— says a letter to this effect from Mr. Otis is in his possession. "In fact" says Mr. D. "the plan of '84 was so very imperfect that it could not be mended to answer any purpose nor could materials be found in it to form the 1/13 part of the ordinance of '87. The remainder of the letter relates to Nullification and as a new view is taken of the subject I will extract the whole of it." I go back to the foundation and beginning of the Genl. and State Govts. I begin at Jan. '74 and find evidence in public records clearly proving that the Genl. Govt. was first completely established by the people in their original sovereign capacity as early as Sept. '74 certainly as early as June '75— As the Commissions of Washington and others then given by Congress continued in full force through the War—as did the army congress then established / These measures were void if the Genl. Govt. was not

1. Nathan Dane (1752–1835), a Massachusetts representative to the Continental Congress, helped draft the Northwest Ordinance of 1787. His observations about Thomas Hart Benton (1782–1858; Democratic senator from Missouri, 1821–51), Thomas Jefferson, and the origins of the ordinance appear in *A General Abridgment and Digest of American Law* . . . , 9 vols. (Boston, 1823–29), 9:74–75. *DAB*, 2:210–13, 5:63–64.

2. John Hay Farnham (1791–1833) was an attorney from Salem, Ind., and a founder of the Indiana Historical Society. A partial copy of the letter, dated May 12, 1831, appears in the *Indiana Historical Society Publications* 1 (1897): 69–74. Elizabeth Tucker Cauble, "John Hay Farnham," *Indiana Magazine of History* 20 (June 1924): 154–59.

3. David Howell (1747–1824), a delegate to the Continental Congress. *Bio. Dir. U.S. Cong.*, 1220.

4. Massachusetts politician and congressional delegate, Rufus King (1755–1827). *DAB*, 10:398–400.

5. Harrison Gray Otis (1765–1848), a U.S. senator from Massachusetts; Daniel Brent, chief clerk in the U.S. Department of State, 1817–33. Ibid., 14:98–100; Samuel Flagg Bemis, *John Quincy Adams and the Union* (New York, 1965), 158.

then well established— If well established then a correct principle of Mr Jefferson stated in the app. sec. 4. applies i.e. if the source of power the people remain the same they may change their form of Government, and yet retain their form laws and delegated power &c— In the app. (to Vol. 9. Dig. Am Law.) I view it as a point of immense importance that the Genl. Govt. was first so established, and long before the Declaration of Independence that the source of power the same people and their allegiance have ever remained the same since they created Congress in '74–'75—that Congress under the authority of the people in fact created the foundation of the 13 States which could come into existence *only after* that Independence was declared. Applying said principle it seems clear that the States have come into existence during and in subordination to the Genl. Govt. as allowed by Mass in 1780. This was new at least not well understood by myself until I carefully examined the federal and State records. These few thoughts may be material in reading the appendix. Your obt. Sert. N. Dane—
To J. H. Farnhame Esq.

DEC. 7.[6] Today I wrote the following lines addressed to a young and lovely friend of mine who had requested me to write in her album.

For C. . . . . L. . . . .[7]

Some verses for a Lady's Album;—well;—
What subject shall I take? "Herself, be sure;
"Tell her, her eyes enchant as by a spell,
"Her lips are like pomegranate seeds, but fewer;
"Her voice like Heavens own music, rich & pure,
"Tell her she steps most goddesslike: Declare
"Though many louder praise, that none are truer,
"And that you live upon her smiles and bear
"Deep graven on your heart the memory of her hair!—"

No: She's too sensible for stuff like this,
Although she has an album; and, indeed,
In it no little poetry, I wis,
"For which a cap and bells were fitting meed.
Beside my humour doth not that way lead.—

---

6. Between Aug. and Nov. 1831, Chase made a trip that took in Boston, Hopkinton, N.H., Philadelphia, New York, and Baltimore. Chase to Joseph A. Denison, Jr., Nov. 15, 1831 (Chase Papers, L.C.); Chase to Hamilton Smith, Aug. 5, Nov. 10, 1831 (Smith MSS, Indiana Univ.).

7. Catherine Longworth.

February 1832 { 61 }

"Then wake a loftier note, and tell of Love
"To whose supremacy all passions cede
"Love that refines illumines, lifts above
"This earthly earth what soul its power divine may prove."

   Oh no! that word too often men profane
   With most unworthy lips: And I am grown
   Colder than once I was; and will not feign
   That which I feel not.— I perchance have known
   Something of Love's Strange virtue; and alone
   Or in the press of crowds have recognized
   The presence of a motion, look, or tone
   That like the magic of a spell sufficed
To clothe with Love's own hues even what was most unprized.

   But that is of the past: or, it may be,
   It was a dream and now the dream hath fled,
   No matter whe'r 'twere fact or fantasy:—
   The heart is whole again if once it bled,
   The dream if it were such hath vanished;
   And it's illusions with it: and I feel
   Stirring within me manlier thoughts instead
   Fame ringeth in mine ear a wakening peal
And glorious hopes on high their glittering scroll reveal!

   Ill might I then the page of gay sixteen
   Stain with the colouring of thoughts like mine;—
   And she, the Lady, is too rich, I ween,
   Too miss the votive wreath from her bright shrine
   That my unskilful hands might haply twine.—
   I will return the volume therefore free
   From an uncherished name, and worthless line
   And doubt not that the Lady pleased will be
The page, unsullied now, unsullied still to see.

1832

FEBY. 14 A few days ago the Ohio began to rise rapidly.[8] After reaching its ordinary height, when reckoned at full flood, the noble stream, as if satisfied with that display of strength, flowed steadily on for awhile, without increase or abatement. After a few hours

---

   8. In margin: "The Deluge."

however it began to subside and continued slowly falling for some time. It then rose again and higher than before. Merchants, whose warehouses fronted on the river, began to remove their goods, from the lower story to the level of the bank. The river, like an animal eager in pursuit, as its antagonist retires, pushed closely on; and forced them to remove their stores still farther to the second story. This morning I went down to look at the stream. As I passed down Broadway across Columbia street, I looked towards the Eastern termination of the latter. It was covered with water. At the foot of Broadway the river had filled the space between the two Hotels, and covered the floor of the western store in Cassilys buildings[9] / I stepped from the pavement (sidewalk) on board a woodboat from which I passed to a steamboat of the largest class, which lay so that its side was parralel with the Western front of Cassilly's buildings. I mounted the hurricane deck and walked to the stern of the vessel. My position afforded me a commanding view. I saw the water pouring into the fourth story of the steam'mill, reckoning from the top.[10] Newport & Covington were both in a measure flooded: a great part of the former being under water. The Ohio, now swelled to an immense flood, more than a mile from shore to shore, and seventy feet in depth, rushed on almost without a ripple. It was sublime. It was power mighty, terrible, yet unostentatious. It was simple grandeur; a calm putting forth of gigantic energy. I looked to the west. The whole quay, lately so dry, was now covered with steamers riding majestically on the bosom of the water, crowded together, in close neighbourhood. One was just about to start, and her engine was working and throwing out vast volumes of steam. I returned to the sidewalk and went on board another boat from which I had a complete view of the land side of the scene. The boats were receiving and discharging their cargo, directly on the sidewalk, being lashed for the first time, I suppose, to the trees which had been planted to shade it. The space between the steamboats and the range of buildings was crowded with busy men. I have seen the busiest streets of New York, but never have I beheld a scene of such activity. The water was at the curbstone, & (at the foot of Sycamore and Broadway over the curbstone. On Commercial Row the water was 6 inches deep, in Owen's store; and the same nearly at Broadwell's, corner

9. The Cincinnati Hotel was located at Broadway and Front Street, and the Broadway Hotel at Broadway and Second Street. Michael P. Cassilly was a local dry goods merchant. *Cinc. Dir.* (*1831*), 31, 176; ibid. (1834), 33.

10. Probably a flour mill, located on East Front Street near Broadway. *Cinc. Dir.* (*1831*), 178.

of Syc. & Front.[11] I went to my office; but after a while determined to visit the West End of the town to see what had been done there. I passed along fourth street to it's termination   The whole western part of the city, except a ridge of land, immediately on the bank of the river was inundated. Of one house I could on see the roof, while others were visible from the second story upwards. I went down Elm street until my progress was stopped by the water. I then hired a waterman, with whom I embarked. The boat under the impulse of a strong and skilful arm, shot swiftly down Elm until we reached Columbia street. We continued our course along Columbia street to Western Row; down Western Row to Front street, along Front to Elm, up Elm to Columbia, along Columbia to Vine, on which street, at the distance of about a square from Columbia we were landed after sailing, in deep water, in the midst of the most populous part of the city for nearly an hour. On Columbia street from Vine to its western termination the water was from four to six feet deep / The depth on Front street between the same limits was from 2½ to 6 feet. Every thing that could float and sustain a man was pressed into service. And multitudes were busied in saving the wreck of their furniture. Many of the houses which we passed had been abandoned. In others the inhabitants still remained; but had retreated to the second story. As I passed the dwelling of a friend between Elm & Plumb streets, (on front) I recognized some of the young ladies of the family at a window in the second story. I ordered the boatman to stop and conversed a few moments with them from the street. The door was open into the hall, the floor of which with that of the parlours, was deeply submerged. On Columbia street lumber was floating away in vast quantities, and in one instance a small dwelling house had been uplifted from its foundation

At the moment when I write the water yet prevails & is rising!

18. SATURDAY. The water after rising for more than a week, began to subside today.[12] The flood has been unprecedented. The whole of the city south of Lower Market street has been completely inundated. With several friends I took a boat this afternoon for the purpose of observing the scene. We embarked on Main street a little below Lower Market, and proceed through Columbia street, through the whole length of which a strong current was running,

---

11. Commercial row occupied the southwest corner of Main and Water Streets. Allison O. Owen and Alfred H. Hayden were commission merchants; Jacob and C. Broadwell were grocers. Ibid., vii, 24, 119.

12. In margin: "The flood."

to Broadway. Passing the theatre we observed that the water was upon the platform of the steps.[13] We sailed down Broadway into the current of the Ohio on the outside of the steamboats. The water covered the first pane in the windows of the second story belonging to Cassillys buildings / As we passed along down the Ohio we observed that the doors of the buildings at the corner of water street and the Quay were hardly visible. We entered the city again at Plumb street. As our boat turned round I had a full view of the magnificent stream. It was a rushing ocean. The water at the corner of Front & Elm was nearly at the tops of the doors. Many frame buildings in this quarter were removed from their foundations and some of them descended the river. Others still remained, blocking up the streets or lying close to where they formerly stood. On Walnut street the water approached within a few feet of Pearl street House and on Vine within a few feet of Third street. Almost the population of the inundated part of the town abandoned their habitation. The consequent distress among the poor is very great though the citizens, with their usual prompt humanity, are exerting themselves to relieve it as far as possible / Our party landed at Main street: and I probably shall never again pass in the same manner over the same ground. At all events I hope no similar deluge will ever again present an occasion for a like excursion.[14]

APRIL 10. I this day formed a law partnership with Genl. E. King and T. Walker.[15] We are to divide the proceeds of the business equally: I am to be cashier: Walker and I are to purchase what additional books are wanted and to pay the expence of rent, fuel light and servants.

JUNE 4. 1832 "When you have found me a woman[16] who prefers

---

13. The Cincinnati Theatre, on Columbia between Main and Sycamore Streets. *Cinc. Dir. (1834),* 254.
14. The flood, which peaked in Pittsburgh at 64 feet 3 inches, remained unsurpassed on that section of the Ohio River until 1883. Chase's detailed knowledge of the flood was related to his service on a special Committee of Relief organized by the mayor of Cincinnati. *History of Cincinnati and Hamilton County, Ohio: Their Past and Present . . .* (Cincinnati, 1894), 302; notes of relief efforts, Feb. 1832 (Chase Papers, Hist. Soc. of Pa.).
15. Edward King (1795–1836) had previously served as state senator and speaker of Ohio's House of Representatives. The other partner, Timothy Walker (1802–56), was a recent Harvard graduate. Charles Robson, ed., *The Biographical Encyclopædia of Ohio of the Nineteenth Century* (Cincinnati, 1876), 178; *DAB,* 19:363; Walter Theodore Hitchcock, "Timothy Walker: Antebellum Lawyer" (Ph.D. diss., University of Mississippi, 1980), 128–31.
16. In margin: "Woman."

eloquence to youth, beauty & pomp, "place me on Sunium's marbled Steep, there Swan-like let me sing and die";—and my last notes shall be a pæan in her praise! But before you *do* find me such a woman, you will have assembled the unicorn the salamander and the phœnix in one cage, to which let me recommend you to add your lady who prefers eloquence to youth, beauty and pomp and what a menagerie you'll have!" New Orleans paper

JUNE 9. Genl. King went to Columbus today and left me in charge of our whole business.

JUNE 12. Wrote to Dr. Lindsly today enclosing the name of a subscriber to his projected periodical & expressing my regret that more cd. not be obtained[17]

JUNE 13 Wrote to King communicating the substance of a letter on business from R. Biddle of Pittsburgh.[18]

JUNE 16. 1832 On subjects of mutual interest[19]—the Review—Miss C &c—the times—political movements—the progress of the city &c &c—

Recd. our new bookcases today—and made quite a change in our office.[20] Feel now rather more at my ease than for some months past.

JUNE 18 Wrote to J. Longworth at New Haven and sent a prospectus of the Review[21]—asked his exertions for it—congratulated him on his college honors, &c—

---

17. In margin: "Dr. Lindsly." Harvey Lindsly (1804–89), a physician, was an acquaintance from Washington, D.C. Neither the letter nor the nature of the proposed periodical have been discovered. Harvey Lindsly to Chase, June 19, 1830, Mrs. E. C. Lindsly to Chase, July 5, 1830 (Chase Papers, L.C.); *Nat. Cyc.*, 12:205–6.

18. In margin: "Letter to E. King." Richard Biddle (1796–1847) was an author and attorney. *Appletons'*, 1:258.

19. In margin: "Letter to T. Swann." Chase and Timothy Walker were trying to start a periodical entitled the *Western Quarterly Review*. They abandoned the project in Sept. 1832 after an unsuccessful campaign to generate interest among potential contributors and subscribers. Thomas Swann, Jr., had previously expressed interest in a Miss Carleton, of New Orleans, and announced his engagement later in the year. *Bio. Dir. U.S. Cong.*, 1899; *Liberty Hall and Cincinnati Gazette*, Sept. 18, 1832; Walker to Chase, June 8, 1832, Swann to Chase, Sept. 6, 1832 (Chase Papers, Hist. Soc. of Pa.).

20. In margin: "Bookcases."

21. In margin: "To J. Longworth." Joseph Longworth (d. 1883), the second son of Nicholas Longworth, had recently graduated from Yale University. *Catalogue of the Officers and Graduates of Yale University in New Haven, Connecticut, 1701–1924* (New Haven, 1924), 164; DeChambrun, *Nicholas Longworth*, 40.

{ 66 }   *The Journals of Salmon P. Chase*

JUNE 22   Letter[22]—declined loaning him money—urged him to exertion & self-reliance under Providence. The truth is I am much in want of money myself: business is dull and I hardly know which way to look.

Letter.[23] Enquired as to William's standing, proficiency &c—as to the amount of pecuniary assistance which ought to be afforded him &c.

JUNE 23   Letter[24]—Acceded to his proposition that I shd. become the guardian of Helen: requested the immediate remittance of her portion of Mother's property & of what is due her from the estate: requested general information as to the condition of the estate &c.

JUNE 25   Letter[25]—regretted he did not see the Wirts—made some remarks on concession [act nul]fication—told him of the failure of the late attempt to unite the Claymen & Antimasons; of the recent tariff meeting, of the cholera; urged him to exertion for the Review; foretold its success &c &c.

JULY 3   Agreed to superintend the publication of the Ill. M. M. and do what I can for the work.[26] Mentioned that Tannehill had

22. In margin: "to W. F. Chase." William Frederick Chase (1813–52) was Chase's youngest brother. William eventually became an attorney in St. Louis, but developed profligate ways which continued throughout his life. He married Mary Gillespie. Child, *Cornish*, 2:65; entry for Nov. 3, 1852, below; *St. Louis Dir. (1842)*, 23; A. W. Corey to Chase, July 16, 1837, Lewis F. Thomas to Chase, Jan. 17, 1840, William Greenleaf Eliot to Chase, June 9, 1840, and "Family Memoranda" (Chase Papers, L.C.).

23. In margin: "to H. Paine." Henry Paine (1793–1868) was the principal of Waterville Academy, a preparatory school which William attended. Chase's letter to Paine remains unlocated. The principal's reply acknowledged William's "good talents," but noted also his lack of "close application" to studies. William had been granted provisional acceptance to Waterville College, the predecessor to Colby College, where anticipated expenses for the coming year were $75 or $80. *General Catalogue of Officers, Graduates and Former Students of Colby College . . .* (Waterville, Maine, 1920), 25, 247; Paine to Chase, Sept. 1, 1832 (Chase Papers, L.C.).

24. In margin: "to E. Parker." Elijah Parker (1776–1858), an attorney from Keene, N.H., executed the will of Chase's mother, Jannette Ralston Chase, after her death in Apr. 1832. The letter about Helen, Chase's sister, has not been located. Abigail Colby to Chase, Apr. 21, 1832 (Chase Papers, Hist. Soc. of Pa.); Emerson, *General Catalogue*, 216.

25. In margin: "to T. Walker." An earlier letter from Timothy Walker, written in Washington, D.C., had mentioned rumors of Southern rebellion due to the tariff of 1832 and told of his inability to find new subscribers for the *Western Quarterly Review*. Walker to Chase, June 8, 1832 (Chase Papers, Hist. Soc. of Pa.).

26. In margin: "to J. Hall." Chase and James Hall (1793–1868), a former judge and editor of the *Illinois Monthly Magazine*, had previously corresponded about moving Hall's publication from Vandalia, Ill., to Cincinnati. In Jan. 1833, the magazine reappeared in Cincinnati as the *Western Monthly Magazine, A Continuation of the Illinois Monthly Magazine*. It merged six months later with the *Western Literary Journal and Monthly Review* to form the *Western Monthly Magazine and Literary Journal*. Robson,

been requested to come here[27] and expressed a hope that the Judge wd. not give up the idea of editing the Quarterly

Requested him[28] to pay what is due me about 40.48 to Dryden & Hunt. Advised him to leave his school & commence the practice of law.

AUGUST 24   As I went to dinner today I saw [word canceled] "pouring his leprous distillation" into the ear of a "workie" whom he was probably enlightening as to his superior fitness as a Candidate for Congress to [word canceled].[29]

——— His face, Sir, is an assault and battery upon physiognomy.[30] He was educated in a college where ignorance was taught as a Science; and he took the first honours as a proficient when he was graduated.

NOV. 1.   Dissolved partnership with King & Walker & formed a new one with D. J. Caswell[31]—I am to give a bonus of 1475 in a note payable in 90 days & to share equally in all business, including that of the Agency of the Bank U. States for which Caswell is solicitor

1833

JANY. 18.   On Tuesday, the 18th. ultimo, I was attacked by a violent headache, which proved to be a rheumatic affection. I had exposed myself much to the weather the Saturday and Sunday previous; And on the evening of Sunday felt the approaches of the disease. Thinking I was suffering from ordinary headache I paid little attention to my symptoms, until the neglected disease so

---

Biographical Encyclopædia, 660–61; Chase to Hamilton Smith, May 29, 1832 (Smith MSS, Indiana Univ.); Hall to Chase, May 2, June 23, 1832 (Chase Papers, L.C.); Mott, *American Magazines*, 1:387, 595–97.

27. Probably Wilkins Tannehill (1787–1858), a Louisville lawyer and editor. *Appletons'*, 6:31; W. Woodford Clayton, *History of Davidson County, Tennessee* . . . (Philadelphia, 1880), 231–33.

28. In margin: "to H. Smith" (Hamilton Smith).

29. There is also a heavily canceled notation in the margin. The major candidates in the election were Nathaniel Greene Pendleton (1793–1861), a Whig and former state senator, and Robert Todd Lytle (1804–39), a Jackson Democrat and U.S. congressman, 1833–35. The second canceled word in the entry is probably "Pendleton"; the first is neither "Pendleton" nor "Lytle." *Bio. Dir. U.S. Cong.*, 1404; *The Biographical Cyclopædia and Portrait Gallery with an Historical Sketch of the State of Ohio* (Cincinnati, 1883–95), 2:528; *Cincinnati Advertiser and Ohio Phoenix*, Oct. 13, 1830.

30. In margin: "Descriptive Eulogy."

31. Chase's agreement with Daniel J. Caswell anticipated a four-year partnership. The arrangement was actually dissolved in Jan. 1834. Chase to Caswell, Nov. 1, 1832, Jan. 25, 1834, Caswell to Chase, July 7, 1834 (Chase Papers, L.C.).

increased in violence that I was forced to my bed on the day first mentioned. For two or three days the disease made little progress & I felt hopes of a speedy recovery. These hopes however were not to be realized. One morning after an unquiet night, the disease had left me free from pain. Dr Colby had left the house thinking that I was doing well & required but little care.[32] But before noon a fever supervened. I felt myself rapidly becoming worse: and when the Doctor returned in the evening I described to him my symptoms. He seemed somewhat alarmed—bled me & remained with me to a late hour that night. The next day I was very sick. My strength declined rapidly &, in a short time I could with difficulty support myself. The medicines I took had no effect. Finally a consultation of physicians was called, & a different plan of treatment was determined on. From that time I began to recover & in the course of a few days was able to leave my bed. During this illness I was seriously alarmed, as were also my friends lest I should never recover. I was led by this circumstance to review my life: & in how different a light did many things appear to me from that in which I had once regarded them. Some things which I had thought almost venial now appeared exceedingly sinful. Yet I trust I was willing to depart in the hope that I should be with Christ. I felt a confidence that though my transgressions were multiplied & aggravated yet the blood of Christ was sufficient to wash away all sin. And I resolved if I should recover to try to do more for God than I had before done—to live a more godly life—& to be near instant in prayer & more abundant in good works.

During my illness[33] I received a letter from Mr Fairbank at Columbus informing me that the Senate had subscribed for two hundred copies of our proposed new Edition of the Statutes & that the House of Representatives wd. probably concur. The resolution however failed in the House by one or two votes & was amended afterward, by reducing the number to one hundred & then passed.[34]

---

32. Isaac Colby, M.D. (1793–1866), a leading member of the Cincinnati Anti-Slavery Society, was the husband of Chase's sister, Abigail Corbet Chase Colby. The Colbys had moved to Cincinnati from Hopkinton, N.H., the previous June. Emerson, *General Catalogue*, 488; *Philanthropist*, Jan. 23, 1838; Chase to Hamilton Smith, Nov. 14, 1832 (Smith MSS, Indiana Univ.).

33. In margin: "Revised Edition of the Statutes of Ohio."

34. Chase planned to edit Ohio's previously uncollected statutes. Daniel Fairbank, partner with A. W. Corey in a Cincinnati bookselling and publishing firm, evidently traveled to Columbus to lobby in the edition's behalf. The final House resolution passed on Dec. 26, 1832, 35 to 29. The Senate concurred two days later, 32 to 3. Corey and Fairbank published Chase's efforts as *The Statutes of Ohio and of the Northwestern Territory . . .* , 3 vols. (Cincinnati, 1833–35). Ohio General Assembly, House of

JAN. 21 Rose this morning without any strong consciousness of the presence & Government of God—dressed and breakfasted—after breakfast retired to my chamber, read the scriptures & prayed—went to my office—several friends called to congratulate me on my recovery, & Mr. Horton,[35] a young member of the bar, well-informed, of fine natural endowments & of prepossessing appearance & manners, who has left a good practice in the smoky city of Pittsburgh to come & settle among us, returned a call I made on him some days since— I read Judge Ware's opinion on assignment lately pronounced in the District Court of Maine[36]—the courts seem to be setting their faces against preferences effected thro' assignments: but will it avail anything to cut off one head of the Hydra?—partially arranged our library—returned homeward—the acquaintances I met on the Sts seemed glad to see me once more abroad—on my way home called on Mrs King, and thanked her for the kindness she shewed me during sickness[37]—dined & returned to my office—completed the arrangement of our library, a tedious & laborious business—Mr. Cope called & conversed a good while[38]—read article in the Am. Jurist on the Mistakes of the Westminster Review[39]—returned home—took tea—heard Helen's lesson in French—studied the history &c of the Federal Convention preparatory to a lecture on that subject[40]—commenced an examination of the Ohio Reports, with a view to a new Edition of the Statutes of the state which I am to edit—studied the new Testament half an hour—reviewed the occurrences of the day—found

---

Representatives, *Journal*, 31st Assem., 1st sess., 1832, 147–48; Ohio General Assembly, Senate, *Journal*, 31st Assem., 1st sess., 1832, 155–56; Fairbank to Chase, Dec. 19, 1832 (Chase Papers, L.C.); *Cinc. Dir. (1834)*, 41, 59.

35. In margin: "V. B. Horton." Valentine Baxter Horton (1802–88), U.S. congressman, 1855–59, 1861–63. *DAB*, 9:238–39.

36. "Assignment by an Insolvent Debtor," an opinion by U.S. district judge Ashur Ware, in *American Jurist and Law Magazine* 8 (Oct. 1832): 284–97.

37. Sarah Anne Worthington King Peter (1800–1877), the wife of Chase's former partner, Edward King, and later the wife of William Peter, British consul in Philadelphia. She became noted as a charitable worker, linguist, and benefactor of the arts. *DAB*, 14:500–501; Edward T. James et al., eds., *Notable American Women, 1607–1950*... (Cambridge, 1971), 3:54–56.

38. Herman Cope (1789–1869), a local agent and former solicitor for the Bank of the United States. *Cinc. Dir. (1831)*, 38; Cope deposition, Sept. 20, 1842 (Chase Papers, L.C.); Wiltse et al., *Papers of Daniel Webster*, Corres., 5:89.

39. "Mistakes of the Westminster Review on the Subject of American Jurisprudence," *American Jurist and Law Magazine* 8 (Oct. 1832): 275–83.

40. The major sources available to Chase were the *Journal, Acts and Proceedings of the Convention, Assembled at Philadelphia, Monday, May 14, and Dissolved Monday, September 17, 1787*... (Boston, 1819); John Lansing, Jr., ed., *Secret Proceedings and Debates of the Convention Assembled at Philadelphia, in the Year 1787... from the Notes Taken by the Late Robert Yates*... (Albany, 1821).

a lamentable forgetfulness of God's presence goodness & providence & shall now after prayer, retire to bed. 11 P.M.

APL. 22 Received notification of membership H. C. Ag. So.[41] Meetings first Saturdays March, June, September & December—

APL. 27 I heard today that I had had a violent quarrel with a gentleman of my acquaintance.[42] There was not a word of truth in the story; but it had been sent into circulation by some forger of slanders & had by this time I know not how many endorsers. I mentioned the thing to the gentleman concerned who was amused by the tale though displeased by its circulation. In the evening heard Revd. Mr. Peabody lecture at the Mechanics Institute[43]—lecture extempore without much preparation— The Institute has done & is doing much good. More than a hundred scholars are receiving instruction in various branches of useful knowledge. They pay $3. a year: which money goes to increase the funds of the Institution. The best teachers in the City render gratuitous services in instructing every evg. all who will come.

After the lecture I called on Mrs. Townsend[44] & had a long talk on matters principally interesting to myself alone.

In the afternoon Mr. G——[45] invited me to join his party in riding. Declined the invitation & rode with J Longworth & Mr. Young. Met Mr. G——'s party while out.

APL. 27[46] Attended Dr. Beecher's Church[47]— Sermon by Dr. B—— on the Christian Character— Text "Except ye be converted & become as little children ye shall, in no case, enter the Kingdom of Heaven."[48] The christian sustains a filial relation to God; & must discharge the duties, & possess the feelings belonging to that re-

---

41. Hamilton County Agricultural Society. *Cinc. Dir.* (*1834*), 255–56.
42. In margin: "Slander."
43. In margin: "Mechs. Institute." Ephraim Peabody (1807–56) presided over Cincinnati's Unitarian Church. *Cinc. Dir.* (*1834*), 134, 259; *Appletons'*, 4:688.
44. In margin: "Mrs Townsend."
45. Cincinnati businessman John P. Garniss, Chase's future father-in-law. Garniss resided in New York City beginning in the 1840s. Chase to Pliny Bliss, June 18, 1834 (Chase Papers, L.C.); Garniss to Chase, Oct. 12, 1849, Mar. 5, 1864 (Chase Papers, Hist. Soc. of Pa.); *Cinc. Dir.* (*1836–37*), v; *New York Dir.* (*1852–53*), 199; Warden, *Chase*, 223.
46. In margin: "Dr. Beecher's Sermon." Chase may have written the date as *28* originally, then changed it to 27. April 28, 1833, was a Sunday.
47. Lyman Beecher (1775–1863), previously of Litchfield, Conn., and Boston, was the pastor of Cincinnati's Second Presbyterian Church and president of Lane Theological Seminary. *DAB*, 2:135–36.
48. Matt. 18:3.

lation. The child has no separate interest from its parents is careful of their honour, resents aspersions on their characters—reposes implicit trust in their wisdoms—obeys unhesitatingly their commands—regards them with affectionate love—& resorts to them with confidence in every difficulty. So feels so acts a Christian towards his God.

Today I have been at Dr. Colby's & Mrs. Foote's.[49]— Mr Young came in before church.

I have read an Essay on the Progress of society.[50] The Author believes that the human race have, on the whole, been in constant advance since the beginning. He regards Revolutions as the great landmarks of human progress. He begins with the moral revolution occasioned by the Introduction of Christianity—next he discusses the revolution which produced the downfall of the Roman Empire & the institution of the Feudal System—then the Reformation— then the English Revolution in which Cromwell played so conspicuous a part—then and last our own American Revolution. All these he views as connected events, following each other naturally & almost necessarily. The style of the Essay is too ambitiously florid & too declamatory. But the ideas seem generally just & the views striking and comprehensive. I have also read a Review of Bunyan's Life & of Bp. McIlvaine's Evidences of Christianity[51]—neither of them peices of much merit—though the subject of the former possesses much interest.

APL. 2[8][52]   Called to see J. Longworth in the eveng.—spent an hour and a half in chat—then went to the fair—spent about five dollars—attended Helen to Mrs Foote's— Came home.

APL. 29 TUESDAY.[53]   Rose at 6—read newspapers—attended to the preparation of the Statutes till dinner—wrote to Judge Turner

---

49. John Parsons Foote (1783–1865), president of the Cincinnati Water Works, and his brother, Samuel Edmund Foote (1787–1858), a director of the Ohio Insurance Company, were two of the city's leading citizens. Chase probably refers either to Jane Warner Foote (1789–1864), John's wife, or to Elizabeth Betts Foote (1807–78), Samuel's wife. *Cinc. Dir.* (*1831*), 57; Abram William Foote, *Foote Family, Comprising the Genealogy and History of Nathaniel Foote* ... (Rutland, Vt., 1907–32), 2:201–2.

50. In margin: "Progress of Society." The article appeared as a review of Edgar Quinet, *Idées Sur la Philosophie de l'Histoire de l'Humanité par Herder* ... (Paris, 1827), in *The North American Review* 36 (Apr. 1833): 418–48.

51. Reviews of Robert Southey, *The Pilgrim's Progress, With a Life of John Bunyan* (London, 1830), and Charles Pettit McIlvaine, *The Evidences of Christianity; in Their Exact Division* ... (New York, 1832), were published in ibid., 345–58, 449–72.

52. Chase may have changed the *8* in the date to a *9*, or vice versa. The entry probably refers to Monday, April 29.

53. This entry probably describes Tuesday, April 30.

requesting information as to the history of the Territory &c[54]—prepared case for Sup. Court—called on Longworth—coming away called back by E—— C—— came to the door[55]—retired—returned—brought me glass of water—conversed awhile—goodnight—went to see Helen—gave her money—called on Miss G——[56]—returned home—went to bed unwell—

[APL] 30 WEDNESDAY[57] After breakfast said to Mr. G—— that if Miss G—— would like to attend the May Day Exhibition of Mrs Hentz's pupils I should be happy to attend her[58]— She assented & we went on horseback— The Exhibition took place on a dusty side hill over which a few bushes were sparsely scattered— An arbour was provided to screen the throne from the ardors of the blazing sun. Thither the elected Queen was conducted & crowned. Several addresses were then delivered—some good—some bad & some indifferent. We came home under a broiling sun & agreed upon a ride in the evg. & by moonlight.[59] In the meantime I was busy professionally. At six we started—ten in company—four ladies & six gentlemen. I abominate large parties. The dust was intolerable & the sultry air was almost suffocating. The party generally however was in high spirits. For myself I felt languid & unwell & said little: nor said that little well. I was reproached for my dullness but reproaches had no effect on me. Having at length arrived at home I took tea at Mr. G's rooms— Thence proceeded to Mr Edmands' wedding.[60] Found bride & groom walking on the pavement / Joined them & chatted awhile— Went into the house—chatted awhile came home & went to bed. Must think more & eat less, tomorrow.

54. George Turner (1750–1843) was a Revolutionary War hero from Morris Farm, Ohio, commissioned judge of the Northwest Territory in 1789. Lanman, *Biographical Annals*, 434; Turner to Chase, May 8, 1833 (Chase Papers, L.C.).

55. Eliza and Catherine Longworth.

56. Chase's first wife, Catharine Jane ("Kitty") Garniss (1811–35), the daughter of John P. and Amelia Garniss. Catharine and Chase were married by Lyman Beecher on Mar. 4, 1834, at the Garniss residence on the corner of Broadway and Fourth Streets in Cincinnati. "Family Memoranda" (Chase Papers, L.C.); Schuckers, *Chase*, 3.

57. In margin: "May Celebration." Chase wrote both *Apl* and *May*, one on top of the other, but left the date unaltered as *30*. This entry probably describes Wednesday, May 1, 1833.

58. Caroline Lee Whiting Hentz (1805–56) and her husband, N. M. Hentz, presided over Hentz's Female Academy. *Celebration of the Forty-Fifth Anniversary of Cincinnati and the Miami Country, December 26, 1833* (Cincinnati, 1834), 20; *Cinc. Dir. (1834)*, 82, 250; Isaac Appleton Jewett, "'Cincinnati is a Delightful Place': Letters of a Law Clerk, 1831–34," edited by James Taylor Dunn, *Bulletin of the Historical and Philosophical Society of Ohio* 10 (Oct. 1952): 265.

59. In margin: "Moonlight ride."

60. In margin: "Edmands Wedding." Horace S. Edmands was a partner in the Cincinnati bookselling and publishing firm of Hubbard and Edmands. *Cinc. Dir. (1834)*, 56.

May 2 Thursday   Meant to call on Edmands & Miss Elliott this morning but did not— Went to Clerks Office & examined Docket—spent some time after return upon the new Edition of the Statutes— Mr. Cr[ee]d called— In the afternoon read a few pages of Reports & took notes— Read a little miscellaneously— Called on J. Longworth talked half an hour principally on the effect of the Affections on the happiness & true glory of human life— Saw the young ladies but a moment at the gate[61]— E. Miller & his sister were conversing with them—called on Miss Casilly[62]— spent an hour—came home & now after having read something in the Word & having commended myself to the keeping of my Greatest & best & only true friend I shall lay down to sleep—

May 3 Friday   Rose rather late—attended to making a report of Bank business—was engaged for awhile on the Statutes—went to Court in the afternoon—Judges Lane & Wright[63]— Called to see Longworth—found him almost well—saw Miss E—— Miss C. indisposed— Called on the Judges— Spent an hour & a half very agreeably— Called at Mr. G's rooms—heard as usual not a little slander— Came home.

May 4 Saturday   Made out & presented Report to Bank U. States— Wrote to Mr. Peters asking his kind offices in reference to an arrangement proposed with the Bank[64]— Wrote to Mr. Swan to enquire whether any law of the Territory has probably been lost.[65] In the afternoon wrote to Judge Pease[66] to Mr James of Urbana— bought some Psalms & Hymns of Corey & Fairbank— After tea called at Mrs Foote's—

---

61. Catherine and Eliza Longworth.
62. Mary, daughter of Michael P. Cassilly. Warden, *Chase*, 238.
63. Ebenezer Lane (1793–1866) and John C. Wright (1783–1861), justices of the Ohio Supreme Court. *Appletons'*, 3:606, 6:624–25; *Cinc. Dir. (1834)*, 220.
64. Chase and Caswell wanted Richard Peters (1780–1848), a Philadelphia lawyer and U.S. Supreme Court reporter, to help secure a raise in pay from $600 to $1,200 per year for services as solicitors of the Bank of the United States. In return, Chase offered to assume responsibility for cases which fell outside their duties as solicitors but involved the bank's Cincinnati branch. *Appletons'*, 4:744; Chase to Peters, May [4], 1833 (Chase Papers, Hist. Soc. of Pa.).
65. Probably either Judge Gustavus Swan, of Columbus, or his nephew, Joseph Rockwell Swan (1802–84), future judge of the Franklin County Court of Common Pleas and justice on the Supreme Court of Ohio. *DAB*, 18:234–35.
66. The letter to Calvin Pease (1776–1839), a former justice on the Ohio Supreme Court, announced Chase's intentions to edit the state's laws and inquired about the location of early judicial records. Chase to Calvin Pease, May 4, 1833 (Charles E. Rice Collec., Ohio Hist. Soc.); *DAB*, 14:368.

MAY 5 SUNDAY   I have this day deviated very far from the paths in which a Christian should walk on the sabbath. In the morning, after my usual devotional exercises & the cursory perusal of a chapter in the Bible I went to breakfast. The morning of the day of rest had awakened no fitting sentiments of grateful love in my bosom, nor did the bounties which spread the board have that effect. After breakfast I read a Review of Chatham's Letters[67] & a sermon by Doctor Beecher. The first was badly chosen employment for a holy day. The second was good & I hope did me good. After this I went to church with my sister.[68] Mr Root preached but I listened so negligently that I do not even remember the subject of his sermon.[69] After this I went to dine with Mr. Cope. No other person was invited, &, as I have no other than a boarding house I did not scruple to accept the invitation: but instead of directing the conversation to suitable topics I suffered myself to bed[70] into worldly & frivolous talk without bearing on any thing good. After dinner I went to church. Dr. Beecher preached on the unreasonableness of unbelief. After the sermon the communion was administered. I did not participate having never communed in a Presbyterian Church. After church I accompanied Judge Lane to his room, where after something said on matters connected with religion, the conversation took a literary & political turn. From the Judge's room I went to tea— Thence to my brother in law's & thence to my room having spent a sabbath as unprofitably & vainly & sinfully as I have done for years. May the Lord pardon me, & arm with sufficient resolution to avoid such conduct in future.

MAY 7   This morng. I rose with very serious reflections & earnest determinations to act with more system & consistency than have marked my conduct of late.

After breakfast I walked to the Court House where I remained about an hour. I then came home & furnished some copy to the Printer & spent a little time on the book.[71] I then went to dinner. After dinner I worked awhile. Then called on Mr. Jenks—then went to Mr. G's rooms where I was cheated of time until sundown. After tea I called at Mr. Longworth's whence I have just returned.

---

67. See the review of *Letters Written by the Late Earl of Chatham, to His Nephew Thomas Pitt, Esquire* . . . , 2nd ed. (London, 1804), in *The Edinburgh Review* 4 (July 1804): 377–86.
68. Abigail Chase Colby.
69. David Root (1790–1873), pastor of Cincinnati's Second Presbyterian Church. *Appletons',* 5:319; *Cinc. Dir. (1831),* 203.
70. Chase may have intended to write, "to be led."
71. Probably Chase's *Statutes of Ohio.*

May 1833   { 75 }

MAY 11   Aroused this morng. by an alarm of fire[72]—rose & went to the window it was raining but a broad red glare was spread over the N.W. quarter of the city— Not belonging to any fire company I returned to my bed—& remained there for an hour—then rose, dressed, walked & bathed. After breakfast read a book of Milton P.L—a chapter in the N.T.[73]—then called on Judge Lane & invited him to accompany me to church. He declined & I went alone. Dr Beecher preached a plain & very powerful sermon.[74] His object was to show that no man who will not *now* repent & be converted has the slightest reason to hope that he ever will. He enforced this topic by arguments from experience & scripture with great earnestness & force. He said he did not wish his hearers to resolve that hereafter they would become Christians. He wanted to cut off that deceitful hope. He wanted to sever that strongest of the cords of sin. He wanted to show that neither the promises of God, nor the analogies of moral government, nor the experience of men justified any reliance upon resolutions of future obedience. While men delay habit strengthens & ties multiply & by & by the sinner will struggle, but he can't get loose / I listened to the greater part of the sermon with much attention & hope it will be blessed to my soul.

MAY 18   Sent precipe for sundry executions in favor B.U.S. to Columbus

MAY 20   Wet & covered with mud on a ride.

MAY 21   Was much amused by the following passage from the "Malade Imaginaire" of Moliére.[75] "Mais sur toute chose, ce qui me plait en lui, et en quoi il suit mon exemple, c'est qu'il s'attache aveuglément aux opinions de nos anciens, et que jamais il n'a voulu comprendre, ni écouter les raisons et les expériences des prétendues découvertes de notre siécle, touchant la circulation du sang, et autres opinions de la même farine."[76]

    72. In margin: "Fire!" Entry probably describes Sunday, May 12.
    73. *Paradise Lost*, by John Milton, and the New Testament.
    74. In margin: "Dr. Beecher Sermon."
    75. In margin: "Extrait du Malade Imaginaire."
    76. Molière, *Le Malade Imaginaire*, act 2, scene 6. "But, that which above all pleases me in him, and in which he follows my example, is that he attaches himself blindly to the opinions of the ancients, and that he never would understand or listen to the reasonings and experiments of the pretended discoveries of our age in reference to the circulation of the blood, and other opinions of the same kind." Henri Van Laun, trans., *The Dramatic Works of Molière* (Boston, n.d.), 6:191.

MAY 22 Note Hills due 3rd. July[77]—will probably be paid—please send receipt for 161.62 formerly remitted— Shall I send proceeds of note ($150.) by mail?

AUGUST 2 The following shews the mortality in Cincinnati from the first of up to this time from cholera & other diseases[78]— 1st. week June—24. 2nd week June 46— 3rd. week June 43— 4th week June 40— 1st week July 42— 2nd week July — 3rd week in July — Week ending July [23]rd 99— Week ending July 30—122[79]

{AUG. 6.}[80] To W. F. C. stating cause why Helen did not come to Lockport; and giving general counsel[81]— to N. G. Enclosing note for renewal—funds at the Yellow Springs—state of health improving in town &c &c[82]

AUG. 7. Reply to his of July 25 or thereabouts[83]—new Edition of Statutes—loan of money—advice & promises as to settlement in Cincinnati—Cholera Drs. Smith & Staughton victims[84]— Remembrances &c

---

77. In margin: "Letter to T. Belden." Thomas Belden was a director of the Ætna Insurance Company in Hartford, Conn. Previous correspondence suggests that Belden had employed Chase to collect money owed by William Hills, a bookkeeper at the Cincinnati dry goods firm of Wade, Hills and Company. Belden to Chase, Jan. 4, 1832 (Chase Papers, L.C.); *Cinc. Dir. (1836–37)*, 82, 180; *Hartford Dir. (1828)*, 14.

78. In margin: "Cholera &c in Cinti."

79. According to physician Daniel Drake, Cincinnati's cholera epidemic of 1832–34 destroyed 4 percent of the city's population. "The aspect of things was fearful," Chase wrote at the beginning of the crisis. "The streets were deserted at night: and, in the day few ventured forth." Chase to Hamilton Smith, Nov. 14, 1832 (Smith MSS, Indiana Univ.); E. W. Mitchell, "Cholera in Cincinnati," *Ohio State Archaeological and Historical Quarterly* 51 (Oct.–Dec. 1942): 289.

80. In margin: "Letters to W. F. Chase & N. Guilford." In the original, this entry follows that for August 7.

81. Chase's letter to his younger brother has not been found. William's reply from Lockport, N.Y., did not reveal the nature of Chase's counsel, but did indicate that Helen, their sister, was needed in Cincinnati to care for their ailing brother-in-law, Dr. Isaac Colby. William F. Chase to Chase, Aug. 26, 1833 (Chase Papers, L.C.).

82. Nathan Guilford (1786–1854) was an attorney, bookseller, and former state senator from Cincinnati. *Cinc. Dir. (1834)*, 74; *DAB*, 8:43.

83. In margin: "Letter to H. Smith." Hamilton Smith was considering the possibility of practicing law in Cincinnati. Chase to Smith, Aug. 7, 1833 (Smith MSS, Indiana Univ.).

84. Cincinnati physicians Jesse Smith (1793–1833), a former professor of anatomy and physiology at the Medical College of Ohio, and James M. Staughton (1800–1833), editor of the *Western Medical Gazette* and professor of surgery at Miami University. Otto Juettner, *1785–1909. Daniel Drake and His Followers: Historical and Biographical Sketches* (Cincinnati, 1909), 117, 133, 142–43, 145, 251–52; *Cinc. Dir. (1831)*, 192–93.

December 1833 {77}

AUG. 8. Letter[85]—introduction of Mr. Thal—foreigners—cholera in the west   Inquires for Miss Cobell— Reminiscences—Mr. Wirts family—Mr Swanns family—Miss Maxcy & Collins Lee—rectification of mistake about answer of letter from Fredericksburg &c

SEPT. 4.   Wrote for information in relation to Attachment Sampson & Tisdale vs McBride & Co[86]

SEPT. 4   Wrote urging payment of judgment $87.21[87]— Stated intention to forward transcript to lawyer if no answer within six weeks.

NOV. 20[88]   To rise at ½ past six—not done—breakfast moderately—fuld.[89]—read newspapers—fuld.—finish brief B & R ads B.C. & W—get Letter book & Judgt. Book from C. & F[90]—dine sparingly—look over docket & arrange cases—tea—hear Bishop McIlvaine[91]—Write agricultural address[92]—read—bed—

DECR. 3   Did not leave the house till after breakfast— [I then] went to the office & before I had occasion to leave it Smith came[93]— I walked with him towards the Courthouse— He left me & I went alone— After remaining a few moments at the C.H. I returned, & was encountered by several Dutchmen by whose business I was obliged to return to the C.H—after spending some time in

---

85. In margin: "T. Swann." Chase's letter to Thomas Swann, Jr., has not survived. Previous correspondence from Swann had introduced Mr. Thal as a traveler from Russia who intended to visit Cincinnati. Swann to Chase, May 28, 1833 (Chase Papers, Hist. Soc. of Pa.).

86. In margin: "W. Forward." Chase represented New York merchants John Sampson and Samuel T. Tisdale in a claim against another firm. Attorney and politician Walter Forward (1786–1852) was involved with the case at Pittsburgh, where goods of McBride & Co. had been attached. Chase to Sampson and Tisdale, Nov. 21, 1833, letterbook memorandum (Chase Papers, L.C.); *New York Dir. (1833)*, 526, 594; *DAB*, 6:537–38.

87. In margin: "S. F. Bonfils." St. Sauveur François Bonfils (c. 1795–1849), a native of France, taught for a time at the University of Alabama and, late in the 1830s, operated a school in Cincinnati. The nature of Chase's dispute with him remains unknown. Charles Boewe, "Who's Buried in Rafinesque's Tomb?" *Pennsylvania Magazine of History and Biography* 111 (Apr. 1987): 220; Bonfils to Chase, July 14, 1832, Dec. 8, 1838 (Chase Papers, L.C.).

88. In margin: "Intentions."

89. That is, "fulfilled."

90. Booksellers A. W. Corey and Daniel Fairbank.

91. Charles Pettit McIlvaine (1799–1873), a former chaplain to the U.S. Senate, was the Episcopal Bishop of Ohio. *DAB*, 12:64–65.

92. Chase's lecture focused on useful knowledge as a foundation of free institutions. "An Address delivered before the Agricultural Society of Hamilton County. Decr. 7. 1833" (Chase Papers, Hist. Soc. of Pa.).

93. Possibly Hamilton Smith. Earlier in the year, Chase had invited Smith to visit Cincinnati. Chase to Smith, May 29, 1833 (Smith MSS, Indiana Univ.).

examining papers in the clerk's office I returned to the office & then went to see Smith— He came with me to my office & after parting with him I went to dinner— After dinner I returned to my office & was closely occupied until dark. In the course of this day I lost my specs. I am confident I had them in the morning. I went nowhere in the morng. before seeing Smith except to the Post Office. When I went to the C.H I think I did not have them. They must have been mislaid then either at the office or at home before I left the house.

1834

11 JAN. 1834 Recd. your letter[94]—off accepted—wish to retain proceeds 100 dys if you can spare the money *with perfect convenience*—otherwise it shall be sent as soon as paid. My letter about things in general & Elisha Mills in particular has doubtless reached you ere this— If M. ever goes over to Indiana & arrangements can be made then to apprehend him upon a capias I have no doubt the money could be got out of him— Please pay particular attention to this matter. It will be *business* at any rate & may ultimately produce a good fee. Yrs Ever S. P. C.

FEBRUARY 8. 1834[95] I awoke this morning and remembered that the day belonged to God, and gratefully acknowledged the benevolence which provided a special season for thought on eternal things. I felt resolved that the day should be more appropriately employed than my Sundays have lately been. At about 7 I rose & dressed & breakfasted sparingly.[96] After breakfast I returned to my room and read, but with too little attention a chapter in Romans.[97] I then offerd my thanksgivings for past mercies & supplications for needed Aids & blessings to the great All Giver. I then put my bible in my pocket and went to my office. An accidental reference had determined me to read the book of Deuteronomy, and I occupied the hours till church time in reading the first chapters. I was much affected by what I read and I hope instructed. The perversity and punishment of the Israelites—their peculiar privileges—their singular institutions—the earnest prayer of Moses that he might be permitted to enter the promised land & his final exclusion affected & interested me. I thought I would look into Milman's history of the Jews to see how he treats these matters, and to procure the book

---

94. In margin: "To H. Smith Louisville."
95. In margin: "Morning thoughts." Feb. 8, 1834, was a Saturday. This entry, which describes a Sunday, probably refers to Feb. 9.
96. In margin: "Breakfast."
97. In margin: "Devotion."

went up to Mr. Perkins office.[98] While there I conversed principally on secular topics. At length I went to church. When near Dr. Beecher's I met Mr. G—— and went with him to hear Mr. Lynde.[99] The sermon was indifferent. The style was low—the ideas sometimes ludicrous and seldom impressive. On the whole it was far below Mr. L's average. Leaving the church I walked home with Mr. G——. In conversation with him and afterwards I fell into the common fault, of dwelling upon the defects of the sermon without adverting at all to the instructive thoughts thrown out in it. At Mr. G's I found Mr. H[1] sitting with Miss G——. She had Bulwers Engd. & the Engh. in her hand.[2] We conversed on ordinary topics. Miss G—— remarked on the eccentricity of Mr. H—— and mentioned a striking instance. She also told me that she dreamed of me last night—that we were together at Mr. Longworth's—that I perceived a drop of water on her cheek & attempting to wipe it off discovered that she was rouged—that I upbraided her with deception—that she declared it was the first time she had ever used paint, but that I would believe her—that finally after endeavoring in vain to restrain her feelings she burst into tears, and actually sobbed so violently that her mother heard her & came into the room and wakened her[3]—when they both laughed heartily at the incident. After sitting about half an hour I declined an invitation to dine & went over to Mr. Longworth's. Here I was kindly & cordially greeted. Miss E—— who had been sick for the past week came into the room. After we were seated at the dinner table Mr. Jones came in and introduced Gen. Clarke.[4] This gentleman resides far up the Missouri, between the State of that name & the Rocky Mountains. He was attired in a brown hunting shirt, which opened a little upon the breast. It was

98. Chase sought Henry Hart Milman, *The History of the Jews* . . . , 3 vols. (London, 1829), at the office of James Handasayd Perkins (1810–49), Cincinnati attorney, editor, and future Unitarian minister. Coggeshall, *Poets and Poetry of the West*, 154–57.

99. Samuel W. Lynd, a local Baptist minister, served on the Committee of Agency for the Baptist Board of Foreign Missions for the Western States. Chase accompanied John P. Garniss to the service. *Cinc. Dir. (1831)*, 203; ibid. (1834), 203, 242; Goss, *Cincinnati*, 1:499.

1. Mr. Hamilton, apparently a suitor of Catharine Jane Garniss. See Chase's description of his early acquaintance with Catharine Garniss in Journal II, below.

2. Edward George Earle Lytton Bulwer-Lytton, *England and the English* . . . , 2 vols. (London, 1833).

3. Amelia Garniss (d. 1864) was the wife of John P. Garniss and the mother of Catharine Jane Garniss. Chase to J. P. Garniss, Feb. 18, 1864, Garniss to Chase, Mar. 5, 1864 (Chase Papers, Hist. Soc. of Pa.); entry for Nov. 18, 1835, below.

4. Military officer, younger brother of George Rogers Clark, former governor of Missouri Territory, and partner of Meriwether Lewis in exploration to the Pacific, William Clark (1770–1838) had for many years been superintendent of Indian affairs in the West. He was probably introduced by George W. Jones, president of the Cincinnati Savings Institution and director of the Cincinnati, Columbus, and Worcester Turnpike Company. *DAB*, 4:141–44; *Cinc. Dir. (1831)*, 184; ibid. (1834), 257.

furnished with a small cape which was copiously fringed. A quantity of fringe also lined the back of the sleeve from the shoulder to the wrist. The skirts were also fringed. The whole was confined to the body by a crimson sash which was tied at one side and the ends hung down to the thigh. The whole dress was extremely picturesque and the whole appearance of the old veteran highly interesting. He was asked if there was a post office in his neighbourhood, & answered with perfect naiveté, that there was one about a hundred miles off to which he sent twice a month. He described several peculiar plants & flowers, & proved as interesting in conversation as he was in appearance. After dinner I went to church. Dr. Beecher preached. His subject was the urgent necessity and the best adapted means of moral & religious culture. He dwelt with great force upon the inadequacy of mere intelligence to the salvation of the nation. Enlightened Greece had gone down— Rome, who borrowed her light, had perished—America, too, must perish unless she can improve upon their example. He adverted to the various [sources] of corrupting influence—the influence of infidel publications and organized infidel exertion—the struggles of papacy to establish an influence in the West—the tide of European emigration augmented by existg. agitation—& the theatre and other amusements of the same class. He then adverted to the change of condition in the country from the time when every thing was regulated in law to the present time when everything must be accomplished by associated effort, and declared himself glad of the change. He then spoke of the means of renovation—of infant school Sunday Schools, bible societies &c—declared them to be ample if rightly managed, and concluding by urging upon his hearers the duty of active personal effort— After the sermon I went to my brother in law's where I took tea[5]— Thence I returned to my office—read Robert Hall on the Excellency of the Chn. Depensation[6] & wrote these lines—

FEB. 13[7] Partnersp. with Caswell dissolved before this date— probably within a month—appd. Solr. of Agy. U.S. Bk at that time— As to dissn of pshp v. l. to Wood & Oliver Feb. 13, 34

NOV. 12–22 Elected Solr. & Dir. of Laf. Bk—(l to H Smith Nov. 22)[8]

5. Isaac Colby's.
6. *The Excellency of the Christian Dispensation* (London, [1825?]).
7. This entry, and that for November which follows it, are from memoranda at the end of Journal I. In the original journal the two entries appear in reverse order.
8. See entry of Nov. 1, 1832 (above) for precise dates of the partnership. Chase's "v. l." means "vide (see) letter"; he mentioned the dissolution of the partnership in a business letter to Philadelphia merchants Oliver and Wood. The letter to Hamilton

1835

MARCH 12. Within a few days I have become acquainted with the Hon. Isaac Blackford, one of the Judges of the Supreme Court of Indiana[9]

JUNE 12 Resolved from & after this date for the period of one year I will not ask a discount of any note (except renewals & except as endorser for Mr. Garniss if he request it) either drawn or endorsed by me, unless in the meantime I shall have sold the St Clair property.[10]

JOURNAL II

The first time I ever saw Miss Garniss was at the house of M. P. Cassilly.[11] I had just returned from the Eastern States, whither I had been on a visit to my friends and relatives. It was, I think, in the month of November, 1831. I was paying a morning visit to Miss Mary Cassilly when Miss Garniss came in. Her appearance did not please me. I thought her features large and her face plain. I had little conversation with her, and have no recollection of that little.

Not long after this, I was invited to a party, on Front Street, at Mr. Henry Emerson's,[12] whose niece, Miss Mary Smith, had recently arrived in the city from New England. I asked the favor of being permitted to escort Miss Cassilly, and it was arranged that a party should go from her house. At the appointed hour, Miss Garniss, with her father and one or two young gentlemen, came in, and we all went together.

Shortly after, or perhaps before this, I called on Miss Garniss, at Mr. Hamilton's, with Mr. Young. She received us very politely. I

Smith reconciled personal accounts and announced Chase's selection as director and solicitor of the Lafayette Bank of Cincinnati, incorporated in Feb. 1834 with a capital stock of $1 million. Chase to Oliver and Wood, Feb. 13, 1834, Chase to Smith, Nov. 22, 1834 (Chase Papers, L.C.); *Phila. Dir. (1835)*, 196; *Cinc. Dir. (1834)*, 239.

9. Isaac Newton Blackford (1786–1859). *Appletons'*, 1:273.

10. Property in Cincinnati previously owned by Arthur St. Clair (1737–1818), Revolutionary War general and governor of the Northwest Territory. Chase was involved in a transaction with John Flavel Wright and Leroy Swormstedt, Cincinnati agents for the Methodist Book Concern. *DAB*, 16:293–95; *Cinc. Dir. (1840)*, 375, 414; H. C. Jennings, *The Methodist Book Concern: A Romance of History*, (New York, 1924), 99–100; Wright to Chase, June 13, 1836, Wright and Swormstedt to Chase, July 12, 28, 1836 (Chase Papers, L.C.).

11. This journal, which includes Chase's recollections of his first wife, is described at pp. lvii–lx above.

12. A Cincinnati wholesale auctioneer and merchant. *Cinc. Dir. (1834)*, 57; ibid. (1846), 156.

conversed a little with her. I can not recollect the subjects of conversation, but I believe we talked a little about books. I remember that Miss Garniss sat almost in front of the door into the hall, about one-third of the distance from the door to the fire-place. The impressions then made upon me were favorable.

I had, at this time, I know not how, taken up an impression that the Garniss family were pretenders to style, and were ambitious to lead the fashions here. My idea of Miss Garniss was that she was an affected and shallow girl—with little real delicacy or refinement of character. Oh! how mistaken was I in this estimate! How vastly did I underrate her! What genuine delicacy and depth of feeling, what devotedness and self-sacrifice, did she afterward evince!

I do not remember—yes I do—I did see her again that winter. It was on New Year's Day. I was coming out of a house on Broadway—I think Mr. Lawler's[13] or Mrs. Wood's. A large sleigh, drawn by four fine horses, stopped at the door, and a half dozen laughing, merry girls came dancing into the house. Among them, and most conspicuous, was Miss Garniss. She looked beautiful. Her countenance was full of animation, and she moved along with light and elastic tread. I merely bowed to her as she passed me; but I frequently saw that party of sleigh-riders in the streets that day, and never without a feeling of half regret that I was not among them.

I do not remember that I saw her again that winter. She went to New Orleans in February, where she reigned as a belle, for a season, and then returned to Cincinnati. The family, on their return, took lodgings at the Broadway House. I do not remember seeing her during the spring. Early in the summer she went to the White Sulphur Springs, of Virginia, whither I also had a strong inclination to go, and talked of doing so with Mr. Armstrong.[14] I did not, however, go. When Miss Garniss returned from the Springs, her family took lodgings at the Cincinnati Hotel. Here also, for a short time, lodged Mr. and Mrs. and Miss Carlton, of New Orleans. I called on Miss Carlton several times—never on Miss Garniss. Miss Carlton, at this time, was the affianced bride of my friend, Thomas Swann.[15]

13. Davis B. Lawler, director of the Ohio Insurance Company. *Cinc. Dir.* (*1831*), 185; ibid. (1836–37), 102.
14. White Sulphur Springs was one of several popular resorts located in what is now Monroe County, W.Va. James Smith Armstrong (b. 1798) served as director, and later president, of the Commercial Bank of Cincinnati. *Cinc. Dir.* (*1834*), 238; ibid. (1840), 93, 143; Oren F. Morton, *A History of Monroe County West Virginia* (Staunton, Va., 1916), 205–6.
15. The marriage did not take place. *DAB*, 18:237–38.

November 1835

In the fall of 1832, while Miss Carlton was in Cincinnati, Miss Ruhamah Pike was married to Mr. Kenner, of New Orleans.[16] I was at the wedding party, and so was Miss Garniss. I merely remember speaking to her. I have a vague idea of her personal appearance then, but it floats in my mind like mist. Nothing is distinct. Miss Carlton was at this party, and I paid much attention to her. She gave me a bouquet of flowers, of which I was silly enough to be vain.

In December, 1832, I was attacked by a violent disease, which nearly terminated my existence. Shortly after my recovery, Dr. Colby was taken ill, and my cousin Dunbar and myself, who then boarded together at Dr. Colby's, were compelled to seek new lodgings.[17] Dunbar went to Mrs. Eaton's. I went to the Pearl Street House[18]— sometime late in January or early in February—a new establishment which had been opened the preceding spring, and was then kept by Dexter & Alexander.[19] Dexter afterward died of cholera, as did also one of his daughters, soon after child-birth. Mr. Garniss and his family also, at this time, boarded at the Pearl Street House; and I had not been there long before I called at his rooms. I found Kitty and her mother seated at the the table, and Kitty was engaged in animated conversation with a Mr. Warfield.[20] I was much pleased with her this evening, and repeated my visits frequently. One evening, when we were sitting at the table together, talking of I know not what—but trifles surely—I wrote on the blank side of a card these lines:

> "Young love presided o'er thy birth
> And named thee, then, the Queen of Mirth;
> While on thy head the smiling Hours
> Placed, fittest crown, a wreath of flowers.
> And oft Love would implore to be
> A dweller in those eyes of thine,

---

16. Warden probably misread Chase's handwriting here, reading "Riske" as "Pike." Ruhamah Riske was apparently a half-sister of Cincinnatian James C. Ludlow. Her husband, William Butler Kenner (1810–73), owned Oakland plantation in Jefferson Parish, La. Stanley Clisby Arthur, *Old Families of Louisiana* (New Orleans, 1931), 159–60; unpublished guide to Ludlow-Dunlop-Chambers Collection, Western History Research Center, University of Wyoming.

17. William E. Dunbar was the son of Keene, N.H., attorney Elijah Dunbar and Mary Ralston Dunbar, Chase's aunt on his mother's side. W. Dunbar to Chase, Sept. 11, Dec. 5, 1833 (Chase Papers, Hist. Soc. of Pa.); Simon Goodell Griffin, *A History of the Town of Keene* . . . (Keene, N.H., 1904), 587, 638.

18. At the corner of Pearl and Walnut Streets. Mary Eaton ran a boarding house at the corner of Third and Ludlow Streets. *Cinc. Dir. (1834)*, 55, 256.

19. Cincinnati merchants Edmund Dexter and Joseph Alexander. Ibid., 8, 30.

20. Perhaps this was Joshua Warfield, a local carpenter. Ibid., 181.

And oft he promised, nay, he swore,
Wouldst thou but list to his request,
That he would be a harmless guest.—
BUT."[21]

These lines were slightly altered from some which I had written, three or four years before, for and of a young friend of mine, one of the daughters of Mr. Wirt. Since the death of my dear Kitty I have found the card on which these lines were written. She preserved it from that time. In giving it to her I intended nothing more than a piece of gallantry, the import of which I purposely left doubtful.

While I boarded at this place, Mr. Drake and Mr. Bullitt, of Louisville, visited Cincinnati, and a few friends were invited to Mr. G.'s rooms, to meet them. I was charmed this evening by the grace with which she received her visitors. But I was most interested by observing her when standing perfectly quiet, with her fine countenance in repose. Her face then assumed a pensive and almost melancholy expression, which, to me, was extremely interesting. The singing was delightful, and the evening passed pleasantly away. There was a settee, cushioned, on the west side of the room, and I have a vague remembrance of sitting there with my Kitty and having some very pleasant conversation; but it is extremely indistinct.

At this time, we used to assemble frequently in the parlor of the hotel after tea, and spend some time in conversation..[22] Miss Townsend used to play and sing, sometimes.

I used to sit near Kitty, at table. On one occasion, she gave me one-half of a double Almond as a Phillipina, and having, at our next meeting, anticipated me in the utterance of the magic word, I gave her a book. It was the *Percy Anecdotes,* and, on a blank leaf, was written: "Phillip to Phillipina."[23] Some time after this, I gave her half of a double Almond in the same way, and brought her in my debt.

---

21. Possibly an extract from the writings of English poet Samuel Butler (1612–80). *DNB*, 3:526–29.

22. So punctuated in the original, and most likely a printer's error. The spacing of this double period does not resemble that of the ellipsis points which Warden used to show omissions in other extracts from the journal.

23. Thomas Byerley and Joseph Clinton Robertson wrote *The Percy Anecdotes . . .* (London, 1821–23), a series of humorous stories supposedly compiled by two Benedictine brothers named Sholto and Reuben Percy. The philopena was "a small present made in accordance with a custom said to have been introduced from Germany. A person who in eating almonds, finds one containing two kernels, presents one of them to a person of the opposite sex, and whichever, when they next meet, shall first say *Philopena,* is entitled to receive from the other a present bearing his name." Noah Webster, *An American Dictionary of the English Language . . .* (Springfield, Mass., 1853); *DNB*, 3:562, 16:1303.

I looked with considerable anxiety for the result, hoping that, from the nature of her present, I could gather some idea of the state of her feelings toward me. I hoped that her present would indicate preference. I was disappointed; for, with the maidenly delicacy and propriety which characterized every action of her life, she gave me a blank album. I turned its leaves, hoping to find something written there. There was nothing.

About this time, my friends began to rally me upon my attentions to Miss G., and rumors began to be circulated of our approaching wedding at the Pearl Street House. I had not, however, at this time, any fixed purpose of addressing her, nor do I think that she had learned to regard me in any other light than that of a friend, and, perhaps, that word is too strong.

Some time about the middle of April, I remember riding out with my dear Kitty, her father, and Mrs. Lawler. I rode with Kitty; Mr. G. rode with Mrs. L. We went down the river, and returned over the hill below Mill Creek. We rode several miles, and, as we were returning, my fair companion and I trotted on rapidly before the rest of our company, until we were induced to diminish our speed by the repeated calls of her father, who now came up, quite heated. He was very severe in the reproof of his daughter, and uncivil in his language to me. I took no notice of it, however, at the time, nor afterward, but I felt it deeply; and, but for my partiality to Miss G., my visits to his family would then probably have ceased.[24]

On the evening of Saturday, the 14th of November, 1835, I came home to tea in the evening and found that my dear wife had been extremely busy all day in household affairs.[25]

At half-past two, or, perhaps, nearer three in the morning, her labor terminated in the safe delivery of a little daughter.[26] When she was informed that it was over, she lay back in the bed and exclaimed, "Oh, Heavenly Father! I thank thee!"

I did not go to court in the morning. I walked down to my office, however, and mentioned the birth of my babe to Mr. Caswell, whom I overtook on the way. At night, about half past nine or ten, Kitty suddenly became delirious. I had gone up stairs to bed; but, hearing something unusual below, I hastened down stairs, and found my

---

24. The memoir, as printed by Warden, contains nothing more about Chase's courtship of Catharine Garniss and resumes at a point over a year and a half after their wedding.
25. "Most of the remainder of this very interesting entry I have felt at liberty to withhold from readers," Warden noted, observing only that "it is full of evidence that he who made it was a fond, devoted husband." Warden, *Chase*, 252.
26. Warden's version of the memoir has resumed on Nov. 16, the birthdate of Chase's first daughter, Catharine Jane ("Kate") Chase (1835–40), who died of scarlet fever before her fifth birthday. "Family Memoranda" (Chase Papers, L.C.); Chase to C. D. Cleveland, Feb. 7, 1840 (Chase Papers, Hist. Soc. of Pa.).

dear wife talking incoherently. I ran for the doctor, who soon came, and, having ascertained her condition, requested a consultation. Her father and I objected, fearing to alarm her. The doctor observed that he was satisfied as to the nature of the attack, and as to the course to be prescribed; but that he had proposed a consultation in deference to our feelings. I told him, if he was satisfied, to go on. I was greatly alarmed, and trembled violently. He said he thought he ought to bleed. He went home and procured his lancet, but when he returned the delirium had passed off.

At this time, or before, I went to the bedside and asked Kitty if she would like to have another physician. She replied, "No," saying that she had the greatest confidence in Dr. Colby, and when I urged it farther she said, "Do n't you talk so, you will hurt his feelings." Her father then interposed, saying that the doctor had himself proposed it, and I, fearing lest, if she knew that the proposition had emanated from the doctor, that she might be injuriously alarmed, dropped the subject. I followed the doctor out of the room, however, and, as he went down stairs, said to him that, as Kitty did not seem to be alarmed by the idea of having another physician, I would go for Dr. Eberle if he still thought it expedient.[27] He thought it unnecessary, and I did not go. After the delirium passed off, the doctor concluded not to bleed her. After charging the nurse to call me if any thing should happen, I went to bed again.

When I went up stairs, I knelt down and earnestly implored God to spare the life of my dear wife; to give wisdom to the physician, and efficacy to his remedies; and especially to prepare her for all His holy will. Nothing farther occurred that night.[28]

[WEDNESDAY, NOVEMBER 18] It was on the evening of this day, I think, that a serious controversy took place about the name of the child. I wished to have it called Catherine Jane, after its mother. Kitty wished to have it called Amelia Catherine or Amelia Janette, after its two grandmothers. Mrs. Garniss wanted to have it named after herself. I felt thoroughly disinclined to this, but was willing that it should be called Catherine Amelia; and this, indeed, was the name we had agreed upon before its birth. Mrs. G. then said that she did n't care how it was called—that she would not take any more notice of it, and a great deal of the same import, and in the same temper. I made no reply, but felt much displeased.

27. John Eberle (1787–1838), professor of theory and practice of medicine at the Medical College of Ohio and a founder of the *Western Medical Gazette. Cinc. Dir.* (*1834*), 55, 247; *DAB*, 5:615–16.
28. Warden here noted: "I must omit much other matter, the presentation of which affected delicacy might condemn." Warden, *Chase*, 257.

[THURSDAY, NOVEMBER 19]   I remember very little of Kitty's appearance this day, but she seemed much improved.

[FRIDAY, NOVEMBER 20]   Kitty seemed to be getting better today, also, quite fast; so much, that, in a conversation with the president and cashier of the Lafayette Bank,[29] I expressed a willingness to go to Philadelphia on the business of the bank should there be nothing at home to prevent it. At noon, I went home and suggested the possibility of my being sent to Philadelphia. Kitty seemed pleased with the idea of my going, and, on my remarking that probably I should not get any compensation for going, she observed, "but you will get reputation by it."
   Shortly after this she spoke to me about naming the child. I told her that I should leave it entirely to her. She said, "No, it rested with me. The name should be as I pleased." "Well," I replied, "it shall be as you have said." She wished me to have the name of Amelia Janette placed on the child's bracelets. I tried to evade a promise; but she insisted on it, saying that if I promised I should be sure to do it. At length I promised, and, immediately on going out after dinner, went to the jeweler, Mr. McGrew's, and gave him the proper directions.[30] By some accident, however, the jeweler did not execute my order; and my dear Kitty, seeing the bracelets returned unmarked, never knew that I had complied with her request. I did not see my Kitty again till I came home to tea, having been engaged all the afternoon, arguing a cause at court.

[SATURDAY, NOVEMBER 21]   On going to the bank this morning, the cashier inquired of me if I had concluded to go to Philadelphia. I replied that I had, if it was desired. He said that it was urgently desired. I then went immediately home, and found the doctor in my wife's room. I asked him if it was safe and prudent for me to go. He said that it was. I asked him if there was no danger that something might go wrong in my absence. He said he could not say that there was *no* danger; but there was no probability of any thing amiss. I then turned to Kitty. She did not seem as bright as yesterday. She had taken morphine the previous evening. I had a vague idea that she did not wish me to go. I expressed it. "Yes," said she, "I do want you to go." "Kitty do n't want me to go," said I to her mother. "Yes, she does," was the reply. I then concluded to go, but reluctantly. Kitty seemed to take an interest in the preparations for my departure.

---

29. Josiah Lawrence, a local grocer, served as president; the cashier was W. G. W. Gano. *Cinc. Dir.* (*1834*), 103; ibid. (1836–37), 65, 102.
30. Cincinnati silversmith Alexander McGrew. *Cinc. Dir.* (*1834*), 115.

She told me to clothe myself warm—to take my overshoes—not to ride over the inclined plane, etc.[31] It was near four in the afternoon when I kissed her, and bade her farewell. Little did I dream that it was for the last time!

Came on the "Philadelphia" with the intention of going to Philadelphia.[32] The P. is a boat of the middling class, with an upper cabin. A large number of passengers (about forty) were already on board, and I had some difficulty in procuring a berth. I secured one, however, but it was near the wheel. The passengers were nearly all strangers to me, but I was introduced by Mr. Lytle to Mr. Greene, of Richmond, and Mr. Bainbridge, of Louisville.[33] We left the landing at Cincinnati about six o'clock. It was twilight, then, and twilight soon deepened into darkness, relieved by a faint starlight. The weather was cold and cheerless, and I was fain to remain in the cabin and while away the time by reading, and by a game of chequers with Mr. B., of Portsmouth. My antagonist was easily vanquished at the first evng, (?)[34] and did not seem disposed to renew the contest.

Mr. B. had been visiting Cincinnati, and had been introduced into the family of Mr. Moore. He was pleased with the young ladies. I rallied him on his state of unblest singleness. He confessed that he did not find much pleasure in it, and expressed a firm determination to wed before spring. He said that he had lately journeyed from Cincinnati to Portsmouth with Mrs. A——, of whom he spoke in such terms that I was induced to tell him that I had heard authentically that the fair lady was engaged to Mr. M——, of Cincinnati. He received the intelligence with absolute consternation, and could not be persuaded that the report was correct. He left the boat at Portsmouth.

About nine, I sought my berth, and, except that the jar of the wheels and noise of stopping, etc., frequently disturbed me, passed a comfortable night.

31. The Portage Railway between Hollidaysburg and Johnstown, Pa., crossed the Allegheny Mountains to connect the eastern and western divisions of the Pennsylvania Canal. The steepest sections of the railway consisted of ten inclined planes, each powered by a stationary engine. One set of tracks was finished by Nov. 1833. In 1835 double tracks for the full length of the railway were completed, allowing uninterrupted two-way traffic. David Stevenson, *Sketch of the Civil Engineering of North America* . . . (London, 1838), 262–73.

32. Warden labeled the section beginning with this sentence as an entry for "Saturday, November 22d," but Nov. 22, 1835, was a Sunday. This text appears to be a description of Chase's activities on Saturday, Nov. 21, following his goodbye to his wife in the afternoon. Chase probably traveled on the sidewheel steamer *Philadelphia*, which operated out of Pittsburgh. Warden, *Chase*, 258; Lytle, *Merchant Vessels*, 151.

33. Robert Todd Lytle and E. T. Bainbridge, a Louisville merchant. *Louisville Dir.* (*1832*), 10.

34. The (?) is apparently Warden's, to indicate uncertainty over the reading, "evng."

SUNDAY, NOVEMBER 23.[35] I rose early this morning, and, to my surprise, found the guards of the boat and the banks of the river covered with snow. The atmosphere was still charged with mingled rain and snow. I was obliged, with the rest of the passengers, to perform my ablutions in the open air, and to use the common towel. I evaded the disagreeableness of the latter necessity, however, by seizing my opportunity, when the first towel, being completely blackened, was removed and another substituted in its place. Early in the morning I took my Bible and a couple of volumes of Dick's works from my trunk.[36] At first, fear of ridicule had nearly induced me not to take out my Bible. I did not, however, yield to this unworthy feeling, and, in the course of the day, had the pleasure, not only of using my Bible myself, but of seeing it much used by others.

SUNDAY, NOVEMBER 22.[37] There was a violent snow storm to-day. Mr. Garniss wrote to me that Kitty was better, and that the babe was well. She continued to drink the porter.

[TUESDAY, NOVEMBER 24][38] The nurse says Kitty continued to improve. She was not, however, very lively; nor did she, at any time during her illness, manifest much disposition to have her babe with her, though she expressed the liveliest concern about every thing relating to its welfare. She continued to drink the porter.

WEDNESDAY, NOVEMBER 25. Kitty still continued to mend slowly. She continued to take the porter.

THURSDAY, NOVEMBER 26. To-day Kitty complained of a pain in her ear and of deafness, or, rather, of a slight difficulty in hearing. The doctor syringed her ear. Mr. Garniss wrote me that her health continued to improve, but that her spirits were rather low. She continued to take porter.

---

35. This entry probably refers to Sunday, Nov. 22. Warden stated that it "was made before the entries rehearsing the story of the wife's illness and the birth of the child." Evidently the paragraphs which describe Chase's trip on the *Philadelphia* were contemporaneous journal records, written in the same small volume in which Chase later placed his retrospective memoir of his wife. Warden mingled the two kinds of entries to create a chronological narrative. Warden, *Chase*, 259.
36. Thomas Dick (1774–1857), a popular Scottish writer of science, philosophy, and religion, was the author of *The Works of Thomas Dick*, 4 vols. (Philadelphia, 1835). *DNB*, 5:923.
37. This entry and those which follow describe events in Cincinnati during Chase's absence. He reconstructed this narrative after his return.
38. Warden mistakenly called this an entry for "Thursday, November 24." Warden, *Chase*, 259.

FRIDAY, NOVEMBER 27. Kitty commenced taking quinine pills to-day, and kept on drinking porter. She began also to eat the soft parts of oysters as well as to take oyster soup. She took very little, however, of any thing, for her appetite was poor.

SATURDAY, NOVEMBER 28. The same course of medical treatment and diet continued to-day. In the evening, she sat up for some time.

SUNDAY, NOVEMBER 29. This morning Mrs. Garniss came into the room, and wished Kitty to get up, but she did not feel very well, and was disinclined to rise. Her nurse told her if she did not feel as if she wanted to get up to lie still—there was no need of her getting up. About noon she expressed a wish to rise, and the nurse assisted her out of bed into her chair. She leaned back in the chair as usual, and so remained till after dinner. At dinner, two or three oysters and a small piece of boiled turkey was sent up to her. She ate the soft parts of the oysters, and, as the nurse says, a part of the turkey. Two little bits of turkey remained, which the nurse urged her to eat, and she did take them. . . . .[39] A little while after this, she was put back into bed, and the nurse observes that she then noticed that she seemed more helpless than she had before—that she did not help herself so well. But all this seems to have passed without farther attention. Toward evening Mrs. McCandless and Mrs. Emerson came in.[40] She said she felt cold—a kind of crawling sensation, and asked that the bed clothes might be put close around her neck. This was done and she seemed comfortable and conversed with them. In the evening she was up again and was sitting up, reclining back in the chair.

MONDAY, NOVEMBER 30. . . . .[41] It was now morning, and Eliza, one of the servants, came into the room. She told her to call her mother. When her mother came she told her to send her father for the doctor, for she was very sick. Her mother did so immediately and then asked her why she had not sent for her. She answered,

39. The ellipses apparently show an omission by Warden, who indicated that this entry was, "in part, unfit, accordingly to received æsthetic views, for presentation to readers." Ibid., 260.
40. Probably the wives of Henry Emerson and James McCandless, who was a partner in a rolling mill and director of the Commercial Bank of Cincinnati. *Cinc. Dir.* (*1836–37*), 113, 208.
41. The ellipses are Warden's, apparently to show an omission. Warden noted before this entry that he was transcribing the remainder of Chase's retrospective of Kitty "in part." Warden, *Chase*, 260.

"She would n't let me." The doctor soon came . . .[42] About eleven o'clock the doctor came in again. The nurse said that Kitty was doing very well, and, as she had not slept any during the night, the doctor did not disturb her. About two o'clock in the afternoon Mrs. Garniss, who had been very much alarmed by Kitty's unusual manner of breathing, sent for Mrs. Colby, notwithstanding the assurances of the nurse that all was well. As soon as Mrs. Colby came she said that Kitty was very sick, and went home and sent the doctor over. When he came he also pronounced her to be very ill, and requested a consultation. Her father proposed to send for Dr. Drake,[43] who was accordingly summoned immediately. Before he had arrived, Dr. Colby had made preparations for bleeding her, thinking immediate bloodletting necessary, and that a high state of peritoneal inflammation existed. Dr. Drake concurred, and they proceeded to bleed. When six or eight ounces of blood had been abstracted, Dr. Colby, thinking that she had been bled as much as her constitution would bear, and becoming satisfied also, from the effects of the bleeding, that the high state of inflammation supposed did not exist, arrested the flow of blood. Dr. Drake was much dissatisfied, and insisted on a more copious bleeding. The bandage was accordingly removed, and more blood was taken. It was then replaced. Dr. Drake still remained dissatisfied, urging that it was necessary to bleed to fainting. He represented the difference of opinion to Mr. and Mrs. Garniss, and spoke of leaving the house. Mr. Garniss entreated him not to do so. He then suggested that another physician should be sent for, and suggested Dr. Marshall.[44] Mr. Garniss objected to him. He then proposed Dr. Richards.[45] This was acceded to, and Dr. Drake went for Dr. Richards himself. When they came, both soon agreed as to the necessity of bleeding, and she was again bled, contrary to Dr. Colby's opinion and wish. Forty grains of calomel were then administered. Thirty ounces of blood had been taken. Still Drs. Drake and Richards were not satisfied; they thought further bleeding necessary, but postponed it till morning. While this bleeding was going on, Drs. Drake and Colby each counted Kitty's pulse—the latter repeatedly. Dr. Drake affirmed that the pulse was diminished in frequency from one hundred and forty-five to one hundred and twenty, and Dr. Colby was equally confident that it was accelerated from one hundred and forty-five to one hundred and

---

42. Warden's ellipses, apparently to indicate an omission.
43. Cincinnati's leading physician, Daniel Drake (1785–1852). *DAB*, 5:426–27.
44. Vincent Marshall. *Cinc. Dir. (1834)*, 110.
45. Wolcott Richards (1803–71), a general practitioner in Cincinnati. Ibid., 145; Juettner, *Daniel Drake*, 444–45.

seventy. Drs. Drake and Colby remained in the house all night, and Dr. Colby, fearing the result of the bleeding, and, still more, the consequence of a repetition of it, exerted himself to prevent any opinion of its necessity. Warm fomentations and warm drinks were copiously used. Kitty was thrown into a profuse perspiration, which continued through the night, and in the morning all her symptoms were better. . . .[46]

TUESDAY, DECEMBER 1. Such was her condition on the morning of this unhappy day. There was a fair prospect of recovery. All the symptoms boded well. But Drs. Drake and Richards were of opinion that she had not been bled sufficiently, and that the disease was not subdued. They, accordingly recommended further bleeding. Dr. Colby opposed it, saying that all her symptoms were improved, and they ought to watch the result. The other physicians insisted, however. Dr. Colby then urgently recommended that Dr. Eberle should be sent for. Mr. Garniss went for him, and returned with him. On the way, he told him that Kitty was suffering from a violent inflammation. Dr. Eberle remarked that such inflammation rarely, if ever, occurred so late after confinement. When he arrived, Drs. Drake and Richards stated their view to him, and Dr. Colby stated his. He concurred with the majority, and further bleeding was, consequently, resolved upon. It was anticipated that the effect would be to reduce the frequency of the pulse and augment its volume. Kitty was told that the doctors thought of bleeding her again, and was asked if she was willing. She said "Yes, any thing." She was then raised up in the bed, and twenty ounces of blood were taken from her. The effect upon the pulse was the exact contrary of what was anticipated. It became more frequent and more feeble. But, in other respects, she seemed somewhat easier. The physicians seemed to entertain some hope of her recovery, and agreed upon a course of treatment to be adopted.

Her father came into the room, exclaiming, "Thank God! my child! the doctors say there is hope." She said nothing. All hope soon vanished. Her difficulty of respiration returned. It was not painful, but tiresome and wearying. It was plain that she was dying.

Her father came to her bedside and said:
"My daughter, do you know your father?"
"Oh! yes," she said, "I know my father."
"My daughter, do you know that you are dying?"
To this, her father says, she answered "yes." Mrs. Cope,[47] who was

---
46. Warden's ellipses.
47. Probably the wife of Herman Cope.

also at the bedside, thinks she answered "no."

"My daughter, have you thought of God?"

"Oh! yes," she answered, "long and seriously."

"Are you willing to die, my daughter?"

She faintly answered in the affirmative, and seemed to sink, to sink, to sleep. Dr. Drake felt her pulse, and said that she was dead.

"My daughter!" exclaimed her father. She partly opened her eyes, and then closed them again, forever. Those who were near her during those two last awful days, say that her whole demeanor was inexpressibly sweet and gentle. Her faculties were unclouded. Her complexion was clear. Her eyes were larger and more lustrous than usual, and her whole countenance was illumined by an almost celestial radiance. She passed away almost insensibly—without a struggle—without even a sigh.

I was far away. At the moment of her death, I was in Philadelphia, thinking of her, I believe, but little dreaming of her situation. The next morning I left Philadelphia on my return home; arrived in Baltimore the same day. Visited several of my friends in the evening, and, early, on the following morning, Wednesday, continued my journey homeward. My whole soul was occupied by the idea of reaching home, and receiving the welcome embrace of my dear wife. From Baltimore we traveled day and night, and reached Wheeling about midnight between Saturday and Sunday.

Sunday morning, the "Leonidas" came down from Pittsburg, and I, fearing the river would be frozen over, resolved to proced in her without delay.[48] Before leaving the hotel, however, I sent a servant to the post-office, who brought me three letters—one from her father, dated Thursday, the 26th November, stating that Kitty's health was improving, but that her spirits were low; another from Mr. McCandless, dated Monday, 11 o'clock, P.M., stating the sudden and alarming accession of disease; and another, dated the next day, announcing the fatal termination.

My cup of anticipated enjoyment was thus dashed suddenly from my lips, and I was made to drink the dregs of sorrow.

I went immediately on board the steamboat. On Tuesday night, about twelve o'clock, we arrived at Cincinnati. I hurried up to the house, hoping, even against hope. The black crape at the door announced that death was within. I felt afraid to disturb her parents, and determined to return to the boat. I walked several squares through the silent streets. I returned, passed the house, and went to Dr. Colby's. I roused them, and went in, and made some inquiries

---

48. The sidewheel steamer *Leonidas*, also known as the *Dom Pedro*, operated out of Cincinnati. Lytle, *Merchant Vessels*, 111.

about Kitty and about the family. I then went over to the house. After some time, Mr. Garniss was awakened, and opened the door.

I shall not attempt to describe my meeting with him, or with the broken-hearted mother. I went up stairs. There, in our nuptial chamber, in her coffin, lay my sweet wife. "Lovely in death the beauteous ruin lay."[49] She was but little changed in features—but, oh! the look of life was gone. The sweet smile, the glance of affection, the expression, the mind, was gone. Nothing was left but clay.

I kneeled before her, and implored God to restore her to me. My prayer was not heard. I kissed her cold lips. They returned no pressure as they were wont. I pressed her cold, but still noble, forehead. She was dead.

From this time till Thursday I was almost continually by her dead body. It was a mournful satisfaction even thus to have her near me; but it was soon to end. On Thursday we committed her body to the tomb. Since then I have visited her grave every day except twice, when circumstances which I could not control, prevented. She lies, for the present, in the family vault of Geo. W. Jones, Esq., but we shall build one for her (and for ourselves when we may be summoned to join her) in the spring.

JOURNAL I

DECR. 25 I rose at my usual hour this morning. One thought filled my mind one emotion occupied my whole soul— My great— my irreparable loss— My wife—my dear wife—gone—never to return— Oh how I accused myself of folly & wickedness in leaving her when yet sick—how I mourned that the prospect of a little addition to my reputation—a little pecuniary compensation shd. have tempted me away from her at a time of such interest. Yet every one told me there was no danger—the doctor & the nurse—She & her father & mother seemed desirous that I shd. go—I went—alas I took my last leave of my precious wife—I imprinted my last kiss on her conscious lips— She was dead ere I returned

After dressing & offering my morning devotions I went down stairs to breakfast— Before breakfast I prayed with my father & mother in law— We then breakfasted. After breakfast I read awhile then went to my office where I saw Mr. Wiggins[50] & held some

---

49. Edward Young, *The Complaint; or, Night Thoughts on Life, Death, and Immortality* (London, 1742), line 104.

50. Samuel Wiggins, the business partner of John P. Garniss and a director of the Franklin Bank of Cincinnati. Chase to Pliny Bliss, June 18, 1834; *Cinc. Dir. (1834)*, 238; ibid. (1836–37), v.

conversation with him on business—about Heys bill to foreclose mortgage on the leasehold interest of Dawson on premises belonging to G. & W. on Water Street;[51] about debts due from Williams' estate & about payment for stock lately purchased by him for Mr. G. & myself in New York. After Mr. W. left the office I went home & from thence to church— While in the house of God I endeavored to fix my thoughts on the solemn service & prayed for strength so to do, but I was sitting in the same pew, joining in the same service & listening to the same hymns as a year ago when my dear wife was with me. I saw the wife of the clergyman who was not a professor of religion at the time of her marriage go forward to receive the sacrament, & I thought how I had anticipated the pleasure of seeing my dear wife do the same. How mysterious are his ways who ordereth all things after the counsel of his own will! My wife was cut off without the opportunity of publicly testifying her faith in Christ, though not, I trust, without such faith. I kneeled at the Lord's table & renewed my vows of love & obedience. Oh for grace to enable me to keep them. After the communion I returned home to weep & moun. I went to my chamber, whither a year ago I had returned with the partner of my bosom & could not restrain my feelings. After awhile I went down to dinner— I then came up again & again surrendered myself to grief. At length I calmed myself & walked out. I went to the vault which contains the mortal part of my dear departed one. I prayed for grace to sustain me under my bereavement— I came home. I had hardly exchanged my boots for my slippers when Mr. Read the Prosecuting Attorney came in.[52] He informed me that Mcguire, a man who was shot on the 21st by a man named Gedney, who, having been committed for the crime of shooting with intent to kill, was let to bail in $1000—that Mcguire was dying & suggested a new warrant for the apprehension of G[53]— I advised against this course until the event in regard to Mcguire shd. be ascertained, & proposed to go & see. He assented & we went

---

51. *G. & W.* means Garniss and Wiggins. Chase referred to a mortgage claim involving James Hey of Hamilton County and Moses Dawson, editor of the *Ohio Phoenix*, located on Water Street in Cincinnati. See also entries describing May 4–5, 1840, below. Dawson was later editor of the *Cincinnati Daily Advertiser*, and died by June 1845. Chase to Isaac Stevens, Jr., June 20, 1845 (Chase Papers, L.C.); *Cinc. Dir. (1834)*, 187; ibid. (1836–37), 47; ibid. (1840), 156.

52. State's attorney Nathaniel C. Read, later president judge of Hamilton County Court and associate justice of Ohio's Supreme Court, 1842–49. *Cinc. Dir. (1836–37)*, 141; ibid. (1840), 327; Elliot Howard Gilkey, *The Ohio Hundred Year Book: A Hand-Book of the Public Men and Public Institutions of Ohio* . . . (Columbus, 1901), 470–71.

53. The encounter involved Isaac McGuire and city watchman Charles F. Gedney. McGuire died later that day of a bullet wound which "penetrated the lower part of the heart." *Cincinnati Daily Gazette*, Dec. 29, 1835; *Cinc. Dir. (1836–37)*, 66.

together. We found that Mcguire was dead & immediately sent for a magistrate. Two Wing & Wiseman refused to issue a new warrant[54] / Harrison, however, issued it & committed him to prison[55]— I conceived a higher estimate of Read's character this evening than I had previously held. He talked to me of the loss of his two children last summer & of the dangerous illness of his wife & seemed to entertain very correct & even religious views. After leaving the Magistrate's office I came home & after prayer with the family came to my lonely room. I have now no wife to whom I can narrate any incident that concerns or interests me.

DECR. 26. I rose this morning at my usual hour with the one engrossing thought in possession of my soul. My loneliness—my utter desolation— After reading the bible—the 3rd Chap 1st Epistle of John[56]—& praying in my room I went down stairs & read the bible & prayed with the family. I then breakfasted & went to my office. I spent the morning in preparing an answer in Chy. for Messrs G & W[57] & in fruitless attempts to prepare an argument for the Sup—— Court of the U. States.[58] Mr. G. handed me Mr Wiggins' receipt for $10.050. I came home to dinner—returned to my office accomplished nothing—visited the resting place of my dear wife— every thing was still except the clamours of two or three dogs— Came home—took tea—had a long conversation with my motherinlaw about Kitty. Mrs G. thinks that Dr. C—— did not act with sufficient efficiency—that he was not explicit enough with the family—that he was negligent of her the morng. before she died. I think her death was occasiond by excessive bleeding—a measure which was advised by Dr. Drake & adopted against Dr. Colby's wishes—

---

54. Isaiah Wing and John A. Wiseman, justices of the peace. *Cinc. Dir. (1836–37),* 201; ibid. (1834), 190.

55. Ebenezer Harrison, a local constable. *Cinc. Dir. (1836–37),* 76.

56. The chapter begins, "Behold, what manner of love the Father hath bestowed upon us, that we should be called the sons of God."

57. That is, the chancery case for Garniss and Wiggins; see entry for Dec. 25 above.

58. Here, and in other entries to Jan. 9, 1836, Chase referred to the preparation of his argument in *John Voorhees, Jeremiah Letton, Schoney Achley, and Nicholas Longworth v. James Jackson, ex dem. The President, Directors and Company of the Bank of the United States.* In July 1834, Chase represented the bank in this ejectment suit in the U.S. circuit court at Columbus, which decided in the bank's favor. The Supreme Court took the case on a writ of error, heard arguments on Feb. 6, 1836, and affirmed the circuit court's decision on Feb. 15. Chase presented his argument in printed form only. The case hinged on the validity of an attachment proceeding in 1808. *Voorhees v. Jackson,* 10 Pet. 449 (1836); Engrossed Dockets, vol. E, Engrossed Minutes, vol. G, and appellate case file no. 1865 (Records of the Supreme Court, Nat. Arch.); Charles Fairman, *Reconstruction and Reunion: 1864–88, Part One,* v. 6 of Paul A. Freund, gen. ed., *The Oliver Wendell Holmes Devise History of the Supreme Court of the United States* (New York, 1971), 29.

went to my office—did nothing retd. home—alarm of fire—went to the spot 9th St between Sycamore & Main—some frame buildings on fires—two brick buildings & some frames in danger[59]—retd. home—joined in family worship—& came to my room & wrote these lines—& heard David read[60]— He makes slow progress—

DECR. 27. I rose this morning with a heavy heart. I had been dreaming of accompanying my dear wife to church & I awoke to the mournful conviction that never more should we walk to the house of God in company or take sweet counsel together. The day was very fine, and it pressed my heart to think that never more would my dear wife be gladdened by the brightness of the sun. At length I endeavored to seek God in prayer / I read the last chapter in the first epistle of John in which he sets forth so strongly the preeminent necessity & excellence of Christian love[61] & went down stairs where I was soon joined by my mother in law & fatherinlaw & we united in family prayer. Oh that God would give me a deeper sense of my own sinfulness & destitution that I might pray with more earnestness & humility—greater love for others that I might pray for them more heartily. After breakfast I took my little daughter in my arms & held her for some time. Dear remembrancer of thy departed mother, may I supply to thee a mother's care & watchfulness— And may God be to thee better than father & mother. The natural pilot of thy life's barque, God hath taken from thee at the very commencement of thy voyage— May He himself be the pilot & the Saviour— I spent the morning until churchtime chiefly in thinking of my loss & mourning that it was irreparable. What grieves me most is that I was not, while my dear wife lived so faithful with her on the subject of religion as I should have been, and I have now no certain assurance that she died in the faith / I am not, blessed be God, without strong hope—but I have not that clear evidence of her salvation which might reasonably have been expected to result from more faithful & diligent efforts on my part for her conversion. Oh if I had not contented myself with a few conversations on the subject of religion with a few recommendations of religious books, with faint prayers—if I had incessantly followed her with kind & earnest persuasion—if I had ceaselessly brought

59. Notice of the fire appeared in the *Cincinnati Daily Gazette*, Dec. 29, 1835.
60. Eleven-year-old David Whitcombe Thorp. Chase had become David's guardian in March 1835, soon after the death of the boy's father, Andrew. David's older brothers, John F. and Truman B., aged seventeen and fifteen, had passed into Chase's care at the same time. Notice from Hamilton County, Ohio, Court of Common Pleas, Mar. 16, 1835, David Whitcombe Thorp to Chase, Dec. 11, 1842 (Chase Papers, L.C.).
61. 1 John 5.

God's blessing on my efforts—if had ever exhibited before an example of the Christian life—she might have been before her death enrolled among the professed followers of the Lamb. But I procrastinated & now she is gone

I attended church in the morning at St Pauls.[62] Mr. Horrell conducted the service & preached.[63] My thoughts wandered much & once during the sermon I fell asleep. May God pardon these sins. When I returned home I went to my home & read various passages—chiefly such as were calculated to bring my dear wife to remembrance. In the afternoon I went over to my sister's to see my cousin James Denison, who is sick.[64] Found him convalescent. I then went to the grave yard where my Kitty's remains are deposited. Oh how I wished that I could once more see even her lifeless corpse— There are a multitude of graves in the two contiguous yards—most of those who lie there are younger than I am—few much older. May I feel the warning. My afflicted father in law joined me at the grave of my dear wife—who is laid for the present in the family vault of George W. Jones. We returned home together. In the morning we all went to church— Mr. Brooke preached a Sermon on the folly of the common maxim that it is no matter what a man thinks provided he be sincere.[65] My thoughts wandered less than in the morning. After church I attempted to learn David the Lord's prayer but made little progress. I shall persevere however. I then wrote the foregoing journal of the day.

DECR. 28   Before going to bed last night I told David that I would allow him a cent every morning if he wd. make my fire by daylight, to be laid out in books for him: and this morning I had a fire very early / I rose earlier than usual in consequence. I had been dreaming that my beloved wife was dangerously ill & I rose with my mind full of her. After dressing & private prayer I went down stairs, & joined in family prayers. Oh how I mourn that my dear wife cannot join us in our devotions: but I trust she is joining in a purer & more acceptable service than can be rendered on earth, even in that offered by the glorious company of angels & by the spirits of just men

62. St. Paul's Episcopal Church. *Cinc. Dir. (1834)*, 258.
63. Thomas Horrel, assistant minister of Christ Church. Venable, *Christ Church*, 32, 137.
64. Denison, an attorney and later a representative in the Texas House, was one of nine children of Chase's aunt, Rachel Chase Denison, and her husband, Dr. Joseph Adam Denison, Sr., of Royalton, Vt. James Denison worked at this time in Chase's office. Child, *Cornish*, 2:62; James Denison to Chase, Aug. 11, 1834, Joseph A. Denison, Sr., et al. to Chase, Oct. 1, 1835 (Chase Papers, Hist. Soc. of Pa.); Walter Prescott Webb et al., *The Handbook of Texas* (Austin, 1952), 1:490.
65. John T. Brooke was rector of Christ Church. *Cinc. Dir. (1836–37)*, 25, 242.

made perfect. After breakfast I went down to my office, where I found a letter for me from H. Brunot enclosing a note against E. H. Lytle.[66] I wrote a note to Mr. Lytle requesting him to call & pay the note & also the judgment standing against him. He called & agreed to arrange it satisfactorily tomorrow. Mrs Bigelow came in.[67] We conversed about my dear wife & she seemed to sympathize sincerely with me. How much almost any person may become endeared to us by sympathy! I gave her some deeds & leases belonging to her & she went away. Mr. Wm McGuire came in to know if he ought to retain additional counsel in the prosecution of Gedney—I told him I thought it unnecessary. I advised him to send Joiner & Brummel two of his witnesses to me that I might ascertain the exact purport of their testimony— The Revd. Mr. Lynd came in. He wished my advice as to the claim set up by Goodwin & Wilstach[68] against Dr. Staughton's estate. I advised him to reject the claim & leave them to their legal remedy. After I had got through with my morning visitors I applied myself to the preparation of an argument in the case of the Bk U. States vs Longworth & others in the Supreme Court of the United States,[69] & continued engaged upon it until dinner time; after dinner I returned to my work & continued at it till I went to visit the grave of my Kitty. It was twilight—a solemn hour, in a solemn place. I stood at her silent resting place & prayed for strength to perform the will of God & to suffer it. As I came I thought—& Oh how terrible was the thought—of meeting my dear-dear wife as an accusing spirit at the bar of God—that she might reproach me for my unfaithfulness to her in spiritual things as the cause of her misery— But I hope for better things / When I came home I found the family assembled in the parlour. We took tea & I returned to my office & my argument. I spent sometime however before I renewed my labour, in dipping into Dr. Dewees book on Midwifery.[70] I feel extremely sorry that I did not study this subject before the sickness of my wife. It might have prevented me from leaving her. At nine o'clock I came home, bringing Dewees & Good's Study of Medicine with me.[71] After family prayer came to my room, & attempted to learn David the Lord's prayer & heard

---

66. Edward H. Lytle, a business associate. Timothy Walker to Chase, Apr. 1, 1841 (Chase Papers, L.C.).
67. Probably either the wife of H. G. Bigelow, a local wagon maker, or Cincinnati resident Mrs. John Bigelow. *Cinc. Dir. (1834)*, 19.
68. Cincinnati druggists Dr. Oliver Goodwin and C. F. Wilstach. Ibid., 70, 190.
69. *Voorhees v. Jackson.*
70. William Potts Dewees, *A Compendious System of Midwifery, Chiefly Designed to Facilitate the Inquiries of those Who May be Pursuing this Branch of Study*... (London, 1825).
71. John Mason Good, *The Study of Medicine*, 4 vols. (London, 1822).

him read. The child certainly makes some progress. May the Lord enable me to be a blessing to him. I shall spend, by the permission, of God the remainder of this night, until I go to bed in reading Dewees, my bible & in prayer.

DECR. 29 The sun had hardly risen when I left my bed this morning full as usual of sad & mournful recollections. How can I become reconciled to the loss of my chief Earthly treasure? After reading the scripture—the third Epistle of John—& prayer I went down stairs & joined in family devotion. After a while the nurse came down stairs with my dear little motherless child. I ought to be & I hope I am thankful that I have been able to obtain such good nursing for the child & that her health is so good. After breakfast I went to my office & spent the morning, except when interrupted by visitors, in preparing my argument for the Supreme Court of the U. States, until I went to the meeting of the Directors of the Lafayette Bank at 10 oclock. After the Board adjourned I spoke to the President & Cashier about placing funds in New York to enable them to give me a draft to pay for some stock lately purchased by Mr. Garniss & myself. Mr. Lawrence the President promised that it shd. be attended to. I then returned to my office & resumed my argument until dinner time. After dinner I went to work again & continued so employed until evening when I again visited the resting place of my dear wife. Several young wives of about her own age sleep very near her / I returned home but after tea again went to my office where I staid till near nine oclock, when I came home bringing with me Dewees on Females & Eberle on Children,[72] in which books I read with little profit until the approach of midnight sumd. me to devotion.

DECR. 30 David came into my room this morning just after daylight & made a fire: but I did not rise till some time after / When risen I endeavored to offer my morning prayer & praise to God: but my heart was heavey & I felt that I did not pray aright. Oh for a closer walk with God—for greater degrees of conformity to his will. After prayer I went down stairs. After breakfast I went to my office. At eleven Mr. Lytle called & took the amt. of his indebtedness to Brunot, which I gave him. He promised to call & settle tomorrow. I have this day been engaged nearly the whole time in preparing the argument already mentioned. It is heavey work now with me.

---

72. William Potts Dewees, *A Treatise on the Diseases of Females* (Philadelphia, 1826), and John Eberle, *A Treatise on the Diseases and Physical Education of Children* (Cincinnati, 1833).

I have no longer a wife at home interested, in all that I do & gratified by all my success. I am no longer stimulated by a wish to please one whom I love far better than myself / But I have duties to perform, & I ought to exert myself from Love to God & my fellow men. Would that I could feel so devoted to God that I might do every thing with all my might for the sake of pleasing Him. My partner Mr. Eells has been engaged in the preparation of two declarations one in covenant & the other in debt—he is yet a raw hand but will improve by practice.[73]

Towards evening I went to the grave yard. The rain & snow were falling fast & the northwest wind blew chill. It was a melancholy evening but it harmonized well with my feelings. I felt a sad pleasure in standing once more at the spot where her mortal remains are deposited. I offered up a silent prayer to God for more conformity to his will & reluctantly turned my steps homeward.

After writing the above I went to a prayer meeting at Mr. Brooke's church with my father & mother in law. It was held in a room in the basement story. Not many were present. The exercises were to me very solemn & interesting. Short addresses were delivered both by Mr. Horrell & Mr. Brooke—by the former on bringing all our sorrows & sins & laying them at the foot of the cross by the latter on the joy of believing and the inconsistency of Christians in living so far away from God. Deeply & bitterly did I regret that my poor wife could not hear the messages which I heard & join in those solemn services: but I do hope she needs no message now to tell of her Saviour & that she constantly joins in a better service. Oh could I be but sure of this how gladly would I embrace my lot!

This day Genl. Findlay has been borne to his tomb—Genl. James Findlay.[74] He was I believe a native of Pennsylvania but emigrated early to the west where he soon became a conspicuous citizen. He was a member of the first Territorial Council for the Territory Northwest of the River Ohio; afterwards a Col. in the Northwestern Army & present at Hull's Surrender;[75] afterwards a member of Congress from Ohio, & afterwards—a year ago last October—the

---

73. Chase formed a partnership with Samuel Eells (1810–42), a recent Cincinnati arrival, in Nov. 1835. Their agreement lasted until Aug. 1838. *Biographical Cyclopædia*, 1:187; *Cinc. Dir. (1836–37)*, 55; Chase partnership records (Chase Papers, L.C.); entry for Aug. 11, 1848, below.

74. James Findlay (1770–1835), a major general in the Ohio state militia. *DAB*, 6:384–85.

75. Gen. William Hull (1753–1825), the governor of Michigan Territory, had surrendered American forces to Gen. Isaac Brock, the lieutenant governor of Canada, on Aug. 12, 1812. The defeat was a serious blow to American morale at the beginning of the War of 1812. Ibid., 9:363–64.

Whig candidate for Governor of Ohio. He was a kindhearted & most amiable man & had many friends. He has left a widow but no children.

DECR. 31. The last day of the old year! The old year: strange name for a portion of time so lately begun—so speedily terminated. The old year: but yesterday as it seems it was ushered in as the New Year. How little did I then anticipate what has come to pass. This year found me a husband—it has left me wifeless; it found me childless—it has left me charged with a solemn trust—the welfare of the sole pledge of my departed wife's affection—it found me rejoicing in the hope of worldly advancement—it has left me with all such wishes annihilated—it found me receding from God—it has left me I trust drawing nigh to Him—it found me laying up treasures on earth—it leaves me convinced of the vanity of such occupation & anxious, chiefly, to lay up treasures in Heaven. In professional attainment & reputation it found me nearly as it leaves me. I have during this year completed the Edition of the Statutes of Ohio on which I have been so long engaged by publishing the Third Volume. This book my beloved wife used to say she wd. keep for her oldest son. Alas she never saw the third volume.

1836

JAN. 1. This day—the first of the New Year—usually with me a day of gladness has been a day of gloom. My dear wife who shared the joys of the last New Year's has gone. Every thing reminds me of her. Just so gloriously did the unclouded sun ascend the sky last year—just so did he magnificently sink to rest. Just so mild was the temperature of the air—just so serene the expanse of heaven. Here she sat at the breakfast table bidding me admire her New Years gift to her father, & when I remarked that every one in the house had a Gift but me, she said nothing. When I wanted to go out & attempted to draw on my boots I found a difficulty in the way. Something had got into my boot! Half fretfully & half expectingly I drew it out. It was a gold pencil case. On it was inscribed Penzez á moi.[76] It was my wife's new year's gift / Delightful gift yet not half so delightful as the kiss which accompanied it. How often has she adverted since to this little circumstance & said "How bad I should have felt had there indeed been nothing for you! When you complained I could hardly help telling you to look in your boot." Dear—

---

76. "Think of me."

dear Kitty—life of my life is it possible that thou art gone? That I shall no more hear that kind & gentle voice—no more recieve that kind affectionate caress. I can at times hardly realize it— Yet I know it is so. "Penzez á moi" Yes I will think of thee as long as I live.

We all went to church this morning—but Mr. Haight, the Rector being indisposed there was no Service.[77] After leaving the church I walked up to the grave yard where my Kitty lies with her mother.[78] We talked of her all the way going & returning home / When we got home I told her what I thought respecting the management of her disorder by the physicians.

Mrs Anderson with her little baby & Mrs McCandless with her little children came to see us this morning. They passed through childbirth safely—but My Kitty died.

This afternoon I went down to the office with the intention of finishing my argument in the ejectmen case but I did not write a line. Towards evening I walked up to the vault where lies the mortal part of all that was most dear to me on earth. Here I lingered for some time—until the twilight was rapidly merging in darkness.

This evening I went again to my office where I began to copy my argument for the press. Before I went Mr. G. at table told a story about Gov. Root & Elisha Williams & Thos. J. Oakley[79]— How discordantly it struck upon my ears.

JANUARY 2. The same subject continues to occupy my nightly dreams & daily thoughts—my great & irreparabable loss. Oh that I could live over again the last two months—how different would be my conduct. Let this make me enquire May not happen within two months which would make me wish that the conduct of today had been different? My wife is indeed gone. She can no longer be the object of care or kindness. But duties remain. Are they fulfilled?

The day has been very different from yesterday. It has rained nearly all day: and the clouds have completely shut out the sun. Every thing has looked gloomy.

I have attended to little business today. I intended to complete my argument but I have hardly touched it. I have settled a few claims on Thorp's estate[80]—little else. I received a notification to

---

77. Benjamin I. Haight (1809–79), the rector of St. Paul's Episcopal Church. *Appletons'*, 3:27.

78. Chase meant that he walked to the graveyard with Amelia Garniss.

79. Erastus Root (1773–1846) of New York, a Democratic assemblyman, state senator, and former lieutenant governor; Elisha Williams (1773–1833), a Federalist leader in the New York assembly, 1800–1828; and Federalist jurist Thomas Jackson Oakley (1783–1857), who had served as New York assemblyman and U.S. congressman. "Mr. G." was John P. Garniss. *DAB*, 13:604, 16:145–46, 20:257–58.

80. Andrew Thorp.

attend a meeting of the Committee on the Dividend of the Lafayette Bank: but forgot the duty at the hour.

I have repeated my visit to my wife's grave. It was nearly dark and it was raining fast: but I like to go there. I have lately become accustomed to grave yard walks. Oh that the solemn voices which seem to issue from all those tombs might humble & sober every high thought in me.

I walked over to Mrs Colby's after tea & conversed with her a long time about my dear wife. Mrs C. thinks it probable she would not have recovered, even had not the treatment of Dr. C. been departed from. I think otherwise & am agonized by the thought that had I been at home she would have recovered, but I was far from her.

I have been reading lately on medicine. The barbarous jargon makes my progress slow. It is like reading Greek. I am compelled to have a dictionary by & use it constantly.

I have had some talk with David this evening since prayers. His conduct has been quite bad of late. He has been remiss in getting his lessons—insolent and abusive towards the other servants and extremely dirty in his personal appearance. I have warned him that unless he mends his ways I shall be compelled to punish him.

JAN. 4[81] Another day is nearly gone: it is rapidly hastening to a close. Am I nearer Heaven by a day's journey? I rose this morning with less painful feeling than I have lately experienced: but I had hardly risen before the tide of recollection began to flow and wave upon wave of painful memory overwhelmed my soul. I did not I hope repine or murmur against my Heavenly Father, my best & wisest friend, whom I will love and trust though he afflict: but I saw much sinful neglect in myself, so much transgression of God's law, so much ignorance & mismanagement, all combining to produce the disastrous result that I could not contain myself. After awhile I read a chapter in Proverbs & endeavored to pour out my soul in prayer to God for grace to sustain all afflictions & to fulfil all his will. I then went down stairs & joined in family prayer. After breakfast I read for some time in Saturday Evening[82] & then went to church. My thoughts wandered considerably during prayer. The sermon was unusually solemn & interestg. The text was "Man giveth up the Ghost & where is he?"[83] On returning home I resumed my reading

---

81. So dated at the beginning of the entry, but at a page turn in the original journal Chase altered his heading from Jan. 4 to Jan. 3. Since Jan. 3, 1836, was a Sunday, the entry relates to that date.

82. Isaac Taylor, *Saturday Evening. By the Author of Natural History of Enthusiasm* . . . (Boston, 1832).

83. Job 14:10.

in Saturday Evening. In the afternoon we all went to the church, but there was no service. We returned home / Towards evening I walked to the resting place of the mortal part of my beloved wife. It had rained nearly all day and the walking was extremely bad. I passed through the Presbyterian Burying Ground. I noticed many graves without any mark or memorial to indicate the dweller below. Often I remarked graves nearly obliterated & undistinguishable from the surrounding inequalities of surface. In the Episcopal Ground, there are fewer interments & more apparent respect for the dead.

In the evening we attended Mr. Brooke's church. I was remarkably free, blessed be God, from wandering thoughts. The sermon was not so good as Mr. Brooke usually delivers: but was perhaps well adapted to one class of his hearers. It was not prepared with much care & the mind of the speaker seemed often to lose its tension.

Since I returned from Church I have been principally occupied in teaching David the Lord's prayer & in learning him to read. I teaching to read I became too impatient & once even angry / For this I pray to be forgiven & that the Lord may give wisdom in dealing with him. His immortal happiness may depend upon it.

JAN. 5 Yesterday was a wet and cheerless day—only that now & then for a little while the sun would shine out from behind the clouds with cheering beams. Today the weather has been delightful. Today had my dear wife lived she would have called for me at my office & we should have been walking arm in arm & heart in heart beneath the pleasant sun. But she—where is she? Rejoicing I hope beneath the far brighter beams of the Sun of Righteousness.

My little babe continues to improve. She enjoys the most perfect health & now takes considerable notice of many things. She smiles & laughs now & then, awake & in dreams. The servant girl of our next neighbor says that when she smiles in dreams it is because she sees an angel pass by. She begins to endeavour to make her wants known by sounds: at least so I think. She is quite fat or rather plump / Her eyes are blue— Her forehead is slightly depressed just above the eyes. Her hair is brown. Her eyelashes are long & her eyebrows I think will be heavy. Her cheeks are now full. Her mouth is not very pretty. Her lips are too thick & the upper overhangs the lower too much. Her chin sometimes looks a little too pointed then again it is quite round. She is very gentle and mild—seldom crying or fretting. Every body says she is a sweet & very pretty child. Her grandmother grandfather & I think so. May God of his infinite mercy make her his child.

Mrs Yorke has been confined today.[84] Her child was premature & was still born. This is a light affliction compared with mine: but I have no doubt it is deeply felt. May He who is able comfort the parents & preserve the life of the mother.

JAN 9. For three or four days past I have written nothing in this journal, because nothing unusual has occurred. The returning hours have brought with them their appropriate duties; which I have attempted to perform in the strength of one mighty to support & save. Far short indeed have I come of the standard of purity & zeal exhibited in the Gospel. When shall I learn to subdue all hastiness of temper, all petulance, all selfishness? When shall I be thoroughly imbued with a humble, selfdenying, holy spirit? Oh Lord, my Saviour do thou assist & teach me. I have been diligently engaged for two weeks on an argument for the Supreme Court of the United States, which I have finished tonight, in the case of the Bank of the United States vs Longworth & others.[85] My object has been to establish a title made under an order of sale in the course of certain procedings in attachment. The proceedings were extremely irregular & defective: but I attempted to sustain the title on the ground that the order of sale was made by a court of competent jurisdiction & could not in this suit be collaterally questioned. I think I shall succeed. I argued this same case a Year ago last July at Columbus in the Circuit Court. My dear wife was with me then. We roomed at Mrs Robinson, where Judge McLean and his lady also boarded.[86] I remember expressing some anxiety to my wife about this case, telling her that a fee of $150 depended on my success, and that the next day she said playfully to the Judge that he must decide this case for me at any rate, that I might get the fee.

I have attended this evening a meeting of a committee on the subject of obtaining the Public Schoolhouses for the use of the Sabbath Schools.[87] I was appointed one of a Committee to ascertain to whom application for this privilege should be made.

---

84. Possibly the wife of Joshua Yorke, a partner in a wholesale grocery firm. *Cinc. Dir. (1836–37)*, 113, 196.

85. *Voorhees v. Jackson*.

86. Chase probably referred to the Franklin House, operated by J. Robinson and Son at the corner of High and Town Streets. Ohio politician and jurist John McLean (1785–1861) joined the U.S. Supreme Court as an associate justice in 1829. South Carolina native Rebecca Edwards McLean (d. 1840 or 1841) was his first wife. William T. Martin, *History of Franklin County: A Collection of Reminiscences of the Early Settlement of the County* . . . (Columbus, 1858), 311; *DAB*, 12:127–28; Weisenburger, *McLean*, 6, 220.

87. Chase probably referred to the Western Board of Agency of the American Sunday School Union, formed in Jan. 1836. The board, with Chase as one of its members, was expected to promote the formation of Sunday schools and to distribute the publications of the American Sunday School Union. *Cinc. Dir. (1836–37)*, 240–41.

January 1836

JANUARY 17   My little babe was vaccinated yesterday by Dr. Drake. Some days ago my motherinlaw asked me who shd. vaccinate the child. I replied Dr. Colby. To this she strongly objected urging that Dr. Colby had not been as faithful as he ought to have been to my dear wife in her sickness and expressing her strong distrust of his fitness to attend the babe. My objections to Dr. Drake were that he was generally unsuccessful in his practice & that I believed that the death of my dear Kitty was attributable to his mistaken treatment / I said however that I did not think it of much consequence who vaccinated her but that should she be seriously indisposed I should certainly send for Dr. Colby. and she said that she was willing I should select any physician other than Dr. C. On this the conversation terminated. When I came home last night & was about to go to bed I was informed that Dr. Drake had been here & had vaccinated the babe, without my knowledge. I was surprised and displeased: but hardly knew what to say or do. I am unwilling to hurt the feelings of any one much more than of the parents of my dear wife. I am anxious to act kindly towards them: but I foresee that in regard to the babe unpleasant difficulties will arise / I pray for grace to act firmly & conscientiously.

Today I have attended church with little profit. My mind has wandered exceedingly. The incident of yesterday has been suffered to occupy too much of my attention & I have made little or no progress in the divine life. I have attended church three times—twice at Mr. Haight's & once at Mr. Brookes. I have visited as usual the vault where lies the mortal part of her who was to me the life of life. It was misty & rained a little. Oh how ardently I wished as I stood by the silent tomb that the door might open & that she who slept within might be restored to me: but it might not be   And not my will but thine O God be done. I feel that the stroke is just: I feel that I have deserved far more evil than has fallen to my lot. I desire humbly to submit myself to the Divine Will, & magnify the name of the Lord. Yet could I be assured of her salvation much of the bitterness of the cup would be removed. I strongly hope that she is safe—but the evidence is not clear & full.

JAN 18.   I had a conversation this morning with my motherinlaw in regard to the employment of a physician for the child and I grieve to say that I allowed myself to exhibit a very improper spirit. It is my duty to be firm & decided in that course which my conscience approves: but I should remember how much older than I she is: I shd. remember that she is the mother of my dear departed wife and in every way entitled to respect & deference from me. I do hope & pray that I may not thus offend any more. After this conversation I went over to my sister's & told her that I thought I should be obliged to employ another physician and that I should select Dr. Eberle. She said that she should be satisfied to have Dr. Eberle attend the baby. We then conversed much on the circumstances of Kitty's last illness. These conversations unfitted me entirely for the business of the morning. I went down to the Office. Mr. Leslie called to enquire about a claim in my hands & I satisfied him as far as I was able.[88] In the afternoon I wrote to Helen, inviting & urging her to come out here should a suitable opportunity present.[89] This evening I have attended a meeting of our vestry.

JAN 22   For the last two or three days I have been engaged in conducting in aid of the prosecuting attorney, a criminal trial. Charles F. Gedney, lately one of the city watch, was indicted for maliciously & purposely shooting Isaac Mcguire. The charge was for murder in the second degree. The examination of witnesses commenced on Wednesday & was continued until about five oclock last night when I addressed the jury. The examination of the witnesses was extremely fatiguing. The evidence related to a transaction which took place in three or four minutes & was witnessed from different points in the room by different persons. There was of course a good deal of descrepancy in the testimony. Some of the witnesses also were impeached, and a great deal of testimony was introduced in relation to a previous difficulty between M—— & G—— when the former was arrested by the latter & taken to the watchhouse. I spoke about an hour and a half & was listened to with great attention by a crowded audience. I have reason to think that in the judgment of my hearers I acquitted myself well. Today Mr. Fox & Mr. Benham have addressed the jury in behalf of the prisoner.[90] I heard but little of Mr F——'s speech— He is earnest & sometimes ingenious—he is vehement in manner & boisterous in enunciation. His main defect is want of logical consecutiveness. Mr. Benham has a high reputation as a speaker— He is a very portly man—somewhat obese indeed—with a full, long & broad face surmounted by a forehead, high but narrow & pyramidal. He has a

---

88. Andrew and James Leslie were Cincinnati goldbeaters. James, subsequently a dentist, later worked with Chase in the free-soil movement. Ibid. (1840), 260; *History of Cincinnati and Hamilton County,* 725–26.

89. Chase's youngest sister, Helen, was living in Concord, N.H., at the time. Subsequent correspondence suggests that personal tensions between Chase and the Garnisses had increased after the death of Catharine Garniss Chase, and that Chase needed household assistance and the companionship of a close relative. Chase to Helen Chase, Apr. 24, 1836 (Chase Papers, Hist. Soc. of Pa.).

90. Charles Fox (1796–1882) was a partner in the Cincinnati law firm of Fox and Wright and later a judge of the Superior Court. *Cinc. Dir. (1836–37),* 62; Jewett, "Cincinnati," 259; *History of Cincinnati and Hamilton County,* 193.

January 1836 { 109 }

good voice but was today affected by a severe cold. His manner is good. He is perfectly selfpossessed—understands his subject well—is slow & deliberate in his enunciation. He is verbose however & to use a word which I today heard for the first time very repetitionary. He expands, dilates & and repeats a good deal too much, & is of course excessively prolix. He spoke today over five hours. It was his first speech since his return from Louisville & he put forth all his powers. He commenced by a very unwarrantable attack upon me in regard to my appearance there for the state. He said that I had reversed the chivalry of my profession by appearing in the prosecution rather than the defence of criminals. I had, he said, remarked that I could not conscientiously refuse my services when required. He did not envy me such a conscience. This language was highly improper especially as coming from one so much my senior.

I have been quite unwell today, and oh how much do I miss the endearing attentions of my dear wife. How much do I regret that I cannot tell tell her of my speech & impart to her all my feelings. I made my way out of the courthouse while Mr. B was speaking & went to her grave, & ejaculated a brief prayer to God for strength & patience to do & suffer his will.

I have spent this evening at my office reading two articles in the London Quarterly Review—one reviewing brief Reed & Mathesons Tour, Latrobe's Rambler in America, Abdy's Tour &c and another reviewing with some severity Willis' Pencillings by the Way.[91]

JAN. 26 I dreamed last night—as I do almost every night—of my dear departed wife: but I cannot now recollect my dream. It has passed from me like the visions of Nebuchadnizzar. I rose rather rather later than usual this morning for it was intensely cold / After prayer in my room alone, I went down stairs & joined in family prayer. Oh how my heart aches when I think that my dear wife is not permitted to join in these delightful exercises but I do hope that she is worshipping the same God in a better Society. I remember her saying frequently that sin was the only cause of unhappiness in our family; and I am sure it would have gladdened her heart to kneel at the family altar with her father, mother, & husband. After breakfast in conversation her mother remarked that about two

---

91. The *London Quarterly Review* 108 (Sept. 1835): 205–15, 238–44, contained reviews of Andrew Reed and James Matheson, *A Narrative of the Visit to the American Churches, by the Deputation from the Congregational Union of England and Wales*, 2 vols. (London, 1835); Charles Joseph Latrobe, *The Rambler in North America: 1832–1833*, 2 vols. (London, 1835); Edward Strutt Abdy, *Journal of a Residence and Tour in the United States . . .* , 3 vols. (London, 1835); and Nathaniel Parker Willis, *Pencillings by the Way . . .* (New York, 1835).

hours before her death she asked the Doctor if her milk would not return when she should get well, saying that she could not bear the idea of not nursing her own babe. From this it seems that she was not at all aware of her imminent danger or of her approaching dissolution. Surely this was very wrong.

After breakfast I went to my office where I have spent the greater part of the day in arranging my papers, which have been for some time past much deranged.

This morning conversing about a proposed amendment of our Charter Mr. Geo. W. Neff remarked that they must send me to the Senate next year & get it through.[92] I observed that I would have it done if they would send me. "Well" said Mr. N "if you will say you will accept the nomination I will assure you of my efforts in your behalf." "Why" said I "I should like to go there one winter very well if I could make it comport with my business." "Well" said he I shall probably have some influence next year, & I will remember you." *Nous verrons* as Mr. Ritchie says.[93] Who can tell what may happen as another year rolls round? I have heard within a few hours that Mr. Garrard, one of the candidates for the Legislature at the last election lies even now in the grasp of death:[94] and I have just returned from my evening visit to the tomb of my dear wife who was then in full health. Let me study to be ready for the coming of the Lord.

JAN. 27   Today I have been engaged in arranging my letters and in bringing up the arrears of my correspondence. I opened some old letters & read them— Among them were three from my dear & now sainted mother written while I was at college.[95] How precious are these remembrancers of her now / How painfully pleasant to read over her good advice, her lessons of thrift & economy, lessons which she rigidly practiced from an earnest desire to have her children well educated but which I alas too little regarded. How delighted she was to hear that her children had done well: but how much more she was anxious that they might win the favor of God. "I hope that they will be good & that will be great to

92. George W. Neff, a partner in the hardware firm of Neff and Brothers, was a director of the Lafayette Bank, president of the Fireman's Insurance Company, and president of the Cincinnati City Council. *Cinc. Dir. (1836–37),* 126, 201, 209, 211.

93. *Nous verrons* means "we shall see." Thomas Ritchie (1778–1854) was editor of the *Richmond Enquirer. DAB,* 15:628–29.

94. Jeptha Dudley Garrard (1802–36) died from "inflamation of the brain" the following day. Anna Russell des Cognets, *Governor Garrard, of Kentucky, His Descendants and Relatives* (Lexington, Ky., 1898), 29; *Liberty Hall and Cincinnati Gazette,* Feb. 4, 1836.

95. Three such documents have survived. The earliest contains entries from Aug. 14, 1824, July 16, 1825, and an undated entry; the other two are dated July 7, 1825, and Aug. 1825 (Chase Papers, Hist. Soc. of Pa.).

me."[96] How willing she was to spend & be spent for us all! Oh how little I deserved such a mother & such a wife as I have had & lost. Would that they could have been spared to me a little while longer that I might have given more proofs of my affection to them. But God has seen fit to order otherwise and I submit.

I have attended Mr. Brooke's prayer meeting this evening with my father & motherinlaw. The subject of the lecture was Prayer. It was a simple exposition of the importance & general neglect of this duty even by professing Christians.

Dr Drake has been here today & has vaccinated my child again. It is very unpleasant to me to have the physician who I firmly believe was the immediate cause of my wife's death, attending my child: but in this matter of vaccination I must yield my feelings to oblige the grandparents.

FEB. 7. I rose this day at my usual hour and after reading a chapter in Proverbs & offering my morning prayer & praise I went down stairs & joined in family prayer. After prayer & breakfast I came up stairs but did little except read a few pages in Baxter's Saint's Rest until the bell summoned me to church.[97] At church my thoughts wandered a good deal. I endeavored to restrain this wandering, but was not very successful. I shd. have succeeded better had I attempted less in my own strength & relied more on Divine assistance. To Mr. Haight's sermon I was enabled to give pretty close attention. His subject was the unprofitable hearing of preaching. His text was "And as he sowed some fell by the wayside &c."[98] He described the several classes of wayside hearers; the careless, the worldly, the frivolous and he reproved nothing of which my conscience did not accuse me. How often have I heedlessly listened to the preaching of God's word! How often have I suffered wordly thoughts to distract my attention! How often have I indulged in reverie during sermons! Alas even since I have indulged a hope of salvation through Christ how often have I been guilty of all these sins! And have I indeed any title to the inheritance of the saints? I am ashamed of my foolish wanderings; I grieve for the hardness of my heart: I pray for deliverance from all these offences. If I am saved through grace, it is through grace alone. I am totally unworthy. After the sermon I ventured to approach the Lord's table & partake of the Holy Communion. It was painful to see how few out of the congregation remained to testify their love to the Savior by celebrating his Supper. And of those few some doubtless are wanting in the even balances

---

96. A paraphrase from Jannette Ralston Chase to Chase, Aug. 14, 1824, ibid.
97. Richard Baxter, *The Saint's Everlasting Rest: or, a Treatise of the Blessed State of the Saints in their Enjoyment of God in Glory* . . . (London, 1649).
98. Luke 8:5.

of God's judgment. I felt grateful for the privilege I enjoyed & I trust did not fail altogether to discern the Lord's body. After coming home I retired to my room & prayed that God would sanctify to me & to my fellow communicants the solemn services in wh. we had been engaged.

After dinner I took up Foster's Essay on the Importance of Religion[99] & attempted to read. I found myself overcome by sleep induced I think by eating too much at dinner. I heard David's lesson. Towards evening I paid my daily visit to the tomb where lies the body of my dear wife.

This evening I attended Mr. Brooke's church. The funeral of Gen. King was announced to take place on Wednesday next.[1] His career therefore is terminated. Endowed with uncommon genius, full of warm & generous affections, deeply impressed with religious sentiments, favoured by birth & alliance, he has fallen the victim of ill regulated appetite—of an uncontrolled convivial temperament. Could he have but steadily pursued the plain path of duty, he would have been distinguished among men: and he might have accomplished much good.

FEB. 8   This morning I called on Mr. Bates[2] & conversed with him about the investment of a hundred thousand dollars surplus capital belonging to the Lafayette Bank. I told him that I knew three individuals who wd. take it & secure the payment by a note & pledge of stocks. After some conversation he thought such an investment would be a judicious one. I then called on Mr. Lawrence & invited him to become a partner in the loan. He declined on the ground that being Prest. of the Bank it might be said that he had improperly used its funds. I then called on Mr. Neff who acquiesced in my views & agreed to become interested. Mr. Neff has since made enquiries as to the purchase of stocks but finds them higher than we anticipated. Lafayette stock sells at 103 & Trust Co at 117. We shall probably however complete the arrangement in a day or two

I have done no business at my office today except to give a Man some advice in an assault & battery case: and none at the Court House except to make out in part my cases from the general Chancery Docket.

99. Possibly James Foster, *The Usefulness Truth and Excellency of the Christian Revelation* . . . (London, 1731).
1. King had died on Feb. 6, "after a long illness and great suffering." *Liberty Hall and Cincinnati Gazette*, Feb. 11, 1836.
2. John Bates (1798–1870), proprietor of the Exchange Bank and Savings Institution. *Biographical Cyclopædia*, 3:696; *Cinc. Dir. (1836–37)*, 210.

There was a bar meeting this morning to pass resolutions in regard to Genl. King. I was not present not having been notified. I suggested to Judge Wright the appointment of a committee to make arrangements for the attendance of the profession at the funeral & for crape for their arms. This was done & the Sheriff agreed to procure the crape.

This evening after having read over the bylaws for the Western Board of Agency for the American Sunday School Union I went to a meeting of the Committee on Bylaws. None being present except Mr. Seward[3] I requested him to represent me & proceeded to a meeting of the Committee on Sunday Schools within the Diocese of Ohio at Mr. Brooke's. I found Messrs Haight, Brooke & Griswold there but four wd. not form a quorum. After pleasant & interesting conversation for an hour I went to Mr. Neff's.

FEB. 10 Mr. Neff being unwilling to take the money from the Laf. Bk in the present state of the stock market, the plan arranged a day or two since was abandoned— Had no business at Court to day— transacted little at my office. Wrote to Hilliard, Gray & Co enclosing Judge Storys order for a copy of his Commentaries on Equity.[4]

I have assisted this afternoon in committing to the tomb my friend & former partner Gen. King. He died in the hope of a happy resurrection of a disease brought on by his former irregular habits of life. He was a man of distinguished abilities, great versatility, wonderful tact & admirable practical talent. He was in his fortieth year.

Our neighbor Mrs Wood has lost her third daughter, a sweet girl of eighteen by bilious fever. She was laid in the vault by the side of my wife.

I recd. a letter this evening from Mrs Wirt.[5] It was full of kind sympathy for a loss which seems to me greater & greater every day.

FEB. 17 Rose this morning at my usual hour, washed, dressed & breakfasted as usual. My dear little babe grows finely: but I can discover little or no resemblance to her departed mother. She takes a great deal of notice of many things—attends to sounds. Yesterday she observed a picture very attentively. She has been twice vaccinated without effect. She is very good tempered, cries very little &

3. B. J. Seward, an agent for the American Sunday School Union. *Cinc. Dir.* (*1836–37*), 154.
4. Chase's order, to Boston publishers Hilliard, Gray and Company, was for a copy of Joseph Story, *Commentaries on Equity Jurisprudence, as Administered in England and America* . . . , 2 vols. (Boston, 1836). *Boston Dir. (1836)*, 15.
5. A copy of the letter, dated Feb. 3, may be found in Warden, *Chase*, 281.

gives so far as I can observe very little trouble. She was three months old yesterday. Today completes eleven weeks since her mother died. Oh could she have been spared to witness the growth and improvement of our dear babe—how delighted she would have been! How often should I have been called upon to note one & another little feat of infancy! How happy we should have been! And it seems so strange that she should have been taken away. There was no cause for her death in the disease itself, had it not been aided by injudicious treatment.

After breakfast I went to my office & found there a letter from Mr. Calvary Morris informing me that the bill to repeal the Charter of the Trust Co would not get much support in either House[6] / Shortly after Mr. Garniss called to inform me that Mr. Lytle himself in conversation with a friend last night expressed his conviction that the bill could not pass. At the Board of the Laf. Bk I communicated this information to Mr. [Lawrence] & afterwards to the Messrs Neff.[7] After the meeting of the Board I went to the Court House & filed a decree nisi in the case of the Bank vs Wheeler, Lytle & other. Some of my cases were called & I asked the Court to assess damages in one of them. I also asked the Court to appoint a guardian ad litem in the Case of Bank vs Bordens, Ferguson et al. Saml. Borden was appointed.[8]

Going to the Court House this morning I met Mr. Benham on the sidewalk. This individual has manifested a singular feeling of malevolence towards me ever since the trial of Gedney. He avoids meeting my eye—and shuns speaking to me. I do not regret this in itself, because his character is such as to render association with him undesirable: but I am unwilling to be on bad terms with anyone. I cherish no malevolent feelings towards him. On the contrary I sincerely forgive his assault upon me and was willing to speak to him today but he looked the other way as he passed me & we did not speak.

This afternoon Mr. Fox informed [me] that the Baptists would not purchase my Main Street lot. He offered to give $6000 and the house in which he lives. I told him that I would take time to consider of it. Before going to court I prepared an abstract & opinion of the title to Thomas' subdivision & MacAlester Square for Mr. Lawrence.

---

6. Morris (1798–1871), a Whig, represented Athens County in Ohio's lower house. The bill to repeal the charter of the Ohio Life Insurance and Trust Company was indefinitely postponed on Mar. 12. *Bio. Dir. U.S. Cong.*, 1535; Morris to Chase, Feb. 13, 1836 (Chase Papers, Hist. Soc. of Pa.); Ohio General Assembly, House of Representatives, *Journal*, 34th Assem., 1st sess., 1836, 907.

7. George W. Neff and William R. Neff, a partner in the family's hardware business and a director of the Cincinnati branch of the Bank of the United States. *Cinc. Dir. (1834)*, 237–38; ibid. (1836–37), 209, 126.

8. Borden was a Cincinnati grocer. *Cinc. Dir. (1836–37)*, 23.

From the Court House I went to the tomb of my dear wife. She sleeps free from the cares of this life. Oh for an assurance of her blessed immortality. But of that I shall not be assured until the resurrection.

This evening I have attended a meeting of the Western Board of Agency for the American Sunday School Union. We had an interesting meeting & solemnly pledged ourselves to zeal, industry, & prayerfulness in our work. The Lord help us to keep our resolution. From the meeting I came home & have since attended family prayers & am now teaching David to read & spell.

FEB. 21 I rose this morning a few moments after David had kindled my fire. read the chapter narrating the birth of Isaac & the expulsion of Hagar & Ishmael from the family of Abraham[9] & offered my morning sacrifice of prayer & thanksgiving to my Heavenly Father. I then went down stairs & joined the family in prayer. After this I came up stairs & spent my time till the bell rang for church in reading the Ninth Report of the American Sunday School Union.[10] Having become a member of the Western Board of Agency for the A.S.S.U. I wish to make myself more thoroughly acquainted with its constitution, history & plan of operations. I regard the plan of Sunday School Instruction as among the best schemes for diffusing religious knowledge & creating a taste for general information: and feel bound by my Christian profession to aid as much as possible in carrying on this work & I heartily pray that God may add his blessing to our endeavours to promote his glory & the happiness of our fellowmen. At church this morning I was more than usual preserved from wandering thoughts / Mr. Haight preached on the Temptation of our Savior—an excellent sermon full of instructive matter. In the interval between the services I read the same report. In the afternoon Mr. H—— again preached on the everlasting punishment of the wicked. After Church I came home—read awhile—prayed for God's blessing on the Services of the day & then walked up to the resting place of my dear wife. After my return I again attended church. Mr. H preached on Ye cannot serve God & Mammon.[11] When I came home Mrs G—— came into my room & the conversation soon turned upon Kitty. She said that she visited Mrs Conover[12] lasted week who remembered a great deal about her. Kitty visited her when she lost her baby & comforted her. At another

9. Gen. 21.
10. *The Ninth Annual Report of the American Sunday-School Union. May 21, 1833* (Philadelphia, 1833).
11. Matt. 6:24; Luke 16:13.
12. The wife of James F. Conover, editor and publisher of the *Cincinnati Whig. Cinc. Dir. (1836–37)*, 39.

time Kitty held her baby while its gums were lanced, though usually much averse to such things from a natural reluctance to witness pain & from a peculiar nervous temperament. Mrs. Selman[13] adverted to her visit here spoke of the manner in which Kitty met her—of her gentle & affectionate manner—of having icecream in the evening & of Kitty saying "Now I must take some to Mary for she won't like it after it is melted" & then filling a saucer & tripping away to give it to Mary. Mrs. S—— said she have never seen so much sweetness & kindliness in any one except one of her own daughters who died sometime since. Dear Kitty always remembered every one & was ready to share every thing she had with all. Mrs. G—— says that after I went away she said Mother I love my husband very much, but cannot recollect in what connexion she said it. She also says that on Saturday night previous to her death Kittys abdomen was as much enlarged as before her confinement. If this be true it is extraordinary that Dr. Colby was not informed of it or did not discover it.

I have head David lesson tonight. I think he improves steadily both in Spelling & reading.

JULY 23 Paid J. Reese Friy $61 for guitar & case which gave to sister Helen—[14]

1837

JAN 6. Near a year has elapsed since I last wrote in this book: I now resume my journal but perhaps shall again soon intermit it. On the first of this month I was at Columbus.[15] It was Sunday. I attended Mr. Preston's church morning & evening.[16] As I came out of church in the evening I overtook Miss Espy & accompanied her home.[17] She is an interesting young girl: but seems in delicate

---

13. The wife of Carberry Selman, a clerk at wholesale grocer Wright Smith and Company. Ibid., 154.

14. This entry is from memoranda at the end of Journal I. John E. Rees was a cutler in the partnership of Marks and Rees. *Cinc. Dir. (1834)*, 143; ibid. (1836–37), 142.

15. In margin: "Jan. 1." Chase appears to have been lobbying legislators in behalf of the Cincinnati school system, the Lafayette Bank, and entrepreneurs who intended to develop Yellow Springs, in Greene County. Elam P. Langdon to Chase, Dec. 25, 1836, Josiah Lawrence to Chase, Dec. 30, 1836, William Price to Chase, Jan. 16, 1837 (Chase Papers, L.C.).

16. William Preston presided at the Trinity Episcopal Church. William A. Taylor, *Centennial History of Columbus and Franklin County, Ohio* (Chicago, 1909), 1:186.

17. Lovinia Espy (1818–1900), the daughter of Josiah Murdoch Espy, cashier at the Franklin Bank of Columbus. Florence Mercy Espy, *History and Genealogy of the Espy Family in America* ([Fort Madison, Iowa], 1905), 33, 64; Josiah Espy, "A Tour in

health. At my room I spent my time in reading the New Testament, a few pages of Peck's Trial[18] & in conversation with the gentlemen who came. On the following day[19] I left Columbus for Cincinnati in the stage. Judge Burnet was also a passenger. It was too cold to talk much. We arrived at Springfield about dusk. Mr. Worden gave us a room in the new part of his hotel where no fire had been kindled for some time. It was very cold. Mr. Anthony called to see Judge B———[20] Mr. Linn called to see me & paid 375 on the Sherer note & promised that Mr. S. would come to Cin—— soon & pay the balance.[21] With my overcoat & two cloaks on the bed I slept very cold. At five, the next morning[22] we were called & rode to Cin. shut up in a close stage without any occurrence of interest / We arrived about 11 oclock at night. I found some difficulty in getting into the house, but after a while succeeded, and on gaining my room, after returning thanks to God for his protecting care, I betook myself to my bed. On the next morning[23] I did not rise very early. After breakfast went to my Office—shook hands with my partner, miner, & some other friends[24]— Went over to the new Bank[25]—found myself on the Ex: Com. attended to my duties as a member—returned to office went home—shaved & dressed—dined—returned to my office & attended to some business—came home & spent the evening— Heard of the death of Mrs Stettinius.[26] Six years ago last Spring I was groomsman at her bridal. It was a splendid fête. Three years after her husband was no more & now she also is gone. She is gone: but blessed be God, there is hope in her death. She was

---

Ohio, Kentucky and Indiana Territory, in 1805," *Ohio Valley Historical Series, Miscellanies* 1 (1871): v–vii; William P. Gallagher to Chase, Mar. 29, 1839 (Chase Papers, Hist. Soc. of Pa.).

18. Arthur J. Stansbury, *Report of the Trial of James H. Peck, Judge of the United States District Court for the District of Missouri, before the Senate of the United States, on an Impeachment Preferred by the House of Representatives* . . . (Boston, 1833).

19. In margin: "Jan. 2."

20. Springfield attorney Charles Anthony (1798–1862) served in both houses of the Ohio General Assembly during the 1830s. *Biographical Cyclopædia*, 6:1424; Gilkey, *Ohio Hundred Year Book*, 162–3, 198, 204.

21. Possibly Samuel B. Sherer, a Cincinnati resident. *Cinc. Dir. (1840)*, 353.

22. In margin: "Jan. 3."

23. In margin: "Jan. 4."

24. Samuel Eells and John L. Miner (b. 1810), a former student in Chase's office and future judge in the Superior Court of Cincinnati. Robson, *Biographical Encyclopædia*, 355.

25. The Lafayette Bank had recently constructed a new building on Third Street near the Cincinnati post office. *Cinc. Dir. (1836–37)*, 209.

26. Mary Longworth Stettinius (c. 1809–37), the oldest daughter of Nicholas Longworth and the widow of Washington, D.C., merchant John Stettinius, died of typhus. *Cincinnati Advertiser and Ohio Phoenix*, Jan. 11, 1837; *Daily National Intelligencer*, Jan. 14, 1837; DeChambrun, *Nicholas Longworth*, 45; *Wash. Dir. (1830)*, 72.

a follower of Christ & now lives with him. Yesterday morning[27] I called at Mr. Longworth's to tender any service I could render. I found Mr. L composed. He spoke affectionately & admiringly of his daughter. Would that he might follow her example. Attended to my duty at the Bank & to some business at the Office. In the evg. called with Sister Helen at Mr. Walker's found Miss W—— at home & spent quite a pleasant evening with her.[28] It was late when her brother came in & shortly after we took our leave. This morning[29] I awoke after dreaming of committing a very great sin, and O how thankful I was to find it but a dream! and how earnestly did I pray to be guarded against trangression. I felt myself very weak & sinful: & prayed for grace from on high. My little daughter sat next me as usual at the breakfast table. She is a sweet child & so far has enjoyed uncommon health. After breakfast I went to my office, and after attending to some business went to the Bank—where the note of Wright & Swormstedt, Meth. Book Agents in my fav. for 1495.49 was discounted—attended exchange committee—returned to my office: copied letter to Mr. Hubbard of Chicago & put it (enclosing Capt Russell's deed & bond into the Post Office[30]— After dinner returned to my office and found Mr. Wiggins there—conversed with him on business—stocks &c—Mr. J. L. Avery came in;[31] wished me to prepare release of lots sold by him—promised to attend to it— paid sundry bills—attended to various business—took tea—played with my child—called at Dr. Colby's—came to my office & wrote the above—

1837 AUG 24   It was just after day break when I awoke this morning. My little daughter was wide awake and urgent to be taken up. I gratified her wish and she was soon willing to return to bed. Not

---

27. In margin: "Jan. 5."

28. Chase was visiting at the house of Timothy Walker, his former law partner. Walker's sister, Susan (1811–87), later worked as an antislavery activist; as a teacher to freedmen on South Carolina's Sea Islands and in Washington, D.C.; and as a mathematician for the U.S. Coast Survey. Chase corresponded with her frequently over the following years. Hitchcock, "Timothy Walker," 34; *New York Tribune*, Dec. 18, 1887; Willie Lee Rose, *Rehearsal for Reconstruction: The Port Royal Experiment* (New York, 1964; reprint, New York, 1976), 45; Henry Noble Sherwood, "Journal of Miss. Susan Walker, March 3d to June 6th, 1862," *Quarterly Publications of the Historical and Philosophical Society of Ohio* 7 (Jan.–Mar. 1912): 3–48; Chase to S. Walker, Dec. 30, 1869 (Walker Papers, Cinc. Hist. Soc.).

29. In margin: "Jan. 6."

30. Thomas R. Hubbard, a former Cincinnati law student, practiced law in Chicago. He and his partner, Joseph N. Balestier, represented Chase in a real estate transaction with Capt. John B. F. Russell (d. 1861), a U.S. Army officer living in Chicago. *Chicago Dir. (1839)*, 6, 19; Hubbard to Chase, Aug. 2, 1834, Sept. 20, 1836, May 12, 1837, Balestier to Chase, Jan. 19, Feb. 2, Apr. 4, 15, July 8, Aug. 18, 1837 (Chase Papers, L.C.); Cullum, *Biographical Register*, 1:180.

31. John L. Avery, a commission merchant in the Cincinnati partnership of Avery and Athearn. *Cinc. Dir. (1836–37)*, 12.

long however was she quiet. She wanted to go to Grandma and I took her to the door and let her go in. I then washed & dressed myself and attended to my morning devotions: I trust not without profit. I then walked down to my office but did nothing there before I returned to breakfast. Found Helen waiting to see me and urged her to be sure & consult the doctor about her symptoms coughing &c. On returning to the Office saw & conversed with several persons, with E. Bailey the carpenter to whom I gave several copies of my speech in Mathilda's case;[32] with Mr. Morgan the bookseller, with whom I advised as to the best mode of collecting a debt from C. P. Barnes;[33] Dr. Waldo who consulted me as to the expediency of obtaining insurance on his life;[34] which I rather discouraged. I also in the course of the morning prepared a mortgage to be executed by Mr. S. E. Foote to the Lafayette Bank. After dinner I went to the Court House & filed several declarations & searched the appearance docket. After returning to my office settled some business with Mr. Owens the shoemaker[35] & with the assistance of Truman Thorp, arranged my bookcases & books. Since then I have taken supper heard Truman's verses out of The Titles of Christ, read the Philanthropist & Ohio Political Register & written the above, I shall now go home to bed.[36] 10 o'clock

1838

Sometime in Feb. 1838 went to housekeeping: had visited Richmond—proceeded to N.E. and brot out Eliza Whipple to stay with us for awhile[37]

32. Ezra Bailey (b. 1802), a master builder. In Mar. 1837, Chase had made an unsuccessful attempt to obtain the release of Matilda, who had stopped at Cincinnati on a journey with her Virginia master, took employment in the house of James G. Birney, and was seized as a fugitive slave. Chase's argument in the habeas corpus hearing was published as the *Speech of Salmon P. Chase, in the Case of the Colored Woman, Matilda* . . . (Cincinnati, 1837). Chase also defended Birney against charges of harboring a fugitive slave. Chase to John T. Trowbridge, Mar. 16, 1864 (Chase Papers, Cinc. Hist. Soc.); *Birney v. Ohio*, 8 Ohio 230 (1837); Robson, *Biographical Encyclopædia*, 457–58.

33. Bookseller and stationer Ephraim Morgan (1790–1873) was a partner in the firm of Morgan and Saxony. C. P. Barnes ran the Cincinnati bookstore of Barnes and Carpenter. *Biographical Cyclopædia*, 6:1427–28; *Cinc. Dir. (1836–37)*, 16, 122.

34. F. Augustus Waldo, a local physician. *Cinc. Dir. (1836–37)*, 181.

35. Either John or Owen Owens. Ibid., 130.

36. Ambrose Serle, *Horæ Solitariæ; or Essays upon Some Remarkable Names and Titles of Jesus Christ Occurring in the Old Testament* . . . (London, 1776); the *Philanthropist*, begun by Cincinnati antislavery activist James Gillespie Birney in Jan. 1836; and the *Ohio Political Register*, edited in Columbus by John M. Gallagher. *DAB*, 2:292; Martin, *History of Franklin County*, 59.

37. Eliza Chase Whipple, later a schoolteacher and an officer in a Civil War relief society, was the daughter of John Whipple and Chase's sister, Hannah Chase Whipple. These entries for 1838–39 are memoranda from the end of the manuscript

AUG 11— Dissolved ptnship with S. Eells & gave him $650 for his ⅓ interest in two notes at 3 & 6 mos

1839

At beginning of this year lived on Broadway sister Helen being housekeeper Jeannette Skinner was with us—she attended Mr. Bonfils school[38]—paid him March 13 for her semiannual tuition $50. Paid Mad. Blaique for her dancing lessons $12, Feb. 12

1840

MAY 2. After a long interval I resume this journal.— What a change since the last entry was made has a single circumstance wrought. My dear little daughter's death![39] What sorrow and yet, blessed be God! What consolation. My most cherished hopes blasted! but she safe forever.

This day I have done little—almost nothing. Read but little Scripture this morning and have read nothing else of consequence during the whole day. Rode out to Edgeforest in afternoon with wife, Eliza & Mr Gallagher[40]—gathered wild flowers. Mr. Gallagher at supper—after supper wrote to Mrs. Garniss. I go now to prayer and then to bed.

MAY 4. 8 OCLOCK A.M. Yesterday[41] I was greatly troubled with wandering thoughts and my mind was far too little affected by the

---

journal. In the original, the entry for August 11 precedes this paragraph. "Family Memoranda" (Chase Papers, L.C.); James O. Lyford, ed., *History of Concord, New Hampshire* . . . (Concord, N.H., 1903), 1:495–96, 2:1250.

38. Janette (Jenny) Logan Skinner, who in 1852 married J. J. L. C. (Jack) Jewett, was the daughter of Chase's sister and brother-in-law, Janette and Josiah Skinner. Helen Chase and Jenny Skinner were students at an "Institute" directed by St. Sauveur François Bonfils. Bonfils to Chase, Dec. 8, 1838, Jenny Jewett to Chase, May 18, 1859, Chase to Jenny Jewett, Mar. 28, 1867, Chase to J. J. L. C. Jewett, Aug. 24, 1868, and "Family Memoranda" (Chase Papers, L.C.); Janette Logan Chase Skinner to Chase, June 4, 1852 (Chase Papers, Hist. Soc. of Pa.).

39. Catharine Jane Chase had died of scarlet fever on Feb. 6, 1840. "Family Memoranda" (Chase Papers, L.C.).

40. On Sept. 26, 1839, Chase had married Eliza Ann Smith (1821–45), the daughter of Edmund Curtis Smith and Mary Colton Smith of Cincinnati. Eliza Chase Whipple was still a member of Chase's household. William Davis Gallagher (1808–94), Ohio poet, journalist, and Whig and Republican politician, served at this time on the editorial staff of the *Cincinnati Gazette*. During the Civil War he worked as special collector of customs and commercial agent in the upper Mississippi Valley. *Cincinnati Daily Gazette*, Sept. 28, 1839; "Family Memoranda" (Chase Papers, L.C.); Coggeshall, *Poets and Poetry of the West*, 134; DAB, 7:102–3.

41. Entry describes May 3.

sacredness of the day. Was dull at the Sunday school and in church. Young Mr. Gassaway preached & well.[42] Read at home two nos Journal Chris. Education—many valuable ideas suggested worth reflecting on—especially how in common schools can gospel motives be substituted for worldly motives to gain knowledge & perform duty.[43] Read also from Cowper to wife his glowing description of the coming millennium[44]—the Sabbath of the world—

MAY 5. Yesterday[45] was not a busy nor an idle day. I accomplished something but might have accomplished much more. Wrote an argument for the Supreme Court and sent a messenger to Hey about Steven's business.[46] In the afternoon Messrs Neff & Mitchell called to converse with me.[47] Made an appointment for the evg. but afterwards excused myself as obliged to attend council in Evening.[48] Went to Council. Succeeded in carrying all I advocated: but I fear one vote was wrong. If fully satisfied of this I mean to move for a reconsideration next meeting. In the morning read 1st Psalm and parralel passages. Committed the Psalm and referred to it through the day: but alas! how prone to forget God!

MAY 5 Was dull this morning and my thoughts sadly out of order—very insensible in private prayer and not much moved at family devotions. What a spectacle is such a creature as I am loaded with benefits by a gracious Father and rendering such poor returns. Beset in the Street with suggestions as to the proper course to be pursued in council on various questions, which I endeavored to

42. Possibly a relative of Henry Gassaway, former vestryman and warden of Cincinnati's Christ Church. Venable, *Christ Church*, 136–37.
43. "Mistakes in Education" appeared in the Feb., Mar., and Apr. issues of the *Journal of Christian Education, and Family and Sunday School Visitor.*
44. British poet William Cowper (1731–1800) never married. Chase refers here to book five of *The Task, a Poem, in Six Books* (London, 1785), written at the request of "a lady" known now to have been Lady Ann Richardson Austen. *DNB*, 4:1319–27.
45. Entry describes May 4.
46. Chase represented Isaac Stevens, Sr., of Cincinnati and Vevay, Ind., in a claim against James Hey and Moses Dawson. Entry for Dec. 25, 1835 (above); Isaac Stevens, Jr., to Chase, Apr. 11, 1840, Chase to Stevens, Jr., June 20, 1845 (Chase Papers, L.C.); *Cinc. Dir. (1840)*, 369.
47. Probably Ormsby MacKnight Mitchel (1809–62), West Point class of 1829, civil engineer, professor of mathematics at Cincinnati College, and, during the Civil War, a brigadier and major general of volunteers. Mitchel and George Neff were both involved in the development of the Little Miami Railroad. Robson, *Biographical Encyclopædia*, 312–14; *Nat. Cyc.*, 3:440; *Cinc. Dir. (1840)*, 290.
48. Chase, running as a Harrison Whig, had been elected to the Cincinnati City Council in Apr. 1840. He sought reelection the following year, but lost his position when voters repudiated the temperance position which he and other local reformers advocated. Chase to Charles Dexter Cleveland, Aug. 29, 1840 (Chase Papers, Hist. Soc. of Pa.); *Cincinnati Daily Gazette*, Apr. 6, 8, 1840, Apr. 7, 13, 1841.

avoid, saying only in general terms that I would endeavor to do what is right. Was at the Supreme Court—& much annoyed by the reflections of a member of the bar, which irritate me, though the imputations were totally unjust / Presented a petition for rehearing in the case of Stevens vs Dawson fortified by an affidavit. Called to see my friend Eells who is confined by sickness / Spoke to him of the Life of Wilberforce, as a model for young men.[49] He seemed interested and I promised to bring him the book. May its perusal be blessed to him. He is thoughtful on the subject of religion and I know no better mode of making him think more deeply than by placing in his hands such a book.

MAY 13 Was rather a tardy riser this morning, but my thoughts were more than usual on the word of God. After dressing my self and devotions went down stairs and committed the second part of the 119th Psalm—Where with shall a young man cleanse his way,[50] and meditated a little while upon it—then family prayer & breakfast— Went down to my office feeling very happy & cheerful—paid a reduction on an accommodation draft, attended to considerable other business and wrote part of an argument for the Cir. Ct. U States for Indiana— Dined at Mr. Garniss with Brooks, Editor New York Express, pleasing man but nothing uncommon[51]—attended council—maintained silence generally, but used some little exertion to defeat licence to a tavern which I was persuaded ought not to have one & succeeded. Qu. Ought I to vote for licence to any tavern to retail intoxicating drinks? Mr. Garniss at tea—afterwards went to office—wrote a little—home—prayer with wife—read Pathfinder[52] & now to bed—

MAY 20 Met Mr. Hoyt in the Street today but did not recognize him. It is about fourteen years since we were boys at College together. He recognized & spoke to me knowing before he came that I resided here. He has come to take a likeness of Gen. Harrison for a whig association at Boston.[53] In the evening called at Mrs

49. Robert Isaac Wilberforce, *The Life of William Wilberforce* ... (London, 1838).
50. "Wherewithal shall a young man cleanse his way?" Ps. 119:9.
51. James Brooks (1810–73), an attorney and future U.S. congressman, had started the paper with Whig backing four years earlier. *DAB*, 3:77–79.
52. James Fenimore Cooper, *The Pathfinder, or The Inland Sea* ... (New York, 1826).
53. Bostonian Albert Gallatin Hoit (1809–56), Dartmouth class of 1829, painted portraits and landscapes. His painting of William Henry Harrison (1773–1841), who was elected later in 1840 as the ninth president of the U.S., was the last portrait of Harrison painted from life. George C. Groce and David H. Wallace, *The New-York*

Findlay's to see Gen. H—— for Mr. Hoyt but he had gone to Northbend— Went to Mr. Whiteman's room who is confined from a hurt received from being overturned in a stage[54]—determined to go to Northbend tomorrow.

MAY 21   Went down to Northbend with wife, Eliza Whipple & Mr. Hoyt. arrived a little after 12 oclock. Told Gen. H. the object of my visit and he consented to sit for his portrait—wished then to come away but the General insisted on over staying to dinner and we staid. Before dinner visited the tunnel of the Whitewater Canal 1600 feet through a hill.[55] After dinner, which was abundant but plain, we returned home by the way of Cleves & Cheviot. When we arrived at Northbend, as the morning was somewhat raw the General insisted on having a fire made for us, and the Dutch servant being slow and awkward he sent him about his business and built the fire himself / When he had finished he said to wife that she need not be surprised to see him making a fire for it was his habit in winter to make two fires himself every morning before any other member of his family was stirring. The place is very prettily situated. The ground rises gradually from the edge of the river bank to the house, which is itself surrounded with trees. It is composed of several small buildings put together, one of which is constructed of logs. These buildings were formerly the habitations of families when Northbend was something of a village, but, as the danger of savage invasion & the increasing attractions of Cincinnati gradually unpeopled the village, these dwellings were deserted

MAY 23   Attended Sunday school in the morning but did not attend church. In the evening went to church—Mr. Gassaway preached. The sermon was dull or I was sleepy. I find myself much disposed to sleep of late days. I can hardly keep myself awake at night and can hardly get myself awake in the morning.

Historical Society's Dictionary of Artists in America, 1564–1860 (New Haven, 1957), 322; *DAB*, 8:348–51; Albert Gallatin Hoit to Daniel Hoit, May 21, 1840 (Dartmouth College Lib.); Monroe H. Fabian, "A Portrait of William Henry Harrison," *Prologue: The Journal of the National Archives* 1 (Winter 1969): 29–32.

54. Probably Lewis (or Louis) Whiteman (d. 1862), a Cincinnati commission merchant and the future husband of Catherine Ludlow Baker Whiteman, a sister of Chase's third wife. *Cinc. Dir. (1840)*, 403; Charlotte Ludlow Jones to Chase, Dec. 31, 1861, James D. Ludlow to Chase, Nov. 18, 1861, Mar. 4, 1862 (Chase Papers, L.C.); unpublished guide to Ludlow-Dunlop-Chambers Collec., Univ. of Wyoming.

55. The twenty-five-mile Cincinnati and Whitewater Canal, incorporated in 1837, extended from Cincinnati to Harrison, Ohio. Charles Cist, *Sketches and Statistics of Cincinnati in 1851* (Cincinnati, 1851), 142.

{ 124 }   *The Journals of Salmon P. Chase*

MAY 26   At the council in the afternoon. Introduced an ordinance to prescribe the duties of certain offices, made elective by a late act of the Legislature.[56]

MAY 27   Rose rather late being sleepy as usual. Retired to Library where committed to memory part of 119th Psalm also part of Cowper's Poem on his Mother's Picture.[57] How sweet and touching that picture is! How powerfully it awakens the filial affections, and how sweetly it consoles filial sorrows! I also read a chapter of Jer. Taylor's contemplations on the State of Man[58]— The glory & happiness of the just. What a theme for the warm and glowing imagination of the old man eloquent. It was on the whole a delightful hour in my retirement for which I bless God. Was called on to give my deposition in a case in Chy,[59] and I fear was betrayed, at the office where I went into censorious conversation. I find myself prone to this. Let me watch and subdue the disposition. Devoted the principal part of the morning, but too sluggishly, to the examination of a case of guarantee. At noon read a chapter in Philips Life & Times of Whitefield.[60] Like the man but not the book—too crude, hasty, flippant and egotistical. In the afternoon occupied by an arbitration between Messrs Crafts J Wright & Henry Starr.[61] Mr. Storer & myself arbitrators Mr. Walker, counsel, & Judge Wright witness.[62] Made some progress and adjourned. Mr. Garniss came to tea & Mr. Ball after tea.[63] Nothing peculiar said or done.

56. Chase's ordinance implemented state legislation which required the popular election of wharf masters, market masters, city collectors, the city engineer, city surveyor, captain and lieutenant of the night watch, and engineer and collector of the water works. In the same meeting, Chase called for repeal of another ordinance which permitted the city council to appoint other officers whose duties partly overlapped those performed by the newly elected officials. *Cincinnati Daily Gazette*, Mar. 27, May 28, 1840.
57. William Cowper, *Poems. I. On the Receipt of My Mother's Picture. II. The Dog and the Water-Lily* (London, 1798).
58. Jeremy Taylor, *Contemplations of the State of Man in this Life, and in that Which is to Come* . . . (London, 1664).
59. Chancery.
60. Robert Philip, *The Life and Times of the Reverend George Whitefield, M.A.* (London, 1837).
61. Starr and Wright were local attorneys. Crafts James Wright (1808–83), the son of Judge John C. Wright, was also an entrepreneur, assistant editor of the *Cincinnati Gazette*, and, in 1862, colonel in the Union Army. *Appletons'*, 6:625; *Cinc. Dir. (1840)*, 366.
62. John C. Wright. Bellamy Storer (1796–1875), a former Whig congressman, was a partner in the Cincinnati law firm of Storer and Fox. *Cinc. Dir. (1840)*, 371; *Nat. Cyc.*, 11:338.
63. New York native Flamen Ball (b. 1809), a recent graduate of Cincinnati College, was Chase's law partner, 1838–58. During the Civil War, Ball served as U.S. attorney for the southern district of Ohio. In 1867, Chase appointed him a U.S. register in bankruptcy. *Biographical Cyclopædia*, 3:758–59; *Biog. Enc. of Ohio*, 99–100.

MAY 29   It is designed to call a public meeting & I am desired to prepare a set of resolutions expressing the sense of this Community in reference to the Slanders against Genl. Harrison. I have partly promised to do so. I have also called on Mr. Wm Neff and he has consented to act as chairman of the meeting, if no fitter or more acceptable man can be found.[64]

MAY 30   This is the last weekday of a month by no means adequately improved. How little have I done for the Saviour or for souls! With only two or three have I conversed on religious subjects at all with a view to the special benefit of either party. I have been too little watchful of my own heart and too little engaged in the study of the Word. I have however committed about 50 verses of the 119th Psalm and have nearly perused the life of Whitefield. Oh Lord forbid that the truths of thy word and the glorious example of thy servant shall fail utterly to bring forth fruit to the glory of thy name. I feel that I love thee and desire to serve thee. Let me not delude myself with false imaginations. I have done almost nothing this day except to write a little this morning to my brotherinlaw Mr. Walbridge advising as to his coming west.[65] I have suffered much from a headache which has disabled me from much labor— called to see likeness of Gen Harrison by my friend Hoyt—a fine likeness and a good picture—saw Bracketts bust but cd. not recognize the likeness[66]— One of the nightwatch called, apprehending that he was to lose his place—& asked my interference, which, knowing the man, I promised—

JUNE 25   Read this morning some remarks in Todds Manual on the importance of system and endeavored to be systematic, but to no great purpose.[67] Rose early and spent an hour in devotion & in

64. At the Democratic Convention in Baltimore earlier in the month, Felix Grundy had repeated an allegation that William Henry Harrison was an abolitionist. Chase's meeting, held on June 3, criticized Grundy's speech and reaffirmed confidence in Harrison, but said nothing directly about Harrison's attitude toward abolition. Cincinnati *Advertiser and Journal*, May 27, 29, 30, 1840; *Cincinnati Daily Gazette*, June 4, 1840; Washington *Globe*, May 5, 1840.

65. Henry B. Walbridge, an aspiring lawyer and later a Protestant Episcopal clergyman, had married Chase's youngest sister, Helen, in 1839. They came west to reside in Toledo. Clark Waggoner, *History of the City of Toledo and Lucas County, Ohio* . . . (New York, 1888), 484; [Eliza Chase Whipple] to [Jacob W. Schuckers], [1873] (Schuckers Papers, L.C.); H. B. Walbridge to Chase, Apr. 15, 1839 (Chase Papers, L.C.).

66. Cincinnati sculptor Edward Augustus Brackett (1818–1908) had made a bust of William H. Harrison, on display with Hoyt's portrait at the Pearl Street House. *Cincinnati Daily Gazette*, June 2, 1840; *DAB*, 2:547.

67. John Todd, *The Student's Manual: Designed by Specific Directions, to Aid in Forming and Strengthening the Intellectual and Moral Character and Habits of the Student* (Northampton and Boston, 1835).

memorizing and meditating upon the 119 Psalm—I think I can now appreciate much better than ever the pure and spiritual wisdom which inspires that preceptive psalm. I have devoted much time to it but I trust not in vain. I was determined to devote this day to the prepation of a case involving an important question of copyright, and accordingly on reaching my office commenced an argument— was obliged however to attend court where detained by unprofitable wrangling till dinnertime. On going to office after dinner found a letter from clients in copyright case containing intelligence of compromise. After this spent some time in running about on various errands and the residue of the afternoon reading Theory of Rights of Authors,[68] which ingeniously if not conclusively argues that Authors have no right of copy in their works, except so far as the law may grant it to them as compensation for their services to the public. Came home to tea, talked with wife—wrote the above and now mean to read Todd's Manual for an hour—then frame a plan for tomorrow and then to bed—

PLAN FOR JUNE 26[69]
1   ½ past 4 to ½ past 5 Showerbath & dress.
2   ½ past 5 to 6 Bible & devotion—
3   6 to ½ past 6— Commit Cowper
4   ½ past 6 to 7— Sketch Speech for Ward Meeting
5   7 to 8— Breakfast
6   8 to 9— Clients or make list of cases in Supr. Court
7   9 to 10— at Court—make copy of sci. fa. &c
8   10 to ¼ past 11 at Bank & dep. of Conahan[70]
9   ¼ past 11 to 1 P.M— Dep. of Conahan, Clients, list cases Supr. Ct
10 1 to 2 Dinner—
11 2 to 3— Story on Conf Laws[71]—
12 3 to 6— Arbitration of copyright case Perkins[72]

68. Augustin-Charles Renouard, "Theory of the Rights of Authors," trans. Luther Stearns Cushing, *American Jurist and Law Magazine* 22 (Oct. 1839): 39–92.
69. At this point in his journal Chase, apparently inspired by Todd's book to manage his time more efficiently, began a system of planning each day's activities in advance and noting afterward his actual fulfillment of the plan. His "Plan for June 26" breaks the day into fifteen numbered sections, allots a time period to each, and gives a brief indication of what he expected to accomplish. That outline is followed by fifteen sections describing Chase's performance of each part of the day's plan.
70. Evidently a deposition by Charles Conahan, a clerk at the Lafayette Bank. *Cinc. Dir. (1840)*, 143.
71. Joseph Story, *Commentaries on the Conflict of Laws* ... (Boston, 1834). Story (1779–1845), the noted legal scholar and associate justice of the U.S. Supreme Court, 1811–45, appears to have given this volume to Chase more than a half decade earlier. *DAB*, 18:102–8; Story to Chase, Mar. 1, 1834 (Chase Papers, Hist. Soc. of Pa.).
72. Probably James Handasyd Perkins.

13 6 to 8 Tea & conversation at home—
14 8 to 9— Todds Students Manual
15 9 to 10— Journal—devotion—
1   Rose at 10 min p. 5—omitted Showerbath—dressed by 4 min. past 5.
2   Committed 16 verses 119th Psalm & devotion—find it difficult now to recall the verses.
3   Read through & repeated to my self Cowper's beautiful verses on his mothers picture—have it almost perfect—
4   Prepared Sketch—Speech to be on Making public appointments rewards of partizan service to dominant party
5   Breakfast & newspaper—Denial of Judge Wright that he was ever a federalist &c
6   Calls on business at office—list of cases partly made—
7   Went to court at 9—too early by two hours—returning met Broadwell & talked to him about road up the hill and straightening Millcreek—a plan of mine for improving west part of city—then went to office—client wanted me to go to Magistrates—went left Mr. Ball there & went to the Bank—
8   10 to ¼ past 11— At Board of Directors & Exchange Board—some profitable and some unprofitable conversation—dep. not taken
9   Went to court house—copied sci. fa.—took books out of desk to bring home & forgot them—spent greater part of time unprofitably—
10 Dinner—unpleasant incident—
11 2 to 3— Wrote letter enclosing dedimus in Alton case to New York—[Atte]nded to Conahan dep. Vaughan & Smith abt. copy right case[73]—Agreed to see Perkins tomorrow.
12 3 to ½ past 6— Drowsy—too much dinner—read Story on Conf. of Laws—Hughes, Smith & Conahan interrupted me—read two chapters—Some valuable suggestions—too prolix &

---

73. John Champion Vaughan, a partner in the Cincinnati law firm of Vaughan and Cranch, and possibly George R. Smith, the deputy clerk of Hamilton County's Superior Court. Vaughan was active in antislavery politics and served successively on the editorial staffs of Lexington's *True American*, the *Cincinnati Gazette*, Cleveland's *Daily True Democrat* and *Forest City Democrat*, and the *Chicago Tribune*. By 1858 he published the *Times*, a Free State paper, in Leavenworth, Kans. *Cinc. Dir. (1840)*, 359, 390; ibid. (1846), 377; Philip Kinsley, *The Chicago Tribune: Its First Hundred Years* (New York, 1943), 1:36–37, 43, 46, 48, 59, 61; Samuel P. Orth, *A History of Cleveland Ohio . . .* (Chicago, 1910), 1:506; Harold Edward Richardson, *Cassius Marcellus Clay: Firebrand of Freedom* (Lexington, Ky., 1976), 54; William Ganson Rose, *Cleveland: The Making of a City* (Cleveland, 1950; reprint, Kent, Ohio, 1990), 255; George Bradburn, *A Statement, by George Bradburn, of his Connection with the "True Democrat," and John C. Vaughan* (Cleveland, 1853); H. Miles Moore, *Early History of Leavenworth City and County . . .* (Leavenworth, Kans., 1906), 182.

repetionary too much quotation—too much Latin—Blackstone a model who had digested everything made it his own & gave it to reader in his own style & language.[74]

13 ½ p 6 to 8— Family not retd. from ride when came home— read Chronicle—Dr. Price's account of doings at his cocoonery[75]—not wholly intelligible to me—read Jefferson's Manual[76]— Importance of Rules—Legislature—Privilege—tea & conversation.

14 8 to 9— Read Todd—Choice of Books—Value of Time—Excellent—

15 9 to 10— Wrote plan for tomorrow—reviewed 16 verses comd: this morning—now to d. & bed—

JUNE 27.[77]

1 ½ p. 4 to ½ p. 5— Shower bath—repetition of Psalm—dress— 15 m p 4 to ¼ past 5—accomplished all—

2 ½ p 5 to 6— Bible & devotion— done—committed 16 verses & reviewed a little

3 6 to ½ p. 6— Commit Cowper— 6 to ¼ 6 repeated whole of Cowpers verses on his Mother now thoroughly committed—

4 ½ p. 6 to 7— Write Speech for Ward Meeting— ¼ p 6 to ½ p. 6 read a little in Cannings Speeches[78] by way of prep. for writing speech when called to Fam. Prayers—

5 7 to 8. Family Prayer & Breakfast— ½ p 6 to ½ p. 7. Fam. Prayer & breakfast & Gazette[79]—after which till 8 wrote speech—

6 8 to 9— Review Conf. Laws—Clients—arrange papers—ascertain missing books—court &c / Busy with clients & callers Dawson,[80] Vaughan, [Mcleady], Hughes, 5 Slaves emancipated yes-

---

74. William Blackstone, *Commentaries on the Laws of England*, 4 vols. (Oxford, 1765–69).

75. William Price, a Cincinnati physician, had written a letter to the paper which detailed successful attempts to raise silk worms at his Prospect Hill Cocoonery. *Cincinnati Chronicle*, June 27, 1840; *Cinc. Dir. (1840)*, 322.

76. Thomas Jefferson, *A Manual of Parliamentary Practice* . . . (Washington, D.C., 1801).

77. In the entries for June 27–28, Chase continued to plan his daily activities but adopted a different format. He now combined in a single listing the plan for the day and the record of its fulfillment. In these entries, he divided the day into periods, gave a brief indication of what he expected to do in each, and left space between them. Later he returned to those spaces to note his fulfillment of the plan for each period.

78. The major source at the time was R. Therry, *The Speeches of the Right Honourable George Canning. With a Memoir of His Life* . . . , 6 vols. (London, 1828).

79. A Whig paper from Cincinnati founded in 1827, available in daily, tri-weekly, and weekly editions. *Cinc. Dir. (1840)*, 508; Osman Castle Hooper, *History of Ohio Journalism, 1793–1933* (Columbus, 1933), 70.

80. Probably Moses Dawson.

terday—Thompson, Smith &c—none of much importance—arranged papers—did not review—or ascertain misg. books or attend court—

7 1 to 2— Dinner— Dinner & looked over Rochester paper sent by Joseph Faver announcing death of his wife—my cousin[81]—

8 2 to ¼ p. 3— Jefferson's Manual— Didn't read Jefferson's Manual— Spent the time in arranging papers except when interrupted—Dawson called with Hey's receipts—Thompson and and Winter

9 ¼ p 3 to ½ p. 6— Exercise & call on sick man— Exercised as intended & went to Sunday school teachers meeting which pleasant—afterwds arranged benches &c—did not call on sick man—though I might have done so and am without just excuse for having neglected it.

10 ½ p 6 to 8— Tea & conversation— Used this time as designed— Shall I try to remember some topics of conversation in future—

11 8 to [½ p 9]— Call at neighbors— Called at Mr. Garniss' and Mr. Neffs— At the G's talked of proper celebration of Battle of Maumee of wh. we both disapproved[82]— At Mr. Neff's talked of various politics—moral & other matters—

12 ½ p 9 to 10— Journal—devotion— ½ p 9 to ¾ 9 Journal—now plan & then bed

JUNE 28

1 ½ p 4 to 5— dress—repetition of Psalms—meditation— Did not rise till ½ past 5 being much disturbed through the night—then dressed & repeated Psalms with some meditation as I purposed—

2 5 to ½ p 5— Devotion & Bible— ½ p 6 to 7—Committed 16 verses 119th Psalm on review & devotion

3 ½ p. 5 to ½ p. 6— Prepare to remark on 17 Hymn to Sunday School— (Omitted)

4 ½ p 6 to ½ p. 7— Fam. Prayer & Breakfast— ½ p. 7 to 8 Fam. Prayer & breakfast—

---

81. Sarah R. Bond Faver (c. 1820–49) was the wife of Col. Joseph Faver and a first cousin of Chase on his mother's side. *Rochester Daily Democrat*, June 17, 1849; Griffin, *Keene*, 638.

82. Anthony Wayne's victory of Aug. 20, 1794, at the Battle of Fallen Timbers (or Maumee) marked the beginning of William Henry Harrison's military career. Chase's disapproval reflects initial Whig reluctance to use such popular events as campaign devices. Despite this attitude, Cincinnati's Whigs commemorated the occasion later in the summer with a meeting which featured patriotic songs and speeches. *Cincinnati Daily Gazette*, Aug. 20, 22, 1840; Freeman Cleaves, *Old Tippecanoe: William Henry Harrison and His Time* (New York, 1939), 17; Robert Gray Gunderson, *The Log-Cabin Campaign* (Lexington, 1957), 108.

5   ½ p. 7 to 9— Missy. Herald[83]— 8 to ½ past 8—Made some preparation to address children—didn't read My. Hd.
6   9 to 11 Sunday School— ½ p. 8 to ¾ p. 10 Sunday School— confusion incident to new arrangement prevented address—86 in School—
7   11 to 1— Church— At church—many wandering thoughts— little fervor in prayer or praise—listened to Sermon carelessly— Twas on not being ashamed of the cross of Christ[84]—the preacher Mr. Gassaway—quite young.
8   1 to 2 Dinner— Ate too much—little, if any, profitable conversation—
9   2 to 7— Missy. Herald & visit to sick man— 2 to 6. Read N.Y. Evangelist, an excellent religious paper full of valuable matter, not, I trust, without real advantage.[85] I can fix attention much better on my devotions or reading when alone than when at church— Read also in My. Hd. accts of the progress of the Gospel amg. the heathen[86]—some discouraging and some cheering— Mr. Ball came—conversation not very profitable—
10 7 to 8 Tea &c— Mr. Ball at tea
11 8 to ½ p. 9. Church— At church—weather oppressively hot— wife with me—thoughts still wandering—Mr. Johns, our pastor, arrived this evening but did not preach / Is it right for professors of religion or for any one to travel on Sunday?
12 ½ p 9 to to 10— Journal &c— Read My. Hd.—did not write in Journal

JUNE 29.[87] Abt. 40 min p. 5 to ½ p. 6—Dress & repeat Psalms— ½ p. 6 to 7. Bring up Journal & frame plan— 7 to 8—Commit Psalms, private devotions, Fam. Pryr, & Bkft 8 to 10—Read Story on Conf. Laws—Arrange papers & ascertain missg. books— 11 to ½ p 11—at Bank ½ p 11 to 1—Study & prepare cases in Supr.

---

83. *The Missionary Herald*, a publication of the American Board of Commissioners for Foreign Missions. *DAB*, 6:215.
84. Rom. 1:16.
85. *The New-York Evangelist*, founded in 1831 by antislavery leader Joshua Leavitt. *DAB*, 11:85.
86. The May and June 1840 issues of *The Missionary Herald* were filled with such reports.
87. Beginning with this entry, Chase adopted another format for planning his days. He abandoned the numbered list and recorded each day's plan as a précis comprising the first paragraph of the entry. Then at the end of the day he added another paragraph, containing his description of the day's activities. He followed this system, with some exceptions, until mid-August, when he dropped the practice of making a systematic plan for each day.

Ct—visit sick man— 1 to 2 Dinner— 2 to 6—prepare cases in Supr. Ct— 6 to 8—relax & tea— 8 to 9—Todd— 9 to 10 Journal &c

It was so sultry last night and I rested so badly in consequence of my wife's indisposition that I rose late this morning and comparatively unrefreshed.[88] From 40 min p. 5 to ½ past 6 I dressed repeated 24 verses 119th Psalm / I make slow progress in committing this admirable psalm to memory but I feel the value of the exercise in many ways. The example of Wilberforce induced me to attempt it. *½ p 6 to 7* Brought up my Journal & framed plan as delineated above. *7 to 8* did as designed—Committed 16 verses 119th Psalm— *8 to 11* Went to my office—many called on various purposes / Thompson, a lumber man was there talking with Ball when I went in[89]— wanted & obtained writ of replevin—went to Court House to see to fastening my desks in their places—Mr. Gano handed me bill of costs for Laf. Bank—demurred to it in part— Saw Mr. Wright on subject of costs he agreed with me— *½ p. 11 to 1.* Went to the Bank—saw Armstrong, Wiggins, Neff & others— A number of letters from How & Co, N.Y. Prentiss, Keene—Hendee, Boston,[90] Dolan N.Y.—Mr. Loring came in about Dolan business—read Story on Conf Laws— did not arrange papers or ascertain missing books—Mr. Ball indisposed & went home—did not prepare cases in Supr. Court or visit sick man—Blair called to know if money cd. be had from bank—obtd. ch. for $1500 to send Smith[91] / *1 to 2* Dinner & talk— *2 to 6* busy again with clients—prepared precipe for replevin Dunlap vs Craig et al—Woodall of Hogan & Thompson called[92]—Smith & others— Col Davies came in about toasts[93]—went to see Col. Todd.[94] He came

---

88. The specific "indisposition" is unknown. Eliza Chase was pregnant at this time. Two years later she was diagnosed as having tuberculosis. See journal for Aug. 12–13, 1840, below; Noah Worcester to Chase, Sept. 5, 1842 (Chase Papers, L.C.).

89. Probably John Thompson, a local hardware merchant; carpenter James Thompson; or David Thompson, also a carpenter. *Cinc. Dir. (1840),* 380.

90. David How and Company were New York exchange brokers. John Prentiss (1778–1873), a New Hampshire politician and editor of the Keene *New Hampshire Sentinel,* reported to Chase about politics among state Whigs. Charles J. Hendee was a Boston publisher and bookseller. *New York Dir. (1841–42),* 76; Griffin, *Keene,* 636–37; Prentiss to Chase, June 19, 1840 (Chase Papers, L.C.); *Boston Dir. (1840),* 224; Moses King, *King's Hand-Book of Boston* (Cambridge, Mass., 1878), 137.

91. Probably Hamilton Smith.

92. Possibly William Woodall, a local drayman. *Cinc. Dir. (1842),* 412.

93. Mayor Samuel Watts Davies (1776–1843), a colonel in the state militia, was evidently concerned about a reception to be held on July 2 in honor of Gen. Solomon Van Rensselaer. *Cincinnati Daily Gazette,* July 4, 1840; Harry R. Stevens, "Samuel Watts Davies and the Industrial Revolution in Cincinnati," *Ohio Historical Quarterly* 70 (Apr. 1961): 95–98.

94. Charles Scott Todd (1791–1871), a Whig politician, colonel in the U.S. Army, and editor of the Cincinnati *Daily Republican. Appletons',* 6:127.

to my office and we sketched some—paid some attention to case Corey vs Hall[95]—read in Gow on Partp.[96]— Sent ch. to Smith of Louisville—Called to settle up with H. & T. Mr. Woodall not in—went home— $^1/_2$ *p. 6 to 8*—visited sick man who very low & in much pain—tea—evening paper & talk— *8 to 9*. Todd's Manual—excellent thoughts & suggestions on value of time & on conversation— *9 to 10*—Mrs Smith & Frank here[97]—ice cream went home with them—wrote in journal—now to bed—

JUNE 30 ½ p 4 to ½ p 5—Showerbath—Psalms—dress— ½ p 5 to 6—Commit Young[98] & repeat Cowper 6 to ½ p. 6—Commit Psalm & devotion— ½ p 6 to 8—Breakfast, Todds Manual &c— 8 to 10—decree copyright case Cases in Supr. Ct & clients &c— 10 to ½ p 11—Bank— ½ p. 11 to 1—Story on Conf— *1 to 2* Dinner— 2 to 6 Cases Supr. Court—arrange books &c— 6 to 8 Tea &c— 8 to ½ p 9 visit— ½ p 9 to 10 Journal &c

½ p 4 to ½ 5 did as designed— ½ p 5 to 6 did as designed— 6 to ½ p 6—d. as d. ½ p. 6 to 8—d. as d. read in Todds Manual on Politness wh. virtue he strongly recommends— 8 to 10—prepared decree—clients so much engrossed my time that I cd. bestow little attention on cases in court—recd. fees from Messrs Wiggins & Reid & paid note for stable lot $278.28 10 to ½ p 11—Bd. of Directors & Ex. Com.— ½ p. 11 to 1—time engrossed by clients & private business— 1 to 2—Dinner—incident of little bird— 2 to ½ p. 6 Attended to business with Ludlow & Kenner[99]—wrote to Balestier proposing to give note of Johnston & cash in payt. of Edwd's ob. to Follett[1]— ½ p. 6 to ¼ b. 9. Tea & company—Mrs C. Beach,

---

95. Chase represented former Cincinnati publisher and book dealer A. W. Corey, now living in Madison County, Ill., in a suit involving a claim against James Hall. Corey to Chase, Jan. 20, Mar. 13, 1843 (Chase Papers, L.C.).

96. Niel Gow, *A Practical Treatise on the Law of Partnership* (London, 1823).

97. Chase's mother-in-law, Mary Colton Smith, and sister-in-law, Frances Mary Smith (1820–43). James R. Skinner to Chase, Jan. 12, 1841, and "Family Memoranda" (Chase Papers, L.C.).

98. Possibly Edward Young, *The Complaint* (see Dec. 1, 1835, above).

99. James C. Ludlow (1798–1841), a local antislavery activist and the son of Cincinnati founder Israel Ludlow, and William Butler Kenner. Robson, *Biographical Encyclopædia*, 488–89; James C. Ludlow, last will and testament, Mar. 19, 1841 (Chase Papers, L.C.).

1. Chase was corresponding with Chicago lawyer Joseph N. Balestier. The offer involved a debt owed by Cincinnati businessman William S. Johnston (b. 1791) and Wisconsin property which Chase's brother, Edward Ithamar Chase (1810–62), had purchased from Jonathan S. Follett of Galena, Ill. Johnson acted as trustee to the estate of Chase's father-in-law, Edmund Curtis Smith. Edward Ithamar Chase, who in 1861 became U.S. marshal for the northern district of New York, resided in Lockport, N.Y., with his wife, Mary Eliza Chase. Robson, *Biographical Encyclopædia*, 546–47; *Chicago Dir. (1839)*, 6; Balestier to Chase, Mar. 6, 1840, Johnston to Hiram Hart,

July 1840 { 133 }

Mrs M. Beach, Miss C. Picket, children & Mr. Garniss— ¼ b. 9 to 10 Went to Wedding of Miss Adeline Wiggins to Mr. Breese[2]—was greatly pleased by the ceremony—saw Mr. Johns and several other gentlemen of my acquaintance but hardly made a sensible or useful observation during the evening— Came home—prayed with wife read a little in the Life of Chrysostom[3]—to bed—

JUNE 31[4] Plan— 10 m. b. 5 to 20 m. b. 6—Dress— 20 min b. 6 to 6—write Journal— 6 to ½ p. 6. Fam Prayer &c ½ p 6 to ½ p. 7. Breakfast, priv. dev. & com. Psalms— ½ p. 7 to 8 Todd— 8 to 11. Clients & prep. to leave town— 11 to ½ p. 11—Exchge Com. ½ p. 11 to 1 Story on Conf.— 1 to 2. Dinner— 2 to 3 Preparation for Council— 3 to   Council—   to 9—unappropriated— 9 to 10 Journal &c

JULY 1 As I was going to my office after dinner was joined by Mr. Whiteman who wished to secure my vote in council for Mr. James F. Irwin, an old schoolfellow of mine who desires the appointment of secretary of the Waterworks.[5] I told him that I had already determined to cast my vote for Mr. Richards, if no other candidate of superior qualifications presented himself and I thought Mr. Irwin's not superior. If however Mr. Richards should decline & I could do so consistently with my public duty, I should be happy to further Mr. I's views. While we were talking Gen. Harrison came from the opposite direction. We met and exchanged the usual greetings. I saw

---

Sept. 1, 1840, Follett to Chase, Feb. 10, 1841, Mary Eliza Chase to Chase, Oct. 14, 1862, and "Family Memoranda" (Chase Papers, L.C.); Edward I. Chase to Chase, Aug. 2, 1839 (Chase Papers, Hist. Soc. of Pa.); *Register of Officers (1861)*, 190.

2. The bride, a daughter of Samuel Wiggins, married Cincinnati grocer William G. Breese. *Cincinnati Daily Gazette*, July 3, 1840, Jan. 8, 1841.

3. The biography of St. John Chrysostom (c. 347–407), bishop of Constantinople, first appeared in print as *De Vita S. Johannis Chrysostomi Dialogus* . . . (Paris, 1680), by Palladius, bishop of Helenopolis. It was also available in Greek and English editions. F. L. Cross and E. A. Livingstone, eds., *The Oxford Dictionary of the Christian Church*, 2nd ed., (London, New York, and Toronto, 1974), 285, 286, 1024.

4. Apparently on the night of June 30 Chase planned his activities for the next day and forgot that June has only thirty days. Following this entry, perhaps because of the out-of-town trip mentioned in it, his daily journal record was disrupted. An entry for August 3, which appears at its proper chronological place below, follows the "June 31" entry in the original. Then comes an entry for July 1, followed (after two blank pages) by the resumption of daily entries on July 12. This evidence suggests that Chase left four pages blank for the later insertion of entries for July 1–11. He may have opened his journal to the first of those blank pages by mistake when he made the August 3 entry, thinking that it was the first available page after the July 27 entry. Sometime after making the August 3 entry, he made the entry for July 1 which follows this one marked "June 31."

5. Irwin, a produce merchant, received the appointment later in the day. He had probably attended Cincinnati College with Chase. *Cincinnati Daily Gazette*, July 3, 1840; *Cinc. Dir. (1840)*, 233.

that something disturbed the Gen. & was not long left to guess the cause. "Do you know a person named Bailey?" said he addressing me.[6] "Very well," I replied. He then requested me to call on him with Mr. Greene or alone and enquire of him what foundation he had for the charges published against him yesterday morn'g in the Philanthropist.[7] I said I was willing to go alone, but wd. prefer not to be associated in a mission of that sort with Mr. Greene   Mr. Owen, near whose door we stood and who had joined us while we were talking said "let Mr. C go alone," and the Gen. assented. The Gen at the same time said that he had never called on Dr. Bailey but once and had said nothing which could give color to the charges against him, unless it might be a remark he had made that he would as soon appoint an abolitionist to office as any body else if qualified. He said he particularly wanted to know if, in any conversation with Dr. B. he had ever been understood to retract any of the sentiments expressed in the Vincennes or Cheviot Speeches.[8] Soon afterwards I called on Dr. B. I told him what I wanted and made the particular enquiries which the Gen. suggested. He said the speeches were not distinctly named or referred to in the conversation. I remarked that I thought he had dealt with unwarranted harshness by Gen. H. He said I was not more sorry for it, than he was that the occasion had arisen

JULY 12   Formed no definite plan for the employment of this day. Rose about 6—went to the Library; recommitted 16 verses of the 119th Psalm & read the 3rd Chap. Matt. Gr. Test.[9] private devotion— Breakfast—ate moderately—attended Sunday School— about 80 present—two young gentlemen from Texas called to see the School & afterwards sat with me in Church. They were teachers they said in a Sunday School in Austin in Texas. It is said that the Episcopal church is more favorably regarded than any other church in Texas— Can this be owing to the fact that the Episcopal Church has taken no ground against Slavery; but, on the contrary, has a slaveholding ministry? Attended church. Mr. Johns on justification

---

6. Gamaliel Bailey, M.D. (1807–59), lectured at Lane Seminary, assumed the editorship of the *Philanthropist* in 1837, and, from 1847 to 1859, edited the Washington, D.C., *National Era*, a publication of the American and Foreign Anti-Slavery Society. *DAB*, 1:496–97.

7. Bailey's article, "The Crisis—The Duty," criticized William Henry Harrison for alleged duplicity on the issue of slavery and urged abolitionists not to support the Whig ticket. *Philanthropist*, June 30, 1840.

8. Harrison's Vincennes and Cheviot speeches, delivered on May 25, 1835, and July 4, 1833, respectively, supported Southern claims to state sovereignty on the slavery question. Cleaves, *Old Tippecanoe*, 283–84, 296.

9. Greek Testament.

by faith—after church—read Life of Chrysostom till dinner, and after dinner except while asleep in a conversation with wife till tea— after tea church Mr. Johns, same subject, better discourse & I more attentive—Mr. & Mrs Ball came home with us[10]—Mr. Southgate[11] & Miss Post came in—conversation turned on worldly topics, but all soon took leave—came to Library and wrote foregoing & now prayer and bed.

JULY 13   It is not easy to devise a plan for today as court is sitting and I am liable to much interruption—but I will try the following. Having risen at 5 taken a bath, dressed & read some pages of my journal, I will devote from ½ p. 6 to ½ p. 7 to Fam. Prayer & breakfast. ½ p. 7 to 8 to private prayer & study of bible— 8 to 9 business at office 9 to 11 to business at Court— 11 to ½ p 11— Exchange Committee— ½ p 11 to 1 business at office— 1 to 2 dinner
   Performance— Left my plan incomplete designing to finish before dinner— Devoted the time till 8 to the objects mentioned in plan / From 8 to 9 was at office conversing with clients & preparing for court— Took Southgate's deposition—talked with Justice,[12] Vaughan & others— From 9 to ½ p 11 at Court—took list of cases from procedendo & attended to some other small matters— ½ p 11 to 1 when not interrupted studied Conf. Laws with reference to cases to be argued this afternoon—read a case in Peters with same view—Edwards vs Boyce & Henry 4 Pet.[13]— 1 to ¼ p. 2—Dinner &c— ¼ p 2 to 3 at office 3 to ½ p. 6 at Court—read pt. case in Law Reporter for May '40 on Guarantee, Wildes vs Savage[14]—also case in Ohio Rep on rights of Sureties— Read neither with sufficient discrimination & attention—commenced cases to be argued—spoke briefly Walker more at length—am to close tomorrow morning. ½ p 6 to 8—at home—read Philanthropist article on Gen. Harrison & Chronicle— 8 to 10 prepared for tomorrow— 10 to ———— wrote above & now prayer & to bed—

JULY 14   Having risen at ½ p. 5 & employed the time till 20 m p 6 in dressing, private devotions and reading some pages of

---

10. Flamen Ball and his wife Evelina Chandler Ball (d. 1864). Robson, *Biographical Encyclopædia*, 99–100.

11. Probably attorney James Southgate, widower of Jane Smith Southgate (1816–40), a recently deceased sister of Eliza Ann Smith Chase. "Family Memoranda" (Chase Papers, L.C.); *Cinc. Dir. (1842)*, 278.

12. Cincinnati merchant Jesse Justice. *Cinc. Dir. (1840)*, 241.

13. *Boyce & Henry v. Timothy Edwards*, 4 Pet. 111 (1830), a case involving acceptance of a bill of exchange.

14. The summary of the case, decided in the U.S. circuit court for Massachusetts, appeared in *Law Reporter* 3 (May 1840): 1–11.

journal, I now adopt the following *Plan*— ½ p. 6 to ½ p. 7—Study Bible, Fam. Prayer, breakfast &c— ½ p 7 to 9—Prepare for argument at Court— 9 to 12 argument at Court & attendance at Bank— 12 to 1—Prepare business for court— 1 to 2 dinner &c— 2 to 3— Prepare for court— 3 to 7 at court &c— 7 to 8 tea &c— 8 to ½ p 9 Histy. F. Rev[15]— ½ p 9 to 10 Prayer &c

Performance— From ½ p 6 to ½ p. 7, I recommitted 16 verses of the 119th Psalm, using the Septuagint Greek to aid in the right apprehension of the import of words. Never until this *study* of the Psalm did I ever understand it even tolerably. I now wonder at my blindness. At Family Prayer I read a part of the unequalled sermon on the mount[16] & earnestly desired to be imbued with the spirit of its teachings. Afterwards until the expiration of the hour I read the Gazette. The only thing worthy of particular remembrance was the discovery of the Antartic Continent in latitude 66°. Part of Sweden is not more distant from the Equator. If the account be true, what purpose does this great Southern continent, surrounded by a barrier of eternal ice, answer in the economy of Divine Providence?[17]

After the hour I purposed going to my office, but my wife had determined to visit a relative in the country for a few days, and the preparations for her departure delayed me half an hour. After she had gone I went to my office and employed the interval till 9 in preparation for court. At 9 went to court and made the closing in argument on two cases of great importance both as to the amts involved and the questions raised. At ½ past 10 I returned to the office to ascertain the state of my next case for trial. After getting the papers and two books treating the questions arising in the case, and having paid a brief visit at the Bank, where the Ex. Com. had adjd., I went to the Court House and spent the remainder of the morning in preparation of the case. From ½ p. 1 to near 3—I dined, read on the state of France before Rev. & slept. At 3 went to court again but did nothing—a singular and discreditable squabble between Messrs Walker & Storer in regard to an application for continuance. At about ½ past 5 returned to office & spent about an hour and a half in detail business. At 7 came home to tea bringing Mr. Ball with me. Frank and Edmund, my wife's brother & sister[18]

---

15. Adolphe Thiers, *The History of the French Revolution* . . . , 3 vols. (London, 1835). References to the French Revolution which appear in the journal entries from this point to the end of 1840 evidently allude to Chase's reading in this work.

16. Matt. 5–7.

17. The article focused on discoveries by Capt. Charles Wilkes and a U.S. Navy survey along the Antarctic coast, the Pacific islands, and the American northwest. *Cincinnati Daily Gazette,* July 14, 1840.

18. Frances Mary Smith and Edmund Curtis Smith, Jr. (1823–47). Will of E. C. Smith, Jr., 1847, and "Family Memoranda" (Chase Papers, L.C.).

came also to tea—talked with them till ½ p. 8—then read on French Revolution till about 10

Miss Carneal gives a fashionable party tonight[19]—a political meeting is held in the 3rd Ward[20]— Mr. Benham, once a rising star, bright & brightening, distinguished for talent, for oratory, & for personal advantages, afterwards a bankrupt in fortune & fame, both sacrificed to appetite, lies at a public hotel, the victim of disease, near the termination of his mortal career. In an obscure street, nursed by a mother herself rude and uneducated if not intemprate, lies a young man acutely suffering the last agonies of long protracted disease, but cheerful, grateful, supported by a hope that never fails—at least I so judge. What contrasts of fact and of opinion & of emotion are here!

JULY 15 Rose at ½ p. 5—dressed till 10 m. p. 6—without much if any useful reflection— Came then to the Libry & prayed—I now adopt this *plan*

20/m p. 6 to ½ p 7—Bible, Young breakfast, &c.— ½ p 7 to 8. Todd— 8 to 9—Clients or office business— 9 to 1. Court—office & Bank— 1 to 2 dinner— 2 to 7—read Story Conf. Law at least 20 pages attentively—attend court if necessary if not attend council— other business as I can—& exercise— 7 to 8 tea— 8 to ½ p. 9 F. Rev— to 10 Prayer &c— Endeavor thro the whole day to have my heart right with God & man—

Until ½ p 7, I recommitted 24 verses of the 119th Psalm—attended family prayers, breakfasted & read the Gazette—the only article of permanent interest was that the Sultan had given a constitution to the Ottoman Empire— A striking event in the history of the age & probably the herald of events more striking still.[21] Another article was an elaborate vindication by the affidavits of old citizens of Gen. Harrison, the Whig candidate for the Ch. Magistracy of the Republic, from the charge of ancient Federalism from the sin of having agreed with Washington, with Hamilton, with Jay![22] Found no time to read Young— From 20 m. before 8 read Todd Chap. on Exercise— At 8 went to my office, where was engagd

---

19. Probably a relative of Thomas D. Carneal, one of Chase's clients. *Cinc. Dir.* *(1842)*, 160; Carneal to Chase, Aug. 10, 1837 (Chase Papers, L.C.).

20. The Whig meeting, at the corner of Pearl and Walnut Streets, featured speeches by Judge Elisha Mills Huntington of Indiana and Green B. Duncan, a New Orleans attorney. *Cincinnati Daily Gazette,* July 14, 1840.

21. The newspaper article reprinted the constitution, which had been read in Constantinople on Nov. 3, 1839. Ibid., July 15, 1840.

22. The charges had been levied by Jacksonian journalist Amos Kendall. Harrison's defenders included Gen. James Taylor of Kentucky and several former local officials from the Cincinnati area. Ibid.

by a client the greater part of the time—at 9 went to court found nothing to do so read about 10 p. Story's Conf. interrupted by Mr. Carneal about his business with Lawrence & Symmes[23] & 4th Street— Went to Exchange Committee— Occupied residue of morning with various matters, such as investigating case of Daisley ads Dennison, writing to Phelps & Foley about it— From a little b. 1 till near 2 at dinner—employed a moment before in repeating the verses committed in the morning— After dinner till 3 engaged in procuring a note discounted for 3760 in renewal of three others others & in obt'g check on Louisville to pay dft 750 on Smith. From 3 to 7 at Council—several important measures passed for which I voted[24]— Ret'd home to tea & spent the evg. till now in the F. Rev. Now prayer & bed— My wife is absent in the country. Mr. Benham had died & his body has been committed to the tomb.

JULY 16 Formed no plan this day—attended to business as usual—read about 35 pages Conf. Laws— Mr. Clay's Speech[25]—a masterly effort—went into the country in evg. ten miles to see my wife who returned with me— A gentleman handed me the call for an anti slavery convention wishing me to sign it—I declined and reasoned with him on the impropriety of the step at the present time: but I think without much effect.

JULY 17 Rose about 5—took showerbath & dressed—glanced at Georgia Scenes[26]—a poor book—& wrote the few lines above—now ¼ past 6—
Plan ¼ p 6 to 8—Bible—fam. prayer—Young—breakfast—papers— *to 9* prepare for court at office— *to ½ p. 12* Court attending Bank at interval if possible— *to 2*—dinner &c— *to 3*—clients &c at office— to 7 at Court—Conf. Laws—Exercise to 8 tea— *to ½ p 9* F. Rev— *To 10*—Devotion, meditation—

---

23. Peyton Short Symmes (1793–1861), federal land register. *Appletons'*, 6:16; *Cinc. Dir. (1840)*, 375.
24. Most of the city council's work this evening involved proposed improvements to streets and bridges. The major issue was a request from the president of the Little Miami Railroad for $80,000 to assist with construction expenses. Chase had previously moved that city officials invest $60,000 in the railroad and $20,000 in the Cincinnati and Whitewater Canal Company. In this meeting, the council passed his motion, but redirected the smaller portion to an investment in the Cincinnati Water Works. *Cincinnati Daily Gazette*, May 8, July 17, 1840.
25. Henry Clay's speech, delivered June 27 in Taylorsville, Va., endorsed the candidacy of William Henry Harrison and repeated standard Whig criticisms that Andrew Jackson had reached beyond his constitutional authority while serving as president. Ibid., July 16, 1840.
26. Augustus Baldwin Longstreet, *Georgia Scenes, Characters, Incidents, &c., in the First Half Century of the Republic* ... (Augusta, Ga., 1835).

The plan abo[27]

JULY 26 For more than a week I have neglected to frame any plan and though I have continued to read with some diligence I have omitted several duties, through forgetfulness which I think I should have remembered had I looked forward through each day and assigned to each hour its appropriate employment.

This morning I did not rise till past 7 oclock and had time only for family prayer and breakfast after dressing before the bell rang for the Sunday School, which I attended. The number present exceeded seventy. I purposed addressing them but did not. After Sunday School I returned home, not being willing to be absent longer from my wife, in her present state of health. Found her on my return asleep. Spent the morning chiefly in reading various articles of a religious character in the New York Evangelist—was interested particularly by a condensed sketch of the results of missionary enterprize.[28] How few are at any pains to inform themselves on this subject—the most deeply interesting, except one's personal salvation to every true Christian.

After dinner had a most interesting conversation with my dear wife. It was made up of reflections on the providential dealings of our Heavenly Father with us, and especially in relation to our dear little departed one. From every subject of reflection, my mind constantly reverts to my little one in Heaven. Lizzy said that one day as she was sitting on her grandfather's knee he used some harsh expressions in relation an absent individual. She looked up and said "Grandpa is that right—only wicked people call folks such names." Her grandfather's eyes filled with tears and she added "Grandpa won't do so any more; will you grandpa?" When playing with little children, if asked to play any part, as pretending to visit &c she would ask if that was right to say what was not the truth. Not long before her death her grandfather coming into the parlor found her kneeling before her mothers picture and asked her what she was doing. She answered, he told me that she was praying her mother to take her to heaven. I hardly think this was so, for she was always taught to pray only to God and she was much in the habit of praying to him when in any little affliction. She probably said she had been praying to God to take her to heaven to her dear mother. This was a wish she often expressed / On one occasion she came and told me that a meal was ready and I asked some one to see if it was so; she

---

27. So in the original. Chase evidently stopped in mid-word and never completed the sentence.
28. Probably "Christian Missions. The Progress Made in the Missionary Work," in *New-York Evangelist*, July 11, 1840.

seemed hurt and said "Pa! don't you think I tell the truth?" Whenever I denied anything to her, she invariably acquiesced saying "Pa knows what is best for his little daughter." and never fretted or cried on account of it.

After the conversation which revived these reminiscences I reviewed the latter part of the 119th Psalm. This is the third time I have gone over the whole of this Psalm memorizing it in addition to my other Bible reading. I mean to continue to do so until I can repeat it with facility from beginning to end.

JULY 27 MONDAY   Rose at ¼ past 5— Took a bath & while doing so repeated nearly 40 verses of 119th Psalm—dressed & at ¼ p 6 had family prayer—called Warren and told him to hire a carriage for me to go to Lawrenceburgh— It is now half past 6— My plan for the day must be short. From ½ p 6 to 8—Bible, private devotion breakfast &c— 8 to 12 ride to L— 12 to 4—Dinner Conversation with brother &c[29]— 4 to 8—ride home— 8 to 9 tea &c—half an hour Fr. Rev.—till ten review—plan—devotion & bed—

AUGUST 3[30]   Rose at ½ p. 5—repeated about 40 verses 119th Psalm with some meditation, dressed, attended family prayers & private; breakfasted—read & committed a new part of 119th Psalm—plucked first ripe peach for wife who is sick—it is now near 8—I propose to go to my office & attend to business & Story Conf. Laws until 9—then go to court calling at house & stay there till 10 or ½ past—return to house—then to office till 1—not forgetting to pay $320 borrd. money to Mr. Longworth—fr 1 to ½ p 2 dinner & plan for afternoon— after writing this I went to my office and read, amid interruptions, a few pages of Storys Work on the application of foreign law to foreign contracts;—afterwards went to the court house where remained, doing little till ½ p. 10— Returned home found wife asleep—went again to office & attended to busi-

---

29. Formerly a resident of Conneaut, Ohio, Chase's oldest brother, Alexander Ralston Chase (1797–1847), suffered from financial problems, ill health, and, evidently, alcoholism. Alexander worked at times as an attorney and notary public, and in Nov. 1842 patented a device which kept the blades of steamboat paddlewheels in a vertical position as they entered and left the water. He died in Cincinnati, although he did not reside there continuously from the summer of 1840 until his death. He had married Stella King Chase, whose situation during the last years of her husband's life is unknown. Mar. 23, 1847, below; A. R. Chase to Chase, Nov. 9, 1836, July, Sept. 10, 1840, June 11, Sept. 7, 1846, James Allen to Chase, May 5, 27, 1843, and "Family Memoranda" (Chase Papers, L.C.); *Cinc. Dir. (1842)*, 161; patent application file 2845 (Records of the Patent Office, Nat. Arch.).

30. In the original journal, this entry begins a new page after the entry for "June 31." The following note in Chase's hand appears along the left margin: "This should follow the pages which contains the account of July 27."

ness till near one—collected money of Smith[31]—each sd. div. for bankable money; paid 320 due Mr. Longworth—recd. private letters from Mr. Warder,[32] brother Edward came home & staid till ½ p 2 when went again to office— Mr. Collins called about renting house occupied by Fulweiler[33]—Went to court at 3 and continued busily engaged in examining & preparing cases till 7 when came home— read Chronicle[34] tea—read F. Rev. the preparatory steps to the insurrection which dethroned the King—have since written the foregoing—much annoyed by musketoes.

AUGUST 4 How rapidly time fleets—already the 4th day of the last day of summer and but yesterday the summer begun!

Rose, after disturbed night, wife still suffering much pain, at ½ p. 5. fr ½ p. 5 to ½ p. 6—dressing and repeating 119th Psalm—till 7 Memorize Psalm & Prayer—till 8 Breakfast, Family Prayer &c— Till 9 Story and business—till 1 Court, Bank if possible, & office business—till ½ p 2 dinner—till 3 office business—till 7 Court— Story & office business—till 8 tea—till ½ p 9 French Rev—Till 10 Journal, Prayer—

Not much accomplished this day— Memorized before 7 a considerable portion of the 119th Psalm & offered private prayer—but cold & stupid & thoughts wandering—after & until 8 read newspaper, breakfasted, attended F.P.[35]—reading of newspaper very unprofitable hardly ever recollect anything it contains—after 8 went to office—several persons came in & interrupted me—made entries in accounts—read nothing— At 9 went to Court—conversed with Judge about case Bates vs Kellogg et al—procured assent of court to two decrees—just before 10 went to Bank—afterwards home to see wife who was quite comfortable—then to court & prepared decree in Bank vs [Martin] etal—came home at 1—found wife suffering much—dined but did not go out again, except for a moment to the office—occupied leisure moments in reading French Revolutions—Massacres of September—frightful—prayed with wife— bed at ½ p 10

---

31. Probably Hamilton Smith.
32. The letter from Jeremiah Warder, a businessman from Springfield, Ohio, described a local homestead which Chase was interested in purchasing. William M. Rockel, ed. and comp., *20th Century History of Springfield, and Clark County, Ohio and Representative Citizens* (Chicago, 1908), 185, 329, 374; Warder to Chase, July 31, 1840 (Chase Papers, L.C.).
33. Probably either Abraham Fulweiler, a local tanner and currier, or Michael H. Fulweiler, a tailor. *Cinc. Dir. (1840)*, 188.
34. The Cincinnati *Daily Chronicle*. Goss, *Cincinnati*, 2:500.
35. Family prayer.

AUG 12   When I came home this evening I found my dear wife suffering a good deal of pain but sitting up and apparently otherwise well / Her suffering increased however and after tea I insisted on sending for the physician & her mother. The latter came first and it soon became apparent that Lizzy was about to be confined. The servant was sent again to hasten the doctor and I went for Mrs Ball, a kind friend, deservedly dear to us all. She came as soon as she could, but before she arrived I had sent for the nurse and the Dr. (Dr. Rives) had come.[36] The pains continued to increase. I went apart and kneeling down prayed God to support and comfort my dear wife, to preserve the life of the child and save both from sin. I endeavored to give up the child and all into his hands. I went once or twice into the room where my suffering wife lay and occasionally whispered to her words of consolation & encouragement. She bore her pains with great fortitude and I believe was strengthened by her Heavenly Father to endure. At length after full trial of her patience, by a protracted labor of 4 hours, a little daughter was born.[37] Mrs Ball came to announce the tidings to me. But lying in the next room I had heard the pleased exclamation of the kind physician after all was safely over. After a while I went into the room. The birth had taken place at 2 oclock AM on 13th.[38] After I had seen my wife & child I went into the Library & read a few pages in Eberle's book on Children—a judicious treatise. At last I became tired & though it was now day lay down and slept awhile. The babe is pronounced pretty. I think it quite otherwise. It is however well formed and I am thankful. May God give the child a good understanding that she may keep his commandments. I have done little this day besides reading a few pages in Story's Conflict of Laws. Saw Mr Pratt about Raymond's debt to me.[39] Wrote to Mr Johnston about his debt to

---

36. Landon C. Rives (1790–1870), former professor of obstetrics in the medical department of Cincinnati College. Juettner, *Daniel Drake*, 198–99.

37. Catharine Jane ("Kate") Chase (1840–99), daughter of Salmon and Eliza Ann Smith Chase, was her father's second daughter, but the oldest to survive to adulthood. She bore the same name as Chase's first-born child, who had died in Feb. 1840. Kate Chase acted as her father's hostess during the early part of the Civil War and married William Sprague in Nov. 1863. Although her father spelled her name *Catharine* in his notes of family events, she tended to spell it *Katharine*. DAB, 17:473; "Family Memoranda" (Chase Papers, L.C.).

38. In margin: "Aug 13."

39. Robert Raikes Raymond (1819–88) was a student in Chase's office, future editor of the Syracuse, N.Y., *Free Democrat* and *Evening Chronicle*, and professor of elocution and English at Brooklyn Polytechnic Institute, 1857–64. Pratt may have been William Pratt, a local cooper and the only known Cincinnati resident at the time with this surname. *Appletons'*, 5:193–94; *Cinc. Dir. (1840)*, 321, 327; W. Stewart Wallace, comp., *A Dictionary of North American Authors Deceased before 1950* (Toronto, 1951), 373.

me. My wife has been very comfortable today and has slept well. The child has been restless and uneasy. The Dr. directed some Castor oil for her. Since I came home this evening I have repeated the whole of the 119th Psalm being obliged still howreve frequently to refer to the book. I have also written to Mr. Neil on the Subject of property offered me by Mr. Pratt.[40]

I now lay down this plan for tomorrow—

Rise at ½ p. 5—to ¼ p. 6 dress—to 7 repeat Psalm—devotions—to 8 Family Prayer breakfast &c—to 9—Story on Conflict & accidentals—to 1 PM Court house,—office business especially preparation of causes—bank—& business again—to 2—dinner—to 6—office business—private business—to 8 Tea &c—to 10 History of Fr Rev—to ½ p. 11. Journal &c

AUGUST 30[41] I have omitted to form any regular plans for each day as it seems impossible for me to do more than sketch the outline of each days action as it takes place whether planned or no.

This morning I rose about ½ past 6 o'clock—was interrupted in dressing and did not get ready for family prayers until about ½ past 7. Then attended family prayers, but was cold and formal. Neither my thoughts nor my affections seemed free. Repeated as usual while dressing a considerable part of the 119th Psalm & afterwards during the day the whole of the residue—I do hope the word thus hid in my heart will keep me from sinning against God. Nothing saves me from absolute despair, in the contemplation of the [*illeg.*] and guilt of my heart, but the certainty that the atonement is infinite and that the Holy Spirit is pledged to those who ask / After breakfast went to church, when I superintended the Sunday School as usual and addressed the children briefly on topics suggested by the hymn for the day— Must pay more attention to these addresses and try to make them more interesting and instructive. Attended church—a stranger preached sermon sound, but badly composed and delivered. Why cannot clergymen speak to their fellow citizens in a frank, kind & natural manner—as a man would speak to a friend whom he was warning against evil habits & dangerous courses? In the afternoon committed part of 37th Psalm & read Life of Chrysostom— In evg attended church—Mr. Johns preached—text God be

---

40. William Neil (1788–1870) was a Columbus businessman. *Col. Dir. (1845–46)*, 56; Neil to Chase, Aug. 18, 1840 (Chase Papers, L.C.); Taylor, *Columbus and Franklin County*, 1:510.

41. Chase wrote "Aug. 29" in the margin after a page turn within this entry. The Aug. 30 date at the beginning of the entry is correct, however, since the 30th was a Sunday.

merciful to me a sinner[42]—walked to near home with Col. Dudley[43]— found Mrs Garniss with wife—went home with her—wrote foregoing & now to bed—

DECR 25 When I ceased writing in this journal last August, I intended only to omit it for a day or two. The day or two, by procrastination has been extended to near four months. Yet idleness has not been the cause of the omission. I have allowed other things of less real importance to engross the time.

During the interval I have been at Lockport in New York and at Chicago in Illinois.[44] Went to Chicago from Cleveland in Steamboat of that name.[45] Encountered storm on Lake Huron. Read History of Michigan & Cobbett on Paper Money on board the boat.[46]

Since my return have been almost constantly occupied in professional duties & public engagements. Have nevertheless, continued to read Thiers & have commenced De Tocqueville de la Democratie des Etats Unis.[47]

Today I rose too late—attended to private & family prayer afterwards read several chapters in Leviticus—having again begun to read the Scriptures in course intending to read the old testament in private & the new with the family—the 19th chapter analyzed and compared its precepts with the 10 comdts—which it expands & enforces in a most admirable manner. It is my deliberate opinion, that all the writings of all moral & political philosophers do not contain so much practical wisdom, whither applicable to states or persons— While analyzing this chap. my wife came in ready to go to church. We went—an excellent sermon from Mr. Johns on the Divinity of our Savior from Mal. "The Lord whom ye seek &c"[48] After sermon communion. Before church recd. a letter fr several clergymen in reply to a note signed by myself & others as a com. of Young Men's Bible Sy. in answer to a remonstrance on their pt.

---

42. Luke 18:13.
43. Possibly Elias Dudley, originally of Massachusetts, secretary of the Manufacturers Insurance Company; or Ambrose Dudley, profession unknown, originally from Kentucky. *Cinc. Dir. (1840)*, 167.
44. Chase had recently purchased land in Lockport, home of his brother, Edward Ithamar Chase, and his sister, Janette Logan Chase Skinner. His trip to Chicago probably involved real estate transactions there and in Wisconsin. Joseph N. Balestier to Chase, Aug. 27, 1839, agreement between S. P. Chase and E. I. Chase, Sept. 14, 1840, Jonathan S. Follett to Chase, Feb. 2, 1841 (Chase Papers, L.C.).
45. The *Cleveland*, a sidewheel steamer of 579 tons built in Huron, Ohio, in 1837. Lytle, *Merchant Vessels*, 35.
46. James Henry Lanman, *History of Michigan, Civil and Topographical*... (New York, 1839); William Cobbett, *Cobbett's Paper against Gold: Containing the History and Mystery of the Bank of England*... (London, 1810–15).
47. Alexis de Tocqueville, *De la Démocratie en Amerique* (Brussels, 1835).
48. Mal. 3:1.

against the election of Unitarians as Officers or the selection of such as speakers for the Society. Thought the letter weak as an argument.

After church read a few pages in French Revolution & then went to Mr Balls to dine. A small & not very interesting party. Might have made it more interesting and profitable had I taken the proper course.

Coming home called at Mrs Smiths[49] where we had left our baby, who has now grown finely and is very healthy. After coming home went to Mr. Garniss where sat talking some time—then home again to tea—then to my office, whence returned immediately without doing anything. Read Thiers—[Geogy.] of Switzerland[50] & wrote— Wife unwell from cold & retired early—

Wife made XMas presents Margaret, dress, Nancy shawl, Betsey ½ dollar,[51] me, suspenders— I gave Warren silver pencil case—

DEC 26— After a night of disturbed slumber and strange dreams awoke with a head ache, dressed & breakfasted late—no newspapers— Can't we have more conversation & more sociability at table. At family prayers read two chaps of revelations—designing to finish the book before New Years. Going to office after breakfast found Mr. Kirby & others waiting to see me[52]— After getting through with them went to the Bank to assist in counting the cash &c as a member of the Quarterly Committee. Met Gen Stokely at the Bk & invited him to dine with me but he excused himself.[53] Went to work—had some difference with clerk as to mode of making statement—the committee determined to make a full & explicit report. Afterwards, without finishing, adjd. till Monday Morning— Came home—went back to office—employed a few moments on Truman's account & other matters—came home again—read after dinner at 5 a few pages of Thiers then attended a meeting of the Bible Society's

---

49. Chase's mother-in-law, Mary Colton Smith.

50. The reading is problematical. Warden, *Chase*, 293, transcribed the phrase: "Read Thiers' *Geography of Switzerland.*" No book of such title is associated with Adolphe Thiers, however, and it is evident from other references that Chase was reading Thiers' history of the French Revolution. The abbreviation may not be *Geogy.* It is not clear that Chase meant to link the references to Thiers and Switzerland, or that the work in question related to the geography of Switzerland.

51. Possibly Betsey Farington, a twelve-year-old black girl recently freed from slavery in Georgia and recommended to Chase's wife as a servant. John Martin to Chase, Mar. 1, Aug. 10, Nov. 11, 1840 (Chase Papers, L.C.).

52. Timothy Kirby (1797–1874), a land agent for the Bank of the United States. Robson, *Biographical Encyclopædia*, 124–25; *Cinc. Dir. (1840)*, 248.

53. Samuel Stokely (1796–1861), a brigadier general in the state militia, was a Whig congressman from Steubenville. *Bio. Dir. U.S. Cong.*, 1880; John Alexander Caldwell, *History of Belmont and Jefferson Counties, Ohio* . . . (Wheeling, 1880), 440.

Committee. Laid before them letter from large number of clergymen, disapproving course of society in electing one of its officers & appointing one of its Anniversary speakers from the Unitarian Society, & threatening withdrawal of cooperation in consequence. Committee resolved to adhere to the course hitherto pursued by the society. Messrs Blanchard & Nast spoke on the subject & others.[54] Coming home read a few more pages of Thiers & wrote foregoing.

1841

JAN 1. 1841   Here is the New Year. I look back to its commencement: I was then the father of a lovely child, just entering on her fifth year. On New Year's day with what delight did she not receive her little presents! A little more than one month after she died, and my heart was desolate, but she was blest. The New Year which found her with the flush of health upon her cheek, flung its gifts to her and immediately summoned her to part with them and all forever.

Besides this great affliction I have experienced little sorrow during the year. I have suffered no pecuniary losses. My professional practice has increased and I have encountered no serious disappointments.

My wife's health has improved. She has been safely delivered of a little daughter, who lives to be our common delight. I have been able to afford a home to an unfortunate brother, and I hope to render him some essential service.[55]

In public estimation I do not think I have gained much. I have been obliged occasionally to take positions, not acceptable to some, and, perhaps, I have maintained myself in them with unnecessary harshness.

I have read something and have remembered something. Though I have not advanced much in knowledge I have not been quite stationary.

I have reflected but little. I am greatly wanting in the habit of thinking out matters.

And now I begin the year. I have today visited a large number of my acquaintances, tendering to them the gratulations of the season. I have also attended to some little business at the office. Gave little baby, rattle & coral, wife, a muff, & Mrs Garniss, Pilgrims Progress.

---

54. Jonathan Blanchard (1811–92), the pastor of Cincinnati's Sixth Presbyterian Church, and William Nast (1807–99), a Methodist clergyman and editor of Cincinnati's *Der Christliche Apologete. DAB,* 2:350–51, 13:393.

55. Alexander Ralston Chase.

January 1841 {147}

JANY 2. SATURDAY   In the evening of today attended the Council. Spoke on the Vagrant Ordinance & introduced one modifying that on the subject of coffee houses:[56] and procured some presents for Sunday School children. In afternoon meeting at my house to make arrangements for meeting

JANY 3. SUNDAY   Attended Sunday School in morning, few present, distributed presents went to church—afternoon read Channing on Emancipation[57]—church in ev'g—Mr Johns.

JANY 4 MONDAY   Superior Court commenced its term—also Court of Com. Pleas criminal term— Attended former—little business today—after adjournment went into latter & heard part of Judge Read's charge, good but rambling & declamatory— Sent communication to Gazette over Signature of Hammond about meeting of citizens opposed to Slavery in the District of Columbia[58]—called on Gallagher the editor about same matter—he promised to notice meeting editorially— In evening read essays of "Wythe" on Power of Congress over Slavery in District[59]

JANY 5 TUESDAY   Attended court in morn'g—read Jay's view[60]— called on a gentleman who promised to attend the meeting tonight and appeared to be very warm last week, but who has become a little alarmed. He delined being Secretary. Went to the meeting in the evening—a large number present—was called on for a speech which I delivered—people apparently gratified—resolutions reported strong but good—unanimously adopted.[61]

56. The first proposed ordinance, which was amended and tabled, called for "the punishment of all vagabonds, gamblers, vagrants &c." The second, carried over to the next meeting, provided penalties for those who kept, "without license, a house or room furnished and prepared for the sale or distribution of intoxicating liquors." *Cincinnati Daily Gazette*, Jan. 6, 1841.
57. William Ellery Channing, *Emancipation* . . . (Boston, 1840).
58. Chase's letter complimented the paper for advertising a Jan. 5 meeting of those who opposed slavery in Washington, D.C. It also expressed satisfaction that the matter had been brought into the open by "men who are not members of Abolition societies; but who are tired of keeping silent upon a great question like this." *Cincinnati Daily Gazette*, Jan. 5, 1841.
59. Theodore Dwight Weld, *The Power of Congress over the District of Columbia* (New York, 1838).
60. William Jay, *A View of the Action of the Federal Government, in Behalf of Slavery* (New York, 1839).
61. According to one report, Chase "addressed the meeting at considerable length on the power and duty of Congress to prohibit, without further delay, slavery and the slave trade in the District of Columbia; and on the unconstitutionality of the various rules and practices by which Congress had abridged the right of petition on this subject." The resolutions which followed denounced the existence of slavery and the slave trade in the District of Columbia. *Cincinnati Daily Gazette*, Jan. 7, 1841.

JANY 6 WEDNESDAY   Rose late—hurried to court immediately after breakfast—attended to business there—aftwds came to office attended, desultorily, to a little business; informed that Republican refused to insert proceedings & resolutions of the meeting; proprietors of Gazette timid, but consent to publish; the Junior Editor of Gazette, alone, bold, manly, & firm[62]—recd. call from Dr. Bailey requesting me to write out portions of speech for publication—declined doing so—recd. call from Mayor,[63] on subject of a resolution requiring a certain report from him—advised him to make it, but in general terms; in ev'g attended Council; vagrant ordinance passed, ordinance to punish keepers of coffee houses lost—large committee in attendance solicitous for passage of last ordinance—Committee on Night Watch proposed summarily to dismiss an officer; opposed it & moved that the subject be again referred to the committee with instructions to enquire what watchmen have neglected official duty & in what respects. This was carried. Came home read a few pages in De Tocqueville.

JAN 31   This is the last day of the first month of the new year. It has not passed without some incidents of considerable interest to me, but by a fall which sprained my wrist, & from which I yet suffer I have been unable to record them. The close of the month finds me in health &, as to worldly affairs, moderately prosperous—my wife is as well as I could reasonably hope and my little daughter grows finely and displays, every day, new developments of intelligence & activity. I do not forget that just a year ago my little Kate was suffering from her last illness. I cannot but mourn her loss, but I endeavor to imagine her celestial bliss, and check ungrateful repining. I have this month been regular in my attendance at the Sunday School & at the Council chamber, and have endeavored though feebly to aid the cause of truth, justice & righteousness. In my own private business I have been far less active and diligent, than duty required. I have frequently indulged an impatient & captious spirit. I have been greatly deficient in charity & brotherly kindness. I have not done so much for the poor and the distressed as I might have done. Pardon, Heavenly Father, my omissions & other sins & give me a better & holier spirit

Today I rose in tolerable season & after breakfast attended the Sunday School; where more than ninety persons were in atten-

---

62. The *Daily Republican,* Jan. 7, 1841, claimed that publication of the minutes would have only inflamed emotions. The article probably appeared in the *Gazette* as a result of efforts by William Gallagher.

63. Samuel Davies.

dance / After S.S. went to church—Johns—an excellent, though unconnected discourse, on Elijah's appeal to the people at Mt Carmel to choose between God & Baal.[64] Nothing can exceed the sublimity of the narrative of this transaction as recorded in Scripture— And all descriptions of it in uninspired language are comparatively tame. After church came home read Epis. Observer[65]—some excellent articles—editorials good except the feeble imitations of Carlyle—dined & after dinner fell asleep when reading in my chair. At 4 went to meeting of Teachers of Sunday School—prayed & advised with them. They agreed at each monthly meeting hereafter to make verbal reports of the progress &c of their respective classes. Came home & tea / In evg. read voyages of Morrison & Himmaleh for Missionary & benevolent exploration[66]— After a little more reading of these, perusal of scriptures & prayer I shall go to bed—it being now 10 oclock

FEB. 13, 41   Wrote to Gen. Harrison by Maj Clarkson, recommending appointments of C. to post. office in Cincinnati, E. to consulate at Havana or some other suitable post, & G. to consulate in Europe, & advising the Gen. to make no allusions to the subject of slavery in his inaugural address[67]

FEB. 16, '41   Was at polls nearly all day recg. votes on a proposition submitted to the citizens for subscribing $200.000 [more] to stock of Cin. & Whitewater Canal.[68] Voted against proposition myself but it prevailed, in 1st Ward 288 for 99 agst

---

64. 1 Kings 18:42.
65. The *Western Episcopal Observer*, published in Cincinnati and Louisville. Stephen Gutgesell, ed., *Guide to Ohio Newspapers, 1793–1973: Union Bibliography of Ohio Newspapers Available in Ohio Libraries* (Columbus, 1974), 87.
66. *The Claims of Japan and Malaysia upon Christendom: Exhibited in Notes of Voyages Made in 1837, from Canton, in the Ship Morrison and Brig Himmaleh under the Direction of the Owners* (New York, 1839).
67. Chase's letter to William Henry Harrison, apparently ineffective, included recommendations for Charles S. Clarkson, a local client and former assistant district paymaster for the U.S. Army, Samuel Eells, and John P. Garniss. Chase to Harrison, Feb. 13, 1841 (William Henry Harrison Papers, L.C.); *Cinc. Dir. (1840)*, 139; Clarkson to Chase, Dec. 8, 1842 (Chase Papers, L.C.); Heitman, *Historical Register*, 1:308.
68. The Cincinnati and Whitewater Canal, a controversial experiment in mixed enterprise, comprised the last segment of a canal from Cincinnati to the national road at Cambridge, Ind. Cincinnati voters faced the question of whether to redirect $200,000 of city funds previously authorized for investment in the Charleston and Ohio Railroad. Cincinnati *Advertiser and Journal*, Jan. 19, 1841; *Cincinnati Daily Gazette*, Jan. 30, Feb. 17, 1841; Charles Cist, *Cincinnati in 1841: Its Early Annals and Future Prospects*, (Cincinnati, 1841), 86–93; Harry N. Scheiber, *Ohio Canal Era: A Case Study of Government and the Economy, 1820–1861* (Athens, Ohio, 1969), 131.

FEB. 17 Attended meeting of City Council— Exciting debate on ordinance to divide fines on unlicensed selling of liquors with the informant, & on resolution to subscribe $200.000 to stock of Cin. & Whitewater Canal, if so much shd. be needed to complete the work, provided the State will increase her subscription in a similar ratio[69]

FEB. 18 Rose a little before seven; breakfasted about half past 8— Went to office—spent a couple of hours in revising Mr Ball's copy of my letter to Mr. Cope on the subject of resigning the Solicitorship of the Agency of the Bank of the U States[70] and in interviews with clients. Miss Barber called on Mrs Burr's business.[71] Spencer agreed to take charge of brother A's application for patent[72] / At eleven attended meeting of Exchange Committee at Bank—took Clarkson's mortgage to foreclose—went to Court House—dont recollect of doing any thing— Coming home to dinner found Mrs & Miss Este at the door, ushered them in[73]— After dinner returned to office—began to prepare abstract of case Holladays vs Pugh & Duffield— At 3 went to Court House; had decrees in several cases confirmed—B.U.S. vs Matthews, B.U.S. vs Prendergast etal, Conklin vs Bissell[74] etal, Petit Dunning & Co vs Wade Lafayette Bank vs Young etal & perhaps others not recollected— Returned to office & made progress in abstract—after tea at Mrs Smiths resumed my

---

69. The liquor ordinance was recommitted to its author, Whig councilman Moses Brooks. The council unanimously adopted the canal measure, but conditioned the city's subscription on receipt of additional private subscriptions and on assurances that the project would be completed in 1841. *Cincinnati Daily Gazette,* Apr. 6, 8, 1840, Feb. 19, Apr. 13, 1841.

70. Chase's resignation was to be effective April 1, 1841. According to Timothy Kirby, "the immediate cause of the withdrawal of Mr. Chase is a difference of opinion about the compensation for legal services and he claiming the right to fix the amount of his own pay." Kirby to Thomas Dunlap, Feb. 17, 1841 (Chase Papers, L.C.).

71. Miss Barber may have been an employee of Mrs. O. K. Burr, a Cincinnati milliner. Burr to Chase, Mar. 10, 1841 (Chase Papers, L.C.); *Cinc. Dir. (1840),* 126.

72. Alexander Ralston Chase's patent relating to steamboat paddles. Attorney Henry Evans Spencer (1808–82) later served as the Whig mayor of Cincinnati, 1843–1851. *Cinc. Dir. (1842),* 76; Melvin G. Holli and Peter d'A. Jones, eds., *Biographical Dictionary of American Mayors, 1820–1980: Big City Mayors* (Westport, Conn., 1981), 339–40.

73. David Kirkpatrick Este (1785–1875), a judge in the superior court of Cincinnati, is known to have had three surviving daughters by two wives. The oldest (c. 1822–69), a child of Lucy Ann Harrison Este (d. 1826), eventually married Joseph Reynolds of Baltimore. The other daughters, Louisa, the future wife of William Alexander Fisher of Baltimore, and Ursula C., were offspring of Louisa Miller Este. *Appletons',* 2:377; Robson, *Biographical Encyclopædia,* 132; James Landy, *Cincinnati Past and Present: Or its Industrial History, as Exhibited in the Life-Labors of its Leading Men* (Cincinnati, 1872), 24–25; *Nat. Cyc.,* 25:134.

74. Possibly Israel M. Bissell, a Cincinnati exchange broker. *Cinc. Dir. (1842),* 94, 292.

labor— Mr. Johnston called & interview with him as to management of estate of E. C. Smith decd[75] / coming home at 9 read Philanthropist & Bible & now, after prayer, shall retire to bed

FEB. 19, 41   Rose a little before seven—dressed, musing unprofitably—prayed in private—then family prayer, reading portion of Mark—breakfasted having read morning papers—went to office & thence to Court house—was examined as witness in case of Tappin vs Magee—went at ½ past 10 to Bank—attended meeting of Board & of Ex. Committee—nothing of note transpired—returned to office at ½ past 11 & attended to divers matters till ½ past one—when came home to dinner— Mr. Garniss came in & took home Delia Picket who was here[76]— Mr. G., going to Washington on Monday, proposes to leave power of atty with me to transact some business,— I furnished Alexr. with $32 to buy $30 in gold to pay for patent—he carried his model money &c to Mr. H. E. Spencer who engaged to take them to Washington for him—after dinner returned to office— wrote Suydam, Sage & Co & Dudley Chase[77]—former on their case & deps to be taken, latter pleading inability to aid him in getting money as requested— Partly prepared dft of deed Miles to Bell for Texas land—came home at ½ past 5—Mrs Mitchell here. Spoke to her of Miss Post accompanying wife to N.O.—tea at ½ past 6—read in Chronicle a/c of report of Com. on For. Relations on affair of the Caroline[78]— At 7 attended meeting of council took little part in the discussions which arose—voted against reconsidering the vote by which licence was refused to Franklin House—also against reconsidering vote on accepting report of Committee against licence to Pfau—former lost, latter carried—moved to refer Holmes

---

75. Edmund Curtis Smith (c. 1790–1833), the father of Chase's second wife, Eliza Ann Smith Chase. "Family Memoranda" (Chase Papers, L.C.).

76. Chase seems to have referred to Delia Picket, years later, as an "adopted daughter" of John P. and Amelia Garniss. Apparently she married David Austen, Jr., of New York and died by June 1861. It is possible that she was the "Miss C. Picket" mentioned in the journal at June 30, 1840 (above). David Austen, Jr., to Chase, June 4, 1861, John P. Garniss to Chase, Jan. 15, 1850, Apr. 7, 1855 (Chase Papers, Hist. Soc. of Pa.); Chase to Austen, Mar. 16, 1867 (Chase Papers, Hist. Soc. of Pa.).

77. Ferdinand Suydam and Francis P. Sage operated a mercantile firm in New York City. Chase had several relatives named Dudley Chase. Here he probably corresponded with one of uncle Philander's sons, a student of theology preparing for ordination as a Protestant Episcopal clergyman. Philander Chase to Salmon Chase, Nov. 3, 1842 (Chase Papers, L.C.); *New York Dir. (1841–42)*, 125.

78. In Dec. 1837, the *Caroline*, a supply ship owned by American filibusterers, had been sunk by a Canadian raiding party on the Niagara River. Tempers on both sides of the border had flared, but firm action by Gen. Winfield Scott and British officials prevented the incident from escalating into war. David M. Pletcher, *The Diplomacy of Annexation: Texas, Oregon, and the Mexican War* (Columbia, Mo., 1973), 14–15.

application anew to committee carried[79]—have serious doubts whether I ought to vote for licencing any tavern—council elected Mason, marketmaster & Fields woodmeasurer[80] / coming home took up bible & read at first page to which I opened, Woe unto him that establisheth a city by iniquity &c[81]   May not this licence system be an attempt to establish a city by iniquity— Read 3 pages of Joshua & wrote above

FEB. 20, 41   Rose a little before 7—no profitable subject occupied my thoughts while dressing—private & family prayers & then breakfast—went to office about ½ past 8—H Lewis called & went with him[82]—to [see a] certain Street &c / Mr. Patterson of Missi. called for letter wh. I promised him to Mr. Webster[83]—gave it to him—went to Court House—had judgt. entered for deft in Clarkson ads Wagoner agreeably to report of referees—ret'g to office met Mr. Wade who wished to know if I had seen Mr. Lawrence about his matter[84]—said no, but wd. today— Went to Bank for that purpose— Cashr. told me that Mr. L had replied to W's proposition unfavorably—went to office Mansfield came in to ask about Patterson[85]— Johnson for loan—gave Mansfield what information I had & promised J. $45 in afternoon if I got it— Poe came in to ask about his case & also Griffin Watson a cold. man[86]—satisfied both as well as I could— Came to dinner— At abt. ½ past 2 returned to office & spent what time I could command from various interruptions in

---

79. John M. Pfau kept a tavern on Main Street. William Holmes operated Holmes's Hotel at the corner of Broadway and Market. *Cinc. Dir. (1842),* 64, 184; *Cincinnati Daily Gazette,* Feb. 23, 1841.

80. John W. Mason and William M. Field. *Cincinnati Daily Gazette,* Feb. 23, 1841.

81. Hab. 2:12.

82. Cincinnati merchant and pork packer Henry Lewis, a brother of Samuel Lewis. *Cinc. Dir. (1840),* 260; Chase to Lewis Tappan, Oct. 18, 1842 (Chase Papers, L.C.).

83. Chase's letter to Daniel Webster recommended Andrew Patterson, a former Cincinnati hatter, for the position of U.S. marshal for the southern district of Mississippi. *Cinc. Dir. (1834),* 134; Wiltse et al., *Papers of Daniel Webster,* Corres., 5:355.

84. Probably David Wade, a local lawyer; David E. Wade, prosecuting attorney of Hamilton County, 1812–29; or one of two Cincinnati merchants: Stephen J. Wade or Melancthon S. Wade (1802–68), brigadier general of U.S. volunteers, 1861–62. *Appletons',* 6:311; Robson, *Biographical Encyclopædia,* 307–8; *Cinc. Dir. (1840),* 391; Charles Theodore Greve, *Centennial History of Cincinnati and Representative Citizens* (Chicago, 1904), 1:628.

85. Edward Deering Mansfield (1801–80), graduate of West Point, author, editor of the *Cincinnati Chronicle,* professor of history at Cincinnati College, and commissioner of statistics for the state of Ohio, 1858–68. *Cinc. Dir. (1840),* 270; *DAB,* 12:255–56.

86. Probably William Poe, one of Chase's local clients who faced bankruptcy. Griffin Watson was a steward on the steamboat *Ohio Belle.* Poe to Chase, Aug. 13, 1842 (Chase Papers, L.C.); *Cinc. Dir. (1842),* 447; entry for Mar. 14, 1841, below.

March 1841   { 153 }

writing to Judge Burnet & Mr. Kelley in favor Mr. Eells[87]—first however went to Riddle's office[88]—then to L'Hommedieus where settled all outstanding accounts and recd. small balance $12 & some cents in my favor[89]—came home to tea—after tea went to Mr. Garniss who is to go to Washington tomorrow, and who has left me a power of Atty to transact his business, & has undertaken to attend to Alexr's patent for him—played a couple of games of chess with him—went to office made some entries & filed various receipts—returned home—read 3 pages Joshua—little child somewhat unwell—wife gave her some castor oil—wrote the foregoing intend reading a few pages of Carlyle's Fr. Revolution,[90] then prayer & bed—

MAR. 1. It was pretty well acertained today that the Steamboat Independence on which wife, & others proposed going to New Orleans would not be here for some days, and there was a great consultation among those intending to go down as to the best way of going. Maj. Oliver and his family concluded to go on the Swallow:[91] Mr. & Mrs Hewson determined to go on the Mailboat to Louisville and then take the Ambassador[92]— My wife and her sister were undecided but inclined to accompany Mrs Hewson

MAR. 2. This morning we finally determined to take the mail boat to Louisville and after getting every thing ready that we could think of we started about eleven o'clock in the morning. The day was fine

---

87. Chase's correspondence with Jacob Burnet and Alfred Kelley (1789–1859), a Columbus attorney and Ohio legislator, recommended Samuel Eells for the position of U.S. consul in Havana. Chase to Jacob Burnet, Feb. 21, 1841 (Burnet Papers, Cinc. Hist. Soc.); *DAB*, 10:296–97.
88. Adam N. Riddle, a partner in the Cincinnati law firm of Riddle and Roll. *Cinc. Dir. (1840)*, 333.
89. Richard F. L'Hommedieu (d. 1847) and Stephen S. L'Hommedieu (1806–75) published the *Cincinnati Daily Gazette*. Stephen also served as president of the Cincinnati, Hamilton and Dayton Railroad Company, 1848–71. *Biographical Cyclopædia*, 3:797; Robson, *Biographical Encyclopædia*, 519–20; *Cinc. Dir. (1840)*, 261; *Cincinnati Weekly Herald*, Feb. 3, 1847.
90. Thomas Carlyle, *The French Revolution: A History*, 3 vols. (London, 1837).
91. The *Independence* and the *Swallow* were sidewheel steamboats built and based at Cincinnati. A veteran of the War of 1812, William Oliver (d. ca. 1851) speculated in land in the Toledo area, was secretary of the Cincinnati Insurance Co., and served in the Ohio Senate, 1837–39. He resided on the Ohio River below Cincinnati. *Cincinnati Daily Gazette*, Mar. 1, 5, 1841; Lytle, *Merchant Vessels*, 89, 181; Gayle Thornbrough et al., eds., *The Diary of Calvin Fletcher* (Indianapolis, 1972–83), 1:96, 461, 2:107, 7:543; Waggoner, *Toledo*, 326, 370, 819; Bert J. Griswold, *Fort Wayne, Gateway of the West, 1802–1813*, Indiana Historical Collections, v. 15 (Indianapolis, 1927), 58–59, 281, 311; Gilkey, *Ohio Hundred Year Book*, 162, 164.
92. A New Orleans steamboat under the command of J. J. James. Bethuel W. Hewson was a Cincinnati exchange broker. *Louisville Daily Journal*, Mar. 2, 1841; *Cinc. Dir. (1840)*, 218.

and the company tolerably agreeable, but nothing occurred to distinguish the trip from a thousand others. At Madison an old class mate, Revd. Henry Little came on board & accompanied us to Louisville.[93]

MARCH 3   We arrived at Louisville very early and after dressing myself I told my wife that I would walk up into the town and after a while return to the boat again. I walked in the direction of Portland where the Ambassador was lying & the car coming along soon I jumped in & rode down to the place. I found all the staterooms in the ladies cabin engaged except two and returned to the Mailboat in a hack. Having bought a nursing bottle and some little articles in town, we all got into one hack & Mr. Hewson & his family into another and rode to Portland. It was my original intention to return from Louisville but I concluded, on the whole, to accompany my family a little way further down the Ohio. We started about 12 M. with quite a pleasant party on board: Mr. & Mrs Hewson, Mr. C. J Wright, Mr. Owen, Dr. Cobb,[94] Dr Drake, Mr & Mrs Humphrys a newly wedded pair from Louisville[95] & other ladies and gentlemen. This day was also very pleasant, and nothing marred our enjoyment but a cold which the baby had taken the first night on board the Pike.[96] At night this cold was quite troublesome and wife gave the little creature some hive syrup, and the next day she seemed tho' languid & somewhat unwell, considerably better. The Dr., consulted, gave it as his opinion that it was a catarrhal affection only. After dinner, having charged the Capt. & Dr. Cobb with especial watchfulness over my wife and little one I left the Ambassador & came on board the Edwd. Shippen,[97] on her way up the river. From the hurricane deck of the Shippen I waved my handkerchief in farewell to the dear ones I had left, and the next morning found myself again at the landing at Portland

---

93. Little (1800–1882) had graduated from Dartmouth in 1826. Emerson, *General Catalogue*, 239.

94. Jedediah Cobb, M.D. (1800–1860), formerly on the faculty of the Ohio Medical College, was professor of anatomy and dean of faculty at the University of Louisville. *General Catalogue of Bowdoin College . . . 1794–1950* (Brunswick, Maine, 1950), 51; *Louisville Dir. (1848–49)*, 32, 92.

95. Possibly Edward Porter Humphrey (1809–87), the pastor of Louisville's Second Presbyterian Church, 1836–53, and his first wife (d. 1844). Rossiter Johnson, ed., *The Twentieth Century Biographical Dictionary of Notable Americans . . .* (Boston, 1904; reprint, Detroit, 1968), v. 1; J. Stoddard Johnston, ed., *Memorial History of Louisville from Its Settlement to the Year 1896* (Chicago, n.d.), 2:156–57, 162; *Louisville Dir. (1848–49)*, 114.

96. In margin: "Mar. 4." The *Pike*, a 294-ton paddlewheel steamer, was built in 1838. Lytle, *Merchant Vessels*, 152.

97. A sidewheel steamer which operated out of Louisville. Ibid., 54.

MAR. 5   I walked to Louisville, 3 miles, in company with some passengers before breakfast; breakfasted at the Galt House;[98] then went to the office of my friend Ham Smith, where I wrote to my wife, & to Mr. Jewett, Mr. Stetson & Mr. Holmes,[99] and then went on board the Pike for Cincinnati. Before I left Louisville I purchased Miss Martineau's "The Hour & the Man" and was reading it all the way up.[1] It intereste[d] me greatly.

MARCH 6   Again in Cincinnati, but so early that no one was astir at home and I was fain to betake myself to Mrs Garniss' and there, not in most comfortable state await the opening of my own house.[2] In about ½ hour I succeeded in getting in. I suffered too much from my cold to do much today.

MAR. 7   Went to Church, morning St Paul's—Mr Johns, evening Christ, Mr. Brooke / wrote to wife—attended Sunday school. Still suffering much from cold.

MARCH 13—   During this week I have not accomplished a great deal, tho' I have taken some important steps. The first letter, written on Saturday was sent to my wife by the Winchester, which started I think on Monday. The next by Mr. Buchanan, who went on the Independence, I think on Wednesday.[3] I have also during the week written to my brother Edward, to my little nephew James Skinner[4] / On Wednesday evening, at the Council, I openly declared

---

98. A hotel at the corner of Main and Second Street. *Louisville Dir. (1841)*, 36.

99. Chase was asking Isaac Appleton Jewett (1808–53), a New Orleans author and attorney, to guide his wife on a tour of the city. The reasons for Chase's correspondence with Sylvester Holmes, pastor of the North Congregational Church in New Bedford, Mass., and with Charles Stetson, a Cincinnati merchant and official at the Ohio Life Insurance and Trust Company, are not known. *Cinc. Dir. (1840)*, 368; *New Bedford Dir. (1839)*, 24, 85; Jewett to Chase, Mar. 16, 1841, Stetson to Chase, Dec. 8, 1846 (Chase Papers, L.C.).

1. Harriet Martineau, *The Hour and the Man. A Historical Romance*, 3 vols. (London, 1841).

2. Chase's house was on Broadway, between Fourth and Fifth Streets. John and Amelia Garniss lived on the same block, at the corner of Broadway and Fourth. *Cinc. Dir. (1840)*, 136, 190.

3. The *Winchester*, a sidewheel steamboat, operated between Cincinnati and New Orleans. Robert Buchanan (b. 1797) was a partner in the Cincinnati mercantile firm of Buchanan and Shaw. *Cincinnati Daily Gazette*, Mar. 4, 1841; Lytle, *Merchant Vessels*, 205; Robson, *Biographical Encyclopædia*, 62–63; *Cinc. Dir. (1840)*.

4. James Ralston Skinner (d. 1893), commonly called "Ralston," was the son of Chase's sister, Janette Logan Chase Skinner, and her husband, Josiah K. Skinner. Skinner later studied with Chase, managed his property during the early 1850s, practiced law with him, and served as major and judge advocate of U.S. volunteers, 1862–65. *Cinc. Dir. (1850–51)*, 249; ibid. (1855), 201; Heitman, *Historical Register*, 1:890; Skinner to Chase, Jan. 12, 1841, Jan. 15, 1850 (Chase Papers, L.C.).

my resolution to vote for no more licences to sell intoxicating drinks whether to taverns or other houses, and I took some pains to prevent the grant of a licence to a new house proposed to be established on Main Street in which I succeeded.[5] I don't know what the effect may be on me personally, but I believe I have done right— Recd. invitation to address Societies Marietta College, next July[6]—

MARCH 14 Went to church this morning to St Pauls—Mr. Johns preached / Attended Sunday School. Read Keith on Prophecies[7]— Mr. Ball came in—conversation almost wholly unprofitable— Read Missy. Herald & bible.

MARCH 15. Rose somewhat earlier than usual this morning. Private prayer—dull—began letter to Lizzy—family prayer,—breakfast—finished letter to Lizzy read newspapers—went to office. Attended to business of several clients—Mr. Pearton bookkeeper Downes & Haven[8]—sent Mr. Ball to Lebanon—more clients, Col. Dudley, Maj Clarkson—Mr. Justice— Left letter for Lizzy and March No. Repository with Hartwell to be sent on board the Ohio Belle[9]— afterwards, Watson the Steward coming to the office, desired him to take note to Lizzy and see if she wanted any thing which cd. be sent from here. Went to Bank, Exchge Committee—thence to Court house—enquired about injunction against Watson's Ejectment— Notified Morris[10] of intention to take deps in case of Justice vs Plough tomorrow— Went to dinner— Wrote to Revd. Mr. Holmes,

---

5. Chase's declaration corresponded with the wishes of a petition recently presented to the city council by more than three thousand Cincinnatians. *Cincinnati Daily Gazette*, Mar. 12, 1841.
6. The letter also announced Chase's election as an honorary member of the college's Alpha Kappa Society. R. B. Ford et al. to Chase, Feb. 27, 1841 (Chase Papers, Hist. Soc. of Pa.).
7. The best known works of Scottish Presbyterian minister Alexander Keith included *The Evidence of Prophecy* . . . (London, [1830?]); *The Signs of the Times as Denoted by the Fulfillment of Historical Predictions* . . . (Edinburgh, 1832); and *Sketch of the Evidence from Prophecy* . . . (Edinburgh, 1823).
8. Downes and Haven apparently faced allegations of fraud. Flamen Ball to Chase, Aug. 31, 1841; Chase to Ebenezer Lane, June 27, 1844 (Chase Papers, Hist. Soc. of Pa.); Aaron S. Lippincott to Rowland G. Mitchell, Oct. 2, 1841 (Chase Papers, L.C.).
9. A sidewheel steamer which ran between Cincinnati and New Orleans. George H. Hartwell was a partner in the Cincinnati firm of Hartwell and Atherton, merchants and steamboat agents. Chase probably sent his wife *The Universalist and Ladies' Repository* 9 (Mar. 1841): 361–400. *Cincinnati Daily Gazette*, Mar. 11, 1841; Lytle, *Merchant Vessels*, 143; *Cinc. Dir. (1842)*, 179.
10. Probably lawyer and former U.S. Senator Thomas Morris (1776–1844). An antislavery Democrat, he was the Liberty party's nominee for the vice presidency in 1844. *DAB*, 13:226–27; *Cinc. Dir. (1840)*, 295.

March 1841 { 157 }

St Louis, J. Scott Harrison, Northbend[11]—paid milk bill, $25 to Miner[12]—adjustment of Mr's a/c & a long consultation with Downes & Haven closed the afternoon—went to Court house and directed Sheff to meet me with exn. vs D. & H. at my office tomorrow, before 9[13]—tea—visit at Mrs Garniss frightful story about P & girl living with him—read law of admn.—wrote foregoing—now prayer & bed—

MAR. 20   Greatly disappointed—getting no letter from my wife— Miss Hewson having recd. one fr Mr. Hewson, who went in the same boat, dated on the 12th, the boat having arrived on the 10th— Wrote to wife—sent one letter by New Orleans steamboat the other by mail— Went to Mrs Hewson in eve'g hop'g to hear something of her—in vain

MAR. 21 SUNDAY   Rose as early as usual for the last few days but much too late— Attended Sunday School, but did less good than might with reflection & preparation— Hoping to get letter from wife, sent Warren to river—again disappointed— Attended Church—Mr. Johns "Add to your faith, godliness"[14]— After church read on subject of Temperance, with view to oppose farther licencing of houses for sale of liquor by City Council— Also read a little in Missy. Herald & some excellent practical articles in the N.Y. Evangelist— In evg. church—Mr. Johns—"Whose faith follow: considering the end of their conversation—"[15] A memoir of Bishop White with some practical reflections[16]

MARCH 22   The day has been warm & genial, but no letter from my wife and this disappointment is enough to rob the day of half its brightness to me. I am saying to myself all the time, why don't I hear from Lizzy? I wonder what she is doing now!

---

   11. Chase asked Sylvester Holmes to enquire about the welfare of his youngest brother, William F. Chase, while on a visit to St. Louis. Chase wrote John Scott Harrison (1804–78), the son of William Henry Harrison and a future congressman, about money owed to a client. Holmes to Chase, Mar. 30, 1841 (Chase Papers, L.C.); *Appletons'*, 3:98; Harrison to Chase, Mar. 16, 1841 (Chase Papers, Hist. Soc. of Pa.).
   12. Possibly John L. Miner; the Cincinnati wholesale grocery firm of Irwin and Minor; Thomas H. Minor, a partner in that company; or John D. Minor, one of the firm's clerks. *Cinc. Dir. (1840)*, 290.
   13. That is, Chase met the sheriff in regard to an execution against Downes and Haven.
   14. 1 Pet. 1:5–7.
   15. Heb. 13:7.
   16. William White, *Memoirs of the Protestant Episcopal Church in the United States of America* . . . (Philadelphia, 1820).

The foliage has been unusually backward this Spring. The buds are beginning to develope themselves on the trees in the yard and a few days like this will bring out the leaves in abundance.

I have been trying today to prepare a case for argument in the Supreme Court, but have been greatly interrupted. Several clients called & some who were not clients and distracted my attention greatly. Was obliged to go to the meeting of the Exchange Committee. A draft of Ludlow on Scott Harrison was discounted for me, and I paid a note due to morrow for $926

In the afternoon two gentlemen called to ask me to attend a meeting to morrow evening at the Court House. The meeting is called as a meeting of the friends of equal rights and privileges & opponents of the present course of the Council. Many friends of the temperance reform think the call is designed for them. It is in fact promulgated by the enemies of the reform. The gentlemen thought that a majority of the meeting would be friends of temperance and that obnoxious resolutions if their true character should be exposed could be defeated / They wished me to be present & debate the resolutions. I promised to be there and to enter into the debate, if circumstances made it proper to do so.

Yesterday evening Mrs Hinsdale, mother of Mrs Burr, a client of mine, died.[17] A short time ago, calling on Mrs Burr as she was just starting for New York on business, this old lady asked me to stay a short time after her daughter had gone and I was much interested by the simple piety which her conversation displayed. She was then well. She is now gone, I believe to Heaven / Her daughter is not yet returned from New York.

This evening Miles & his brother called to pay the rent of the Clifton farm.[18] After this business done, I went to Mrs Garniss where I remained an hour or two. Having returned wrote foregoing.

MAR. 28 This is Sunday—always a welcome day to me, though in one sense it can hardly be called a day of rest. Rose as usual—after breakfast read a little while Dr. Grant's interesting account of his journey to the Mountain District of the Independent Nestorians[19]—went to Sunday school and after to church—Mr.

---

17. Elizabeth Hinsdale (c. 1780–1841). *Cincinnati Daily Gazette*, Mar. 30, 1841.

18. Clifton was a neighborhood immediately north of Cincinnati in Mill Creek Township. Chase either owned the farm or managed it for the heirs of James C. Ludlow. C. S. Clarkson to Chase, Oct. 23, 1842, July 7, 1848, George Smith to Chase, Jan. 29, 1842, Robert Spiller to Chase, Oct. 31, 1842, memorandum of will of James C. Ludlow, Mar. 19, 1841 (Chase Papers, L.C.); *Titus' Atlas of Hamilton County, Ohio* . . . (Philadelphia, 1869), 7, 63.

19. The article about Asahel Grant (1807–44), a physician and Presbyterian missionary, appeared in *Missionary Herald*, Mar. 1841. *DAB*, 7:485–86.

Johns preached—Dr. Colton read the service[20]— Having come home read further missionary accounts & works of Taylor[21]—in afternoon attended meeting of Sunday School—opened with prayer by Mr. Johns—closed with singing / Afterwards read Dymond's Essays, Temperance Documents & Bible[22]—reading desultory & of course comparatively unprofitable.

Mrs Hinsdale buried today—her daughter Mrs Burr having arrived last night.

APL. 10[23] Today the distressing intelligence of the death of the President of the United States was recd. here. At the courthouse, the Supreme Court being in session, Judge Wright privately suggested to the Judges the propriety of adjourment. They thought it inexpedient & declined. The bar was much disappointed that this customary tribute of respect should be withheld in this very peculiar case and at the request of some members I drew up the following written paper addressed to the Court— "The undersigned members of the bar respectfully suggest to the Court the propriety of an adjournment. The President of the United States is no more. The country suffers a great calamity. This community is bereaved of its most honored citizen." This paper was signed by all the members of the bar (except two) then at the Courthouse and I presented it to the Court. After the conclusion of the case then in hearing the Court adjourned.

When I came down to my office it was proposed to have an extra meeting of the City Council and take proper measures. A special meeting was accordingly held at which I offered sundry resolutions expressing the deep sense of bereavement felt by the council, their high estimation of the public services and private virtues of the deceased and their profound sympathy with mourning family. After this I attended a numerous meeting of citizens held in open air on Third Street opposite the Henrie House. Judge Burnet presided. Appropriate resolutions were adopted and a committee of twenty

---

20. Chauncey Colton, D.D., the rector of Grace Episcopal Church. *Cinc. Dir. (1842)*, x, 375.

21. Jeremy Taylor, *The Whole Works of the Right Rev. Jeremy Taylor . . . with an Essay, Biographical and Critical . . .* , 3 vols. (London, 1835). Chase owned this edition of the works of Taylor, a seventeenth-century Anglican bishop. *Catalogue of a Most Superb Collection of Extremely Rare and Elaborate Furniture . . . Formed by the Late Hon. Salmon Portland Chase*, ([New York, 1900]), 95; *DNB*, 19:422–29.

22. Jonathan Dymond, *Essays on the Principles of Morality, and on the Private and Political Rights and Obligations of Mankind* (London, 1829); American Temperance Society, *Permanent Temperance Documents of the American Temperance Society* (Boston, 1835).

23. Chase's page headings for this entry call it April 8. The entry immediately following is for April 9. Perhaps Chase recorded his description of April 8 (and 9?) on the 10th.

six persons was appointed to act in concert with the committee appointed by the City Council to take further measures for the expression of the general grief. In the evening Mr. Gallagher took tea with me and after tea Judge Burnet called and stated that a portion of the Committee had resolved to cause the bells of the several churches to be tolled tomorrow. Mr. Gallagher agreed to see that the design was carried into effect at some of the churches—Judge Burnet took upon himself to attend to others and I engaged to call upon the Roman Catholic Bishop and ask him to call the bells under his control to be tolled also.[24] After some interesting conversation in relation to the deceased and his successor Judge Burnet took his leave.

AP. 9. '41 Today almost all the shops are closed and the toll of the bells is indescribably solemn. Every countenance wears an anxious expression. The Supreme Court sat, but I was there but a few moments. At Eleven I went to Church the day being Good Friday. Mr. Johns preached. The concluding prayers were framed with reference to the death of the President. In the afternoon I attended a joint meeting of the two committees / It was agreed to request the acting President to appoint a day of fasting humiliation & prayer and to commemorate the sad event by an eulogy on the deceased to be delivered at a time & place hereafter to be designated. It was proposed that Judge Burnet should be the Eulogist. The proposition greatly affected him. "I can't do it" he said "I could as easily pronounce an eulogy on my father or my brother. The utterance would choke me. No man knows the relations which have existed between us. He and I were the last of a band of thirty who were associated here forty five years ago. He is gone and I am left alone." The Judge greatly affected could not proceed. There was hardly an unmoistened eye in the room. It was proposed to ask permission of the family to bring his remains home to be buried in the City or at North Bend. This proposition elicited some discussion but was finally adopted—I rode up to the Court House afterwards with Maj Clarkson.

AP. 12, '41 Tried the case of Kempers Lessee vs Cin. Col. & Wooster Turnpike Co.[25] Court decided that a Co. having, by char-

---

24. Irish-born John Baptist Purcell (1800–1883), consecrated bishop of Cincinnati in 1833, became archbishop in 1850. *DAB*, 15:266–68; *Appletons'*, 5:136.

25. As Chase indicated, the issue was whether a company could take land to construct a toll house outside the chartered right of way for a road. In 1842 Charles Fox argued the case before the state supreme court and won a reversal. *Lessee of Presley Kemper v. Cincinnati, Columbus and Wooster Turnpike Co.*, 11 Ohio 392.

ter, a right to take land for road & to erect toll gates, had also a right to take land whereon to erect a toll house. Thought decision wrong. Commenced examination of witnesses in Lessee of Ludlow's Heirs vs Heirs of Barr.[26]

AP. 13, '41 This day my little Kate is 8 months old—not a tooth yet and hardly an articulate sound. Finished examination of witnesses in Barr case. Court suggested a general verdict for defendant subject to opinion of court on points of law—this course, against my judgment was agreed to. Attended examination of some law students in the evening.

MAY 23, 41 Yesterday, was Sunday.[27] At the Sunday School in the morning was pleased to see so many in attendance—addressed teachers & pupils briefly on order &c— Several new subscribers to Youth's Temp. Advocate[28] among little folks— At home read Bacchus[29]— Am fully persuaded that no alcoholic wine was used at Institution of Lord's Supper and that the use of such ought to be discontinued everywhere— Conversed with my dear wife / She said that if she should die she should have great pain in parting with little Kate, but did not doubt that the Lord would take care of her. "You dont know" said she "how delighted I was when you kneeled down with me after we were married. I thought I should be inexcusable if I did not become pious—all difficulties seemed to be taken out of the way." My dear wife is not well, though, I trust, not in great danger.— It is delightful to feel that she sympathizes with me in religious views and feelings and to believe that she is indeed a renewed child of God. How much sanctity, how much tenderness does this thought add to the marriage relation— At church at night. Mr. Johns preached.

MAY 23, '41[30] Rather late up this morning & slow in dressing—dull in family prayer—read three pages in Chronicles—mostly

---

26. Presumably the continuation of a land title dispute which had reached the state supreme court in 1828. In 1839 Chase agreed to represent the claims of Israel Ludlow's heirs. *Lessee of Ludlow's heirs v. William Barr*, 3 Ohio 388; agreement of Apr. 18, 1839 (Chase Papers, L.C.).
27. This entry pertains to Sunday, May 23, but apparently was written on the 24th.
28. A publication of the American Temperance Union. Emil Christopher Vigilante, "The Temperance Reform in New York State, 1829–1851" (Ph.D. diss., New York University, 1964), 25.
29. Ralph Barnes Grindrod, *Bacchus. An Essay on the Nature, Causes, Effects, and Cure, of Intemperance,* ed. by Charles A. Lee, 3rd ed. (New York, 1840).
30. This entry probably describes May 24.

names—all that is left of "men of renown"[31]—&, at fam. prayer, a chapter of acts[32]—Paul's imprisonment at Jerusalem & transmission to Cæsarea—& Lysias letter—how natural this letter—takes as much credit as he can, suppresses some circumstances & supplies others so as to make himself appear as well as possible in the eyes of the governor—quite in character for a man who "with a great sum obtained this freedom."[33] After breakfast about half past eight went to office—going saw Mansfield & Gallagher told Mansfield to copy "Mary Townes" & strike off extra copies[34]—said he wd this week—

1843

AP. 30, 43   Up late—attended Sunday School—few in attendance on account of bad weather—contribution for missionary purposes small—attended church—more free from wandering thoughts than usual—Winthrop[35]—good sermon on With the heart man believeth unto righteousness & with the mouth confession is made unto Salvation[36]— He distinguished faith working by love & purifying the heart from spurious faith, whether imaginative or intellectual— insisted on vital faith & open profession of religion— Coming home read, before & after dinner Bishop Chase's Reminiscences & D'Aubigne's Reformation[37] / The Bishop had more trials & more pleasures in England than I was aware.[38] His courage, patience, faith & forbearance were exemplary / I exceedingly admire the char-

31. The genealogy appears in 1 Chron. 1–9.
32. Acts 23.
33. Acts 22:28.
34. Townes, a resident of Cincinnati since 1831, was an alleged runaway slave. Earlier in the month, Chase had successfully fought her extradition to Kentucky largely by questioning the validity of the affidavit issued for her arrest. Chase probably wanted either copies of articles related to the case or reprints of the legal argument—items which newspapermen Edward Deering Mansfield and William Gallagher would have been able to provide. Stephen Middleton, "Ohio and the Antislavery Activities of Attorney Salmon Portland Chase, 1830–1849" (Ph.D. diss., Miami University, 1987), 105–7.
35. Edward B. Winthrop, pastor of St. Paul's Episcopal Church. *Cinc. Dir. (1843)*, 381.
36. Rom. 10:10.
37. Philander Chase, *The Reminiscences of Bishop Chase* . . . (Peoria and New York, 1841–43), initially appeared in a series of installments. Jean Henri Merle D'Aubigné, *Réformation du Seizième Siècle*, 5 vols. (Paris, 1835–53), was available in French and English editions.
38. Philander Chase had traveled to England in 1824 in search of money to establish an Episcopal seminary in Ohio. Despite opposition stemming from fears of competition with the church's General Seminary in New York, the bishop gained enough support by late 1824 to establish Kenyon College. Raymond Wolf Albright, *A History of the Protestant Episcopal Church* (New York, [1964]), 204–5; *DAB*, 4:26–27.

acter of Luther. How he endured seeing the invisible! He lived, almost, out of the body. To him the clouds, the winds, the thunders & the lightnings uttered voices. Voices spoke to him from the recesses of his own heart. He saw what no man else saw. He heard what no man else heard. After tea went to church with Mrs Garniss—Winthrop read the service—Lounsbery preached[39]—Christ church—sermon good. "What shall it profit a man if he gain the whole world & lose his own soul or what shall a man give in exchange for his soul."[40] Returning home found Mr. & Mrs Ball—conversation not so christian as it should have been. Spoke harshly of one whom, though I have reason to believe he has injured me greatly, I should rather forgive. After they went read some more of D'Aubigne. & Friend Reynolds[41] called about obtaining process to prevent a woman from taking away a colored child, whose mother, brought here by her mistress has escaped from her. Gave him necessary instructions / Wife has suffered much from pains today, & has coughed some— Little Kate has not appeared to be very well, Jane has been solitary & reserved, making wife feel quite unpleasantly.[42]

MAY 25–6 Attended Liberty meeting at Elkton, Preble Co to nom. for Congress in place of "that miserable doughface J B Weller" on invitation of Lorenzo & Robert Stubbs & Walter R. Wheeler, Com. who were pleased to call on me as "so faithful a champion[43]

---

39. Possibly the Rev. Edward Lounsbury of Toledo. George Franklin Smythe, *A History of the Diocese of Ohio Until the Year 1918* (Cleveland, 1931), 276.

40. Matt. 16:26.

41. Chase might refer to Wiley Reynolds, Cincinnati house painter, antislavery activist, and pastor of the city's African Methodist Episcopal Church. Aside from its use by Quakers, the title "Friend" was also commonly employed by opponents of slavery. Benjamin Stanton to Chase, Oct. 10, 1844, James A. Shedd to Chase, Aug. 30, 1844, William Steel to David Putnam, Jr., Sept. 5, 1843 (Chase Papers, L.C.); *The Address and Reply on the Presentation of a Testimonial to S. P. Chase, by the Colored People of Cincinnati* (Cincinnati, 1845), 35; *Cinc. Dir. (1843)*, 397; ibid. (1846), 316.

42. Jane Chase (b. 1824 or 1825) was the daughter of Chase's brother Alexander and Stella King Chase. Jane, who married Robert Auld, also lived with her uncles Edward and William Chase at times as she grew up. A. R. Chase to Chase, Nov. 9, 1836, June 11, 1846, Isabel R. D. Skinner to Chase, Jan. 19, 1837, Chase to Edward I. Chase, Feb. 5, 1848, "Family Memoranda" (Chase Papers, L.C.); Flamen Ball to Chase, Aug. 5, 1845 (Chase Papers, Hist. Soc. of Pa.); T. J. C. Williams and Folger McKinsey, *History of Frederick County, Maryland . . .* ([Frederick, Md.], 1910; reprint, Baltimore, 1979), 2:1242.

43. This entry is from memoranda at the end of Journal I. Lorenzo Stubbs (b. 1818), Robert Stubbs, and Walter R. Wheeler were Liberty party activists. The convention selected Dr. M. C. Williams of Camden to challenge John B. Weller (1812–75), incumbent Democratic congressman, 1839–45. Weller later became chairman of the U.S.–Mexican Boundary Commission, 1849–50, and Union Democratic senator

JUNE 16 FRIDAY   Went to the office this morning & attended to some business— About half past ten had Message from wife that she wished me to come home—hastened to her—nurse had been sent for—proposed to send for Dr. Rives, but she wished to wait for nurse—after a few moments however sent—Dr. & nurse came & about a quarter before one a little Stranger was ushered into the world: another daughter.[44]

I cannot be sufficiently thankful that my dear wife has passed through the crisis so well—Dr. Rives dined with me—in the afternoon spent about an hour at office.

JUNE 17 SATURDAY   Lizzy spent a very comfortable day—the babe sleeps constantly— Mr. & Mrs Smith, from Hickman Co & Mrs Kents Mrs S's mother arrd. went to Horticultural exhibition[45] with Mr. S. & Mrs K & aft'wds rode

JUNE 18 SUNDAY   Was at Sunday school this morn'g—but did not go to our church— Lizzy well—requires, the Dr. says, no medicine—baby sleeps / In evening went with Mrs G & Mrs Kent— Spent part of afternoon with Mrs Smith who suffers from a hip complaint & is unable to walk but cheerful—heard in morn'g sermon from Lewis at 6th Pres. Church / Text "Woe unto you Scribes &c"[46] Mr. Smith went with me.

JUNE 19 MOND'Y   Mr. & Mrs Smith left the city for Louisville—Dr. Mussey gives Mrs S. some encouragement as to recovery but nothing positive[47]— Mrs Kent came to our house— Sent letter to Judge King[48] & two resolutions by Mr Lewis— Lizzy still improves—baby still sleeps

---

from California, 1851–57. *DAB*, 19:628–29; *History of Preble County, Ohio, with Illustrations and Biographical Sketches* (Philadelphia, 1881), 188, 309, 312; *Philanthropist*, May 3, 24, June 7, 21, 1843.

44. "Lizzie" Chase (1843–44), probably the namesake of her mother, Eliza Ann Chase. She was her father's fourth daughter and the second to be named Lizzie (the elder Lizzie, born in 1842, having died at the age of three months). "Family Memoranda" (Chase Papers, L.C.); *Tri-Weekly Cincinnati Gazette*, July 30, 1844.

45. A display of flowers and fruits grown by Cincinnatians which had opened the previous Saturday. *Cincinnati Daily Chronicle*, June 10, 1843.

46. Methodist clergyman, attorney, educator, and Liberty party activist Samuel Lewis (1799–1854) preached from Matt. 23. *DAB*, 11:223–24.

47. Reuben Dimond Mussey (1780–1866) was professor of surgery at the Medical College of Ohio. *DAB*, 13:372–73.

48. Leicester King (1789–1856), a former state senator and associate judge on the court of common pleas for Trumbull County, was Liberty party candidate for governor, 1842 and 1844. *History of Trumbull and Mahoning Counties with Illustrations and Biographical Sketches* (Cleveland, 1882), 1:309–10.

June 1843 { 165 }

JUNE 20 TUESDAY   Mrs Kent left us on "Montgomery"[49] for Greenupsburgh—amusing scene between French gentleman & Capt of Boat— I have concluded not to attend Anti Slavery Convention at Bloomingburgh[50]— Lizzy still improves—baby opens her eyes a little—Dr. lets Lizzy have some strawberries

JUNE 21 WEDN'Y   Lizzy still continues to improve—baby nurses well when not asleep which is the greater part of the time

JUNE 22 THURSDY   Ditto as to Lizzy & baby— Dr. allows Lizzy a broiled chicken— A meeting of Vestry of St Paul's at my house in evening— I stated that I had recd. letter from Mr. Butler declining our invitation to visit Cincinnati & refusing positively to leave his present charge[51]— A letter from Dr. Upfold recommending Dr. Proal of Utica was laid before the meeting & vestry agreed to authorize committee to correspond further & if satisfied to call Dr. P. to rectorship[52]

JUNE 23 FRIDAY   Ditto as to mother & child—forgot to call at Franklin Bank to take up note to Hinkle[53]—was busy in office greater part of day

JUNE 24 SATY   Tendered amt note to F. Bank except protest—refused—was at court in morning—heard Judge Caldwell pronounce an opinion as to widows right to improve wild land assigned her for dower[54] & an argt. by Messrs Coffin & Pugh as to right to decree for amt. of note not alleged to be due nor otherwise

---

49. A 163-ton steamboat under the command of Elisha Bennett. Charles Henry Ambler, *A History of Transportation in the Ohio Valley*... (Glendale, Calif., 1932), 170.

50. The June 22 anniversary meeting of the Ohio State Anti-Slavery Society. *Philanthropist*, July 5, 1843.

51. Clement Moore Butler (1810–90), rector of St. John's Church, Georgetown, D.C. He was later chaplain of the U.S. Senate, 1849–53, and minister at Christ Church, Cincinnati, 1854–57. *Appletons'*, 1:478; C. P. McIlvaine to Chase, Aug. 12, 1843 (Chase Papers, Hist. Soc. of Pa.).

52. George Upfold (1796–1872) held the position of rector at Trinity Church in Pittsburgh. Pierre Alexis Proal (d. 1857) served as rector of Utica's Trinity Episcopal Church, 1836–57. Chase and the committee were interested in Proal's salary requirements and attitude toward ecclesiastical authority, temperance, and the anti-slavery movement. Upfold to Chase, July 10, 1843 (Chase Papers, L.C.); *Appletons'*, 6:211; Samuel W. Durant, *History of Oneida County* (Philadelphia, 1878), 323; Pomeroy Jones, *Annals and Recollections of Oneida County* (Rome, N.Y., 1851), 572.

53. Either Anthony H. Hinkle, a bookbinder, or Philip Hinkle (1811–80), a carpenter and innovator in the use of woodworking machinery and ready-made houses. *Biographical Cyclopædia*, 6:1347–48; *Cinc. Dir. (1843)*, 163.

54. William B. Caldwell (1808–76) presided at Hamilton County's court of common pleas. *Cinc. Dir. (1843)*, 63; *Nat. Cyc.*, 7:545.

mentioned than by reference to mortgage wh describes it[55]— At office spent time chiefly in preparing a defence for a client sued for the penalty given by fugitive act of 1793[56] / P.M. wrote Dr. Upfold & Bishop McIlvaine about supply of our church & Dr. Proal—in postscript to each letter spoke of the subject of slavery—of the action of the Penn. Convention in exscinding the African Churches & of the prop. of the Spt. of Missions for a McDonough Institute![57] Dr. Aydelotte called—read me letter to be addd. to Trustees Woodwd. Coll.[58] Dr. McIlvaine called abt Dorsey lots[59]— Rode with Mrs Garniss, Jane & Kate to Mrs Ludlow's—took tea—Isl. L. Ludlow & wife & Mr. Chas Jones of N.O. about to be married (pity) to Charlotte Ludlow were there.[60] Came home & called at Dr. Baileys,

55. Cincinnati attorneys Charles Dustin Coffin (1805–80), U.S. congressman, 1837–39, and judge of the Hamilton County Superior Court, 1845–47; and Jordan A. Pugh. *Bio. Dir. U.S. Cong.*, 803; *Biographical Cyclopædia*, 1:83; *Cinc. Dir. (1843)*, 281.

56. In April 1842, John Van Zandt of Hamilton County was discovered transporting a group of fugitive slaves from Kentucky. Wharton Jones, the slaves' owner, brought suit against Van Zandt under the fugitive slave act of 1793. Chase and Thomas Morris represented Van Zandt before the U.S. circuit court in Cincinnati. In the July 1843 court term, the jury awarded Jones $1,200 damages. Another suit, in which Jones sought an additional $500 penalty, went to the U.S. Supreme Court, where Chase and William H. Seward defended Van Zandt. In both courts Chase argued technical points relating to the fugitive slave law, but also contended that the 1793 act was contrary to the Northwest Ordinance of 1787 and the U.S. Constitution. In Mar. 1847 the Supreme Court ruled against Van Zandt. Chase stated that Van Zandt, who died by about mid-1848, was the model for John Van Trompe in Harriet Beecher Stowe's *Uncle Tom's Cabin*. Chase to J. T. Trowbridge, Mar. 18, 1864 (Chase Papers, Cinc. Hist. Soc.); *Western Law Journal* 1 (Oct. 1843): 2–14; ibid., 1 (Nov. 1843): 56–69; *Jones v. Van Zandt*, 5 How. 215 (1847); *Reports of Cases Argued and Determined in the Federal Courts held in Ohio*, v. 2 (Norwalk, Ohio, 1900), 220–23, 652–57; Salmon P. Chase, *Reclamation of Fugitives from Service: An Argument for the Defendant . . . in the Case of Wharton Jones vs. John Vanzandt* (Cincinnati, 1847).

57. In March 1843, *Spirit of Missions*, official publication of the Protestant Episcopal Board of Missions, asserted that outright emancipation was impractical, presented a colonization plan requiring slaves to earn their freedom over fifteen or sixteen years, and proposed that the church establish a special plantation based on this model. According to Bishop McIlvaine, the idea was "universally condemned" at the next Board of Missions meeting. The editor retracted the suggestions in July 1843. "A letter of John McDonough, on African Colonization . . . ," *Spirit of Missions* 8 (Mar. 1843): 68–75; "Proceedings of the Board of Missions," ibid., 8 (July 1843): 228–29; C. P. McIlvaine to Chase, June 29, 1843 (Chase Papers, Hist. Soc. of Pa.).

58. Benjamin Parkham Aydelott, M.D. (1795–1860), was president of Woodward College, a private Cincinnati school founded in 1831. Chase had served as a trustee since Apr. 1841. Aydelott, *An Address on the Origin, Character and Advantages of the Woodward College . . .* ([Cincinnati, 1836?]); *Cinc. Dir. (1843)*, 24; Goss, *Cincinnati*, 2:407; Charles Satterly to Chase, Apr. 16, 1841 (Chase Papers, L.C.); Wallace, *North American Authors*, 18.

59. G. Dorsey was apparently an attorney from New Orleans. John Young to W. G. W. Gano, Feb. 12, 1842 (Chase Papers, L.C.)

60. Josephine Dunlop Ludlow (1797–1841), the wife of James C. Ludlow; her brother-in-law, Israel L. Ludlow, a local farmer; her sister-in-law, Helen A. Ludlow; her daughter, Charlotte Chambers Ludlow; and her future son-in-law, Charles A. Jones (1815–51), an attorney, writer, and poet. *Appletons'*, 3:463; Arthur E. Cooper,

just returned fr. Bloomingburgh Convention—the best yet held in the state—1500 people—excellent speeches, King, Lewis, Morris Hudson[61]—& others—enthusiastic & resolute— Lizzy & baby still doing finely—Lizzy sitting up most of day

JUNE 25 SUNDAY   Up at 6—too late by mu[ch]—private prayer cold & wandering—fam'y Scrip. reading & prayer in library— breakfast Sunday School—Mr. Buehler of Phila called at Sundy school[62]—also young man about meeting on Tuesday of ladies for Bethel S.S Library[63]—gave notice for the meeting to Mr. Winthrop— Mr. B—— in my pew— Mr. Winthrop preached—dinner— short nap—Scripture, temperance tale & life of Chrysostom— meeting of Sunday School Teachers— Mr. Buehler called to tea— Mr B. Mrs Garniss, Jane & self to Christ Church—Mr. Brooke— excellent discourse—home about half past nine—Lizzy after being very well all day now complains of headache—baby still doing first rate—Kate unwell—on Friday & Saty she took turpentine Spts morn'g & eveg for worms & this morn'g dose castor oil—

JUNE 26 MONDY   Rose late—in private & family prayer cold—alas when shall I overcome wandering thoughts & worldly imaginations—breakfast late obliged to send for bread— Mr. Buehler & Mr. Headry (last introduced by Mr. B. F. Wade)[64] called at office / Discussed with him H. principles of Liberty men as distinguished from abolitionists— Went to court house—jury dismissed— Saw Mr. Lewis about Mrs Williams dower case[65]—attended Sale of Ludlow lots west of Elm & not far south of Hamilton road[66]—sale good—all

"Col. Cornelius Ludlow," *Proceedings of the New Jersey Historical Society*, ser. 3, 3 (1898): 50; *Cinc. Dir. (1840)*, 443; unpublished guide to Ludlow-Dunlop-Chambers Collec., Univ. of Wyoming; deed of sale, Israel L. and Helen A. Ludlow to William Green, Apr. 1835 (Chase Papers, L.C.); *A History and Biographical Cyclopædia of Butler County, Ohio* . . . (Cincinnati, 1882), 89.

61. Leicester King; Samuel Lewis; Thomas Morris, who presided over the gathering; and T. B. Hudson. *Philanthropist*, July 5, 1843.
62. William Buehler, Philadelphia merchant and manager of the American Sunday School Union, 1841–42. *Phila. Dir. (1843)*, 35; *The Seventeenth Annual Report of the American Sunday-School Union* (Philadelphia, 1841), 4.
63. Probably related to the Bethel African Methodist Church or the nondenominational Bethel Chapel. *Cinc. Dir. (1843)*, 11–12.
64. Benjamin Franklin Wade (1800–1878), prosecuting attorney of Ashtabula County, 1835–37; Ohio state senator, 1837–38, 1841–42; judge of Ohio's third judicial court, 1847–51; Whig, later Republican, U.S. senator, 1851–69. *Bio. Dir. U.S. Cong.*, 1989; *DAB*, 19:303–5.
65. Probably Mrs. Eunice Williams, a client. *Cinc. Dir. (1843)*, 376; Samuel Lewis to Chase, Jan. 16, 1844 (Chase Papers, Hist. Soc. of Pa.).
66. The sale, ordered by the Hamilton County Court of Common Pleas, featured sixty building lots from the estate of James C. Ludlow. Chase and his partner, Flamen Ball, were attorneys for the transaction. *Daily Cincinnati Enquirer*, June 24, 1843.

over ⅔, some 2ce & some 3ce[67] the appraisement— Came home to dinner— Went to office—idle afternoon—read Natl. Intr. OConnell—Repeal—& Slavery[68]— Mr. Gallagher called—home to tea—arranged papers read Cassius Clay's comments on "A whig"—read Advocate of Peace[69]—prayer—to bed— Wife better today than yesterday—baby still doing well—little Kate unwell—bad cough at night

JUNE 27 TUESDY Rose at ½ past 4—dressed—shaved—marketed—took little Kate to ride in the country—let her walk over the hill & pick clover &c—home by ¼ to 7—prayer—journal of yesterday—

JUNE 28 WEDNY Rode out with Mr. Garniss & Mr. Southgate[70] to Ludlow sale, Consulted by P. Evens[71] as to effect of a written agreement not to bid against each other between himself and another purchaser—told him it would be void—partook of lunch on the ground—after sale came home.

JUNE 29 Attended to sundry business—made some progress in preparation of Vanzandt ads Jones—had decree nisi confirmed, [Fox] vs Johnson etal / attended Commencement of Woodward College—good speaking by Cady—also, as I heard by Morher[72]—did not hear him myself— Excellent address by Dr. Aydelotte[73]

JUNE 30 FRIDAY Transactions of this day did not amount to much— Attended meeting Trustees Woodward Coll. at my house—purchased "the Lawyer" & "Whateleys Kingdom of Christ"[74]—

---

67. That is, "some twice & some thrice."
68. The article, which appeared in the *Daily National Intelligencer,* June 21, 1843, reprinted a speech by Irish politician Daniel O'Connell (1775–1847) expressing support for the American Antislavery Society. *DNB,* 14:815–34.
69. A publication of the American Peace Society. Mott, *American Magazines,* 2:211.
70. Probably James Southgate.
71. Platt Evens, a local mercer and tailor. *Cinc. Dir. (1843),* 115; Greve, *Centennial History,* 1:563, 678.
72. Philander Kinney Cady (1826–1917), a recent graduate who became an Episcopal clergyman and professor at New York's General Theological Seminary; and his fellow student, La Fayette Morher. *Daily Cincinnati Chronicle,* June 30, 1843; *Who Was Who,* H:181; W. G. Williams et al. to Chase, July 8, 1842 (Chase Papers, L.C.).
73. Chase inserted the latter part of this entry, beginning with *attended Commencement,* after he had written the entry for June 30.
74. Edward O'Brien, *The Lawyer: His Character and Rule of Holy Life. After the Manner of George Herbert's Country Parson* (Philadelphia, 1843); Richard Whately, *The Kingdom of Christ Delineated in Two Essays . . .* (London, 1841).

Prest. McGuffey, Mr. Mansfield & Dr. Bailey took tea with me[75]— Attended Exhibition of Woodward Lit. Society—Speaking by & Jones good[76]—compo. of Moore good[77]—speaking without force—Mr. Mansfields address excellent but too indiscriminately eulogistic of American Civilization—

JULY 1. SATY Had judgt. entered Ferris use of Buchanan vs Goodins[78] $2604.82—at office prepared in Vanzandt Case—weather excessively warm for a few days past.

JULY 2—SUN Went to Sunday School—exceedingly dull & sleepy—at church same influence but was enabled to shake it off in some degree— Communion—thought I could give up all for Christ, but alas how feeble are my determinations—how imperfect my self-surrender—more careful about eating at dinner than usual so as not to be drowsy in afternoon—my health is good & my appetite excellent and I am prone to eat too much at meals—in afternoon heard Mr. Cleveland at 2nd Pres. Church[79]—an excellent discourse on 2 Saml. 24. 24. Neither will I offer burnt offerings unto the Lord my God of that which doth cost me nothing. Object to show the sin of giving to God only so much service & so much property as is convenient— Mr. Ball came home with me / Mr. Cleveland in prayer asked for the deliverance of the land from Slavery among other sins & evils & in Sermon spoke of the imprisonment of Butler & Worcester in Geo. Penitentiary[80]— Coming out of Church, Mr. Ewing asked me how I liked their stranger— On my expressing the gratification I felt—He said his anti slavery feelings

---

75. In 1843, William Holmes McGuffey (1800–1873), formerly president of Cincinnati College, left the presidency of Ohio University in Athens and joined the faculty of Woodward College. From 1845 until his death, McGuffey, compiler of the famous McGuffey *Readers*, taught at the University of Virginia. *DAB*, 12:57–58.

76. Probably G. G. Jones, a student official in the society. The exhibition was at the Ninth Street Baptist Church. *Daily Cincinnati Chronicle*, June 24, 1843; W. G. Williams et al. to Chase, July 8, 1842 (Chase Papers, L.C.).

77. Probably La Fayette Morher.

78. Evidently a case involving Robert Buchanan and Cincinnati dry goods merchants James Goodin and S. H. Goodin. *Cinc. Dir. (1843)*, 136.

79. John P. Cleveland, pastor of Cincinnati's Second Presbyterian Church. Henry A. Ford and Kate B. Ford, *History of Cincinnati, Ohio, with Illustrations and Biographical Sketches* (Cleveland, 1881), 152.

80. Elizur Butler (1794–1857), a Massachusetts physician, and Samuel Austin Worcester (1798–1859), a translator from Vermont, had violated Georgia laws which required special permits and oaths of allegiance for whites living among Cherokees. Their imprisonment, 1831–33, ended after William Wirt successfully argued the case before the U.S. Supreme Court. *DAB*, 20:530–31; Robert Sparks Walker, *Torchlights to the Cherokees: The Brainerd Mission* (New York, 1931), 45–49.

stuck out too much for that Congregation—that his allusion to the imprisonment in the Geo. Pen. was evidence of it— "Why" I replied, "that was no allusion to slavery—Butler & W. were the missionaries to the Indians imprisoned by the Geo. authorities for whom Wirt made his great speech"— It seemed that he supposed they were abolitionists imprisoned for some aggression on slavery— And this gent. is one of the most intelligent members of the Church— After Mr. Ball went away— Mr. Mitchell & his two children came in & staid to tea—after they went read Wh[ate]ly 'Kingdom of Christ— "The Lawyer" is missing quite mysteriously—

JULY 3. MON. Read, after dressing, a Psalm the 50th & the 4 first chaps Matt.[81] some earnestness in prayer—was obliged to correct my dear little Kate—prayed with her—brot up the jour—from June 26

JOURNAL III

DEC. 28 At Columbus attending Court (Cir Ct. U.S)— ☛ Morng Herald Jany 1, 44—Dr Worcester was at this time delivering medical lectures in Cleveland.[82]

1844

JANY 2. A Liberty meeting was held at the City Hall or Court House at which Judge King, the Liberty nominee for Governor & I spoke M.H. Jany 6.[83]

JANY 4 Addressed a Liberty meeting at the Court House in Dayton—

JANY 5. Addressed an Irish Repeal Meeting at Dayton in Court House

---

81. Chapters describing the genealogy, birth, and early ministry of Jesus.
82. Chase represented the plaintiff in a patent case. Noah Worcester (1812–47) taught general pathology for a time at Western Reserve College and later practiced medicine in Cincinnati. *Appletons'*, 6:614; *Cincinnati Morning Herald*, Jan. 1, 1844; *Philanthropist*, Jan. 10, 1844.
83. The Columbus meeting, led by Chase and Leicester King, was "fully attended." *Philanthropist*, Jan. 10, 1844; *Cincinnati Morning Herald*, Jan. 6, 1844.

March 1845 {171}

1845

JOURNAL IV

MARCH 1. At court for a short time this morning but no business: Judge Este says no more chy[84] business to be taken up this term: settled a/cs with Trust Co; drew balance & deposited same with Ellis:[85] collected Sundry a/cs & paid some, v. Day book: Mr. Cheney dined:[86] to come on Monday & visit Hardscrabble Hall:[87] afternoon attended funeral of Mrs Wiggins:[88] S. W. Pomeroy,[89] J. P. Foote, S. E. Foote, D. B. Lawler, J. H. Groesbeck,[90] Hy Emerson,[91] self & *unknown* pallbearers: Mr. H. S. Gilmore called; stated receipts from Vanzandt fund, J. W. Alden last summer $86.66:[92] person & time unknown .50: [8]7.16: bot Temperance & Grammar chart: little Kate much amused with it: also bo't *Johnsoniana*.[93] at office in eveng; read paper, *Judge Hitchcock* voted against repealing negro disqualifying testimony law in 1816![94] made entries day book; filed & put away papers in Mersereau case: also retained today in nuisance case, Mitchell ads Schnetz.[95]

---

84. Chancery.
85. Roland Ellis, a partner in the Cincinnati exchange brokerage firm of Ellis and Vallette. The Ohio Life Insurance and Trust Company stood at the corner of Main and Third Street. *Cinc. Dir. (1846)*, 156, 291.
86. Charles Cheney (1803–74), antislavery merchant from Mount Healthy, Ohio. *Nat. Cyc.*, 19:71–72.
87. Chase's new house in Storrs Township, west of Cincinnati. Chase's involvement with craftsmen and artisans during the following months arose largely from construction on the building and from an attempt to contain a landslide behind the structure. A. W. Gilbert to Chase, July 17, Aug. 7, 1845, James Wickes Taylor to Chase, July 14, 1845 (Chase Papers, L.C.); *Titus' Atlas*, 6.
88. Cornelia Wiggins, the wife of Samuel Wiggins, had died on Feb. 26. *Cincinnati Daily Gazette*, Mar. 1, 1845.
89. S. Wyllys Pomeroy, a local agent for Pomeroy Coal Mines. Pomeroy to Chase, Dec. 20, 1862 (Chase Papers, L.C.); *Cinc. Dir. (1846)*, 305.
90. John H. Groesbeck, a Cincinnati banker. *Cinc. Dir. (1846)*, 184.
91. Henry Emerson.
92. Hiram S. Gilmore, a local teacher, served on a committee gathering funds to support the Van Zandt litigation. Joseph W. Alden, at various times a resident of Boston and New York, had a background in business but later worked with Joshua Leavitt producing antislavery publications. Alden to Chase, May 6, 1861 (Hiram Barney Papers, Huntington Lib.); *Boston Dir. (1850)*, 75; *Cinc. Dir. (1846)*, 177; *Philanthropist*, Oct. 11, 1843.
93. *Johnsoniana; or, a Collection of Bon Mots, etc., by Dr. Johnson and Others* . . . (London, 1776).
94. Peter Hitchcock (1781–1853), judge of the Ohio Supreme Court, 1819–32, 1845–52. Robson, *Biographical Encyclopædia*, 575–76; *DAB*, 9:77–78.
95. Possibly Martin Schnetz, associated with a public garden in Cincinnati. The Mersereau case involved Ludlow family land titles. *Cinc. Dir. (1846)*, 333; J. Bartlett to T. Ewing, Mar. 2, 1843, with note by Chase (Ewing Papers, L.C.).

SUNDAY. MAR. 2. At home morning, with wife, who quite ill: read Wilberforce Life &c: Evening at church: Mr. Gillespie, on vows[96]—did not much like it

MON. MAR. 3. Rose rather late—wrote article on Hab. Cor. for Gazette[97]—prepared lease to Higlin & Shaeffer—rode down river with wife & Mrs. Garniss & Kate: while at house Mr. Cheney came—retd. with us & dined: office business afternoon: remitted Mr. Johns bal. due: cold. committee[98] in evening abt. present: told them wd receive whatever & however honorable to themselves & proper to me:[99] letters fr Scoville & Co N.Y. & Snyder Cash. Pitts:[1] Speeech from Brinkerhoff M.C.:[2] news that Benton's bill for Annexation passed Senate 27 to 25: what next

SAT. MAR. 8: Wife quite sick this morn'g, and all day: not much done in office but busy all day: Afternoon interview with Mrs Todd, & uncivil message from Mr. Florer: prepared dft of letter to Smedes abt. Downes & Haven; & of supl. bill Laf. Bk vs Jones: Mr. Jones called, ascertained situation of his property:[3] Taft, about Hodges asseignt of McMillan judgt. to me.[4] Mr. Taylor with me in office, assistant:[5] sensible, industrious & obliging; Gilbert speaks of

---

96. George de Normandie Gillespie (b. 1819), rector of St. Paul's Protestant Episcopal Church. *Appletons'*, 2:651.

97. The article supported proposals to reform Ohio's habeas corpus act. *Cincinnati Daily Gazette*, Mar. 4, 1845.

98. That is, "colored committee."

99. Chase had led a well-publicized effort to secure the release of Samuel Watson, an Arkansas slave who escaped in Cincinnati while traveling on the Ohio River. The resulting case, *State v. Hoppess*, failed to win freedom for Watson, but the presiding supreme court justice, Nathaniel C. Read, recognized the restricted local nature of slavery, as Chase had previously suggested in the Matilda case. Chase was honored for his efforts with a silver pitcher presented on May 6. *Address and Reply; Cincinnati Weekly Herald and Philanthropist*, Feb. 19, 26, 1845; *Daily Cincinnati Gazette*, Feb. 26, 1845; "The State v. Hoppess, in the Matter of Watson, Claimed as a Fugitive from Service," *Western Law Journal* 2 (Mar. 1845): 279–93.

1. John Snyder, cashier of the Pittsburgh Bank, and possibly New York attorney Harris Scovill. *Pittsburgh Dir. (1847)*, 143; *New York Dir. (1841–42)*, 116.

2. Jacob Brinkerhoff, *Speech of Mr. J. Brinkerhoff, of Ohio, on the Annexation of Texas: Delivered in the House of Representatives, January 13, 1845* (Washington, D.C., 1845). An antislavery Democrat, Brinkerhoff (1810–80) served in Congress from Ohio, 1843–47, and sat on the supreme court of the state, 1856–71. *DAB*, 3:49.

3. Probably Charles A. Jones. Chase to Jones, Feb. 26, 1847 (Chase Papers, L.C.).

4. Cincinnati attorney Alfonso Taft (1810–91), U.S. secretary of war and attorney general, 1876–77; Adam Hodge, a partner in the legal firm of Bryant and Hodge; and possibly Archibald McMillan, a local blacksmith. *DAB*, 18:264–65; *Cinc. Dir. (1846)*, 204, 283.

5. James Wickes Taylor (1819–93), one of Chase's law clerks. A Free-Soil activist, he later edited newspapers in Cincinnati and Sandusky; served as special agent of the U.S. Treasury, 1859–69, and State Department, 1869–70; and was U.S. consul

helping:[6] no letters today; vote on Senate bill to amend colored testy disqualifying law in House: disgraceful, 31 nays, Gallagher Speaker one of them.[7]

FRI. MAR. 14: Carey called for sub to Temp. Hall:[8] subscd. $100: he said Bell desired him to put down his name as "no abolitionist": he remarked when asked to subscribe he was "no abolitionist & Bell then said Put that down or equivalent language: Mr. Gilmore called to ask services in selling place for him. agreed to try & make no chge if no sale except for advt.: wife rather better today:

JOURNAL I

AUG 1— Was at Buffalo night July 31/1 Aug with wife & her mother child nurse & driver (Reuben) at Eagle [Talon][9]

JOURNAL IV

1845: NOV. 24: I resume my journal after a long intermission, during which the saddest affliction has fallen upon me. I have recorded its details in separate sheets which with other intervening events I may yet note in this book.[10] If so the preceding page will exhibit a reference to them. This day has been marked by no extraordinary event: rose, as usual of late, before sunrise: breakfasted

---

at Winnipeg, 1870–93. *DAB*, 18:330; James Wickes Taylor, *"A Choice Nook of Memory": The Diary of a Cincinnati Law Clerk 1842–44*, ed. by James Taylor Dunn (Columbus, 1950), vii–xi.

6. Alfred West Gilbert (1816–1900), a civil engineer, studied law in Chase's office. William E. Smith and Ophia D. Smith, eds., *Colonel A. W. Gilbert, Citizen-Soldier of Cincinnati* (Cincinnati, 1934), 13, 17, 33, 34, 44.

7. On Mar. 6, the Ohio House of Representatives declined to advance to a third reading a Senate bill "to allow blacks and mulattos to testify in courts of justice." John M. Gallagher of Clark County was speaker. *Weekly Ohio State Journal*, Mar. 12, 1845; Gilkey, *Ohio Hundred Year Book*, 210, 263.

8. Samuel Fenton Cary (1814–1900), a local attorney and one of Ohio's leading temperance reformers, solicited contributions for the construction of a Temperance Hall in Cincinnati. Cary later served in Congress, 1867–69. *Bio. Dir. U.S. Cong.*, 752; Jed Dannenbaum, "The Crusader: Samuel Cary and Cincinnati Temperance," *Cincinnati Historical Society Bulletin* 33 (1975): 138–39, 142; *Tri-Weekly Cincinnati Gazette*, Mar. 1, 13, 1845.

9. This entry is taken from memoranda at the end of Journal I. Chase put it under a heading for 1835, but he could not have been traveling with a child that summer. The entry relates to 1845. Family members traveling with Chase were Eliza Ann Smith Chase; their daughter, Kate; and Eliza's mother, Mary Colton Smith. Flamen Ball to Chase, Aug. 5, 1845 (Chase Papers, Hist. Soc. of Pa.); Chase to Gerrit Smith, July 31, 1845 (Gerrit Smith Collec., Syracuse Univ.).

10. Chase's account of his second wife's death, Sept. 29, 1845, has not been found. *Daily Cincinnati Gazette*, Sept. 30, 1845; "Family Memoranda" (Chase Papers, L.C.).

with Sister Alice & little Kate—read Scriptures (Job) to little Kate who listened & seemed to be pleased, probably with the solemn rhythm['s] for she certainly can understand very little; then prayer with her: then to town in omnibus, unshaven for want of time: Clark Williams came in to have copies of Munsell bonds prepared[11]— spoke to him of sale of horses &c—Mr. Nye called about son &c—letter from Haven of condolence[12]—very kind & sympathizing—letter from Dr. Brisbane about his litigation with J. M. Staughton[13]—really sorry for him—called at Bailey's office for list of invitees to Lib. Convention[14]—prepared sundry circulars to be sent off with Taylor's help—dined with Dr. Bailey—conversation about Foster & Kelley[15]—Foster in speech said "Liberty men had accomplished nothing but the election of Polk & the defeat of Clay, who would at all events have respected the Constitution"—returned to Office which found locked—went to French & Winslow stovedealers[16]—to Truman's Bookstore, where bo't series of little books for little Kate[17]—met there Gilmore who said $200 on hand of Vansandt fund—in his note to Treasr. without interest—called at Wicker & Routh's painters who to send hand tomorrow to paint gate posts[18]—returned to office—found H. Lewis there—wished suit bro't against Kenner & Brown—gave him preliminary directions—Tompkins called to have suit brought vs Morgan & Co.[19]—

11. Clark Williams, a local attorney, had complained to Chase the previous month that Leander Munsell, a business associate, failed to meet a financial obligation. *Cinc. Dir. (1846)*, 393; Williams to Chase, Oct. 20, 1845 (Chase Papers, L.C.).

12. Charles H. Haven, a St. Louis attorney and former student, offered condolences for the death of Chase's second wife, Eliza. Haven to Chase, Apr. 25, Nov. 16, 1845 (Chase Papers, L.C.).

13. Chase represented the underage son and widow of James M. Staughton in litigation involving a mortgage. The letter from William Henry Brisbane, M.D. (c. 1803–78), a Baptist clergyman and Liberty party activist, asked Chase to facilitate timely resolution of the dispute. The case came before the Ohio Supreme Court in the Dec. 1848 term. Entries for Jan. 6, 8, and 9, 1849, below; *Appletons'*, 1:378; Brisbane to Chase, Nov. 22, 1845, Chase to David Putnam, Jr., July 2, 1845 (Chase Papers, L.C.); 17 Ohio 482; *Cinc. Dir. (1846)*, 103.

14. Chase chaired the Liberty State Convention, which met in Columbus Dec. 30–31. Its delegates asked him to represent the Liberty party as candidate for governor. Chase declined and saw Samuel Lewis nominated instead. *Philanthropist*, Jan. 7, 1846.

15. Abolitionists and reformers Stephen Symonds Foster (1809–81) and Abigail Kelley (1810–87), soon to be married, were famous for their criticisms of established religion and politics. They had given a series of lectures in Cincinnati the previous week. *DAB*, 6:542–43, 558–59; *Cincinnati Weekly Herald and Philanthropist*, Nov. 26, 1845.

16. Maynard French and A. S. Winslow. *Cinc. Dir. (1846)*, 169, 397.

17. Cincinnati bookseller E. D. Truman. *Cincinnati Daily Gazette*, Nov. 22, 1845; *Cinc. Dir. (1846)*, 372.

18. Lawrence S. Wicker and James W. Routh. *Cinc. Dir. (1846)*, 325, 392.

19. E. Morgan and Company, Cincinnati booksellers and publishers; James Tompkins was a local turner. Ibid., 270–71, 370.

November 1845   { 175 }

made some little progress in preparation of Vansandt case—home in omnibus—read newspapers—read Landscape Gardening[20]—heard little Kate read a little poem—also in Bible—& wrote above—a little more time now on Vansandt case & then to bed

TUES. NOV. 25: Up betimes & breakfast: to town in Omnibus: little done at office: to court with Corry: listened to Worthington in Irwin ejectment[21] agst Carneal; very able: to office & then to dinner—before dinner met Taft who infd. me that affair of Newport Mang. Co closed & advised to present bill:[22] after dinner at office all afternoon taking deps as Commr. in Williams vs Thacker—Mr. & Mrs & Miss Taylor home with me[23]—went for little Kate to Major Oliver's—Supper—Kate read Bible—Scriptures & fam prayers conversation & musics till half past 10—ent[ered] some famy. mema.[24]—wrote above & now to bed.

WED. NOV. 26. Rose very early—prayer—breakfast, selves & guests—Taylor & I to town in omnibus Alice & Mrs. T. & Miss T. to follow at their leisure with Kate in carriage—finished taking deps at office for Capt. Thacker—chgd. $10 which he paid—dinner—went to French & Winslow's & bespoke stove— Mr. Lewis called—talk abt. his being candidate for Gov. of Liberty men—he coyly willing— Alice with Kate called for me to go home—went in carriage—Miss Eliza Cotton, dear Lizzie's aunt with us— Hardinge abt. steps & gates[25]—John Friday about steps[26]—$6 to Hardinge 4 to John—supper—prayers—heard Kate read bible— Before coming down called on Whitney rail road king[27]—he full of enthusiasm

---

20. Andrew Jackson Downing, *A Treatise on the Theory and Practice of Landscape Gardening*... (New York, London, and Boston, 1841). "Books in Loveland belonging to Hon S. P. Chase" (Chase Papers, L.C.).
21. Local attorneys William M. Corry (b. 1811); Samuel W. Irwin; and one of three Worthingtons: Benjamin J., John G., or Vachel (b. 1802). Corry later abandoned his legal career for journalism and politics. A state representative from Hamilton County, 1856–57, he assumed the sobriquet "Citizen" and gained a reputation for "independent radicalism." Robson, *Biographical Encyclopædia*, 461–62, 610–11; *Cinc. Dir. (1846)*, 131, 215, 402; Gilkey, *Ohio Hundred Year Book*, 216; Ohio General Assembly, House of Representatives, *Journal*, 52nd Assem., 2nd sess., 1857, appen., 174.
22. The Newport Manufacturing Company, incorporated in Kentucky in 1831, produced a variety of lead, cotton, and wool products. *Cinc. Dir. (1834)*, 235.
23. Possibly James Wickes Taylor; Chloe Sweeting Langford Taylor, who had married Taylor in Oct. 1845; and a female relative. Taylor, *"Choice Nook of Memory,"* ix.
24. Chase kept a record entitled "Family Memoranda" in an undated memorandum book (Chase Papers, L.C.).
25. Christopher Harding, a local painter. *Cinc. Dir. (1846)*, 190.
26. Friday was a workman at Hardscrabble Hall. Chase financial records, 1845 (Chase Papers, L.C.).
27. Possibly Luther Whitney (b. 1817), a contractor and builder from Chillicothe. Robson, *Biographical Encyclopædia*, 305–6.

which he has breathed into Cist, who, now, admits himself mistaken as to the destiny of Cincinnati to be the greatest city in the World, which preeminence is, in his opinion, reserved for the city to be at the Pacific termination of the Railroad[28]— I also deliverd the award of Johnston & myself in favor of U. States against the claim of R. F. L'Hommedieu, to Judge Wright.[29]

SAT. NOV. 29: Have not written for several days—feel this evening rather unwell & disinclined to journalize, but will jot down a few things— Mr. Cheney with us last night—very cold weather thermometer day before yesterday before sunrise 10° above zero—yesterday morning 14—this morning about same—breakfast ¼ past seven—Mr. Cheney & I to town in omnibus—attended to Vanzant case—Mr. Clark Williams called—recd. of H. S. & Co[30] $55—pd. Mr. Stone[31] $20—Dall & other Mason 18.25: Hardinge 5—John Friday $10—Klein[32] $1—OConnell called about job of digging on side hill—walked home / Michael at work on new place for woodshed[33]—tea—prayers with family—very thankful for continued blessings—heard little Kate read Bible as usual—she very well for which I thank God—there must be great distress in Europe from scarcity[34]—flour high here $5.50 to $6 per bbl.

TUESDAY, DECR. 2. I wrote nothing on Sunday or Monday night because I felt too much indisposed: on Sunday however I was at church in morning & in afternoon attended funeral services of

---

28. Charles Cist (1792–1868), a local editor and author, had written in 1841 "that within one hundred years from this time, Cincinnati will be the greatest city in America; and by the year of our Lord two thousand, the greatest city in the world." Cist, *Cincinnati in 1841*, Appendix A, 275; *DAB*, 4:108–9.

29. William Johnston (1804–91), a former member of the Ohio Assembly and an "old friend" of Chase, was a partner in the Cincinnati law firm of Johnston and Jones. Johnston later sat as a judge on the Superior Court of Cincinnati and, at the request of Abraham Lincoln, served on the Commission to Codify the Statutes of the U.S. *Biographical Cyclopædia*, 6:1402–5; *Cinc. Dir. (1846)*, 220; Gilkey, *Hundred Year Book*, 205, 213, 275; Johnston to Chase, Feb. 13, 1839 (Chase Papers, L.C.).

30. Higlin and Schaeffer.

31. Ethan Stone, a local attorney and businessman, owned land in Storrs Township which Chase leased. Lease from T. B. Coffin and Bridget Coffin, Apr. 1, 1845 (Chase Papers, L.C.); Taylor, *"Choice Nook of Memory,"* 78.

32. Probably Herman H. Klein, a local carpenter. *Cinc. Dir. (1846)*, 232.

33. Aaron Michael, a local carpenter, or perhaps Michael Golden or Michael Mitchel, laborers at Hardscrabble Hall. Ibid., 264; financial records, Sept. 20, 1845 (Chase Papers, L.C.).

34. Due to potato blight that swept Europe during the summer and fall of 1845. Woodham Smith and B. F. G. Cecil, *The Great Hunger, Ireland 1845–1849* (London, 1962), 38–43.

Saml. Lewis child at his house on Broadway[35]—he is said to have been a very bright child, just turned of 4. years—only two months younger than my dear little Kate, and destroyed by the same dreadful disease, the scarlet fever.— During the night, Sunday, I was quite ill & much alarmed by my symptoms—sinking faintness, palpitation, violent shaking— Dear Sister Alice wrapped me up warm—made a fire in my room & gave me hot drink & after a while I got better. Monday I was in town & devoted most of my time to stating an account of my debts, which more than I expected—I thought I had reduced them to about $9.000 but found them to exceed $11.000—abstained from dinner in hope of benefit from it—to bed soon after prayers & rather restless night—very cold this morning—rather restless night—thermometer this morn'g 8° above zero—to town in sleigh omnibus—busied chiefly as yesterday but a good deal interrupted—dined temperately at Mrs Capt Smith's[36]—home about 5—much better than for several days—heard dear little Kate read verses, & bible, & pray: talked to her—read conclusion of Job—& wrote foregoing before family prayers—

SATURDAY DECR. 6: Up this morn'g betimes—prayer—breakfast—heard Kate read a little—to town in omnibus—morning somewhat interrupted by callers & a good deal frittered away—read Prest.'s message—able, clear & firm—erroneous I think as to Texas & postage[37]—but creditable to the author as a whole—called on Trust Co abt. Clark Williams' business—recd. of C. & B.[38] fee of Justice Wright for drawing power of attorney—commenced examination of Condict dower case with reference to opinion to be drawn for defendants—dinner at Capt Smith's—called to see Dr. Worcester & at Mr. at Mr. Wiggins—saw no one but Miss Laura[39]—home in Omnibus—Michael has made good progress towards erection of Woodhouse south of house—tea—heard Kate read little book & Bible—read Cheever's Lectures on Bunyan—Sketch of Life of Romilly in Law Reporter—abstract of decisions in the last vol. of Story's

---

35. Samuel Henry Lewis had died on Nov. 27. *Cincinnati Daily Gazette*, Nov. 29, 1845.
36. Perhaps the wife of George G. Smith, a local canal captain. *Cinc. Dir. (1846)*, 345.
37. James K. Polk's State of the Union message included proposals for the admission of Texas and an unspecified increase in postal rates. *Cincinnati Daily Gazette*, Dec. 12, 1845.
38. Chase and Ball.
39. A daughter of Samuel Wiggins. Caroline A. Smith to Chase, Nov. 1, 1845 (Chase Papers, L.C.).

Reports in same[40]—prayer & now to bed—thermometer this morning before sunrise 4° above 0—now 10 P.M. 12° above 0.

1846

SUN FEB. 22: Rose in pretty good season—private devotion in bedroom—I feel so little my sinfulness & so little my obligations for mercies recd. that I am distressed by it: Mr. Fenton, a young lawyer, who staid with me last night breakfasted with me:[41] Alice & Kate in town—Mr. Fenton left at ½ past nine— I spent the morning in reading on Slavery and in perusing Milton's Vindication of the Action of Parliament in executing Charles 1st.[42] dined alone—read Job & other parts of Scripture: my understanding of what I read is very imperfect and, I fear, my spiritual apprehension of the truth still more so— May God enlighten me by His Holy Spirit: took tea alone & wrote above: Have not attended church today chiefly because of inconvenience of getting to town, having no place there for my horses; but partly, also, because I feel doubtful as to my duty arising from the relation of the Church to Slavery. On one side I cannot doubt that it is wrong for the Church to maintain an indifferent if not a hostile attitude to the cause of the enslaved: on the other I feel quite sure that other members of the Church, who do not feel as I do in reference to the Slaves, are far more zealous in other good works and live much nearer to Christ: I am anxious to see the path of duty in reference to the subject of church connexions more clearly than I do.

SUN. [MAR] 1. This is the commencement of another month: I resolve to be more diligent than during the last: I fritter my time too much in a variety of employments and am no diligent enough in any one: my great difficulty is want of concentratdness: I cannot call into exercise the power of abstraction except upon an emergency such as that of delivering an argument. I rose rather late this morning: not earnest enough in devotion. Oh for a sense of nearness to God & for a feeling of communion with Him! I have not been in town today, but have spent my time in reading the Bible,

---

40. George Barrell Cheever, *Lectures on the Pilgrim's Progress, and on the Life and Times of John Bunyan* (New York, 1844); "Sir Samuel Romilly," *Law Reporter* 8 (Nov. 1845): 289–305; William W. Story, *Reports of Cases Argued and Determined in the Circuit Court of the United States for the First Circuit* . . . , 3 vols. (Boston, 1842–47).

41. Joseph B. Fenton, later a resident of Cincinnati. Flamen Ball to Chase, Nov. 11, 1847 (Chase Papers, Hist. Soc. of Pa.); Fenton to Chase, Nov. 9, 1846 (Chase Papers, L.C.).

42. John Milton, *The Tenure of Kings and Magistrates* . . . (n.p., 1649).

March 1846 { 179 }

Job. & Genesis, Miltons Prose Works & Life[43] & Missionary Herald. No one at home but sister Alice & servants: of last none but Vina the colored woman[44] attend Family Prayers: the other two being Catholics & one of them a German unacquainted with our language.

MON. MAR. 2: Too late breakfast this morn'g for omnibus—so to town in wagon—snow on ground & slippery—snow granular— At court Judge Coffin[45] overruled exceptions to my report as trustee in Dorsey case—no other business there—very little done at office / note from Mr. Ball; premature confinement Mrs B—death of child—dangerous condition of mother / rode out to see Mr. & Mrs B—with sister Alice & little Kate— She better—home late & to bed— Note from Sarah Bella Ludlow[46] & sent her $10.

TUES. MAR. 3— Up early—private devotion as usual—why can I not have more freedom & enjoyment in prayer—breakfast with Alice & Kate—to town in Omnibus—went to Court—all litigated cases for jury to be continued in Com. Pleas: Superior occupied for all day with chy[47] case—back to Office, calling at Mrs McLean's to see D. W. Thorp, who not in, saw wife[48]—a pleasant chatty lady / sundry callers at office—Mr. Cheney—Mr. Grow introduced by Mr. Eells of Licking[49]—Mr. Lewis who left Memoirs—Mr. W. Lewis with sub. paper of Epanthean Socy.[50]—subscribed $5—Mr. Northrop

---

43. C. Symmons, *The Prose Works of John Milton; with a Life of the Author* . . . , 7 vols. (London, 1806).
44. Vina Lewis, apparently a runaway slave from Mississippi. She reappears in Chase's correspondence seventeen years later as a servant in New York City. Chase to James Dunlop Ludlow, June 1, 1863 (Chase Papers, Hist. Soc. of Pa.); B. B. Loring to V. Lewis, Sept. 5, 1845 (Chase Papers, L.C.).
45. Charles Dustin Coffin.
46. Chase's future wife Sarah Bella Dunlop Ludlow (c. 1820–52), a daughter of James C. Ludlow and Josephine Dunlop Ludlow. She and Chase married on Nov. 6, 1846. Cooper, "Cornelius Ludlow," 49; *Daily Cincinnati Gazette,* Jan. 15, 1852; quit claim deed, May 13, 1867, and "Family Memoranda" (Chase Papers, L.C.).
47. Chancery.
48. Angeline F. Thorp, wife of David Whitcombe Thorp. In 1842 or 1843, John McLean married his second wife, Sarah Bella Ludlow Garrard (1802–82), Jeptha Dudley Garrard's widow. She was the daughter of Cincinnati founder Israel Ludlow and an aunt of Sarah Bella Dunlop Ludlow. Deed of sale, Thorps to Chase, July 12, 1846 (Chase Papers, L.C.); Des Cognets, *Governor Garrard,* 29; Weisenburger, *McLean,* 220; *Nat. Cyc.,* 2:470.
49. The letter from George W. Ells, a Liberty party activist from Granville, Licking Co., Ohio, introduced George W. Grow, one of his law students. Ells to Chase, Feb. 15, Apr. 7, 1844, Feb. 26, 1846 (Chase Papers, L.C.).
50. William G. W. Lewis, a son of Samuel Lewis and a student at Woodward College, served as corresponding secretary of the society. *DAB,* 11:224; W. G. W. Lewis to S. Lewis, Jan. 9, 1845, in Woodward College papers (Chase Papers, L.C.).

about Berryman's character[51]—called with him at Donaldson's[52]—
D. W. Thorp about business of estate—promised him list of debts—
dined at Mr. Garniss's, who just returned from Columbus, rejoicing
in defeat of Bridge bill[53] / home by omnibus: heard Kate's readg.
& prayer—famy. prayers—read papers—private devotions & now to
bed—finished today statement of debts; whole amt. $12.525—pd.
Michael part & settled—pd. $14 for hay—

THURS. APL. 2 Spent nearly the whole of last week in Miami
County whither I went to try an important replevin case, in which
successful—Messrs Spencer, (O. M.) & W. R. Thomas for deft, Chas
Morris, R. S. Hart, H Hart & self for plff[54]—Morris & I argued
cause to Jury: verdict rendered about 7—left about 8 P.M. and came
to Dayton—cold ride & somewhat dangerous—Spencer, Albt. Lewis
& self— Spent Sunday in Dayton— Monday, came home—have not
accomplished much since—today rose somewhat late—to town in
omnibus—met Col Miner on Street who told me result of expedition
to Ky in pursuit of one kidnapped[55]—found Col Schillinger at office—made out bills agst Greene, Fenton, Bradbury & Hindelbath

---

51. Possibly either Henry A. Northrop, a local carpenter, or W. W. Northrop, an accountant; and James Berryman, a laborer. *Cinc. Dir. (1846)*, 93, 289.

52. A number of Donaldsons lived in Cincinnati. Chase had business dealings later with William Donaldson, a local tailor. Ibid., 147; Donaldson to Chase, Feb. 26, 1848 (Chase Papers, L.C.).

53. John P. Garniss and Samuel Wiggins owned a steam ferry that ran between Cincinnati and Covington, Ky. On Feb. 27, the Ohio State Senate had postponed action on a bill to charter a competing suspension bridge. *Cincinnati Morning Herald*, Mar. 3, 1846; Henry Stanberry to Garniss and Wiggins, Dec. 29, 1846 (Chase Papers, L.C.).

54. Oliver M. Spencer (1809–61), a partner in the Cincinnati law firm of Spencer and Corwine and judge of the city's Superior Court, 1854–61; Charles Morris (b. 1780), an attorney from Troy, Ohio; Ralph S. Hart, later a common pleas judge for the district which included Miami County; and probably Hart's brother, James Harvey Hart (1814–67). *Biographical Cyclopædia*, 2:462, 521–22; *Cinc. Dir. (1846)*, 350; Gilkey, *Ohio Hundred Year Book*, 543, 552; *A Genealogical and Biographical Record of Miami County Ohio . . .* (Chicago, 1900), 231; J. H. Hart to Chase, Jan. 12, 1846 (Chase Papers, L.C.).

55. Col. William Miner was clerk of the U.S. district court in Columbus and a supporter of the Liberty party. He referred to Jerry Finney (or Phinney), a black resident of Columbus for more than a decade, abducted on Mar. 31 by representatives of his former Kentucky master. Soon after, one of Cincinnati's "most respectable citizens" had journeyed to Louisville with two companions from Columbus in an attempt to secure Finney's release. Finney remained in captivity despite this effort and outcries from antislavery activists throughout Ohio. Chase to Miner, May 8, 1835, Mar. 30, 1841, May 22, 1848, June 2, 1850 (Chase Papers, L.C.); *Cincinnati Weekly Herald and Philanthropist*, Apr. 1, 8, 15, 1846; *History of Franklin and Pickaway Counties, Ohio . . .* (Cleveland, 1880), 83, 551; *Weekly Ohio State Journal*, Apr. 1, 8, 15, 29, May 6, 27, 1846.

& Co[56]—sent $80 in dft on Mt. Vernon to E. C. Smith at Gambier[57]—wrote to Ham Smith[58]—cold. man called saying had lost horse, circuit preacher—gave him dollar—he called on others saying that I had sent him which false—dined—arranged some papers—wrote Patterson[59]—also in A.M. Parish[60]—Weeks called with umbrella which I had left at Dayton—unprofitable talk with him—home in Omnibus—delightful chat & play with dear little Kate—a comfortable supper—progressive improvement in grounds—heard Kate read Bible—read myself & wrote above—

JOURNAL I

SEP. 16 Being Candidate for Congress recd. letter from Natl. Ref. Committee asking my views as to grants of land to landless persons & the exemption of a homestead from forced sales & ansd. I was in favor of both objects[61]

---

56. Perhaps attorney William Greene and one of several Bradburys: Cornelius S., proprietor of Bradbury's Mills; John, a clerk; John, a toolmaker; or attorney W. E. Bradbury. *Cinc. Dir. (1846)*, 101, 182.

57. Chase administered funds for Edmund C. Smith, Jr., who was attending Kenyon College. Smith to Chase, Jan. 19, Mar. 20, June 12, 21, 1846 (Chase Papers, L.C.).

58. Hamilton Smith had recently corresponded with Chase about an account between the two men and a case focused on Natchez, Miss. H. Smith to Chase, Mar. 27, 1846, ibid.

59. Chase's correspondence with John S. Patterson, a Logansport, Ind., attorney, involved a bankruptcy sale of land. Chase to Patterson, Nov. 11, 1845, Patterson to Chase, Mar. 21, Apr. 18, 1846, ibid.

60. Chase represented Sandusky attorney and antislavery activist Francis Drake Parish (1796–1886) in a suit brought under the fugitive slave law of 1793. Peter Driskell of Mason County, Ky., sought penalties against Parish for harboring and concealing a runaway slave and her child, and obstructing their arrest. The first trial, in U.S. circuit court at Columbus during the July 1847 term, resulted in a hung jury. In Nov. term of the same year, a new jury found against Parish on two counts, but the court granted a new trial. Chase got the third trial continued in Nov. 1848 (see entry for Nov. 22, 1848, below), but in the Nov. 1849 term a jury found Parish guilty of obstructing the arrest of the runaway. *Western Law Journal* 5 (Oct. 1847): 25–34; ibid., 5 (Feb. 1848): 206–8; ibid., 7 (Feb. 1850): 222–31; Parish to Chase, Oct. 15, 1845, Feb. 14, 1846, and other letters (Chase Papers, Hist. Soc. of Pa.); Chase to Sarah Bella Chase, July 26, 1847, Nov. 14, 1848, Chase to J. T. Trowbridge, Mar. 19, 1864 (Chase Papers, L.C.); Hewson L. Peeke, *A Standard History of Erie County, Ohio . . .* (Chicago, 1916), 1:427–28.

61. Chase was nominated by the Hamilton County Liberty party on Sept. 5, shortly after Samuel Lewis, a perennial Liberty party candidate, signaled his own unwillingness to run due to illness. Nine days later, a letter from a local committee of the National Reform Association asked Chase's opinion on "a Distribution of the Public Lands, in limited quantities, to landless persons" and "the exemption of the Homestead from all future debts, mortgages or liabilities." Chase's response, on

1847

JOURNAL IV

1847: FEB   Several days ago a colored man, John Woodson[62] called on me with a white man John Horton. Woodson's story was that a boy named David Reed lately an immate of the colored orphan asylum had been kidnapped & taken into Kentucky where he had been taken up by Horton while attempting to escape & had been brought by him to Covington ready to be delivered to his friends on this side, on proof of his being a free boy.[63] At Woodson's request Dr. Geo. Mendenhall called at my office,[64] and I prepared an affidavit of Davids Freedom for him, which he swore to and delivered to Horton, who soon after brot the boy over & delivered him to his friends, receiving $20 for his expences & services

After this—several days after the Mayor of the City[65] called at my office for some information in relation to the laws against kidnapping, and I learned from him that he had taken steps to have the kidnapper of David arrested. The next day Woodson again called at my office desiring my services in the examination of Geo. C Buckley who had been arrested on the charge[66] / I promised to see the Mayor &, if best, attend.

Yesterday I went to the Mayor's office. Buckley had been arrested, & was about to be brought out for examination. The Witnesses for the prosecution were not present, in conse. of some misunderstanding. The hearing was put off to the next day, and the Perry, the Marshal of Covington went after the witnesses being paid for doing so by the colored people.

Today the examination came on. John Horton testified that he lives about 3 miles back from Hamilton in Boone Co. a small town about 40 miles below Cin. That riding into the town one morning,

---

Sept. 28, expressed qualified agreement with both proposals, but failed to win either the association's endorsement or a Liberty party victory. J. H. Atkinson to Chase, Sept. 29, 1846 (Chase Papers, L.C.); *Cincinnati Weekly Herald and Philanthropist*, Sept. 9, Oct. 7, 28, 1846.

62. A local carpenter. *Cinc. Dir. (1846)*, 401.

63. An account of the eleven-year-old's kidnapping appeared in the *Cincinnati Weekly Herald*, Mar. 17, 1847. In that account, the name which Chase rendered in his journal as *Horton* was spelled *Haughton*.

64. Cincinnati obstetrician George Mendenhall (1814–74), a future president of the American Medical Association known for his philanthropic work. *Appletons'*, 4:296; *Cinc. Dir. (1846)*, 261.

65. Henry Evans Spencer.

66. The alleged kidnapper, listed elsewhere as George S. Buckley, had faced similar charges in 1842. *Cincinnati Weekly Herald*, Mar. 17, 1847.

Saturday, about 3 wks ago he was applied to Mrs Clark to catch a negro boy who had just escaped from her house—that he went on to town but saw nothing of the boy—that towards night he returned; & was again urged by Mrs C—— to pursue the boy with a promise that he should be paid whatever he might charge—that upon this he again went in pursuit of the boy & caught him—that the boys story made him mistrust something was wrong & he therefore did not give him up to Mrs Clark but took him home, & soon after sent him to his brother Williams: that he came to Cin & satisfied himself by enquiry that the boy was free—returned home—that the prisoner came to his brothers & demanded the boy—said he got him of Woodson—Horton told him he had seen Woodson—prisoner then said not Woodson but [Hersey] Williams—that he brought him from Cincinnati—admitted he was free. Witness had seen prisoner the day before he took the boy at the store of Mr. Freis in Hamilton & had afterwards met him coming into town as he, witness was going out home towards evg.

Fries—testified—keeps store in Hamilton—prisoner called Friday about 3 weeks ago—made some purchases—brought in skiff oars—offered to sell skiff—witness didn't want to buy & prisoners asked witness to sell Skiff for him—afterwards met prisoner in Cincinnati / he said "they needn't make such a fuss about that boy—he is free—I took him from Cin to Hamilton in the skiff.

William Horton— Is brother of John Horton & lives on part of same farm— Dave was left at my house—was there when prisoner came—he wanted to know if I was the man who had been to town—told him no, my brother was— Wife spoke up & said she believed the boy was Stolen—prisoner said Madam I brought him here—said he was free boy—Dave came—prisoner asked him if he wasnt given to him—if he hadn't waited for him at grocery—Dave said no—prisoner pulled his ears to make him say what he wished him to—Dave wouldnt—asked him if he didnt get cap for him—Dave sd. he would rather have his straw hat that he took from him—prisoner finally left him there—

William Huffman— Saw Dave at Woodson's shop the Tuesday before he was Stolen— Counsel for deft. Objected to competency of this witness on a/c of color! He is full white.

Dr. Geo Mendenhall   Knew Dave at orphan asylum about two weeks before disappearance—had home there.

Defendant called

Mrs Clark: Prisoner was at her home 17 Jany—Sunday—she wanted a Servant—he sd. he cd. procure her one in Cincinnati: brot Dave— Dave willing to stay with her for board & clothes—no kidnapping—fair bargain

Crossexd. Employed Horton to go after boy—dont remember how much offered him—when brot him back learned for first time that he might have been stolen.

Prosecut[ion] called

John Horton: Mrs Clark told me Master of boy—understood her Mr. Vernon—had left him for a short time—was to be back on Tuesday.—offered me any price to catch him—when brought him back ordered him [*illeg.*]—said he shd. have fifty lashes & when his master came he should be dealt with as he thought proper / is widow—has husband.—

Mayor required Buckley to find bail in $500 & in default committed him to Jail

Returning to my office a colored man applied to me to prepare some evidence of freedom for his wife as he was about to return to Nashville having married [here]

47 FEB.   Nashville colored man called with his wife—a rather pretty young Mulatto recently married— She stated she was born in Cincinnati had lived with Lieut ___ who now at Hamilton—and with a lady now in town but sick—could not therefore get their affidavits of her freedom. Told her I could do nothing for her, but make a memorandum of these particulars & if she got into trouble she might write me & I would see what cd. be done.

47 MARCH 1:   John Smothers called having been at my office before in reference a cousin of his wife's confined in Calaboose at New Orleans—proof he says has been made of her freedom, but she cannot be discharged until her jail fees are paid— Told him to leave the money with me & I would write to New Orleans & have payment made if available & woman discharged— He had not money enough and I prepared a statement as to his character to be signed by Mr. Ware who gave me a high character of him, and a subscription paper appended

Took Dr. Worcester home with me to see my brother who sick my house:[67] Dr's account unfavorable—disease dropsy

47 MAR. 2:   Recd. from Gov. Seward opinion of Supreme Court of New York in case of Freeman[68]— Wrote Fox after conversation

---

67. Alexander Ralston Chase.
68. Whig, later Republican, politician William Henry Seward (1801–72) served as governor of New York, 1838–42, U.S. senator, 1849–61, and secretary of state, 1861–69. In 1846, he had unsuccessfully defended William Freeman, an impoverished black of limited mental capacity who faced murder charges. Seward's letter to Chase announced that the New York Supreme Court had granted Freeman another

with H. Lewis—to whom gave copy argt. in Vanzandt case—sent copy to Albert Lewis— Mr. Denman called—spoke of Triplett purchase[69]—offered 5000 acres at 20c. Dinner— Read Pres. Church case— C. Williams called—commenced drawing his answer to Bartlett's bill[70]— Home in buggy with Luke[71]— Omitted to mention Carter, prosg. atty called in morning with subpœnas for witnesses to attend examining court kidnappers case[72]—sent for Bates cold.[73]—gave them to him & told him to have them served. Perry, Marshal Cowington called having been sent for through Bates—sent him to Prosg. Atty.

1847 MAR. 3: Rose this morning at 7—having gone to bed last night about 11—private devotion before breakfast—to town in buggy—looked over papers—Mr. C. Williams called—agreed to have his ansr. to Bartlett's bill ready by morning—Mr. I. D. Wheeler called—conversed on his transactions with Meriweather[74]—Thos. Hurst called[75]—agreed to attend Court for him tomorrow & see to application to be made for injunction against him: Woodson & another colored man called to see if I cd. attend exn. of Buckley—told them case was in hands of prosg. atty & wd. go & see him—went but he not in his office—called at Desilver's coming down[76]—saw Judge Coffin there—met Mr. Starr invited by him to meet Mr.

---

trial, and requested additional copies of Chase's Van Zandt argument. *DAB*, 16:615–21; George E. Baker, ed., *The Works of William H. Seward* (New York, 1884), 1:lxxi–lxxx, 409–75; Seward to Chase, Feb. 18, 1847 (Chase Papers, L.C.).

69. Possibly Edward H. Denman, a local carpenter. On Feb. 16, Robert Triplett of Fleming County, Ky., had sold 3,838 acres to Chase, Augustus I. Brown, George H. Bates, George Milne, and Noah Worcester. *Cinc. Dir. (1846)*, 142, 356; deed of sale, George H. Bates et al. to Chase, May 10, 1847 (Chase Papers, L.C.).

70. Probably Jonathan Bartlett, a Cincinnati resident later involved with Chase in land transactions. Bartlett to Chase, Nov. 17, 1847, I. P. Taylor to Bartlett, Nov. 10, 1847 (Chase Papers, L.C.).

71. Luke Ren (or Wren), one of Chase's servants. Ren to Chase, Nov. 8, 1847, ibid.

72. Alfred George Washington Carter (1819–85), Hamilton County prosecuting attorney and later a common pleas judge. The case was that of David Reed discussed in the first entry for Feb. 1847 above. William Coyle, ed., *Ohio Authors and Their Books: Biographical Data and Selective Biographies for Ohio Authors, Native and Resident, 1796–1950* (Cleveland, 1962), 101; *Cinc. Dir. (1846)*, 118.

73. Apparently Wilson Bates, a black barber. *Cinc. Dir. (1846)*, 88; entry for July 5, 1848, below.

74. Wheeler operated a local hardware store. Meriweather was possibly W. Meriweather, Jr., a worker in Wheeler's store; J. H. Meriweather, proprietor of a dry goods business; William Meriweather, occupation unknown; or F. Merriweather, an agent for Boardreth's Pills. *Cinc. Dir. (1846)*, 261–62, 389.

75. Thomas Hurst, a constable. Ibid., 213.

76. John Ford Desilver, a partner in the Cincinnati bookselling firm of Desilver and Burr. Ibid., 111, 143; Desilver to Chase, Aug. 28, 1842 (Chase Papers, L.C.).

Stevenson & others at his house tonight[77]—engaged to prepare plea in Dr. Beechers case[78]— Commenced answer of C. Williams—had to make general examination of documents connected with his transactions with Colby[79] & with Bartlett & Bartletts with Swain— dinner at Ritters[80]—resumed & finished rough draft answer for Clark Williams—called at Coffin & Mitchells[81]—corrected proof of handbill of Admrs. sale of Ludlow lands in Butler Co—came home wife had been unwell all day— Supper—prayers—journal.— Omitted that Dr. Worcester called in morning about A. R's[82] sickness— Brown to see Worcester & spoke of Ky lands— Donogh to dun for balance bill[83]—agreed to deduct what I thought unreasonable—had letter today from Lewis Tappan about Vanzandt argument—wants me to write a book on Constitution & Slavery[84] / Handsome notice of Vanzandt argt. in W. Law. Journal—sent argts to Theodore Sedgwick, C. C. Felton and others[85]

MAR. 23: Rose this morning as usual—went into brother Alexander's room who has been growing worse for sevl. days—he seemed much as usual but weaker—wanted Luke to assist George, his regular attendant in some service—I proposed to act instead of Luke—but he said he would wait for Luke— Went to breakfast but had hardly begun the meal when I heard him breathing hard: hastened up stairs—at first thought him asleep, but soon began to fear

77. Henry Starr and, probably, John White Stevenson (1812–86), a Covington, Ky., lawyer and state legislator who later became a Democratic member of Congress, 1857–61, governor of Kentucky, 1867–71, and U.S. senator, 1871–77. *DAB*, 17:633–34.

78. Chase was one of the attorneys representing Lyman Beecher, Calvin E. Stowe, and Diarca Howe Allen in suits intended to remove them from the faculty of Lane Seminary for their lack of adherence to "Old School" Presbyterianism. *State ex rel. Kemper v. Beecher*, 16 Ohio 358; *Kemper v. Trustees of Lane Seminary*, 17 Ohio 293; Fairman, *Reconstruction and Reunion*, 28.

79. Probably either Isaac Colby or Samuel Colby, local tailors. *Cinc. Dir. (1846)*, 126.

80. Anthony Ritter operated a Cincinnati tavern. Ibid., 319.

81. Thomas G. Mitchell was the son-in-law and law partner of Charles Dustin Coffin. *Biographical Cyclopædia*, 1:83; *Cinc. Dir. (1849–50)*, 64, 202.

82. Alexander Ralston Chase.

83. Joseph B. Donogh and Robert P. Donogh were local printers. *Cinc. Dir. (1849–50)*, 147.

84. New York merchant and abolitionist Lewis Tappan (1788–1873) wanted Chase to write in behalf of the American and Foreign Anti-Slavery Society. Chase accepted the offer, but evidence of the book's publication has not been found. *DAB*, 18:303–4; Chase to Tappan, Mar. 18, 1847 (Chase Papers, L.C.); Tappan to Chase, Feb. 24, Mar. 11, 1847 (Chase Papers, Hist. Soc. of Pa.).

85. Notices of the Van Zandt case appeared in the *Western Law Journal* 4 (Mar. 1847): 286, and 4 (Apr. 1847): 321–28. Theodore Sedgwick (1811–59), author and U.S. diplomat, practiced law in New York. Cornelius Conway Felton (1807–62) served as Eliot Professor of Greek Literature at Harvard College. *DAB*, 6:317–18, 16:551–52.

he was dying, which fear the result proved too well founded:—he expired in a few moments at about nine o'clock, having manifested no consciousness after I came into the room:— Mr. & Mrs Folger, Mrs Coffin,[86] & Mrs Nye assisted us in the last duties to his remains— Wrote to Brothers Edwd. & Wm & Sister Hannah

MAR. 24: Today we committed the body of my departed brother to the vault in the Presbyterian ground— Mr. Gillespie performed the funeral service—the attendance of friends in consequence of the dangerous condition of the bridge the shortness of the notice & other causes was small— Messrs H. Hall, J. C. Vaughan, T. K. Smith, & Dunlop Ludlow acted as pall bearers.[87]

MAR. 28. Rose this morning as usual—breakfasted—prepared to go to town to Church, but driver sent word he cd. not wait—other circumstances making it seem best not to retain him told him I would find someone to take his place—read Old Testament in Coarse— Went with wife & Kate to Mr. Bushnells church[88]—much interested & I hope profited by his discourse, wh. a plain & affecting exhibition of the necessity of the sinner's complete surrender to God & of the reality of religion— After dinner read Cudworth a little, but drowsy[89]—read also Krummacher[90]— After tea went to Mr. Bushnell's prayermeeting—again much interested— May God enable me to make an unreserved surrender of self, time, property & powers to his service & disposal— After return read Krummacher & wrote this date & two preceding—

MON. MARCH 29: Rose as usual & breakfasted but too late for the Omnibus. Plumber came down to fix cistern pipes & pump: to

---

86. Harriet Eliza Wooster Coffin (d. 1870), the wife of Judge Charles Dustin Coffin. *Biographical Cyclopædia*, 1:83.

87. Harvey Hall, a Cincinnati attorney; John C. Vaughan; Thomas Kilby Smith (1820–87), one of Chase's former law students, U.S. marshal for the southern district of Ohio, 1855–56, and, during the Civil War, from lieutenant colonel to major general of U.S. volunteers; and Chase's brother-in-law, James Dunlop Ludlow (1820–86), a son of James C. Ludlow and Josephine Dunlop Ludlow. *Appletons'*, 5:590–91; *Nat. Cyc.*, 8:275; *Cinc. Dir. (1846)*, 187; Cooper, "Cornelius Ludlow," 49; unpublished guide to Ludlow-Dunlop-Chambers Collec., Univ. of Wyoming.

88. Asa B. Bushnell was a local "city missionary." *Cinc. Dir. (1849–50)*, 14.

89. Chase owned at least one title by seventeenth-century English divine Ralph Cudworth: *The True Intellectual System of the Universe* . . . , 2 vols. (New York, 1837–38). *Catalogue of a Most Superb Collection*, 72; *DNB*, 5:271–72.

90. A number of works by Protestant theologian Friedrich Adolf Krummacher (1767–1845), a native of Westphalia, were available in German or English. Chase owned at least one, *Cornelius the Centurion*, a translation first printed in Edinburgh in 1838 and in New York in 1841. "Books in Loveland belonging to Hon S. P. Chase" (Chase Papers, L.C.); *Allgemein Deutsche Biographie* (Leipzig, 1883), 17:240–43.

town in buggy: found several persons waiting to see me: went to Court House: did nothing there but take copy of bill of exchange sued on in Robertson et al v Ludlow: returned to office: went up to see Dr. Worcester: none permitted to see him: W. H. Mussey says his situation quite critical[91]—Dr. Mussey thinks he has a chance of Life: the other physicians think little or no hope—I pray God to Spare his life—he is much beloved—left answers of Hughes Trustees with Brough[92]—to dinner—a little soup & rice pudding—back to office—attended meeting of Commissioners on Estate of Mr. T. Williams more than two hours[93]—called at Mrs Smith's—Ed. out riding but came home just as I was coming away[94]—looks badly—thence to Dr. Worcester's—he a little better but very dangerously ill right lung much inflamed & left, which much weakened & injured heretofore burdened with whole of respiration—paid due bill $165 & int 176.55—home in buggy: Dunlop Ludlow, Kenner Garrard, Ben Ludlow came down in Omnibus[95]—tea—family prayers—wrote above—read—private prayer, bed

TUES. MAR 30: Rose as usual—breakfast—to town in Omnibus—called to enquire for Dr. W—then to office—looked at papers—wife came in gave her $5—singular feeling of numbness in upper part of head—walked to get rid of it—saw H. & A. Lewis while out[96]—A Lewis divorce matter—came back to office better— Sent McDougal

---

91. William Heberdon Mussey (1818–82) studied medicine under his father, Reuben Dimond Mussey. *Appletons'*, 4:471–72; Ford and Ford, *History of Cincinnati*, 423.

92. Probably either Charles H. Brough (1813–49), an attorney in the firm of Brough and Zinn who became presiding judge of Ohio's ninth circuit court of common pleas, or his brother, John Brough (1811–65), Republican governor of Ohio, 1864–65. The Broughs, both former members of the Ohio House, also owned and published the Democratic *Cincinnati Daily Enquirer*, 1841–49. *Cinc. Dir. (1846)*, 105; *DAB*, 3:94–95; *Appletons'*, 1:391; Gilkey, *Ohio Hundred Year Book*, 246, 541; Osman Castle Hooper, "John Brough," *Ohio Archaeological and Historical Quarterly* 13 (Jan. 1904): 41, 55.

93. Apparently the case of one Thomas Williams, whose estate seems to have included property in Britain. John Williams to Chase, Mar. 2, 1847 (Chase Papers, Hist. Soc. of Pa.).

94. Mary Colton Smith and Edmund Curtis Smith, Jr.

95. Kenner Garrard (1827–79), U.S. Military Academy class of 1851, was a son of Jeptha Dudley Garrard and Sarah Bella Ludlow Garrard. Benjamin Chambers Ludlow (1832–98), the son of James C. Ludlow and Josephine Dunlop Ludlow, was Chase's brother-in-law and Garrard's cousin. Both men later received brevets as major generals in the U.S. Army. Cooper, "Cornelius Ludlow," 49; *Biographical Cyclopædia*, 5:1220–21, 6:1494–96; Des Cognets, *Governor Garrard*, 31–32; Heitman, *Historical Register*, 1:447–48, 646.

96. Albert Lewis, a Cincinnati pork packer, was a brother of Samuel and Henry Lewis. Chase to Lewis Tappan, Oct. 18, 1842 (Chase Papers, L.C.); *Cinc. Dir. (1846)*, 245.

to enquire for Wade[97]—Mr. Sampson called—wants title exd. & had drawn— Mrs Ball came in—told her thought we shd. be out there this week—dinner at Ritter's—to Mrs Smith's to see Ed—took him to ride—to our house—Belle[98] kind to him nice lunch—took him home—& returned, calling to enquire again for Dr. Worcester—glad to hear that he is better— Mem. Col. Dudley in office about ejectment costs—tea with wife & Kate—then family prayers—worked on Ed & Carries a/cs[99]—wrote above— Met Mr. Wright in Street & explained about Jonas.[1]

SUNDAY, APL. 4: Rose late this morning—past 7—which I confess with shame, & resolve to amend with Divine help—after breakfast went to town to enquire after Dr. Worcester—the crape on the door announced that all was over—went in & learned that he had expired a few minutes before, at ten o'clock—offered my services in anything I could do & returned— Dr. Mussey told me that Dr. W—— had some conversation with him about religion, & expressed to his brother his confidence in Christ for salvation— He was a man of real religious sentiments, as I judge from a long acquaintance. He had some peculiar views which I never clearly understood. His mind was active & inquiring, & resolutely honest. I never knew a franker or sincerer man. Emphatically he was faithful & true. I loved him as a brother; & have now no friend left for whom I feel the same attachment. He was greatly beloved & honored in the community; and has left no one who can supply his place. Learned, without pretension, cheerful, without levity, earnest, without fanaticism, he was a good physician, a good citizen, and a good friend.— I wish his Christian character had been more open to observation. I am sure he was a sincere believer, And, I trust, he has found acceptance with God. I mourn for him not at all without hope—but where shall I find a friend like him. He, more than any one else thought as I did on many things, & felt as I did. I had entire confidence in him. His heart knew no guile. He was incapable of deceit

---

97. Joseph McDougal was one of Chase's law students. Wade may have been Benjamin Franklin Wade or his brother Edward (1802–66), a Liberty party activist from Cleveland and a Free-Soil and Republican congressman, 1853–61. *Bio. Dir. U.S. Cong.*, 1989; Chase to E. Wade, June 23, 1847, Henry McDougal to Chase, Aug. 24, 1863 (Chase Papers, L.C.); *Cinc. Dir. (1846)*, 379.
98. Sarah Bella Dunlop Ludlow Chase.
99. Chase apparently served as guardian for Caroline ("Carrie") A. Smith (b. 1829), Chase's second wife's sister, and her brother, Edmund Curtis Smith, Jr. C. Smith to Chase, Jan. 26, Mar. 21, 1846, E. Smith to C. H. James, Jan. 14, 1846, E. Smith to Chase, Feb. 27, 1846, and "Family Memoranda" (Chase Papers, L.C.).
1. Joseph Jonas, a Cincinnati resident. *Cinc. Dir. (1846)*, 221.

or hypocrisy.² Went this morning to Mr. Bushnells sermon.— Sermon on Evidences of Christian Character, plain, practical & persuasive. When I look back upon the twenty years which have rolled away since I professed faith in Christ & see what inconsistencies, what sins, what omissions have marked my course & stained every day, I am overwhelmed with confusion, & am forced to cry God! be merciful to me a sinner. All these years have been crowded with mercies, intermingled with severe chastisements intended, also, doubtless as mercies. And how evil & unthankful I have been! If I do not despair, it is only because Christ has died,³ nay, rather has risen again, & ever liveth to make intercession for me.

TUES. APL. 6. Attended the funeral of Dr. Worcester at Judge Burnets this afternoon at 3 o'clock. A large assemblage was present. Every man seemed to feel as if he had lost a near friend. All were sad—many wept. Tears flowed freely from eyes unused to weeping. The good old Doctor Beecher spoke, with deep earnestness, of the virtues of the deceased—of his established faith in Christ—of his readiness to depart—of his regret that he had not made a public profession of religion—of his dying messages to his friends; and exhorted all to lay hold on the hope which sustained him. Every carriage to the grave was occupied & many went on foot. His remains were deposited for the time in the family vault of Judge Burnet. The artist Baker⁴ took a cast of his head & will furnish busts to his friends. It will be something—yes much to have such a memorial of such a man.

WED. APL. 7: Rode out this afternoon with my brother in law Ed. C. Smith / He is following all the elder members of his family to the grave. He is much wasted by consumption & cannot survive very long. He said that he had become reconciled to die, & that, if it was the will of God he was willing to go. [We] rode as far as my house, where I got some refreshment for him & returned with him to town. Home in omnibus & in the evening after family prayers, at Mr. Yeatman's, where saw Messrs Yeatman, Aubrey & Thompson, & Meses Yeatman & Aubrey⁵—

---

2. A double *x* follows this sentence in the original, then the next sentence continues on the same line.
3. The comma appears to have been written over an exclamation point.
4. Cincinnati sculptor Nathan F. Baker (b. ca. 1822). Groce and Wallace, *Dictionary of Artists*, 22.
5. Chase called on the family of Thomas H. Yeatman (b. 1805), Cincinnati banker and industrialist, and his wife, Elizabeth Hartzell Yeatman. During the Civil War, Yeatman served as Treasury agent in Memphis and government purchasing agent

APRIL 12: W. H. Mussey called at the office to deliver a message—
a dying message from my dear friend Worcester. He said that about
one oclock in the morning of Sunday, his strength failing visibly,
Frank Mussey & Dr. Potter, who alone were with him, his brother
David having retired to take some rest,[6] thought it best to acquaint
him with the fact that he could not survive many hours. He either
said 'I am surprised' or 'I'm not surprised'; but they thought the
latter as he at once proceeded to speak in reference to his approaching end. He spoke of his past life; of his trials; of his omissions of
duty. He said he had been sometimes irritable, but he had more
excuse for it than many would think, for he had suffered more than
anyone had an idea of. He confessed freely his unworthiness, and
said that his only reliance was in Christ for salvation. "I believe" said
he "in God the Father, God the Son, & the Spirit." He then offered
a most beautiful & touching prayer. "Father in Heaven," he prayed
"receive a wanderer from thee for thirty five years." William Mussey
said he cd. not remember the words of the prayer, but it was the
most affecting & beautiful he had ever heard. He, also, addressed
some words of admonition to Dr. Potter & Dr. Frank Mussey, who
were both much affected. His brother David came in and they were
alone together a short time. He sent messages to several of his
friends; and spoke particularly of me. He told them to give his love
to me, & spoke strongly of his regard for me & his confidence in
me. After he had specially named several of his friends, he said he
could not mention all—he had not time or strength but desired to
be remembered to all. He then lay quiet, seeming to be engaged
in meditation and prayer; and after a while exclaimed "Oh death
where is thy victory: oh grave where is thy sting?"[7] As the morning
approached he seemed to revive a little and said to Doctor Potter
"Doctor, I shall see the sun rise again." To which the Doctor answered "if you do, you will probably live through the day. The sun
did rise & he was living, and so much easier that Drs Potter & F.
Mussey & his brother went away to breakfast leaving him with
William Mussey. He lay quite tranquilly for a time; when he seemed
to rouse a little, & expressed some solicitude lest what he had said
had given offence to Dr. P. & F. M. William assured him that he had

---

at Vicksburg. Aubrey may have been John F. Aubrey, a local carpenter, or W. Aubrey, an employee at Cincinnati grocers Place, Traber and Co. *Meses* is for "Mesdames," as a plural for "Mrs." Robson, *Biographical Encyclopædia*, 253–54; *Cinc. Dir. (1846)*, 81, 304.

6. Francis Brown Mussey, M.D. (1819–1900), was one of Reuben Dimond Mussey's sons. Joseph F. Potter, an allopathic physician, taught at the Ohio College of Dental Surgery. David F. Worcester operated a local oil mill. *Cinc. Dir. (1846)*, 401; ibid. (1849–50), 229; Emerson, *General Catalogue*, 258; Juettner, *Daniel Drake*, 91–92.

7. "O death, where *is* thy sting? O grave, where *is* thy victory?" 1 Cor. 15:55.

not, & that both were much affected. He said "It is all true, every word." Soon after he began to fail, & William M. sent for his brother & the doctors. They came soon; but he continued to fail, and soon became nearly unconscious. His brother spoke in his ear "Do you know your brother." A pressure of the hand was the only token of recognition: and soon after, about a quarter before ten on Sunday morning this excellent & accomplished man ceased to breathe, leaving a void, which as Judge Burnet justly remarked, "no man can fill"

APRIL 17: John Frink, of New York, husband of Cousin Charlotte Wallace, was with me last night, & went to town with me in the omnibus this morning.[8] I remember a levity of conversation which I deplore: Forward came in—proposes to rent mill at $300 per annum—put in breast wheel, 300 feet trench for race & complete repair—lease for 6 years[9]— At Court—made docket entries from minutes—to see bust of Worcester—pleased with it—at Melodeon for Carries photograph[10]—not prepared / dinner—after, to see Edmund—found him quite low—spent some little time on Clarkson case at office—home in omnibus— There is to be a meeting tonight to nominate Gen. Taylor for the Presidency.[11]

APRIL 23: Edmund Smith, my late wife's brother died today. He was conscious almost to the last moment, and perfectly resigned. He had made his will giving the larger part of his small property to his only surviving sister, & leaving some bequests to his mother, two aunts & some other relatives. He expressed himself as ready to depart, trusting in Christ for salvation. He was singularly upright & amiable. I never knew him do a wrong act. To his mother & sister he was a kind and affectionate son & brother. He was not a member of the church, but had been thoughtful on the subject of religion, and found, I trust, acceptance through Christ.

---

8. Charlotte ("Lottie") Wallace Frink was a cousin of Chase's first wife, Catharine Jane Garniss Chase. Amelia Wallace Smith to Chase, Sept. 25, 1846, Feb. 15, 1864 (Chase Papers, L.C.).

9. The mill was part of the estate which Chase oversaw for the Ludlow heirs. Forward, who may have been William Forward, a Cincinnati cabinetmaker, "succeeded very ill" in the venture. *Cinc. Dir. (1850–51)*, 100; James Dunlop Ludlow to Chase, Oct. 8, 1847, statement of account with Catherine Ludlow Baker, [1852?] (Chase Papers, L.C.).

10. The Melodeon was a three-story structure built in 1846 on the corner of Fourth and Walnut Streets. Its tenants included a dentist, a music publisher, an apothecary, and a daguerreotypist. Cist, *Sketches and Statistics*, 163.

11. Zachary Taylor (1784–1850), twelfth president of the U.S. *DAB*, 18:349–54.

APRIL 25: In the city at church—Mr. Gillespie on selfishness—unprofitable—dinner at Judge McLean's. Attended Edmund's funeral in afternoon—many present / This evening little Kate disobeyed her stepmother & made untrue representation: admonished her, & promised to punish her, if I cd. not otherwise induce her to amend.

1848

JANY 1. Went to my office this morning intending to make some New Years calls but found a letter from Thos H. Hewes of New Orleans asking my aid in obtaining evidence to establish the claim of Samuel Brown, to freedom. He states that a Judge in New Orleans handed him some affidavits, purporting to have been made in Feby. last before Wm H Skerritt, late mayor of Chillicothe, to the effect that Samuel Brown was a free born inhabitant of Chillicothe, where his parents, both free, had lived for many years. Mr. Hewes wishes me to write to Mr. Skerritt that his (Hewes') statements may be depended on; and says the negro's story is that he was hired to go as a waiter into Virginia, where he was sold, and had not exhibited his papers before he shewed them to the Judge, for fear of the trader.[12] I recd. also a letter from Cassius Clay, a noble letter.[13] I called at once on Col. Bond on Hewes business.[14] Found him still confined to his bed by the effects of the injury he received in November. Col. Bond says that he did not know Samuel, but knew the old people well & has no doubt that Samuel is their son & free. He referred me to Mr. Ligget, bookkeeper L. D. Leach & Co.[15] Went to Mr. Leach's store but found it closed. Returned to my office &

12. Hewes, an attorney who had dealt with Chase on other legal matters, had agreed to represent Brown gratis in spite of finding his client "an accomplished scoundrel." Skerritt, a Chillicothe merchant, had served in 1838 as the city's first mayor. Henry H. Bennett, ed., *The County of Ross: A History of Ross County, Ohio* . . . (Madison, 1902), 224; Lyle S. Evans, ed., *A Standard History of Ross County, Ohio* . . . (Chicago, 1917), 1:277; Hewes to Chase, July 11, 1848, Mar. 10, 1849 (Chase Papers, Hist. Soc. of Pa.).

13. Cassius Marcellus Clay (1810–1903) of Kentucky published the abolitionist newspaper *True American* and served as U.S. minister to Russia, 1861–62, 1863–69. Clay's letter explained his decision in 1846 to serve with the U.S. Army in Mexico as an attempt to "to convince the *people* that I was not *their* enemy but the enemy of *slavery* of *slaveholders* if you please." Clay to Chase, Dec. 27, 1847 (Chase Papers, Hist. Soc. of Pa.); *DAB*, 4:169–70.

14. Attorney William Key Bond (1792–1864), former resident of Chillicothe, militia officer, U.S. congressman, 1835–41. *Bio. Dir. U.S. Cong.*, 641; Lanman, *Biographical Annals*, 47.

15. Local commercial merchants. The firm's bookkeeper might have been John Liggett. *Cinc. Dir.* (*1849–50*), 173, 176.

wrote Mr. Skerrit & Mr. Hewes. Home to dinner. Afternoon read Sumner's Address on Fame & Glory to wife[16]— And an admirable production it is. Towards evening Gallagher called & insisted on my spending evening [a]t his house. After tea went to G's—found Vaughan, Shreve, Drake, Butler, Matthews, Billings of Nashville, Cassidy, Jewett and one or two more[17]—good oysters & pleasant evening except that punch which Gallagher introduced after most of us had left the supper room—good yankeeism by Jewett & good gallicism by Cassidy: took Butler home with me.

JANY 2: SUNDAY: At home all day—read Warburton Church & State—& Phelps God's Method with great social wrongs.[18] Butler left for home, with his friends on evening boat.

JANY 3. Went to Court to attend call of docket—called at Leach & Co's to see Liggett—he said he knew nobody from Chillicothe, now in New Orleans—knew Brown rather a bad character— in a scrape at St Louis last Spring from which extricated by Mr. Johnson[19] with considerable difficulty: returned to office & thence to dinner—after dinner Mr. Ligget called at office—gave me names of two persons from Chillicothe in New Orleans—more particulars of scrape at St Louis— Recd. letter from Mr. Hewes who Says "Brown in custody of Sheriff—afraid he is imposter & has colluded with seller whose name, assumed, Barber—real, Buckley." Sent for Wesley Brown who came. He tells me Saml., after scrape in St Louis, was barber here; left with Buckley, notorious kidnapper, knowing [torn] character & practices: not too good to collude with seller: Wrote to Mr. Hewes, substance of what I learned:

---

16. Charles Sumner, *Fame and Glory. An Address before the Literary Societies of Amherst College, at their Anniversary, August 11, 1847* (Boston, 1847). Sumner (1811–74) gained reputation as a Boston attorney and orator and served in the U.S. Senate as a Free-Soiler, later a Republican, from Massachusetts, 1851–74. *DAB*, 18:208–14.

17. Louisville author and businessman Thomas H. Shreve (1808–53); Stanley Matthews (1824–89), Cincinnati attorney and editor, clerk of the Ohio House, 1848–49, state senator, 1856–58, U.S. senator, 1877–79, associate justice of the U.S. Supreme Court, 1881–89; possibly James J. S. Billings, a member of the editorial staff at Nashville's *Daily Orthopolitan;* Peter Cassidy, a local grocer. *Appletons'*, 5:517; *DAB*, 12:418–20; Gilkey, *Ohio Hundred Year Book*, 170, 214; Clayton, *History of Davidson County*, 232; *Cinc. Dir. (1849–50)*, 57.

18. William Warburton, *The Alliance between Church and State, or, the Necessity and Equity of an Established Religion and a Test-Law Demonstrated* . . . (London, 1736); Amos A. Phelps, *Letters to Professor Stowe and Dr. Bacon: On God's Real Method with Great Social Wrongs* . . . (New York, 1848).

19. The slave trader who had detained Samuel Brown. Thomas H. Hewes to Chase, Mar. 10, 1849 (Chase Papers, Hist. Soc. of Pa.); entry for Jan. 1, 1848, above.

Colored man, James M. Bell,[20] called for advice about claim on Orphan Asylum—gave it to him. Various other callers. Sent Mr. Hoadly & Mr. McDougal to ascertain matters enquired of by C. M. Clay.[21] Vaughan called with letter from Clay, authorizing him to draw at sight for $800 to cover expences of supplying subscribers to True American.[22] Vaughan asked me to endorse draft, that he might get the money. Told Ball to write to Hamilton after seeing Judge Burgoyne, about payt. Ludlow taxes in Butler Co.[23] Judge Burgoyne called about Insurance arbitration. Called at office Coffin & Mitchell—some talk about matter in arbitration. Home to tea: Aunt Adela with us.[24] After tea attended Dr. Aydelotte's lecture which very good, "Christianity grand Conservative Principle of Human Progress: much just & striking thought. Home & wrote foregoing: now to prepare Answer of Alden ads Alden.

JANY 4: Nothing of much interest transpired today. Engaged almost wholly in professional matters of no special consequence. Taylor came in about dark & read Cass' non interference letter—expressing strong disapprobation.[25] Telegraph from Cushing, wishing to know when I wd. be at Columbus.[26] Aunt Adela here in morning & at dinner: told Belle to speak to her about Texas slaves. Mary Murphy at tea. All evening upon Alden's answer: Not finished: now 11 oclock to bed.

20. A Cincinnati plasterer. *Cinc. Dir. (1849–50)*, 32.
21. George Hoadly, Jr. (1826–1902), a judge of the superior court of Cincinnati, 1851–55, 1859–65, and Democratic governor of Ohio, 1884–86, was a student in Chase's law office. Ibid., 139; *DAB*, 9:84–85; Gilkey, *Ohio Hundred Year Book*, 328.
22. John C. Vaughan had recently assumed the editorship of Cassius Clay's newspaper. Richardson, *Cassius Marcellus Clay*, 54.
23. John Burgoyne (1801–81), at various times justice of the peace in Mill Creek township, judge of Hamilton County's court of common pleas, and judge of probate. *Biographical Cyclopædia*, 5:1250–51; *History of Cincinnati and Hamilton County*, 560.
24. Adela Ludlow, apparently a relative of Sarah Bella Dunlop Ludlow Chase. Chase to James Ralston Skinner, Feb. 27, 1850 (Chase Papers, L.C.); Chase to Kate Chase, Aug. 4, 1853 (Chase Papers, Hist. Soc. of Pa.).
25. Democratic politician Lewis Cass (1782–1866), a former soldier and former governor of Michigan Territory, served as U.S. senator from Michigan, 1845–48, 1849–57, and as U.S. secretary of state, 1857–60. His *Letter from Hon. Lewis Cass, of Michigan, on the War and the Wilmot Proviso* (Washington, 1847) anticipated the doctrine of "squatter sovereignty" by suggesting that federal authorities lacked authority to regulate slavery in the territories. *DAB*, 3:562–64; *Bio. Dir. U.S. Cong.*, 754–55.
26. Benjamin Tupper Cushing (1825–49), a Columbus attorney, had previously studied in Chase's office. They were discussing formation of a legal partnership which apparently never materialized. Chase to Cushing, Jan. 3, 1848, Cushing to Chase, Jan. 4, 8, 1848 (Chase Papers, L.C.); Coggeshall, *Poets and Poetry of the West*, 489; Goss, *Cincinnati*, 2:493.

JULY 5: Many & striking events since last entry above—the most important so far as I am concerned the call of a Convention in Ohio made in advance of the National Whigs, & Democratic Conventions to assemble after the adjt. of those, to nominate if those do not, Free Territory candidates.[27] I prepared the circular & obtained the signatures of a few, Messrs Starr, Guilford, Gregory, Shields, &c & sent it out inviting signatures to a call which I also prepared[28]— The calls were returned with three thousand names / This movement greatly encouraged the Friends of Freedom in other states, & the results are now developing themselves

Walked to town this morning—thinking most of the way of Calhoun's speech in defence of Slavery delivered last week in the Senate[29]—went to court & attended to call of submitted docket—took judgt. Dumont v Gilbert—argued dems. Lewis ads —took judgment nonsuit Bartlett ads Winans &c— Judge Key promises to do very well[30]—called on Bates the barber to get him to make enquiries about colored boy & wife, supposed to be kidnapped &c by Ficklin M.C. of Illinois[31]— Went to Fox's to cross examine in Wheeler ads Merreweather—called on V. Worthington with Wheeler to learn what he would testify to—disappointed—Vaughan called just from Dayton—wrote Hamlin urging Paper forward &c[32]—also Wrote Stanton Editor Chronicle New Garden,[33] views about Van Buren &c & saying Vaughan & I wd. probably

---

27. Chase's arrangement for simultaneous conventions of the Ohio Liberty and Free Territory parties, meeting in Columbus on June 21, 1848, was part of an attempt to form a political coalition opposed to slavery in the territories. The combined gathering severed ties with the Whigs and Democrats and called for a national convention, to meet in Buffalo on Aug. 8, of opponents to the presidential candidacies of Lewis Cass and Zachary Taylor. Columbus *Weekly Ohio State Journal*, June 22, 28, 1848; Stephen E. Maizlish, *The Triumph of Sectionalism: The Transformation of Ohio Politics, 1844–1856* (Kent, Ohio, 1983), 105–6.

28. The final enumeration, solicited by Hamilton County antislavery activists Henry Starr, Nathan Guilford, E. M. Gregory, James W. Shields, and others, appeared in *Cincinnati Gazette Extra*, Apr. 1848.

29. Calhoun's speech of June 28 argued against the restriction of slavery in the territories. *Cong. Globe*, 30th Cong., 1st sess., 1848, 875–76.

30. Thomas Marshall Key (1819–69), a future Ohio state senator and aide to Gen. George B. McClellan, was judge in Hamilton County's commission court. *Appletons'*, 3:530; *Cinc. Dir. (1849–50)*, 162; Heitman, *Historical Register*, 1:595.

31. Democrat Orlando Bell Ficklin (1808–86). *Bio. Dir. U.S. Cong.*, 993.

32. Attorney and Free-Soil activist Edward Stowe Hamlin (1808–94), U.S. congressman, 1844–45, published the Cleveland *True Democrat*. During the late 1840s and early 1850s, Hamlin served as president of Ohio's Board of Public Works and, with Israel Garrard, operated the *Ohio Standard*, a Free-Soil newspaper in Columbus. *Bio. Dir. U.S. Cong.*, 1122; Gutgesell, *Ohio Newspapers*, 127; Chase to Stanley Matthews, Mar. 1, 1849, Matthews to Chase, Mar. 12, 1849 (Chase Papers, L.C.).

33. Benjamin Stanton of New Garden, Ind. Stanton to Chase, Oct. 10, 1844 (Chase Papers, L.C.).

attend meeting at Centreville—coming home read my speech made Saty evg. to wife.

NOV. 22: Returned yesterday (Monday) Morn'g from Columbus where I spent near a week in attendance on the Circuit Court, arriving there Tuesday Morning at 1 & leaving Sunday Evening at 7 P.M. I did little in court except to continue some cases, among them Parish ads Driskell, which we thought it inexpedient to try on account of the complexion of the Jury & the state of public feeling immediately after a contested Presidential Election— Argued a question, as to the right of the Lafayette Bank to certain shares of stock held as collateral, arising in the Mahard Case—Gholson[34] & Judge Wright *contra*. Attended by invitation a meeting of State Free Dem. Committee. They agreed to make an effort to raise 5000 for the cause—I subscribed $200. They agreed also to call a State Convention of delegates,—one for each County & one for every 500 votes given for Van Buren in each County & one for any fraction over 250—to assemble at Columbus, Thursday Decr. 29:[35] Many friends think it probable I shall be elected to the U.S. Senate. It is possible, but not, I think, probable. Wrote to Brown at Cleveland;[36] also to Snodgrass at Baltimore, in ansr. to letter from him about compensation for visit to Ohio.[37]

Yesterday, after return, attended to getting Hathaway Case (Inquest of Lunacy) under way[38] & commenced brief on questions between Franklin & Lafayette Banks in Mahard case, on which engaged till half past ten: Vaughan (who said he had letter from

---

34. Cincinnati attorney William Yates Gholson (1807–70), Princeton class of 1825, a future justice on the Ohio Supreme Court. *Appletons'*, 2:634; *DAB*, 7:234.
35. The committee's meeting was in Columbus. On Dec. 30, the 180-member convention, also in Columbus, ratified the Aug. 1848 national Free-Soil platform adopted in Buffalo and established a state platform which, among other provisions, called for the repeal of Ohio's "Black Laws," disapproved of state cooperation with federal fugitive slave acts, and issued a plan to reform the state constitution. *Cincinnati Weekly Globe*, Nov. 23, 1848; *Daily Ohio State Journal*, Jan. 3, 1849.
36. Attorney Thomas Brown (1819–67), Free-Soil activist, founder of the Cleveland *True Democrat*, and special agent for the U.S. Treasury, 1861–67. *Appletons'*, 1:411.
37. Joseph Evans Snodgrass (1813–80), a physician and editor of Baltimore's *Saturday Morning Visitor*, an antislavery newspaper, had accused Chase of reneging on an offer to finance a recent trip to Ohio, where Snodgrass had spoken in behalf of the Free-Soil and temperance movements. Scharf, *History of Baltimore*, 617; Wallace, *North American Authors*, 427; Snodgrass to Chase, Sept. 26, Oct. 6, Nov. 12, 1848 (Chase Papers, L.C.).
38. The case, also mentioned below at May 14–15, 1849, involved disputed ownership of property in the family of Cincinnatian Henry Hathaway, one of Chase's clients. Chase brought the litigation to a successful conclusion early in 1850. Henry Hathaway, Jr., to Chase, Dec. 19, 1848, May 21, 1849, Apr. 17, 1850 (Chase Papers, L.C.).

Briggs cordial to me) Taylor, Disney J Goesbeck & others called in the course of day[39]—wrote article on Convention—

Today, did not get to office till past nine—engaged on Brief (commd yesterday) till half past 12, when finished & mailed it, with Exceptions & Reports of Sale & Liens, to Judge McLean at Columbus—home to dinner—wife out—read Waddy Thompson's Mexico[40]—dinner—back to office—went to Court House to see about Hathaway case— Saw Judge Saffin[41] & Buckingham, Deputy Sheriff— Told Judge cd. not consent to continuance & why— Saw number of lawyers, some of whom mentioned my probable election as Senator— Might believe it myself if it did not seem so absolutely out of the question whenever I seriously think of it— Saw Donn Piatt of Logan who says he will be at Columbus at opening of session[42]— He reports that Judge Read says the Free Soilers may have the Senator if they will give the Democrats the other offices. Told him I hoped the Free Soilers wd. act with conscientious regard to right, & let consequences take care of themselves— Met Judge Key as I came down— Said he wd. hear argument on Lewis' Case— Some talk about his sitting with Judge Saffin in Lunacy case— Matthews called—arranged papers—home to tea— Chat with wife in Parlor—read Shelford on Lunacy[43]—wrote foregoing—

JOURNAL I

Lived on River Road—Wm Forsyth was gardner[44]—paid him in full & dischd. 4 [Aug.] 48—$14 per mo.

---

39. Probably John H. Groesbeck and William Disney, city treasurer, or David Tiernan Disney (1803–57), former member of the Ohio House and Senate and a U.S. congressman, 1849–55. James A. Briggs was a Cleveland attorney, businessman, Whig (subsequently Republican) political activist, and orator. He later acted as the Ohio state agent in New York. *Bio. Dir. U.S. Cong.*, 913; *Cinc. Dir. (1849–50)*, 82; Elroy McKendree Avery, *A History of Cleveland* . . . (Chicago, 1918), 1:217; William R. Coates et al., *A History of Cuyahoga County and the City of Cleveland* (Chicago, 1924), 1:445; Rose, *Cleveland*, 145, 175–76, 216, 245, 307; *New York Dir. (1863)*, 106.

40. Waddy Thompson, *Recollections of Mexico* (New York, 1846).

41. James Saffin, associate judge, Hamilton County Court of Common Pleas, and former city marshal. *Cinc. Dir. (1846)*, 328; ibid. (1850–51), 234; Gilkey, *Ohio Hundred Year Book*, 537.

42. Piatt (1819–91), an attorney and author, had recently moved from Cincinnati to his homestead near West Liberty, Ohio. He later pursued careers as a judge of Hamilton County's Court of Common Pleas, 1852–53; from captain to lieutenant colonel in Union service, 1861–65; member of the Ohio House, 1866–67; and co-editor of the Washington, D.C., *Capital*. *DAB*, 14:555–56; Gilkey, *Ohio Hundred Year Book*, 295.

43. Leonard Shelford, *A Practical Treatise on the Law Concerning Lunatics, Idiots and Persons of Unsound Mind* . . . (London, 1833).

44. A Quaker who apparently worked for Chase the entire summer before moving to New Orleans. Chase's residence in this period was in Storrs Township. This

1849

JOURNAL IV

M. JANY 1. Begin the New Year at Columbus—engaged on argument in Lane Seminary case,[45] but subject to a good many interruptions. The argument of the disputed seats from Hamilton County in the Ohio H. Reps commences today—Geo E. Pugh for himself and Peirce; O. M. Spencer for himself & Runyan.[46]

T. JAN. 2. Went over to the House today to hear Spencer & Pugh. At noon wrote out proposition or rather engagement to be signed by such gentlemen of the Dem. Party as might see fit to the effect that in case Pugh & Peirce should be admitted, no attempt should be made to keep in Sheldon, a Democratic Member from Portage,[47] having the Clerks certificate, given to him in consequence of a mere mistake, through which a number of votes making a majority for his opponent were not counted. Saw Judge Smart, of Highland, in company with Dr. Townshend.[48] He assured us that he would give no countenance to any attempt to keep Sheldon in, but would unite with the Freesoilers against the Dem. candidate for Speaker, unless he wd. pledge himself to make a fair Committee on Elections. This interview was before the House met in the morning. Handed the

---

entry is from memoranda at the end of Journal I. Forsyth to Chase, Feb. 13, 1849 (Chase Papers, L.C.); *Cinc. Dir. (1846)*, 121.

45. *Kemper v. Trustees of Lane Seminary*.

46. Democrat George Ellis Pugh (1822–76) was a partner in the Cincinnati law firm of Pugh and Pendleton. He later served in the Ohio House, 1848–50, and U.S. Senate, 1855–61. Pugh and Alexander N. Pierce had recently been chosen as Democrats to the Ohio House. Their election was challenged by Spencer and Cincinnati builder George W. Runyan, both Whigs, who also claimed victory due to a Jan. 1848 reapportionment act engineered by the Whig majority in Ohio's previous general assembly. This contested election, combined with a near-even split between Democrats and Whigs in the new assembly, offered Ohio's eleven newly elected Free-Soil legislators an opportunity to wield the balance of power and to strike political bargains favorable to the coalition's agenda and leaders. *Bio. Dir. U.S. Cong.*, 1678–79; *Cinc. Dir. (1849–50)*, 246; *Cincinnati Weekly Globe*, Nov. 23, 1848; *DAB*, 15:258–59; A. G. Riddle, "Recollections of the Forty-Seventh General Assembly of Ohio, 1847–48," *Magazine of Western History* 6 (Aug. 1887): 342; *Weekly Ohio State Journal*, Jan. 7, 1849; Francis P. Weisenburger, *The Passing of the Frontier, 1825–1850*, v. 3 of Carl Wittke, ed., *The History of the State of Ohio* (Columbus, 1941), 470–71.

47. George Sheldon, Ohio state representative, 1848–50. Gilkey, *Ohio Hundred Year Book*, 218, 304.

48. Hugh Smart (b. 1800), a state representative from Highland County, 1848–49, was a former associate judge of the county's court of common pleas. Norton Strange Townshend, M.D. (1815–95), a resident of Lorain County and a member of the Free-Soil coalition, had recently been elected to the Ohio House as a Liberty party candidate. He later served as a Democratic congressman, 1851–53. Ibid., 305, 312, 522; *Bio. Dir. U.S. Cong.*, 1950; *History of Ross and Highland Counties, Ohio...* (Cleveland, 1880), 418; Riddle, "Recollections," 343.

paper written at noon to Dr. T. just before the P.M. sitting. Pugh concluded his argument, wh. was both able & eloquent. Dr. T. moved an adjournment. It was lost. I told Disney who was near me that if the question on the right to seats should be taken now, P. & P. wd. be excluded. He went over to speak to the Dems. Breslin consulted Dr. T. He, thinking Van Doren wd. vote for P. & P. said adjournment unnecessary.[49] Question then taken on P. & P.'s right. Ayes 35 Nays 35. only Townshend voting with Dems; Van Doren voting against them. Next on Spencer & Runyons right Ayes 32 Nays 38. Among the latter Townshend, Morse, Van Doren, Riddle, Smart.[50] The Democrats were much excited—charged bad faith on Freesoilers— Several came to see me: told them to keep cool: Many threatened to go home & break up Legislature, but finally concluded to take another day for consideration, if enough Freesoilers would vote with them to adjourn next day without electing Speaker &c which they agreed to do.

W. JAN'Y 3. There was a good deal of consultation today: the Democrats still much excited & inclined to break up the Legislature. The adjournment took place as agreed. Starr came up tonight, arriving abt. one A.M. 4th.[51]

TH. JANY 4. This morning it was finally understood that the Dem. candidate for Speaker should be elected—Stanley Matthews Freesoiler Clerk—& that a Committee on Priv. & Elec. should be constituted of one Freesoiler, 2 Dems. & 2 Whigs.[52] The House met at 10. Breslin, Dem. was elected Speaker—Matthews, Clerk,—& House after several ballots for Sergt. at Arms adjd. I was not present at

---

49. John G. Breslin (1824–92) was editor of the *Seneca Advertiser*, 1842–54, a Democratic member of the Ohio House, 1848–50, and Ohio state treasurer, 1852–56. At this time, he was enmeshed in negotiations which, among other results, secured his election as Speaker of the House on Jan. 3. Isaac Van Doren, a Free-Soiler from Ottawa County, had recently been elected to the Ohio House as a Democrat. *A Biographical Record of Fairfield County, Ohio* . . . (New York, 1902), 266–71; *Daily Ohio State Journal*, Jan. 4, 1849; Gilkey, *Ohio Hundred Year Book*, 214, 313, 453; Riddle, "Recollections," 343.

50. John Flavel Morse (1801–84), a Whig with Free-Soil sympathies, represented Ashtabula and Lake Counties. Later, he served as an Ohio state senator and, from 1862 to 1876, as a special agent for the U.S. Treasury. Albert Gallatin Riddle (1816–1902), another Whig member of the Free-Soil coalition, had recently been elected to the Ohio House from Geauga County and, between 1861 and 1863, was one of Ohio's Republican congressmen. Riddle, "Recollections," 343; *Biographical Cyclopædia*, 3:730; *DAB*, 15:591; Gilkey, *Ohio Hundred Year Book*, 290, 299.

51. Chase may have inserted the last sentence of this entry after the succeeding entry was written.

52. The Committee on Privileges and Elections, charged with seating members of the assembly. *Daily Ohio State Journal*, Jan. 9, 1849.

either morning or afternoon session, but busy at my argument except when interrupted by callers— Monfort & Long called in even'g, to ask if it was desired to elect Purdy Free Soil nominee by Dem. votes[53]—cd. not tell— Submitted argt. in Lane Seminary case.[54]

FRI. JANY 5: Had long walk & conversation with Lucien Swift, Senator from Portage.[55] He intimated his desire of my election as Senator—talking of printing—of expected election to fill vacancy from Clinton. I suggested expediency of Dems aiding Election of Free Soiler—he concurred. We parted I promising to write note recommending this to Dems of Clinton, to be signed by Dems in Legislature. Wrote it & went over to Senate & handed it to him— met Purdy—said Watts Whig had been elected Sergeant at Arms[56]— all Dems voting for him & no freesoilers though he Freesoil Candidate— Subd. argt.

6. SAT.[57] Submitted argument to Supreme Court in Staughton ads Brisbane. Prepared some resolutions on the subject of the public printing at the request of a member of the Senate.

7. SUN Spent this day in my room preparing bill for separate schools for colored children, embracing a clause for the repeal of all the Black Laws. If this law can be carried, I thought, it would be an ample reward for all our labor in the last election: Not willing to devote Sunday to such a labor, but having so little other time, and believing I could in no way do so much good, did set myself at it,—also prepared in part bill to prevent kidnapping.[58] Riddle

---

53. Luther Monfort of Darke County, a member of the Ohio House of Representatives; Alexander Long (1816–86), a Cincinnati attorney and future Democratic congressman who at this time represented Hamilton County in the legislature; and John H. Purdy of Columbus, publisher of the *Ohio Land Seller* and a candidate for the position of sergeant at arms in the Ohio House. *Bio. Dir. U.S. Cong.*, 1386; Gilkey, *Ohio Hundred Year Book*, 281; William Alexander Taylor, *Ohio Statesman and Hundred Year Book, from 1788 to 1892, Inclusive* (Columbus, 1892), 231; *Col. Dir. (1848)*, 166; *Daily Ohio State Journal*, Jan. 4, 1849.
54. The last six words of this entry are in the margin, possibly added after the next entry was written.
55. Lucian Swift of Akron, an attorney, represented Summit and Portage counties in the Ohio Senate, 1848–50. Gilkey, *Ohio Hundred Year Book*, 168, 310; Swift to Chase, Apr. 24, 1849 (Chase Papers, L.C.); *Nat. Cyc.*, 6:286.
56. Democrat David Watt. Gilkey, *Ohio Hundred Year Book*, 214.
57. Chase probably added the last two words of the preceding paragraph sometime after he had completed the body of that entry. He also probably added the dates and days of the week for the Jan. 6–9 entries, which are squeezed into available space at the beginnings of paragraphs, sometime after writing the entries' text.
58. The proposed modifications to Ohio's Black Laws would have allowed blacks to enter the state, testify in court against whites, and receive public education in segregated facilities. Final passage of the motions occurred on Feb. 10, after Chase's

called. Most willingly would I forego every hope of personal distinction if I could secure the adoption of the great principles of Right, Justice & Humanity for which we are contending, by retiring myself to complete obscurity, recognized of none but a few friends & God.

8. MON.   Court decided Brisbane avs Staughton against defendant our client— I not present when decision announced— Called to see Mr. Randall[59]—dealt frankly with him as to Senatorial Election— The Democrats celebrated 8th Jan'y by Supper at American as usual[60]—I not there— At House when resolution adopted to count votes for Governor—went home thinking proceeding would be dull & formal—but afterwards heard that quite a scene occurred[61]—

9 TUES.   In evening Read, Judge,[62] called & Hamlin—the former visits me much—he talked this evening of various matters—said he dissented from court in Brisbane vs Staughton—approved of platform of Free Democracy, especially of resolution in relation to repeal of Black Laws—regretted I & other Free Democrats had not been invited to 8th Jan'y supper. Judge Read evidently, is almost persuaded to be a free democrat—and would be alotegether such doubtless if the body of the old democracy was quite ready to take our platform.

Court this morning decided Lane Seminary case for the defendants— My Court in Bank business now ended and I at liberty to go home, and very glad to be so at liberty— This evening attempted

---

Free-Soil allies agreed to vote for the seating of G. E. Pugh and A. N. Pierce in return for Democratic support on the race measures. The "kidnapping" bill, which failed to pass the assembly, would have prevented state and local officials from cooperating with federal fugitive slave laws. Entries for Jan. 10, 24, and 25, 1849, below; Maizlish, *Triumph of Sectionalism*, 133–34; *Ohio Acts*, 47th Assembly, 17–18; Ohio General Assembly, House of Representatives, *Journal*, 47th Assem., 1st sess., 1849, 736; Ohio General Assembly, Senate, *Journal*, 47th Assem., 1st sess., 1849, 581; Frank Uriah Quillan, *The Color Line in Ohio* . . . (Ann Arbor, 1913), 36–37.

59. Brewster Randall of Ashtabula County, a member, 1847–50, and speaker, 1848–49, of the Ohio Senate. Gilkey, *Ohio Hundred Year Book*, 298; Taylor, *Ohio Statesman*, 168.

60. The American Hotel, at the corner of High and State Streets. *Col. Dir. (1848)*, 89.

61. The outburst, which extended into the following day, arose when Hard-Money Democrats learned of a partial defection by members of the Free-Soil coalition which permitted supporters of Whig candidate Seabury Ford to declare premature victory. *Daily Ohio State Journal*, Jan. 9, 1849; Maizlish, *Triumph of Sectionalism*, 130–31.

62. Nathaniel C. Read.

January 1849 { 203 }

publication of votes for Governor—Archbold[63]—Randall—Judge Tappan[64]

10 WED. Called, this morning, on Cousin Rachel Denison and invited her to go home with me this evening to which she agreed[65]— Called also on Cousin Elizabeth Matthews and found Cousin Mary Ann Wilson with her— Received a pleasant scolding letter from my dear wife & telegraphic despatch from Lincoln wishing to know when I would return[66]—wishing professional consultation— Hamlin called to take leave— Matthews said Rœdter wanted interview[67]—went over to House, where wasting time on unavailing motions to adjourn &c—said goodbye to Townshend, Morse, Riddle, Van Doren, Lee[68] & some others—had a few words with Capt. Rœdter— Left Bill to prevent kidnapping with Hamlin to be put in charge of Riddle— Started for home with Cousin Rachel in company at ½ past 6.

11. THURS. Arrived home after fatiguing night ride— All well and all glad to see me.[69]

21. SUN. At St Pauls morning— Stranger preached—at home in afternoon read Job & Genesis— Evening Vaughan called & mentioned interview with Edwards from Warren[70]—

22. MON. Recd. letter from Riddle

---

63. Edward Archbold of Belmont County, a state representative. Gilkey, *Ohio Hundred Year Book*, 239.
64. Free-Soil activist Benjamin Tappan (1773–1857), Democratic member of the U.S. Senate, 1839–45, and former president judge of Ohio's fifth circuit court of common pleas. *DAB*, 18:300–301.
65. Rachel Denison was evidently a daughter of Chase's aunt, Rachel Chase Denison, and Dr. Joseph A. Denison, Sr. Child, *Cornish*, 2:62.
66. Cincinnati attorney Timothy Danielson Lincoln (1815–90). Greve, *Centennial History*, 2:619–22.
67. Henry Rœdter (1805–57), a German editor and antislavery Democrat, represented Hamilton County in the lower house of the assembly. Ford and Ford, *History of Cincinnati*, 129, 130; Gilkey, *Ohio Hundred Year Book*, 300.
68. Isaac Lee, a state representative from Warren, Ohio. Gilkey, *Ohio Hundred Year Book*, 280.
69. Chase wrote the dates for Jan. 12–24, leaving space between, apparently with the intention of filling in entries for those days. He made brief entries for Jan. 21–24, but wrote nothing for January 12–20.
70. Probably John Miller Edwards (1805–86), attorney, Democratic politician, and editor of the *Mahoning Index*. *Catalogue of Officers and Graduates of Yale University*, 156; *History of Trumbull and Mahoning Counties*, 1:441–42.

23. TUES. Wrote Riddle[71]—

24 WED. Brough (C. H.)[72] called and said that democrats or some of them had bolted from their agreement to repeal the Black Laws and named Cockerill, Rœdter & Mott as most active[73]— A. B. Coleman called for advice about Burnet House[74]— Vaughan agreed to go up to Clinton tomorrow.

THURS. 25. Late up this morning as usual—am ashamed of myself & yet make little improvement— At office after nine— various callers—Vaughan, Brough, Donn Piatt—sent off letters to Hamlin, Stanley Matthews, Dr. Bailey & Eli Nichols[75] Recd. letters from Hamlin, Matthews & Swift, the last enclosing bill to establish separate colored schools &c repealing black laws. H. & M. report progress in Legislature towards repeal of Black Laws and admission of Pugh & Peirce[76]—no notice of bolting from engagement to repeal black laws reported yesterday— Brough found some fault with Swifts bill— Vaughan wanted endorsements $176.75—gave it—furnished him $12 to go to Clinton—expected to go this afternoon— D. Piatt home with me to dinner—left him with ladies—he spoke of new Free Soil Paper at West Liberty[77]— Vaughan at office—did not go to Clinton on a/c message from

---

71. Albert G. Riddle's letter expressed admiration for Chase and discussed the political prospects of James Wickes Taylor, John C. Vaughan, and other state activists. Riddle noted that he had received "all manner of threats" after introducing a bill for the repeal of Ohio's Black Laws. Chase's response relayed news of mutual friends and outlined a proposal for regulating interest rates in the state. Riddle to Chase, Jan. 21, [1849] (Chase Papers, Hist. Soc. of Pa.); Chase to Riddle, Jan. 23, 1849 (Riddle Papers, Western Reserve Hist. Soc.).

72. Charles Henry Brough.

73. Daniel Cockerill (1792–1864) and Samuel R. Mott (b. 1818) represented Adams and Auglaize Counties, respectively. Nelson Wiley Evans and Emmons B. Stivers, *A History of Adams County, Ohio* . . . (West Union, Ohio, 1900), 914, 915; Gilkey, *Ohio Hundred Year Book*, 290; *Portrait and Biographical Record of Auglaize, Logan and Shelby Counties, Ohio* . . . (Chicago, 1892), 216–18.

74. Abraham B. Coleman operated the Burnet House, a hotel at the corner of Third and Vine Streets in Cincinnati. *Cinc. Dir. (1850–51)*, 49, 61; ibid. (1857), 51.

75. Eli Nichols (1799–1871), an attorney, farmer, and former state representative from Belmont County. William J. Bahmer, *Centennial History of Coshocton County, Ohio* (Chicago, 1909), 2:236–40; Gilkey, *Ohio Hundred Year Book*, 292.

76. Hamlin also discussed strategies to appoint state supreme court justices suitable to Democrats in the legislature. In addition, both Hamlin and Matthews offered opinions on prospects for Chase's election to the U.S. Senate. Hamlin to Chase, Jan. 24, 1849 (Chase Papers, Hist. Soc. of Pa.); Matthews to Chase, Jan. 24, 1849 (Chase Papers, L.C.).

77. Piatt had previously edited the West Liberty *Democratic Club*. *DAB*, 14:555; *History of Logan County and Ohio* . . . (Chicago, 1880), 570–73; Robert P. Kennedy, *The Historical Review of Logan County* (Chicago, 1903), 212–14.

W. B. Smith[78]— J. V. Smith called[79]—gave up my endorsements $400 & took endorsements on 2 notes 100 30 dys & 300 60 dys— prepared dft ptnsp Coleman & Freedley[80]— Vaughan called again—goes to Clinton tomorrow— A. B. Coleman called for advice abt. Burnet House— At Globe office few moments— Gave Taylor copy of Swifts bill—read his article on Apportionment law— insufficent[81]— Judge Walker called about 4 to enquire if I going to Columbus to argue for Pugh & Peirce—said despatch recd. that Committee had reported in their favor—told him did not expect to go— Home to tea—after tea, wrote letter to Thomas Hibben Wilmington, matters in Legislature & necessity of Freesoilers from Clinton[82]—wrote above—now ½ past 9.

26: Up at 8—to bed at 11—nine hours—too bad—office after breakfast— J. H. Coleman called about suit against Judge Wright for monument[83]—letter from Hamlin—fears of Morse's firmness in determination to vote for admission of Pugh & Peirce, he besieged by Whigs and many promises made— Wrote Hamlin, Matthews, & Townshend[84]—home to dinner—called at King's office to see about

---

78. Cincinnati publisher Winthrop B. Smith (1808–85), developer of the popular McGuffey reader. Mauck Brammer, "Winthrop B. Smith: Creator of the Eclectic Educational Series," *Ohio History* 80 (Winter 1971): 45–59.

79. Around this time Joseph Vial ("Victor") Smith (c. 1826–65) was publisher of the Cincinnati *Globe,* a weekly Democratic newspaper. Smith, who had studied law in Chicago, was later connected with the Cincinnati *Commercial* and also speculated in real estate. During the Civil War he had a controversial tenure as collector of customs at Puget Sound. Marian Parks, "A Man For His Season: Victor Smith, 1826–1865" (M.A. thesis, Claremont Graduate School, 1981); "Reminiscence of Norman R. Smith" (Oreg. Hist. Soc.); *Cinc. Dir. (1849–50),* 265; Gutgesell, *Ohio Newspapers,* 72.

80. John H. Coleman and Edwin Troxell Freedley (1827–1904), who became an author and economist, operated a steam marble works. *Appletons',* 2:539; *Cinc. Dir. (1849–50),* 65, 106; Wallace, *North American Authors,* 158.

81. During this period James Wickes Taylor wrote articles for the Cincinnati *Weekly Globe* and the Cincinnati *Chronicle.* Taylor to Chase, Feb. 3, 1849 (Chase Papers, L.C.).

82. Thomas Hibben of Wilmington, a Clinton County antislavery leader and former member of the Ohio House, was working on the coalition between Free-Soilers and Democrats discussed on Jan. 5, 1849, above. Albert J. Brown, *History of Clinton County, Ohio* (Indianapolis, 1915), 352; Gilkey, *Ohio Hundred Year Book,* 270; Hibben to Chase, Jan. 24, 1849 (Chase Papers, L.C.).

83. The dispute between John H. Coleman and John C. Wright concerned payment for construction of a mausoleum for the Wright family in Cincinnati's Spring Grove Cemetery. Chase to Stanley Matthews, Jan. 27, 1849 (Chase Papers, State Hist. Soc. of Wis.).

84. Norton S. Townshend, the only Free-Soil member of the Committee on Privileges and Elections, had voted the previous day in favor of recognizing Democrats George E. Pugh and Alexander N. Pierce as representatives from Hamilton County. Hamlin was concerned that Whigs in the assembly, alarmed at prospects of a dominating alliance between Democrats and Free-Soilers, would attempt to regain legislative power by enticing Whig John F. Morse from the Free-Soil coalition with

Ia[85] Bank claim v. Mears & Hunt for which I responsible— (Mem. In Morning called at Ins. Office for Kates Interest $79.80 wh. recd.—at Smiths about payt. for Vaughan on 31st— Abraham called to enquire abt. store[86]—& Myers & Ale about Mill, wrote Forward on subject[87] / Judge Walker called; starts for Columbus at 2—) Called on Fox to see when he wd. go on with deps in Wheeler & Merreweather—said perhaps tomorrow— Spent sometime at Globe office unprofitably— King called— Wrote note to Birkem, Prest. Ia Bank & sent it to King & Anderson— Conversation with Ball abt. Gano's business &c— At dinner time wrote subscription paper for poor black woman who wants aid to buy son & gave her $2[88]— Sent in morning $100 to Carrie Smith— Home to tea— After tea prepared scraps for Book—read Mr. Harris Sermon, Church's Duty & World's Need[89]—quite eloquent & striking—wrote foregoing

27. Up as yesterday—no better—not at office till ½ past 9— Myers & Ale called—arrangt. with Forward completed—they to have immediate possession—to pay $225 or 305 arrears rent—gave them written memo. of agreet. Harrington called about course of Globe[90]— Went over to Globe office—conversation with Taylor— Hoadly came in saying he hoped there was at least one Free Soil Paper which would defend the only two Free Soil Men in the Legislature—Morse & Townd. in their vote for Pugh & Peirce, of which news this morning—told Taylor I thought they shd. be vigorously defended & promised hints— Saw article in true Democrat, saying Giddings would be Free Soil Candidate for Senator—commending

---

promises to elect Congressman Joshua Reed Giddings, another Free-Soil Whig, as Ohio's next U.S. senator. Chase's response expressed hope that Morse would continue to vote with Free-Soilers in the assembly. Chase to Hamlin, Jan. 26, 1849 (Chase Papers, L.C.); *Daily Ohio State Journal*, Jan. 9, 1849; Hamlin to Chase, Jan. 25, 1849 (Chase Papers, Hist. Soc. of Pa.); entry for Jan. 4, 1849, above.
    85. Indiana.
    86. Joseph Abraham (1817–94), a local clothier and attorney, had previously leased part of a store owned by Chase. Chase to Abraham, June 12, 1844 (Chase Papers, L.C.), *Cinc. Dir. (1849–50)*, 17; Greve, *Centennial History*, 2:462–63.
    87. Myers and Ale took over the rental of the mill belonging to the Ludlow estate and succeeded no better than Forward had at making the operation profitable. Myers may have been John Myer, a Cincinnati millwright. *Cinc. Dir. (1849–50)*, 210; statement of account with Catherine Ludlow Baker, [1852?] (Chase Papers, L.C.).
    88. Chase later described the woman as "an old negress, grimy black, fat and squat & *odorous*" who needed a total of $300 to $350. Chase to Stanley Matthews, Jan. 27, 1849 (Chase Papers, State Hist. Soc. of Wis.).
    89. Probably one of many sermons by John Harris, D.D. (1802–56), principal of New College, London, and a popular advocate of practical Christianity. *DNB*, 9:15–16.
    90. Possibly Eben Harrington, a partner in the Cincinnati law firm of Harrington and Burnett. *Cinc. Dir. (1849–50)*, 127.

January 1849 { 207 }

me & quoting Taylor's Article[91]—quite a change of tone— Found Israel Garrard at office when returned[92]— Received letters Hamlin & Matthews[93]— Wrote to Riddle & enclosed interest bill[94]—comments on bill, & admission of P. & P.—shd have voted so, law not being repealed—regretted not postponed as desired— Smith called—talk about Globe— Garrard home with me to dinner—folks all out— G & I sat down alone—folks came before souped—before dinner over James Skinner came with little Kate, who very well— went to office—sent up 30 for Mrs Chase— Taylor came in with Article from Hoadly which read to me—furnished him with suggestions for articles on Morse & Townshend— Apportionment Act[95]— Beaver & Co certificate to Jones— Smith came in while Taylor with me[96]—said nothing— Taylor left— Harrington came complaining of Taylor & course of paper— Wheeler called—Fox not ready to take deps—will Monday / Vaughan returned from

---

91. Joshua Reed Giddings (1795–1864) was a congressman (Whig, Free-Soil, Republican) from Ashtabula County, 1838–59, and U.S. consul general to Canada from 1861 to his death. Chase apparently read two articles in the Jan. 24 edition of the *Daily True Democrat*, a Free-Soil newspaper from Cleveland. One discussed Giddings and Chase as U.S. senatorial candidates. The other quoted from a defense of Chase which James Wickes Taylor had evidently written for the *Cincinnati Globe*. *DAB*, 7:260–61; *Daily True Democrat*, Jan. 24, 1849; Gutgesell, *Ohio Newspapers*, 113; Taylor to Chase, Feb. 3, 1849 (Chase Papers, L.C.).
92. Israel Ludlow Garrard (d. 1901), a Harvard-trained editor and Cincinnati attorney, was a son of Jeptha Dudley Garrard and Sarah Bella Ludlow Garrard. He later served as colonel of volunteers and, in 1865, as brevet brigadier general. Des Cognets, *Governor Garrard*, 29–30; *Quinquennial Catalogue of the Officers and Graduates of Harvard University, 1636–1915* (Cambridge, Mass., 1915), 697; Heitman, *Historical Register*, 1:447; Whitelaw Reid, *Ohio in the War: Her Statesman, Her Generals, and Soldiers* (Cincinnati, 1868), 943.
93. Both letters told of continuing attempts by Whigs to entice John F. Morse away from the coalition of Free-Soilers and Democrats, and reported on maneuvering for the seat in the U.S. Senate. Matthews declared victory virtually assured for repeal of the state's Black Laws since Free-Soil members had agreed to support the admission of Democrats Pugh and Pierce as Hamilton County's representatives. E. S. Hamlin to Chase, Jan. 26, 1849 (Chase Papers, Hist. Soc. of Pa.); S. Matthews to Chase, Jan. 26, 1849 (Chase Papers, L.C.); Riddle, "Recollections," 349.
94. The letter to A. G. Riddle explained Chase's proposal to limit interest rates and commented approvingly on the admission of Pugh and Pierce as members of the Ohio House. Chase to Riddle, Jan. 27, 1849 (Riddle Papers, Western Reserve Hist. Soc.).
95. The Jan. 1848 apportionment act (see Jan. 1, 1849, above). George Hoadly, Jr., had written an article for the Columbus *Daily Standard* defending John F. Morse and Norton S. Townshend. Chase to [Morse], Jan. 19, [1849] (Chase Papers, L.C.).
96. Possibly a reference to John F. Beaver, a state senator from Trumbull County, and Alanson Jones, a Democrat from Clinton County and the victorious candidate for the House election mentioned by Chase on Jan. 1, 24, and 25. Smith was probably Joseph Vial (Victor) Smith or Winthrop B. Smith. Gilkey, *Ohio Hundred Year Book*, 242, 275; *Cinc. Dir. (1850–51)*, 30; Thomas Hibben to Chase, Jan. 24, 31, 1849 (Chase Papers, L.C.).

Clinton— Tillinghast, member Free Soil Central Committee[97]— Hibben says all right— Coleman called[98]—difficulty with Burnet House Trustees nearly arranged—gave him some advice— Commd. letter to S. Matthews— Home to tea—talk with little Kate after tea—teeth in bad condition—finished letter to S. Matthews / Law books—mechanic & tomb proprietor—old negress—Morse & Townshend, noble conduct, but regret not postponed—especially on Riddle's account—Clinton election—prospect fair—must have seat by M. & Townshend[99]— Wrote Hamlin,[1] Morse & Townshend—must not leave Columbus—no false delicacy shd. make you forbear to draw— Enclosed this in Matthews envelope— Wrote Thomas Hibben, Wilmington[2]—importance of true men to stand by M. & T.—better Whig than any other than such—care nothing for Senatorial election in comparison—will give T.[3] if elected notes to M. & T. by whom he will probably wish to sit—sent letters to Office by Ralston[4]—wrote above—now ¼ to 12—

JOURNAL V

MAR. 6. Called with Dr Bailey on Senator Corwin; he offered to present my credentials[5]— Senator Hale called to accompany me to Capitol— Went with him to Senate Chamber— Introduced to Senators Upham, Vt, Phelps Vt, Dawson, Ga. Butler, S.C. Borland Ark

---

97. Joseph G. Tillinghast, a member of Clinton County's Free-Soil central committee and the unsuccessful competitor of Alanson Jones. Hibben to Chase, Jan. 24, 31, 1849 (Chase Papers, L.C.).
98. Abraham B. Coleman.
99. Chase's letter to Stanley Matthews discussed the law books beside his desk, problems of a client seeking payment for building a tomb, and Chase's Jan. 26 encounter with a black woman. He approved the votes of John F. Morse and Norton S. Townshend to seat Pugh and Pierce despite A. G. Riddle's desire to postpone debate. Chase closed with an optimistic assessment of the election in Clinton County, hoping that Free-Soiler Joseph G. Tillinghast, whom Chase incorrectly assumed had won, would sit beside Morse and Townshend in the House. Chase to Matthews, Jan. 27, 1849 (Chase Papers, State Hist. Soc. of Wis.).
1. Chase expressed the opinion that his election to the U.S. Senate was preferable to that of J. R. Giddings, his major competitor, since Giddings already represented the Free-Soil movement in the House of Representatives. Chase to Edward S. Hamlin, Jan. 27, 1849 (Chase Papers, L.C.).
2. Surrounding correspondence suggests that Chase and Hibben were working together on the Clinton County election mentioned on Jan. 1, 24, and 25. Hibben to Chase, Jan. 24, 31, 1849 (Chase Papers, L.C.).
3. Tillinghast; "M. & T." were Morse and Townshend.
4. James Ralston Skinner.
5. Thomas Corwin (1794–1865), former governor of Ohio, Whig senator, and future secretary of the U.S. Treasury. *DAB*, 4:457–58.

Houston, Tex. Shields, Ills. Badger N.C. & others[6]— Met also Senators Seward N.Y. Corwin, O. Benton, Mo., Fillmore V.P.,[7] Webster, Mass; also Messrs Wever,[8] Mitchell, Col, Drake, Vinton,[9] I. Wright & others— Corwin presented my credentials—sworn in & took my seat— Douglass, Ill.[10] insisted on Gen Shields being sworn—objected to—but finally agreed unanimously— Cabinet nominations submitted—adjd.—went into Sup. Ct.—saw Judge McLean—Gilpin speaking[11]—long & feeble—called on Mrs McLean—home— Went to Willards to see Col. Jo P. Taylor—& Dr. & Mrs McCormick[12] / Col Jo —— at dinner—Dr. & Mrs McC. dining out—home dinner— recd. letters, Wm Larrimer, Pitts[13]—Jno Van Buren & B. F. Butler N.Y. H. B. Stanton, Seneca Falls, Josh. Leavitt, N.Y. S. Matthews Columbus, A. G. Riddle, Columbus;[14] T. D. Lincoln; B. F. Hoffman

6. Independent Democrat and future Republican John Parker Hale (1806–73); William Upham (1792–1853), Samuel Shethar Phelps (1793–1855), and William Crosby Dawson (1798–1856), all Whigs; Democrats Andrew Pickens Butler (1796–1857), Solon Borland (1808–64), Samuel Houston (1793–1863), and James Shields (1806–79) of Illinois, who served a brigadier general of volunteers, 1861–63; and Whig George Edmund Badger (1795–1866). Ibid., 1:485–86, 2:464–65, 3:355–56, 5:154–55, 8:105–7, 9:263–67, 17:106–7; *Appletons'*, 6:213, 4:752–53.

7. Millard Fillmore (1800–1874) became thirteenth president of the U.S. in 1850. *DAB*, 6:380–82.

8. Caspar W. Wever (d. 1861), an engineer on the National Road and uncle of Sarah Bella Dunlop Ludlow Chase. Chase to Sarah Bella D. L. Chase, Mar. 6, 1849 (Chase Papers, L.C.); unpublished guide to Ludlow-Dunlop-Chambers Collec., Univ. of Wyoming.

9. Samuel Finley Vinton (1792–1862), Whig congressman from Gallipolis, Ohio. *DAB*, 19:284–85.

10. Illinois Democrat Stephen Arnold Douglas (1813–61). *DAB*, 5:397–403.

11. Probably Henry Dilworth Gilpin (1801–60), former attorney general of the U.S., arguing the case of *Veazie v. Williams*. *Appletons'*, 2:659; *DAB*, 7:315–16; *Daily National Intelligencer*, Feb. 27, 28, Mar. 2, 1849.

12. Col. Joseph Pannel Taylor (1796–1864), Zachary Taylor's brother and the husband of Eveline Aurilla McLean Taylor, John McLean's daughter; and Charles McCormick (d. 1877), an assistant surgeon in the U.S. Army. Mrs. McCormick was the former Ellen Tazewell Wirt. Willard's Hotel stood on Pennsylvania Avenue. *Appletons'*, 6:55; Heitman, *Historical Register*, 1:659; Weisenburger, *McLean*, 218; *Wash. Dir. (1853)*, 56.

13. William Larimer, Jr., a Pittsburgh exchange broker. *Pittsburgh Dir. (1847)*, 88.

14. Free-Soil activists and politicians John Van Buren (1810–66), Benjamin Franklin Butler (1795–1858), Henry Brewster Stanton (1805–87), and Joshua Leavitt (1794–1873) congratulated Chase on his recent election to the U.S. Senate. Stanley Matthews offered suggestions for rejuvenating the troubled *Ohio Standard*, a Free-Soil newspaper, and discussed Ohio Free-Soil politics. Albert Gallatin Riddle explained his reasons for not voting for Chase's election. Chase to Butler, Mar. 8, 1849 (Butler Family Papers, Princeton Univ.); Stanton to Chase, Feb. 24, 1849, Matthews to Chase, Mar. 1, 1849 (Chase Papers, L.C.); Van Buren to Chase, Feb. 23, 1849, Riddle to Chase, Feb. 27, 1849, Leavitt to Chase, Mar. 2, 1849 (Chase Papers, Hist. Soc. of Pa.); *DAB*, 3:356–57, 11:84–85, 17:524–25, 19:151–52.

Edwards Pierrepont, New York; Eliza Chase, Lockport;[15]— Wrote J. R. Gidding, Mrs Chase, S. Matthews, A. G. Riddle, Jno Van Buren[16]—read Newspapers & wrote above

JOURNAL I

APL. 22 Near six years have passed since I last wrote in this book—six eventful years— Some mema. of events &c have been written in another volume but they are few and imperfect.[17] This morning I rose rather late—my old habit still cleaving to me— After prayer in closet and family prayer breakfast—think I have more feeling in family prayer than formerly—have commenced practice of committing some scripture every day—but have not persevered as I should have done— Confirmation at St Paul's today—Bishop McIlvaine preached admirable sermon on Inheritance of saints and meetness for it. Have read during most of the day Life of Wilberforce— How his example shames me! Let me strive to follow him as he followed Christ. Our circumstances very different—he so easy in his circumstances—I comparatively poor & indebted, and obliged, besides public duties to continue practice of my profession.

MAY 12 Spent last night, as also the night previous, with my wife in the country with Mr Burrows[18]—came in this morning, & stopped at house—looked at papers, abounding with notices of Cholera, now prevalent in our City but not nearly so fatal as in 1832[19]— Gave some directions about repair of hydrant &c & then, calling for a moment at the Office, went to the Court House to join the Bar in attending the funeral of Chs H Brough, elected last

---

15. Mary Eliza Chase, the wife of Chase's brother, Edward Ithamar Chase. Benjamin F. Hoffman (b. 1812), a Free-Soil attorney from Warren, Ohio, congratulated Chase on his election to the Senate and asked for assistance in a legal case. Edwards Pierrepont (1817–92) was a New York attorney and judge. "Family Memoranda" (Chase Papers, L.C.); Robson, *Biographical Encyclopædia*, 347; *History of Trumbull and Mahoning Counties*, 1:447–48; Hoffman to Chase, Feb. 24, 1849 (Chase Papers, Hist. Soc. of Pa.); *DAB*, 14:587.

16. Chase was attempting reconciliation with Giddings, his major competitor in the recent senatorial election. Chase explained his cooperation with Ohio Democrats and urged Free-Soil Whigs to continue working with the alliance as attention turned to Hamilton County's apportionment problems. The letter to Sarah Bella Chase described Chase's journey to Washington, D.C., and his initial activities as a senator. Chase to Giddings, Mar. 6, 1849 (Giddings Papers, Ohio Hist. Soc.); Chase to Sarah Bella Chase, Mar. 6, 1849 (Chase Papers, L.C.); entry for Jan. 1, 1849, above.

17. Journal IV.

18. Probably John A. Burrows, a Clifton resident and wholesale grocer in Cincinnati. *Cinc. Dir. (1849–50)*, 51.

19. According to later reports, the epidemic reached its peak between April and June, killing at least 4,600 of the city's 116,000 inhabitants. Edward Deering Mansfield, *Memoirs of the Life and Services of Daniel Drake, M.D. . . .* (Cincinnati, 1855), 98.

winter a Judge of the Court of Common Pleas of the 9th Circuit, (this County) soon after my election to the Senate, and by the same votes, with perhaps not more than one exception. Judge Brough died of Cholera, day before yesterday, after a very short illness, of about six hours. He had been previously indisposed, but not enough to induce him to keep the house; in fact I had been in conversation with him the evening before at the Court House. I was greatly shocked hearing of his attack and imminent danger, when engaged in the argument of a case before the Supreme Court, in which we were associated before he went to Mexico as a Col. of volunteers. I was so much affected that I could hardly proceed. Today we have committed his remains to the Earth. He was an earnest able, & indefatigable man; a zealous partizan, but zealous, I believe, from conviction; correct in his deportment; and, though so recently elected, already possessed, in a remarkable degree, of the confidence & respect of the Bar, as a Judge. He attended the Universalist Church. Beyond this, I know nothing of his religious sentiments. His brother, his widow and some other relatives attended the funeral, which was large & imposing. His brother a stern & resolute man, could hardly repress his tears. Judge Key walked with me and we had much interesting conversation. From the funeral Mr. Ball came with me to dinner. After dinner to Office— Offered bill at M. & Traders Bank[20]— Wrote cancellation so far as interested of Brown's mortgage on Cheviot land, sold him 3 years ago and now worth twice what I sold it for[21]— Wrote several letters, Ballard Smith, Louisville, Gov. Ford & W. B. Jarvis, Columbus[22]— Paid some bills— Recd $5 pt [from] from Mr. Ball—directed large number of documents— Home to tea—read Wilberforce— Have found advantage of committing Scripture, having chapters in Memory when Bible not at hand— Dr. Pulte came in at tea & talk of homoepathy &c &c[23]

20. The Mechanics' and Traders' Branch Bank on Main Street in Cincinnati. Cist, *Sketches and Statistics*, 88.
21. Possibly Augustus I. Brown, one of Chase's business associates. Mar. 2, 1847, above.
22. William Ballard Smith (1821–66) was the half brother of Chase's friend, Hamilton Smith, and an Indiana judge and politician. He had previously asked Chase for assistance with the appointment of John C. Bullitt, a friend and partner, as commissioner from Pennsylvania to the state of Ohio. Seabury Ford (1801–55) served as governor of Ohio, 1849–50. W. B. Jarvis was a Columbus attorney and former associate in Liberty party politics. *Appletons'*, 2:501; Chapman, *Sketches of the Alumni*, 313; *Col. Dir. (1850–51)*, 144; Jarvis to Chase, May 18, 1848, Mar. 17, 1849, B. Smith to Chase, May 10, 17, 1849 (Chase Papers, L.C.); Rebecca A. Shepherd et al., comps. and eds., *A Biographical Directory of the General Assembly. Volume 1 1816–1899* (Indianapolis, 1880), 361.
23. Cincinnatian Joseph Hippolyt Pulte, M.D. (1811–84), a founder of the American Institute of Homeopathy. *DAB*, 15:264.

MAY 13 SUNDAY Was up rather late this morning though not much later than usual / Dressing, repeated to myself, the first two & most of the 3rd Chapters of Proverbs / After private & family prayer & breakfast read Life of Wilberforce— How his example shames & humbles me— Went to Trinity Church[24]—Dr. Aydelotte on Sunday Schools & particularly Am Sunday School Union—collection for the Church Sunday School— Home to dinner—walked down for church with Mr. Todd[25]— Afternoon & evening, with exception of that walk Wilberforce & Bishop Chase Reminiscences— Some little time unprofitably on Library Address & this Journal— now to bed after prayer— May God enable me to keep diligent watch of myself during the next week & to be diligent in efforts to do good & promote his glory—

MAY 14 MONDAY Up too late again, &, though repeated Scripture, too little time allowed for morning prayer—during day have not been bold for Christ as I should have been—too uncertain and vague in my speech—Lord help me— Parable of Prodigal Son & Unjust Steward at family prayer[26]— I am exceedingly defective in the power of exposition & consciousness of the defect generally deters me from attempt. At Supreme Court in morning after looking at papers quite unprofitably—only one matter of interest—expedition of Ranald McDonald to Japan[27]— Nothing done at Court— Judge Avery indisposed[28]—Judge Caldwell in his place— Certificates for Candidates for Clerkship for E. M. Stanton[29]—at office Matlack called about title—Cist about same[30]—Cable abt. Missy. Meeting too curt with him[31]—but, though a good man, prolix & tiresome—letters from Judge Stevens, C Sumner & M. Sutliff—sent

24. Trinity Protestant Episcopal Church. *Cinc. Dir. (1851–52)*, 310.
25. Possibly Alexander Todd, a local attorney. Ibid. (1849–50), 285.
26. Luke 15:11–32, 16:1–13.
27. Ranald McDonald (1824–94) was a Canadian-American adventurer who had recently been released from imprisonment in Japan, where he had gone in 1841 disguised as a shipwrecked sailor. *DAB*, 12:18–19.
28. Ohio Supreme Court justice Edward Avery (1790–1866). Dexter, *Biographical Sketches*, 6:298.
29. Pittsburgh attorney and former Ohioian Edwin McMasters Stanton (1814–69), U.S. attorney general, 1860–61, and secretary of war, 1862–68. *DAB*, 17:517–21.
30. Possibly Bowen Matlack, a partner in the Cincinnati wholesale dry goods firm of Day and Matlack, and either Charles Cist; Charles E. Cist, librarian of the Young Men's Mercantile Library Association; Francis J. Cist, a local clerk; or Lewis Jacob Cist (1818–85), a teller in the Ohio Life and Trust Company. *Appletons'*, 1:617; *Cinc. Dir. (1849–50)*, 60, 78, 194.
31. The Rev. Jonathan Cable, at times a resident of Kentucky, Indiana, Ohio, and Philadelphia, was active in various missionary and philanthrophic endeavors. Cable to Chase, Mar. 8, July 7, 1849, Dec. 9, 1864 (Chase Papers, L.C.); Chase to Cable, Mar. 7, 1864 (Chase Papers, Hist. Soc. of Pa.).

last & others, Fremonts Maps[32]— Wrote Sumner & Stanton, enclosing certificates to last.[33] Somewhat earnest with him on religion—God grant good fruits— At Court afternoon—commenced Ewing v. Borden[34]—walked down Street with Spaulding[35] & Caldwell—handed report on Steam Boat Explosions to Walker[36]—sent copies to Shields, Wiley & Wash. McLean, Harkness, & Krauth[37]— prepared partly plan of Hathaway Compromise—obtained subs. $100 towards Globe—home to tea—after with wife who indisposed—then read Stanton, article on India & Geo. Thompson— good—but somewhat inaccurate—Benton's Railroad Speech at Pitts—Albany Atlas on Gen. Taylor's course[38]—part Ham. Smith's

32. John Charles Frémont, *Geographical Memoir upon Upper California, in Illustration of his Map of Oregon and California*, 30th Cong., 1st sess., 1848, S. Misc. Doc. 148. Stephen C. Stevens, an antislavery activist from Madison, Ohio, and formerly an Indiana state supreme court judge, had recently requested a copy of Chase's argument in the Van Zandt case. Charles Sumner's letter speculated about the reelection of Massachusetts Free-Soil congressman John G. Palfrey. Milton Sutliff (1806–78), a Free-Soil state representative from Warren, Ohio, complained of criticisms against Chase in Whig newspapers. Thornbrough et al., *Diary of Calvin Fletcher*, 1:152, 3:92; Sutliff to Chase, May 5, 1849, Sumner to Chase, May 9, 1849, Stevens to Chase, May 12, 1849 (Chase Papers, L.C.); Robson, *Biographical Encyclopædia*, 128–29; *History of Trumbull and Mahoning Counties*, 1:178–81.

33. Chase informed Sumner of the publication, in the *National Era*, of a Chase letter explaining the circumstances of his election to the Senate. Subsequent correspondence suggests that Chase was urging Edwin M. Stanton to seek election as governor of Ohio. Chase to Sumner, May 14, 1849 (Vertical File, Ohio Hist. Soc.); *National Era*, May 3, 1849; Stanton to Chase, May 27, 1849 (Chase Papers, Hist. Soc. of Pa.).

34. James U. Borden, a Cincinnati grocer, and James H. Ewing, a local attorney. *Cinc. Dir. (1849–50)*, 39, 95.

35. Possibly Rufus Paine Spalding (1798–1886), a former Ohio state legislator; judge of the state supreme court, 1849–52; and Republican U.S. congressman, 1863–69. At this time, Spalding, a resident of Trumbull County, was one of Ohio's leading Free-Soil politicians. Robson, *Biographical Encyclopædia*, 319–20; *Nat. Cyc.*, 5:224; July 13, 1849, below.

36. *Report of the Commissioners, to the Senate of the United States, on the Subject of Steam Boiler Explosions*, 30th Cong., 2nd sess., 1849, S. Ex. Doc. 18.

37. Wiley may have been Austin Willey (1806–96), antislavery activist and editor of the Brunswick, Maine, *Advocate of Freedom*. Washington McLean (1816–90) was a local boilermaker, future owner of the *Cincinnati Enquirer*, and eventually one of Ohio's most influential Democrats and an opponent of Chase. Anthony and William Harkness constructed steam engines in Cincinnati. John B. Krauth was state representative from Hamilton County, 1854–55. Willey to Chase, July 10, 1848, McLean to Chase, June 30, 1861 (Chase Papers, L.C.); *Cinc. Dir. (1849–50)*, 126, 188; Thomas E. Powell, ed., *The Democratic Party of the State of Ohio . . .* (n.p., 1913), 2:295–96; *Appletons'*, 6:518; Wallace, *North American Authors*, 506; Gilkey, *Ohio Hundred Year Book*, 278.

38. Henry B. Stanton's article on India and British antislavery advocate George Thompson (1804–78) appeared in the *National Era*, May 7, 1849. The same issue also contained a speech by Sen. Thomas Hart Benton supporting extension of the Pennsylvania and Ohio R.R. through St. Louis to the Pacific Ocean, and reprinted an *Albany Atlas* article criticizing the political appointments of President Zachary Taylor. *DNB*, 19:691.

Essay on Resources of Indiana[39]—all interesting— Now scripture, prayer & bed—

MAY 15 TUESDAY Up late again—dressing repeated Proverbs first three chapters in part—am trying to familiarize myself with language and thought—private & family prayer—too cold alas, when shall I feel the glow & flame I would fain realize, and which, one would think, the very slightest contemplation of God's goodness through christ and our infinite obligation could not fail to kindle— After breakfast, went to office—read letters & papers & then to court—finished Ewing & Borden—made tolerable argument but only tolerable—argued or rather stated Urmston ads Nolan, Judge Read & Mr. Thompson contra[40]— Ewing & Borden decided except as to one point for my client who gets within ⅙ All he claimed— Back to office—walked down with young man some conversation on religion but not definite enough— If I had more spiritual life myself, I could more easily speak to others. Wasted time till dinner, newspapers &c— Ball to dinner with me—back to office—directed many "Reports on Steamboat Explosions"—called on Washn.-McLean he gives $25 to Globe to pay within 60 dys— Saw Judge Caldwell—some talk with him on Free Democracy— He is not earnest enough—too general & too little special application, with decision— Returning to Office found Hathaway & Lewis—prepared plan of Hathaway Compromise—agreed to meet Judge Walker at ½ past 8 tomorrow morning—drew decree Borden & Ewing— home—talk with wife—tea—Dr. Aydelotte came in—long talk—interesting reminiscences of Hammond &c. &c—

JUNE 30 Came up from Louisville whither I went to argue motion for Injunction by Morse & Co v OReilly & others[41]— I for defts with

---

39. Hamilton Smith, "Indiana—Her Resources and Prospects," *The Commercial Review (DeBow's)* 1, n.s. (Sept. 1849): 246–61.

40. *Mary Nolan v. Samuel Urmston*, a land title case in which Chase represented Urmston. E. A. Thompson was a local attorney. 17 Ohio 170, 18 Ohio 273; *Cinc. Dir. (1849–50)*, 283.

41. In 1847, former newspaper editor Henry O'Reilly (1806–86), who had constructed telegraph lines for Samuel Finley Breese Morse (1791–1872) and his associates, began to build his own lines in competition. Chase became one of O'Reilly's counsel in an effort to overturn an injunction preventing O'Reilly from putting lines through Kentucky on the grounds that he infringed on Morse's patents. O'Reilly's attorneys argued that Morse tried to use his patents to protect not just specific devices, but all use of electromagnetism for long-distance communication. The complex suit was argued before the U.S. Supreme Court in Dec. 1852. The court, in Jan. 1854, gave Morse's patents relatively broad coverage and declared that O'Reilly's equipment infringed on them. The court did not, however, allow Morse's patent to

Judge Pirtle[42]— Came up river with Mr. Bain, with whom conversed on subject of modification of contract with Mr. OReilly[43] / He declared himself so far as then advised satisfied with proposed modification—

JULY 1 SUNDAY Arrived at Cincinnati at daylight—walked up Broadway with Mr. Bain pointed out Henrie House to him— Coal fires burning at all intersections—a preposterous remedy for cholera—giving an aspect of gloom to every thing hardly to be surpassed—found all at home well, blessed be God—

JULY 2 MONDAY At office this morning—cholera report—frightful mortality[44]—did nothing of consequence—read & arranged papers— LHommedieu called—agreed to wait for my payment to his brothers estate till next year— In evening my dear wife confined— another little daughter[45] & mother doing well—fresh occasion for thankfulness to God our Preserver— Physician—Dr M. B. Wright— Nurse, Miss Townley.[46]

JULY 3 TUESDAY Nothing of special interest occurred today— It was the Fast appointed by the City Authorities[47]—attended Dr. Aydelottes church—gave [Nye] $5 to be used in relieving distress.

---

include the underlying principle of electromagnetic telegraphs. *DAB*, 13:247–51, 14:52–53; *Henry O'Reilly et al. v. Samuel F. B. Morse et al.*, 15 How. 62 (1854); *The Electric Telegraph. Substance of the Argument of S. P. Chase before the Supreme Court of the United States, . . . in the case of H. O'Reilly, and Others, vs. S. F. B. Morse, and Others . . .* (New York, 1853); Carl B. Swisher, *The Taney Period, 1836–64*, v. 5 of Paul A. Freund, gen. ed., *The Oliver Wendell Holmes Devise History of the Supreme Court of the United States* (New York, 1974), 488–504. For Chase's role see Chase Papers, L.C.; O'Reilly Papers, New York Hist. Soc.; O'Reilly Papers, Rochester Public Lib.; Appellate Jurisdiction Records, case file 2898 (Recs. of Supreme Court, Nat. Arch.).

42. Kentucky attorney and former Louisville judge Henry Pirtle (1798–1880). *Appletons'*, 5:30.

43. Alexander Bain had invented telegraph equipment which O'Reilly hoped would not be covered by the injunction protecting Morse's patents. Swisher, *Taney Period*, 491–93.

44. "The cholera is absolutely fearful in its ravages here," Chase wrote to one correspondent two days later. "Nine hundred died last week, and the number of deaths this week will probably exceed a thousand." Chase to George Bradburn, July 4, 1849, in Francis H. Bradburn, comp., *A Memorial of George Bradburn* (Boston, 1883), 174.

45. Josephine Ludlow Chase (1849–50), also known as "Zoe." Chase to Sarah Bella Chase, July 28, 1850, and "Family Memoranda" (Chase Papers, L.C.).

46. Marmaduke Burr Wright (1803–69) taught obstetrics at Cincinnati College. Miss Townley might have been a relative of Cincinnati attorney Asa Townley. *Cinc. Dir. (1849–50)*, 285; Juettner, *Daniel Drake*, 174–76.

47. Observed because of the cholera epidemic. *Cincinnati Daily Gazette*, July 4, 1849.

JULY 4 WED   At office most of day writing letters—among others one to Lucas County Free Democracy[48]— Miss Townley called to Mrs Irvin[49] & Mrs C obliged to obtain another nurse—could obtain none except a fat colored woman—but well pleased with her, preferring her on the whole to Miss Townley.

JULY 5 THURSDAY   Col Doane came up from Louisville on his way to Pittsburgh to arrange Mr. OReillys matters[50]—had full conversation with him—went over Burnet House with him & Coleman—really a fine structure & capacious & convenient. Met Beard on the Street & went with him to see his new picture[51]—a beautiful creation of genius—told me his design of picture of deluge & of primitive christian assembly or martyrdom— Lent him Martyr of Antioch & Valerius[52]— A man calling himself called & asked loan of $2 to bury child—gave him money of course, though not certain but he an imposter—of whom numbers now.

JULY 6 FRIDAY   Prepared full letter to Col Doane, giving my views of things necessary to be done at Pittsburgh—read it to him & delivered it— He agreed to all in it— Sent copy to Mr. OReilly.[53]

JULY 7 SATURDAY   Col. Doane left for Pittsburgh today—really hope he may succeed in his undertaking

JULY 8 SUNDAY   At church morning & evening—Dr. Aydelotte who always preaches edifying discourses— Gave $5 to be used by him for relief of sick and distressed.

JULY 9. MONDAY   Going home this afternoon, hailed, as passing Engine House, "Well you'll make no more speeches in old box—"

---

48. Chase had recently been asked to address a convention of Lucas County's Free Democrats. Chase to C. R. Miller, July 4, 1849, in Schuckers, *Chase*, 100–101; Miller to Chase, June 26, 1849 (Chase Papers, L.C.).

49. Possibly Eilen Irvin, proprietor of a local boarding house. *Cinc. Dir. (1849–50)*, 151.

50. Charles Doane of Burlington, Vt., was involved with the O'Reilly telegraph interests. Correspondence of Doane to Chase (Chase Papers, L.C.).

51. Cincinnati portrait painter James Henry Beard (1812–93). *Cinc. Dir. (1849–50)*, 31; *DAB*, 2:94.

52. Henry Hart Milman, *The Martyr of Antioch: A Dramatic Poem* (London and New York, 1822); and John Gibson Lockhart, *Valerius, a Roman Story*... (Boston, 1821).

53. Chase's letter to O'Reilly was dated July 7. Doane went to Pittsburgh to examine accounts of O'Reilly's telegraph company to arrange a settlement with creditors. Chase to Henry O'Reilly, July 7, 1849 (O'Reilly Papers, New-York Hist. Soc.); O'Reilly to Chase, July 9, 1849, Doane telegrams and letters, July–Aug. 1849 (Chase Papers, L.C.).

July 1849 { 217 }

"Why?" "The Court House is burning" / Never saw the firemen so slow in getting out their Engines— Every body glad that the old Nuisance abated.[54]

JULY 11 WEDNESDAY   Met Hutchings of Louisville[55] at Rail Road Office this morning where I went to find why omnibus did not call for me—had ris[en] & breakfasted by 4 expecting to start for Sandusky at 5[56]— Learned that R.R. track broken by storm and one or more bridges made impassible— Train to start in afternoon— Left accordingly at 3— Hutchings & Dr. Cobb of Louisville—Sargent, Adams & others—Heaton & family of Cincinnati[57]—delayed by injuries to road—at one place baggage had to be packed by hand over breach to an extra train on the other side & passengers had to walked over—failed to reach Springfield in time for connection Mad River train had left— Slept at National Hotel.

JULY 12.   At breakfast this morning gratified to meet T. C. H Smith, a hearty Free Democrat and a most reliable and true hearted man[58]— Judge & Mrs McLean also at table—found Mrs Greene & daughter had come up with us from Cincinnati, wishing to go to Urbana where they had heard that Mr. Greene was detained by indisposition[59]— Went to livery stable & engaged hack to take them over, but learned incidentally from Smith that he had seen Greene who had recovered & gone home—Mrs G of course delighted to hear it & to turn homeward instead of going to Urbana. I understand Mr Greene has been particularly severe in his comments on my election, & was pleased with this opportunity of doing him a good turn— Left Springfield for Sandusky at ½ past 11— Judge & Mrs McLean / R. Burnet, N. C. McLean & wife,[60] Mr. & Mrs Lee

54. The courthouse, completed in 1816, had supposedly outlived its usefulness. Cincinnatians welcomed the fire as an excuse to construct a new building. Alfred George Washington Carter, *The Old Court House: Reminiscences and Anecdotes of the Courts and Bar of Cincinnati* (Cincinnati, 1880), 13–14; *Cincinnati Enquirer*, July 10, 1849.
55. Eusebius Hutchings, a Louisville exchange broker. *Louisville Dir. (1848)*, 101.
56. A mark, possibly another 5, appears above the line and to the left of this numeral.
57. The family of Daniel Heaton, proprietor of Cincinnati's Heaton House. *Cinc. Dir. (1849–50)*, 131.
58. Cincinnati attorney Thomas Church Haskell Smith (1819–97) a founder of the Morse telegraph system and future brigadier general of the U.S. Army. *Appletons'*, 5:590; Johnson, *Twentieth Century Biographical Dictionary*, v. 9.
59. William Greene married Abby Lyman (d. 1862) of Northampton, Mass., in 1821. They had two daughters, Annie Jean and Catharine Ray Greene. *Nat. Cyc.*, 8:193.
60. Cincinnati attorneys Robert Burnet and Nathaniel Collins McLean (1815–1905), who was a son of John and Rebecca Edwards McLean; and Nathaniel

& other Cincinnatians in cars— Had a rather earnest talk with Mrs McLean about Mr. Hamlin & his connexion with Israel Garrard[61]— Arrived at Sandusky and slept at Townsend House[62]

JULY 13. FRIDAY Awoke this morning with looseness of bowels— got into bed again & covered myself up & took some camphor pellets—perspiration followed & felt better—breakfasted very light & after some talk with Mr. Dean, of New Orleans, whom I found decidedly antislavery in his views, went on board boat—diarrhea returned but slightly & laid down on couch—after a while felt better & got up & was shaved—some conversation with Mrs Burke of N.O. Mrs Heaton & others— Adams & Sargent very kind— At Cleveland met by Committee of Convention, Bolton, Vaughan & Hoadly[63]— Went to Mr. Hoadly's (Sen.) for dinner & after light repast went to Weddell House,[64] where I saw Col Swift & Dr. Townshend— Invited into Committee Room on Resolutions—found Mr. Ellsworth, Judge Spalding & E. T. Tappan[65]—they read resolutions to me— suggested some amendments which concurred in— Judge Spalding's resolution on Dis. of Col. preferred to Mr. Tappans— I drew Resolution approving Union of Free & Old Line Democracy in Vermont which adopted & reported.[66]— Went with John Van Bu-

---

McLean's wife Caroline Thew Burnet McLean (d. 1856), a daughter of Jacob Burnet. *Appletons'*, 4:144; *Nat. Cyc.*, 2:470; Weisenburger, *McLean*, 219.

61. E. S. Hamlin had drawn criticism from the *Ohio State Journal* for allegedly neglecting his duties as president of Ohio's Board of Public Works. Garrard, Hamlin's associate at the *Ohio Standard*, also faced criticism for delays in fulfilling a state printing contract. Sarah Bella Ludlow Garrard McLean might have been concerned that her son's involvement with Hamlin would embarrass John McLean. Chase to Hamlin, July 26, 1849 (Chase Papers, L.C.); *Daily Ohio State Journal*, Jan. 6, 8, 1849; *Weekly Ohio State Journal*, July 4, 25, 1849.

62. At the corner of Market and Decatur. *Sandusky Dir. (1858–59)*, 77, 109.

63. John Van Buren was keynote speaker of the convention of Free Democrats celebrating passage of the Ordinance of 1787. Committee members greeting Chase were: Cleveland attorney and politician Thomas Bolton (1809–71); John C. Vaughan; and George Hoadly (1780–1857), mayor of Cleveland and father of Chase's law student, George Hoadly, Jr. *Cleveland Daily Plain Dealer*, July 12–14, 1849; David D. Van Tassel and John J. Grabowski, eds., *The Encyclopedia of Cleveland History* (Bloomington, 1987), 113, 513.

64. At the corner of Bank and Superior Streets. Van Tassel and Grabowski, *Encyclopedia of Cleveland*, 1035.

65. Henry Leavitt Ellsworth (1791–1858), former mayor of Hartford, Conn., U.S. commissioner of patents, 1835–45, and, at the time of this entry, a resident of Lafayette, Ind.; Rufus Paine Spalding; and Eli Todd Tappan (1824–88), a Columbus attorney and editor of the weekly *Ohio Press*. *DAB*, 6:110–11, 18:301; *Cleveland Daily Plain Dealer*, July 13, 1849.

66. As adopted, the first resolution urged the election of senators and congressmen "who will vote unhesitatingly for the abolition of slavery and the slave trade in the District of Columbia, or for the removal of the seat of Government to a place consecrated to Free Soil." The other resolution expressed support for efforts in Ver-

ren to stand—kindly greeted—Giddings, Judge Tappan, Gray[67] & others— Judge Spalding spoke after report of Resolutions, well & handsomely— John Van Buren followed, & I was to follow him—but becoming very unwell was obliged to leave stand & go home with Geo. Hoadly— Sent for Dr. Williams[68]—& then for Dr. Townshend— Dr. T. came—took camphor & covered & soon in perspiration—Dr. Williams came, also, and gave me some medicine—Dr. Townshend with me till eleven—George Hoadly all night giving me medicine as directed—

JULY 14 SATURDAY Wrote wife[69]—better than yesterday but not rid of diarrhea—kept quiet all day—despatch from Townshend to Hoadly enquiring for me—Hoadly ansd.

JULY 15 SUNDAY. Quiet all day—read Scriptures and endeavored to commit portion as I have been in the practice of doing for some time past.

JULY 16 MONDAY. Dr. Williams, who thought on Saturday I might be well enough to leave for home today, forbid me to think of it— Bates, Mr. H's soninlaw started for Cin. this day[70]—some friends called.

JULY 17 TUESDAY In the Afternoon rode out with George Hoadly to Water Cure Establishment & walked around premises with him, Dr. Seelye & Heaton[71]— Have a good deal of faith in

---

mont and elsewhere "to bring up the old Democracy to the Platform of Freedom," as outlined in the Buffalo Free-Soil Convention of 1849, and "dissolve the bonds of its unnatural alliance with the slave power." Cleveland *Daily True Democrat,* July 14, 1849.

67. Joseph William Gray (1813–62), Democratic editor of the Cleveland *Plain Dealer. DAB,* 7:522; Van Tassel and Grabowski, *Encyclopedia of Cleveland,* 466; Archer H. Shaw, *The Plain Dealer: One Hundred Years in Cleveland, 1842–1942* (New York, 1942), 51.

68. Charles D. Williams, M.D. (d. 1882), dean of Cleveland's Homeopathic Hospital College. James Harrison Kennedy, *A History of Cleveland: Its Settlement, Rise and Progress. 1876–1896* (Cleveland, 1896), 339; Orth, *History of Cleveland,* 1:196.

69. Chase's letter discussed his illness and mentioned plans to remain in Cleveland with Mayor George Hoadley until Monday. Chase to Sarah Bella Chase, July 16, 1849 (Chase Papers, L.C.).

70. Joshua Hall Bates (1817–1908), U.S. Military Academy class of 1837; partner in the Cincinnati law firm of Bates and Scarborough; brigadier general of volunteers, 1861; son-in-law of George Hoadley. *Appletons',* 1:194; *Cinc. Dir. (1849–50),* 29; Goss, *Cincinnati,* 4:220; George Irving Reed, ed., *Bench and Bar of Ohio: A Compendium of History and Biography* (Chicago, 1897), 1:134–35.

71. Dr. Thomas T. Seelye operated a large hydropathic clinic in a landscaped setting near a spring. Rose, *Cleveland,* 214.

hydropathy— The establishment is large, well situated, said to be well managed & will doubtless prosper.

JULY 18 WEDNESDAY   Walked, in the Morning down Euclid St to Public Square, and up Superior Street to a Cross St which brought me again into Euclid & so home— But little fatigued— Afternoon walked down town with Mr. Hoadly—stopped at Hitchcock, Wilson & Wade's Office to rest[72]—met all of them & Gen. Ahaz Merchant[73]— Mr. Hoadly procured buggy & took me to site of Naval Hospital[74]—on bank of Lake & I fear insecure—afterward, rode through several parts of town— Sent $25 to Bp Purcell for Catholic poor & $25 for Hospital 1st Ward.

JULY 19 THURS.   Read Typee most of day[75]—a curious & interesting story—founded on how much fact I know not— In evening according to promise went with Severance & Vaughan to former's house, where met Vaughan & Dr. Williams at tea[76]— Judge Hitchcock[77] called before I left Mr. Hoadlys—also Wade & Bolton & Tiffany evening before[78]—& Wade & Tiffany this morning— Coming home after tea learned that Gray of Plaindealer had called—

JULY 20 FRIDAY   Rained hard early in Morning—sorry to learn at breakfast that Mrs Woolsey sister & next door neighbor of Mrs Hoadly's was Attacked by Cholera Symptoms last night & was quite ill this morning.[79]— Arranged my papers & some little matters—

---

72. The law office of Reuben Hitchcock (b. 1806), Free-Soil activist and future judge in Cleveland's Court of Common Pleas; Hiram V. Willson (1808–66), lawyer, civic promoter, and federal judge for the northern district of Ohio, 1855–66; and Edward Wade. *Biographical Cyclopædia*, 2:398–99, 3:730–31.

73. Ahaz Merchant (1794–1862), surveyor of Cuyahoga County and a general in the state militia. Van Tassel and Grabowski, *Encyclopedia of Cleveland*, 677–78.

74. Construction of the hospital, at the corner of Erie and Lake Streets, had started in 1847. It passed into city control in 1875. Avery, *History of Cleveland*, 1:546–47.

75. Herman Melville, *Typee: A Peep at Polynesian Life. During a Four Months' Residence in the Valley of the Marquesas* ... (New York, 1846).

76. Reformer and Liberty party activist Theodoric Cordenio Severance was a teller at Cleveland's Canal Bank and, during the early 1860s, assistant agent for the U.S. Treasury at Hilton Head, S.C. *Cleve. Dir. (1848)*, 166; James et al., *Notable American Women*, 3:265–68; *OR*, ser. 1, v. 47, pt. 2:158.

77. Peter Hitchcock.

78. Joel Tiffany was a member of the board of trustees for Cleveland's Homeopathic Hospital College. Kennedy, *History of Cleveland*, 339.

79. Probably the spouse of John M. Woolsey, a Cleveland land agent who appears to have been the brother of George Hoadley's wife. *Cleve. Dir. (1848)*, 200; *DAB*, 9:84; Van Tassel and Grabowski, *Encyclopedia of Cleveland*, 513.

July 1849 {221}

pd. Dr. W. 9.50 G. H. Jr,[80] sums expended for me $4.80—Servant $1.00— Left Mr. H's hospitable mansion after 12 in Omnibus, in a real downpour of rain— Saratoga not in when arrived at Pier[81]— glad to meet Dr. & Mrs Chase in Omnibus on their way to Cincinnati[82]— Boat soon arrived & went on board— Cabin deluged with water— '.50 to Omnibus Mr. Woodbury & Lane on board,[83] both of Sandusky & very attentive—arrived in Sandusky about 4— Fare $2— Went to Townshend House where met Taylor, Mills, Parish, Stone, Farwell, McGee & E. H. Haines—staid at Townsend all night.[84]

JULY 21 SAT. Left Sandusky at ¼ past 5 for Cincinnati—fare $6.50— Met Breslin at Republic—introduced to Joseph Shoemaker[85] & others—breakfasted on a cracker & cup of tea at Tiffin— before arriving at Urbana became quite ill— Dr. Chase intending to stop at Urbana urged me to do so also, but could not— He then agreed to go with me to Springfield after leaving Mrs Chase at Mr. Bouchers[86]— Took a couple of crackers & a cup of strong green tea & felt much better— Dr. Chase did not get back before cars started—went on to Springfield & feeling still better concluded to keep on home—met T. C. H. S[87] at Springfield— Detained between Morrow & Cincinnati by injury to tire of locomotive—arrived home at 11 at night, walking up from the Depot & not much fatigued by it—and, blessed be God, found all well—

80. George Hoadly, Jr.
81. The 661-ton sidewheel steamer *Saratoga* operated out of Cleveland. Lytle, *Merchant Vessels*, 172.
82. Possibly S. H. Chase, a Cincinnati physician and Free-Soil activist, and his wife. *Cinc. Dir. (1849–50)*, 59; *Cincinnati Weekly Globe*, Dec. 6, 1848.
83. At this time Ebenezer Lane lived in Sandusky and managed railroad companies. *Biographical Cyclopædia*, 2:400–401.
84. The Townsend House stood at the corner of Market and Decatur. Among the people Chase met there were James Wickes Taylor; William S. Mills, the editor of Sandusky's *Democratic Mirror;* Francis Drake Parish; probably Walter F. Stone (1822–74), a Free-Soil attorney from Sandusky and an associate justice of the Ohio Supreme Court, 1872–74; and Moors Farwell, a local antislavery leader. Peeke, *Standard History of Erie County*, 1:260, 415, 416, 420; *Biographical Cyclopædia*, 3:619–20; *Sandusky Dir. (1858–59)*, 109.
85. Described later as a "pillar" in the local Methodist church. Abraham J. Baughman, *History of Seneca County, Ohio* ... (Chicago, 1911), 1:388.
86. Probably Joshua Boucher, a Methodist preacher and a friend and political ally of S. P. Chase. J. M. Barker, *History of Ohio Methodism* (Cincinnati, 1898), 419–20; Rockel, *Springfield and Clark County*, 477; *Philanthropist*, June 25, 1845; Boucher to Chase, Oct. 18, 1855, July 7, 1862, Lucinda Boucher to Chase, Dec. 2, 1863 (Chase Papers, L.C.).
87. Thomas Church Haskell Smith.

JULY 22. SUN   At home all day—but I hope not altogether unprofitably employed— Cholera evidently decreasing—

JULY 23. MON.   Spent day in house & at office doing little except look over papers & letters received during absence—

JULY (26) THURS   Wrote B. F. Butler, N.Y[88]—Jno Corby, Mo— Dd. Putnam, Harmer, O;[89] W. F. Chase, St Louis, Mo.—Cornwall & Bro. Louisville, Ky.[90]

JULY 27, FRI   Wrote T. Bolton, Cleveland; J. R. Giddings, Jefferson; Judge Caldwell, Lower Sandusky;[91] Hutchings & Co Louisville, enclosing check $1000— Ed. I. Chase, Lockport; Thomas Lee, Cadiz, O[92]— E. Nichols, Walhonding, O. Recd. $40 div. on Carrie Smith's Laf. Bk Stock.

JULY 28. SAT.   Wrote A. Bain, N.Y. E. M. Stanton & C. Doane, Pitts;[93] Dr. J. K. Skinner N.Y. J. S. Patterson, Logansport, H. Smith Louisville[94]

---

88. Chase wrote of his concern about rumors of a possible union between New York's mainline Democrats, the "Hunkers," and members of the party who supported the Free-Soil Buffalo Convention of 1848—a group Chase called the "Free Democracy." He approved the idea of party unity, but warned about sacrificing antislavery principles or Free-Soil cohesiveness. Chase to Benjamin F. Butler, July 26, 1849 (Butler Family Papers, Princeton Univ.).

89. David Putnam, Jr., a Harmar, Ohio, resident with antislavery sentiments, faced legal action for allegedly harboring nine fugitive slaves. Putnam to Chase, July 18, 30, 1849 (Chase Papers, L.C.).

90. Cornwall and Brother were wholesale grocers and commission merchants in Louisville. *Louisville Dir. (1848–49),* 96.

91. Chase dated his letters to Thomas Bolton and Joshua R. Giddings as July 26. The letter to Bolton supported the reelection of Free-Soil Whig legislator John F. Morse. To Giddings, Chase repeated his concern over unity with the "Hunkers," offered a favorable assessment of cohesiveness among Ohio's Free-Soilers, and urged Morse's reelection. William B. Caldwell had warned Chase of Norton S. Townshend's need to pursue mainline Democratic support in Lorain County in order to secure reelection. Caldwell to Chase, July 16, 1849 (Chase Papers, L.C.); Chase to Bolton, July 26, 1847 (Chicago Hist. Soc.); Chase to Giddings, July 26, 1849 (Giddings Papers, Ohio Hist. Soc.).

92. Lee was an associate judge in the Harrison County Court of Common Pleas. Gilkey, *Ohio Hundred Year Book,* 531.

93. The letters to Alexander Bain, Edwin M. Stanton, and Charles Doane all probably involved Henry O'Reilly's telegraph business. Stanton assisted with financial and legal aspects of a reorganization of O'Reilly's ventures. Chase to Stanton, July 2, 1849 (Stanton Papers, L.C.); Stanton to Chase, July 10, Aug. 9, 1849 (Chase Papers, Hist. Soc. of Pa.); Chase to Stanton, June 17, July 7, 1849 (letterbook abstracts), and Stanton to Chase, June 21, July 12, 14, 17, 18, Aug. 1, 1849 (Chase Papers, L.C.).

94. Josiah K. Skinner, a Lockport, N.Y., physician, was married to Chase's sister, Janette Logan Chase Skinner. Chase apparently gave John S. Patterson instructions for the sale of land in Logansport, Ind. Hamilton Smith and Chase were involved

JULY 29 SUN. At Trinity Church in Morning—Dr. Aydelotte preached funeral sermon for Mrs Beresford & Mrs Ho[lden]

JULY 30 MON Wrote J. W. Taylor, Sandusky, C. C. Convers, Zanesville;[95] J. G. Breslin, Tiffin;[96] A. G. Dimmock Millersburgh;[97] Geo Fisher ; N. S. Townshend, Elyria[98] / Recd. from James $15 rent Pugh & Pendleton;[99] pd. Mrs C. $20— Despatch to Hamlin .40—from Hamlin .30— Pd. Mrs C. Marketing $5— Drew from M. & T.[1] $10—

1850

MAY 18 Left Washn. at 6 AM—self, wife, Kate Ludlow,[2] two children & nurse—Cath. McDonald accompanied us to cars, grieved to part with her little Nettie whom she had nursed so long[3]—arrived

---

in a financial transaction whose nature remains unknown. Pool, *Landmarks of Niagara*, 136, 374, 386–88; Patterson to Chase, May 9, Aug. 2, 1849, Smith to Chase, July 30, Aug. 3, 6, 9, 11, 1849 (Chase Papers, L.C.).

95. Attorney Charles C. Convers (1810–60), a state senator from Muskingum County, 1849–52, speaker of the Ohio Senate, 1850–52, and justice of the Ohio Supreme Court, 1855. Previous correspondence suggests that Convers represented a client who wanted to help finance antislavery activities in Kentucky. *The Biographical and Historical Memoirs of Muskingum County, Ohio* . . . (Chicago, 1892), 191; Gilkey, *Ohio Hundred Year Book*, 168–69, 252, 473; Convers to Chase, July 26, 1849 (Chase Papers, L.C.).

96. Chase advocated a general coalition between Independent and mainline Democrats based on opposition to the geographic expansion of slavery. Chase to John G. Breslin, July 30, 1849, *Cong. Globe*, 31st Cong., 1st sess., 1850, 135–36.

97. Chase sent a copy of his argument in the Van Zandt case to Asa G. Dimmock, editor of the *Ohio Farmer* and a member of the Ohio Senate representing Holmes and Knox counties, 1848–50. Chase urged Dimmock to write against those who accused Democrats of advocating nonintervention on the slavery issue. Warden, *Chase*, 332–33; Gilkey, *Ohio Hundred Year Book*, 168.

98. Chase, writing at the request of William B. Caldwell, urged Townshend to solicit the assistance of Lorain County Democratic leaders to insure reelection to the legislature. Chase to Norton S. Townshend, July 30, 1849 (Chase Papers, Hist. Soc. of Pa.).

99. The Cincinnati legal partnership of George Ellis Pugh and Edmund Pendleton. "James" was James Ralston Skinner. *Cinc. Dir. (1849–50)*, 225, 231; Chase to Skinner, June 19, July 8, 1850 (Chase Papers, L.C.).

1. The Mechanics' and Traders' Branch Bank.

2. Catherine (Kate) Ludlow Baker Whiteman (1828–1905), a daughter of James C. Ludlow and Josephine Dunlop Ludlow and sister of Sarah Bella Dunlop Ludlow Chase. Unmarried at the time of this entry, she later married first a Mr. Baker and subsequently Lewis Whiteman. Unpublished guide to Ludlow-Dunlop-Chambers Collec., Univ. of Wyoming; Catherine Ludlow to Chase, Sept. 29, 1850, C. C. Clopper to Chase, June 30, 1852, James D. Ludlow to Chase, May 30, 1860 (Chase Papers, L.C.).

3. Janet ("Nettie") Ralston Chase (1847–1925) was the younger of Chase's two daughters who survived to adulthood. She became an illustrator of children's books and married William Sprague Hoyt in Mar. 1871. In his record of family births and deaths Chase spelled her name *Janette*, but later both he and his daughter spelled

in New York at Irving House[4] at ½ past 9 much fatigued— Rode to Mr. Garniss myself.

MAY 19   Went to Church with Mrs G. & Kate Ludlow—in afternoon we all went to Mr. Garniss & staid all night

MAY 20   Mr. Garniss went at 8 with Mrs C, Kate &c to Northampton—in evening I returned to Washington where arrived Tuesday Morning.

Mrs Chase spent a part of the Summer at Morristown N.Y.[5] While there she obtained daguerreotypes taken in Aug. of Mr. Israel Day & his wife, who is a near relation of her father & grandfather. The receipt for the daguerreotypes bears date Chatham Aug 23, '50 & is signed B. L. Burnett. While at M, Mrs C. boarded with Mrs Margaret Crowell[6] & Kate Ludlow was with her—dear little Josie died there & her remains were sent to Cin[7]— Mrs C—— left & came to Washn. early in Sep. whence after Congress adjd to Weberton— whence with her brother Dun[8] on horseback to Cincinnati.

1851

JOURNAL IV

AUG [9] 1851:   Wrote Judge Spalding, C. M. Clay, Jac. Brinkerhoff, B. F. Hoffman, J. R. Giddings,[9] John A. Reed, Isaac H. Hill

---

it *Janet*. "Family Memoranda" (Chase Papers, L.C.); *New York Tribune*, Mar. 24, 1871; *New York Times*, Nov. 20, 1925; Chase to Catherine Ludlow Whiteman, Oct. 21, 1865 (Chase Papers, Hist. Soc. of Pa.).

4. On Broadway. *New York Dir. (1850)*, 137.
5. This paragraph is from memoranda at the end of Journal I. Chase meant Morristown, New Jersey, not New York. Earlier in the year Sarah Bella Chase, who suffered from tuberculosis, had sought treatment or rest at the Parkeville Institute, near Woodbury, N.J., and at Northampton, Mass. She went to Morristown during July. George T. Dexter to Chase, Jan. 2, 1850, J. D. Ludlow to Chase, Feb. 6, 1850, Chase to Lewis Tappan, May 21, 1850, Chase to Sarah Bella Chase, May 22, 1850, Chase to J. R. Skinner, July 8, 1850 (Chase Papers, L.C.).
6. Perhaps a relative of David A. Crowell, later the owner of a hotel at Schooley's Mountain, a popular health resort in Morris County, N.J. Chase to Sarah Bella Chase, Aug. 9, 1850, ibid.; *History of Morris County, New Jersey* . . . (New York, 1882), 380.
7. Chase's daughter, Josephine, died on July 28. "Family Memoranda" (Chase Papers, L.C.).
8. James Dunlop Ludlow.
9. Chase's "Private & Confidential" letter to Joshua R. Giddings commented favorably on the moderate antislavery position taken by Ohio Democrats in their 1850 convention. He expressed concern that Free-Soilers in the state were not yet prepared to operate on their own as an independent political party and recommended fusion with Democrats. Chase to Giddings, Aug. 9, 1851 (Chase Papers, L.C.); Eugene H. Roseboom, *The Civil War Era, 1850–1873*, v. 4 of Carl Wittke, ed., *The History of the State of Ohio* (Columbus, 1944), 257–58.

enclg $5, about dem. conv. & course to be pursued— Recd. letters from Gt. Smith & Jos. Lyman, Comh. & Emanr. bill $4[10]—

AUG. 10, 51. Wrote Aaron Pardee, Wadsworth, W. T. Tillinghast, Wilmington, W. A. Rogers Springfield[11]— Recd. letters Pardee, & Wilson abt. Stateman $13 due unless Secy. pays— Thomas says he must cease— Dr. Brisbane called—also Rd. Gaines abt. Free Dem. Conv.[12] Gaines right ideas—

AUG. 26, 51: Wrote Edwd. Archbold,[13] C. R. Miller, Toledo,[14] G. Hoadly Sen. Cleveland; Swayne & Bates Columbus;[15] D. Putnam Jr Harmar; E. M. Stanton Pittsburgh; D. M. McKinley, Millersburgh— J. F. Asper, Chardon;[16] Miss H. B. Haines[17]— Recd. despatch Miller abt. sale Repn. & ansd

10. Reformer and antislavery leader Gerrit Smith (1797–874) sat for one term as an independent congressman from New York, 1853–54. The *Commonwealth and Emancipator,* a Boston weekly, appeared under that title during the first half of 1851. *DAB,* 17:270–71.

11. Aaron Pardee (b. 1808), a prominent lawyer from Medina County, served in the Ohio Senate, 1850, 1852–54. William Allen Rogers (1809–55), a Free-Soil Whig from Springfield, Ohio, became a common pleas judge, 1851–55. William A. Duff, *History of North Central Ohio* . . . (Topeka, Kans., 1931), 3:1255; Gilkey, *Ohio Hundred Year Book,* 168, 171, 294, 553; *The History of Clark County, Ohio* . . . (Chicago, 1881), 912–13.

12. Richard Gaines was a Cincinnati grocer and a political ally. He and Chase apparently conferred about the National Free Democratic Convention, also called the National Convention of Friends of Freedom, to be held in Cleveland, Sept. 24–25, 1851. *Cinc. Dir. (1850–51),* 105; *National Era,* Oct. 2, 9, 1851; Chase to Gaines, May 5, 1868 (Chase Papers, L.C.).

13. Archbold had asked Chase to enquire about the fate of Jonathan Zane Hayward, a young man who disappeared shortly after enlisting for military service during the Mexican War. Archbold to Chase, Aug. 20, Sept. 17, 1851 (Chase Papers, L.C.).

14. On Aug. 25, Chase wrote a long letter to Charles R. Miller, publisher and editor of the Toledo *Commercial Republican,* a free-soil Democratic newspaper. Chase explained his support for the Democratic party ticket, rather than that of the independent Free-Soilers, in the coming state election. He had the letter printed for distribution; it is the "Toledo letter" mentioned in entries for Sept. 2 and 4, below. Chase to C. R. Miller, Aug. 25, 1851 (printed copy, Cinc. Hist. Soc.); Waggoner, *Toledo,* 342, 494, 640.

15. Noah Haynes Swayne (1804–84), a Columbus attorney and justice of the U.S. Supreme Court, 1862–81; and his partner, James Lawrence Bates (1815–90), judge of Ohio's fifth district Court of Common Pleas. *DAB,* 18:239–40; Gilkey, *Ohio Hundred Year Book,* 558; Reed, *Bench and Bar of Ohio,* 2:225.

16. Attorney Joel Funk Asper (1822–72), Iowa Free-Soil activist, editor of the *Chardon Democrat,* and U.S. congressman, 1869–71, had written to express disapproval of the Democratic position on slavery and to urge continued independence for the Free-Soil movement. Asper to Chase, Aug. 23, 1851 (Chase Papers, L.C.); *Bio. Dir. U.S. Cong.,* 551–52.

17. Henrietta B. Haines operated a school in New York City which Chase's daughter, Kate, attended. J. P. Garniss to Chase, Jan. 7, 1850 (Chase Papers, Hist. Soc. of Pa.); Haines to Chase, July 5, 1851 (Chase Papers, L.C.); *New York Dir. (1851–52),* 231.

AUG 27, '51 Wrote H Smith Louisville & telegraphed him abt. accepts[18]— Recd. 2d. despatch from Miller—ansd. yesterday— Wrote L. W. Hall encg. $5[19]— ☞ Perl. a/c— C. H. Haven, St Louis & I. G. Burnet, Walnut Hills[20]

AUG 29, 51: Wrote A. L. Robinson, Evansville;[21] C. R. Miller, Toledo; Wm H Day, Cleveland;[22] Thos Hibben, Wilmington; Israel Garrard, Boston, enclosing Intron. to C. F. Adams;[23] Mr. Howe, Mt Pleasant, Iowa, enclosing letter to H. L. Preston: recd. Wm H. Day abt. B. B. Chapman[24] & Storer— wrote J. W. Taylor, enclosing Addison Art. Nat Conv. friends of Freedom; Dr. Bailey, enclosing same & Ohio Dem. Resolutions—James Mackenzie, Kalida[25]

AUG 30. Recd. C. M. Clay White Hall—will go to Conv.[26]—G. Hoadly Sen Cleveland (abt Hosmer School[27]—C. R. Miller, Toledo abt. sale Repn. Wrote J. C. Vaughan, Cleveland, Clay comg. &c &c—

---

18. Chase's letter informed Hamilton Smith that $2,200 in drafts had matured on the previous day: "I telegraphed you this morning that you may be prepared tomorrow to take up the drafts on their return." Chase to Smith, Aug. 27, 1851 (Smith MSS, Indiana Univ.)

19. Lyman W. Hall apparently edited the *Ohio Star,* a Free-Soil newspaper in Ravenna. Gutgesell, *Ohio Newspapers,* 307; Hall to Chase, May 7, 1851 (Chase Papers, L.C.).

20. Isaac G. Burnet was clerk of the Ohio Supreme Court. *Cinc. Dir. (1850–51),* 49.

21. Robinson, a supporter of the antislavery movement, operated a collection business in Evansville, Ind. During the Civil War, he served in Evansville as U.S. surveyor of customs. *Register of Officers (1863),* 92; Robinson to Chase, Nov. 30, 1857 (Chase Papers, L.C.).

22. William Howard Day (1825–1900) was a black abolitionist later noted for his work with fugitive slaves in Canada and the U.S. and, following his ordination in 1866, his leadership of the African Methodist Episcopal Zion Church. He edited the Cleveland *True Democrat,* 1851–53. Day to Chase, Apr. 5, 1862 (Chase Papers, L.C.); Van Tassel and Grabowski, *Encyclopedia of Cleveland,* 335.

23. Chase's letter of introduction recommended Garrard to Charles Francis Adams (1807–86), Free-Soil nominee for the vice presidency in 1848 and U.S. ambassador to Britain, 1861–68. *DAB,* 1:40–48.

24. Bird Beers Chapman (1821–71), an attorney from Lorain County, Ohio, and Democratic congressman, 1855–57. *Bio. Dir. U.S. Cong.,* 765.

25. James Mackenzie, who served in the Ohio House, 1854–55, edited the *Kalida Venture,* a Democratic newspaper. Gilkey, *Ohio Hundred Year Book,* 286; Gutgesell, *Ohio Newspapers,* 212; *The Putnam County Atlas 1895* . . . (Ottawa, Ohio, n.d.), 129.

26. Cassius M. Clay, writing from his Kentucky home called White Hall, planned to attend the National Free Democratic Convention in Cleveland on Sept. 24. Clay to Chase, Aug. 27, 1851 (Chase Papers, Hist. Soc. of Pa.).

27. Elbridge Hosmer (1807–52), Dartmouth class of 1831, was principal of Cleveland's Young Ladies' Institute. *Cleve. Dir. (1848),* 22, 110; Emerson, *General Catalogue,* 258.

September 1851 {227}

C. R. Miller, Toledo agst sale & abt. prospects—C. Sumner, Boston;[28]—Dr. Bailey, Washn.; C. J. Chase, East Hampton.[29]

SEP. 1. Wrote C. M. Clay, will *go 22nd:*

SEP 2: Recd. Bingham's Cer. Commr. Pensions & fowd.[30]— Gen Jones Letter abt. Hayward & Wrote Archbold[31]— My Letter in Toledo Republican & wrote Smith, Statesman,[32] enclosing one & Dr. Bailey enclosing one— Recd. letter B. F. Hoffman: Wrote N. K. Hall PM Genl.[33] abt. *Edin Rev.* &c: H Smith enclosing ch. $1750:

SEP 4. Wrote *B. F. Hoffman,* enclosing Toledo Letter; W. W. Stapp, Frankfort Ky enclosing Vanzandt argt., Union & Freedom Speech, & Toledo Speech;[34] John Van Buren, with Toledo Letter; T. H. Benton, Washn. with do— Krauth & Myers called abt. pub. Toledo letter in Enquirer[35]— Mr. Garniss to Enquire abt. Omnibus to Mt.

28. Chase inquired if Sumner planned to attend the Cleveland convention. Chase to Charles Sumner, Aug. 30, 1851 (Houghton Lib., Harvard Univ.).

29. Chase's daughter Kate (Catharine Jane) was apparently on vacation from the boarding school of Miss Henrietta B. Haines, in New York City. Chase scolded her for not writing clearly and more often, reported on the health of his wife, and relayed miscellaneous pieces of family news. Chase to Kate Chase, Aug. 30, 1851 (Chase Papers, Hist. Soc. of Pa.).

30. Kinsley S. Bingham (1808–61) served as U.S. representative from Michigan. Chase, a member of the Senate's Committee on Revolutionary Claims, was apparently helping Bingham with a transaction which involved James Ewell Heath (1792–1862), U.S. commissioner of pensions, 1850–53. *Appletons',* 1:264; *List of Committees of the Senate of the United States for the Second Session of the Thirty-First Congress,* 31st Cong., 2nd sess., 1850, S. Misc. Doc. 1; *DAB,* 8:489.

31. Chase's letter to Edward Archbold reported the inability of Roger Jones (1789–1852), adjutant general of the U.S. Army, to find any military record of Jonathan Zane Hayward, the missing person brought to Chase's attention on Aug. 26. Archbold to Chase, Sept. 17, 1851 (Chase Papers, L.C.); *Appletons',* 3:470.

32. Columbus attorney James Haddock Smith (1822–62) was an editor of the Democratic *Ohio Statesman;* member of the Ohio House, 1847–49, 1856–57; and, at his death, clerk of the Court of Common Pleas of Franklin County. Reed, *Bench and Bar of Ohio,* 2:57–58; *Columbus Gazette,* Jan. 30, 1857; Gilkey, *Ohio Hundred Year Book,* 211, 306.

33. Nathan Kelsey Hall (1810–74), U.S. postmaster general, 1850–52. *DAB,* 8:140–41.

34. On Mar. 26–27, 1850, Chase made an address in the Senate opposing any extension of slavery into western territories under Henry Clay's compromise plan. That speech and a political address made in Toledo were printed as pamphlets for distribution: *Union and Freedom, without Compromise. Speech of Mr. Chase, of Ohio, on Mr. Clay's Compromise Resolutions* (Washington, D.C., 1850); *Speech of Senator Chase, delivered at Toledo, May 30, 1851, before a Mass Convention of the Democracy of North-Western Ohio* (Cincinnati, 1851); *Cong. Globe,* 31st Cong., 1st sess., 1850, appen., 468–80.

35. John B. Krauth and James Myers (1795–1864) of Toledo, a canal and road contractor; former county judge; C. R. Miller's partner on the *Republican;* state senator and legislator, 1848–52, 1862–63; and lieutenant governor, 1854–56. On

Auburn— Luke [Wren], abt. lot— *Recd* letters L. W. Hall, Ravenna— James Myers Enclosing dft C. R. Miller $75— Wrote C. R. Miller, encld. certif. dep. C. R. M to cr. J. Myers $75 M & T. Br. Bk.[36]—David Wilmot, Towanda; Preston King, Ogdensburgh;[37] K. S. Bingham, Kensington, *each* copy *letter* Toledo:

SEP. 5. Recd. C. R. Miller: Judge G. Beach, [Perrys]burg O— Wrote both—

SEP 9. Recd. Miller, Clay Giddings & others[38]— Wrote Clay, Giddings, *Scott, Maysville, autograph;* C. C. Bonney Bulletin off. Bloomington, Ill,[39] Miss Haines infg. letter yesterday with $200 ch. enclosed fear mislaid— Taylor[40]— Firemans Parade[41]—didn't see it—made propositions to Ball[42]—

SEP. 10. Letters from P. Kelley Dayton[43]—surpd. by Centre Hall Resolution—C. R. Miller, abt. sundries—E. M. Stanton *do.*[44]— Recd. Norwalk Experiment Letter publd. & kind & flattering notice[45]—

Sept. 9, the *Cincinnati Enquirer* carried a notice of Chase's recent expulsion from Hamilton County's Free-Soil convention and extracts of his explanatory letter to Miller (see Aug. 26 above). Waggoner, *Toledo,* 494, 640, 694–95; *Gilkey, Ohio Hundred Year Book,* 168, 291.

36. The Mechanics' and Traders' Branch Bank of Cincinnati.

37. David Wilmot (1814–68), of Towanda, Pa., and Preston King (1806–65), of Ogdensburg, N.Y., were Free-Soil congressmen and future Republican U.S. senators. *DAB,* 10:396–97, 20:317.

38. Giddings expressed outraged outrage over allegations that he and Chase had conspired to promote the presidential candidacy of Sam Houston, and requested Chase's help refuting the charges. Cleveland *Daily True Democrat,* Sept. 2, 1851; J. R. Giddings to Chase, Sept. 9, 1851 (Chase Papers, Hist. Soc. of Pa.).

39. Peoria, Ill., educator Charles Carroll Bonney (1831–1903), later a Chicago attorney. The *Illinois State Bulletin* was published under that title in Bloomington, Ill., 1850–53. *DAB,* 2:439.

40. From Sandusky, James Wickes Taylor had warned Chase of growing dissatisfaction with Ohio's Free-Soil leaders and of local plans for a separate Liberty party organized by Francis D. Parish and others. Taylor to Chase, Sept. 5, 6, 1851 (Chase Papers, L.C.).

41. The annual parade, three miles long, included companies from Cincinnati and from as far away as Louisville and Nashville. *Cincinnati Daily Gazette,* Sept. 10, 1851.

42. Chase offered Flamen Ball several options to reorganize or dissolve their legal partnership. Chase to Ball, Sept. 9, 1851 (Chase Papers, L.C.).

43. Patrick Kelly was a Dayton merchant. Kelly to Chase, Jan. 6, 1846, ibid.; A. W. Drury, *History of the City of Dayton and Montgomery County, Ohio* . . . (Chicago, 1909), 2:597.

44. Stanton discussed politics and told of pressing duties which prevented him from meeting with Chase and from assisting with the defense of David Putnam, Jr. E. M. Stanton to Chase, Sept. 7, 1851 (Chase Papers, Hist. Soc. of Pa.); Chase to Stanton, July 16, 1850 (Stanton Papers, L.C.).

45. The *Norwalk Experiment* was a Democratic newspaper published in Norwalk, Ohio. Gutgesell, *Ohio Newspapers,* 279.

Wrote P. Kelley—saw Myers abt. printing letter[46]—gave him Foster & Whitney's Rep— Went with Belle to Boat—she concluded not to go today.[47]

JOURNAL I

In Nov. I furnished Mrs Burrows house at Clifton which I had rented in order to give Belle a pleasant home in the country, thinking it best she should not accept Mrs Clarksons invitation to spend the winter with her[48]— The bedsteads &c were bot of H. Boyd the cold. mechanic[49]

1852

JOURNAL IV

Washington.

DECR. 10.   I recd. today the following announcement of the death of my brother William at St Louis, on the 30th ulto.
"Your brother William is no more. He died last night in full possession of his mind and with all the consolations of religion. The Rev. Mr. Leach of the Episcopal Church attended him. His death was so gentle, it was as though he fell asleep asking forgiveness of all to whom he might have acted amiss—for all errors of omission & commission—he said he was going home, and, with a tear, bid all farewell. But he died in the full faith of a Saviors atonement.
The letter was written by Mr. J. Delafield Jr and dated Dec 1. '52.[50] Thus I have lost my youngest brother: and of five brothers, myself and my brother Edward, of Lockport, alone remain. Of our

---

46. Chase consulted with James Myers about printing the "Toledo Letter." See Aug. 26 and Sept. 4, above.

47. Sarah Bella Chase had planned a week-long vacation in Clermont County, forty miles up the Ohio River, but found the boat crowded with travelers leaving the previous day's Fireman's Parade. Chase to Kate Chase, Sept. 10, 1851 (Chase Papers, Hist. Soc. of Pa.).

48. This entry for Nov. 1851 is from memoranda at the rear of Journal I. Charlotte Dunlop Clarkson was Sarah Bella Chase's aunt and the wife of Charles S. Clarkson. Mrs. Burrows was probably John A. Burrows's wife. Unpublished guide to Ludlow-Dunlop-Chambers Collec., Univ. of Wyoming.

49. Henry Boyd, a noted black entrepreneur, manufactured bedsteads at the corner of Broadway and Eighth Street. *Cinc. Dir.* (*1849–50*), 41; Martin Robison Delany, *The Condition, Elevation, Emigration, and Destiny of the Colored People of the United States Politically Considered* (Philadelphia, 1852; reprint, New York, 1968), 98.

50. John Delafield, a partner in the St. Louis law firm of Delafield and Kribben. *St. Louis Dir.* (*1854–55*), 43, 107.

family of ten, five & our father & mother, also, have departed.[51] A few years and we shall follow.

Wrote my neice Eliza Whipple, my sister Helen Walbridge, my brother Edward, Mr. Delafield & my sister in law Mary, widow of my brother William.[52]

DEC. 11. No incident of much interest occurred. Called on Mr. Everett Secy. of State; on Mr. Markoe, State Dept;[53] on Sumner, with whom talked about committees, proper course of policy &c. Walking down avenue joined by Bodisco, Russian Minister,[54] who invited Sumner & myself to call; agreed to do so. Mr. Rockwell called and staid to dinner,[55] with whom interesting talk about Benton. Sympathizing note from S. Walker about brother Williams death.

Wrote E. S. Hubbard, Cin; W. Birney, Phila; L. C. Munn, Boston;[56] T. Walker, Cin; Isaac Fisher Huntingdon, Pa; M. M. Southworth, (Dem League) Lockport;[57] Eliza Whipple, Concord; Ralston Skinner Cin; Heath, Commr. (Gilberts Patent 40 acres) Pension Bureau.

DEC. 13. Prepared before going to Capitol resolutions for revision of rules & repeal of resolution for election of officers—also bill granting public lands in Ohio to the State.[58] In Senate Bright moved

51. Besides Chase, family members still living included Alice, Edward, Helen, and their sister Janette. Those who had died were Abigail; Alexander; Dudley Heber Chase (1801–20), who went to sea at an early age and died in the Caribbean; Hannah; William; and their parents, Jannette Ralston Chase and Ithamar Chase (1762–1817), a farmer, justice of the peace, and businessman. Child, *Cornish*, 2:64–65; Griffin, *Keene*, 373; "Family Memoranda" (Chase Papers, L.C.); Chase to John T. Trowbridge, Dec. 27, 1863, Jan. 19, [1864] (Chase Papers, Hist. Soc. of Pa.).

52. The former Mary Gillespie of St. Louis. "Family Memoranda" (Chase Papers, L.C.); *St. Louis Dir. (1854–55)*, 31.

53. Educator, orator, and politician Edward Everett (1794–1865), U.S. secretary of state, 1852–53; Francis Markoe, chief clerk in the diplomatic bureau of the State Department and husband of Chase's friend, Mary Galloway Maxcy Markoe. *DAB*, 6:223–26; Hammond, *Colonial Mansions*, 142; *Wash. Dir. (1853)*, 103.

54. Waldemar de Bodisco (d. 1878). *Appletons'*, 1:299.

55. Possibly Julius Rockwell (1805–88), Whig congressman from Massachusetts, 1843–51. *Bio. Dir. U.S. Cong.*, 1733.

56. Edwin S. Hubbard, a local attorney; William Birney (1819–1907), a former Cincinnati attorney, later a Philadelphia lawyer and editor of that city's *Register*, and brigadier and major general of U.S. volunteers, 1863–65; and Lewis C. Munn, a Boston printer. *Cinc. Dir. (1853)*, 189; *DAB*, 2:294; *Boston Dir. (1850)*, 244.

57. Mortimer M. Southworth held various local offices in Lockport, N.Y. Pool, *Landmarks of Niagara*, 114, 374–75.

58. Chase, excluded from significant committee assignments, opposed the Democratic majority's control of Senate committees. His motion to postpone the vote on committee appointments was rejected, 38–6. His other proposal regarding revisions failed to reach the floor. The public land measure was actually a resolution from the Ohio legislature which called for "a law granting land to actual settlers at the cost of surveying and locating the same." *Cong. Globe*, 32nd Cong., 2nd sess., 1852, 40–43; U.S. Senate, *Journal*, 32nd Cong., 2nd sess., 1852, 31–32.

to dispense with rule for appointment of Committees by ballot[59]—Hale asked for statement of mode of appt. Bright said appointed by Caucuses of respective parties, excluding Senators outside of the healthy political organizations of the country. Hale replied. Walker, Wis. complained of his treatment in appts. of Committee[60]—Hale suggested it might be owing to fanaticism of his state. Walker thought Wisconsin had improved in that respect. after brief speech I moved to postpone till tomorrow and asked ayes and noes—ordered—only 6 ayes—Walker excused from his appointments—Committees in other respects appointed as proposed—Hale objected to Chair filling vacancies—ballotted—no quorum—again & no quorum—Hale having gone out without leaving word & I supposing he had withdrawn objection, no objection to Chair appointing— I then presented Resolutions of Ohio in favor of Land Reform with speech in favor & reference to fact that doctrine in no national platform except that of Pittsburgh Convention[61]— Underwood spoke in favor of Dixon[62]— Evening free democrats & Howe of Pa met at my house; a good deal of talk and little done.[63] Mr. Adams C. F. present.

Heard a day or two since characteristic anecdote of Benton. A gentleman remarked to him "You must have had a hard struggle Mr. Benton in Missouri, with two parties against you". "Sir" replied Old Bullion "Did you ever read Gullivers Travels." "When I was a boy," answered the gentleman. "Then, Sir" said Benton you remember that when Gulliver arrived in Lilliput, the inhabitants were seized with consternation lest he should cause a famine in the land. A dozen chickens hardly made a mouthful for him. Well, Sir, when he was asleep whole armies of Lilliputians marched against him. They planted scaling ladders against his sides. They mounted by tens of thousands. They bound him with millions of cords hands, arms & feet. But Sir when Gulliver awoke he barely turned over on his side, and he killed forthy thousand of them Sir. Yes, Sir, forthy thousand Sir; by simply turning over, Sir; Sir I played Gulliver in Missouri Sir.

59. Democrat Jesse David Bright (1812–75), U.S. senator from Indiana, 1845–62. Expelled from the Senate in 1862 for acknowledging Confederate legitimacy, Bright moved to Kentucky in 1863. *DAB*, 3:45–46.

60. Isaac Pigeon Walker (1815–72), Democratic member of the U.S. Senate, 1848–55, and member of the Committees on Revolutionary Claims, Agriculture, and Indian Affairs. *Bio. Dir. U.S. Cong.*, 1995.

61. The National Free-Soil Convention, which met in Pittsburgh, Aug. 10–13, 1852. *Daily National Intelligencer*, Aug. 11–14, 1852.

62. U.S. Senators Joseph Rogers Underwood (1791–1876) and Archibald Dixon (1802–76), Whigs from Kentucky. *DAB*, 19:114–15; *Appletons'*, 2:185–86.

63. The group, which included Free-Soiler John W. Howe (1801–73), a congressman from Pennsylvania, 1849–53, met at Chase's house on the south side of C, between 3d and 4th Streets. *Bio. Dir. U.S. Cong.*, 1219; *Wash. Dir. (1853), 48.*

Recd. letters from Day T. C.[64]

DECR. 15; Dined at Presidents—assigned to Mrs Phelps—Mrs Gwin on Prest's right[65]—I next—next Mrs Phelps—not so pleasant as on some former occasions—told Prest. what Sartige French Minister[66] said of his wife— Elle est charmante—admirable femme pour un diplomat[67]— Would you believe? She did ask me Was Mr. Fillmore Whig or Democrat? He laughed heartily. Asked Prest. if true he had received communication from his late Secy. Mr. Webster in Spirit world[68]— Said he had but did not read—talk with Corcoran, Reverdy Johnson Com. Morris, Gen Jesup & others[69]—brot Mr. Butler home with me.[70] Recd. F. Ball

DEC. 16. FRIDAY— Senate did not sit—called on S. W[71]—indiscreet & wrong—sat for daguerreotypers Whitehursts Gallery[72]— one for Picture of Senate—one for Gleason Pictures[73]

---

64. Timothy Crane Day (1819–69), an editor and proprietor of the *Cincinnati Enquirer*, 1849–52, Republican member of Congress, 1855–56. *Bio. Dir. U.S. Cong.*, 886.
65. Mary Whitney Phelps and Mary Bell Gwin, wives of Democratic Congressman John Smith Phelps of Missouri and Senator William McKendree Gwin of California. The president was Millard Fillmore. *Bio. Dir. U.S. Cong.*, 1641–42; *DAB*, 8:64–65, 14:530.
66. Le comte Eugène de Sartiges (b. 1809), envoy extraordinary and minister plenipotentiary of France. *Wash. Dir. (1853)*, 28; Gustave Vapereau, ed., *Dictionnaire Universel des Contemporains: Contenant Toutes les Personnes Notables de la France et des Pays Étrangers*, 5th ed. (Paris, 1880), 1621.
67. "She is charming—admirable wife for a diplomat."
68. Daniel Webster, Fillmore's secretary of state, had died on Oct. 14. *DAB*, 19:585.
69. William Wilson Corcoran (1798–1888), financier, philanthropist, and partner in the Washington banking firm of Corcoran and Riggs; Reverdy Johnson (1796–1876) of Baltimore, Whig and later Union Democrat U.S. senator, 1845–49, 1863–68, minister to England, 1868–69, and, later, an attorney noted for defending Southerners accused of disloyalty; Maj. Gen. Thomas Sidney Jesup (1788–1860), quartermaster general of the U.S. Army. Morris may have been Commander Henry W. Morris of the U.S. Navy or Charles Morris (1784–1856), naval officer, former member of the Board of Navy Commissioners, and at this time chief of the Bureau of Ordnance and Hydrography. Henry Cohen, *Business and Politics in America from the Age of Jackson to the Civil War: The Career Biography of W. W. Corcoran* (Westport, Conn., 1971), 3, 6, 224; *DAB*, 10:62–63, 112–14, 13:202–3; *Letter from the Secretary of the Navy transmitting Tabular Statements showing the Pay & Allowances of Officers of the Navy*, 32nd Cong., 2nd sess., 1853, H. Ex. Doc. 35, 7.
70. Probably Clement Moore Butler.
71. Susan Walker.
72. The gallery of Jesse H. Whitehurst (c. 1820–75) on Pennsylvania Avenue. Beaumont Newhall, *The Daguerreotype in America* (New York, 1961; rev. ed., 1968); *Daily National Intelligencer*, Dec. 16, 1852.
73. Chase apparently had a photograph taken to serve as the basis for an engraved portrait in *Gleason's Pictorial Drawing-Room Companion*, v. 4, no. 6 (Feb. 5, 1853): 88.

January 1853   { 233 }

DECR. 17—SATY.— Read newspapers—went to Gallery with Dr. Townshend—one portrait good—others indifferent— Called on Mr. & Mrs Cope & Mr. & Mrs Hale & Judge Grier[74]— Home / Judge Peters called—F. P. Blair[75]—Gangewer[76]—dinner—walk with Dr. Bailey— Wrote B. Tappan F. Ball, two letters—R. Skinner[77]—Dr. John Paul—Woolsey Welles[78]—Ralph I. Leet—Miss Haines—Belle Skinner[79]—Mr. Garniss— Recd. E. Nichols Walhonding—R. Skinner—

1853

JANY 9. SUNDAY. Day not well spent—read variously in the morng.—after dinner Uncle Tom's Cabin[80]— What a character & the book what a sermon! I cannot read it without tears. Surely it is "tuba, mirum spargens sonum."[81] Walked—met my classmate

---

74. Probably Herman Cope and his wife; Sen. John Parker Hale and Lucy Lambert Hale; and, Robert Cooper Grier (1794–1870), an associate justice of the U.S. Supreme Court. Chase to Cope, Nov. 8, 1845 (Chase Papers, L.C.); *DAB*, 7:612–13, 8:105–7.

75. Washington, D.C., and Maryland politician and journalist Francis Preston Blair, Sr. (1791–1876). *DAB*, 2:330–32.

76. Allen M. Gangewer of Columbus, Ohio, editor and publisher of the *Ohio Columbian* and, starting in 1859, Chase's secretary. During the Civil War, Gangewer worked as a clerk in the U.S. Treasury. *Col. Dir. (1856–57)*, 87; *Detailed Statement of the Receipts and Disbursements of the Public Money*, Ohio Exec. Docs. for 1859, 2:462; *Wash. Dir. (1862)*, 86; ibid. (1865), 202.

77. James Ralston Skinner.

78. John Paul (c. 1805–72), a Defiance, Ohio, physician and Liberty party activist, was a longtime supporter of Chase; a collector of state revenue, 1856; and, later, a resident of LaSalle County, Ill. Woolsey Welles, a resident of Lorain County, had previously worked with Chase in the Liberty party. *Annual Report of the Secretary of State*, Ohio Exec. Docs. for 1856, 2:361; *The Past and Present of LaSalle County, Illinois* . . . (Chicago, 1877), 290–91; Paul to Chase, Oct. 24, 1855, July 5, 1864 (Chase Papers, Hist. Soc. of Pa.); Welles to Chase, Apr. 2, July 5, Oct. 12, Nov. 4, 1844 (Chase Papers, L.C.).

79. Ironton, Ohio, attorney and Free-Soil politician Ralph Leete (b. 1822) became a Republican party leader in Lawrence County. Chase's niece, Isabel ("Belle") R. D. Skinner, was a daughter of Janette Logan Chase Skinner and Josiah K. Skinner. After marrying George Walbridge she lived in Toledo, Ohio. "Personal History Department Lawrence County," in *Historical Hand-Atlas . . . and Histories of Lawrence and Gallia Counties, Ohio* (Chicago and Toledo, 1882), 42–43; Leete to Chase, June 18, 1855, J. R. Skinner to Chase, May 10, 1861, G. Walbridge to Chase, Apr. 4, 1861, and "Family Memoranda" (Chase Papers, L.C.); Chase to Isabel Skinner Walbridge, May 4, 1864 (Chase Papers, Hist. Soc. of Pa.).

80. Chase read Harriet Beecher Stowe's famous novel as it first appeared in the *National Era* from June 1851 to Apr. 1852, and had just purchased an illustrated copy of the book. Chase to Sarah Bella Chase, Dec. 10, 1851, Lewis Clephane receipt, Jan. 1, 1853 (Chase Papers, L.C.).

81. "Bugle, spread the wonderful sound."

Allen, of Texas, who turned & walked with me.[82] Met Shields[83] & Judge & Mrs McLean—Shields stopped & chatted a moment. Allen told me a good deal about Texas—Germans settling Western Texas; not anti-slavery—buy slaves as soon as able—poor people from Illinois, Indiana, & other states coming in. Extensive timber lands between N. & Rio G.[84] Mexican Ranches there inhabitants hardly know what governmnt. they live under—ranches unknown to American population— Allen came home with me & sat few minutes— gave him letter from Moses Kimball our classmate[85]—read bible— went to Church—stranger preached—read Bible, 1st Period Townsend's Arrangement[86]— He thinks Messiah & Lord God equivalent terms—that the Messiah appeared to our first parents in the garden—warned Noah to build the ark—watched over the Church—is the God of Mankind. Is not this substantially the Arian idea? Read Wiseman's Lectures[87]—arranged some Miscellanies & wrote above—now past 12:

JANY 11. News that Dem. Conv. Ohio laid Balte. Platform on table—good but dashed by account of resolutions adopted, it not appearing that antislavery resolution among them.[88] Ex. session of Senate abt. removing injunction of secrecy from Clayton-Bulwer treaty[89]—injn. removed 25 to 2[1]—Sumner & I aye Hale no. Gerrit

---

82. Ebenezer Allen (1795–1863), Dartmouth class of 1826, attorney general of Texas, and future radical secessionist. Emerson, *General Catalogue*, 238; Webb et al., *Handbook of Texas*, 1:30.
83. Senator James Shields.
84. The Nueces and Rio Grande rivers.
85. Moses Kimball (1799–1868) was graduated from Dartmouth in 1826 and from Andover Theological Seminary in 1830. He acted as supply minister at East Weathersfield, Vt., beginning in 1850. Emerson, *General Catalogue*, 239; Chapman, *Sketches of the Alumni*, 231–32.
86. George Townsend (1788–1857) was a British author and clergyman. His most noted works included *The Old Testament Arranged in Historical and Chronological Order* . . . , 8 vols. (London, 1821); and *The New Testament Arranged in Historical and Chronological Order* . . . , 8 vols. (London, 1826). *DNB*, 19:1031–32.
87. Cardinal Nicholas Patrick Stephen Wiseman (1802–65), Irish Catholic archbishop of Westminster. Wiseman's works included *Four Lectures on the Offices and Ceremonies of Holy Week* . . . (London, 1839); *Lectures on the Principal Doctrines and Practices of the Catholic Church* . . . , 2 vols. (London, 1836); *Three Lectures on the Catholic Hierarchy* . . . (London, 1850); and *Twelve Lectures on the Connection between Science and Revealed Religion* . . . (London, 1836). *DNB*, 21:714–17.
88. The Democratic National Convention, meeting in Baltimore on June 5, 1852, had denounced antislavery activists, denied the power of Congress to interfere with slavery, and expressed support for the Compromise of 1850—including its provisions for a strengthened fugitive slave law. The Ohio State Democratic Convention had repudiated the national platform in Columbus on Jan. 8, 1853. *Daily National Intelligencer*, June 7, 1852; *Ohio State Journal*, Jan. 11, 1853.
89. The Clayton-Bulwer Treaty, ratified by the U.S. Senate in 1850, forbade Great Britain and the U.S. from colonizing Central America and guaranteed the neutrality of any future Isthmian transportation route. At this time, the controversial agreement was under attack by Chase and others who criticized the British for maintaining

Smith with me—came yesterday—was today in Senate— After dinner Mr. Goicuria, a Cuban refugee, called[90]—much interesting conversation about Cuba & slavery there— He related an amusing anecdote of negress—her mistress had hard labor—she exclaimed— Well—I'm thankful we can't do dat for Misses—if I could Mass'd set me at it— Enfranchisement by [baptism] $25— Afterwards on appraisement. Aguéro y Aguero emancipated just before revolt at Puerto Principe.[91] Creoles favor emancipation— Related incident at Madrid— Wished to make intreat with certain high magistrate—was told apply to wife of Senora's lover or to husband of Senor's mistress— Cartter,[92] Hale, Bailey came in—after gone wrote awhile argt.—tea at Baileys Corwin & Smith[93] there—home—argt. & now bed.

JANY 17. Finished Argt. in Tel: Case Saty. night[94]—had sent two parcels of it & now balance— Attended to sundry matters this morning—read articles—wrote at Senate Dr. Colby, Miss Haines,—at home morng. G. Smith, P.M. Washn—at home evg. Moses Kimball with a/c life—Ed Everett for letter for Mr. Pierrepont— Read article on Gov. Ramsey conduct in Sioux matter—looks bad for Ramsey[95]— Read Free Dem. Resolutions in Statesman, good: kind article on me in Elevator[96]— Went with Baileys to

---

a protectorate over the Mosquito Indian tribe of eastern Honduras. *Cong. Globe,* 32nd Cong., 2nd sess, 1853, 237–38, 253, 414–18, 567; Mary Wilhelmine Williams, *Anglo-American Isthmian Diplomacy, 1815–1915* (Washington, D.C., 1916), 97–100.

90. Domingo Goicouria (1804–70), at this time a resident of Mississippi, participated in several filibustering expeditions in Latin America during the late 1840s and early 1850s. Francisco Calcagno, *Diccionario Biografico Cubano* (New York, 1878), 302; Francis Drake, *Dictionary of American Biography* . . . (Boston, 1872), 366–67.

91. Cuban reformer Joaquin de Agüero (1816–51) freed eight slaves in 1843, pledging to educate them in their rights and responsibilities as free persons. He was executed in 1851 for his part in a revolt in the province of Puerto Príncipe (Camagüey). Calcagno, *Diccionario Biografico Cubano,* 17–19.

92. David Kellogg Cartter (1812–87), Democratic congressman from Ohio, 1849–53; U.S. minister to Bolivia, 1861–62; and chief justice of the Supreme Court of the District of Columbia, 1863–87. *Bio. Dir. U.S. Cong.,* 751.

93. Gerrit Smith.

94. Chase had his argument before the U.S. Supreme Court in the O'Reilly telegraph case printed as a pamphlet. The Morse group countered by issuing one of their counsel's arguments in pamphlet form. *The Electric Telegraph;* Swisher, *Taney Period,* 499–500; entry for June 30, 1849, above.

95. Alexander Ramsey (1815–1903), governor of Minnesota and later a U.S. senator, faced charges of misappropriating funds intended to fulfill treaty obligations with the Sioux. The Senate eventually exonerated him. *DAB,* 15:341–42; *Report . . . of the Investigation of the Charges of Fraud and Official Misconduct Alleged against Alexander Ramsey, Superintendent of Indian Affairs in Minnesota,* 33rd Cong., 1st sess, 1854, S. Ex. Doc. 61.

96. *Swan's Elevator,* a general newspaper from Columbus, Ohio. On Jan. 12, 1853, a state Free Democratic convention at Columbus adopted a set of twenty-one resolutions, which among other things denied the power of the federal government to

Kennedy's[97]—[illeg.] Ball with me— Met there Phelp's new Senr. fr. Vt. vice Upham decd.[98]—Downs & Mallory[99]—Corcoran, Ct. Reichenback, Kennedy Supt.[1] & divers—Mrs Preston, Misses Fillmore / Lindsley from whom flower; Meses. Marshall, Hale, Lindsley.[2] Heard today that James R.I. at first against—aftwds for Collins Line— Check E. K. Collins $5000, to his credit in Providence Bank immediately after vote—also that he said he cd. get two votes for Badger's confn., if two votes cd. be given to him for another purpose.[3]

JOURNAL VI

APRIL 11. Senate adjourned—much show of goodwill.

12. Called on P.M.G. behalf Muse[4]—did not see Muse after—left note for him—sent boxes to Miss Ellicott[5]—started at 5—disgraceful rowdyism in cars b. Pha. & N.Y. Time rolls on—

---

sanction slavery and attacked the Fugitive Slave Act of 1850. Gutgesell, *Ohio Newspapers*, 121; *Daily Ohio State Journal*, Jan. 14, 1853.

97. Probably John Pendleton Kennedy (1795–1870), author, biographer of William Wirt, former Whig congressman from Maryland, and secretary of the navy, 1852–53. *DAB*, 10:333–34.

98. Samuel Phelps, former U.S. senator from Vermont, was reappointed to fill the vacancy caused by the death of William Upham. *Bio. Dir. U.S. Cong.*, 1642.

99. Senators Solomon Weathersbee Downs (1801–54), Democrat of Louisiana, and Stephen Russell Mallory (1813–73), a Florida Democrat who became secretary of the Confederate navy. Ibid., 928, 1416; *DAB*, 12:224–26.

1. Joseph Camp Griffith Kennedy (1813–87), superintendent of the seventh and eighth censuses. *DAB*, 10:335.

2. Margaret Howard Wickliffe Preston, the wife of William Preston (1816–87), a Whig congressman from Kentucky; Mary Abigail Fillmore (1832–54), the president's daughter; possibly the wife of Edward Colston Marshall (1821–93), Democratic congressman from California; and Lucy Lambert Hale. Mrs. Lindsley may have been the wife of William Dell Lindsley (1812–90), Democratic congressman from Ohio; or Emeline Colby Webster Lindsly (1808–92), Dr. Harvey Lindsly's wife. *Meses.* is short for "Mesdames." *Bio. Dir. U.S. Cong.*, 1375, 1425; *DAB*, 15:205–6; John J. Farrell, ed., *Zachary Taylor, 1784–1850/Millard Fillmore, 1800–1874: Chronology Documents Bibliographical Aids* (Dobbs Ferry, N.Y., 1971), 51, 65; *Nat. Cyc.*, 9:433.

3. Democrat Charles Tillinghast James (1805–62) represented Rhode Island in the U.S. Senate, 1851–57. Edward Knight Collins (1802–78) was primary owner of the government-subsidized United States Mail Steamship Company, or "Collins Line," an early rival to Britain's Cunard Line. Millard Fillmore had nominated George Edmund Badger for a place on the U.S. Supreme Court, but the Senate did not confirm the appointment. *DAB*, 1:485–86, 4:305–6, 9:572–73.

4. Chase was visiting James Campbell (1812–93), U.S. postmaster general, 1853–57, in behalf of R. W. P. Muse, editor of the Zanesville, Ohio, *Aurora*, with reference to a federal appointment. Muse to Chase, Apr. 27, July 12, 1853 (Chase Papers, L.C.); *DAB*, 3:454–55; *History of Muskingum County, Ohio* . . . (Columbus, 1882), 207.

5. Elizabeth Ellicott, a friend from Avondale, Pa., who in 1855 married James Shepherd Pike. *DAB*, 14:596; Chase to Kate Chase, Aug. 4, 1853, Elizabeth Ellicott Pike to Chase, June 29, [1855] (Chase Papers, Hist. Soc. of Pa.).

13. Breakfast at Austen's[6]—saw Kate—called on Miss Haines. dined with Barney at N York Hotel[7]—saw Breese & wife—

14. Called at Judge Jays but not in[8]—left N.Y at 5 by H. River Road[9]—Brayton on cars

15. Syracuse—Wheaton very kind & attentive—home with Raymond—tea at C. B. Sedgwicks—Rev. Mr. May & Dr Clay & wives there[10]

17. Hear Mr. Pierpont at Unitarian Church morng. Evg. to Epis. Ch. with Amelia Smith & Lotty Frink[11]—Ashley preacher

18. To Lockport— Met bro. Ed. at depot—home with him—tea at Dr. Skinners—

19. Recd. letters Spaulding, Judge McLean, Vaughan—dined Skinners—slept, Edwards—John Roberts, true fellow & clear headed, called.

20 to Cleveland by Lake Shore R.R.[12]—saw Belle & Jenny at Buffalo[13]

6. David Austen, Jr., evidently the husband of Delia Picket, was thus connected to the Garniss family. Originally from a Staten Island family of dry goods auctioneers, Austen became involved in the petroleum and kerosene business. Austen to Chase, Apr. 19, June 4, 1861, Jan. 28, 1862, Jan. 11, 1864, John P. Garniss to Chase, May 27, 1854, Aug. 12, 1855 (Chase Papers, Hist. Soc. of Pa.); Chase to Austen, Mar. 16, 1867 (Chase Papers, L.C.); *New York Dir. (1853–54)*, 48; *New York Times*, July 17, 1917; *Nat. Cyc.*, 13:92.

7. Hiram Barney (1811–95), attorney, antislavery leader, and collector of customs for the port of New York during the Civil War. The New York Hotel stood on Broadway. Johnson, *Twentieth Century Biographical Dictionary*, v. 1; *New York Dir. (1853–54)*, 81.

8. William Jay (1789–1858), antislavery leader and former judge of Westchester County, N.Y.; he was a son of John Jay, first chief justice of the U.S. Supreme Court. *DAB*, 10:11–12.

9. The Hudson River Railroad, chartered in 1846. Henry V. Poor, *History of the Railroads and Canals of the United States of America* . . . (New York, 1860), 259.

10. Horace Wheaton (1803–82), former Democratic congressman and mayor of Syracuse, 1851–53; Robert Raikes Raymond; Charles Baldwin Sedgwick (1815–83), Syracuse attorney and Republican congressman, 1859–63; and Samuel Joseph May (1797–1871) Unitarian minister and antislavery leader. *Bio. Dir. U.S. Cong.*, 1787, 2032–33; *DAB*, 12:447, 448.

11. Syracuse resident Amelia Wallace Smith, the sister of Charlotte ("Lottie") Frink and a cousin of Chase's first wife, Catharine Jane Garniss Chase. Amelia Wallace Smith to Chase, Sept. 25, 1846, Feb. 15, 1864 (Chase Papers, L.C.).

12. Along the southern shore of Lake Erie. Henry V. Poor, *Manual of the Railroads of the United States, for 1872–73* . . . (New York, 1872), 485.

13. Isabel Skinner Walbridge and Janette Skinner Jewett. Jenny, who like Belle was a daughter of Josiah K. Skinner and Chase's sister Janette Logan Chase Skinner,

21. R. F. Paine & Bradburn called—called at T. D. office[14]—saw Vaughan & Brown—met J. A. Briggs, Wilson, Wade[15] & others.

MAY— In course of last of Apl. & first of May sent Globe containing Debate with Weller to a considerable number of Ohio papers[16]— It was published by the I.D.[17] papers generally and by a few Old Line papers in part or noticed.

9 Spoke at Xenia in evg with Gid. & Lewis[18]—good meeting—Gid & Lewis praised my speech.

10. Spoke at W'n with same—pleasant visit at Hibbens—I promd. to use influence for Morse[19]—

23. To Indianapolis—saw Dunham, Mace & others[20]—spoke to large audience very fully—Pierce with me[21]—Gov. Wright very polite[22]—invited me to dine—could not.

---

had recently married Jack Jewett, apparently of Lockport, N.Y. Janette Skinner Jewett to Chase, May 18, 1859, and "Family Memoranda" (Chase Papers, L.C.); Janette Chase Skinner to Chase, June 4, 1852 (Chase Papers, Hist. Soc. of Pa.).

14. Robert F. Paine (1810–88), an antislavery attorney from Cleveland, had previously held a seat in the Ohio House. In 1861 he served as U.S. district attorney for the northern district of Ohio, and between 1869 and 1874 as judge of the state's fourth district Court of Common Pleas. George Bradburn (1806–80) was a former editor and owner of the Cleveland antislavery newspaper, *True Democrat*. Bradburn, *Memorial of George Bradburn*, 1, 237; Bradburn, *A Statement;* Coates et al., *History of Cuyahoga County*, 1:443, 477–78; Gilkey, *Ohio Hundred Year Book*, 293, 557; Reed, *Bench and Bar of Ohio*, 2:212–15.

15. Probably Hiram V. Willson and Edward Wade.

16. The debate with John B. Weller on Apr. 9 started over a proposal to provide financial support for the publication of Senate proceedings in the *National Intelligencer*, but degenerated into a heated exchange over the legitimacy of the Independent Democrats, the mental soundness of antislavery activists, and the ethical propriety of Chase's election to the Senate. *Cong. Globe*, 32nd Cong., 3rd sess, 1853, 323–30.

17. Independent Democrat.

18. Joshua Giddings and Samuel Lewis. Chase to E. S. Hamlin, May 7, 1853 (Chase Papers, L.C.).

19. Isaiah Morse, a resident of Wilmington, Ohio. Notebook, 1857 election, ibid.

20. Democrats Cyrus Livingston Dunham (1817–77) and Daniel Mace (1811–67), congressmen from Indiana. *Bio. Dir. U.S. Cong.*, 936–937, 1405–6.

21. Harvard-trained attorney Edward Lillie Pierce (1829–97) of Massachusetts, a protégé of Charles Sumner. Pierce was active as a Democratic, Free-Soil, and Republican politician. In 1862, Chase appointed him a U.S. Treasury agent supervising freedmen's affairs at Port Royal, S.C. Pierce served as collector of internal revenue at Boston, 1864–66, and held a variety of civil offices in Massachusetts. *DAB*, 14:575–76; *Daily Indiana State Sentinal*, May 26, 1853.

22. Democrat Joseph Albert Wright (1810–67), U.S. congressman, 1843–45, governor of Indiana, 1849–57, U.S. senator, 1862–63. *DAB*, 20:559–60; *Bio. Dir. U.S. Cong.*, 2091.

June 1853 {239}

24— Left by way of Madison—Judge Stevens along / Met Bright just from Washington—

JUNE 3— At Martinsville—Father Betts first rate man—

JUNE 4. Wilmington—good meeting—good feeling—tea with Judge Hinkson—Chaffin very sick[23]
Mem[24] visit to St Louis—Fred. Holmes, formerly in Cin. very polite[25]—also John How, Mayor Rev. W. G. Eliot, H. S. Geyer, F. P. Blair,[26] Wm L McKee C. H. Haven—Alexr. Kayser[27]

18— Detroit met Hamlin—several called—Fox—Baker[28] / called on Gen. Cass—left P.M. for Toledo

19. SUNDAY Toledo—

20. Toledo—Hamlin spoke P.M. I even'g—small attendance very hot—staid with b. in law Walbridge

21. TU. Perrysburgh—Judge Beach attentive & kind[29]—Parmalee went up with us—small meeting—notice poor—Dr. White with us.[30] Evg. at Maumee City—good audience

---

23. Benjamin Hinkson (d. 1877), former secretary of state of Ohio and common pleas judge; and possibly J. W. Chaffin, a Free-Soil activist from Champaign County. Brown, *History of Clinton County*, 135; *Weekly Ohio State Journal*, Sept. 9, 1851.
24. Memorandum.
25. Attorney Frederick B. Homes, secretary of the Missouri State Mutual Insurance Company. *Cinc. Dir.* (1846), 207; *St. Louis Dir.* (1854–55), 89.
26. John How (1813–85), local merchant, Democratic mayor of St. Louis, 1853–55, 1856–57; William Greenleaf Eliot (1811–87), Congregational clergyman and founder of Washington University in St. Louis; Henry Sheffie Geyer (1790–1859), U.S. senator (Whig) from Missouri; Francis Preston Blair, Jr. (1821–75), attorney, soldier, and Free-Soil and Republican politician. Holli and Jones, *Biographical Dictionary of American Mayors*, 171; *DAB*, 2:332–34, 6:82–83, 7:231.
27. Alexander Kayser (b. 1815), a prominent St. Louis attorney and Democrat. William McKee later edited the *Missouri Democrat*. Richard Edwards and M. Hopewell, *Edwards's Great West and Her Commercial Metropolis* . . . (St. Louis, 1860), 564; Roy P. Basler, ed., *The Collected Works of Abraham Lincoln* (New Brunswick, N.J., 1953–55), 6:325.
28. Jabez Fox, the pastor of Detroit's New Jerusalem Church, editor of *The Medium*, a Swedenborgian magazine, and future editor of the *Free Democrat;* and S. A. Baker, former editor of *Western Evangelist*. Silas Farmer, *History of Detroit and Wayne County* . . . , 3rd ed. (Detroit, 1890), 625, 675–76, 683.
29. Gilbert Beach, a common pleas judge from Wood County. *Commemorative Historical and Biographical Record of Wood County, Ohio* . . . (Chicago, 1897), 73.
30. Oscar White, M.D. (1809–83), a longtime resident of Lucas County. John M. Killits, ed., *Toledo and Lucas County, Ohio, 1623–1923*, 3 vols. (Chicago and Toledo, 1923), 1:650.

22. W. Dr. White took us to Sylvania—another poor meeting—

22. Judge Pease with us to Delta—whence H & I to Ottokee— S. M. Huyek, Saml. Durgin & others called[31]—pretty good meeting but small place—returned to Delta good meeting—

23. Dr. & Mrs Paul met us with carriage at Delta & with them to West Unity—Hunter recd. us very kindly—at Dr. Thorns for tea—queer man & queer advt.—good meeting & good feeling—Morrison against us.[32]

24. Dr. Thorn with us to Bryan—Blakeslee met us / good fellow—spoke in C.H[33]—fair audience—Artesia wells.[34]

25— Judge Ensign who met us at Bryan & took us to his house at Williams Centre, accomd. us to Farmer Centre where good audience[35]—returned to Williams evening

26 SUNDAY— To church P.M. at Wms Centre—good man but dull preacher

27— Williams Centre spoke evg. good audience

28— Hicksville with Dr. Ensign—good audience—Dr. Rakestraw—Edgerton lives here[36]—

---

31. Sanders M. Huyek, a local Free-Soil Democrat, and Samuel Durgin, a state representative from Lucas County, 1854–56. Gilkey, *Ohio Hundred Year Book*, 217, 258; Huyek to Chase, Aug. 28, 1853 (Chase Papers, L.C.).
32. William Hunter, editor of the Williams County *Democrat*; possibly J. Thorn, previously a Greene County physician and a longtime acquaintance of Chase's family; and Thomas S. C. Morrison, state representative from Paulding County, 1852–54. Gilkey, *Ohio Hundred Year Book*, 213; Paul to Chase, Jan. 7, 1853 (Chase Papers, Hist. Soc. of Pa.); Thorn to Chase, Jan. 8, 1843 (Chase Papers, L.C.).
33. Courthouse. Schuyler E. Blakeslee (b. ca. 1809) of Williams County was an attorney, Free-Soil activist, and Ohio state representative, 1856–58, 1870–74. Ohio General Assembly, House of Representatives, *Journal*, 52nd Assem., 2nd sess., 1857, appen., 174; Gilkey, *Ohio Hundred Year Book*, 224, 244; John Paul to Chase, Feb. 19, 1849, Jan. 7, 1853 (Chase Papers, Hist. Soc. of Pa.); William Henry Shinn, *The County of Williams: A History of Williams County, Ohio* . . . (Madison, Wis., 1905), 176.
34. The area around Bryan, Ohio, was famous for its artesian wells. Shinn, *Williams County*, 138–39.
35. William O. Ensign of Defiance County served as a court of common pleas judge, 1845–50. Gilkey, *Ohio Hundred Year Book*, 536; *History of Defiance County, Ohio* . . . (Chicago, 1883), 91.
36. Local dentist, physician, and antislavery advocate B. M. Rakestraw (b. 1818) and Democrat Alfred Peck Edgerton (1813–97), a former state senator who served in Congress, 1851–55. *History of Defiance County*, 305–6; *DAB*, 6:19–20.

August 1853 { 241 }

29— Defiance with young Paul[37] whom sent by Father for us—staid at Dr. Pauls—good meeting—Greene fearful—Judge Taylor cordial & son—Leland, Gibson & others to dine[38]—consulted abt. land sales—good audience—Steedman in town—Ashley came down from Toledo[39]—staid all night at Dr. P——'s.

JUNE 30— Left Defiance at night in rain storm—

JOURNAL IV

AUG. 13.[40] At Kygersville, Gallia Co—Lewis did not speak—I did—contrast of Ohio & Baltimore platforms— Indt. Demy. nothing but Ohio Demy. made national—Balte. platform pledges party to despotism— Quoted Lowell "We begin to think its nater" &c[41]

AUG. 15— Lewis stopped at Chesterfd.—I to Malta with S. C. Beckwith[42]— Spoke to good audience at McConnelsville—as democrat but not as partizan—prin. of demy. to be found in declar. of

37. John Paul, Jr., the only known son of Dr. John Paul. Chase to Paul, July 11, 1864 (Chase Papers, Hist. Soc. of Pa.).
38. Jacob J. Greene (b. 1821) edited the Defiance *Democrat*. John Taylor (b. 1796), a former common pleas judge, held a seat in the Ohio Senate, 1852–55. He had four sons: William (1820–64); James (b. 1821); David (1825–78), who became one of Chase's political allies and during the Civil War served as a military paymaster with the rank of major; and Benjamin (b. 1831). Erastus H. Leland represented Defiance and Paulding Counties in the Ohio House, 1854–56. *Biographical Cyclopædia*, 1:112–13; Gilkey, *Ohio Hundred Year Book*, 218, 310, 526; *History of Defiance County*, 233, 344–45; Heitman, *Historical Register*, 1:946; D. Taylor to Chase, Oct. 19, 1859, Dec. 24, 1860 (Chase Papers, Hist. Soc. of Pa.); same to same, May 22, 1860 (Chase Papers, L.C.).
39. Toledo residents James Blair Steedman (1817–83), a Douglas Democrat, former Ohio state legislator, Union general during the Civil War, and collector of internal revenue at New Orleans, 1866–69; and James Mitchell Ashley (1824–96), Free-Soil attorney, merchant, and Republican member of Congress, 1859–69. *Bio. Dir. U.S. Cong.*, 550; *DAB*, 1:389–90, 17:554–55.
40. These entries for August 1853 are from some miscellaneous notes of the 1850s in Journal IV. In the original, the entry for Aug. 13 comes between those for Aug. 15 and 16.
41. Them thet rule us, them slave-traders,
   Haint they cut a thunderin' swarth,
   (Helped by Yankee renegaders,)
   Thru the vartu o' the North!
We begin to think it's nater
   To take sarse an' not be riled;—
Who'd expect to see a tater
All on eend at bein' biled?

Thomas Wortham, ed., *James Russell Lowell's* The Biglow Papers *[First Series]: A Critical Edition* (DeKalb, Ill., 1977), 51.
42. Beckwith (b. ca. 1803) was a resident of McConnelsville, Ohio, and apparently one of Chase's supporters. Beckwith to Chase, Apr. 23, 1861 (Chase Papers, L.C.).

Independ.— Society divided into progressives & conservatives—debates in Consl. Convn. revealed this division &c

AUG 16 At Rutland— Great meeting—people assembled from all quarters— Spoke twice— Am before my constituents—bound to represent them or resign—have endd. by speech & vote to do so faithfully— American Govt. founded on great ideas—

AUG 17— At Albany—large meeting—procession—banners— Lewis spoke first—I followed— Lewis gave thanks for greeting— stated doctrine of State rights—exhibited tendency to consolidation— Quoted Pickens, Calhoun & Harper for doctrines of oppression[43]—

I[44]— Two great principles of d[ec]larn. of Ind.—Equal Rights & Governt to maintain them
 Our country responsible for fidelity to these—all nations observing her[45]
 Now subjugated by Slave Power & incapable of illustrating principles
 In Legislation 90 Reps unit for Slavery—& 30 Senators
 In Political Party Conventions 120 delegates unit for Slavery
 In Electoral Colleges 120 votes unit for Slavery
 Hence control of nominations—& so President—& through Reps & Senators aided by Perst.[46] influence rule of legislation & through Prest. appoint judges
 Government patronage all over the land in hands of Slave Power
 Ohio can redeem the nation— Once free herself her example will influence other states

JOURNAL I

Boarded during part of spring & summer & part of fall (till went to Washn) with Mrs Hamil[ton] on Broadway[47]

---

43. Samuel Lewis referred to South Carolina states' rights activists Francis Wilkinson Pickens (1805–69), John C. Calhoun, and William Harper (1790–1847). *DAB*, 8:286–87, 14:559–61.

44. This is the personal pronoun *I*, to indicate that what follows is the outline of Chase's own speech.

45. In the original, Chase followed each heading of the speech with a short double stroke aligned with the left edge of the text.

46. Apparently an error, in haste, for "Prest." (President).

47. This entry, and that for "Feb or Mar." 1854 which follows, is from memoranda at the end of Journal I. Eliza Hamilton operated a boarding house in Cincinnati. *Cinc. Dir. (1853)*, 161.

1854

FEB OR MAR. Immediately after passage of Nebraska bill I prepared a call for a Convention in Ohio to organize a "Demy. of the People" in oppn. to the Servile Demy. Wade joined me in a letter inviting signatures & the letter & call were sent to many in Ohio; but a movement for a similar Convention less definite in object, originated in Columbus & supported by Judge Swan & Mr. Andrews superceded that which we proposed.[48]

JOURNAL IV

AUG. 7, Wrote Shelman agreeing to take $100 for $200 advanced for True Democrat if recd. in check on N.Y. or Cin by 1st proxo

G. Brewster George Brewster called to ask subscription in aid of proposed publication in Kansas[49]—agreed to contribute $10 when publication actually established.

S. W. Fisher Matagorda Sent to Commr. Gen Land Office[50] S. W. Fisher's letter with mem. of land located by S. R. Fisher in Indiana. Mr. Fisher requests me to return letter of A. Pachet & Co. wrote him

Illinois & Eastman— Wrote Z. Eastman Chicago[51] agreeing to speak in that state from 12 to 19 Oct will not receive compensation

---

48. Chase, B. F. Wade, and others in Ohio's congressional delegation called for meetings to oppose the Kansas-Nebraska bill. The state's important "fusion" gatherings, however, including a convention in Columbus in July 1854, were controlled by a group that included Independent Democrat Joseph Rockwell Swan and Democrat John W. Andrews, a Columbus attorney. Roseboom, *Civil War Era*, 279–86; William E. Gienapp, *The Origins of the Republican Party, 1852–1856* (New York, 1987), 114–18; Chase to E. L. Pierce, Jan. 21, 1854 (Houghton Lib., Harvard Univ.); Chase to William Schouler, May 28, 1854 (Schouler Papers, Mass. Hist. Soc.); Chase's draft resolutions for July convention (Chase Papers, Hist. Soc. of Pa.); *Col. Dir. (1856–57)*, 13.

49. Brewster (1800–1865), an educator, published the *Western Literary Magazine* at Detroit, Columbus, and Lawrence, Kans. Coyle, *Ohio Authors*, 75.

50. John Wilson (c. 1808–76), commissioner of the General Land Office, 1852–6; head of the land department of the Illinois Central R.R.; appointed third auditor of the U.S. Treasury in 1864. Paul Wallace Gates, *The Illinois Central Railroad and Its Colonization Work* (Cambridge, Mass., 1834; reprint, New York, 1968), 177, 236; Lanman, *Biographical Annals*, 471.

51. Zebina Eastman (1815–83), Chicago antislavery journalist. *New York Times*, June 15, 1883.

1855

MAR. 24, SATY. At Hillsborough this morng.—talk with Nettie— her tree prettily drawn[52]—Dr. Sams came in—wanted Pat. Rep.[53]— down to Cin. in P.M. train—saw Gordon at Lovelands who intrd several[54]—Nelson, son of J. M. in cars from Hillsboro— Dickson wanted to see me as soon as I reached office[55]—told me of Slave Case & Pendery[56]— P—— wanted to borrow $10 of D.—said he wd. be able to return it on Monday you know where Ill get it—lent him money but told him did not want it again from that source[57] / Tried to convince him he should decide for liberty & distinguish himself— he seemed impressed with the idea of distinguishing himself—told Dickson my opinion of Pendery unfavorable enough in wh. he concurred. Farther conversation about Slavery. Dickson related incident about Mrs Preston[58]—shortly before she started for Washington first time she compelled a mulatto woman whom she wished to take with her to give up her own child, a babe of three weeks old, who was placed in the charge of an old colored man & died in conse-

---

52. Janet Chase was staying with the family of Catharine Wever Collins, a cousin of Sarah Bella Chase who gave Nettie drawing lessons during her visit. Chase to Kate Chase, Mar. 23, 1855 (Chase Papers, Hist. Soc. of Pa.); unpublished guide to Ludlow-Dunlop-Chambers Collec., Univ. of Wyoming.

53. C. C. Sams (d. 1865) graduated from the Medical University of Maryland and practiced primarily at Hillsboro, Ohio. He evidently wished to obtain the *Report of the Commissioner of Patents for the Year 1854*, 33rd Cong., 2nd sess., 1855, S. Ex. Doc. 42. J. W. Klise, *The County of Highland: A History of Highland County, Ohio* ... (Madison, Wis., 1902), 205–6; *History of Ross and Highland Counties*, 163.

54. Possibly Cleveland merchant William J. Gordon (1818–92). Van Tassel and Grabowski, *Encyclopedia of Cleveland*, 459–60.

55. Cincinnati lawyer William Martin Dickson (1827–89) became a Republican political writer. In 1859, by Chase's appointment, he served briefly as a common pleas judge in Hamilton County. Reed, *Bench and Bar of Ohio*, 1:144–46.

56. At Columbus in early Mar. 1855, antislavery activists had sixteen-year-old slave Rosetta Armstead, in transit from Kentucky to Virginia with an agent of her owner, freed on a writ of habeas corpus. On Mar. 23, Rosetta was captured and taken to Cincinnati by a deputy marshal acting under authority of John L. Pendery, a Cincinnati attorney empowered, as a U.S. commissioner under the provisions of the Fugitive Slave Act of 1850, to hear cases involving alleged fugitives. Chase, Timothy Walker, and Rutherford B. Hayes obtained Rosetta's release a second time by means of a writ of habeas corpus presented in a state court. *Cinc. Dir. (1855)*, 171; *Daily Ohio State Journal*, Mar. 12, 16, 24, 27–29, 1855; Chase to John T. Trowbridge, Mar. 19, 1864 (Chase Papers, Hist. Soc. of Pa.).

57. Pendery, whom Chase later described as "notoriously venal," stood to collect a $10 fee if he ruled to return Rosetta to her owner, but only $5 if he set her free—hence Dickson's refusal of Pendery's intended repayment "from that source," and his urging of Pendery to "decide for liberty." Later, after Chase's successful implementation of the writ of habeas corpus in her case, Rosetta was brought before Pendery again and he released her. Chase to John T. Trowbridge, Mar. 19, 1864 (Chase Papers, Hist. Soc. of Pa.); *Statutes at Large*, 9:464.

58. Margaret Wickliffe Preston.

quence—this because she wanted the woman as a servant & did not wish her to be encumbered by her child. I could hardly believe this; but Dickson had it from his father in law Dr. Parker who was personally cognizant of the facts[59]—so he said. D—— also said when he lived in Kentucky near Lexington he made his home in the family of Dr. Sharp—a member of the Church / Mrs Sharp a devoted Presbyterian.[60] D. was teacher— A female slave had several children. One day one was taken suddenly ill & died—afterwards another & another till all were dead, also a child of the womans dead sister. Afterwards the House was burnt. The woman had killed all the children by poison & had finally set fire to the House— She killed the children to save them from the dreadful life she led herself & burnt the House from revenge. Her mistress would frequently punish her—often by burning her hands or face with a red hot iron, & if she would resist Dr. Sharp wd. whip her till she would submit or at least pretend to submit— About a year after the house was burnt she tied her hands & feet & a stone to her neck & threw herself into a small stream near the place & was drowned. The rest of the family of negroes was sold down the river. Dr. & Mrs Sharp passed for kind master & mistress— Mrs S—— was a delicate woman, very soft in her manners like Mrs St Clare somewhat[61]—if one should go into neighborhood would be told of horrid family of negroes, but no word of mistress's cruelty. Dickson also talked of election—thought of withdrawing from Kn—didn't like secrecy—stated Kn plan for nominating Bhoff for Govr. to catch Reserve & fill out ticket with proslave, Kns— I told him if he could prevent nomination of Kn's he would do a good work— Said he thought he wd. be delegate to Cleveland Conv. in June.[62] Fishback Member of State Kn Comee. Letter from Dr. Paul—says V. & Medill right

59. In 1852, Dickson had married Anna Maria Parker, a daughter of Dr. John Todd Parker of Lexington, Ky. Dr. Parker was an uncle of Mary Todd Lincoln. Reed, *Bench and Bar of Ohio*, 1:144; Basler, *Collected Works*, 3:491.

60. Ebenezer Sharp (or Sharpe), professor of languages and medicine at Transylvania University, married Eliza Lake of Lexington in 1805. He was remembered as "a strong Presbyterian." Robert Peter and Johanna Peter, *Transylvania University: Its Origin, Rise, Decline, and Fall*, Filson Club Publications, No. 11 (Louisville, 1896), 88, 110–11; Charles R. Staples, *The History of Pioneer Lexington (Kentucky), 1779–1806*, (Lexington, 1939), 218, 255, 263.

61. Marie St. Clare, a character in Harriet Beecher Stowe's *Uncle Tom's Cabin*.

62. Chase succeeded in blocking the separate nomination of Jacob Brinkerhoff as the Know-Nothing candidate for governor at the party's council meeting at Cleveland in June by suggesting, near the end of May, that he would endorse Brinkerhoff at the Free-Soil and Know-Nothing coalition convention in July if the Know-Nothings made no prior nomination. This stratagem hindered the Know-Nothings from operating as a bloc at the Republican convention and enabled Chase to win the gubernatorial nomination through a compromise of Free-Soil and Know-Nothing interests. Maizlish, *Triumph of Sectionalism*, 207–17.

& Reserve right[63]—V. & M. ready to come out if Toledo folks advise. Donaldson called abt. Slave case[64]—tea at Burnet House

SUNDAY MAR. 25. At breakfast Judge Key talked of Dennison's affidavit before Penderey that slave had escaped from Kentucky when in fact brought by authorized agent from Ky[65]—thought oath very rash—did not see how he could escape charge of perjury—certainly only by throwing on his lawyers responsibility of advising him that transaction at Columbus constituted Escape from Ky into Ohio— After breakfast to my room read Benton's speech against new Regiments—horrible injustice towards the Indians[66] / went to Church Mr. Boynton's[67]—he preached excellent Sermon necessity of death in the Christian Economy—back to my room—regulated table & wrote several letters and article for Columbian about the army & Indians, reprobating the unwise & criminal course taken towards the latter—dinner at Burnet House before this last sentence—it was at dinner I think the talk with Judge Key occurred— Ralston came to my room—gave him Sumner's speech[68]—tea at Burnet House— Church evg. Mr. Butler preached[69]—good—Highway of Redemption—sat in LHommedieu's pew—wrote this page & last.[70]

63. Joseph Medill (1823–99), Free-Soil and Republican editor best known for his conduct of the *Chicago Tribune*, published, with John Vaughan, the *Cleveland Leader*, 1853–55. *DAB*, 12:491–92; *Nat. Cyc.*, 1:131–32.

64. Possibly Andrew Donaldson, a commission merchant, or Alexander Donaldson, a machinist. *Cinc. Dir. (1855)*, 63.

65. The Rev. Henry M. Dennison (or Denison), rector of St. Paul's Protestant Episcopal Church in Louisville, 1853–57, and later rector at St. Peter's in Charleston, S.C., swore an affidavit that Rosetta had escaped from him in Kentucky. This statement conflicted with other testimony that Rosetta came to Ohio with Dennison's agent. Johnston, *Memorial History*, 2:146; *Daily Ohio State Journal*, Mar. 28, 1855.

66. Thomas Hart Benton, "On the Proposition to raise four new Regiments for the Regular Army," *Cong. Globe*, 33rd Cong., 2nd sess., appen., 334–41. Benton believed that troops raised locally put down Indian resistance on the frontier more effectively than regular army soldiers led by political appointees.

67. Antislavery advocate and author Charles Brandon Boynton, D.D. (1806–83), pastor of Cincinnati's Second Orthodox Congregational Church, 1846–56, and chaplain of the U.S. House of Representatives, 1865–69. *DAB*, 2:536–37; *Appletons'*, 1:342–43; *Cinc. Dir. (1855)*, 278.

68. Chase apparently gave James Ralston Skinner a copy of Sumner's speech of Feb. 23, 1855, on a bill relating to the Fugitive Slave Act. Charles Sumner, *The Demands of Freedom. Speech of Hon. Charles Sumner . . .* (Washington, 1855); Edward L. Pierce, *Memoir and Letters of Charles Sumner, 1845–1860*, 2nd ed. (Boston, 1894), 3:410–12.

69. Clement Moore Butler.

70. Following this entry in the original journal are miscellaneous memoranda and copies of several letters. Material in this section of the journal bears dates from Aug. 1853 to Mar. 1860. Those entries resembling journal entries in form have been included here at their proper chronological places. The other memoranda and the letters have not been transcribed.

1857

JOURNAL VII

THURSDAY, JANUARY 1. Happy New Year to every body— After breakfast presents—Nettie and Katie well pleased— Mrs Snowden gave each Bible & Prayer Book— Mr. S. Gloves to me— Maria S.—beautiful Ink stand & tray[71]— Finished Message before dinner[72]—after dinner with Coggeshall[73] called Parsons', Galloway's, Kelsey's, Kelley's, Dr. Andrew's, Nevin's, Wrights, Bakers, Schoulers, Swayne's Mattoon's[74]—pleasant time— Evg. party at Dr. Andrews.

FRIDAY, JANUARY 2. Did little today but correct proof of Message wrote long letter to S W[75] in answer to one receivd Wedy. but did not like it on a/c of some allusions & did not send it.

---

71. Chase probably boarded at the house of P. T. Snowden, a Columbus dealer in silks and embroideries who moved to Baltimore by 1862. Maria J. Southgate was the daughter of James Southgate of Covington, Ky., and Jane Smith (d. 1840), a sister of Chase's second wife. Maria married James Morrison Hawes on Feb. 3, 1857. Entries for Jan. 4 and Feb. 3, 1857, below; "Family Memoranda" (Chase Papers, L.C.); *Col. Dir. (1855)*, 107; ibid., (1856–57), 186; *Daily Cincinnati Gazette*, Feb. 4, 1857; Snowden to Chase, Apr. 16, 1862 (Chase Papers, L.C.).

72. Chase's annual gubernatorial message for 1857, which elaborated on economic conditions in Ohio with emphasis on agriculture and railroads, had kept him "very busy." *Message of the Governor of Ohio, to the Fifty-Second General Assembly, at the Adjourned Session, Commencing January 5*, 1857 (Columbus, 1857); Chase to Edward L. Pierce, Jan. 1, [1857] (Houghton Lib., Harvard Univ.).

73. William Turner Coggeshall (1824–67), journalist, author, and Ohio state librarian, 1856–62. *DAB*, 4:272–73.

74. George M. Parsons (b. ca. 1818), lawyer, civic leader, state representative, 1856–57; Samuel G. Galloway (1811–72), educator, lawyer, Republican congressman, 1855–57; William Kelsey, proprietor of the American Hotel, 1836–70; Alfred Kelley; probably John Andrews (1805–c. 1866), physician, farmer, businessman, president of the State Bank of Ohio Board of Control; Richard Nevins, state printer; Francis Mastin Wright (1810–69) of Champaign County, state auditor, 1856–60; James Heaton Baker (1829–1913), Ohio's secretary of state, whose later political and military career in Minnesota was more noteworthy; William Schouler (1814–72), editor of the Republican *Ohio State Journal*, 1856–58, better known as a Massachusetts editor; Noah Haynes Swayne; and Calvin S. Mattoon, first clerk in the secretary of state's office, or perhaps his brother Willis (d. 1857), an early Liberty party supporter, then Republican. *DAB*, 1:521–22, 7:117–18, 16:460–61, 18:239–40; Ohio General Assembly, House of Representatives, *Journal*, 52nd Assem., 2nd sess., 1857, appen., 175; *Col. Dir. (1856–57)*, 17, 87, 125, 155, 191, 205; Alfred Emory Lee, *History of the City of Columbus, Capital of Ohio* (New York, 1892), 1:288, 888–89, 2:421; Joseph P. Smith, *History of the Republican Party in Ohio*, 2 vols. (Chicago, 1898), 1:45; *History of Franklin and Pickaway Counties*, 61, 162–63, 469, 554, 569, 571; Gilkey, *Ohio Hundred Year Book*, 349; *Columbus Gazette*, Apr. 17, 1857.

75. Susan Walker.

SATURDAY, JANUARY 3. Spent some time correcting proof Message— Sent Sleigh for Mr. Rice & gave instructions about proof[76]— went to office got State Journal &c 1839 contg. proceedings laying corner stone 1839[77]— Sleigh came for me & went home— Burick's friends abt. pardon[78]— After dinner sleepy & rested on sociable[79]— rheumatic when got up—went to office & rooms in New S. House not ready yet[80]— Becket, Elliott, Schouler, Howells, & others at office[81]— Retg. home read Virgil 6th Book, the Prophecy.[82] wrote 2d. letter to S W & destroyed first—marked it "mailed 4 Jany"

SUNDAY, JANUARY 4. Too lame & sore to go to church—read Sept. Ex. 28[83]—Kate & N. went to church—sent letter to P.O. for S. W.—read prophecy of Anchises in Virgil—dinner—Dr. Coulter came in afternoon[84]—prescribed for rheusm.— Called at Galloways / Sam. sick of Typd. fever better[85]— G—— says all fds at Wn[86] think

---

76. Lewis Lippett Rice, secretary to Chase 1856–58, former Ohio antislavery newspaper editor, and later supervisor of public printing in Ohio, had long been one of Chase's political correspondents. *History of Franklin and Pickaway Counties*, 164; Harriet Taylor Upton, *History of the Western Reserve* (Chicago, 1910), 1:650; Jacob H. Studer, *Columbus, Ohio: Its History, Resources, and Progress* (Washington, D.C., 1873), 199–202; Lee, *Columbus*, 1:463; Rice to Chase, Apr. 20, 1846 (Chase Papers, L.C.); *Annual Report of Secretary of State*, 1856, 2:360; *Detailed Statement of Receipts*, 1859, 2:462.

77. *Ohio State Journal*. A celebration on July 4, 1839, marked the laying of the cornerstone for the new Ohio State House. Taylor, *Columbus and Franklin County*, 1:316.

78. In 1854 William Burdick had been sentenced to six years imprisonment as an accomplice to grand larceny. Chase pardoned him on May 26, 1857. Burdick file (Pardon Records, Ohio Hist. Soc.).

79. An S-shaped couch designed for two people to sit facing opposite directions.

80. The building, under construction for eighteen years, opened officially on Jan. 5. Martin, *History of Franklin County*, 312–16.

81. William Beckett (1821–95), businessman and real estate agent; probably James Elliott, a lawyer and canal collector who assisted Chase with his personal business affairs; William Cooper Howells (1807–94), Ohio newspaper editor and assistant clerk of the Ohio House of Representatives, 1856–57. *History and Biographical Cyclopædia of Butler County*, 344; Stephen D. Cone, *Biographical and Historical Sketches: A Narrative of Hamilton and Its Residents from 1792 to 1896* (Hamilton, Ohio, 1896), 396–98; *Cinc. Dir. (1857)*, 99; Chase to Elliott, Nov. 23, Nov. 30, 1858, Elliott to Chase, Nov. 29, 1858 (Chase Papers, L.C.); William Cooper Howells, *Recollections of Life in Ohio From 1813 to 1840*, ed. by Edwin H. Cady (1895; reprint, Gainesville, Fla., 1963), v–xii; *History of Ashtabula County, Ohio* . . . (Philadelphia, 1878), 103–4; *Columbus Gazette*, Jan. 23, 1857.

82. In the sixth book of the *Aeneid*, Aeneas meets the shade of his father, Anchises, who forecasts the rise of Rome.

83. Exodus, chap. 28, of the Septuagint, the Greek version of the Old Testament. English translations were available, but Chase evidently read the Greek original. Janet Chase Hoyt, "A Woman's Memories: Salmon P. Chase's Home Life," *New York Tribune*, Feb. 15, 1891.

84. James H. Coulter, homeopathic physician. *Col. Dir. (1856–57)*, 53.

85. Samuel Buchanan Galloway, eldest son of Samuel G. Galloway, died on Jan. 17, 1857, aged nine years and eleven months. *Daily Ohio State Journal*, Jan. 6, 19, 1857.

86. Friends at Washington.

January 1857

nom. of F.[87] Mistake— Gid.[88] sd. he sd. write Howells / Capt Hawes called on Maria Southgate[89]—saw him—hd Nettie say hymn—told her stories.

MONDAY, JANUARY 5. Went down early—remd. in old office till recd. joint Com. of G.A.[90] anng. met & ready— Sent Message immediately—directed things to be taken over to New Office & printed Reports to be brought there—sent them to Sergt. Arms of Each House not to be deled. till authorized by message—both Houses adjd. till tomorrow. dined—&c. Mr. Kelley called with his remarks for Festival[91]

TUESDAY, JANUARY 6. Remained in room all day preparing remarks for Festival[92]—Mr. Coggeshall came P.M. & made copy for Cin. papers—went in evg with Nettie and Katie—great crowd on steps—hemmed in—finally got out & went to Old office— Mr. Gibson[93] & several ladies came in— By & bye Sen. Hamilton[94] announced so. door open—got in—found Dr. Hoge[95] & Mr. Kelley waiting—got through better than I expected—vast crowd—many friends

WEDNESDAY, JANUARY 7. Went to office early to be ready to send Message to Senate but that body met & adjd. immediately— Mr. &

---

87. John Charles Frémont (1813–90), soldier, explorer, Republican presidential candidate in 1856, and major general, 1861–62. *DAB*, 7:19–23.

88. Joshua Reed Giddings.

89. James Morrison Hawes (1824–89), a West Point graduate, married Maria Southgate on Feb. 3, 1857. John L. Wakelyn, ed., *Biographical Dictionary of the Confederacy* (Westport, Conn., 1977), 221–22; *Daily Cincinnati Gazette*, Feb. 4, 1857; entry for Feb. 3, below.

90. Committee of General Assembly.

91. This festival on the evening of Jan. 6, 1857, celebrated the dedication of the new Ohio State House. State Senator Alfred Kelley made remarks. *Daily Ohio State Journal*, Jan. 6, 7, 1857.

92. Chase's remarks at the capitol dedication sketched the settlement of Ohio and development of state government. Two incomplete drafts exist (Chase Papers, Ohio Hist. Soc. and Chase Papers, Hist. Soc. of Pa.); printed versions are in *Daily Ohio State Journal*, Jan. 7, 1857, and *Daily National Intelligencer*, Jan. 14, 1857.

93. William H. Gibson (1821–94), lawyer, politician, acclaimed speaker, and Civil War officer, had been elected treasurer of Ohio in 1855 on the same ticket with Chase. He served until his forced resignation in June 1857. Reed, *Bench and Bar of Ohio*, 1:202–4; David Dwight Bigger, *Ohio's Silver-Tongued Orator: Life and Speeches of General William H. Gibson* (Dayton, Ohio, 1901).

94. Cornelius Springer Hamilton (1821–67), lawyer and Ohio state senator. *Bio. Dir. U.S. Cong.*, 1120.

95. James Hoge, D.D. (1784–1863) pastor of the First Presbyterian Church in Columbus, abolitionist, and temperance advocate. *Appletons'*, 3:230; *Daily Ohio State Journal*, Feb. 28, 1857.

Mrs Ernst[96] & Mr. & Mrs [Ralstram] & many other friends called—home to dinner b. 1 & 2—no school this afternoon—took a little rest in room—to Office at 3—busy until night writing letters—sending Messages— Correcting Address Festival &c &c—home wrote H. J. Adams[97] J. R. Giddings & others. Judge Green handed letter resn. today[98] / Shaw, Edson & others called[99]—

THURSDAY, JANUARY 8. Office b. 9 & 10—several petitions for pardon—many callers—Nelson Rush, Briggs of Fayette[1]—Paul—Brazee—Follet / Adair of Morgan[2]—Worthington, who says I must be candidate for reelection[3]—dined—directed Messages to many—Wrote sypathizingly to young man enquiring about Alby Man. Lab. Coll[4]—w. Molitor[5] abt. Message & Elliott— Very kind notice of Mess

---

96. Possibly William Ernst (1813–95), a Covington, Ky., banker, philanthropist, and Republican party supporter, and his wife Sarah A. Butler Ernst. George Mortimer Roe, ed., *Cincinnati: The Queen City of the West* (Cincinnati, 1895), 69–70; Greve, *Centennial History*, 1:237–39.

97. Henry Joseph Adams (1816–70), educator and lawyer, moved from Cincinnati to Leavenworth, Kans., in 1855 and became prominent in the Free State movement. *Nat. Cyc.*, 13:586–87; Chase to Adams, May 11, 1857, Adams to Chase, May 30, 1857 (Chase Papers, L.C.).

98. John L. Green of Columbus had been judge of the common pleas court since 1852. Green to Chase, Jan. 7, 1857 (Chase Papers, Ohio Hist. Soc.); Gilkey, *Ohio Hundred Year Book*, 559.

99. Probably John Shaw (b. ca. 1820), farmer and representative from Van Wert County, and Charles P. Edson, Van Wert lawyer and politician. Ohio General Assembly, House of Representatives, *Journal*, 52nd Assem., 2nd sess., 1857, appen., 176; Thaddeus S. Gilliland, ed., *History of Van Wert County, Ohio* . . . (Chicago, 1906), 92, 283; Gilkey, *Ohio Hundred Year Book*, 259.

1. Nelson Rush (b. ca. 1814), lawyer and state senator from Fayette County, and Robert M. Briggs (1831–69), an attorney from Washington, Fayette County. Ohio General Assembly, House of Representatives, *Journal*, 52nd Assem., 2nd sess., 1857, appen., 173; Gilkey, *Ohio Hundred Year Book*, 301; *History of Ross and Highland Counties*, 143; Frank M. Allen, ed, *History of Fayette County, Ohio* . . . (Indianapolis, 1914), 161.

2. Dr. John Paul; John Trafford Brasee (1800–1880), lawyer, state senator from Fairfield County, and political informant for Chase in the 1857 gubernatorial campaign; Oran Follet (1798–1894), journalist, politician, businessman, Republican promoter, editor of the *Ohio State Journal*, 1853–56; and James A. Adair (b. 1814), a lawyer and local politician who edited the McConnelsville *Herald* for more than twenty years. *Biographical Cyclopædia*, , 1:201–2; Gilkey, *Ohio Hundred Year Book*, 245; Brasee to Chase, Aug. 28, 1857 (Chase Papers, L.C.); Coyle, *Ohio Authors*, 217–18; Charles Robertson, *History of Morgan County, Ohio* . . . (Chicago, 1886), 266.

3. Probably Gen. James Taylor Worthington (b. 1802), son of an Ohio governor, who served in 1857 as advisory commissioner for the Ohio State House and as a member of the state board of agriculture. Anna [Shannon] McAllister, *In Winter We Flourish: Life and Letters of Sarah Worthington King Peter, 1800–1877* (New York, 1939), 20, 332; *Col. Dir.* (1856–57), 46, 50.

4. The Albany Manual Labor University in Athens County, which solicited Chase for state assistance on at least one occasion. *National Era*, Jan. 22, 1857; J. Cable to Chase, Feb. 18, 1857 (Chase Papers, Ohio Hist. Soc.).

5. Stephen Molitor (1806–73), German-born publisher of the Cincinnati *Volksblatt*, converted the paper about 1856 from a Democratic to a Republican organ. Greve,

in Cleved. Herald[6]— Collins home with me to tea[7]—read able article by Hazard on Language[8]—

FRIDAY, JANUARY 9. At office soon after 9— Went to Neil House to call on Gen. Worthington & Mrs W—pleasant call—Judge Bostwick called at Office[9]—expressed himself warmly my friend— home to dinner Judge Brayton with me[10]—many callers afternoon—had Messages sent to M—— Congress[11] & others— Dr. Paul called today or yestery. talk abt Hamlin[12]—

SATURDAY, JANUARY 10. Near 10 before reached office—no one there—after read'g letters & attending to appln. for Mansfield as city & talk with Greiner went to Senate[13]—saw Burnet, Beatty Cattell, Kelley, Matthews, & others[14]— Mem. rode to off. this morng.

Centennial History, 1:812; Henry John Groen, "A History of the German-American Newspapers of Cincinnati Before 1860" (Ph.D. diss., Ohio State University, 1944), 53–54, 80–82, 289–91.

6. The *Cleveland Herald* notice of Chase's annual message appeared in the *Daily Ohio State Journal*, Jan. 8, 1857.

7. Probably William Oliver Collins (1809–80), Hillsboro lawyer, businessman, and Ohio senator, 1860–61, who served during the Civil War as colonel of a cavalry regiment in the Far West. He married Catharine Wever, a cousin of Chase's third wife. Klise, *County of Highland*, 196–97; *General Catalogue of Amherst College . . . 1821–1910* (Amherst, Mass., 1910), 35; Catharine W. Collins to Chase, Sept. 21, 1854 (Chase Papers, L.C.); unpublished guide to Ludlow-Dunlop-Chambers Collec., Univ. of Wyoming.

8. Rowland Gibson Hazard, *Essay on Language, and Other Papers, . . . Edited by E. P. Peabody* (Boston, 1857).

9. Probably Samuel W. Bostwick, former representative from Harrison County and judge of the Ohio court of common pleas. Gilkey, *Ohio Hundred Year Book*, 244, 563.

10. Isaac Brayton (b. ca. 1801), merchant and representative from Cuyahoga County, 1856–57, elected to the court of common pleas from Portage County in 1850. Upton, *Western Reserve*, 1:709; Ohio General Assembly, House of Representatives, *Journal*, 52nd Assem., 2nd sess., 1857, appen., 174; Gilkey, *Ohio Hundred Year Book*, 543.

11. Members of Congress.

12. In an investigating committee report released the following week, E. S. Hamlin was censured for his management of contracts while a member of the Ohio Board of Public Works. See Jan. 16, 19, and 24 below. Ohio General Assembly, House of Representatives, *Journal*, 52nd Assem., 2nd sess., 1857, 41.

13. The petition for the village of Mansfield to become a city of the second class was approved within a few weeks. John Greiner (1810–71) edited the *Columbus Gazette*. *Annual Report of the Secretary of State*, Ohio Exec. Docs. for 1857, 1:598; G. F. Carpenter to Chase, Jan. 25, 1857 (Chase Papers, Ohio Hist. Soc.); *Appletons'*, 2:761; *Columbus Gazette*, Jan. 9, 1857.

14. Edmund Burnet (b. 1814), Tuscarawas County businessman; John Beatty (b. ca. 1805), Carroll County manufacturer; J. D. Cattell (b. ca. 1814), Columbiana County farmer; Alfred Kelley, Franklin County; and Stanley Matthews, Hamilton County, all sat in the Ohio Senate, 1856–57. Ohio General Assembly, House of Representatives, *Journal*, 52nd Assem., 2nd sess., 1857, appen., 172–73; *The History of Tuscarawas County, Ohio . . .* (Chicago, 1884), 740–41.

in sleigh with children & Mr. Snowden—poor sleighing—home to dinner walked—saw Col. Schouler before dinner abt. State Journal & Galloway— Visit from Deaf Mutes[15]— Pat Thomson called[16]— Morris of Monroe[17]—Hutchins & Wife[18]—Mrs Sisco could not pardon husband[19]—Wrote Stambaugh, will pardon Dicks[20]—issued warrt. on requisition fr. Illinois / Letter, Message & Gaz. & Jour. with my Cap Speech to S. W.[21]—

SUNDAY, JANUARY 11. Rose as usual—private prayer—breakfast—wild drifting snow—no church today—read Espousals[22]— Storm ceased and sun shone out—carriage & to church with Kate & Nettie—good sermon Mr. Reynolds[23]—dinner—after read Espousals through—calm gentle pure—church evg—home read Bible Adam Clarke's Comy.[24]

MONDAY, JANUARY 12. Awake early—Sd. morng. hymn & repeated Pollio[25]—up dressed & pp.[26]—breakft. & Office—

15. The Ohio State Institution for Deaf Mutes opened in 1829 at Columbus. Gilkey, *Ohio Hundred Year Book,* 710.
16. Patrick Thompson (b. ca. 1817), farmer and representative from Coshocton County. Ohio General Assembly, House of Representatives, *Journal,* 52nd Assem., 2nd sess., 1857, appen., 176.
17. Attorney and editor James Remley Morris (1819–99) received the Democratic nomination for state treasurer in Aug. 1857. Morris, who served as a Democratic congressman, 1843–47 and 1861–65, practiced law at Woodsfield. *Bio. Dir. U.S. Cong.,* 1535–36; *Columbus Gazette,* Aug. 7, 1857.
18. John Hutchins (1812–91), lawyer and antislavery politician, and Rhoda M. Andrews Hutchins (1817–90), daughter of Connecticut pioneers in the Western Reserve. *Bio. Dir. U.S. Cong.,* 1239; *Biographical Cyclopædia,* 2:354, 4:969; Coates et al., *History of Cuyahoga County,* 3:60.
19. Amelia M. Sisco sought pardon for her husband James, sentenced to eight years imprisonment in Nov. 1854. Sisco file (Pardon Records, Ohio Hist. Soc.).
20. New Philadelphia resident D. W. Stambaugh had written an earnest letter in favor of Harrison Dicks, serving a three-year prison term for horse theft. Dicks file (Pardon Records, Ohio Hist. Soc.); "Report on Pardons, Governor Salmon P. Chase to the General Assembly," in Ohio General Assembly, House of Representatives, *Journal,* 52nd Assem., 2nd sess., 1857, 163.
21. Chase wrote this notation, about an unlocated letter sent to Susan Walker with newspaper copies of his annual message to the assembly and his state house dedication speech, as an interlineation above *Visit from Deaf Mutes.* The insertion probably belongs at the end of the entry, where he had run out of space.
22. The second section of Coventry Kersey Dighton Patmore, *The Angel in the House* (London, 1854–56).
23. The Rev. Charles Reynolds, pastor of Trinity Protestant Episcopal Church. *Col. Dir. (1856–57),* 34, 172.
24. Adam Clarke, *The Holy Bible . . . with a Commentary and Critical Notes . . .* (London, 1810–25).
25. Paraphrases of the *Magnificat* and the Lord's Prayer by Symphorianus Pollio, a Strasbourg hymn writer, were translated into English during the sixteenth century. Many hymns had "Morning" as a title or theme; for one perhaps known to Chase, see *Hymns of the Protestant Episcopal Church, in the United States of America* (Philadelphia, 1827), 35. John Julian, *A Dictionary of Hymnology* (London, 1908), 899–900.
26. Here, and at Jan. 13, 15, and 18, *p.p.* and *pp.* mean "private prayer."

Blackwell[27]—to Neil House with him to see books—introduced him to Baker & others— Paul came in to insist I shd. be candidate—Sd. my fds. wd. announce determination to nominate—to Van Slyke's with Kate & Nettie[28]—rubbers for N.—dinner— Office again Wolcott called[29]—thinks I shd. announce purpose—Gibson / called on Stanton at American[30]—home—after tea called at Galloway's— child better—read Hyperion[31] & Pollio—

TUESDAY, JANUARY 13. Repeated M. Hymn & Pollio before rising—p.p.—to Office after children— Supreme Court room—Bartley's opinion sound[32]— Hall of Rep. got militia bill from Slough[33]— met Townshend & wife[34]—& other fds—little done at Office—many applications for pardon—tea told folks today my birthday— May I be wise—

27. Former Cincinnati resident Henry Browne Blackwell (1825–1909), businessman, publisher, and social reformer, worked for Chase's gubernatorial nomination in 1855. *Nat. Cyc.*, 20:294–95; Leslie Wheeler, ed., *Selected Letters of Lucy Stone and Henry B. Blackwell, 1853–1893* (New York, 1981), 141.
28. Lewis G. Van Slyke, president of the Ohio Penitentiary and fugitive slave benefactor, operated a shoe and leather store. *Col. Dir. (1856–57)*, 196; Taylor, *Ohio Statesmen*, 2:32; Stanley W. Campbell, *The Slave Catchers: Enforcement of the Fugitive Slave Law, 1850–1860* (Chapel Hill, 1968), 141.
29. Antislavery advocate Christopher Parsons Wolcott (1820–63) studied law in Steubenville with Edwin M. Stanton. He married Stanton's sister and practiced law in Akron before becoming attorney general of Ohio in 1856. He served in that office until 1862, when he accepted the post of assistant secretary of war under Stanton. Ill health forced him to resign that position shortly before his death. Samuel A. Lane, *Fifty Years and Over of Akron and Summit County* (Akron, 1892), 553; Benjamin P. Thomas and Harold M. Hyman, *Stanton: The Life and Times of Lincoln's Secretary of War* (New York, 1962), 46, 208; *Daily National Intelligencer*, Apr. 7, 1863.
30. Likely Edwin M. Stanton, at Columbus' American Hotel. *Col. Dir. (1856–57)*, 209.
31. Henry Wadsworth Longfellow, *Hyperion, a Romance* (New York, 1839).
32. Thomas Welles Bartley (1812–85) dissented in *Ross County Bank v. Henry S. Lewis*, a case involving taxation of bank stocks. Bartley, a former Ohio governor and a brother-in-law of William Tecumseh Sherman and John Sherman, was a state supreme court justice, 1852–59, then practiced law in Mansfield, Cincinnati, and Washington, D.C. Robert Sobel and John Raimo, eds., *Biographical Directory of the Governors of the United States, 1789–1978* (Westport, Conn., 1978), 3:1202–3; *Daily Ohio State Journal*, Jan. 15, 1857; Anna [Shannon] McAllister, *Ellen Ewing: Wife of General Sherman* (New York, 1936), 327.
33. The Militia Bill sought reorganization of the Ohio militia. The House of Representatives on Jan. 13 committed the measure for consideration to the committee of the whole rather than to the committee on the militia. John P. Slough (1829–67), Cincinnati lawyer and Democratic state representative, was expelled from his seat on Jan. 29, 1857. See entry for that date, below. Ohio General Assembly, House of Representatives, *Journal*, 52nd Assem., 2nd sess., 1857, 20, 23; *Appletons'*, 5:552; Gilkey, *Ohio Hundred Year Book*, 305.
34. Margaret A. Bailey of Columbus married Norton S. Townshend in 1854. Robson, *Biographical Encyclopædia*, 472.

WEDNESDAY, JANUARY 14. Many callers at office—Reemelin, Foot, Ladd Hoadly & others[35]— Hoadly & R. think I must be a candidate— Mr. C. Prentiss with me to dinner[36]—intg. a/c of affairs at Phila Conv[37]—dined—sent Jenkins[38] to Bk with certif. of dept too late—laid it on table & forgot it / Evg to Denison's—Field with me—large party political friends—Brayton & Mills back with me in sleigh[39]— Carey attack because no recom. of Temp. Law in Mess[40]

THURSDAY, JANUARY 15. Repd. Pollio before rising / p.p.—to Office in sleigh— Mrs Clark for pardon of son[41]—Lewis for pardon of relative afflicted with fits[42]— Telh. to Cin. abt. certif. dep wh. lost— Victor Smith called—says Halsted & other friends say I must

35. Charles Gustav Reemelin (1814–c. 1891), an important voice within the Cincinnati German community, prospered as a grocer, farmer, lawyer, and journalist, sat as a Democrat in the General Assembly during the 1840s, and later held several state appointments. John A. Foote (1803–91) was a Cleveland lawyer, businessman, reformer, and politician. Ladd was probably James D. Ladd of Jefferson County, who joined Reemelin and Foote in planning the Ohio Boys' Industrial School at Lancaster, but may have been William H. Ladd, president of the Ohio State Board of Agriculture. Robson, *Biographical Encyclopædia*, 70–71; Coyle, *Ohio Authors*, 519; *Life of Charles Reemelin . . . From 1814–1892, Written by Himself . . .* (Cincinnati, 1892); Van Tassel and Grabowski, *Encylcopedia of Cleveland*, 413–14; Gilkey, *Ohio Hundred Year Book*, 720; *Col. Dir. (1856–57)*, 50.

36. Probably Cyrus Prentiss from Portage County, who appears in Chase's notebook related to the 1857 Ohio state election with an indication that he supported Chase for the presidential nomination in 1856. Notebook, 1857 election (Chase Papers, L.C.).

37. The 1856 Republican convention in Philadelphia.

38. Josiah H. Jenkins, a clerk in the Ohio executive office, 1856–57. *Col. Dir. (1856–57)*, 119; *Detailed Statement of the Receipts and Disbursements of the Public Money*, Ohio Exec. Docs. for 1857, 2:363.

39. William Dennison (1815–82), lawyer, bank president, Republican governor of Ohio, 1859–61, and U.S. postmaster general, 1864–66; probably William Field, justice of the peace in Columbus; and Jonathan Mills (1813–69), farmer and state representative from Tuscarawas County, who gained prominence as a Methodist Episcopal preacher. A Republican state convention at Columbus was responsible for the surge of political callers on Jan. 14–15. *DAB*, 5:241–42; *Col. Dir. (1856–57)*, 61, 77; *History of Tuscarawas County*, 963–64; Ohio General Assembly, House of Representatives, *Journal*, 52nd Assem., 2nd sess., 1857, appen., 175; *Daily Ohio State Journal*, Jan. 15, 1857.

40. Samuel Fenton Carey participated in the state temperance convention held this day in Columbus. A newspaper account stated that "abuse of politicians and politics seemed to be the principal ingredients" of the discussions. Chase's recent message to the assembly had not recommended a state temperance law. *Daily Ohio State Journal*, Jan. 14, 1857; *Columbus Gazette*, Jan. 16, 1857.

41. Samuel Clark was in the middle of a seven-year prison sentence for malicious assault. Chase pardoned him on Sept. 14, 1857. Among Chase's reasons for this act were the earnest solicitations of Clark's mother, who appealed to Chase in person. Clark file (Pardon Records, Ohio Hist. Soc.).

42. On this date Chase pardoned Solomon Lewis, sentenced to one year in prison for manslaughter, because "he was subject to violent epileptic convulsions" and needed care that could not be provided in the penitentiary. "Report on Pardons," 163; Lewis file (Pardon Records, Ohio. Hist. Soc.).

not run[43]—Taft called sensible & true—Prentiss fr. Comee. Meeting—[Col.] Derringer with engravings—home to dine / Evg. with Kate to Nevins—Ella Watts,[44] Miss Dickey Mrs Moore who spoke of Mrs Holt[45]— Home before supper & bed—K. wltzd with Chambers—forbid[46]—

FRIDAY, JANUARY 16. Office rather later than usual— Hamlin called—brought him to dinner—long talk about his & partners affidavits respecting contract—advised clear & full statement of exact facts so as to remove all doubt—back to office. Kate came in & home in sleigh—snow—

SATURDAY, JANUARY 17. At office as yesterday—nothing unusual in morning—letter from Mrs Bailey[47]—home to dinner—afternoon Paul & Hamlin came in—nothing of interest—took Brayton & Mendenhall[48] with Kate in sleigh—M—— to tea—to Judge Swan's[49] for Kate—K. & Louise Jones short ride[50]— Carrington's[51]—pleasant—home—week unprofitable

43. Murat Halstead (1829–1908), part-owner since 1854 of the *Cincinnati Commercial*, enjoyed a long career as a journalist. *DAB*, 8:163.
44. Ellen Worthington Watts (d. 1863), daughter of an Ohio governor and wife of Arthur Watts, a Chillicothe physician. McAllister, *In Winter We Flourish*, 86, 333.
45. Chase identified Mrs. Moore as "Florence Greenhow that was." She evidently related that Addie Smith Holt, a Washington acquaintance of Chase, had decided to remain in the East and let her husband go to California alone. Chase to E. L. Pierce, Jan. 1, [1857] (Houghton Lib., Harvard Univ.); Addie Smith letters to Chase, 1854–56 (Chase Papers, L.C.).
46. Probably Col. Francis T. Chambers, Kentucky-born Cincinnati lawyer. A contemporary described him as "possessed of much peculiar chivalry" as well as "of much awful superciliousness, and absolute arrogance, sometimes not to be endured." One of Chase's nieces later recalled that Chase "would let us dance a plain quadrille but never a walt[ze]." *Cinc. Dir. (1857)*, 298; Carter, *Old Court House*, 341–46; Jed Dannenbaum, *Drink and Disorder: Temperance Reform in Cincinnati from the Washingtonian Revival to the WCTU* (Urbana, Ill., 1984), 119; [Eliza Chase Whipple] to [Jacob W. Schuckers], [1873] (Schuckers Papers, L.C.).
47. Virginia-born Margaret Lucy Shands Bailey (1812–88), antislavery writer and wife of journalist Gamaliel Bailey. Her letter recounted news of family and friends and commented on politics. Bailey to Chase, Jan. 11, 1857 (Chase Papers, L.C.); Stanley Harrold, *Gamaliel Bailey and Antislavery Union* (Kent, Ohio, 1986), 13, 215.
48. Either Moses Mendenhall (b. ca. 1808) of Columbiana County or Cyrus Mendenhall (b. ca. 1811) of Jefferson County. Both were state representatives. Ohio General Assembly, House of Representatives, *Journal*, 52nd Assem., 2nd sess., 1857, appen., 175.
49. Joseph Rockwell Swan.
50. Louise Jones, daughter of Dr. I. G. Jones, later married Baldwin Gwynne. Ruth Young White, ed., *We Too Built Columbus* . . . (Columbus, Ohio, 1936), 114; *Daily Ohio State Journal*, Mar. 20, 1857.
51. Author and lawyer Henry Beebee Carrington (1824–1912) became adjutant general of Ohio and a Union officer during the Civil War. *DAB*, 3:520–21; *Col. Dir. (1856–57)*, 41.

SUNDAY, JANUARY 18. Up too late—no time to read before church—good sermon fr. Mr. Reynolds—home—dined—read awhile Life of Morris[52]—finished letter to Mrs Goldsborough[53]—tea—heard Nettie say hymn—conversed with children—read sermon by Mr. Conway, "Lesson of Defeat"[54]—Seyffarth's Lecture on Egyptian Antiquities"[55]—p.p. bed at 10½

MONDAY, JANUARY 19. Up rather late but early to office—Latty called[56]—doubts as to my being candidate on persl. grounds—wrote Wilson, Hale & Seward[57]—cold in room—ther. 55° 40′—manager tried to rectify—Kate's Report— Home with children—uneasey on a/c slight cough Kate—dinner[58]—attended funeral Sam Galloway ten years old—walked to State House with Dennison[59]—Hamilton called (think P.M. but perhaps A.M.)—Talked to him about Hamlin[60]—he regretted that H. had not made same explanation to him as to me—nothing more of consequence—home—heard Netties lesson, read Bingham's speech[61]

---

52. Benjamin Franklin Morris, ed., *The Life of Thomas Morris: Pioneer and Long a Legislator of Ohio* . . . (Cincinnati, 1856).

53. Elizabeth Wirt Goldsborough later acknowledged a "kind and friendly" letter from Chase dated Jan. 17, 1857. Goldsborough to Chase, May 19, 1857 (Chase Papers, L.C.).

54. Moncure Daniel Conway, "Virtue *vs.* Defeat: A Discourse, preached on November 9, 1856 (the First Sunday After the Presidential Election), in the Unitarian Church, Cincinnati, Ohio" (Cincinnati, 1856).

55. German archaeologist and theologian Gustavus Seyffarth (1796–1885) wrote extensively on ancient Egypt. His most recent works included a *Summary of Recent Discoveries in Biblical Chronology, Universal History and Egyptian Archæology* . . . (New York, 1857). *DAB*, 17:4–5.

56. Alexander Sankey Latty, judge on the Ohio Court of Common Pleas, 1857–62, 1872–77. Gilkey, *Ohio Hundred Year Book*, 554; Nevin O. Winter, *A History of Northwest Ohio* . . . (Chicago, 1917), 1:534–35; Latty to Chase, Jan. 15, 1861 (Chase Papers, L.C.); Chase to Friedrich Hassaurek, Apr. 7, 1857 (Hassaurek Papers, Ohio Hist. Soc.).

57. U.S. Senators Henry Wilson (1812–75), Republican of Massachusetts, 1855–73; John P. Hale; and William H. Seward. Chase acknowledged Seward's "kind note of commendation" regarding his annual message. *Bio. Dir. U.S. Cong.*, 2067; Chase to Seward, Jan. 19, 1857 (Seward Papers, Univ. of Rochester Lib.); *DAB*, 20:322–25.

58. The remainder of this entry originally read simply, *at office again in afternoon—heard Netties Latin—* Chase struck through those phrases. He originally wrote the section beginning with *attended funeral* in the space for Jan. 20, with somewhat different wording and arrangement. He drew lines to link that text to Jan. 19, then finally lined through it (along with the printed heading for Jan. 20) and rewrote the clauses as the conclusion to Jan. 19.

59. William Dennison.

60. Cornelius Springer Hamilton was chairman of a legislative committee investigating E. S. Hamlin and the state canal contracts. *Cincinnati Daily Gazette*, Aug. 26, 1857.

61. John Armor Bingham, "Remarks on the President's Message," *Cong. Globe*, 34th Cong., 3rd sess., appen., 135–40. Bingham's speech addressed the question of Congressional authority over slavery in the territories.

January 1857   { 257 }

TUESDAY, 20[62] Meditated much before rising—resolved to live to God—repeated Pollio—to office walking with children—extremely cold— Mrs Dr Smith, Miss Anthony & others called[63]—afterwards Mr. [Hurley] & Miss Scott—wrote Ralston Skinner—drew sketch of proclamation of Bank Charter result[64] / dinner—Pennington called[65]— Morton with letter from Sherman who wishes me to be candidate[66]— Mr. Hutcheison with R. W. Emerson[67]—home with Mr. Mot[68]—arranged for French lessons— Dr. Coulter called—thinks nothing ails K.

WED. 21— Nothing of importance except Mr Mot commd. French Lessons, Kate, self & Nettie $24 per quarter.[69]

THURSDAY, JANUARY 22. Profitable reflections—rose rather late—intensely cold—at office after nine—near 10 indeed—read Picciola[70] & other books—read Septuagint—did not accomplish much at office on a/c of cold—dined— Saw Mrs Cooper at Senate Cham. who expressed wish to see Nettie[71]—promised to send her—after tea called Galloways—Mr. Langarl there—letter from Th.

---

62. This entry occupies the space under the printed heading for Wednesday, Jan. 21, which Chase crossed out, substituting his own heading for Tuesday the 20th.
63. Susan H. Anthony, eldest daughter of Charles Anthony, married Samuel Mitchel Smith in 1843. Anna J. ("Annie") Anthony was her sister. Robson, *Biographical Encyclopædia*, 400; A. Anthony to Chase, Nov. 21, 1860, Apr. 28, May 31, 1862 (Chase Papers, L.C.).
64. Chase was responding to *State of Ohio ex rel. Noah L. Wilson and others v. Salmon P. Chase*, a case involving creation of a Cincinnati branch of the State Bank of Ohio. *Daily Ohio State Journal*, Jan. 9, 13, 15, 30, 1857.
65. Attorney Robert Gill Pennington (1816–92), identified with Republican and business interests in Tiffin, Ohio. *Biographical Cyclopædia*, 2:455–56; *A Centennial Biographical History of Seneca County, Ohio* . . . (Chicago, 1902), 100–104.
66. T. P. Morton was a post office clerk. John Sherman (1823–1900) of Ohio served as a Republican in Congress, 1855–61, and the U.S. Senate, 1861–77. *DAB*, 17:84–88; *Col. Dir. (1856–57)*, 160.
67. Joseph Hutcheson, a banker, was also a director of the Columbus Atheneum, where essayist and poet Ralph Waldo Emerson (1803–82) delivered addresses on Jan. 19 and 20. *Columbus Gazette*, Jan. 2, 23, 1857; *DAB*, 6:132–41; Susan Sutton Smith and Harrison Hayford, eds., *The Journals and Miscellaneous Notebooks of Ralph Waldo Emerson*, vol. 14, *1854–1861* (Cambridge, Mass., 1978), 448; *Col. Dir. (1856–57)*, 117; Lee, *Columbus*, 1:414.
68. French-born Adolphus Mot (b. ca. 1814) resided until 1862 in Columbus, moved to Fernandina, Fla., where he served in local government, and relocated later to Washington, D.C. Brooks D. Simpson et al., eds., *Advice After Appomattox: Letters to Andrew Johnson, 1865–1866: Special Volume No. 1 of the Papers of Andrew Johnson* (Knoxville, 1987), 36.
69. Chase inserted this entry at the top of a page, above the printed heading for Jan. 22.
70. Joseph Xavier Boniface Saintine, *Picciola* (Paris, 1836).
71. Perhaps Mrs. Mary Cooper. *Col. Dir. (1856–57)*, 53.

Spooner[72]—bed about 10½. Wm. Stanberry called today[73]—also Mr. Moore fr. Canada[74]

FRIDAY, JANUARY 23. Up late—intensely cold—water frozen in pitcher before fire all night—p.p.[75] & 2pp Septu—to office—very cold—cd. do little—tried to prepare proclation[76]—did not succeed—dinner—read Picciola—office again—Ball called—astonished to hear of judgment & execution on Miner debt—wrote D. P. Evans, King & Marshall & R. Skinner[77]— Judge Myers, Bassett & McBain called[78]—tea— French Lessons— Party at Dr. Ide's[79]—

SATURDAY, JANUARY 24. To office after breakfast—very cold still—for sevl. days past singular roughness on back— Mr. Ball called at office—home with me to dinner—afternoon mail letter from Levi Coffin wh read to Ball & asked him to see Coffin[80]— He walked out as far as D & D Asylum with me—requested him to write—reading after tea—Netties Latin. read Rep. Conc. Investigation Pub. Wks[81]—able—

72. Thomas Spooner (b. 1817), recently an Ohio Know-Nothing leader, held the office of Hamilton County clerk. *Cinc. Dir. (1857)*, 244; Henry B. Teetor, *The Past and Present of Mill Creek Valley*... (Cincinnati, 1882; reprint, Knightstown, Ind., 1977), 268–69; Maizlish, *Triumph of Sectionalism*, 214–17, 222, 226.
73. William Stanbery (1788–1873), lawyer and former congressman. *Bio. Dir. U.S. Cong.*, 1860; Norman N. Hill, Jr., ed., *History of Licking County, Ohio*... (Newark, Ohio, 1881), 275–76.
74. Probably Canadian-born Thomas Moore (1822–93), lawyer, social reformer, and Republican. *History and Biographical Cyclopædia of Butler County*, 351; Cone, *Biographical and Historical Sketches*, 357.
75. Here and in the entry for Jan. 25 below, *p.p.* and *pp* mean "private prayer."
76. That is, "proclamation"; Chase split the word over two lines and omitted a syllable.
77. James Ralston Skinner. The Farmers' Branch of the state bank at Ripley had obtained a judgment against John L. Miner, in whose behalf Chase had a surety obligation. Daniel P. Evans (d. 1877) helped found the Farmers' Branch and was its cashier. George W. King (1797–1879) and John G. Marshall (1823–78), lawyers from Georgetown, Ohio, handled legal matters related to the Miner debt case. In Apr. 1857, Chase saw an advertisement offering some of his Cincinnati property at a sheriff's sale and learned to his astonishment that Miner had not honored their agreement. Chase to Chambers Baird, Apr. 21, 1857, Baird to Chase, Apr. 27, 1857 (Chase Papers, L.C.); *The History of Brown County, Ohio*... (Chicago, 1883), 1:446, 2:23, 28–29, 62.
78. James Myers; Edward P. Bassett (b. 1818), Toledo lawyer and Republican politician; and probably Daniel McBain, a Toledo political figure associated with the *Toledo Blade*. Robson, *Biographical Encyclopædia*, 622; Harvey Scribner, ed., *Memoirs of Lucas County and the City of Toledo*... (Madison, Wis., 1910), 1:120–21; Waggoner, *Toledo*, 314, 322, 365, 385, 638.
79. William E. Ide, physician and a director of the Columbus Atheneum. *Col. Dir. (1856–57)*, 117.
80. Levi Coffin (1789–1877), antislavery activist and benefactor of fugitive slaves, lived at this time in Cincinnati. *DAB*, 4:268–69.
81. *Report of Investigating Committee on Public Works* (Columbus, 1857). A special legislative committee prepared this report documenting frauds and irregularities in

January 1857 {259}

SUNDAY, JANUARY 25. Rose as usual— Meditation pleasant and I hope profitable—p.p. Church—Mr. Reynolds excellent sermon on prayer—after dinner read Life of Morris—Septuagint—after tea Seyffarth on Egyptian Antiquities—heard Nettie say hymn & talked with her before tea—bed about ten after pp.

MONDAY, JANUARY 26. Repeated M.h.[82] & Pollio before rising— breakft—walked with children to 4 & State—office cold had table moved into Sec'y's— Dr. Paul abt. contracts—Cattell called & Taylor[83]—C. to ask about contracts—dinner—Paul & Blakesly[84]— began letter to Barney ans. to his recd. today[85]—to Meeting Bd Directors P.C. & L. adjd. till tomorrow at 10[86]—tea—heard Nettie Latin in pt.— Prof. Mot & French— Galloway & talk—says F. Wade for Fremt.[87]

TUESDAY, JANUARY 27. Office in morning as usual—letter from S. Walker very interesting giving account of Meeting with Emperor & Emperess at toy shop—nothing else noteworthy till afternoon when Mr. Harlan of Iowa called on his way to Washington having been promptly reelected[88]—in the evening went after French with Mr. Mot to small evg party at Mr. Dwight Stones[89]—home by 11¾ & bed—

---

canal contracts let by the State Board of Public Works. R. R. Bowker, ed., *State Publications: A Provisional List of the Official Publications of the Several States of the United States* . . . (New York, 1908), 215; *Daily Ohio State Journal,* Jan. 9, 27, 1857; *Xenia Torch-Light,* Jan. 14, 1857.

82. Morning hymn.

83. Possibly Lester Taylor (b. ca. 1798), farmer and state senator from Geauga County. Gilkey, *Ohio Hundred Year Book,* 310; Ohio General Assembly, House of Representatives, *Journal,* 52nd Assem., 2nd sess., 1857, appen., 173.

84. Schuyler E. Blakeslee.

85. Hiram Barney's letter thanked Chase for a copy of his 1857 gubernatorial message and urged Chase's candidacy for president of the U.S. in 1860. Barney to Chase, Jan. 19, 1857 (Chase Papers, Hist. Soc. of Pa.).

86. Chase had received stock in the Pittsburgh, Cincinnati, and Louisville Telegraph Company as compensation for legal services in Henry O'Reilly's litigation with S. F. B. Morse. He kept minutes of this directors' meeting in his own hand. O'Reilly agreement, Oct. 29, 1849, Stanhope S. Rowe to Chase, Apr. 21, 1851, and "Meeting of Directors of P.C. & L. Telegraph Company, Jany. 26 and 28, 1857, Proceedings" (Chase Papers, L.C.); "Senator Chase's proposition for Stock," Jan. 13, 1851, and Chase to O'Reilly, June 29, 1852 (O'Reilly Papers, Rochester Public Lib.).

87. Benjamin Franklin Wade, called "Frank" before he became known as "Ben," supported Frémont for president in 1856. Hans L. Trefousse, *Benjamin Franklin Wade: Radical Republican from Ohio* (New York, 1963), 18, 104.

88. Republican James Harlan (1820–99), just reelected to his seat in the U.S. Senate, which had declared the place vacant due to irregularities relating to Harlan's election in 1855. He served in the Senate, 1855–65, 1867–73, and as secretary of the interior, 1865–66. *Bio. Dir. U.S. Cong.,* 1134–35.

89. Stone was a Columbus dry goods merchant. *Col. Dir. (1856–57),* 189.

WEDNESDAY, JANUARY 28. Dr. Townshend called at office—Mr. Eaton artist then with me[90]—talk about art—Eaton desirous of order to paint for pannel in Rotunda[91]— Galloway went to Washn. this morng.— Tel. Meeting & appropriations / trouble at dinner thro' Kate asking if Mary cd. not sit in my [r]oom—more trouble after about Nevins walking with K—took Nettie & Kate to Sunday School Anniversary—called at Neil House—saw several—called Judge Bartley.

THURSDAY, JANUARY 29. At office this morning Mr. Eaton called—wished me to sit[92]—consented— Flowers about pardon of ONeill[93]—walked with Dr. Jewett on way to dinner[94]—vote on expulsion substitute resolution in Slough's case[95]—after dinner sitting to Eaton—beautiful portrait of his wife[96]—some work at office—tea—french with Prof Mot—party at Robt. Neils[97]—very pleasant—talk with Sally Sullivant[98]—letter from S. W. dated 11th Janry today.

90. Ohio native Joseph Oriel Eaton (1829–75). *DAB*, 5:610–11.
91. Many artists sought commissions for work in the new state capitol. One journalist lamented the "crowd of sign painters, lately arrived, who wish to disfigure the walls of the State House with their miserable daubs, which they facetiously call historical paintings." *Columbus Gazette*, Feb. 27, 1857.
92. Eaton had traveled to Columbus from his home in Cincinnati to solicit commissions for portraits. *Daily Ohio State Journal*, Jan. 28, 1857; *Cincinnati Daily Gazette*, Jan. 30, 1857.
93. Dr. Franklin L. Flowers (b. ca. 1812), representative from Perry County, spoke on behalf of his constituent, Patrick O'Neill, an "old man" of "quiet disposition" sentenced to two years in prison for manslaughter. Chase pardoned O'Neill on Jan. 30. Ohio General Assembly, House of Representatives, *Journal*, 52nd Assem., 2nd sess., 1857, appen., 174; O'Neill file (Pardon Records, Ohio Hist. Soc.).
94. Mendall Jewett (b. 1815), an assemblyman from Summit County, graduated from Willoughby Medical College in Cleveland. William Henry Perrin, *History of Summit County* . . . (Chicago, 1881), 313–14; Ohio General Assembly, House of Representatives, *Journal*, 52nd Assem., 2nd sess., 1857, appen., 175.
95. On this day the Ohio House of Representatives adopted a resolution expelling John P. Slough for striking Republican member Darius Cadwell on Jan. 14. An effort to pass a replacement resolution that only would have reprimanded Slough and censured Cadwell for "disorderly language" then failed. A final vote for Slough's expulsion carried. The incident stemmed from a dispute over mileage and per diem payments to legislators during adjournments. *Daily Ohio State Journal*, Jan. 22, 29, 30, 1857; Ohio General Assembly, House of Representatives, *Journal*, 52nd Assem., 2nd sess., 1857, 12, 30–31, 42–43, 52–53, 58–59, 70–71, 97–99, and "Case of Messrs. Slough and Cadwell," appen., 78–84.
96. Emma Jane Goodman Eaton of Cincinnati married Joseph Oriel Eaton in 1855. *DAB*, 5:610; *New York Times*, Feb. 9, 1875.
97. Either Robert Neil (1796–1883) or his nephew Robert Elkin Neil (b. 1819). Both were Columbus businessmen. *Col. Dir. (1855)*, 86; ibid. (1856–57), 161; *Biographical Cyclopædia*, 4:973; Taylor, *Columbus and Franklin County*, 1:514, 2:208–13.
98. Possibly Sarah McDowell Sullivant (b. 1837), daughter of Michael Lucas Sullivant and Sarah Lapsley McDowell Sullivant of Columbus. Chase's rendering is ambiguous, here and elsewhere in his journal, and the name could be Lally (Lallie). In that case the nickname may refer to Pamela B. Sullivant, later Neil (b. 1836).

FRIDAY, JANUARY 30. Busy all morning getting ready to go to Cin—prepared advance decision in ONeills case—despatch from Hanna[99]—agrees with my views as to Salary &c— Ansd. it & telegd to Burnet House & R. Skinner— Haines called[1]—Ball—Hamlin—borrd. $50 of Paul— Took cars [about] one P.M.— Brough Jim Lane, Gurley, Bickham, Loomis & others[2]—Sallie Sullt. & her family—arrid. Burnet House after 6[3]—suppd.— R. Skinner called—has called on gentlemen bound with me on Miner—all will pay—but must lose $500[4]—

SATURDAY, JANUARY 31. Up late—to breakt. with children—Kate $3 Netties rubbers &c—to C House[5]—Spencer, Storer, Gholson[6]—Parker[7]—fine rooms—Law Library—children went to

---

Pamela was a daughter of Michael Sullivant's brother Joseph and his second wife, Mary Eliza Brashear Sullivant. Joseph Sullivant, *A Genealogy and Family Memorial* (Columbus, 1874), family tables for Michael L. and Joseph Sullivant; White, *We Too Built Columbus*, 115.

99. Joshua Hanna, a Pittsburgh banker and businessman who later moved to New York. Hanna to Chase, Mar. 27, 1857, Aug. 31, 1865 (Chase Papers, L.C.).

1. Probably Seth S. Haines (b. ca. 1824), merchant and representative from Warren County. Ohio General Assembly, House of Representatives, *Journal*, 52nd Assem., 2nd sess., 1857, appen., 175.

2. John Brough; James Henry Lane (1814–66), former lieutenant governor of Indiana, soldier, Kansas Free State leader, U.S. senator, 1861–66; John Addison Gurley (1813–63), retired Universalist pastor, Cincinnati newspaperman, and Republican congressman, 1859–63; William Denison Bickham (1827–94), correspondent for Cincinnati newspapers and later editor and proprietor of the Republican *Dayton Journal;* and probably B. J. Loomis, Ohio journalist, for several years the Columbus correspondent of the *Cincinnati Commercial*. *DAB*, 10:576–78; Chase to Henry J. Adams, May 11, 1857 (Chase Papers, L.C.); *Bio. Dir. U.S. Cong.*, 1105; *The History of Montgomery County, Ohio* . . . (Chicago, 1882), 191–92; Frank Conover, ed., *Centennial Portrait and Biographical Record of the City of Dayton and Montgomery County, Ohio* . . . (Logansport, Ind., 1897), 403–4; Lee, *Columbus*, 1:490; *History of Ashtabula County*, 40.

3. A numeral 5 appears above the line and to the left of the 6.

4. Chase originally began his description of Jan. 30 in the space intended for Jan. 31 in his pocket diary. Under the heading for the thirty-first, he wrote, then lined through, an incomplete account of Jan. 30. There are some differences between the two versions, but both describe the same general sequence of activities. The aborted start at Jan. 31 contains one significant clause absent from the final version of the entry: "told Lane plan of rescuing free state prisoners." This statement refers to a clandestine proposal Chase had made to Gov. James W. Grimes of Iowa, whereby a group of Free State men held by the Lecompton government in Kansas would be forcibly rescued and taken into Iowa, where U.S. authority (and troops) supporting the Kansas territorial government could not reach them. Chase to Grimes, Nov. 8, 1856 (copy, Chase Papers, Hist. Soc. of Pa.); Chase to John W. Geary, Dec. 3, 1856 (Chase Papers, L.C.); Geary to Chase, Jan. 6, 1857 (Chase Papers, Cinc. Hist. Soc.).

5. Courthouse.

6. Superior Court judges Oliver M. Spencer, Bellamy Storer, and William Yates Gholson.

7. Probably Judge James Parker or his son James, Jr., a notary public. *Cinc. Dir. (1857)*, 213.

Clifton—dined solus—evening to Emerson's lecture with Paul Anderson[8]—then to Literary Club[9]—rather dull—drank some eggnog wh. against conscience—another wrong act before going to lecture—home—reading—pp[10]—bed—

SUNDAY, FEBRUARY 1. Up 7½—breakfast—Mrs Dominick[11] & others at brkft. Attended Mr. Conway's[12]— Excellent sermon except some theological points—went to Clifton—Dined at Mr. Balls with family & staid all night—Eva[13] at Washington—saw children at Judge McLean's—family in Washn.—C. L. Jones & Josie there.[14]

MONDAY, FEBRUARY 2. Rode to town with Mr. Ball—he stopped at C. House— Huston & Meredith[15]—to room with H—he anxious for union of opponents of Admn.—suggested plan—children came in fr. country in afternoon—Spent their time with Maria Southgate— Huston & Col. Watson called[16]—expressed themselves agst Amnt. of Cons. requiring residence after naturn. before voting[17]—

---

8. Ralph Waldo Emerson lectured at the Cincinnati Unitarian Church on the subject of "Beauty." General Paul Anderson boarded at the Burnet House and was a prominent Cincinnati social figure. *Daily Cincinnati Gazette*, Jan. 31, Feb. 2, 1857; Smith and Hayford, *Journals of Emerson*, 448; *Cinc. Dir. (1857)*, 13; William Prescott Smith, *The Book of the Great Railway Celebrations of 1857* . . . (New York, 1858), 1:199.

9. The Literary Club of Cincinnati, of which Chase was a member, was organized in 1849 and limited its membership to distinguished professionals. The club's library held only the writings of club members. *History of Cincinnati and Hamilton County*, 154.

10. "Private prayer" (also at Feb. 6 and 7 below). Chase wrote this entry between the struck-through lines of the Jan. 30 entry he began, then canceled, under the heading for Jan. 31.

11. George Dominick, curer and dealer in provisions, boarded at the Burnet House. *Cinc. Dir. (1857)*, 91.

12. Moncure Daniel Conway (1832–1907), antislavery clergyman and author, was associated with the First Congregational Church of Cincinnati, 1856–62. *DAB*, 4:364–65.

13. Evelina Chandler Ball.

14. Charlotte Ludlow Jones and her daughter Josephine Jones. C. L. Jones to Chase, Mar. 12, Sept. 30, 1863 (Chase Papers, L.C.).

15. Alexander Botkin Huston (b. 1829), a Cincinnati lawyer with Democratic political inclinations, and John R. Meredith (1820–80), who practiced law in Steubenville and Cincinnati until he relocated later in 1857 to Omaha, Neb. *Cinc. Dir. (1857)*, 166, 198; Greve, *Centennial History*, 2:373–75; Reed, *Bench and Bar of Ohio*, 2:456–59; James W. Savage and John T. Bell, *History of the City of Omaha Nebraska* (New York, 1894), 233; Meredith to Chase, Aug. 11, 1857 (Chase Papers, L.C.).

16. Possibly James Watson, Henrie House proprietor. *Cinc. Dir. (1857)*, 271.

17. This proposed amendment to the Ohio Constitution passed the General Assembly in late Jan. 1857 and required naturalized citizens coming to Ohio to reside in the state one year after receiving their final naturalization papers before being eligible to vote. *Daily Ohio State Journal*, Jan. 2, 23, 28, 1857.

February 1857 { 263 }

called on Molitor—boy Adolph[18] / party at Mr. Lord's—Miss Groesbeck & Mrs Bates[19]—very pleasant—bed abt. 12.

TUESDAY, FEBRUARY 3. Up betimes—dressed & b'kft—to church with Maria Southgate & Nettie—Kate with Capt Hawes— Capt took Maria into church—married by Rev. Mr. Butler— Another couple married at 8^{20}—to Columbus by 10 AM. cars—three couples in same car all married this morn'g—Rev. Mr. Co[ur]t[21] talked with me on cars— Colums. after 3—dined—papers & letters—tea—Mr. Mot came—talked French—to Neil House for Kate—home—bed

WEDNESDAY, FEBRUARY 4. To Neil House after bkft with Kate & Nettie & accompanied Maria to cars—then I to Office—girls to school— Mrs S—— gave [me] note she had found in afternoon— Sat to Eaton 2d. sitting—has painted while I gone likeness of S. Matthews— Ball came up from Cin— Mr. Mot came after tea—I tired & sleepy—

THURSDAY, FEBRUARY 5. Up as usual & after breakft to office— many callers—no time for real business—before bkft Kate asked how she had offended—told her by false conduct—after dinner she anxious to know what—could not then explain— Pruden about Slavin[22]—Franklin & Renick abt Pro. Judge in place of Bierce[23]—

18. Adolph Molitor, probably the son of Cincinnati *Volksblatt* editor Stephen Molitor. *Cinc. Dir. (1864)*, 272.
19. Henry C. Lord was a Cincinnati attorney. Olivia Groesbeck (d. 1868), daughter of a Cincinnati banker, married Gen. Joseph Hooker in 1865. Elizabeth Dwight Hoadly (d. 1911), sister of George Hoadly, Jr., married Joshua Hall Bates in 1844. *Cinc. Dir. (1857)*, 135, 187; Walter H. Hebert, *Fighting Joe Hooker* (Indianapolis, 1944), 291, 293–94; Greve, *Centennial History*, 2:117–19; Goss, *Cincinnati*, 4:220.
20. Joseph S. Morris of Louisville and Miss Matties, daughter of Gideon Burton of Cincinnati. The Rev. Clement Moore Butler officiated in Christ Church. *Daily Cincinnati Gazette*, Feb. 4, 1857; Goss, *Cincinnati*, 4:220.
21. Possibly Rev. Lucian Court. *Col. Dir. (1856–57)*, 53.
22. A. J. Pruden (b. 1818), lawyer, Democratic politician, and Cincinnati police judge. He probably called about the pardon application of Patrick Clavin, sentenced in 1855 to life imprisonment for second degree murder. Chase pardoned Clavin on Feb. 7 because of previous good character, new evidence, the general circumstances of the case, and fears that continued imprisonment would cause Clavin's insanity. Greve, *Centennial History*, 2:880–81; Clavin file (Pardon Records, Ohio Hist. Soc.); "Report on Pardons," 163–64.
23. William W. Bierce resigned as probate judge of Pickaway County in Feb. 1857. Seymour G. Renick, a Circleville banker, secured the appointment to fill the vacancy (see entry for Mar. 5, 1857). Chase's other visitor was probably either Nelson Franklin (b. ca. 1803), a state representative from Pickaway County, or his son, identified as "young Franklin," who promoted Renick's appointment. Bierce to Chase,

Mr. Mot in evg—after he was gone long conversation with Kate—she sincerely sorry apparently read & bed

FRIDAY, FEBRUARY 6. Rose as usual—p.p.— Office—"Friends" from Belmont, Dowdney & others—say Rep. vote will increase there—Sat to Eaton—young artist there—home to dinner—Kate did not go to school today—seems really penitent— Ball with me to dinner—Grant v Laf. Bk decided today adversely[24]— Afternoon sat again—Spooner gave me Life of Lewis[25]—Smith of Mont[26] with Sallie & Lu Sullivant[27] called—tea—began lecture[28]—

SATURDAY, FEBRUARY 7. Rose early—read Sep[29] & pp before breakft—to office & then Eaton's with Kate—Mrs John Neil, Mrs Rob. Neil & Mrs Dennison came in[30]—retd. to Office—determd. to pardon Pat Clavin—talk with Ball abt. successor to Slough— H. J. Adams of Leavenwth City with me to dinner—Nevins called before & long talk of Snowdens &c—few words to Hamilton abt. contracts— Canfield called abt. naturaln amendt.[31]—Spencer called—not in favor of it— Prof Mot & French.

Feb. 4, 1857, W. P. Darst to H. H. Hunter, Feb. 1857, Jonathan Renick to Chase, Feb. 7, 1857, and John Cochran to Franklin, Feb. 7, 1857 (Chase Papers, Ohio Hist. Soc.); *Columbus Gazette*, Mar. 6, 1857; *History of Franklin and Pickaway Counties*, 47–48, 53, 104, 166, 180–82, 193, 199, 200–207, 343; Ohio General Assembly, House of Representatives, *Journal*, 52nd Assem., 2nd sess., 1857, appen., 174.

24. *Samuel Grant v. Lafayette Bank, the Administrator of James C. Ludlow et al.*, a mortgage case heard by the state supreme court. *Cincinnati Daily Gazette*, Feb. 8, 1857; *Daily Ohio State Journal*, Apr. 28, 1857.

25. William G. W. Lewis, *Biography of Samuel Lewis, First Superintendent of Common Schools for the State of Ohio* (Cincinnati, 1857).

26. Either Thomas J. S. Smith (1806–68), lawyer, railroad promoter, and Democratic politician representing Montgomery County in the legislature, or his son, Samuel B. Smith (b. 1836), who later became adjutant general of Ohio. *History of Montgomery County*, 484–85.

27. Possibly Lucy Jane Sullivant, later Hopkins (b. 1839), Michael Lucas Sullivant's daughter and the younger sister of Sarah McDowell Sullivant. Sullivant, *Genealogy*, family table for Michael L. Sullivant; White, *We Too Built Columbus*, 115.

28. Chase refers to his preparation for a lecture on the life and scientific accomplishments of Galileo Galilei, which he delivered in Cleveland on Feb. 19. *Cleveland Daily Plain Dealer*, Feb. 19, 20, 1857; "Galileo" (Chase Papers, L.C.).

29. Septuagint.

30. Mrs. John G. Neil and Jane Marshall Sullivant Neil (b. 1824), the latter a daughter of William Starling Sullivant and the spouse of Robert Elkin Neil, were sisters-in-law of Anne Eliza Neil Dennison, William Dennison's wife and the daughter of Columbus businessman William Neil. Taylor, *Columbus and Franklin County*, 1:514; Sullivant, *Genealogy*, 238, W. S. Sullivant family table; *DAB*, 5:241–42; White, *We Too Built Columbus*, 111–12.

31. Herman Canfield (b. ca. 1817), lawyer and state senator from Medina County, 1856–60. Ohio General Assembly, House of Representatives, *Journal*, 52nd Assem., 2nd sess., 1857, appen., 172; Gilkey, *Ohio Hundred Year Book*, 171.

February 1857

SUNDAY, FEBRUARY 8. Up at 7½—attended Church—Mr. Reynolds—dined—read P.M. Dr. Seyffarths Lectures on Egyptian Antiquities—very instructive After tea heard Nettie say hymns—talked to her—wrote part of lecture—bed at 12.

MONDAY, FEBRUARY 9. Up at 7—after bkft walked to office—with children to 4th St. Mr. Phillips[32] & another called—home early—wrote part of lecture—dinner to office again—various unimportant matters—home—tea— Mr. Mot & french—Mr. M. related interesting anecdote of LeVerier[33]—wrote lecture from 8.15 to 12.15. bed.

TUESDAY, FEBRUARY 10. Mr. Pierce came today & brought letter from Vaughan, very kind—usual business at office—Mrs Andrews about pardon of son[34]—gave her all encouragement I could—afternoon wrote several pages of lecture— Evening attended exhibition of young men at high school[35]—Rice had excellent piece—Pierce home with me to stay.

WEDNESDAY, FEBRUARY 11. To office in morning as usual—nothing unusual there—afternoon wrote lecture two or three hours—evening to Franklinton small party at M. Sullivants[36]—P. P. Lowe,[37] H. G. Phillips, & others from Dayton—Judge Thurman & others[38]—Sallie & Lou Sullivant Eliza Sullivant—Mrs Collins[39]—all

32. Probably Horatio Gates Phillips (1783–1859), Dayton merchant and businessman (see Feb. 11 below). *History of Montgomery County*, 389–93; Drury, *Dayton and Montgomery County*, 1:120.
33. French astronomer Urbain Jean Joseph Leverrier (1811–77). *Nouvelle Biographie*, 31:32–35.
34. Mrs. O. M. Andrews beseeched Chase for the pardon of her son Joseph, sentenced to six months' labor on a chain gang for larceny. In his Feb. 26 entry (below), Chase wrote, "pardoned Mrs Andrews son," but no evidence of the pardon has been found. Andrews file (Pardon Records, Ohio Hist. Soc.).
35. The Columbus High School Literary Society gave an exhibition of original orations and essays "to the delight and admiration of a large and respectable audience." *Daily Ohio State Journal*, Feb. 12, 1857.
36. Michael Lucas Sullivant (1807–79), a son of Columbus pioneers, managed extensive farm properties in Ohio and later in Illinois. *Appletons'*, 5:743; Sullivant, *Genealogy*, 160–68, M. L. Sullivant family table; White, *We Too Built Columbus*, 99–100.
37. Peter Perlee Lowe (1801–86), Dayton lawyer, businessman, civic promoter, and (after 1856) Republican. *Biographical Cyclopædia*, 3:729–30; Johnson, *Twentieth Century Biographical Dictionary*, v. 7.
38. Allen Granberry Thurman (1813–95) was a Columbus lawyer, Democratic politician, and chief justice of the Ohio Supreme Court, 1854–56. From 1869 to 1881 he served in the U.S. Senate. *DAB*, 18:515–16; *Bio. Dir. U.S. Cong.*, 1938–39.
39. Eliza G. Sullivant (b. 1838), a daughter of William S. Sullivant, married Andrew Denny Rogers in 1858. Mrs. Collins may have been Helen K. Collins, wife of Bryan Collins and daughter of Alfred Kelley. Sullivant, *Genealogy*, W. S. Sullivant family table; White, *We Too Built Columbus*, 112; *Daily Ohio State Journal*, Jan. 22, 1857.

very pleasant—home by ½ p. 10—read Picciola & bed— Mr. Pierce with us & much pleased—

THURSDAY, FEBRUARY 13.[40] Talked today with Pierce about book—he half disposed to undertake it[41]—sat to Eaton in morning as I have done for several morn'gs past for a portrait—he succeeding very well— Evening Mr Mot came—had written 5 pp. lecture— French with children—after French went with Kate to Mr. Stones— pleasant party—Annie Anthony & Sallie Sullivant—home after 12—Pierce not till two.

FRIDAY, FEBRUARY 12.[42] Up at 7½—before rising read 2 lessons Pinney[43]— Pierce & I to Capitol after bkft—talked about 1860—he told conversation with Denison, & said Vaughan with me—callers / Cadwell with me to Eaton[']s[44]— Pierce came in—A. S Sullivan there[45]— Ball called & consulted about Grant case[46]—dinner / Pierce left— Ansd. inv. of Y.M. Cath. Institute Cin. to celebration of Washns. birthday[47]—declined courteously— Corwine to tea[48]— Nettie to Mrs Stones—Mr. Mot & French / Pierce left today—

---

40. This entry occupies the space under the printed heading for Friday, Feb. 13, which Chase altered to read *Thursday* without correcting the date.

41. Edward L. Pierce had begun a biography of Chase a few years earlier but ceased work in 1855 after Chase expressed reservations about the project. Chase also corresponded with Pierce at that time about publishing a collection of Chase's Senate speeches with a memoir. No publications resulted from these initiatives, but Pierce's manuscript biography served as the basis for sketches of Chase's life in later publications. It is unclear whether Chase's discussion with Pierce in Feb. 1857 involved the renewal of former efforts or a new project. Despite at least one later allusion to the idea of a book, nothing came to fruition. Pierce biographical essay, [1855], Pierce to Chase, Nov. 9, 1855 (Chase Papers, L.C.); Chase to Pierce, Oct. 27, Nov. 13, 1855, Oct. 15, 1857, Jan. 18, 29, 1860, Sept. 23, 1863 (Houghton Lib., Harvard Univ.); William D. Gallagher to Pierce, Dec. 16, 1872 (Gallagher Papers, Cinc. Hist. Soc.).

42. This entry appears under the printed heading for Thursday, Feb. 12, which Chase altered to read *Friday* without correcting the date.

43. Norman Pinney, *The First Book in French; or, a Practical Introduction to Reading, Writing, and Speaking the French Language* (New York, [c. 1848]).

44. Darius Cadwell (1821–1905) was an Ashtabula County lawyer and the Republican state representative whose comments had provoked John P. Slough to assault him on the floor of the Ohio House (see Jan. 29 above). Joseph Oriel Eaton and his family, Cincinnati residents, had taken temporary rooms in Columbus. Van Tassel and Grabowski, *Encyclopedia of Cleveland*, 150; *History of Ashtabula County*, 93; *Daily Ohio State Journal*, Jan. 28, 1857; *Cincinnati Daily Gazette*, Jan. 30, 1857.

45. Algernon Sydney Sullivan (1826–87), lawyer, resided in Cincinnati, 1855–59, and then moved to New York. *Appletons'*, 5:740.

46. See Feb. 6 entry, above.

47. The Cincinnati Young Men's Catholic Literary Institute, organized in 1852, met at St. Thomas Church. *Cinc. Dir. (1859)*, Appendix, 18.

48. Richard M. Corwine, a Cincinnati lawyer who later moved to Washington, D.C., maintained a professional association with Chase. *Cinc. Dir. (1857)*, 73; Corwine to Chase, Apr. 18, 1857 (Chase Papers, Hist. Soc. of Pa.); *Wash. Dir. (1873)*, 140.

February 1857 {267}

SATURDAY, FEBRUARY 14. At office today in morn'g—afternoon worked hard on my lecture on Galileo—had more freedom in writing than at first—finished it—nothing else important today—

SUNDAY, FEBRUARY 15. To church morng—Mr. Reynolds—children with me— Ev'g Mr. Reynolds also to the young—read some in Sep. & Clarks Commy.[49]—

MONDAY, FEBRUARY 16. Today Special election in Cincinnati to fill vacancy[50]—much interest felt—gentleman called [in] behalf of Mr. Aubery painter[51] / reproached him for not being at home to vote— Evg Mr. Mot & French—

TUESDAY, FEBRUARY 17. At Office as usual—papers from Cincinnati leave election in doubt—but probabilities in favor of Hosea[52]—

WEDNESDAY, FEBRUARY 18. At office as usual— Corwine called—talk abt. Hosea & result in Cincinnati[53]— Evg. French & Mr. Mot— Nettie took Slough part but abandoned him on learning he was proslavery— Call fr. Matthews today abt. Summons[54]—

49. That is, Chase read in the Septuagint and in Clarke, *Holy Bible . . . with Commentary*.
50. John P. Slough's expulsion from the Ohio House of Representatives necessitated a special election to fill the seat. Chase to L. L. Rice, Jan. 30, 31, 1857, and Richard Mathers, Hamilton Co. sheriff, receipt of proclamation for special election, Jan. 31, 1857 (Chase Papers, Ohio Hist. Soc.); *Daily Cincinnati Gazette*, Feb. 16, 1857.
51. German-born Jean Aubery (1810–93), portrait and religious painter, had settled in Cincinnati by 1853. Groce and Wallace, *Dictionary of Artists*, 15.
52. Robert Hosea (b. 1811), a Cincinnati merchant and civic promoter running on "strictly independent grounds," narrowly won the special election for the vacancy created by Slough's expulsion. *Biographical Cyclopædia*, 5:1165–66; *Daily Ohio State Journal*, Feb. 10, 1857; *Daily Cincinnati Gazette*, Feb. 17, 18, 1857; Ohio General Assembly, House of Representatives, *Journal*, 52nd Assem., 2nd sess., 1857, 203, 205–6, appen., 102–9.
53. Corwine had turned down a request to run in the special election, leaving the candidacy open for Hosea. Hosea's unofficial majority over Slough on the morning of Feb. 18 stood at ten votes. *Daily Cincinnati Gazette*, Feb. 6, 18, 1857.
54. Stanley Matthews called about the pardon application of James Summons, which had excited general interest. Summons was indicted in 1849 for the murder and attempted murder of family members by means of arsenic-poisoned tea. He came to trial four times before being convicted and sentenced to death in 1852. His conviction hinged on the questionable testimony of a servant girl, and the jury issued its verdict with a recommendation for executive clemency. Chase ended extended judicial appeals and saved Summons, who was in ill health, from hanging on Mar. 10, 1857, by commuting his sentence to life imprisonment. Chase thought highly of this decision and welcomed its wide publicity. "Report on Pardons," 165–66; *Daily Ohio State Journal*, Jan. 16, Feb. 17, 26, Mar. 11, 1857; *Daily Cincinnati Gazette*, Jan. 20, Feb. 16, Mar. 6, 10, 1857; Chase to Col. F. T. Chambers, Mar. 10, 1857, and Chase to T. A. O'Connor, same date (Chase Papers, L.C.); Chase to E. L. Pierce, Mar. 13, 1857 (Houghton Lib., Harvard Univ.).

THURSDAY, FEBRUARY 19. Only stopped at office on Bowler called[55] way to Cars for Cleveland— Wilson conductor very polite[56]—Mr. Powell of Del. & others on cars[57]—reached Cleveland after 3—Angier House[58]—read Lecture—Bradburn—Chase & others called[59]—to Hall with Parsons & others[60]— Lecture well received—gentlemen to Hotel with me—$50—long talk with Bradburn—to bed— Hosea came up today—met him just before taking cars.

FRIDAY, FEBRUARY 20. Awake at 4 with sick headache—quite sick—some vomiting & purging—up little after 6—dressed breakft.—met Mr. Howard of Conn[61]—& Bowler at table— Cars for Cin— Bp. McIlvaine & most interesting conversation— Mr. Livermore & others[62]—read Picciola quite unwell when reached home & remained in house all afternoon & evg— No french tonight

SATURDAY, FEBRUARY 21. At office rather late—nothing unusual there—towards noon Mr. Briggs called—went to dinner with me—talked of sundry matters but nothing of much interest. Mr. French called[63]—wishes me to attend meeting of Board of Wilber-

---

55. Chase inserted the words *Bowler called* above the line, perhaps intending them as a parenthetical comment after *office*. The insertion is located here according to the placement of the words themselves and Chase's caret below them. Nodiah Potter Bowler (b. 1820) was a Cleveland industrialist who became an active Republican after leaving the Democrats in 1856. *Biographical Cyclopædia*, 5:1315–16.
56. Possibly J. S. Wilson, a railroad engineer. *Col. Dir. (1856–57)*, 203.
57. Thomas Watkins Powell (1797–1882), a lawyer and businessman from Delaware, Ohio, had served in the Ohio General Assembly during the 1840s. Taylor, *Columbus and Franklin County*, 2:188–90.
58. A hotel, noted for its cuisine, which opened in 1854. Historical Records Survey, Ohio, *Historic Sites of Cleveland: Hotels and Taverns* (Columbus, 1942), 366–67.
59. George Bradburn and probably James E. Chase (1824–1900), farmer and distant relative of Salmon P. Chase, who served as a Democratic state representative from Stark County, 1858–61. George W. Hill, *History of Ashland County, Ohio* . . . (n.p., 1880), 173; A. J. Baughman, *History of Ashland County, Ohio* . . . (Chicago, 1909), 712.
60. Chase presented his Galileo lecture in the evening at Melodeon Hall. An aide-de-camp on Chase's military staff, Cleveland attorney and Republican politician Richard Chappel Parsons (1826–99) later became collector of internal revenue at Cleveland, 1862–66, marshal of the U.S. Supreme Court, 1867–72, and member of Congress, 1873–75. He and Chase maintained a long friendship. *Cleveland Daily Plain Dealer*, Feb. 19, 20, 1857; Rose, *Cleveland*, 175; *Bio. Dir. U.S. Cong.*, 1614; *Annual Report of Secretary of State*, 1856, 2:359.
61. Mark Howard, Connecticut insurance agent and political figure. Forrest Morgan, ed., *Connecticut As a Colony and As a State* . . . , 4 vols. (Hartford, 1904), 4:219; Howard K. Beale, ed., *Diary of Gideon Welles: Secretary of the Navy Under Lincoln and Johnson* (New York, 1960), 1:78, 81–82, 235, 239, 246; Basler, *Collected Works*, 6:122–23.
62. Possibly Abiel Abbot Livermore (1811–92), a Unitarian clergyman and editor who resided in Cincinnati, 1850–56. *DAB*, 11:303–4.
63. Mansfield French (1810–76), a Methodist Episcopal clergyman and educator, worked at this time as agent for Wilberforce University. He moved to New York in

force University— Contd. $100 to it payt. of sub made some time ago[64] / 50 to Lutheran Ch. $25 to Booth & $25 to Cleveld. Liby. Asso.[65] Pd. Dr. Coulters bill 51.75—Dr. Paul to tea—Mr. Mot & french

SUNDAY, FEBRUARY 22. Rose too late & every thing out of place in consequence—this must not be— Church with Kate & Nettie— Mr. Taylor preached[66]—read Sep. & Clarks Commy.[67]—hope usefully— Church evg. with Kate sermon by Mr. Taylor— Yesterday Mr. French sd. he had felt himself impressed to send me a text of scripture—that many are praying for me—that many hope much from me— God help me to do right.

MONDAY, FEBRUARY 23. At office morning—recollect nothing especial—despatch from Judge Bierce that he will come on Tuesday—callers as usual— Evg. Mr. Mot & French—am making considerable progress. The fête of the Fencibles took place this eve'g[68]—Kate & I there—long talk with Miss Anthony—Deshler invited to refreshments[69]—oysters bad.

TUESDAY, FEBRUARY 24. Passed some time at office this morng—attending to various matters—took 1.05 train for Xenia— Giddings & daughter on cars[70]—also Mr. & Mrs Rice of Boston

---

1858. During the Civil War, French was general agent of the National Freedmen's Relief Association and took a leading role in the instruction of freed slaves at Port Royal, S.C. *Appletons'*, 2:548–49.

64. The abbreviated words are "Contributed," "payment," and "subscription."

65. Chase's letter accompanying his contribution to lawyer Sherman M. Booth appeared in the *Milwaukee Free Democrat* and was reprinted in the *Daily Ohio State Journal*, Mar. 13, 1857. Booth defended fugitive slaves. The Cleveland Library Association, chartered in 1848, numbered five hundred subscribers by 1858 and operated the largest library in the city. *Nat. Cyc.*, 4:305; Van Tassel and Grabowski, *Encyclopedia of Cleveland*, 247.

66. J. Rice Taylor, rector of St. Paul's Church of Mount Vernon, was in Columbus to deliver the seventh and last of a course of "Sermons to the Young" at Trinity Church. *Daily Ohio State Journal*, Feb. 21, 1857; Norman N. Hill, Jr., ed., *History of Knox County, Ohio* . . . (Mt. Vernon, Ohio, 1881), 414.

67. The reference is to the Septuagint and to Clarke, *Holy Bible . . . with Commentary*.

68. The Fencibles, a Columbus military company, received a banner from the "ladies of Columbus" at their armory and marked the occasion with speeches and dancing. *Daily Ohio State Journal*, Feb. 23, 24, 1857.

69. Columbus banker William Green Deshler (1827–1916) became a major Ohio financier and philanthropist. Chase regarded him as a personal friend and enlisted his aid while governor and secretary of the U.S. Treasury. *Nat. Cyc.*, 17:391.

70. Joshua Giddings had two daughters: Lura Maria (1825–71), an antislavery reformer, and Laura (1839–84), who married George Julian in Dec. 1863. George W. Julian, *The Life of Joshua R. Giddings* (Chicago, 1892), 25–26.

introduced by Mr. Wood[71]—carriage from Xenia to Wil. University— Found there Revs Merrick French, Hypes, Wright & others[72]—Bishop Paine[73] & Anderson cold.—meeting of Trustees— Bp Paine spoke well—Prof. Merrick & I occupied same room

WEDNESDAY, FEBRUARY 25. Up very early & breakfast before 7—to Xenia with Revs. Merrick & Dustin[74]— Cars to Columbus— found Rev. Mr. Livermore & Wife[75]—Drake E. F. & Clemets[76] / reached Columbus a little after 10— Office—home to dinner— Messrs Haines Carlisle & Ball called A.M.[77] Ball dined with me— Office in afternoon— Evg. Mr. Mot & French—ride with Ford[78]—& call on Mrs Ford.

71. Possibly William Wood (b. 1808), Cincinnati merchant, Methodist Episcopal benefactor, and one of the incorporators of the Wesleyan Female College in 1852. *Biographical Cyclopædia*, 2:472–74; *Fourth Annual Report of the State Commissioner of Common Schools*, Ohio Exec. Docs. for 1857, 2:158–59.

72. Frederick Merrick (1810–94), Methodist Episcopal clergyman, social reformer, and educator at Ohio Wesleyan University; Mansfield French; probably an unidentified relative of Henry Hypes (1775–1854), a Methodist resident of Xenia; and John Flavel Wright, who chaired the committee that in 1854 had proposed the founding of Wilberforce University. *DAB*, 12:555–56; William Warren Sweet, *Religion on the American Frontier: 1783–1840*, vol. 4, *The Methodists* (Chicago, 1946), 178; Jennings, *Methodist Book Concern*, 99; Daniel A. Payne, "Historical Sketch of Wilberforce University," in *Historical Sketches of the Higher Educational Institutions . . . of the State of Ohio* (n.p., 1876).

73. Daniel Alexander Payne (1811–93), African Methodist Episcopal bishop, served as a trustee of Wilberforce University and became its president in 1863. Alfred Anderson, a member of the African Methodist Episcopal Church at Hamilton, Ohio, was among the original trustees of Wilberforce University. *DAB*, 14:324–25; Daniel A. Payne, *Annual Report and Retrospection of the First Decade of Wilberforce University, June 18, 1873*, reprinted in Payne, *Sermons and Addresses, 1853–1891*, ed. Charles Killian (New York, 1972).

74. M. Dustin (d. 1896), antislavery Methodist Episcopal minister. Conover, *Centennial Portrait*, 1:239.

75. Possibly Elizabeth Dorcas Abbot Livermore (d. 1879), author and wife of Abiel Abbot Livermore. *DAB*, 11:304.

76. Elias Franklin Drake (1813–92), politician and capitalist with an interest in the Columbus & Xenia R.R., continued his career in Minnesota after 1860. William Henry Clement (1815–87), civil engineer and railroad manager, superintended the Columbus & Xenia line. *Nat. Cyc.*, 6:92–93; *Biographical Cyclopædia*, 5:1230; Smith, *Railway Celebrations*, 2:7–9.

77. E. S. Haines, lawyer and for many years surveyor general of the Cincinnati Land Office; George Carlisle (1797–1863), merchant and president of the Lafayette Bank; Flamen Ball. *Cinc. Dir. (1857)*, 139; Carter, *Old Court House*, 90–91; Greve, *Centennial History*, 2:923–25.

78. Thomas H. Ford (1814–68), lawyer and lieutenant governor of Ohio, 1856–58, fought in the Mexican War, supported the American party before becoming a Republican, and commanded an Ohio regiment in the Civil War. A. J. Baughman, *History of Richland County, Ohio, from 1808 to 1908*, 2 vols. (Chicago, 1908), 1:289–90; Duff, *History of North Central Ohio*, 1:626.

February 1857 { 271 }

THURSDAY, FEBRUARY 26. Office in morng—directed invitations to be given to divers—at noon read Picciola & Practical Read[79][—] P.M. Office—pardoned Mrs Andrews son[80]—home towards evg. to dress— Mr. Hubbard came in very early[81]—tea with me—Jewett, Needham[82] & Hubbard first in parlor—company soon arrived—many—some to Kelzey's for liquor—oysters poor—company all gone soon after eleven[83]— Today Pictures self & Sumner for Kate & others for Nettie—

FRIDAY, FEBRUARY 27. Rose 7½—having first read P.R. & repeated hymn—walked far as 4th & State with children— Mendenhall called—at his instance & on papers pardoned Johnson[84]— wrote Mrs Peter[85] & Judge Storer—noon read Picciola— P.M. refused pardon to Fr. Frank[86]—rode with Kate—looked at Mr. Gills house[87]—well built & handsome but not suited to me— Mr. Mot & French—

SATURDAY, FEBRUARY 28. Col Chambers came up today to see me about Summons—of whose various trials he gave me a long & interesting account[88]—Dr. Coulter came in during our conversation / Summons' case interests me much & I think I shall commute his sentence— Studied my French as usual today.

79. Pinney, *First Book in French*. See Feb. 13, above.
80. See Feb. 10, 1857, above.
81. William Blackstone Hubbard (1795–1866), Ohio lawyer, state legislator, banker, capitalist, and Freemason. *Biographical Cyclopædia*, 5:1219–20.
82. Erasmus Needham (b. ca. 1804), farmer and member of the Ohio House from Portage County. Ohio General Assembly, House of Representatives, *Journal*, 52nd Assem., 2nd sess., 1857, appen., 175.
83. "The Governor held a grand Levee last evening at which the Members of the Legislature, State officers, and a large number of our prominent citizens, and several distinguished strangers were present." *Columbus Gazette*, Feb. 27, 1857. "Kelzey's" was apparently William Kelsey's American Hotel.
84. Cyrus Mendenhall urged pardon for Samuel Johnson of Defiance County, sentenced in 1853 to five years in prison for horse theft. Johnson's conviction had been based not on an actual theft but on an intention to steal a horse. Johnson file (Pardon Records, Ohio Hist. Soc.).
85. Sarah Anne Worthington King Peter.
86. Francis Frank, sentenced in 1853 to a five-year sentence for horse theft. Chase refused pardon because of irregularities in the application and the absence of character certification for the two men vouching for Frank's innocence. Frank file (Pardon Records, Ohio Hist. Soc.).
87. Possibly inventor and manufacturer John Loriman Gill (1806–95). *Nat. Cyc.*, 4:89–90.
88. Col. Francis T. Chambers had defended James Summons in a recent appeal before the Ohio Supreme Court. *Daily Cincinnati Gazette*, Jan. 20, 1857; *Daily Ohio State Journal*, Feb. 27, 1857.

SUNDAY, MARCH 1. Was not out at all today—intended going to Church at night but a storm came up & the weather was inclement— Read life of Sam. Lewis & wrote his son[89]— What a noble man he was—but he had infirmities which are held back from view— perhaps best so & who are we that judge—

MONDAY, MARCH 2. To the office this morning as usual & in thee afternoon—nothing but routine business— Ev'g Mr. Mot came—& we had our French reading & talk—there is manifest improvement I think.

TUESDAY, MARCH 3. Today at office nothing unusual—recd. letters from Trumbull & Wade—former abt election of Judges to Congress—latter fulminating his discontent with existing state of things.[90] Trumbull is cool, logical, sagacious— Wade earnest, strong in perception, & bold— Swayne's this ev'g—pleasant—Mr. Mot & Mr. Corrie[91]—conservative & radical.

WEDNESDAY, MARCH 4. To office as usual— Mr. McAllister & Col Dickey called[92]—former confidential friend of Gov. Geary[93]—latter Pierce & Douglass emigrant fr. N.H. to Kansas now Republican— former said he shd. demand of Mr. Buchanan fulfilt. of promises by Pierce or withdrawal of U.S. forces & leave people to fight it out

---

89. William G. W. Lewis thanked Chase for expressing a "favorable" opinion of his *Biography of Samuel Lewis,* although Chase evidently questioned the absence of a clear endorsement of his own conduct. Lewis enunciated his authorial aim "not to bring charges against others (or to defend them), but to vindicate my father's position and course." He noted that his father gave Chase "full credit for purity of purpose, & integrity of principle." W. G. W. Lewis to Chase, Mar. 16, 1857 (Chase Papers, L.C.).

90. Lyman Trumbull (1813–96), Democratic and later Republican U.S. senator from Illinois, 1855–73, and a justice of the state supreme court before his election, wrote Chase about the election of state judges to Congress and discussed the situation in Kansas. It is uncertain whether the "fulminating" Wade was Benjamin, agitated over Democratic party manuevers and the recipient of appeals from Ohio Republicans requesting his help in the next state campaign, or Edward. Trumbull to Chase, Feb. 28, 1857, Edward Wade to Chase, Nov. 21, 1857 (Chase Papers, Hist. Soc. of Pa.); *DAB,* 19:19–20; Trefousse, *Benjamin Franklin Wade,* 104–6, 337.

91. Doubtless William M. Corry.

92. Richard McAllister, deputy secretary in the Kansas Executive Office, foiled an assassination attempt on John Geary. Milton C. Dickey, a colonel under a commission from the Executive Committee of the Kansas Territory, was prominent in the settlement of Topeka. Both men represented free state interests. *Kansas Historical Collections,* 4:656, 708, 6:257, 9:468, 13:138, 150, 156, 166–258, 16:765, 773; F. W. Giles, *Thirty Years in Topeka: A Historical Sketch* (Topeka, Kans., 1886), 20–22, 88, 266, 334; John H. Gihon, *Geary and Kansas, Governor Geary's Administration in Kansas . . .* (Philadelphia, 1857), 233–35.

93. Soldier and Pennsylvania politician John White Geary (1819–73), who on this day resigned the territorial governorship of Kansas. *DAB,* 7:203–4.

on pain of Demc. displeasure[94]—tea at Mr. Kelsey's— Mr. Mot & french conversan. no reading—

THURSDAY, MARCH 5. Med. &c before rising— Very pleasant & I hope beneficial / Not much done at office—too many callers—am'g them Corwine & Hosea— Evening went to Mr. Conways' lecture on Success which very good but not the best he can[95]—Kate with me— bro't Kate home—went for Mr. Eaton & took him to small party, at Mr. Halls[96] Mr. Case & his daughter & grd dr Mrs Willets & Miss W of Auburn N.Y.— Appd. Seymour G. Renick Judge / letter today fr S. W.[97]

FRIDAY, MARCH 6. Up as usual after some med. &c & reading a little French—to Office abt. 9—little done—m'nt to dispose of Summons case but did not— Judge Palmer called[98]—Mr. Conway & Mr. Mrs & Miss Hosea[99]—long talk with Judge P—thinks I shd. have increased vote in N.W. counties—Mr. Conway dined with me— to office finished letter to Mrs Rantoul[1]— Recd. Mrs Eastmans letter[2] / at J. H. Smith's[3] ev'g &c—Miss Anthony—pleasant time.

94. This passage touching on the Kansas situation refers to the policies of Stephen A. Douglas and Democratic presidents Franklin Pierce (1804–69) and James Buchanan (1791–1868). *DAB*, 3:207–14; 14:576–80.

95. Moncure D. Conway discoursed on the subject of "Success" upon the invitation of Chase and many members of the General Assembly. *Daily Ohio State Journal*, Mar. 4, 6, 1857.

96. Possibly Frank Hall, proprietor of the Broadway Exchange, who resided eight miles north of Columbus. *Col. Dir. (1856–57)*, 99.

97. Susan Walker. In the original, the words *letter today fr. S. W.* appear above the words *him to small party, at*. Chase probably inserted the phrase there because he had run out of space at the bottom of the entry and found the next closest place with sufficient room for an interlineation.

98. John M. Palmer, court of common pleas judge in northwestern Ohio, 1852– 57. Notebook, 1857 election, and Palmer to Chase, June 17, 1861 (Chase Papers, L.C.); Gilkey, *Ohio Hundred Year Book*, 554.

99. Harriet Newell Moore Hosea (d. 1875), artist and miniaturist, married Robert Hosea in 1836. The couple had ten children. *Biographical Cyclopædia*, 5:1165; Groce and Wallace, *Dictionary of Artists*, 328; Greve, *Centennial History*, 1:932.

1. Jane Elizabeth Woodbury Rantoul (1807–70) of Beverly, Mass., widow of Robert Rantoul (1805–52), Massachusetts attorney, reformer, and antislavery Democrat. Robert S. Rantoul, "Some Material for a History of the Name and Family of Rentoul-Rintoul-Rantoul," *Essex Institute Historical Collections* 21 (1884): 268; *DAB*, 15:381–82.

2. Charlotte ("Lottie") Sewall Eastman was the widow of Ben C. Eastman (1812– 56), a Wisconsin attorney who served in Congress, 1851–55, as a Democrat with free-soil leanings. Both he and her husband had New England antecedents. Chase maintained an affectionate correspondence with her, and also saw her in Washington, D.C., where she sometimes spent the winter, and at Beverly, Mass., where she made extended visits to the home of her friend Jane Rantoul. Guy S. Rix, *History and Genealogy of the Eastman Family of America* (Concord, N.H., 1901), 463; *Bio. Dir. U.S. Cong.*, 946; *Dictionary of Wisconsin Biography* (Madison, Wis., 1960), 113; John R. Berryman, ed., *History of the Bench and Bar of Wisconsin* (Chicago, 1898), 2:186–87; B. Eastman to Chase, Oct. 20, 1855 (Chase Papers, L.C.).

3. James Haddock Smith.

SATURDAY, MARCH 7. At office as usual   Committee came to invite me with other state officers to attend meeting in Senate Chamber in reference to receiving remains of Dr. kane[4] / attended— Committees appd.—conversation with Mr. Kelley—determd. by meeting that Remains be placed in Senate Chamber arr Sunday—& that Committees go to Xenia to meet them—Mr. Dennison tendered free tickets on Railroad—recd. & ansd. despatches from Cin on this subject.

SUNDAY, MARCH 8. At Church, Trinity in morning—very few present most hearing Mr. Conway or attending Services at Senate Chamber—glad I went—Miss Louise Jones walked home with us— her father very ill[5]—went to see Kanes at Neil House—Col. T. L. Mr. R. P. & Dr. Mr. Morton also with them[6]— Ev'g Mr. Conway & Mr. Eaton called—after tea went to Church Universalist & heard Mr. Conway[7]

MONDAY, MARCH 9. Children went down to witness ceremonies—followed soon in another carriage (Mr. Nevins)—rode in process[ion] Gen. Haris with me—Mr. Rice with Gen. Glenn[8]— Officers called from Cin Mr. Jones, Mr. Weisner Mr. Thorp—with them C.

---

4. Elisha Kent Kane (1820–57), physician and Arctic explorer, gained fame during the 1850s for his polar explorations. His second trip broke his health, and he died in Cuba. An elaborate funeral journey that transported his remains up the Mississippi and Ohio rivers and overland by railroad from Cincinnati to Philadelphia elicited numerous tributes. *DAB*, 10:256–57; George W. Corner, *Doctor Kane of the Arctic Seas* (Philadelphia, 1972), 252–57; William Elder, *Biography of Elisha Kent Kane* (Philadelphia, 1858), 285–387.

5. I. G. Jones (1807–57), a Columbus physician, died six days later on Mar. 14. *Daily Ohio State Journal*, Mar. 14, 20, 1857.

6. Three of Elisha Kent Kane's brothers accompanied the funeral party at its stop in Columbus: Thomas Leiper Kane (1822–83), Philadelphia lawyer, Free-Soil party activist, Mormon advocate, and Civil War general; Robert Patterson Kane (1827–1906), Philadelphia lawyer; and John Kintzing Kane, Jr. (1833–86), a physician who lived principally in Wilmington, Del. William Morton (b. 1822?), Artic explorer, had been Kane's personal aide. Corner, *Doctor Kane*, 7, 16–17, 126, 252, 254, 275; *DAB*, 10:258–59.

7. Moncure D. Conway preached on this day at the Columbus Universalist Church. *Daily Ohio State Journal*, Jan. 21, Feb. 28, Mar. 7, 1857.

8. The obsequies in Columbus for Kane included a sermon preached in the Ohio Senate Chamber where the body lay in state and a procession of officials and citizens that conducted the casket to the railroad depot. Chase rode in the procession with his staff, including Adjutant General Sullivan D. Harris, editor and proprietor of the *Ohio Cultivator*, and Quartermaster General Alexander Ewing Glenn (1811–72), who came to prominence in Ohio as a leader of the Odd Fellow's Society and published *The Ark*, its weekly journal. *Daily Ohio State Journal*, Mar. 7, 9, 1857; *History of Franklin and Pickaway Counties*, 164, 553–54; Lee, *Columbus*, 1:471; *Col. Dir. (1856–57)*, 40, 46, 91, 103.

Anderson[9]— P.M. not at office busy preparing decision in Summons case—asked through Mr. Rice Col Swayne for opinion—he thinks Reprieve Stat shd. be followed[10]

THURSDAY, APRIL 16. Up late not having heard the first bell—to office unshaved—J. M. Brown called[11]—& divers others—sent messages to Senate appg Reemelin, Foot & Ladd Comms Reform School[12]— Engaged whole morng in talk—Brown to dinner with me—pardoned Glass sent pardon to Mrs Janney & wrote Kebler[13]— Mattoon called abt house A.M. Talked with Swayne abt. Snowdens

FRIDAY, APRIL 17. Up a little earlier—shaved—spent sometime in H R urging passage Statistics Bill—& advising with members as to slaveholding & kidnapping bill & arsenal bill & other matters[14]—

9. Cincinnatians John D. Jones (1797–1878), dry-goods merchant associated with the Lafayette Bank, railroad development, and charitable work; Thomas H. Weasner, city council member and lumber merchant; and probably William A. Thorp, real estate broker, escorted Kane's remains to Columbus. Charles Anderson (1814–95), who formally presented the remains to the Columbus funeral committee, championed black rights as a lawyer in Dayton and Cincinnati and as a state senator. He commanded a regiment during the Civil War, was elected lieutenant governor in 1863, and completed the term of deceased Gov. John Brough. *Cincinnati Daily Gazette*, Feb. 3, Mar. 7, 11, 1857; *Cinc. Dir. (1857)*, 255, 271; *Biographical Cyclopædia*, 3:704–5, 6:1506–8; Sobel and Raimo, *Biographical Directory of Governors*, 3:1210–11.

10. For Summons's case see Feb. 18, 1857, above. There are no entries in Journal VII for Mar. 10 through Apr. 15. Instructions for a medicinal dosage, not in Chase's hand, fill the space for Mar. 14.

11. Northwestern Ohio merchant James Monroe Brown (1818–67) was an antislavery advocate and Liberty and Republican party activist. *Biographical Cyclopædia*, 3:792–93; Brown to Chase, Feb. 6, 1860 (Chase Papers, L.C.).

12. Chase's message, dated Apr. 17, appointed Charles Reemelin, John A. Foote, and James D. Ladd commissioners under the act to provide for the establishment of reform schools. Ohio General Assembly, Senate, *Journal*, 52nd Assem., 2nd sess., 1857, 465–67; Chase to Reemelin, Apr. 21, 1857 (Chase Papers, L.C.).

13. German immigrant William Glass of Hamilton County had been convicted of arson in 1851 and sentenced to ten years in prison. His Sunday school teacher, Mrs. R. A. S. Janney, and his Cincinnati attorney, John Kebler, had both urged his pardon. Kebler later managed business affairs for Chase's friend, Susan Walker. Glass file (Pardon Records, Ohio Hist. Soc.); "Report on Pardons," 167–68; *Cinc. Dir. (1857)*, 172; Kebler to Chase, Mar. 4, 1862 (Chase Papers, L.C.).

14. On this day the Ohio House of Representatives passed a bill establishing a state commissioner of statistics, action urged by Chase in his annual message, and the Senate approved the measure. The House also passed bills to "prevent slaveholding and kidnapping in Ohio" and for construction of a state arsenal. Other significant legislation considered on this final full day of the session addressed the code of civil procedure, the organization of cities and incorporated villages, the duties of county commissioners, the property rights of women, and the U.S. Supreme Court's Dred Scott decision. Ohio General Assembly, House of Representatives, *Journal*, 52nd Assem., 2nd sess., 1857, 550–72; "Draft of Message to the Ohio General Assembly," [Jan. 1857] (Chase Papers, Hist. Soc. of Pa.).

called on Col. Benton at Neil House—Corry with him[15]— Appd. Coggeshall Librarian, Anthony, Director S. Lun Asym[16]—pardoned Dowes, Alder & Dent[17]— Bennet says Bingham warm for me[18]— *Night*—bills passed—appointed Dennison, Townshend & Cook Comms Idiots[19] & Mansfield Commr. Statistics[20]—home near midnight after very busy day

SATURDAY, APRIL 18. Members going off today—Several came in to get portraits which gave them—Hunter[21] Jewett, Brayton & others—several democrats called to take leave. [Beekman] about Ha[ynes] case[22]—

FRIDAY, MAY 1. Bad morn'g—troubled by vain imagining—began letter to Sumner before going to Capitol—finished it there[23]—

15. Thomas Hart Benton delivered a public lecture in Columbus on the evening of Apr. 17. His other visitor may have been William M. Corry. *Daily Ohio State Journal,* Apr. 14, 17, 1857.
16. Charles Anthony accepted his unanimous appointment as trustee of the Southern Lunatic Asylum. Ohio General Assembly, Senate, *Journal,* 52nd Assem., 2nd sess., 1857, 466; Anthony to Chase, Apr. 21, 1857 (Chase Papers, Ohio Hist. Soc.).
17. William Dowes, "seventy years of age, and very feeble," had been sentenced in 1853 to life imprisonment for second degree murder. Thomas Alder had been convicted of rape and sentenced in 1851 to ten years in prison. Chase pardoned him because circumstances disclosed since his trial cast doubt upon his guilt. In 1854 Alfred W. Dent had been sentenced to fifteen years imprisonment for assault with intent to kill. Chase pardoned him upon evidence that the other party had provoked his actions. "Report on Pardons," 168; Dowes, Alder, and Dent files (Pardon Records, Ohio. Hist. Soc.).
18. Probably a reference to John Armor Bingham (1815–1900), a Tuscarawas County lawyer, Republican congressman, 1855–63, 1865–73, judge advocate of the army and special judge advocate in the trial of the Lincoln assassination conspirators, and U.S. minister to Japan, 1873–85. *DAB,* 2:277–78.
19. The Senate confirmed the appointments of William Dennison, Jr., Norton S. Townshend, and Asher Cook (1823–92), lawyer, education advocate, and leading Republican in Wood County, as trustees of the Ohio State Asylum for idiots, which opened in Columbus in rented buildings. *Men of Northwestern Ohio: A Collection of Portraits and Biographies . . .* (Bowling Green and Toledo, 1898), 42; Cook to Chase, Apr. 24, 1857, and Dennison to Chase, Apr. 25, 1857 (Chase Papers, Ohio Hist. Soc.); Gilkey, *Ohio Hundred Year Book,* 713; Ohio General Assembly, Senate, *Journal,* 52nd Assem., 2nd sess., 1857, 467.
20. Edward D. Mansfield, after some indecision, accepted his appointment as Ohio's commissioner of statistics. Mansfield to Chase, Apr. 22, 1857 (Chase Papers, L.C.); Mansfield to Chase, Apr. 25, 1857 (Chase Papers, Ohio Hist. Soc.); Ohio General Assembly, Senate, *Journal,* 52nd Assem., 2nd sess., 1857, 466–67.
21. John Hunter (b. ca. 1818), collier and representative from Columbiana County. Ohio General Assembly, House of Representatives, *Journal,* 52nd Assem., 2nd sess., 1857, appen., 175.
22. Possibly a reference to Daniel A. Haynes (1815–c. 1896), lawyer, politician, and judge of the state superior court of Montgomery County, 1856–70. *History of Montgomery County,* 478–79; Conover, *Centennial Portrait,* 1:177–78; Drury, *Dayton and Montgomery County,* 1:780–81.
23. This letter discussed the situation in Kansas, political ramifications of the Dred Scott case, and Chase's views on running for reelection. Chase to Charles Sumner, May 1, 1857 (Houghton Lib., Harvard Univ.).

also wrote S. W.[24] amid interruptions— Tompkins called with Bascomb[25]—also Walker with Robeson of Lafayette[26]—wrote Wiswell N.Y. & Roosevelt & Co[27]—Courier d'Etats Unis with list of books[28]— P.M. Wright called abt portrait for banknote—also Jones & Morton same[29]— French with Pr. Mot—rd. today Spencer, French & Papers[30]—little office work ex routine

SATURDAY, MAY 16. Came up from Cincinnati on cars[31]—with Kate—arrived at 10—transacted usual business at office—no occurrences of special note—found Mr. Pierce awaiting my arrival— pleasant talk with—going East to publish law book[32]

SUNDAY, MAY 17. To church with Katie & Mr. Pierce—Sermon from Mr. Reynolds & passed Dr. Morton coming home[33]—"Why were you not at Church—dinner—siesta— Kate & Mr. P—— talked about me & various persons—Kate sprightly & intelligent & right

24. Susan Walker.
25. Cydnor Bailey Tompkins (1810–62) was an attorney, Ohio Republican politician, and U.S congressman, 1857–61. Vermont native William T. Bascom (b. ca. 1813), lawyer, clerk of the Ohio senate, 1856–58, and an Ohio Republican party secretary in 1857, edited the *Ohio State Journal*, 1849–56. *Bio. Dir. U.S. Cong.*, 1946; Ohio General Assembly, House of Representatives, *Journal*, 52nd Assem., 2nd sess., 1857, appen., 173; *History of Franklin and Pickaway Counties*, 160; Lee, *Columbus*, 1:463, 489; Robertson, *History of Morgan County*, 265; *Daily Ohio State Journal*, Aug. 12, 13, 1857.
26. James Walker, a Rhode Island political friend of Chase, maintained a business interest at Lafayette, Ind. He probably introduced John Peter Robison (b. 1811), a merchant and banker trained in medicine who moved from Lafayette to Cleveland in 1857. Walker to Chase, Oct. 3, 1859 (Chase Papers, L.C.); *Biographical Cyclopædia*, 2:330–32.
27. Probably William Wiswell, who maintained a free art gallery in Cincinnati during the 1850s. Roosevelt & Son, Importers of New York, had supplied information on British plate glass at the request of a state investigating committee examining construction contracts for the Ohio State House. Robert C. Vitz, *The Queen City and the Arts: Cultural Life in Nineteenth-Century Cincinnati* (Kent, Ohio, 1989), 48; *Columbus Gazette*, Jan. 23, 1857.
28. Chase was probably ordering a list of French books from the New York foreign-language newspaper. *Courrier des États-Unis*, May 1, 1857.
29. Chase's visitors were likely James Wright, banknote engraver engaged with Danforth, Wright & Co; George T. Jones (b. ca. 1818), engraver, who worked as a banknote company agent in Cincinnati, 1849–59; and Edmund Morton, miniaturist, or J. N. Morton, engraver. Groce and Wallace, *Dictionary of Artists*, 164, 357, 456–57, 705; *Daily Ohio State Journal*, May 30, 1857; Jones to Chase, Apr. 4, June 24, 1863 (Chase Papers, L.C.).
30. In the back of this diary, Chase copied twenty-one quotations from Edmund Spenser's *The Faerie Queene*, Book V, Cantos ix–xii, and Book VI, Cantos iii, v, vii–x.
31. Chase left Columbus on May 6 "for a brief visit to Cincinnati." *Daily Ohio State Journal*, May 7, 1857.
32. Edward Lillie Pierce, *A Treatise on American Railroad Law* (New York, 1857).
33. Dr. George R. Morton, from Sandusky City, was corresponding clerk in the state auditor's office. *Annual Report of Secretary of State*, 1856, 2:360; notebook, 1857 election (Chase Papers, L.C.).

minded—they to church / I read Spencer & Bossuet[34]—tea—much talk with Mr P on various subjects—

MONDAY, MAY 18. Mr. Pierce left this morning—seems afd. to do much for me for fear of being called Chase's hanger on— Dennison & Platt called abt. Arsenal & Peny. lot[35]— Neeramer & Savage abt. guns / sold parcel pay $1100 to Savage[36]—read Choquet[37]—Bible—Spencer— Follet called—talk abt. Gov [&c]— seems to think I shd. have declined last winter—perhaps so—began letter to S. W.[38]— Follet[t] says Bowen at old tricks[39]—tea—Mr. Mot—french talk & reading—read Dialogues[40]—devotion as usual—bed—

TUESDAY, MAY 19. To office pretty early after usual devotion, reading &c / rode down with Kate who not quite well but went to school— Crosson & Dr. Meng from Paulding called—wanted

34. The entry for July 12, 1857 (below) and a notation among Chase's miscellaneous memoranda at the end of this journal indicate that he was reading the *Oraisons Funèbres* (Funeral Orations) of Jacques-Bénigne Bossuet, originally published in the 1600s.

35. In Mar. 1856 the General Assembly authorized the governor to sell "portions of the Old Penitentiary Lot in the City of Columbus." Chase appointed Columbus businessman and civic promoter William Augustus Platt (1809–82) one of three appraisers of the parcel in June 1857. The property sold at auction in August, its proceeds to assist construction of a new state arsenal. Taylor, *Columbus and Franklin County*, 2:181–82; Chase to Platt et al., June 5, 1857, C. P. Wolcott to L. L. Rice, Sept. 9, 1857 (Chase Papers, Ohio Hist. Soc.); Thomas Comstock, "To Vacate certain Streets and Alleys in the Old Penitentiary Lot" (Chase Papers, L.C.); *Columbus Gazette*, May 29, July 17, Aug. 28, 1857.

36. John F. Neereamer, confectioner and superintendent of the state arsenal, oversaw an effort to collect state armaments. William Montgomery Savage (1814–92), a jeweler, assisted with this collection and purchased parcels of unwanted weapons. See, for example, May 21, 1857, below. *Col. Dir. (1856–57)*, 161, 178; Chase to Neereamer, May 2, 27, 1857 (Chase Papers, L.C.); Lee, *Columbus*, 2:805–7.

37. Apparently a reference to Gustave Choquet, author of *First Lessons in Learning French* (New York, 1857) and *Easy Conversations in French* (New York, 1858). A memorandum at the end of Journal VII associates the name Choquet with the title "Rhetoric," although a work by Choquet with that title has not been located. Other entries from this period mention "Rhetoric" or "French Rhetoric," and it seems likely that those references are to a volume by Choquet which Chase used in his study of French.

38. Susan Walker.

39. In June 1856, Chase appointed Ozias Bowen (1805–71), president judge of the Ohio Court of Common Pleas, 1838–51, to a vacancy on the Ohio Supreme Court. Bowen voted for Lincoln as a delegate at the 1860 Republican convention. *Biographical Cyclopædia*, 3:731–32; *History of Seneca County, Ohio*... (Chicago, 1886), 300; Gilkey, *Ohio Hundred Year Book*, 473.

40. Exact title unknown. Two copies of French *Dialogues*, otherwise undescribed, were on a list of Chase's books which may date from the early 1860s. "Books in Loveland belonging to Hon S. P. Chase" (Chase Papers, L.C.).

Commn. as Notary for F. S. Cable[41]—J. Cable at Van Wert[42] / Dr. Prime & others from N.Y.[43]—dined—read Spencer 3 canto[es] today / to depot for Nettie—did not come—Wilson [Mass] at office to tea with me[44]—bid him goodbye at Schoulers—called Dr. Smiths[45]—Miss Anthony—l fr. S. W. w. her[46]—also R. & [M]

WEDNESDAY, MAY 20. After usual morning duties & occupations went to office where very little was accomplished—some letters written & some recd.—newspapers—callers &c &c—dinner—read a little after—then Katie & I to depot for Nettie who did not come—to office & little done—tea—Mr. Mot & french in evening

THURSDAY, MAY 21. Pain Quotidien[47]—Bible—prayer—breakft Spencer—with Katie to office—correspondence—few callers— Bascom abt Circular[48]—suggested modifications—l. fr Mansfield abt Sci. & Hockg. Valley R.R. Co.[49]—sold for state lot old arms to

---

41. John Crosson, hotel keeper, and Dr. A. P. Meng, dry goods merchant, started businesses about this time at Paulding, Ohio. Crosson, who transported a convict to the Ohio Penitentiary, made this trip to Columbus on official state business. Fielding S. Cable edited or published two different newspapers in Paulding, 1856–65. Winter, *Northwest Ohio*, 1:536, 540; *Detailed Statement of Receipts*, 1857, 2:424.

42. Joseph Cable (1801–80), Ohio newspaper publisher and Democratic member of the U.S. House of Representatives, 1849–53, relocated in 1857 to Van Wert. *Bio. Dir. U.S. Cong.*, 724; Lewis Cass Aldrich, ed., *History of Erie County, Ohio . . .* (Syracuse, N.Y., 1889), 182.

43. Probably either Samuel Irenæus Prime, D.D. (1812–85), a Presbyterian clergyman who edited the *New York Observer* from 1851 until his death, or his brother Edward Dorr Griffin Prime (1814–91), also a Presbyterian clergyman, who once studied medicine and contributed for many years to the *New York Observer*. *DAB*, 15:227–28; *Appletons'*, 5:122–23.

44. Henry Wilson was on a "Western tour." *Daily Ohio State Journal*, May 20, 1857.

45. Physician Samuel Mitchel Smith (1816–74), active in antislavery and Republican politics, served during the Civil War as surgeon general of Ohio. For eighteen years, beginning during Chase's tenure as governor, Smith sat as a trustee of the Central Ohio Lunatic Asylum. Robson, *Biographical Encyclopædia*, 400–401; *Col. Dir. (1856–57)*, 186.

46. Chase meant that he received a letter from Susan Walker and also wrote her.

47. Literally, "Daily Bread." This is the first of several references in this journal to *Pain Quotidien*, apparently meaning a French devotional work with passages for each day, such as *Pain Quotidien pour les Chrétiens* (New York, [1851]) or *Pain Quotidien de la Conscience, ou, Passages de l'Ecriture Sainte, Choisis pour s'Examiner Tous les Jours de l'Année* (Toulouse, 1853).

48. This comment refers to a response being prepared to a "circular of the 10th instant" from the secretary of the U.S. Treasury. The secretary's annual report included information about the states that may have been gathered through the circular. ——— to Howell Cobb, May 20, 1857 (Chase Papers, Ohio Hist. Soc.); *Report of the Secretary of the Treasury, on the State of the Finances, For the Year Ending June 30, 1857*, 35th Cong., 1st sess., 1857, S. Ex. Doc. 1.

49. Edward D. Mansfield, in his capacity as commissioner of statistics, reported on the Scioto and Hocking Valley Railroad. The company responsible for building this line between Newark and Portsmouth, chartered in 1849, had not completed

Savage— Neereamer made report abt. collection[50] / dinner—nap— Spencer—French Rhetoric[51]—office— Rice handed me certif deposit proceeds arms—w. Arthur Wiley Washn. Co[52]—Ralston Sk. not protest Allston note &c[53]—tea at Dr. Smiths—Notre Dame de Paris[54]—bed

FRIDAY, MAY 22. P. Qn.— B— p[55]— repeating hymns while dressing—need better thoughts on awaking & before rising— Spencer— Office Messrs Wood & Pond abt commuting sentence[56] / Deshler abt deposit—will give 5% & bond— Neereamer made rept.—dinner—read Rhet. & Notre Dame—office—wrote short Article on Demy. in morning—copied now— Called Schouler's handed it to him[57]—recd. Squatter Sovn fr McBratney[58]—tea—Mr. Mot & Fr.

---

the work and was in financial trouble. Mansfield to Chase, May 20, 1857 (Chase Papers, L.C.); Albert Adams Graham, comp., *History of Fairfield and Perry Counties, Ohio* (Chicago, 1883), 83–85.

50. William Savage purchased $1267.82 worth of state arms. J. F. Neereamer received $39.50 for "25 days labor and drayage" related to the "storage and care of public arms." Chase to Savage, May 21, 1857 (Chase Papers, Ohio Hist. Soc.); *Detailed Statement of Receipts*, 1857, 2:442.

51. See the note on Gustave Choquet at May 18 above.

52. Chase apparently asked Arthur Wiley, collector at Harmar for the Muskingum Improvement, to file proper documentation for his bonds. Wiley to Chase, May 26, 1857 (Chase Papers, Ohio Hist. Soc.); *Annual Report of Secretary of State*, 1856, 2:361; *Detailed Statement of Receipts*, 1857, 2:324.

53. By a mortgage agreement between Montgomery P. Alston and Chase, Alston could void the transfer of some Butler County property to Chase by presenting two promissory notes for $333.33, one in May 1857 and the other a year later. Alston and Chase, mortgage documents, Dec. 30, 1856, Jan. 8, 1857 (Chase Papers, L.C.).

54. Victor Marie Hugo, *Notre-Dame de Paris* (Paris, 1836).

55. "Pain Quotidien— Bible— prayer—"

56. Frederick W. Wood, a McConnelsville lawyer later active in Ohio Republican politics, and Francis Bates Pond (1825–83), Morgan County prosecuting attorney, 1852–61, saw Chase on the subject of clemency for the brothers Jonas and Phillip Fouts. See May 25, 1857, entry. Robertson, *History of Morgan County*, 258–61; Fouts file (Pardon Records, Ohio Hist. Soc.).

57. This almost certainly refers to an article which appeared the following day in the *Daily Ohio State Journal* under the heading "Men Change Often—Principles Never!" The piece focused on national politics and attacked "the present administration party" for using the name "Democracy." *Daily Ohio State Journal*, May 23, 1857.

58. Robert McBratney (d. 1881), an editor of the *Xenia Torch-Light* until Jan. 1857, purchased the *Squatter Sovereign* of Atchison, Kans., and converted it from a proslavery to a Free State newspaper. He sold his interest later in 1857, then participated in Kansas politics and business ventures. McBratney to Chase, Aug. 3, 1849, June 7, 1850, June 20, 1851 (Chase Papers, L.C.); *Xenia Torch-Light*, Jan. 7, 1857; *Daily Ohio State Journal*, May 23, 1857; *Transactions of the Kansas Historical Society . . . 1875–1881*, 164; ibid., 1901–1902, 376–77; *Collections of the Kansas State Historical Society 1923–1925 . . .* , 674.

May 1857   { 281 }

SATURDAY, MAY 23. Rose ½ p 5— r. h. d— Pn. Q— B[59]— resolved to do more official work—to office after b. Deshler called—with bond—attended to correspondence—read papers—far from fulfilling resolutions—dined—read Rhet. & N.D.—office—nothing done— Schouler called—rode with him—says Wilson said he told [Seward] Chase strongest—tea—read—to Mrs Parsons French circle[60]—lemonade—headache—soda—bed.

SUNDAY, MAY 24. Up late & with remains of headache—thoughts not clear— After b. took up Bo.[61] Surprised most agreeably by entrance of my old friend Elliott[62]—he to church with us—dinner long talk after not so profitable as might—tea— Schouler & Walker came in—more talk & less profitable—after they went read Bo—[pr]—lamented misapplication of time.

MONDAY, MAY 25. Rose early r. h.—d.— P. Q— B— b. R. 8 pa[63] wrote two last days mema.—to office—made some progress in examining Fouts application but much interrupted[64]—sent word to Journal abt. going to Marietta[65]—wrote Parsons & others / dinner—reading after—office late— Eliot went away in morn[']g— Mot & French evg. read several chapters Notre Dame—

TUESDAY, MAY 26. Rose later than yesterday— r. h. d— P. Q.— B— R——— seven or 8 pages— office—nearly same employments as

59. "Repeated hymns while dressing— Pain Quotidien— Bible—"
60. Jane Swan Parsons, wife of George M. Parsons, was the daughter of an Ohio judge. *History of Franklin and Pickaway Counties,* 65, 528.
61. "Breakfast" and "Bossuet."
62. Thomas Dawes Eliot had arrrived in Columbus on May 23. *Daily Ohio State Journal,* May 25, 1857.
63. "Repeated hymns while dressing— Pain Quotidien— Bible— breakfast." According to Chase's memoranda at the end of the journal, *R* means "Rhetoric Choquet" (see May 18 above).
64. In April, Jonas and Phillip Fouts had been convicted of first degree murder and sentenced to death. Their case caused a sensation because the victim had been a notorious rake known to have had sexual liaisons with the wife of Jonas Fouts. The brothers, widely regarded as "ignorant," allegedly had acted in response to inducements from a third party who escaped indictment. The Ohio Supreme Court handed down a writ of error a few days before their scheduled execution, obviating a final decision by Chase on the question of clemency. Fouts file (Pardon Records, Ohio Hist. Soc.); *Daily Cincinnati Gazette,* June 26, 1857.
65. The following day, the *Daily Ohio State Journal* announced that Chase would travel later in the week to Marietta by way of Zanesville and the Muskingum River to receive government officials and other visitors at "The Great Railroad Celebration." This June celebration commemorated the completion of a railroad chain from Baltimore to St. Louis and included festivities at many sites. *Daily Ohio State Journal,* May 26, 1857; Smith, *Railway Celebrations,* esp. 1:v–vi.

yesterday—letters &c—dinner—& reading as usual—disappointed about Dr. Smiths coming out—went for Nettie—disappointed—tea—reading &c

WEDNESDAY, MAY 27. Same morning as usual—Dr. Smith came out advice about eyes—nothing of much interest today—

FRIDAY, MAY 29. Very busy today without accomplishing much—teld. to ascertain when meeting Stckhdrs PC & L[66]—learned it will be Monday / Expected Mr. Hanna by evg train—did not arrive—talk with A. P. Stone abt. proceedings stckhdrs[67] / wrote Hanna— Schouler, Coggeshall & Caldwell left for Zanesville by boat train[68]—

SATURDAY, MAY 30. To Zanesville by 1 AM train—arrived soon after 4—lay down ½ hour—bkft—boat Charley Bowen,[69] Ck old man Dexter— Schouler, Caldwell, Coggeshall with me—Kauffman & others to see us off[70]— Misty, rainy cold trip[,] glimpses of warm sunshine— Lewis Putnam. Huntington of Waterford & others— gave decision in Fouts case to attorneys— Marietta—David Putnam—Mayor Whittelsey and others[71]—quartered with B. Gates— called Kendrick[72]— Many callers evg.

SUNDAY, MAY 31. At Church morng congl.—good sermon old church edifice—almost coeval with settlement—wrote some of address—PM Church Episcopal[73]—excellent discourse—Character Christ—tea with Prof Kendrick / home abt 8—wrote a little & bed—

---

66. Pittsburgh, Cincinnati, and Louisville Telegraph Company.
67. In June 1857, Chase appointed dry goods merchant and former Democratic congressman Alfred Parish Stone (1813–65) treasurer of Ohio. *Bio. Dir. U.S. Cong.*, 1881; *Col. Dir. (1856–57)*, 189.
68. Prominent Cincinnatian John D. Caldwell (1816–1902) covered the railroad celebrations in Ohio as editor of the *Cincinnati Gazette*. Greve, *Centennial History*, 2:895–96; Smith, *Railway Celebrations*, 1:184.
69. A sternwheel steamboat of 152 tons built in 1856. Lytle, *Merchant Vessels*, 30.
70. S. H. Kauffman, Ohio Canal collector at Zanesville, later became a U.S. Treasury clerk. *Annual Report of Secretary of State*, 1856, 2:360; Kauffman to Chase, Sept. 9, 1861 (Chase Papers, L.C.); *Register of Officers (1863)*, 18.
71. William Augustus Whittlesey (1796–1866), Marietta politician and former congressman, 1849–51. *Bio. Dir. U.S. Cong.*, 2046; *History of Washington County, Ohio . . . 1788–1881* (Cleveland, 1881), 122.
72. Beman Gates, (b. 1818), vice president of the Marietta & Cincinnati R.R., edited the *Marietta Intelligencer*, 1839–56. John Kendrick (1804–89) graduated from Dartmouth with Chase in 1826. He began an association with Marietta College in 1840 that lasted until his death. *History of Washington County*, 414–15; *Columbus Gazette*, June 12, 1857; Emerson, *General Catalogue*, 239.
73. The Congregational Church in Marietta, Thomas Wickes, pastor, was first organized in 1796. The edifice was built 1807–9. St. Luke's Protestant Episcopal

June 1857 {283}

MONDAY, JUNE 1. Finished Address[74]—but had to write nearly all day—dined with Prest. Andrews[75] / read Address to Gates who approved—tea / Col. Mills—called before on Mr. Ward—visited his Church[76]— Wilson suggested printing address / read parts to him & he much pleased—sent it to office—reception—evening at Gates—good many people—Leavitt, NY &c[77]—

TUESDAY, JUNE 2. Revised print of address— D. Putnam called— with him to Harmar—pleasant visit Mrs Putnam & children[78]— returned—went to top of Mound in Cemetery visited grave of Commodore Whipple[79]—recd. neat Copy from printer and pasted it on small slips fools cap for convenient reading—dinner—to landing with Mayor W— Cass, Swann, Sartiges, McMullen & others[80] / Address—responses— Cars to Chillicothe—Jewett at Athens[81]— Supper & bed with N. H. Wilson.[82]

WEDNESDAY, JUNE 3. To Cin by morning train—talk with Sartiges on cars—called out at Blanchester responded briefly[83]—great

---

Church, John Boyd, rector, was organized in 1826. *History of Washington County*, 381–82, 387–88.

74. Chase gave a welcoming address on June 2 at the railroad celebration in Marietta. The speech applauded railroads for promoting "that larger Union ... which forms the best assurance & guaranty of the permanence and enlargement of our precious heritage of Free Institutions." Speech at Marietta, June 2, 1857 (Chase Papers, Hist. Soc. of Pa.); *Columbus Daily Gazette*, June 12, 1857.

75. Israel Ward Andrews (1815–88), Marietta College president, 1855–85. *DAB*, 1:293.

76. Ohio militia veteran and financier John Mills (1795–1882) helped found and administer Marietta College. Nahum Ward (1785–1860), Marietta landowner and developer, financed the church of the First Unitarian Society of Marietta, dedicated on June 4, 1857. Martin R. Andrews, ed., *History of Marietta and Washington County, Ohio* . . . (Chicago, 1902), 903–4; Smith, *Railway Celebrations*, 1:91; *History of Washington County*, 391, 476–79.

77. Joshua Leavitt covered the railroad celebrations for the New York *Independent*. Smith, *Railway Celebrations*, 1:116; *Cincinnati Daily Gazette*, June 4, 1857.

78. Either Douglas or David Putnam. Douglas Putnam married his second wife, Eliza Tucker (d. 1862), in 1844. Five of his children survived infancy. *Biographical Cyclopædia*, 1:230–31.

79. Abraham Whipple (1733–1819), naval officer during the American Revolution, died at Marietta after emigrating from Rhode Island. *DAB*, 20:66.

80. William Augustus Whittlesey, Lewis Cass, Thomas Swann, Eugène de Sartiges, and Fayette McMullen (1805–80), former Democratic congressman from Virginia. Smith, *Railway Celebrations*, 1:89–90, 129; *Cincinnati Daily Gazette*, June 4, 1857; *Bio. Dir. U.S. Cong.*, 1482.

81. Probably Hugh Judge Jewett (1817–98), a lawyer, Democratic politician, and president of the Central Ohio Railroad Co. *DAB*, 10:68–69.

82. Noah L. Wilson, Chillicothe banker and president of the Marietta & Cincinnati R.R. *History of Ross and Highland Counties*, 199–200; *Columbus Gazette*, June 12, 1857.

83. A reporter on the train from Chillicothe to Cincinnati did not mention a stop at Blanchester in his published account. *Daily Ohio State Journal*, June 3, 1857.

crowd at Cin—Mayor Thomas recd.[84] Cass, myself, Mayor & another in carr[ia]ge—[crowd chered]—Cass & me—intd. Gen Cass at Burnet House also afterwards Mayor Swann— Recd. despatch May 30 from Pros. Atty Clarke Co about Rescue cases[85]—invited to Gen Haines[86]—staid at Burnet—

THURSDAY, JUNE 4. Many callers at Burnet—exhibition of Fire Engines 5th St. yesterday[87]— Gen Cass left this morn'g—repeated my speech introducing Swann to precede his[88]— Excursionists generally left— Douglas & wife[89]—dined with them & Swann / Douglas talked of his investments—left in even[']g with Swann for Columbus, having teld. Mason & Goode to meet me tomorrow morng.[90]

---

84. Nicholas W. Thomas (1810–64), meatpacker and Republican mayor of Cincinnati, 1857–59, received the guests arriving for the railroad celebration with a "neat speech." *Cincinnati Daily Gazette*, June 4, 1857; Holli and Jones, *Biographical Dictionary of American Mayors*, 359–60.

85. In late May, U.S. marshals had beaten the sheriff of Clark County after he attempted to serve them with a writ of habeas corpus. The marshals had arrested Ohioans from Champaign County for harboring a fugitive slave and obstructing federal officers acting under the Fugitive Slave Law of 1850. Subsequently, officials in Greene County, in concert with nearby counties, arrested the federal marshals on charges of assault and battery with intent to kill. Trial of the "Clark County (or Greene County) rescue case" began June 9 in federal district court at Cincinnati. Campbell, *Slave Catchers*, 161–64; Benjamin Franklin Prince, "The Rescue Case of 1857," *Ohio Archæological and Historical Society Publications* 16 (Jan. 1907): 292–309.

86. Possibly E. S. Haines.

87. This demonstration by the city's fire department on June 3 showed how swiftly fire fighters using steam engines could stream water onto the roofs of five-story buildings at the Fifth Street market. The carriage carrying Chase and others accidently received a dousing near the end of the demonstration. *Cincinnati Daily Gazette*, June 4, 1857.

88. On the evening of June 3 a crowd outside the Burnet House heard Chase repeat at least the substance of his "Address of Welcome at Marietta." He also introduced Thomas Swann for a speech that celebrated the new railway connection between Cincinnati and Baltimore. Ibid.

89. Stephen A. Douglas and his wife arrived in Cincinnati about June 4 and, like Chase, stayed at the Burnet House. Rain kept Douglas and Chase from taking a planned drive to Clifton. Adèle Cutts Douglas (1835–99), society belle in the District of Columbia and a devout Catholic, married the widower Douglas in Nov. 1856 and frequently accompanied him on his political trips. After his death in May 1861 she resided in Washington. She married Robert Williams, an army officer, in 1866. *Cincinnati Daily Gazette*, June 5, 1857; James et al., *Notable American Women*, 1:509–10.

90. Rodney Mason and James S. Goode (1823–91), Springfield lawyers involved in the Clark County rescue case, wanted the Ohio attorney general to participate in the upcoming trial because the matter embodied "a direct conflict" of federal and state jurisdiction. Chase reportedly met with Mason and Goode "at the earliest possible moment" after returning to Columbus on June 5 and directed the attorney general to appear with them in court. Rockel, *Springfield and Clark County*, 518, 525; Mason and Goode to Chase, [June 3, 1857], Mason to Chase, June 18, 1857 (Chase Papers, Ohio Hist. Soc.); *Daily Ohio State Journal*, June 6, 1857.

June 1857 { 285 }

SATURDAY, JUNE 6. Despatch from Wolcott—will be here at nine tonight[91]

WEDNESDAY, JUNE 10. p.[92] Breakfast with Prof. Merrick & some friends / family prayer—visited Library Building[93]—admirably adapted—marched in procession with Prest. Thomson— Commencement Exercises pretty good—some very good—dined with Prof ——excellent baccalaureate fr. Prest. Thomson[94]—reunion chez lui[95]—cars to Cols.— Wright at depot—deficit in Treasury $550.000—amazed but manifested little feeling[96]— Gibson gone but to return tomorrow.

THURSDAY, JUNE 11. p— Telegraphed Attorney Gen.[97] to come up from Cin—telegrap[h] by Wright to Gibson at Tiffin to return—answered "will be down tomorrow" / consulted Mr. Kelley & Mr. Dennison about steps proper to be taken—appointed Mr. Dennison to examine treasury—objected to act unless G. shd. resign—Wolcott tels. "will be up tonight—much excitement & uneasiness in town

FRIDAY, JUNE 12. p. B.[98] Met Wolcott & Wright early in morning— Gibson not returned— W—— fearful he never will—agreed

---

91. Chase left five lines blank under the date's heading before writing this sentence. He may have intended to fill in more information about the day later. An aborted start, perhaps a *T* or an *F*, appears on the first line below the heading.
92. "Prayer." Like similar abbreviations at June 11 and 12, this notation appears as an interlineation, apparently added as an afterthought.
93. This entry describes a visit to Delaware, Ohio. Ohio Wesleyan University's Sturgis Library was dedicated in 1855. Henry Clyde Hubbart, *Ohio Wesleyan's First Hundred Years* (Delaware, Ohio, 1943), 302.
94. Edward Thomson (1810–70), president of Ohio Wesleyan, 1842–60, elected a Methodist Episcopal bishop in 1864. Eighteen student addresses were presented at the commencement exercises. *DAB*, 18:482–83; *Xenia Torch-Light*, June 17, 1857.
95. That is, a gathering at Thomson's.
96. State Auditor Francis M. Wright met Chase. The two prior state treasurers, both Democrats, accumulated this deficit through failed personal speculations undertaken with state funds. John G. Breslin, William Gibson's brother-in-law and immediate predecessor as treasurer, bore principal responsibility for the shortfall. Gibson shared blame by hiding the true condition of the treasury over the previous eighteen months. The treasury defalcation prompted much administrative activity over the next weeks and burdened Chase through the rest of his tenure as governor. *Daily Ohio State Journal*, June–Oct. 1857; *Columbus Gazette*, June–Oct. 1857; *Annual Report of the Treasurer*, Ohio Exec. Docs. for 1857, 1:253–78; *Special Report on the Condition of the Treasury, Nov. 15, 1857*, ibid., 2:5–20; *Report of the Investigating Commission Appointed to Enquire into the Causes of the Defalcation in the State Treasury . . . April 12, 1858* (Columbus, Ohio, 1859); *Special Message from the Governor*, Ohio Exec. Docs. for 1859, 2:650–52; Bigger, *Ohio's Silver-Tongued Orator*, 274–83.
97. Christopher Parsons Wolcott.
98. "Prayer" and "Bible."

he should resign—if not must be arrested—which will create disability— Mr. Dennison's note declining to examine treasury—tendered appt. Examr. Treasury to Mr. Perry who declined—then insisted Mr. Dennison shd. accept[99]—reunion at Mr. Heyls[1]— Gibson retd. late—interview with him & other State officers at 11½—no definite talk—determined to see him early & insist on resignation,

SATURDAY, JUNE 13. prayed earnestly for strength & guidance— went to Treasury at 7½—found G—— there—talked with him— other State officers came in but no progress made—resolved to talk to him alone—did so—urged resignation—wished to see friends—I said he could see Thurman—he sent for him—left them together taking with me keys of safes—after dinner returned—unwilling to resign—I mentioned alternatives—called in Wright—resigned—I appointed Stone whose bonds given, oath taken & in office 11½[2]

WEDNESDAY, JUNE 17. Up 6½— B— ND[3]— Office—Gibson— [denies] business relations with Breslin

FRIDAY, JUNE 19. p. B. Office—Barr called by request abt Director Peny—recommends Breyfogle[4]— Tel from Wolcott—up tonight—fr Gibson, [do.][5]—saw Treasurer about progress mak-

---

99. William Dennison and probably Aaron Fyfe Perry (1815–93), Ohio lawyer, politician, and at this time receiver of the Mechanics and Traders Bank of Cincinnati, refused appointment as examiner of the state treasury. Dennison finally agreed to accept, but resigned on June 23. *Daily Ohio State Journal,* June 13, 1857; *Columbus Gazette,* June 19, 1857; Dennison appointment, June 10, 1857, Dennison to Chase, June 23, 1857 (Chase Papers, Ohio Hist. Soc.); *Bio. Dir. U.S. Cong.,* 1634; Perry to Chase, Apr. 16, 1857, Chase to Perry, May 12, 1857 (Chase Papers, L.C.).

1. Either Christian Heyl (1788–1878), a German immigrant who grew wealthy as a hotelkeeper before moving to a farm outside Columbus, or his son Lewis Heyl, principal of a female seminary. *History of Franklin and Pickaway Counties,* 583; *Col. Dir. (1856–57),* 109.

2. Gibson resigned as state treasurer. Alfred P. Stone resigned the directorship of the Ohio Penitentiary to accept Chase's appointment as treasurer. *Daily Ohio State Journal,* June 16, 1857; Gibson to Chase, June 13 1857, Stone to Chase, same date, and James H. Baker, acknowledgement of Stone's bond and oath, June 15, 1857 (Chase Papers, Ohio Hist. Soc.).

3. "Bible" and "Notre Dame."

4. Robert N. Barr, physician, officer in the Columbus Republican Club, and Ohio's surgeon general during the latter part of the Civil War, recommended Charles Breyfogle (1815–84) for the vacancy on the board of directors of the Ohio Penitentiary. Breyfogle was a tailor and an officer in the Republican Club. Chase appointed Breyfogle on June 29. *Daily Ohio State Journal,* Aug. 22, 1857; *Col. Dir. (1856–57),* 21; Rose, *Cleveland,* 320; Reid, *Ohio in the War,* 1:247; *Portrait and Biographical Record of Fayette, Pickaway and Madison Counties, Ohio* . . . (Chicago, 1892), 577–78; A. P. Stone et al. to Chase, June 16, 1857 (Chase Papers, Ohio Hist. Soc.).

5. "Will be up afternoon or Tonight." William H. Gibson to Chase, June 19, 1857 (Chase Papers, Hist. Soc. of Pa.).

ing in examination— Eveng at Vedettes Entertainment for few moments[6]— Wright & Wolcott called about 11 PM—nothing of special importance— Read some French with Prof Mot

SATURDAY, JUNE 20. p. B— Gibson came out just as I was going in—rode in with him—says regrets resignation—has paper from Breslin but cannot shew it— B—— cannot & will not make full avowals— Conversation with Atto Genl abt prosecutions—also with Prosg Atto. gave him full particulars, he thinks exn. best next week before Grand Jury / Spoke to Audr. abt making affidt. to [Buttles] vs Breslin[7]— Instructions for Audr. in NY ☞ A[ppd] 24

SUNDAY, JUNE 21. reached Cin at 2 AM—Burnet House 2½ up at 7[8]— Swayne to see Leavitt at 12½[9] I to church—Nicholson—Bp assisting[10]—Col & Mrs Haines[11]—dined Judge Hoadley's—talk abt habeas corpus case—thinks best to read written application for time— Swayne reports Leavitt gives till Thursday— Military gentlemen called—saw Potter of Coml.[12]—called Col Haines—packed for start

MONDAY, JUNE 22. Came up from Cincinnati by 6 AM train—met Dennison at Depot—sd. Wright just starting for NY wh letters &c[13]—

---

6. The Columbus Vedettes, a recently organized "corps of young soldiers," presented "a grand Levee and Strawberry Festival" at Concert Hall. *Columbus Gazette*, June 19, 1857.
7. Chase apparently consulted Auditor Wright about the possibility of giving Albert B. Buttles, Franklin County clerk of courts, an affadavit against Breslin. *Col. Dir. (1856–57)*, 39.
8. Chase had telegraphed George Hoadly that he and Noah Swayne would come to Cincinnati "by night train." He asked Hoadly to reserve rooms at the Burnet House. Chase to Hoadly, June 20, 1857 (Chase Papers, Ohio Hist. Soc.).
9. Humphrey Howe Leavitt (1796–1873), a federal judge from 1834 to 1871, was at this time judge of the U.S. district court in Cincinnati. Despite personal sentiments against slavery, he upheld the constitutionality of federal fugitive slave laws. In the Clark County rescue case he decided in favor of the U.S. marshals. Immediately after this decision the U.S. district attorney pressed charges against the Ohio officials and citizens who had hindered the marshals in the performance of their duty. *DAB*, 11:83–84; *Cincinnati Daily Gazette*, June 22, 23, 1857; Campbell, *Slave Catchers*, 163–64; Chase to Joseph C. Brand, June 20, 1857 (Chase Papers, L.C.).
10. William Rufus Nicholson (1822–1901) was rector of St. John's Protestant Episcopal Church. The bishop was C. P. McIlvaine. *Who Was Who*, 1:898; *Appletons'*, 4:516; *Cinc. Dir. (1857)*, 208.
11. Possibly E. S. Haines and his wife.
12. M. D. Potter (d. 1866) managed the *Cincinnati Commercial*. Greve, *Centennial History*, 1:1036.
13. Drafts on Ohio banks were being protested in New York City after the revelation of the treasury defalcation. The state auditor went to New York to try to restore the state's credit. Chase to F. M. Wright, June 22, June 23, 1857 (Chase Papers, L.C.).

WEDNESDAY, JUNE 24. p— Office 8—vexed by article in Cin Gaz & displayed headings—discrediting Sen Co. Bk & impeaching Gibson[14]—called on Treas. & advised caution in communication—despatch from Wright at New York—dfts paid & interest provided for / suggested to Treas. & Atto. G. statement about Bonds—prepared & sent to papers[15]—convn. with Atto. Gen. about case at Cincinnati.[16]

THURSDAY, JUNE 25. Atto. Gen. in Cincinnati today—letter from Slade about biennial unions—wishes to know if I desire to be a candidate—ansd. no[17]—letter from Walker who wants his money[18]—called at Bk. & fd. myself overdrawn—went out afternoon to Mrs Neils—spent eveng at office—Wolcott returned makes good report / calculated amounts due fr H. Smith

14. The article in the Republican *Cincinnati Daily Gazette* questioned official reports about the size of the deficit in the state treasury and probed the operations of the Seneca County Bank. Some of the headings preceding the article read: "More Astounding Developments! . . . A Portion of the Missing Bonds Hypothecated in New York.—$100,000 of the Securities Attached by the State! . . . Gibson Claims the Bonds as Private Property! . . . Bogus Drafts Passed to the State by Gibson!!" Gibson, who had gone to New York City to help Ohio officials account for state assets, wrote Chase: "There is too much talk at Columbus and the *Gazette* man should be enjoined. His statements are false unfounded and malicious, I care not who he is." *Cincinnati Daily Gazette,* June 24, 1857; Gibson to Chase, June 27, 1857 (Chase Papers, L.C.); *Daily Ohio State Journal,* July 6, 1857.
15. F. M. Wright informed Chase that he had met the state interest payments due on July 1, 1857, and advised immediate publication of an official notice to prevent currency depreciation. Wright met the state's obligations with loans Chase secured from Ohio state branch banks. Treasurer Stone and Attorney General Wolcott indicated publicly that the state had assumed responsibility for bonds supporting the circulation of the Seneca County Bank despite the absence of legal obligation. Many of Breslin's speculations had been transacted through the Seneca County Bank, and not until 1864 would the confused affairs of that institution be resolved. Wright to Chase, June 24, 1857 (Chase Papers, Hist. Soc. of Pa.); Chase to John Andrews, [June 18, 1857], Andrews to Chase, June 20 and 27, 1857 (Chase Papers, Ohio Hist. Soc.); *Daily Ohio State Journal,* June 24, 25, 1857; *Annual Report of the Treasurer,* 1857, 1:264–65; *Annual Report of the Treasurer,* Ohio Exec. Docs. for 1858, 1:412–19; *Report of the Investigating Commission,* 65–67; William Lang, *History of Seneca County* . . . (Springfield, Ohio, 1880), 336–38.
16. The Clark County rescue case. Chase wrote the beginning of this entry in pencil, as he did other entries in this section of the journal. From *called on Treas.* through the end of the entry is in ink.
17. William Slade, Jr., son of a Vermont governor, held firm antislavery principles and regarded himself as Chase's "personal and political" friend. He and Chase corresponded about whether Chase should run for reelection in the fall. C. M. L. Wiseman, *Centennial History of Lancaster Ohio* . . . (Lancaster, Ohio, 1898), 245; Slade to Chase, July 2, 1857 (Chase Papers, Hist. Soc. of Pa.).
18. Attorney and abolitionist James Walker (1826–85) helped organize the Republican party in Logan County and received appointments from Chase during the Civil War. He had loaned Chase seven thousand dollars in May 1857 which Chase promised "to return on demand." *History of Logan County,* 615; Kennedy, *Historical Review of Logan County,* 116–17, 736–38; Chase to Walker, voucher dated May 5, 1857, Walker to Chase, June 30, 1857 (Chase Papers, L.C.).

FRIDAY, JUNE 26. Wrote H Smith asking amt. to reduce balance Lewis & Wilkes to $700—also payt. balance Badger or arrangement[19]—little accomplished in Treasury matters—Cin papers speak warmly of Wolcott's speech[20]—

SATURDAY, JUNE 27. Conversation with Deshler abt money [for] Walker / agrees to let me have $2000 on check & balance on Bill— took Mem. abt. Bartlett & Smith's purchases[21]— Despatch from Wright about payt. of Claims against bonds in N York / much relieved by this— Despatch from Scott Toledo—"Mott absent—cannot leave"[22]—wished him to examine Seneca Co Bank

SUNDAY, JUNE 28. At church morning—stranger preached— Katie did not go—Nettie went home from Sunday School instead of attending—tried to write a little on address in afternoon—

MONDAY, JUNE 29. Very busy at office in morning—a great deal to do—left at 2.20 with children for Cincinnati—they stopped with Mr Febiger— Mr Reemelin [brot] in report—called at Febigers— Mrs Feb. Jones there[23]—pleasant visit—back to Hotel—& bed—

FRIDAY, JULY 3. Gibson expected today but did not come[24]

SATURDAY, JULY 4. Reamy says Breslin certainly gone[25] / Coggeshall went down to Cincinnati told him to bring up children—l

---

19. Chase had paid on a note given to secure Hamilton Smith's debt to Lewis & Wilkes. He asked Smith to collect money from other notes to enable payment on the "old Badger bill," which Chase had endorsed for Smith six years earlier. Chase to H. Smith, June 27, 1857 (Chase Papers, L.C.).

20. On June 25 Attorney General Christopher Wolcott spoke for the state in the Clark County rescue case. His two-hour speech in defense of state jurisdiction rested upon the reserved powers clause of the U.S. Constitution. *Cincinnati Daily Gazette,* June 26, 1857; *Cincinnati Daily Enquirer,* June 26, 1857.

21. John F. Bartlet and Benjamin E. Smith operated a private bank. *Col. Dir. (1856–57),* 21, 185; Martin, *History of Franklin County,* 324.

22. Maurice A. Scott (b. 1830) headed the Toledo telegraph office during the 1850s. The dispatch undoubtedly referred to Richard Mott (1804–88), Toledo merchant and antislavery congressman, 1855–59. Scribner, *Lucas County and the City of Toledo,* 1:231; 2:28–29; *Bio. Dir. U.S. Cong.,* 1545; Waggoner, *Toledo,* 497–99.

23. George L. Febiger was the widower of Caroline Smith, Chase's sister-in-law by his second marriage. Mrs. H. Febiger Jones was apparently George Febiger's mother. Chase to Elizabeth F. Febiger (deed), Nov. 22, 1852, G. Febiger to Chase, June 25, 1862, Jones to Chase, Nov. 16, 1862 (Chase Papers, L.C.); Chase to Jones, Oct. 16, 1865 (Free Library of Philadelphia).

24. This sentence appears near the bottom of the space available for the entry, as if Chase intended to insert more text above it.

25. Franklin County prosecuting attorney J. O. Reamey attempted to have John G. Breslin arrested. Breslin, who had visited Columbus shortly after the defalcation became public, fled to Canada. Chase made extended but vain efforts to have him

fr. S. W[26] with description of Hotel de Ville ball for Kate / Ansd. don't see why great gulph between us—to picnic with Mrs Parsons—pleasant there—Geiger made Speech[27]—home read Notre Dame &c

SUNDAY, JULY 5. Read ceci tuera cela—finished Hiawatha[28]—walked—tried to write address—could not—wrote letter to teachers Association excusing non attendence &c[29]—walked with Galloway—read Common School History[30]—doubtful if time *best* employed though not ill employed

TUESDAY, JULY 7. Called on Deshler abt. money—he gone to Grand Jury[31]—but gave check 4000 to Overdier who promised to send package to McMahon[32]— Wolcott returned & comd. investigation before Grand Jury—letter from Gibson & sheets of

---

extradited. Breslin's flight encumbered attempts by Democrats to absolve him of wrongdoing and pin blame for the defalcation on Gibson and Chase. *Daily Ohio State Journal,* June 17, July 20, 22, 1857; Chase to Lewis Cass, July 27, Aug. 15, 1857, Mar. 30, 1859, Chase to Edmund Head, Mar. 9, 1859 (Chase Papers, Ohio Hist. Soc.); "Deposition of John G. Breslin, taken in Hamilton, C.W., 23rd and 24th of Dec., 1857," *Ohio Exec. Docs.,* 1857, 2:290–92; *Report of the Investigating Commission,* 233–56; Reamey receipt, July 27, 1857 (Chase Papers, Ohio Hist. Soc.); *Col. Dir. (1856–57),* 171.

26. Susan Walker.

27. Chase went with Jane Swan Parsons to a picnic at Sullivant's Hill replete with music, games, and speeches. The speech of Joseph H. Geiger (b. ca. 1817), Ohio lawyer, political figure, and popular lecturer, was reported as a "burlesque" upon the "fire-eating, world-thrashing proclivities" of the U.S. *Columbus Gazette,* July 10, 1857; *Franklin County at the Beginning of the Twentieth Century...* (Columbus, 1901), 275–76; *History of Franklin and Pickaway Counties,* 79.

28. Henry Wadsworth Longfellow, *The Song of Hiawatha* (Boston, 1855). Literally "this will kill that," the French phrase is a chapter title from Hugo's *Notre-Dame de Paris.*

29. Chase had been invited to address the Ohio State Teachers' Association at Steubenville on July 8. He sent a letter dated July 6, explaining that pressing public duties prevented his attendance and expressing his commitment to state support for education. *Columbus Gazette,* Jan. 9, July 17, 1857; *Daily Ohio State Journal,* Jan. 1, June 19, July 10, 11, 1857; "Fragment of intended Address before Teachers Association 1856 or 1857" (Chase Papers, Hist. Soc. of Pa.).

30. Samuel Goodrich Griswold, *Peter Parley's Common School History* (Philadelphia, 1853).

31. The grand jury of the Franklin County Court of Common Pleas indicted Breslin and Gibson for embezzlement on July 16, 1857. Reportedly, Chase pursued the indictments after rejecting an offer that would have released Breslin's securities and freed him from arrest in exchange for a payment of $250,000. *Daily Ohio State Journal,* June 26, 27, July 15, 16, 17, 23, 1857; *Report of the Investigating Commission,* 357–64.

32. David Overdier was a bank bookkeeper. James McMahon, a resident of Cumberland, Ohio, associated with the Cambridge Agency, State Bank of Ohio, collected Chase's repayment of his loan from James Walker. Walker to Chase, June 30, 1857 (Chase Papers, L.C.); *Col. Dir. (1855),* 89; ibid. *(1856–57),* 165.

statement[33]— Thrall appd to examine Seneca Co Bank by Commi[ssioners][34] / read ND— Nevins in evg. children retd.

WEDNESDAY, JULY 8. Recd McMahons despatch of yesterday— ansd. sent 2000 yesterday—send 2000 today— Pennington[35] called says friends Gibson fear he may leave country / Patterson & Naylor gone after him[36]—borrd Nevins carriage & took ride. Winans J J & ―― called—say Corwin exd tomorrow & Lewis Saturday / want State represented—Atto. Genl does not wish to appear at prelimy examn.[37]—

THURSDAY, JULY 9. h. B p. D. b. Off. $8\frac{1}{4}$[38]— Watson called[39]— but before him Pennington— P―― down on Gibson— Watson on Pennington—Conversan with Stone & Wolcott as to Sen. Co Bank—to Mrs Neils—fear of rain—tea there—Mrs King[40] / pleasant— home with us— Saw Baltzell, Johnston, Watson &

33. Gibson, confident that he could "square accounts with the State" and feeling "most keenly the wrongs done by professed friends," criticized Treasurer Stone and the Republican press in Ohio. W. H. Gibson to Chase, July 4, 1857 (Chase Papers, Hist. Soc. of Pa.).
34. William Barlow Thrall (1798–1873), Ohio journalist and politician, had experience as a bureau head in the U.S. Treasury. In 1858 Chase appointed him comptroller of the state treasury. *History of Franklin and Pickaway Counties,* 218–26.
35. Robert Gill Pennington.
36. Tiffin Republicans J. M. Patterson, mayor, and John M. Naylor (b. 1822), hardware merchant and financier. *Daily Ohio State Journal,* Apr. 10, 1857; *Centennial Biographical History of Seneca County,* 536–39.
37. James January Winans (1818–79), Xenia lawyer and politician, appealed to Chase for state intervention in behalf of his client, Greene County sheriff Daniel Lewis (1797–1863). Lewis and Ichabod Corwin, a nephew of Thomas Corwin, were indicted for interfering with federal officers in the Clark County rescue case and were examined by a U.S. commissioner at Cincinnati. Neither man came to trial because a compromise between Ohio and the U.S. government, involving reimbursement to the owner of the fugitive slave through private subscription, halted litigation. *Bio. Dir. U.S. Cong.,* 2072–73; Winans to Chase, July 4, 1857 (Chase Papers, Ohio Hist. Soc.); George F. Robinson, *History of Greene County, Ohio* . . . (Chicago, 1902), 164; *Cincinnati Daily Gazette,* July 11, 1857; *Appletons',* 1:751; Campbell, *Slave Catchers,* 164.
38. Here and in succeeding entries, *h* means "hymns"; *B*, "Bible"; *p*, "prayer"; *d*, "dressed"; *b*, "breakfast." $8\frac{1}{4}$ denotes the hour of Chase's arrival at his office. According to his memoranda at the end of the journal, a capital *D* represents Hugo's *Notre-Dame de Paris.* From context here, "dressed" seems possible also.
39. Cooper Kinderdine Watson (1810–80), lawyer and Free-Soil congressman, 1855–57, settled in Tiffin, Ohio, about 1850. *Bio. Dir. U.S. Cong.,* 2015; Lang, *History of Seneca County,* 372–73.
40. Probably Elizabeth Jane Neil King (b. ca. 1824), a daughter of wealthy Columbus pioneers who was considered "a stately beauty" and "highly accomplished." She married Thomas Worthington King and was widowed in 1851. McAllister, *In Winter We Flourish,* 137–38, 150.

Wolcott at Treasurers Office[41] / Appd. Pro Judges, Wood & Brown Cos[42]

FRIDAY, JULY 10. h. B. p. d. 8¼— Sent for Gen Harris declined to interfere as to Maj. Gen Ham Co—thought no Sur. Genl. Division cd. be appd. except by [Gov] after Dept. Organized[43]— Appd. H. B. Carrington, Judge Adv. Gen & David L. Wood, Eng in Chf[44]— long talk with Watson—who in liquor— Wolcott called— Platt abt. furniture—don't want table & wardrobe— Mrs Dennison's with Kate—Mrs King & Miss Anthony very agreeable

SATURDAY, JULY 11. h. B. p. D— 8¼—found Mr. Longwth at office[45]—went with him to see Mrs. L— Watson called—sore abt. yesterdays conversation—dinner / D—— S—— O4[46]— Watson has despatch from Gibson at Buffalo—on his way home—consulted Wolcott abt Swayne or Galloway going to Tiffin—saw Galloway— urged him to go— Ford came from LaCrosse[47]—retired very early— Despatches from Swann abt visit to Baltimore[48]—

SUNDAY, JULY 12. Galloway called on way to Sunday School returned & I went with him to Westminster Church—Smith[49]—good

---

41. Lewis Baltzell owned stock in the Seneca County Bank. "Johnston" was likely Charles L. Johnson, cashier of that bank from July 1854 to May 1857, but possibly R. Rhodes Johnston, a deputy sheriff from Columbus. *Report of the Investigating Commission*, 323, 346; *Col. Dir. (1856–57)*, 121.

42. John A. Kelley of Wood County and John W. King of Brown County resigned as probate judges. Chase appointed Josiah F. Price and James H. King as replacements. Kelley to Chase, June 12, 1857, King to Chase, July 3, 1857 (Chase Papers, Ohio Hist. Soc.); *Daily Ohio State Journal*, July 10, 1857.

43. Chase spoke to Sullivan D. Harris about a disputed election of the major general of militia in Hamilton County. A second election followed a court challenge, and William H. Lytle emerged with the commission. Chase commissioned a Surgeon General on July 15. July 16, 1857, below; *Daily Ohio State Journal*, July 2, Aug. 21, Sept. 22, 1857; Chase to Harris, July 10, 1857 (Chase Papers, Ohio Hist. Soc.).

44. Carrington was given the office of judge advocate general, created by the new militia law, with the rank of colonel. In Oct. 1857, Chase appointed David L. Wood an agent to collect the state's arms. Wood later became quartermaster general of Ohio. ——— to "Dear Sir," July 10, 1857, Wood to Chase, Oct. 2, 1857, Chase to Wood, Oct. 16, 1857 (Chase Papers, Ohio Hist. Soc.); *Daily Ohio State Journal*, July 13, 1857; *OR*, ser. 3, v. 1:4–5; entry for Oct. 14, 1857, below.

45. Nicholas Longworth was then involved in a dispute with an inspector of liquors. *Cincinnati Daily Gazette*, July 20, 1857.

46. According to Chase's key at the end of the journal, these abbreviations mean "Notre Dame— Siesta— Office at 4."

47. Thomas H. Ford.

48. Railroad festivities in Baltimore in mid-July were to continue the commemoration, begun in June, of the railway link between Baltimore and the West. *Baltimore Sun*, July 15, 1857.

49. Josiah D. Smith (d. 1863) became pastor of the Westminster Presbyterian Church upon its organization in 1854. *Daily Ohio State Journal*, Feb. 28, 1857; *Col. Dir. (1856–57)*, 185; *History of Franklin and Pickaway Counties*, 516.

July 1857 { 293 }

ideas but commonplace & not effectively stated—read Longfellow & Bossuets sermon for Henrietta, queen of Chs 1st[50]—also Bible Clarke's Commentaries—called at Dr. Smiths—Miss Anthony, Dr. McMillan &c[51]   Talked with G abt his going for Gibson

MONDAY, JULY 14.[52]   Swayne & Galloway went to Tiffin this morning to see & bring Gibson—Watson went with them—nothing of special interest today that I now (Washington July 23) remember

TUESDAY, JULY 14.   To office early and very busy all day without accomplishing much—afternoon rode out by Mrs Neils with Kate & Mrs Wolcott[53]—going out met Gibson just arrived—after tea called on him and earnestly urged him to keep nothing back & disguise nothing—

WEDNESDAY, JULY 15.   Gibson examd in part before Sparrow my appointee[54]—in afternoon before Grand Jury[55]—glad to find from Atto. General that good impression made on Grand Jury & from Sparrow that good impression made on him—rode out to Mrs. Neils with Kate & Net & left shawl— Dr. McMillan & Mr Carrington agreed to accompany me east

50. In 1669, Bossuet delivered the first of the funeral orations for which he became noted, commemorating Henrietta Maria, French-born widow of Charles I of England. E. K. Sanders, *Jacques Bénigne Bossuet: A Study* (London, 1921), 103–4; E. E. Reynolds, *Bossuet* (Garden City, N.Y., 1963), 68–69.
51. Columbus physician William Linn McMillen, M.D. (1829–1902) had been a surgeon in the Russian army during the Crimean War. *Appletons'*, 4:150; *Who Was Who*, 1:821; *Col. Dir. (1855)*, 81.
52. Chase wrote this entry in the space intended for Wednesday the 15th; his entry for Tuesday the 14th in the space intended for Monday; and his entry for Wednesday in the space intended for Tuesday. In each case he altered the printed heading to show the new day and date, but he dated both Monday and Tuesday as July 14. Alongside the original printed heading for Monday he placed a pointing hand with the note "Wed 15" to indicate that Monday's entry could be found in the space meant for Wednesday. As shown by his comment at the end of the Monday entry, at least some of this text was written on the 23rd, when he was in Washington.
53. Pamphilia Stanton Wolcott, sister of Edwin M. Stanton, married Christopher Parsons Wolcott. Thomas and Hyman, *Stanton*, 5, 46.
54. Columbus attorney Thomas Sparrow (1818–71), a Democrat, assisted William Dennison in examining the state treasury. On June 22, Chase appointed Sparrow examiner to succeed Dennison, who had been reluctant to accept the position and formally resigned June 23. Chase to Sparrow, June 22, 1857, Dennison to Chase, June 23, 1857, Sparrow receipt, [Sept. 24, 1857] (Chase Papers, Ohio Hist. Soc.); Chase to F. M. Wright, June 22, June 23, 1857 (Chase Papers, L.C.); *History of Franklin and Pickaway Counties*, 73–74; *Daily Ohio State Journal*, July 23, 1857.
55. Chase originally wrote *Sparrow* here, then sometime later, with a different pencil, lined through the word and inserted *Grand Jury*.

THURSDAY, JULY 16. Commissioned yesterday Dr. McMillan as Surgeon General—despatched some routine business—teld. Swann & Mrs Goldsborough—off at ten[56]— Dr McM—— Carrington, Kate & Nettie made party— Pruden, Gerrard, & other excursionists on cars—Ferguson, among them[57] / met Chy Brooks, Prest. B & O[58] at River—passed Cheat River after dark having supped at Grafton

FRIDAY, JULY 17.[59] Not much sleep in cars—but all pretty smart—hungry but no breakfast till Baltimore— Swann, Garret & Crowley met us at cars[60]—children & staff in one carriage—Swann Crowley & I in another to Gilmor House[61]—brkfst at 10 30— About 2 Swann called & Net Kate & I went to his house—beautifully furnished—fine painting / Mrs Swann[62]—Louise,[63] Lizzie,   / worked on response to reception speech[64]

SATURDAY, JULY 18. Up at 5 to finish response—got through about 9—bkft—Carrington came—returned to his hotel—to Depot Swann Staff & I—no speaking there & no ch[eer]ing—Swann Staff & I in open carriage fine white horses long march—speeches at Md. Institute[65]— Mr. & Mrs Dennison,[66] Mrs King &c— Lee, Kemp &

56. Chase was leaving for the railroad celebration in Baltimore. Accounts of the trip may be found in the *Baltimore Sun*, July 20, 1857, and *Daily Ohio State Journal*, July 18, 21, 22, 1857.
57. A. J. Pruden represented the mayor of Cincinnati at the Baltimore ceremonies. John H. Gerard, county commissioner, and S. C. Gerard were among the Cincinnati excursionists. Cincinnati lawyer and Democratic politician Edward Alexander Ferguson (1826–1906) later promoted the Cincinnati Southern Railroad. *Baltimore Sun*, July 20, 1857; *OR*, ser. 2, v. 2:280; *Nat. Cyc.*, 26:135–36.
58. Chauncey Brooks (1794–1880). *Nat. Cyc.*, 18:2–3.
59. Chase wrote text similar to the beginning portions of this entry, with some variations, under the printed heading for June 30, then crossed it out.
60. John Work Garrett (1820–84) rose through the ranks of Baltimore & Ohio R.R. investors and assumed the presidency of the firm in 1858. He remained loyal to the Union during the Civil War and expanded his railroad and financial activities in the postbellum period. F. C. Crowley, Esq., of Baltimore helped with arrangements to greet the western visitors. *DAB*, 7:163–64; *Baltimore Sun*, July 15, 16, 1857.
61. The six-story Gilmor House opened in late 1855. Scharf, *History of Baltimore*, 516.
62. Elizabeth Gilmor Sherlock Swann (d. 1876) had married Thomas Swann, Jr., in 1834. Wilbur F. Coyle, *The Mayors of Baltimore* (Baltimore, 1919), 97.
63. Swann's daughter Louise later married Baltimore lawyer and politician Ferdinand C. Latrobe. *Nat. Cyc.*, 9:309, 427; Holli and Jones, *Biographical Dictionary of American Mayors*, 209–10.
64. Chase was to deliver a speech on July 18 at the Maryland Institute. In it he thanked Baltimoreans for their hospitality and elaborated on railroads as "bonds of union." He reiterated themes from this address in a toast at a closing dinner on July 20. *Baltimore Sun*, July 20, 1857; Smith, *Railway Celebrations*, 2:67–70, 88–90.
65. Garrett, Swann, and officials from Cincinnati, St. Louis, and Chillicothe, as well as Chase, gave speeches. *Baltimore Sun*, July 20, 1857.
66. William and Anne Eliza Neil Dennison. Smith, *Railway Celebrations*, 2:40.

August 1857 { 295 }

Nichol[as] at dinner with me[67]—Lee liberal but timid—fireworks at night—

WEDNESDAY, AUGUST 5. Off. 8.30—walked with Galloway—talk about Warden[68]— Tod called[69]— Nettie & Mary Galloway—15c to N— Gibson called— Baldwin, abt. Klinck Asst. Inspr. Toledo[70]— L fr Pierce—w him[71]— Renick & Fulton from P[72]— R. thinks chance good in P[73]— Miller & Bates dels / Lytle & J. H. Smith—F Linck & Smith, [*illeg.*] / Wilson, fory of Clevd.[74]— Panorama evg Mrs King[75]

67. Baltimore Superior Court judge Zadoc Collins Lee (1805–59), like Chase, had studied law under William Wirt. John Spear Nicholas (b. 1823) was a Baltimore lawyer, director of the Baltimore and Ohio R.R., and Democratic partisan. Drake, *American Biography*, 540; Lanman, *Biographical Annals*, 255–56; Scharf, *History of Baltimore*, 717; *Baltimore Sun*, July 21, 1857; *The Biographical Encyclopedia of Representative Men of Maryland and District of Columbia* (Baltimore, 1879), 247–48.

68. Columbus attorney Robert Bruce Warden (1824–88) renounced his allegiance to the Democratic party about this time and came out "boldly and flat-footed on the side of the Republicans." A former judge and reporter of the Ohio Supreme Court, Warden had studied law in Cincinnati and returned there after the Civil War. Upon suffering financial reverses in early 1873 he moved to Washington, D.C., and engaged himself as Chase's "private Secretary" and biographer. *DAB*, 19:444; *Daily Ohio State Journal*, Aug. 8, 1857; *Columbus Gazette*, Aug. 14, 1857; Warden to Chase, Apr. 2, 1873 (Chase Papers, Cinc. Hist. Soc.); check stub, Mar. 26, 1873 (Chase Papers, L.C.).

69. David Tod (1805–68), Western Reserve lawyer, industrialist, and politician, was in Columbus for the Ohio Democratic convention. He served as Union governor of Ohio, 1861–63, and in 1864 refused a chance to become secretary of the U.S. Treasury. *Daily Ohio State Journal*, Aug. 7, 1857; *DAB*, 18:567–68.

70. Hiram Baldwin, chief clerk, Department of Public Works, Auditor of State's Office, calling in regard to John G. Klinck, a Lucas County Republican who worked in the Canal Office at Toledo. *Col. Dir. (1856–57)*, 17; *Annual Report of Secretary of State*, 1856, 2:360; Waggoner, *Toledo*, 315, 342, 368, 721–22; *Daily Toledo Blade*, July 13, Aug. 8, 10, 1857.

71. Pierce discussed the completion of his lawbook, Chase's political prospects, Republican politics in Massachusetts, and social matters. Chase endorsed the letter "ansd Aug 5, 57," but his reply has not been found. Pierce to Chase, Aug. 3, 1857 (Chase Papers, L.C.).

72. Possibly Seymour G. Renick, or one of his relatives, and W. H. Fulton from Monroe Township, Pickaway County. *History of Franklin and Pickaway Counties*, 309.

73. The text from *Renick* through *good in P* is in lead pencil. The portions of the entry before and after are in blue pencil.

74. Alexander P. Miller (b. ca. 1811), Butler County farmer and state representative, 1857–58, and John Bates of Wood County were vice presidents of the Ohio Democratic convention gathering in Columbus. William Haines Lytle (1826–63), Cincinnati lawyer, soldier, and poet, won the 1857 Democratic nomination for lieutenant governor. James Haddock Smith assumed editorial charge of the *Ohio Statesman* near this date. Francis Linck, Cincinnati brewer and delegate to the convention, served with fellow delegate John M. Smith, a former representative from Adams County, on a committee to select the Ohio Democratic party's central committee. Both Richard Wilson, assemblyman from Marion County, 1858–60, and E. M. Wilson served on the convention's committee on rules. *Daily Ohio State Journal*, Aug. 3, 5, 6, 8, 1857; Ohio General Assembly, House of Representatives, *Journal*, 52nd Assem., 2nd sess., 1857, appen., 175; *DAB*, 11:538; Gilkey, *Ohio Hundred Year Book*, 217, 282, 306, 318; *Cinc. Dir. (1857)*, 185.

75. A Panorama of the Bible painted by J. Insco Williams was on exhibit in Columbus. *Daily Ohio State Journal*, July 31, Aug. 1, 3, 4, 6, 1857.

THURSDAY, AUGUST 6. Off with Galloway—thinks Payne ahead[76]—l. fr Ford violent &c—several members Fed Conv. called[77]—Payne nominated on 1st ballot—have thought this nomn. best for us—but possibly Ranney's might have been better—clear triumph of Douglas interest[78]—Lytle, Lt. Gov Morgan for Treasr beaten badly—Morris nominated—Reinhard Secr State, Backus PW[79]

SATURDAY, AUGUST 15. Office at 9—much office work—reqn. fr. Pa which declined to grant—Bascom & Buttles called abt. campaign[80]—meeting at New London 29th Aug. at Groveport Sat. 22[81]—Req fr N.Y. granted[82]—children with Coggeshall to Hillsboro

76. Cleveland lawyer, businessman, and politician Henry B. Payne (1810–96) became the 1857 Democratic nominee for governor. *DAB*, 14:325–26; *Daily Ohio State Journal*, Aug. 6, 1857.
77. The 1857 Ohio Democratic State Convention, with 340 delegates, met in Columbus on Aug. 6. Democratic support for the federal Fugitive Slave Law prompted use of the label "Federal" to designate the Ohio Democratic party. The first resolution in the state party's 1857 platform reaffirmed such a "Federal" sentiment. *Daily Ohio State Journal*, Aug. 8, 1857.
78. Rufus Percival Ranney (1813–91), lawyer, Democratic politician, and Ohio Supreme Court justice, 1851–56, polled 89 votes to 187 for Payne and 64 for a third candidate. Ranney sat again on the state's high court during the Civil War, then resigned and returned to the practice of law in Cleveland. A Republican assessment of the Democratic nominations published the day after the convention labeled the Democratic nominations "a Buchanan defeat and a Douglas triumph." *Daily Ohio State Journal*, Aug. 6, 7, 1857; *DAB*, 15:376–77.
79. William D. Morgan, editor of the *Newark Advocate* and state auditor during Breslin's tenure as treasurer, lost the Democratic nomination for treasurer to James Remley Morris on the sixth ballot by a vote of 209 to 131. Jacob Reinhard (b. 1815), banker, Columbus city council member, and a founder of the German-language newspaper *Der Westbote,* won the nomination for secretary of state on the first ballot. Abner L. Backus (1818–95), a civil engineer for state canal projects and later a Toledo businessman and civic promoter, easily won nomination to the Board of Public Works. Backus was the only Democratic state nominee to win in the 1857 general election. *Daily Ohio State Journal*, Aug. 6, 8, 1857; Gilkey, *Ohio Hundred Year Book,* 349; Hill, *Licking County,* 543; *Biographical Cyclopædia,* 1:210–11; Lee, *Columbus,* 1:492; *History of Franklin and Pickaway Counties,* 542–43; Scribner, *Lucas County and the City of Toledo,* 1:124–25.
80. Lucian Buttles was a former Columbus city council member associated with the Republican state central committee at this time. *Col. Dir. (1855),* 6; ibid. (1856–57), 39; *Daily Ohio State Journal,* Aug. 13, 1857.
81. Chase, renominated by acclamation on Aug. 12 as the Republican candidate for governor, planned to speak on Aug. 29 at a mass meeting at New London in conjunction with the Madison County Republican convention. On Aug. 22 he spoke for three hours to an audience of "substantial farmers and free white laborers" at Groveport in Franklin County. *Daily Ohio State Journal,* Aug. 12, 15, 17, 24, 1857.
82. The requisition from the governor of New York pertained to George See, a fugitive charged with forgery. Chase to sheriff of Lake County, Aug. 15, 1857 (Chase Papers, Ohio Hist. Soc.).

August 1857 {297}

10.50 AM / tea Dr Smiths—rode out with Miss Anthony / Nevins called at house abt. Report—sd. he cd. print [83]

JOURNAL IV

Canvass of 1857. [84]

The canvass of 1857 was somewhat remarkable. I had been nominated for reelection by acclamation, and with remarkable manifestations of enthusiasm & confidence. But we were surrounded by great difficulties. We were responsible for all the action of a Legislature, by no means harmonized by devotion to a common principle or unanimous in their views of public measures. The Whig & American elements were largely preponderant over the Democratic & Antislavery even among those who acted together as Republicans. Hence amid much legislation that was wise & beneficial was some which was neither wise nor beneficial, resulting from demands on one side & compliances, in fear of alienating needed support from Antislavery measures, on the other. Of all the mistakes real & imputed our adversaries were prepared to take every advantage. Then the Defalcation, committed by one of their own party, was to be charged upon ours, under cover of the false representations of Gibson, for whose acts I was to be held responsible. Then the cries of negro equality, amalgamation & the like were to employed to the uttermost to prejudice us with the ignorant. Then the financial troubles which arose soon after the nomination were also pressed into their service. [85] These things presented formidable difficulties & it soon became apparent that I was to have little aid in the canvass. no man had been nominated who was a speaker. The members of Congress on our side, by the policy of the State Committee, were directed to labor in their respective districts; which operated in [several] instances as a direction not to labor at all. Several presses & many of the electors repudiated one of the nominations of the State

---

83. Two days later Chase supplied state printer Richard Nevins with "the manuscript copy of Mr. Sparrow's Report on the State Treasury, to be printed pursuant to law." Nevins receipt, Aug. 17, 1857 (Chase Papers, Ohio Hist. Soc.).
84. This memorandum is from a collection of miscellaneous entries toward the rear of Journal IV.
85. The Ohio Life Insurance and Trust Company failed on Aug. 24, 1857, after the collapse of its New York branch. This failure and resulting litigation seriously hindered all banking operations in Ohio. *Report of the Investigating Commission . . . April 12, 1858*, 172–98; C. C. Huntington, "A History of Banking and Currency in Ohio Before the Civil War," *Ohio Archaeological and Historical Publications* 24 (1915): 470–72; *Daily Ohio State Journal*, Aug. 25, Sept. 30, 1857.

Convention, that of Mr. Blickensderfer.[86] Mr. Wade, Senator, & Judge Warden, alone, except Judge Welker who visited a few with me, accepted appointments to speak in the difft. counties.[87] And their appointments together did not equal mine alone. Thus the main burden of the general canvass was thrown upon me, contrary to my expectation when I received the nomination, which only extended to speaking in twenty eight or thirty counties. On the other hand the most active canvassers of the other party were constantly engaged—Payne himself, Lytle the nominee for Leiut Gov, E. B. Olds,[88] G. E. Pugh & many more.

Under these circumstances I have thought it worth while to set down here as sort of itinerary of my canvass as worth remembrance & hereafter perhaps interesting

I was nominated on the 12th of August 1857 & accepted the nomination in a brief speech.[89] In the evg. I addressed the people from the steps of the State House.[90]

On the 13, 14, 15 & 16 & pt. of 17th I remained at Columbus: 17th P.M. went to Morrow with Carrington 83 miles; staid overnight; 18th to Washington Fayette Co, 41m, where addressed meeting[91]—staid with Rush—[P.]M & night returned to Columbus 124m—remained at Cols. 18 & 19 & part of 20th—20th 10.50 A.M. to Cincinnati 120m with Warden & spoke 6th St Market[92]—21st

---

86. Jacob Blickensderfer, road and canal contractor from Tuscarawas County and incumbent member of the Ohio Board of Public Works, won renomination for his seat at the state Republican convention in Columbus on Aug. 12. Subsequent charges of improprieties in the letting of contracts drew repudiations from some Republican quarters and compromised his candidacy. Blickensderfer was the only Republican state candidate to lose in the 1857 election. *Col. Dir. (1856–57)*, 46; *Daily Ohio State Journal*, Aug. 7, 12, 13, 20, 31, Sept. 18, 22, Oct. 19, 1857.

87. The Republican nominee for lieutenant governor was Martin Welker (1819–1902), a Wooster resident and state judge. Welker later became a U.S. congressman, 1865–71, and a federal judge. *Bio. Dir. U.S. Cong.*, 2025.

88. Edson B. Olds (1802–69), Democratic congressman, 1849–55, and chairman of the 1857 Ohio Democratic convention. *Daily Ohio State Journal*, Aug. 6, 1857; *Bio. Dir. U.S. Cong.*, 1588.

89. Chase delivered this acceptance speech during an apparently unanticipated appearance at the Republican convention on Aug. 12. He put forth no "new principles" but reaffirmed support for "the rights of mankind" and opposition "to oppression in every form." *Daily Ohio State Journal*, Aug. 12, 13, 1857.

90. Chase's partisan address, to "two or three thousand persons" who greeted him with "loud huzzas," remarked upon the slave question, states' rights, and the treasury defalcation. Ibid., Aug. 13, 1857.

91. A local correspondent placed Chase and Carrington at Washington on Aug. 19. Chase spoke for two hours to an audience that "more than filled the court-room." Ibid., Aug. 20, 1857.

92. Chase's speech of nearly two hours covered the treasury defalcation, the situation in Kansas, states' rights, and slavery. Robert B. Warden addressed the meeting after Chase. Ibid., Aug. 20, 25, 1857; *New York Times*, Aug. 29, 1857.

returned to Cols. 120—22d. to Groveport 11m—stopped at McCormicks—addressed people in hall 2 P.M. & retd. to Cols. 11m Sunday & pt. of Monday at Columbus—24th Mon. to Lancaster 28m in carriage with Dennison—stopped at Tallmadge House[93]—addressed full Court House in evg.[94]—Dennison followed briefly—25th Tuesday to Logan 18m with Beatty in buggy[95]—spoke at night in Court House full—26th Wedy—to McArthur 22m—spoke there in afternoon Court House, pretty well filled—27th Thurs—to Greenfield by cars 60m. & addressed full meeting in Church—Galloway came over from Hillsborgh & spoke also[96]—Carey Trimble nominated for Senate[97]—staid while at G—— at Mr. Moore's[98]—red. present Life of Rev. S. Crothers[99]—

JOURNAL VII

THURSDAY, SEPTEMBER 17. Left Cin at 6 AM—goodbye to Dr Sams / change for check at B House[1]—Dayton—met Gen Spiece, Judge Young, Mr. Comly at P Hou[se][2] / Sidney—met at depot by Mathers & others / saw Judge Cummins & son, Conklin

---

93. The Tallmadge House at Lancaster opened in May 1857. *Columbus Gazette*, May 8, 15, 1857.

94. In response to a Democratic accusation that this meeting was a "failure," the *Daily Ohio State Journal* reprinted a report from the American party newspaper in Lancaster: "A large majority in attendance appeared to be delighted with the Governor's treatment of matters and things in general." *Daily Ohio State Journal*, Aug. 29, 1857.

95. William M. Beatty (b. 1820), Logan County lawyer and "stalwart Republican." Notebook, 1857 election (Chase Papers, L.C.); *History of Logan County*, 271–72, 316–17; *Portrait and Biographical Record of Auglaize, Logan and Shelby Counties*, 159–61.

96. A newspaper dispatch credited Chase and Samuel Galloway with speaking to "a large meeting of Republicans." *Daily Ohio State Journal*, Aug. 28, 1857.

97. Carey Allen Trimble (1813–87), Chillicothe doctor and Republican congressman, 1859–63, was nominated for state senator by acclamation at the 1857 convention of Ross and Highland counties. *Bio. Dir. U.S. Cong.*, 1954; *Daily Ohio State Journal*, Aug. 28, 1857.

98. Possibly farmer and mill owner Thomas Moore (1786–1870), a longtime resident of Highland County. *History of Ross and Highland Counties*, 434.

99. Andrew Ritchie, *The Life and Writings of Rev. Samuel Crothers, D.D.* . . . (Cincinnati, 1857).

1. Chase had attended the Ohio State Fair at Cincinnati, and stayed at the Burnet House. *Daily Ohio State Journal*, Sept. 18, 1857; Chase to Burnet House, Sept. 14, 1857 (Chase Papers, Ohio Hist. Soc.).

2. The Phillips House opened in 1850. Chase saw: Major General Adam Spiece, commander in chief of the Ohio militia; George Murray Young (1802–78), merchant and temperance reformer, who moved in 1851 from Cincinnati to Dayton and became a prominent Republican politician; and James M. Comly (1832–87), who studied law with Christopher P. Wolcott and worked as a correspondent for the *Cincinnati Gazette*. Comly entered the army in 1861 and emerged from the Civil War as a brigadier

& others[3]—speech—old man & humbugging / to Bellefontaine with Stanton & West[4]—speech there at night / slept at Stanton's— very well

FRIDAY, SEPTEMBER 18. Left for Marion—fast run—44 miles 50 min / stopped at Mr. Williams—handsome landscapes in parlor— pleasant wife &c— Speech at CH. to large crowd—outside[5]— Started immy for Findlay with Mr Porch[6]—reached Up. Sandy abt 8— Col M. H. Kirby [&] others met me[7]—insisted on speech—went to CH & spoke about an hour inside—supper at Hotel, with Judge Wilkinson of Worthn. & wife, after speech then bed—sheets used & not very comfortable—

SATURDAY, SEPTEMBER 19. Left early for Findlay—reached Carey to bkft[8]—at Hotel by Crook—his wife good repubn as well as he— Judge Carey took me to Findlay—spoke of Breslin who

---

general. *History of Montgomery County*, 256, 393, 402; Conover, *Centennial Portrait*, 2:1032–35; *Nat. Cyc.*, 12:465; Taylor, *Columbus and Franklin County*, 2:810; Lee, *Columbus*, 2:479–80; Heitman, *Historical Register*, 1:319.

3. John H. Mathers (1830–75), Sidney lawyer; Joseph Cummins, resident of Shelby County and judge of the Ohio Court of Common Pleas; and Jacob S. Conklin (1815–87), Sidney lawyer, former Ohio legislator, and Republican presidential elector in 1856. A. B. C. Hitchcock, *History of Shelby County, Ohio and Representative Citizens . . .* (Chicago, 1913), 325–26, 439–40; Gilkey, *Ohio Hundred Year Book*, 252, 543; *History of Shelby County . . .* (Philadelphia, 1883), 372.

4. Chase inserted the words *old man & humbugging* above the line with a different pencil from that used for the body of the entry. Benjamin Stanton (1809–72), Whig and then Republican congressman, 1851–53, 1855–61, practiced law at Bellefontaine. He was lieutenant governor of Ohio in 1862 and later moved to West Virginia. William H. West (1824–1911), Bellefontaine lawyer, helped organize the Republican party in Ohio and served as a state representative, 1858–65. *Bio. Dir. U.S. Cong.*, 1861; *Who Was Who*, 1:1324; Kennedy, *Historical Review of Logan County*, 73–74, 699–701; Gilkey, *Ohio Hundred Year Book*, 316.

5. A newspaper notice that placed Chase in Marion County on Saturday reported that he "addressed a large meeting." Chase may have visited Benjamin Williams and his wife, who were among the organizers of a Methodist church in Marion. *Daily Ohio State Journal*, Sept. 21, 1857; Winter, *Northwest Ohio*, 1:500.

6. Henry Porch of Findlay, a delegate to the 1857 Ohio Republican convention. Memorandum, rear of Journal VII; *Daily Ohio State Journal*, Aug. 12, 1857.

7. Ohio lawyer and politician Moses H. Kirby (1798–1889) of Upper Sandusky, known as "Colonel," lost the Whig gubernatorial nomination in 1850. He had a long tenure as prosecuting attorney of Wyandot County. *Biographical Cyclopædia*, 5:1099; Gilkey, *Ohio Hundred Year Book*, 278.

8. John Carey (1792–1875), associate judge of the Crawford County court of common pleas, 1825–32, Republican politician, and railroad promoter, established the town of Carey at a rail junction in Wyandot County. *Bio. Dir. U.S. Cong.*, 742–43; Gilkey, *Ohio Hundred Year Book*, 249, 516.

September 1857 { 301 }

asked him to be security &c—stopped with Mr. Gage[9]— Judge Carey & others to dinner—raining & obliged to speak in C.H. which much crowded— Mr. Spear & others called[10]—started for Fremont with Tillotson & Clapp[11]—reached Fostoria where had to speak at night.

SUNDAY, SEPTEMBER 20. rose 6½— p[12]— Clapp first, aftwds Tillotson called—sd. I wd. not go morn'g but wd. evening if necessary for Clapp / attended M.E. church[13]—afternoon started at 4—arrived Fremont about 8—stopped with R. [P.] Buckland, Sen. & candidate for reelection[14]—bed 10 30 & good rest / stool before bed.

MONDAY, SEPTEMBER 21. Up 6.15—dressing & p—breakfast excellent / stool after—w. letter to Bascom—many callers—went to Buckland's office—saw number of workingmen—also Homer Everett, B's partner, who cand. for p. atty[15] / Dr. Harkness & wife to dinner[16]—speech at 2 near 3 hours—audience large & attentive[17]—symptoms diarr—stool immy after speaking—felt weak—to Toledo at night warm reception at depot[18]—

9. Probably James L. Gage, a lawyer who built his reputation at McConnelsville, Ohio, and moved to northern Ohio around 1850. Robertson, *History of Morgan County,* 256; *History of Defiance County,* 91–92.
10. Samuel A. Spear edited the Findlay *Jeffersonian* in 1857. Winter, *Northwest Ohio,* 1:440; *Daily Ohio State Journal,* Oct. 15, 23, 1857; notebook, 1857 election (Chase Papers, L.C.).
11. Memoranda by Chase at the back of this journal refer to George M. Tillotson, identified as a captain, and Theodore Clapp, Esq., of Fremont.
12. Prayer.
13. The Methodist Episcopal Church in Fostoria, organized in 1833. *History of Seneca County,* 607–9.
14. Ralph Pomeroy Buckland (1812–92), Fremont lawyer, Republican state senator, 1855–59, Civil War general. *DAB,* 3:230.
15. Fremont lawyer and politician Homer Everett (1813–87), was Republican candidate for prosecuting attorney of Sandusky County. *Commemorative Biographical Record of the Counties of Sandusky and Ottawa . . .* (Chicago, 1896), 325–26; *Daily Toledo Blade,* Sept. 23, 1857.
16. Probably Lamon G. Harkness (b. 1801), formerly a practicing physician, now a merchant and businessman in Bellevue, Ohio, and his wife, Julia Follett Harkness (d. 1870). W. W. Williams, *History of the Fire Lands, Comprising Huron and Erie Counties, Ohio . . .* ([Cleveland], 1879), 414–15; Basil Meek, ed., *Twentieth Century History of Sandusky County, Ohio and Representative Citizens* (Chicago, 1909), 205.
17. A report reprinted from the *Fremont Journal* said that Chase "held the crowded listeners in a chained silence and attention." *Daily Ohio State Journal,* Sept. 26, 1857.
18. Most of this entry is in blue pencil. The portion from *immy* to the end of the entry is in standard lead pencil, as is the entry which follows.

TUESDAY, SEPTEMBER 22. Slept last night at Geo Walbridge's. Sister Alice, & Ed & Alice Skinner there—Belle's children Carrie & Jenny[19]—this morng. called Jane Auld—she & chil. well[20]—called H. B. Walbrid[ge] / spoke at Union Hall[21]— U. Pease Chn.[22]— Audience large—hard speaking—insisted on my going to Perrysburgh—warm greeting, music & cannon / speech—returned at night[23]—bed at G W's

WEDNESDAY, SEPTEMBER 23. Left for Bryan with Mott, Ashley & others[24]— Mr. [Hanks] Treasr. Paulding says I shall have 400 maj in P. Lannam, Whiteley[25] & Latty came into cars at Wauseon—Latty fears for Paulding— Friends in Fulton promise increase over Fremont—arrd. Bryan—stopped with Mr. Mallory[26]—spoke—good audience—much exhausted—to Deacon Ensigns with Dr. Paul—old gentleman near his end but full of faith[27] / symptoms of sickness.

THURSDAY, SEPTEMBER 24. started for Defiance after breakfast & parting words from Deacon—stopped with Mr. Brown interesting

---

19. George Walbridge (d. 1861) was married to Chase's niece Isabel (Belle) Skinner Walbridge. George, whose relationship (if any) to Chase's brother-in-law Henry B. Walbridge is unclear, obtained an appointment as postmaster of Toledo shortly before his death. Edward R. Skinner and Alice Skinner were siblings of Belle Skinner Walbridge and offspring of Chase's sister Janette. J. Ralston Skinner to Chase, Mar. 2, May 10, 1861, G. Walbridge to Chase, Apr. 3, 1861, H. B. Walbridge to Chase, May 11, 1861, Mar. 5, 1864, A. Skinner to Chase, Nov. 22, 1862, H. S. Walbridge & Co. to ———, Mar. 26, 1864, and "Family Memoranda" (Chase Papers, L.C.); Chase to Isabel Skinner Walbridge, May 4, 1864 (Chase Papers, Hist. Soc. of Pa.).

20. Chase's niece Jane Chase Auld was now a widow with three daughters, probably born in the later 1840s and early 1850s: Jane (known as "Jenny" or "Jennie," d. late 1864–early 1865), Alice, and Amy, who married Edward Yerburg Goldsborough in 1874. "Family Memoranda" (Chase Papers, L.C.); entry for Jan. 8, 1865, below; Chase to Kate Chase, July 4, 1853 (Chase Papers, Hist. Soc. of Pa.); Williams and McKinsey, *History of Frederick County*, 2:1242.

21. "Governor Chase began speaking soon after two o'clock, and held the audience in unremitted attention till five o'clock." *Daily Toledo Blade*, Sept. 22, 23, 1857.

22. John Usher Pease (1796–1870), merchant, led Lucas County Republicans during the 1857 campaign. Scribner, *Lucas County and the City of Toledo*, 1:149; *Daily Toledo Blade*, Aug. 10, 1857.

23. Chase, escorted by about seventy-five people and a band, was taken by steamboat to Perrysburg, up the Maumee River from Toledo, where he delivered an evening address at the courthouse. *Daily Ohio State Journal*, Sept. 25, 30, 1857.

24. Richard Mott and James Mitchell Ashley.

25. Possibly William Lannam of Bellefontaine or Rev. John Lannam, an editor from Montgomery County; and possibly M. C. Whiteley, a political correspondent and court of common pleas judge in northwestern Ohio, 1857–62. Notebook, 1857 election (Chase Papers, L.C.); Whiteley to Chase, Nov. 22, 1851 (Chase Papers, L.C.); Gilkey, *Ohio Hundred Year Book*, 555.

26. Perhaps C. W. Mallory, who about 1848 opened a store in Montpelier, Williams County. Winter, *Northwest Ohio*, 1:621.

27. Chase probably visited the father of William O. Ensign.

children[28]—spoke—audience best I ever had in defiance—much interest—crowd at depot on leaving—cheers—off for Ft Way[ne] met Mr. Colton on cars—model for steam plough[29]—slept at Rockhill House—first rate house and excellent room[30]

FRIDAY, SEPTEMBER 25. Dr. Paul returned to Defiance—I went to Van Wert with Committee—stopped at tavern Holmes landlord[31]—wretched room—many callers— Submitted to daguerreotype—good meeting—good feeling—in grove—old soldiers on stand— Committee from Delphos—Talbert[32] & another insisting on speech—went with them—stopped with Clark?—met Nichols—he spoke—I would not—Nichols & I in same room for night.[33]

SATURDAY, SEPTEMBER 26. Up after Nichols—washed, dressed & p—cars to Lima—stopped with Nichols—pleasant wife & fine boy—went to his office—saw many—some friends & some opponents—Col Jim Cunningham now among latter[34]—speech to good crowd in grove—tea with Nichols— Cars to Forest—Gorman spoke to me—good repn.—to Crestline & Columbus—arrived 2.20—

SUNDAY, SEPTEMBER 27. Remember now (Oct. 20) nothing of how this day was passed—

28. Four children of William A. Brown (1815–75), Defiance grain merchant and local officeholder, survived infancy: Frank (b. 1841), Helen (b. 1847), Mary (b. 1849), and Alfred (b. 1853). *History of Defiance County*, 230–31.

29. Chase may have met Alexander M. F. Colton (c. 1818–96), a Chicago architect associated with agricultural implement inventor Cyrus McCormick. *Who Was Who*, H:116; *Chicago Tribune*, Mar. 14, 17, 1896.

30. The sixty-five room Rockhill House in Fort Wayne, considered among the finest hotels in Indiana, opened in 1843. Charles R. Poinsatte, *Fort Wayne During the Canal Era, 1828–1855: A Study of a Western Community in the Middle Period of American History* (Indiana Historical Bureau, 1969), 223.

31. A "hewed-log house" in Van Wert, called the Eagle Tavern, then the American House, was managed for a time by Samuel Holmes (1812–89). Gilliland, *History of Van Wert*, 235, 398.

32. Probably Smith Talbott, local officeholder from Delphos, Allen County. Winter, *Northwest Ohio*, 1:611; notebook, 1857 election (Chase Papers, L.C.).

33. Clark may have been Israel D. Clark, a Van Wert lawyer elected probate judge in 1855. Lima attorney Matthias H. Nichols (1824–62) served in Congress, 1853–59, and converted from the Democratic to the Republican party after his first term. Gilliland, *History of Van Wert*, 284; notebook, 1857 election (Chase Papers, L.C.); *Bio. Dir. U.S. Cong.*, 1569; *Daily Ohio State Journal*, Oct. 2, 1857.

34. James Cunningham held local offices in Lima and Allen County. William Rusler, ed., *A Standard History of Allen County, Ohio . . .* (Chicago, 1923), 1:254–55, 258, 267, 2:291.

MONDAY, SEPTEMBER 28. Passed morng at office attending to sundry duties—in the afternoon or rather at night went to Xenia expecting to take Springfield down train in the morning / found train taken off—good room at Hotel[35]—

TUESDAY, SEPTEMBER 29. Up at 4 & cars to Deerfield— Denny & with Rob. G. Corwin waiting to take me to Lebanon / breakfast at Lebanon House—went to Corwins / agreeable lady Mrs C— military escort to Hall[36] / large audience—spoke over 2½ hours— retd to Corwin's—tea—buggy with him to Dayton arrived b. 9 & 10—talk on way—he desired my nomn at Phila.[37] & desires it now in 1860. with Parsons, Carrington and other staff[38]—bed—

MONDAY, OCTOBER 12. Saw number of friends at office—Dennison, Bascom & Wood at Com. Room[39]—dined— Cars to Zanesville, Dennison with me— Duvall, Applegate & crowd with band met me at depot & escorted me to Hotel[40]—to Hall to speak / crowded— adjd. to front of Court House— Congos[41] came from Market House

---

35. Chase's secretary telegraphed a friend at Xenia: "Governor comes by nine o'clock train. Have room ready at Hotel." L. L. Rice to William B. Fairchild, Sept. 28, 1857 (Chase Papers, Ohio Hist. Soc.).

36. The Warren Guards escorted Chase from the Corwin residence. Ohio editor and Republican politician William H. P. Denny (b. 1811) published the *Western Star* at Lebanon, 1846–58. Robert G. Corwin (b. 1815), a Lebanon attorney, operated a stock farm until 1859, when he resumed the practice of law at Dayton. He had married Eliza Bruen Corwin of Dayton in 1839. *History of Brown County*, 2:11–12; notebook, 1857 election (Chase Papers, L.C.); *The History of Warren County, Ohio* . . . (Chicago, 1882), 731–32; *Daily Ohio State Journal*, Oct. 1, 1857.

37. The 1856 Republican national convention, which had nominated John C. Frémont for president. George H. Mayer, *The Republican Party, 1854–1966*, 2nd ed. (London, 1967), 42–44.

38. Chase reviewed militia units from across the state at Dayton during their annual gathering on Sept. 30. *Daily Ohio State Journal*, Sept. 21, 25, 29, Oct. 1, 1857.

39. Very likely William W. Wood, a vice president of the 1857 Ohio Republican convention. *Daily Ohio State Journal*, Aug. 12, 1857.

40. "Duvall" may have been a descendant of Jonathan Duval, who built a mill near Zanesville in 1798. Daniel Applegate was a Zanesville businessman, Republican partisan, and member of the board of control of the state bank. Samuel P. Hildreth, *Pioneer History: Being an Account of the First Examinations of the Ohio Valley* . . . (Cincinnati, 1848), 442; Smith, *Railway Celebrations*, 1:113; *History of Muskingum County*, 87, 100, 262; *Daily Ohio State Journal*, Aug. 12, 1857; *Annual Report of Secretary of State, 1856*, 2:357.

41. A term which Republicans derisively applied to Democrats during the 1857 campaign for their efforts to make issues of race and slavery the focus of debate. The usage derived from a dispute over the actual origins of a statement which the Democratic *Ohio Statesman* printed as "The Congo Creed," allegedly from Republican sources: "We believe a negro is human—he has a soul—he has an intellect—and so far as the right of suffrage or any other right of citizenship is concerned, he should be placed on an equality with the rest of mankind." *Daily Ohio State Journal*, Sept. 4–Oct. 6, 1857.

to stand near bye / drums & speeches—made my speech notwithg to satisfn of our fds—slept at Stacey House[42]

TUESDAY, OCTOBER 13. Tired & rose rather late—bkft with Goddard[43] / Cars to Columbus— Duvall came in just before starting—says gained 46 amg. his hands— Van Slyke on cars—conft. of success—called at office & got tickets for him & me—voted for Bk Charter & all constl. amendments—except Bank & Indivd. Taxatn[44]—home to dinner— Snowden says our friends in good spirits & all going well— At night some apprehn. abt. Franklin Co.

WEDNESDAY, OCTOBER 14. Office pretty early—heavy losses from Fremonts vote reported from Reserve— Franklin county 5 or 600 against me—danger of deft. but still a large margin to overcome— Greene reported 1200 for me—a bright spot— Col David L. Wood called abt. collection of arms—talk with him abt. his appointment—

THURSDAY, OCTOBER 15. Election prospects still rather discouraging though by no means decisive agst me Evidence of coalition b. Hunkers & KNs— Van Trump reported through Culver as advising to vote for Payne[45]— Steedman through Paul as boasting of perfected arrangement [certain] defeat Chase not completed till within few days—more talk with Wood—wrote

---

42. Stacy's Hotel, a brick building erected in Zanesville during the 1840s. *History of Muskingum County,* 94.

43. Likely Charles Backus Goddard (1796–1864), Zanesville lawyer; state representative, 1838–39; and state senator, 1845–49. *Biographical Cyclopædia,* 3:591–92; Gilkey, *Ohio Hundred Year Book,* 166, 168, 205.

44. Ohio voters considered a bank bill and five amendments to the Ohio Constitution at this election. The amendments involved the frequency of legislative sessions, district courts, taxation, special laws for the relief of corporations, and legislative districts. All six measures lost. *Daily Ohio State Journal,* Feb. 23, Apr. 4, 14, July 7, Sept. 11, Oct. 6, 24, 1857.

45. Philadelph Van Trump (1810–74), editor, lawyer, and politician, received the American party (Know-Nothing) nomination for governor in 1857. Republicans believed that Van Trump had urged his few thousand supporters to vote for the Democratic ("Hunker") ticket, although Van Trump denied collusion with the Democrats. Culver was likely either Lucius H. Culver (d. 1881), a lawyer who later pursued business interests in Pennsylvania; or his brother, Charles Vernon Culver (1830–1909), who worked as a cashier in his father's bank, then also moved to Pennsylvania, where he became a Republican congressman, 1865–67. *Bio. Dir. U.S. Cong.,* 856, 1978; *Daily Ohio State Journal,* Aug. 6 and Oct. 14, 22, 1857; *Cincinnati Daily Gazette,* Oct. 12, 1857; John J. Brasee to Chase, Aug. 28, 1857 (Chase Papers, L.C.); *Biographical Cyclopædia,* 1:242–44; notebook, 1857 election (Chase Papers, L.C.).

Hickox askg acceptance appt. Director Northern O Lun. asylum— Scarborough appd Exr. Treasy.[46]

FRIDAY, OCTOBER 16. No certain news of election still—but evidently great losses—Congos rather sanguine of success— Appd. Wood agent to collect arms—referred Armstrong to him[47]—wrote Collins will come for children Monday[48]—all counties in except Monroe which at last reported 2100 for Payne— This seems almost decisive against us.

SATURDAY, OCTOBER 17. Better news—Hamilton County formerly reported 3500 Payne now only 3245—Monroe corrected from 2100 to 1225—this seems to settle question in our favor—Congos give up and send swearing telegrams[49]— Sent in morng. commission to Wm M. Wilson Judge vice Clark resigned[50]—

SUNDAY, OCTOBER 18. Up pretty early & p.[51]—read Gibbon's Rome—with Milmans instructive notes[52]— Church—Mr. Reynolds morng. about deceitfulness of riches— Galloway called to enquire

46. Chase appointed Charles Hickox (1810–90), a Cleveland resident of antislavery sympathies, to fill a vacancy on the board of the Northern Ohio Lunatic Asylum. William W. Scarborough (b. 1814), Cincinnati banker and businessman and half brother of George Hoadly, Jr., declined appointment as special examiner of the state treasury. Chase apparently wrote Scarborough again on Oct. 21 and asked him to reconsider, but Alfred Kelley eventually accepted the position. Orth, *History of Cleveland*, 2:1036–39; R. P. Spalding to Chase, Oct. 13 1857, Chase to Hickox, Oct. 15, 1857, Chase to Scarborough, Oct. 15, 1857, Scarborough to Chase, Oct. 17, 1857 (two letters same date), (Chase Papers, Ohio Hist. Soc.); Robson, *Biographical Encyclopædia*, 599; *The Third Annual Report of the Trustees and Superintendent of the Northern Ohio Lunatic Asylum*, Ohio Exec. Docs. for 1857, 2:64; *Special Report on the Condition of the Treasury*.
47. Possibly William Armstrong, Columbus city treasurer, 1843–61, or William Wallace Armstrong (1833–1905), editor and Ohio Democratic politician whose father had been a major general in the Ohio militia. Taylor, *Columbus and Franklin County*, 1:133; *Nat. Cyc.*, 24:352; Van Tassel and Grabowski, *Encylcopedia of Cleveland*, 50; Lang, *History of Seneca County*, 412–14.
48. William O. Collins.
49. Chase's reelection remained doubtful virtually until the Democrats conceded. *Daily Ohio State Journal*, Oct. 14–20, 1857.
50. Greenville lawyer William Martin Wilson (1808–64), commissioned common pleas judge for the second judicial district to succeed James Clark (1830–81). Clark, who later moved to New York, resigned before he intended to step down from the bench, setting in motion an examination of the gubernatorial appointment power. *Daily Ohio State Journal*, Oct. 17, 1857; *A Biographical History of Darke County* . . . (Chicago, 1900), 234–35; *The History of Darke County, Ohio* . . . (Chicago, 1880), 230–31; E. B. Taylor to Chase, Aug. 30, 1857, Clark to Chase, Aug. 25 and Oct. 7, 1857; C. P. Wolcott to Chase, Sept. 12, 1857 (Chase Papers, Ohio Hist. Soc.); Gilkey, *Ohio Hundred Year Book*, 551, 553; *History and Biographical Cyclopædia of Butler County*, 260; Cone, *Narrative of Hamilton*, 241.
51. "Prayer" or "prayed."
52. Edward Gibbon, *The Decline and Fall of the Roman Empire*, with notes by the Rev. H. H. Milman (London, 1838–39).

October 1857 {307}

abt. PM or evg. service—sd. correction from Hamilton increases Payne[']s Majority abt. 200—from Washn mine abt. same— Evg. Church with Mr. Snowden / Mills formerly act[ive][53]— If righteous scarcely &[c]—loose declamation but great truths—bed late.

MONDAY, OCTOBER 19. To office about nine after p. & readg. Gibbon / dreamed last night of defeat by maj. in Ia. agst me[!] Rice, at office, reported gains, certainly electing me / several calling to congratulate—w. Hanna abt. P.C. & L. divd.—*Case* congg. him on election[54]—Ensign (Judge W.O.) on his father's death— Cars to Loveland—night at Victor Smith's—songs very pleasantly sung by Miss Annie Rogers—Miss Mary Smith, V's sister[55]

TUESDAY, OCTOBER 20. Up early & p—bkft at Smith's—wagon & fast drivers to cars with Victor S—gave him letter for Halsted[56]— met divers in cars & at Blanchester—Doddridge Circleville—Marley, Hillsboro[57]—& others—much gratn. amg. Reps on a/c of victory— heard Collins defd. & also Carey Trimble with great regret—fd. children at Collins well except Kate's cold—dinner—met Mrs Sams—went to Female College—Mr. Matthews Miss Kerr[58]—I. S. Dickey, Briggs—Rothrock & others called[59]—Doran & Hibben locos[60]—

53. Evidently the reference is to Jonathan Mills, who had been a preacher.
54. Charles Case (1817–83), Indiana lawyer and Republican congressman, Dec. 1857–61. *Bio. Dir. U.S. Cong.*, 752–53.
55. Victor Smith's household now occupied a farm in Loveland. Annie Rogers, Smith's wife's sister, was a daughter of New Hampshire abolitionist Nathaniel Peabody Rogers. *Nat. Cyc.*, 2:320; Ezra S. Stearns, *History of Plymouth, New Hampshire* (Cambridge, Mass., 1906), 2:577–79; Parks, "A Man For His Season," 7, 20.
56. Murat Halstead.
57. Hillsboro resident Joseph K. Marley served as a provost marshal during the Civil War. James H. Thompson, *The History of the County of Highland* . . . (Hillsboro, Ohio, 1878), 29.
58. Mrs. Sams was possibly Marianna Stuart Sams (d. 1885), wife of a Hillsboro businessman active in the local Episcopalian church. The Hillsboro Female College, established in 1855 under Methodist Episcopal auspices, completed its building in 1857. The Rev. Joseph McDowell Matthews was the college's first president. Miss Kerr was perhaps a daughter of either James Kerr (1786–1870), a farmer, or S. F. Kerr (1805–81), lawyer and judge from Fayette County. Winter, *Northwest Ohio*, 3:1759; Klise, *County of Highland*, 212, 360; Thompson, *County of Highland*, 58–62; *History of Ross and Highland Counties*, 376; R. S. Dills, *History of Fayette County* . . . (Dayton, Ohio, 1881), 1031–32.
59. Possibly Alfred S. Dickey (1812–73), a Greenfield lawyer whom Chase appointed judge of common pleas in 1858; Robert M. Briggs; and James Harvey Rothrock (1829–99), a Greenfield lawyer who emigrated to Iowa in 1860. *History of Ross and Highland Counties*, 143–44; *Nat. Cyc.*, 12:336; Klise, *County of Highland*, 197.
60. That is, "locofocos." Democratic journalist John G. Doren (b. ca. 1833) edited the *Hillsboro Gazette*, 1854–58. Hibben was probably Samuel E. Hibben (b. 1804), Hillsboro merchant and former state senator, or one of his sons. Chase wrote most of this

WEDNESDAY, OCTOBER 21. Up at 6—bkft & to cars— Gen & Mrs McDowell[61]—Rothrock & Briggs on cars—K left box wh. Collins promd. to send up—chgd cars at Loveland—Maj or Col somebody intd.[62] Met Hosea on L. Mi. Road[63]—also Col. Patterson, Dr. Thomson with whom was Ed fr. Auburn[64]—found many letters congratg. [Wine] Corwine, Heaton Gurley Plants & others[65]— Judge Brayton home from Capital with me—dinner with chiln. at 4—present slippers fr. Miss Anthony—wrote her thanks also Thayer[66] Scarborough abt. Exn.—Humphreys,[67] Bierce[68]

---

entry in pencil. The text beginning *met Mrs Sams* is in ink, as is the entry which follows. *History of Montgomery County*, 712–13; *History of Ross and Highland Counties*, 363, 391; Gilkey, *Ohio Hundred Year Book*, 270.

61. Sarah A. McCue McDowell, daughter of Virginia Presbyterian clergyman John McCue, and her husband Joseph Jefferson McDowell (1800–1877), Hillsboro lawyer, Democratic politician, and former militia general. *Bio. Dir. U.S. Cong.*, 1461; *Biographical Cyclopædia*, 6:1471–72.

62. Introduced.

63. The Little Miami R.R. provided service between Cincinnati and Columbus through its connection at Xenia with the Columbus & Xenia R.R. Robert L. Black, *The Little Miami Railroad* (Cincinnati, n.d.).

64. Philadelphia businessman William Chamberlain Patterson (1813–83) had been president of the Pennsylvania R.R., 1849–52. He served as an officer during the war with Mexico and briefly in 1861 as an aide to his brother, Gen. Robert Patterson. Edward Thomson's companion was likely either William Hosmer, who in 1856 broke from the Methodist Episcopal *Northern Christian Advocate* of Auburn, N.Y., to found the more zealously antislavery *Northern Independent*, or Hosmer's former editorial partner, Freeborn Garrettson Hibbard (1811–95), who continued to edit the *Northern Christian Advocate* until 1860. *Nat. Cyc.*, 13:334; Smith, *Railway Celebrations*, 1:134; Elliot G. Storke, *History of Cayuga County, New York* . . . (Syracuse, N.Y., 1879), 52–53, 57; *DAB*, 8:612; *Historical and Statistical Gazetteer of New York State* (Syracuse, N.Y., 1860), 198–99.

65. Probably Richard M. Corwine; David Heaton (1823–70), Ohio Republican and state senator, 1856–57, who moved in Sept. 1857 from Ohio to Minnesota and during the Civil War served as a special agent of the U.S. Treasury Department at New Bern, N.C.; John A. Gurley; and Homer G. Plantz, son of Ohio politician Tobias Avery Plants and at this time apparently a student at Urbana University. (Spelling of the Plantz/Plants family name seems to have varied.) As a Treasury clerk during the Civil War, Homer Plantz served as one of Chase's secretaries. In 1863 he became U.S. district attorney at Key West, Florida. Gurley to Chase, Oct. 19, 1857 (Chase Papers, L.C.); *Appletons'*, 3:155; *Daily Ohio State Journal*, Aug. 12, Sept. 17, 1857; Ohio General Assembly, House of Representatives, *Journal*, 52nd Assem., 2nd sess., 1857, appen., 173; memoranda, rear of Journal VII; *Bio. Dir. U.S. Cong.*, 1652–53; Frederick J. Blue, *Salmon P. Chase: A Life in Politics* (Kent, Ohio, 1987), 218–19.

66. Perhaps William Sydney Thayer (1829–64), a member of the staff of the New York *Evening Post* who had written Chase in Aug. to request biographical information for a "new American Encyclopaedia." Thayer to Chase, Aug. 4, 1857 (Chase Papers, L.C.); William Cullen Bryant II and Thomas G. Voss, eds., *The Letters of William Cullen Bryant: Volume III, 1849–1857* (New York, 1981), 373.

67. Possibly Joseph Bloomfield Humphreys (b. 1802), assistant to the Hamilton County auditor, 1849–63. Robson, *Biographical Encyclopædia*, 48; *Cinc. Dir. (1857)*, 165.

68. Lucius Verus Bierce (1801–76), Akron lawyer, Republican politician, and once a state militia general. Chase apparently wrote to decline attending a political dinner. Bierce to Chase, Oct. 20, 1857 (Chase Papers, L.C.); Lane, *Akron and Summit County*, 414; Coyle, *Ohio Authors*, 56–58; Perrin, *History of Summit County*, 307.

Gurley—Plants[69] Heaton—Briggs—read Gibbon—bed

THURSDAY, OCTOBER 22. Very little done today except routine and not much of that— Kate engaged in putting her room to rights / I wrote Ralston Skinner to send up furniture—read Gibbon—

SUNDAY, OCTOBER 25. Hard rain & inclement—did not go to Church—read— Evg. went with Nettie & Katie & found church closed—heard afterwards that reason was want of wood— Mr. Pinneys funeral afternoon at Church—held not suicide because insane[70]

MONDAY, OCTOBER 26. Rose as usual—mailed letter to Mrs. Eastman—read some pages Gibbon before dinner—at office—little done morng.—after dinner—went to office again—saw Mr. Carrington about house also had note from him—Dr. Carter will take $12000[71]—thinks it & so do I too much[72]—

JOURNAL IV

OCT. 30— Tried foolish expert. & was duly rewarded.[73]

NOV. 10— Looked at Dr. Carters house—half inclined to buy—much pleased with it.

---

69. Chase thanked Homer G. Plantz for his "kind note of congratulations." Chase to Plantz, Oct. 21, 1857 (Chase Papers, Cinc. Hist. Soc.).

70. A. H. Pinney, (b. ca. 1805), a contractor, died a few days earlier in Michigan. His funeral took place at Trinity Church in Columbus. A report that Pinney had committed suicide assigned the act to "pecuniary embarrassment and ill health." *Columbus Gazette*, Oct. 23, 30, 1857; *Daily Ohio State Journal*, Oct. 26, 1857.

71. Henry B. Carrington evidently assisted Chase with matters related to the occupation of a house. Francis Carter, a graduate of Kings and Queens College of Dublin and a member of the Starling Medical College faculty, resided in a "mansion" on the northeast corner of Sixth and State Streets until he built and moved into another house nearby. Chase occupied the corner mansion later in 1857. White, *We Too Built Columbus*, 103–4; *Col. Dir.* (1856–57), 41; *History of Franklin and Pickaway Counties*, 566; Chase to Kate Chase, Dec. 4, 1857 (Chase Papers, Hist. Soc. of Pa.).

72. In the original journal, the pages with printed headings for Oct. 27 through Nov. 26 have no entries. Pages intended for Nov. 27 through Dec. 20 entries are missing. Pages with printed headings for Dec. 21–31 are present, but Chase made no entries on them. Following them are nine pages of miscellaneous memoranda, including names, addresses, notes, and over three pages of quotations from Spenser's *Faerie Queene*. Some financial accounts occupy the final pages of Journal VII.

73. These entries for fall 1857, and those for 1859 which follow them, are from miscellaneous memoranda toward the end of Journal IV.

Nov. 11. Asked Stone to rent Kelseys if possible at $1000 & to go to $1200 if necessary—determd. to buy Carters if cannot rent. Met Reemelin on cars who says that dems made bargain with Fries to cover dft in Ham Co Treasy. & then Americans voted whole dem ticket[74]—otherwise Payne's maj wd. not have been over 1000

1859

FEB. 17, 1859. My dear sister Alice died today. She had been apparently in perfectly good health for some months—going out so freely & taking such part and interest in all that went on that I had no uneasiness about her. I knew indeed & she knew that she was liable to attacks of heart trouble, but so uniform had been her health that I had almost ceased to fear it & as well as herself had relaxed the precautions I formerly shewed, such as seeing myself that she did not walk any considerable distance or do any thing which might unnecessarily fatigue or startle her. So last evening, when after tea she said she was going to church (the Wed. evg. Lecture) I let her go without enquiring how she was going or indeed making any enquiry at all / On her return she left her escort at the yard gate & must have been seized with an apoplectic fit immediately after for she had just strength enough to reach the door where she fell on the threshold. My daughter Katie heard some one groaning there & ran to the Library & called me. I hastened to the door & found my dear Sister. I got her into the house without delay & sent for medical aid. In a very few moments Dr. Carter came & soon after Dr. Smith. Her suffering from head ache was dreadful for some time. At last she seemed to get relief & her symptoms became more favorable. The improvement however was but temporary about 2 o'clock this morning she began to sink & continued to fail gradually until about half past one when her spirit departed. Thus have I lost a dear & good sister; and with the painful circumstances that from the attack to her death she was not able to converse with any of us; so great was for part of the time her suffering, or during the remainder, her delerium or unconsciousness. She had been long a member of the Episcopal church & was, I trust & believe a true Christian. Doubtless our loss is far overmatched by her gain. All our friends have been very kind. Dr. Smith with Mr. Gangewer took upon himself the charge of arrangements for

---

74. George Fries (1799–1866) was a physician, Democratic congressman, 1845–49, and Hamilton County treasurer, 1860–62. *Bio. Dir. U.S. Cong.*, 1029.

the funeral. Mr. Gangewer & Mr. Simkins[75] sit up tonight in the Library, while Miss Anth[on]y & Mrs Wright watch the body.

FEB. 18.— Many friends called— Mr. Jones the sculptor took a cast of the face[76] / Mr. Norton the Episcopal Minister called.[77] He said that Mr. James Bates who walked home last night with Sister[78] Alice—(I wrote "Aunt" for we commonly called her Aunt Alice) told him that she talked pleasantly all the way home—that when they reached the gate she invited him to come in, which he declined— that on leaving her a few steps from the door he observed her stretch out her hand to take hold of the branch of a tree, but supposed she was only putting it out of the way as it overhangs partially the path. He bid her good night & went home. He does not know whether she replied to his goodnight but thinks she did not— Nothing however then struck him as unusual, although it now seems probable that this was the commencement of the attack & that she was only able to reach but not to open the door before she was prostrated. The opinion of the physicians is that the immediate exciting cause was indigestion, she having partaken of a supper on the night of the 16th of which she vomited undigested portions and having eaten at tea on the night of the attack some ham which was vomited quite undigested.

I wrote yesterday to Eliza Whipple, brother Edward, Sister Helen Jennie Jewett & Susan Walker announcing our loss, & sent despatches to Mr. Walbridge & recd. for answer that Belle W—— & Helen Skinner wd. come down today.[79] Today I have sent to a number of friends copies of the State Journal announcing her death.[80]

---

75. Possibly F. A. B. Simkins, who in 1857 assumed editorial control of the Hocking Valley *Republican*. *Daily Ohio State Journal*, Sept. 30, 1857.

76. Thomas Dow Jones (1811–81), portrait sculptor and medallionist. In 1858 a group of Cincinnati citizens commissioned Jones to make a bust of Chase. Groce and Wallace, *Dictionary of Artists*, 358; Coyle, *Ohio Authors*, 345; N. W. Thomas et al. to Chase, Apr. 7, 1858, Chase to Thomas et al., Apr. 17, 1858, Chase to Jones, Feb. 23, 1864 (Chase Papers, Hist. Soc. of Pa.); Chase to Jones, Nov. 2, 1868 (Chase Papers, L.C.).

77. George Hatley Norton (1824–93), rector, Trinity Church in Columbus, 1858–59. *Appletons'*, 4:538; *History of Franklin and Pickaway Counties*, 520; Wallace, *North American Authors*, 331.

78. *Sister* is written over something else, apparently, from Chase's explanation in the text, *Aunt*.

79. Helen Skinner was Chase's niece and a sister of Isabel (Belle) Skinner Walbridge. "Family Memoranda" (Chase Papers, L.C.).

80. The newspaper noted that Alice Chase's "amiable virtues had endeared her to many friends. Active in good works, earnest in deeds of charity, her consistent Christian life gave evidence of that strong abiding faith in the Savior whose sure fruits are holy deeds." Funeral services took place at Chase's home on Feb. 19 at half past two o'clock. *Daily Ohio State Journal*, Feb. 18, 19, 1859.

SEP. 29— Spoke to a good audience at Toledo in front of C.H. Dennison followed.[81] Staid with Geo. Walbridge

" 30   Instead of going to Defiance as I intended, went, on request & in conformity with arrangement of friends to Ottawa. Bassett accompanied me. Met Laskey candidate for Senator on cars— Agl. Exhibition just closed at Ottawa—racing—spoke under Exhibition shed—pretty fair audience.[82] Went in night from Ottawa to Lima by Dayton & Mich. Road & arrived about 3 A.M. 1st Oct.[83]

1861

JOURNAL VIII

MONDAY, DEC. 9TH., 1861. Had conversation with Messrs. *Stevens and Vail* about reimbursement.[84] They contended that the Banks were entitled to be reimbursed, in coin, for all Two Years' Bonds and 60 Day Notes received in payment of Subscriptions, whether paid by the Banks themselves on account of deposits, or by individuals for Bonds. I denied the right of the Banks to reimbursement for Bonds paid by them, but promised to take the other into consideration.

Mr. Cisco telegraphed that the Banks had paid the first instalment of the 7 per cent Loan[85]

---

81. Chase spoke at Toledo with Republican gubernatorial candidate William Dennison. *Daily Ohio State Journal*, Sept. 27, 1859.

82. This meeting at Ottawa, where the Putnam County fair was held Sept. 29–30, was a late change to the campaign schedule. Chase attended with Edward P. Bassett. George Laskey (b. 1824), merchant and agriculturist from Wood County, won election in 1859 to the Ohio senate as a Republican and served one term. *Daily Ohio State Journal*, Sept. 29, 1859; *Portrait and Biographical Record of the City of Toledo and Lucas and Wood Counties, Ohio* . . . (Chicago, 1895), 259–60; *Ohio Cultivator* 15 (Aug. 1859), 240.

83. Chase traveled on the Dayton and Michigan Railroad to reach his scheduled campaign meeting the next day in Lima. *Daily Ohio State Journal*, Sept. 27, 1859; *History of Montgomery County*, 465.

84. In margin: "Reimbursement of the Banks." John Austin Stevens (1795–1874) and Henry F. Vail were president and cashier, respectively, of New York's Bank of Commerce. The copyist, Homer Plantz, underlined names in the early portion of this journal. *DAB*, 17:616; *New York Dir. (1863)*, 883; Vail to Chase, Dec. 27, 1861 (Chase Papers, Hist. Soc. of Pa.).

85. In margin: "The 7% Loan." John Jay Cisco (1806–84) served as assistant treasurer at New York, 1853–64. *New York Times*, Mar. 24, 1884; Cisco file (Presidential Appointments, Gen. Recs. Treasury Dept., Nat. Arch.).

Gov. Fish, Mr. Case and many others called in the evening.[86] The Annual Report went to Congress to-day[87]

TUESDAY, DEC. 10TH., 1861. *Mr. Haight*, M.C. from N.Y., called and stated results of Bank Meeting yesterday.[88] Mr. Gallatin only opposed payment of first instalment;[89] objecting that the Secretary had recommended a tax on Bank circulation, and so had broken his agreement.

A number of gentlemen called at the office on applications for office and otherwise.[90]

At 12, went to President's to Cabinet Meeting.[91] A deputation from New York, consisting of *Judge Davies, Mr. O'Gorman* and *Mr. Savage*,[92] represented the importance of an exchange of prisoners, with special reference to the case of Col. Corcoran.[93] After their withdrawal some conversation took place on this subject. *Mr. Blair* favored exchanges generally. *Mr. Bates* objected to the recognition of the Confederates as belligerents by regular exchanges.[94] *Mr. Seward* thought

---

86. Hamilton Fish (1808–93), Whig congressman, 1843–45, governor of New York, 1849–50, U.S. senator, 1851–57, and secretary of state, 1869–77; and possibly Eliphalet Case, an editor and friend of Chase from Portland, Maine, and Patriot, Ind. Case to Chase, Nov. 23, Dec. 16, 1861 (Chase Papers, L.C.); *DAB*, 6:397–400.

87. In margin: "Annual Report." *Report of the Secretary of the Treasury on the State of the Finances, for the Year Ending June 30, 1861*, 37th Cong., 2nd sess., 1861, S. Ex. Doc. 2.

88. In margin: "Payment of First Instalment, 7% Loan." Edward Haight (1817–85) was president of New York's Bank of the Commonwealth and a Democratic congressman, 1861–63. *Bio. Dir. U.S. Cong.*, 1109.

89. James Gallatin (1796–1876), president of New York's Gallatin National Bank. *New York Dir. (1863)*, 315; *New York Times*, June 27, 1876.

90. In margin: "Callers."

91. Abraham Lincoln (1809–65) was now in his ninth month as president of the U.S. *DAB*, 11:242–61.

92. Henry Ebenezer Davies (1805–81), of New York's Court of Appeals; attorney Richard O'Gorman (1821–95), an ardent supporter of the Union; and possibly James W. Savage, another New York lawyer. *Nat. Cyc.*, 3:26; *New York Dir. (1863)*, 762; *New York Times*, Mar. 2, 1895.

93. In margin: "Exchange of Prisoners." Michael Corcoran (1827–63) of the 69th New York State Militia, later a brigadier general of volunteers, had been wounded and taken prisoner at Bull Run, July 21, 1861. Union officials were concerned about Corcoran's possible abuse as a prisoner of war. Corcoran regained freedom through an exchange of prisoners in Aug. 1862. *Nat. Cyc.*, 4:54; *OR*, ser. 2, v. 2:1113, v. 4:394–95.

94. Postmaster General Montgomery Blair (1813–83), a son of Francis P. Blair, Sr., had been mayor of St. Louis and a judge. Attorney General Edward Bates (1793–1869) was formerly a Missouri legislator, judge at St. Louis, and Whig congressman, 1827–29. *Appletons'*, 1:193; *DAB*, 2:48–49, 339–40.

best to take the matter under consideration and defer a conclusion; urging that it would be bad policy to abandon the position taken as to privateers, which he thought had been effectual in protecting our commerce from general depredation.[95] My own view was that we had already acknowledged the rebels as belligerents by the institution of the blockade, but not as National belligerents; that we were therefore at liberty to adopt what course we pleased in respect to privateers; that Mr. Seward's view was correct at the time the policy was proclaimed; that now, with a stronger and better built Navy to protect our commerce, we could well afford to allow privateering, provided they could get ships and men, precisely as we allowed War on land; and that I would not object to sending Smith, who had been convicted of piracy at Philadelphia, to Fortress Monroe, and let Gen. Wool exchange him for Corcoran.[96] I thought it would be a very good bargain. In fact, the system of exchanges did not seem to me to be attended by the difficulties which embarrassed other gentlemen; but I thought the whole thing could be done without recognition of the rebels as National belligerents, by allowing the exchanges to take place between Gen. Wool and Gen. Huger.[97] Nothing was decided, but the matter is still reserved for further consideration.

It was proposed to invite *Gen. McClellan* to a meeting of the Cabinet tomorrow, to learn his plans.[98] Objection made by *Mr. Blair,* and *the President* took it into consideration.

Gen. Hunter's application for authority to muster a Brigade of Indians was considered, in connection with a proposition of Gen McClellan to invade Western Texas from the North and from the Gulf simultaneously.[99] I expressed my approval of the latter, and my disapproval of the former for want of power, the President

---

95. In margin: "Privateers."
96. In margin: "Exchange of Prisoners." William Smith, of the Confederate privateer *Jeff. Davis,* had been convicted on Oct. 25. John Ellis Wool (1784–1869) commanded the Department of Virginia. *DAB,* 20:513–14; *OR,* ser. 2, v. 3:58–121, 130–31.
97. Confederate Benjamin Huger (1805–77) of the Department of Norfolk. *DAB,* 9:343.
98. In margin: "Genl. McClellan's plans." George Brinton McClellan (1826–85) had served as general-in-chief of Union armies since Nov. *DAB,* 11:581–84.
99. In margin: "Brigade of Indians." In Nov., David Hunter (1802–86), commander of the Western Department and, later, of the Department of the South, had requested permission to raise a brigade of Kansas Indians. McClellan's plan, presented in Aug., proposed an invasion through Kansas and Nebraska "for the purpose of protecting and developing the latent Union and Free-state sentiment." Annie Heloise Abel, *The American Indian as Participant in the Civil War* (Cleveland, 1919), 74–75; *DAB,* 9:400–401; *Letter of the Secretary of War, Transmitting Report on the Organization of the Army of the Potomac . . .* , 38th Cong., 1st sess., 1864, H. Ex. Doc. 15, 4–5.

having already exhausted the authority, given him by Congress, to raise men. This view was generally concurred in and the subject dropped.

I directed the attention of the President to complaints made against *Gen. Smith* at Paducah, and was glad to learn that Gen. McClellan had already directed him to be superseded.[1]

Some conversation took place in respect to organizing courts at Beaufort; and it was agreed that I should see certain Southern gentlemen and then confer with *Judge Bates* as to what should be done.[2]

Sent copies of Report to Messrs. *Ketchum, Williams, Gallatin* and *Coe,* with letters expressing the hope of their concurrence in its views.[3]

WEDNESDAY, DEC. 11TH., 1861. A multitude of callers at the office this morning, among them *Wade* of the Senate and *Ashley* of the House, Chairmen of the Territorial Committees in their respective houses.[4] To both of them I gave my views in brief as to the relations of the insurrectionary States to the Union; that no State nor any portion of the people could withdraw from the Union or absolve themselves from allegiance to it; but that when the attempt was made, and the State government was placed in hostility to the Federal Government, the State organization was forfeited and it lapsed into the condition of a Territory with which we could do what we pleased; that we could form a Provisional Government, as was done in Western Virginia, or, when we occupied any portion of a rebellious State, such as Beaufort, we could organize territorial Courts and, as soon as it became necessary, a Territorial Government;[5] that those States could not properly be considered as States in the Union but must be

---

1. In margin: "Charges agt. Gen. Smith." Brigadier General Charles Ferguson Smith (1807–62) commanded the District of Western Kentucky from Paducah. *DAB,* 17:247; McClellan to D. C. Buell, Dec. 10, 1862, *OR,* ser. 1, v. 7:487–88.

2. Edward Bates. In margin: "Courts at Beaufort."

3. In margin: "Copies of Report sent." Chase transmitted copies of his annual report to New York bankers Morris Ketchum (c. 1796–1880), of Ketchum, Son and Co.; John E. Williams, president of the Metropolitan Bank; James Gallatin; and George Simmons Coe (1817–96), president of the American Exchange Bank. Chase proposed to issue small amounts of demand notes and to secure funding through three-year, 7.75% Treasury notes to be purchased for resale by bankers in Boston, Philadelphia, and New York. Bray Hammond, *Sovereignty and an Empty Purse, Banks and Politics in the Civil War* (Princeton, 1970), 73; Chase to Williams, Dec. 10, 1861 (Lincoln Collec., John Hay Lib., Brown Univ.); *DAB,* 4:261; *New York Dir. (1863),* 471; "City Register," in ibid., 8; *New York Times,* Jan. 3, 1880.

4. In margin: "Status of rebel States."

5. In margin: "Courts and Government."

readmitted from time to time, as Congress should provide. Messrs Wade and Ashley expressed their concurrence.

Senator Johnson of Tennessee called, and gave an account of the military operations in Kentucky during the summer, of which he was a witness.[6] He said there was nothing to prevent a march into Tennessee and the possession of Knoxville immediately after the Battle at Camp Wild Cat; but that Gen Sherman was so intimidated by Buckner's alleged strength and purposes that he was much of the time incapacitated for command.[7]

Mr. Speed of Louisville called my attention to restrictions placed by our Special Agent upon shipments of provisions to Louisville.[8] I told him that Louisville, being a loyal city, stood upon the same footing as Washington, and that Mr. Mellen should be instructed accordingly.[9]

Mr. Hooper, M.C. from Boston, expressed a cordial approval of my report.[10]

Genl. Meigs and Judge Advocate Lee[11] called at my request, the former more especially with reference to to the collection and disposition of Cotton at Port Royal.[12] He promised to place bagging, bale-rope etc for 1000 Bales at the disposal of the Agent of the Treasury Department there. I proposed to transfer the whole business to him; but we did not determine whether the transfer should be made. With Maj. Lee and also with Gen Meigs, I had some conversation about government for seceded States. *Maj. Lee* seemed to favor Mil-

---

6. In margin: "Summer campaign in Kentucky." Democrat Andrew Johnson (1808–75) of Tennessee was U.S. senator, 1857–62, military governor of Tennessee, 1862–65, vice president of the U.S., 1865, and president, 1865–68. *DAB,* 10:81–89.

7. Union general William Tecumseh Sherman (1820–91) and Confederate officer Simon Boliver Buckner (1823–1914). *DAB,* 3:234–36, 17:93–97.

8. In margin: "Trade with Louisville." Joshua Fry Speed (1814–82) was a Louisville merchant and real estate magnate. *Appletons',* 5:626; Speed to Chase, Aug. 22, 1861 (Chase Papers, Hist. Soc. of Pa.).

9. William P. Mellen, the Treasury's special agent at Cincinnati, had restricted shipments of pork. Chase instructed him to exercise less caution "unless you are satisfied that the supplies are intended for disloyal parties." Mellen served through the war as a special agent and supervising special agent, primarily in the Mississippi and Ohio valleys. Chase to Mellen, Dec. 13, 1861 (General Agent, Recs. of Civil War Special Agencies, Nat. Arch.).

10. In margin: "Approval of Report by Mr. Hooper." Boston merchant Samuel Hooper (1808–75) was a Republican congressman, 1861–75, and a supporter of Chase's financial policies. *DAB,* 9:203–4.

11. Montgomery Cunningham Meigs (1816–92), quartermaster general, 1861–82, and John Fitzgerald Lee (d. 1884), judge advocate general, 1849–62. Cullum, *Biographical Register,* 1:448, 3:101; *DAB,* 12:507–8; Heitman, *Historical Register,* 1:625.

12. In margin: "Collection and disposition of Cotton."

itary Commissions for the trial of questions not cognizable by Courts Martial.[13] He promised to send an order of Gen Scott, issued in Mexico, which might serve as a precedent.[14]

Wrote to Messrs *Aspinwall, Sprague and Minturn*, giving them the substance of what Gen Meigs had said about the Cotton business, and telling them that, should I retain the management, I should be glad to avail myself of their counsel and support.[15]

THURSDAY DEC. 12TH., 1861. *Judge Key* called this morning and read draft of Bill for the emancipation of slaves in the District of Columbia.[16]

Col. Sullivan of Ohio called, being here on business connected with the B. & O. R.R., and represented his interviews with Genl McClellan as highly satisfactory.[17] Among other things he stated that when Gen. Kelley advanced upon Romney, the rebels supposed he designed to attack Winchester—that they called upon Johnston for help[18]—that he at first refused to send any, and finally only sent a Regiment of raw recruits, who had recently gone to Manassas from Winchester; thus showing that, important as Winchester was, no troops could be spared from Manassas.

Genl. McClellan called at 12 M. and remained about an hour and a half [19]

[THE SECRETARY *was absent in New York from Dec. 18 to Dec. 21st.* H. G. P.][20]

13. In margin: "Military Commissions in Rebel States."
14. Winfield Scott (1786–1866), general-in-chief of the U.S. Army, 1841–61. *DAB*, 16:505–11.
15. In margin: "Cotton." Chase wrote to New York shipping magnates William Henry Aspinwall (1807–75) and Robert Browne Minturn (1805–66), officers of the city's Union League Club; and William Sprague (1830–1915), Rhode Island cotton manufacturer, governor, 1860–63, aide to Gen. Ambrose Burnside, 1861, and U.S. senator, 1863–75. On Nov. 12, 1863, Sprague married Chase's daughter Kate. Chase to Aspinwall, Sprague, and Minturn, Dec. 11, 1861 (Misc. Letters Sent, Gen. Recs. Treasury Dept., Nat. Arch.); *DAB*, 1:396, 13:32–33.
16. In margin: "Emancipation in D.C."
17. In margin: "Kelley's advance on Romney." John H. Sullivan, general transportation agent for the Baltimore and Ohio R.R., had written two days earlier with a detailed analysis of the military situation around Romney and Harpers Ferry in the area that would soon become West Virginia. *OR*, ser. 1, v. 5:587; Sullivan to Chase, Dec. 12, 1861 (Chase Papers, L.C.).
18. Benjamin Franklin Kelley (1807–91), brigadier and later major general of U.S. volunteers; and Confederate Gen. Joseph Eggleston Johnston (1807–91). *Appletons'*, 3:504; *DAB*, 10:144–46; *Nat. Cyc.*, 6:165.
19. In margin: "Interview with McClellan."
20. In margin: "Absence of Secretary." The initials are those of Homer G. Plantz, in whose hand this journal was recorded. Chase was in New York negotiating with bankers for a new loan of fifty million dollars. Hammond, *Sovereignty*, 154.

DECEMBER 25TH., 1861.
The "Trent" Affair.[21]
Remarks of Secretary Chase at the Cabinet Meeting.

In my judgment, the case stands precisely thus: In taking the rebel Envoys and their Secretaries from the "Trent," without invoking or proposing to invoke the sanction of any judicial tribunal, Capt. Wilkes clearly violated the Law of Nations,[22] and in that very principle which the United States have ever most zealously maintained. Great Britain, therefore, has a right to ask from us a disavowal of the act, and the restoration of the persons to the condition in which they were when taken; and, if this right be insisted on, it is our duty, however disagreeable, to do what is thus asked.

On the other hand, the circumstances under which the act of Capt. Wilkes was done, not only repel the imputation of agressive or unfriendly intent, but entitle him to commendation for the motives by which his conduct was governed and reduce the seizure and removal from the "Trent" of the Rebel Commissioners, to a mere technical violation of the neutral rights of England. Mason and Slidell were Commissioners bearing despatches from the rebel government to Europe, and their character and charge were known to the commander of the "Trent."[23] At the time of the seizure, therefore, the "Trent" was knowingly employed, in violation of English Law, of the Royal Proclamation, and of her duty to the United States as a friendly nation.[24] Conscious of the fact, the commander refused, when requested, to exhibit his passenger List. The capture was, of course, warranted, and Capt. Wilkes, in making it, performed only his plain duty to his Government. He had a right to break up the voyage and send the steamer as prize into a port for

---

21. The USS *San Jacinto* had stopped the British mail packet *Trent* on Nov. 8 and seized two Confederate commissioners en route to England and France. Chase's journal records his comments as the cabinet discussed a course of action in the diplomatic crisis triggered by the incident.

22. U.S. naval officer and explorer Charles Wilkes (1798–1877) commanded the *San Jacinto*. *DAB*, 20:216–18.

23. James Murray Mason (1798–1871) of Virginia and John Slidell (1793–1871) of Louisiana, both former U.S. senators, were the Confederate representatives taken from the *Trent*. *DAB*, 12:364–65, 17:209–11.

24. Queen Victoria's Proclamation of Neutrality, May 13, 1861, accepted the Union blockade of Southern ports, forbade U.S. and Confederate warships from being equipped in British ports, and called for Britons to refrain from non-neutral activities, but also granted the Confederacy status as a belligerent. Gordon H. Warren, *Fountain of Discontent: The Trent Affair and Freedom of the Seas* (Boston, 1980), 70–71.

trial and condemnation. But the steamer was employed in the conveyance of mails and passengers; and Capt. Wilkes was desirous to avid the public injury of delaying the transmission of the former, and the private hardship likely to result from interrupting the voyage of the latter.

Governed mainly by these motives, he obeyed what seemed to him the dictates of humanity and friendly consideration for a friendly nation, by removing the contraband persons from the "Trent" with the least possible inconvenience to all concerned, and suffering the vessel with her other passengers and mails to proceed to her destination. In doing this, he surrendered a prize which might have tempted cupidity, without a thought that, by the self-same act, he was depriving himself of the only means of justifying the capture, either of persons or vessels, through a judicial decision.

Certainly it was not too much to expect of a friendly nation, and especially of a nation of the same blood, religion and characteristic civilization as our own, that, in consideration of the great rights, she would overlook the little wrong; nor can I now persuade myself that, were all the circumstances known to the English Government, as to ours, the surrender of the rebel Commissioners would be insisted on.

The technical right is undoubtedly with England. As rebels or as traitors to our Government, the pretended Commissioners would have been safe on a neutral ship. It was only in their character as Envoys that they were subject to arrest as contraband. As contraband, they could not rightfully be taken from the ship until after the judicial condemnation of the ship itself, for receiving and carrying them. However excused or even justified by motives, the act of removing them as prisoners from the "Trent," without resort to any judicial cognizance, was in itself indefensible. We cannot deny this without denying our history. Were the circumstances reversed, our Government would, I think, accept the explanation, and let England keep her Rebels; and I cannot divest myself of the beleif that, were the case fairly understood, the British Government would do likewise.

But we cannot afford delays. While the matter hangs in uncertainty, the public mind will remain disquieted, our commerce will suffer serious harm, our action against the rebels must be greatly hindered, and the restoration of our prosperity, largely identified with that of all nations, must be delayed. Better, then, to make now the sacrifice of feeling involved in the surrender of these rebels, than even avoid it by the delays which explanations must occasion. I give my adhesion, therefore, to the conclusion to which the Secretary of State has arrived.[25]

It is gall and wormwood to me. Rather than consent to the liberation of these men, I would sacrifice everything I possess. But I am consoled by the reflection that while nothing but severest retribution is due to them, the surrender, under existing circumstances, is but simply doing right; simply proving faithful to our own ideas and traditions under strong temptations to violate them; simply giving to England and to the world the most signal proof that the American Nation will not, under any circumstances, for the sake of inflicting just punishment on Rebels, commit even a technical wrong against neutrals.

1862

WEDNESDAY, JANUARY 1ST., 1862. Went to President's at 11, with my two daughters and Miss Walker. Prodigious crowd around the gates. Afterwards received at our own house. Mrs Genl McDowell, Mrs. Bridge and Miss Walker assisted Kate.[26] All the Diplomatic Corps except Stoeckel,[27] and many officers of the Army, called. When Lord Lyons came in, I saluted him with "Pax esto Perpetua";[28] and he expressed the hope that his conduct had always been that of a Peacemaker.

THURSDAY, JANUARY 2D., Resumed ordinary duties at Department, Mr. Harrington still absent.[29]

---

25. Seward maintained that Wilkes had captured Mason and Slidell legally, but had forfeited the right to claim the prisoners by neglecting to seize the *Trent* and adjudicate the case before a court of admirality. Ibid., 183–84; *ORN*, ser. 1, v. 1:177–87.

26. Helen Burden McDowell (d. 1891), wife of Irvin McDowell; Charlotte Marshall Bridge, wife of Navy Department official Horatio Bridge; and Susan Walker. The Bridges had been neighbors of Chase and his daughters when the Chases first moved to Washington in 1861. *Nat. Cyc.*, 4:50; William Charvat et al., eds., *The Centenary Edition of the Works of Nathaniel Hawthorne*, 20 vols. (Columbus, Ohio, 1962–88), 16:165, 166; Janet Chase Hoyt, "A Woman's Memories: Washington in War Time," *New York Tribune*, Mar. 8, 1891.

27. Édouard de Stoeckl (b. ca. 1808), Russian minister to the U.S., 1858–65. Frank A. Golder, "The American Civil War through the Eyes of a Russian Diplomat," *American Historical Review* 26 (Apr. 1921): 454–55.

28. "Peace is everlasting." Richard Bickerton Pemell Lyons (1817–87) was British minister to the U.S., 1857–68. *DNB*, 12:358–59.

29. George Harrington (1815–92) became assistant secretary of the Treasury in 1861 after long service as a clerk. He was U.S. minister to Switzerland, 1865–69. *Nat. Cyc.*, 12:337.

January 1862 { 321 }

In the evening Kate had big Turkey, and Mr Sumner and Genl. McDowell dined with us[30]

FRIDAY AND SATURDAY 3D–4TH   Routine.

SUNDAY, JANUARY 5TH.   Attended church at The Trinity in the morning.[31]

In the evening received a despatch from Mr. Garrett, President of the B. & O. R.R., stating that the enemy had advanced to Hancock and were shelling the town—that the Union troops had fallen back to the Maryland side—and that the enemy was in possession of a considerable portion of the newly prepared Road. Sent the despatch by Col. Barstow to Genl McClellan. Wrote to Lander who had been ordered to the command at Romney.[32]

Senator Chandler came in to converse about Gen McDowell being put in command of the Army of the Potomac and of military affairs generally; and evinced an excellent spirit.[33]

MONDAY JANUARY 6TH.   Received a note from McClellan's Aid, saying that the General had read the despatch sent him last night, and would take immediate measures to protect the Road; that reinforcements would be immediately sent to Hancock; and that Genl. Banks had been ordered to support Lander.[34]

In fulfillment of engagement with the President of the American Bank Note Company, went to Ulke's, who took a number of Photographs.[35]

Cabinet Meeting held at night to confer with the Joint Committee of the two Houses of Congress on the Conduct of the War. The

---

30. Ohio-born professional soldier Brig. Gen. Irvin McDowell (1818–85), promoted to major general of volunteers in Mar. 1862. *DAB*, 12:29–30.

31. Trinity Episcopal Church, at the corner of West Third and North C Streets. *Wash. Dir. (1862)*, 255.

32. Simon Forrester Barstow (d. 1882), actually a captain, served as acting aide-de-camp for Frederick West Lander (1821–62), brigadier general of volunteers. *DAB*, 10:569–70; Heitman, *Historical Register*, 1:195–96; *OR*, ser. 1, v. 5:630–31.

33. Republican Zachariah Chandler (1813–79) of Michigan, chairman of the Committee on Commerce, 1861–75, member of the Joint Committee on the Conduct of the War, and future U.S. secretary of the interior. *DAB*, 3:618.

34. Major general of volunteers Nathaniel Prentiss Banks (1816–94), former Speaker of the U.S. House and governor of Massachusetts. He commanded U.S. troops at New Orleans and vicinity, late 1862–65. Banks sat in Congress again, 1865–73, and after. *DAB*, 1:577–80.

35. The request to visit the studio of Henry Ulke (1821–1910), a photographer and portrait painter on Pennsylvania Avenue, had come from Tracy Robinson Edson (1809–81), an engraver and founder of the American Bank Note Company. *Nat. Cyc.*, 19:394; *Wash. Dir. (1862)*, 173; *Who Was Who*, 1:1263.

members of the Committee, especially Messrs. Chandler Wade, Johnson, Odell and Covode,[36] were very earnest in urging the vigorous prosecution of the War, and in recommending the appointment of Genl. McDowell as Major-General, to command the Army of the Potomac.

A great deal of discussion took place. I expressed my own views, saying that, in my judgment, Genl. McClellan was the best man for the place he held known to me—that, I believed, if his sickness had not prevented he would by this time have satisfied every body in the country of his efficiency and capacity—that I thought, however, that he tasked himself too severely—that no physical or mental vigor could sustain the strains he imposed on himself, Often on the saddle nearly all day and transacting business at his rooms nearly all night—that, in my judgment, he ought to confer freely with his ablest and most experienced Generals, deriving from them the benefits which their counsels, whether accepted or rejected, would certainly impart, and communicating to them full intelligence of his own plans of action, so that, in the event of sickness or accident to himself, the movements of the army need not necessarily be interrupted or delayed. I added that, in my own opinion, no one person could discharge fitly the special duties of Commander of the Army of the Potomac, and the general duties of Commanding General of the Armies of the United States; and that Genl. McClellan, in undertaking to discharge both, had undertaken what he could not perform.

Much else was said by various gentlemen, and the discussion was concluded by the announcement by the President that he would call on Genl. McClellan, and ascertain his views in respect to the division of the commands.

WEDNESDAY, JAN. 8TH., Special Loan Committee from New-York here.

Gave the usual dinner to Committees of Finance of the two Houses. Present, Messrs. Fessenden, Simmons, Sherman, Howe and Pearce, of the Senate,[37] and Messrs. Stephens, Morrill, Spaulding,

---

36. Zachariah Chandler; Benjamin F. Wade; Andrew Johnson; Moses Fowler Odell (1818–66), Democratic congressman from New York, 1861–65; John Covode (1808–71), Republican congressman from Pennsylvania, 1855–63, 1867–71. *Bio. Dir. U.S. Cong.*, 1584; *DAB*, 4:470.

37. Maine Republican William Pitt Fessenden (1806–69), chairman of the committee, secretary of the U.S. Treasury, 1864–65; James Fowler Simmons (1795–1864) of Rhode Island; John Sherman; Timothy Otis Howe (1816–83), Republican of Wisconsin; and Democrat James Alfred Pearce (1805–62), senator from Maryland, 1843–62. *Bio. Dir. U.S. Cong.*, 1813; *DAB*, 6:348–50, 9:297–98, 14:352–53.

January 1862 {323}

Corning, Horton, Stratton, Hooper and Maynard, of the House.[38] Messrs. Bright and McDougall, of the Senate, and Mr. Phelps, of the House, were absent.[39] Mr. Jay Cooke, of Philadelphia, was also present.[40]

After dinner, Messrs Coe, Russell and Vermilye came in.[41] Messrs C. & V. were very desirous that I should cancel so much of the Loan as remained unpaid; for which I promised consideration but declined giving any definite answer

THURSDAY, JAN. 9TH. Mr. Russell came to breakfast. After breakfast we discussed somewhat his Financial Suggestions. He proposes a Board of Exchequer, to be appointed by the President and Senate, to whom Bonds of the U.S. shall be issued, and by whom 80 per cent of the amount shall be returned in circulating Notes; that similar Bonds shall be issued by the Board and 75 percent of the amount issued to any depositor and redeemed by the U.S. if necessary; that Associations for Banking purposes shall be authorized, to whom 90 per cent of Bonds deposited may be issued, with provisions for reserves of specie, etc.

Called at Ulke's coming to Department. At Dept. attended to the usual business and made appointment with Committees from Philadelphia and New-York to come to my house at Eight this evening.

Went to the Capitol and heard Mr. Sumner's speech, which was, in the main, admirable in manner and matter.[42] Told him I thought he had better omit the word *"penitent"*, applied to England in

---

38. Committee of Ways and Means chairman Thaddeus Stevens (1792–1868), Pennsylvania Republican; Justin Smith Morrill (1810–98), Republican congressman from Vermont, 1855–67, U.S. senator, 1867–98; New Yorkers Elbridge Gerry Spaulding (1809–97), a Republican, and Erastus Corning (1794–1872), a Democrat; Ohio Republican Valentine Baxter Horton; New Jersey Republican John Leake Newbold Stratton (1817–99); Samuel Hooper; and Horace Maynard (1814–82), Tennessee Unionist. *Bio. Dir. U.S. Cong.*, 1887; *DAB*, 4:446–47, 9:238–39, 12:460–61, 13:198–99, 17:436–37, 620–25.

39. Democrats James Alexander McDougall (1817–67) of California and John Smith Phelps (1814–86) of Missouri. *Bio. Dir. U.S. Cong.*, 1460; *DAB*, 14:530.

40. Cooke (1821–1905), a native Ohioan and close friend of Chase, was a partner in the Philadelphia banking house of Jay Cooke and Co. He oversaw government loan subscriptions during the war. *DAB*, 4:383–84.

41. Charles Handy Russell (1796–1884), a director of New York's Bank of Commerce, merchant, and Unionist who maintained business interests in his native state of Rhode Island and owned property in Newport; and probably either Washington R. or William G. Vermilye, bankers in the New York firm of Vermilye and Co. *New York Tribune*, Jan. 22, 1884; Antoinette F. Downing and Vincent J. Scully, Jr., *The Architectural Heritage of Newport, Rhode Island, 1640–1915*, 2nd ed., rev. (New York, 1967), 137–38; *New York Dir. (1863)*, 892; ibid., "City Register," 8.

42. Sumner's remarks on the *Trent* Affair introduced a Jan. 6 letter from the president to the Senate Committee on Foreign Relations. *Cong. Globe*, 37th Cong., 2d sess., 1862, 241–45.

connection with her implied recantation of ancient pretensions by her demand for Mason & Slidell; and that it would have been well to omit the argument against the right to capture and bring in the ship for having Commissioners or Despatches on board, inasmuch as that argument contradicted the position taken by Mr. Seward on the same question. Most of the foreign Ministers were present, and full galleries.

Returning to the Department, received a visit from General McDowell, who showed me his map, and the relative position of our own and the enemy's forces near Washington.

Kate and Mr. Cooke came in, saying that Nettie was ill, but doing well, at Philadelphia. Kate determined to go by this evening's train with Mr. Cooke, and promised to telegraph me to-night.

FRIDAY, JAN 10TH. Bank Committees here.

SATURDAY, JAN. 11TH. Many callers at Department—among them Genl. McDowell and Col. Key. Genl. McD. enquired about McClellan's plans, and I told him what I knew of them, in strict confidence. Col. Key was about to have an interview with Genl. McClellan, and wanted to know what I would recommend. I replied that McC. should (1st.) Relieve himself of the imputation of Nepotism and favoritism in the selection of his staff; (2d.) That he should not allow the President to wait on him, but should honor the office by sending one of his aids regularly to the President; and (3d.) That he should call into his counsels the most experienced and able men in the army, and should insist on the appointment of McDowell as Major-General at once.

Had conversation with Edwin M. Stanton about Lander, McClellan &c. Requested Col. Sullivan to see War Department about B. & O. R.R.

Finance Committees and Bank Committees met at office at 3 P.M.

JOURNAL IX

1862, JANUARY 12TH.— At church in the morning. Good, plain sermon. Wished much to join in communion, but felt myself too subject to temptation to sin. After church went to see Cameron by appointment;[43] but being obliged to meet the President, etc., at one, could only excuse myself. At President's found Generals McDowell,

---

43. Simon Cameron (1799–1889) of Pennsylvania, U.S. secretary of war, 1861–62; also U.S. senator, 1845–49, 1867–77, and U.S. minister to Russia, 1862–63. *DAB*, 3:437–39.

Franklin,[44] and Meigs, and Seward and Blair. Meigs decided against dividing forces, and in favor of battle in front. President said McClellan's health was much improved, and thought it best to adjourn till to-morrow, and have all then present attend with McC. at three. Home, and talk and reading. Dinner. Cameron came in. Advised loan in Holland, and recommended Brooks, Lewis,[45] and another whom I have forgotten. Then turned to Department matters, and we talked of his going to Russia and Stanton as successor, and he proposed I should again see the President. I first proposed seeing Seward, to which he assented. He declared himself determined to maintain himself at the head of his Department if he remained, and to resist hereafter all interference. I told him I would in that event stand by him faithfully. He and I drove to Willard's, where I left him, and went myself to Seward's. I told him at once what was in my mind—that I thought the President and Cameron were both willing that C. should go to Russia. He seemed to receive the matter as new, except so far as suggested by me last night. Wanted to know who would succeed Cameron. I said Holt[46] and Stanton had been named; that I feared Holt might embarrass us on the slavery question, and might not prove quite equal to the emergency; that Stanton was a good lawyer and full of energy; but I could not, of course, judge him as an executive officer as well as he (S.) could, for he knew him when he was in Buchanan's Cabinet. Seward replied that he saw much of him then; that he was of great force—full of expedients, and thoroughly loyal. Finally he agreed to the whole thing, and promised to go with me to talk with the President about it to-morrow. Just at this point Cameron came in with a letter from the President proposing his nomination to Russia in the morning! He was quite offended, supposing the letter intended as a dismissal, and, therefore, discourteous. We both assured him it could not be so. Finally he concluded to retain the letter till morning, and then go and see the President. Seward was expecting General Butler, and Cameron said he ought to be sent off immediately. I said, "Well, let's leave Seward to order him off at once." C. laughed, and we went off together, I taking him to his house. Before parting, I told him what had passed between me and Seward concerning Stanton, with

44. Brig. Gen. William Buel Franklin (1823–1903), later major general of volunteers. *DAB*, 6:601–2.

45. Possibly Joseph Jackson Lewis (1801–83), a Republican politician from Pennsylvania and U.S. commissioner of internal revenue, 1863–65. Samuel Reeves Brooks of New York pressed Chase for authorization to negotiate a loan in Europe. *Nat. Cyc.*, 27:413; Brooks to Chase, July 21, Aug. 4, 18, Nov. 19, 1862 (Chase Papers, L.C.).

46. Joseph Holt (1807–94), former U.S. commissioner of patents, postmaster general, and secretary of war; judge advocate general of the army, 1862–75. *DAB*, 9:181–83.

which he was gratified. I advised him to go to the President in the morning, express his thanks for the consideration with which his wishes, made known through me as well as by himself orally, had been treated, and tell him frankly how desirable it was to him that his successor should be a Pennsylvanian, and should be Stanton. I said I thought that his wish, supported as it would be by Seward and myself, would certainly be gratified, and told him that the President had already mentioned Stanton in a way which indicated that no objection on his part would be made. I said also that, if he wished, I would see Seward, and would go to the President after he had left him, and urge the point. He asked why not come in when he should be there, and I assented to this. We parted, and I came home. A day which may have—and seemingly must have—great bearing on affairs. Oh, that my heart and life were so pure and right before God and I might not hurt our great cause! I fear Mr. Seward may think Cameron's coming into his house pre-arranged, and that I was not dealing frankly. I feel satisfied, however, that I have acted right, and with just deference to all concerned, and have in no respect deviated from the truth.

JOURNAL VIII

MONDAY, JAN 13, 1862 To-day Genl. Cameron resigned his place as Secretary of War, and E. M. Stanton, of Penna., was appointed in his stead. Many callers, among them both Messrs Cameron & Stanton.

TUESDAY JAN 14, 1862 The day was occupied wholly in conferences with Members of the Bank Committees and Boards of Trade of the three cities who are here consulting on Financial matters, and with Senators and others who called in regard to the change in the Cabinet.

Mr. Fessenden of the Senate, and Mr. Stanton, were together with the Secretary, for more than an hour.

Mr Rodman, Chief Clerk of the Department, died suddenly this morning, and at 2 o'clock, I attended the funeral services. His remains were taken to Philadelphia.[47]

WEDNESDAY, JANUARY 15, 1862 The consultations with Bankers and Members of the Boards of Trade from New-York, Boston

---

47. According to newspaper accounts, the death of Gilbert Rodman (1800–1862) actually occurred on Jan. 15. *Daily National Intelligencer*, Jan. 16, 1862.

and Philadelphia were terminated to-day, and the result was reduced to writing, as follows:—

1st.— The general views of the Secretary of the Treasury are assented to

2d.— The Banks will receive and pay out the U.S. Demand Notes freely, and sustain, in all proper ways, their credit.

3d.— The Secretary will, within the next two weeks, in addition to the current daily payment of a Million and a half of Dollars in U.S. Notes, pay the further sum of at least Twenty Millions of Dollars in 7.30 Three Years Bonds to such public creditors as desire to receive them, and thus relieve the existing pressure upon the community.

4th.— The issue of U.S. Demand Notes not to be extended beyond the Fifty Millions now authorized; but it is desired that Congress will extend the provisions of the existing Loan Acts,[48] so as to enable the Secretary to issue in exchange for U.S. Notes or in payment to creditors, Notes payable in one year, bearing 3.65 per cent interest, and convertible into 7.30 Three Years Bonds, or to borrow under the existing provisions to the amount of Two Hundred and Fifty or Three Hundred Millions of Dollars.

5th.— It is thought desirable that Congress should adopt a general Law relating to the Currency and Banking Associations, embracing the general provisions recommended by the Secretary in his Report.

6th.— It is beleived that this action and legislation will render the making of U.S. Demand Notes a legal tender, or their increase beyond the Fifty Millions now authorized, unnecessary.

The gentlemen assenting to these propositions were, from New-York, Messrs Coe,

Boston, Mr. Walley,[49]

Philadelphia

About an hour after this understanding was arrived at (each gentleman agreeing to urge the plan embodied in it upon the adoption of the Banks of his city, and expressing his belief that it would be cordially sustained) a sub-Committee from the House Committee of Ways & Means, consisting of Messrs Spaulding, Hooper and Horton, called at the Department. Mr Hooper expressed his decided opinion that the U.S. Notes must necessarily be made legal tender. Messrs Spaulding and Horton expressed no opinion and it was agreed that the Secretary should confer with Mr Stevens,[50] Chairman of the Committee, this evening.

---

48. The National Loan Act of July 17, 1861, and a supplementary act of Aug. 5. *Statutes at Large*, 12:259–61, 313–14.

49. Samuel Hurd Walley (1805–77), president of the Revere National Bank and U.S. congressman, 1853–55. *Bio. Dir. U.S. Cong.*, 2000.

50. Thaddeus Stevens.

THURSDAY, JANUARY 16TH. The Bankers left for home to-day, news having first reached Washington of the rise in the value of Stocks in New-York, consequent upon the receipt there, by Telegraph, of the result of the Financial Conferences of the past few days.

FRIDAY, JAN. 17TH., 1862 Wrote to Mr. Stevens[51] expressing the hope that the arrangement adopted on Wednesday would meet his approval and be sanctioned by the banks.

MONDAY, JANUARY 20, 1862. Mr. Stanton took formal possession of the War Department to-day. Paid respects to the out-going and in-coming Secretaries.

Mr. Walley telegraphed that Boston Banks would not assent to proposed arrangment, and advised the immediate making of U.S. Notes legal tender.

WEDNESDAY, JANUARY 22D, A Committee from the Chamber of Commerce of Cincinnati waited on me this morning, to urge the location of the proposed new Armory at Cincinnati. They also represented the earnest feeling of the People of Cincinnati and the West in favor of greater energy and decision in the conduct of the War, and alluded to the state of politics in Ohio. Told them that Cincinnati, "never very kind, was always very dear to me," and that I had already presented her claims for the Armory and should continue to do so. As to the conduct of the War, I gave them every assurance, and especially expressed confidence in Mr. Stanton, as a man who would be master of his Department, and yield to no one save the President. On Politics, I said that the Democratic Party must be reconstructed as a party of Freedom.

Messrs Cisco, Barney and Andrews[52] came from New-York to confer about Government property there. Mayor Opdyke accompanied them, but returned to-day.[53] He favors a Legal-tender Law.

MARCH 6TH., 1862. To-day the President sent a Message to Congress, recommending coöperation by Federal Government with States in abolition of Slavery within their limits[54]

---

51. Probably John Austin Stevens.
52. Rufus F. Andrews, surveyor of customs at New York. *Register of Officers* (*1863*), 81.
53. George Opdyke (1807–80), merchant, former Free-Soil politician, and Republican mayor of New York, 1862–64. Holli and Jones, *Biographical Dictionary of American Mayors*, 274–75; *Nat. Cyc.*, 11:464–65.
54. Lincoln's message proposed "pecuniary aid . . . to compensate for the inconveniences" of gradual abolition. Basler, *Collected Works*, 5:144–46.

March 1862 {329}

The following is a draft of a Message on this subject, prepared and submitted to the President during the last week of December.

Message.

In my Annual Message communicated to Congress at the commencement of the present session, I took occasion to say:—

"The Union must be preserved; and hence all indispensable means must be employed. We should not be in haste to determine that radical and extreme measures, which may reach the loyal as well as the disloyal, are indispensable."

Reflecting since, with great solicitude, upon the condition of the country, and sharing, in full proportion, the desire which pervades the whole community for a speedy suppression of the rebellion, I have reached the conclusion that it is my duty to submit to the consideration of Congress some suggestions which seem to me to deserve their most serious attention.

It is known to all that the most potent falsehood by which the fomentors of discontent and promoters of insurrection inflamed the minds of citizens of the slaveholding States, and prepared them for rebellion under the guise of secession, was the assertion that the party by which I was chosen President of the United States designed to interfere, through the agency of the Federal Government, with the institution of slavery in the States where it existed. It is equally well known to all who have taken any pains to inform themselves, that such interference was never designed or sanctioned by that party; but was, on the contrary, in all its declarations, whether by National or State Conventions, distinctly and emphatically disavowed and repudiated. No well-informed person can reasonably doubt that, under an Administration conducted upon the prinicples set forth in those declarations, the Institution of Slavery, existing under State Constitutions and Laws, would have been as absolutely safe from Federal interference, as it has been under any Administration since the establishment of the Union.

It is true that the majority of the people, by whose suffrages the existing Administration was called to the concerns of government, cherishing on this subject the sentiments of Washington and Jefferson, of Franklin and Adams, opposed the extension of Slavery beyond State limits, and proposed to afford it no Governmental support within the sphere of exclusive National jurisdiction. But it is equally true that they regarded Slavery within State limits, as beyond that sphere and meant to perform fully, in reference to Slaves held under State laws, as well as in reference to every other matter of duty to every citizen of every State every Constitutional obligation.

The rebellion, therefore, except so far as its chiefs and some of their more deluded followers were concerned, was inspired and is sustained by a delusion. Were the people of the rebellious districts even now to reject the counsels of their misleaders; reorganize loyal State governments; and again send Senators and Representatives to Congress; they would find themselves at peace, with no institution changed, and with their just influence in the National Councils unabridged and unimpaired. With peace so restored, prosperity and happiness would return.

A pacific conquest of this delusion having been made impossible by the bombardment of Sumter, it became necessary to preserve the Union by War; and the question now most imperatively demanding attention and solution is, by what means can this War be best abridged without sacrificing its object.

Without now adverting to the military measures demanded for the suppression of rebellion, it seems fit to direct your attention to one of another nature. I have already observed that the rebellion, so far as the people of the Slave States participate in it, is prompted by a delusion—by the groundless fear of interference with State concerns, and especially in the matter of Slavery, by Federal authority. The real motives with its chiefs and the initiated are, first, resentment at defeat of their schemes for the subjection of the Federal Administration to the permanent supremacy of slaveholders as a separate ruling class; and, secondly, ambition to found a government, either consolidated or federal, Republican or Monarchical, of which Slavery shall be the central idea, and which they themselves may administer and control.

To dispel the illusion of the masses, and to deprive the leaders of the hope of success in their cherished schemes, will go far towards extinguishing the rebellion, by withdrawing its aliment.

I suggest, therefore, for the consideration of Congress, the expediency of offering by Joint Resolution, to the acceptance of the several States within whose limits Slavery exists under sanction of loyal State governments, a compensation, not exceeding a certain sum for each person held as a slave according to the last Census, to be paid to the States and distributed to individuals in proportions ascertained by their own legislation, in case the people thereof, through their own Conventions or Legislatures, shall see fit to accept such compensation and make provision for emancipation.

Such a proposition on the part of Congress, submitted frankly to the free acceptance or rejection of the loyal States, would be a distinct and emphatic repudiation of all pretence of Federal authority to interfere with slavery within State limits, by referring the whole subject to the States and people immediately interested; it would afford clear evidence of fraternal sentiments, by manifested readiness to assume as a common burden the cost of a benefit shared by all, but by none more largely than by the enfranchising States; and it would, so far as accepted by the loyal Slaveholding States, strengthen the bonds of Union between themselves and their brethren, while it would, in the same degree, destroy the hope of bringing these loyal States into their scheme of extending Slaveholding empire yet cherished by the leaders of the rebellion; compel them to see for what wretched husks of sovereignty they have prodigally wasted their rich inheritance of safety, honor, prosperity and power under the Federal Constitution; and arouse, in the minds of the misled masses, irresistible desires to return to the Union from which, in an evil hour, under coercion or delusion, they have attempted to withdraw.

MARCH 10TH., 1862. This morning Judge [Col.] Key came into the office, dressed for the march towards Manassas, which the Army of the Potomac is making. He bade me Good bye most cordially— thanking me repeatedly for my kindness, by which, he said, I had won his faithful and life-long friendship; there was no man in the country for whom he had so high a respect and regard—no man whose advancement he so much desired, nor whom he so wished to serve.

MARCH 13TH. Revd. Dr. Fuller, of Baltimore, called, and asked advice as to the course he should pursue in regard to his plantations and slaves at Port Royal.[55] He wished to know what were his rights in respect to them.

Told him that, as a loyal man, he was Proprietor of the *land*. How about the negroes? he asked. They were free, I replied. He thought his right to them was the same as his right to the land. Told him opinions would differ on that point, but that, for one, I should never consent to the involuntary reduction to Slavery of one of the negroes who had been in the service of the Government. Told him further what I thought of the character of the rebellion and its results, etc.

He said he was willing to acquiesce in the experiments of the Government, but expressed grave doubts of the success of the undertaking at Port Royal. Quoted Machiavelli's saying "Next to making freemen slaves, it is most difficult to makes slaves freemen."[56]

---

55. Originally from Beaufort, S.C., Richard Fuller, D.D. (1804–76) was pastor of Baltimore's Seventh Baptist Church, 1847–71. *DAB*, 7:62–63; *Appletons'*, 2:560–61.

56. *Discourses*, Book III, 8:7. As secretary of the Treasury, Chase had jurisdiction over "contraband" cotton and slaves seized by Federal forces after the capture of South Carolina's Sea Islands in Nov. 1861. Chase, his agent on the scene, Edward L. Pierce,

MARCH 14TH., 1862. To-day the vote was taken in the Senate on the confirmation of General McDowell as Major-General of Volunteers. Senator Wade sent me the vote, which was as follows:—

For confirmation.

Messrs. Anthony, Browning, Chandler, Clark, Cowan, Davis, Dixon, Fessenden, Foot, Foster,[57] Harris, Henderson, Howe, King, Latham, Morrill, Saulsbury, Stark, Sumner, Wade, Willey, and Wilson of Mass.[58]—22.

Against confirmation.

Messrs. Carlile, Grimes, Harlan, Howard, Lane of Indiana, Lane of Kansas, McDougall, Nesmith, Pomeroy, Rice, Ten Eyck, Trumbull and Wilkinson[59]—13

Absent or Not Voting

Messrs. Bayard, Collamer, Doolittle, Hale, Johnson, Kennedy, Pearce, Powell, Sherman, Simmons, Thomson, Wilmot, Wilson of Mo. and Wright.[60]—14.

---

and Northern philanthropists had recently initiated a program of social reform and education—the "Port Royal Experiment"—designed to prepare former Sea Island slaves for the transition to freedom. Rose, *Rehearsal for Reconstruction*, 3–31.

57. Senators Henry Bowen Anthony (1815–84), a former governor of Rhode Island and editor of the *Providence Journal;* Orville Hickman Browning (1806–81) of Illinois; Zachariah Chandler; Daniel Clark (1809–91) of New Hampshire; Edgar Cowan (1815–85) of Pennsylvania; Garrett Davis (1801–72) of Kentucky; James Dixon (1814–73) of Connecticut; William Pitt Fessenden; Solomon Foot (1802–66) of Vermont; and Lafayette Sabine Foster (1806–80) of Connecticut, who was president *pro tempore* of the Senate, 1865–67. *Bio. Dir. U.S. Cong.*, 1020; *DAB*, 1:316–17, 3:175–76, 4:125–26, 470–71, 5:113–14, 328–29, 6:498–99.

58. Ira Harris (1802–75) of New York, a former member of that state's supreme court and a U.S. senator, 1861–67; John Brooks Henderson (1826–1913) of Missouri; Timothy Otis Howe; Preston King; Milton Slocum Latham (1827–82) of California; Lot Myrick Morrill (181–83) of Maine; Willard Saulsbury (1820–92) of Delaware; Benjamin Stark (1820–98) of Oregon; Charles Sumner; Benjamin F. Wade; Waitman Thomas Willey (1811–1900) of Virginia; and Henry Wilson. *Bio. Dir. U.S. Cong.*, 1139, 1534, 1862, 2053; *DAB*, 8:310, 527–29; 11:13; 16:379.

59. John Snyder Carlile (1817–78) of Virginia; James Wilson Grimes (1816–72) of Iowa; James Harlan; Jacob Merritt Howard (1805–71) of Michigan; Henry Smith Lane (1811–81) of Indiana; James H. Lane; James Alexander McDougall; James Willis Nesmith (1820–85) of Oregon; Samuel Clarke Pomeroy (1816–91) of Kansas; Henry Mower Rice (1816–94) of Minnesota; John Conover Ten Eyck (1814–79) of New York; Lyman Trumbull; and Morton Smith Wilkinson (1819–94) of Minnesota. *Bio. Dir. U.S. Cong.*, 1921; *DAB*, 3:493, 7:631–32, 9:278–79, 10:574–75, 13:430–31, 15:54, 540–41, 19:19–20.

60. James Asheton Bayard (1799–1880) of Delaware; Jacob Collamer (1791–1865) of Vermont; James Rood Doolittle (1815–97) of Wisconsin; John P. Hale; Andrew Johnson; Anthony Kennedy (1810–92) of Maryland; James Alfred Pearce; Lazarus Whitehead Powell (1812–67) of Kentucky; John Sherman; James Fowler Simmons;

MARCH 17, 1862 W. D. Bickham, of the Cincinnati Commercial, called having just returned from Manassas—

He reports that the stories of Wooden Guns and absence of fortifications are fully sustained by the facts,[61] that the rebels must have been evacuating for weeks; that they left neither a cannon nor a good gun behind them—that we left more property to be wasted and destroyed in our own camps when we made the movement, than we found at Manassas. He says that what was left shows that the rebels have lived well—having molasses, sugar, rice, corn-meal in abundance. They did not leave more than $20.000 worth of property behind them—consisting of clothing, and useless guns and some swords.

FRIDAY, APL. 11TH., 1862. The House of Representatives, after a long and exciting Session passed the Senate Bill, abolishing Slavery in the District of Columbia, without amendment.

The vote in the Senate was— Yeas.— 29
Nays.— 14
The vote in the House was— Yeas— 92
Nays.— 38

WEDNESDAY, APL 16, The President signed the Emancipation Bill this morning.

THURSDAY, MAY 1ST. This has not been an eventful day, though it has brought information of great events

Genl. Saxton came to breakfast, and the Rev. Mr. French, just arrived from Port Royal, happened in.[62] We talked over Port Royal matters, inter alia. Mr. F. don't like many things—thinks the Unitarians don't get hold of the work in the right way. The negroes are mostly Baptists, and like emotional religion better than rational, so called. They " to Jesus", and cannot understand a religion that is not founded on His Divinity. Many marriages have been "confirmed" among them, He had laid much stress on the duty of regular marriages between those who have been living together without

---

John Renshaw Thomson (1800–1862) of New Jersey; David Wilmot; Robert Wilson (1803–70) of Missouri; and Joseph Albert Wright. *Bio. Dir. U.S. Cong.*, 1936, 2070; *DAB*, 2:66–67, 4:300, 5:374–75, 15:148–49.

61. Wooden, or "Quaker," guns were occasionally used by the Confederates to give a deceptive impression of their strength. Kenneth P. Williams, *Lincoln Finds a General: A Military Study of the Civil War* (New York, 1949), 1:123–24.

62. Mansfield French and Rufus Saxton (1824–1908), brigadier general of volunteers, quartermaster at Port Royal, S.C., and military governor of the Department of the South, 1862–65. *Appletons'*, 5:410; *Nat. Cyc.*, 4:219–20.

that sanction. On some plantations, the masters had allowed and encouraged marriages by ministers—on others, little was cared about it. A good deal of cotton had been planted, and more corn. The work of cultivation was going on as well as could be expected. Mr. F. thought Mr. Snydam would make a good Collector.[63] I talked to Gen. S. about the work before him. He said the Secretary of War had authorized him to procure one or two thousand red flannel suits for the blacks, with a view to organization. No arms to be supplied as yet.

Gov Dennison, with Col Milliken & Messrs Donaldson[64] & Butler of Columbus, called. Gov. D. commended Col. M. to me.

To Department and usual morning business—applications for office from Senators, Representatives and others. Promised nothing to nobody. Wilmot most urgent for McKean, but Dunn quite so for his nephew.[65] Col Milliken came in and related case—read his letters—wrongfully dismissed—my old friend T. C. H. Smith mixed up in it. Endorsed strongly his statement to Secretary of War. R. J. Walker and F. P. Stanton came in with argument in Porter Case, which I took and promised to examine.[66] Saxton and French came in—had seen Secretary of War, and S. had received Instructions—read them and found them nearly same as had been written, omitting reference to my Instructions to Agents of Treasury Department.[67] Went over to War Department about 5 P.M.—Stanton gone to dinner—read despatches. Banks thinks his work done in Shenandoah Valley and wishes to advance. McDowell reports

---

63. Probably J. A. Snydam, who had given "valuable assistance in the Collection of Cotton, & other property" at Hilton Head, S.C. William H. Reynolds to Chase, Feb. 18, 1862 (Chase Papers, L.C.).

64. Minor Millikin (1834–62), 1st Ohio Cavalry; Luther Donaldson, of Miller, Donaldson and Co., a Columbus banker. Lester J. Cappon, " 'The Soldier's Creed,' " *Ohio Historical Quarterly* 64 (July 1955): 320–27; *Col. Dir. (1856–57)*, 65, 157.

65. Probably S. M. McKean, disbursing clerk of the U.S. Treasury; William McKee Dunn (1814–87) was a Republican congressman from Indiana, 1861–63. *Register of Officers (1863)*, 18; *DAB*, 5:521–22.

66. Robert John Walker (1801–69), former U.S. senator from Mississippi, 1835–45, and secretary of the U.S. Treasury, 1845–49; and Frederick Perry Stanton (1814–94), U.S. congressman from Tennessee, 1835–55. Both men had served as governors of Kansas Territory in 1857. The case was evidently *James D. Porter et al. v. Bushrod W. Foley*, a litigation over land titles in Covington, Ky. *DAB*, 17:523–24, 19:355–58; David Donald, ed., *Inside Lincoln's Cabinet: The Civil War Diaries of Salmon P. Chase* (New York, 1954), 284; *Porter v. Foley*, 21 How. 393, 24 How. 415.

67. Chase's instructions had been issued on Mar. 3, in compliance with congressional authorization given the previous July. Rules and Regulations Concerning Internal Commercial Intercourse, Mar. 3, 1862 (Letters Sent Relating to Restricted Commercial Intercourse and Captured and Abandoned Property, Gen. Recs. Treasury Dept., Nat. Arch.); *Statutes at Large*, 12:255–58.

May 1862 { 335 }

force in front, on authority of deserters from Yorktown—impressed men who had got away & were trying to reach their homes—4 Regiments & some cavalry & artillery under Smith (Gus.) say 3000—abt. 3000 more under   —Jackson coming to join them with, say, 5. to 10.000[68]— Whole force not over, I judge, from 12. to 16.000 & mostly raw & badly armed. Smith's force in large part detailed from Yorktown, where I do not believe the rebels now have 60.000 men—not equal to 40.000 good troops. Strange that McClellan dallies & waits in eternal preparation. Strange that the President does not give McDowell all the disposable force in the region & send him on to Richmond. Telegram from McD. copies extracts from Richmond papers, giving correspondence between Mayor of N.O. & Com. Farragut.[69] Mayor's letter insolent. Also gives account of fall of Ft. Macon, where rebels were permitted to retire with honors of war, wh. I think wrong.[70]

Home abt. 6 to dinner. Judge Lane dined with me.[71] Knew McClellan when Superintendent of Central R.R. Was good Supt. but had no occasion for display of abilities needed now. Knew John Wilson well—unscrupulous in action agt. persons he disliked—sanguine—not always judicious—but capable where work & energy & not much breadth & solidity required.

[Mr Lathrop came in at Dept.[72]—told him he had been appd. Coll. at N.O. & wd. have Instructions as soon as confirmed. Chandler came in & introduced him to Mr. L. Asked him to have confn. & Bill extending powers to prevent aid to rebels passed—wh. he promised]

---

68. Gustavus Woodson Smith (1822–96), former New York City street commissioner and a major general in the Confederate army; and Thomas Jonathan "Stonewall" Jackson (1824–63). *DAB*, 9:556–59, 17:272–73.

69. Captain—soon to be Rear Admiral—David Glasgow Farragut (1801–70) had taken New Orleans on Apr. 25, calling for unqualified surrender and the removal of Confederate colors. Mayor John T. Monroe (1823–71) had reluctantly agreed to Farragut's first demand, but had refused to comply with the second. "The man lives not in our midst," he defiantly answered, "whose hand and heart would not be palsied at the mere thought of such an act." *DAB*, 6:286–90; *Daily Richmond Whig*, Apr. 30, 1862; Holli and Jones, *Biographical Dictionary of American Mayors*, 257–58.

70. On Apr. 26, Confederate troops at Ft. Macon, N.C., had surrendered to U.S. forces under Ambrose E. Burnside, who had granted paroles and released the prisoners with their personal property. *OR*, ser. 1, v. 9:275–76.

71. Ebenezer Lane.

72. Chase had recently appointed Charles C. Lathrop a special agent for the Mississippi Valley. Objections were raised that blocked Lathrop's confirmation as collector at New Orleans. Chase to Lathrop, Apr. 29, 1862 (Letters Sent to Special Agents, Recs. of Bureau of Customs, Nat. Arch.); Lathrop to Chase, May 19, 1862 (Chase Papers, L.C.); Basler, *Collected Works*, 5:188.

Letters from Gov Chase to Miss Nettie.[73]
The taking of Norfolk.
I.
Revenue Steamer "Miami"[74]
Off Fortress Monroe, May 7, 1862.

My darling Nettie[75]

I write to you from the cabin of the Steamer Miami, just outside of two steam transports loaded with troops embarked for a proposed attack on Norfolk.

We came here night-before-last, having left Washn. on Monday evening, Our party consisted of the President, Secretary Stanton & Gen Viele,[76] who had just returned fr. Port Royal where he had commanded a Brigade chgd. with most impt. duties in the reduction of Ft. Pulaski. Our staunch little Steamer bore us rapidly & pleasantly down the River until we were some 10 or 15 miles below Alexandria, when the night wh. had come on with a drizzling rain became so thick & dark that the Pilot found himself unable to discern the right course. We were, therefore, obliged to cast anchor & wait for clearer sky. By 3 of Tuesday morng. we were again on our way. We passed Aquia abt. day, & found ourselves abt. noon tossing on the Chesapeake. It wd. have amused you to see us take our luncheon. The President gave it up almost as soon as he began, & declaring himself too uncomfortable to eat, stretched himself at length on the locker. The rest of us persisted; but the plates slipped this way and that—the glasses tumbled over & slid & rolled abt.—& the whole table seemed as topsy-turvy as if some Spiritualist were operating upon it. But we got thro, & then the Secy. of War followed the example of the Prest. & Gen V. & I went on deck & chatted.

Bet. 8 & 9 we reached our destination. Mr. Stanton at once sent

---

73. Regarding these three letters from Chase to his younger daughter, see the description of Journal VIII, p. lxiv above. In each case there is an extant original of the letter in Chase's hand. The originals differ in varying degrees from the versions given in the journal. The "letter" versions will be printed in a subsequent volume with other correspondence from 1862. The differences between them and these "journal" versions are noted below in general terms only.

74. Previously the British steamer *Lady Le Marchant*. U.S. Department of Transportation, *Record of Movements: Vessels of the United States Coast Guard, 1790–December 31, 1933* (Washington, D.C., 1989), 417.

75. Chase's draft of this letter is in the Chase Papers, Hist. Soc. of Pa. In addition to other differences between the two texts, eleven passages of more than five words each which appear in the draft are not in this version from the journal.

76. Egbert Ludovicus Viele (182–1902), brigadier general of volunteers, second in command at Port Royal, then military governor of Norfolk, Va., May–Oct. 1862. *DAB*, 19:267–68.

a message to Gen Wool notifying our arrival & after a while the Genl. & a number of his staff came on board. It was now near 10; but after a short conference it was determd. that the Prest., Mr. S., Gen. W., & myself with Genl. V. shd. visit Com. Goldsborough & talk with him abt the condition of thgs. & the thgs to be done.[77] As it was not easy to get along side the Minnesota[78] in the night on the Rev. Steamer, we took a tug & were soon within hail. As directed in response to our hail, we went to the port side. And there were the narrow steps up the lofty side, with the guiding ropes on either hand hardly visible in the darkness. It seemed to me *very* high & a little fearsome. But etiquette reqd. the Prest. to go first and he went. Etiquette reqd. the Secy. of the Treasy. to follow & I followed. We got up safely of course, & when up it did not seem so vy. much of a getting up stairs after all.

But I must not stop to describe the Minnesota though the noble ship is worth description; nor shall I tell you of the conference except that it related to military & naval movements in connection with the dreaded "Merrimac."[79]

The next morning—yesterday—Wednesday—we of the Miami were up pretty early, for it isn't easy somehow to sleep late on shipboard. We were to breakfast at 9 with Gen. W. & Mr. S. proposed we shd. visit the Vanderbilt first.[80] She was already for her encounter with the Merrimac, enormously strengthened abt. the bow with timbers so as to be little else for many feet (say 50) from the prow than a mass of solid timber plated outside with iron. We stood a moment on her wheel-house & looked down thro. the immense diameter of her wheels, the frame-work of wh. seemed slight & curiously interlaced; but was in fact of the strongest wrought iron bars & adjusted carefully to the greatest strength. The weight of one wheel was 100 tons & the diameter thro wh we looked 42 ft. From the Vanderbilt we sailed round the Monitor & Stevens & then back to the wharf;[81] but I must omit in this letter the breakfast—the visit

---

77. Louis Malesherbes Goldsborough (1805–77), a flag officer (later rear admiral), U.S.N., commanded the North Atlantic Blockading Squadron. He had married Elizabeth Gamble Wirt in 1831. *DAB,* 7:365–66; *ORN,* ser. 1, v. 1:417, v. 7:131–33.

78. The USS *Minnesota,* a 3,307-ton wooden screw steamer. *ORN,* ser. 2, v. 1:145.

79. So called when built by the federal government (officially *Merrimack*), but captured in 1861 and renamed the CSS *Virginia.* On Mar. 8 and 9, the 3,200-ton ironclad ram had terrorized Hampton Roads during engagements which had damaged the USS *Monitor, Minnesota,* and *St. Lawrence,* and destroyed the *Cumberland* and *Congress. ORN,* ser. 2, v. 1:270–71.

80. The 1,770-ton USS *Vanderbilt,* a wooden side-wheel steamer given to the U.S. government by Cornelius Vanderbilt. Ibid., ser. 2, v. 1:230.

81. The USS *Stevens Battery,* originally named the *Naugatuck,* was an experimental 192-ton twin-screw steamer recently contributed to the U.S. government by Edwin

to the Monitor & Stevens—to the Rip Raps—Com. G's coming & discussion—the appearance of the Merrimac & disappearance—the Review—the visit to ruined Hampton[82]—the determination to direct Com. G. to send the Galena[83] & 2 gunboats up the river—how it was determd. to attempt the reduction of the batteries at Sewalls Pt next morning—how we went to the Rip Raps—how the fleet moved to the attack—how the great guns of the Rip Raps joined in the fray throwing shot & shell more than 3 miles—how the Merrimac came down & out—how the Monitor moved up & quietly waited for her—how the big wooden ships got out of the way, that the Minnesota & Vanderbilt mt. have fair sweep at her & run her down—how she wd.n't come where they cd.—how she finally retreated to where the Monitor alone cd. follow her—all this & much more I must leave untold this morning, for since I wrote the first half & more of this letter, a night is past & the sun of the 8th of May has risen splendidly over Ft Monroe.

Your affec. Father.
S. P. C.

II

Head-quarters, Dept. of Va.
Ft. Monroe, Va., May 8, 1862.

My darling Nettie[84]

I was obliged to close my letter to you this morning quite abruptly—with a mere synopsis of events. I will now give you a little better idea of what took place yesterday. Bu[85]

Augustus Stevens (1795–1868), a New Jersey engineer and inventor. The *Stevens* could be turned end-for-end in less than two minutes and lowered three feet below loadline for lessened visibility. The USS *Monitor* was inventor John Ericsson's famous ironclad single-turret steamer. *Appletons'*, 5:675; *DAB*, 17:608–9; *ORN*, ser. 2, v. 1:148–49, 215.

82. Earlier in the day, the presidential party had reviewed troops at Camp Hamilton, Va., and visited the town of Hampton, Va., which had burned on the night of Aug. 7–8, 1861. Earl Schenck Miers, ed., *Lincoln Day by Day: A Chronology, 1809–1865* (Washington, D.C., 1960), 3:110; *ORN*, ser. 1, v. 6:66.

83. The USS *Galena*, a 738-ton ironclad steamer. *ORN*, ser. 2, v. 1:90.

84. The original of this letter, in Chase's hand, is in the Chase Papers, Hist. Soc. of Pa. Unfortunately is incomplete, breaking off in mid-sentence after four pages. Most of the text of the original was omitted from the version copied in the journal, which after two sentences jumps to a point midway down the last surviving page of the original. Thus most of the incomplete original is not included in the journal, and most of the journal version contains text that comes after the point where the original breaks off.

85. This is a false start; the original letter continues here with the word *But*. The version of this letter in the journal skips approximately three pages of Chase's original text at this point.

Yesterday morning we came ashore early. Com. G. came at the same time, on a summons from the Prest. & it was then that the attack on Sewalls Pt. Batteries was determined on. After the orders had been given, the Prest., Mr. S., & myself went over to the Rip Raps in a tug to observe its execution. It was not a great while before the great ships were in motion. The Seminole took the lead, the San Jacinto & the Dakota[86] & finally[87] the Susquehenna followed, whose Capt., Lardner, was the commg. officer of the vessels engaged.[88] With these ships were the Monitor & little gunboat Stevens, wh. Com. Stevens[89] presented to the Tr. Dep. & wh I christened the "Stevens" in honor of him. By & by the Seminole reached her position & a belch of smoke, followed in a few seconds by a report like distant thunder, announced the beginning of the cannonade. Then came the guns from the Rip Raps where we were & soon the Monitor & the Stevens joined. In a little while the small battery at the extreme point was silenced, and the cannonade was directed on a battery inside the point a half-mile or a mile nearer Norfolk. While this was going on, a smoke curled up over the woods on Sewell's Pt. 5 or 6 miles fr. its termination, & each man, almost, sd to the other, "There comes the Merrimac;" & sure enough it was the Merrimac. But before she made her appearance we had left the Rip Raps & had reached the landing on our way to Head-Quarters. Just as we were going ashore, the Monster came slowly abt. fr. behind the Pt. & all the big wooden vessels began to haul off. The Monitor & Stevens, however, held their ground. The M. still came on slowly & in a little while there was a clear sheet of water bet. her & the Monitor. Then the great rebel terror paused—then turned back—& having finally attained what she considered a safe position, became stationary again. This was the end of the battle. Its results were on one side nobody & nothing hurt, with a certainty that the battery at the extreme Pt. was useless to the rebels & the battery on the inside much less strong and much less strongly manned than had been supposed. The results on the rebel side we can't tell but only know that their barracks were burnt by our shells. Another certainty is that the rebel Monster don't *want to* fight,—& *won't* fight if she can help it, except with more advantage than she is likely to have. Enough for one day.

---

86. The 801-ton *Seminole*, 1,567-ton *San Jacinto*, and 996-ton *Dacotah*, wooden screw steamers of the U.S. Navy. *ORN*, ser. 2, v. 1:70, 200, 204.

87. Here the original letter breaks off, its remainder apparently lost. The journal contains the only surviving version of the rest of the letter.

88. James Lawrence Lardner (1802–81) of the USS *Susquehanna*, a 2,450-ton wooden side-wheel steamer. *DAB*, 10:615–16; *ORN*, ser. 2, v. 1:217.

89. Edwin Augustus Stevens.

III.
Steamer Baltimore, May 11, 1862

My darling Nettie.[90]

I beleive I closed my last letter to you with an account of the bombardment. That was tho't to have shown the inutility of an attempt to land at Sewall's Pt. while the Merrimac lay watching it; & it at once became a question, what shd now be done? Three plans only seemed feasible; to send all the troops that cd. be spared around to Burnside & let him come on Norfolk fr. behind[91]—that is, fr. the South; to send them up James River to aid McC; or to seek another landing place out of reach of the Merrimac. In this state of thgs., I offered to take the Miami, if a tug of less dft. & capable, therefore, of getting nearer shore cd. accompany me, & make an examination, in company with an officer, of the coast East of the Pt. Col. Cram offered to go & Gen. W. sd. he wd. accompany us.[92] We started accordingly & being arrived opp. a pt. wh. I mark "a" on the poor dft. I send you,[93] sent a boat's crew on shore to find the depth of water. We had already approached within some 500 yds. in the Miami, & the tug had approached within perhaps 100, of the shore. The boats went vy. near the shore & then pulled off, somewhat to my surprise. But when they returned to the boat the mystery was explained. They had seen an enemy's picket & a soldier standing up & beckoning to his companions to lie close: & they had inferred the existence of an ambush & had pulled off to avoid being fired upon. When the officer of the boat & Col Cram came on board, they cd. still see the picket on horseback, & pointed his position out to me; but I being near sighted, cd. not see. It was

---

90. Chase wrote this letter on board the USS *Baltimore*, a 500-ton side-wheel wooden steamer. Both Chase's autograph original and a copy signed by him, but in Homer Plantz's handwriting, are in the Chase Papers, Hist. Soc. of Pa. The version in Plantz's hand was that received by Janet Chase. As her father explained in a postscript, he considered the original letter too difficult to read and had Plantz copy it for his signature. Plantz probably made the copy in Journal VIII from Chase's original, not from the version sent to Nettie. There are several places where text in the original was omitted from the journal version, although no omitted section is longer than a sentence. *ORN*, ser. 2, v. 1:42.

91. At this time, Ambrose Everett Burnside (1824–81), major general of volunteers, commanded Union troops on the coast of N.C. after his successful expedition in early 1862. *DAB*, 3:309–13.

92. Thomas Jefferson Cram (1807–83) served as aide-de-camp to Gen. John Ellis Wool. *Appletons'*, 1:767.

93. Chase apparently meant to accompany the letter with a diagram, but then did not do so. He explained to his daughter: "The Chart is missing—but a map will answer. Our landing was at the head of Willoughby bay." Chase to Janet Chase, May 11, 1862 (Chase Papers, Hist. Soc. of Pa.).

plain enough that there was no use in landing men to be fired upon & overcome by a superior force, & so the order was given to get under way to return to Ft. M. We had, indeed, accomplished our main purpose, having found the water sufficiently deep to admit of landing without any serious difficulty. But just as we were going away, a white flag was seen waving over the sand-bank on shore, & the Genl. ordered it to be ansd. at once, wh. was done by fastening a bed-sheet to the flag-line & running it up. When this was done, several colored people appeared on shore—all women & children. Fearing the flag and the appearance of the colored people might be a cover intended to get our people within rifle-shot, I directed two boats to go ashore, with full crews well armed. They went; & pretty soon I saw Col. Cram talking with the people on shore, while some of the men were walking abt. on the beach. Presently, one boat pulled off towards the ship, & when she had come quite near, I observed the colored people going up the sand bank & Col Cram preparing to return with the other boat. It occurred to me that the poor people mt. have desired to go to Ft. M. & mt. have been refused. So I detd. to go ashore myself, &, jumping into the returned boat, was quickly on the beach. The Col. reported his examinn. entirely satisfy. & I found fr. the cold. people (one of whom, however, turned out to be a white woman living near by) that none of them wanted to leave & we all retd. to the ship. These women were the soldiers who had alarmed our folks.

We had made an important discovery—a gd. & convenient landing place, some 5 or 6 miles fr. Ft. M., capable of receiving any No. of troops & communicating with Norfolk by quite passable roads, with a distance by one route of 8 or 9 & by another of 12 or 13 miles.

When I got back to Ft. M. I found the Prest. had been listening to a Pilot & studying a chart & had become impressed with a conviction that there was a nearer landing & wished to go & see abt. it on the spot. So we started again & soon reached the shore, taking with us a large boat & some 20 armed soldiers fr. the Rip Raps. The Prest. & Mr. S.[94] were on the tug & I on the Miami. The tug was, of course, nearest shore & as soon as she found the water too shoal for her to go farther safely, the Rip Raps boat was manned & sent in. Meantime, I had the M. got ready for action & directed the Capt. to go ashore with both boats & all the men they cd. take fully armed. Before this cd. be done, however, the other boat had pulled off shore & several horsemen who appeared to be soldiers of the enemy were

---

94. Stanton.

seen on the beach. I sent to the Prest. to ask if we shd. fire on them & he replied negatively. We had again found a gd. landing, wh. at the time I supposed to be bet. 2 & 3 miles nearer Ft. M. but wh proved to be only ½ to ¾ of a mile nearer.

Returning to Ft. M. it was agreed that an advance shd. at once be made on N. fr. one of these landings. Genl. W. preferred the one he had visited & it was selected. It was now night but the preparations proceeded with grt. activity. 4 Regts. were sent off & orders given for others to follow. Col. Cram went down to make a bridge of boats to the landing, & Genl. W. asked me to accompany him the next morning.

Next morning (yesterday) I was up early, & we got off as soon as possible. As soon as we reached the place, I took the tug wh. bro't us down & went up the shore to where the Prests. boat had attempted to land the eve'g. before. I found the distance to be only ¾ of a mile & retd. to the Miami where I had left the Genl. He had gone ashore & I at once followed. On shore, I found Gen. Viele with an orderly behind him. He asked if I wd. like a horse & I sd. Yes. He thereupon directed his Orderly to dismount & I mounted. I then proposed to ride up where the pickets had been seen the night before. He complied. We found a shed where the pickets had staid & fresh horse-tracks in many places, showing that the enemy had only withdrawn a few hours. Meantime Mr. S. had come down & on my return to Genl. W. asked me to go with the expedition, & I finally detd. to do so. Accordingly I asked Genl. W. for a squad of dragoons & for permission to ride on with Genl. V. ahead of him. He granted both requests. After going abt. 5 miles Genl. V. & myself came up with the rear of the advance (wh. had preceded us 3 or 4 hours) & soon heard firing of artillery in front. We soon heard that the bridge wh we expected to cross was burnt—that the enemy's artillery was posted on the other side—& that Gens. Mansfield & Weber were returning.[95] Abt. ½ or ¾ of a mile fr. the burning bridge we met them, & of course turned back. Returning we met Genl. W. who detd. to leave a guard on that route & take another to N. There was now a gd. deal of confusion, to remedy wh. & provide for contingencies, Gen. W. sent Gen. M. to Newport News to bring ford. his Brigade & brigaded the troops with him, assigning Gen. V. to command of one & Gen. Weber to commd. of the other. Things now went much better. The cavalry & Maj. Dodge were in

---

95. Brig. Gen. Joseph King Fenno Mansfield, U.S.A. (1803–62), later a major general of volunteers; and Max Weber (1824–1901), brigadier general of volunteers. Both served at Fort Monroe under Gen. John Ellis Wool. *Appletons'*, 6:405; *DAB*, 12:257; *Nat. Cyc.*, 12:264.

advance[96]—Gen. W. & staff next—then a body of sharpshooting skirmishers—then the main body of V's brigade—& then Weber's. We stopped everybody fr. whom we cd. obtain information & was not long before we were informed that the intrenched camp, where we expected the rebels wd. fight if any where, had just been evacuated & that the barracks were fired. This pleasant intelligence was soon confirmed by the arrival of one of Dodge's dragoons who told us that the cavalry were already within it.

We kept on & were soon within the work—a very strong one—defended by many heavy guns of wh. 21 still remained in position. The troops as they entered gave cheer after cheer & were immy. formed into line for the further march, now only two miles, to N. Genl. Wool now invited Gen. V., Gen Weber, & Maj. D. to ride with us in front & so we proceeded until we met a deputation of the city authorities, who surrendered the city in form. Genl. W. & myself entered one carriage with two of the deputation & Gen. V. another with others, & so we drove into town & to the City Hall, where the Genl. completed his arrangements for taking possession of the City. These completed, & Gen. V. being left in chg. as Mil. Govr., Genl W & myself set out on our return to Ocean View, our landing place, in the carriage wh. had brot. us to the City Hall; wh. carriage, by the way, was that used by the rebel Genl. Huger & he had, perhaps, been riding in it that very morning.

It was sundown when we left N.—abt. 10 when we reached Ocean View—& near 12 when we reached Ft. M. The Prest. had been greatly alarmed for our safety by the report of Genl. M. as he went by to Newport News; & you can imagine his delight when we told him N. was ours. S. soon came up to his room & was equally delighted. He fairly hugged Gen. W.

For my part, I was very tired & glad to get to bed.

This morning, as the Prest. had detd. to leave for Washn. at 7, I rose at 6 & just before 7 came into the parlor where Com. G. astonished & gratified us that the rebels had set fire to the Merrimac & had blown her up. It was detd. that, before leaving, we wd go up in the Balto., wh was to convey us to Washn., to the point where the suicide had been performed & above the obstructions in the channel if possible, so as to be sure of the access to Norfolk by water wh had been defended by the exploded ship. This was done; but the voyage was longer than we anticipated, taking us up to the wharves of N. where, in the Elizabeth River, were already lying the Montor, the Stevens, the Susquehenna & one or two other vessels.

96. Major Charles Cleveland Dodge (b. 1841) of New York's mounted rifles. *Appletons'*, 2:192; Heitman, *Historical Register*, 1:376.

Genl. W. & Com. G. had come up with us on the Balto. & as soon as they were transferred to the Susquehenna, our prow was turned down steam & touching for a moment at the Ft. we kept on our way towards Washn., where we hope to be at Breakfast tomorrow.

So has ended a brilliant week's campaign of the Prest., for I thk. it quite certain that if he had not come down, N. wd. still have been in possession of the enemy & the M. as grim & defiant & as much a terror as ever. The whole coast is now virtually ours. There is no port wh. the Monitor & Stevens cannot enter & take.

It was sad & pleasant to see the Union flag once more waving over N. & the shipping in the harbor & to think of the destruction accomplished there a little more than a year ago.

I went to Norfolk last night by land with the army; this morning by water with the navy. My campaign too is over

SATURDAY, MAY 16, 1862. Wrote, on leaving for Philadelphia, the following Letter to the President.[97]

"Washington, May 16, 1862
"My dear Sir.
"Obliged to go to Philadelphia this afternoon, I cannot confer with you as I wish in relation to the Military Order of Maj. Gen. Hunter, enfranchising the Slaves in his Department.[98]

"Of course, I do not assume to judge of the military necessity; but it seems to me of the highest importance, whether our relations at home or abroad be considered, that this Order be not revoked. It has been made as a military measure, to meet a military exigency, and should, in my judgment, be suffered to stand upon the responsibility of the Commanding General who made it.

"It will be cordially approved, I am sure, by more than nine-tenths of the people on whom you must rely for support of your administration.

"Pardon this brief and hurried note, and beleive me
"Most cordially and respectfully yours,
"S. P. Chase."
To the President

---

97. In the journal, this letter to Abraham Lincoln precedes the three letters to Janet Chase, although they have earlier dates. The original of the May 16 letter to Lincoln, written in Chase's hand, is in Lincoln's papers at the L.C. The version in the journal differs from the autograph letter in punctuation and capitalization, in the use of *and* for the original's *&*, and in the substitution of *To the President* for *The President* at the end of the letter.

98. On May 9, Maj. Gen. David Hunter freed slaves under his jurisdiction as commander of the Department of the South. Ten days later, President Lincoln disavowed the order and issued a reminder of his Mar. 6 call to Congress for gradual emancipation. Basler, *Collected Works*, 5:222–23.

May 1862

Narrative of Operations
[Dictated June 26]

On Sunday morning, May 11, the Prest., becoming uneasy on acct. of his long absence from Washn., determined to return forthwith. The explosion of the Merrimac, however, detained him long enough to go to the spot, ascertain the exact condition of things & return to Ft. M., whence we proceeded immediately towards Washn. On our way up, I remarked on the probability that a small force, say 5000 men, embarked on transports & convoyed by gun boats, mt. contribute largely to the taking of Richmond, if sent immediately up James R. But nothing was determined on. After our return to Washn. I frequently spoke of this matter & urged the sending of Gen Wool up Jas. R. with all his disposable force. It was tho't Gen. McClellan cd be reinforced more effectually in another direction.

Gen. McD. was ordered to concentrate his whole corps, including Shields' division,[99] at Fredericksburgh, with a view to march upon Richmond fr. that pt. Shields' division, wh. had been in the valley of the Shenandoah, was marched across the country & joined McD.

On Friday, May 23d., the Prest. & Secy. of War visited the Army at Fredericksburg & retd. to Washn. on Saturday morning, highly gratified by the condition of the troops and anticipating an imposing & successful advance on the Monday following. On the afternoon of the same Saturday I was sent for to the War Dept. & found that intelligence had been recd. of the taking of Front-R. & the annihilation of Kenley's Regt. on the preceding day.[1] The enemy was reported to have pushed forward to Middletown & cut off the retreat of Banks, supposed to be at Strasburg. An order was immy. dispatched to Gen. Frémont to advance to Harrisonburg, & do all in his power for the relief of Banks. An Order was also sent to Genl. McD. to detach 20.000—or one-half his force—sending them partly by land to Catlett's station & partly by water to Alexdria. & Washn. To expedite these movements, I was directed to proceed immy. to Fredk.bg. & confer personally with Gen. McD. I left accordingly the same afternoon, & reached Fredk.bg. abt. 1 o.c A.M., Sunday. I found that Gen. McD. had given all the necessary Orders for the movements directed by the Prest. The march began early the next morning, & successive divisions & regts. followed, until, during the

99. James Shields.
1. On May 23, Confederate troops under Stonewall Jackson defeated Federal forces at Front Royal, Va. Col. John Reese Kenly (1822–91), commander of the 1st Maryland Regiment and future major general of volunteers, was severely wounded and taken prisoner. *Appletons'*, 3:515; *Nat. Cyc.*, 6:144; *OR*, ser. 2, v. 12, pt. 1:536–37, 778–80.

course of the day, the whole 20.000 were on their march. I retd. to Washn. Sunday night accompanied by Gen. Shields, & found the Prest., with the Secy. of War, Secy. of State, & several Senators & Representatives, at the War Dept. By this time intelligence had been recd. that B. had retreated early on Saturday morning from Strasbg., reaching Winchester the same night, & that his retreat had been continued thro. Sunday, & that a portion of his troops had already arrived at Williamsport. Gen. Saxton had been ordered to Harper's-Ferry, & reinforcements had been & were still rapidly being pushed forward to that point.

On Monday, Shields' divn. arrived at Catlett's Station, & Geary's divn.,[2] wh. had been stationed along the line of the Manassas Gap R.R., had fallen back to Manassas. Ord's divn. followed, partly by water & partly by land, &, with Shields, was concentrated within a day or two at Manassas. McD. came from Fredk.bg. at the instance of the Prest. & took command in person, having ordered King's divn. to advance towards Martinsbg. as a supporting column. Shields pushed forward to Fr.-R., wh. place he reached on Friday. McD. followed, also reaching Fr.-R. on Saturday. The object of this movement was to cut off the retreat of Jackson thro. Fr.-R.

Meantime Frémont, observing the spirit though not the letter of his Orders, had marched to Moorfield & thence to Wardensville a few miles distant fr. Strasbg.—his directions being to occupy Strasb. & cut off the retreat of Jackson by that road. Unfortunately Frémont did not reach Strasbg. until Jackson, defeated by Saxton on Friday in his attack upon Harper's-F., & being apprised no doubt of the movements in his rear, had passed thro. Strasbg. on his retreat down the valley.

While this combined movement, intended to capture Jackson & his force, was in progress, Gen. McC. was constantly asking for reinforcements at Richmond. I had no confidence in his ability to handle a great army, but inasmuch as the Prest. was unwilling to give the command to any other Genl. I thought it of great importance that he shd. be reinforced as far as possible. To this end, in the course of the week, I urged on several occasions that one-half of the McCall's divn. be sent down to form a junction with McClellan's army, & that Gen Wool, with 10.000 of his force, be sent up from Ft. Monroe & Norfolk by Jas. R. to effect, if possible, the capture of Ft. Darling, or at least to cooperate with McClellan,

---

2. At the time, John White Geary was brigadier general of the 28th Pennsylvania.

whose lines, I supposed, cd be extended from Bottom's Bridge to the Jas. R. These reinforcements were not sent, partly, as I suppose, because the Prest. was unwilling to weaken the advance at Fredk.bg., & partly because he was unwilling to order Gen W., who was at variance with McC., to a coöperation wh. mt. lead to collision bet. the Gens. & so to unpleasant results.

I also urged that, inasmuch as McDowell's force had been drawn over into and near the Shenandoah Valley, his three divisions—Shields', Ord's & King's—shd be massed & ordered forwd. to Charlottesville & Lynchbg. This movement had been proposed by Gen. Shields, as a movement to be executed fr. Fredk.bg. Gen. McD. also had proposed the same. As much reluctance was manifested agt. undertaking this movement, as had been in resp. to the reinforcement of McClellan.

On Friday, June 14, the Prest. detd. to send 20.000 men to McCl. To effect this object, he directed the embarkation of the whole of McCall's division at Fredk.bg. & annexed the Dept. of Va., wh. had been under Genl. Wool, to the command of McCln. Wool was transferred to Balto. and Dix to Ft. Monroe,[3] to avoid the apprehended difficulties from placing the Dept., while under the command of Genl. W., also under the command of McClellan. Most of the drilled troops at Ft. M—of whom there were abt. 14.000,—were sent to McClellan & their places supplied mainly with new levies. Thus, long after I had proposed the reinforcement, the arrangment was made by whi they were sent.

On the same day, upon the President expressing his gratification that the reinforcements had been sent to McClellan, I replied to him that his satisfaction wd. be much increased if he wd. order McD., with his three divisions, strengthened if necessary by portions of Banks and Fremont's commands, on the southward expedition to Charlottesville & Lynchburgh. I endeavored to impress upon him the idea that this movement wd. be of grt. importance to McC. by creating a diversion in his favor & by cutting off the supplies wh. reached Richmond through Lynchburg, fr. E. Tenn. I was not successful in impressing the President with the correctness of my views. I suppose that his difficulty arose, partly from a desire to have McD. in a position fr. wh. he cd. directly reinforce McC. & partly fr. apprehension of disagreement bet. the Maj. Gens. commg. the separate bodies wh. it might be necessary to combine in the

---

3. John Adams Dix (1798–1879) was U.S. senator from New York, 1845–49, secretary of the Treasury, 1861, major general in the Union army, 1861–65, and governor of New York, 1873–75. *DAB*, 5:325–27.

Charlottesville Expedition. This, of course is mere conjecture. What is certain is, that the Expedition was not organized or attempted.

Subsequently (June 24) the Prest., having become convinced of the necessity of combining these three bodies under one command, created the Army of Virginia, to consist of these three bodies) & placed it under the command of Genl Pope,[4] who was junior in rank, though of the same grade, as Maj. Gens. Frémont, Banks & McDowell, who were made subject to his orders.

I understood that the object of this consolidation was, to make the movement upon Charlottesville wh. I had been so anxious to see attempted.

JOURNAL X

MONDAY, JULY 21, 1862. Early this morning, Count Gurowski called and told me that, yesterday, at a great dinner at Mr. Tassara's[5]—the only Americans present being Gov. Seward and Senator Carlile—Gov. Seward remarked that he had lately begun to realize the value of a CROMWELL, and to appreciate the *Coup d'etat;* and that he wished we had had a Cromwell or a Coup d'etat for our Congress. The Count said that the diplomats present were very much disgusted, and that the language of Gov. Seward injured the Administration much in the estimation of all intelligent foreigners.

After the Count left, I received a notice to attend a Cabinet meeting, at 10 o'clock. It has been so long since any consultation has been held that it struck me as a novelty.[6]

I went at the appointed hour, and found that the President had been profoundly concerned at the present aspect of affairs, and had determined to take some definitive steps in respect to military action and slavery. He had prepared several Orders, the first of which contemplated authority to Commanders to subsist their troops in the hostile territory—the second, authority to employ negroes as laborers—the third requiring that both in the case of property taken and of negroes employed, accounts should be kept with such degrees of certainty as would enable compensation to be made in

---

4. Maj. Gen. John Pope (1822–92). *DAB,* 15:76–77.
5. Polish revolutionary and author Count Adam Gurowski (1805–66) acted as a translator for the U.S. State Department, 1861–63. Gabriel García y Tassara (1817–75) served as Spanish minister to the U.S., 1857–67. *Appletons',* 3:14; Kinley J. Brauer, "Gabriel García y Tassara and the American Civil War: A Spanish Perspective," *Civil War History* 21 (1975): 5–27; Mario Mendez Bejarano, *Tassara: Nueva Biografía Crítica* (Madrid, 1928).
6. The most recent cabinet meeting had taken place on July 19. Miers, *Lincoln Day by Day,* 3:128.

proper cases—another provided for the colonization of negroes in some tropical country

A good deal of discussion took place upon these points. The first Order was universally approved. The second was approved entirely; and the third, by all except myself. I doubted the expediency of attempting to keep accounts for the benefit of the inhabitants of rebel States. The Colonization project was not much discussed.

The Secretary of War presented some letters from Genl. Hunter, in which he advised the Department that the withdrawal of a large proportion of his troops to reinforce Genl. McClellan, rendered it highly important that he should be immediately authorized to enlist all loyal persons without reference to complection. Messrs. Stanton, Seward and myself, expressed ourselves in favor of this plan, and no one expressed himself against it. [Mr. Blair was not present.] The President was not prepared to decide the question, but expressed himself as averse to arming negroes. The whole matter was postponed until tomorrow.

After the meeting of the Cabinet, Messrs. Speed, Holloway and Casey—the first, a distinguished lawyer of Louisville, a State Senator, and now Postmaster of the city; the second, a large slaveholder in South-western Kentucky; the third, M.C. from the Southwestern District[7]—called at the Department. Messrs. Speed and Casey were decided in favor of the most decided measures in respect to Slavery and the employment of negroes in whatever capacity they were fitted for. Messrs. Speed and Casey assured me that Mr Holloway (though a large slaveholder) was in favor of every measure necessary for success and that he held no sacrifice too great to insure it. He would cheerfully give up slavery if it became necessary or important.

Mr. Casey, Mr. Horton and Genl. Pope dined with me. Mr Horton condemned severely the conduct of the campaign on the Peninisula and the misrepresentations made to the public in regard to it. Genl Pope expressed himself freely and decidedly in favor of the most vigorous measures in the prosecution of the war. He beleived that, in consequence of the rebellion, Slavery must perish, and with him it was only a question of prudence as to the means to be employed to weaken it. He was in favor of using every instrument which could be brought to bear against the enemy; and while he did not speak in favor of a general arming of the slaves as soldiers, he advocated their use as laborers, in the defence of fortifications, and in any way

7. John J. Speed (b. 1816), postmaster of Louisville, was actually a physician. Samuel Lewis Casey (1821–1902) was a Unionist congressman from Kentucky. *Biographical Cyclopedia of the Commonwealth of Kentucky* (Chicago, 1896), 563; *Bio. Dir. U.S. Cong.*, 754.

in which their services could be made useful without impairing the general tone of the service. He said he was now waiting, by request of the President, the arrival of Genl. Halleck;[8] and he regarded it as necessary for the safety and success of his operations that there should be a change in the command of the Army of the Potomac. He beleived that Genl. McClellan's incompetency and indisposition to active movements were so great, that if, in his operations, he should need assistance, he could not expect it from him. He had urged upon the President the importance of superseding Genl. McClellan before the arrival of Halleck, representing the delicacy of Halleck's future position, and the importance of having the field clear for him when he assumed the general command. The President, however, had only promised that he (Genl. Pope) should be present at his interview with Genl Halleck, when he would give the latter his opinion of McClellan.

TUESDAY, JULY 22D., 1862. This morning, I called on the President with a letter received some time since from Col. Key, in which he stated that he had reason to beleive that if Genl. McClellan found he could not otherwise sustain himself in Virginia, he would declare the liberation of the slaves; and that the President would not dare to interfere with the Order. I urged upon the President the importance of an immediate change in the command of the Army of the Potomac, representing the necessity of having a General in that command who would cordially and efficiently coöperate with the movements of Pope and others; and urging a change before the arrival of Genl. Halleck, in view of the extreme delicacy of his position in this respect, Genl. McClellan being his senior Major-General. I said that I did not regard Genl. McClellan as loyal to the Administration, although I did not question his general loyalty to the country.

I also urged Genl. McClellan's removal upon financial grounds. I told him that, if such a change in the command was made as would insure action to the army and give it power in the ratio of its strength, and if such measures were adopted in respect to slavery as would inspire the country with confidence that no measure would be left untried which promised a speedy and successful result, I would insure that, within ten days, the Bonds of the U.S.—except the 5–20s.[9]—would be so far above par that conversions into the

---

8. Henry Wager Halleck (1815–72), general-in-chief of the Union army since July 11. *DAB*, 8:150–52.

9. Five hundred million dollars' worth of U.S. bonds issued in 1862, callable in five years and maturing in twenty. Hammond, *Sovereignty*, 289.

latter stock would take place rapidly and furnish the necessary means for carrying on the Government. If this was not done, it seemed to me impossible to meet necessary expenses. Already there were $10.000.000 of unpaid Requisitions, and this amount must constantly increase.

The President came to no conclusion, but said he would confer with Gen. Halleck on all these matters. I left him, promising to return to Cabinet, when the subject of the Orders discussed yesterday would be resumed.

Went to Cabinet at the appointed hour. It was unanimously agreed that the Order in respect to Colonization should be dropped; and the others were adopted unanimously, except that I wished North Carolina included among the States named in the first order.

The question of arming slaves was then brought up and I advocated it warmly. The President was unwilling to adopt this measure, but proposed to issue a Proclamation, on the basis of the Confiscation Bill, calling upon the States to return to their allegiance—warning the rebels the provisions of the Act would have full force at the expiration of sixty days—adding, on his own part, a declaration of his intention to renew, at the next session of Congress, his recommendation of compensation to States adopting the gradual abolishment of slavery—and proclaiming the emancipation of all slaves within States remaining in insurrection on the first of January, 1863.[10]

I said that I should give to such a measure my cordial support; but I should prefer that no new expression on the subject of compensation should be made, and I thought that the measure of Emancipation could be much better and more quietly accomplished by allowing Generals to organize and arm the slaves (thus avoiding depredation and massacre on the one hand, and support to the insurrection on the other) and by directing the Commanders of Departments to proclaim emancipation within their Districts as soon as practicable; but I regarded this as so much better than inaction on the subject, that I should give it my entire support.

The President determined to publish the first three Orders forthwith, and to leave the other for some further consideration.[11] The impression left upon my mind by the whole discussion was, that while the President thought that the organization, equipment and

---

10. A copy of Lincoln's first draft of the Emancipation Proclamation appears in Basler, *Collected Works*, 5:33–37.

11. The first three orders were published later the same day as Chase had described them on July 21. *Daily National Intelligencer*, Aug. 16, 1862.

arming of negroes, like other soldiers, would be productive of more evil than good, he was not unwilling that Commanders should, at their discretion, arm, for purely defensive purposes, slaves coming within their lines.

Mr. Stanton brought forward a proposition to draft 50.000 men. Mr. Seward proposed that the number should be 100.000. The President directed that, whatever number were drafted, should be a part of the 300.000 already called for. No decision was reached, however.[12]

FRIDAY, JULY 25 No Cabinet to-day. Went to War Department in the morning, where I found the President and Stanton. We talked about the necessity of clearing the Mississippi, and Stanton again urged sending Mitchell. The President said he would see him. Stanton sent for him at Willards, and sent him to the President.[13]

In the evening I called for Mitchell to ride, with H. Walbridge.[14] Asked him the result. He said the President had asked him with what force he could take Vicksburgh and clear the river, and, with the black population on its banks, hold it open below Memphis; and had bid him consider. He had replied that, with his own division and Curtis' army,[15] he could do it he thought, but he would consider and reply.

I told him now was the time to do great things.

SATURDAY, JULY 26. Sent order to close and encrape the Department, in respect to ex-President Van Buren, just deceased.

The President came in, to talk about the controvery between the Postmaster General and 6th Auditor, in regard to rooms.[16] Agreed to see the Attorney General, for whom I afterwards sent. The Attorney General had not heard of Rabe's removal, of which I spoke

---

12. The administration was acting here in accordance with the militia act of July 17, 1862. *Statutes at Large,* 12:597–600. In the original journal, entries for Aug. 1–3 follow this entry.

13. Despite discussions on July 25–27, Stanton's plans for Ormsby M. Mitchel never materialized. In Sept., Mitchel was given command of the Department of the South, where he commanded from Hilton Head, S.C., until his death the following month. *DAB,* 13:39.

14. Possibly Hiram Walbridge (1821–70), a former Democratic congressman from New York and personal friend of Lincoln. *Appletons',* 6:319.

15. Samuel Ryan Curtis (1805–66), former Republican congressman from Iowa, was brigadier general, and later major general, of volunteers. *Bio. Dir. U.S. Cong.,* 861; *DAB,* 4:619–20.

16. Postmaster General Montgomery Blair and Green Adams (1812–84), Whig and Opposition party U.S. congressman from Kentucky, 1847–49, 1859–61, judge of the circuit court of Kentucky, 1851–56, and sixth auditor of the U.S. Treasury, 1861–64. *Bio. Dir. U.S. Cong.,* 512.

to him, and I directed Mr. Harrington to telegraph Rabe that the removal had been made without my knowledge or that of the Attorney-General.[17]

Genl Pope came in about 1 P.M., and went to Photographer's with me and Col. Welch.[18] He talked as if McClellan might be retained in command and retrieve himself by advancing on Richmond, which was now quite feasible there being but few troops on the North side of the James. I replied that no such advance would be made; or, if made and successful, would only restore undeserved confidence and prepare future calamities.

Mitchell called. He had seen the President, who had postponed his decision until he could consult Halleck. Mitchell had all his orders ready for rapid movement. Told him his only course was to wait and see.

Talked with Pope about Mitchell, who inclined to think him visionary. Asked him to get acquainted with him which he promised.

Wrote Mrs. E.[19] in reply to letter received from her

SUNDAY, JULY 27. A telegram from Genl. Morgan this morning apprised me of his resignation, and of his wish that I would secure its prompt acceptance.[20] I went, therefore, to the War Department, wishing to oblige him, and also to secure Garfield's appointment in his place.[21] Mr. Stanton was not in, but saw Watson.[22]

Talked with Watson about the state of things. He mentioned two conversations with McClellan in November of last year, in both of which Watson expressed the opinion that the rebels were in earnest—that peace, through any arrangement with them, was not to

---

17. William Rabé, a San Francisco druggist and secretary of the California Republican committee, was U.S. marshal for the northern district of the state. In Apr. 1862, political opponents had accused Rabé of packing juries against the government and, soon after, successfully lobbied Lincoln for his removal. Basler, *Collected Works*, 4:304–5; G. Harrington to Rabé, July 26, 1862 (Telegrams Sent, Gen. Recs. Treasury Dept., Nat. Arch.); Rabé to Ogden Hoffman, Nov. 18, 1862, Rabé to Chase, Nov. 22, Dec. 4, 1862 (Chase Papers, L.C.).

18. Benjamin Welch (c. 1818–63), one of Pope's aides, formerly treasurer and commissary general for the state of New York. Heitman, *Historical Register*, 1:1015; *New York Times*, Apr. 15, 1863.

19. Charlotte Eastman.

20. George Washington Morgan (1820–93), brigadier general of volunteers and a Democratic congressman from Ohio, 1869–73, was ill and disagreed with the federal policy of using black troops. *DAB*, 13:170–71.

21. James Abram Garfield (1831–81) was at this time brigadier general of volunteers. He became major general, then a Republican congressman from Ohio, 1863–80, and president of the United States, 1881. *DAB*, 7:145–50.

22. Assistant Secretary of War Peter H. Watson, a prominent patent attorney before the war. Lanman, *Biographical Annals*, 452; Thomas and Hyman, *Stanton*, 63–64, 152–53.

be hoped for—and that it would be necessary to prosecute the war, even to the point of subjugation, if we meant to maintain the territorial integrity of the country. McClellan differed. He thought we ought to avoid harshness and violence—that we should conduct the war so as to avoid offence as far as possible;—and said that if he thought as Watson did, he should feel obliged to lay down his arms.

It was during the same month that he told me of his plan for a rapid advance on Richmond, and gave me the assurance that he would take it by the middle of February; which induced me to assure the capitalists in New-York that they could rely on his activity, vigor and success.

From the War Department I went to the President's, to whom I spoke of the resignation of Morgan and of substituting Garfield, which seemed to please him. Spoke also of the financial importance of getting rid of McClellan; and expressed the hope that Halleck would approve his project of sending Mitchell to the Mississippi. On these points he said nothing. I then spoke of Jones, the Sculptor,[23] and of the fitness of giving him some Consulate in Italy, which he liked the idea of. He read me a statement (very good) which he was preparing in reply to a letter from   , in New-Orleans, forwarded by Bullitt.[24]

After some other talk and reminding him of the importance of a talk between me and Halleck about finances as affected by the war (by the way, he told me he desired Halleck to come and see me last Saturday,[25] but he did not come) I returned home. Was too late for church. Read various books—among others, Whitfield's life.[26] What a worker!

Spent evening with Katie and Nettie, and read H. W. Beecher's last sermon in the Independent.[27]

Not a caller all day.— O si sic omnes dies![28]

---

23. Thomas Dow Jones.
24. Cuthbert Bullitt, who in 1863 became acting collector of customs at New Orleans, had forwarded a letter written by Louisiana loyalist Thomas Jefferson Durant (1817–82). Durant complained of federal "police regulations" in occupied sections of the state. Lincoln promised to withdraw military rule when Louisiana reestablished a Unionist government. Durant, a New Orleans attorney and politician, practiced law in Washington, D.C., after the war. Lincoln to Bullitt, July 28, 1862, in Basler, *Collected Works*, 5:344–46; *DAB*, 5:543–44; *Register of Officers (1863)*, 95.
25. *Saturday* is in Chase's hand, inserted in a blank left by the clerk.
26. Philip, *George Whitefield*.
27. The sermon, by Henry Ward Beecher (1813–87), pastor of Brooklyn's Congregational Plymouth Church and editor of the *Independent*, cautioned against hasty criticism of U.S. political leaders, particularly President Lincoln. *DAB*, 2:129–35; *Independent*, July 24, 1862.
28. "If every day could be this way!" In the original, the entries for Aug. 15–Sept. 9 follow this entry.

August 1862 {355}

FRIDAY, AUG. 1, 1862. No events of much importance to-day.— A Cabinet Meeting was held and a good deal of talk took place, but no results.— Blair sent me his paper on Colonization to which he referred in our long talk of yesterday.[29]— A nice letter from my friend Mrs. Eastman.— Spent a few moments at the War Department—telegram came that the enemy has been shelling McClellan's position from Point Coggin.— Wrote to Genl. Pope and Genl. Butler, touching, in both letters, the Slavery question.[30]— Called on Genl. Halleck in the evening, and talked a good while with him. Judged it prudent not to say much of the war / He spoke of Buell as slow but safe; of Grant, as a good general and brave in battle, but careless of his command. Of Thomas, he spoke very highly.[31]

SATURDAY, AUG 2D. At Department all day—went neither to the President's nor the War Department.

Genl Shields called and talked over movement up the Shenandoah. He told me that when he received peremptory orders to return, he had held communication with Frémont and Jackson's capture was certain. I told him of my urgency that McDowell should be ordered forward with his entire command from Warrenton, and from[32] Front Royal, to Charlottesville and Lynchburg; that the President was not ready to act; that McDowell himself was apparently disinclined, preferring concentration at Manassas and then advance to Richmond. Plain enough now, he said, that this was the true movement. He had himself telegraphed McDowell that Jackson

---

29. Chase received a copy of comments which Montgomery Blair prepared on Lincoln's proposed emancipation proclamation, but that paper was not concerned with colonization. In a speech on Apr. 11, Blair's brother, Francis Preston Blair, Jr., had supported Lincoln's proposal for compensated emancipation and advocated colonization in Central America. M. Blair to Lincoln, July 23, 1862 (Chase Papers, L.C.); *Cong. Globe,* 37th Cong., 2nd sess., 1862, 1631–34.

30. Chase urged Pope, the new commander of the Army of Virginia, to "deal genuinely and kindly by the blacks. . . . If I were in the field I would let every man understand that no man loyal to the Union could be a slave." Maj. Gen. Benjamin Franklin Butler (1818–93) was Union commander at New Orleans, May–Dec. 1862, and later a Republican congressman from Massachusetts, 1867–75. Chase advised Butler to stop returning any fugitive slaves to their masters, even when the masters had taken an oath of allegiance, and suggested that public opinion would support a call for blacks to serve in "the defence of the Union." Chase to Pope, Aug. 1, 1862 (Chase Papers, Hist. Soc. of Pa.); Chase to Butler, July 31, 1862 (Butler Papers, L.C.); *DAB,* 3:357–59, 15:76.

31. Don Carlos Buell (1818–98); future U.S. President Ulysses Simpson Grant (1822–85); and George Henry Thomas (1816–70). At this time, all were major generals of volunteers. *DAB,* 3:240–41, 7:492–501, 18:432–35.

32. *And from* is in Chase's hand, replacing the clerk's *per.*

would be Pattersonized by recall of troops from pursuit.[33] The troops were, nevertheless, recalled; and, by peremptory order from the President himself, those of Shields were directed to return to Manassas and those of Frémont to resume position as a corps of observation.

Here was a terrible mistake. It would have been easy to take Charlottesville and Lynchburgh—very easy; the capture of Jackson, though not at the time seen at Washington to be practicable, was, nevertheless, within easy possibility; his defeat and the dispersion of his force certain. Our troops were called off when they were just upon him. The course of the whole movement was changed, for no reason that I could see. Charlottesville and Lynchburgh were saved to the enemy, with their stores and the Rail Roads on which they are situated, forming the great East and West communication of the rebels. A wide door for Jackson to Richmond was opened—the very door through which, a little later, he passed; fell, in coöperation with the rebel army at Richmond, on McClellan's right, left unsupported as if to invite disaster; defeated it; and then, with the same army, pursued the Union main body to the James. Sad! sad! yet nobody seems to heed. Genl. Shields and I talked this all over, deploring the strange fatality which seemed to preside over the whole transaction. He dined with us; and, after dinner, rode out with brother Edward and Nettie.

In the evening, several callers came in. Beebe, from Ravenna, a faithful friend[34]—John R. French—Smith Homans—Chas. Selden—and some others.[35] Selden says that at Cincinnati, old Mr. Molitor and Revd. Edw. Purcell spoke very kindly of me.[36]

---

33. Prior to the First Battle of Bull Run, Maj. Gen. Robert Patterson (1792–1881), commander of Union forces around Washington, D.C., had received orders to block the army of Joseph E. Johnston while Irvin McDowell moved into Virginia. Patterson's failure to check Johnston and cooperate with McDowell was considered a major cause of the Union defeat. *DAB*, 14:306–7.

34. Horace Y. Beebe of Portage Co., Ohio, soon to become, on Chase's recommendation, a federal assessor of internal revenue. Chase to A. Lincoln, Aug. 16, 1862 (Lincoln Papers, L.C.); *Register of Officers (1863)*, 39.

35. John R. French, a former state legislator from Lake Co., Ohio; Isaac Smith Homans (d. 1874), a New York publisher of business books and periodicals currently holding a clerkship in the Treasury; and Charles Selden, a clerk in the treasurer's office of Hamilton Co., Ohio. *Cinc. Dir. (1861)*, 310; Gilkey, *Ohio Hundred Year Book*, 262; *Nat. Cyc.*, 30:549; Homans to Chase, June 10, 1862 (Chase Papers, L.C.); Chase to Sheppard Homans, Jan. 30, 1864 (Chase Papers, Hist. Soc. of Pa.); *Letter from the Secretary of the Treasury, Transmitting List of Clerks Employed in the Treasury Department during the Year ending December 31, 1862*, 37th Cong., 3rd sess., *1863*, H. Ex. Doc. 70, 3; *Letter from the Secretary of the Treasury, Transmitting a List of Clerks and other Persons Employed in the Treasury Department for the Year 1863*, 38th Cong., 1st sess., 1864, H. Ex. Doc. 62, 2.

36. Stephen Molitor and Edward Purcell, editor of Cincinnati's *Catholic Telegraph*. *Cinc. Dir. (1862)*, 263.

August 1862

SUNDAY, AUG. 3. Genl. Shields came to breakfast and to visit the Ohio men of his command in the Cliffburne Hospital.[37] He told me he desired greatly to have a command of 5000 men, and be allowed to dash as he could, breaking the lines and communications of the enemy. My daughters went with him to the Hospital.

Soon after they left, I received a summons to a Cabinet Meeting. The President spoke of the Treaty said to have been formed between the Cherokees and Confederates,[38] and suggested the expediency of organizing a force of whites and blacks, in separate Regiments, to invade and take possession of their country. Statistics of the Indians were sent for, from which it appeared that the whole fighting force of the Cherokees could hardly exceed 2500 men. Mr. Usher, Assistant Secretary of the Interior was not in favor of the expedition.[39] He thought it better to deal indulgently with deluded Indians, and make their deluders feel the weight of the Federal authority. Most, or the whole, seemed to concur with him.

Mr. Usher mentioned a report that the Louisville Democrat had come out openly for disunion, saying that it was now manifest that the Government was in the hands of the Abolitionists. The President said, this was equivalent to a declaration of hostility by the entire Douglas Party of Kentucky, and manifested much uneasiness.

There was a good deal of conversation on the connection of the Slavery question with the rebellion. I expressed my conviction for the tenth or twentieth time, that the time for the suppression of the rebellion without interference with slavery had long passed;— that it was possible, probably, at the outset, by striking the insurrectionists wherever found, strongly and decisively; but we had elected to act on the principles of a civil war, in which assuming that[40] the whole population of every seceding State was engaged against the Federal Government, instead of treating the active secessionists as insurgents and exerting our utmost energies for their arrest and punishment;—that the bitternesses of the conflict had now substantially united the white population of the rebel States against us;—that the loyal whites remaining, if they would not prefer the Union without Slavery, certainly would not prefer Slavery to the Union;—that the blacks were really the only loyal population worth counting; and that, in the Gulf States at least, their right to

---

37. The word *Cliffburne* appears twice, once in the clerk's hand and once in an interlineation by Chase in pencil. Cliffburne was one of many federal hospitals in the vicinity of Washington, D.C. *Daily National Intelligencer*, July 23, 1862.

38. Signed Oct. 7, 1861. *OR*, ser. 4, v. 1:669–87.

39. John Palmer Usher (1816–89) became secretary of the interior, 1863–65. *DAB*, 19:134–35.

40. *Assuming that* is in Chase's hand, written above the clerk's *in which*.

Freedom ought to be at once recognized, while, in the Border States, the President's plan of Emancipation might be made the basis of the necessary measures for their ultimate enfranchisement;—that the practical mode of effecting this seemed to me quite simple;—that the President had already spoken of the importance of making of the freed blacks on the Mississippi, below Tennessee, a safeguard to the navigation of the river;—that Mitchell, with a few thousand soldiers, could take Vicksburgh;—assure the blacks freedom on condition of loyalty; organize the best of them in companies, regiments &c., and provide, as far as practicable, for the cultivation of the plantations by the rest;—that Butler should signify to the slaveholders of Louisiana that they must recognize the freedom of their workpeople by paying them wages;—and that Hunter should do the same thing in South-Carolina.

Mr. Seward expressed himself as in favor of any measures likely to accomplish the results I contemplated, which could be carried into effect without Proclamations; and the President said he was pretty well cured of objections to any measure except want of adaptedness to put down the rebellion; but did not seem satisfied that the time had come for the adoption of such a plan as I proposed.

There was also a good deal of conversation concerning the merits of Generals. I objected pretty decidedly to the policy of selecting nearly all the highest officers from among men hostile to the Administration, and continuing them in office after they had proved themselves incompetent, or at least not specially competent, and referred to the needless defeat of McClellan and the slowness of Buell. Seward asked what I would do. I replied, Remove the men who failed to accomplish results, and put abler and more active men in their places. He wished to know whom I would prefer to Buell. I answered that if I were President, or Secretary of War authorized to act by the President, I would confer with the General in Chief; require him to name to me the best officers he knew of; talk the matter over with him; get all the light I could; and then designate my man.

As much as anything, the clearing of the Mississippi by the capture of Vicksburgh was discussed. I reminded the President that after the evacuation of Corinth it would have been an easy matter to send down a few thousand men and complete our possession of the river; and of his own plan of putting Gen. Mitchell at the head of his own division and Curtis' army, and sending him to take Vicksburgh, almost adopted more than two weeks ago. Mr. Usher suggested that since Genl. Halleck had decided against this plan, on the ground that Mitchell's division could not be spared from Buell's command, and Curtis' army was needed to prevent a foray from

Arkansas into Missouri, it might be well to raise a special force by volunteering for this one object, of taking Vicksburgh, opening the Mississippi and keeping it open. I heartily seconded this idea and it was a good deal talked over.

At length, the President determined to send for Genl. Halleck and have the matter discussed with him. The General came, and the matter was fully stated to him both by Gov Seward and myself. He did not absolutely reject the idea, but thought the object could be better accomplished by hastening the new levies; putting the new troops in the positions now occupied by the old regiments; and setting these last to the work of opening the Mississippi. He expressed the strongest convictions as to the importance of the work, and his desire to see it accomplished at the earliest possible period. At this moment, however, the necessary troops could not be spared for the purpose / Taking into consideration the delay incident to raising a special force, equal, perhaps, to that demanded by Gen. Halleck's plan, and the other disadvantages it was thought best to drop the idea.

In connection with this subject, Genl. Halleck spoke of the distribution of troops in the West. He said that Hardee had broken up his camp south of Corinth, and transferred his army to Chattanooga, where he now had probably 40 or 50.000 men; that Price had attempted to cross the river into Arkansas, but had as yet failed to accomplish his purpose;[41] that a considerable force was, however, advancing northward into Missouri; and that he had sent a division and brigade, say 7000 men, to Curtis (making his whole force about 17.000) and instructed him to prevent the invasion of Missouri; that he had also detached from Grant about 15.000 men, say three divisions, to take position at Decatur to support Buell if necessary; that Grant had still under his command about 43.000, of whom 7000 under Jackson had been ordered to the   to watch Price; that Buell had 60.000, with which force he was approaching Chattanooga. These numbers give the whole force in the West; exclusive of troops occupying St. Louis and various Posts and Camps north of the Ohio;—Buell, 60.000—Grant, including detachments, except Curtis', 58.000.—Curtis 17.000—in all, 135.000 men, excellent troops. He stated McClellan's army at present and fit for duty at 88.000; absent on leave 33.000; absent without leave, 3.000; present but sick, 16:000—in all, say, 140.000. Another statement makes the number fit for duty 91.000, and the total 143.000.

41. Confederate Major Generals William Joseph Hardee (1815–73) and Sterling Price (1809–67), commander, Army of the West. "Jackson" below means James S. Jackson (1823–62). *Appletons'*, 3:388, 5:118–19; *DAB*, 8:239–40, 15:216–17.

The President read a communication from Genl. H. proposing that 200.000 militia should be drafted for 9 months, and that the 300.000 men to fill old and form new regiments should be obtained without delay; and to prevent the evil of hasty and improper appointments and promotions, that a Board of Officers should be organized, to which all proposed action of that sort should be referred. The General condemned, respectfully but as decidedly, the inconsideration which has hitherto marked the action of the Government in this respect, and stated one case where a Colonel had been tried and convicted of gross misconduct and was on the point of being dismissed, when he came on to Washington and returned with a Brigadier's Commission!

The General commanded my sincere respect by the great intelligence and manliness he displayed, and excited great hopes by his obvious purpose to allow no lagging and by his evident mastery of the business he has taken in hand. I cannot agree with him as to the expediency of retaining McClellan and Buell in their important commands; and I was sorry to hear him say, in reply to a question of the President, as to what use could be made of the black population of the borders of the Mississippi, "I confess, I do not think much of the negro."

Neither Mr. Stanton nor Mr. Blair were present at the meeting to-day.

When the Cabinet Council broke up, I proposed to Mr. Usher, who made a most favorable impression on me, to ride home in my carriage; but he was called back by the President, and I, finding my carriage had not come, rode home with Mr. Bates.[42]

WEDNESDAY, AUGUST 6, 1862. Nothing much thought of to-day except the great War Meeting—which was immense. None of the Cabinet there except myself and Mr. Bates. The President, after Mr. Chittenden had finished, said to me (the people clamoring for him) "Well! Hadn't I better say a few words and get rid of myself?" Hardly waiting for an answer, he advanced at once to the stand. He was received with most uproarious enthusiasm. His frank, genial, generous face and direct simplicity of bearing, took all hearts. His speech is in all the prints, and evinces his usual orginality and sagacity.[43]

---

42. In the original, the entries for July 25–27 follow this entry, and the entries for Aug. 6–8 follow that for Sept. 9.

43. The massive patriotic meeting, in front of the Capitol building, expressed support for the war but acknowledged "apprehension" over "want of readiness and determination to employ, decisively, crushingly, the full power of the nation." After the speech by Lucius Eugene Chittenden (1824–1902), register of the U.S. Treasury,

August 1862 { 361 }

Prof. Read and his son, Capt. Read, and Assistant-Secretary Usher dined with me.[44] Mr. Bates and Dr. Schmidt came from meeting with me and stopped at my house.[45] After Mr. Bates went, I played chess with the Doctor, who was far my overmatch—he beating me with ease two or three times, while I only, by accident, beat him once.

THURSDAY, AUG. 7. Very little accomplished as yet, though much, I hope, in the train of accomplishment. Engaged nearly all day on selections for recommendation of Collectors and Assessors. Prepared letter to President, containing names &c. of candidates, with my recommendations, for Connecticut; made up in very small part on my own personal Knowledge, but mainly on the representations and advice—sometimes agreeing and sometimes not—of the Senators, Representatives, State Officers and Secretary Welles.[46]

In the evening, went to War Department, where I saw Curtis' dispatch from Helena, urging the clearing out of the Mississippi before attempting inland operations; and McClellan's, announcing advance of the enemy on Malvern Hill, and his purpose to order the retirement of Hooker's Division; and those of various Governors, announcing progress of volunteering and preparations for drafting—on the whole, very encouraging and denoting the greatest possible earnestness and determination among the people.

Home. Taylor, Davis and Hopper (all Clerks) called.[47]— Wrote my friend E.[48] and sent some pencil scribblings.— Mr. Gest called, but not able to see him.[49]

Lincoln discounted rumors of a rift between Gen. McClellan and Secretary of War Stanton. *Daily National Intelligencer,* Aug. 7, 8, 1862.

44. Probably former Ohioan Daniel Read (1805–78), professor of philosophy at the University of Wisconsin, 1856–66, and then president of the University of Missouri, 1866–77. His son Theodore Read (1836–65) became a general of volunteers before dying in battle, Apr. 1865. *Appletons',* 5:196–97; *DAB,* 15:421–22.

45. Charles F. Schmidt of Ohio was a clerk in the Treasury Department, one of Chase's political supporters, and apparently a liaison with the German-American community. Chase to Schmidt, Aug. 12, 1864 (William Howard Taft Papers, L.C.); *Letter from the Secretary . . . Clerks . . . 1862,* 6; Schmidt to Chase, Nov. 3, 1863 (Chase Papers, Hist. Soc. of Pa.); Schmidt to Chase, Aug. 28, 1864 (Chase Papers, L.C.).

46. Gideon Welles (1802–78), Connecticut editor, politician, and secretary of the U.S. Navy, 1861–69. *DAB,* 19:629–32.

47. Probably David Taylor, either Jesse L. Davis or William H. Davis, and J. C. Hopper, all of whom were clerks in the Treasury Department. *Register of Officers (1863),* 41; *Wash. Dir. (1862),* 68–69, 102; ibid. (1863), 195.

48. Charlotte Eastman.

49. Probably Joseph G. Gest of Greene Co., Ohio, a member of the Ohio House, 1852–56, 1882–86. Gilkey, *Ohio Hundred Year Book,* 212, 216, 226, 230; entry for Aug. 19, 1862, below.

FRIDAY, AUGUST 8, 1862. Sent letter and scrap to my friend E., and sundry other letters to sundry people—particularly Gen. Pope's recommendation of young Perkins, with my heartiest endorsement, to Gov. Tod. Also sent Gen. Pope, by Maj. Johnson, some photographs of himself and Col. Welch, taken by the Treasury artist before he went to the field.[50]

Attended Cabinet Meeting. Autograph letter from Queen Victoria announcing marriage of Princess Alice.[51]— Seward gave account of Order prepared by Gen. Halleck, Secretary Stanton and himself, forbidding changes of domicil and granting of passports, until after the draft.— Nothing proposed and nothing done of any moment.

Directed Connecticut Abstract and my letter of recommendation to be sent to President.[52]

FRIDAY, AUGUST 15, 1862. p. and r. un peu de Marius.[53]— Saw in *"Republican"* account of interview invited by President with colored people, and his talk to them on Colonization.[54] How much better would be a manly protest against prejudice against color!—and a wise effort to give freemen homes in America! A Military Order, emancipating at least the slaves of South-Carolina, Georgia and the Gulf States, would do more to terminate the war and ensure an early restoration of solid peace and prosperity than anything else that can be devised.

Commissioner Boutwell breakfasted with me.[55] After breakfast

---

50. Chase enclosed photographs of Pope and Welch in his Aug. 1 letter to Pope. See July 26 and Aug. 1 above.

51. In a letter addressed to Lincoln on July 4, 1862, Queen Victoria (1819–1901) announced that her daughter, Princess Alice Maud Mary (1843–78), had married Prince Frederick William Louis of Hesse on July 1, 1862. *DNB*, 1:285–86, 22:1261–1372; Basler, *Collected Works*, 5:363.

52. Chase was in the process of nominating collectors and assessors for every congressional district in accordance with the Internal Revenue Act of July 1, 1862. On Aug. 7 he had sent his first set of recommendations for Connecticut to Lincoln, who replied that most of the appointments for that state were "fiercely contested." In the original journal, the series of entries beginning Sept. 10 follows this entry. Chase to Lincoln, Aug. 7, 1862 (Lincoln Papers, L.C.); Basler, *Collected Works*, 5:361–62, 375.

53. The *p. and r.* may mean *prayed & read; un peu de* means "a little of." As noted in Donald, ed., *Inside Lincoln's Cabinet*, 292, "Marius" probably refers to the third part of Victor Hugo's *Les Misérables*, first published in 1862.

54. Lincoln was unsuccessfully urging colonization on the Isthmus of Chiriqui in Central America. Copies of the Aug. 14 interview evidently appeared in a number of newspapers, including the Washington *National Republican*. Basler, *Collected Works*, 5:370–75.

55. Former governor of Massachusetts George Sewall Boutwell (1818–1905) was commissioner of internal revenue, 1862–63, a Republican congressman, 1863–69, and secretary of the Treasury, 1869–73. *Bio. Dir. U.S. Cong.*, 648; *DAB*, 2:489–90.

took up tax appointments in Indiana and Ohio; and arranged both substantially to my satisfaction, and, I hope, of all concerned.— President sent for me about the Connecticut appointments. Found there Collector Babcock, State Senator Pratt (or Platt) and Secy. Welles.[56] Arranged the business. The State Senator got a Mr. Wright, of Middlesex, with Mr. Welles' consent, vice Cowles.[57]— Mr. Dix, by general consent, was substituted for Hammond.[58]— Hollister was agreed to in place of Matherson, whom Burnham recommended.— Howard was retained at Hartford.[59] The President said he felt much releived. Returned to Department, and instantly engaged on other tax appointments.

No Cabinet to-day. Went to War Department. Stanton said Halleck had sent Burnside to James River, to act as second in command—or as adviser of McClellan, in reality to control him. He thought the experiment would fail, and wished I would go and see Halleck. Went. Asked about the mission of Burnside. Halleck said he could not disclose it as it was uncertain what it would really turn out to be. Asked him what was the hostile force at Richmond? He thought 75.000 to 80.000 men.— Before Pope? About 60.000.— Whole army in Virginia? About 150.000. I thought it not possible, unless Western force was much reduced. He thought a levy en masse had been made, and that it was possible for the enemy to bring 600.000 to 700.000 into the field. I thought the whole number could not at this time exceed 300.000 to 350.000; of which at least 180.000 to 230.000 were in the West, South-West and South-East.— I enquired about East Tennessee and the Mississippi River, but got no satisfactory information on either point. He said, however, that 15.000 men had been sent from Decatur to reinforce Buell, and 15.000 from Grant to Decatur; and that Curtis was needed to

56. James F. Babcock (1809–74), of New Haven, former editor of the *Palladium* and collector of the port; and Orville Hitchcock Platt (1827–1905), who became a U.S. senator from Connecticut, 1879–1905. *DAB*, 15:2–4.

57. John B. Wright of Clinton became assessor of internal revenue for Connecticut's second district. Chase originally recommended Laman Cowles for the position. *Register of Officers (1863)*, 38; Chase to A. Lincoln, Aug. 7, 1862 (Lincoln Papers, L.C.).

58. John B. Mix, according to Chase's letter outlining internal revenue appointments for Connecticut; and Henry Hammond, a friend of Sen. James Dixon later commissioned as a federal marshal. Chase to Lincoln, Aug. 7, 1862 (Lincoln Papers, L.C.); Basler, *Collected Works*, 5:375, 385–86, 7:82–83, 8:242.

59. David F. Hollister of Bridgeport, who became collector of internal revenue in Connecticut's fourth district; Rufus S. Matherson, whom Chase originally recommended as collector of the third district; Alfred Avery Burnham (1819–79), Republican congressman from Connecticut, 1859–63; and Mark Howard, recommended as collector of Connecticut's first district. Basler, *Collected Works*, 5:375; *Bio. Dir. U.S. Cong.*, 709; *Register of Officers (1863)*, 38; Chase to Lincoln, Aug. 7, 1862 (Lincoln Papers, L.C.).

prevent further inroads into Missouri. The whole interview was very unsatisfactory, though the General was very civil.— Left with him Memoranda in behalf of Col. Carrington.[60]

The papers show that the rebels mean to execute their threat of treating Pope's officers and soldiers as felons, and not as prisoners of war. This cannot be permitted without shameful disgrace. When will the Administration awake to its duty.

Rode out with Parsons.[61]— Judge Harris called at night when Boutwell and I were engaged on Tax appointments.[62] Invited him to breakfast in the morning.

SATURDAY, AUGUST 16, 1862   Nothing in public affairs of special note to-day. New regiments begin to arrive, but what reason to hope more from new levies than old? None, that I see, except Genl. Halleck;—if he fails, all fails.— Pope telegraphs that his whole force is as near the Rapidan as the nature of the country will permit, and that he is pushing strong reconnoissances beyond.— Grant telegraphs that 15.000 men have gone to Decatur to replace 15.000 sent to reinforce Buell—that he is now weak and may be attacked, though there is no indication yet of more than feints towards Missouri.— Nothing from Burnside or McClellan.

Sent Katie $150. and Varnum, rent, $375.[63]

Mr. Harrington brought in the Postage Currency.[64] I directed that it should be received as furnished by the P.O. Department—i.e. perforated instead of clipped, perforation being considered partial safeguard against counterfeiting.

Judge Roselius, Dr. Cottman and Mr. C. Bullitt, of New-Orleans, dined with me.[65] Also, Messrs. Usher, Assistant Secretary of the Interior; Maj. Smith, First Auditor;[66] Meline, Clerk in Treasury

---

60. Henry B. Carrington, at this time recruiting in Indianapolis, desired command over a division. Carrington to Chase, Aug. 31, Oct. 19, Nov. 10, 1862 (Chase Papers, L.C.).

61. Richard C. Parsons. Parsons to Chase, July 29, 1862 (Chase Papers, L.C.).

62. Ira Harris.

63. New York attorney Joseph Bradley Varnum, Jr. (1818–74), owned the house in which Chase resided in Washington. *Appletons'*, 6:262; Varnum to Chase, May 7, 1862 (Chase Papers, L.C.).

64. On July 17, Congress had authorized Chase to issue "postage and other stamps" for use as currency. *Statutes at Large*, 12:592.

65. Christian Roselius (1803–73), previously a Louisiana state legislator and attorney general; former secessionist Thomas Cottman, a New Orleans physician who resigned from the U.S. Congress soon after his election in 1863; and Cuthbert Bullitt. Jefferson Davis Bragg, *Louisiana in the Confederacy* (Baton Rouge, 1941); Cottman to Chase, June 19, 1863 (Chase Papers, L.C.); *DAB*, 16:164–65.

66. Thomas L. Smith (d. 1871), first auditor of the Treasury, 1849–71. Lanman, *Biographical Annals*, 394; Washington *Daily Morning Chronicle*, Dec. 5, 1871.

Department;[67] Col. R. C. Parsons; Reverdy Johnson and Col. Seaton.[68] Sumner came in after dinner. Retired when he went away.

SUNDAY, AUGUST 17, 1862 At home all day, except when at church.

MONDAY, AUG. 18, 1862 Busy, except when interrupted by callers, with list of Collectors and Assessors. Saw Chandler and Gov. Blair at President's, and closed Michigan appointments.[69] President insisted on Stanley, to save Trowbridge's feelings, instead of Mills, whom I recommended as best man; and Chandler and Blair concurred—none of us, however, knowing Stanley.[70]

Thurlow Weed dined with me.[71] Parsons was at home but had dined, and went away. After dinner, left Weed at Willard's, where I went to call on Colonels Corcoran and Wilcox, returned yesterday from their long captivity in Richmond.[72] They had gone to dine at the President's; and I went to Mr. Cutts' and spent an hour with Mr. C. and Mrs. D.[73]

TUESDAY, AUG. 19, 1862. Col. Corcoran and Mr. Mellen breakfasted with me. Col. C. gave interesting particulars of rebeldom, and thinks their force larger than I have supposed. He says, however, that their rolling-stock and roads are in such bad order that no more than 300   can be moved at a time

R. G. Corwin, J. G. Gest and Rep. Steele[74] called—all about Collectorships. Went to Department, and sent Ohio appointments to the President.

67. T. M. Meline, appointed from Ohio. *Register of Officers (1863)*, 30.
68. William Winston Seaton (1785–1866), former reporter for Congress and editor, with Joseph Gales, of the *National Intelligencer*. His military title was from the Virginia state militia. *DAB*, 16:541–42.
69. Austin Blair (1818–94) was Republican governor of Michigan, 1861–65, and a U.S. congressman, 1867–73. *DAB*, 2:329–30.
70. Luther Stanley of Birmingham was named assessor of internal revenue for Michigan's fifth district in place of William S. Mills of Lexington, whom Chase knew and had recommended. Rowland Ebenezer Trowbridge (1821–81) was a Republican congressman from Birmingham. *Register of Officers (1863)*, 40; Chase to Lincoln, Aug. 5, 1862 (Lincoln Papers, L.C.); *Bio. Dir. U.S. Cong.*, 1956.
71. Weed (1797–1882), a Republican politician from New York and ally of William H. Seward, edited the *Albany Evening Journal*. *DAB*, 19:598–600.
72. Like Michael Corcoran, Orlando Bolivar Willcox (1823–1907), later a brigadier general of volunteers, had been captured at the First Battle of Bull Run. *DAB*, 20:243; *OR*, ser. 2, v. 4:394–95.
73. James Madison Cutts, second comptroller of the Treasury, 1857–63, and his daughter, Adèle Cutts Douglas. Lanman, *Biographical Annals*, 106; *Register of Officers (1861)*, 16.
74. Either John Benedict Steele (1814–66), Democrat of New York, or William Gaston Steele (1820–92), a Democrat from New Jersey. *Bio. Dir. U.S. Cong.*, 1865–66.

Went to Cabinet. President uneasy about Pope. He sent to War Department for telegrams. There was one from Pope, at Culpepper, retiring across Rappahannock, while the force of the enemy was beyond the Rapidan at Gordonsville; one from Burnside, at Falmouth, saying that the first division of the Army of the Potomac will reach Aquia this evening. Nothing more of immediate importance.— Troops coming in to-day—11.000 already arrived. Money wanted for Bounties.

Returning to Department, telegraphed Cisco to negotiate three or four millions at rate not more than One per cent below market.[75] Stock telegram states sales to-day at 5 3–8 to 5 1–2.

Closed Indiana appointments. Signed letter transmitting Pennsylvania recommendations to President. Spent much time with Weed over New-York appointments. Ely called, and I advised him to come tomorrow.[76] Thomas Brown called and gave interesting personal history.

Dined, at 7, with Messrs Roselius, Cottman and Bullitt—only guests, Col. Seaton, Reverdy Johnson and myself.— Went to War Department. Met Stanton in the hall, and took him in my carriage to his house. He was much dissatisfied with the President's lack of decision, especially as to McClellan. Thinks Burnside too partial to McClellan to be safe.

Home. Read a little

FRIDAY, AUG. 29, 1862   The Secretary of War called on me in reference to Genl. McClellan. He has long beleived, and so have I, that Genl. McClellan ought not to be trusted with the command of any army of the Union; and the events of the last few days have greatly strengthened our judgment.— We called on Judge Bates, who was not at home.— Called on Genl. Halleck, and remonstrated against Gen. McClellan commanding.— Secy. wrote & presented to Genl. H. a call for a report touching McC's. disobedience of orders & consequent delay of support to Army of Va. Genl. H. promised answer tomorrow morning.[77]

SATURDAY, AUGUST 30, 1862   Judge Bates called, and we conversed in regard to Genl. McClellan—he concurring in our judg-

---

75. "Three or four Millions are needed to pay bounties and advances so as to bring troops rapidly into the field— . . . See Banks and Capitalists and if possible conclude negotiation to day and report." Chase to Cisco, Aug. 19, 1862 (Telegrams Sent, Gen. Recs. Treasury Dept., Nat. Arch.).

76. Alfred Ely (1815–92) was a Republican congressman from New York. *Bio. Dir. U.S. Cong.*, 965.

77. The last two sentences of this entry may have been added after the entry for Aug. 30 was recorded.

ment. Afterwards, I went to the War Department where Watson showed me a paper expressing it. I suggested modifications. Afterwards saw Stanton. He approved the modifications, and we both signed the paper. I then took it to Secy. Welles, who concurred in judgment but thought the paper not exactly right, and did not sign it. Returned the paper to Stanton.[78]

Promised report from Genl. Halleck was not made.

SUNDAY, AUG. 31, 1862. Much busied at Department to-day, although it is Sunday; and spent much time with the President, endeavoring to close appointments under Tax Law.

David Dudley Field called and said we had sustained a serious defeat yesterday, and that the Secretary of War wished to see me.[79] Went to the Department and found that Gen. Pope had, in fact, been defeated partially, and had fallen back to Centreville. Fitz John Porter was not in the battle, nor was Franklin or Sumner, with whose corps the result would have probably been very different.[80] Little fighting to-day.— Clerks went out to battlefield as nurses, Mr. Harrington with them.

MONDAY, SEPT. 1ST., 1862. This has been an anxious day. An Order appears declaring command of his corps in Burnside; of that portion of the Army of the Potomac not sent forward to Pope, in McClellan; of the Army of Virginia and all forces temporarily attached, in Pope; of the whole, in Halleck. Reports from Pope's Army state that its losses are heavy, but in good spirits—confirm that neither Franklin nor Sumner arrived,—and that McClellan failed to send forward ammunition.

On suggestion of Judge Bates, the remonstrance against McClellan, which had been previously signed by Smith, was modified; and, having been further slightly altered on my suggestion, was signed by Stanton, Bates and myself, and afterwards by Smith. Welles declined to sign it, on the ground that it might seem unfriendly to the President—though this was the exact reverse of its intent. He

---

78. The last one or two sentences of the Aug. 30 entry also may have been inserted after the entry that follows it was recorded. For another account of the cabinet intrigues against McClellan, Aug. 30–Sept. 1, see Beale, *Diary of Gideon Welles*, 1:93–104. The Sept. 1 version of the written protest, stating that "at this time, it is not safe to entrust to Major General McClellan the command of any Army of the United States," is in E. M. Stanton's papers, L.C.

79. Field (1805–94) was a Republican politician and legal reformer from New York. *DAB*, 6:360–62.

80. Brig. Gen. Fitz John Porter (1822–1901) was cashiered for his role at Second Bull Run and only reinstated long after the war. Edwin Vose Sumner (1797–1863) was major general of volunteers. *DAB*, 15:90–91, 18:214–15.

said he agreed in opinion and was willing to express it, personally. This determined us to await the Cabinet Meeting tomorrow.

Meantime, McClellan came up on invitation of Halleck, and held personal conference with him and the President. Soon after, a rumor pervaded the town that McClellan was to resume his full command. Col. Key called at my house and told me that he supposed such was the fact.

TUESDAY, SEPT. 2, 1862. Cabinet met, but neither the President nor Secretary of War were present. Some conversation took place concerning Generals. Mr. F. W. Seward (the Secretary of State being out of town) said nothing.[81] All others agreed that we needed a change in Commander of the Army. Mr. Blair referred to the report he had constantly given McClellan, but confessed that he now thought he could not wisely be trusted with the chief command. Mr. Bates was very decided against his competency, and Mr. Smith equally so. Mr. Welles was of the same judgment, though less positive in expression.

After some time, while the talk was going on, the President came in, saying that not seeing much for a Cabinet Meeting to-day, he had been talking at the Department and Head Quarters about the War. The Secretary of War came in. In answer to some inquiry, the fact was stated, by the President or the Secretary, that McClellan had been placed in command of the forces to defend the Capital—or rather, to use the President's own words, he "had set him to putting these troops into the fortifications about Washington," beleiving that he could do that thing better than any other man. I remarked that this could be done equally well by the Engineer who constructed the Forts; and that putting Genl. McClellan in command for this purpose was equivalent to making him second in command of the entire army. The Secretary of War said that no one was now responsible for the defense of the Capital;—that the Order to McClellan was given by the President direct to McClellan, and that Genl. Halleck considered himself releived from responsibility, although he acquiesced, and approved the Order;—that McClellan could now shield himself, should anything go wrong, under Halleck, while Halleck could and would disclaim all responsibility for the Order given. The President thought Gen. Halleck as much responsible as before; and repeated that the whole scope of the Order was, simply, to direct McClellan to put the troops into the fortifications and command them for the defence of Washington. I remarked that

---

81. Frederick William Seward (1830–1915), the son of William Henry Seward, was assistant secretary of state, 1861–69, 1877–79. *DAB*, 16:612–13.

this seemed to me equivalent to making him Commander in Chief for the time being, and that I thought it would prove very difficult to make any substitution hereafter, for active operations;—that I had no feeling whatever against Genl. McClellan;—that he came to the command with my most cordial approbation and support;—that until I became satisfied that his delays would greatly injure our cause, he possessed my full confidence;—that, after I had felt myself compelled to withold that confidence, I had (since the President, notwithstanding my opinion that he should, refrained from putting another in command) given him all possible support in every way, raising means and urging reinforcements;—that his experience as a military commander had been little else than a series of failures;—and that his omission to urge troops forward to the battles of Friday and Saturday, evinced a spirit which rendered him unworthy of trust, and that I could not but feel that giving the command to him was equivalent to giving Washington to the rebels. This and more I said. Other members of the Cabinet expressed a general concurrence, but in no very energetic terms. [Mr. Blair must be excepted, but he did not dissent.]

The President said it distressed him exceedingly to find himself differing on such a point from the Secretary of War and Secretary of the Treasury; that he would gladly resign his place; but he could not see who could do the work wanted as well as McClellan. I named Hooker,[82] or Sumner, or Burnside—either of whom, I thought, would be better.

At length the conversation ended and the meeting broke up, leaving the matter as we found it.

A few Tax Appointments were lying on the table. I asked the President to sign them; which he did, saying he would sign them just as they were and ask no questions. I told him that they had all been prepared in accordance with his directions, and that it was necessary to complete the appointments. They were signed, and I returned to the Department.

WEDNESDAY, SEPT. 3. The getting the Army into the works, and making general arrangements, went on to-day. Gen. McClellan assumed the command and returned to his old Head Quarters, as if the disastrous expedition of near eight months had been only the absence of a few days, unmarked by special incident; and, with the same old Staff, except the French Princes, Mr Astor and Mr. Gantt,

---

82. Joseph "Fighting Joe" Hooker (1814–79), major general of volunteers, soon to be brigadier general in the regular army. Hooker later commanded the Departments of the North, East, and Lakes from Cincinnati, New York City, and Detroit, respectively, before retiring in 1868. *DAB*, 9:196–98.

he went out, as of old, to visit the fortifications and the troops.[83]— Pope came over and talked with the President, who assured him of his entire satisfaction with his conduct; assured him that McClellan's command was only temporary; and gave him some reason to expect that another army of active operations would be organized at once which he (Pope) would lead

In my Department nothing especial occurred; but the expenses are becoming enormous[84]

THURSDAY, SEPT. 4, 1862. McDowell came over to-day and gave me a circumstantial account of the recent battles—attributing our ill success to the conduct of McClellan in not urging forward reinforcements, and especially to the conduct of Porter and his division on the day of the last battle. He stayed all night.

FRIDAY, SEPT. 5, 1862 The President, at Cabinet Meeting, read Pope's Report, which strongly inculpates McClellan, Porter, Franklin and Griffin;[85] and asked opinion as to its publication. All against it, on the score of policy under existing circumstances. President stated that Porter, Franklin and Griffin would be releived from command and brought before a Court of Inquiry; and also, I think, that the Order had been made.

The President had previously, at the Department, told me that the clamor against McDowell was so great that he could not lead his troops unless something was done to restore confidence; and proposed to me to suggest to him the asking for a Court of Inquiry. I told him I had already done so, and would do so again. So, availing myself of a Messenger from Gen. Pope who came during the meeting, I sent a note to McDowell, asking him to come over. He accordingly came in the evening, and I suggested the matter to him. He thought it hard to make the demand when there were no

---

83. François Ferdinand Philippe Louis Marie d'Orléans (1818–1900), Prince de Joinville, and his nephews Louis Philippe Albert d'Orléans (1838–94), Comte de Paris, and Robert Philippe Louis Eugène Ferdinand d'Orléans (1840–1910), Duc de Chartres, were volunteer aides on McClellan's staff. John Jacob Astor (1822–90) and Thomas Tasker Gantt (1814–89) were aides with the rank of colonel. *Appletons'*, 4:589–90; Paul Augé, ed., *Larousse du XXe Siècle en Six Volumes* (Paris, 1928–33), 2:161, 4:186, 5:381; *The Bench and Bar of St. Louis* . . . (St. Louis and Chicago, 1884), 435–37; *DAB*, 1:399–400; Heitman, *Historical Register*, 1:444.

84. Between Jan. 1861 and Jan. 1862, the U.S. national debt quadrupled, growing from $69 million to $293 million. By Jan. 1863, it expanded again nearly two and half times to $722 million. *The American Annual Cyclopædia and Register of Important Events of the Year 1862* (New York, 1867), 466.

85. Simon Goodell Griffen (1824–1902), colonel of New Hampshire's 6th Regiment, under Pope's command, was appointed brigadier general in 1864. Griffen later became a New Hampshire state politician and manufacturer. *DAB*, 7:621–22.

charges. I told him I thought he could assume the charge made by the Michigan Officer who, when dying, scrawled a letter saying he died a victim to Pope's imbecility and McDowell's treachery. He reflected, and then said he would make the demand. He staid again all night.[86]

SATURDAY, SEPT. 6. Genl. and Mrs. Worthington breakfasted with me;[87]—also Gen. McDowell and Mr Haven[88]

After Breakfast, Genl McDowell read me the draft of his letter, which I thought excellent, but suggested one or two modifications which he adopted.[89] I then went to the Department.

Soon after, the President came in, and asked what McDowell had determined to do. I told him. "Where is the letter"? "He took it, intending to have it copied I suppose". "Well, it ought to be done immediately, for the corps must march, and Gen. Halleck feels that he must be releived, at all events, from command. Where can he be found?"— "I cannot tell. An orderly, no doubt, can find him."— The President went away, and, later in the day, I heard that Gen. McDowell had been relieved at his own request. He came in himself, afterwards, stating the fact and adding, "I did not ask to be relieved—I only asked for a court." I explained as well as I could, and he left me.

Afterwards, I started to War Department, but met Seward, who said Stanton was not there. Went to President's,—where Stanton was. He spoke of McDowell's letter, and praised it in the strongest terms.

Mr. Barney came this morning about the labor Contract in New-York, about which quite a difference of opinion and interest exists— one or two of our most influential journals being concerned in its continuance. The question was, whether the Contract, by its own terms, was not limited to three years, and whether an extension of it beyond that time would be, in reality, a new Contract. Doubting

---

86. As shown below, McDowell requested the court of inquiry the following day. The allegations, which he successfully answered, included treachery, negligence, and drunkenness. *DAB*, 12:29; *OR*, ser. 1, v. 12, pt. 1:41–43.

87. James Taylor Worthington and his wife, Martha Piatt Read Worthington. McAllister, *In Winter We Flourish*, 67, 297–98.

88. Franklin Haven, Jr. (1835–1908), a Bostonian and Harvard graduate, assisted McDowell as aide-de-camp with the rank of captain. Haven became a lieutenant colonel of cavalry in 1865. After the war he was a banker and U.S. assistant treasurer at Boston, 1868–79. *Who Was Who*, 1:535; Andrew Hilen, ed., *The Letters of Henry Wadsworth Longfellow* (Cambridge, Mass., 1966–82), 5:477; Heitman, *Historical Register*, 1:512.

89. McDowell's letter to Lincoln requested a court of inquiry. A few days later Chase had the letter printed in the *National Intelligencer*. Entry for Sept. 10, below; *Daily National Intelligencer*, Sept. 12, 1862.

on the point, I referred it to the Attorney-General, who returned an answer expressing a decided opinion that the Contract was so limited and could not be extended without a new Contract.[90]— Before receiving this opinion, I telegraphed Mr. Field to come on, if he desired to say anything further.[91]

In the evening, Gen Pope came in. He expressed strong indignation against Fitz-John Porter and McClellan, who had, as he beleived, prevented his success. He wanted his Report published, as an act of justice to himself and his army. I stated my objection to present publication, on the ground of injury to service at this critical time; but said that a General Order, thanking his Army for what they had done ought to be promulgated. He said this would be satisfactory, (partially so, at least) but that Halleck would not publish one. I said, I would see the President and urge it.

Mr. Barney and others also called,—B. having declined invitation to breakfast, but said he would come at nine, to meet Field who telegraphed he would come and call at that hour.— Maj. Andrews came in and spoke so of Col. Crook, that I agreed to ask that he be made a Brigadier-General.[92] Major Andrew wrote a statement of what Crook did in Western Virginia

SUNDAY, SEPT. 7, 1862. Mr. Field called after breakfast, and proposed to go to War Department, and we went together. Met Gurowski, who denounced what he called military usurpation, saying that Franklin's corps, marching out, cheered McClellan. Found Stanton, Pope, and Wadsworth,[93] uneasy on account of critical condition of affairs. Spoke to Stanton about Crook, and he promised to give him a Commission. Saw Halleck, and he approved.

90. Hiram Barney was empowered to let a contract to haul, unpack, and repack sample imports and exports taken to the New York Custom House to test the honesty of invoices. In May 1861, Barney awarded the unexpired part of the three-year agreement to his own firm of Barney, Parsons, and Butler. The task, criticized for the abuses it encouraged, was reassigned directly to the collector of customs when the contract expired. William J. Hartman, "Politics and Patronage: The New York Custom House, 1852–1902" (Ph.D. diss., Columbia University, 1952), 103–5.

91. Chase to David Dudley Field, Sept. 6, 1862 (Telegrams Sent, Gen. Recs. Treasury Dept., Nat. Arch.).

92. Major Ebenezer Baldwin Andrews (1821–80), who later became a professor of geology at Marietta College, was praising George Crook (1829–90), a fellow officer in the 36th Ohio Infantry. Crook later received the brevet rank of brigadier general for unrelated action in West Virginia during the opening months of 1864. Andrews to Chase, Sept. 16, 1862 (Chase Papers, L.C.); *Annual Report of the Adjutant General, to the Governor of the State of Ohio: for the Year 1861* (n.p., n.d.), 214; *Appletons'*, 1:74; *DAB*, 4:563–64; *History of Washington County*, 242–43.

93. Brig. Gen. James Samuel Wadsworth (1807–64), commander of Union forces around Washington, D.C., and a Republican candidate for governor of New York. *DAB*, 19:308–9.

September 1862

Went to President's, and spoke of General Order commending Pope's Army. He thought it due, and said he would speak to Halleck.

Coming home met McDowell and T. C. H. Smith. Smith came home with me and spoke of battles,—eulogizing in strong terms both Pope and McDowell. Referring to my omission to reply to his letter of a year ago, I explained it as well as I could.— Field and Barney came, and I sent for Harrington. Had long talk about Labor Contract, and dissatisfaction of our friends with Mr. Barney. So far as I could see, the dissatisfaction was unreasonable. I said I could not hold the contract to be continuing, unless the Attorney-General should reverse his opinion, of which there was too little probability to warrant postponement of action, and so virtual continuance, until his review of his decision. Said I would gladly oblige party friends, but not at the expense of any breach of public duty.— Field and Barney left together, and soon after Harrington.

Received to-day telegram from Paymaster-General of New-York:[94] "Cannot forward troops for want of means to pay State bounty. Will you exchange smaller U.S. Notes for $1000s and 500s., to enable State to do it?"— Answered, "Yes! Be as prompt in sending your troops;" and sent necessary directions to Mr. Cisco.

In the afternoon, McDowell called to say Good bye. The Court of Inquiry demanded by him had been postponed, and he had fifteen days leave of absence. He went away feeling very sad indeed.

In the night, a large part of the army moved northward, following the force already sent forward to meet the rebels invading Maryland. Generals Burnside, Hooker, Sumner and Reno in command (Burnside chief) as reported.[95]

MONDAY, SEPT 8, 1862. Jay Cooke came to breakfast, after which we talked on financial matters. He thought gold could be easily obtained on deposit at 4%; and that, by and by, on a more favorable turn of affairs, 5–20s could be negotiated.— Clay[96] came in, and Cooke left. Clay and I rode towards Department in wagon. Clay said he had made up his mind to take Department and that the President and Stanton were willing he should take that beyond the Mississippi. "Would I go with him to see Halleck?"— "Certainly."— Halleck received us kindly, but was unwell. Showed no favor to the new Department project.

Returned to Department and attended to general business. Nothing of special financial moment. Barney came in, and said that

94. Col. George Bliss (1830–97). *DAB*, 2:373–74.
95. Maj. Gen. Jesse Lee Reno (1823–62) commanded the 9th Corps under Burnside. *DAB*, 15:504.
96. Cassius Marcellus Clay.

Stanton and Wadsworth had advised him to leave for New-York this evening, as communication with Baltimore might be cut off before tomorrow. He would be governed by my advice. Told him I did not think the event probable, but he had best govern himself by the advice received.

After he had gone, Gen. Mansfield came in and talked very earnestly about the necessity of ordering up, from Suffolk, 1st. Delaware and 3 and 4 New-York, trained and disciplined now 14 months, each 800 strong, say 2400 men; and from Norfolk 19th. Wisconsin and 48th. Pennsylvania, say 1600 men; leaving, at Suffolk, Forey's[97] Brigade of four diminished Regiments, say 1800 men in all, late of Shields' division;—11th Pennsylvania Cavalry (a full and good Regiment) say 900 men;—and Dodge's Regiment of mounted Rifles[98] except one Company; and at Norfolk, 99th New-York, and one Company of Dodge's, sufficient for military police. He favored leaving Keyes and Peck at Yorktown.[99]— He said the defences of the city were weak on the Eastern side; and that there ought to be at least 65.000 good men to hold it if McClellan is defeated—to improve victory, if he is successful.— He referred to old times. Was in Texas the Winter before Rebellion broke out. Saw Twiggs, who hated him because he was on Court-Martial.[1] Was then told by officer in Council of War of K.G.C. that Floyd and Cobb, in Cabinet, and Jeff Davis and Breckinridge, were members.[2] In this Council of War, Orders were given to seize Navy-Yards, Forts, &c., while its

---

97. Actually, Orris Sanford Ferry (1823–75), Republican congressman from Connecticut, 1859–61, brigadier general of volunteers, 1862–65, and U.S. senator, 1867–75. *Appletons'*, 2:442–43; *DAB*, 6:342–43; *OR*, ser. 1, v. 18, pt. 3:123.

98. The regiment of Maj. Charles Cleveland Dodge.

99. Erasmus Darwin Keyes (1810–95), major general of volunteers, brevet brigadier general of the regular army, commander of the 4th Army Corps during McClellan's Peninsular campaign; and John James Peck (1821–78), major general of volunteers. *DAB*, 10:365–66, 14:380–81.

1. In Feb. 1861, David Emanuel Twiggs (1790–1862), a U.S. brigadier general in charge of the Department of Texas, surrendered his command to the Confederates. He was dismissed from the U.S. service and became a major general in the Confederate Army. *DAB*, 19:83.

2. Cincinnatian George Washington Leigh Bickley founded the Knights of the Golden Circle as a secret society in 1851. Throughout the Civil War the group was inaccurately rumored to have been a source of proslavery subversion. John Buchanan Floyd (1806–63) and Howell Cobb (1815–68) were U.S. secretaries of war and the Treasury, respectively, under James Buchanan. Jefferson Davis (1808–89), former U.S. senator and secretary of war, became president of the Confederacy in Feb. 1861. John Cabell Breckinridge (1821–75), Buchanan's vice president, served the Confederacy as major general, 1862–65, and secretary of war, 1865. Frank L. Klement, *Dark Lanterns: Secret Political Societies and Treason Trials in the Civil War* (Baton Rouge, La., 1984), 7–33; *DAB*, 3:7–10, 4:241–44, 5:123–31, 6:482–83.

members were yet Cabinet officers and Senators. The Order of the K.G.C. ramified throughout the South. First offered services to Juarez, who refused them because too dangerous.³ They then plotted the invasion of Cuba, which failed. Then declared themselves Protectors of Southern Rights and levied a contribution upon all planters and slaveholders—some giving $5 and some $10, and some more or less. In this way they got large sums and commenced operations. They designed to seize Washington and inaugurate Breckinridge; and with reference to this Mason wrote Faulkner advising him not to resign⁴—this letter being now in Seward's possession. This plot only failed through the bringing of troops to Washington, and the unwillingness of leaders to make a bloody issue so early.— He spoke of Gen Scott. Said he had not treated him well—had placed McDowell in command over the river last year, superseding himself, and when he had asked for explanation he simply replied that his orders had been given. He felt himself wronged, but did his duty to the best of his ability. He was afterwards treated badly by Gen Wool, who did not like him, though he treated him civilly. Had lately been in command at Suffolk (an insignificant post) until summoned here to Court of Inquiry.— Wanted active employment but was unable to get any. Had sent for his horses, and proposed to visit all the fortifications around the city on his own account.— I was a good deal affected by the manifest patriotism and desire to do something for his country manifested by the old General; and could not help wishing that he was younger, and thinking that, perhaps, after all, it would have been better to trust him.

After the General left, went to War Department, where found the President, Stanton and Wadsworth. The President said he had felt badly all day. Wadsworth said there was no danger of an attack on Washington, and that the man ought to be severely punished who intimated the possibility of its surrender. The President spoke of the great number of stragglers he had seen coming into town this morning; and of the immense losses by desertion.

Returned home. Maj. Andrews and others called

TUESDAY, SEPT. 9, 1862. Maj. Andrews came to breakfast. Told him I had seen Secretary of War, who had assured me that Col. Crooks' commission as Brigadier had been sent him.

3. In the late 1850s, Benito Pablo Juárez (1806–72) was leading a liberal revolution, the War of the Reform, in Mexico. *Appletons'*, 3:478–80.
4. James Murray Mason; Charles James Faulkner (1806–84), U.S. congressman from Virginia, 1851–59, and minister to France, 1859–61. *DAB*, 6:298.

Went to Department. Directed Commission for 10th. New-York district to be sent to Hyatt.[5] Directed Mr. Rogers to proceed to New-York and expedite alterations in Exchange and Custom House, and make proper contracts for the same.[6]

Went to President's to attend Cabinet Meeting, but there was only a talk. I proposed the creation of a Department beyond the Mississippi and that Clay be placed in command, with whom Frank P. Blair should be associated; and that an Expedition should be organized to Petersburgh and afterwards to Charleston.

Genl Van Ransellaer called to ask my interest for him as Paymaster-General; and Mr Carroll, to ask the same for Genl. Griffin.[7]— Went to War Department, where Watson told me that Gen. McClellan had telegraphed expressing doubt if there was any large rebel force in Maryland, and apprehension that their movement might be a feint.— Watson dined with me. Read him Denison's letter from New-Orleans about evacuation of Baton Rouge—Butler's black Regiment—&c., &c.[8]

Just after dinner, Capt. _____ came in with Mr. Gr[eaves], who had been arrested near Soldiers' Home as a suspicious character— taken before Gen Wadsworth, to whom he said he was known to me—sent by Gen. W. to me—identified and discharged. He is an Englishman of a Manchester House, who brought a letter from Mr. Layard to Acting Minister Stuart, by whom he had been commended

---

5. Abram Hyatt of Sing Sing (Ossining), newly appointed assessor of internal revenue. *Register of Officers (1863)*, 38.

6. Isaiah Rogers (1800–1869) was supervising architect of the Treasury, 1862–65. *DAB*, 16:98–99.

7. A former Whig congressman from New York, Henry Bell Van Rensselaer (1810–64) served as chief of staff with rank of brigadier general under Winfield Scott in 1861 and as inspector general of the U.S. Army, 1862–64. William Thomas Carroll (d. 1863), clerk of the U.S. Supreme Court, 1827–62, was probably acting in behalf of his son-in-law, Charles Griffin (1825–67), a brigadier and future major general of volunteers, who after the war was a colonel in the regular army. *Appletons'*, 1:539, 6:252; *Bio. Dir. U.S. Cong.*, 1977; *DAB*, 7:617–18.

8. Vermont native George Stanton Denison (1833–66), the son of Chase's cousin, Joseph Adam Denison, Jr., practiced law in Texas before the Civil War. From May 1862 he was special agent of the U.S. Treasury acting as a customs and internal revenue officer at New Orleans. Denison's letter discussed the Federal evacuation of Baton Rouge on Aug. 21 and the unit of free black soldiers recently formed by Benjamin F. Butler. Denison to Chase, Aug. 26, 1862 (Chase Papers, L.C.); *General Catalogue of the University of Vermont and State Agricultural College, Burlington, Vermont, 1791–1900* (Burlington, Vt., 1901), 101; James H. Padgett, ed., "Some Letters of George Stanton Denison, 1854–1866: Observations of a Yankee on Conditions in Louisiana and Texas," *Louisiana Historical Quarterly* 23 (1940): 1132–1240; *Letter of the Secretary of the Treasury, Transmitting . . . A List of the Special Agents of the Treasury Department and their Assistants*, 38th Cong., 1st sess., 1864, S. Ex. Doc. 31, 3; Hans L. Trefousse, *Ben Butler: The South Called Him Beast!* (New York, 1957), 131.

to me.[9] Riding around to gratify curiosity he had fallen into trouble.[10]

WEDNESDAY, SEPT. 10   Mr. Skinner at breakfast.[11]— Soon after, Mr Hamilton (James A.) came, and we conversed about the condition of things. He said the Committee from New-York had arrived, representing the views of the five New-England Governors who met lately; and that they would insist on the resignation of Messrs. S. and B.[12]— I told him I thought the mission vain—that it might be useful if all the Heads of Departments were to resign, and that I was not only ready but anxious to do so, either with my associates or alone.— He criticized severely some passages in Mr. Seward's Diplomatic Correspondence—especially those in the Letter of April 10, to Mr. Adams, which concede the proposition that the Federal Government could not reduce the seceding States to obedience by conquest, and affirm that "only an imperial or despotic Government could subjugate thoroughly disaffected and insurrectionary members of the State."[13] He said in them was the key to the whole temporizing policy, civil and military, which had been pursued. I could make no repy to this, except to say that I had never known Mr. Seward object to any *action,* however vigorous, of a military nature; though his influence had been cast in favor of harmonizing the various elements of support to the Administration, by retaining Genl. McClellan in command, and by avoiding action which would be likely to alienate the Border States. I added that in his wishes for harmony I concurred; and that I credited him with good motives in the choice of means to ends, though I could not always concur with him in judgment as to their adaptation.

After this conversation, I went to the Department and transacted the routine business. I also examined the Tax Law for insurgent

---

9. William Stuart was secretary of the British legation in Washington. Sir Austen Henry Layard (1817–94), British undersecretary of foreign affairs, identified Greaves as "a Partner in a large cotton manufacturing house in Lancashire" who wished to follow Union forces "with a view of ascertaining what quantity of cotton is likely to be exported during the ensuing season." *Wash. Dir. (1862),* 240; Layard to Stuart, July 3, 1862, Stuart to Chase, Aug. 29, 1862 (Chase Papers, L.C.).
10. In the original, the entries for Aug. 6–8 follow this entry.
11. James Ralston Skinner.
12. William H. Seward and Montgomery Blair.
13. "This federal system of ours is of all forms of government the very one which is most unfitted for such a labor," Seward had written to Charles Francis Adams, the U.S. minister to Great Britain, before the outbreak of war at Ft. Sumter. "Happily, however, this is only an imaginary defect. The system has within itself adequate, peaceful, conservative, and recuperative forces." Seward to Adams, Apr. 10, 1861, in Baker, *Works of William H. Seward,* 5:205.

States;[14] sent for Commissioner Boutwell; read and approved Regulations drafted by Judge Smith;[15] and determined to overcome the difficulties in the way of putting the law into operation, arising from the omission of any appropriation for the purpose by Congress, by applying, so far as the District of South-Carolina is concerned, the necessary amount from a small fund legally at my disposal.

Received letter from Birney, desiring that his brother should command Kearney's corps, and sent it to War Department with strong commendation.[16]

Genl. Kane called to thank me for my support to his appointment as Brigadier, to which I answered, most sincerely, that he "was indebted for the appointment, not to my support, but to his own merits."[17] Indeed, while I will most gladly aid merit to place, and seek it out in order to give it place, I am resolved never from sympathy or weak compliance, to help unfit persons to position. The condition of the country is too critical for it now, were it ever excusable.

At dinner, Mr Hamilton told me of the interview between the New-York Committee and the President. The Committee urged a change of policy. The President became vexed, and said, in substance, "It is plain enough what you want—you want to get Seward out of the Cabinet. There is not one of you who would not see the country ruined, if you could turn out Seward."[18]

After dinner, rode to Mr. Cutts', proposing to invite Mrs. D.[19] to ride; and was very sorry to learn from her mother that she was much indisposed.— Went to the War Department. No satisfactory information yet from army and no satisfactory account of numbers or position of the enemy.— David Taylor[20] called with Mr. North-

14. "An Act for the Collection of Direct Taxes in Insurrectionary Districts, June 7, 1862," *Statutes at Large*, 12:422–26.

15. Probably Abram D. Smith of Wisconsin, who became a U.S. direct tax commissioner for South Carolina. Rose, *Rehearsal for Reconstruction*, 202; Smith to Chase, Nov. 5, 1862 (Chase Papers, L.C.).

16. James Birney (1817–88), a judge of Michigan's 18th judicial circuit and a son of antislavery leader James Gillespie Birney, was writing in behalf of Brig. Gen. David Bell Birney (1825–64) of the 23rd Regiment of Pennsylvania Volunteers. Maj. Gen. Philip Kearny (1814–62) had lost his life in battle at Chantilly, Va., Aug. 31, 1862. D. B. Birney replaced him and was promoted to major general in May 1863. *DAB*, 2:290–91, 10:271–72.

17. Thomas Leiper Kane (1822–83) previously served as lieutenant colonel of the Pennsylvania "Bucktails." Kane had received the promotion for gallant service on Sept. 7. *DAB*, 10:258–59.

18. As originally written by the clerk, this phrase was *ruin Seward*. A faint pencil interlineation, probably by Chase, reads *turn out*. Either Chase or the clerk, working in ink, made *ruin* into *turn* and inserted *out*, to produce *turn out Seward*.

19. Adèle Cutts Douglas.

20. Maj. David Taylor.

cott, of Champaign, who wants to be Commissary. Endorsed his paper, *"Recommended"*

Received telegram from McDowell, asking if it was not just to publish his letter. Answered, "Will see it done".[21]

THURSDAY, SEPT 11TH., 1862. Two weeks since Hooker drove Ewell at Bristow Station[22]—and what weeks! *Ten*[23] days of battle, and then such changes.—changes in which it is difficult to see the public good! How singularly all our worst defeats have followed Administrative cr—no, blunders! McDowell defeated at Bull Run, because the Administration would not supersede Patterson[24] by a General of more capacity, vigor and devotion to the cause. McClellan defeated at Richmond, because the Administration recalled Shields and forced Frémont to retire from the pursuit of Jackson, in order that McDowell's force might be concentrated at Manassas to be sent to McClellan before Richmond. Pope defeated at Bull Run because the Administration persisted in keeping McClellan in command of the Army of the Potomac, after full warning that, under his lead and influence, that army would not coöperate effectively with Pope.

After breakfast this morning Mr. Hamilton took leave of me, and I prepared to go to Fairfax Seminary to visit Butterfield, who, according to the papers, is sick there.[25] Before starting, however, I thought it best to send Bannister to the War Department to learn if anything of importance had occurred.[26] He returned with a note to the effect that nothing important had come from the army but that an important question was for consideration and decision, and if I would come up he would send for Genl Halleck and the President. Went up immediately. It rained. On arriving at the War Department, found Gen Wright, of Penna., there; with a request from Gov. Curtin to call into active service all the able bodied men of the

21. See Sept. 6 above regarding McDowell's letter to Lincoln.
22. Hooker's victory over Maj. Gen. Richard Stoddert Ewell (1817–72), C.S.A., had occurred on Aug. 27 at Bristoe Station, Va. *DAB*, 6:229–30; *OR*, ser. 1, v. 12, pt. 2:437–39, 456–57, 720–21, 743.
23. Word underlined in pencil, possibly by Chase when he made pencil interlineations elsewhere in this journal.
24. Robert Patterson.
25. Daniel Butterfield (1831–1901), brigadier general of volunteers under the command of Fitz John Porter, and later Joseph Hooker's chief of staff. Sick with a fever, Butterfield was resting at the home of Philip Kearny near Alexandria, Va. Julia Lorriland Butterfield, ed., *A Biographical Memorial of General Daniel Butterfield* . . . (New York, 1904), 99; *DAB*, 3:372–74.
26. Maj. Dwight Bannister of Ohio, paymaster under Irvin McDowell. In the 1860s and early 1870s Bannister managed property for Chase in Columbus. Heitman, *Historical Register*, 1:189; *OR*, ser. 1, v. 51, pt. 1:61; Bannister to Chase, Apr. 6, June 7, 1861, May 17, 1867, Oct. 14, 1872 (Chase Papers, L.C.); Chase to Bannister, Mar. 30, 1864, Jan. 31, 1867 (Chase Papers, Hist. Soc. of Pa.).

State.[27] The President, Gen. Halleck and Mr. Stanton submitted the question, "What answer shall be returned to Gov Curtin?"— Gen H. thought the important thing was to mass all the force possible on this side the enemy, and defeat him; and that a general arming of Pennsylvania would not be sufficiently available to warrant the vast expenses sure to be incurred.— Mr. Stanton expressed no opinion as to defeat of the enemy from this side, but thought Gov. Curtin's proposal too large to be entertained, and stated that the arms for a general arming could not be furnished.— I asked Gen. H., "What force, in your opinion, has the enemy?"— "From the best evidence I have—not satisfactory, but the best—I reckon the whole number in Maryland and the vicinity of Washington, at 150.000."— "How many in Maryland?"— "Two-thirds probably, or 100.000"— "What in your judgment as a soldier, are the designs of the enemy?"— "Impossible to judge with certainty. Suppose he will do what I would do if in his place—rest, recruit, get supplies, augment force, and obtain all possible information; and then strike the safest and most effectual blow he can—at Washington, Baltimore or Philadelphia. If not strong enough to strike a blow, he will, after getting all he can, attempt to re-cross into Virginia."— "You think, then, there is no probability of an advance into Pennsylvania at present."— "None, unless a raid."— Upon these statements, I expressed the opinion, that, considering the situation of our troops sent out to attack the rebel army, it was not impossible that a raid, at least, would be attempted into Pennsylvania, and that Gov. Curtin was wise in making provision for it; that the proposition to arm the whole people was, however, too broad; and that I thought it would be well to authorize the Governor to call out as many troops as could be armed with the arms he reported himself as having—say 30.000. The President said he was averse to giving the order, on the score of expense; but would think of it till tomorrow.

The President and Secy. Stanton having left the room, I took occasion to ask Gen. Halleck what, in his judgment, were the causes of the demoralization of the troops. He replied, there were several causes; first, the incapacity of officers from inexperience, or want of ability or character; second, the want of proper discipline; third,—a political cause—, the action of the late Congress in its abolition and confiscation measures, which were very distasteful to the Army of the West, and, as he understood, also to the Army of the Potomac. I expressed my conviction that the influence of the last was exaggerated, and dropped the subject.

27. Col. John A. Wright was on the staff of Andrew Gregg Curtin (1817–94), governor of Pennsylvania, 1861–67. *DAB*, 4:606–8; *OR*, ser. 1, v. 19, pt. 2:247–51, 267.

I abandoned the idea of visiting Butterfield and returned to the Department, where I transacted usual routine business.

In the evening, called to enquire for Mrs. Douglas, taking some

FRIDAY, SEPTEMBER 12. Breakfasted alone. After breakfast went to Department, putting carelessly in my pocket a roll of papers, consisting, in part, of some sheets of an Account of McClellan's Course till the junction of the Army of the Potomac with that of Virginia, and of others containing the first draft of my Journal of the 10th. and in part of the 11th.[28] On reaching the Treasury, I was a little alarmed on missing my roll; and still more annoyed when, on sending Thomas[29] and Mr. Plants to look along the street and at the house, nothing could be found of it. What if it should fall into the hands of somebody who will make public what is not designed for publication, but simply in memoriam?

Fortunately the roll was picked up in the street and brought to me.

Little of interest occurred at the Department to-day. Expenses are enormous, increasing instead of diminishing; and the ill-successes in the field have so affected Government Stocks that it is impossible to obtain money except on temporary deposit, and these deposits very little exceed   . We are forced, therefore, to rely on the increased issue of U.S. Notes, which hurts almost as much as it helps; for the omission of Congress to take any measures to restrict bank-note circulation, makes the issue of these notes a stimulant to its increase so that the augmentation of the currency proceeds by a double action and prices rise proportionably. It is a bad state of things; but neither the President, his counsellors nor his commanding general seem to care. They rush on from expense to expense and from defeat to defeat, heedless of the abyss of bankruptcy and ruin which yawns before us—so easily shunned, yet seemingly so sure to engulf us. May God open the eyes of those who control, before it is too late!

Went over to the War Department about two. Found that no important intelligence of rebel movements had been received. The

---

28. What Chase calls here "an Account of McClellan's Course" is an undated draft in Chase's hand (Chase Papers, Hist. Soc. of Pa.) entitled "Notes [*or* "Mema."; *one word has been written over the other in the original*] on the Union of the Army of the Potomac & the Army of Virgin[ia]." This memorandum is printed in Schuckers, *Chase*, 445–50. The editors have not located a "first draft" of Chase's journal for Sept. 10–11.

29. Possibly Henry L. Thomas, a messenger in the office of the second comptroller of the U.S. Treasury. *Wash. Dir. (1862)*, 169.

Secretary informed me that *he had heard* from Genl. H.[30] that the President is going out to see Gen. McClellan; and commented with some severity, on his humiliating submissiveness to that officer. It is, indeed, humiliating; but prompted, I believe, by a sincere desire to serve the country, and a fear that, should he supersede McClellan by any other commander, no advantage would be gained in leadership, but much harm in the disaffection of officers and troops. The truth is, I think, that the President with the most honest intentions in the world, and a naturally clear judgment and a true, unselfish patriotism, has yielded so much to Border State and negrophobic counsels that he now finds it difficult to arrest his own descent towards the most fatal concessions. He has already separated himself from the great body of the party which elected him; distrusts most those who most represent its spirit; and waits. For what?

Before I left the Department, the Secretary kindly promised me a Paymastership for Wm. D. Bickham; which will, when given be a great gratification to a very worthy friend.— We talked also of Port Royal and matters there. I advised the removal of Brannan, who is hostile to the plans of the Department and the measures of Saxton.[31] He said he would be ordered to the North; but did not seem inclined to talk much about it.

Speaking of the number of rebels, he said he thought it could not exceed 100.000; but that his judgment was founded upon possibilities of supplies and transportation—not on reports.

Called at President's, and spoke to him of Leave of Absence to Cameron. He referred me to Seward, to whom I went, and was informed that Leave was sent by last steamer.[32]— We talked on many things—Barney's appointments, conduct of the war, &c., &c.— Engaged to go together tomorrow, and urge expedition to Cn.[33]— He said some one had proposed that the President should issue a Proclamation, on the invasion of Pennsylvania, freeing all the Apprentices of that State, or with some similar object. I thought the jest ill-timed.

Judge Adams (6th. Auditor), Mr. Burnam (of Kentucky Legislature, now a refugee from his home) and Mr. Case, (formerly of

---

30. Henry Halleck.

31. John Milton Brannan (1819–92), brigadier general of volunteers, commanded the Department of Key West, Fla., and later served in the Army of the Cumberland. *DAB*, 2:600–601.

32. Simon Cameron, U.S. minister to Russia since Jan., had asked Chase to intervene in his behalf. "I must leave here," Cameron wrote. "The climate is killing my wife, and is breaking me down. . . ." Cameron to Chase, Aug. 18, 1862 (Chase Papers, Hist. Soc. of Pa.).

33. Charleston.

Patriot, Ia., now of Portland, Me.) dined with me.[34] The Kentucky Slaveholders were more against Slavery than the Northern Conservative. Strange, yet not strange!

In the evening, Maj. D. Taylor, Mr. O'Harra and Mr. Cooke called[35]—later Mr. Cummings.[36] General talk and not very profitable. Cooke and O'Harra want introduction to Gen. Mitchell[37] for Pitt Cooke and O'Harra, who want to buy cotton at Port Royal.[38]— Col. Kane called and left note about McDowell.— Mr. Cummings talked about *"Bulletin"*—about removal of one of the Editors from Custom House—about support to himself for Assembly—about distribution of stamps, &c.[39]— I got tired.

SATURDAY, SEPT. 13, 1862. Breakfasted alone. What has become of Mr. Skinner?[40] Went to Department and attended to some matters of routine.

Went to Navy Department with Gov. Seward, according to appointment, about expedition to Charleston. Examined chart with Secretary Welles and Asst. Secy. Fox.[41] Learned that the *"Ironsides"* and *"Passaic"* will be ready for sea by the 1st. October;[42] which is more than two weeks longer than Mr. Welles gave me to understand ten days ago. Fox thinks that James Island ought to have been held and that Hunter was wrong in withdrawing our force from it; but it is now commanded by our gunboats, so that a landing upon it is easy,

---

34. Green Adams; Curtis Field Burnham (b. 1820), Yale class of 1840, assistant secretary of the U.S. Treasury, 1875–76; and Eliphalet Case. H. Levin, ed., *The Lawyers and Lawmakers of Kentucky* (Chicago, [1897]), 524–25.

35. George F. O'Harra, an employee in the Columbus, Ohio, staple and fancy dry goods firm of A. P. Stone and Co.; and Jay Cooke. O'Harra to Chase, Nov. 19, 1863 (Chase Papers, L.C.); *Col. Dir. (1856–57)*, 163, 189.

36. Alexander Cummings (1810–79), founder of the Philadelphia *Evening Bulletin* and controversial governor of Colorado Territory, 1865–67, served ineptly as special purchasing agent for the War Department after his appointment in Apr. 1861. Thomas A. McMullin and David Walker, eds., *Biographical Directory of American Territorial Governors* (Westport, Conn., 1984), 69–70; Chase to Cummings, Oct. 14, 1862 (Chase Papers, Hist. Soc. of Pa.).

37. Ormsby MacKnight Mitchel.

38. Pitt Cooke (1819–79) was a brother and business associate of Jay Cooke. Ellis Paxson Oberholtzer, *Jay Cooke: Financier of the Civil War* (Philadelphia, 1907), 1:5, 2:17–21, 537.

39. The Internal Revenue Act of July 1, 1862, required stamp duties, beginning Oct. 1, on legal papers, banking documents, telegrams, express shipments, and certain goods such as pharmaceuticals, cosmetics, and playing cards. *Statutes at Large*, 12:475–85.

40. James Ralston Skinner.

41. Gustavus Vasa Fox (1821–83), assistant secretary of the U.S. Navy. *DAB*, 6:568–69.

42. The USS *New Ironsides*, a 3,486-ton ironclad screw steamer commissioned in Philadelphia on Aug. 21, and the USS *Passaic*, an 844-ton single-turreted wood and iron monitor recently constructed by John Ericsson. *ORN*, ser. 2, v. 1:159, 170.

and a force of 10.000 or 15.000 men would suffice for the reduction of Charleston. A land force, however, would have to act mainly independently of the naval; and no naval force but ironclads could act with any efficiency, because the harbor being a *cul de sac*, wooden vessels entering it to bombard the town would be exposed to fire from all sides, and could not pass and repass the enemy's batteries, as at Port Royal, and, by motion, make the enemy's fire comparatively ineffectual. Ironclads, however, such as the *"Passaic"* and the *"Ironsides"*, could go right into the harbor, with little or no risk, and destroy the Forts, batteries, and the town itself if not surrendered. After all, it seemed to me that it would contribute greatly to the certainty of the result if a land force should be organized, and I determined to confer with the Secretary of War on the subject, as soon as possible. No time should be lost in making every arrangement for such overwhelming blows, just as soon as the ironclads are ready, as will effectually annihilate the possibility of rebel success.

From the Navy Department, we went to Head Quarters where we found Genl. Cullum,[43] who said: "We have got whipped again. We have just received a telegram that the rebels have defeated our people in Fayette County, Va., and are driving them down the Kanawha. The trouble is that our men won't fight." The style of remark did not suit me; but it is too common among our generals. In my opinion, the soldiers are better than the officers.— Genl. Halleck came in, and we asked the situation. There was nothing new, he said, except confirmation that Burnside drove the rebels out of Frederick yesterday, and had renewed the fight to-day. Heavy firing had been heard from the direction of Harpers Ferry and the Frederick and Hagerstown Road. We left Headquarters, and I returned to the Department.

Gave O'Harra and Pitt Cooke letter of introduction to Gen. Mitchell. Visited Mr. Clark's Sealing and trimming Machines for the ones and twos and found them a perfect success;[44] and the ones and twos are sealed and trimmed by machinery, attended for the most part by women, with such prodigious advantage to the Government, that it seems difficult to imagine that coining, except in large masses, can be of much utility hereafter.

Jay Cooke writes that he has visited New-York and conversed with Bankers; and thinks that $10.000.000 in Gold will be gladly deposited at 4%. I think that, in this way, all the Gold needed can be

---

43. Brig. Gen. George Washington Cullum (1809–92), Henry W. Halleck's chief of staff. *DAB*, 4:589–90.
44. Spencer Morton Clark was chief of the National Currency Bureau. Chase to Clark, Feb. 6, 1865 (Chase Papers, Hist. Soc. of Pa.); *Register of Officers (1863)*, 42; *Wash. Dir. (1864)*, 127.

September 1862 { 385 }

obtained at very small cost and without affecting the market in any way. If it succeeds, it will form not the least remarkable chapter in the history of the financial success which has attended me thus far.

Wrote to Katie and Nettie, and to Horton—to Katie, advising her not to return immediately; to Horton about Pope.[45]

In the evening, went to Willard's to call on Genl. Schenck, but did not see him.[46] Met Weed, and went to his room and talked of sundry matters. He says I have done as well in the New-York appointments as was possible, and advises care as to securities taken; which advice I think very good. He thinks the time has come for vigorous measures South; and is for freeing the slaves, and arming them as far as useful, without noise or excitement. He saw Hunter[47] in New-York; who says that if he had been sustained, he would have emasculated the rebellion South-Carolina before now—which he seemed to believe and which I believe absolutely.

Went to War Department. Telegraph men[48] told me that telegraph was built to Point of Rocks and several miles beyond the Monocacy towards Frederick, and that heavy continuous firing was heard, by the operator at the former place, from the direction of Harpers Ferry, till between three and four this afternoon; and that firing, though not so heavy, was also heard from the direction of Middleton, between Frederick and Hagerstown. There was also a rumor that we had captured a large wagon-train, with a considerable number of prisoners. The inference from the firing heard is that an attack has been made on Harpers Ferry by a large rebel force, and a stout defense with unknown result; and that a less important conflict has taken place between the advance under Burnside and the rebel rear falling back towards Hagerstown or Harpers Ferry, (probably the former) and that the rebels have been worsted.

Telegram from Gov Curtin yesterday states that a reliable gentleman of Maryland, who had opportunities to converse freely with officers of the rebel army, says that the rebel force in Maryland is 190.000, and on the other side of the Potomac 250.000—in all 440.000. This is a specimen of information collected and believed!

---

45. Subsequent correspondence indicates that Chase's letter to Valentine B. Horton defended Gen. John Pope from criticism he faced after losing the Second Battle of Bull Run, Aug. 27–30. *DAB*, 15:77; Horton to Chase, Oct. 4, 1862 (Chase Papers, L.C.).

46. Robert Cumming Schenck (1809–90), Whig and Republican congressman from Ohio, 1843–51, 1863–71; U.S. minister to Brazil, 1851–53; brigadier and major general of volunteers, 1861–63; and U.S. minister to Great Britain, 1870–76. *Bio. Dir. U.S. Cong.*, 1774; *DAB*, 16:427–28.

47. David Hunter.

48. The word *men* was inserted above the line, possibly by Chase.

Came home and Cooke called with Mr. Davis, General Birney's partner, who wants him made a Major-General with command of Kearney's corps.[49] I think this should be done. We must advance all our Republican officers who have real merit, so as to counterpoise the too great weight already given to Democratic officers, without much merit. They have been more pushed than the Republicans and we have been more than just—more than generous even—we have been lavish towards them. It is time to change the policy

SUNDAY, SEPT. 14, 1862. Went to Methodist Church. Mr. Brown preached good sermon.[50]— Afterwards called to enquire for Mrs. Douglas, who, I found, had passed a bad night, but was better.

Went to War Department. Despatches from McClellan to the President—also to Gen. Halleck. First, complimentary—respects to Mrs. Lincoln; ladies enthusiatic welcome of McClellan and his army "us". The second states getting possession of Lee's Order to Hill of 10th.[51]—troops from various directions to attack Martinsburgh and Harpers Ferry on the 12th.—capture both—and then reünite at Hagerstown;—White had anticipated the enemy by joining Miles at Harpers Ferry, where the enemy made vigorous attack yesterday;[52]—courier from Miles says he can hold out two days, but enemy is in possession of Maryland Heights;—McC. hopes before two days to relieve Miles—is already in possession of of Middleton and Jefferson;—estimates rebel force in Maryland at 125.000;— thinks defeat of his army would be ruinous, and therefore better to spare all troops from Washington than suffer it;—anticipates great battle tomorrow, Monday;—enemy don't mean to go back to Virginia, but thinks Lee has blundered, and hopes to make him repent of it.— Watson[53] rode with me.

Read several books, especially article in "Revue des deux Mondes" on the soul.[54]— In the evening, Mr. Case called and talked

---

49. Oliver Wilson Davis, a Philadelphia attorney and former partner of David Bell Birney. Oliver Wilson Davis, *Life of David Bell Birney* . . . (Philadelphia, 1867); *Phila. Dir. (1859)*, 52, 158, 160.

50. Either Benjamin N. Brown, an employee in the Second Auditor's office and minister of the Capitol Hill Methodist Episcopal Church, or B. Peyton Brown, pastor of Wesley Chapel. *Wash. Dir. (1863)*, 53, 295.

51. Robert E. Lee (1807–70), commander of the Army of Northern Virginia, actually issued the order to Maj. Gen. Daniel Harvey Hill (1821–89) on Sept. 9. *DAB*, 9:27–28, 11:120–29; George B. McClellan, *McClellan's Own Story* . . . (New York, 1887), 573.

52. Julius White (1816–93), brigadier and later major general of volunteers, served in the Department of the Shenandoah. Col. Dixon Stansbury Miles (1804–62), U.S.A., commanded the post at Harpers Ferry. *Appletons'*, 4:321; *Nat. Cyc.*, 4:335–36.

53. P. H. Watson.

54. Émile Saisset, "Recherches Nouvelles sur l'Ame et sur la Vie," *Revue des Deux Mondes*, 40 (Aug. 15, 1862): 957–87.

of Politics and Spiritualism—especially the last, in which he is a firm believer. Says he receives letters from the inhabitants of the Sixth and other Spheres, among whom are Calhoun, Brutus and others; that there is a Council in the 6th., presided over by Washington, to which the control of this war is committed; that Richmond will be taken about Dec. 1st., and Charleston early in the Spring.— Dr. Rabe called and talked over California matters. Seems to have been very unfairly and unjustly dealt with. Thinks Hoffman an excellent man—also Sharp, Dist. Atty.[55] Thinks Phelps or   , a partizan of Frémont, will be elected Senator.[56] Rand, new Marshal, is one of Palmer, Cook & Co. set.[57] Advised him to examine papers, and, if possible, refute charges and be restored.

Mr. Varnum, of N.Y., and his cousin, from Mass., came in and talked a little. Nothing important

MONDAY, SEPT. 15, 1862. Went to Department soon after nine, stopping at Franklin's to buy glasses.[58] Got a pair, not I fear exactly the best for me. Received letters from John Sherman, O. Follett, Horace Greeley, and others.[59] Greeley's assured me that the "Tribune" had no interest in the Labor Contract, which I was very glad to learn.— Called on Attorney-General about citizenship of colored men. Found him averse to expressing official opinion.[60]— Met Eliot

---

55. San Franciscans Ogden Hoffman, Jr. (d. 1891) and William H. Sharp (1824–88), respectively U.S. judge and U.S. attorney for the northern district of California. *The Bay of San Francisco . . . A History*, 2 vols. (Chicago, 1892), 2:269; *Catalogue of Officers and Graduates of Columbia University . . .* (New York, 1916), 107; *Register of Officers (1863)*, 270.

56. Timothy Guy Phelps (1824–99), Republican congressman from California, 1861–63. *Bio. Dir. U.S. Cong.*, 1642.

57. C. W. Rand was the newly appointed U.S. marshal for the northern district of California. Palmer, Cook and Company was a San Francisco banking firm. Dwight L. Clarke, *William Tecumseh Sherman: Gold Rush Banker* (San Francisco, 1969), 160, 362; *Register of Officers (1863)*, 270.

58. M. J. Franklin, an optician on Pennsylvania Avenue. *Wash. Dir. (1862)*, 84.

59. John Sherman described defensive measures in Cincinnati and urged preemptive military action against Confederate forces massed south of the Ohio River. He also expressed frustration with the management of the war. Oran Follett reported from Sandusky, Ohio, that public faith in the administration's conduct of the war was "pretty nearly exhausted." *New York Tribune* editor Horace Greeley (1811–72) was a radical politician and unsuccessful presidential candidate on the Liberal Republican and Democratic tickets, 1872. Sherman to Chase, Sept. 10, 1862 (Chase Papers, Hist. Soc. of Pa.); Follett to Chase, Sept. 11, 1862 (Chase Papers, L.C.); *DAB*, 7:528–34.

60. Chase pressed the issue nine days later, when he officially requested Attorney General Bates to declare whether a schooner could be lawfully detained "because commanded by a 'colored man,' and so by a person not a Citizen of the United States." Over two months later Bates made a lengthy reply, concluding "that the *free man of color*, mentioned in your letter, if born in the United States, is a citizen of the United States, and, if otherwise qualified, is competent, according to the Acts of Congress, to be master of a vessel engaged in the coasting trade." Chase to Bates, Sept. 24, 1862 (Attorney General's Papers, General Recs. of Dept. of Justice, Nat. Arch.); Bates to

and Tabor, Mayor of New Bedford, and invited them to dine with me.[61]— Commenced letter to Greeley; when I was reminded of my promise to accompany Mr Case to the President's. Went with him. Found Eliot and Tabor in ante-chamber. Went in, and found Blair with the President discussing affairs. Told him of the gentlemen outside, and was permitted to bring them in. Did so. Introduced Case, who shook hands, and we two came away.

Parted from Case at Department. Finished letter to Greeley, and wrote Judge Mason about Rodney, promising to do what I could for trial.[62] Several callers—among them, Col Lloyd of   Ohio Cavalry, and Col Mason of   Ohio Infantry,[63] with two Captains. Lloyd said that the cavalry was very badly used; that forage was insufficient and irregular, and needlessly wasted; that sometimes a squadron, company or regiment, was ordered out early in the morning, and left all day without any further orders. Pope, he said, had nominally about 2000 cavalry when he went South, and when he returned had not 500 fit for duty. Sometimes the cavalry was ordered to march, when five or six horses in a Company would die from sheer exhaustion. Artillery horses better cared for. Lloyd desired Mason to be made Brigadier-General. Promised to make inquiries, and if found all right, promote object.

Mr. Wetmore called about Cotton and Tobacco.[64] Proposed that Government should take all cotton at 20 cents and tobacco at   cents—pay this price—send it to New-York—sell it for Gold—keep account with each owner, and, at the end of the war, pay him the difference, if loyal. The idea struck me very favorably, and I promised to see him again tomorrow.

Chase, Nov. 29, 1862 (Letters Received from Executive Officers, Gen. Recs. Treasury Dept., Nat. Arch.).

61. Thomas Dawes Eliot and Isaac C. Tabor, mayor of New Bedford, 1860–62. Duane Hamilton Hurd, ed., *History of Bristol County, Massachusetts* . . . (Philadelphia, 1883), 114.

62. Samson Mason (1793–1869), a former congressman, U.S. attorney for Ohio, and state legislator, had asked Chase for help in behalf of his son Rodney, whom Chase knew personally from the Clark County rescue case in 1857 (see June 4, 1857, above). Rodney Mason, a colonel in the 71st Ohio Vol. Inf., had been cashiered on Aug. 22 for surrendering his command to Confederate guerrillas at Clarksville, Tenn. Four years later, the War Department dropped the charges against Mason and honorably mustered him out of service. *Bio. Dir. U.S. Cong.*, 1435; *OR*, ser. 1, v. 16, pt. 1:865; S. Mason to Chase, Sept. 10, 1862 (Chase Papers, L.C.); John Y. Simon et al., eds., *The Papers of Ulysses S. Grant* (Carbondale, Ill., 1967–), 5:321–23, 327.

63. Probably William R. Lloyd and John Sanford Mason (1824–97), officers in the 6th Ohio Cavalry and 4th Ohio Infantry, respectively. *Ohio Adjutant General's Report, 1861*, 242; *Nat. Cyc.*, 12:262–63; *OR*, ser. 1, v. 12, pt. 2:97–98.

64. James Carnahan Wetmore (b. 1813) was military agent for the state of Ohio. *OR*, ser. 1, v. 29, 2:468, ser. 2, v. 6:264–65; Wallace, comp., *Dictionary of North American Authors*, 496; Wetmore to Chase, Oct. 10, 1861 (Chase Papers, L.C.).

September 1862 { 389 }

Weed called and we had a long talk. He expressed again his conviction that more decided measures are needed in an Anti-Slavery direction; and said there was much dissatisfaction with Seward in New-York because he is supposed to be averse to such measures. I told him, I did not doubt Mr. Seward's fidelity to his ideas of progress, amelioration and freedom; but that I thought he adhered too tenaciously to men who proved themselves unworthy and dangerous, such as McClellan; that he resisted too persistently decided measures; that his influence encouraged the irresolution and inaction of the President in respect to men and measures, although personally he was as decided as anybody in favor of vigorous prosecution of the war, and as active as anybody in concerting plans of action against the rebels. Mr. Weed admitted that there was much justice in my views, and said he had expressed similar ideas to Mr. Seward himself. He said he would see him again, and that Seward and I must agree on a definite line, especially on the Slavery question, which we must recommend to the President. We talked a good deal about our matters—about the absence of proper Cabinet discussion of important subjects—about Tax appointments in New-York, with which he is well satisfied,—&c., &c.

Went to War Department between 3 and 4, and saw telegrams of McClellan. They state that the action of yesterday resulted in a decided success—that the enemy, driven from Mountain Crest,[65] did not renew the action this morning but retreated in disorder—that Lee confessed himself "shockingly whipped", with loss of 15.000 killed, wounded, missing and prisoners—that he has 700 prisoners at Frederick, and that 1000 have been taken by Hooker and held—that he proposed pursuit as rapidly as possible—that Franklin on the right in advance towards Harpers Ferry, had succeeded as well as the troops on the right. News from the West also good. Nothing from Miles at Harpers Ferry but it is believed that he still holds out.

Returned to the Department, closed the business of the day, and went home. Eliot, Tabor and Harrington dined with me. After dinner, rode with Harrington. Stopped at Mr. Cutts, to enquire for Mrs. Douglas—glad to hear she was better. Stopped also at War Department. No further news. Stanton thinks Halleck begins to realize his mistake. Said he intended to make Birney Major-General, but Halleck (or rather McClellan) had designated Stoneman.[66] Told him

---

65. Apparently the battle of South Mountain, fought on Sept. 14.
66. Brig. Gen. George Stoneman (1822–94), future governor of California, promoted to major general and given command of the 3rd Corps in Nov. *Appletons'*, 5:706; *DAB*, 18:92.

that Birney had sent his letter of resignation to me, but I had declined to present it. Nothing new from the army, except report from Operator at Point of Rocks of firing apparently between that place and Harpers Ferry—which may indicate Franklin or Miles in that position. Nothing from McClellan since noon.

Dropped Harrington at Ebbitt House,[67] and called on General Schenck at Willards. Helped dressed his wound which looked very bad, but the surgeons say he is improving rapidly and will be able to sit up in two or three days.[68] His daughter is with him, and most assiduous and devoted.

Home. Friend Butler and Benedict called, wishing to be introduced to the President, in order to present Petition for exemption of society from draft. Promised to go with them, or write note, tomorrow morning.— Gov Boutwell called and we talked of Tax Law, Stamp distribution, etc.

TUESDAY, SEPT. 16. Bannister at breakfast. Went to Department, and from Department with deputation of Friends from Mt. Pleasant, O., and Wilmington, Del., to the President and introduced them.— Asked, for Bishop McIlvaine, the appointment of Revd. Mr. Tolford as Chaplain at Camp Chase—which the President directed.[69]

Went to Navy Department and advised Expedition up the James River; and said if Gen Wool or other good General could be sent I would go myself as Volunteer Aid. Mr. Welles seemed pleased with the idea; and said the "Ironsides" and "Passaic" would be ready by the time troops could be, and might take Richmond as preliminary to Charleston.— Spoke to the Secretary of Commodore Barbhead's remark to Harrington, that the Government ought to be superseded by McClellan.[70]— Went to War Department / Surrender of Harpers Ferry is confirmed. McClellan's victory of Sunday was probably over the rear of Longstreet's Division, which made a stand.[71]

Weed called with Morgan,[72] who wished to enquire about Texas Bonds issued under authority of the Rebel Government. Told him

---

67. On F North, between 13th and 14th West. *Wash. Dir. (1862)*, 76.

68. Schenck had been wounded in the right wrist during the Second Battle of Bull Run. *DAB*, 16:428.

69. David Wilson Tolford (d. 1875), a chaplain in Iowa's 10th Vol. Inf., was actually requesting an appointment to Camp Dennison, in Hamilton County, Ohio. Heitman, *Historical Register*, 1:964, 2:495; Tolford to R. G. Corwin, Aug. 5, 1862 (Chase Papers, L.C.).

70. According to Gideon Welles, the conversation actually referred to comments made by John Pine Bankhead (1821–67), commander of the USS *Monitor*. *Appletons'*, 1:158; Beale, *Diary of Gideon Welles*, 1:131.

71. James Longstreet (1821–1904) was at this time major general in the Confederate army. *DAB*, 11:391–93.

72. Edwin Denison Morgan (1811–83), Republican governor of New York, 1859–62; major general of volunteers, 1861–63; and U.S. senator, 1863–69. *DAB*, 13: 168–69.

September 1862 { 391 }

they would not be recognized and promised him copies of papers relating to the subject, from files and records of the Department. Told Weed that we must have decided action and that he could ensure it. Was going to Meeting of Heads of Department, not to Cabinet. Went over to White House. Met Seward, who said the President was busy with Gen Halleck and there would be no meeting.

Returned to Department. Rode out to Sigel's Camp, by way of Chain Bridge, with Harrington and Dr. Schmidt.[73] Saw Sigel and Schurz.[74] They want to have corps organized for operations in the field. Sigel said scouts returned from Drainesville report large rebel force at Leesburgh.

Home to late dinner—Harrington with me. Sent message to War Department for news. Nothing of importance.

WEDNESDAY, SEPT. 17, 1862. Bannister breakfasted with me.— At Department finished Proclamation declaring States in insurrection, without the exceptions formerly made, with view to taking exclusive control of all purchases of cotton, sugar, tobacco and rice in insurgent States

Judge Hoadley came.[75] Went to War Department with him. Stanton promised the Generals he wanted, but could promise nothing else.— Went also to Genl. Halleck's. Found the President and Reverdy Johnson there, talking with a Union Captain who was at Harpers Ferry at the time of its surrender. Says Maryland Heights were surrendered to the surprise of every one; that Miles was struck by a shell after surrender of the post, just as he had put the white flag in the hands of an orderly,—that there was no necessity whatever for the surrender, and that the officers were very indignant.

Warrants to-day enormous—over $4.000.000—and unpaid Requisitions still accumulating—now over $40.000.000. Where will this end?

Gen Hunter came to dine with me. Expressed his decided opinion that if his Order had not been revoked, he would now have had the whole coast lined with disciplined loyal Southern men—black, to be sure, but good soldiers and true.[76]

---

73. German-American politician and editor Franz Sigel (1824–1902), served as major general of volunteers in the Army of the Potomac. Chain Bridge crossed the Potomac four miles above Washington. *DAB*, 17:153–54; Keim, *Washington and Its Environs*, 53.

74. At this time a brigadier general of volunteers, German-born Carl Schurz (1829–1906) was an editor and orator; former U.S. minister to Spain; and Republican senator from Missouri, 1869–75. *DAB*, 16:466–70.

75. George Hoadly, Jr.

76. Regarding Gen. David Hunter's attempt to emancipate slaves under his jurisdiction in the Department of the South, see entries for May 16 and Sept. 13, 1862, above.

FRIDAY, SEPT 19   Recd letter from Robt. Dale Owen (addressed to the President) eloquently urging General Emancipation;[77] which I handed to the President at Cabinet.[78]

—Stanton showed me Halleck's telegram to McClellan, dated Aug. 31, which was substantially as follows:—

"I do not know the terms of Order. I expected to leave you in full command, except of troops temporarily detached to Pope. I beg you to come up and give me the benefit of your talents, experience and judgment at this critical moment. Am completely tired out."[79]

This telegram announced the surrender of Halleck to McClellan. It saddens me to think that a Commander in Chief, whose opinion of his subordinate's military conduct is such as I have heard Halleck express of McClellan's, should, in a moment of pressure, so yield to that very subordinate. Good may come of it, but my fears are stronger than my hopes. How differently old Gen. Scott would have acted! When up all night at the critical period immediately following the first Battle of Bull Run, he was never heard to complain of being "completely tired out", or known to try to shift any part of his responsibility upon another.

SATURDAY, SEPT. 20.   Katie came home this morning, looking very well.— Nothing of special importance in any Department.— Mr. Garrett called expressing great uneasiness about the B. and O. R.R., and the probable invasion of Western Virginia if the enemy is not followed up.— Genl. Mason dined with me. He is extremely anxious to have a trial in the case of Rodney Mason, who was lately

---

77. Owen gave practical, legal, and constitutional arguments in favor of general emancipation and enclosed a draft proclamation. He addressed the letter to Lincoln, but left it unsealed and sent it to Chase, with whom he had corresponded about the emancipation issue. Chase, following Owen's instructions, showed the letter to Stanton before closing it and handing it to the president. A copy of the appeal to Lincoln appeared in the *New York Daily Tribune*, Oct. 23, 1862. Owen to Lincoln, Sept. 17, 1862 (Lincoln Papers, L.C.); Owen to Chase, Sept. 12, 15, 17, 23, 1862, and Chase to Owen, Sept. 20, 1862 (Chase Papers, Hist. Soc. of Pa.).

78. In the original, the entry for Sept. 19 breaks off at this point, with a note by the clerk indicating that the remainder of the entry is located twelve pages farther along, between the entries for Sept. 22–23. The splitting of the Sept. 19 entry may indicate that it was recorded after the entries for Sept. 20–22, the clerk beginning the entry for the nineteenth on available space below the end of Sept. 17 and continuing on the next available full page. The Sept. 19 entry has been consolidated here.

79. Chase paraphrases the telegram, which Halleck sent immediately after John Pope's defeat at the Second Battle of Bull Run. McClellan had complained that a War Department order of Aug. 30 left him in actual command of only a tiny contingent of men. *OR*, ser. 1, v. 2, pt. 1:102–3.

dismissed the service for the surrender of Clarksville.— Received letter from Mr. Hamilton. He will come on Monday to see the President about Proclamation.

Received a letter from Miss Virginia Smith, asking my interest for Col. Bulow's appointment as Brigadier; to which I replied that I would say a good word for the Colonel, and thought the prospect not desperate as no man is safe, now-a-days, from being made a Brigadier—not even a man of merit.

SUNDAY, SEPT. 21. At home to-day, under orders from Dr. F.[80]— Mr. Montgomery of Philadelphia dined with us.— Called on Harrington, to have Dr. F. go to see Gen. Hooker, if possible. Harrington made arrangements.— Towards sundown, called at Mrs. C's. to enquire for Mrs. D.,[81] and was much gratified to find her so far recovered as to be in the parlor.— Mr. Montgomery went to church with Katie.— Bannister, Taylor[82] and others called.— Dr. F. spoke of having been to the President's, who, being very busy writing, could not see him.

Thought to myself, "Possibly engaged on Proclamation"

MONDAY, SEPT. 22D., 1862 To Department about nine. State Department messenger came, with notice to Heads of Departments to meet at 12.— Received sundry callers.— Went to White House.

All the members of the Cabinet were in attendance. There was some general talk; and the President mentioned that Artemus Ward[83] had sent him his book. Proposed to read a chapter which he thought very funny. Read it, and seemed to enjoy it very much— the Heads also (except Stanton) of course. The Chapter was "High-handed Outrage at Utica"[84]

The President then took a graver tone and said:—

"Gentlemen; I have, as you are aware, thought a great deal about the relation of this war to Slavery; and you all remember that, several weeks ago, I read to you an Order I had prepared on this subject, which, on account of objections made by some of you, was not issued. Ever since then, my mind has been much occupied with this subject, and I have thought all along that the time for acting

80. Cincinnatian Samuel W. Forsha, a manufacturer of family medicines. Sept. 23, 1862, below; Chase to Abraham Lincoln, Sept. 28, 1862 (Chase Papers, L.C.); *Cinc. Dir. (1862)*, 138.
81. Mrs. Cutts and Mrs. Douglas.
82. Probably Maj. David Taylor.
83. The pen-name of U.S. humorist Charles Farrar Browne (1834–67). *DAB*, 3:162–64.
84. This sentence is an insertion in Chase's hand. The chapter appeared in *Artemus Ward His Book* (New York, 1862), 34–35.

on it might very probably come. I think the time has come now. I wish it were a better time. I wish that we were in a better condition. The action of the army against the rebels has not been quite what I should have best liked. But they have been driven out of Maryland, and Pennsylvania is no longer in danger of invasion. When the rebel army was at Frederick, I determined, as soon as it should be driven out of Maryland, to issue a Proclamation of Emancipation such as I thought most likely to be useful. I said nothing to any one; but I made the promise to myself, and (hesitating a little)—to my Maker. The rebel army is now driven out, and I am going to fulfil that promise. I have got you together to hear what I have written down. I do not wish your advice about the main matter—for that I have determined for myself. This I say without intending any thing but respect for any one of you. But I already know the views of each on this question. They have been heretofore expressed, and I have considered them as thoroughly and carefully as I can. What I have written is that which my reflections have determined me to say. If there is anything in the expressions I use, or in any other minor matter, which anyone of you thinks had best be changed, I shall be glad to receive the suggestions. One other observation I will make. I know very well that many others might, in this matter, as in others, do better than I can; and if I were satisfied that the public confidence was more fully possessed by any one of them than by me, and knew of any Constitutional way in which he could be put in my place, he should have it. I would gladly yield it to him. But though I believe that I have not so much of the confidence of the people as I had some time since, I do not know that, all things considered, any other person has more; and, however this may be, there is no way in which I can have any other man put where I am. I am here. I must do the best I can, and bear the responsibility of taking the course which I feel I ought to take."

The President then proceeded to read his Emancipation Proclamation, making remarks on the several parts as he went on, and showing that he had fully considered the whole subject, in all the lights under which it had been presented to him.

After he had closed, Gov. Seward said: "The general question having been decided, nothing can be said further about that. Would it not, however, make the Proclamation more clear and decided, to leave out all reference to the act being sustained during the incumbency of the present President; and not merely say that the Government 'recognizes', but that it will maintain, the freedom it proclaims?"

I followed, saying: "What you have said, Mr. President, fully satisfies me that you have given to every proposition which has been made, a kind and candid consideration. And you have now expressed the conclusion to which you have arrived, clearly and distinctly. This it was your right, and under your oath of office your duty, to do. The Proclamation does not, indeed, mark out exactly the course I should myself prefer. But I am ready to take it just as it is written, and to stand by it with all my heart. I think, however, the suggestions of Gov. Seward very judicious, and shall be glad to have them adopted."

The President then asked us severally our opinions as to the modifications proposed, saying that he did not care much about the phrases he had used. Everyone favored the modification and it was adopted. Gov. Seward then proposed that in the passage relating to colonization, some language should be introduced to show that the colonization proposed was to be only with the consent of the colonists, and the consent of the States in which colonies might be attempted. This, too, was agreed to; and no other modification was proposed. Mr. Blair then said that the question having been decided, he would make no objection to issuing the Proclamation; but he would ask to have his paper, presented some days since, against the policy, filed with the Proclamation. The President consented to this readily. And then Mr. Blair went on to say that he was afraid of the influence of the Proclamation on the Border States and on the Army, and stated at some length the grounds of his apprehensions. He disclaimed most expressly, however, all objection to emancipation *per se,* saying he had always been personally in favor of it—always ready for immediate Emancipation in the midst of Slave States, rather than submit to the perpetuation of the system.

After this matter was over, I stated to the Cabinet that it had been strongly recommended that all Cotton, Sugar, Tobacco and Rice should henceforward be purchased only by Government officers, paying to the owners, loyal or disloyal, a certain proportion of the price in New-York amounting to nearly or quite the full price in the producing States; and giving a Certificate which would entitle the owner to the remainder of the proceeds, deducting taxes and charges, at the end of the rebellion, if loyal. Having made this statement, I said I would like to have the matter reflected on, and that I should bring it up at our next meeting.

Before going to Cabinet, and on my walk to Mr. Seward's room, I met Judge Pierrepont, and invited him to dinner. Coming from Cabinet, I found a letter from Barney about Wadsworth's nomination and Weed's willingness to make it unanimous, if it is not to be considered as a triumph over him;[85] and wrote a note to the General, asking him also to dine. Both he and the Judge came, and

---

85. Chase may refer to a letter from Hiram Barney dated Sept. 15, 1862 (Chase Papers, Hist. Soc. of Pa.).

we had a pleasant time. Wadsworth had but one objection to saying he would be Governor, if at all, of the State and not of a section of a party; which was, that it might be considered as in some sort a pledge, which he would not give to anybody. Told Wadsworth, in confidence, that the Proclamation might be expected tomorrow morning—which surprised and gratified him equally.

Mr. Smith, Chief-Clerk of the Third Auditor's Office; his brother, associated with Fowler;[86] and Dr. Schmidt, called. Also Donn Piatt. A good deal of speculation about Proclamation, of which some said a rumor was current a day or two since. I said I thought we need not despair of one yet. Chief Clerk Smith said he had eagerly looked at the newspapers one morning lately, on the strength of the rumor, for it, and was really disappointed. I told him to keep looking.

Donn Piatt wanted young Esté made Clerk.[87] Told him I would be glad to do so, but could not promise. Mr. Platt called to learn about Col Hays, and Dr. Harkness about his son-in-law.[88]

TUESDAY, SEPT. 23, 1862 At breakfast this morning, I proposed to Katie to ride over to the Insane Asylum and see Genl. Hooker, to which she agreed; and she having provided a basket of grapes, peaches, &c., we went. We were very kindly received by Mrs. Nichols, who ushered us into the General's room.[89] He was lying on a couch, but suffering no pain. He talked very freely, as far as time would permit, of the recent events. He said that at Richmond, when the order came to withdraw the army, he advised McClellan to disobey,

---

86. Delano T. Smith of Minnesota was chief clerk in the third auditor's office. In Sept. 1863 he became a U.S. direct tax commissioner for Tennessee. Austin Fowler worked in the office of First Auditor Thomas L. Smith. *Register of Officers (1863)*, 24; *New York Daily Tribune*, Sept. 14, 1863; *Letter of the Secretary of the Treasury, Communicating . . . Officers Appointed . . . for the Collection of Direct Taxes in Insurrectionary Districts . . .* , 38th Cong., 1st sess., 1864, S. Ex. Doc. 35, 3; Fowler to Chase, Oct. 7, 1862 (Chase Papers, L.C.).

87. Possibly Lt. William Miller Este (d. 1900), of Ohio's 26th Vol. Inf., or David K. Este, Jr., an aide to Gen. John McAllister Schofield. Both were sons of Cincinnati's David K. Este. Heitman, *Historical Register*, 1:408; Landy, *Cincinnati Past and Present*, 25.

88. In the original journal, the last three paragraphs of the Sept. 19 entry intervene between the entries for Sept. 22–23. William A. Platt of Columbus, Ohio, was the brother-in-law of Rutherford Birchard Hayes (1822–93), future president of the U.S. Hayes, lieutenant colonel of the 23rd Ohio Vol. Inf., had been wounded at the battle of South Mountain in mid-Sept. Lamon G. Harkness had four sons-in-law: Henry M. Flagler (1830–1913), a founder, with John D. Rockefeller, of the Standard Oil Company; D. M. Harkness; Cleveland businessman G. S. Wheaton; and B. H. York. Charles Richard Williams, ed., *Diary and Letters of Rutherford Birchard Hayes . . .* (Columbus, 1922), 2:199; *DAB*, 8:446–51; Heitman, *Historical Register*, 1:515; Williams, *History of the Fire Lands*, 415.

89. Ellen G. Maury Nichols (d. 1872) was the wife of Charles Henry Nichols, M.D. (1820–89), superintendent of the hospital at the Washington Asylum, corner of 19th East and C South. *DAB*, 13:489; *Wash. Dir. (1863)*, 298.

and proposed a plan for an advance on Richmond. McClellan gave him the order to advance, but before the time for movement came recalled it, and gave orders for evacuation. When Hooker expected to march to Richmond, therefore, he found himself, to his surprise, compelled to fall back to the Chickahominy on his way to Aquia. I said to him, "General, if my advice had been followed, you would have commanded after the retreat to James River[90] if not before"— He replied, "If I had commanded, Richmond would have been ours".— He then spoke of the Battle of Antietam, where he received his wound, and expressed his deep sorrow that he could not remain on on the field three hours longer. "If I could have done so", he said, "our victory would have been complete; for I had already gained enough and seen enough to make the rout of the enemy sure." After he had been carried off, he said, McClellan sent for him again to lead an advance. The General impressed me favorably, as a frank, manly, brave and energetic soldier, of somewhat less breadth of intellect than I had expected, however, though not of less quickness, clearness & activity[91]

While we were conversing, Dr. Nichols came in and I had some talk with him in an adjoining room. He said the General's wound was as little dangerous as a foot-wound could be, the ball having passed through the fleshy part just above the sole and below the instep, probably without touching a bone. I suggested the trial of Dr. Forshés Balm. He made no special objection, but said the wound was doing as well as possible, without inflamation and with very little matter; and he thought it unnecessary to try any experiments. I could not help concurring in this, and postponed Dr. F. and his Balm.— The Doctor said he first knew him when encamped below him last year; that he became deeply interested in him; that when he heard he was wounded, he went up to Frederick, seeking him; that he missed him; but that his message reached him, and he came down to the Asylum himself. I asked, "What is your estimate of him?"— "Brave, energetic, full of life, skilful on the field, not comprehensive enough, perhaps, for plan and conduct of a great campaign; but at least equal in this respect, if not superior, to any General in the service.

Mr. Rives (of the Globe) his daughter and son-in-law came in and we took our leave;[92] Dr. Nichols having first strongly recommended

---

90. *To James River* is an insertion, possibly by Chase.
91. The word *energetic* in this sentence is Chase's insertion, in a space left by the clerk. The last part of the sentence, beginning with the comma after *however*, is also Chase's insertion.
92. John Cook Rives (1795–1864), publisher of the *Congressional Globe*, had two daughters: Caroline, the wife of Samuel T. Williams of Prince Georges County, Md.,

to me to secure the appointment of Col. Dwight, of Mass., as a Brigadier-General.[93]

Returned home and went to Department. Found Genl. Robinson, of Pittsburgh,[94] there: and Mr. Platt and Dr. Harkness. Got Harrington to go with P. & H. to War Department.— Mr. Welles came in, about appointment of Pease, in Wisconsin,[95] and I asked him to write a note about it.— Attorney-General Bates called, with Mr. Gibson of St. Louis, about pecuniary aid to Gov. Gamble[96]—both telling a very different story from Farrar and Dick.[97] Promised to look at papers and answer tomorrow.— Stanton came in about payment of paroled soldiers at Camp Chase, which I promised to provide for. Said that he proposed to make the Department of Florida, with Thayer as Governor and Garfield as Commanding General, if I approved of Garfield.[98] I said I approved heartily. Said he had insisted on removal of Buell, and leaving Thomas[99] in command. I could not disapprove of this, though I think less highly of him than he seems to think.— He went, and Barney came in / Asked him to dine. Declined, but promised to call in the evening.— Mr. Hamilton, on invitation, came to our house to stay while in town.

In the evening, many callers—Miss Schenck,[1] Genl. and Mrs. McDowell, Genl. Garfield, and others. Young Mr. Walley came, with letters from his father, and I brought him in and introduced him to Katie and our guests.[2]

---

and Lucy, whose spouse is unknown. James Rives Childs, *Reliques of the Rives...* (Lynchburg, Va., 1929), 388; *DAB*, 15:635.

93. William Dwight (1831–88), a native of Massachusetts, became brigadier general of the 70th New York Volunteers in Nov. *Appletons'*, 2:280; *DAB*, 5:578.

94. Jesse H. Robinson, an officer in the U.S. military telegraph service. *History of Pittsburgh and Environs* (New York, 1922), 244.

95. J. J. R. Pease, a resident of Janesville, Wis., and a political associate of Gideon Welles. Beale, *Diary of Gideon Welles*, 2:398, 3:639.

96. Charles Gibson (1825–99) was U.S. solicitor for the court of claims. Hamilton Rowan Gamble (1798–1864) served as Unionist governor after secessionist officials fled Missouri in June 1861. *DAB*, 7:120–21; *Nat. Cyc.*, 5:114–15.

97. Benjamin Farrar, assistant U.S. treasurer at St. Louis, and Lt. Col. Franklin A. Dick, provost marshal general of the Department of Missouri. Basler, *Collected Works*, 6:8; *Register of Officers (1863)*, 33.

98. Educator and reform politician Eli Thayer (1819–99) was a U.S. Treasury agent, 1861–62, and promoted military colonization in Florida. He did not become governor of a Department of Florida, nor James A. Garfield its commanding general. Thayer was a railroad land agent in New York, 1864–70. *DAB*, 18:402–3.

99. George H. Thomas.

1. Probably a daughter of Robert Cumming Schenck.

2. Henshaw Bates Walley, the son of Samuel H. Walley, was conducting a campaign, ultimately successful, for appointment as paymaster in the U.S. Army. Chase to E. M. Stanton, Oct. 4, 1862 (Chase Papers, Hist. Soc. of Pa.); Heitman, *Historical Register*, 1:999; H. B. Walley to S. H. Walley, Oct. 10, 1863 (Chase Papers, L.C.).

WEDNESDAY, SEPT. 24. The President called a special meeting of the Cabinet to-day, and asked our judgments on two questions:

First, as to the expediency of Treaties with Governments desiring their immigration, for voluntary colonization of blacks.

Second, As to the proper answer to be returned to the letter from John Ross, excusing the Treaty of the Cherokees with the Rebels, and asking the protection of the United States and the fulfilment of old Treaties.[3]

On the first question, there was the usual diversity of opinion. I, not thinking Colonization in itself desirable, except as a means of getting a foothold in Central America, thought no Treaties expedient; but simple arrangements, under the legislation of Congress, by which any persons who might choose to emigrate would be secured in such advantages as might be offered them by other States or Governments. Seward rather favored Treaties, but evidently did not think much of the wisdom of any measures for sending out of the country laborers needed here. The President asked us to think of the subject, and be ready to express our opinions when we next come together.

As to the Cherokee question there seemed to be a general concurrence that no new pledges should be given them, but that, at the end of the war, their condition and relations to the United States should have just consideration.

After Cabinet, went with Stanton to War Department, and laid before him sundry applications for positions, with such verbal support as I thought due to them. Returning to the Department, I found there young Mr. Walley, and gave him an earnest recommendation to Stanton; and was surprised, an hour or so after, to receive a note from him, thanking me for my kindness, but saying that Mr. Stanton told him there was no likelihood of his receiving an appointment; and that he was going to enlist as a private. Wrote note to Mr. Walley (his father) expressing my regret.

Nothing at Department but routine—except direction to Cisco to receive deposits of Gold,[4] and a call from Eli Thayer about his project for colonizing East Florida, with which I sympathize.

---

3. In a letter to Lincoln on Sept. 16, Chief John Ross (1790–1866) claimed that U.S. unwillingness to afford protection under existing treaty obligations had encouraged the Cherokee Nation to sign its Oct. 1861 pact with the Confederacy. In his reply on Sept. 25, Lincoln offered to study the matter and, meanwhile, to extend U.S. protection to "Cherokee people remaining practically loyal to the federal Union." *DAB*, 16:178–79; Ross to Lincoln, Sept. 16, 1862, Lincoln to Ross, Sept. 25, 1862, in Basler, *Collected Works*, 5:439–40; entry for Aug. 3, 1862, above.

4. Chase instructed Cisco to receive deposits of gold at 4 percent. Chase to Cisco, Sept. 23, 1862 (Loan Division, Letters Sent, Recs. of Bureau of Public Debt, Nat. Arch.).

Had proposed to Gen. Garfield to take him over and call on Genl. Hooker but it rained and he did not come. After dinner, however, the sky cleared somewhat and Katie and I rode out and called on him. He was still improving.

An hour or two after our return, a band of music, which had just serenaded the President by way of congratulation on the Proclamation, came to my house and demanded a speech—with which demand, I complied briefly. Gen. Clay, who was with me, responded more at length.[5] After the crowd had passed on, Gen. Clay; Mr Clarke, of Mercer, Penna.; Genl. Robinson, of Pittsburgh; and Mr. Wm. D. Lewis, of Philadelphia, came in and spent a little time with me.[6]

THURSDAY, SEPT. 25. At Department as usual. The President sent for me to meet the Secretary of War. Found he had nothing to talk about except the supply of an additional sum to Gov. Gamble, of Missouri, to be used in defending the State against invasion and guerillaism. Agreed to confer with the Secretary of War on the subject.— Enquired as to progress of the war. No information, and nothing satisfactory as to what is to be expected. Coming out, Stanton told me that McClellan wants bridges built across the Potomac and Shenandoah, as preliminaries to movement; to which Halleck won't consent. Dan helps Zeke doing nothing.

Delighted this morning by news of Genl Wadsworth's nomination for Governor of New-York, on the first ballot.

In the afternoon, went with Garfield to see Hooker, who was very free in his expressions about McClellan. He said it was not true that either the army or the officers were specially attached to him;—that only two corps, whose commanders were special favorites and whose troops had special indulgences, could be said to care anything about him; that other officers—he himself, certainly—thought him unfit to lead a great army; that he is timid and hesitating when decision is necessary; that the Battle of Antietam was near being lost by his way of fighting it, whereas, had the attack been simultaneous and vigorous on the enemy's right, centre and left, the rout would have been complete; that our force in the battle exceeded the enemy's

---

5. Chase and Cassius M. Clay praised Lincoln's recent decision to issue the Emancipation Proclamation. *Daily National Intelligencer*, Sept. 26, 1862.

6. "Clarke" may have been William F. Clark, appointed to the collectorship of Pennsylvania's twentieth internal revenue district. William David Lewis (1792–1881), a merchant and authority on Russian literature, was collector of the port of Philadelphia, 1849–53. In Journal XI (text below, beginning Sept. 26) a notation for Sept. 24 contains only the names *Hamilton* and *Barney*, followed by two or three illegible words. Chase to Lincoln, Aug. 19, 1862 (Lincoln Papers, L.C.); *Register of Officers (1863)*, 39; *Appletons'*, 3:707.

by 30.000 men, and that the defeat of the enemy should have been final. He said, also, that when Pope had drawn off a large part of the rebels from Richmond and orders came to McClellan to withdraw, he urged him to give, on the contrary, orders for advance; that the orders were actually given and then revoked, much to his chagrin. This recalled to my mind a conversation with Gen Halleck at that time. I said to him, that it seemed to me our people could now certainly take Richmond by a vigorous push, as Pope had 60.000 of the rebels before him, and at least half of the remaining 60.000 were South of the James, leaving only 30.000 with the fortifications on the North side; to which Gen Halleck replied, that it was too dangerous an undertaking. I said, "If this cannot be done, why not return to Fredericksburgh, leaving Richmond on the left?" "This", he said, "would be quite as dangerous—a flank movement, in which our army would be exposed to being cut off and totally lost." Gen Hooker said that the movement I suggested could have been executed with safety and success. He said, also, that he was somewhat reconciled to leaving the Peninsula, by being told that it was a plan for getting rid of McClellan, and the only one which it was thought safe to adopt. This he thought so essential, that anything necessary to it was to be accepted

Returning from Gen Hooker's, as well as going, Genl. Garfield gave me some very interesting portions of his own experience. This fine officer was a laborer on a canal in his younger days. Inspired by a noble ambition, he had availed himself of all means to acquire knowledge—became a Preacher of the Baptist Church—was made the President of a flourishing Literary Institution on the Reserve—was elected to the Ohio Senate, and took a conspicuous part as a Republican leader. On the breaking out of the War he became a Colonel—led his regiment into Eastern Kentucky—fought Humphrey Marshall near Prestonburgh[7]—gained position rapidly—was made, at my instance, a Brigadier—fought under Buell at Shiloh—and was now in Washington by direction of the Secretary of War, who proposes to give him the Department of Florida. A large portion of his Regiment, he said, was composed of students from his College.

Went to Seward's to dinner, where I met the Marquis of Cavendish, and his brother, Col. Leslie of the British Army;[8] Mr. Stuart

---

7. Marshall (1812–72), a former Whig and Know-Nothing congressman from Kentucky, held the rank of brigadier general in the Confederate army. *DAB*, 12:310–11.

8. English politician Spencer Compton Cavendish (1833–1908), the marquis of Hartington and later duke of Devonshire, and his brother Lord Edward Cavendish (1838–91), who was stationed with a British regiment in Canada, had recently

and Mr Kennedy of the British Legation;[9] Genl. Banks, and Mr Everett.[10] Genl Banks earnest against more separation of forces until the rebel army is crushed

Home. Found there Genl. and Mrs McDowell. Soon after, Capt. and Mrs Loomis came in.[11] Could not help the Captain who wished to be Quartermaster of Genl. Sigel's Corps.

To bed, tired and unwell.

JOURNAL XI

SEPT. 26—[12] called on Governors—saw Yates with whom Usher, McClernand, Moses & others— Kirkwood with whom interesting convn.— Solomon at Willard, who said wd. call [tomorrow] at Dept.[13]

JOURNAL X

FRIDAY, SEPT. 26. Received note from Gov. Seward, asking me to name Consul to Rio. Named James Monroe.[14] Another note from Fred Seward asked me to call at State Department before going to Cabinet. Called, but Gov. Seward had already gone.

Went to Cabinet. Talk about Colonization. I said nothing. All the others except Welles (Stanton not present) in favor of treaties

---

embarked on a six-month tour of the United States. Col. Leslie was a member of their party. *DNB*, 2nd supp., 1:323–24; Bernard Holland, *The Life of Spencer Compton, Eighth Duke of Devonshire* (London, 1911), 1:40–54; Washington *Evening Star*, Sept. 26, 1862.

9. John Gordon Kennedy, third secretary of the British Legation. *Wash. Dir. (1863)*, 125.

10. Edward Everett.

11. Possibly M. D. W. Loomis, an assistant quartermaster in the U.S. Army, and his wife. Heitman, *Historical Register*, 1:641.

12. Journal X, in a clerk's hand, and Journal XI, in Chase's hand, correspond closely from Sept. 26 through Oct. 12. In this period, Journal XI probably served as the basis for Journal X, so the Journal XI entry is given first for each day.

13. The Northern governors had completed their famous Altoona, Pa., wartime conference on Sept. 22. Chase saw Richard Yates (1815–73), Republican governor and later U.S. senator from Illinois; John Palmer Usher; John Alexander McClernand (1812–1900), former Democratic congressman from Illinois and Union general, 1861–64; attorney John Moses (1825–98), private secretary to Yates, 1861–63; Samuel Jordan Kirkwood (1813–94), Republican governor and later U.S. senator from Iowa; and Edward Salomon (1830–1909), Republican governor of Wisconsin. *DAB*, 10:436–37, 11:587–88, 20:599–601; *Nat. Cyc.*, 12:75; Newton Bateman, Paul Selloy, and J. Seymour Currey, eds., *Historical Encyclopedia of Illinois with Commemorative Biographies*, 2 vols. (Chicago, 1925), 388.

14. Monroe (1821–98), a professor at Oberlin College and an Ohio state legislator, was consul at Rio de Janeiro, 1863–69, and a U.S. congressman, 1871–81. *Appletons'*, 4:358; *Bio. Dir. U.S. Cong.*, 1519; Chase to Seward, Sept. 26, 1862 (Chase Papers, Hist. Soc. of Pa.).

Several of the loyal Governors came to-day, and in the evening I called on them. Saw Yates at the National, and left card for Berry of N.H.— Saw Kirkwood at Kirkwood House.[15]— Saw Salomon at Willard's and left cards for Andrew, Bradford, Sprague, Tod, Blair and Pierpont.[16] At Gov. Yates' room saw Genl. McClernand, of Ills., who made a very favorable impression on me.

JOURNAL XI

SEP. 27— Gov Andrew at bkft— Col Andrews & Lt. [Barber] came in[17]— Andrews said Col Clark killed at Sharpsburg[18]— Gov. A mentd visit to Hooker—Stanton & Tod called on him together— Hooker very [firm] in condn. of McClellans timidity—

At dept. McClernand called—explained his idea of Wn operations— [*illeg.*] called &c

Saw Prest.—asked his opinion of McCd.—thought him brave & capable but too desirous to be indt. of every body else— Telgm. fr Bliss[19]

JOURNAL X

SATURDAY, SEPT. 27. Gov Andrew came to breakfast. Laughed— vexed too—at Report in Herald of proceedings of Governor's at Altoona, which he ascribed to the exclusion of reporters.[20] While at breakfast, Col. Andrews and Lieut. Barber, both of Marietta, came in from battle-ground. The Colonel handed me Cox's Report, and informed me that Col Clark was killed, which left him Lieut.-Colonel in actual command / He gave a very interesting account of the conduct of Cox's (late Reno's) corps, both at South Mountain

---

15. The National Hotel, operated by F. Tenny & Co., was on Pennsylvania Ave. at the corner of 6th West. The Kirkwood House of Alfred W. and John H. Kirkwood stood on the same avenue at 12th West. *Wash. Dir. (1862),* 113.

16. Nathaniel Springer Berry (1796–1894), Republican of New Hampshire; John Albion Andrew (1818–67), Republican of Massachusetts; Augustus Williamson Bradford (1806–81), Unionist of Maryland; William Sprague; David Tod; Austin Blair; and Francis Harrison Pierpont (1814–99), Unionist of the "restored" state of Virginia. *DAB,* 2:227–28, 279–81, 2:553–55, 14:584–85.

17. Probably Ebenezer B. Andrews and 1st Lt. Levi Barber, a regimental quartermaster who later became a provost marshal in the U.S. Army. U.S. Adjutant-General's Office, *Official Army Register of the Volunteer Force of the United States* (Washington, D.C., 1865–67), 5:108; *OR,* ser. 3, v. 5:902.

18. Melvin Clarke (d. 1862), 36th Ohio Infantry. Reid, *Ohio in the War,* 2:231.

19. George Bliss.

20. The New York *Herald* depicted the meeting as a secretive assembly, with John A. Andrew as one of several participants intent on removing McClellan, "superseding the President, and making Frémont the 'great man.'" *Herald,* Sept. 25, 1862.

and Antietam.[21] The Reports, however, were more full, and reflected the highest credit on Cox and the officers and men of his troops. Andrews said that McClellan and Burnside would recommend Cox for Major-General—an object which I assured Col. A. I would most gladly promote.

Gov Andrew said he had called on Gen. Hooker the evening before, and met Stanton and Tod. Hooker was unequivocal in condemnation of McClellan's inactivity. At Department, McClernand called and my favorable impression of last evening was strengthened. Many things in a plan of campaign which he urged seemed admirable, especially the Eastern movement from the Mississippi River.

Saw the President, and asked him his opinion of McClernand. Said he thought him brave and capable, but too desirous to be independent of every body else.

Later in the day, received telegram from Bliss, Paymaster General of New-York, asking for $300.000 in small notes in exchange for the same amount of large ones to enable him to forward eight regiments. It occurred to me that, by having these regiments sent to Louisville and Mitchell's and Garfield's brigades brought from Louisville and sent to Port Royal, with one or two brigades in addition, a successful expedition against Charleston might be immediately organized; and I determined to speak to Stanton in relation to it tomorrow. Garfield spent the evening with me and accepted invitation to make my house his home while in town.

[The Chapter in Artemus Ward's Book, read by the President as introductory to his Proclamation, was "Highhanded Outrage in Utica."][22]

JOURNAL XI

SEPT. 28 SUN— At Dr. Pynes' morning[23]—excellent Sermon— home afternoon—evg. went to War Dt. abt. expedition to Charleston— My idea to have the new N.Y rgts. sent to Louisville Mitchels & Garfields Brigades brought to N.Y.—another or two added forthwith & all sent to [Port] Royal with Gd. & immediate attack on Chn. wh. sure to fall—did not find Stanton at Dt. went to Hallecks—fd. [him there] had some general talk—infd by H—— that Enemy mov-

---

21. After the death of Jesse Lee Reno on Sept. 14, Burnside's 9th Corps was briefly commanded by Jacob Dolson Cox (1828–1900), a former Ohio state legislator; brigadier, later major general, of volunteers, 1861–66; governor of Ohio, 1866–68; secretary of the interior, 1869–70. *DAB*, 4:476–78, 15:504.

22. This note by the copyist refers to Sept. 22, where Chase made his own insertion to this effect.

23. St. John's Episcopal Church, under the care of the Rev. Smith Pyne. *Wash. Dir. (1862)*, 145, 255.

ing to Martinsburgh—how many? 150000—how many McC—— abt. 1[0]0.000— where Pa troops said to have joined him though raised only for emergency? "all gone back"—talk abt draft— H—— showed [the] letter to Gamble insisting that all officers of drafted militia above regimental shd. be appd. by Prest.— I expressed opinion that principle of drafting [mil. an error]— Law shd. have provided for drafting from the people for an army of U.S.—he agreed—askd. his opinion of McClernand—he said he is brave, & capable, but no disciplinarian—his camp always full of disorder—at Corinth he pitched his tents where his men had buried our dead just below the ground & with dead horses lying all round—[when] disease [*two words illeg.*]—witht. effort to bury the horses— The cause of the evil was that officers & men were his constituents— Leaving Halleck Stanton & I rode together out to Cola. Coll.[24] & back to his house— I stated my wish concerning the two brigades & Charleston—he said nothing cd. be done—the NY regits must go to McClellan—who absorbs & is likely to absorb every thing & do nothing— At Stantons saw for first time Gen. Harney,[25] who mentioned several circumstances to show Frank Blairs['] misconduct in Mo. matters[—]said it was not [a necy] to have fired a gun to keep Mo. in the Union— I thot the General [entirely] mistaken.

JOURNAL X

SUNDAY, SEPT. 28. At Dr. Pyne's in morning—sermon excellent. Home in afternoon. In the evening went to War Department, about Expedition to Charleston; my idea being to have New York regiments sent to Louisville, and Mitchell's and Garfield's brigades withdrawn thence and sent to Port Royal with Garfield; when an immediate attack should be made on Charleston which would be sure to fall. Did not find Stanton at Department. Went to Halleck's and found him there. Had some general talk. Was informed by Halleck that the enemy was moving to Martinsburg. "How many?"— "150.000." "How many has McClellan?"— "About 100.000."— "Where Pennsylvania troops, said to have joined him though raised only for emergency?" "All gone back".— Had talk about draft. He showed me a letter to Gamble, insisting that all officers of drafted militia above Regimental[26] should be appointed by the President. I expressed the opinion that the principle

---

24. Columbian College. *Wash. Dir. (1863)*, 296.
25. Brig. Gen. William Selby Harney (1800–1889) commanded the Department of the West, 1859–61. *DAB*, 8:280–81.
26. Originally *Sergeants*. The word has been struck through and *Regimental* inserted above, possibly by Chase. Journal XI for this date (above) has *regimental*. It is likely that *Sergeants* was the clerk's misreading of Chase's draft.

of drafting militia was erroneous—that the law should have provided for drafting from the people an army of the United States. He agreed.— I asked him his opinion of McClernand. He said he is brave and able but no disciplinarian; that his camp was always full of disorder; that at Corinth he pitched his tents where his men had been buried just below ground, and with dead horses lying all around. The cause of the evil was that his officers and men were his constituents.

Leaving Halleck, Stanton and I rode together to Columbia College and back to his house. I stated my wish concerning the two brigades and Charleston. He said nothing could be done. The New-York Regiments must go to McClellan, who absorbs and is likely to absorb everything and do nothing. At Stanton's saw, for the first time, Genl. Harney who mentioned several circumstances to show Frank Blairs' misconduct in Missouri matters. He said it was not necessary to fire a gun to keep Missouri in the Union. I thought him evidently mistaken.[27]

JOURNAL XI

SEP 30. TUES. Papers this morng confirm news of Nelsons death—he died as the fool dieth—how sad![28] His early services to the Union cause in Ky,—his generous & manly nature,—his fine talents & great energy,—compelled my admiration & esteem—while his cruelty & passion & tyranny especially when excited by drink often excited my indignation[—] Nothing from any quarter of much importance in a military point of view

Gen. Garfield at breakfast related this— When Gen Buells army was on the march to Nashville a regiment passed in front of the house of Gen Pillows brother, where was a spring of good water & a little stream issuing from it[29]— As the soldiers quenched their thirst &, filled their canteens & watered their horses at the stream, Pillow came out & cursed the men, forbidding them to take water and saying if he were younger he would fight against the Yankees till the last man of them was killed or driven home. A Lieut commanding the company then passing expostulated with him without effect & finding the army likely to be delayed by his interference

---

27. In Journal XI, Chase made a heading for Monday, Sept. 29, as if he intended to make an entry for that day, but the rest of the page is blank.

28. William Nelson (1824–62), Kentucky Unionist and brigadier general of volunteers, had died on Sept. 29 as the result of an altercation in Louisville with Brig. Gen. Jefferson C. Davis, one of his subordinates. *DAB*, 13:426.

29. Probably the house of Jerome Pillow, near Columbia, Tenn. *Nat. Cyc.*, 9:279; *OR*, ser. 1, v. 16, pt. 2:107, 183.

directed him to be put under arrest & sent him to the Colonel. It happened that this Colonel was an admirer of Miss Stevenson a young lady of Nashville, a niece of Pillow & a violent secessionist & had been in the habit of sending the regimental band to serenade her, with Dixie & the like, not playing any National Airs. As soon as he understood who Pillow was therefore he discharged him from arrest and apologized for it. At the same time he ordered the young lieut under arrest. Pillow returned to his house—mounted his horse—& rode to Gen. Buells Head Quarters & complained that a slave of his had escaped & was somewhere in the army. Buell gave him leave to hunt for him & with this warrant he rode where he pleased. After fully satisfying himself he went on to Corinth & gave Beauregard[30] an exact account of Buells force and rate of advance. This information led to the attack on Grants division which Beauregard hoped to destroy before Buell should come & almost succeeded in doing it[.]

At Department nothing unusual in the business—recd. note from Sew with mem by Stuart, Actg Bh. Minister of conversations with Seward abt. cotton fr. wh it appears that Butlers order of Aug. authg. free purchases even from Slidell & Grant's order annulling Sherman's prohibition of payments in gold were if not motived[31] by Seward fully approved by him & made the basis of assurances that no hindrance to purchase & payment for cotton fr rebels wd. be interposed by this govt.[32]— Aftwds or abt. the time of these orders Seward proposed the same general policy of substantially unrestricted purchase for money to me & I was at first, in view of the importance of a supply of cotton inclined to adopt it: but reflection & infn. from Special Agents in Mi. Valley changed my views. The subject was also bro't up in cabinet & Seward proposed liberty to purchase 500.000 bales. Stanton opposed & I & the Prest. sided with us, and the subject was dropped. I then proceeded to

30. Brig. Gen. Pierre Gustave Toutant Beauregard, C.S.A. (1818–93). *DAB*, 2:111–12.

31. Homer Plantz, Chase's amanuensis for Journal X, underlined this word and wrote "139" above it. This section of the Sept. 30 entry appears on p. 139 of the manuscript Journal X.

32. William H. Seward sent Chase a package of papers (evidently including memoranda by British diplomat William Stuart) which concerned exports of cotton and their payment in gold. On July 21, 1862, Benjamin F. Butler had offered assurances of "safe conduct, open market, and prompt shipment" for all merchandise sent to New Orleans, "and the owner, were he Slidell himself, should have the pay for his cotton if sent here under this assurance." Also in July, William Tecumseh Sherman, in an effort to limit the ability of the Confederates to purchase arms and ammunition, prohibited payments in specie. Ulysses S. Grant, in accordance with instructions from the War Department, reversed the order on Aug. 11. Seward to Chase, Sept. 29, 1862 (Letters Received from Executive Officers, Gen. Recs. Treasury Dept., Nat. Arch.); *OR*, ser. 1, v. 17, pt. 2:140–41, 150, 163, ser. 3, v. 2:239.

frame regulations for trade to & from insurrectionary districts in which was included a prohibition of payts in gold

To this prohibition Stuart now objects as a contravention of Sewards assurances connected with Butler's & Grant[']s orders

After considering the whole subject I addressed a letter to Gov Seward declining to change the [*illeg.*] regulation as to gold[33]—

Recd. a letter fr. Mellen stating diff. b. himself and agent Gallagher as to confiscation—he thinking that antecedents of cotton, as to liability to confiscation in prior hands and notice to present hands, shd. not be investigated as a general [*illeg.*]— Gallagher contra— Wrote Mellen that his view is approved, thinking this may relieve Seward[34]—

JOURNAL X

TUESDAY, SEPT. 30. The papers this morning confirm the news of Nelson's death. He died as the fool dieth. How sad! His early services to the Union cause in Kentucky—his generous and manly nature—his fine talents and great energy—compelled my admiration and esteem; while his cruelty and passion and tyranny, especially when excited by drink, often excited my indignation. Nothing from any quarter of much importance in a military point of view.

Genl. Garfield, at breakfast, related this: When Gen. Buell's Army was on the march to Nashville, a Regiment passed in front of the house of Gen Pillow's brother, where was a spring of good water and a little stream issuing from it. As the soldiers quenched their thirst and filled their canteens and watered their horses at the stream, Pillow came out and cursed the men, forbidding them to take water and saying that if he were younger he would fight against the Yankees until the last man of them was killed or driven home. A Lieutenant commanding the Company then having expostulated with him without effect and finding the army likely to be delayed by his interference, directed him to be put under arrest, and sent him to the Colonel. It happened that this Colonel was an admirer of Miss Stevenson—a young lady of Nashville, a niece of Pillow, and a violent Secessionist—and had been in the habit of sending the Regimental Band to serenade her with "Dixie" and the like, not playing any National Airs. As soon as he understood who Pillow was, there-

---

33. Chase revised this letter and sent it the next day; see Oct. 1, below.

34. William P. Mellen's dispute with William Davis Gallagher related to the Confiscation Act of July 17, 1862, which authorized seizure of "all the estate and property, moneys, stocks, and credits" owned by persons "engaged in armed rebellion." *Statutes at Large*, 12:589–92; Chase to Mellen, Oct. 1, 1862 (General Agent, Recs. of Civil War Special Agencies, Nat. Arch.); Mellen to Chase, Sept. 26, 1862 (Misc. Letters, Gen. Recs. State Dept., Nat. Arch.).

fore, he discharged him from arrest and apologized for it; and at the same time arrested the young Lieutenant. Pillow returned to his house, mounted his horse and rode to Genl. Buell's Head Quarters and complained that a slave of his had escaped and was somewhere in the army. Buell gave him leave to hunt for him and with this warrant he rode where he pleased. After fully satisfying himself, he went on to Corinth and gave Beauregard a full account of Buell's force and rate of advance. This information led to the attack on Grant's division, which Beauregard hoped to destroy before Buell should come—and he almost succeeded in doing it.

At Department, received a Note from Seward, with Memorandum by Stuart, Acting British Minister, of Conversations with Seward about cotton. From this Memorandum, it appears the Butler's Order of August authorizing free purchases even from Slidell, and Grant's Order annulling Sherman's prohibition of payments in gold, were, if not motived by Seward, fully approved by him and made the basis of assurances that no hindrance to purchase and payment on cotton from rebels would be interposed by this government. Afterwards, or about the time of these Orders, Seward proposed the same policy of substantially unrestricted purchase for money, to me; and I was at first, in view of the importance of a supply of cotton, inclined to adopt it; but reflection and information from Special Agents in the Mississippi Valley changed my views. The subject was also brought up in Cabinet, and Seward proposed liberty to purchase 500.000 bales. Stanton and I opposed this, and the President sided with us; and the subject was dropped. I then proposed to frame Regulations for trade to and from Insurrectionary Districts, in which was included prohibition of payments in gold.

To this prohibition Stuart now objects, as in contravention of Seward's assurances connected with Butler's and Grant's Orders.

After considering the whole subject, I addressed a letter to Seward declining to change the existing Regulation as to payments in gold.

Received letter from himself, stating difficulty between himself and Agent Gallagher as to Confiscation—Mellen thinking that antecedents of cotton, as to liability to confiscation in prior hands and notice to present holders, should not be investigated; Gallagher contra. Wrote Mellen that his view is approved—thinking this may relieve Seward.

JOURNAL XI

OCT. 1 WED Mr. Seward came to Dept & we talked over foreign relations particularly as connected with cotton— Showed him my reply to his note yesterday—he thought it wd. not answer as his assurances coupled with Butlers & Grants orders committed us too far— I said I wd modify it—after he left altered close of letter & sent it.[35] Examined Regulations concg. trade with blockaded ports & coal orders.

JOURNAL X

WEDNESDAY, OCTO. 1, 1862. Seward came to Department and we talked over foreign relations, particularly as connected with cotton. Showed him my Reply to his Note of yesterday. He thought it would not answer, as his assurances, coupled with Butler's and Grant's Orders, committed us too far. I said I would modify it. After he left, altered my reply and sent it.

Examined Regulations concerning trade with blockaded ports, and War Orders.[36]

JOURNAL XI

OCT. 2—THURS Seward came to my house with letter to Mr. Stuart, vindicating course of ty Dt. concerning Trade orders & regulations— I approved the whole but suggested that as regulations embraced coal order substantially & Gt. Britain took except[ion] to last as particularly intended for her, he might say that to prove the absence of such intention and as a proof of the entire absence of any wish to vex trade the Coal order wd. be rescinded[.][37]

JOURNAL X

THURSDAY, OCTO. 2, 1862. Seward came to my house with Letter to Stuart, vindicating the course of the Treasury Department

---

35. In his letter, Chase justified the restrictions on the use of specie to buy Southern products; maintained that the rule was not intended to stop British firms from buying cotton and other goods, but only to prevent the flow of gold into the Confederacy; and suggested means by which British traders could convert their gold into notes or bills to be used for the purchase of goods in "insurrectionary districts." Chase to Seward, Oct. 1, 1862 (Misc. Letters, Gen. Recs. State Dept., Nat. Arch.).

36. Should be *coal* orders. Apparently the clerk misread Chase's handwriting.

37. On Sept. 25, William Stuart of the British legation in Washington complained of the refusal of Hiram Barney, collector of customs at New York, to clear certain shipments to the Bahama Islands. In a lengthy reply dated Oct. 3, Seward stated that there would be no change in regulations which authorized customs officers to stop shipments or require bonds to prevent contraband from reaching the Confederates through neutral ports. The U.S. did agree, as Chase suggested, to rescind Treasury Department orders of Apr. and May 1862, which had placed additional prohibitions on the export of anthracite coal to Atlantic and Caribbean ports. Seward to Stuart, Oct. 3, 1862 (Notes to Foreign Legations, Gen. Recs. State Dept., Nat. Arch.).

concerning Trade Orders and Regulations. I approved the whole; but suggested that as the Regulations embraced the Coal Order substantially, and as Great Britain took exception to that as particularly intended for her, he might say that, to prove the absence of such intention and as as a proof of the entire absence of any wish to vex trade, the Coal Order would be rescinded.

JOURNAL XI

OCT. 3 FRI   The President still absent at McClellan[']s Army— I expect little good from this visit—

JOURNAL X

FRIDAY, OCTO. 3.   The President still absent at McClellan's Army. I expect little good from this visit

JOURNAL XI

OCT. 4 SAT.   Mr. Harrington left this morng for N. York &c— instructed to hasten increase of issue of Postage Currency: to $100.000 per day— Expects to go in Miami to Boston.

JOURNAL X

SATURDAY, OCTO. 4.   Mr. Harrington left this morning for New-York. He is instructed to hasten increase of issue of Postage Currency to $100.000, per day. Expects to go to Boston in "Miami"

JOURNAL XI

OCT. 5—SUN.—   At home to favor foot—much better in afternoon & rode over to Insane Asylum to see Hooker—glad to find him much improved— He said we had plenty of good officers and that all the courage, ability, & genius we needed to make excellent generals could be found in the Colonels of our volunteer regiments. Mentd. that aid of McClellan had been to see him with McC——s enquiry how soon he wd. be able to take the field, expressing [a] confidence, and hints of important command of army moving from Washington— He expressed the belief that no decisive victory wd. be achieved so long as McClellan had command.

Before starting on this visit John A. Stevens Jr called, wishing me to see Col. Hamilton abt Texas & I asked him to bring him to dinner[38]—

Accg. both came— Secy. Stanton also from accident, & Mr. Montgomery by Katies inn.—

After dinner Col. H—— spoke fully of Texas—described his escape & hiding in the woods—said that many hundred loyal Texans were now concealed in Texas or refugees—declared that the war was a war of the Oligarchy upon the people—that slavery was the base of the Oligarchy but the perpetuation of slavery not their grand object, but despotic power of the class over the mass. I entered fully into his feelings & promised to go with him to the Presidents tomorrow— After he went Gov Morton came in & spoke very earnestly of the condition of matters in Indiana[39]—apprehends state defeat on the 14th and loss of all congl. districts except Julians Colfax's & perhaps Shanks[40] / wants Ia regts in the State furloughed so that they can vote—thinks Buell utterly unfit for command of the great army under him—is slow, opposed to the proclamation, & has bad influence every way—wishes me to go with him to Presidents about regts which I promd. tomorrow morng $9\frac{1}{4}$[41]—

JOURNAL X

SUNDAY, OCTO. 5. At home to favor foot. Much better in the afternoon, and rode over to Insane Asylum to see Hooker / Was glad to find him much improved. He said we had plenty of good officers, and that all the courage, ability and genius we needed could be found among our Volunteer Colonels. He then said that an *aide* of

---

38. Stevens (1827–1910), son of the banker of the same name, was a New York merchant and Republican activist. Texas Unionist Andrew Jackson Hamilton (1815–75) received a commission as brigadier general of volunteers in Nov. 1862 and an appointment as military governor of Texas soon afterward. After the war, he served as provisional governor and state supreme court justice. *Appletons'*, 3:64; *DAB*, 8:182–83, 17:617.

39. Oliver Hazard Perry Throck Morton (1823–77), Republican governor of Indiana, 1861–67, and U.S. senator, 1867–77. *Bio. Dir. U.S. Cong.*, 1542; *DAB*, 13:262–64.

40. Indiana Republicans George Washington Julian (1817–99), in Congress, 1849–51, 1861–71; Schuyler Colfax (1823–85), in Congress, 1855–69, Speaker of the House, 1863–69, and vice president of the U.S., 1869–73; and John Peter Cleaver Shanks (1826–1901), in Congress, 1861–63, 1867–75. *Bio. Dir. U.S. Cong.*, 1795; *DAB*, 4:297–98, 10:245–46.

41. This entry breaks after the words *After he went* and resumes seven pages farther along in the manuscript journal with *Gov Morton*. The intervening pages contain entries for Oct. 6–7 and Nov. 8–9. If the leaves of the manuscript were bound in the order indicated by Chase's page numbers, then Chase may not have written the last quarter or more of the Oct. 5 entry until well into Nov.

McClellan had been down to see him with an equiry as to how soon he would be able to take the field, and expressing his confidence with hints of important command of army moving from Washington. He expressed the belief that no decisive victory would be achieved so long as McClellan had command.

Before starting on this visit, John A. Stevens, jr., called wishing me to see Col. Hamilton about Texas; and I asked him to bring him to dinner. Accordingly both came. Secretary Stanton also, by accident, and Mr. Montgomery, by Katie's invitation. After dinner, Col. Hamilton spoke fully of Texas—described his escape and hiding in the woods—said that many hundred loyal Texans were now concealed in Texas or refugees—declared that the War was a war of the Oligarchy upon the People—that Slavery was the basis of the Oligarchy, but that the perpetuation of Slavery was not more their object, than the despotic power of the Class over the Mass. I entered fully into his feelings; and promised to go with him to the President's tomorrow.

After he went, Gov. Morton came in and spoke very earnestly of the condition of matters in Indiana. Apprehends State defeat on the 14th., and loss of all the Congressional Districts except Julian's, Colfax's, and perhaps Shanks'. Wants Indiana Regiments in the State furloughed so that they can vote. Thinks Buell utterly unfit for command of the great army under him—is slow, opposed to the Proclamation, and has bad influence every way. Wishes me to go with him to President's about the regiments which I promised to do tomorrow.

JOURNAL XI

OCT. 6. MON.   Maj. Garrard called to speak abt N.C. & Foster[42]— F—— [has] now 3d. NY Cav Inf 17, 24, 25 Mass—9 NJ & 2d. Md 5 RI—supported by Albemarle & Pamlico fleet—say ten gunboats— F—— wants reenforcements; Sevl. regimts infy & another regiment of cavalry— Maj. G. desires, if another regt. cavalry is sent that Col Mix should be made Brigadier.[43]

Gen. Keyes & Maj. Bannister with Gen Garfield & Maj. Garrard formed our bkft party. Gen. Keyes spoke of disp[n]. in army

---

42. Jeptha D. Garrard (c. 1835–1915), an officer in New York's 3rd Cavalry, was a son of Jeptha Dudley Garrard and Sarah Bella Ludlow Garrard. Garrard had called to discuss John Gray Foster (1823–74), major general of volunteers and commander of the Department of North Carolina. *Appletons'*, 2:511–12; *DAB*, 6:549–50; Des Cognets, *Governor Garrard*, 33–34; *New York Times*, Dec. 17, 1915; *Who Was Who*, 1:441.

43. Simon H. Mix (d. 1864), of New York's 3rd Cavalry Regiment. U.S. Adjutant-General's Office, *Official Army Register*, 2:108.

(Gen. McClellan &c) to disfavor Repn. officers— Gen. Garfield mentioned the case of a young officer (Rep) ordered to a Regt. in Kansas in 1856 who was told by his Col. that he wd. not allow him to remain in the Regt. if he remained a Repn / Gen K—— spoke of Chapn.[44] at W. Pt. as the most perfect specimen of a northern man with southern principles he knew and said that when new regts were organized under Jeff Davis as Secy of War to Pierce that 11 of 15 officers were appd. from south, & when he remarked on it he was challenged to select 11 better men!

Went to Dept & with Gov Morton to see Prest. about furlough to enable Ina soldiers [in] camp to vote wh. he promd.—left Gov. with President—saw Col Hamilton & arranged for his interview— Met Wadsworth & Cochrane[45]—asked C—— to bkft.

JOURNAL X

OCTO. 6—MONDAY. Maj. Garrard called to speak about North-Carolina and Genl Foster. Foster has now 3d. N.Y. Cav.; and of Infantry, 17, 24 and 25 Mass, 9 N.J., 2 Md., and 5 R.I.; supported by Albemarle and Pamlico Fleet, say Ten Gunboats. Foster wants reinforcements,—several Regiments of Infantry and another Regiment of Cavalry. Maj Garrard desires that if another Regiment of Cavalry is sent, Col Mix should be made Brigadier.

Genl Keyes and Maj. Bannister, with Genl. Garfield and Major Garrard formed our breakfast party. Genl. Keyes spoke of the disposition in the army (McClellan &c.) to disfavor Republican officers. Genl. Garfield mentioned the case of a young Republican officer ordered to Kansas in 1856, who was told by his Colonel that he would not allow him to remain in the Regiment if he remained a Republican. Genl Keyes spoke of the Chaplain at West Point, as the most perfect specimen of a Northern man with Southern principles he ever knew; and said that when the new Regiments were organized under Jeff Davis, as Secretary of War to Pierce, eleven out of fifteen officers were appointed from the South, and when he remarked upon it he was challenged to select eleven better men.

Went to Department, and with Gov Morton to see the President about furlough to enable Indiana soldiers in camp to vote; which he promised. Left the Governor with the President. Saw Col. Hamil-

---

44. Homer Plantz underlined this word and wrote "146" above it, evidently as a cross-reference as he copied Journal X. This portion of the Oct. 6 entry appears on p. 146 of the manuscript Journal X.

45. John Cochrane (1813–98), Democratic congressman from New York, 1857–61, brigadier general of volunteers, 1862–63, and state attorney general, 1863–65. *Bio. Dir. U.S. Cong.*, 801; *DAB*, 4:252–53.

ton and arranged interview for him. Met Wadsworth and Cochrane. Asked Cochrane to breakfast.

JOURNAL XI

OCT 7 TUES— ☛ (1)[46] At Cabinet President spoke of his visit to army at Sharpsburgh & to the battlefields of Antietam and South Mn. He said he was fully satisfied that we had not over 60000 men engaged—described the position of the enemy & our own—enemy's much the best, his wings & center communicating easily by the Sharpsburgh road parallel with stream— Said Hookers attack was on enemys left, flanked. Expressed no opinion as to generalship, nor of results— Seward asked what now of expedition to Charleston[?] I said I was glad to have this subject brot up (2)

(1) [General] Cochran breakfasted with me and after breakfast conversed freely abt. McClellan. Said McC—— wd. like to retire from active comd if without disgrace wh. cd. be accomplished & a more active general secured by restoring him to Chief Command, where he wd. now act in unison with myself and those like me anxious for more decisive action— I expld. frankly my relations to McClellan—my original admiration & confidence—my disappointment in his inactivity & irresolution—my loss of confidence & conviction that another [general] shd. replace him—my constant endeavour to support him by supplies & reinforcements notwithstanding my distrust, when the Prest determined to keep him in command—my present belief that I had not judged incorrectly but my entire willingness also to receive any correction which facts wd. warrant—& my absolute freedom from personal illwill and entire readiness to do any thing which wd. ensure the earliest possible suppression of the rebellion— He said that Col. Key had often expressed his regret that Gen McC. had not conferred with me & acted in concert— I replied that if he had I thought the rebellion wd. be ended now,—but I feared concert between us impossible, our views, dispositions & principles harmoning so little. He said he wd. talk with McC. & write me. I answered that I shd be glad to hear from

---

46. See the Oct. 7 entry from Journal X (below) for the proper sequence of paragraphs. The entry from Journal XI appears here as it is found in the original. After writing some or all of the entry, Chase added notations to change the order of the paragraphs. The pointing hand and *(1)* at the top of the entry indicate that the paragraph beginning *[General] Cochran* should come first. Then follows the section beginning *At Cabinet* (the opening paragraph as originally written). Then two notations of *(2)* mark a transition from *this subject brot up* down to *Secy. Welles*. In the original of Journal X, the entry for Oct. 7 follows the sequence prescribed by Chase's notations in Journal XI.

him & was quite willing he should repeat to McC whatever I said to him

(2) Secy. Welles said the necessary ironclads could not be ready in less than a month / I was much disappd by this Statement, remembering the 10 days of a month ago & said at once that I hoped then we should not wait for the Navy but at once organize a land force sufft. to take the city from James Island—

Mr. Stanton agreed in the importance of this & proposed to order Mitchells & Garfields Brigades from the West— Send Garfield immy down with them & two more & let Mitchell go to work immediately— He said also that he proposed at once, to organize an expedition to open the Missi. & give the command of it to McClernand— The Prest. seemed well pleased with both movements—but Halleck remained to be consulted— Wd. he oppose the P & S[47]— I thought not— I left the cabinet with more hope than I have felt for months—

At the Presidents I met W. H. Aspinwall & invited him to come and dine with me which he did— In conversation I enquired what he thought of the idea of selling some 50.000.000 of 5–20s at about the market rate— He thought it should be done, but doubted whether more than 97½ could be obtained— I said I hoped 99 or 99½. He then spoke of his visit to McClellan & seemed greatly to desire my cooperation with him— Mentd that Burnside had heard that I blamed him for having Porter restored to command, but think I wd. not if I understood all the circumstances.

JOURNAL X

TUESDAY, OCTO. 7. Genl. Cochrane breakfasted with me, and after breakfast conversed freely about McClellan. He said McClellan would like to retire from active command if he could do so without disgrace—which could be accomplished and a more active General secured by restoring him to the chief command, where he would now act in unison with myself. I explained frankly my relations to McClellan—my original admiration and confidence—my disappointment in his inactivity and irresolution—my loss of confidence and conviction that another General should replace him—my constant endeavor to support him by supplies and reinforcements, notwithstanding my distrust when the President determined to keep him in command—my present belief that I had not judged incorrectly, but my entire willingness, also, to receive any correction

---

47. President and Stanton.

which facts would warrant; and my absolute freedom from personal ill-will, and my entire readiness to do anything which would ensure the earliest possible suppression of the rebellion / He said that Col. Key had often expressed his regret that McClellan had not conferred with me, and acted in concert with me. I replied that I thought, if he had, the rebellion would be ended now; but that I feared concert between us impossible, our views, dispositions and principles harmonizing so little. He said he would talk with McClellan and write me. I answered that I should be glad to hear from him, and was quite willing he should report to McClellan what I had said.[48]

At Cabinet, the President spoke of his visit to the Army at Sharpsburgh, and the battle-fields of Antietam and South Mountain. He said he was fully satisfied that we had not over 60.000 men engaged; and he described the position of the enemy and our own—the enemy's being much the best, his wings and centre communicating easily be the Sharpsburgh road parallel with the stream. He expressed no opinion as to Generalship, nor of results.

Seward asked what new of the Expedition to Charleston? Secretary Welles the necessary iron-clads could not be ready in less than a month. I was much disappointed by this statement, remembering that ten days of a month were up; and said at once that I hoped then we should not wait for the Navy but at once organize a land force sufficient to take the city from James' Island. Mr. Stanton agreed in the importance of this, and proposed to order Mitchell's and Garfield's Brigades from the West—send Garfield at once to South Carolina with these Brigades and two more regiments—and let Mitchell go to work immediately. He said also that he proposed at once to organize an Expedition to open the Mississippi, and give the command of it to McClernand. The President seemed much pleased with both movements—but Halleck remained to be consulted. Would he oppose the President and Stanton? I thought not.

I left the Cabinet with more hope than I have felt for months.

At the President's, I met W. H. Aspinwall and invited him to come and dine with me; which he did. In conversation I enquired what he thought of the idea of selling some $50.000.000 of Five-twenties at about the Market rate? He thought it should be done

---

48. On Oct. 9, Cochrane reported that McClellan had reaffirmed his dedication to the destruction of slavery. Cochrane offered assurances that McClellan was concerned only with military matters. "He bade me write to you fully upon these subjects," Cochrane continued, "and to assure you of the cordiality with which he would cooperate with you." Cochrane to Chase, Oct. 9, 1862 (Chase Papers, Hist. Soc. of Pa.).

but doubted whether more than 97½ could be obtained. I said I hoped to get 99 or 99½. He then spoke of his visit to McClellan and seemed greatly to desire my coöperation with him. He mentioned that Burnside had heard that I blamed him for having Porter restored to command; but thinks I would not if I understood all the circumstances

JOURNAL XI

OCT 10 FRI. Went to Cabt. taking Mr. Whittlesey to Dept[49]— found Prest. reading telegs fro. Ky—McCook's Division engaged with Bragg's army on 8th Wedy. and hard pressed but reinforced & enemy repulsed[50]— All the corps up at night & in position— Slight engagemt. with enemy's rear guard yesterday but main body retreated to Harrodsburgh This from Buell at Perryville yesterday morn'g— Stager[51] fr. Cleveland telegraphs "another great battle yesterday & no mistake abt victory this time— This this morng at 10— So we hope best— Nothing of much importance discussed except Norfolk—I favd. opening port—nothing decided. Asked Stanton what had been done abt. McClernands army for clearing the Missi. & he replied "Nothing" / Seward said he thought something had been done & the Prest. that something had been agreed on— It turned out that orders for organization of Expn. had been given but nothing of importance yet done [regarding] them— Home— signed official letters & warrants—directed regulations of trade with opened ports to be sent to Secy of War / [Butler dined]— Evg. Gen Hunter, Maj. Halpine,[52] Mr. Cowan, Judge & Mr. Maxwell[53] of N.Y., Gen McDowell, Maj David Taylor & others called— Before dinner Bannister came abt. Col Hamilton ([A] J of [Texas]) going to Ohio— urged him to have [him] go if possible— See Schenck & have [*illeg.*] go with him. Directed 10.000 Postage Cy sent to Cincinnati[.]

49. Elisha Whittlesey (1783–1863), congressman from Ohio, 1823–38; sixth auditor of the U.S. Treasury, 1841–43; and first comptroller of the Treasury, 1849–57, 1861–63. *Appletons'*, 6:495; *Bio. Dir. U.S. Cong.*, 2046.
50. Alexander McDowell McCook (1831–1903), major general of volunteers, soon to be breveted brigadier general, U.S.A., commanded the 1st Army Corps against Maj. Gen. Braxton Bragg, C.S.A. (1817–76) at the Battle of Perrysville. *Appletons'*, 4:92; *DAB*, 2:585–87, 11:600–601.
51. Col. Anson Stager (1825–85), general superintendent of the Western Union Telegraph Co. at Cleveland, oversaw U.S. military telegraphs during the war. *DAB*, 17:492–93.
52. Journalist Charles Graham Halpine (1829–68) served on David Hunter's staff. Halpine was famous at the time for creating the character of "Miles O'Reilly," a fictional Irish private who communicated with the press about his experiences in the Union army. *DAB*, 8:160–61.
53. Judge Maxwell may have been New York attorney Hugh Maxwell (1787–1873), a former assistant judge advocate general of the army. *DAB*, 12:441.

October 1862 {419}

JOURNAL X

FRIDAY, OCTO. 10, 1862. Went to Cabinet, taking Mr. Whittlesey to Department. Found the President reading telegrams from Kentucky. McCook's division engaged with Bragg's Army on the 8th. and hard pressed, but was reinforced and the enemy repulsed. All the Corps up at night and in position. Slight engagement with enemy's rear guard yesterday, but main body retreated to Harrodsburgh. This from Buell at Perryville yesterday morning. Stager p. Cleveland telegraphs another great battle yesterday, and no mistake about victory this time. This came this morning at ten. So we hope the best.

Nothing of much importance was discussed except Norfolk. I favored opening the Port. Nothing was decided.— Asked Stanton what he had done about McClernand's Army for clearing the Mississippi, and he replied "Nothing". Seward said he thought something had been done, and the President that something had been agreed on. It turned out that orders for the organization of the expedition had been given but that nothing of importance was yet done.

Home. Signed official letters and Warrants— Directed Regulations of Trade with open ports to be sent to the Secretary of War.

In the evening, Genl Hunter, Maj. Halpin, Mr. Cowan, Judge and Mr. Maxwell of N.Y., Genl. McDowell, Maj. D. Taylor and others called. Before Dinner, Bannister came about Col. A. J. Hamilton, of Texas, going to Ohio. Urged him to have him go if possible.

Directed $10.000 Postage Currency sent to Cincinnati

JOURNAL XI

OCT 11. SAT. Surprised to read this morng that Stuarts cavalry have taken Chambersburgh in Pa[54]—what next—

Recd. letter fr. John Cochrane that McC—— appreciates my support while not approving his command—and wd. gladly cooperate with me & see me—no substantial diff. between us on Sly question[55]—also fr Aspinwall abt. 5/20 Loan which he advises—thinks 98 may be obtained—equivalent to say 75 for gold[56]—also fr Cisco

---

54. Brig. Gen. James Ewell Brown "Jeb" Stuart, C.S.A. (1833–64) finished his destructive raid on Oct. 12 by returning to Virginia with 1,200 Federal horses. *DAB*, 18:170–72.

55. That is, "Slavery question." John Cochrane to Chase, Oct. 9, 1862 (Chase Papers, Hist. Soc. of Pa.).

56. William H. Aspinwall anticipated that the government's 5–20 bonds might bring bids of 95–98% of value. Aspinwall to Chase, Oct. 10, 1862, ibid.

sending $10 Ty note purloined fr. Nat. Bk Note Co. & falsely filled & sealed— Wrote Cisco, abt. detective;[57] enclosed Aspinwalls note, & asked opinion;—sundry other letters recd. & answered, Geiger,[58] Plumb,[59] Bliss of Dakotah[60] &c;—Needham called; accepted Williams declination as Assessor Louisville District & agreed to appoint Needham in place; N—— to resign Collectorship[.][61] signed official letters & warrants—

Gen Hunter, Maj. Halpin, Mr Jay,[62] Gen. Garfield (still our guest) at dinner—Maj. H—— mentnd. that McC—— had telegd. Head Qrs that not one of the rebels who have invaded Pa shall return to Va— Hope it may be so, faintly—too many bills of same sort protested for the credit of drawer— After dinner talked a good deal with H—— who very well read— Asked his opinion of Halleck— He said he has ability and knowledge, but does not make it an earnest study of the war—does not *labor* to get clear ideas of positions[,] conditions, & possibilities so as to seize & press advantages or remedy evils— "What think of Prest." A man irresolute but of kind intentions—born a poor white in a slave state and of course among aristocrats—Kind in spirit & not envious but anxious for approval especially of those to whom he has been accustomed to look up—hence solicitous for support of the slaveholders in the border states & unwilling to offend them.—without the large mind necessary to grasp great question— uncertain of himself.—and in many things ready to lean too much on others— What of Secy Stanton— Know little of him—saw him but

---

57. Chase wanted Cisco to investigate a suspected case of counterfeiting. Chase to Cisco, Oct. 11, 1862 (Letters Sent Relating to Subtreasury System, Gen. Recs. Treasury Dept., Nat. Arch.).

58. Joseph H. Geiger was apparently encouraging Chase to intervene in behalf of Brig. Gen. James Cooper (1810–63), a former U.S. senator from Pennsylvania who had expressed dissatisfaction with his position as the commander of Camp Wallace, near Columbus, Ohio. Cooper to Chase, Oct. 14, 1862 (Chase Papers, Hist. Soc. of Pa.); *DAB*, 4:400; Geiger to Chase, Sept. 29, 1862 (Chase Papers, L.C.).

59. At this point, Ralph Plumb (1816–1903), a future Republican congressman from Illinois, 1885–89, was a captain in the Union army. Heitman, *Historical Register*, 1:795; *Bio. Dir. U.S. Cong.*, 1655; Plumb to Chase, Nov. 1, 1862 (Chase Papers, Hist. Soc. of Pa.).

60. Philemon Bliss (1813–89), presiding judge of Ohio's fourteenth judicial district, 1848–51; Republican congressman, 1855–59; chief justice of the Territory of Dakota, 1861–63; and associate justice of the Missouri supreme court, 1868–72. He desired an appointment as governor of Dakota Territory with the military commission of colonel. Bliss to John C. Underwood, Oct. 27, 1862 (Chase Papers, L.C.); *Bio. Dir. U.S. Cong.*, 634; *DAB*, 2:375–76.

61. English-born Edgar Needham of Louisville was a former merchant of marble and stone and had been a promoter of the Liberty party in Kentucky during the 1840s. He was appointed assessor of internal revenue for Kentucky's third district in the place of Harrison A. Williams. *Register of Officers (1863)*, 36; *Louisville Dir. (1848–49)*, 184; ibid. (1865–66), 199; Needham to Chase, Aug. 12, 1844 (Chase Papers, L.C.); Chase to Lincoln, Aug. 29, 1862 (Lincoln Papers, L.C.).

62. Possibly John Jay (1817–94), Republican activist from New York and the son of Chase's friend, William Jay. *DAB*, 10:10.

once & so treated that I never desired to see him again—think from facts which have come to my knowledge he is not sincere—he wears two faces, but has energy & ability—though [not] steady power— The conversation then turned on Douglas,[63] whose ardent friend Mr. H—— had been & constant supporter; also on other persons & things. I found him well read and extremely intelligent— Gen. Hunter tells me that he desires to retire from army & have some position in New York which will enable him to resume his special vocation as a writer for the Press— He says he has written lately some [leaders] for the Republican & has *aided* the propr. of Wilkes [Spt of Times][64]

JOURNAL X

SATURDAY, OCTO. 11 Surprised to read this morning that Stuart's Cavalry have taken Chambersburgh, Penna. What next?

Recd. letter from John Cochrane, saying that McClellan appreciates my support while not approving his command, and would gladly coöperate with me and see me; and that there is no substantial difference between us on the Slavery question.— Also received letter from Aspinwall about Five-twenty Loan, which he advises— He thinks 98 may be obtained—equivalent to, say, 75 in gold.— Also a letter from Cisco sending a $10 U.S. Note, purloined from National Bank Note Company and falsely filled and sealed.— Wrote Cisco about detective; and enclosed Aspinwall's note and asked his opinion.— Sundry other letters received and answered.— Needham (Ky) called. I accepted Williams' declination as Assessor Louisville District, and agreed to appoint Needham in his place—he to resign Collectorship.

Genl. Hunter, Maj. Halpin, Mr. Jay and Genl. Garfield (still our guest) at dinner. Maj. Halpin mentioned that McClellan had telegraphed Head Quarters that not one of the rebels who have invaded Pennsylvania shall return to Virginia. Hope it may be so, faintly. Too many Bills of the same sort protested for the credit of the Drawer.

After dinner talked a good deal with Genl. Hunter, who is very well read. Asked him his opinion of Halleck. He said, "He has ability and knowledge, but does not make an earnest study of the War— does not *labor* to get clear ideas of positions, conditions and possibilities, so as to seize and press advantages or remedy evils."— I then asked what he thought of the President? "A man irresolute but of honest intentions—born a poor white in a Slave State, and, of course,

---

63. Stephen A. Douglas. *H——* means Halpine, not Hunter.
64. The Washington, D.C., *National Republican,* and the sensationalist New York paper, *Wilkes' Spirit of the Times,* whose owner, George Wilkes (1817–85), covered major engagements of the war. *Wash. Dir. (1862),* 260; *DAB,* 20:218.

among aristocrats—kind in spirit and not envious, but anxious for approval, especially of those to whom he has been accustomed to look up—hence solicitous of support of the Slaveholders in the Border States, and unwilling to offend them—without the large mind necessary to grasp great questions—uncertain of himself, and in many things ready to lean too much on others." What of Stanton?— "Know little of him. Have seen him but once, and was then so treated that I never desired to see him again. Think from facts that have come to my knowledge that he is not sincere. He wears two faces; but has energy and ability, though not steady power." The conversation then turned on Douglas whose ardent friend and constant supporter Hunter was—also on other persons and things. I found him well read and extremely intelligent.

Gen Hunter tells me that he desires to retire from the army, and have some position in New-York which will enable him to resume his special vocation as a writer for the Press. He says he has written lately some leaders for the *"Republican"*, and has *aided* the Proprietor of *"Wilkes' Spirit of the Times."*

JOURNAL XI

OCT. 12 SUN. At home all day—reading—nursing my inflamed foot—& conversing with Katie & friends

JOURNAL X

SUNDAY, OCTO. 12. At home all day, nursing inflamed foot—reading, and conversing with Katie and friends.[65]

JOURNAL XI

NOV. 10 SAT.—[66] Mr Watson[67] came in & showed telegram announcing removal of McClellan— So that is over. Mr. [Case] & Mr. Campbell called[68][—]& we had interesting talk on Finance

---

65. This final entry in Journal X marks the last day for which there are parallel entries in Journals X and XI.
66. This entry refers to Saturday, Nov. 8, 1862, and the entry which follows it is for Sunday, Nov. 9. In the original, these two entries follow that for Oct. 7. Chase was confused about his dates during this part of Nov. He made headings for *Nov 7 Thurs* (presumably Thursday the sixth) and *Nov 8 Fri* (presumably Friday the seventh), but wrote no entries under those headings.
67. Peter H. Watson.
68. Alexander Campbell (c. 1820–83), a partner in the New York banking house of Ward, Campbell, and Co., an affiliate of London's Baring Brothers. Campbell to Chase, Nov. 12, 1862 (Chase Papers, L.C.); *New York Times*, Sept. 17, 1883.

November 1862 {423}

Nov [9] Sun. [C. k. fr.] Gen Cochran at breakfast—he thinks reorganization of parties inevitable—agrees in my view that name shd. be democratic Republican & principles democratic— Stated to him three points which should form our policy 1. Banking System, govt. furnishing notes—Banks receiving them on depg. bonds [as] security & circulating them: 2. Provl. govts in rebel states: 3. No slavery in rebel states— He agreed. He spoke of Bennett & attacks of NY. Herald on me[69]—thought these cd. be prevented—told him I felt they were gratuitous & groundless but cd. not go out of my way to attend to them—that I had told one of those connected with the paper long ago in reply to some intimations of the power of the Herald that newspapers did not make me & could not un-make me / He expressed his wish to be military Govr. of Washn. in case Wadsworth shd. go into field— I liked the idea & promd aid—

Nov. 12—[70] Engaged on report till noon—called at Head Qrs— Gen. H—— not in—at War Dept—saw Stanton—talked of necessity of paper not afraid to vindicate us from underhand assaults of the [oos]—agreed to consult Cameron on arrival—asked how he liked Burnsides plan of campaign / "Well" "The massing at Warrenton & advance from Fgh.[71] without battle"? That changed—ordered to get at enemy by shortest route & quickest time" At White House saw President— Asked about Gen.   "Had recd. letter & sent to War Dept." Talk abt. National Banking System—promised to send him Websters Speeches[72][—]attended to [usual] business at Dept.— home to dinner—in evening Mr. [Homer] of [Boston],[73] Wilkes of Spirit & others—Wilkes talked of newspaper in N York & I promised if this attempted to help.

Nov. 13. Thurs. Engaged in reading with reference to rept. till 12—went to dept— Weed called—but I did not see him—sent

---

69. James Gordon Bennett, Sr. (1795–1872), publisher of the *New York Herald*, had attacked Chase, a leading supporter of New York gubernatorial candidate James S. Wadsworth, as "the Mephistophiles of this war ... who has sacrificed the lives and the health of thousands of our brave soldiers to his intrigues against McClellan and in favor of incompetent generals." The paper declared that Chase "has so mismanaged the Treasury Department as to reduce the value of the dollar bill in a working man's pocket to about seventy-five cents. In voting for Wadsworth you vote for Chase." *New York Herald*, Nov. 3, 1862; *DAB*, 2:195–99.

70. Earlier entries from Nov. 1862 show a discrepancy in day/date agreement. This entry presumably refers to Wednesday, Nov. 12. The next entry, describing Thursday, Nov. 13, shows the correct day of the week for the date given.

71. Fredericksburg, Va.

72. Edward Everett, ed., *The Works of Daniel Webster*, 6 vols. (Boston, 1851).

73. Possibly either Charles C. Homer, a broker, or Henry Homer, who worked in the Suffolk Co., Mass., Superior Court. *Boston Dir. (1864)*, 184.

Websters Speeches to President— Garfield left us today— Goicouria, Judge Wayne,[74] Chandler & Barney to dinner—nothing of importance / G—— talked of Lopez,—Cuba, Slavery &c[75]— Judge W—— of ordinary matters— Chandler delighted with results in Michigan[76]— In evg. Gen Hunter & Major Halpine came in—the Major to talk of Wilkes project & his own connexion with it—thinks it best to try Times which he says Raymd[77] [w]ants to leave— Mr. Cummings & Bishop Simpson came in.[78] The Bp just from Cala., Oregon, Washn. through homewards Utah & Nevada gave much interesting information—

1863

JOURNAL XII

JANY 1. The new year arrives with its new duties. May I find strength and will for them.

The day has been given as usual to the social duties of paying & receiving visits. In the morning I went with my sister Mrs Walbridge, my daughters Katie & Nettie & Netties schoolmate & friend Lizzie P[*illeg.*] to call on the President. The Prest. & Mrs L—— had not made their appearance when we arrived and I took my sister into the reception room & found a pleasant seat for her where she could witness every thing [with the] least inconvenience from her lameness[79] and then mingled with the crowd in the Antechamber, composed chiefly of the foreign legation & the Heads of the Departments with their families. The news from Murfreesboro had cleared up in favor of our army & we were confident that Vicksburgh had been taken & we all felt quite cheerful. So every thing went

---

74. James Moore Wayne (c. 1790–1867), Georgia politician and jurist; associate justice of the U.S. Supreme Court, 1835–67. *Bio. Dir. U.S. Cong.*, 2018; *DAB*, 19:565–66.

75. Domingo Goicouria helped Venezuelan-born revolutionary leader Narciso Lopez (1798–1851) organize expeditions to Cuba in 1850–51. Calcagno, *Diccionario Biografico Cubano*, 302, 373–75; *Appletons'*, 4:22; Drake, *American Biography*, 366.

76. According to reports, the Republicans had recaptured the governor's mansion and won four of the state's six congressional seats. *Daily National Intelligencer,* Nov. 7, 1862.

77. Henry Jarvis Raymond (1820–69), editor of the *New York Daily Times* and Republican U.S. congressman, 1865–67. *DAB*, 15:408–12.

78. Chase's friend Matthew Simpson (1811–84), a prominent Methodist Episcopal clergyman and staunch Unionist, had been editor of the *Western Christian Advocate*. Alexander Cummings may have been his companion during the call on Chase. *DAB*, 17:181–82.

79. Chase's youngest sister, Helen Chase Walbridge, suffered from paralysis. She was visiting Chase after a recent series of medical treatments in New York. Helen Walbridge to Chase, Jan. 26, 1864, Henry Walbridge to Chase, July 2, Sept. 22, Oct. 7, 1862 (Chase Papers, L.C.).

January 1863 {425}

pleasantly. After the Presidents reception was over we received at home. It tired me a good deal but the children enjoyed it greatly.

JANY 23. Washburne came to breakfast[80]—explained that he abandoned his motion for a select Committee & moved reference to Ways & Means on advice of Hooper—is decided for Banking bill.[81]

Attended to various matters of business before going to Cabinet. There not much done of importance—some talk on Finance Bills—all agreed in [favor] banking bill—Seward to see Pomeroy / all glad of safety of Weehawken & Nahant, the loss of which in the recent storm had been seriously apprehended[82]— It was stated that Grant with his army must be now at Vicksburgh cutting canal. I have not much faith in this digging, but hope the best. To illustrate the sometimes unexpected results of new ways for water the President told the story of the man with the mill supplied from a lake at the top of the hill on the side of which the mill was built. He opened the sluice a trifle & the water rushed out, widening the passage until its volume swept off mill & miller. In some other connexion he told the story of the man at the muster who sold cider at one end of his barrel while a rogue who had tapped it at the other end outside the shanty was underselling him from his own barrel. And Seward told a story [of] which, I examining a map, did not catch the drift. Then the President talked to me about some bales of cotton confiscated by a decree of court which he was asked to set aside— It seemed to me very clear that he had no power to do so: and such appeared to be the general opinion. No large question was discussed, except the little talk about finances. In some talk with Stanton he insisted that I knew that Butler was to be superceded by Banks. This surprised me greatly, for I did not dream of it until two or three weeks before it was done when I wrote to Gen. Butler begging him to remain under Banks. I told him so & he said we differed in our recollection.[83]

---

80. Elihu Benjamin Washburne (1816–87), Whig and Republican congressman from Illinois, 1853–69, and U.S. minister to France, 1869–77. *DAB*, 19:504–6.

81. The bill, which provided for a system of national banks, was known formally as a "national currency act" and became law on Feb. 25. Its provisions were amended by a second act, approved June 3, 1864. *Statutes at Large*, 12:665–82, 13:99–118.

82. USS *Nahant* and USS *Weehawken* were new ironclad monitors traveling from New York to assignments with the South Atlantic Blockading Squadron. Both ships were caught in a gale on Jan. 20–21 but came through without major damage. *ORN*, ser. 1, v. 8:366–71, 13:504, ser. 2, v. 1:153, 238.

83. Banks sailed from New York on Dec. 4, 1862, and formally relieved Butler in New Orleans on Dec. 17. Butler wrote Chase on Nov. 29, indignant over newspaper stories that Banks was to have "an independent Command." Butler declared his intention to resign if the reports proved correct. On Dec. 14, Chase replied that it

Ordinary business at the Department— A good many callers and a good deal of talk about finances. There seems an increasing disposition to favor my bill for banking—but much diversity and a good deal of fluctuation. In the evening a number of invited guests at dinner—Judge Collamer, Gen Cameron Mr. Olcott (Albany), Mr. Bancroft,[84] Mr. Jay, Mr. Nixon, Mr. Harrington, Judge Thomas[85] Mr Shellabarger, Mrs, Mr. Noell, Mr. Hickman, Mr. Edwards,[86] Gen. Moorhead, Mr. Barney, Mr. Potter, Mr. Sheffield[87] / Every thing went off quite pleasantly.

JULY 1. This is an anxious day. Meade's army seems to be drawing right to the rebel positions.[88] Is he not too far to the right? May not Lee turn his left and so get between him and Washington? These are questions much discussed. Gen Halleck and the President both seem uneasy. Every thing in Meades despatches—neither frequent or long however—indicates prudence, courage & activity— I trust all will go well.

---

was only after receiving Butler's letter "that I learned from Mr. Stanton the real destination and instructions of Gen. Banks." Chase urged Butler to stay on in New Orleans under Banks's command. B. F. Butler to Chase, Nov. 29, 1862 (Chase Papers, Hist. Soc. of Pa.); Chase to Butler, Dec. 14, 1862 (Butler Papers, L.C.); Bragg, *Louisiana*, 136–37.

84. Jacob Collamer; Simon Cameron; Thomas Worth Olcott (1795–1880), president of the Mechanics and Farmers Bank of Albany, N.Y., who gave Chase suggestions on the pending national banking bill and was Chase's original nominee as comptroller of the currency; and historian and diplomat George Bancroft (1800–1891). *Bio. Dir. U.S. Cong.*, 809; *DAB*, 1:564–70; *Nat. Cyc.*, 18:204; H. Barney to Chase, Jan. 15, 1863, Olcott to Chase, Feb. 10, 1863 (Chase Papers, Hist. Soc. of Pa.); Chase to Olcott, Mar. 4, 1863 (Misc. Letters Sent, Gen. Recs. Treasury Dept., Nat. Arch.).

85. John Jay; John Thompson Nixon (1820–89), Republican congressman from New Jersey, 1859–63, and U.S. judge, 1870–89; George Harrington; and Benjamin Franklin Thomas (1813–78) of Massachusetts, a graduate of Brown University, judge of the Massachusetts Supreme Court, 1853–59, and Unionist congressman, 1861–63. *DAB*, 13:531–32; *Bio. Dir. U.S. Cong.*, 1925–26.

86. Samuel Shellabarger (1817–96), Republican congressman from Ohio, 1861–63, 1865–69, 1871–73; John William Noell (1816–63), Democrat and Unconditional Unionist congressman of Missouri, 1851–55, 1859–63; John Hickman (1810–75), Douglas Democrat, later Republican, congressman from Pennsylvania, 1855–63; Thomas McKey Edwards (1795–1875), Republican congressman from New Hampshire, 1859–63. *Bio. Dir. U.S. Cong.*, 954, 1573, 1800; *Appletons'*, 3:195.

87. James Kennedy Moorhead (1806–84), former adjutant general of Pennsylvania and Republican congressman, 1859–69; Hiram Barney; John Fox Potter (1817–99), Republican congressman from Wisconsin, 1857–63, and U.S. consul general at Montreal, 1863–66; and William Paine Sheffield (1820–1907) of Rhode Island, Republican congressman, 1861–63, and U.S. senator, 1884–85. *DAB*, 13:147–48; *Bio. Dir. U.S. Cong.*, 1528–29, 1665, 1799–1800.

88. Maj. Gen. George Gordon Meade (1815–72) commanded the Army of the Potomac, 1863–65. On this day his army was involved in the opening movements of the battle of Gettysburg. *DAB*, 12:474–76.

August 1863   {427}

Rosecrans is moving—not rapidly enough I fear.[89] His delay has been greater than expected. But he is the best judge of what his circumstances require, and his faithfulness and capacity are least questioned by those nearest to him and most capable of judgment.

Grant moves steadily to the end of his immediate work the capture of Vicksburgh—the beginning of a much greater work I hope.

Banks seems in some danger; but he is cool & capable & has excellent generals. Grant too will help in case of need.

Gilmore is busy near Charleston, with good prospects.[90]

The log books of the Tacony and the Florida have come. How promptly Collector Jewett & Lieut. Merryman acted.[91]

JOURNAL XIII

SATURDAY, AUGUST 29. 1863.[92] Received from A. C. Wilson, President of the Continental Bank Note Company, his charges against Mr. Clark, and referred them to Mr. C. for explanation or answer.[93] The charges seem to be inspired by no public reason, but

---

89. William Starke Rosecrans (1819–98), at this time major general of volunteers and commander of the Army of the Cumberland, faced the army of Braxton Bragg in Tennessee. After the war Rosecrans was U.S. minister to Mexico, 1868–69, and a member of Congress, 1881–85. *DAB*, 16:163–64.

90. Quincy Adams Gillmore (1825–88), soon to be promoted to major general of volunteers, commanded the 10th Army Corps and the Department of the South. *DAB*, 7:295.

91. During May 1863, 2nd Lt. Charles William Read (1840–90) and a crew from the Confederate cruiser *Florida*, operating from captured prize vessels, raided shipping off the eastern seaboard. On the night of June 26–27, Read seized a revenue cutter at Portland, Maine. Collector of Customs Jedediah Jewett and 1st Lt. (later Capt.) James H. Merryman of the Revenue Service commandeered local vessels and captured Read. They reclaimed the logs of two of Read's prizes, including the bark *Tacony*, which Read had operated briefly as CSS *Florida No. 2*. The CSS *Florida* itself, with its official log, was far from the scene. *DAB*, 15:420; *ORN*, ser. 1, v. 2:322–26, 330–32, 336–37; Clarence Hale, "The Capture of the 'Caleb Cushing'," *Maine Historical Society Collections*, 3d ser., 1 (1904): 191–211; *Register of Officers (1863)*, 46, 60; ibid. (1865), 68; Basler, *Collected Works*, 6:214.

92. In the original, the clerk placed the date heading for this entry at the end, rather than the beginning, of the entry's text.

93. In margin: "A. C. Wilson's Charges against Mr. Clark; inspired by no regard for the public interest." Alexander C. Wilson had recently been managing editor of the *New York Times*, and before it the Philadelphia *Inquirer*. His bank note company was engaged in contracts to print government currency. In 1864, S. M. Clark faced allegations of trying to "defraud the government" through an experimental printing process which critics said was impractical. Clark's supporters claimed that established bank note companies like Wilson's had encouraged an investigation to undermine Clark and create business opportunities for themselves. Wilson to Chase, Aug. 27, 1863, 38th Cong., 1st sess., H. Rep. 140, 381–85; J. Cutler Andrews, *The North Reports the Civil War* (Pittsburgh, 1955), 23; L. C. Baker, *History of the United States Secret Service* (Philadelphia, 1868), 260–92; H. W. Beecher to Chase, Jan. 20, 1863, Wilson to Chase, Aug. 13, 17, Oct. 6, 1863 (Letters Received from Executive Officers, Gen. Recs.

by hostility to Mr. Clark because of his supposed animosity and injustice to the Company.

Conferred with Mr. McCulloch on the subject of deposits with the National Banks, and determined that the clerk having special charge of this business and its correspondence, shall take a desk under Mr. McC. and be attached to his Bureau.[94]

Mr. Smith Chief Clerk of the 3d. Auditor's Office,[95] was consulted on the subject of the selection of the Chief Clerk in his place, in view of his probable appointment to some outside position.[96]

In the afternoon the President came in with letters from Generals Grant and Banks in relation to the arming of negro troops, and read them to me.[97] Gen. Banks stated that he had already about 12.000 in about 25 regiments of 500 each, which number he regarded as most likely to secure good discipline and drill, and the greatest efficiency of the regiments when filled to their maximum, which he expected to accomplish by degrees. He tho't he had now organized about all the blacks who could be obtained till a larger extent of country should be occupied. Gen. Grant's was much to the same effect, except that he did not contemplate any other original organization as to numbers than that of the white regiments, nor did he specify the numbers actually enlisted. Both Generals express confidence in the efficiency of these troops and clear opinions in favor of using them.[98] These letters gave much satisfaction to the President, and I suggested to him that not only was the public sentiment of the loyal people of Louisiana in favor of negro troops, but also in favor of the revocation of the exception in his Proclamation of the two Districts,[99] including New Orleans, from its operation, and told him that some weeks ago, after talking with him on this subject, tho' more particularly in reference to the excepted Virginia

---

Treasury Dept., Nat. Arch.); Chase to Wilson, Aug. 15, 27, Oct. 2, 1863 (Misc. Letters Sent, ibid.); Chase to Wilson, Oct. 8, 1863 (Chase Papers, Hist. Soc. of Pa.); *Printing Bureau of the Treasury Department. . .* , 38th Cong., 2nd sess., 1865, H. Ex. Docs. 50, 64.

94. In margin: "Deposits with National Banks; conference with Mr. McCulloch." Indiana banker Hugh McCulloch (1808–95) was comptroller of the currency, 1863–65, and secretary of the Treasury, 1865–69, 1884–85. *DAB*, 12:6–8.

95. Delano T. Smith.

96. In margin: "Consultation with Mr. Smith of 3d Auditor's Office."

97. In margin: "Visit from the President; Negro troops in Generals Grant's and Banks' Departments."

98. Banks to Lincoln, Aug. 17, 1863 (Lincoln Papers, L.C.); Grant to Lincoln, Aug. 23, 1863, in Simon et al., *Papers of Ulysses S. Grant*, 9:195–97. Both officers acted in accordance with Lincoln's wishes. On Aug. 9, the president had written that he considered the recruitment of black troops "a resource which if vigorously applied now, will soon close the contest—It works doubly, weakening the enemy & strengthening us." Lincoln to Grant, Aug. 9, 1863, ibid., 9:197.

99. In margin: "Public sentiment in La. as to revocation of excepted Districts."

Districts, I had prepared the draft of a Proclamation revoking the exceptions, which, with his permission, I would hand to him. He received it kindly, and said he would consider it further.¹

In the evening Mr. Mellen and Mr. Risley came to my house, and we read through the new Regulations of trade and concerning abandoned property, and completed their revision.² Mr. Mellen will now return to his Agency, and Mr. Risley will supervise the printing of the new Regulations.

SUNDAY, AUGUST 30, 1863. Mr. Covode called at my house after church and desired to know my opinion as to the proper course to be taken in Pennsylvania.³ I replied that there seemed to me but one course to be taken, and that was to give a hearty support to the re-election of Gov. Curtin. He thought Gov. Curtin and his friends designed that he should be brought forward as a candidate for the Presidency, and that, if elected Governor he would shape matters in Pennsylvania so as to secure its delegates in the Convention,⁴ while a majority of the loyal men of Pennsylvania preferred me, and that the vote of the State controlled by Curtin would not be given to me unless under some arrangement which would pledge to Gov. Curtin and his friends the patronage in Pennsylvania. To this I replied that no speculations as to Gov. Curtin's future course could excuse the loyal men from supporting him now; that the future must take care of itself; that I was not anxious for the Presidency; that there was but one position in the Government which I really w'd like to have, if it were possible to have it without any sacrifice of principle or public interest, and that was the Chief Justiceship, and that should the wishes of our political friends incline to me as a nominee for the Presidency, those wishes must be entirely of a public nature, for I certainly would never consent under any circumstances to make pledges as to appointments to office,⁵ but would insist upon being left entirely free to avail myself of the services of the best men in the country. Mr. Covode approved of

---

1. Certain parishes of Louisiana and counties of Virginia, as well as all of West Virginia, were excepted from the provisions of the Emancipation Proclamation. Chase had drafted an executive order to eliminate all the exceptions but that for West Virginia. Letterpress copy, [Aug. 1863] (Chase Papers, Hist. Soc. of Pa.). Chase and Lincoln discussed the president's reaction on Sept. 17 (see below).

2. In margin: "Mess. Mellen and Risley; Revision of Gen. Regulations." Hanson A. Risley, the Treasury's supervising special agent for Virginia and the eastern part of West Virginia, was the father of William H. Seward's adopted daughter, Olive Risley Seward. *Letter of the Secretary . . . Special Agents,* 2; Maunsell B. Field, *Memories of Many Men and of Some Women: Being Personal Recollections . . .* (New York, 1874), 285–87.

3. In margin: "Visit of Mr. Covode; Gov. Curtin for the Presidency, etc.—"

4. In margin: "Preference for Mr. Chase."

5. In margin: "Will make no pledges for office."

these sentiments, and said that he would confer with a number of prominent citizens opposed to Mr. Curtin to-morrow evening, at Philadelphia, and endeavor to secure united action in his favor. After he left, Mr. Mellen came in and dined with me.[6] We had some conversation in relation to the duties of his Agency from which I hope some good. He is active, intelligent, and faithful,[7] and if any one can accomplish the work of regulating trade without prejudice to military operations, and at the same time to the satisfaction of honest people engaged in it, and for the benefit of the people of the of the rebel states within our military lines, I think he will do it.

MONDAY, AUGUST 31, 1863. Business at the Department for to-day was chiefly routine. Wrote to Mr. Cisco directing him to ascertain whether the Banks and Bankers of New York would subscribe 35.000.000$ for 5 per cent. Treasury Notes payable in a year and made a legal tender for their face.[8] Addressed similar letters to the Assistant Treasurers at Boston and Philadelphia,[9] asking for a subscription of ten millions at Boston and five millions at Philadelphia. I am not at all sanguine in the expectation that success will attend these applications. It is substantially a proposition to the capitalists to loan money to the Government for a year at about $5\frac{1}{4}$ per cent., with a privilege, however, of being repaid at any time after 30 days when the Treasury Notes can be delivered.

A note from Senator Henderson apprised me that a delegation from St. Louis desired to call upon me with reference to the regulations of the River trade. I replied that I would see them to-morrow at 10 or 2 o'clock as best suited them. I afterwards received a note from the Senator, saying they would call at 2 to-morrow afternoon.

In the afternoon I called at the President's, and found him listening to representations of Senator Bowdoin and Representatives Chandler and Segur of Virginia,[10] and Dr. ———, of Northampton

---

6. In margin: "Mr. Mellen."

7. In margin: "A faithful officer, etc."

8. In margin: "Loan of 35 millions of 5 per cent. notes for one year: letters to Assistant Treasurers." Chase intended to raise a total of $50 million. Chase to Cisco, Aug. 31, 1863 (Loan Division, Letters Sent, Recs. of Bureau of Public Debt, Nat. Arch.).

9. At Boston, Theophilus P. Chandler (1807–86), and at Philadelphia, Archibald McIntyre, who also acted as treasurer of the Philadelphia mint. *Register of Officers (1863)*, 31, 33, 45; Beverly Wilson Palmer, ed., *The Selected Letters of Charles Sumner* (Boston, 1990), 2:7.

10. Lemuel Jackson Bowden (1815–64), Republican of Virginia, 1863–64, and Joseph Eggleston Segar (1804–80), Unionist congressman, 1862–63. Lucius H. Chan-

county, concerning the tax imposed by order of the War Department on the people of that county to pay for the re-building of a Light-house lately destroyed by rebels. The object of these gentlemen was to induce the President to revoke that order, on the ground that the people of Northampton were thoroughly loyal, and that the destruction of the Light-house was without the least privity of theirs, but by rebels who came from that portion of Virginia still controlled by rebels. After these gentlemen took their leave, the President said to me that he felt inclined to suspend the order. I suggested that perhaps it would be well to revoke the exception of Northampton and the other counties of Virginia from his Proclamation, and accompany that revocation by the revocation of the order imposing the tax, inasmuch as the first revocation would insure the loyalty which the people of the county professed.

Turning from this subject I asked the President to appoint Mr. Shellaberger Governor of Dacotah if he should determine not to give that place to Judge Bliss,[11] and if he should then to give the Chief Justiceship to Mr. Shellaberger; and I also asked him in case Mr. Bingham should decline the Judgeship at Key West to give it to Judge Lawrence of Logan county, Ohio.[12] He received these requests favorably, but promised nothing.

I then called at the War Department, and not finding the Secretary, left a request that he would call at the Treasury Department, and went myself to the Navy Department, to inquire if there was any immediate necessity for a Judge at Key West. Secretary Welles was absent at the North, but Assistant Secretary Fox informed me that the want of a Judge at Key West occasioned great inconvenience and risk of public and private injuries, but that he thought Judge Marvin would hold the Court if requested until his successor could arrive in November.[13] Mr. Fox informed me that there were now between sixty and seventy naval vessels undergoing repairs at New York,—and the loss in consequence of the poor timber necessarily employed in their construction was enormous. I inquired if any steps had been taken toward purchasing tar, pitch, turpentine and ship

---

dler claimed to have been elected to Virginia's second congressional district, but was refused the seat due to election irregularities. *Bio. Dir. U.S. Cong.*, 177, 649, 1788; *Lucius H. Chandler*, 38th Cong., 1st sess., 1864, H. Report 59, 1–2.

11. Philemon Bliss.

12. John Armor Bingham and Ohio attorney William Lawrence (1819–99), who was a former judge in Logan County and served as a Republican congressman, 1865–71, 1873–77. Lawrence received the appointment, but declined to serve. *DAB*, 11:52–53.

13. William Marvin (1808–92) served as judge of the U.S. District Court for Southern Florida, 1839–63, and as provisional governor of the state in 1865. *Nat. Cyc.*, 11:379.

timber in North Carolina, the export of which I had prohibited in order to give the Navy Department an opportunity to buy at reasonable rates. He replied that orders had been given to purchase except as to ship timber. I inquired the cause of such frequent violations of the blockade at Wilmington, to which he answered that the blockade there was now weak in consequence of the withdrawal of so many of the ships for Charleston and for repairs, but that in a few days be greatly strengthened. After I returned to the Department, Mr. Stanton came in and I suggested to him to propose to the President the revocation of the Proclamation exceptions in Virginia in connection with the suspension or revocation of the Northampton tax order. He seemed disinclined to connect the two, but was disposed to insist on the tax. We discussed the question briefly and left it unsettled. I represented to him the great importance of prompt and vigorous military action, that to-morrow the amount of suspended requisitions, including the pay of the whole Army for July and August would approach 35.000.000$, of which I could not command in ordinary ways over 5.000.000$, and that unless the war could be pushed more vigorously and with greater certainty of early and successful termination there was cause for serious apprehension of financial embarrassment. He replied that the delay of Gen. Rosecrans was the principal cause of difficulty; that he commanded a full third of all the effective force of the country, and did nothing comparatively with it. That in a week's time he could if he would penetrate those portions of Georgia and Alabama in which the negroes had been taken by their masters, and where the gathering of large bodies of negro troops would be easy. He said that he had represented these things to the President, but so far without much effect.

At the house in the evening Major Taylor, Doctor Schmidt, and Mr. Wright of California,[14] called. Dr. Schmidt warned me, in his way, against Mr. Clark and Dr. Gwinn; to which I answered that if facts were presented to me instead of vague generalities, they would be considered.[15]— Mr. Wright said he should like some position at

---

14. San Francisco banker George Washington Wright (1816–85), Independent congressman, 1850–51, later an attorney for the Choctaw Indians and private scientific investigator. *Bio. Dir. U.S. Cong.*, 2090.

15. Stuart Gwynn, a civil engineer and Treasury Department contractor, was the mastermind behind much of the Treasury's currency-printing operation supervised by Spencer Morton Clark. Early in 1864, investigations into Gwynn's dealings with the government led to his temporary confinement in Old Capitol Prison. Chase later expressed regret that he had approved of Gwynn's imprisonment. Baker, *United States Secret Service*, 265; Chase to A. G. Browne, Jr., Jan. 20, 1865 (Chase Papers, Hist. Soc. of Pa.); Chase to J. A. Garfield, May 30, 1864 (Letters Received from Sec. of Treasury, Recs. of Solicitor of the Treasury, Nat. Arch.); *Wash. Dir. (1863)*, 103.

my hands some fourteen months hence, to which I replied that at that time it was not likely I should have any to give. He then went into a statement of his connection with the Fremont campaign in '56, and of the election of Mr. Lincoln in '60, and expressed his conviction that I would be the nominee in '64, and that it was his wish to promote that result. I replied that nothing could be more uncertain than the currents of popular sentiment; that I was by no means anxious that they should turn towards me, and that if they did, and the result should be such as he predicted, it must be without any pledges from me in relation to appointments, for no man could honorably take charge of the administration under any other obligations than those of duty, and exercise its powers for the best good of the whole country in conformity with the principles upon which, and in general with the aid of the best men by whom, he had been elected.

TUESDAY SEPTEMBER 1, 1863. The Committee from Saint Louis called, and after some conversation on the subject of the Regulations of Trade Mr. Breckinridge who appeared to be their chairman, handed me a letter and they withdrew.[16] On reading the letter I found it an indictment against the course of the Government in respect to Western trade with a demand that the river be opened to the same freedom of trade as in times of peace, except so far as restriction might be necessary at points of distribution within the rebel States. I sent for Mr. Barnitz and consulted with him on this subject.[17] He prepared a draft of a of Reply to the Committee.[18]

I directed Mr. Plantz to prepare an abstract of the papers relating to the compensation of Jay Cooke as General Subscription Agent for the Sale of "Five Twenties."[19]

NOTE.—This draft was not used.

16. The letter from Samuel Miller Breckinridge (1828–91), a Republican politician and jurist, Barton Able, Charles L. Tucker, and J. H. Alexander also asked that trade in the area be placed "exclusively under military control." Breckinridge et al. to Lincoln, Sept. 1, 1863 (Lincoln Papers, L.C.); Johnson, *Twentieth Century Biographical Dictionary*, v. 1.

17. David G. Barnitz was deputy supervising special agent in the Mississippi Valley. *Letter of the Secretary . . . Special Agents*, 2.

18. Chase's reply, dated Sept. 3, explained that existing trade policies had been formulated in accordance with action taken by Congress and the president, and predicted changes only after the "rebellion" was "speedily and permanently suppressed throughout the land." Chase to Breckinridge et al., Sept. 3, 1863 (Lincoln Papers, L.C.); printed in *New York Times*, Sept. 25, 1863.

19. The question of appropriate compensation for Jay Cooke and his agents in the sale of U.S. 5–20 bonds caused much controversy. Oberholtzer, *Jay Cooke*, 1:267–73; Henrietta M. Larson, *Jay Cooke: Private Banker* (Cambridge, Mass., 1936), 14–51; *Cong. Globe*, 38th Cong., 1st. sess., 1864–65, 1046.

WEDNESDAY, SEPT. 2, 1863. Nothing of note transpired during the day.

In the evening General Schenck called and conversed fully about the Court of Inquiry called nominally to investigate the conduct of General Milroy,[20] but which subjected to its investigations *his* conduct as well as all the circumstances connected with the evacuation of Winchester. He was much dissatisfied with these proceedings which gave him no notice and allowed him no opportunity for proper defence. He said he should call upon the President and have the matter set right. I tendered him my services so far as they might be useful.

THURSDAY, SEPTEMBER 3, 1863. Mr. Risley came to breakfast, bringing with him the still unfinished regulations. I could give but little attention to them, being compelled to prepare an answer to the Saint Louis Committee, which I wrote after breakfast and took to the Department to be copied.— Gov. Pierpont called and talked about Virginia affairs. He thought a majority of the members of the Legislature would be in favor of calling a Convention to amend the Constitution so as to make it a free-labor State. He said he had not yet sent a written request to the President for a revocation of the exception of the South Eastern counties in his Proclamation, and that though he had originally asked for this exception, he become fully satisfied that it was unwise, and had represented to the President his wish to have it revoked. I told him that if he would put this wish in writing, and place his request on grounds of military necessity, the revocation would probably be made; and I suggested to him some grounds of military necessity which seemed to me important. He replied that if I would make a draft of a letter he would use it in framing a request to the President for the revocation. I told him I would do so within the next half hour. At the expiration of that time he called, and I handed him the draft.[21]

Judge Whittaker of New Orleans dined and afterwards took a ride with me.[22] We conversed fully about the state of things in Louisiana, and he expressed himself as being satisfied that Slavery was

---

20. The subject of the inquiry was Maj. Gen. Robert Huston Milroy (1816–90), commander of the second division in the 8th Army Corps. Milroy, subsequently exonerated, had sustained disastrous losses during Robert E. Lee's invasion of Pennsylvania earlier in the year. *DAB*, 13:20–21.

21. Chase's draft letter for Francis H. Pierpont has not been found. Early in 1864, Pierpont sponsored a constitutional convention within the jurisdiction of the reorganized Virginia government which abolished slavery in the state. Charles H. Ambler, *West Virginia: The Mountain State* (New York, 1940), 340.

22. John S. Whitaker (b. 1817) was a New Orleans Unionist politician and municipal judge who worked for the *New Orleans Times*, circa 1864–65. Edwin L. Jewell, *Jewell's Crescent City Illustrated* (New Orleans, 1873).

virtually abolished, and that the Constitution of the State should be so framed as to prohibit it permanently. He was not at first as decided in these sentiments as he became towards the end of our conversation. Indeed, I had expected to find him, from the representations of Mr. Denison and Mr. Plumley,[23] much further advanced than I did.

In the evening, Messrs. McJilton, Meredith, Turner and Snowden, called to converse about matters in Maryland.[24] They stated that Mr. Swan would probably be a candidate against Mr. Davis,[25] on the part of the Conservative Union men, and that on the other hand the Radicals would probably nominate candidates in the several Districts where the Conservatives had succeeded in carrying the Conventions. All these gentlemen seemed to belong to the Conservative side, but were desirous that Mr. Swan should not be a candidate, and on the other hand that the candidates who had been nominated by the Conservatives should not be opposed. I expressed my great regret that the division had occurred, but said that I felt it was founded in differences too radical to be overcome. I could see no remedy, unless both sides could agree to call a Convention upon a platform satisfactory to each and support the candidates that were already or might be nominated and accept it in good faith. Mr. McJilton thought if some of the leaders would come together and talk matters over in a patriotic spirit of accommodation that some good might come of it, and some common ground be found. I begged him to do what he could to accomplish this result, and especially to call with some others of Mr. Swan's friends and represent to him the impossibility of supporting him if he should be

---

23. George S. Denison and Benjamin Rush Plumly (1816–87), an antislavery advocate and writer formerly on the staff of John C. Frémont. Plumly, who had been corresponding with Chase throughout the war, had recently resigned as "general appraiser," in which position he recruited black soldiers in Louisiana for Gen. Banks's Corps d'Afrique. He was also involved in the supervision of abandoned plantations in the lower Mississippi Valley. *Appletons'*, 5:43; Plumly to Chase, Aug. 1, 28, 1863 (Chase Papers, L.C.); Chase to Plumly, Feb. 26, 1864 (Chase Papers, Hist. Soc. of Pa.).

24. John F. McJilton, customs surveyor at Baltimore, 1861–65, and editor of the Baltimore *Patriot;* John F. Meredith, general appraiser of customs at Baltimore since 1861; possibly either Robert Turner of Baltimore, who had written Chase about redemption of certificates of indebtedness, or Lewis Turner (b. 1810), a Baltimore butcher and Unionist leader; and P. T. Snowden. Scharf, *History of Baltimore*, 380–81, 497–98; McJilton to Chase, Aug. 28, 1863 (Chase Papers, L.C.); Chase to McJilton, Aug. 29, 1863 (Chase Papers, Hist. Soc. of Pa.); Chase to Robert Turner, Apr. 4, 1863 (Misc. Letters Sent, Gen. Recs. Treasury Dept., Nat. Arch.); *Proceedings and Speeches at a Public Meeting of the Friends of the Union . . .* (Baltimore, 1861), 3.

25. Henry Winter Davis (1817–65) of Maryland, American party and Unconditional Unionist congressman, 1855–61, 1863–65, and a leading Radical critic of the Lincoln administration. *Bio. Dir. U.S. Cong.*, 878; *DAB*, 5:119–21.

a candidate, and induce him, if possible not to consent to such a use of his name.— He promised to do this, and the gentlemen left me.

Mr. Taft and Mr. French of Cincinnati also called to talk over Ohio affairs and political matters generally.— Mr. Parker of St. Louis also called about his Express Company, with a letter from Mr. McKee.[26] Sent word to him to call at the Department to-morrow.

FRIDAY, SEPTEMBER 4, 1863. At the meeting of the Cabinet (so-called) to-day, Mr. Bates stated that the restrictions on trade created a great deal of inconvenience; that he thought the River should now be free to trade as in times of peace except at points occupied by our troops, and that care should be taken that supplies did not reach rebels. He admitted that some few thousands of dollars worth of goods would get to them under the system he proposed, but he thought this evil would be trivial compared with the evils of restriction. I stated briefly the law and the executive action on the subject and that the change proposed by Mr. Bates was disapproved by Generals Banks and Grant. I added that I had been revising the Regulations, and hoped soon to have them complete; that they had been modified in favor of trade as far as the improved condition of affairs will allow, but w'd. not, I feared, meet the sanction of the Generals, whose views and wishes were entitled to the greatest consideration. Mr. Stanton stated that a letter had been recently received from General Grant, in which he proposed to prohibit all trade except in certain articles through Post-Sutlers; that he did not agree with General Grant in this view, believing that Sutlers should be confined to furnishing supplies to the Army, and that all trade with citizens should be under the Regulations of the Treasury Department. After some observations from the President and others the subject was dropped.

The President then called the attention of Mr. Stanton to the order prohibiting the export of arms, and after some conversation, it was agreed that all arms imported into the country should be allowed to be exported to the place from which they were shipped. I then called Mr. Stanton's attention to the order prohibiting the exportation of live stock, and he consented that the order should be modified so far as to allow exportation from ports on the Pacific. On returning to the Department, in order to avoid delay I drew up an executive order, modifying the former order so as to allow exportation of imported arms to the place from which they were orig-

26. J. W. Parker evidently oversaw Parker's Express Company until its demise following the Civil War. Alvin F. Harlow, *Old Waybills: The Romance of the Express Companies* (New York, 1934), 60, 296, 301.

Portrait of Salmon P. Chase as a young man.
Courtesy of the Chase Manhattan Archives.

Chase (above) and his first wife, Catharine Garniss (facing page), posed for these portraits by Samuel Lovett Waldo and William Jewett in 1834.
From the Taper Collection; photographs courtesy of the Tapers.

Catharine, known as Kitty, died shortly after childbirth in 1835, which affected Chase deeply. His memoir of their relationship and her death begins on page 81.

Sarah Bella Dunlop Ludlow, or "Belle," married Chase in 1846.
This third and last marriage for Chase ended with Belle's death in 1852.
Courtesy of the Cincinnati Historical Society (B-83-275).

Only two of Chase's daughters lived to adulthood. At left is Janet ("Nettie"), born in 1847 to Chase's third wife Belle. At right is Catharine ("Kate"), born to Chase's second wife Eliza Ann Smith in 1840.
Courtesy of the Cincinnati Historical Society.

While he was secretary of the Treasury, a likeness of Chase, similar to this, was used on paper money, or greenbacks, issued during the Civil War.
Courtesy of the Chase Manhattan Archives.

Chase's image was used as the identifying statement by the Chase National Bank in New York City for many years. This gold note was issued in 1878. *Courtesy of the Chase Manhattan Archives.*

Chief Justice Salmon P. Chase (center) with members of the Supreme Court. *Courtesy of the Cincinnati Historical Society (B-93-218).*

inally shipped, and the exportation of live stock from the ports of the Pacific, and sent them to Mr. Stanton for his approval, and then to the President for his signature; and I then telegraphed the Collector at San Francisco that the exportation of live stock was permitted.[27]

Mr. Scudder, of Memphis, called; to whom I read the letter of the St. Louis Committee and my reply. He approved the letter and expressed the opinion that no greater liberty of trade than I proposed could at present be safely allowed.

Mr. Tilton, of the New York *Independent*, came to dinner, and rode with me afterwards.[28] I endeavored to impress upon his mind that there were but too practical ways of reconstructing the Proclamation States so as to them against the re-establishment of Slavery: One, by the organization of Provisional Governments; the other, by encouraging the loyal citizens to re-establish State Governments under constitutions prohibiting Slavery. He inquired much concerning men and things, and I endeavored to give him correct information. The Rev. Mr. Turner (colored) called for a letter to Mr. Stanton recommending him as Chaplain; which I gave him.[29] Professor Hedrick also called to talk about North Carolina matters.[30]

SATURDAY, SEPTEMBER 5, 1863. Telegraphed the Collector at San Francisco, congratulating him on the result of the California election.[31]

Received a telegram from Judge Bond desiring to have an interview arranged with the President for Mr. Goldsborough, and

---

27. On Sept. 3, Chase received a telegram from W. B. Farwell, acting collector of customs at San Francisco, reminding Chase of unhappiness in California over restrictions preventing the shipment of livestock to British Columbia. Lincoln signed the order amending the regulations later on Sept. 4. Chase to F. F. Low, July 14, 1863, Farwell to Chase, Sept. 2, 1863, Chase to Farwell, Sept. 4, 1863 (Telegrams Sent, Gen. Recs. Treasury Dept., Nat. Arch.); Low to Chase, July 23, 1863 (Letters Received from Executive Officers, ibid.); Basler, *Collected Works*, 6:432.

28. Theodore Tilton (1835–1907), New York Radical Republican and editor of the Congregationalist periodical, the *Independent*. *DAB*, 18:55–53.

29. Henry McNeal Turner (1834–1915), bishop of the African Methodist Episcopal Church and pastor of Washington, D.C.'s Israel Church, became the first black chaplain in the U.S. Army later in 1863. *DAB*, 19:65–66.

30. Antislavery leader Benjamin Sherwood Hedrick (1827–86) was chair of analytical and agricultural chemistry at the University of North Carolina, 1854–56, principal examiner in the U.S. Patent Office, 1861–86, and professor of chemistry and toxicology at Georgetown University, 1872–76. *Nat. Cyc.*, 9:127–28.

31. Chase's brief congratulatory telegram was to Frederick Ferdinand Low (1828–94), California banker and Union Republican politician. Low, who a few days earlier resigned from a short tenure as collector of customs at San Francisco, had just been elected governor of California. Chase to Low, Sept. 4, 1863 (Telegrams Sent, Gen. Recs. Treasury Dept., Nat. Arch.); Chase to A. Lincoln, Aug. 10, 1863 (Letters Sent to the President, ibid.); *DAB*, 11:445–46.

other Maryland gentlemen.³²— Sent to the President a commission for Mr. Stewart, in place of Mr. Ridgeley, who was removed, because of his hostility to the President's policy.³³

SUNDAY, SEPTEMBER 6, 1863. Mr. Heaton³⁴ came to breakfast, and gave me a full account of the progress of the emancipation sentiment in North Carolina. He represents the hostility to the Proclamation to be confined principally to the former slave owners, who wish to re-enslave the Emancipees, but the poorer classes, and many of the middle class, desire freedom, and with it, education and progress. On talking with men who came in to sell a barrell of turpentine, sometimes bringing it in a boat for several miles, or to sell water-melons from an old cart, he found them always quick to understand the cause of their troubles, and their poverty, and anxious for the removal of slavery in order that their children might have the advantages of education, which had been denied to them by the aristocracy.

In the afternoon Mr. Stickney called.³⁵ He had just arrived from Florida, and lastly from Morris Island. He says that it is easy now to take possession of Florida; that five thousand men can accomplish it. Gen. Saxton desires the command, and Gen. Gilmore³⁶ approves the Expedition, and is willing to spare one or two regiments to aid it. If the business can be promptly taken hold of, and pushed vigorously, Mr. Stickney is confident that Florida can be restored as a Free State by the first of December.

FRIDAY, SEPTEMBER 11, 1863. Mr. Galloway breakfasted with me.³⁷ We talked of Ohio affairs. He speaks encouragingly of our political prospects at home.

32. Hugh Lennox Bond (1828–93) served as judge of Baltimore's judicial court, 1861–67, and justice of the fourth U.S. circuit court, 1870–93. He may have communicated with Chase regarding either Henry H. Goldsborough, a Unionist state senator, or Edward Yerbury Goldsborough (b. 1839), also a Unionist, who became state's attorney of Maryland in 1864 and U.S. marshal in 1869. E. Y. Goldsborough married Chase's grandniece, Amy Auld, in 1874. *DAB*, 2:431–32; Basler, *Collected Works*, 5:285–86, 402; *OR*, ser. 2, v. 1:679–80, 712–13, v. 4:63–64; Williams and McKinsey, *History of Frederick County*, 2:1241–42.

33. Joseph J. Stewart of Baltimore was replacing James Lot Ridgely as collector of Maryland's second internal revenue district. Ridgely (1807–81), a Baltimore author, attorney, and politician, had failed to support Lincoln's Emancipation Proclamation adequately. *Appletons'*, 6:250; Basler, *Collected Works*, 7:75–76, 8:348; *Register of Officers (1863)*, 39.

34. David Heaton.

35. Lyman D. Stickney was a U.S. direct tax commissioner in Florida. Stickney to Chase, Apr. 16, 17, 1863 (Chase Papers, L.C.).

36. Quincy Adams Gillmore.

37. Samuel G. Galloway.

Called on the President immediately after breakfast to obtain his approval of the revised Regulations of Trade.[38] He referred me to the Secretary of War, wishing that the Secretary's order to officers to observe the Regulations, should precede his approval. Going then to the War Office,[39] I obtained Mr. Stanton's order, and at the Navy Department obtained that of Secretary Welles. Returned to the President's. He read me the rough draft of a letter to Andrew Johnson of Tennessee, urging immediate measures to re-constitute that State, and to so amend the Constitution as to insure emancipation, and promising him that the re-constituted State Government, so framed as to exclude the possibility of rebels regaining the ascendancy, would be recognized and sustained by the National Government.[40] Immediately after this, Secretaries Stanton and Fox, and General Halleck, came in. Some conversation took place about the further steps for the reduction of Charleston. Fox expressed the opinion that the harbor outside of Charleston had been closed by the rebels so as to be inaccessible to our ships, except through a narrow passage in which they kept a ship ready to be sunk, so as to close it completely. He said he thought that if such proved to be the fact, the only course would be to reduce the batteries on Sullivan's Island, so as to command that portion of the inner harbor outside of the obstructions. Gilmore had told him, he said, before going on the expedition, that he could reduce Fort Moultrie from Cumming's Point. Mr. Stanton doubted the existence of the obstructions, and said that the Admiral should try immediately what could be done. After Fox left, the President mentioned the resignation of General Burnside, received yesterday.— He said he was not willing to accept it at present, at any rate, as Burnside was now doing very well, and was very loyal and true-hearted. He proposed to say to him that he could not be spared at present, but that after awhile, should success still attend us and his private affairs should make his retirement necessary, his resignation would be accepted. Gen. Halleck then spoke briefly of affairs in and near Tennessee. He thought Rosecrans should advance so as to hold the mountains between him and Atlanta, but not attempt to advance on Atlanta until the movements of the rebels were more fully developed. That Burnside should also hold the country towards the eastern limits of

---

38. Issued to accompany circular instructions to special agents of the Treasury, Sept. 11, 1863. 38th Cong., 1st sess., 1863, H. Ex. Doc. 3, 408–22.

39. At this spot the clerk inserted an asterisk with the marginal note, "See first paragraph on page 91." The reference is to the next paragraph, set off in brackets by the clerk, which relates to this visit by Chase to the War Department.

40. A copy of the letter appears in Basler, *Collected Works*, 6:440–41.

Tennessee, but not attempt a further advance till more certain intelligence concerning the enemy and their designs.

[While I was at the War Department, Mr. Stanton told he should endeavor, to-morrow, to prevail on the President to revoke his exceptions in Virginia, and to adopt some settled principles respecting the enlistment of negroes held as slaves, and that he wanted me to be present. He wished me also to see Seward, and ask him to use his influence with the President to have Farragut sent to Charleston.]

After Stanton and Halleck had left, I explained briefly the Trade Regulations to the President, who said: "You understand these things: I do not," and signed the approval.

At the department, little of interest occurred.— Gen. Blair called with Col. Sanford, and I promised to speak to the Secretary of War in Sanford's behalf.[41] Gen. Cameron called, and told me he was about leaving town, and could not dine with me. I gave him a designation for Mr. Minor.[42] Directed payment of the ten per cent. gold loan in full.[43] Called on Gov. Seward. Spoke to him about sending Farragut to Charleston, and he promised to see the President on the subject.

In the evening, several callers as usual. Among others, Reese, who promised to bring Judge Edmunds,[44] which I told him to do at any time; and Brand, whom I promised to assist in obtaining promotion if practicable,[45] and Field who gave me an account of the Bank discussions in the Bank Meeting about the Loan.[46]

---

41. Francis Preston Blair, Jr., and possibly Edward Sewall Sanford (d. 1882), former president of the American Telegraph Company and, at this time, military supervisor of telegrams. David Homer Bates, *Lincoln in the Telegraph Office* . . . (New York, 1939), 108; Heitman, *Historical Register*, 1:859.

42. Chase appointed Charles S. Minor, an attorney from Honesdale, Pa., clerk in the third auditor's office. *Letter from the Secretary . . . Clerks . . . 1863*, 21; Minor to S. Cameron, Sept. 17, 1863 (Chase Papers, Hist. Soc. of Pa.).

43. Chase had been negotiating for a loan from New York banks (see Aug. 31, 1863, above). The loan was to take the form of bank subscriptions for new interest-bearing legal tender notes. The printing of those notes was now far enough advanced for Chase to order John J. Cisco to draw ten percent of the loan. Chase to Cisco, Aug. 31, Sept. 9, 1863 (Loan Division, Letters Sent, Recs. of Bureau of Public Debt, Nat. Arch.).

44. Probably John Worth Edmonds (1799–1874), a former New York supreme court justice and a member of the National Freedmen's Relief Association. *DAB*, 6:23–24; Edmonds to Chase, Mar. 4, 1862 (Chase Papers, Hist. Soc. of Pa.); same to same, Mar. 22, 29, 1862 (Chase Papers, L.C.).

45. Probably Joseph C. Brand, Jr., or Louis Brand, clerks for the register of the Treasury and the commissioner of customs, respectively. *Register of Officers (1863)*, 21, 34.

46. Maunsell B. Field (1822–75) was deputy assistant treasurer at New York, 1861–63, assistant secretary of the Treasury, 1863–65, collector for the sixth internal revenue district of New York, 1865–69, and judge of the state's second district court, 1873–74. *New York Times*, Jan. 25, 1875.

September 1863

JOURNAL III

1863. SEP. 14[47]   Gov. Andrew breakfasted with me: went with him to President—then saw Stanton about Scotty to whom a medal is to be given for his extraordinary gallantry.[48] Then went to Presidents & talked over order to Officers

JOURNAL XIII

MONDAY, SEPTEMBER 14, 1863. Governor Andrew came in to breakfast. Afterwards I went with him to the President, where I found Secretary Stanton, to whom I recommended "Scotty" for a medal, as I had promised him. Stanton said he would order one engraved, as soon as I sent him the name and inscription. At eleven a meeting of Heads was held. The President said that the applications for discharges by drafted men and deserters were very numerous, and were granted under circumstances which show that the Judges are disposed to defeat the objects of the law. He expressed the opinion that State Courts had no authority to issue a Writ of Habeas Corpus for any person in the custody of United States officers,—claiming to act under the national law. He proposed, therefore, to direct officers holding persons in such custody, to make a return of the fact that they were so held, and to refuse to obey the writ; and if force should be used to overcome it by force. Mr. Seward favored this action, and there was no expression against it, till I remarked that I had always been accustomed to regard the Writ of Habeas Corpus as a most important safeguard of personal liberty. "It has been generally conceded," I went on to say, "or at least such has been the practice, that State Courts may issue Writs of Habeas Corpus for persons detained as enlisted soldiers, and to discharge them. Several cases of this kind have occurred in Ohio, and the proceeding of the State Court was never questioned, to my knowledge. Of course, a proper exercise of the power does not justify its improper exercise. If the Writ is abused with a criminal purpose of breaking up the Army, the persons who abuse it should be punished as any other criminals are. But before taking any action, which even seems to set aside the writ, a clear case should be made, which will command the concurrence of the people and their approval. I suggest, therefore, that the Secretary of War should make a statement of the number of persons discharged from military service under

---

47. This is the first of seven days for which entries appear both in Journal XIII (in the clerk's hand) and in Journal III (in Chase's hand).

48. John Gray, a native of Scotland serving with Ohio's 5th Volunteers, had "captured a field piece, killed three men with the but of his musket—and performed several other daring feats." *OR*, ser. 3, v. 4:810–11, 814; James C. Wetmore to Chase, Oct. 24, 1863 (Chase Papers, L.C.).

the Writ, with such notes of the circumstances as will show the abuse of it. After which such action can be taken as the case requires." Mr. Blair[49] and Mr. Usher coincided substantially with these views, Mr. Blair remarking that he had often, when a judge in Missouri, discharged soldiers on Habeas Corpus. The President thought there was no doubt of the bad faith in which the Writ was now being used; Mr. Seward thought it indispensable to assert the authority of the Government at once; and Mr. Bates expressed the opinion that the President as head of the Army could not be interfered with by any civil authority, whatever; but was in his action as Commander-in-Chief superior to any process, and might properly instruct his officers and disregard such process; and this without any suspension of the Writ of Habeas Corpus, except as incidental to the exercise of his legitimate authority.— Mr. Stanton thought prompt action necessary. The President ended the discussion by saying he would prepare such an order as he thought best, and would see us again to-morrow at half-past two. The conversation then turned upon Writs of Habeas Corpus issued from Federal Courts, when it appeared that the number of discharges made by two Federal Judges in Pennsylvania, Cadwalader at Philadelphia, and McCandless at Pittsburgh, largely exceeded the number discharged by all the State Courts put together.[50] So it at once became evident that an order to reach the State Courts only would be inefficient.

After leaving the President I returned to the Department, and attended to its ordinary duties; the principal to-day being that of drawing upon the Banks for ten per cent. of their subscription for Treasury Notes, and the beginning of the distribution of the revised regulations concerning trade.

JOURNAL III

SEPT. 15 Heaton & Field breakfasted with me—then to Presidents. He read order & we had some talk about it

JOURNAL XIII

TUESDAY, SEPTEMBER 15, 1863. Went to the President's at half-past nine, and met there young Mr. Steven, nephew to the English lawyer, and Mr. Gillespie, of Illinois.[51]

49. Montgomery Blair.
50. John Cadwalader (1805–79) and Wilson McCandless (1810–82), judges of the U.S. district courts for eastern and western Pennsylvania. *Appletons'*, 4:76; *DAB*, 3:398–99.
51. Sir Leslie Stephen (1832–1904), a Cambridge don, writer, and Union supporter, was touring the U.S. His impressions of the meeting were later published in

Most all the Heads of the Departments having come in, the President read his order. It was a diriction to the military officers holding persons in custody as soldiers, deserters or drafted men, to make return to the Writ of Habeas Corpus from any Court, that the principal in the Writ was so held and refuse obedience; and that if force should be used to compel obedience, to overcome it. After the order was read, the Secretary of War made a statement showing the great number of persons discharged by Habeas Corpus principally by the two Federal Judges Cadwalader and McCandless, and stated some very gross proceedings under color of judicial authority, manifestly intended to interfere with the recruiting and maintenance of the Army. The President remarked that the order he had read was the same he had proposed yesterday, only modified so as to apply to Federal as well as to State courts. I then remarked: "This is an important matter. The statement made by the Secretary of War clearly shows a design to defeat the measures which Congress and the Executive have thought necessary to maintain the Army. The only question then is, in what mode should this attempt be met. You, Mr. President, have believed that you have the power to suspend the writ of Habeas Corpus without being authorized by Congress, and in some cases have acted on this belief. After much consideration I have come to the conclusion that your opinion and action are sanctioned by the Constitution. Whatever doubt there may have been as to your power to suspend the Writ, it has been removed by express legislation. The Act of the 3d March last, approved by you, authorizes you to suspend the Writ in any case during the existing rebellion when in your judgment the public safety may require it. The order you have just read does not suspend the Writ in terms, though it probably does in effect.— It leaves the question of suspension open to debate, and will lead to serious collisions probably, with the disadvantage on the side of the Federal authority. In my judgment, therefore, instead of this order there should be a Proclamation distinctly suspending the Writ of Habeas Corpus so far as may be necessary to prevent the great evil of virtually disbanding the Army, and when once issued any attempt to interfere with the organization should be punished under the Act

---

Frederick William Maitland, *The Life and Letters of Leslie Stephen* (London, 1906), 119–20. Leslie Stephen's uncle, Sir Alfred Stephen (1802–94), served at this time as chief justice of New South Wales. Gillespie was likely Joseph Gillespie (1809–85), Illinois state circuit judge, 1861–73, and an old political associate of Abraham Lincoln. *DNB*, 18:1044–45, 2nd Supp., 398–405; Newton Bateman, ed., *Historical Encyclopedia of Illinois, with Commemorative Biographies*, 2 vols. (Chicago, 1925), 1:201; Basler, *Collected Works*, 1:237, 249, 6:463.

of Congress promptly and decisively, no matter who the offender may be, whether Governor or Judge, or any less conspicuous personage. By this bold and direct action, I think you will command the confidence of the public, avoid collisions upon uncertain grounds, and secure most completely the great objects you have in view." This I said in substance. The President seemed to be struck with the force of it; took the law to which I had referred, and came to the conclusion that the best mode was to issue a Proclamation under it, suspending the Writ.[52] Some conversation then took place as to the proper return to be made by the officer to whom the Writ was addressed. As this matter, however, seemed to be sufficiently provided for by the law, the subject was not pursued. I was surprised to find that in a matter of this importance no one but myself seemed to have read the Act of March 3d with reference to the subject under discussion, and that its provisions were unfamiliar to all.[53]

Mr. Field left for New York to-day. I offered to make him Chief Clerk, with $3.000 a year, and to make him Second Assistant Secretary in case Congress would give me such an officer. He will consider it and reply.

I was much gratified to find by reports of the proper officers that the arrearages in the issue of 5–20 bonds was nearly made up, and that there was reason to expect that in the course of the present month we shall be prepared to issue fractional currency and Treasury Notes in sufficient quantities for the public demand.

JOURNAL III

SEP 16— Many callers & little done—tried to examine & decide Jay Cooke's business but made little progress—disposed of claim for cotton represented by Col Leathers.[54] Mr. Moore of New Jersey who desires to be appointed Collr. Int. Rev. Puget Sound District called[55]

SEP 16[56] Whole time consumed by callers, except necessary for routine work.

---

52. Lincoln issued the proclamation which suspended the writ of habeas corpus later the same day. Basler, *Collected Works*, 6:451–52.

53. The act authorized the president to suspend the writ of habeas corpus "whenever, in his judgment, the public safety may require it." *Statutes at Large*, 12:755–58.

54. Possibly D. M. Leatherman, an attorney who had recently approached Lincoln regarding property claims of a Tennessee woman whose husband served in the Confederate army. Basler, *Collected Works*, 6:431.

55. Philip D. Moore became collector of internal revenue for Washington Territory. *Register of Officers (1863)*, 41.

56. Journal III contains more than one entry, at different locations within the manuscript volume, for some days. In such cases, the day's entries appear here in succession, in the order in which one finds them in Journal III (although in the original they might be some distance apart).

JOURNAL XIII

WEDNESDAY, SEPTEMBER 16, 1863. Nearly my whole time was consumed by callers. Endeavored to examine the papers in relation to Jay Cookes Agency, but made small progress. Some claims for cotton surrendered to Yeatman, the Agent,[57] the largest of which was represented by Colonel Letherman, came in. Mr. Moore, from Washington Territory, called. He is a candidate for the Collectorship vacated by Major Goldsborough.[58] He explained the transaction relating to the *Herald of Progress* and Dr. Allyn, showing that Victor Smith had no connection with Dr. Allyn's contribution to the *Herald*.[59] His explanation was entirely satisfactory on this point. He also denied positively on behalf of Mr. Smith, the statement of Henry and others, that Smith asserted that I was indebted to him.[60] In the evening, Mr. Pierce and Mr. McKim called.[61] Also Major Smith[62] and Mr. Green, the latter of whom said that he was requested by Judge Balcom of the Court of Appeals of New York[63] to tender his respects to me and say that the Court had agreed upon a decision in the legal tender cases, before them, affirming the Constitutionality of the law. Major Giddings and Captain Ilgis also called, who, in the course of conversation made these remarkable statements about the condition of the Regular Regiments.[64] They said that the Twelfth, now in New

---

57. Thomas H. Yeatman.

58. Hugh A. Goldsborough, collector of internal revenue for Washington Territory, was upset with factional political disputes in the territory and had been requesting permission to resign since April. In the early 1870s he was chief clerk of the Navy's bureau of construction and repair. Chase to A. Lincoln, July 29, 1862 (Lincoln Papers, L.C.); Goldsborough to Chase, July 27, 1863 (Chase Papers, L.C.); Chase to Goldsborough, Sept. 17, 1863 (Chase Papers, Hist. Soc. of Pa.); Parks, "A Man for His Season," 87; *Wash. Dir. (1872)*, 205; ibid. (1873), 210.

59. Chase's reference is to one of various accusations made by opponents of Victor Smith, whom Abraham Lincoln had removed from his position as collector of customs in the Puget Sound area. According to one of his critics, Smith had awarded John Allyn a contract to operate the local marine hospital, and reached an unwritten agreement that $100 of the physician's profits each month would be sent to the New York *Herald of Progress*, a spiritualist periodical which Smith admired. Anson G. Henry to Abraham Lincoln, Mar. 14, 1863 (Chase Papers, Hist. Soc. of Pa.); Mott, *American Magazines*, 2:210; Parks, "A Man for His Season," 36–102.

60. One of Victor Smith's strongest critics was Anson G. Henry (d. 1865), a Springfield, Ill., physician and close associate of Abraham Lincoln, who had appointed Henry surveyor general of Washington Territory. Basler, *Collected Works*, 1:77–78, 6:111, 202, 215; Parks, "A Man for His Season," 96.

61. Edward Lillie Pierce and Pennsylvania antislavery leader James Miller McKim (1810–74), founder of the Philadelphia Port Royal Committee and co-founder of *The Nation*. *DAB*, 12:103–4.

62. Thomas L. Smith, the third auditor.

63. Ransom Balcom (1818–79), an admirer of Chase from Binghamton, N.Y., was a justice on the state supreme court. Balcom to Chase, June 6, 1863 (Chase Papers, L.C.); H. P. Smith, *History of Broome County, New York* . . . (Syracuse, N.Y., 1885), 125–26.

64. Grotius Reed Giddings (d. 1867) and Guido Ilges were officers in the 14th U.S. Infantry. Heitman, *Historical Register*, 1:454, 562.

York, had 600 men, and about twenty-seven officers; that the Fourteenth at 400 men, and seventy seven officers, the full complement. These two regiments are of the new organization, 2400 men each; that the Third had 180 men and eight officers; the Fourth 22 men and nineteen officers; the 6th 130 to 140 men and fifteen officers; the 10th 31 men and nearly a full complement of twenty-seven officers. The 3d, 4th, 6th and 10th are old regiments.

JOURNAL III

" 17 Went to Presidents—found Gov. Newell & others interceding for pardon of deserters[65]—urged countenance to free state movement by loyal men in Florida—

SEP 17 See Prest. about Hamilton[66]— Suspension of Habeas Corpus— Ridgely, Assessor— General Davies[67]— Florida government.

JOURNAL XIII

THURSDAY, SEPTEMBER 17TH, 1863. Went to the President's immediately after breakfast— Found Governor Newall and other New Jersey gentlemen interceding with the President for the pardon of a deserter. Said to the President that I feared some injustice had been done in removing Mr. Ridgeley, who had in conversation with me the day before expressed the most decided support of the Administration, saying that the ground of complaint against him was that he had supported Mr. Webster for nomination to Congress, and that Mr. Webster was as decided a friend to the Administration as himself.[68] Mr. Ridgeley had asked me for a pass to go to the Army to see Col. Webster, and I suggested to the President the propriety of allowing him to go. The President said he could go after a few days, but that just now the Army might be moving. I mentioned to the President the message of Judge Balcom, and he said that Judge Davies had given him similar information. I again referred to the case of Gen. Hamilton, and he told me that General Hamilton had

---

65. William Augustus Newell, M.D. (1817–1901), Whig and Republican congressman, 1847–51, 1865–67, governor of New Jersey, 1857–61, and territorial governor of Washington, 1880–84. *DAB*, 13:459–60.

66. Andrew Jackson Hamilton.

67. Col. Henry Eugene Davies (1836–94), the son of Judge Henry Ebenezer Davies, was appointed brigadier general of volunteers, Sept. 16, 1863. *DAB*, 5:101–2.

68. Col. Edwin Hanson Webster (1829–93), Maryland Volunteer Infantry, 1862–63, American party, Unionist and Unconditional Unionist congressman, 1859–65, and collector of customs at Baltimore, 1865–69, 1882–86. *Bio. Dir. U.S. Cong.*, 2021.

been sent for, and wd probably return to Texas, as Brigadier General and Military Governor. Referred again to the subject of revoking the exceptions of the South-Eastern counties of Virginia from his Proclamation, and he read to me the draft of an unfinished letter he had begun to me on that subject, the argument of which was very strongly put, but based entirely upon the idea that the military necessity which justified the Proclamation did not now exist in regard to these counties.[69]— I questioned the correctness of this view and referred to the letter of Gov. Pierpont,[70] urging the revocation upon the distinct grounds of military necessity. He then remarked that the revocation, at all events, was not expedient at present, and should be deferred until after the Fall elections. We then talked on the suspension of the Habeas Corpus. He said that I was quite right in recommending it rather than the order which had been prepared, and that he had been convinced of it as soon as he heard my statement of the law. I also spoke to him about the promotion of Col. Davies, saying that I thought he deserved it by his gallantry and ability, and that I should be particularly glad to have it done because of the Judges' steady support of the Government. He intimated that it had been already decided upon, which I was very glad to hear.

I then went to the War Department. Mr. Stanton stated a curious circumstance. Yesterday, he said, a shot or shell from the Navy Yard fell into a cavalry camp on the Maryland side of the Potomac, killing one man and doing considerable injury to the Camp. He directed a report of the facts to be made to Secretary Welles, with a request to change the direction of the guns; to which the Secretary replied that he paid $200 a year for the privilege of firing on that piece of ground! Mr. Stanton said that he was going to offer him $600 a year to make such a change as would save his camp.—

After returning to the Department, Mr. Plumley called to talk about matters in Louisiana, and I invited him to breakfast tomorrow morning.

JOURNAL III

18. Maj. B. R. Plumly breakfasted with me—went with him to War Dept & introduced him to Mr. Stanton & commended him—

---

69. A copy of the letter, dated Sept. 2, appears in Basler, *Collected Works*, 6:428–29.
70. Francis Harrison Pierpont; see Sept. 3, 1863, above.

SEP 18 S. E. Stroughn, Edr. Cambridge Intr, recommended for Assessor vice Russum[71]— F Curr[72] $5000 50s Wed. $2000 to Garrett[73]—$5000 25s by Saturday—for 10s & 5s will have 7 presses at work on Wednesday & 15 on Wednesday following (2)

(2) refers to distribution of fractional currency to Railroads to facilitate making change & to ensure general circulation[74]

JOURNAL XIII

18TH OF SEPTEMBER, 1863. Mr. L. E. Straughn, of the Cambridge (Maryland) Intelligencer, called. He had been recommended for Assessor in place of Russell,[75] and naturally thought the change a desirable one. He impressed me very favorably: indeed, I had already been satisfied by his paper, of his activity and patriotism, and should be very glad to show my sense of it, but am not prepared to make the desired removal.—

Plumly breakfasted with me, and gave quite a clear inside view of military and civil affairs at New Orleans. He represents General Banks as very friendly to me.

Gen Hamilton called and bid me "good bye," being about to leave for his new position in Texas. Shurz also called.

20TH OF SEPTEMBER, 1863. Having been impressed, by somewhat careful study, with apprehensions for the condition of Rosecran's Army, I was a good deal alarmed by the telegrams in the morning papers,[76] and went immediately to the War Department after breakfast, where I found two telegrams, one from Rosecrans himself, and one from Dana,[77] both dated at Chattanooga, and both reporting serious disaster. Later in the day another telegram came

---

71. "Stroughn" was L. E. Straughn. George M. Russum was assessor of Maryland's first internal revenue district. Straughn did not replace Russum, but later in the year Lincoln appointed him to hear claims by Marylanders whose slaves had enlisted with Union forces. Chase to Lincoln, Aug. 27, 1862 (Lincoln Papers, L.C.); *Register of Officers (1863)*, 39; OR, ser. 3, v. 3:938; Straughn to ———— Humphreys, Oct. 1861 (Chase Papers, Hist. Soc. of Pa.).

72. Fractional Currency.

73. John Work Garrett of the B & O Railroad.

74. The text following the (2) is Chase's footnote, at the bottom of the page in the original journal. Chase called this note 2 because an entry for Oct. 1, 1863, written higher on the same page, had a footnote which he had labeled *1*.

75. George M. Russum.

76. Sept. 20, 1863, was a Sunday. Chase probably referred to news from the Battle of Chickamagua which appeared in the Monday morning papers. *Daily National Intelligencer*, Sept. 21, 1863.

77. New York newspaperman Charles Anderson Dana (1819–97) had recently received an appointment as assistant secretary of war. *DAB*, 5:49–52.

from Dana, saying that Thomas[78] had successfully resisted the enemy's advance, but left room for serious forebodings

JOURNAL III

SEP. 21. At War Dept.—Rosecran's & Dana's telegrams look bad—Chickamauga

SEP. 22. Harrington left for Europe today. May he come back fully restored![79] Went to Hallecks Headquarters—President spoke of recent battle—of Thomas, Granger[80] & Garfield as distinguished for gallantry.

JOURNAL XIII

22D OF SEPTEMBER, 1863. At the meeting of the Heads of Departments, the President gave an account of the battle of Sunday. Results are less unfavorable than was feared, although the losses are great in killed, wounded and prisoners, and some fifty guns captured by the enemy on the center and right. On the left Thomas and Granger and Garfield, who had joined Thomas at great personal risk, had distinguished themselves greatly.

Received a letter from Shurz, enclosing a printed scheme for a Testimonial to McClellan, which was being circulated in the Army for subscriptions, with the sanction of the Commanding General and his Staff.[81] Called Stanton's attention to it, who agreed with me in thinking it an insult to the President. I also showed the letter and the paper to the President, who took the paper and promised to see Stanton about it.— Harrington left to-day for Europe, hoping to recover his health, impaired by over-exertion.— Received a telegram from Mrs. Charles Jones that her brother, and my brother-in-law, Lieut. Ludlow, was wounded and a prisoner at Chickamauga.[82] I

---

78. George Henry Thomas.

79. Harrington suffered from some unspecified "trouble" involving his head. He remained in Europe until Feb. 1864. Maunsell B. Field was assistant secretary of the Treasury in the interim, and remained as a second assistant secretary after Harrington's return. Harrington to Chase, Oct. 4, 1863 (Chase Papers, Hist. Soc. of Pa.); Chase to Harrington, Feb. 26, 1864 (Harrington Papers, Mo. Hist. Soc.).

80. Career soldier Gordon Granger (1821–76), a major general of volunteers, commanded the Army of Kentucky. *DAB*, 7:484–85.

81. The subscription for McClellan resulted in nothing of consequence. H. J. Eckenrode and Bryan Conrad, *George B. McClellan: The Man Who Saved The Union* (Chapel Hill, 1941), 265–66.

82. Charlotte Ludlow Jones was communicating news of her brother, Israel Ludlow.

telegraphed Garfield, at Chattanooga, and received a reply confirming the report, and urging prompt reinforcements.

23D OF SEPTEMBER, 1863. Spoke to Stanton about promoting Charles A. Cooledge, who enlisted as a private and has been promoted Lance Sergeant in the Sixteenth Regulars.[83]

JOURNAL III

SEP. 23. I shall not soon forget the events of the night of this day.[84] Our news from Chattanooga was more hopeful—but it was evident that Rosecran's army was in great peril. Meade was in the neighborhood of [Manassas], following Lee, and, it was hoped, about to win a decisive victory over him— But he was cautious & it was uncertain if he would strike at all. I went home from the Department thinking over the state of things—with great anxiety. It was about midnight & I had just retired, when[85] the door bell rang & the message was brought to me "The Secretary of War desires that you will come to the Department immediately & has sent a carriage for you." "What can be the matter" I said to myself as I hastily rose & dressed. "Has the enemy attacked Rosecrans?' Has he captured him & his army? Has he driven our men across the Tennessee"?— When I reached the War Dept I found Mr Stanton there, silent & stern. "Is there any bad news" I asked. "None" was the brief reply— General Halleck was present; and the President either was there already or soon came in; Mr. Seward also came.

At length when we five were assembled Mr. Stanton began: "I have invited this meeting because I am thoroughly convinced that something must be done & done immediately to ensure the safety of the army under Rosecrans; & wish to have it considered & decided whether any thing & if any thing what shall be done."

Then turning to General Halleck he asked:

What force can Burnside send to Rosecrans at Chattanooga? General Halleck replied, "20.000 men"

---

83. Charles Austin Coolidge (1844–1926), who later earned a medical degree, was promoted to the position of second lieutenant, 16th Infantry, in 1864. He eventually achieved the rank of brigadier general by the time of his retirement in 1903. *Who Was Who*, 1:256–57.

84. This entry, although dated Sept. 23, describes the night of Sept. 23–24. The midnight conference is also described in Journal XIII, under date of Sept. 24 (below).

85. In the original journal, the entry breaks at this point and continues twenty-two pages farther along. The intervening pages contain entries from July to September 1864, evidence which strongly implies that Chase put this entry for Sept. 23, 1863, into the journal at least a year after the events it describes. (See the description of Journal III, pp. lx–lxii above.)

September 1863 {451}

Stanton— How soon.
Halleck— In ten days if not interrupted.
President— Before ten days Burnside can put in enough to hold the place
Halleck— He can bring up 12 000 perhaps in eight days
President— When Burnsides men begin to arrive the place will be safe; but the pinch is now.
Stanton— If the enemy presses or attacks Burnside what then?
Halleck— Burnside must take his measures accordingly—fight, or act defensively.
Stanton— If Enemy has enough to detach a force against Burnside & also attack Rosecrans?
Halleck— Rosecrans must be relieved otherwise.
Stanton— When can Sherman relieve him?
Halleck— In about ten days if already marched from Vicksburgh— If not marched should come up the River & overland from Memphis—he has 20 000 or 25 000 men—every available man is ordered forward & boats have gone down the river from Cairo to bring them up.
Stanton— Then your estimate of what can be done by Sherman is only conjectural?
Halleck— Of course it is impossible to speak definitely on such a matter.
Stanton— Can men be had from any other quarter?
Halleck— Perhaps a few from Kentucky—don't know how many— all are already ordered to Rosecrans.
Stanton— Mr. President, I think it perfectly clear from what has been said that no certain or even probable relief will reach Rosecrans from any quarter that has been named. I do not believe a man will get to him from Burnside or Sherman in time to be of any use in the emergency which is upon us. The Army of the Potomac is doing nothing important; nor is it likely to be more actively employed. I propose, therefore, to send #20.000 men from the Army of the Potomac to Chattanooga, under the command of Gen Hooker.

This proposition was objected to quite strongly both by Gen Halleck & the President both expressed the belief that the troops could not be got through to Chattanooga or near enough to be of essential service to the army of Rosecrans as soon as troops could be furnished from Burnside's or Sherman's command & both were unwilling to withdraw troops from Meade.

Mr. Stanton said that he had fully considered the question of practicability & should not have submitted his proposition had he not fully satisfied himself on that head by conference with the ablest railroad men of the country. [Gen.] Halleck had give no definite assurance as to the time in which relief could be given by Sherman or Burnside. His nearest approach to definiteness was eight days by Burnside, if uninterrupted by the enemy? Was not the enemy sure to interrupt? & Was it not well known that relief by Burnside would involve the abandonment of East Tennessee to which Burnside was strongly opposed—therefore extremely unwilling to move. Whereas if it should be determined to send men from the army of the Potomac the order for the two corps could be given in the morning—by night the column would be entering Washington—the troops could be put in cars at once & in five days the advance might be entering Nashville.

"Why" said the President "you cant get one corps into Washington in the time you fix for reaching Nashville"; and he illustrated his idea of the impossibility by some story which I have forgotten.

Stanton was greatly annoyed & made some remark to the effect that the danger was too imminent & the occasion to serious for jokes; but added that as he saw himself overruled he would give up the point; & invited us all into the adjoining room where he had caused a light collation to be prepared.

I then remarked that I hoped the proposition would not be abandoned: that it seemed to me exceedingly important; & that we could resume its consideration with advantage after a little refreshment. I added a very brief resumé of Mr. Stantons arguments already urged—expressed my entire confidence in his ability to do what he proposed—& declared it to be my deliberate judgment that to refuse to adopt it was to refuse to adopt the only plan [by] which the Army of Rosecrans [w]ould with any certainty be saved.

We, then, went to the collation. On returning to the Secretarys room Mr. Seward took up the subject & supported Mr. Stantons proposition with excellent arguments.

The scale was now turned. Every objection was abandoned except that of weakening Meade & finally the President said that he wd. telegraph Meade in the morning & if he did not propose an immediate movement, the order for the two corps to move should be given at once by Gen Halleck. It was near morning when we went home. Two or three hours later the telegram was sent—the answer recd—the order for the movement given.

The result is well known. The advance of Hooker's command reached Nashville in a week—frustrated the attempt to break up Rosecrans' communications; & his army was saved; and Chattanooga was saved; & the future was saved. Neither Shermans column nor Burnsides came up in time to be of any use in this special work. Burnsides did not come up at all. Sherman's came; but came after the peril was past; though in time for the glorious achievements which soon afterwards electrified the country. The country does not know how much it owes Edwin M. Stanton for that nights work.

JOURNAL XIII

24TH OF SEPTEMBER, 1863. Having gone home last evening very weary, was called up from my bed about midnight by a messenger from the War Department, who said I was wanted there immediately. The Summons really alarmed me. I felt sure that disaster had befallen us; that the army of Rosecrans had been attacked before his defences were completed, and had been compelled to surrender, or had been defeated with great loss in another bloody battle, and its remains driven across the Tennessee. Great was my relief when, reaching the War Department and asking "more bad news?" Stanton replied, "No, what there is, is favorable." He then handed me a telegram from Garfield to myself, which stated that Rosecrans could hold out ten days where he was, but earnestly urged reinforcements.[86] Other telegrams from Rosecrans and Dana gave encouraging expectations that he could hold out still longer time. Both also urged re-inforcements. After a little while the President and Mr. Seward also came in.— General Halleck was already there. Mr. Stanton then opened the conference by inquiring of Gen. Halleck, what reinforcements Burnside could add to Rosecrans and in what time. Halleck replied twenty thousand men in ten days, if uninterrupted. The President then said, "before the ten days Burnside will put in enough to hold the place (Chattanooga).

Stanton to Halleck— How many in eight days?

Halleck— 12000.

The President— After Burnside begins to arrive, the pinch will be over.

Stanton.— Unless the enemy, anticipating reinforcements, attacks promptly.—(To Halleck)—When will Sherman's reach Rosecrans?

Halleck.— In about ten days, if already moved from Vicksburg. His route will be to Memphis, thence to Corinth and Decatur, and a march of a hundred or a hundred and fifty miles on the north side of the Tennessee River. Boats have already gone down from Cairo, and every available man ordered forward, say from twenty to twenty-five thousand.

Stanton.— Are any more available elsewhere?

---

86. Garfield to Chase, Sept. 23, 1863 (Chase Papers, L.C.).

Halleck.— A few in Kentucky; I dont know how many.— All were ordered to Burnside.

Stanton.— I propose then to send 30.000 from the Army of the Potomac. There is no reason to expect that General Meade will attack Lee, although greatly superior in force; and his great numbers where they are, are useless. In five days 30.000 could be put with Rosecrans.

The President.— I will bet that if the order is given tonight, the troops could not be got to Washington in five days.

Stanton.— On such a subject I don't feel inclined to bet; but the matter has been carefully investigated, and it is certain that 30.000 bales of cotton could be sent in that time by taking possession of the railroads and excluding all other business, and I do not see why 30.000 men cannot be sent as well. But if 30.000 cannot be sent, let 20.000 go.

Much conversation followed, the President and Halleck being evidently disinclined to weaken Meade's force, whilst Seward and myself were decided in recommending the re-inforcement of Rosecrans. It was at length agreed that Halleck should telegraph Meade in the morning, and if an immediate advance was not certain, the Eleventh and Twelfth Corps, supposed to make about 13.000 men, should be sent Westward at once, under Hooker, with Butterfield as his Chief of Staff.

SEPTEMBER 25, 1863. By telegram after we separated last night, the Secretary of War called the officers of the Baltimore and Ohio, the Philadelphia and Baltimore, and the Pennsylvania Central Railroads to Washington.[87] They were in conference with him the greater part of the day. The movement of the troops was arranged. It was found that the number would exceed 15.000, but no doubt was expressed that the movement would could be accomplished promptly, though not quite so soon as Stanton had anticipated. In the Evening I found myself quite unwell.

SEPTEMBER 26TH, 1863. Having been kept awake most of the night, with severe pains, I telegraphed Garrett and Smith that I could not come to Baltimore and visit Mr. Hopkins[88] as I had pro-

---

87. John Work Garrett, president, and William Prescott Smith (c. 1822–72), master of transportation for the Baltimore and Ohio; Samuel Morse Felton (1809–89), president of the Philadelphia, Wilmington and Baltimore; and Thomas Alexander Scott (1823–81), first vice president of the Pennsylvania Railroad. *DAB*, 6:318–19, 16:500–501; Hungerford, *Baltimore and Ohio Railroad*, 2:51; *New York Times*, Oct. 2, 1872.

88. Baltimore entrepreneur and philanthropist Johns Hopkins (1795–1873). *DAB*, 9:213–14.

posed. A little before 11 I received a reply from Mr. Smith to the effect that Mr. Hopkins had notified some twelve or fifteen of the leading financial men to meet me at dinner, and that the disappointment would be great if I did not come.[89] I concluded therefore to risk the journey, and answered that I would come on the 11:15 train. I arrived in Baltimore; met Mr. Garrett and Mr. Smith, who insisted that I should take a ride with them through Federal Hill and Fort McHenry before going to Mr. Hopkins's: to which I consented. We reached Mr. Hopkins's about four o'clock. Only two or three of the guests had arrived, and Mr. Hopkins proposed to show us his place. We therefore accompanied him on a walk around the grounds, which are very spacious and beautiful. Extensive graperies with every variety of grapes in rich clusters; a pleasant fruit orchard, the trees of which were loaded with fruit; a vegetable garden, conveniently situated, with commodious and handsome farm buildings near, together with a lake so artistically contrived with islands, trees and shores, as to give it the appearance of great extent,—formed the principal features of this beautiful place. The whole extent of the grounds is about four hundred acres, of which perhaps sixty are used for the purpose just mentioned, while the rest are devoted to farm cultivation. Mr. Hopkins insists that though a gentleman farmer, he contrives to make both ends meet, at the close of each year. His dinner was simple, but excellently prepared and in the best taste. His dessert of grapes exceeded in beauty and variety and flavor anything I had ever seen. My indisposition condemned me to almost total abstinence, much to my regret. The guests were intelligent and substantial men, constituting, as Mr. Hopkins said, the best part of the Baltimore merchants and capitalists. And all of them earnest Union men. And nearly all, if not all, decided Emancipationists. It was about nine o'clock when we left his hospitable mansion and returned to the City, where I soon found myself established in comfortable quarters at Mr. Garrett's.

SEPTEMBER 27TH, 1863. I slept better last night than the night before, tho' still far from well. A slight fever made me fancy myself beset with matters of public concern, when I was sure I was not so engaged; and would try to dispel the illusion, and sometimes succeeded for a moment, only to find it coming back the next. This was unpleasant enough, and I was glad when the morning came to my relief. After breakfast, of which I partook very slightly, I found myself sufficiently well to accompany the family to Church; where I heard an excellent sermon and spent two pleasant hours.— On

---

89. William Prescott Smith also offered to put a special train at Chase's disposal. Smith to Chase, Sept. 26, 1863 (Chase Papers, Hist. Soc. of Pa.).

coming out, Judge Bond asked us to go with him to see a dress parade of a colored regiment at Camp Birney.[90] They asked Mr. Garrett if he would go, and he assented. A little after five o'clock we rode to the Camp. The regiment was already in line, nine hundred strong, besides the guards on duty. Behind it was another line; three or four hundred new recruits. These were rough and rugged in their negro clothes, fresh from the plantations. I directed Mr. Garrett's attention to the spectacle, saying that the front line in uniform and the rear line in negro clothes soon to come forward also into the front ranks in uniform, was very suggestive. Mr. Garrett looked and said nothing. The sight could hardly be palatable to one so recently, if not still, thoroughly pro-slavery in his sentiments. After some conversation with Col. Birney, in charge of the recruiting service, and Col. Duncan[91] (whose graduation I witnessed some years ago at Dartmouth College), commanding the uniformed, we returned to the city.

28TH OF SEPTEMBER, 1863. I slept pretty well last night under the hospitable roof of Mr. Garrett. After breakfast he and Mr. Smith accompanied me to Mr. Swann's, with whom I exchanged kind greetings; thence to the hat-store of Mr. Smith's father-in-law, Mr. Van Zandt,[92] where I supplied myself with something more suitable to the season than my "straw;" thence to the Custom House where I exchanged salutations with the officers and clerks, and thence to the cars where I found Judge JEWETT,[93] with whom I proceeded to Washington; and resumed my duties at the Department.—

Mr. Garrett informed me that the movement of the troops was going on successfully, which was confirmed by Mr. Stanton, who is greatly delighted by its success. He told me that the number to be moved had been found to reach 20.000, and yet the whole had been

---

90. The camp, apparently located at the end of Madison Avenue in Baltimore, was operated by William Birney, who served at this time as colonel with the 4th Regiment of U.S. Colored Troops. Birney had been recruiting black soldiers in the area since the middle of July. Recently, he had antagonized Maryland loyalists by accepting slaves and forming black recruiting parties. On Oct. 1, Lincoln issued temporary orders for Birney to cease enlistments in the state. *Baltimore Sun*, Sept. 18, 1863; Ira Berlin, ed., *Freedom: A Documentary History of Emancipation 1861–67. Series II, The Black Military Experience* (Cambridge, 1982), 184–85; Donn Piatt, *Memories of the Men Who Saved the Union* (New York, 1887), 44–46; *OR*, ser. 3, v. 3:767–68, 881–82, 1111–14.

91. Samuel Augustus Duncan (1836–95), Dartmouth class of 1858, of the 4th U.S. Colored Infantry. Emerson, *General Catalogue*, 297; Heitman, *Historical Register*, 1:388.

92. Joshua Van Sant (1803–84), Baltimore hat manufacturer and Democratic congressman, 1853–55. *Bio. Dir. U.S. Cong.*, 1978; *Baltimore Dir. (1842)*, 382.

93. Probably Thomas Lightfoot Jewett (1810–75), previously a judge in the courts of Steubenville, Ohio, and at this time president of the Steubenville and Indiana Railway Co. *Appletons'*, 3:433; *Nat. Cyc.*, 7:548; *OR*, ser. 1, v. 23, pt. 1:673–74.

put in motion without disturbance and in perfect order. The last were expected to reach Washington to-day, and would be immediately sent forward. Thus in five days the men who, as the President was ready to bet, could not be got to Washington, would be already past that point on their way to Rosecrans, while their advance had reached the Ohio River. If this whole movement is carried through to the end as well as it has been thus far, it will be an achievement in the transportation of troops unprecedented, I think, in history.

29TH OF SEPTEMBER, 1863. Nothing occurred of much interest to-day. At the President's neither Mr. Seward nor Mr. Stanton were present. They seemed, reasonably enough, to have given up attendance on these meetings of the Heads of Departments as useless. And for aught I see I may as well follow their example.— Received a note from Miss Walker, asking the promotion of Bryant Walker to be an Assistant Adjutant General with the rank of Captain, and sent a note to Mr. Stanton, begging that the favor might be done, which was promptly and kindly done.[94]

30TH OF SEPTEMBER, 1863. Received a note from Mr. Stanton, notifying me that young Walker's commission would be sent to him as soon as possible. I enclosed the note to Miss Walker, New York. There was the usual number of callers, and the usual variety of talk and business, but nothing of special importance.

In the evening, I entertained at my house, a delegation of "Radicals" from Kansas and Missouri, with Mr. Charles D. Drake as their Chairman,[95] come hither to ask of the President such a change in the conduct of military affairs in that Department as shall better secure the loyal men in their rights and homes.

JOURNAL III

OCT. 1. Mr. Field takes his place as Asst Secretary.[96]

---

94. Susan Walker had written in behalf of her nephew James Bryant Walker (d. 1874), an attorney and the son of Chase's former law partner, Timothy Walker. Chase's letter asked Stanton to appoint Walker, who was currently an officer with the 20th Ohio Volunteers, assistant adjutant general under Maj. Gen. Manning Ferguson Force. Chase either misdated his letter or recorded the matter under the wrong date heading in his diary. Chase to Stanton, Sept. 27, 1863 (Chase Papers, Hist. Soc. of Pa.); *Quinquennial Catalogue*, 226.

95. St. Louis attorney Charles Daniel Drake (1811–92), a leading member of the radical wing in Missouri's Unionist party, later served as U.S. senator, 1867–70, and as chief justice of the U.S. Court of Claims, 1870–85. *DAB*, 5:425–26.

96. At the end of this entry in the original journal there is a sketch of a pointing hand with Chase's notation, "next page." This note refers to the second entry for Oct. 1, separated from this one in the original by entries for two other days.

OCT. 1 Genl. de Ahna called with strange story[97]— He says a letter came from Richmond, with $3000 from Benjamin.[98] The money was to be used by one Chs. d'Arnaud formerly on Fremont's staff to corrupt Col. Percy Wyndham an officer of one of our cavalry regiments & induce him to betray his command to the enemy[99]—for which he was to receive some addl. compensation— This letter came to a Mrs Van Camp, wife of a Mr. Van Camp said to have the confidence of the Prest. & to claim to hold a licence to buy cotton granted by him[1]—thro' some mistake of personal identity this letter of Benj. came to de Ahna; who communicated with Hogan, a detective employed by the Treasy. Dept;[2] who communicated to me; & I to the Secry of War: who agreed with me that I should see de Ahna & hear his story. It was little else than above—he showed me Benjamins note which promd. compensation for "articles" meaning I suppose "horses"—he also paid over to Hogan $2000 of the money sent by Benjamin which I directed Hogan to deposit with Jay Cooke & Co. De Ahna was told to discover, if he could, what was being done in complicity with the rebels, & advise me or the Secy. of War[3]

Mr. Field entered on his duties as Asst. Secy. today

OCT. 1. While during the past month I was very busy in aiding as far as I could the work of others, my own was very arduous & important. Every day had its various & complicated demands. The

---

97. Henry C. De Ahna of Missouri, a veteran of military service in Germany, was actually a colonel. In 1862, the U.S. Senate had rejected his appointment as a brigadier general of volunteers. Basler, *Collected Works*, 5:368–69; De Ahna to Lincoln, Jan. 31, 1864 (Lincoln Papers, L.C.).

98. Judah Philip Benjamin (1811–84), a former U.S. senator from Louisiana, 1853–61, served as Confederate attorney general, 1861; secretary of war, 1861–62; and secretary of state, 1862–65. *DAB*, 2:181–86.

99. Charles D'Arnaud had previously spied for John Charles Frémont. Sir Percy Wyndham was an English officer in New Jersey's First Cavalry who had previously seen military service with the British, French, and Italian armies. Allan Nevins, *Frémont: Pathmarker of the West* (New York, London, and Toronto, 1955), 491–92; Henry R. Pyne, *Ride to War: The History of the First New Jersey Cavalry*, ed. by Earl Schenck Miers (rev. ed., New Brunswick, 1961), xiii–xiv.

1. Aaron Van Camp practiced dentistry in Washington, D.C. In Dec. 1861, he had been arrested as a Confederate spy and detained three months in the Old Capitol Prison. *OR*, ser. 2, v. 2:562, 572–74; *Wash. Dir. (1862)*, 174.

2. Christopher V. Hogan, employed from Dec. 1862 through Sept. 1863 to investigate counterfeiting. Chase to Hogan, Dec. 27, 1862 (Letters Sent to Special Agents, Recs. of Bureau of Customs, Nat. Arch.); Hogan to Chase, Sept. 31, 1863 (Applications and Recommendations for Positions in the Washington Offices of the Treasury Dept., Gen. Recs. Treasury Dept., Nat. Arch.).

3. De Ahna later accused Chase of failing to follow through with an adequate investigation. De Ahna to Lincoln, Jan. 31, 1864 (Lincoln Papers, L.C.).

October 1863

trade between the loyal states & those parts of the rebel states of which our forces were in possession required careful attention & had it. The forming of the necessary regulations was a work of great labor & devolved largely on me.

OCT. 1. Chs. [S]herrill (1) for Supervising Agent—Opdyke— — M. C. Stanley (1) Plumly, Wilkes for Chf Clerk 3d Audr.[4] Gangewer (1) now has $1800 [Mc]Daniel (1) has 1400 Carleton (1) has 1400[5] (1) Persons recommended for place—to be considered[6]

OCT. 2.— Camp called with letter from Greeley,—proposed plan for collecting public sentiment in my favor as candidate for Presy.[7]— told him that people must do as they pleased in this matter—I could not interfere. Sickles,[8] Cartter & others also called—had pretty hard nights work on business of Dept.

OCT. 3. Mr. Camp called introduced by Mr. Greeley—proposes plan for collecting public sentiment in reference to next Presidency— Told him I could take no part—people must do as they pleased.

OCT. 4— Mr. Barney came—went to church with me— Sermon on Christ in us—grand theme ill handled— Much talk on coming

---

4. The person being recommended may have been Marcus Cicero Stanley, a North Carolina native living in New York who in 1861 had been arrested and imprisoned briefly on the charge of dissuading men from enlisting. His recommenders were probably George Wilkes, who vouched for Stanley after his arrest in 1861, and either B. Rush Plumly, who was traveling through New York about this time, or Alexander R. Plumley, a weigher in the New York Custom House. Chase knew Alexander Plumley, a Vermont native, from years before in Washington, when Chase had tried to establish himself as a schoolmaster and Plumley had let him take over a class of Plumley's students. *OR*, ser. 2, v. 2:766–71; *New York Dir. (1864)*, 822; B. R. Plumly to Chase, Oct. 3, 1863 (Chase Papers, L.C.); *Register of Officers (1863)*, 75; Chase to J. T. Trowbridge, Feb. 10, 1864 (Chase Papers, Hist. Soc. of Pa.).

5. Chase's former secretary Allen M. Gangewer, Osborne Macdaniel, and John L. Carleton were all clerks in the third auditor's office. Gangewer got the promotion to chief clerk. *Register of Officers (1863)*, 25; *Letter from the Secretary . . . Clerks . . . 1863*, 20.

6. Chase wrote this sentence as a footnote at the bottom of the page. He wrote the *(1)* notations above the names to which they refer, so it is likely that he inserted the explanatory footnote and reference numbers after he had completed the body of the entry.

7. New York builder Benjamin F. Camp was a friend of Horace Greeley and a stockholder in the *Tribune*. Greeley had written to Chase that "if in 1864 I could *make* a President (not merely a candidate) you would be my first choice." Greeley to Chase, Sept. 29, 1863 (Chase Papers, Hist. Soc. of Pa.); *New York Dir. (1863)*, 137.

8. Maj. Gen. Daniel Edgar Sickles (1825–1914), of the 3rd Corps; military governor of the Carolinas, 1865–67; U.S. minister to Spain, 1869–73; and Democratic congressman from New York, 1857–61, 1893–95. *DAB*, 17:150–51.

home with Barney—is my friend certainly—but does not like to show preference if Mr. L—— desires renomination.

OCT. 5— Mr. Barney breakfasted with me—Mr. Risley came with Trade Regulations as proposed—looked over them & made corrections

OCT. 5. Barney called at breakfast—seems not exactly to know his own mind—but will go for Mr. Lincoln if he desires reelection— Risley came in with Trade forms which I revised

OCT. 7 Have Wilkins bond sent for correction. Has Yeatman leave of absence? Colvin, Randolph[9] Th. S. Meux

OCT 8 Morrill suggests Index to Commerce & Navigation Report

OCT 9.— Promote J. J. Piatt if possible[10]

DEC. 1. In November on my memorandum book occur such entries as these

NOV. 17 Enquire of Clark[11] as to printing notes for 1 year & two years (1)— See the fractional currency now furnished— Enquire of Qr. Mr. General comparative contract prices last fall & since 8 March (1) These were the first interest bearing legal tenders for which I ever substituted the 6% compound [rate] notes

NOV. 18 Speak to Pacific members about the currency—attend to seizure of the Light Ships at New Bedford[12]

NOV. 19— Papers say steamer exploded at San Pedro[13]—Captain not licenced— What officer this—naval or merchant? Boats char-

---

9. Possibly James W. Colvin, a printer, and William B. Randolph, chief clerk in the treasurer's office. *Wash. Dir. (1865)*, 167; *Register of Officers (1865)*, 30.

10. Ohio poet and editor John James Piatt (1835–1917) was a Treasury clerk, 1861–67, assistant clerk and librarian of the House of Representatives, 1871–75, and U.S. consul at Cork, Ire., 1882–93. *DAB*, 14:556–57.

11. Spencer Morton Clark.

12. During the summer of 1863, three government lightships undergoing final outfitting at New Bedford were placed under a sheriff's lien for unpaid claims against the contractor. The case came before the supreme court of Massachusetts during the autumn. At least two of the vessels were later placed into service. *Report of the Secretary of the Treasury, on the State of Finances, for the Year ending June 30, 1863*, 38th Cong., 1st sess., 1863, H. Ex. Doc. 3, 160; *Report of the Secretary of the Treasury on the State of the Finances, for the Year 1864*, 38th Cong., 1864, H. Ex. Doc. 3, 167.

13. Chase may refer to the *Ada Hancock*, a steamer that exploded off San Pedro, Calif., in May 1863. *New York Times*, May 31, 1863.

tered by govt. do not conform to licence & inspection law—great losses in consequence— — Commr. of Customs thinks Collectors bonds &c should be referred to him[14]

About this time I was very busy on my Report & made many mema. to aid in its preparation.[15]

1864

JOURNAL XIV

JUNE 24—[16]   Another anxious day. What will be the result of the summer campaign? Can we keep Grant & Sherman so furnished with men & means that they can inflict decisive blows on the rebellion?

My part is to supply if possible the means—and where am I to find them. The currency is depreciated less—though much—by surcharge than by the distrust which seems to be gradually pervading the public mind; especially the mind of that class whose conclusions,—half instinctive, half reasoned,—determine the degree of confidence in Governments and Institutions

Under these circumstances, to increase the circulation will merely aggravate our greatest financial [curse]—that of disordered commerce & prices unnaturally high. It should be diminished rather than increased. Can this be done? Not without large taxes or large loans.

A committee from New York, introduced by Senator Morgan, called this morning to urge modification or repeal of the Gold Act.[17] Their arguments should, I said, be addressed to Congress rather than to me; but I was glad to hear their views. Some, especially Mr. James Brown, of Brown Brothers & Co, Mr. Hoffman, of Colegate & Hoffman, & Mr. Ward, of Ward Campbell & Co argued for

---

14. Attorney and journalist Nathan Sargent (1794–1875) was U.S. commissioner of customs, 1861–71. *DAB*, 16:368.

15. *Report of the Secretary . . . 1863.*

16. Chase's heading for this entry includes the notation, "copied from a loose sheet written June 24." The entry shows some alterations, so Chase did more than simply copy it from elsewhere. When he wrote the entry into Journal XIV he may have added the "Note" forming the entry's last paragraph, which, as indicated below, he could not have written before the end of June. Although the Journal XIV entries are presented here in chronological sequence, in the original the June 24 entry follows those for June 26 through July 6. Chase made a brief notation at June 26 calling attention to the entry for the 24th farther along in the journal.

17. On June 17, Congress had passed legislation to prohibit speculation in gold futures. The statute, which required that gold be delivered to a buyer no later than the date of the sales contract, was repealed by a one-sentence act approved July 2, 1864. Ernest A. McKay, *The Civil War in New York City* (Syracuse, N.Y., 1990), 249–50; *Statutes at Large*, 13:132–33, 344.

repeal;[18] if repeal impossible for modification. Their arguments were substantially these (1.) Absolute freedom of trade secures lowest prices. True in certain conditions of market individuals or combinations may monopolize whole supply & exact their own prices from those who must have the article monopolized as gold for example but this evil less than restrictive regulation. (2) Convenience to merchants of public sales even those of gold gambling room as giving a standard of price. The complaints of practical inconvenience were principally of the supposed necessity to pay notes in hand for gold bought when check would be much more convenient and of the supposed prohibition against buying exchange for gold. I could not see that licence to gambling was essential to freedom of trade; and said that under the act as I understood it there could be no objection to *public* sales; or to the use of checks, if real checks on actual deposits & paid during the day; to to direct purchases of exchange for gold. One gentleman suggested that Congress should expressly authorize loans of gold to be repaid in gold & sales not of exchange only but of all merchandise for gold. I saw no objection to loans of gold for gold but sales such as proposed would repeal the legal tender law.[19] The conversation was good tempered on both sides & to me instructive.

The Internal Revenue bill remains with the Committee of Conference; but it is expected they will report tomorrow.[20] It is apprehended that the bill will not impose taxes enough to bring the residue of expences within the reach of loans. Mr. Orton came tonight from New York at my request & will devote himself to careful examination of the bill & amendments & estimate the probable revenue as nearly as possible.[21]

Spent some time with Mr. Taylor[22] who by my direction has been engaged in preparing a bill or measure to authorize the sale of gold & silver lands. I cannot but think that fee simple titles in mines will tend powerfully to their most productive working. He has conferred with Senator Conness, Commissioner Edmonds &

---

18. New York bankers James Muncastor Brown (1820–90); Charles Burrall Hoffman of Colgate and Hoffman; and George Cabot Ward (1828–87), founder of Ward, Campbell & Co., the New York agency of London's Baring Brothers. *Nat. Cyc.*, 5:558–59, 8:14–15; *New York Dir. (1864)*, 170, 404.

19. The measure, signed into law on Feb. 25, 1862, which made "greenbacks" a legal tender. *Statutes at Large*, 12:345–48.

20. Lincoln signed the legislation on June 24. Ibid., 12:223–306.

21. William Orton (1826–78), collector of internal revenue at New York, 1862–65, U.S. commissioner of internal revenue, 1865, and from vice president to president of the Western Union Telegraph Company, 1866–78. *DAB*, 14:65–66.

22. James Wickes Taylor.

June 1864 { 463 }

others & has finally proposed a bill which seems to me adequate.[23] I directed him to put it into the form of a section to be added by way of amendment to a bill authorizing sales of lands embracing coal mines which has passed the Senate & is in the House. This was done & I prepared letters to Mr. Julian Chairman of the Public Lands Committee & to Senator Conness[24] & instructed Mr. Taylor to confer with Senator C—— and the California delegation & if they approved the amendment take it with my amendment to Mr. Julian & try to have the bill adopted. If the measure succeeds it will work quite a revolution.

Note. The amendment was approved & came very near success. It is possible,—had not the necessity for my resignation arisen—I might have carried it through. It will probably engage the attention of Congress at the next Session & become law.[25]

SUNDAY, JUNE 26. This day was given to what seemed necessary labor. It was extremely important to know whether a gentleman invited to accept the Asst. Treasr. ship at New York would consent to do so[26] & to set in motion the advertising for the New loan & to prepare for an appeal to Congress to make up the deficiencies in taxes. The day was therefore mainly devoted to these objects. Dr. Elder came in & dined with me[27]—no one at home besides myself.

MONDAY. JUNE 27. Called on Senator Morgan to consult about Asst. Treasurer at New York—told him I had concluded to recommend Mr. Field.[28] He thought I had better name Mr. Gregory

---

23. California Republican John Conness (1821–1909) was a U.S. senator, 1863–69. James Madison Edmunds (1810–79) served as commissioner of the U.S. land office, 1861–66. *Bio. Dir. U.S. Cong.*, 818; Johnson, *Twentieth Century Biographical Dictionary*, v. 3.

24. Chase to George Washington Julian, June 24, 1864 (Letters Sent to Committees of Congress, Gen. Recs. Treasury Dept., Nat. Arch.); Chase to John Conness, June 24, 1864 (Chase Papers, Hist. Soc. of Pa.).

25. Lincoln accepted Chase's resignation on June 30, 1864, and the second session of the 38th Congress began on Dec. 5, 1864, so Chase must have composed this "Note" between those dates.

26. Chase had offered the position to New York banker Denning Duer, who had already turned down the invitation. Chase to Duer, June 20, 1864 (Chase Papers, Hist. Soc. of Pa.); Duer to Chase, June 22, 1864 (Chase Papers, L.C.); *New York Dir. (1863)*, 247.

27. William Elder (1806–85), originally from Pennsylvania, was a physician, attorney, free-soil advocate, and writer on political economy. During the Civil War he compiled financial statistics within the Treasury Department and wrote pamphlets on the subject of the national debt. *DAB*, 6:68.

28. Maunsell B. Field.

or Mr. Blatchford[29]— I replied that either gentleman would be entirely acceptable to me personally but I thought the public interests would on the whole be best consulted by the appointment of Mr. F. He said that Mr. Jones of Brooklyn Chairman of the Union Committee[30] had brought a list of clerks & officers under Mr. Cisco and that there were but some half dozen Union men among them— all the rest being[31] democrats / I replied that I thought the statement erroneous and that on fair enquiry it would be found that of the persons called democrats the largest proportion are of the same class with Andrew Johnson—but I would think the matter all over & decide today. At the Dept. Mr Freeman Clarke called & I talked the matter over with him.[32] He seemed to prefer Mr. Field. I told him if he would take it I would send his name to the President at once. He said his health would not allow him to do so & [even if] it would he could not on other grounds. I asked him to confer with the Senators & report, telling him I must decide today. Having waited to hear from him till about four & having in the meantime conferred fully with Mr. Field, whom I found even a more decided supporter of the Admn. than Johnson was at the time of his nomination, I went to the Capitol to see him. He was neither in the House nor Senate & I then sent to the Department thinking that in the meantime he might have gone thither. The Messenger returned reporting that he had not been there & I at once sent Mr. Fields name to the President, about half past four

In the course of the morning, Mr. Orton whom I had summoned from New York to examine the Internal Revenue bill and ascertain what revenue might be expected & to give me also his judgment as to the sources from which the deficiencies if any might be raised made his report.[33] He estimated the net product at 220 mills for

29. New Jersey banker Dudley Sanford Gregory (1800–1874), Whig congressman, 1847–49; and Richard Milford Blatchford (1798–1875), New York attorney and U.S. representative to the States of the Church at Rome, 1862–63. *Bio. Dir. U.S. Cong.*, 1093–94; *DAB*, 2:359.

30. Charles Jones, of New York's Union State Committee. Jones to A. Lincoln, Aug. 21, 1864 (Lincoln Papers, L.C.); Basler, *Collected Works*, 8:43.

31. A stroke, possibly intended as underlining but evidently added after the text was written, appears below the words *rest being*. A similar stroke appears below *largest* in the next sentence.

32. Freeman Clarke (1809–87) of New York was a Republican congressman, 1863–65 and 1871–75, and comptroller of the currency, 1865–67. *Bio. Dir. U.S. Cong.*, 786.

33. Chase included Orton's suggestions in recommendations to the financial committees of Congress and the president (see June 29–30 below). Chase also advised the committees to interview Orton. Orton to Chase, June 27, 1864, and undated [probably of same date] (Ways and Means, Treasury Dept. Papers, 38th Cong., Recs. of the House of Representatives, Nat. Arch.); Chase to T. Stevens, June 29, 1864, and to W. P. Fessenden, same date (Chase Papers, Hist. Soc. of Pa.).

the next fiscal year and submitted a paper showing how the deficiency of eighty millions would be made up. I directed him to have a bill prepared for the taxes suggested by him. I have repeatedly assured the Committee and the President that we cannot [even] sustain the existing or even somewhat reduced rate of expenditure without a revenue from taxes & duties of $400 000 000. In a recent letter upon the assumption, admitted to be improbable that expenditure might be reduced to 750.000,000 I fixed the amount with which we might get along at one half or 375 000 000. I mean to send the bill for the additional taxes to Congress & the President & insist on it.

These were the most important matters of the day. Talk about Trade regulations, various applications for permits and positions, revision of Spragues proposed remarks about Blairs charge against him of Cotton Speculations;[34] correspondence & conversation about gold bill occupied most of the day.

One thing merits record. Having received a telegram from Mr. Barney about 6 P.M. enquiring when the operation of the Joint Resolution increasing duties for 60 days[35] would cease, & having satisfied myself that, on the construction already given that it took effect on the day of its approval, it would cease today at midnight I conferred with Mr. Hooper who happened to be with me, &, having ascertained that Congress had taken no step to extend its operation except to put such a provision in the Tariff bill not yet passed, requested him to introduce a Joint Resolution to extend the time till the first of July— He drew one immediately & promised. The result was the introduction of this Joint Resolution—its passage through the House & Senate—its approval by the Senate & its communication by telegraph to all the Collectors before midnight.

JUNE 28, TUESDAY— How beautiful & excellent is the order and progress which St Paul enjoins & illustrates in his letter to the Ephesians![36] Oh if the world could but learn that lesson, how anxieties, & perplexities would lighten & pass away with the clashes, & jars, & wars which bring them. May God in His infinite mercy send us peace with union and freedom.

34. The charges by Francis Preston Blair, Jr., had been made on Apr. 23 as part of wholesale attack on Chase and the policies of the U.S. Treasury. According to Blair, Chase had given Sprague a permit to buy Southern cotton which was expected to yield a profit of $2 million. Sprague answered the charges on the Senate floor on July 4. *Cong. Globe*, 38th Cong., 1st sess., 1864, 34, pt. 2:1831; William Ernest Smith, *The Francis Preston Blair Family in Politics*, 2 vols. (New York, 1933), 2:256–60.
35. *Statutes at Large*, 13:411.
36. Especially Eph. 4–6.

This morning I read part of Paul to the Ephesians & as usual endeavored to seek God in prayer. Oh, for more faith & clearer sight! How stable is the City of God! How disordered is the City of Man!

At the Department received a note from the President, saying that Senator Morgan strongly opposed the nomination of Mr. Field in place of Mr. Cisco—replied asking an interview—but received no answer. He may not wish one or what is more probable allows himself to forget the request. He asks the nomination of R. S. Blatchford or Dudley S. Gregory, neither of whom, I fear, is the proper man to take charge of the office at this critical juncture; though either would be entirely acceptable to me personally. I fear Senator Morgan desires to make a political engine of the office, and loses sight in this desire of the necessities of the service

Received a note from Senator Morrill informing me that the Trade Bill has passed the Senate, & from Mr. Hooper that the Loan bill passed the House by concurrence in all the Senates amendment.[37] He had vainly endeavored to procure a modification of one, so as to let the Govt. pay for stock used in engraving its notes instead of allowing the same stock to be used, if it had been previously so used, in preparation of other circulation, & to exclude the use of green pigment from all notes & bonds, letting Govt. remunerate any patentee. Congress preferred to risk the evils to the National Note Circulation.

Went to House & talked with Mr. Hooper & Mr. Washburne[38] about Trade Bill & urged importance of it. I do this reluctantly because of the labor it will impose on me & because of the odium which its interference with private speculation & naval [*illeg.* prize] will be sure to excite against me. I wish we could have good Commissions to manage these things & also Loans. But the President would almost certainly put in men from political considerations and after all the responsibility would still be on me.

Returning to Dept. conferred with Mr. Orton & Actg. Comm. Rollins[39] (Int. Rev.) about supplementary tax bill. Both agreed that the Revenue for fiscal year commencing next Friday would not exceed 220 or 225 millions whereas 300 mills at least is nec-

---

37. The trade bill, which passed both houses of Congress on July 2, provided "for the Collection of captured and abandoned Property, and the Prevention of Frauds in States declared in Insurrection." The Loan Act of June 30 authorized the U.S. Treasury to borrow $400 million. *Statutes at Large*, 13:218–22, 375–78.

38. Elihu Benjamin Washburne.

39. Edward A. Rollins, formerly cashier of the internal revenue division. *Register of Officers (1863)*, 35; ibid. (1865), 50.

essary. In accordance with my instructions they had prepared a new bill which with their statements & a letter of my own I propose to send to Congress tomorrow—another great & painful responsibility!

Telegraphed Mr. Cisco urging him to withdraw resignation & serve at least another quarter;[40] & wrote to President what I had done & why I could not honestly, in duty to him or the country, recommend at this time either of the names he had suggested.[41]

In the evening went up to the Capitol. The Senate was holding an eveng session & Garrett Davis was making a rambling, violent speech for slavery, abusing the President, against the Freedmens-Bureau Bill then under consideration.[42] Talked to some of the Senators—found that the House was not in Session & so came home.

The 3d. Auditor Mr. Atkinson resigned today. Mr. Sills of Iowa is to take his place.[43] Atkinson has been an excellent officer; but has been much disliked by our friends on account of his politics. I advised him to resign therefore, proposing to use his services in another place where the same hostility wd. not manifest itself / His health too requires a change. Hence his resignation.

The day has been one of great anxieties & distress— What can be done to arrest the decline of public credit? I see nothing effectual except taxation which will make excessive borrowing unnecessary & military success which will make necessary borrowing possible on reasonable terms. Had the first object of this Campaign been the suppression of rebellion west of the Mississippi I think our prospects now would have been much brighter. Had artificial reconstruction by amnesty proclamations & military power been let alone & actual reconstruction left to the loyal people—loyal enough to recognize in every real loyalist a man & a citizen—and had the Army of the Gulf been put under a real military but at the same time thoroughly loyal leader—the trans-Mississippi rebellion might & probably would have suppressed with the force actually engaged.

---

40. Chase to Cisco, June 28, 1864 (Cisco Papers, L.C.).
41. Chase also drew up a memorandum promoting Maunsell B. Field's appointment to succeed Cisco, and wrote a brief note asking for a personal interview on the subject. All three documents are dated June 28, 1864 (Lincoln Papers, L.C.).
42. "An Act to establish a Bureau for the Relief of Freedmen and Refugees" finally passed Congress on Mar. 3, 1865. *Statutes at Large*, 13:507–9.
43. Robert J. Atkinson had held the position since 1854. His potential replacement was Elijah Sills, who in fact did not succeed Atkinson as third auditor. Lanman, *Biographical Annals*, 14; *Wash. Dir. (1863)*, 37; Basler, *Collected Works*, 7:392; *Register of Officers (1865)*, 29.

I must not omit to mention that the President & faculty of Otterbein College, travelling together in Vacation called on me this evening.[44]

JUNE 29. Last evening I received Mr. Ciscos reply to my telegram consenting to withdraw his resignation. This morning I received the Presidents reply to my note.[45] He says he did not accede to personal interview because useless—complains of the difficulties occasioned by his retention of Mr. Barney & the appointment of Judge Hogeboom,[46] both considered as of the radical side and says he cannot go farther in that direction by the appointment of Mr. Field desires appt. made acceptable to Gov Morgan & those who think as he does— Will await Mr. Cisco's action. I replied that I made no general distinction in appointments except friend & opponents of his administration and among the former none except degrees of fitness—that Mr. Cisco's reply relieved the present difficulty; but as I could not [that], help feeling that my position here was not agreeable to him & there was nothing in my office making me wish to retain it, I enclosed my resignation & should feel really relieved by its acceptance. I added that I would give my successor all the aid I could on his entrance upon the duties of the office. With this note I enclosed my resignation.[47]

All the time I could command today was devoted to the preparation of a letter to the Chn. of the Com. of Ways & Means urging additional taxes[48]—sufficient to ensure a revenue from Internal Duties of 300.000.000, I representing strongly the necessity of such provision in order to reduce circulation & diminish the increase of debt—the former depreciating currency & the latter damaging public credit. It was finished & sent with letters & statements supporting it from Collector Orton of New York, about six 'oclock in the afternoon. I also directed copies of the letter & all the documents to be prepared for the Chn. of the Com. on Finance (Senate)[49] and

---

44. Rev. Lewis Davis, D.D., was president of the United Brethren institution located at Westerville, Ohio. George W. Knight and John R. Commons, *The History of Education in Ohio* (Washington, 1891), 140–44; Willard W. Bartlett, *Education for Humanity: The Story of Otterbein College* (Westerville, Ohio, 1934), 41–42.

45. Cisco to Chase, June 28, 1864 (Lincoln Papers, L.C.); Lincoln to Chase, June 28, 1864 (Lincoln Collec., John Hay Lib., Brown Univ.).

46. John T. Hogeboom was general appraiser in the New York Custom House. *Register of Officers (1865)*, 105.

47. Chase to Lincoln, June 29, 1864 (Lincoln Papers, L.C.). Copies of the correspondence between Chase and Lincoln appear in Basler, *Collected Works*, 7:413–14.

48. Chase to Thaddeus Stevens, June 29, 1864 (Ways and Means, Treasury Dept. Papers, 38th Cong., Recs. of the House of Representatives, Nat. Arch.).

49. Chase to William P. Fessenden, June 29, 1864 (Finance Committee Papers, 38th Cong., Recs. of the Senate, Nat. Arch.).

of all except the bill & the letters of Collector Orton & Rollins to be prepared for the President.[50]

One of the last acts today was to send to the President nominations of Captains & other officers in the Revenue Service.

Coming home Mr. Day & his daughter called—the former asking influence for the latter— I was vexed & I fear rude which was wrong. The man however does not impress me as true & honest.

Risley called & Orton came to the House to spend the remainder of his time while in the city with me. Risley & Harrington went to the House to promote, if possible, the passage of the Insurrecting District Trade Bill[51] / Washburn of Ill[52] told me today that it would be very difficult to get the bill before the House.

JUNE 30. Immediately after breakfast this morning I went to see Gen Schenck about the enrollment law; & found him with Gen Garfield and a gentleman who was a stranger to me at breakfast. In view of the difficulties which embarrassed the action of the Senate & House I suggested & somewhat earnestly pressed the expediency of leaving the whole subject very much to the discretion of the President, authorizing him to draft for not less than one or more than two years and to allow commutation, if he should deem it expedient, at rates not less than $300 nor more than $500. Under this law the discretion would I thought be judiciously exercised by the Secretary of War & the Lieutenant General who would doubtless be allowed to act upon their own judgment, and the rule being flexible could be adjusted to circumstances with great advantage.[53] This idea seemed to strike both gentlemen favorably, & as they are both on the Military Committee some good may come of it.

On going to the Department I found that Mr. Fessenden had been there & left word that he desired to see me at the Capitol. So after signing a letter to the President, commending to his attention my letter to the Committee of Ways & Means & the Statements & estimates of Mr. Orton,[54] I went to the Capitol. Fessenden had not

---

50. See June 30 for the letter to Lincoln. Rollins, like Orton, had provided information on internal revenues. Rollins to Chase, June 28, 1864 (Ways and Means, Papers on Taxation, 38th Cong., Recs. of the House of Representatives, Nat. Arch.).

51. The "Trade Bill" mentioned on June 28.

52. Elihu Benjamin Washburne.

53. The enrollment act, which passed Congress on July 4, authorized Lincoln to draft any number of volunteers for one to three year terms, but forbade commutation. Recently, Congress had engaged in heated debate over the possibility that the law would encourage the recruitment of substitute black soldiers from states still technically in rebellion. *Cong. Globe*, 38th Cong., 2nd sess., 1864, 34, pt. 4, 3484–91; *Statutes at Large*, 13:379–81.

54. Chase to Lincoln, June 30, 1864 (Lincoln Papers, L.C.).

yet returned; but I had read on my way a letter he had left for my perusal from a Mr. Dole urging the repeal of the gold bill. When he came in we talked on this subject, & he desired my views. I told him that I never expected great benefits from such legislation; but that I thought it hardly wise to yield to the clamor of the opponents of this particular act; that the rise of gold did not in my judgment come from this law as a permanent cause, though doubtless its tendency in the particular condition of the market was to cause a rise; & that as there was no prohibition of sales in it nothing but simple restrictions upon gambling & restraint of operation to legitimate channels, I thought it best to let it alone at this session; but should be entirely satisfied whatever the Committees and Congress might do.

Mr. Morrill of Vt. came in during our conversation & spoke of the proposition I had made to increase taxes. He was adverse to it. In his opinion the bill already passed would yield some 30 millions more than Orton's Estimate. I replied that admitting there might be such improvement or increase, still the revenue would fall far short of half the expenditure & it would be impossible to borrow the remainder for terms. On conversation with Mr. Orton afterwards I found that Mr. Morrill had omitted to take into the account the important circumstance that the increase he expects [would] not even if realized go into the next fiscal year but into the year following.

While we were talking a messenger came in to summon Mr. Fessenden to the Senate. The messenger said something privately & he came back to me saying "Have you resigned. I am called to the Senate & told that the President has sent in the nomination of your successor. I told him I had tendered my resignation but had not been informed till now of its acceptance. He expressed his surprise & disappointment & we parted— He to the Senate & I to the Department. There I found a letter from the President accepting my resignation, & putting the acceptance on the ground of the difference between us indicating a degree of embarrassment in our official relations which could not be continued or sustained consistently with the public service.[55] I had found a good deal of embarrassment from him but what he had found from me I could not imagine, unless it has been created by my unwillingness to have offices distributed by spoils or benefits with more regard to the claims of divisions, factions, cliques and individuals, than to fitness of selection. He had never given me the active & earnest support I was entitled to & even now Congress was about to adjourn without

---

55. A copy of the letter appears in Basler, *Collected Works*, 7:419.

passing sufficient tax bills, though making appropriations with lavish profusion, and he was notwithstanding my appeals taking no pains to ensure a different results.

Among those who called during the day was Mr. Hooper who related a conversation with the President some days ago, in which the President expressed regret that our relations were not more free from embarrassment, saying that when I came to see him he felt awkward & that I seemed constrained. At the same time he expressed his esteem for me & said that he had intended in case of vacancy in the Chief Justiceship to tender it to me & would now did a vacancy exist. This he said, he remarked, to show his real sentiments towards me; for he remembered that not very long after we took charge of the administration I had remarked one day that I preferred judicial to administrative office & would rather if I could be Chief Justice of the United States than hold any other position that could be given me. Mr. Hooper said that he thought this was said to him in order to [be] repeated to me and that he had sought an opportunity of doing so but had not found one. I said it was quite possible had any such expressions of good will reached me I might, before the present difficulty arose, have gone to him & had a frank understanding which would have prevented it: but I did not now see how I could change my position.[56]

Indeed if such were the real feelings of Mr. Lincoln he would hardly have refused a personal interview when I asked it or have required me to consult local politics in the choice of an officer, whose character & qualifications were so vitally important to the Department. Besides I did not see how I could carry on the Department without more means than Congress was likely to supply & amid the embarrassments created by factious hostility within & both factious & party hostility without the Department.

So my official life closes. I have laid broad foundations. Nothing but wise legislation—and especially bold yet judicious provision of taxes—with fair economy in admn. and energetic yet prudent military action, (the last of which seems to be ensured by the position of Grant at the head our armies—oh may he have troops & supplies enough!) seems necessary to ensure complete success. The Insurrectionary District Trade bill will give the Department the power to regulate trade more efficiently than heretofore & to take to the use of the Government the profits of purchase & sale of the Staples of the Rebel States. Not only can many abuses be now corrected—but a pecuniary benefit can be derived to the Govt. of not less I think

---

56. Originally there was no paragraph break here. Chase inserted a paragraph symbol to indicate the beginning of a new paragraph after this sentence.

than $25.000.000. The Tax bill it is true is inadequate but Congress may give to my successor, under the alarms created by the change, what would not be yielded to me. And even if taxes are not increased a tolerable showing can be made. The provisions I have secured with so much difficulty in the Tax bill requiring monthly returns of banks & monthly collection of taxes & high taxes on excess beyond existing circulation, or any circulation beyond ninety per cent of capital, will, I think, certainly prevent increase of bank note circulation & secure some slight reduction. This to be sure leaves almost the whole burden of reduction upon loans; but something at least can be done in this way also: for the next six months when Congress will have been again in session a month & will have had an opportunity to supply what is now lacking. With these advantages & with all the great work of administration already inaugurated & blocked out, and especially with the still greater advantage of [not] having the inside & outside hostility to encounter, which I have been obliged to meet, my successor, I think, can get on pretty well. If he fails any where, without his own fault, it will be on the side of loans or under the pressure of military disaster. What I can do to help him, I will, for the country's sake, do most gladly.

JULY 1. This morning the papers contained telegrams announcing that Gov Tod[57] declines to take the Treasury Department. On receiving this information the President sent to the Senate the name of Mr. Fessenden—a wise selection. He has the confidence of the country & many who have become inimical to me will give their confidence to him & their support. Perhaps they will do more than they otherwise would to sustain him in order to shew how much better a Secretary he is than I was. If so the country will gain even by hostility to me transmuted into friendship for him.

Gen Moorhead called & related briefly an interview between himself & Mr. Williams,[58] & the President. They had attempted to induce him to send for me with a view to my return to the Department; but he would not consent to this. He thought we could not agree & it was without use: and in this he was I think right. I cannot sympathize with his notion notion[59] more than once expressed to me & others that the best policy is to have no policy & he cannot sympathize with my desires for positive & energetic ac-

---

57. David Tod.
58. Thomas Williams (1806–72), Republican congressman from Pennsylvania, 1863–69. *Bio. Dir. U.S. Cong.*, 2060.
59. Chase wrote *notion* on top of the false start of another word (perhaps "id" for "idea"). The original *notion* is difficult to read, and Chase wrote the word again, very clearly, above the line.

tion. It is best that he try somebody else. They had then mentioned to him Mr. Howe of Pittsburgh as a proper person for Secretary;[60] but found him not inclined to this. The conversation preceded Tod's declination; [and] had reference to the possibility that the Senate might not confirm the nomination.

The day was given to writing letters & to conversation with others who called. In the evening Fessenden came in immediately after dinner, or rather just before finishing dinner. Nobody but Senator Sprague & myself were at the table & he [introduced] the subject of his nomination. He expressed an extreme aversion to acceptance—fears of inability to carry on the Department—& especially strong apprehensions that his health would give way. He had he said begun to a note declining, but had been prevented from finishing it by constant interruptions—& had received so many & such urgent appeals to accept that he was greatly embarrassed & wanted my advice. I told I thought he ought to accept—that all the great work of the Department was now fairly blocked out & in progress—that the organization was planned; in many parts complete, and in all in a state which admitted completion—that is so far as completeness could be said of any thing needing constant supervision & allowing constant development & improvement. His most difficult task would be to provide money. He would now see, I thought, how important sufficient taxation was & that the Department ought to have been helped by some legislation, asked but denied. But he would have advantages which I had not. I had been obliged to inaugurate the National Banking System & to claim the circulation for the whole country through their Association & had necessarily encountered the ill will of those whose prejudices or interests bind them to the support of the old System. And I had necessarily also given offence to many whose counsels I had not been able to follow or whose wishes I had not been able to gratify. These persons would have no cause of ill will against him: and would very probably come to his support with zeal increased by their ill will to me. So my damage would be his advantage, especially with a certain class of capitalists & Bankers; and I thought nothing more probable than that he would be able to obtain loans easier than I could. At any rate this would be his chief & so far as I could see the only real difficulty in his administration. He expressed great apprehension lest his health might give way and said that if he took the place to which he was much urged in Congress & by callers & telegrams from

---

60. Pittsburgh merchant and manufacturer Thomas Marshall Howe (1808–77), assistant adjutant general of Pennsylvania and Whig congressman, 1851–55. *Bio. Dir. U.S. Cong.*, 1219.

various parts of the country, he should look to me for counsel & all the help I could give. I told him that I thought he would want very little of either; but that all I could give was at his service. He referred to the long standing relations of confidence & friendship between us & said he felt he had a right to depend on me. And I told him that I would stand by him & with him and whether he needed me or not that my friendship & affection would continue the same as ever. Judge Spalding came in[61]—& we all three rode to the Capitol together—Fessenden stopped at the Senate Wing, but Spalding and I rode a few minutes longer together, talking of the resignation of Todds appointment & declension &c when I left him also at the Capitol & returned home

SATURDAY JULY 2. The bill giving the Secretary of the Treasury effective control control over trade in rebel states and power to purchase their products for resale for the benefit of the Government, & authority to lease abandoned property and care for the freedmen passed the House today having previously passed the Senate.[62] How much good I expected to accomplish under this bill! Will my successor do this work? I fear not. He had not the same heart for this measure that I had.

I spent the day in writing letters & in receiving calls, not going out at all. My letters to the Com of Ways & Means appeared in the Intellig[encer] & Chronicle.[63] I am glad of it. It will prove at least that I desired no inflation.

SUNDAY JULY 3— Attended Church at Wesley Chapel where I heard an excellent Sermon on Orphanage, suggested by the death of a young girl member of the Church killed lately with twenty others by an explosion of powder at the Arsenal.[64]

MONDAY JULY 4. Cries of all kinds except cries of pain filled the air this morning, with explosions of cannon, ringing of bells, and whiz-whiz snap-snap of crackers & awaken me. It is the Anniversary of the Independence of the United States! How little most of those who celebrate it are thinking of the difference between the United

---

61. Rufus Paine Spalding.
62. The "Trade Bill" mentioned on June 28–29.
63. Chase refers to the correspondence sent to Thaddeus Stevens on June 29. *Daily National Intelligencer*, July 2, 1864.
64. B. P. Brown presided at the church, located at 5th and F, N.W. The girl, Susan Harris, had perished on June 17 in an explosion at the Washington Arsenal. *Daily National Intelligencer*, June 18, 20, 1864; *Wash. Dir. (1864)*, 88.

States which declared it & the United States which [now] celebrate it—then thirteen United States—just resolved no longer to be colonies—& battling for Independence & Union—now twenty three of the United States struggling, with divided counsels, to compel to obedience to the National Constitution & laws, eleven others, in which counting all classes & colors there is a majority of loyalists, but a majority controlled by the master class, and, so far as the colored portion of it is concerned, treated by the Government of the Union as inferiors & aliens rather than as equals in natural rights & as citizens. What will be the end? It is hidden from me. The Twenty three are vastly stronger than the Eleven, & must prevail if they persevere unless Divine Providence takes sides against them. Surely if the Government had been willing to do justice & had used its vast powers with equal energy & wisdom the Struggle might have been happily terminated long ago.

Congress adjourned today without having passed an additional tax bill except five percent on incomes, which may produce 22 mills. There must be great reduction of expenditure, or better success in borrowing than I anticipate or inflation must continue. The President pocketed the great bill providing for the reorganization of the rebel states as loyal states. He did not venture to veto, & so put it in his pocket. It was a condemnation of his Amnesty Proclamation & of his general policy of reconstruction, rejecting the idea of possible reconstitution with Slavery; which neither the President nor his Chief advisers have, in my opinion, abandoned.[65]

Called at Mr. Hoopers & found nobody in; but left a note inviting Gov. Andrew & himself to come down & dine with me. Mr. Sumner called & remained to dinner with Mr. Hooper & Gov. A. He said Gov. Sprague had made a statement of great force & power in relation to the Blair charges which was listened to with breathless attention.[66] He said also that there was intense indignation against the President on account of his pocketing the Winter Davis or Reconstruction bill. Gov. Andrew hopes to have the controversy about

---

65. On Dec. 8, 1863, Lincoln had offered liberal terms for the pardon of former Confederates and presented his famous ten percent plan for Reconstruction. The congressional proposal, sponsored by Benjamin F. Wade and Henry Winter Davis, would have permitted reorganization only after a majority of qualified voters in each state had sworn allegiance and formed a government acceptable to Congress and the president. Basler, *Collected Works*, 7:53–56; *DAB*, 5:120; *Daily National Intelligencer*, July 9, 1864.

66. On the floor of the Senate earlier in the day, Sprague had accused Francis Preston Blair, Jr., of raising the issue of special privileges in cotton dealings "to strike the Secretary of the Treasury." Sprague asserted that he had not for any reason "asked or received any special privileges to buy cotton or anything else." *Cong. Globe*, 38th Cong., 1st sess., 1864, 34, pt. 4:3543.

pay of Negro troops enlisted by Massachusetts settled on just principles. This justice has been too long & too cruelly withheld.[67]

After dinner many others called. Mr. Fessenden came in about nine. He had already been with me in the morning and had told me that he had received a letter from a certain individual (the same who proclaimed the most indecent joy in my leaving the cabinet) recommending Gov Morgans special choice for the successor of Mr. Cisco & he expressed his intention not to have either of those from whom it was sought to make me choose appointed & had told me that he should call on the President & before acceptance have it distinctly understood that the appointment of Subordinates in his office, for whom he was to be responsible, must be made only with his full consent & approval, if not made directly on his own nominations. He now came in to say that the President had at once acceded to this, only reserving that should he himself desire any particular appointment made that his wishes in that regard should be fully considered. He said too that he hoped Mr. F―― would not without a real necessity remove any friends of Gov. Chase. Had the President [in] reply to my note tendering his resignation expressed himself as he did now to Mr. F――n, I should have cheerfully withdrawn it. Why did he not? I can see but one reason, that I am too earnest, too antislavery, &, say, too radical to make him willing to have me connected with the Admn., just as my opinion that he is not earnest enough; not antislavery enough; not radical enough,― but goes naturally with those hostile to me rather than with me,― makes me willing & glad to be disconnected from it.

We parted—I promising to meet him at the Department in the morning and introduce him to his work & his Chief Officers.

JULY 5—TUESDAY. Called on Fessenden & took him to the Department & spent some time in explaining the State of the Finances and the general working of business. About half past ten Judge Wayne came in & administered the oath of office.[68] Fessenden read it from the printed form from the State Department very distinctly & pronounced the adjunction so help me God! with great earnestness. The conclusion of the oath struck me "I will faithfully ad-

---

67. At this time, different pay scales existed for black and white soldiers in Union service. On June 15, Congress had passed legislation to redress the inequality, but not until Aug. 1 did the attorney general render a decision which enabled implementation. Berlin, *Freedom*, 21; *Statutes at Large*, 13:129–30; George W. Williams, *A History of the Negro Troops in the War of the Rebellion* . . . (New York, 1888; reprint, New York, 1969), 153.

68. Justice James Moore Wayne administered the oath.

minister perform[69] the duties of the office on which I am about to enter". There was no such clause as is commonly added "to the best of my ability." At eleven or a little after the Heads of the Bureaus came in & I introduced them to the new Secretary. Most of them were already known to him & the greeting on both sides was cordial. After this was over I left him promising to call again in the morning & confer about the practical business of borrowing money.

From the Department I returned home; and used the remainder of the day in writing letters & receiving visitors. Mr. Durant called & talked over La matters.[70] Garfield Schenck & Wetmore rode with me—all [*illeg.*] bitter against the timid & almost proslavery course of the President. Strange story by Garfield about Col. Jaques.[71]

JULY 6. WEDNESDAY— Senator Pomeroy came to breakfast—he says there is great dissatisfaction with Mr. Lincoln, which has been much exasperated by the pocketing of the reorganization bill. Garfield said yesterday that when the news of the intention of the President to pocket this bill came to the House on Monday, Norton of Ills. the special friend of the President said it was impossible & would be fatal.[72] G—— told him, if he desired to prevent it he should go to him at his room in the Capitol at once & remonstrate. Norton started, almost running; but returned after a little. "Did you see him". "Yes" "Will he sign". "No—great mistake but no use trying to prevent it." Pomeroy says he means to go on a Buffalo hunt & then to Europe. He cannot support Lincoln, but wont desert his principles. I much of the same sentiments; though not willing now to decide what duty may demand next fall. Pomeroy remarked that on the news of my resignation reaching the Senate several of the democratic Senators came to him & said "well go with you now for Chase." This meant nothing but a vehement desire to overthrow the existing Administration: but might mean much if the Democrats could only cut loose from Slavery & go for freedom & the protection of labor by a national currency. If they would do that I would cheerfully go for any good man they might nominate.

69. Originally *faithfully administer the duties*. Chase added *perform* above *administer* without canceling the latter word.

70. Thomas Jefferson Durant was at odds with other members of Louisiana's pro–Union Free State party. Durant, at this time the state's attorney general, had the responsibility of registering voters. *DAB*, 5:543–44; Joseph G. Dawson III, *Army Generals and Reconstruction: Louisiana, 1862–1877* (Baton Rouge and London, 1982), 15–17.

71. James Frazier Jaquess (1819–98), a Methodist clergyman and colonel in the 73rd Illinois Volunteers, was known for personal efforts during 1863–64 to negotiate a peaceful settlement to the war. *DAB*, 9:615–16.

72. Jesse Olds Norton (1812–75) was a Whig and Republican congressman from Illinois, 1853–57, 1863–65. *Bio. Dir. U.S. Cong.*, 1576.

Several other gentlemen called while Pomeroy was with me, but about nothing of much consequence.

Went to Department & talked about loans with Fessenden. The problem to provide means without further inflation & with gradual reduction. Condition, Immediate demands in requisition about $94.000.000. &c &c &c— Means (1) proceeds of late loan received mainly in 5% Coupon Legal Tenders (2) receipts from temporary loan also most in same Legal T. (3) & receipts from Internal Revenue— 4 Miscellaneous receipts sales of exchange &c—

The condition is by no means so difficult or rather by no means so apparently difficult as at the close of the [last] Session of Congress. Then the unpaid requisitions amounted to $72.171,189,41; and the funds on hand were   . At the close of the recent Session the requisitions amounted to   Then Congress had passed the National Banking act & had repealed the conversion clauses of the loan act;[73] but had provided no essential increase of revenue. But with those aids, notwithstanding a very unpromising Military condition I succeeded in disposing so rapidly of public securities that within four months the whole amt. of unpaid requisitions had been discharged & all demands were promptly met. The same can be done now, but Mr. Fessenden will be obliged to pay higher interest for less value. The Tax Legislation is better than then—far better—though not what it should be. The power of the Department over the Trade in Insurrectionary Districts is more complete & may be made very productive. The Military situation is far better. All things combine to make financial success comparatively easy.

Left Ty Dept. & went to see Stanton at War. Found him concerned about Raid to Martinsburgh & Harpers Ferry—thinks Sigel inefficient & that Hunter went too far off. Hunter however yesterday at Parkersburg & will probably today reach the vicinity of the rebels— I [can] not see from the statements made why they may not be cut off & signally defeated or captured. Told Stanton that every thing looked favorable to me only I wished Grant could have more men. Sherman at Marietta & rebels forced back on the Chattahoochie—Danville Railroad broke up & Grant holding fast & on the whole gaining—Hunter soon to drive the reb[els] again from Shenandoah Valley & the glorious victory of the Kearsarge in the combat with the Alabama, which came ought to fight & went to the

---

73. Under both the original legal tender act of Feb. 25, 1862, and an act of July 11, 1862, authorizing additional issues of greenbacks, legal tender notes could be exchanged for 5–20 bonds bearing six percent interest. A provision in the ways and means act of Mar. 3, 1863, made July 1 of that year the last date on which such exchanges would be possible. *Statutes at Large*, 12:345, 532, 711.

bottom.⁷⁴ All looked well— The last event particularly worth millions in the improvement of our prestige & credit in Europe.

Walked home under an intensely hot sun. Soon after Mr. Wetmore came in & we went to Freedmens Village.⁷⁵ What a striking result of the war & illustration as well as result it is. There it stands; a semicular Village extending round a [*illeg.*] of [*illeg.*]; [wooden] houses—about 1800 people—mostly old & infirm or women & children—with schools—a church—good order—though much sickness & poverty—all refugees from slavery & not one wishing to return, unless free after the war.

Evening, Ashley, Hosmer,⁷⁶ & Taylor called— H is going as Chief Justice to Montana. Taylor just from Northwest Ohio⁷⁷—says opinions there much divided about my resignation & some inclined to blame me.

Reid came in with letters from Greeley who wishes me to succeed Pendleton.⁷⁸ Told him I thought nothing gained unless we could have radical change of men & policy. He goes to New York soon. People, of course, think little of any thing in comparison with the war.

JOURNAL III

1864. JULY 13. Half of my fifty seventh year is ended—today I leave Washington a private citizen. Saw Stanton before leaving, warm & cordial as ever—no other Head of Dept. has called on me since my resignation. Stanton said the rebels have left & have probably gone towards Baltimore. There were probably 30.000 in front of City & 5000 more in the region roundabout,— Breckinridge, Early & Gordon dined above Rockville Saturday & were here⁷⁹—& of course their main body. He mentioned a

---

74. On June 19, the USS *Kearsarge* sank the Confederate steam sloop *Alabama* off Cherbourg, France. *ORN*, ser. 1, v. 3:64–65, ser. 2, v. 1:118–19, 247.

75. The village, located in Arlington, Va., had been founded in May under jurisdiction of the Quartermaster's Department. Margaret Leech, *Reveille in Washington, 1860–1865* (New York, 1941), 251–52.

76. Hezekiah Lord Hosmer (1814–93), former editor of the *Toledo Blade;* secretary of the House committee on territories, 1861–64; and chief justice of the Montana territorial supreme court, 1864–68. *DAB*, 9:243–44.

77. James Wickes Taylor.

78. Cincinnati peace Democrat George Hunt Pendleton (1825–89) was a member of Congress, 1857–65, and George McClellan's vice-presidential running partner in the 1864 election. Whitelaw Reid (1837–1912), who during the war was a correspondent for the Cincinnati *Gazette*, became editor of the New York *Tribune* in 1872. *DAB*, 14:419–20, 15:482–86.

79. Confederate officers John Cabell Breckinridge; Lt. Gen. Jubal Anderson Early (1816–94); and Brig. Gen. John Brown Gordon (1832–1904), who in 1873 became a U.S. senator from Georgia. *DAB*, 5:598–99, 7:424–25.

curious misunderstanding. Capt. Paddock (of Cleveland,[80] commanding at Fort Lincoln sent message to Dept.—"The enemy is approaching I desire instructions"— Stanton sent the message to Gen. Halleck & to Gen. Augur.[81] Three hours later another message, of similar purport, came which was sent to the same Generals. But becoming uneasy Stanton desired Col Fry to go out to the Fort & ascertain exact condition of things.[82] He went & found Gen Gillmore[83] whom he supposed to be in command & enquired what was the state of affairs in the Fort—Gillmore replied he did not know—he was not in charge of the defences in that quarter & had no orders / Fry replied the Secretary understands that you are in command at this part of the line— Gillmore produced his orders which simply assigned him to command of 23d. Corps. "About 800 are here," said he, "this is my whole command." Secy. sent for Gen. Augur on this report from Fry & sharply reprimanded him for negligence. Had Enemy known the real state of things he could easily have entered Washington at that point.[84] Bid go[od]bye to Mr. & Mrs Stanton. Harrington accompanied me to Tiger.[85] Off at 10.30— Clark (S. M.) Woodside Pay Mr. B & O. RR[86] & R. W. Tayler 1st Comptroller with me[87]— Woodside had been out with engine half a mile beyond Bladensburgh this morng—found enemys pickets there & returned— Going down the river passed a number of transports going up to Washn. heavily laden with troops—probably 5000 Infy. & 400 Cavalry— Passed Point Lookout in the night—met Norfolk boat in Bay & put Woodside on board for Baltimore. He took from me letter to Harrington asking him to have Portfolio & bonds &c in it lodged in First National Bank. I had carelessly left it in my library & coupon bonds might be easily stolen.[88]

---

80. T. S. Paddock. *OR*, ser. 1, v. 32, pt. 2:241.

81. Christopher Columbus Augur (1821–98), major general of volunteers, commanded the 22nd Army Corps. *DAB*, 1:427–28.

82. Provost Marshal General James Barnet Fry (1827–94), designated colonel in Mar. 1863 and breveted brigadier general in Apr. 1864, provided military advice and assistance during this Confederate advance on Washington. *DAB*, 7:47–48; Heitman, *Historical Register*, 1:439; *OR*, ser. 1, v. 37, pt. 2:224, ser. 3, v. 4:493.

83. Quincy Adams Gillmore.

84. Here, perhaps to signal a change of subject, Chase made two x markings before beginning the next sentence.

85. A U.S. revenue cutter. Chase to Edward Bates, Sept. 24, 1862 (Attorney General's Papers, Gen. Recs. of Dept. of Justice, Nat. Arch.).

86. Probably William S. Woodside. Hungerford, *Baltimore and Ohio Railroad*, 1:270.

87. Robert Walker Tayler (b. 1812), former mayor of Youngstown, Ohio; state senator, 1855–57; and auditor of Ohio, 1860–63. Lanman, *Biographical Annals*, 418.

88. Chase to Harrington, July 13, 1864 (Harrington Papers, Mo. Hist. Soc.).

JULY 14— Sent another letter to Harrington, same tenor, by Capt. of Tiger who returned from Perryville[89]—obliged to go in open boat from Tiger to Perryville abt. 3 miles—Tiger drew too much water to get nearer. Steamer Baltimore, which had passed us coming up the bay, lay out as we passed; but soon came up to the landing bringing Senator Sumner, Gen Franklin, Adml. Porter,[90] F. P Blair Sen. & Mrs Montgomery Blair & others— Old Blair came to me, but I did not talk much with him—perhaps was too rude— Franklin told me about his capture by Gillmore & his escape.[91] Sumner full as usual of interesting talk[92]— Jay Cooke met me at Depot & leaving Clark to look after baggage, rode out with him to Chelten Hills—went to supper at Wm G. Moorheads[93]

JULY 15 To New York— Clark & Jay Cooke with me—Clark having charge of State Dept. foreign Mailbags—on arrival went to Sub Treasury—found Fessenden— He has made no arrangement yet for loan—thinks banks will agree on terms

JULY 16— Breakfast with Jay Cooke—then to Astor House[94] & with Cisco & Fessenden to Subtreasury— Cisco thinks banks will not agree on terms—told me Morgan had called[95]—& he had charged him with false representations about his Clerks—in using document representing them as nearly all democrats when he knew that among the most prominent so represented especially Mr. Dunning

---

89. Confederate operations in Maryland jeopardized land communication around Washington. To be certain that his message reached Harrington, Chase sent three versions of his July 13 letter by different routes: one by way of the Point Lookout guard boat, one to Baltimore with Woodside, and one "by Capt. Baker"— apparently John G. Baker of the revenue cutter service. Ibid.; Chase to Harrington, two letters of July 13, 1864 (Huntington Lib.); *Register of Officers (1865)*, 68.

90. Rear Adm. David Dixon Porter (1813–91), commander of Union naval forces on the lower Mississippi; superintendent of the U.S. Naval Academy, 1865–69. In 1870, Porter became an admiral. *DAB*, 15:85–88.

91. William Buel Franklin had been captured on July 11 by Confederate Maj. Harry Gilmor (1838–83) while en route to Washington, D.C., from Louisiana. Franklin had escaped the following night. *DAB*, 6:602, 7:309.

92. As he did at a spot within the previous day's entry, Chase followed this sentence with two small x marks, perhaps to show a change of subject.

93. Philadelphia railroad financier William G. Moorhead, brother of James Kennedy Moorhead, formed a partnership in 1861 with his brother-in-law, Jay Cooke. Moorhead's Chelten Hills residence some eight miles north of Philadelphia was called "Rockwood." Oberholtzer, *Jay Cooke*, 1:40–42, 101–2, 2:447.

94. On Broadway. *New York Dir. (1864)*, 41.

95. Edwin Denison Morgan.

{ 482 } *The Journals of Salmon P. Chase*

Supt. of Mint & Dr. Torrey never belonged to that party[96]— Called at Bank of Commerce & saw Mr. Stevens & Mr. Vail. dined at Astor House with Katie & Nettie—left in evening for Newport.[97]

JULY 17   At Newport attended Dr. Mercer's church—very pleasant & a very good sermon—at table'd'hote met Mr. Otis of Boston & Count Giorgi the Austrian Minister.[98]

" 18.   Mr. Sheffield, Mr. Belmont, & others called[99]—Katie & I called at Whiting's & Barréda's[1]

" 19—   Rode with Russell of New York[2]—to Club with him—little of interest.

" 20.—   Dined at Mr. Russell's—Mr. Royal Phelps & others guests[3]

" 21.   Howe came from Boston.[4]

96. George Freeman Dunning (1817–1910), a mint service employee since 1838, supervised the New York assay office, 1862–77. Botanist and mineralogist John Torrey, M.D. (1796–1873), was assayer in the New York office, 1853–73. *Who Was Who*, 1:348; *DAB*, 18:596–98.

97. Chase wrote the last five words of this entry with a pen nib and in a handwriting more similar to the entries for July 17–23 than to the main body of the July 16 entry. The July 24 entry resumes with a nib and style similar to those of the body of the July 16 entry. Chase may have left space between the entries for July 16 and July 24, returning at another time to insert the last five words under July 16 and the entries for July 17–23.

98. Alexander G. Mercer was pastor of All Saint's Chapel, an Episcopal congregation in Newport. Nicholas George, or Count Giorgi, Austrian minister to the U.S., died unexpectedly at New York later in 1864. Chase may also have met William C. Otis, a Bostonian who kept a house in Newport. *Wash. Dir. (1864)*, 81; *Papers Relating to Foreign Affairs*, 38th Cong., 2nd sess., 4:113; *Newport Dir. (1863)*, 104, 173, 179.

99. William Paine Sheffield and banker August Belmont (1816–90), former U.S. minister to Austria, 1844–50, and the Netherlands, 1853–57. *DAB*, 2:169–70; *Newport Dir. (1863)*, 117.

1. Augustus Whiting of New York and Federico L. Barreda, who was the Peruvian minister to the U.S. at various times during the 1860s, both had houses in Newport. *Newport Dir. (1865)*, 221; *Papers Relating to Foreign Affairs, Accompanying the Annual Message of the President to the 2d. Session Thirty-Ninth Congress. Part II* (Washington, D.C., 1867), 664–65; *Wash. Dir. (1863)*, 283; *Enciclopedia Universal Ilustrada Europeo-Americana* (Barcelona, 1907–30), 7:910; Downing and Scully, *Architectural Heritage of Newport*, 138–39.

2. Charles Handy Russell.

3. Phelps (1809–84) was a New York merchant and former Democratic state legislator. *Appletons'*, 4:752; *Newport Dir. (1863)*, 183.

4. Frank E. Howe (1829–83), Massachusetts state agent at New York City and assistant quartermaster general with the rank of colonel, had invited Chase to visit his home in Brookline. Howe had looked into Treasury matters at New Orleans earlier in 1864. *New York Times*, May 24, 1883; Henry Greenleaf Pearson, *The Life of John A. Andrew: Governor of Massachusetts, 1861–1865* (Boston, 1904), 1:253–55; Heit-

" 22   Went to Boston with Howe—met Pierce at depot—rode to Howe's fathers—beautiful place.

" 23—   Many callers—

JULY 24—SUNDAY—   Went with Mr. & Mrs Endicott to Beverly to church[5]—stopped at Mrs Rantouls & accompanied her to church—home with her— Saw Mrs Eastman—pleasant talk and a walk on the little piece of land across the road & between it & the sea—say an acre & a half—which she calls her farm

JULY 25 M.   Passed the day at Mr. Endicotts— Started in rain for Lynn to keep promise to Dana to meet him there & go to Nahant— recd note from him that Mrs D—— had been obliged to leave N—— & concluded not to go[6]— Very heavy rain.

JULY 26—T.   Went to Boston with Mr. Endicott & stopped at Revere House[7]— Haven,[8] Dana, Pierce & others called—rode to Milton with Pierce & walked over the pretty place which he has lately bought.

JULY 27—W.   To Lynn— Alley met me at Depot & had me to dinner where I met Gov. Kent and others[9]—visited shoe factories— amazing applications of machinery—since war begun new inventions save ¾th, of human labor. Called at Mrs Lander's but did not find her at home— In evening many called—lawyers, ministers, manufacturers—among them my old friend Gen. Schouler.[10]

---

man, *Historical Register*, 1:547; Howe to Chase, June 20, 1864 (Chase Papers, Hist. Soc. of Pa.); Chase to Howe, Feb. 20, 1864 (Chase Papers, L.C.); Chase to Howe, Mar. 30, 1864 (Misc. Letters Sent, Gen. Recs. Treasury Dept., Nat. Arch.).

    5. William Endicott (1826–1914), Massachusetts businessman and Republican, attended the First Unitarian Church at Beverly. He married Annie Thorndike (d. 1876) in 1856. Robert S. Rantoul, "Memoir of William Endicott," *Proceedings of the Massachusetts Historical Society, 1914–15*, 48:243–52.

    6. Boston author and antislavery activist Richard Henry Dana, Jr. (1815–82) was U.S. attorney for the district of Massachusetts, 1861–66. He had married Sarah Watson Dana (1814–1907) of Hartford, Conn., in 1841. *DAB*, 5:60; Robert F. Lucid, ed., *The Journal of Richard Henry Dana, Jr.* (Cambridge, Mass., 1968), 3:1141.

    7. On Bowdoin Square. *Boston Dir. (1864)*, 427.

    8. Franklin Haven, Sr. (1804–93), president of Boston's Merchants Bank and a public official. Wiltse, *Papers of Daniel Webster: Correspondence*, 5:72; *Boston Dir. (1864)*, 171.

    9. John Bassett Alley (1817–96) was a Republican congressman from Massachusetts, 1859–67. Edward Kent (1802–77), former Whig governor of Maine, held positions as U.S. consul to Rio de Janeiro, 1849–53, and justice of Maine's supreme judicial court, 1859–73. *Bio. Dir. U.S. Cong.*, 529; *DAB*, 10:343–44.

    10. William Schouler.

JULY 28. T. Mr. & Mrs Alley took me to Cherry Hill—took up my friend & Host, R P. Waters,[11] between Salem & Cherry Hill— walked over farm—Alley told me that general opinion of our friends was that I had erred in resigning.

JULY 29—F At Cherry Hill— Prof Alpheus Crosby[12]—Junior at Dartmouth when I was Senior—called & staid to dinner— A. G. Brown & Vincent Brown called[13]—proposed center excursion which I declined— Went to Mrs Rantouls—Robt. S & Charles Rantoul called / latter with his young & pretty wife[14]—long & agreeable talk with Mrs E.[15]

JULY 30. S. Mr. Haven called at Mrs R—— where I met him by appt. & took me to his house at West Beach—a lovely place

JULY 31. SUN. Passed day at Mr. Havens—Sumner dined.

AUG 1. (M) Passed day at Mr. Haven's—Dr. Palfrey Dr. Lothrop and others dined[16]

AUG 2. T. Called at Beverly with Mrs Haven on Mrs R—— & Mrs E——[17] returned to West Beach & took cars for Lynn—young Warren, *en route* to New York, accompanying me / Hooper[18] & Dana met me at Lynn & took me to Nahant—Agassiz, Thomas H Perkins, Amos A. Lawrence & others met me at dinner & we had a pleasant

11. Richard Palmer Waters (1807–87), Salem merchant, Massachusetts politician, and U.S. consul to Zanzibar, 1837–45. *General Catalogue of Bowdoin College*, 428.
12. Alpheus Crosby (1810–74), principal of the normal school at Salem, 1857–65. He had graduated from Dartmouth in 1827, taught Greek there for many years, and was emeritus professor from 1849 until his death. Emerson, *General Catalogue*, 139–40; *Appletons'*, 2:16.
13. Salem native Albert Gallatin Browne, Jr. (1835–91), lawyer, journalist, and private secretary of Gov. John A. Andrew during the Civil War; and J. Vincent Browne, U.S. collector of internal revenue at Salem. *Nat. Cyc.*, 19:316; *Register of Officers (1865)*, 58.
14. Attorney Robert Samuel Rantoul (1832–1922), the son of Robert Rantoul and Jane Woodbury Rantoul, was U.S. collector of customs at Salem, 1865–69. His recently married younger brother, Charles William Rantoul (b. 1839), moved to Florida after the Civil War. *Nat. Cyc.*, 41:228; "Rantoul Genealogy, &c.," *Essex Institute Historical Collections* 5 (1863): 147; Duane Hamilton Hurd, ed., *History of Essex County, Massachusetts* . . . (Philadelphia, 1888), 1:43.
15. Charlotte Eastman.
16. John Gorham Palfrey (1796–1881), historian, Unitarian clergyman, and former U.S. congressman, served at this time as Boston's postmaster. Samuel Kirkland Lothrop, D.D. (1804–86) presided over Boston's Brattle Square Church. *Appletons'*, 4:32; *DAB*, 14:169–70.
17. Jane Rantoul and Charlotte Eastman.
18. Samuel Hooper.

time[19]— After dinner we all played croquet with Mr. Danas young daughters[20]—very merry—Agassiz in particular entered into the sport with great zest.

AUG 3. Hooper & I went to dine with A. A. Lawrence, who has a pretty place in a most romantic situation—the house almost overhanging the sea— Recd. letter from Mellen at Washn enclosing one to him from Carson at Cincinnati[21] saying that there would be opposition to my nomination for Congress in First District but that it could be overcome by active exertion[22]— Wrote telegram to Mellen "Unanimous nomination would command acceptance but cannot compete & must not be regarded as competitor." No telegraph from Nahant

AUG. 4. Left Nahant with Hooper for Boston—sent telegram to Mellen— Met Pierce at depot—Forbes joined me & Hooper & off for New Bedford[23]—saw Eliot there[24] & asked him to accompany us but he could not—embarked on Azalea Mr. Forbes' yacht at 1.30 P.M. Gen Barlow & Col. Russell on board[25]—reached Naushon at 6.30— Ladies met us in row boat as we came in to the little harbor.

---

19. Jean Louis Rodolphe Agassiz (1807–73), the famous Swiss-American geologist, taught at Harvard. Thomas H. Perkins was a local stockbroker. Amos Adams Lawrence (1814–86) was a Massachusetts commission merchant, textile manufacturer, philanthropist, and supporter of antislavery causes. *Boston Dir. (1864),* 286; *DAB,* 1:114–22, 11:47–48.

20. Richard Henry Dana, Jr., and Sarah Watson Dana had five daughters: Sarah Watson (1842–1902); Ruth Charlotte (1844–1903); Elizabeth Ellery (1846–1939); Mary Rosamund (1848–1937); Angela Henrietta Channing (1857–1928). Lucid, *Journal of Richard Henry Dana,* 3:1140.

21. Enoch Terry Carson (1822–99), a merchant and surveyor of customs for the port of Cincinnati, 1861–65. *Cinc. Dir. (1864),* 79, 253; Greve, *Centennial History,* 2:613–15; *Register of Officers (1863),* 89.

22. Friends in Cincinnati wished to nominate Chase as a candidate for Congress, an initiative which he did not promote. Failure to withdraw his name from consideration before the district convention at Cincinnati resulted in a two-to-one defeat that caused Chase embarrassment. William Stanton to Chase, July 9, Aug. 29, 1864 (Chase Papers, L.C.); W. P. Mellen to Chase, Aug. 10, 13, 1864 (Chase Papers, Hist. Soc. of Pa.); Chase to Mellen, Aug. 5, 17, 1864 (Clara H. Mellen Papers, Bowdoin College); Chase to Charles S. May, Aug. 31, 1864, in Warden, *Chase,* 628–29.

23. Massachusetts merchant and railroad magnate John Murray Forbes (1813–98), an ardent supporter of the Union war effort, owned a summer home on Buzzard's Bay. *DAB,* 6:507–8.

24. Thomas Dawes Eliot.

25. Francis Channing Barlow (1834–96) was a major general of volunteers and future secretary of state and attorney general for New York. Henry Sturgis Russell, husband of John Murray Forbes's daughter Mary Hathaway Forbes, served as colonel of the 5th Massachusetts Cavalry. *DAB,* 1:608–9; Sarah Forbes Hughes, ed., *Letters and Recollections of John Murray Forbes* (Boston, 1900), 2:4; Heitman, *Historical Register,* 1:853.

{ 486 }   *The Journals of Salmon P. Chase*

AUG. 5— Explored Island—about 7 miles long & 1 or ½ wide—beautiful & picturesque—wonderfully so—the only deer in Massachusetts are found on it—saw one—drove Mrs Forbes,[26] a most charming lady, home—played "tactics" with Hooper & Chess with George S. Hale who also a guest[27]—occupied the Gov.'s Room—

AUG. 6—SAT. Went a fishing & caught nothing—went deer hunting & Forbes shot buck—I was twice *posted* & watching vigilantly but not a deer ventured to show himself where I was!

AUG. 7. SUN. Went to Cotuit in the Azalea with Mr. Hooper & Mr. Forbes—Mr. Hooper's summer residence is at Cotuit & we found there Mrs Hooper the widow of his son & spent the day quietly.[28]

AUG. 8—M. Left Cotuit with Messrs F. & H. and Col. Godman for Nantucket & reached that famous island about 1 P.M[29]—welcomed by a crowd of ragged boys, one of whom found out who I was & made me at once an object of marked [attention]. Visited Siasconset—in the evg attended a fair where I took a chance in a raffle by way of giving the good folks a little money— After fair went to Sanford's where we had a cordial welcome, a nice supper, & agreeable gentlemen.[30]

AUG. 9. T. Visited Museum[31]— Macy gave me history of Nantucket[32]—walk with him—found man taking down house to be

26. The former Sarah Swain Hathaway of New Bedford had married John Murray Forbes in 1834. *DAB,* 6:508; *Nat. Cyc.,* 35:332.
27. Boston attorney George Silsbee Hale (1835–97). *Nat. Cyc.,* 13:21.
28. Alice Mason Hooper (1838–1913) was the widow of Samuel Hooper's son, William Sturgis Hooper, and the future wife of Charles Sumner. Palmer, *Selected Letters of Charles Sumner,* 2:373.
29. Boston attorney Charles Russell Codman (1829–1918) served as colonel of the 44th Massachusetts Regiment, 1863–64, and as a Massachusetts state senator, 1864–65. He owned a summer home at "peaceful yet commanding Bluff Point" in Cotuit. M. A. DeWolfe Howe, ed., *Later Years of the Saturday Club, 1870–1920* (Boston, 1927), 303–7.
30. Likely Nantucket shipmaster Frederick C. Sanford. Edward K. Godfrey, comp., *The Island of Nantucket* . . . . (Boston, 1882), 25, 343; *New York Times,* May 5, 1880.
31. The Nantucket Athenæum, incorporated in 1834, contained curiosities and a library. Alexander Starbuck, *The History of Nantucket, County, Island and Town* . . . (Boston, 1924), 337; Elias Nason, *A Gazetteer of the State of Massachusetts* (Boston, 1890), 480–81.
32. Probably William Henry Macy (1805–87), a Nantucket merchant and banker. The standard local source at the time was Obed Macy, *The History of Nantucket* . . . (Boston, 1835). *Nat. Cyc.,* 22:34.

sent to Mainland— This is now a common thing in Nantucket— the house I saw going down was sold for $600 & it would cost say $700 to take it to Mainland & put it up again—it was a good sized double house—before leaving went to the house & shop of Miss Coffin, a nice, plump, (not to say fat), pleasant old maid where I [bought] some shells & specimens of moss[33]—about noon we took leave of the island & returned to Cotuit— I forgot to note that I called on Miss Emily Shaw & saw her father & sisters[34]—

" 10, WED.[35] Letters; Courtlandt Parker, Newark, N.J.[36] Lauren Drury, Mt. Pleasant Iowa.[37] Mrs. R. B. Spring Valley, Falls, R.I.; E. T. Carson, Cinti., O. Wm. Stanton, Cinti., O.[38] W. P. Fessenden, Washn.

" 11, TH. Went to Col. Codman's croquet, Chase & Sturges[39] v. Codman & Mrs Hooper—to Boston with Hooper in Cars fr W. Barnstable met Mr. Francis Lowell on cars; very hot. Boston abt. 6 P.M. walked to Union Club; met Mr. Ward & other gentlemen.[40]

---

33. Chase more than likely met a descendant of Tristam Coffin (1605–81), one of Nantucket's first English settlers. *Nat. Cyc.*, 6:258; *Appletons'*, 1:677; Starbuck, *History of Nantucket*, 697–730.

34. Emily Shaw, evidently a public reader, knew Chase from Gamaliel Bailey's social circle and had sought him as a professional reference. The Shaws may have kept a home in Providence, R.I., as well as on Nantucket. Chase to Shaw, May 23, 1863 (Chase Papers, Hist. Soc. of Pa.); Shaw to Chase, May 18 and July 13, 1863 (Chase Papers, L.C.).

35. Beginning with this date, the entries are in the handwriting of an unidentified amanuensis. Chase, however, made numerous additions and changes to the clerk's text. The clerk left some gaps which Chase filled in, and Chase made corrections to the clerk's rendering of some proper nouns and other words. These clues suggest that the clerk worked from a draft by Chase and had difficulty reading Chase's handwriting. The text presented here is in the final form after Chase's editing (see description of Journal III, pp. lx–lxii). With the entry for Sept. 21, 1864, Chase resumed writing the entries entirely in his own hand.

36. John Cortlandt Parker (1818–1907) was a Republican politician and attorney from New Jersey. *DAB*, 14:233–34.

37. Evidently Lauren Dewey, formerly connected with Iowa Wesleyan College. *Historical Sketch and Alumni Record of Iowa Wesleyan College* (Mount Pleasant, Iowa, 1917), 113.

38. Stanton, a Cincinnati attorney, had urged Chase to run for Congress. *Cinc. Dir. (1864)*, 323; Stanton to Chase, July 9, Aug. 29, 1864 (Chase Papers, L.C.).

39. Charles Russell Codman was married to a daughter of Russell Sturgis, a banker, and Samuel Hooper was married to a daughter of shipper William Sturgis. Howe, *Later Years of the Saturday Club*, 304; *DAB*, 9:203; Hughes, *John Murray Forbes*, 1:145.

40. Samuel G. Ward was an agent for Baring Brothers, the English banking firm. *Boston Dir. (1864)*, 369; Aug. 18, 1864, below.

" 12, F. Letters; Geo. Harrington enclosing McGilvra &—C. F. Schmidt[41] Col. Morse, (Mrs. Auld, empt &c.)[42] A. C. Graham, Cashr. N.O.[43]—at Boston all day; S. T. Dana, E. L. Pierce & others very kind.[44]

" 13, SAT. Letters to Katie & others,[45]—at 8.30 left Boston for Hartford, via Worcester—at 11—met Mr. Noyes at depot[46]—dined at Hotel—Mr. Howard, Mr. Day, & others called:[47] they seem to be not satisfied with Lincoln or prospects; to Litchfield with Mr. Noyes; arrived 8–30 or 9 P.M.; changed dress; pleasant tea with Mrs. Noyes & Miss Emily.[48]

" 14, SUN. Church morning service; preacher plain but sensible; seventy years old—evening walk to Prospect Hill Dr. Beecher's house, N.W. Cor. Prospect & North St.—read part of his biography.[49]

 41. John Jay McGilvra (1827–1903), a personal friend of Lincoln, had served as U.S. attorney for the territory of Washington since 1861. McGilvra apparently wanted access to some Treasury documents. Chase also asked Harrington to send statements of the public debt for Chase's use and requested prompt attention to the accounts of Charles F. Schmidt, who had recently traveled to California on Treasury business. To Schmidt, Chase expressed lukewarm support for Lincoln in the upcoming Presidential election. "My own relation to the canvass," Chase wrote, "must be that of a private citizen having no interest in it except that which any other private citizen has." Chase to Harrington, Aug. 12, 1864 (Harrington Papers, Mo. Hist. Soc.); Chase to Schmidt, Aug. 12, 1864 (Cinc. Hist. Soc.); *Nat. Cyc.*, 14:473–74.
 42. John Flavel Morse had written to Chase about recent investigations of U.S. custom houses in New Orleans and Philadelphia, and about efforts to find housing and teaching employment for Chase's niece, Jane Chase Auld, in Painesville, Ohio. Morse to Chase, Aug. 2, 1864 (Chase Papers, L.C.).
 43. A. C. Graham, apparently a political contact of Chase, served as president of the First National Bank of New Orleans from 1864 until a million dollar defalcation discovered in 1867 threw the institution into receivership. A. C. Graham to Chase, Sept. 30, 1864 (Chase Papers, L.C.); *New Orleans Dir. (1866)*, 203; Henry Rightor, ed., *Standard History of New Orleans* . . . (Chicago, 1900), 603.
 44. Samuel Turner Dana (1810–77) was a Boston merchant. *Boston Dir. (1864)*, 99; Hilen, *Letters of Henry Wadsworth Longfellow*, 5:294.
 45. Chase told of plans to visit Litchfield, Boston, and Concord. Chase to Kate Chase Sprague, Aug. 13, 1864 (Chase Papers, Hist. Soc. of Pa.).
 46. William Curtis Noyes (1805–64), a New York attorney and judicial reformer. *DAB*, 13:592.
 47. Hartford dry goods merchant Calvin Day (c. 1799–1884), like Mark Howard, was a close friend and political associate of Chase's former colleague on the cabinet, Gideon Welles. *New York Times*, June 12, 1884; John Niven, *Gideon Welles: Lincoln's Secretary of the Navy* (New York, 1973), 155, 242, 504, 569.
 48. Julia F. Tallmadge Noyes and daughter Emily Caroline Noyes (1842–1939), who became a noted painter, author, and the wife of New York attorney John Arent Vanderpoel. *Nat. Cyc.*, 18:94; 29:205.
 49. *The Autobiography, Correspondence, etc. of Lyman Beecher, D.D.* (London, 1863), had recently been edited by his son, Charles.

August 1864 { 489 }

" 15, MON. Election held today to adopt or reject proposed amendment of Constitution, allowing soldiers to vote;—several gentlemen called—Mr. Raymond son of R. R. Raymond[50]—Ex Gov. Dutton—Judge Woodruff of N.Y. Judge W.—— of last Congress. Mr. Hubbard of present Congress.— Judge Seymour and others[51]— evng. serenade & short speech—war just & necessary—justice to the colored man indispensable—ballots as well as bullets.— Mr. White & suite of pretty daughters of N.Y. pleasant singing at Mr. Seymour's by young Woodruff[52] & the young ladies—gave Miss Noyes the mosses I brought from Nantucket—agreeable & interesting ride round the Lake with Mr. Noyes.

" 16, TU. Breakfast at Mr. Noyes', whose guest I was—Mr. Hubbard—Mr. Hollister,[53] Rev. Mr. Parmley, Mr. Olmstead,[54] Judge Woodruff & others—very pleasant—afterwards read Beecher Book & wrote letters—evng. a ride to the lake—a row on it & water lilies— some calls in the evng—Tallmadge house occupied by Mr. Noyes, old mansion belonged to Col. Tallmadge of revolutionary army— grandfather of Mrs Noyes.[55]

" 17, WED. Rose very early—Mr. Noyes and I to station in Wagon at 6.30 left station abt. 7.20—at Hartford abt. 9.30— Mr. Howard at Depot who took us to his house—raining—but a number of prominent gentlemen called, among them Prof. Stowe[56]

---

50. Rossiter Worthington Raymond (1840–1918), the son of Robert Raikes Raymond, was a mining engineer and former aide-de-camp for John C. Frémont. He became U.S. commissioner of mining statistics, 1868–76. *DAB*, 15:414–15.
51. Henry Dutton (1796–1869), governor of Connecticut, 1854–55, and judge of the state's supreme court of errors and superior court, 1861–69; Lewis Bartholomew Woodruff (1809–75) of New York's city court of common pleas and superior court, 1850–69; George Catlin Woodruff (1805–85), former judge of probate in Litchfield and a Democratic congressman, 1861–63; John Henry Hubbard (1804–72), Republican congressman from Connecticut, 1863–67; and Origen Storrs Seymour (1804–81), Democratic congressman, 1851–55, Connecticut superior court judge, 1855–63, and attorney in Litchfield, 1863–70. Ibid., 5:555–56; *Nat. Cyc.*, 29:340–41; *Bio. Dir. U.S. Cong.*, 1223, 1793, 2085; Lanman, *Biographical Annals*, 476.
52. Presumably George M., son of George C. Woodruff. *History of Litchfield, Connecticut* . . . (Philadelphia, 1881), 36.
53. David F. Hollister.
54. Likely Connecticut native Aaron B. Olmstead, a deputy collector of customs at New York City. *New York Dir. (1864)*, 661; *Register of Officers (1863)*, 71; A. B. Olmstead to Chase, Mar. 22, 1862 (Chase Papers, L.C.).
55. Benjamin Tallmadge (1754–1835) was a major in the Continental Army and Federalist congressman from Connecticut, 1801–17. *DAB*, 18:284–85.
56. Calvin Ellis Stowe (1802–86), formerly professor at Lane Theological Seminary in Cincinnati, Bowdoin College, and Andover Theological Seminary. *DAB*, 18:115.

& several German gentlemen—Col. Bissell,[57] Prest. Loyal League—nice lunch & agreeable talk—reached Boston abt. 6 & drove to Mr. Hooper's—found them just at dinner—Hooper,—Sumner & Gray[58]—we joined them.

" 18, TH. Fessenden at Breakfast—insists on my going to Europe[59]—I promised to come to Washn. in about two weeks—called on Pierce who went with me to make some purchases. called at Merchant's Bank—met Peter Harvey, old friend of Webster, now strong in opposition[60]—Mr. Amory Davis, Prest. Suffolk Bank;[61]—Mr. Haven, Mr. Davis & another talking with Fessenden; after he went out talked some time with Mr. Haven—recd. from Harrington letter & Statement of Public Debt,[62]—returned to house with Hooper & Fessenden & talked for a time— Fessenden expressed at breakfast his astonishment at the immense work of organization, which I had done—took dinner at Union Club—Emerson, Lowell[63]—Gov. Andrew—Agassiz—Chas. G. Loring,[64] Geo. S. Hale, Brimmer,[65] Judge E. R. Hoar,[66] Sumner, Longfellow, Hooper S. G.

---

57. George P. Bissell of Connecticut's 25th Infantry Regiment. Horace J. Morse, *Catalogue of Connecticut Volunteer Organizations* . . . (Hartford, 1864), 730.

58. Probably Horace Gray (1828–1902), former reporter of the supreme court of Massachusetts; associate and chief justice of the state's supreme court, 1864–73; and associate justice of the U.S. Supreme Court, 1882–1902. *DAB*, 7:518–19.

59. Fessenden wanted Chase to market U.S. Treasury bonds in Europe, but soon abandoned the plan. Frances Fessenden, *Life and Public Services of William Pitt Fessenden* . . . (Boston, 1907), 1:352–53; Fessenden to Chase, Sept. 6, 1864 (Chase Papers, Hist. Soc. of Pa.); Chase to Fessenden, Sept. 8, 1864, Fessenden to Chase, Sept. 11, 1864 (Fessenden Family Papers, Bowdoin College).

60. Boston merchant and railroad magnate Peter Harvey (1810–77), author of *Reminiscences and Anecdotes of Daniel Webster* (Boston, 1877). *Appletons'*, 3:108.

61. J. Amory Davis, president of Boston's Suffolk Bank. *Boston Dir. (1864)*, 102.

62. The letter also expressed frustration over loan negotiations with New York bankers. "Had I the power," Harrington wrote, "I would bring those selfish gentlemen to their Knees or put receivers into their establishments in a week." George Harrington to Chase, Aug. 15, 1864 (Chase Papers, Hist. Soc. of Pa.).

63. Ralph Waldo Emerson and Massachusetts author James Russell Lowell (1819–91), editor of the *Atlantic Monthly*, 1857–61, and diplomat, 1877–85. *DAB*, 11:458–64; Emerson to John Murray Forbes, Aug. 17, 1864 in Ralph L. Rusk, ed., *The Letters of Ralph Waldo Emerson, Vol. 5* (New York, 1939), 381; Lowell to C. E. Norton, Aug. 18, 1864 in Charles Eliot Norton, ed., *Letters of James Russell Lowell, Vol. 1* (New York, 1894), 339–40.

64. Charles Greeley Loring (1794–1868) Republican politician and actuary of the Massachusetts hospital life insurance company, 1857–68. *Appletons'*, 4:27.

65. Boston attorney and Massachusetts politician Martin Brimmer (1829–96). Edward Waldo Emerson, *The Early Years of the Saturday Club, 1855–1870* (Boston, 1918), 366–75.

66. Ebenezer Rockwood Hoar (1816–95), judge of the Massachusetts court of common pleas, 1849–55, and of the state supreme court, 1859–69; U.S. attorney general, 1869–70; unconfirmed nominee to the U.S. Supreme Court, 1869; and Republican congressman, 1873–75. *DAB*, 9:86–87.

Ward, W. C. Noyes, J. M. Forbes, Mudge,[67] Endicott— Home to Hooper's abt. 11 & to bed.

" 19, F.   Mr. Noyes went to N.Y.—wrote by him to Opdyke & Ford—he promised to write me result of meeting—I have little or no faith in it[68]—letter from Jay Cooke with Chronicle article—what does it mean? he asks—I ask—all ask—wrote him briefly—sell Ph. & Cd. Bonds & buy certificates[69] / to Merchants Bank where cashed check $200, (on J.C. & Co Phila.) Hooper with me— Wanted Hair Restorative & he proposed to call at his barbers which we did—took cars to Beverly;—Mr. Haven in seat with me Capt. Whitney took me to Mrs. R——s. pleasant hour with her & Mrs. E.[70]— Waters came after tea—to Cherry Hill with him—cool & pleasant night.

" 20, SAT.   Rode with Waters to Camp Meeting ground—meeting closed last night & broke up this morning at 11—when we reached the ground most had gone—some of the principal men Mr. Gee of Book Concern, Boston,[71] Waite of Essex County and a few other such men remained & recd. us very kindly—Story of committee years ago to get Fremont to come attempt failed—home to dinner—afternoon stroll to top of Brown's Hill or Folly Hill—where there is a grand view— Evening Dr. Cheever & Mrs. C. came[72]—retired early.

---

67. Charles F. Mudge was superintendent of the U.S. Sanitary Executive Committee. *Boston Dir. (1864),* 261.

68. A group of Republicans dissatisfied with Lincoln's candidacy met secretly in New York on Aug. 18 to discuss the prospects of drafting an alternative candidate such as Chase. George Opdyke had telegraphed Chase to invite him to another meeting on the nineteenth. Chase sent Noyes as his representative and replied coyly to Opdyke that "my views are, by no means, as clear as I could wish, and I should be very glad to have the advantage of the clearer & better knowledge of other & better informed gentlemen." Ford may have been Brooklyn antislavery politician Gordon Lester Ford (1823–91). Chase to Opdyke, Aug. 19, 1864 (John Austin Stevens Papers, New-York Hist. Soc.); Pearson, *Life of John A. Andrew,* 2:148–73; Donnal V. Smith, *Chase and Civil War Politics* (1930; reprint, Freeport, N.Y., 1972), 148–59; *DAB,* 6:514–15; Chase to Ford, Jan. 21, 1864 (Chase Papers, Hist. Soc. of Pa.).

69. Chase asked Cooke to sell corporate bonds from Chase's portfolio and reinvest the proceeds in one-year Treasury certificates. What Chase, here and elsewhere, called the "Pittsburgh & Cleveland" company may have been the Cleveland & Pittsburgh Railroad. Chase to Cooke, Aug. 19, 1864, Cooke to Chase, same date (Chase Papers, Hist. Soc. of Pa.); Van Tassel and Grabowski, *Encyclopedia of Cleveland,* 296.

70. Charlotte Eastman, staying in Beverly with her friend, Jane Rantoul.

71. Possibly Nathaniel Gee. *Boston Dir. (1864),* 147.

72. George Barrell Cheever (1807–90), doctor of divinity, doctor of laws, and former reformist pastor of Salem's Howard Street Congregational Church, presided at this time over the Church of the Puritans in New York City. *DAB,* 4:48–49.

" 21, SUN. To church in Beverly with Mrs. R. & Mrs. E.—dined with them & Mr. Putnam, the minister[73]—dissented from his sermon as to necessity of war—to Cy. Hill with Mrs. E. & to Wenham to church—Dr. Cheever preeched—some striking illustrations but doubt general scope—back to Cy. Hill—Mrs. E. returned to Beverly—reading—prayer—bed. During afternoon Reed, Brown[74] & Post called—walk with Waters

AUG. 22, MON. Rain—writing letters & reading morning—walked alone—rain returning and a little wet—dinner—to Beverly in gig—saw Mrs. E. & pleasant talk—got my letters which I forgot & left yesterday—returned to C. Hill.

" 23, TU. Rode with Waters to Danvers—called at Putnams where Gen. Israel P.[75] was born (1)[76]—saw Rev Alfred P. at Danvers[77]—rode P.M. with Mrs. Cheever to Mrs. R——s. Dr. C. & Mr. Waters came in buggy—retd. to Cherry Hill—wrote Bannister to sell for $8000 or $7.500 Columbus property.[78]

---

73. Either Alfred Porter Putnam (1827–1906), a native of North Danvers who presided over the Mount Pleasant Unitarian Society in Roxbury, or J. W. Putnam, a local minister. Aug. 23, 1864, below; *Nat. Cyc.*, 9:269–70; A. P. Putnam to Chase, Dec. 7, 1864 (Chase Papers, L.C.); *Who Was Who*, 1:1001; Hurd, *Essex County*, 1:532, 547–52.

74. Probably Albert Gallatin Browne, Jr., or his father, Albert Gallatin Browne, Sr., who may have been home on leave from his position as the supervising special agent of the Treasury Department at Beaufort, S.C. *Register of Officers (1865)*, 66; Chase to Browne, Sr., June 9, Aug. 24, 1863 (Chase Papers, Hist. Soc. of Pa.); Chase to Browne, Sr., Sept. 23, 1863 (Letters Sent Relating to Restricted Commercial Intercourse and Captured and Abandoned Property, Gen. Recs. Treasury Dept., Nat. Arch.); Browne, Sr., to Chase, June 6, 1864 (Chase Papers, L.C.).

75. Israel Putnam (1718–1790), who had made his home at Pomfret, Conn., and was a veteran of both the last colonial war against France and the American Revolution. Putnam's legendary courage and self-reliance were supposedly illustrated in a story which recounted his single-handed capture of a wolf. *DAB*, 15:281; Sidney Perley, "Hathorne, Part of Salem Village in 1700," *Essex Institute Historical Collections* 53 (1917): 332–44.

76. In the original journal, Chase's description of his visit to the Putnam home, given here as the next paragraph of text (beginning *(1) contd.*), is located a dozen pages beyond the entry for Aug. 23. Chase added the *(1)* after *born* to show where he intended this later passage, which he wrote entirely in his own hand, to belong. The body of the Aug. 23 entry, like those for the days surrounding it, is in the clerk's hand with Chase's emendations.

77. Alfred Porter Putnam.

78. Chase wanted to sell a warehouse in Columbus which he owned and Dwight Bannister managed. Bannister to Chase, May 4, Aug. 16, 1864, Feb. 24, 1865 (Chase Papers, L.C.).

August 1864 { 493 }

(1) contd. Maria P. Putnam, a pretty young girl of about 18 apparently,[79] with a modest mixture of pride & sorrow showed me her brother's wooden sword, which had more interest for me than the native room of the old wolf-hunter.[80] "*He* used to sleep in that room" she said "and when the President first called for troops to save Washington & put down the rebellion he wanted to go so much. This was just after Fort Sumter was taken; but he was too young only about sixteen— Afterwards he would go & sit out doors in the summer nights & by the moonlight he carved this wooden sword." And she handed it to me. It was a rude imitation; but on one side of the blade there was this New England boy's thought "Not to be drawn without right" &, on the other side, this "Not to be sheathed without honor"; and then these Victory or Death! Death to Traitors." "Sometime afterwards" she told me "when Gov. Andrew said the President wanted more men he couldn't be kept back. He said he must go to defend the Constitution & the old Flag & he went. He was wounded in one of the terrible battles before Richmond in July 1862 & was taken prisoner and died in Libby Prison. Brief record & sad! And, of how many, true! The memorials of the old wolf hunter, hung round the chamber or carefully preserved in drawers;—the old rude pictures;— the worn wood engraving, so curiously colored of Wolfes Death at Quebec;[81] the memorials from Pomfret & the Wolfs cave—the Inkstand & Sand box—all faded away— There was nothing in the low ceiled chamber, with its old beams almost touching your head, except the Memory of the brave boy who died in Libby a prisoner that his Country might live & live free forever.[82]

" 24, WED. At home all the morning—reading, writing &c.— Whittier spent the day[83]—much pleasant talk— Evening took him to Beverly & to horse car—called at Castle R[84]—saw R. S. R. & Mrs.

---

79. Maria Phelps Putnam (b. 1843) married Wendell Phillips Hood of Danversport in 1866. Jennie Hood Bosson, "John Hood of Lynn, Massachusetts and some of his Descendants," *Essex Institute Historical Collections* 45 (1909): 154.

80. Maria's brother may have been Robert W. Putnam, whose name is listed on the Danvers Civil War monument. Hurd, *Essex County*, 1:536–37.

81. Probably a hand-colored engraving of Benjamin West's painting depicting the death of Maj. Gen. James Wolfe at Quebec in 1759.

82. Chase incorporated the story of young Putnam into a speech which he gave in Cincinnati on Sept. 24, 1864. *Chicago Tribune*, Sept. 30, 1864.

83. Massachusetts poet and abolitionist John Greenleaf Whittier (1807–92). *DAB*, 20:173–76.

84. The Rantoul home. Robert S. Rantoul's grandfather built this seaside house circa 1805. Hurd, *Essex County*, 1:728; "Rantoul Genealogy," 147, 242; Robert S. Rantoul, "Three Hundred Years of Beverly," *Essex Institute Historical Collections* 55 (1919): 105.

E.[85]—she is agreeable as always—fixed halter for me when I came away fearing danger from Arab horse!—

" 25 TH. W. P. Phillips called;[86] soon after he left, Dr. Schmidt from Washn. with message to write letter advising support of Lincoln with assurance of French mission this from Johnston & Corwin with apparent sanction of President[87]—told him I could do nothing now:—wrote G. B. Senter & others:[88]—told Waters Schmidts affair & to R. Castle evng.—saw Mrs. E. who told me what had been said to her about me—& seemed quite distressed without reason—returned to C. Hill.— Invitation to tea at Cy. Hill declined by Mrs R & Mrs E.— Wrote Gov Sprague & Nettie & Tomeny.[89]

AUG. 26, FRI. Letters from Katie; B, Wilson, N York Dainese, Egypt[90]—G. S. Denison, N. Orleans; I. Washburne Jr. Portland[91] & W. Ried, Washington,[92]—replied to each.[93]— Sent Dainese's letter to Fessenden with my reply / Wrote E. P. Powell, Adrian, Mich. can't

---

85. Charlotte Eastman.
86. Collector of customs at Salem, 1861–65, Willard Peele Phillips (1825–1901). David Mason Little, "Documentary History of the Salem Custom House," *Essex Institute Historical Collections* 67 (1931): 267–68.
87. Probably William Johnston (1819–66), Democratic congressman from Ohio, 1863–65, and Thomas Corwin. *Bio. Dir. U.S. Cong.*, 1275; entry for Sept. 3, 1864, below.
88. George B. Senter (1827–70) was mayor of Cleveland, Ohio, 1859–61, 1864–65. Holli and Jones, *Biographical Dictionary of American Mayors*, 327.
89. To his daughter, Chase described a social visit to Beverly. J. M. Tomeny was an assistant special agent for the Treasury Department in the Mississippi Valley. Chase to Janet Chase, Aug. 25, 1864 (Chase Papers, Hist. Soc. of Pa.); *Letter of the Secretary . . . Special Agents*, 2.
90. Francis Dainese, a controversial acting U.S. consul general in Egypt, wanted Chase to publish a list of individuals living under U.S. protection in Egypt who had subscribed to a fund for widows and orphans of U.S. soldiers killed in the Civil War. Francis Dainese, *The History of Mr. Seward's Pet in Egypt* . . . (Washington, 1867), 44–45; *New York Times*, Aug. 17, 1864; *DAB*, 8:97.
91. Israel Washburn (1813–83), a brother of Illinois congressman Elihu Benjamin Washburne, was a former Republican congressman from Maine, 1851–61; governor of the state, 1861–62; and collector of customs at Portland, 1863–78. *Bio. Dir. U.S. Cong.*, 2012; *DAB*, 19:502–3.
92. Whitelaw Reid expressed concern about rumors that Chase might support Lincoln's supposedly doomed reelection campaign in return for an appointment as U.S. minister to France. "Confound their foreign missions!" he advised. "Isn't it wise to wait for the Chicago Convention; & for the speedy crystallization of elements that is likely to follow?" Reid to Chase, Aug. 22, 1864 (Chase Papers, Hist. Soc. of Pa.).
93. To his daughter Kate, Chase expressed concern for her health, told of plans to visit Concord, N.H., and issued an invitation for a brief trip to the White Mountains late the following week. Chase acknowledged Dainese's letter and, as noted in his journal, forwarded it to William Fessenden. Chase to Kate Chase Sprague, Aug. 26, 1864 (Chase Papers, Hist. Soc. of Pa.); Dainese, *Mr. Seward's Pet in Egypt*, 45.

August 1864 {495}

decide abt. lecturing at present—will some time next month[94]—letter fr. Tho. Brown abt. Quicksilver mine &c. wrote part of financial letter to Fessenden[95]—rode with Mr. Waters—went to Beverly & spent Evng. with Mrs. R. & E.[96]

" 27, SAT. Rose very early—unwell and after going down returned to bed—up again—breakfast & finished letter to Fessenden—goodbye to all the kind folks—Dr. C.[97] & W. rode to depot with me—to Boston just in time to miss Concord train—went to Revere House.—sent note to Mr. Pierce—rewrote letter to Fessenden—met Mr. ——— ——— of N.Y. who told me that Mrs W. G. Moorhead & her family were in the House[98]— Overseer Southron & flunkey northerner at dinner—met Wm. Hatch & J. R. Gilmore of Cinti.— G. presented his two boys—bid them stand by freedom[99]— Pierce came—saw Mrs. Moorhead, Will, Dora and with them Mrs Smith of N.Y.[1]— Cars to Concord—met Mr. Duncan of Hanover[2]—Tucker at depot.[3]

94. Edward Payson Powell (1833–1915) later gained fame as a religious apologist for the theory of evolution. At this time, he was pastor of the Adrian Congregational church. On Aug. 18, Powell had invited Chase "to our Lecture Course for the Coming Winter." *DAB*, 15:144–45; Powell to Chase, Aug. 18, 1864 (Chase Papers, L.C.).

95. Chase was offering Fessenden his assessment of U.S. Treasury finances and suggesting possible sources of revenue. The letter went through at least two versions before Chase sent it the following day. Chase to Fessenden, Aug. 27, 1864 (Chase Manhattan Archives); Aug. 27 entry, below. An incomplete copy of the letter also appears in Schuckers, *Chase*, 414–17.

96. Jane Rantoul and Charlotte Eastman.

97. George Barrell Cheever and Richard Palmer Waters.

98. In 1833, Sarah E. Cooke (1816–c. 1869), Jay Cooke's oldest sister, had married William G. Moorhead, her brother's eventual business partner. Oberholtzer, *Jay Cooke*, 1:3, 40, 2:16, 146.

99. William S. Hatch was one of Chase's political associates and Hamilton County's former representative in the Ohio House, 1841–42, and Senate, 1850, 1858–60. Gilmore was probably James Gilmore (1814–97), a founder of the Cincinnati banking house of Gilmore, Dunlap and Company. One of Gilmore's sons, Virgil G., served as French consular agent in Cincinnati, 1876–85. Another, Clarence D., was a Cincinnati banker. Chase to Hatch, Mar. 2, 1868 (Hatch Papers, Cinc. Hist. Soc.); Gilkey, *Ohio Hundred Year Book*, 168, 170, 205; *Cinc. Dir. (1865)*, 160; Greve, *Centennial History*, 2:531–32.

1. William E. C. Moorhead was the son of William G. and Sarah Moorhead. Dora was evidently his sister. Oberholtzer, *Jay Cooke*, 1:102, 2:206.

2. William Henry Duncan (1807–83), lawyer, Dartmouth class of 1830. Chapman, *Sketches of the Alumni*, 252; Emerson, *General Catalogue*, 244.

3. Josiah Prentice Tucker had married Hannah Ralston Whipple, the daughter of Chase's sister Hannah. Tucker had served as assistant surveyor of customs at Boston and, at this time, was on leave from his position as surveyor of customs at New Orleans. Chase to J. P. Tucker, Oct. 20, 1863 (Chase Papers, Hist. Soc. of Pa.); *Register of Officers (1863)*, 65; Tucker to Chase, July 21, 1863, June 30, 1864, and "Family Memoranda" (Chase Papers, L.C.).

" 28, SUN. To church with family—new edifice since I was here last & very pretty but some inconveniences and too dark—Minister from N.Y. preached a very good sermon[4]—reading and talk rest of day except short nap. Evening—Judge Harvey, Dr. Robinson, & Judge & Mrs. Perley called[5]—talk not very profitable—retired to Chamber & read First Epistle of John & to bed.

" 29, MON. Called at Gov. Gilmore's, who was out—saw Mrs. G.[6]— to Hopkinton with Eliza—Aunt Ellen very glad to see me[7]—now 89—sight failed & quite lame but still clear in mind & faith—visited Mother's Grave plucked a young locust growing upon it & transcribed inscription Mrs. Jannette Chase, relict of Hon. Ithmr. Chase, aged 54, died apr. _____ 1832: And now Lord what is our hope— Truly our hope is even in thee— Returned to Concord; Evening— several called—Mr & Mrs. Chandler[8] / Mr & Mrs. Foster[9]—latter charming—Mr. Perkins Ham. E. formerly of Hopkinton[10]—of rich family & object of my boyish envy—now respectable and well to do citizen—father of Mrs. Foster—Prof. Hadley of Dartmouth, now member of Legislature[11]— Pierce came from Boston—advised

---

4. The guest speaker at St. Paul's Episcopal Church was Francis E. Lawrence (d. 1879), rector of New York City's Church of the Holy Communion. *Concord Daily Monitor*, 2nd ed., Aug. 28, 1864; *New York Times*, June 14, 1879.

5. Matthew Harvey (1781–1866), former governor of New Hampshire and congressman, was U.S. district judge, 1831–66; Abraham Hazen Robinson (d. 1898) had practiced medicine since 1859; former New Hampshire legislator Ira Perley (1799–1874) sat as an associate justice of the state's superior court, 1850–52, then as chief justice of the state's supreme judicial court, 1855–59, 1864–69; Mary S. Nelson Perley was his wife. *Bio. Dir. U.S. Cong.*, 1148; Lyford, *History of Concord*, 2:1169–70, 1380; *Catalogue of Officers and Graduates of Yale University*, 167; *DAB*, 14:478; Duane Hamilton Hurd, ed., *History of Merrimack and Belknap Counties, New Hampshire* (Philadelphia, 1885), 14.

6. Joseph Albree Gilmore (1811–67), Concord merchant, New Hampshire state senator, 1858–59, and Republican governor, 1863–65; and his wife, Ann Page Whipple Gilmore. *DAB*, 7:311.

7. Chase went with his niece, Eliza Chase Whipple, to call on Ellen Wiggin Chase, the wife of Chase's uncle Baruch Chase. Child, *Cornish*, 2:62.

8. The inscription paraphrased Ps. 39:7. William Eaton Chandler (1835–1917) and his wife Ann Caroline Gilmore Chandler (d. 1871). William Chandler was a New Hampshire editor and Republican politician, assistant secretary of the U.S. Treasury, 1865–67, and secretary of the navy, 1882–85. *DAB*, 3:616–18.

9. Concord attorney and New Hampshire politician William Lawrence Foster (b. 1823) had served as commissioner of the U.S. Circuit Court, 1854–62, and sat on the state's supreme judicial court, 1869–74. His wife was Harriet Morton Perkins Foster (b. 1834). Hurd, *Merrimack and Belknap Counties*, 27–28; Ezra S. Stearns, comp., *Genealogical and Family History of the State of New Hampshire* (New York, 1908), 242.

10. Mrs. Foster's father, Hamilton E. Perkins (1806–86), a local merchant and probate judge. Stearns, *Genealogical History of New Hampshire*, 242.

11. Possibly Dartmouth graduate Amos Hadley (1825–1908), a Concord, N.H., attorney, educator, and editor of the *State Capital Reporter*. Chapman, *Sketches of the Alumni*, 349; Emerson, *General Catalogue*, 269.

September 1864   { 497 }

friendly conference between Union Men & Governor G. about differences between them

" 30, Tu.   Gov. G.—called & took me to ride—talked abt. differences with Leg. Gov. censured Chandler & Rollins—thought Lincoln & Stanton had behaved badly[12]— Soldiers coming home will vote for McClellan—left with Pierce on cars for White Mountains—dined at Plymouth—stage to Profile House[13] arrived abt. ½ past 7—met Mr. Bloodgood & daughters & talked finance & a little politics[14]—

" 31, Wed.   Report that McClellan is nominated at Chicago[15]—left Profile at 8—outside seat—grand prospects—towards Littleton abt. [8] miles—passed on right of it—along the Ammonoosuc—Mr. Strong and another lady & gentn. on upper seat—Mr. Pomeroy & I with driver—I tired of this & got inside at last—Pierce in another coach—arrived Crawfords abt. 2 P.M. dull & rainy[16]—bear, chief resource for guests—tenpins with Pomeroy agnst. Pierce & Somebody / we victors—thanks to P.—bed in two hollows & so hard—

Sept. 1 Thus.   Left at 8 for North Conway—Pierce & I outside—Notch scenery magnificent—arrived at C. 1.30—took off flannels & dressed for dinner—after dinner Miss Haven came & spoke to me[17]—introduced Mr. P. to her—she, me to several, among others to Mrs. Caldwell, Mrs. Miller—Miss West—Capt. Miller.— P. & I with Miss H. & Mrs. C. drove to Echo Lake, Diana's Bath & Cathedral[18]—

12. At the Jan. 1864 New Hampshire Republican convention, Congressman Edward Henry Rollins (1824–89) and William Eaton Chandler supported a resolution in favor of Lincoln's reelection. The proposal, contrary to the wishes of "older men" in the party, "passed unanimously amid great enthusiasm." *DAB*, 16:120; James O. Lyford, *Life of Edward H. Rollins: A Political Biography* (Boston, 1906), 163–75.

13. A hotel which opened in 1853 near the natural feature "Old Man and the Mountain." Federal Writers' Project, *New Hampshire: A Guide to the Granite State* (Boston, 1938), 326.

14. Likely New York merchant and author Simeon DeWitt Bloodgood (1799–1866), with whom Chase had corresponded about financial matters through the Civil War. *Appletons'*, 1:296; *New York Tribune*, July 16, 17, 1866.

15. The Democrats did not actually nominate McClellen as their presidential candidate until the thirty-first. *Chicago Tribune*, Sept. 1, 1864.

16. The Crawford House resumed operations in 1859 after a fire in 1854 destroyed the original hotel. Federal Writers' Project, *New Hampshire*, 393.

17. Perhaps a daughter of Franklin Haven, Sr. Chase to Haven, June 8, 1869 (Misc. Letters, Southern Hist. Collec., Univ. of North Carolina).

18. A ten-foot waterfall fed Diana's Bath, a "deep and rounded basin" with a striking rock floor visible during low water. The Cathedral was a recess in the cliffs shaped like a cathedral arch. M. E. Eastman, ed., *East of the White Hills* (North Conway, N.H., 1882), 15, 17–18; Wallace Nutting, *New Hampshire Beautiful* (Framingham, Mass., 1923), 34, 37; Samuel Adams Drake, *The Heart of the White Mountains* . . . (New York, 1882), 46.

a delightful drive / evng. same party to Juggler & ventriloquist—first ridiculous latter amusing—

" 2 FRI. left North Conway at 6 after very early breakfast— Mrs. C. & Miss. H. up & with us at breakfast— Bishop Duggan, of Detroit was asked to take a buggy which was to go back to Centre Harbor which he did and asked me to take a seat with him[19]— I drove the horse & we had very pleasant ride—he seemed to favor McClellan— asked me about Pendleton[20]—we reached Centre Harbor abt. 12.30 dined—met Stover & wife—Stover spoke to me—I rather cold not liking him— Camp meeting party on board Chocura[21]— P. intcd. me to Mr. Guild, Unitarian Minister, who was formerly of Marietta[22]—at Alton Bay took cars for Boston—arrived a little after 8—to Revere House—Sumner & Hooper called—Sumner spoke of meeting at New York[23]—recd letter from Fessenden & copy of one sent him[24]—also from Thayer & Schmidt & call from Stevens[25]— very embarrassing.

" 3, SAT. Pierce to Breakfast—gave him $30 my part of expenses over abt. $5 paid direct—presented him my sleeve buttons / Called at Hoopers— Dana called & Howe—Pierce with me to the Depot— left 11.10, Sprague met me at Depot—in Providence—letters—

19. Chase's traveling companion may have been James Duggan (1825–99), fourth bishop of Chicago, 1858–66, whose behavior became "wayward" and "variable" during the 1860s. In 1870 he was committed to an asylum in St. Louis for the remainder of his life. John Gilmary Shea, *A History of the Catholic Church Within the Limits of the United States* . . . , 4 vols. (New York, 1886–92), 4:620–24; *Appletons'*, 2:250; *Chicago Tribune*, Mar. 28, 1899.
20. George Hunt Pendleton.
21. The *Chocorua*, a new paddle-wheel steamer that ran out of Portsmouth, N.H. Lytle, *Merchant Vessels*, 32.
22. Edward Chipman Guild (1832–99), Harvard class of 1853. *Nat. Cyc.*, 19:329.
23. Charles Sumner had declined an invitation to an Aug. 30 meeting at New York to consider a replacement candidate for Lincoln, but knew about its discussions, including the prospects for Chase's candidacy, from a confidential letter. Aug. 19, 1864, above; Palmer, *Selected Letters of Charles Sumner*, 2:251–52; August Lieber to Sumner, Aug. 31, 1864 (Sumner Papers, Houghton Lib., Harvard Univ.).
24. Chase had not been able to make his own copy of the July 27 letter. Fessenden, unhappy at the country's political and financial situation, commented on Chase's proposals for handling national finances and told of his desire to consult with Chase. Chase to Fessenden, Aug. 27 (Chase Manhattan Archives); Fessenden to Chase, Aug. 31, 1864 (Chase Papers, Hist. Soc. of Pa.).
25. Chase may refer to his friend Eli Thayer and to John Austin Stevens of New York, or possibly to Albert G. Stevens, an employee at the Boston Custom House. On Aug. 28, Charles F. Schmidt wrote with a request that Chase clarify his position regarding a potential presidential nomination. Schmidt was to see Lincoln the next day. Chase to Schmidt, Aug. 12, 1864 (Cinc. Hist. Soc.); Schmidt to Chase, Aug. 28, 1864 (Chase Papers, L.C.); *Boston Dir. (1864)*, 340; Chase to J. A. Stevens, July 20, 1864 (Stevens Papers, New York Hist. Soc.).

Anthony on cars to Greenwich[26] / Chapin intcd. to me, a Providence man spending summer at Stonington[27]—two colored gentlemen— Mr. Halsey of N.Y. came in[28]—talk of indifferent subjects,—Nantucket, Tom. Corwin &c—at Kingston station at 1.24 found Katie & Nettie waiting for me—dusty ride to Narragansett—delightful place—found Maj. Baldwin—Mr. Coleman, Miss Claire Albrecht, Ida Nichols, Annie Winthrop[29]—a housefull—a merry game of croquet—Mrs. Potter called on Kate[30]—dinner at 7.

SEPT. 4, SUN. To church at Wakefield—good sermon—afternoon went to rocks—grand roll of the ocean.

" 5, MON. Gov. S.[31] & Ida to Providence— Easterly storm which began in night—continued with intermission all day—quite chilly— afternoon went to rocks—Nettie & I to Indian rock—dash of waves magnificent.

" 6, TU. All the folks went to Providence—I bought the tickets for 8—Maj. Baldwin & Mr. Coleman, Katie & Nettie, Claire & Annie Winthrop, Josephines[32] & myself. Went to Mrs. Sprague's—then with Mrs. S. & Katie to Centennial[33]—gentlemen took charge of ladies & put me in procession—Mr. Bancroft, my Co-Walker[34]—

---

26. Probably Henry Bowen Anthony.
27. Josiah Chapin (1788–1881) had acquired a fortune in the cotton business. At this time, he served as president of the Merchants' National Bank of Providence. *The Biographical Cyclopedia of Representative Men of Rhode Island* (Providence, 1881), 1:222.
28. Possibly George Armstrong Halsey (1827–94), actually of New Jersey. He was an assessor of internal revenue, 1862–66, and U.S. congressman, 1867–69, 1871–73. *Appletons'*, 3:53; *Bio. Dir. U.S. Cong.*, 1117.
29. Robert B. Coleman (c. 1804–81), a proprietor of hotels in New York City and Baltimore, once operated steamboats serving Providence. Ida Nichols was William Sprague's niece. Annie Neilson Winthrop was a daughter of Benjamin Robert Winthrop, a New York capitalist, and later married Boston banker Horatio Greenough Curtis. *New York Times*, Nov. 2, 1881; *Daily National Intelligencer*, Nov. 13, 1863; *Nat. Cyc.*, 29:384.
30. Probably Eliza Palmer Potter, wife of James Brown Mason Potter (1818–1900), a textile manufacturer from South Kingston, R.I., who was at this time an officer in the U.S. Army. *Representative Men and Old Families of Rhode Island* . . . (Chicago, 1908), 1:56–57.
31. William Sprague.
32. Chase may refer to Josephine Jones, the daughter of his sister-in-law, Charlotte Ludlow Jones. Charlotte Jones to Chase, Sept. 30, 1863 (Chase Papers, L.C.).
33. Sept. 6 marked Brown University's centennial. *Celebration of the One Hundredth Anniversary of the Founding of Brown University, September 6th, 1864* (Providence, 1865); *Providence Daily Journal*, Sept. 7, 8, 1864.
34. George Bancroft owned a summer home in Newport.

intcd. me to Prof. Goldwin Smith[35] & Mr. Stanley a young Englishman—saw Bp. Clark,[36] Mr. Pierce, Bp. Smith of Ky.[37] Chas. James & many other leading men in procession—in church sat next to Prof. Smith—asked what most struck him—expected him to say absence of indications of war—but he did not—forget what he did say—I said what I thought—he said England did not exhibit more such indications in time of Crimean War—yes, but that not a civil war— Dr. Sears delivered an address which was plain & rather dry but quite good[38]—after address dinner—John Henry Clifford presided—excellent opening address—very clever clever poems by Judge Thomas & Mr. Thurber[39]—good speech by Goldwin Smith— I called on to respond & well recd[40]—obliged to leave the table after which Gen. Burnside & Geo. Wm. Curtis spoke[41]— Evng. some young folks at Mrs. Sprague's. Pierce among them—

" 7, WED. With Gov. S. & Maj. Baldwin to commencement some very good pieces—to Powell's picture[42]—home to dinner—late 3 instead of 2—before going to commencement, went through Mrs Spragues Garden with Bp. Clark & the Rochester's after dinner to President Wayland's with Katie[43]—met General Underwood & many others there[44]—then rode to Mr. Davis'—saw him & Mrs.

---

35. Goldwin Smith (1823–1910), professor of history at Oxford University and recipient of an LL.D. from Brown. *DNB*, 2nd supp., 328–40.

36. The Protestant Episcopal bishop of Rhode Island, Thomas March Clark (1812–1903). *DAB*, 4:139–40.

37. Benjamin Bosworth Smith (1794–1884), first Protestant Episcopal bishop of Kentucky, was a Rhode Island native and graduate of Brown University. *Nat. Cyc.*, 3:466–67.

38. The speech by Barnas Sears (1802–80), Baptist minister and president of Brown University, 1855–67, was later published in the *Celebration of the One Hundredth Anniversary*. *DAB*, 16:537–38.

39. John Henry Clifford (1809–76), Brown University class of 1827, former attorney general and governor of Massachusetts; Benjamin Franklin Thomas; and Charles Thurber (1803–86), Brown University class of 1827, inventor, manufacturer, and former Massachusetts state senator. *Appletons'*, 1:657; *DAB*, 4:215–16, 18:513.

40. Chase's brief address expressed hope that cessation of hostilities with the Confederacy would also improve relations between Great Britain and the U.S. *Providence Daily Journal*, Sept. 8, 1864.

41. Curtis (1824–92), the editor of *Harper's Weekly*, was also a famous orator. *DAB*, 4:614–15.

42. *Perry's Victory on Lake Erie*, by William Henry Powell (1823–79), a painting completed for the state of Ohio in 1863, was on display at Dyer's Hall, Westminster Street. *DAB*, 15:153–54.

43. Baptist minister Francis Wayland (1796–1865) had been president of Brown University, 1827–55. *DAB*, 19:558–60.

44. Adin Ballou Underwood (1828–88), Brown University class of 1849, advanced from major to major general of volunteers, 1861–66. *Appletons'*, 6:209.

D.[45]—who quite ill & dejected—back to tea—after with Gov. S. to President Sears' reception—introduced to many & rather lionized—escaped soon & long talk with Gov. S. abt. Mills, business &c. Mrs. Nichols & Miss. Sprague returned v 10 & 11 as we were talking[46]

" 8 THUR.   Went out with Katie to make some purchases bought only a couple of books—& staid at Gov.'s Office till hour for starting—then returned to Pier—Katie & Nettie, Claire, Josephine & Annie Winthrop & myself—croquet &c

" 9, FRI.   Ida Nichols & Miss. Carruth came down in the morning and afternoon Gov. S——;—he & Katie had misunderstanding that evening

" 10, SAT.   Talk with Katie—walk with S. to next farm on Narrow River—then back to house—grand rollers / croquet—Nettie & I agst. S. & Claire— Clambake—very nice—back to house—supper—afterwards to Point Judith & visit to Light House.

" 11, SUN.   Rain—all staid at home—I read testament & Misanthrope[47]

" 12, MON.   Spent morning in writing to Mr. French—(but did not send letter) & packing— Went to Providence in 3 P.M. train—met Mr. Barnard at Kingston station[48]—Eliot in cars—called at Mrs. Sprague's—letters from Schuckers at Albany;[49]—Milliken,

---

45. Probably John Chandler Bancroft Davis (1822–1907), lawyer, diplomat, and assistant secretary of state, 1869–74. He was a nephew of George Bancroft. Frederica Gore King Davis, daughter of a New York financier and railroad president, married Davis in 1857. *DAB*, 5:133–36, 10:392–93.

46. The *v* is very likely the clerk's misreading of Chase's *b* (for "between"). Mary Ann Sprague Nichols, whose first husband was John E. Nichols, was the oldest sister of Gov. William Sprague. She later married Frank W. Latham. Almira Sprague, another sister, married Providence politician Thomas Arthur Doyle in 1869. Thomas W. Bicknell, *The History of the State of Rhode Island and Providence Plantations: Biographical* (New York, 1920), 493; Warren Vincent Sprague, *Sprague Families in America* (Rutland, Vt., 1913), 299; Johnson, *Twentieth Century Biographical Dictionary*, v. 3.

47. Molière's comedy, *Le Misanthrope* (Paris, 1667).

48. Possibly educator Henry Barnard (1811–1900), former Rhode Island commissioner of education. *DAB*, 1:621–25.

49. Ohio native Jacob William Schuckers, who had worked as a Treasury clerk in Chase's office, graduated in 1865 from Albany Law School in New York. In Aug. 1870, he patented a "Harvester-rake," and later that year became Chase's secretary again for a short period. Schuckers later acquired notoriety as an economist and early Chase biographer. Dec. 16, 1870, below; Wallace, *North American Authors*, 403; *Circular and Catalogue of the Law School of the University of Albany, for the Year 1864–5* (Albany, N.Y., 1865); *Annual Report of the Commissioner of Patents for the Year 1870*, 41st Cong.,

Hamilton, O.; Rose Matthews, Secy. Ladies Association, Oberlin;[50] Edwd. Harris Woonsocket;[51] L. S. Bayley, Chicago, W. A. Packard, Secy. O.P.K. Dartmouth[52]— Geo. Francis Train[53]—went on boat Electra for New York.—sat forward till passed Point Judith.[54]

" 13, TUES. Jar of boat kept me waking every few minutes—up at 6—shaved & dressed—reached New York—10 min past 7.—talk with gentleman who thought Lincoln very wise—if more radical would have offended conservatives—if more conservative the radicals—will this be judgment of history?—called at Bk. of Commerce—talked with Stevens & Vail abt. sales of 5.20s. by Barings—they thought best to make power to sell at limit—I approved. Stevens congratulated me on Freedom from official responsibilities—met Mr. Duer & others—all kind—some more than kind—Barney dined with us—Mr. H   & also Orton called[55] & Stevens, Jr.—talked with him—advised to disconnect himself from new convention project—left for Washn. Frank Moore on board who said future Volumes of Rebellion Record would contain more finance.[56]

3rd sess., 1870–71, H. Ex. Doc. 89, 204; *The National Union Catalog: Pre-1956 Imprints* (London, 1968–81), 531:48; *Register of Officers (1863)*, 18; *New York Times*, Mar. 6, 1882; *Wash. Dir. (1862)*, 154; ibid. (1863), 178.

50. Rose Mathews Holway (d. 1871), Oberlin class of 1865, probably invited Chase to address the Young Ladies' Literary Society, formerly known as the Young Ladies' Association of the Oberlin Collegiate Institute. *General Catalogue of Oberlin College, 1833–1908* (Oberlin, Ohio, 1909), 651; Robert Samuel Fletcher, *A History of Oberlin College...*, 2 vols. (Oberlin, Ohio, 1943), 2:761–62, 781.

51. Edward Harris (1801–72), the founder of Harris Woolen Company, wanted Chase to visit Woonsocket, R.I. Harris to Chase, Sept. 9, 1864 (Chase Papers, L.C.); *Nat. Cyc.*, 12:99.

52. *O.P.K.* is probably the clerk's misreading of ΦBK in a draft version of the entry by Chase. William Alfred Packard (1830–1909), professor of Greek Language and Literature at Dartmouth College, 1863–70, notified Chase that he had been appointed orator of the Phi Beta Kappa Society at the 1865 Dartmouth College commencement. *Who Was Who*, 1:927; Packard to Chase, Sept. 3, 1864 (Chase Papers, L.C.); *General Catalogue of Bowdoin College*, 97.

53. Train (1829–1904), a Boston transportation magnate, author, and champion of radical causes, kept a villa in Newport. *DAB*, 18:626–27.

54. The *Electra*, a 1,300-ton steam vessel launched in 1864, operated out of Providence. Lytle, *Merchant Vessels*, 54.

55. New York merchant Benjamin H. Hutton (c. 1809–84) argued a tariff question. Hiram Barney to Chase, Sept. 17, 1863 (Lincoln Papers, L.C.); *New York Times*, Feb. 19, 1884.

56. Moore (1828–1904) was author, editor, and compiler of *The Rebellion Record: A Diary of American Events...*, 11 vols. (New York, 1861–68). *DAB*, 13:122.

September 1864 {503}

" 14, WED. Arrived at Washn. Marshall & Cassie in house[57]—quite out of order—repairing &c. Mr. Harrington called—went to Treasy. Dept.—reiterated advice to Fessenden to organize Agency System in Europe—or facilitate sales there—danger from fluctuations of exchange / examined rules cotton trade—called on Mr. McCulloch—both he & Fessenden advised taking part in Campaign—F—— calling at Presidents talked with him—he wished me to call—McC. said he wd. call—Gov. S. & K.[58] determined to return to R.I. & went at ½ p. 6.—Stanton & several others called.

" 15, THURS. Called at War Dept.—also on Prest.—he recd. me quite cordially—Stanton as kind as always—at Dept. talked with Harrington & Risley abt. Cotton Trade—advised against interference beyond lines—let military control there—dined with Fessenden—called at Howe's room—also at Ames', when met Roselius of New Orleans[59]—met M. O. Roberts & J. M. Forbes at Howes[60]—difference between them—R. spoke strongly agnst. F.—Gov. Andrew—out—spoke with Fessn. favor Howe—he disinclined—

" 16, FRI. At Dept. & sundry matters— Cooke told me he had invited Forney to dine with me to-morrow[61]— Wetmore called asking me to speak with Gov. Andrew at flagraising tomorrow—declined to speak—but promised to be present— Cooke handed me statement of Ferry Co. stock[62]—$20,000 augmented from $10.000 original—says are to be worth par & produces 12%—$9000 & over due—interest from sundry dates— Went to War Dept. & rode with

---

57. Marshall, whose full name remains unknown, was evidently a member of Chase's household staff. For other references to him, see May 1 and 25, 1865, below. Catherine ("Cassie") Vaudry, a former slave, was Chase's housekeeper in Washington until his death. Vaudry account with J. B. Varnum, Jr., Feb. 1, 1862, Chase to Vaudry, July 6, 1864 (Chase Papers, L.C.); cash accounts, rear of Journal XIX; Warden, *Chase*, 804.

58. William Sprague and Kate Chase Sprague.

59. Chase called on Timothy Otis Howe and Massachusetts industrialist Oakes Ames (1804–73), who served as a Republican in Congress, 1863–73. *DAB*, 1:251–53.

60. New York shipping magnate Marshall Owen Roberts (1814–80), a founder of the United States Mail Steamship Company, was a leading Republican financier. *DAB*, 16:11–12.

61. Pennsylvania journalist John Wien Forney (1817–81) was clerk of the U.S. House, 1851–55 and 1859–61, editor of the Washington, D.C., *Daily Morning Chronicle*, and secretary of the U.S. Senate, 1861–68. He was frequently addressed as "Colonel." *Appletons'*, 2:503; *DAB*, 6:526–27; *Nat. Cyc.*, 3:268.

62. The Washington Ferry Company. Chase to Jay Cooke, Oct. 19, 1864 (Chase Papers, Hist. Soc. of Pa.)

Stanton to Soldiers Home[63]—called on Mrs. Stanton nice children[64]—took tea with the family—superb evening Surg. Gen. Barnes there & Mrs B. with him[65]—called at Prest's. Corwin & C. J. Wright there—they went after some talk—talk with President indifferent but cordial—home from War Dept.

" 17, SAT. Tried to give some time to speech at Cinti.—but poor success—

" 18, SUN. Church—Dr. Nadal on Sunday observance—excellent, though as I thought defective in proof that 4th Commandment applies to Christian Sunday[66]—dined alone—read Spencer & other books[67]—Evng. Mr. Goodloe & others called[68]—G—— favors compensation to rebel slave-holders for slaves as peace measure— Young man from Chronicle Office abt. speeches at flag-raising yesterday—promised substance of mine & furnished it.[69]

" 19, MON. Rose earlier than usual—read Testat. &c—speeches at flag raising— Wrote Maj. Milliken Hamn. O. Paid Hooe & Bros. $9.13[70]—wrote P. T. Snowden—Balto. enclosing check on Jay Cooke & Co. Washn. for $68.50 amt. of Raymond & Benton's acct. of shirts paid by him[71]—paid C. S. Magruder's bill coal &c. Sept. & Oct.

---

63. The Home was a favorite summer residence of President Lincoln. It stood about three miles north of the Capitol. Keim, *Washington and Its Environs*, 221–22.

64. Edwin M. Stanton and his wife, Ellen M. Hutchison Stanton, had four surviving children: Edwin Lamson Stanton (1842–77), Eleanor Adams (b. 1857), Lewis Hutchison (b. ca. 1860), and Bessie (b. 1863). *DAB*, 17:521; *Nat. Cyc.*, 20:137; Thomas and Hyman, *Stanton*, 75, 393, 638.

65. Joseph K. Barnes, M.D. (1817–83), surgeon general of the U.S. Army, 1864–82; and his wife, Mary T. Fauntleroy Barnes. *DAB*, 1:631–32; *Nat. Cyc.*, 4:359.

66. The Fourth Commandment (Exod. 20:8–11) pertains to observation of the seventh day of the week as the Sabbath. Bernard Harrison Nadal, D.D. (1812–70) was pastor of the Wesley Chapel. *Appletons'*, 4:475.

67. Chase is known to have read Edmund Spenser's *The Faerie Queene*, and apparently owned *The Poetical Works of Edmund Spenser* (Boston and New York, 1855). *Catalogue of a Most Superb Collection*, 86; May 1, 1857, above.

68. Daniel Reaves Goodloe (1814–1902) was a journalist, former editor of the antislavery *National Era*, and U.S. marshal for North Carolina, 1865–73. *DAB*, 7:390–91; *Nat. Cyc.*, 10:71.

69. Chase's brief remarks at a flag raising ceremony upon the opening of the Ohio and Massachusetts Agency in Washington combined patriotic sentiments with an appeal to vote for the Republican ticket in the November elections. *Chicago Tribune*, Sept. 22, 1864.

70. The Washington, D.C., dry goods store of Robert A. and Peter H. Hooe, on Pennsylvania Avenue. *Wash. Dir. (1863)*, 114.

71. Months earlier Chase had asked Snowden to have shirts made for him. Chase to Snowden, Mar. 15, 1864 (Chase Papers, Hist. Soc. of Pa.).

September 1864 {505}

'63—$29.50[72] / Wrote Prof. W. A. Packard Dart. College; John Fitch, N.Y.; A. C. Sands, Cinti. O; Wm. A. Darling Chn. N.Y.[73] Edgar Conkling Cinti., Horace Greeley, N. York.,[74] Mrs. Eastman Beverly, Prof. Grauert, N.Y.[75] at home all day— Maj. Way called abt. trade at Norfolk[76]—Frank Howe—Col. Forney & Mr. Salladee[77]—Forney spoke abt. Henderson[78]—is thoroughly frightened abt. Pa. & N. York.—thinks Lincoln's chances very bad—promised him to speak to Fessenden abt. Henderson—dined with Fessenden—spoke abt. H.—— as promised—he said he had examined papers & was convinced he ought not to restore him—spoke also abt. Frank Howe & Flanders[79]—earnestly desired Howe's apptm. as purchasing Agent, became obliged to disappoint his reasonable expectation of appt as Sup. Agt. vice Flanders—he declined—had promised another—returned home found note from Goodloe—serenade evng.

72. Chase probably meant Samuel C. Magruder, a partner in the Washington, D.C., wood and coal business of Magruder and Stone. *Wash. Dir. (1863)*, 142.

73. Fitch, a New York attorney, and William Augustus Darling (1817–95), a New York merchant who was at this time a Republican congressman, both wrote Chase on Sept. 16. They invited him to address a Sept. 27 meeting of New York City's combined Union organizations, a coalition of which Darling was the chairman. The gathering was intended to ratify the nomination of Lincoln and other candidates. According to his filing endorsements on their letters, Chase informed Fitch and Darling that he would be in Ohio and could not attend the assembly. Chase corresponded with Alexander C. Sands, U.S. marshal at Cincinnati, about the congressional seat for which Chase had been suggested as a possible nominee. Fitch to Chase, Sept. 16, 1864, Darling et al. to Chase, Sept. 16, 1864, Sands to Chase, Sept. 30, 1864 (Chase Papers, L.C.); *New York Dir. (1864)*, 287; *Cinc. Dir. (1865)*, 336; *OR*, ser. 2, v. 2:127; *Bio. Dir. U.S. Cong.*, 871.

74. Cincinnati financier and land speculator Edgar Conkling, on behalf of Ohio's National Union Association, had invited Chase to deliver an address at Cincinnati's Mozart Hall. Horace Greeley had also written about potential speaking engagements. *Cinc. Dir. (1862)*, 106; Conkling to Chase, Dec. 6, 1861, Jan. 15, 1862, Sept. 17, 1864 (Chase Papers, L.C.); Greeley to Chase, Sept. 12, 1864 (Chase Papers, Hist. Soc. of Pa.).

75. Chase wrote to a Prof. Grauert in Jan. 1864, thanking him for a Portuguese grammar written by Grauert's brother (almost certainly E. F. Grauert, *A New Method for Learning the Portuguese Language* [New York, 1863]). Chase to —— Grauert, Jan. 26, 1864 (Chase Papers, Hist. Soc. of Pa.).

76. George Brevitt Way (d. 1868), a former paymaster of volunteers from Ohio. Heitman, *Historical Register*, 1:1010; *Wash. Dir. (1864)*, 273; Way to Chase, Jan. 5, 1861 (Chase Papers, L.C.).

77. Andrew M. Salade was a Washington, D.C., attorney. *Wash. Dir. (1865)*, 315.

78. Gustavus A. Henderson, a clerk in the Treasury Department. Earlier in the year, he faced allegations of accepting bribes and, with Spencer M. Clark, was accused of corrupting young female employees. Baker, *United States Secret Service*, 293–307; *Wash. Dir. (1864)*, 172.

79. Benjamin Franklin Flanders (1816–96), Unionist congressman from Louisiana, 1862–63; in 1863, appointed supervising special agent for the U.S. Treasury, lower Mississippi Valley; military governor of Louisiana, 1867–68; mayor of New Orleans, 1870–72; and assistant U.S. treasurer at New Orleans, 1873–83. *Bio. Dir. U.S. Cong.*, 1004.

Capt. Brand & son & Reynolds called[80] also Maj. Taylor— Serenade & speech which took well—promised to speak in behf. of Reynolds for chf. clk.

" 20, TUES. Coleman called & spoke abt. Clark & his Office— also Col. Cobb, who desired to be appointed to place vacated by death of Jenner[81]—who was killed— Went to Fessenden & urged him to have new regulations put in force in Clark's division—at once—Harrington sent for—said Dummer the clk. expected immediately[82]—& then new arrangement—knew nothing of Jenner's employment.— Saw Stanton at Fessenden's—called at his Dept. to his house—good-bye—talked with McCulloch who promised to see President & to breakfast with me to-morrow morning— Recd. telegram from Gov. S. that Katie & Nettie will join me at Eutaw House[83] Wednesday evening or Thursday morng— telegraphed Jay Cooke to stop them in Phila.— While at Treasury Department heard shouting of Clerks—enquired cause & was told Sheridan had captured Early & 2500 of his men—called at Mrs Goldsborough's[84]—heard Mrs. G—— read beautiful letter from Mr. Wirt, while 100 guns were being fired in honor of Sheridan's victory— Dined with Fessenden & bid him good bye.[85]

SEPT. 21. Left Washington for Cincinnati intending to speak there ☞ Vol 1, p. 181

---

80. Joseph Carter Brand (d. 1897) of Champaign County, Ohio, formerly of the state's 66th Volunteer Infantry, had previously served as Ohio state representative and state senator. His son was probably Joseph Brand, Jr. L. D. Reynolds, a Treasury clerk from Ohio, earlier had courted Chase's favor. Gilkey, *Ohio Hundred Year Book*, 245; Heitman, *Historical Register*, 1:240; *Register of Officers (1863)*, 34; *Wash. Dir. (1864)*, 235; Chase to L. D. Reynolds, Sept. 19, 1863 (Chase Papers, Hist. Soc. of Pa.).

81. Amasa Cobb (1823–1905), previously with the 5th Wisconsin volunteers, had temporarily retired from service as a Republican congressman, 1863–71. Jenner was probably William H. Jenner, former chief clerk of the National Currency Bureau. *Bio. Dir. U.S. Cong.*, 797; *Nat. Cyc.*, 6:191; *Wash. Dir. (1864)*, 183.

82. Charles Dummer, appointed from Maine, began employment in Nov. 1864 as a first class clerk in the Treasury Department. *Letter from the Secretary . . . Clerks . . . 1863*, 3.

83. A Baltimore hotel opened in 1835 and managed by Robert B. Coleman during the Civil War period. Scharf, *History of Baltimore*, 516.

84. Elizabeth Gamble Wirt Goldsborough.

85. This is the last entry made by the amanuensis. The latter part of the entry, beginning with *While at Treasury Department*, is entirely in Chase's hand. After this entry Chase drew a pointing hand indicating a page number some seven pages farther along in the original journal. On that page entries resume in Chase's hand, beginning with Sept. 21, and the clerk's handwriting does not appear again. The intervening pages contain Chase's description of Gen. Putnam's birthplace (see Aug. 23, 1864, above) and entries from fall 1863 and Nov. 1864.

SEP. 24, SAT   Spoke at Mass Meeting in Market Space[86]—most cordially received—rode down to Burnet House on engine with Flat Iron boys.

SEP. 28—WED   By rail to Aurora—spoke in Market ground—attentive audience

SEP. 29. THURS   Back to Cincinnati—late—but LHommedieu[87] sent special car to Hamilton. found Stanton there—both spoke.

OCT. 1. SAT.   To New Albany by way of St Louis—great crowd—heavy rain—Gov. Lane spoke admirably[88]—I, also, but not admirably.

OCT. 3. MON   Spoke at Louisville at City Hall—a large & attentive audience—spoke very plainly.[89] Many callers Judge Henry Pirtle, Gen Schofield, James Speed G. D. Prentice & others[90]

OCT 6. THURS   Went to Chillicothe & spoke there though quite unwell

OCT. 7. FRI   Spoke at Jackson to large audience—Col. Thomas of Phila there[91]—Bundy & others[92]—all went off well—felt nearly well.

---

86. Chase, addressing a large gathering of Union adherents, spoke in support of the Lincoln administration's conduct of the war. *Chicago Tribune,* Sept. 28, 30, 1864.

87. Stephen S. L'Hommedieu.

88. James Henry Lane.

89. According to one hostile newspaper, the room was not full, people "were continually passing in and out," and Chase's speech was met with "no enthusiasm at all" due to "a general and deep antipathy to the bad cause he defends." *Louisville Daily Journal,* Oct. 4, 1864.

90. John McAllister Schofield (1831–1906), brigadier general of volunteers, at this time commanded the 23rd Corps and the Department and Army of the Ohio. Early in 1865 he was promoted to major general in the regular army and given command of the Department of North Carolina. Kentucky Unionist, later Republican, lawyer James Speed (1812–87) became attorney general of the U.S. in Dec. *1864,* serving until July 1866. George Dennison Prentice (1802–70) was editor of the *Louisville Daily Journal. DAB,* 15:186–87, 16:452–54, 17:440–41.

91. William B. Thomas was U.S. collector of customs at Philadelphia and an officer in Pennsylvania's 192nd Vol. Inf. Regt. *Register of Officers (1865),* 109; Frank Hamilton Taylor, *Philadelphia in the Civil War, 1861–1865* (Philadelphia, 1913), 219, 247, 277.

92. Hezekiah Sanford Bundy (1817–95), former Ohio state legislator and future Republican member of the U.S. House, 1865–67, 1873–75, 1893–95. *Bio. Dir. U.S. Cong.,* 700–701.

OCT 8. SAT   Spoke at MacArthur & returned same eveng to Chillicothe

OCT. 9. SUN.   To Church with Dr. & Mrs. Trimble, whose guest I was & who were very kind.

OCT. 10 M.   Returned to Cincinnati— Many callers John K Green, H Kessl[er], Judge Hoadly &c &c &c[93]

OCT. 11 T.   Election—voted for Republican State Ticket

OCT. 13. WED—   Spoke in Covington Ky—reminded audience of my speech there in 1860

OCT. 14, 15, 16   Th. to Sun. inclusive remained in Cincinnati

OCT. 17. MON.—   To Toledo to attend Sister Helen's silver wedding—very pleasant & all quite happy. Atempts to force me out but I stuck to car.

OCT. 18 TUES.   Returned to Cin.

OCT. 19 & 20 WED & THURS   In Cincinnati

OCT 21. FRI.   Cars to Lexington—crowded—day before cars stopped & robbed by guerrillas[94]—Monty. Blair, on them bu[t] escaping.

OCT. 22 SAT.   Spoke in Lexington—Wade spoke also at same meeting[95]

OCT. 23, SUN.   Went to Dr. Breckinridge's near Lexington[96]— (not quite sure of these exact dates)

   93. Green was a partner in the Cincinnati lumber yard of Thomas W. Farrin and Company. At the time, Cincinnati had two residents named Henry Kessler. One operated a tanyard, the other was president of the Eagle Insurance Company. One or both of them later served in the Ohio General Assembly. *Cinc. Dir. (1864),* 131, 166; ibid. (1865), 233; Gilkey, *Ohio Hundred Year Book,* 173, 176, 221, 277.
   94. According to one report, the capture had actually taken place on Oct. 18. *Chicago Tribune,* Oct. 20, 1864.
   95. Benjamin Franklin Wade, of Ohio. *Chicago Tribune,* Oct. 19, 1864.
   96. Lawyer, Presbyterian clergyman, and educator Robert Jefferson Breckinridge (1800–1871) vigorously supported Lincoln in Kentucky. Chase found Breckinridge "as full of hope & zeal as the best." *DAB,* 3:10–11; Andre Van Vranken Raymond, *Union University: Its History . . .* (New York, 1907), 3:37 (Appendix); Chase to Hugh McCulloch, Oct. 25, 1864 (McCulloch Papers, L.C.).

OCT 24 MON.   Returned to Cincinnati & left next night for Phila.

OCT. 26 WED.   Reached Phila & cordially recd.—next night (27th) addressed great meetings—Gen Cameron with me at one—Mr. J. H. Orne very cordial[97]

OCT. 28 FRI   Went with McVeigh to West Chester[98] & spoke to a very much interested audience—left immediately afterward in carriage with McVeigh & another gentleman to intercept cars on Central Railroad for Pittsburgh.

OCT. 29. SAT.   Took cars a little after midnight & reached Cleveland by way of Pittsburgh in the eveng.

OCT. 30 SUN.   Attended Church at Cleveland with my friends the Parsons[99] who exceedingly anxious that I may be Chief Justice

OCT. 31 MON.   Spoke at Cleveland,[1] & took boat at once for Detroit.

NOV. 1 TU.   Spoke at Detroit—Lyman Tremain there & spoke also.[2]

NOV. 2. WED.   Spoke at Holly—with Wm A Howard[3]

---

97. Chase spoke in support of Lincoln's reelection to "two enormous audiences" in the Union League and National Halls. Carpet dealer James H. Orne, chairman of Philadelphia's Union Committee, had invited Chase to speak. Philadelphia *North American and United States Gazette,* Oct. 28, 1864; Orne to Chase, Oct. 14, 1864 (Chase Papers, L.C.); *Phila. Dir. (1864),* 567, 842.

98. Pennsylvania politician and statesman Isaac Wayne MacVeagh (1833–1917), district attorney for Chester County, 1859–64; chairman of the Republican State Committee, 1863; major of cavalry in the Pennsylvania militia; later U.S. minister to Turkey, ambassador to Italy, and U.S. attorney general. *DAB,* 12:170–71.

99. Richard C. Parsons and his wife, Sarah Starkweather Parsons, had two children, Julia and Richard C., Jr. Chase to Richard C. Parsons, Sept. 17, 1866 (Chase Papers, Hist. Soc. of Pa.); *Nat. Cyc.,* 6:251.

1. Chase spoke in support of Lincoln's reelection and claimed that Democratic presidential candidate George McClellan, if elected, would tolerate the continued existence of slavery. *Cleveland Plain Dealer,* Nov. 1, 1864.

2. For a hostile account, see *Detroit Free Press,* Nov. 2, 1864. New York state Republican politician Lyman Tremain (1819–78) later served a term in Congress, 1873–75. *Bio. Dir. U.S. Cong.,* 1953.

3. William Alanson Howard (1813–80), Republican congressman from Michigan, 1855–61; postmaster of Detroit, 1861–66; land commissioner for railroad corporations, 1869–78; governor of Dakota Territory, 1878–80. *Bio. Dir. U.S. Cong.,* 1218–19; *DAB,* 9:282–83.

Nov 3 Thurs. Spoke at Adrian[4]—Directors car—collision when returning to Detroit (this yesterday)[5]

Nov. 4. Fri. Spoke at Chicago[6]—Gen. Farnsworth there & spoke also[7]—both most kindly recd. took cars immediately after closing for St Louis.

Nov. 5. Sat. Spoke at St Louis[8]—to a great, & attentive and enthusiastic audience—unfortunate division here between the friends of the regular union nominee & Mr. Knox[9]—

Nov. 6—Sun. To Church with Mr. Blow in morng[10]—met Gratz Brown & others[11]—after Church to Carondelet with Blow to dinner.

Nov. 7. Mon. Cars early for Cin.—met on return persons who had just been captured by the rebels on the [Train]—reached Cincinnati in eveng

Nov. 8 Tues. Presl. election—voted for Lincoln & Johnson.

Nov. 9, 10, 11, Wed—Thurs & Friday— At Burnet House & Carsons.[12]

4. "Hon. S. P. Chase addressed the people for one hour in a speech of great fervor and eloquence, which is commended for its support of the Administration and a vigorous prosecution of the war for freedom." *Chicago Tribune*, Nov. 4, 1864.
5. Chase was riding in the director's coach of the Detroit and Milwaukee Railroad on the night of Nov. 2 when an axle broke on one of the train's cars. No serious injuries resulted. Chase gave his speech at Adrian on Nov. 3. *Detroit Free Press*, Nov. 4, 1864.
6. Chase's speech in support of the Union presidential ticket received full coverage in the *Chicago Tribune*, Nov. 5, 1864.
7. John Franklin Farnsworth (1820–97), Republican congressman from Illinois, 1857–61, 1863–73; officer of volunteers, 1861–62. *DAB*, 6:284–85.
8. Chase's speech lasted "for about an hour and a half. His arguments were the same that have been promulgated by all the Republican speakers and papers during the present campaign," claimed one report. *Missouri Republican*, Nov. 6, 1867.
9. In the election for the first congressional district, St. Louis' Republican and Union voters split their support between Charles J. Johnson and one-term Unconditional Unionist incumbent Samuel Knox (1815–1905). The split enabled John Hogan (1805–92), the "Irish-Secession-McClellan candidate," to win the election. *Chicago Tribune*, Nov. 9, 1864; *Bio. Dir. U.S. Cong.*, 1324–25; *DAB*, 9:119–20.
10. St. Louis merchant Henry Taylor Blow (1817–75), U.S. minister to Venezuela, 1861–62; Unconditional Unionist and Republican congressman from Missouri, 1863–67; U.S. minister to Brazil, 1869–71. *DAB*, 2:391–92.
11. Missouri politician Benjamin Gratz Brown (1826–85), former colonel of Missouri volunteers; U.S. senator (Unconditional Unionist), 1863–67; Liberal governor of Missouri, 1871–73, and vice-presidential running partner with Horace Greeley on the Liberal Republican ticket of 1872. *DAB*, 3:105–7.
12. Enoch T. Carson.

1864 Nov. 26. SAT Took Ball's carriage & went to town— Stopped at Carsons got letters—among them a telegram from McCulloch to come to Washington—he wants me to make some explanations or assurances in order to secure appointment of Chief Justice, I suppose— Ansd. Can't come[13]— Wrote Fessenden

Nov. 27, SUN At Mr. Hosea's—wrote several letters—one to Fessenden in addition to yesterday / At Church heard Mr. Mayo[14]— good on selfishness & benevolence—evil & good—met Miss Walker Mr. Kebler & other friends—Mr. Mayo back to Hosea's with us— young Ca[r]t Hosea came home[15]

Nov. 28— To town with Hosea—old rooms ready at Carson's— called on S. W & gave her port monnaie instead of one lost[16]—bot Chess man for Sister Kate Whiteman[17] Mr. Mo[rs]e gave me Blannerhassett Papers[18]

1865

JOURNAL XV

SUNDAY, JANUARY 1. My dear sister Helen—all that was mortal of her—is entombed today at Toledo—I cannot be there except by my sorrow.— Ralston came to my room before church & resumed the story wh. he begun last night—went to Methodist Ch. & heard Dr. Nadal—an excellent sermon on redeeming the time—on return after dinner R—— resumed & finished his story a very strange one—his delusions began nearly twelve years ago in '53—supposed himself implicated in Geo. Ludlows death[19]—then married—

---

13. Chase refused to go "lest I might be thought willing personally to solicit the President for the appointment of Chief Justice. I cannot do this, nor am I willing to have it supposed that I can." Chase to Hugh McCulloch, Nov. 27, 1864 (McCulloch Papers, L.C.).

14. Amory Dwight Mayo (1823–1907) presided over Cincinnati's Universalist Church of the Redeemer. *Cinc. Dir. (1865)*, 284; *DAB*, 12:461–62.

15. Although Chase did not clearly write *Capt.* Hosea, he evidently saw Robert Hosea's son, Lewis Montgomery Hosea (b. 1842), at this time captain of the 16th U.S. Inf., who later became a Cincinnati lawyer and judge. June 17, 1865, below; Greve, *Centennial History*, 2:645–49; Heitman, *Historical Register*, 1:543; *OR*, ser. 1, v. 49, pt. 2:444, 565.

16. *S. W* was Susan Walker. *Porte-monnaie* means "purse."

17. Catherine Ludlow Baker Whiteman.

18. William Harrison Safford, *The Blennerhassett Papers, Embodying the Private Journal of Harman Blennerhassett, and the Hitherto Unpublished Correspondence of Burr . . . and others . . .* (Cincinnati, 1861).

19. In Aug. 1853, James Ralston Skinner hurried from Cincinnati to the Buffalo, N.Y., deathbed of George Ludlow, who was evidently a member of Adela Ludlow's family. Other details about the incident are lacking. Skinner had become acquainted

business—failure—clerkship at Washn.—service as Judge Advocate in army visit to Cincinnati—delusion concerning his wife and her relatives[20]—sojourn with Dun. Ludlow—visit to Belle & Jennie[21]— residence in Insane Asylum—visit to Georgetown—delusion about Charley C—— &c promised to attend to army matter for him— advised him to go to Duns—promd. to get leave of absence for Ed to go with him[22]—sent Mrs Myer $25—

MONDAY, JANUARY 2. On account of sisters death did not receive today—nor go to Presidents with Judges—wrote him brief note of best wishes[23]— Katie & Nettie with Ida Nichols went to Philadelphia— Mr. McCullough, R. W. Tayler, Mr. Huntington & Mr. Wilson insisted on seeing me & I received them[24]—they very kind & interview pleasant—read on various subjects not very profitably— Ralston called with his brother Edward—has resolved to go to Ludlow's at Pera—promised to see to his business & wrote him—poor fellow, how much to be pitied—conscious of delusion yet unable to *assure* himself of it— Evg. read Circassion case till near 12[25]—then prayer & bed & Testament as usual[26]

TUESDAY, JANUARY 3. Much thought of God & Providence on waking / to Court at 10½—many admitted to bar—must reform

---

with members of the Ludlow family when he assisted Chase with business affairs in Cincinnati. Chase to Skinner, Feb. 27, 1850 (Chase Papers, L.C.); Chase to Kate Chase, Aug. 4, 1853 (Chase Papers, Hist. Soc. of Pa.).

20. Eunice Louisa Wiggins Skinner. Her husband believed that she had acquiesced in a scheme to keep him away from Cincinnati. James Ralston Skinner to Chase, Oct. 4, 1852, and warranty deed, Feb. 24, 1858 (Chase Papers, L.C.); Chase to Louisa Skinner, Jan. 10, 1865 (Chase Papers, Hist. Soc. of Pa.).

21. James Dunlop Ludlow, Isabel Skinner Walbridge, and Janette Skinner Jewett.

22. "Ed" was Edward R. Skinner. James Ralston Skinner, who had undergone treatment at the Pennsylvania Hospital for the Insane, had left the house of a friend with whom he was staying because of a fear that he might be held responsible for the illness of the friend's son (possibly the "delusion about Charley C——"). Chase promised to obtain certification of Skinner's disability so that he could resign from the army, and advised Skinner to visit James Dunlop Ludlow in Illinois to recuperate. Chase to Louisa Skinner, Jan. 10, 1865, Chase to Thomas S. Kirkbride, same date (Chase Papers, Hist. Soc. of Pa.); *DAB*, 10:429–30.

23. The president replied with condolences. Lincoln to Chase, Jan. 2, 1865 (Lincoln Collec., John Hay Lib., Brown Univ.).

24. Possibly M. S. McCullough, Treasury clerk; Robert W. Tayler; William S. Huntington (d. 1872), cashier of the First National Bank of Washington; and John Wilson. *Wash. Dir. (1865)*, 234, 271; *Daily National Intelligencer*, Jan. 3, 1865; entry for Apr. 17, 1872, below.

25. *The Circassian*, a blockade case argued Dec. 19–20, 1864. Chase delivered the opinion, his first as chief justice, on Jan. 30, 1865. 2 Wall. 135 (1865); Minutes of the Supreme Court (Recs. of Supreme Court, Nat. Arch.); Chase to Edwin M. Stanton, Jan. 28, [1865] (Stanton Papers, L.C.).

26. Very likely a French version of the New Testament (see Jan. 15 and Apr. 2, 1865, below).

January 1865 {513}

application & admission—took up Court of Claims Case[27]—qun. is Court one from whence cases appeal can be constitutionally provided for? New York Bank Cases tomorrow[28]—walked home with Judge Field[29] & then with him to Willards whence I went to War Dept— Found President there— Spoke to Stanton abt. Skinner— said he had told Dana[30] to see me & do what I thought best— Abt. Este—said there was no vacancy—abt. Israel—said exn. had been made & what I wanted cd. not be done.[31] Prest. & Stanton spoke of Butler—disagreement b. B. & Porter—rebels did not even know of explosion—told my experiment of drying up pond— Prest. thought it good illustration— He & S—— both wished that assault had been made though neither disposed to censure[32]—all three to White House—left P there—then to Stantons—left him— then home

WEDNESDAY, JANUARY 4. As usual today— Argt. of Bank cases begun—question involved is a Statute of New York making monied corporations liable to taxation on amount equal to their capital constitutional?, if capital is invested in bonds of U. States? Argued today by Mr. Bradford & Mr. Lord, Mr. Brady & Mr. Develin[33]

27. *Gordon v. United States*, 2 Wall. 561 (1865).
28. *Bank Tax Case*, 2 Wall. 200 (1865), a group of twenty-five cases involving New York banks.
29. Stephen Johnson Field (1816–99), U.S. Supreme Court justice, 1863–97. *DAB*, 6:372–76.
30. Charles Anderson Dana.
31. Dartmouth alumnus and former Toledo lawyer George Peabody Este (1829–81), an officer serving in the Army of the Cumberland, had asked Chase for help in securing promotion. He became brigadier general of volunteers in June 1865. Israel Ludlow (1840–73), a captain in the 5th Regular U.S. Artillery, was the brother of Chase's third wife, Sarah Bella Dunlop Ludlow Chase. In Nov., Chase had asked Stanton to reassign or promote Ludlow, a former prisoner of war, following his release from Libby Prison. Heitman, *Historical Register*, 1:408, 646; Este to Chase, July 12, Nov. 10, 1864 (Chase Papers, L.C.); Johnson, *Twentieth Century Biographical Dictionary*, v. 4; Robson, *Biographical Encyclopædia*, 629; Chase to Stanton, Nov. 29, 1864 (Stanton Papers, L.C.); unpublished guide to Ludlow-Dunlop-Chambers Collec., Univ. of Wyoming.
32. On Dec. 23–25, 1864, Federal land forces under Benjamin F. Butler and naval forces under David D. Porter had attempted without success to take Fort Fisher, N.C. Detonation near the fort of a boat loaded with tons of explosives had no effect. U.S. troops were landed, then withdrawn without attempting an assault. When he was a boy, Chase had tried to evaporate a small pool of water by floating a burning raft on its surface, an experiment which, like Butler's exploding ship, was unsuccessful. E. B. Long, *The Civil War Day by Day: An Almanac, 1861–1865* (Garden City, N.Y., 1971), 614–15; Chase to John T. Trowbridge, Jan. 19, 1864 (Chase Papers, Hist. Soc. of Pa.).
33. Alexander Warfield Bradford (1815–67); Daniel Lord (1795–1868); James Topham Brady (1815–69); and John Edward Develin (1820–88). According to the Court's minutes, Benjamin Douglas Silliman (1805–1901), not Lord, joined Bradford in opening the banks' argument on Jan. 4; Lord argued in the banks' behalf on Jan.

THURSDAY, JANUARY 5. Nothing unusual morn'g— Ashley tells me he thinks Consl. Amendt. prohibiting slavery will be carried— several dems have determined to vote for it. Argt. in Bank causes resumed and concluded as to Bank of Commerce & Bank of Commonwealth—and begun for other banks, abt half of New York Banks being represented— Mr. Dana came to dinner—promised Skinner should be restored on certifs of disability—that Marcel shd. be promoted if possible[34]—spoke well of Ben & Israel Ludlow & told me Stanton had gone to Savannah— Our talk was very pleasant— After he had gone wrote Charlotte Jones, Mrs Bailey, R. Skinner & J. D. Ludlow.[35]

FRIDAY, JANUARY 6. This motion day at Court but no motions— Argt. in Bank Cases resumed & concluded— The cases have been exhaustively presented, but with too much repetition—adjd about two.

SATURDAY, JANUARY 7. A wet day—rain, sleet, snow but altogether a drizzle— At Consultation— Pilot case affd. I not having sat on it[36]— Consultation on Circassion case—captd. May 4 on voyage to run blockade to New Orleans, but N.O. then occupied by Butler—also on Mary Bangs case chartered for voyage Calcutta to Boston— Some talk of Tobey case & adjd.[37] Judge Field dined with me—we two alone— After dinner Hitchcock of Nebraska came in[38]— Field told interesting incidents of his life in Cala. difficulty with Judge at Marysville & might have been duel at Sacramento—Broderick his true & most useful friend[39]— Hitchcock,

---

5. *DAB*, 2:551–52, 583–84, 11:404–5; *New York Times*, Feb. 24, 1888; *Appletons'*, 5:529–30; *Catalogue of Officers and Graduates of Yale University*, 156; Minutes, Jan. 4–5, 1865 (Recs. of Supreme Court, Nat. Arch.).

34. Marcellus Bailey (b. 1840) was the son of Gamaliel and Margaret Bailey and an officer in a regiment of black soldiers. Heitman, *Historical Register*, 1:181–82; Harrold, *Gamaliel Bailey*, 42.

35. Charlotte Ludlow Jones, Margaret L. Bailey, James Ralston Skinner, and James Dunlop Ludlow.

36. *Pacific Mail Steamship Co. v. Joliffe*, 2 Wall. 450 (1865).

37. The steamer *Circassian* was captured by the U.S. Navy on May 4, 1862, three days after Gen. Benjamin F. Butler officially took control of New Orleans. *Lowber v. Bangs* was a contract dispute involving the ship *Mary Bangs*, and *Tobey v. Leonards* involved a land conveyance. 2 Wall. 135, 423, 728 (1865); Fairman, *Reconstruction and Reunion*, 34–35.

38. Republican politician, U.S. marshal, 1861–64, and territorial delegate to Congress, 1865–67, Phineas Warrener Hitchcock (1831–81). *DAB*, 9:78; *Bio. Dir. U.S. Cong.*, 1193.

39. Like Field, David Colbreth Broderick (1820–59) lived in New York before moving to San Francisco in 1849. Broderick, a Democratic politician, gained national

after Field left, told me Stanton recd. him coldly / Advised him to arrange with Daley & see President— Dr. & Mrs Lindsley called[40]—

SUNDAY, JANUARY 8. Went to church this morning—Dr. Nadal— *well*, as usual, on "Therefore we glory in tribulation"—read Testament— Barney came after church & staid till after dinner—then Ashley & staid till after supper— He means to take vote on Constl. Amendt. tomorrow—says Yeaman of Ky & Rollins & King of Mo will vote for it[41]—Yeaman will speak & so will King—expects to carry it— Judge Field came in & left Ashton's argt. & took his bill & Nelson's opinion[42]— Hassaurek & Judge Johnston,[43] H—— going to Gen Grant abt exchange of his brother Markbreit[44]— Mr. Bridge[45] & a young friend also called—letter fr. Jane Auld—"Jennie is released from suffg." wrote sympathy & enclosed $150.[46]

MONDAY, JANUARY 9. Nothing unusual today, went to President's in evg.—a large crowd there— Our party, Gov. & Mrs Sprague, Nettie, Ida Nichols, & myself— Katie & I followed Prest. intending to speak to him—unluckily went in advance of Mrs. Lincoln, who

---

attention in the late 1850s for his opposition to the party's proslavery element in California. *DAB*, 3:61–62.

40. Harvey and Emeline Colby Webster Lindsly.

41. Nadal's text was Rom. 5:3. Kentucky Unionist George Helm Yeaman (1829–1908), Missouri Unionist James Sidney Rollins (1812–88), and War Democrat Austin Augustus King (1802–70) favored submission of the Thirteenth Amendment to the states. *Bio. Dir. U.S. Cong.*, 2096; *DAB*, 10:382, 16:121–22.

42. Joseph Hubley Ashton (1836–1907) was assistant attorney general of the U.S. The reference is likely to his argument in the *Venice* case, 2 Wall. 258 (1865), which concerned definitions of neutral and enemy property. The opinion may have been that which Samuel Nelson (1792–1873), a member of the Supreme Court from 1845 to 1872, wrote for *Hathorn v. Calef*, 2 Wall. 10 (1865). Entry for Jan. 16, 1865, below; *Who Was Who*, 1:34; *DAB*, 13:422–23.

43. Judge William Johnston. Friedrich Hassaurek (1831–85), born in Vienna, Austria, was a Cincinnati journalist, attorney, and Republican activist serving at this time as U.S. minister to Ecuador. *DAB*, 8:383–84.

44. Leopold Markbreit (1842–1909), Hassaurek's half brother, was Rutherford B. Hayes's law partner just before the Civil War. An officer of the 28th Ohio Infantry, he was captured late in 1863 and remained in Confederate prisons until Feb. 5, 1865. After the war he was a diplomat and corporate director. *Nat. Cyc.*, 12:467–68; *Who Was Who*, 1:777.

45. Probably Horatio Bridge (1806–93), who served as chief of the Navy's bureau of provisions and clothing, 1853–69, and as chief inspector of the bureau, 1869–73. *Nat. Cyc.*, 4:358–59.

46. During the previous year, Chase had offered to help arrange medical care for Jennie Auld, the daughter of Chase's niece Jane Chase Auld. Jennie's ailment is unknown. Chase to Jane Auld, Jan. 2, June 22, 1864, Chase to Jennie Auld, Feb. 3, June 22, 1864 (Chase Papers, Hist. Soc. of Pa.).

swept by on our left—with Gov Morgan[47] / Aftwds met Prest. & paid respects—then Mrs L & apologized for apparent rudeness / She either misunderstood or chose to appear very ungracious—at home abt. half past eleven—having met many warm greetings

TUESDAY, JANUARY 10. Nothing unusual today—regular routine of business & a rain which prohibited going out much—

WEDNESDAY, JANUARY 11. Dined at Mr. Hoopers with very pleasant party—Seward told of Footes arrest & his going down to Alexa. to bring Mrs Foote up[48]—talked of Foote—said good understanding always between them—Foote wd. abuse him & he wd. subscribe for Footes speeches. I said I was less fortunate—I spoke myself & took what others said in earnest— Mr. Forbes who sat next me has a Mail steamship scheme between San Francisco & Japan on hand— Adl. Farragut at the dinner—a charming old salt & full of sense as of courage. Mr. Speed the new Atto Genl. a warm hearted, earnest anti slavery man[49]—the dinner on the whole very pleasant.

THURSDAY, JANUARY 12. Adjourned the Court early today for consultation—after consultation went to Presidents & took cane sent by Geo. C. Miller[50]—met Th. A. Scott there who spoke of his great petroleum adventure in California.[51]

FRIDAY, JANUARY 13. No court today—met for consultation at eleven & sat till 3—read at home very diligently as I do always now—seldom retiring till eleven or twelve. Parsons came—said he

47. Mary Todd Lincoln (1818–82), with Edwin D. Morgan. *DAB*, 11:265–66.
48. Chase evidently made this entry under the wrong day's heading, since events he related did not take place until Jan. 13. With the intention of negotiating terms to end the war, Confederate Congressman Henry Stuart Foote (1804–80) fled Richmond for Washington early in Jan. 1865. Confederate authorities arrested him en route and returned him to Richmond. Mrs. Foote (probably Rachel D. Smiley, Foote's second wife) was paroled and arrived in Alexandria on the morning of Jan. 13. Seward accompanied her to Washington later that day. Henry Foote had represented Mississippi in the U.S. Senate, 1847–52. *DAB*, 6:500–501; *OR*, ser. 1, v. 46, pt. 2:109–10, 123–24, 126, ser. 2, v. 8:68–69; Washington *Evening Star*, Jan. 13, 14, 1865; *Daily National Intelligencer*, Jan. 14, 1865.
49. James Speed.
50. George C. Miller (1789–1872), a manufacturer of carriages and farm implements in Cincinnati, sent Lincoln a cane of white oak pieces held together by an iron rod, symbolizing what Miller hoped would be a restored union. Basler, *Collected Works*, 8:222; Landy, *Cincinnati Past and Present*, 31–34.
51. Commercial oil production began in California during the 1860s but did not achieve significance until the 1880s. John Walton Caughey, *California*, 2nd ed. (New York, 1953), 418–21.

was going into Petroleum with Brown & that they proposed I should have an interest.[52] Kate had a dinner for Mr. Laugel, who brot letter from Count de Paris, his wife, & his wifes sister[53]—Mr. Sumner, Mr Hooper, Miss Motley, Mr. [& Mrs] Dana[54] & others—quite pleasant but Kate becoming suddenly indisposed was obliged to leave the room, & did not return until dinner was over & company had gone to parlor—this damped enjoyment.

SATURDAY, JANUARY 14. Kates dinner which I have put inadvertently on last page was given today.[55]

Court met for consn. at 1 P.M & remained until 3.30.

Judge Wayne walked from consultation room with me—I feared it might hurt him—it was so chilly & he had taken off the thick coverings from his chest.

Read nearly all afternoon & evg.

SUNDAY, JANUARY 15. At church morning & night—Nettie with me— Orphans—$30 for them $25 to help improve access & egress of church—recd. nobody today. read Espousals & Fr. Testament[56]—

MONDAY, JANUARY 16. At capitol at ½ past ten— Judges Swayne & Nelson read opinions— Clifford read sharp dissent from Swayne[57]— I of same general opinion as C but declined to dissent thinking that except in very important causes dissent inexpedient. Argt. in Patent Case comd.[58]—after adj. went to Treasy. Dept.—

52. Richard Chappel Parsons and Thomas Brown.
53. Antoine Auguste Laugel (1830–1914), a French mining engineer and writer who became acquainted with Charles Sumner in Paris in 1857; Louis Philippe Albert d'Orléans; and Elizabeth Bates Chapman Laugel and Anne Greene Chapman, daughters of Massachusetts abolitionist Maria Weston Chapman. In 1867 Anne Chapman married English journalist Edward Dicey. Vapereau, *Dictionnaire Universel,* 1094–95; Auguste Laugel, *The United States during the Civil War,* ed. by Allan Nevins (New York, 1969), x, xxiv–xxv; Pierce, *Memoir and Letters of Charles Sumner,* 3:532, 535, 540; James et al., *Notable American Women,* 1:324; Hilen, *Letters of Henry Wadsworth Longfellow,* 4:466–67; *New York Times,* July 8, 1911.
54. Elizabeth Cabot Motley (b. ca. 1840) was the eldest daughter of John Lothrop Motley and later the wife of the English politician Sir William Vernon Harcourt. Eunice MacDaniel Dana (c. 1824–1903) married Charles Anderson Dana in 1846. Susan St. John Mildmay and Herbert St. John Mildmay, eds., *John Lothrop Motley and His Family* (New York, 1910), 20, 28, 222–25; *DNB,* 2nd supp., 211; *New York Times,* July 2, 1903; *DAB,* 5:52.
55. Auguste Laugel's diary confirms that the dinner at the Spragues' was Jan. 14. *The Nation,* v. 75, no. 1936 (Aug. 7, 1902): 108.
56. French Testament.
57. Swayne: *Lowber v. Bangs;* Nelson: *Hathorn v. Calef.* Nathan Clifford (1803–81) joined the Supreme Court in 1858. Minutes, Jan. 16, 1865 (Recs. of Supreme Court, Nat. Arch.); *DAB,* 4:216–18.
58. *Case v. Brown,* 2 Wall. 320 (1865).

Spoke to Fessenden of Blow, highly; of Victor Smith, do.; of Stuart who removed without cause fr Balte. Collectorship[59]—and of others— F—— don't think well of Boutwell as Secy. of Ty.—I thought McCulloch or Gov. Andrew or Mr Hooper or Mr Sherman wd. make good officer—called on Judge Wayne found him better—home—comd. opinion in Circassion case.

TUESDAY, JANUARY 17. At breakfast found neither Sprague nor Katie & very uneasy—fearing illness or other trouble—went to Capital under this fear—there argt. in patent case concluded & also argt. in contract case[60]—cold air on head made me unwell— Johns[on][61] sent in from Senate Chamber despatch to Navy Dept announcing capture of Fort Fisher—heard that Butler at time news came was before Com on conduct of war demonstrating impossibility of it—am very sorry for Butler, who has great abilit[ies]—this morning Ben. Ludlow left us for home—promd. him what I have always given my best offices to make his brevet full rank— Ashley came down with me—he thinks passage of resolution prop[g]. amendt. prohibiting slavery pretty certain—& has good hopes concerning negro suffrage— I have been earnestly laboring for this & think it very important— Will God prosper us if we fail to enable these meritorious people to protect themselves by ballots? At home studied blockade case—

WEDNESDAY, JANUARY 18. Little of interest today—nothing [not] routine except my reception in the evg. wh. not very well known & attended by about fifty ladies & gentlemen—among them Mr. & Mrs Laugel—declined invitation to dine at Usher's.

THURSDAY, JANUARY 19. Today as yesterday—very busy with cases—

FRIDAY, JANUARY 20. At Court as usual—no event worth mentioning—how monotonous my life—I try to do a little good by writing nearly every day to somebody to stir him up to support of universal suffrage in reconstituted states so as to protect the blacks from wrongs & the country from future dangers.

59. Chase and Fessenden discussed Joseph J. Stewart and, apparently, Henry T. Blow.
60. *John T. Whitaker et al. v. Calvin D. Read.* Minutes, Jan. 17, 1865 (Recs. of Supreme Court, Nat. Arch.).
61. Vice President Andrew Johnson.

January 1865 {519}

SATURDAY, JANUARY 21. Consultation today—Judge Nelson stated fully his views in tax cases in which we all concurred: Miller wished reargument on point of constitutionality of taxing U.S. securities by States to same extent as other property wh. he inclined to favor—no one agreed with him.[62] I mentioned that I was informed that motion for admission [to bar] of colored lawyer of Massachusetts wd be made and asked advice[63]—no one inclining to speak I said I would take silence as indicating willingness to leave the matter to my discretion as Ch. Justice, intimating that I shd admit without hesitation—then one after another nearly all expressed the opinion that the rule must govern & that in it there was no disqualification on ground of color— One queried as to citizenship & I said I wd. direct the motion to be made for admission & [h]ave it argued: but this not being insisted on, we adjd. with the understanding that colored men qualified could be admd without regard to complexion—progress!

SUNDAY, JANUARY 22. To church this morning—very slippery— heard Dr. Nadal—at home read.

MONDAY, JANUARY 23. At court Nelson, Grier, & Miller read opinions—blockade case argued[64]—at home nothing unusual / in evg. a number of gentlemen called among them Mr. Evarts[65] & Judge Pierrepont & used up my time.

At home consulted Dr. Hall about ailments[66]—sharp rheumatism back & loins this morning & [urinal] non-retention—he gave blue pill & magnesia—seems intelligent & self reliant

---

62. Samuel Freeman Miller (1816–90) served on the Supreme Court from 1862 to 1890. *DAB,* 12:637–40.
63. John Swett Rock (1825–66), who was also a dentist and physician, was the first black attorney admitted to the bar of the Supreme Court (see entry for Feb. 1, 1865, below). Charles Sumner sponsored Rock's admission. John A. Garraty, ed., *Encyclopedia of American Biography* (New York, 1974), 916–17; Sumner to Chase, Dec. 21, 1864 (Chase Papers, Hist. Soc. of Pa.), printed in Palmer, *Selected Letters of Charles Sumner,* 2:259–60; Chase to Sumner, Dec. 21, 1864, Sumner to Chase, Jan. 5, [1865], with reply on same sheet (Houghton Lib., Harvard Univ.).
64. The blockade case was *The Andromeda,* 2 Wall. 481 (1865). Nelson's opinions: *Drury v. Foster,* 2 Wall. 24 (1865); *Gregg v. Forsyth,* 2 Wall. 56 (1865). Grier's: *Florentine v. Barton,* 2 Wall. 210 (1865). Miller's: *Marine Bank v. Fulton Co. Bank* (and three related cases), 2 Wall. 252 (1865); *Merriam v. Haas,* 3 Wall. 687 (1865). Minutes, Jan. 23, 1865 (Recs. of Supreme Court, Nat. Arch.).
65. New York attorney William Maxwell Evarts (1818–1901), who became U.S. attorney general, 1868–69; secretary of state, 1877–81; U.S. senator, 1885–91. *DAB,* 6:215–18.
66. Probably James C. Hall, physician. *Wash. Dir. (1865),* 216, 431.

TUESDAY, JANUARY 24. Nothing of much interest, at court as usual—heard argt.—leaving court attention was called to Smithsonian which seemed on fire—went to it with Judge Miller & found centre building in flames—no water or very little & no adequate provision for extinction—could have been put out in ten minutes at Cincinnati[67]—came home very much vexed & [peeved]—rheumatism & cold which attacked me yesterday increased by my exposure—wrapped myself in blanket & lay down—& had my back rubbed—& repeated it at night when went to bed— C—— very kind but must not allow myself to avail of it—

TUESDAY, JANUARY 31. Court adjourned earlier than usual today in consequence of illness of Counsel— went to the House, debating the Constl. Amendt. & about to take final vote—great excitement—rumors of arrival of peace commissioners & loss in consequence of expected democratic votes—vote not taken at 3 as understood & I left for Baltimore with Sprague & LHommedieu[68]— recd. at depot by Albert, Bond & Hoffman[69]—went to Alberts—dinner—then to Maryland Institute—Beecher already speaking—when he closed I was persistently called & at length said a few words—wh well received[70]— Supper at Albert's & quite a party—Mrs Turnbull, Mr Sterling,[71] Mr. Hoffman & many more—spoke to a group around room of the duty & necessity of giving the blacks the right of suffrage & glad to find what I said approved—what a change.

WEDNESDAY, FEBRUARY 1. Rose early—Sprague, I & L'Hommedieu to cars in Alberts carriage—Mr. Stanton & Mr. Beecher there—pleasant ride to Balte.—Stanton related to me interview be-

---

67. Flames became visible at the Smithsonian building about 2:45 P.M. Fire fighting efforts restricted damage to the central and upper portions of the structure. Washington *Evening Star*, Jan. 24, 25, 1865.
68. Probably Stephen S. L'Hommedieu.
69. Baltimore corporation director, banker, and prominent Unionist William Julian Albert (1816–79); Hugh Lennox Bond; and Henry W. Hoffman (1825–95), attorney, politician, and collector of customs at Baltimore, 1861–c. 1865. *Who Was Who*, H:17; *Bio. Dir. U.S. Cong.*, 1198; *Register of Officers (1863)*, 86.
70. Henry Ward Beecher spoke for the benefit of the Baltimore Association for the Moral and Educational Improvement of the Colored People. His address touched upon emancipation, slavery, education, and the anticipated end of the war. Chase, in his impromtu remarks, expressed his pleasure to learn that earlier in the day Congress had passed a constitutional amendment abolishing slavery. He also commended the future prospects of Maryland. *Baltimore Sun*, Jan. 31, Feb. 1, 1865.
71. Mrs. Alexander Turnbull, president of the Women's Maryland Branch of the U.S. Sanitary Commission, and Baltimore attorney and Unionist politician Archibald Stirling, Jr. (d. 1892). *Baltimore American*, Mar. 31, 1865; Scharf, *History of Baltimore*, 718–19; *General Catalogue of Princeton University, 1746–1906* (Princeton, 1908), 182.

tween Sherman & himself and the Cold. delegation at Savannah—said spokesman, old man truly eloquent gave most correct exposition of the causes of the war[72]— Went to capitol—told that Sumner was in the Court Room with cold. lawyer whose admission he was about to move. when Judges seated Sumner made the motion—& introduced Mr. Rock[73]—I recognized the introduction as usual & said "the clerk will administer the oath to Mr. Rock." He then introduced Mr. Balch whom I took to be another cold. man. I recognized him also & said "Mr. Balch will proceed to the clerk's desk & be qualified"—I purposely avoided the slightest deviation from my usual formula in admitting whites—Mr. Balch was as I learned, a white man[74]

SUNDAY, FEBRUARY 19. Mistake in time & missed church—obliged to prepare opinions in motions decided yesterday to be read tomorrow morning[75]—

Just before tea Senator Saulsbury came in about some matter wh. he wished to be considered confidential.

MONDAY, FEBRUARY 20. Copied opinions prepared yesterday & read them in Court— Argument in Sutter case continued—home & worked on Venice case[76]— Mr. Breckinridge of Texas & Maj. Taylor called[77]—Mr. B says Gen Hamilton, Judge Duvall, & Gen Davis & other loyalists of Texas favor universal suffrage as measure of safety[78] / advised him to see Collamer & others—walked with

72. Stanton visited Savannah in Jan. 1865. At his request, Gen. Sherman invited a group of blacks, most of them clergymen, to give their views of emancipation and other topics. The group's spokesman was named Garrison Frazier. William Tecumseh Sherman, *Memoirs of General W. T. Sherman* (New York, 1990), 722–27.

73. John Rock. See Jan. 21 above.

74. Massachusetts attorney Francis Vergnies Balch (1839–98), formerly Charles Sumner's secretary, managed Sumner's legal affairs. Palmer, *Selected Letters of Sumner*, 2:357–58, 387; Pierce, *Memoir and Letters of Charles Sumner*, 4:342; *Quinquennial Catalogue*, 223.

75. *Ex parte Milwaukee & Minnesota R.R. Co.* and *Milwaukee & Minnesota R.R. Co. v. Soutter*, cases arising from a mortgage foreclosure. 2 Wall. 440, 443 (1865); Minutes, Feb. 20, 1865 (Recs. of Supreme Court, Nat. Arch.).

76. *United States v. Sutter*, a case involving California land grants, and *The Venice*, concerning the seizure of a ship and cargo. The *Venice* case was argued in December 1864. Chase delivered the Court's opinion on Feb. 27, 1865. 2 Wall. 258, 562 (1865); Minutes, Dec. 29–30, 1864, Feb. 20, 27, 1865 (Recs. of Supreme Court, Nat. Arch.).

77. Very likely George W. Brackenridge, a Texas Unionist whom Chase had appointed an assistant special agent in the lower Mississippi Valley in 1863; and Maj. David Taylor. James Marten, *Texas Divided: Loyalty and Dissent in the Lone Star State, 1856–1874* (Lexington, Ky., 1990), 93, 128, 175; Chase to Brackenridge, Oct. 29, 1863 (3rd Special Agency, Recs. of Civil War Special Agencies, Nat. Arch.).

78. Andrew Jackson Hamilton; Thomas H. Duval (1813–80), judge of the U.S. court for the western district of Texas, 1857–80; and Edmund Jackson Davis

Sprague to Seaton Square—letter fr. Parsons about Iron Co. Stock[79]—worked all time I could command on Venice case—wrote Miss Walker—can I have rooms at Parsons—Kent Jarvis thanking him for congratulations[80]—

WEDNESDAY, MARCH 15. Worked today without accomplishing much—desultory work— Nettie came in, greatly distressed by trouble with her sister—talked with her quietly & affectionately—hoped good from it—she is a dear but thoughtless child & as sensitive as she is thoughtless

FRIDAY, MARCH 17. Gov. Sprague & Miss Sprague[81] left for R.I. this morning—cook left us suffering from bad cold & I fear dangerous / gave her $20 to make good her loss in coming[82]— Mr. Simmons the Sculptor nearly finished cast for Medallion[83]—Katie & Nettie think it good—wrote Miss Walker—Wm Price Balte.—come & dine Monday at 5 & bring Judge Giles if agreeable to him[84]

SATURDAY, APRIL 1. Prepared for going to Baltimore in the morning & went at 4.30 P.M: found rooms ready at Eutaw House & was made very comfortable—no one calling, read till bedtime

JOURNAL XVI

1865 APRIL 1ST. Went to Baltimore hoping to meet some members of the bar and get a little acquainted with them before opening

---

(1827–83), lawyer, judge, and Republican governor of Texas, 1869–73, who had raised a cavalry regiment for the Union. James D. Lynch, *The Bench and Bar of Texas* (St. Louis, 1885), 160–64; *DAB*, 5:112–13; Heitman, *Historical Register*, 1:357; Marten, *Texas Divided*, 128–31.

79. William W. Seaton kept a garden on a square bounded by Fifth, Sixth, L, and M Streets, N.W. On advice from Richard C. Parsons, Chase invested in the Cleveland Iron Mining Co., which extracted iron ore from the Upper Penninsula of Michigan. Henry E. Davis, "The Seaton Mansion," *Records of the Columbia Hist. Soc.* 29–30 (1928): 294; Chase to Parsons, Sept. 17, 1866 (Chase Papers, Hist. Soc. of Pa.); Van Tassel and Grabowski, *Encyclopedia of Cleveland*, 222–23.

80. Kent Jarvis of Massillon, Ohio, and Chase corresponded on personal and political matters. Chase to Jarvis, Feb. 24, 1863 (Chase Papers, Hist. Soc. of Pa.); Jarvis to Chase, May 28, Nov. 28, 1860, Feb. 20, 1863 (Chase Papers, L.C.).

81. Almira Sprague.

82. Addie Matthews was the cook. Cash accounts, Journal XV.

83. In 1865 and 1866, American sculptor Franklin Simmons (1839–1913) made portrait medallions of prominent people in Washington. His brass alloy medallion of Chase is in the collections of the Union League of Philadelphia (see also July 13, 1865, below). *DAB*, 17:169; Maxwell Whiteman, *Paintings and Sculpture at the Union League of Philadelphia* (Philadelphia, 1978), 116.

84. Most of this entry is in pencil. The latter portion, beginning *Wm Price*, is in ink. William Price was district attorney, and William Fell Giles (1807–79) district

April 1865   {523}

court, for first time as Presiding Justice. I had sent word of my coming to Mr. Price the District Attorney; but he went to Annapolis without informing the bar & so nobody knew of my coming & I saw nobody.

JOURNAL XV

SUNDAY, APRIL 2. At home all day—or rather, what is very different, in my room. Read Article on Sun; its influence as Motor & its sources of renovation—quite instructive & interesting—read also Nouv. Test. several chapters in John.[85] How absolute the purity which Christ requires! Thank God that pardon may be had through faith!

Mr. Hopkins called with Maj Gen Barlow[86]— The news of Lee's repulse intensely interesting— Gen. B—— anxious to go to the army of Potomac, & yet having to be sent to Shenandoah

JOURNAL XVI

1865 APL. 2. Remained in my room all day—read Testament and an article in the Companion to the British Almanac on the Subject of the Sun & its supply. The theory was that innumerable asteroids are continually revolving round the Sun in diminishing orbits until at length they fall into it & thus supply its fires. It was quite plausibly argued. Can it be so?

Towards evening Gen Barlow & Mr. Hopkins came in & passed a few minutes / Gen. B—— had recently returned from Europe & seemed entirely recovered of his wounds at Cold Harbor. He was under orders to join Hancock in the Shenandoah Valley,[87] but had appealed to the War Dept. to allow him to go to Grant, & expected an answer today.

JOURNAL XV

MONDAY, APRIL 3. Judge Giles & Mr. Price, Dis. Atto. called accompanied them to Court Room & took my seat as Presiding Judge   Judge Giles called the docket— Only a few lawyers

---

judge, of the U.S. district court at Baltimore. *Register of Officers (1863)*, 266; *Bio. Dir. U.S. Cong.*, 1060.

85. *Nouveau Testament*, the New Testament in French.

86. Johns Hopkins and Francis Channing Barlow, who was awaiting orders. On Apr. 6, Barlow took command of a division in Virginia. *OR*, ser. 1, v. 46, pt. 1:758–59, pt. 3:460.

87. Maj. Gen. Winfield Scott Hancock (1824–86). *DAB*, 8:221–22.

present—some I am told absent themselves because of the new oath[88]— Adjd. after very short sitting—not over an hour— News fr. Richmond—city taken this morng.

JOURNAL XVI

1865 APL. 3 Judge Giles and Mr. Price, the District Attorney called & accompanied me to the Court Room. Judge G—— had kindly prepared a note of what was proper to be said on opening the Court, and I gladly availed myself of it. There was nothing to be done except call the docket which was done & we adjourned. I walked with Judge G—— to his residence on Franklin Street where I was made acquainted with Mrs G—— and a young lady visiting them.[89] The Judge seems very intelligent and very considerate & kind: and Mrs G—— seems to be an agreeable, well informed lady. She used to know my uncle Bishop Chase very well. From Judge G——'s I went to Swanns, my old friend of lang syne, now Governor elect of the Free State of Maryland / I found no one at home but his daughter Jenny—Virginia I suppose—a sweet girl of 17 or 18 perhaps.[90] After a few minutes of pleasant talk with her I returned to my hotel. In the afternoon [& eveng] quite a number of gentlemen called. The news of Grants victories & capture of Richmond came.

APL. 4. TU— Called docket to see what cases were ready— marked some for trial—Gen. Este called & we went over to Washington together;[91] &, with my daughters, drove through the city to see the illumination in honor of Grants victories—it was superb.[92]

---

88. On Jan. 24, 1865, Congress passed an act which required any attorney practicing at the bar of a federal court to take an oath certifying, in effect, that he had never served under the Confederacy or given aid or encouragement to rebels. Chase supported this controversial measure, which had been promoted by Charles Sumner, although in Jan. 1867 the majority of his colleagues on the Supreme Court, ruling in *Ex parte Garland,* deemed the oath unconstitutional on the grounds that it was an ex post facto punishment. Fairman, *Reconstruction and Reunion,* 58–59, 136–37, 240–48.

89. William Fell Giles married twice: first, in 1831, Sarah Wilson of Baltimore; second, date unknown, Catharine Donaldson. *Biographical Encyclopedia . . . of Maryland,* 670–71.

90. Evidence has been found of two daughters of Thomas Swann, Jr.: Louise Swann Latrobe and Jane Byrd Swann, the future wife of Thomas Barker Ferguson. *DAB,* 6:333.

91. Probably William Miller Este, who had been stationed at Baltimore in Jan. 1865 and appointed judge advocate. He never attained a rank, however, higher than major. *OR,* ser. 1, v. 46, pt. 2:51; Landy, *Cincinnati Past and Present,* 25; Heitman, *Historical Register,* 1:408.

92. Lighting schemes accented decorations on many buildings as part of the demonstration in honor of the capture of Richmond. The jubilee also included fireworks, music, and speeches. Washington *Evening Star,* Apr. 5, 1865.

APL. 5. WED. Returned to Baltimore leaving Este behind—called the trial docket in Court—found no case ready.

JOURNAL XV

TUESDAY, APRIL 4.[93] No business at the court—afternoon dined with Dr. Fuller— The Doctor occupies a very handsome residence; very handsomely though not extravagantly furnished on Park St just north of Franklin St, No 97 / The only persons at the table were Mr. Swann Gov. Elect, Mr. Kennedy author of Swallow Barn & Life of Wirt, formerly Secy of Navy, Dr. Buckler & myself[94]— Mrs Fuller[95] & Miss Hill & a little [boy] / conversation pleasant— asked Kennedy who sat for Swallow Barn characters. He said no body particularly; though several professed to recognize themselves or acquaintances— After dinner talk on Slavery— I expressed myself in favor of reconstruction by universal suffrage— Dr. F—— agr[ee]d— He said I rejoice with my whole heart in emancipation. I had 200 slaves— They were a great burden on my conscience—I did not want to die leaving them slaves—now I am free—friend say I have lost $200,000—I say I have 200000 pounds of iron taken off my soul—I am happy. I am more enfranchised than my slaves.

APL. 7, 65 *Mema. Thoughts*[96]— May not the enfranchisement of America lead to the regeneration of Africa?

Is not the deposit of 56. Mill. chiefly in National Banks a source of serious danger?

JOURNAL XVI

APL. 7 FRI— Dined at Dr. Fuller's— The guests were Ex Secretary Kennedy, Gov. Elect Swann, Dr. Buckler, a practising physician; & no ladies except Mrs Fuller and a neice of the Doctor. The dinner was good—no wine—& the talk pleasant. After dinner, in the parlor, only Messrs Swann, Kennedy, Dr. Fuller & myself being

---

93. Chase wrote this entry on a page with a printed heading for Apr. 4, but the entry actually describes Apr. 7.

94. John Pendleton Kennedy and Baltimore physician Thomas Hepburn Buckler (1812–1901). In 1861 Buckler had married a daughter of Richard Fuller. His wife died within a year of their marriage. *DAB*, 3:230–31.

95. Charlotte Bull Stuart married Richard Fuller in Aug. 1831. J. H. Cuthbert, *Life of Richard Fuller* (New York, 1879), 56–61.

96. Chase wrote these questions, with their heading dated Apr. 7, on the page of the original journal bearing the entry for Jan. 4, 1865.

present, I expressed in the course of conversation my opinion that the only solid foundation of social order & political prosperity was universal suffrage. Gov. Swann said nothing; Mr. Kennedy intimated dissent; Dr. Fuller qualified assent. I said I thought that the nation was bound to secure the right of voting to the loyal blacks of the rebel states, upon reorganizations, not only as a measure of simple justice; but also on grounds of domestic & foreign policy. To deny to those who had been loyal to the country—& eminently loyal—a right to a voice in the affairs of the country they had helped to save would be condemned by all impartial men; while the securing to them of the ballot would save us from much discord, violence & disorder, unfriendly or rather pernicious to regular industry; and would, in possible foreign complications, avert the danger of divisions in our own population. Dr. Fuller spoke of his own relations to Slavery. He said "Formerly I felt bound to sustain the burden of the institution, but was never easy under it. My slaves were my continual anxiety. How could I die & leave them? To what? To whom? I thank God for emancipation—it has taken a great burden off my mind. My friends tell me "You have lost a hundred & fifty thousand dollars!" I tell them Say rather that I have had one hundred & fifty thousand weight of iron taken from my conscience." I was very glad to hear this; and hoped for more progress not only in the mind of the good Doctor, but in those of the other gentlemen.

APL. 8. SAT. Nothing of material interest today. Went to Washington in the afternoon train.

APL. 9. SUND. Attended the Methodist Church—Dr. Nadal preached as usual.

APL. 10. MON. Returned to Baltimore and attended Court— In the evening dined with Judge Giles— Among the guests were Mr. Kennedy, Mr. A. S. Ridgely, a young lawyer of good abilities, but too much inclined to potables;[97] Mr. Price, now District Attorney, quite an old gentleman, over sixty, and a very kind & worthy though not very efficient man; Mr. Schley, about as old as Mr. Price, very

---

97. Andrew Sterett Ridgely (c. 1822–77) was Reverdy Johnson's son-in-law. In 1866, he represented Dr. Samuel A. Mudd, who had given medical treatment to John Wilkes Booth after the assassination of Abraham Lincoln. Ridgely to Chase, Feb. 25, 1864, Dec. 28, 1866 (Chase Papers, L.C.); Scharf, *History of Baltimore*, 806; Fairman, *Reconstruction and Reunion*, 238–39; Beale, *Diary of Gideon Welles*, 3:55–56, 58, 59.

able, and very agreeable & courteous.[98] Many anecdotes were related of prominent members of the bar of Maryland & particularly of Chief Justice Taney & his habit of inveterate smoking.[99]

APL. 11. TU. Ordinary business at Court—dined in the evening, (at 6 P.M.) with Henry Winter Davis— A different set of guests— mostly the radicals, such as Stockbridge & Sterling prominent lawyers[1]—Bond, Judge of the Criminal Court, a thorough able & earnest man—Mr. Ridgely[2] & others of the Conservative side— I took Mrs Davis to table and talked a good deal with her:[3] wrote letter to Prest. Lincoln[4]

APL. 12, WED. Read in American President Lincoln's speech at the White House on Reconstruction in which he refers to my dissatisfaction with the exceptions in his proclamation[5]—began a letter to him—glad that he at length openly avows his wish that the very intelligent & those who have been soldiers, among the loyal blacks, should be allowed to vote but sorry that he is not yet ready for universal or at least equal suffrage[6]—attended Court— Dined in evening with Mr. Albert—a mixed company, Gov. Swann, Admiral Farragut, Jerome Bonaparte, General Morris,[7] the brilliant Davis,

---

98. Baltimore lawyer William Schley (1799–1872). Williams and McKinsey, *History of Frederick County*, 1:306–11.
99. Roger Brooke Taney (1777–1864) of Maryland, a member of Andrew Jackson's cabinet and Chase's predecessor as chief justice, 1836–64. *DAB*, 18:289–94.
1. Archibald Stirling, Jr., and attorney and Republican politician Henry Smith Stockbridge (1822–95), who was instrumental in the dismantling of slavery in Maryland. *DAB*, 18:37.
2. Probably James Lot Ridgely.
3. Nancy Morris Davis (b. ca. 1825), a woman of "keen wit and intelligence" and daughter of a prominent Baltimore attorney, married widower Henry Winter Davis in Jan. 1857. Gerald S. Henig, *Henry Winter Davis: Antebellum and Civil War Congressman from Maryland* (New York, 1973), 90–91.
4. Chase's letter contained suggestions for Reconstruction policy. He advised Lincoln to support Gov. F. H. Pierpont's administration in Virginia. Chase also advocated universal suffrage for blacks and made suggestions for applying that principle in Louisiana and Arkansas. Chase to Lincoln, Apr. 11, 1865 (Lincoln Papers, L.C.).
5. Lincoln praised the Union Army for its successes and discussed Reconstruction measures. Without naming Chase, he referred to Chase's urging, in 1863, that Lincoln apply the Emancipation Proclamation to excepted parts of Virginia and Louisiana. *Baltimore American*, Apr. 12, 1865.
6. Chase recounted his views on the question of universal suffrage for blacks, with particular reference to the administration's policies in Louisiana. Chase to Lincoln, Apr. 12, 1865 (Lincoln Papers, L.C.).
7. Jerome Napoleon Bonaparte (1805–70), the son of Jerome Bonaparte (Napoleon's brother) and Elizabeth Patterson of Baltimore; and Bvt. Brig. Gen. William Walton Morris (1801–65). *Appletons'*, 1:310–11, 4:420.

Gen. Foster, Mayor Chapman,[8] Judge Bond, Mr. Stockbridge, Mr. Sterling & others—finished letter to President.

APL. 13. THURS. Copied & mailed letter to President—home by evening train— Katie & Nettie went out to see illumination—tired & declined to go[9]—

JOURNAL XV

FRIDAY, APRIL 14. Wrote, Mrs Carey A. Trimble, Mrs Jones Mrs Auld, Gen Worthington, Mr. Mansfield, Judge Hall, Mr. [L]Hommedieu, Mr. Hosea, & Mr. Yeatman sending seeds to each, 2 envelopes full of packages to Mrs Auld[10]— Depd. salary with Jay Cooke & Co, 1551.25— Notes to Spinner, Spofford—Newton[11]—

Rode with Nettie afternoon—intending to stop at Presidents—but concluded to postpone it till tomorrow—wishing to talk with him abt. reorganization and universal suffrage but still uncertain how he would take it & so rather shrinking from the duty—returned home half an hour after dusk—a few called—read & wrote a little & to bed—

Abt. 11 the door bell rang—& a servant came up saying that a gentleman wished to see me on very important business—I told him to bring up his card which he did. The name was that of a stranger to me

JOURNAL XVI

APL. 14. FRI. At home morning—afternoon rode out with Nettie intending to have myself left at President & talk with him about universal suffrage in reorganization—felt reluctant to call lest my

---

8. John Gray Foster and John Lee Chapman (1812–80), the moderate Republican mayor of Baltimore, 1862–67. Holli and Jones, *Biographical Dictionary of American Mayors*, 64.

9. Large crowds gathered in the streets of Washington to view another spectacular illumination of public buildings and private residences, which marked the Confederate surrender at Appomattox. Washington *Evening Star*, Apr. 14, 1865.

10. Chase had received a quantity of garden seeds from the commissioner of agriculture, and used William Sprague's franking privileges to send packages to Mrs. Trimble, Charlotte Ludlow Jones, Jane Auld, James T. Worthington, Edward D. Mansfield, James Hall, Stephen S. L'Hommedieu, Robert Hosea, and Thomas H. Yeatman. The editors have located the following letters, all dated Apr. 14, 1865: Chase to Auld, Chase to Trimble (Chase Papers, Hist. Soc. of Pa.); Chase to Hosea (Houghton Lib., Harvard Univ.); Chase to L'Hommedieu (Lincoln Collec., John Hay Lib., Brown Univ.).

11. Francis Elias Spinner (1802–90), treasurer of the U.S.; Ainsworth Rand Spofford (1825–1908), librarian of Congress, who before the Civil War was a Cincinnati bookseller and newspaper editor; Isaac Newton (1800–1867), U.S. commissioner of agriculture. Chase wrote the first paragraph of this entry in ink, the remainder in pencil. *DAB*, 13:472–73, 17:460, 463–64.

talk might annoy him & do harm rather than good—home a little
after dark having postponed my intended call—retired to bed about
ten—sometime after a servant came up & said a gentleman, who
said the President had been shot, wanted to see me— I directed that
he should be shown to my room— He came in, an employé in the
Treasury Department, and said he had just come from the theatre—
the President had been shot in his box by a man who leaped from
the box upon the stage & escaped by the rear— He could give no
particulars & I hoped he might be mistaken—but soon after Mr.
Mellen, Mr. Walker the Fifth Auditor[12] & Mr. Plantz came in &
confirmed what I had been told & added that Secretary Seward had
also been assassinated, and that guards were being placed around
the houses of all the prominent officials, under the apprehension
that the plot had a wide range. My first impulse was to rise immediately & go to the President, whom I could not yet believe to
have been fatally wounded; but reflecting that I could not possibly
be of any service and should probably be in the way of those who
could, I resolved to wait for morning & further intelligence. In a
little while the guard came—for it was supposed that I was one of
the destined victims—and their heavy tramp-tramp was heard under my window all night. Mr. Mellen slept in the house. It was a
night of horrors.

APRIL 15. SAT. Up with the light—a heavy rain was falling, and
the sky was black. Walked up with Mr. Mellen to Mr. Sewards crossing the [Street] (13th I believe) on which is Fords Theatre &, opposite, the house to which the President had been conveyed—was
informed at that point that the President was already dead—continued on to Mr. Sewards—found guards before the house & in the
Street denying access, but the officer allowed me & Mr Mellen to
pass—was admitted to lower hall of the house—learned from assistant surgeon that Mr. Seward had partially recovered his senses
& though in a very critical might live—but that Mr. Frederick
Seward's case was hopeless—his scull having been penetrated to the
brain by what seemed to be a blow from the hammer of a pistol[13]—
returned home full of horror & sorrow—all day long rumors flew—
Booth was the Assassin[14]—he had shot the President & had made
his way to Sewards instantly after—but this could not be—the deed

12. Charles Manning Walker (b. 1834), a Treasury clerk, 1861–62, then fifth
auditor, 1862–69. *Appletons'*, 6:325–26.
13. Frederick W. Seward, injured in a struggle with his father's intended assassin,
remained in danger for weeks but survived. Glyndon G. Van Deusen, *William Henry
Seward* (New York, 1967), 413–15.
14. Maryland native John Wilkes Booth (1838–65), well known for his roles on
the stage in Washington and other cities. *DAB*, 2:448–52.

on Mr. Seward was by a different man—every body had something to repeat or some question to ask— Soon after leaving Mr. Sewards I went to see the Vice President & found him at his hotel, calm apparently but very grave. Soon after Secretary McCulloch & Atto. Gen. Speed came in—they said they were on their way to my house to ask my attendance for Administering the oath of office as President to the Vice President— Some consultation followed as to time & place & it was agreed that it should be in the parlor where we then were & at 10 oclock. I then went with the Atto General to his office to look into the precedents in the cases of Vice Presidents Tyler & Fillmore—and to examine the Constitution & laws— On our way the topic was the late President— Mr. Speed said he had never seen him in better spirits than [on] yesterday. He met the Cabinet very cheerfully & talked with them fully on the subject of reorganization. "He [never] seemed so near our views" said Mr. Speed. "Before the meeting of the Cabinet he had showed me your letter from Baltimore, which, I must say, was a very clear & compact statement of the case. At the meeting he said he thought he had made a mistake at Richmond in sanctioning the assembling of the Virginia Legislature & had perhaps been too fast in his desires for early reconstruction. The matter was referred to Mr. Stanton to draw up a programme for North Carolina." All Mr. Speed said deepened my sorrow for the Country's great loss. After examining the precedents & the Constitution we returned to the Hotel where, at the entrance, I encountered old Mr. Blair & his son Montgomery. I had determined I could bury resentments, & greeted both kindly. We entered the room together—the parlor of the hotel,—where were assembled, some twelve or fourteen gentlemen, Mr. McCulloch, Secy. of the Treasury, Mr. Speed the Atto Gen, the Messrs Blair, Mr. Hale and others. I administered the oath, which the Vice President solemnly repeated after me. He was now the successor of Mr. Lincoln. I said to him May God guide, support & bless you in your arduous duties. The others came forward & tendered their sad congratulations. He asked me if he ought to say anything to those present. I answered that I thought it wd. be better to make a brief announcement to the people in the public prints. He asked me to prepare something & I left the room for that purpose.[15] Returning with it an hour or so later I found that the new President had gone

---

15. Chase drew up a statement announcing Lincoln's assassination and Andrew Johnson's taking of the oath of office, to be published over Johnson's name. Johnson did not use the address. Chase sent it to him the next day. Address to "Fellow Citizens of the United States," [Apr. 15, 1865], and Chase to Johnson, Apr. 16, 1865 (Johnson Papers, L.C.).

to a room at the Treasury Department to meet the Cabinet. In the evening I saw a report of what he had said after I had left the room.[16]

APL. 16. SUN. At Church—Dr. Nadal preached— Bishop Simpson was in the pulpit but took no part in the exercises— Called at Gov. Sewards—a little apparent improvement & but a little. Wrote Judge Giles, Gen Ashley & Gov. Andrew. ☛Letter Book[17]

APL. 17. MON. Gov. Sprague came this morning. Every body seems overwhelmed— The Governor & I went to the Kirkwood to call on Prest. Johnson.[18] He was just leaving to go to a meeting of Heads of Departments at the Treasury.

APRIL 18 TUES. Called on President at Kirkwood & had a long talk with him—he seems thoroughly in earnest & much of the same mind with myself.

APL. 19, WEDY. Called on Gov. Brough and other friends at Willards—they were out & I left cards.

APRL. 20, THURS. Called at Treasy Dept. & saw McCulloch and Prest. Johnson— On the Street heard rumors of an officer with news from Sherman of Johnston's Surrender.[19]

---

16. Second edition columns of the Washington *Evening Star* quoted Johnson: "The duties of the office are mine; I will perform them—the consequences are with God." He closed with an appeal to the cabinet members for their support. *Evening Star,* Apr. 15, 1865.
17. Chase wrote to William F. Giles about a habeas corpus application in the circuit court at Baltimore; to James M. Ashley about the political situation in the aftermath of Lincoln's assassination; and to John A. Andrew concerning Chase's endorsement of a request to Hugh McCulloch, recently appointed secretary of the Treasury. By *Letter Book,* Chase meant the volume of letterpress copies in which the three letters may be found. Chase to Giles, to Ashley, and to Andrew, Apr. 17, 1865 (Chase Papers, Hist. Soc. of Pa.).
18. Andrew Johnson kept his rooms at the Kirkwood House hotel until several weeks after Lincoln's assassination. Hans L. Trefousse, *Andrew Johnson: A Biography* (New York, 1989), 194–95.
19. Gen. William T. Sherman met Gen. Joseph E. Johnston in North Carolina on Apr. 17 and discussed terms for surrendering Johnston's army. The two signed a surrender agreement the following day that also broached matters related to civil reconstruction. President Johnson, acting upon the advice of Gen. Grant and Edwin Stanton, refused the terms. Grant then carried orders to Sherman to resume hostilities. These events resulted in a political furor over the next few weeks and caused open animosity between Sherman and Stanton. Johnston formally surrendered his forces on Apr. 26. Long, *Civil War Day by Day,* 678–79, 681–83; Simon et al., *Papers of Ulysses S. Grant,* 14:417–20, 423–26, 430–35; Sherman, *Memoirs,* 834–56; A. K. McClure, *Abraham Lincoln and Men of War-Times* . . . (Philadelphia, 1892), 216–28.

APL. 21, FRI. Governor Brough called—asked him to breakfast with me on Monday & he agreed—talk about the news from Sherman & Grants' leaving at 2 this morning—Brough said he had predicted it in talk with Stanton—thinks it doubtful if Union Party will carry Ohio at next election—should be more democratic & more liberal to democrats. does not expect himself to be candidate for reelection—

SAT. APL. 22— Called at Willards—met Rosecrans, Campbell & others[20]—invited them to breakfast Monday—went to see McCulloch & talked to him about Dennisons removal—said Prest. Lincoln made a special point of it.[21]

APL. 24, MON. Worked on opinions on cases argued at Baltimore[22]—letter from Jay Cooke—result of investment a net profit of 1232.63—wrote him.[23] At breakfast were Gov. Brough, H. D. Cooke,[24] Gen. Butler, Gen. Rosecrans, H. D. Cooke, W. P. Mellen, L. D. Campbell, Whitelaw Reid, Mr. Wetmore our State Agent, & Col Mussey.[25] It seemed to go off well. wrote Mrs Eastman[26]

APL. 25 TUES. Went to Balte. & read opinions—left cards at Dr. Fullers & Mr. Bonapartes—called on Dr. Collins—returned to Washington in the afternoon. wrote Flanders & Denison at New Orleans[27]

20. Gen. William S. Rosecrans and Ohio politician Lewis Davis Campbell (1811–82). *DAB*, 3:461–62; *Daily National Intelligencer*, Apr. 21, 1865.
21. McCulloch told Chase that Lincoln had considered George S. Denison's continuation as a special agent in New Orleans to be "a great embarrassment." Chase attributed Denison's removal to factional politics in Louisiana. Chase to Denison, Apr. 25, 1865 (Denison Papers, L.C.).
22. For brief summaries of April term proceedings of the U.S. circuit court at Baltimore, see *Baltimore Sun*, Apr. 3–8, 11–14, 1865.
23. Chase's letter concerned his personal investments. He requested Cooke to take back an investment made in Chase's name but without using his own funds. Chase to Cooke, Apr. 24, 1865 (Chase Papers, Hist. Soc. of Pa.).
24. Before the Civil War, Henry David Cooke (1825–81), Jay Cooke's younger brother, was a journalist in Ohio and elsewhere. During the war he headed the Washington offices of his brother's banking firm, promoted bond sales, and established Washington's First National Bank. Later he was a railroad lobbyist and territorial governor of the District of Columbia, 1871–73. *DAB*, 4:382–83.
25. Reuben Delavan Mussey (1833–92), Dartmouth class of 1854, colonel of the 100th U.S. Colored Infantry, and private secretary to President Johnson, Apr. to Nov. 1865. Chapman, *Sketches of the Alumni*, 411; Emerson, *General Catalogue*, 288; Heitman, *Historical Register*, 1:739; Leroy P. Graf et al., eds., *The Papers of Andrew Johnson* (Knoxville, 1967–), 7:199.
26. Chase's letter to Charlotte Eastman detailed his actions on the night of Lincoln's assassination and the following morning. Chase to Eastman, Apr. 14, 1865 (Chase Papers, Hist. Soc. of Pa.).
27. Chase had learned of accusations against the performance of Benjamin F. Flanders as the Treasury's supervising special agent at New Orleans, and wrote with

April 1865

APRIL 26 WED. Took a ride with Nettie in the evening—in the morning called on McCulloch, Speed, & Prest. Johnson.

APL. 27 THURS. Recd. a letter from Col. Key about Semmes case & sent petition to the President with note commending Col. K to his esteem & consideration[28]

AP. 28. FRI. Wrote Col. Key[29]—made some arrangements for starting South—& fixed the day for Monday.

APL. 29 SAT. Wrote a note to Stanton asking for such a general letter as he might think best to enable me to get on conveniently & see all I could see on my southern journey & recd. one from him well adapted to the purpose.[30] Wrote a note to Prest Johnson saying that Johnstons surrender put a new face on affairs & suggesting further conference before going south,[31] & received a request that I would come up to his room. Went taking with me the rough draft of an address in which I had embodied the substance of what I thought ought to be now said to the People on the subject of the reorganization of the rebel States preparatory to their resumption of loyal relations to the Union. See Letter Book page 629.[32] In this address I incorporated a distinct recognition of the loyal colored

---

advice. His letter to George S. Denison concerned the recent removal of Denison from his post as special agent and acting customs officer at New Orleans. Chase to Flanders, Apr. 25, 1865 (Special Collec., Dartmouth College Lib.); Chase to Denison, Apr. 25, 1865 (Denison Papers, L.C.).

28. Thomas M. Key acted as counsel for Richard T. Semmes (b. ca. 1842), a Maryland-born Chicago lawyer. Earlier in 1865, Semmes and seven others had been tried by a military commission in Cincinnati for a supposed conspiracy to free Confederates held prisoner at Camp Douglas, Ill., and devastate the city of Chicago. Despite the absence of evidence linking him to any plot, Semmes was convicted and sentenced to three years of hard labor. In May, Andrew Johnson remitted Semmes's sentence. Graf et al., *Papers of Andrew Johnson*, 8:58, 315; *Message from the President . . . Transmitting Papers relative to the Case of George St. Leger Grenfel*, 39th Cong., 2nd sess., 1867, H. Ex. Doc. 50; *OR*, ser. 2, v. 8:502–3, 573, 644–46; Klement, *Dark Lanterns*, 187–217.

29. Chase informed Key that he had forwarded Semmes's petition. He also wished for national unity and voluntary Reconstruction of Southern states "without distinction of color & without any other agency of the National Government than that of support, encouragement, & protection." Chase to T. M. Key, Apr. 28, 1865 (Chase Papers, Hist. Soc. of Pa.).

30. Chase requested a letter to use on his Southern journey. He also pointed out the need to reduce government expenditures. Stanton provided an order to commanders to assist Chase on his trip. Chase to Stanton, Apr. 29, 1865 (Stanton Papers, L.C.); Warden, *Chase*, 642.

31. Chase to Johnson, Apr. 29, [1865] (Chase Papers, Hist. Soc. of Pa.).

32. "An Address to the People of the United States," a five-page document in Chase's hand (Johnson Papers, L.C.). A copy of the "Address" occupies pp. 629–33

men as citizens, entitled to the right of suffrage. I read it to Mr. Johnston & at his request a part of it more than once. He said I agree to all you say, but I dont see how I can issue such a document now. I am new & untried and cannot venture what I please. I said Mr. President If you will just put forth not this, but some simple declaration that the colored people are free & are citizens & therefore entitled to vote in reorganization & to be protected in that right you will have on your side all the young brain & heart of the country & You will have, of course, all those who feel bound to sneeze when the President takes snuff—no small number—and you will be irresistible. Besides this your declaration will be reprinted in every language under heaven civilized & uncivilized, and it will excite the admiration of all men & the gratitude of all good men, & give you a name & fame equal to that acquired by the Proclamation of Emancipation. Much more was said & much on both sides. I almost hoped the Presidents reluctance was conquered & that the new & [crowning] proclamation wd be issued securing equal & universal suffrage in reorganization. Wrote to Mr. Hastings & Mr. Shuckers at Albany expressing my regret that I cannot attend graduation of Law Class:[33] and to W. G. Deshler, Columbus, enclosing subscription to Sherman Fund & some words of what I thought just praise & defence.[34] Recd. a letter from Gov Sprague somewhat harsh on Sherman.

APL. 30, SUN.   Wrote Gov. Sprague anxious about Katies cough.[35] Wrote a parting note to the President (☞ Letter Book p. 640) en-

---

of Chase's volume of letterpress copies of correspondence for Apr. 14, 1864–Oct. 14, 1865 (Chase Papers, Hist. Soc. of Pa.).

33. Samuel Dexter Hastings, Jr. (1841–1931), the son of an antislavery and temperance reformer, and Jacob W. Schuckers were members of the 1865 class of the University of Albany Law School. Hastings became a Wisconsin attorney and judge. Chase's plans for his Southern trip prevented him from accepting the invitation. Chase to Schuckers, Apr. 29, 1865, and to Hastings, same date (Chase Papers, Hist. Soc. of Pa.); Berryman, *Bench and Bar of Wisconsin*, 2:551–52; *Circular and Catalogue of the Law School . . . 1864-5;* alumni files, Albany Law School; *Nat. Cyc.*, 10:142.

34. William G. Deshler was collecting money for a testimonial in honor of William Tecumseh Sherman. Deshler had Chase's letter printed in the *Ohio State Journal* and cited Chase's contribution as one of the largest yet made. Chase downplayed the controversy surrounding Sherman since his convention with Gen. Johnston and praised him for his "splendid services," patriotism, and valor. Chase to Deshler, Apr. 29, 1865 (Chase Papers, Hist. Soc. of Pa.), printed in *Daily Ohio State Journal*, May 4, 1865.

35. Chase's letter to William Sprague defended Gen. Sherman and gave Chase's expectations for Andrew Johnson's Reconstruction policies. He also noted that he was "very uneasy" due to his daughter Kate's reported cough, and advised Sprague to "make health your care." Chase to Sprague, Apr. 30, 1865 (Chase Papers, Hist. Soc. of Pa.).

May 1865   { 535 }

closing the Bible on which he was sworn into office with passage marked which was pressed by his lips[36]

JOURNAL XV

MONDAY, MAY 1. Very busy all day getting ready to start—wrote divers letters to L'Hommedieu and others[37]—set Marshall to packing & directed him—after all forgot many things books on War—maps—dressing gowns, hair restorative &c— Gov. Sprague came—also earlier Dr. Fuller & between them Lowell[38]—off at last baggage in one carriage, Nettie Gov. S., Katie, Dr. Fuller & I in another—to the Northerner lying at Navy Yard Bridge[39]— Mussey came with regards & best wishes of the President—then adieus— Gov. S. Katie & Mussey left us & we got off about 8.30 P.M—got aground when off arsenal & in some danger of collision with tow boat & convoy—escaped—got off—& went on—beat W. Mellen Jr three games of chequers went to bed—Nettie & I having after cabin—quite comfortably[40]

---

36. Chase also urged Johnson to support citizenship and suffrage for all Southern blacks. *Letter Book* refers to the location of the letter among Chase's letterpress copies of his correspondence from this period. Chase to Johnson, Apr. 30, 1865 (Chase Papers, Hist. Soc. of Pa.), printed (from a typed copy) in Graf et al., *Papers of Andrew Johnson,* 7:672–73.

37. Stephen S. L'Hommedieu had sent railroad passes and promised the use of a special car at the conclusion of Chase's Southern journey. L'Hommedieu to Chase, Apr. 24, 1865 (Chase Papers, L.C.).

38. Richard Fuller was a member of Chase's party for the early portions of the journey along the Southern coast. Russell R. Lowell, formerly deputy U.S. marshal at Syracuse, N.Y., performed special assignments for the Treasury Department, c. 1862–66, and accompanied Chase's party during the Southern trip. He afterwards worked as a private detective in Rochester, N.Y., maintaining a friendship with Chase, and later moved to Kansas. *OR,* ser. 3, v. 2:556–59, ser. 3, v. 3:579; Chase to Lowell, Dec. 8, 1862 (Letters Sent to Members of Judiciary, Gen. Recs. Treasury Dept., Nat. Arch.); Chase to Lowell, Dec. 30, 1862 (Harrington Papers, Mo. Hist. Soc.); Chase to Lowell, Mar. 15, 1867, Apr. 20, 1867, and Lowell to Chase, Oct. 18, 1862, June 15, 1868 (Chase Papers, L.C.); N. Sargeant to Geo. M. Abell, Sept. 24, 1866, and Lowell to ——— Hawley, Jan. 1, 1879 (Division of Appointments, Gen. Recs. Treasury Dept., Nat. Arch.).

39. The *Northerner* was a steamer sold to the U.S. Revenue Cutter Service in Apr. 1864. Lytle, *Merchant Vessels,* 141; U.S. Department of Transportation, *Record of Movements,* 216–19.

40. Secretary of the Treasury Hugh McCulloch ordered William P. Mellen, as supervising special agent, to visit Southern ports and oversee implementation of trade regulations. This arrangement made it possible for Chase and his daughter Janet (Nettie) to travel by revenue steamers for much of their journey. "W. Mellen Jr" was William P. Mellen's son, William S. Mellen, evidently acting as his father's clerk. McCulloch to Mellen, May 1, 1865 (Letters Sent to Special Agents, Recs. of Bureau of Customs, Nat. Arch.); *Cinc. Dir. (1865),* 285; *Charleston Courier,* May 13, 1865.

JOURNAL XVI

MAY 1, MON. Wrote Tilton Sorry I cannot come to Meeting of Cong. Ministers[41]—sent copies of my two letters to Prest. Lincoln[42]—gave briefly my views of the situation—& bid goodbye—Recd. letters from President & Secy. Welles in furtherance of my journey[43]

JOURNAL XV

TUESDAY, MAY 2. Arrived at Fortress Monroe abt. 12—Major James met us & was very kind / He is Chief Qr. Mr. here—married [dtr.] of John Janney of Columbus[44]—I & Nettie with him—Dr. Fuller, Mellen & Reid in another carriage[45]—visited Cold. School under Mr. Raymond[46]— Most of the scholars from mission school under Mr. Day—admirable order some boys very bright—visited Hampton, old church—went to Norfolk—recd. by Genl Gordon—

---

41. Theodore Tilton had telegraphed earlier in the day, asking Chase to preside at an interdenominational gathering at the Brooklyn Academy of Music on May 11. Chase sent his regrets, and also outlined his views on Reconstruction and the importance of suffrage for blacks. Tilton to Chase, May 1, 1865 (Chase Papers, Hist. Soc. of Pa.); Chase to Tilton, same date (New-York Hist. Soc.).

42. Chase had fifty copies of his April 11–12 letters to Lincoln printed to send to friends (copy in James Shepherd Pike Papers, Univ. of Maine). *"For obvious reasons I do not want them published,"* he informed Tilton, but he enclosed extra copies for Tilton to hand to Horace Greeley of the *New York Tribune* and William Cullen Bryant of the *Evening Post.* Chase to Tilton, May 1, 1865 (New-York Hist. Soc.). In June Chase gave the two letters to the *Cincinnati Gazette* for publication, and other newspapers followed suit. Chase to Charles Sumner, June 25, 1865 (Chase Papers, L.C.); *New York Times,* June 30, 1865.

43. On Apr. 29, Johnson wrote a general order to federal officers instructing them to aid Chase on his journey. Welles authorized the commanding officer of the West Gulf blockade squadron at New Orleans to furnish a gunboat, if one were available, for Chase's trip up the Mississippi River. Warden, *Chase,* 642; Welles to Henry Knox Thatcher, May 1, 1865 (Chase Papers, Cinc. Hist. Soc.).

44. William Levis James of Pennsylvania was an assistant quartermaster and officer of volunteers. John Jay Janney (b. 1812) was secretary of the board of control of the state bank of Ohio, 1851–65; secretary and treasurer of Ohio's State Union Executive Committee during the Civil War; later an officer of the Columbus & Hocking Valley R.R. Heitman, *Historical Register,* 1:570; *OR,* ser. 3, v. 5:346; Robson, *Biographical Encyclopædia,* 469–70; Janney to Chase, June 10, 1863 (Chase Papers, L.C.).

45. Whitelaw Reid, who accompanied Chase on this journey, sent dispatches to the *Cincinnati Gazette* (using his pen name, "Agate"), and published an account of his visit to the South as *After the War: A Southern Tour. May 1, 1865, to May 1, 1866* (New York, 1866). Reid also kept a manuscript journal during the trip (Reid Family Papers, L.C.).

46. Charles A. Raymond, U.S. Army chaplain and superintendent of public education for the District of East Virginia, oversaw a model school where on one floor seven hundred children could be kept under "the view and voice of the Superintendent." *Freedmen's Journal* 1 (1865): 9.

who in comd. of District[47]—talked abt. policy of govt.—told him loyal Govt. was & wd. be recognized & sustained—advised him to write Gov. Pierpont & get copy of amended Constitution & ask Gov. to have large edition printed—spoke to him in favor of negro suffrage—he not dissenting nor approving / visited, entrenched camp[48]—returned to boat & Fortress Monroe & were transferred to Wayanda[49]—first impressions not agreeable—wrote Prest. Johnson. Will Mellen copied.[50]

WEDNESDAY, MAY 3. When I rose this morning the Wayanda was under weigh— The wind, after we passed Cape Henry was [behind][51]—the sails were spread and we went on merrily for awhile—how beautiful!—how grand! What delicious air were the frequent exclamations. I was on the ocean for the first time—on the right the Coast of North Carolina, no longer rebel, nor yet wholly reclaimed from rebellion—on the left the broad Atlantic across whose broad waters fancy could discern the coasts of Perfidious Albion & unfriendly France— Soon Mr [Reid] & young Mr. Mellen began to grow seasick / Nettie too suffered greatly though she rose early & went on deck hoping to escape seasickness— She stood it bravely for a while; but was obliged to surrender & went below. I suffd little & enjoyed the new scenes & circumstances greatly[52] / The day passed & night closed in. The moon rose bright & clear & we were still on the ocean, passing Cape Hatteras, seldom so little vexed.[53]

---

47. George Henry Gordon (1823–86), brevet major general of volunteers, commanded the eastern district of Virginia, Mar.–June 1865. *DAB*, 7:421–22.

48. Gordon later claimed that Chase justified his view regarding black suffrage by saying of the freedmen: "their hearts are right, if their heads are empty." Gordon took Chase's party "to the outskirts of Norfolk, where Mr. Chase viewed with much interest the outer line of defenses." George H. Gordon, *A War Diary of Events in the War of the Great Rebellion, 1863–1865* (Boston, 1882), 417–18.

49. A revenue steamer built in 1863. U.S. Department of Transportation, *Record of Movements*, 172.

50. William S. Mellen. Chase wrote the body of the entry in pencil, later adding the final six words in ink. He made the addition to the wrong day's entry: there is no other evidence of a May 2 letter to Andrew Johnson, but Chase did write to the president on May 4 from Beaufort, N.C. An extant copy of that letter, with Chase's filing note, may be the copy made by the younger Mellen. Chase to Johnson, May 4, 1865 (Johnson Papers, L.C.); copy (Chase Papers, Cinc. Hist. Soc.); letter printed in Simpson et al., *Advice After Appomattox*, 17–18.

51. Apparently Chase wrote both *ahead* and *behind*, one on top of the other. It is uncertain which word was Chase's final intention.

52. "'O si sic omnes!' punned the Chief Justice." Reid, *After the War*, 22.

53. Chase began this entry in pencil. The latter portion, beginning with the word *seasickness*, is in ink.

THURSDAY, MAY 4. When I went on deck we were steaming up towards Beaufort & soon came to anchor in the harbor,—Mr. Mellen & a party went over to the town— Capt. West, commg. station soon after came on board & I & Nettie went with him to his ship the Orletta & thence to his quarters on the beach[54]—most kindly recd. by Mrs. West—formerly Miss Jamison of Md—visited Fort Macon— saw effects of Burnside's fire[55]—returned to Wayanda—party fr. Beaufort retd—Capt. W—— arranged transportation to Newberne—visit from Dr. Arundel, Senator rebel Legis & Mr. Rumley Clerk of County Court[56]—went to Morehead City & thence to Newberne by rail—saw pines & sands of N. Carolina—flat & only historically interesting—passed scene of battle—passed the Trent[57]— found Col. Heaton & Gen. Palmer awaiting us at depot[58]—Col. H. took charge of Mr. Mellen & his party—Gen. Palmer of me & mine—visited fortifications—village of cold refugees—quarter of white refugees—latter far most helpless—tea at Gen. P——'s—visit to Col H——s—rebel Col. hotel keeper at Charlotte—talk with Heaton who afraid of cold. suffrage.

FRIDAY, MAY 5. The sun rose bright—the air was delicious— birds seemingly without number & of all notes sang like mad— cheerful good mornings fr Gen Palmer & Dr. Fuller—a nice breakfast with capital coffee & cream—an old hen & chickens as I went out into the yard—thus begins this day—7.30 am. a good breakfast[59]—then to depot & off—message fr Gen Sherman—wd. be glad to see me on Russia[60]—found her at Morehead City wharf— General very cordial—greatly offended with Halleck—says left en-

---

54. Lt. Comdr. William C. West commanded the USS *Arletta*, a wooden mortar schooner on station at Beaufort, N.C. *ORN*, ser. 1, v. 12:133, 143, ser. 2, v. 1:38–39.

55. In 1862 Ambrose Burnside had commanded an expeditionary force that drove Confederate forces from the area around New Bern and Beaufort. *DAB*, 3:310.

56. Former North Carolina state senator Michael F. Arendell (b. 1819), a graduate of the medical department of the University of New York City, had opposed secession but supported the Confederacy during the war. Whitelaw Reid described James Rumley (b. ca. 1813) as "a functionary of near thirty years' service." *Cyclopedia of Eminent and Representative Men of the Carolinas* . . . (Madison, Wis., 1892; reprint, Spartanburg, S.C., 1973), 2:563–65; Simpson et al., *Advice After Appomattox*, 18; Reid, *After the War*, 24–25.

57. Trent River.

58. David Heaton and Innis Newton Palmer (1824–1900), brevet colonel of cavalry and major general of volunteers. *DAB*, 14:184–85.

59. Chase began this entry in pencil. The text beginning with *a good breakfast* is in ink.

60. Sherman made no reference to his meeting with Chase in his military report, but mentions the incident in his *Memoirs*. The *Russia* was a former blockade runner put into service as an army transport under the command of Capt. A. M. Smith. *OR*,

tirely without instructions—except what Prest. Lincoln said abt. Davis & did abt Va Legislature—order Mar 3d to Grant never commd. to him / very wrong to publish his projet of Convention[61]— He accd. me to Wayanda & went on board— Staff Majors Dayton, formerly of Lancaster, Ohio; McCoy of Columbus, & Audenreid of N.Y. devoted to him & no wonder[62]—head wind—useless to go out— Fish fr. Russia with compts of Capt—evening but before dark visited Capt. & Mrs West—Gen Sherman came in—some talk back to Wayanda & sleep after a most agreeable day.

JOURNAL XVII

MAY 6 SATURDAY— At Beaufort N.C. found curious entry in Old Record— It consisted of a copy of a Record from Barnstable Mass beginning "Barnstable [*illeg.*] Anno Regne Geo II July 7, 1730"— It purports to be the sentence of one Jude Porrig alias James Marko to service for having runaway—8 years or twice unexpired term and four years for having stolen a coat valued at 12 shillings— To this was added a conveyance 6 Nov. 1730 apparently in Barnstable of Jude Porrig or James Marko to a Mr. Rooks—and another enscribed in Beaufort to Enoch Bell[,] one of his Majestys Justice[s] of the Peace.

Did Jude survive his servitude[?] Among the best men I met at Beaufort was Col James H Taylor, a gentleman of 60—devotedly Union, intelligent, formerly slaveholder—now for universal freedom & inclined to universal suffrage.[63]

---

ser. 1, v. 47, pt. 1:29–41; Sherman, *Memoirs*, 858, 862; Lytle, *Merchant Vessels*, 167; *ORN*, ser. 1, v. 11:431.

61. In framing his surrender agreement with Gen. Johnston, Sherman relied on a meeting he had with Pres. Lincoln and other officers on Mar. 28, 1865, to discuss the question of ending the war, and on Lincoln's authorization of Apr. 6, 1865, to reconvene the Virginia Legislature under the control of Union supporters. The order from Secretary of War Stanton to Gen. Grant on Mar. 3, which was not sent to Sherman, instructed Grant that Lincoln wished him to "have no conference with General Lee, unless it be for the capitulation of Lee's army or on solely minor and purely military matters," and to avoid political issues. Stanton, without Sherman's knowledge, released an account of the cabinet deliberations that resulted in the rejection of the Johnston surrender terms, and its publication on Apr. 24 infuriated Sherman. Sherman, *Memoirs*, 847–56; Long, *Civil War Day by Day*, 658–59, 668; McClure, *Abraham Lincoln*, 218–21.

62. Lewis Mulford Dayton (d. 1891); James Culbertson McCoy (c. 1830–75); and Joseph Crain Audenried (1839–80) all continued as staff officers for Gen. Sherman after the war. Heitman, *Historical Register*, 1:175, 362, 660; *New York Times*, May 30, 1875; *Appletons'*, 1:117.

63. Taylor (b. ca. 1802) was a North Carolina planter. Simpson et al., *Advice After Appomattox*, 21.

JOURNAL XV

SATURDAY, MAY 6. Wind still "Sou' Sou' West" & strong—no use to go out says Capt. Merryman[64]— The Russia also remains— Gen. Sherman sent me copies of his orders & letter to Gen. Grant, wh. I think Grant, loving Genl. Sherman will keep to himself[65]—sent me also copy of proposed order to Troops[66]— Our party went to Beaufort—met by Dr. Arundel[67] & others—went to Clerks office— Mr. Rumley Clk showed me old records 1724 and forward—singular entry about Jim [Porrig] or James Marko—Dinah sentenced to 39 lashes for having mulatto child—sentence executed—several others baseborn— Rev. Mr. Rumley came—Meth. Minister—Col. Tayor, James H. 61, respectable, thoroughly loyal—ready for reorganization with universal Suffrage— Visited Turpentine distillery— returned to boat—Mr. [Strech] N.Y. merchant there—wrote Gen Sherman strongly agst pubn. of order—recd. answer from him "must publish"[68]— Went ashore for ride on beach—too late for best ride but started—left carriage too heavy for horses, & strolled with Dr. Fuller—magnificent surf—he spoke of the great movement like the tide—[irristable]—I of all movemt like the tides limited & guided by Inspired Intelligence

SUNDAY, MAY 7. Early up—not feeling very well—but going on deck felt better— Asked Capt. Merryman to notify Gen Sherman & Capt. West that Dr Fuller wd. preach at Beaufort— Capt W. ansd. thanks but unwell— Gen. S—— busy with despatches—send that —————— preacher out of harbor or we shall never get away. Our party

---

64. James H. Merryman, commanding the *Wayanda*. William Handy to Merryman, Apr. 25, 1865, and abstract journal of *Wayanda* (Recs. of U.S. Coast Guard, Nat. Arch.).

65. Sherman probably referred to orders given on Apr. 21 for Grant to "proceed immediately to the headquarters of Major General Sherman, and direct operations against the enemy," and Grant's order on the same day for Sherman to end his truce with Johnston and resume hostilities. In his letter to Grant on Apr. 28, 1865, later transmitted to the adjutant general for publication, Sherman defended his own actions and cast aspersions upon Edwin M. Stanton. Sherman, *Memoirs*, 847–49, 854–56; Simon et al., *Papers of Ulysses S. Grant*, 14:424–26, 15:12–15; *OR*, ser. 1, v. 47, pt. 3:334–36.

66. Sherman's proposed order to his troops was meant "to counteract the effect of the insult so wantonly and unjustly, and so publicly inflicted on me by the Secretary of War." Sherman believed the order would lead to the closing of his military career. Sherman to Chase, May 6, 1865 (Sherman Papers, New-York Hist. Soc.).

67. Michael F. Arendell.

68. Chase wrote: "I cannot see that any good will come of it; but I fear some evil." No evidence has been found that Sherman issued the order. Chase to Sherman, May 6, 1865 (W. Sherman Papers, L.C.).

all to Beaufort—met by Col. Taylor & others / Among them Mr. Davis who invited us to his house till Church time—accpd.—met Miss D—— an intelligent young lady, just returned from Epis. Sun. School & a sweet little girl daughter of Col. Taylor— Mr. Rumley the preacher came in & we went to his church Methodist—Dr Fuller preached very good sermon / Ad[vi]d. congregation of the necessity of patience, charity & wisdom—that Slavery was extinct—that the condition of the enfranchised must now be considered in a right Spirit— After he closed a Chaplain Mr. Balloch rose & made a short address[69] / returned to Wayanda— Sent letters to Stearns, Prest & Schofield to Russia which soon went out of Harbor & Wayanda followed.[70]

MONDAY, MAY 8. No chance for doing anything today—a strong head wind—the steamer rolling & pitching badly—Nettie very sick—I very uncomfortable—such seemed our prospect when I awoke or rather when day came for I slept little during the stormy night—but about eight o'clock we came abreast of Fort Fisher— A pilot boat came off & said water too low to cross the bar—and the sea ran too high to allow the boat to come along side—but as the [detention] was inevitable & we desired to visit Fort Fisher we went on bd. the pilot boat—examined the Fort thoroughly under escort of Major Prince who commaned regiment in final charge— great strength—Butler might have gone in—retd. left horses at Capt Johnson's—went on Pilot boat to Fort Caswell & exd it under escort of Capt Carroll[71]—retg. met [Gen] Hawley, Gen Dodge &

---

69. Probably James Balloch, hospital chaplain, 1864–65. Heitman, *Historical Register*, 1:188.

70. George Luther Stearns (1809–67) was a New York merchant and manufacturer with a long involvement in antislavery activities. During the Civil War he received the rank of major and recruited black soldiers. Chase's letter to President Johnson noted Gen. Sherman's unhappiness with the censure he had received from his handling of Johnston's surrender, gave Chase's view of the situation in North Carolina, and urged the president to issue a statement supporting the enrollment of Southern blacks as citizens. Chase sent Maj. Gen. John M. Schofield suggestions on Reconstruction in North Carolina. Chase considered himself authorized to summarize Andrew Johnson's opinions on the subject. *Appletons'*, 5:655; Chase to Johnson, May 7, 1865 (Johnson Papers, L.C.), printed in Simpson et al., *Advice After Appomattox*, 19–20; Chase to Schofield, May 7, 1865 (Schofield Papers, L.C.).

71. Frederick W. Prince led a detachment from the 16th New York Heavy Artillery during the assault on Fort Fisher and was given command of the post in Mar. 1865. James B. Caryl and Peter W. Johnson were officers in the 16th New York Heavy Artillery. *OR*, ser. 1, v. 46, pt. 1:404, 624, v. 47, pt. 2:696, 709; *Annual Report of the Adjutant General of the State of New York* (Albany, 1865), 347.

staff & invited them to Waya.[72]—Mr. Moore & Mr. Pennington,[73] Col. Baker Mr. [McCub] & Mr. Wallace with them to meet us[74]— reception at Gen Hawleys—slept at Gen Dodge

JOURNAL XVII

MAY 9, WILMINGTON—
Met Brig. Gen. E. L. Hayes of Wauseon, Fulton Co[75]—have seen him there but cannot identify him in memory—
Colored delegation called—
1. Rev. Jona. C Gibbs, Pastor 1st Presbyterian Colored Church of Phila—who was gradd. at Dart College when I attended Commt. there—I think in 1855 after nomn. & before election as Governor—he is now here on commission from a benevolent association.[76]
2 Alfred Howe, a carpenter about 48 years old—has followed trade 30 years—bot himself for 1200 & wife & two children for 1800— 3000 in all—was conveyed to White friend & relied on integrity for freedom—has house & lot—never legally free—
2. Henry D. Sampson—carpenter also much younger man perhaps 30 or 35—has followed trade many years—not free till made free by the war—

---

72. Republican editor and politician Joseph Roswell Hawley (1826–1905), brigadier general of volunteers in command at Wilmington, N.C.; and Bvt. Brig. Gen. George S. Dodge (b. 1839), chief quartermaster at Wilmington. *DAB*, 8:421–22; *Appletons'*, 3:123–24; Simpson et al., *Advice After Appomattox*, 22; Heitman, *Historical Register*, 1:376; *OR*, ser. 1, v. 47, pt. 3:396.

73. Bartholomew Figures Moore (1801–78), legal authority and unionist, assumed a leading and often combative role in the Reconstruction of North Carolina. Chase conveyed Moore's views on the political situation in North Carolina to President Johnson on May 12. J. L. Pennington edited the *Raleigh Progress*. *DAB*, 13:114–15; Chase to Johnson, May 12, 1865 (Johnson Papers, L.C.), printed in Simpson et al., *Advice After Appomattox*, 23–25; Reid, *After the War*, 42–44; Raleigh *Weekly Progress*, Apr. 4, 1865.

74. John A. Baker, colonel of a North Carolina cavalry regiment, was captured in June 1864 and took the oath of allegiance to the U.S. in Mar. 1865. He opened a law office at Wilmington but soon departed for the West Indies. Wallace may have been S. D. Wallace, who before the Civil War was involved in efforts to improve Wilmington's public schools. Simpson et al., *Advice After Appomattox*, 25–26; Reid, *After the War*, 43; *OR*, ser. 2, v. 7:899, v. 8:332; Wilmington *Herald of the Union*, May 4, 1865; M. C. S. Noble, *A History of the Public Schools of North Carolina* (Chapel Hill, 1936), 251, 253; Guion Griffis Johnson, *Ante-Bellum North Carolina* . . . (Chapel Hill, 1937), 277.

75. Bvt. Brig. Gen. Edwin L. Hayes of Wauseon, Ohio. *OR*, ser. 1, v. 45, pt. 1:419–20, v. 47, pt. 2:694, 927, ser. 2, v. 7:805–6; Winter, *Northwest Ohio*, 1:425.

76. Jonathan C. Gibbs (c. 1827–74) was a graduate of Dartmouth College and the Princeton Theological Seminary. He taught freedmen in North Carolina and Florida, and in the latter state became secretary of state, 1868–73, and superintendent of public instruction, 1873–74. Chase probably attended Gibbs's Dartmouth graduation, but it was in 1852. John F. Ohles, ed., *Biographical Dictionary of American Educators* (Westport, Conn., 1978), 2:505–6; Emerson, *General Catalogue*, 283; Chase to Kate Chase, July 25, 1852 (Chase Papers, Hist. Soc. of Pa.).

3. Allen Evans—a smart young fellow barber by trade—bought himself & had conveyance made to his wife who was free.

These men fully understand the situation as far as the unsettled policy of the government allows anybody to understand it

They are members of the Union League of which there are three associations at Wilmington numbering 200 members each ⅓ women—there are four at Newbern & 2 or 3 more in the state— these Leagues are societies of a National League which held its Convention at Syracuse Oct 4, 64 & proposes to hold its next [annual] meeting in Tennessee. John M. Langston is President[77] / They seek Education, Improvement & suffrage

JOURNAL XV

TUESDAY, MAY 9. Breakfasted with Gen. Dodge—went to Gen Hawley's & met Mr. Moore & Mr. Pennington—talked abt. reorgn.— Mr. Moore, an old & prominent lawyer of Raleigh stated his views— wants legislature assembled & convention called—opposed to negro suffrage / Mr. P—— willing to accept policy of Govt— Many other gentlemen called—Mr. Baker, recently Col. in rebel service, now for radical reorgann, Mr Russell large slaveholder before rebellion, thinks south ruined by civil war & Emancipation;[78] Mr. Sinclair, Presbyn. & Mr. Burkhead, Meth. ministers;[79] many & difft. views— lunch at 2— Cold deputation called—Mr. Gibbs, Presbn. Min 1. P. Ch. Phila, grad. Dart. Coll. Messrs Howe, Carpenter, Sampson do[80] & Evans barber / They wanted my opinion as to condition & duties of Cold. people,—the elective franchise—the probable rights to leased property— Very interesting talk— They repd. Union Col.

---

77. John Mercer Langston (1829–97), lawyer, politician, educator, and diplomat, took a prominent part in the National Convention of Colored Men held at Syracuse, N.Y., Oct. 4–7, 1864. Black leaders at the conference elected Langston president of the National Equal Rights League, a new organization committed to self-improvement and the attainment of full citizenship for blacks. *DAB*, 10:597–98; William and Aimee Lee Cheek, *John Mercer Langston and the Fight for Black Freedom, 1829–65* (Urbana and Chicago, 1989), 425–36.

78. North Carolina planter and businessman Daniel L. Russell (1804–71) owned 25,000 acres and 150 slaves in 1855. He and his son favored the Republicans after the Civil War. W. McKee Evans, *Ballots and Fence Rails* . . . (Chapel Hill, 1966), 118–19, 312; Johnson, *Ante-Bellum North Carolina*, 487, 523; Roberta Sue Alexander, *North Carolina Faces the Freedmen* . . . (Durham, N.C., 1965), 115–18; *Nat. Cyc.*, 13:356.

79. James Sinclair, a Scottish immigrant, became a Union chaplain and North Carolina Republican politician after being ousted from the Confederate army for treasonous conduct. Liryum Skidmore Burkhead (1824–87) was a Methodist minister, North Carolina Conference. J. G. DeRoulhac Hamilton, *Reconstruction in North Carolina* (1914; reprint, Gloucester, Mass., 1964), 179, 211, 359–60, 430–31; Evans, *Ballots and Fence Rails*, 93, 189; *Nat. Cyc.*, 7:315.

80. That is, "ditto"—Howe and Sampson were both carpenters (see Journal XVII entry for May 9, above).

League— Left with kind farewells[—] Gen. Hawley, Gen Abbott & Mrs A. & others accompd. us, on Jas Christopher to Wayanda[81]— sent letter to President by Gen Dodge who goes tonight.[82]

WEDNESDAY, MAY 10. Got under way early—touched ground coming over the bar—then out in the ocean. Never felt better—air delicious—pleasant breeze. The ocean rolling in gentle though mighty waves smooth almost & equally beautiful & grand— This has been a pleasant—a very pleasant day—the only drawback being Netties seasickness & this is less than it has been— We are about to enter Charleston Harbor and I have been reading Russells letters when he first came to America.[83] I found them more impartial than I thought them three years ago— No wonder he thought the *old* Union could never be restored—it never cd. be restored— It has not been nor will be—but there will be a better & more glorious Union representing a higher civilization and more perfect freedom— How like a dream the past seems as I read—*Wigfall, Anderson, Pickens,* Whiting, Beauregard—Sumter—the bombardment the surrender— the call for 75,000—for Congress—the war![84]

THURSDAY, MAY 11. A little after 6 the pilot came & the str. got under way—bright sky—large cotton ship—passed the light ship— Folly Island / entered the channel along Morris Island—Keokuk buoy—Fort Wagner—Weehawken in chl.—Fort Sumter sand batteries—formidable batteries on Sullivan Isld. Patapsco sunk near

---

81. New Hampshire newspaper editor Joseph Carter Abbott (1825–81), a brevet brigadier general of volunteers, settled in Wilmington at the end of his military service. His wife, whose name is not known, died of typhoid fever contracted while assisting during an epidemic the month following Chase's visit. The paddlewheel steamer *James Christopher* operated in the Wilmington area at this time. *DAB*, 1:23–24; Evans, *Ballots and Fence Rails*, 107; *OR*, ser. 1, v. 47, pt. 2:520, ser. 3, v. 5:479; Lytle, *Merchant Vessels*, 95.

82. Chase wrote Andrew Johnson on May 8 with two procedural suggestions to assist the reorganization of former rebel states, and advising that trade be reopened. Chase to Johnson, May 8, 1865 (Johnson Papers, L.C.), in Simpson et al., *Advice After Appomattox*, 21–22.

83. William Howard Russell, *Pictures of Southern Life: Social, Political, and Military* (New York, 1861). The first edition contained letters, dated between Apr. 30 and June 30, 1861, originally written for the London *Times* from various places in the South.

84. Reading Russell's *Pictures* moved Chase to reflect upon people involved in the secession crisis and the start of the war: Louis Trezevant Wigfall (1816–74), U.S. senator from Texas, 1860–61, who advocated secession of the South; professional soldier Robert Anderson (1805–71), the Federal commander who surrendered Fort Sumter in Apr. 1861; Francis Wilkinson Pickens; William Henry Chase Whiting (1824–65), the Confederate officer who devised new defenses for Charleston; and P. G. T. Beauregard, who commanded Confederate forces around Charleston at the commencement of hostilities. *DAB*, 1:274–75, 2:111–12, 20:136–37, 187–88.

May 1865 {545}

Fort—by Torpedo[85]— Palmatto on Sullivan—batteries Gregg & Putnam, our fleet, Steamers & Monitors—Pawnee, Passaic, Adml. Dahlgren's flagship Philadelphia[86]—passed Castle Pinkney, Fort Ripley, into Cooper River, by batteries on bar & finally came to anchor, a few rods fr. flgship— Soon after Adml. came on board with Capt. Bradford his fleet captain[87] / [Browne][88]—went up Cooper—raised ram—torpedo boat—[illeg.][89] / & with them we visited Fort Sumter now an immense earthwork—thence to Fort Moultrie—long line of batteries on Sullivan—retd. to f. ship—lunch / Plantation diary of Gregory of Greenwood— Herald favor Negro suffrage May 2 to 8[90]—ashore—carriages—Gen Hatch took me[91]—Mrs. [M]artell Nettie[92]—race course, Martyrs[93]—[Meeting rooms] / King St—Meeting House St—Burnt [distt—Shells—Statue][94] / Charleston House—

---

85. *In chl.* means "in channel." The ironclads USS *Keokuk* and USS *Weehawken* sank off Morris Island at the entrance to Charleston Harbor in Apr. 1863 and Dec. 1863, respectively. The USS *Patapsco,* another monitor, sank near Ft. Sumter in Jan. 1865. *ORN,* ser. 2, v. 1:120, 170–71, 238.
86. USS *Pawnee,* wooden twin-screw steamer; USS *Passaic,* monitor; and USS *Philadelphia,* iron side-wheel steamer. Rear Admiral John Adolphus Bernard Dahlgren (1809–70), an expert in naval ordnance, commanded the South Atlantic Blockading Squadron. *ORN,* ser. 2, v. 1:170, 172, 177; *DAB,* 5:29–31.
87. Joseph M. Bradford (1824–72), career naval officer and fleet captain of the South Atlantic Blockading Squadron, 1863–65. *Appletons',* 1:348.
88. Albert Gallatin Browne, Sr.
89. Chase added the nine words from *[Browne]* through this word as an interlineation. "Cooper" refers to the Cooper River. The "raised ram" was a sunken Confederate ironclad being salvaged by the U.S. Navy. Reid, *After the War,* 60; Reid diary, May 11, 1865 (Reid Family Papers, L.C.).
90. Articles addressing Reconstruction appeared in the *New York Herald* each day between May 2 and 8, 1865.
91. Bvt. Brig. Gen. John Porter Hatch (1822–1901), a career soldier in command at Charleston and vicinity. *DAB,* 8:392–93.
92. Nettie Chase was escorted by Maggie Marthell, wife of an army supply officer and evidently a Canadian by birth. Entries for "Friday, May 13," and Sept. 20, 1866, below; Whitelaw Reid diary, May 11, 1865 (Reid Family Papers, L.C.); memorandum book, 1864–69 (Chase Papers, Hist. Soc. of Pa.), 207; Chase to Andrew Johnson, Sept. 22, 1866 (Johnson Papers, L.C.).
93. A racetrack near Charleston had been used during the war as a prison, and an enclosure contained the graves of Northerners who died there. "Sympathizing hands have cleared away the weeds, and placed over the entrance an inscription . . . 'The Martyrs of the Race Course.'" Reid, *After the War,* 69.
94. *Burnt [distt]* probably means "Burnt district." A fire that began accidentally on the night of Dec. 11, 1861, laid waste to 540 acres of Charleston. One postbellum observer considered the ruins "picturesque." Whitelaw Reid's notes of this ride mentioned walkways of the arsenal grounds lined with various types of artillery shells, and two statues, one of John C. Calhoun, the other of William Pitt. Reid diary, May 11, 1865 (Reid Family Papers, L.C.); *New York Times,* Dec. 15, 16, 1861; Thomas Petigru Lesesne, *Landmarks of Charleston . . .* (Richmond, Va., 1932), 93; John Townsend Trowbridge, *The Desolate South 1865–1866 . . .* , ed. Gordon Carroll (Boston, 1956), 274–75.

at Pillsbury's where Browne—company all northern [& official]—Gen Saxton Gen Hatch, Col Gurney &c[95]

JOURNAL XVII

LIBERAL & WISE PLANTER

One an expedition one of our officers brought back the diary of Mr. Gregory of Greenwood, S.C. I saw it on the table of Adml. Dahlgren on board his flagship Charleston Harbor May 13, 1865.[96] I was so struck with some of the remarks that I copied two of them as follows:[97]

"Dec. 20," 1860 "This day at 12½ o'clock this state ceased to be a member of the Union. No other state has as yet left & I fear she will stand alone for some time. Think we were wrong to draw out of the Union—it will be the downfall[98] of slavery."

Nov. 22, 61— "It is my opinion from present appearances that slavery has recd. a blow that it will never recover from. Even if we should be able to conquer our Independence (for we will never obtain it in any other way) the Institution will be so crippled & demoralized that it will never recover."

Other entries in the same book (Gen Hatch told me) state that his slaves were allowed to raise eggs & chickens & that he paid them 1 cent per dozen for the former & 6¼ cents per dozen for the latter—& that one year at Christmas having netted 30.000 from his crop he entered the fact with thanks for the goodness of God & the memo. that he had distributed to his slaves 6¼ cents each cash as a gratuity!

In one case to a very faithful slave in consideration of his excellent conduct & service he paid 18 cents for a dozen of chickens.

---

95. Chase saw John H. Pillsbury, assistant special agent for the U.S. Treasury at Charleston, and Albert Gallatin Browne, Sr. William Gurney (1821–79), soon to be made a brevet brigadier general of volunteers, commanded the post at Charleston. *Register of Officers (1865)*, 66; *Charleston Courier*, May 12, 13, 1865; *Appletons'*, 3:14; Heitman, *Historical Register*, 1:484.

96. According to Journal XV, Chase saw the Gregory diary on May 11 and left Charleston harbor on the night of May 12.

97. Chase also copied the two dated extracts from Gregory's diary on a memorandum page in the rear of Journal XV. The extracts there differ in minor details from the version in Journal XVII. It is uncertain whether Chase copied either version directly from Gregory's diary. Journal XV does not include the additional information from the Gregory diary that follows the extracts in Journal XVII.

98. Chase originally wrote *death blow*, then struck through that phrase and substituted *downfall* above the line. The extract of Gregory's entry in Journal XV has *downfall*.

May 1865   {547}

JOURNAL XV

FRIDAY, MAY 13.[99] Slept at Gen Hatch's—breakfasted with him at Capt. Martels, where Nettie slept—Capt a Prussian / Mrs M—— Canadienne, charming[1]— Several Charleston gent called—John Phillips, lawyer, Col. R. W. Seymour, do. Geo. Williams merct. James Lynah,[2] 71 father in law of Norris of Phila, L. F. Potter, R.I. specr., John S. Ryan do. Isaac E. Holmes,   Macbeth, late Mayor, all anxiou[s] to know policy of govt.[3]—expld. it as far as warranted / Cold. delegation called with address[4]—all free & all able to read & write—education of free blacks never prohibited in Charleston—some of those present quite well instructed—Union League begun—want right to vote— Gen. Gillmore called—also Adml Dahlgren & Capt. Bradford—tried with Gen. Gillmore to reach Fort Wagner in Mr. Getty's boat[5]—too slow & failed—retd. went to cold meeting Zion Church—immense—Maj Delaney speaking—I addressed it[6]—back to Gen Hatch's saw Nettie safe at Mrs M——s—to Col. Gurney's for dinner—Mr. & Mrs Pillsbury, Adl. Dahlgren,

---

99. Chase wrote this entry, which describes Friday, May 12, on the diary page intended for Saturday the 13th. He changed the day of the week in the printed page heading to *Friday*, but left the rest of the heading, including the date, unaltered.

1. Capt. Emil Marthell was chief of the subsistence department and depot commissary at Charleston. He later worked in the New York Custom House. For his wife, see May 11 above. "Official Directory," *Charleston Courier*, May 5, 1865; Heitman, *Historical Register*, 1:691; Chase to Andrew Johnson, Sept. 22, 1866 (Johnson Papers, L.C.).

2. John Phillips (b. ca. 1815); Robert W. Seymour (b. ca. 1805); and wholesale grocer, banker, and businessman George Walton Williams (1820–1903). James Lynah led a group of Charleston residents eager to restore civil government in South Carolina. Simpson et al., *Advice After Appomattox*, 31; *Nat. Cyc.*, 6:494, 47:439; *Who Was Who*, 1:1352; *Charleston Courier*, May 10, 1865; Lillian Adele Kibler, *Benjamin F. Perry: South Carolina Unionist* (Durham, N.C., 1946), 376–77.

3. John S. Ryan assisted charitable activities in Charleston; Isaac Edward Holmes (1796–1867) was an attorney and former congressman; Charles Macbeth (b. ca. 1807) was a lawyer and local politician. *Charleston Courier*, May 22, 1865; *DAB*, 9:165; *New York Times*, May 22, 1865; Chase to Andrew Johnson, May 17, 1865, (Johnson Papers, L.C.), printed in Simpson et al., *Advice After Appomattox*, 26–27.

4. The Charleston free black community, generally supportive of the Confederacy during the Civil War, declared loyalty to the Union at a mass meeting on Mar. 30, 1865, initiating a period of concerted political agitation. Thomas Holt, *Black Over White: Negro Political Leadership in South Carolina during Reconstruction* (Chicago, 1977), 11–15.

5. Charleston dry goods merchant Archibald Getty. *Charleston Courier*, May 3, 1865.

6. Free black physician and antislavery activist Martin Robinson Delany (1812–85) recruited black troops, then went to Charleston in 1865 to serve in the Freedmen's Bureau and as a customs inspector. He and Chase spoke at a large meeting of blacks and whites held in the Zion Church. Chase told the blacks that the elective franchise would come to them most quickly if they were "honest, temperate, industrious and faithful." *DAB*, 5:219–20; *Charleston Courier*, May 13, 1865.

Capts. Bradford & [Pickg][7] et al—to Wayanda—Reid came from printing office—off abt 1[1]

SATURDAY, MAY 12.[8] Left Charleston at 11 last night—past the Glide—Gen Gillmores boat near Sumter[9]—out again on the ocean—all left the deck except Dr. Fuller & myself who sat talking— then I. this morning rose early to see Forts Walker & Beauregard & remember Dupont—passed between them thro' Port Royal Entrance into Port Royal harbor—followed a few miles off by the Glide & a few miles further by a large str. wh. afterwards proved to be the Fort Donelson[10]— Capt Almy sent on board to tender me a salute at 8 & accordingly, at that hour, the yards were manned and the salute fired from every ship in the harbor[11]— All looked beautifully in their colors—the Houghton in signals[12]— Capt Almy came on board with his officers—Capts Belknap, Nichols & others[13]— Gen Gillmore came soon after with his staff—& we went ashore— rode to & thro Mitchellville[14]—fine Magnolia—contented people church—schools—back to Nemeha[15]—waited for party on horseback—to Beaufort—saw Gen. Saxton & Mr. French[16] promised to come up tomorrow

SUNDAY, MAY 14. Breakfasted with Mr. Severance[17]— Ambulance at door at 7.45—called for Gen. Gillmore—on Nemeha at

---

7. Charles Whipple Pickering (1815–88), a career naval officer, commanded the *Vanderbilt*. *Appletons'*, 5:1; *Charleston Courier*, May 13, 1865.
8. This entry describes Saturday, May 13, but Chase wrote it under the heading for Friday the 12th. He altered only the day of the week of the printed heading.
9. Quincy Adams Gillmore had arrived at Charleston on May 12 in the recently launched steamer *William P. Clyde*. *Charleston Courier*, May 13, 1865; Lytle, *Merchant Vessels*, 204.
10. Naval officer Samuel Francis Du Pont (1803–65); USS *Fort Donelson*, en route to duty with the West Gulf Squadron. *DAB*, 5:529–33; *ORN*, ser. 1, v. 12:139, ser. 2, v. 1:85.
11. Career naval officer John Jay Almy (1815–95) spent the war commanding vessels in the blockading squadrons. *DAB*, 1:226–27.
12. USS *Houghton*, sailing bark stationed at Port Royal, S.C. *ORN*, ser. 1, v. 16:327, ser. 2, v. 1:29.
13. George Eugene Belknap (1832–1903), a career officer, commanded the monitor *Canonicus*, and Lt. Smith W. Nichols temporarily commanded the *Passaic*. *DAB*, 2:146–47; *ORN*, ser. 1, v. 16:327, 332.
14. A village of freed slaves named for Gen. Ormsby M. Mitchel. Reid, *After the War*, 89–91.
15. *Nemaha*, a revenue service vessel on station at Port Royal. The *Nemaha* shuttled Chase and his party around the Sea Islands, May 13–15. Chase and his daughter spent Saturday night on shore at Hilton Head and Sunday night at Beaufort. U.S. Department of Transportation, *Record of Movements*, 418; transcript journal of *Nemaha*, May 1865 (Recs. of U.S. Coast Guard, Nat. Arch.).
16. Mansfield French.
17. Theodoric Cordenio Severance.

8—called for Dr. Fuller & rest on Wayanda at Beaufort by 10— Met Gen. Saxton & Mr. French—crossed the river to Ladies' Isld.— Gen. G―― myself Gen Saxton & Mr. Reid in one carriage—Dr. Fuller, Mr French Nettie & others in another &c—through plantations of cotton roads bordered by trees & shrubs, live oak, bayonet palmattos, across a bridge to St Helena—culture still improving—to Church, old—schoolhouse new opposite—between several huge live oaks festooned with moss & underneath these a great crowd of cold. people— Mr. French conducted the services—a cold. minister prayed—Dr. Fuller spoke & I followed[18]—rode afterwds to Saxtonville[19]—then returned—dined Gen S――'s—then to grove near town—immense congregation—Dr. Fuller spoke & I again followed—afterwards the people thronged Dr. Fuller & some of the women broke into the "shout"[20]— All party returned to H―― Head except self & Nettie who remd. at Gen Saxtons

MONDAY, MAY 15. breakfast very pleasant then ride to John Smiths plantation—visited trees where Dr Adams wrote Southside Views[21]—charming spot—pomegranates in blossom—old Spanish Fort—visited Praise House with Miss Botume—then school house where Miss Langford taught[22]—singing—some exercises—back to Beaufort & visited School in Library Building—four rooms, with four schools—remarkable memory—lion & hunter—exercises in Arithmetic—left & went to tax commrs—Negroes getting certifi-

---

18. Fuller and Chase both urged industriousness and expressed confidence in the freed slaves' ability to adapt to their new situation. The assemblage saluted Chase and Fuller, who formerly lived, preached, and owned slaves at St. Helena, with several verses of "Roll, Jordan, Roll." Reid, *After the War*, 99–111.

19. Almost 30,000 freed slaves had settled in the area under Gen. Saxton's authority. Ibid., 117.

20. Whitelaw Reid described the scene: one of the women who rushed toward Fuller "struck up a wild chant, and in a moment half a hundred voices had joined her. She stood ... balancing from one foot to the other in a sort of measured dance, sometimes stopping a moment to shout 'glory.'" The "shout" was a religious practice among Sea Island blacks that involved singing and dancing and invariably provoked a response from white observers. Ibid., 118–21; *The Nation*, v. 4, no. 100 (May 30, 1867): 432–33; Rose, *Rehearsal for Reconstruction*, 90–93.

21. John Smith had owned a plantation on the Sea Islands known as Otaheite. Congregational clergyman Nehemiah Adams (1806–78) wrote *The South-Side View of Slavery; or, Three Months at the South, in 1854* (Boston, 1854), a sympathetic account of slavery that brought Adams notoriety. Elizabeth Hyde Botume, *First Days Amongst the Contrabands* (Boston, 1893), 171; *DAB*, 1:93–94.

22. A Praise House could be any structure used by blacks for religious purposes. Elizabeth Hyde Botume, who kept a journal of her experiences as a teacher of freed blacks, and Fanny S. Langford hailed from Massachusetts. Rose, *Rehearsal for Reconstruction*, 90–91; Botume, *First Days Amongst the Contrabands*; Henry Lee Swint, *The Northern Teacher in the South, 1862–1870* (Nashville, Tenn., 1941), 178, 189.

cates[23]—goodbye back to H—— Head & the Coit[24]—& off for Savannah / Gen Gillmore, Major Gray & Capts. James & Talcott added to our party[25]—all in Gen G——s boat—visited Pulaski[26]—saw effects of bombardment—in wh. Gen Viele seems to have had no share—found Capt. Hale with a company of a N.H. regiment in occupation—salute from fort—3d. R.I. Heavy Art—graves of men & monument—rebel graves by side—reembarked & a few miles above anchored—obstructions—

TUESDAY, MAY 16. Awaked by blowing off steam—found we were close alongside another steamer—suppd we were in Savannah—rose / Mr. Lowell rapped at my Door—"Jeff. Davis is here—he's caught"[27] Soon after Gen. Gillmore rapped—"You can see Jeff Davis if you wish. Any of this party can see him if they want to—" I don't want to see him, unless he expresses a wish to see me. I wouldt let any body see him unless you or myself—wouldnt make a show of him[28]—boat moved on soon after—reached Savannah—went to bkft at Pulaski House rode out to Buonaventura—live oak avenues—Clinch tomb[29]—cemy. private property—rode through town—recd. dep. cold. men—then another[30] / dined on board

23. U.S. tax commissioners were engaged in collecting real estate taxes and issuing certificates of sale for properties with unpaid taxes under legislation passed on Mar. 3, 1865. This act augmented previous legislation on the subject of taxation within insurrectionary districts and made it possible for freedmen to purchase lands formerly under white ownership. *Charleston Courier,* May 20, 1865; *Statutes at Large,* 12:422–26, 640–41, 13:501–4.

24. Steamer *W. W. Coit,* used as a dispatch boat. *OR,* ser. 1, v. 47, pt. 2:202, v. 49, pt. 1:537.

25. John Chipman Gray (1839–1915), Harvard Law School graduate and judge advocate with the rank of major on Gen. Gillmore's staff. Garth Wilkinson James (1845–83), 54th Massachusetts (Colored) Inf., 1863–65, and Edward N. Kirk Talcott (1840–1901), 1st Regt., New York Vol. Engineers, 1862–65, were aides-de-camp to Gen. Gillmore. *DAB,* 7:520–21; Jane Maher, *Biography of Broken Fortunes: Wilkie and Bob, Brothers of William, Henry, and Alice James* (Hamden, Conn., 1986), 1, 52, 163; *Who Was Who,* 1:1214; *OR,* ser. 1, v. 47, pt. 2:792, pt. 3:237.

26. For an account of this visit to Fort Pulaski, see Reid, *After the War,* 131–33.

27. Jefferson Davis had been captured at Irwindale, Ga., on May 10. *DAB,* 5:130.

28. As it is written, part of the text not enclosed in quotation marks could be a rejoinder by Gillmore. Chase's letters confirm, however, that the text beginning *I don't want* and ending *make a show of him* was in fact all part of Chase's comment to Gillmore. Chase to Andrew Johnson, May 17, 1865 (Johnson Papers, L.C.); Chase to Kate Chase Sprague, May 17, 1865 (Chase Papers, Hist. Soc. of Pa.).

29. Bonaventure cemetery contained numerous avenues lined with impressive live oak trees. Duncan Lamont Clinch (1787–1849), soldier and politician, was father-in-law of Gen. Robert Anderson. The Clinch tomb had been vandalized. Writers' Project, Georgia, *Georgia: A Guide to Its Towns and Countryside* (Athens, Ga., 1940), 262; Chase to Kate Chase Sprague, May 17, 1865 (Chase Papers, Hist. Soc. of Pa.); Reid, *After the War,* 138–41; *Nat. Cyc.,* 12:63–64.

30. Chase received one deputation of black citizens from Savannah and another from the interior. He noted that their "chief want is votes." Chase to Kate Chase Sprague, May 17, 1865 (Chase Papers, Hist. Soc. of Pa.); Reid diary, May 16, 1865 (Reid Family Papers, L.C.); Reid, *After the War,* 143–46.

Coit— Visited schools in [Messes] / talked to them—retd.—two deputations of White citizens, 1st Judge Law & others (2d) Mr. Clark & others—talk abt. suffrages &c[31]—boats with rebel prisons[32]— [cheering]—walk in town with Mellen—back—Thompson, (Doesticks)[33] & [Clemet]

WEDNESDAY, MAY 17. Left Savannah this morning for Hilton Head—arrived before 12—went to Hd. Quarters & wrote letters one & paper of suggestions to President[34]—one long letter describing visit to Savannah to Katie[35]—sent Prest. copy of Gillmore's order against rebel Govrs & for wages to black citizens[36]— Mail went to Arago,[37]—Dr. Fuller took leave to go passenger in her to Fortress Monroe— She steamed off abt. 5—watched her receding form half wishing I was on her— We followed after dinner at Hd. Quarters [on] the Coit, Gen. Gillmore & staff again taking charge of us— night on the boat—no incident worth noting

THURSDAY, MAY 18. Off St Johns River bar this morning & soon steaming up it—most beautiful green of trees & grass on shore— save where the latter of sedgy brown—every now & then a porpoise put his snout & back above water & seemed to tumble back again— arrived Jacksonville met Judge Stickney— Went to Gen. Vogde's

31. Members of the first deputation objected to suffrage for blacks and to educating blacks and whites in the same schools. Members of the second, and larger, group expected to resume state government with all former rights and privileges except the power to hold slaves. William Law was a Savannah attorney, judge, and politician. Chase to Kate Chase Sprague, May 17, 1865 (Chase Papers, Hist. Soc. of Pa.); Reid diary, May 16, 1865 (Reid Family Papers, L.C.); Reid, *After the War*, 152–55; Richard Harrison Shryock, ed., *Letters of Richard D. Arnold, M.D., 1808–1876* . . . (Durham, N.C., 1929), 24, 143; I. W. Avery, *The History of the State of Georgia From 1850 to 1881* . . . (New York, 1881), 127; *OR*, ser. 1, v. 47, pt. 3:594–96.

32. On the late afternoon of May 16 a steamer arrived at Savannah with approximately 500 paroled Confederate officers and soldiers. *Savannah Daily Herald*, May 17, 1865.

33. Journalist and humorist Mortimer Neal Thompson or Thomson (1831–75) often wrote under the pseudonym "Q. K. Philander Doesticks, P. B." Preston Wheeler, *American Biographies* (New York, 1940), 1010–11; Reid, *After the War*, 148–49.

34. Chase reported on what and whom he saw in South Carolina and at Savannah. The "Suggestions" which he enclosed concerned trade, the role of military commanders, and the enrollment of citizens in former rebel states. Chase to Andrew Johnson, May 17, 1865 (Johnson Papers, L.C.), in Simpson et al., *Advice After Appomattox*, 26–31.

35. Chase to Kate Chase Sprague, May 17, 1865 (Chase Papers, Hist. Soc. of Pa.).

36. On May 14, Gillmore issued a general order for the Department of the South nullifying actions of the governors of South Carolina, Georgia, and Florida. The order also declared that blacks were U.S. citizens, and "that it is the manifest and binding duty of all citizens, whites as well as blacks, to make such arrangements and agreements among themselves for compensated labor as shall be mutually advantageous to all parties." *OR*, ser. 1, v. 47, pt. 3:498–99.

37. An ocean steamer which had been brought into official service during the war. *OR*, ser. 1, v. 47, pt. 1:1001, pt. 2:525, pt. 3:202; Chase to Kate Chase Sprague, May 17, 1865 (Chase Papers, Hist. Soc. of Pa.).

Head quarters[38]—mentioned to him swearing negro-child Mayor—
said he doubted abt. such things—a pleasant, fat, short, darkfaced
man— Gen Gillmore & I walked abt. town—old trees & many—
mostly water oaks—colored troops on duty—white troops also in
town—Col. Tilghman 3 U.S. C I[39]—drunken Captn. Navy, from
Zanesville / tea at Hd. Qrs— Yulee called[40]—Gen. G—— showed
him recent order— Y—— seemed disappd—said he had been appointed one of several Commrs to visit Wash. & confer with President—told him President wd. not recognize officials of rebel
origin—wanted forced labor & reorganization left to whites—mentd
reasons to contrary—slept on Coit—

FRIDAY, MAY 19. Left Jacksonville a little before 8 so as to have
tide over bar at mouth of St. Johns—no incident going down the
river—no alligators—hardly a porpoise—reach St. Augustine bar
near two—lay off and off waiting for pilot & watching the penguins[41]—pilot came at length—row boat creeping down beach—
signalled us—we followed in shore & pilot came on board—"how
long" said I visiting pilot house have you been pilot"— "Since
change of flag"—& flag was changed in 1821[42]— In a few moments
St Augustine showed itself a multitude of penguins ranked on
shore[43]—hidden behind a green little peninsula, with long sea-
wall built by kind Uncle Sam—and old Spanish fort; a plaza—two
churches fronting upon it—a monument inscribed Plaza de la Constitution"— We visited Fort & ancient dungeon—old gateway where
Oglethorpe cd. not pass.[44] Hay's Orange Grove[45]—Demars place

38. Israel Vogdes (1816–89), a career army officer, commanded the District of
Florida with headquarters at Jacksonville. *Appletons'*, 6:304–5; Heitman, *Historical
Register*, 1:988; *OR*, ser. 1, v. 53:109, ser. 2, v. 8:658.
39. Benjamin Chew Tilghman (1821–1901), an inventor, received command of
the 3rd U.S. Colored Infantry in July 1863. *Nat. Cyc.*, 15:263–64; Heitman, *Historical
Register*, 1:961; *OR*, ser. 1, v. 47, pt. 1:167, ser. 2, v. 8:563, 634–35.
40. David Levy Yulee (1810–86), Southern railroad promoter and former U.S.
senator from Florida, had been taken into federal custody and was imprisoned in
June 1865 at Fort Pulaski, Ga. *DAB*, 20:638; *OR*, ser. 2, v. 8:658.
41. Twice in this entry Chase wrote *penguins*, but he surely meant pelicans. On
the previous day, Whitelaw Reid noted "Pelicans & swans that we do see, & alligators
that we do *not* see." Reid diary, May 18, 1865 (Reid Family Papers, L.C.).
42. Spain formally relinquished control of Florida to the U.S. in 1821. Charlton
W. Tebeau, *A History of Florida* (Coral Gables, Fla., 1971), 114.
43. Chase wrote the phrase *a multitude . . . on shore*— as an interlineation. Its
location within the sentence is conjectural.
44. James Edward Oglethorpe (1696–1785), founder and governor of the Georgia
colony, led troops against St. Augustine, the capital of Spanish Florida, in 1740 and
1743. Both invasions failed after reaching the gate of the city. *DAB*, 14:1–3; Thaddeus
Mason Harris, *Biographical Memorials of James Oglethorpe . . .* (Boston, 1841), 221–42,
271–73; Phinizy Spalding, *Oglethorpe in America* (Chicago, 1977), 110–26.
45. John Milton Hay (1838–1905), one of Abraham Lincoln's private secretaries,

May 1865   {553}

Frenchman of 73— Olivary & bot basket &c / cemetery of Florida War soldiers[46]—most interesting day—nap after dinner—talk after nap with Gen. G—— & others—retd. at 11:30

SATURDAY, MAY 20. Left St Augustine early—crossed bar abt 5—reached Fernandina at 10.45—left soon after for Dungeness[47]— Mayor Mot[48] & Mr. Kenney on board—wrote Katie, Miss Walker & President while running over[49]— Mr. Reid copied letter to President—wrote Mr. Stanton, conviction that much discontent will exist & voting of blacks essential to pacification—Gen Gillmore best & ablest & most in sympathy with policy you & I have advocated[50]— went over Dungeness a magnificent estabt. in ruin & disorder— every variety of flower & fruit & tree live oaks, water oaks, locusts, orange trees, olive trees, cherry trees, wild olives, oleanders, mimosas, pomegranates, and as many more—stately avenues, agreeable walks, a spring house, a clear spring / I was told the whole place can now be bot for $10.000 & authd. Judge Stickney to make purchase[51]—retd. to Coit & back to Fernandina—final talk with Gen G—— who says he will issue order sanctg. Fena. election & direct similar elections in Charleston & elsewhere / bid all goodbye—to Wayanda & off—brilliant sunset—

---

bought Florida property on speculation in 1864 at a tax sale. *DAB*, 8:430–36; Reid, *After the War*, 171–72; William Roscoe Thayer, *The Life of John Hay* (Boston, 1908), 1:271.
    46. Chase refers to battles in 1565 incident to the founding of St. Augustine. Tebeau, *History of Florida*, 34–35; Reid diary, May 18, 1865 (Reid Family Papers, L.C.); Reid, *After the War*, 171.
    47. An island ceded by the state of Georgia to Gen. Nathanael Greene for his military services during the Revolutionary War. Reid, *After the War*, 174–77.
    48. Adolphus Mot.
    49. To his daughter Kate, Chase reported on his visits to Jacksonville, St. Augustine, and Fernandina. Chase's letter to Andrew Johnson was dated Fernandina, May 21, although it seems most likely that he wrote Johnson on the 20th. Chase described for Johnson the form of self-government of blacks at Hilton Head, the widespread formation of Union Leagues, and the participation by blacks in local elections at Fernandina. Chase to Kate Chase Sprague, May 20, 1865 (Chase Papers, Hist. Soc. of Pa.); Chase to Andrew Johnson, May 21, 1865 (Johnson Papers, L.C.), in Simpson et al., *Advice After Appomattox*, 34–35. The copy made by Whitelaw Reid was also dated May 21 (Chase Papers, Cinc. Hist. Soc.).
    50. Chase wrote to Stanton that Southern whites would not resist universal suffrage if the policy "is clearly announced, & firmly but kindly pursued." He also praised Generals Gillmore and Saxton. Chase to E. M. Stanton, May 20, 1865 (Stanton Papers, L.C.).
    51. Stickney's indictment for frauds about this date probably aborted Chase's plan to purchase the property. Jerrell H. Shofner, *Nor Is It Over Yet: Florida in the Era of Reconstruction, 1863–1871* (Gainesville, Fla., 1974), 15; William Watson Davis, *The Civil War and Reconstruction in Florida* (New York, 1913), 352, 528

SUNDAY, MAY 21. Last night water all ablaze in ships wake & at her sides—porpoises sporting & leaving luminous tracks—sparkles[52]—retd at nine—did not rise this morning till after 7—fellow passengers all seasick save self Mr. Lowell & Mr Stickney—W. P. M.[53] tried to bkfast but retired discomfited—very quiet on board—read "St Paul" by Mr. Butler[54]—about half past twelve all alarmed by ship striking on shoal—two three pretty severe thumps & water dashed over side this about 20 m. above Cape Carnaveral / (2) read Stickneys History of Florida to End of DeSoto—(1) worked off shoal soon & steamed north & then east outside of shoals[55]—dinner at 5— Only three besides Captain at table—dolphin caught—changing hues—read Butler on St Paul—Sainte Bible—Nettie sick all day but not quite so sick as yesterday—

MONDAY, MAY 22. Passed Jupiter Inlet Light 7.30—very clear & pleasant—but Mr. Mellen unwell— Nettie still somewhat seasick—Steamer wh. followed us all the morning passed abt. noon—side wheel supposed the Bibb[56]—about 5 hailed by Tug from Beaufort with despatches—out of coal—had met high wind day before—could not supply her but took officer on board with despatches—abt. 6 passed [Cape] Florida well out at sea—at 8 made Carys fort Light—grounding yesterday has destroyed confidence in pilot & made us all anxious—happily the weather was all that cd. be desired and we went on quite pleasantly—hope to be at Key West tomorrow at 11.

TUESDAY, MAY 23. Expectation to reach KW at 11, seen not be fulfilled on coming on deck this morning—we had drifted out into the Gulf Stream—but steering West we made Sombrero light about 9.45—the weather, though warm was still delightful & Nettie nearly well— Abt. 6 we came in sight of Sand Key Light House—and at dusk this Light & the Key West Light were both visible— Our pilot was of little or no account & the Cap. undertook the conduct of the ship—having before dark displayed signal for pilot—none coming Capt. determined to cast anchor & wait till morning—but schooner which had been seen bearing down for us now flashed [their] light & soon after pilot came from her—we went on safely to our an-

---

52. Whitelaw Reid also made note of "the playful porpoises in the phosphorescent gleam of the water." See also May 30, 1865, below. Reid diary, May 21, 31, 1865 (Reid Family Papers, L.C.).
53. William P. Mellen.
54. Clement Moore Butler, *St. Paul in Rome: Lectures Delivered in the Legation of the United States of America, in Rome* (Philadelphia, 1865).
55. Chase inserted the (2) and (1) above the line, apparently to indicate the order in which the events actually occurred.
56. Possibly a U.S. Coast Survey steamer. *ORN*, ser. 1, v. 16:295–96.

chorage which we reached at 9—not much incln. to go ashore & cd. not if we had, for obliged to wait visit from Health Officers in morning

WEDNESDAY, MAY 24. Capt Handy of Dale, with Engineer Tarton & Paymaster Harris called[57]—also several citizens Mrs Plantz—Mr. Patterson, and others[58]—took carriages & rode over island—vegetation peculiar—cocoa trees—palm trees &c—visited Sandy[59]—farm or orchard or garden of 19 acres—formerly slave—bot himself at Tallahassee [$]3000—sold notwithstanding—cut himself desperately fingers, muscles above ancle, side &[,] declared wd. open abdomen if made a slave again—unmolested after that—saved [money] was held as slave by Baldwin but with understanding that he was free & owner of his gettings / is now in 73d. year—has all sorts of trees & fruits—is man of property—has advanced [$]1500 to church / visited Officers Hd. Qrs.—admirable rooms—fort Taylor salute[60]— Harris (Gen) & McCullough, Prof. taken yesterday & confined[61]—dined at Mr. Plantzs—very pleasant—wrote letters Prest. & Katie to be mailed at Havana[62]— Gen. Newton well spoken of by Mr. P—— absent but will return by Sunday.[63] Went aboard—stopping at shell store—off about 9 [P]M

57. Robert Handy commanded the ordnance ship USS *Dale*, stationed at Key West. Jeremiah George Harris (1809–c. 1895) was a Navy disbursing officer. *ORN*, ser. 1, v. 17:430, 844, ser. 2, v. 1:71; Graf et al., *Papers of Andrew Johnson*, 1:28, 8:205–6.

58. Alexander Patterson, a Key West merchant, politician, and Unionist. Jefferson B. Browne, *Key West: The Old and The New* (St. Augustine, 1912; reprint, Gainesville, Fla., 1973), 12, 27, 36, 214–15, 221; *ORN*, ser. 1, v. 16:767.

59. Sandy Cornish operated "the best fruit grove and garden on the island" and assisted in the establishment of the local African Methodist church. Whitelaw Reid's account of Sandy, which includes a picture, differed from Chase's sketch in some details. Sandy's owner probably was John P. Baldwin, a Key West businessman and Democratic politician with Southern sympathies. Browne, *Key West*, 12, 53, 90, 172, 217, 223; Reid, *After the War*, 183–85; Chase to Kate Chase Sprague, May 24, 1865 (Chase Papers, Hist. Soc. of Pa.); Reid diary, May 24, 1865 (Reid Family Papers, L.C.).

60. Reid noted: "Visit to Fort at Key West, tremendous salute thundering out as we cross the moat." Reid diary, May 24, 1865 (Reid Family Papers, L.C.).

61. The prisoners were Thomas Alexander Harris (1826–95), a brigadier general in the Missouri State Guard and former Confederate congressman, and Prof. R. S. McCulloh, a Confederate agent authorized to capture or destroy U.S. military property. McCulloh allegedly concocted a combustible material to carry out his designs. Harris was soon paroled, but McCulloh remained imprisoned until paroled in Mar. 1866. Wakelyn, *Biographical Dictionary of the Confederacy*, 218–19; *OR*, ser. 2, v. 8:566–68, 816, 850, 893, ser. 4, v. 3:37–38, 1079.

62. Chase's letter to President Johnson, which he dated May 23, recommended the use of commissions to grant amnesty and commented on the army's commanders in Florida. His letter to his daughter described the voyage from Fernandina to Key West and gave Chase's impressions of Sandy Cornish. Chase to Andrew Johnson, May 23, 1865 (Johnson Papers, L.C.), in Simpson et al., *Advice After Appomattox*, 36–37; Chase to Kate Chase Sprague, May 24, 1865 (Chase Papers, Hist. Soc. of Pa.).

63. John Newton (1823–95), a career officer and engineer in command of West Florida. *DAB*, 13:473–74.

THURSDAY, MAY 25. When I came on deck found ourselves in sight of Cuban Coast, about 7 AM. Abt 11 passed in between Moro Castle & Fort Cabañas, a narrow entrance[64]— Castle not so formidable as new fort at New York— Health Officer—passed "Carmen"[65]—anchored / Havana beautiful from water—officer came on board—hard to understand either the other— American flag at consulate—one over vessel—boats alongside—pineapples—cigars &c— Capt to consuls— Consul Minor & Vice Consul Savage came on board[66]—arranged to go on shore to Mrs Almy's Hotel—found every thing quite agreeable / Rev. Mr. McLain & Miss McLain from Washn.— Cigars & compts fr W. H. Watts, New York[67]—ride with Nettie & Mr. Savage—Plaza de Armas—Cap. Genls country Villa[68] / ladies & Volantes—Mr. S—— concerned for Nettie's dress[69]—the Cerro—Puentes Grandes—Marianao—church[70]—return to Hotel—magnif. palms P. de Armes—cocoas— Capt de

---

64. The Castillo de los tres Santos Reyes del Morro and the Fortress of San Carlos de la Cabaña, at the entrance to Havana's harbor. Samuel Hazard, *Cuba with Pen and Pencil* (Hartford, 1871), 31, 72–74, 239–48.

65. Described elsewhere by Chase as "the Spanish flagship Carmen." Chase to Kate Chase Sprague, May 29, 1865 (Chase Papers, Hist. Soc. of Pa.).

66. William Thomas Minor (1815–89), former governor of Connecticut, was U.S. consul general at Havana, 1864–67. The vice consul was Thomas Savage, born in Cuba of American parents. *Appletons'*, 4:337; *Catalogue of Officers and Graduates of Yale University*, 166; *OR*, ser. 1, v. 50, pt. 2:904–6; *Register of Officers (1863)*, 2; A. G. Riddle to Chase, Jan. 26, 1864 (Chase Papers, Hist. Soc. of Pa.).

67. Mrs. Almy's establishment was on the Plaza de San Francisco. Theodore Parker and Samuel Gridley Howe were among its guests before the Civil War. Chase described the hotel in a letter to his daughter Kate, May 29, 1865 (Chase Papers, Hist. Soc. of Pa.). The Rev. William McLain was a traveling agent for the American Colonization Society. Watts may have been W. H. Watts, a New York City tool dealer, or William Watts, a provisions merchant. Hazard, *Cuba with Pen and Pencil*, 43–44; Richard Henry Dana, *To Cuba and Back. A Vacation Voyage* (Boston, 1859), 45–46; *Wash. Dir. (1865)*, 274; P. J. Staudenraus, *The African Colonization Movement, 1816–1865* (New York, 1961), 239–40; *New York Dir. (1864)*, 905, commercial register p. 53.

68. The Plaza de Armas was a public square in front of the governor's palace. The governor's summer residence (or *Quinta*) was situated among elaborate gardens out the Paseo Tacon from the older part of the city. Maturin M. Ballou, *History of Cuba; or, Notes of a Traveller in the Tropics* (Boston, 1854), 84–85; Dana, *To Cuba and Back*, 36, 48–49; Hazard, *Cuba with Pen and Pencil*, 138–41.

69. A *volante* was a vehicle with two large wheels, driven by a rider mounted astride one of the horses. Savage thought that Janet Chase, dressed in a "black spencer & little cap," might feel out of place among the elaborately dressed women taking drives along the *paseo*. Nettie "declined to have our course changed." Chase to Kate Chase Sprague, May 29, 1865 (Chase Papers, Hist. Soc. of Pa.); Ballou, *History of Cuba*, 131–32; Dana, *To Cuba and Back*, 34, 48.

70. El Cerro ("The Hill") was a street where many fashionable residences were located. Puentes Grandes and Marianao were villages near Havana. The church which Chase noted was at Marianao. Chase to Kate Chase Sprague, May 29, 1865 (Chase Papers, Hist. Soc. of Pa.); Hazard, *Cuba with Pen and Pencil*, 142–43, 260–63.

May 1865 {557}

Bernade of Carmen called[71]—will take me to Stonewall at 9[72]— Marshall[73] had adventure with [*illeg.*] men

FRIDAY, MAY 26. Nettie off shopping early with Mr. Reid & Judge Stickney— Capt. M.———[74] & I went to shears—found Capt B & boat / pulled to Stonewall—introduced to officers on board— exd. boat[75]—2 turrets fore & aft—2 guns fore 72s—1 aft 300 Armstrong[76]—each foregun two portholes looking forwd. & after— aft gun 3—astern, & port & starbd. / plating of turrets $3\frac{1}{3}$ inc.— porthole [doors]—ram long but heavy for ship—slowed to 2 miles to use it—engine very good—ship not formidable—retd. to hotel after thanking officers, Capt B landing us near hotel— At 12 went with Consul Miner & V.C. Savage to pay respects to Capt. Gen Dulce at palace or villa in country recd. cordially talk abt. Stonewall[77]—false rept. of her getting out—Tassara states wishes of Amn. govt. wh. exceeded— Capt Gen favor Emann. but also impn of coolies[78] / Mr. Lowell bot umbrella & hdkfs for me—rode with Nettie & Mr. Reid—bot photographs— Consul & V.C. called—also two Havana gentlemen[79]—invited Mr. Savage to accompany us to Matanzas & he ac[c]d. Consul consenting—train starts at 6—so says clerk

---

71. José Polo de Bernabé (1821–95), a Spanish naval officer. In 1872–74, holding the rank of rear admiral, he was Spain's minister to the United States. Memorandum book, 1864–69 (Chase Papers, Hist. Soc. of Pa.); *Enciclopedia Universal*, 46:66.

72. The Confederate ironclad ram *Stonewall* entered Havana harbor in need of engine repairs on May 11, and was surrendered to the Spanish government on May 19. *ORN*, ser. 1, v. 3:747–48, 17:850, ser. 2, v. 1:267; *OR*, ser. 1, v. 49, pt. 2:756.

73. Probably Chase's servant.

74. Merryman.

75. That is, "examined boat."

76. English inventor Sir William George Armstrong (1810–1900) developed the advanced Armstrong rifled cannons. The *Stonewall* battery consisted of three Armstrong rifles—one 300 pounder and two 150 pounders. *DNB*, 22:62–70; *ORN*, ser. 2, v. 1:267.

77. Domingo Dulce y Garay (1808–69), a Spanish soldier, became captain general (governor) of Cuba in Dec. 1862. Calcagno, *Diccionario Biografico Cubano*, 248–51.

78. *Emann.* means "emancipation," *impn* is "importation." The captain general "expressed the belief that Coolie labor would be gradually substituted for slave labor, and that slavery itself would come to an end in Cuba within ten years." As captain general, Dulce had attempted to curtail the slave trade to Cuba, and with the close of the American Civil War there were various suggestions for the abolition of black slavery on the island. Chinese workers had been imported since 1847 on a contract labor basis that, especially in its early years, was similar to outright slavery. Reid, *After the War*, 589; Arthur F. Corwin, *Spain and the Abolition of Slavery in Cuba, 1817–1886* (Austin, Tex., 1967), 109–11, 133–34, 137–38, 147–51, 184; Calcagno, *Diccionario Biografico Cubano*, 249.

79. Whitelaw Reid's diary indicates that these men may have been named Mutterfeldt and Barnes. Reid diary, May 26, 1865 (Reid Family Papers, L.C.).

JOURNAL XVII

MAY 26.[80] Left Guiness at 11.30—fare 350 each for for 37 miles—small knobs one or two miles to right—royal palms every where—country rich, rolling—cultivated—no rain for week or more & fields parched—handsome walls of limestone, waterworn—on left two or three miles a brook & shrubbery reminder of New England—Mr. Savage reads from El Siglo paragraph abt. New York speculations concerning my visit to the South[81]—reached Matanzas about 2—volantes to hotel—

We were called this morning at Havana at 4—coffee & roll—Mr. Savage came at 5—Nettie had lost her keys—[cord] put in requisition—reach depot at 5.40 having been informed that cars left [ab] at 6 & meaning to be in good time—but Express had gone already at 5.30—took accommodation at 5.45 rather than return to hotel—this train stops at Guiness at 8 whence another at 11.30 takes passengers to Matanzas—road goes through beautiful grounds of Captain General then through beautiful Scenery—royal palms, mango trees, cocoa & other tropical growths abound—at 12.25 Mr. Savage seated just in front of me is quietly reading El Siglo—Nettie, just in front of him, quite upright, looks pensive or vacant, Mellens Sen. & Jr. on next back to back with Nettie—Mr. Reid on opposite side Mr. Lowell behind me—all quiet— I looking at the sugar estates—with cane just in its first vigor—looking also at the scenery around & thinking how beautiful—

JOURNAL XV

SATURDAY, MAY 27. [Mr.] S—— came—coffee & rolls—to cars—fd. express train gone—misinformed as to hour, 5.30 vice 6—took accomn. at 5.45 for wh. just in time—passed Cerro—all the trees of the island on [routed]—royal palms & cocoas most conspicuous—sugar plantations— Guiness breakfast— American Engineers[82]—Nettie bot artifl. bird— Savage, Reid & self walked into town—plaza church—long street—dwellings & shops—returned to depot—naked baby—cars 11.30— Matanzas abt 1.15—2 volantes to hotel & 1 carriage—Nettie & I in one— El Leon de Oro[83]—below billiards

---

80. So dated by Chase, but this entry describes May 27.

81. The Havana newspaper *El Siglo* reported a rumor that the object of Chase's Southern journey was to build political alliances in anticipation of a run for the presidency in 1868. *El Siglo*, May 27, 1865.

82. Whitelaw Reid noted the presence of a "Yankee engineer," but provided no additional information. Reid diary, May 27, 1865 (Reid Family Papers, L.C.).

83. "The Golden Lion," considered by many travelers to be the best hotel in Cuba. There was, as Chase noted, a café for local people on the lower floor. Hazard, *Cuba with Pen and Pencil*, 272–76; Richard Davey, *Cuba Past and Present* (New York, 1898), 152–57.

May 1865 {559}

& coffee house—long flight of stairs—hotel for strangers on 2 floor—sitting room—2 rugs—6 chrs on each side[84] / Netties room on right—mine on left of it—Mr Hall called[85]—arranged drive to valley of Yumuri—Victoria[86] / old negress—& negro—magnif. prospects—Mr. Hall & I, Nettie Mr. Savage volantes—negro driver— white jacket &c shoes & spurs—returning brot boquet & fireflies fr. Victoria / Mr. Jenckes called—father at Concepcion—Dr. his brother also called[87]—arranged visit to Cave tomorrow invited Capt M—— Lt Mitchell & Lt Bailey[88]

SUNDAY, MAY 28. Went to the Cueva de Bellamar—6 volantes I with Mrs Hall—Mr. Hall with Nettie—Messrs Savage, Mellen, Mellen Jr., Lowell, Reid, Capt Merryman, Lts Mitchell & Bailey— vast Entrance Hall, Chapel of Virgin, Bishop's Chapel, stalactites, stalagmites, every variety of form— Mr. Martinez the proprietor gave me, Nettie & Mr. Savage specimens[89]—returned to El Leon de Or—bkft— Mr. Sanchez, Engineer, a Mexican called— Read & napped—telegram from Mr. Jenckes who recd. son's advice too late for train—wrote him note—Alcalde Jenckes & his bro. in law Dr.   sent their carriages[90] / Mr. Reid with Mrs Hall & Nettie, & Mr. Savage & I rode round Plaza de Armes & through the drive to the landing—where Wayanda's boat met us & we all went on board— There Mr. [H] Mrs Hall & Miss Goddard & Mr. Savage took

84. This sitting room is also briefly described in Hazard, *Cuba with Pen and Pencil,* 276. The arrangement of rocking chairs in two facing rows was the custom in Cuba. Dana, *To Cuba and Back,* 49–50; Henry Ashworth, *A Tour in the United States, Cuba, and Canada* (London, 1861), 50; Eliza McHatton-Ripley, *From Flag to Flag: A Woman's Adventures and Experiences in the South during the War, in Mexico, and in Cuba* (New York, 1889), 136–37.
85. Henry Cook Hall, U.S. consul at Matanzas. *Register of Officers (1865),* 5; *Nat. Cyc.,* 5:551; A. G. Riddle to Chase, Jan. 26, Feb. 26, 1864, and Chase to W. S. Jenckes, Mar. 11, 1864 (Chase Papers, Hist. Soc. of Pa.).
86. La Victoria, a sugar estate often visited by tourists along the route of a scenic drive from Matanzas to an overlook of the valley of the Yumurí. Dana, *To Cuba and Back,* 163–64; Hazard, *Cuba with Pen and Pencil,* 292–94; Whitelaw Reid diary, May 27, 1865 (Reid Family Papers, L.C.).
87. The Jenckes (or Jencks or Jenkes) family owned La Victoria, and at least one family member was also a merchant. The senior Jenckes, who was away from Matanzas at this time and with whom Chase exchanged messages on May 28 (below), was apparently William Scott Jenckes. He corresponded with Chase in 1864 recommending Hall's appointment as consul. The doctor, Dr. Santo, was actually the brother-in-law of the younger Jenckes. Chase to William Scott Jenckes, Mar. 11, 1864 (Chase Papers, Hist. Soc. of Pa.); Dana, *To Cuba and Back,* 163–64; Hazard, *Cuba with Pen and Pencil,* 292, 293; Whitelaw Reid diary, May 28, 1865 (Reid Family Papers, L.C.).
88. James H. Merryman and 2nd Lts. John C. Mitchell and George W. Bailey of the Revenue Cutter Service. *Register of Officers (1865),* 68, 69.
89. The cave (*cueva*) of Bellamar, much visited by travelers, was described by Hazard in *Cuba with Pen and Pencil,* 288–92. According to Whitelaw Reid, the cave's proprietor was originally from Majorca. Reid diary, May 28, 1865 (Reid Family Papers, L.C.).
90. Dr. Santo. *Alcalde* is usually translated as "mayor."

leave— Mrs H, a charming & intelligent & very patriotic young woman— Mr. Savage & Mr. Hall seem excellent officers—sailed 7.20 coasted along shore a few miles—set our course N.N.W & bid good bye to Cuba—new moon—clear bright & pleasant but a considerable sea & Nettie somewhat sick

MONDAY, MAY 29. Came on deck about 6.30—Key West light house in sight— Keys scattered here & there—green spots or with scattered trees—came to wharf about 8.30—Mr. Plantz there— Adml. Stribling called[91]— P invited self, Nettie, Mellen, Reid & Stickney to bkft—accepted—Mrs P—— & little Sybel greeted us cordially—(Net & I to house in wagon with negro driver as nina bonita between us[92]—) nice bkft Capital Steak &c— Judge Boynton, who impresses me very favorably called—also Mr. Howe, Collector, excellent man[93]— Mr. Allen, Clerk[94]— Col comg. at Fort & Maj. called to ask advice as to disposal of Prof. McCullough & Gen. Harris, arrested a few days ago & implicated in plot to burn northern cities[95]—said Govt. must direct but believed it wd. approve the sending of them north imy— Sandy Cornish came—captd by P & R[96]—& told his story wh. P. phonographed & R. wrote out—lunch—Dr. Sweet & Mrs S. called[97]—thanked Dr. for kindness—he took Nettie to see his Australian parroquets—promised parrot / gave direction to Wakefield[98]— Judge B. Mr Stickney, Dr. Sweet & Mr. Allen took leave—Col Potter on fr shore—abt. 8 miles out got fast aground 7

---

91. Acting Rear Adm. Cornelius Kinchiloe Stribling (1796–1880) commanded the East Gulf Blockading Squadron Feb.–July 1865, with headquarters at Key West. *Appletons'*, 5:718–19; *ORN*, ser. 1, v. 17:853–54.

92. *Niña bonita* means "pretty girl" in Spanish: perhaps a reference to a Cuban *volante*, in which three women often sat on the one seat, "the youngest and prettiest always between and a little in front of the other two." *Rambles in Cuba* (New York, 1870), 12; Ashworth, *A Tour*, 50.

93. Thomas Jefferson Boynton, originally of Missouri, became a federal judge at Key West in 1863. Charles Howe, Key West businessman and collector of customs, 1861–69, had resided in Florida at least since the 1830s. Browne, *Key West*, 13, 65, 113, 210, 211, 223; Walter C. Maloney, *A Sketch of the History of Key West, Florida*, ed. Thelma Peters (1876; reprint, Gainesville, Fla., 1968), xii–xiii.

94. Either William S. Allen (1823–91), businessman and politician who came to Key West in 1862, or his brother, George D. Allen, likewise active in Key West business and civic concerns and noted locally for idiosyncratic mannerisms. Both men served terms as clerk of the U.S. court. Browne, *Key West*, 176–77, 211, 221, 224–25.

95. R. S. McCulloh and Thomas Alexander Harris.

96. That is, Cornish was "captured" by Homer Plantz and Whitelaw Reid.

97. George J. Sweet of the U.S. Marine Hospital Service and his wife Emma Johnson, who was a member of a Key West family. Browne, *Key West*, 192–93; *Register of Officers (1865)*, 70.

98. Wakefield, R.I., near the estate which William and Kate Chase Sprague were developing at Narragansett Pier (see July 6, 1865, below).

foot water—tug alongside sunset 6.35—sun dropt down very rapidly—clear but misty

TUESDAY, MAY 30. We lay aground till near twelve—the tug alongside—I reading—at last we moved—scraping the bottom—I came on deck—we were afloat moving cautiously a lantern placed by one of our officers off the port bow—all at once we went hard aground again—the lines which fastened the tug gave way—snapping like twine one after another & starting the bulwark forward— the tug then fell astern & came up on portside & acted in some sort as guide—a few moments after we passed the light on the starboard sight—the man at the lead sung out 11 feet, twelve feet, 3 fathoms— & the Captain of the tug hailed you are all right our Capt gave him a thousand thanks—got his name Capt _____ & soon our course was set N.N. West for Mobile / I went below & to sleep—bef 12.30— bkft this mg at 8.30—about 1 caught a skipjack—saw school of porpoises—and my first flying fish—½ p 4 large school of porpoises 20 or 30—backfin, 2 side fins—[leaping] running diving most fantastically. Reid asleep—sat on deck till 11 talking—looking at phosforescence &c

WEDNESDAY, MAY 31. Another beautiful day—cool & delightful air—coffee & cracker on rising—bkft ½ past eight—clothing distributed to sailors—some not liking to take it—not the best state of feeling among officers or men—at noon lunched sapotes or sapodillos, oranges, cracker & cheese—looked into navigation a little—read Bermuda case[99]—men caught a fish wh. turned out old rag—dined—quite an *embarras de richesses*—chickens—ham—excellent sweet potatoes, baked & fried—Irish do—claret—bread—looked at "Kedge Anchor"[1]—very useful to one ignorant of navigation & sea terms—must get it—coffee half hour after dinner wh. abt. 5 as usual—our rule, officers breakft 7—we 8—offrs. dine 3 we 5—after coffee read Macaulay's Warren Hastings, lying, on boat cushions till dark[2]—talk with Reid & Mellen abt. Science & preachers—till near ten—then turned in— Nettie very well today except some headache in morning—on deck all the time—every body very quiet—made abt 7 miles an hour— So ends May—thanks for health & opportunities

---

99. *The Bermuda*, 2 Wall. 514 (1866), a set of three related cases involving the capture of the steamer *Bermuda* for blockade violation, was argued before the Supreme Court in Jan. 1866. Minutes, Jan. 8–9, 1866 (Recs. of Supreme Court, Nat. Arch.).

1. William N. Brady, *The Kedge-Anchor; or, Young Sailors' Assistant*, 2nd ed. (New York, 1847).

2. Thomas Babington Macaulay, *Warren Hastings* (London, 1852).

THURSDAY, JUNE 1. Another month begins—thoughts evil & not repelled—why do I allow this—dressed & shaved—on deck abt. 8— lovely morning—abt. 60 miles fr Mobile Point—90 fr City—bkft— read Russells account of his visit to Monty. Mobile 1861—Quantum mutata![3] Ate a couple of oranges & drank glass of claret punch for lunch— At 2.30 Mr. Hill from aloft sang out—Land ho! Capt. M—— respd. "Whereaway"[.] "Off Starboard bow Sir!" Nettie made sketch of Capt asleep—every thing very quiet almost dreamy—sun hot but pleasant breeze & air delightful—two sails in sight at 2— Abt. 1 smoke or waterspout, Capt says "smoke" Mr. Hill "spout"— Abt same time caught Spanish Mackerel—pretty soon caught another fish nondescript—another Sp. Mackl.—dinner on do.—came in sight of Dauphin Island—of Fort Gaines—of Fort Morgan—took pilot on board—crossed bar—passed fleet—Lackawanna flagship Capt Emmons[4] / kept on up bay wh wide & beautiful—proposed to anchor 8 or 10 miles out as we cd. not go to town—pilot thought 5 miles better & anchd. accy.

FRIDAY, JUNE 2. Under way early—but soon got aground— Capt went ashore in gig, four or five miles—we waited in broiling sun— took refuge below—abt. 12 boat came down with Gen. Gordon Granger, & several members of his staff—Mr. Dexter & Mr. Kellogg Treasury Agents[5]— Gen. T. Kilby Smith—who says he is appd. to commd. in Mobile— Nettie disinclined to go to town acct. of heat & I at first same mind—but officers insisted & we went—found change fr Waya to officers boat delightful—brisk breeze from land— passed up in sight of Spanish Fort & Fort Blakeley—between batteries Gladden &   through the obstructions by the floating batteries wh. wd. not float & were sunk & made part of stationed defences—rooms at Battle House windows shattered by great expln. on 25—more than a hundred lives lost & vast amt. propy[6]— Mad. Le Vert called—invited us to dinner—accd., This lady formerly op-

---

3. That is, "how much they have changed." For Russell's *Pictures of Southern Life*, see May 10, 1865, above.

4. George Foster Emmons (1811–84) commanded a division of the West Gulf Blockading Squadron from the *Lackawanna*, a screw steamer. *DAB*, 6:149–50; *ORN*, ser. 1, v. 22:213, ser. 2, v. 1:123.

5. Granger commanded Union forces that captured Mobile in Apr. 1865. T. C. A. Dexter was supervising special agent at Mobile. Francis William Kellogg (1810– c. 1879), Republican congressman from Michigan, 1859–65, became collector of internal revenue at Mobile in 1865. *DAB*, 7:484; *Appletons'*, 3:505; *Bio. Dir. U.S. Cong.*, 1294–95; *Register of Officers (1865)*, 62, 66.

6. The main U.S. ordnance depot in Mobile exploded on May 25, flattening several square blocks and causing damage to much of the city. About 300 people died in the disaster. Authorities never determined the cause of the blast. *New York Times*, May 30, June 4, 8, 1865; Reid, *After the War*, 214–16.

ulent now supported by boarding U.S. soldiers—daughters pretty & interesting[7]—Miss McKinstry very smart[8]—ride after dinner— Made. & Misses LeVert, Nettie & I—shell road—call on Gen. Hawkins[9]—back to Hotel—[*illeg.* & muskitoes—bad]—

SATURDAY, JUNE 3. Up early—Staff Officers conduct me to Gen Grangers Hd. Qrs. on Govt. St in fine mansion— Nettie goes to ride on horseback with Miss Octaa. Walton LeVert & 2 young officers— I mount—shoes & no straps—& ride with Gen G—— to review— made, I fear, rather awkward figure—long lines which it seemed I should never get by—but at last took station near Hotel & troops marched by—in splendid condition—2 divisions & part of another—Gen. Andrews, Gen Hawkins & Gen. Benton[10]—abt 15,000 men—only one regiment cavalry & abt a dozen batteries Artillery / Hawkins division cold. appeared very well—after review rode back to Hd. Qrs.—then in buggy with Gen G—— to call on Mrs LeVert— then to Hotel—many citizens called R. H. Slough Mayor & others[11]—all anxious abt. future & nearly all ready to accept any plan of reorgann.—rode with Gen Andrews to see ruins by expln.— 8 to 10 squares completely destroyed— Visited Hospital house & tent—dinner—to "Peerless" abt. 5[12]—[aff] 5.30—Me. LeVert & others—reached Wayanda abt 9[—]Capt Emmons [pleasant off at] 12

    7. Author and social figure Octavia Celeste Walton Le Vert (1811–77) incurred the enmity of her Mobile neighbors by her willingness to entertain Northern officers, and later in 1865 she moved her family to New York City. Two of her four daughters reached adulthood: Octavia Walton, the oldest, died unmarried; and Celeste Annette, the youngest, eventually married Regyle Reab, of Augusta, Ga. James et al., *Notable American Women,* 2:394–95; Thomas McAdory Owen, *History of Alabama and Dictionary of Alabama Biography* (Chicago, 1921), 4:1039.
    8. Evidently either Louise Dade McKinstry, Virginia Dade McKinstry, or Mary Ingersoll McKinstry, all daughters of Alexander McKinstry (1822–79), a Mobile lawyer and politician who served in the Confederate army. Whitelaw Reid diary, June 3, 1865 (Reid Family Papers, L.C.); *DAB,* 12:110; Owen, *History of Alabama and Dictionary of Alabama Biography,* 4:1125–26.
    9. John Parker Hawkins (1830–1914), brigadier general of volunteers, earned citations for his role in the Mobile campaign. Heitman, *Historical Register,* 1:513; *Who Was Who,* 1:536; *Appletons',* 3:121.
    10. Minnesota lawyer, politician, and author Christopher Columbus Andrews (1829–1922) and Indiana lawyer and judge William Plummer Benton (1828–67) participated in the Mobile campaign as brigadier generals of volunteers. Reid, *After the War,* 214; *DAB,* 1:284–85; *Appletons',* 1:243; Heitman, *Historical Register,* 1:166, 213.
    11. R. H. Slough, mayor of Mobile, 1861–65, called on Chase with the city council. Slough had surrendered the city quietly after the Confederate military evacuated. Owen, *History of Alabama and Dictionary of Alabama Biography,* 4:1573; Whitelaw Reid diary, June 3, 1865 (Reid Family Papers, L.C.); *OR,* ser. 1, v. 49, pt. 1:144–46.
    12. The *Peerless* was a river steamer on U.S. army service in Alabama. *OR,* ser. 1, v. 49, pt. 2:48, 115, 728.

SUNDAY, JUNE 4. Up late—on deck abt 8.30—made light Pass a l'eutre bkft—pilot came on board 10.20—then 125 m fr. N. Orleans— Nettie up at 10.30—very-very hot—all decks covd with awning & heat carried back to Qr. deck—11.40 passed Lt. & Lt. House Pass a Leutre / pilot says large increase of marsh islands in 18 years—snags around which collect—low shores either hand—reedy—light green—12 passed wreck of Gen Taylor burnt here, bound out, six or seven years ago—brig sunk on snag—a little further up pilot town four companies now here & at S.W. Pass wh alone used—abt 50 inhabs—some pilots have families—revenue officer & river pilot came on bd.—Capt telegd. Collector[13] "inside, C.J. on bd.—up tomorrow morning—went on past town—abt. 15 m p. one passed monitor anchd. & a little above Cubitts'-Hill hailed Mon. 'do you want to board—No Sir' & we kept on—passed Fort Jackson on right & Fort Philip on left— Abt. 5 reached Quarantine—delayed—Telegraphed Gen Canby[14]—order to allow us to pass—hove anchor and on way abt 10 P.M.

MONDAY, JUNE 5. Came on deck abt. 7.30—18 miles below N.O.—found boiler had sprung a leak & moving slowly—passed some fine plantations—some wholly neglected—crevasse & workmen completing repairs some 8 miles below town—passed Jackson's battle ground[15]—met just below levees by boat with Messrs Denison, Flanders, May, Whitaker & Tucker on board[16]—they came to Wayanda wh. anchored of   St—not able to get in to wharf—went ashore— Nettie & I & Reid to Mr. May's— Randall Hunt & Ammie called[17]—tried to persuade her to go up river with us—weather extremely warm—no rain here for four weeks— Several gentlemen

13. The collector of customs at New Orleans was William Pitt Kellogg (1830–1918), later a U.S. senator from Louisiana and controversial governor of the state. *DAB*, 10:305–6.
14. Maj. Gen. Edward Richard Sprigg Canby (1817–73) commanded the final Federal campaigns in the Gulf Coast region. *DAB*, 3:468–69.
15. The site of Andrew Jackson's victory over the British in Jan. 1815.
16. George S. Denison; Benjamin F. Flanders; Assistant Treasurer Thomas P. May, (b. 1842), a wealthy sugar planter who embraced Unionist sentiments and founded the *New Orleans Times* in 1863; John S. Whitaker; and Josiah Prentice Tucker. *New Orleans Times*, June 6, 1865; Rightor, *New Orleans*, 276; *Register of Officers (1865)*, 45; Ted Tunnell, *Crucible of Reconstruction: War, Radicalism and Race in Louisiana, 1862–1877* (Baton Rouge, 1984), 221; Fred Harvey Harrington, *Fighting Politician: Major General N. P. Banks* (Philadelphia, 1948), 101, 148–49; Reid, *After the War*, 227–28, 268–78.
17. Randall Hunt (1825–92) of New Orleans was professor of law, 1847–67, and president, 1867–83, of the University of Louisiana. His wife, Ruhamah ("Ammie") Ludlow Hunt (1833–1913), was a daughter of James Chambers Ludlow and Josephine Dunlop Ludlow, and a sister of Chase's third wife, Sarah Bella Dunlop Ludlow. Johnson, *Twentieth Century Biographical Dictionary*, v. 1; Israel Ludlow to Chase, June 5, 1863 (Chase Papers, L.C.); unpublished guide to Ludlow-Dunlop-Chambers Collec., Univ. of Wyoming.

called—rode with Mr. May & Mr. Reid about the town after dark—impress[ion] indistinct but pleasing—saw Custom House, unfinished, St Charles Hotel,[18] Jackson & Clay statues for first time Mr. Ames & Rev. Mr. Andrus Mr. Roudanez and others called[19]—Gen. Sheridan [at dinner][20] / Mr. Roselius & Durant[21]—Gen. Banks called— Miss di Mortié called to ask attend. at fair tomorr[22]—

TUESDAY, JUNE 6. A very late breakfast & a very hot morng—Gen. Canby called—proposed to call tomorrow with Staff— Mr. Barker called—a wonderful old man[23]— Members of bar with Mr. Roselius at their head—not very much impressed though some of them seem quite able—some really strong—Mr. R—— had previously called with his daughter[24] / delegation of loyal ministers called—most of them ministering in churches of deprived rebels—went to Mr. Hunts with Nettie—met Phil Kenner two Misses Eulong's Mr. Wm. Hunt[25]—rather southernish all—but Messrs Hunt talented & accomplished / dined—Mr. Graham with

---

18. The cornerstone of the New Orleans Custom House was laid in 1847 and work on the granite and marble structure continued, except for a break during the Civil War, until funding ceased in 1884. Described as "a conspicuous edifice, with white-pillared porticoes and a spacious rotunda," the second St. Charles Hotel was built after a fire in 1851 destroyed the equally famous original. Rightor, *New Orleans*, 428–30; Survey of Federal Archives, Louisiana, *A History of the U.S. Custom House at New Orleans* ([New Orleans], 1940), 5–21; Trowbridge, *Desolate South*, 207–8; Federal Writers' Project, *New Orleans City Guide* (Boston, 1938), 313.

19. Possibly G. W. Ames, commissioner of direct taxes; C. Andrus of the Union Ministerial Association of New Orleans, a member of a committee that addressed resolutions to Chase regarding "equal civil and political rights" for "American citizens of African descent"; and black leader Joseph B. Roudanez, editor and proprietor of the *New Orleans Tribune*, a leading advocate of black suffrage, and a founder of the New Orleans Freedmen's Aid Association. *New Orleans Dir. (1866)*, 62, 384; *New Orleans Tribune*, June 7, 1865; C. Peter Ripley, *Slaves and Freedmen in Civil War Louisiana* (Baton Rouge, 1976), 173, 175; Roger A. Fischer, *The Segregation Struggle in Louisiana, 1862–1877* (Urbana, Ill., 1974), 29, 68; John W. Blassingame, *Black New Orleans, 1860–1880* (Chicago, 1973), 57.

20. Maj. Gen. Philip Henry Sheridan (1831–88), just taking command west of the Mississippi. *DAB*, 17:79–81; Simon et al., *Papers of Ulysses S. Grant*, 15:43–45, 116.

21. Christian Roselius and Thomas J. Durant, concerned that "Rebels" might return to political control in Louisiana. Reid, *After the War*, 260–62.

22. Louise De Mortie, a popular black lecturer and public reader, was president of the Orphan's Industrial and Educational Home for the Children of Freedmen. The organization held a benefit fair, May 26–June 6. Blassingame, *Black New Orleans*, 141–42, 146, 170–71, 266; *New Orleans Tribune*, May 2, 1865.

23. Jacob Barker (1779–1871), a Quaker merchant and capitalist originally from New York, had professed Unionist sentiments for pecuniary reasons. *DAB*, 1:602–3; Reid, *After the War*, 230–31; Harrington, *Fighting Politician*, 100.

24. Christian Roselius had three children and at least one daughter. *DAB*, 16:165.

25. St. Charles Parish sugar and rice planter Philip Minor Kenner, the son of W. B. Kenner and nephew of Louisiana politician Duncan Farrar Kenner; and William Henry Hunt (1823–84), New Orleans lawyer, Unionist, and brother of Randall Hunt. Arthur, *Old Families*, 158–59; *DAB*, 9:396–97, 10:337–38.

us[26]—took a nap or rather tried to after dinner—too hot—went to Fair in Soulé Mansion[27]—met there a number of acquaintances— Gen Banks & Mrs B—— went as we entered[28]— Fair of Colored people under supervision of Miss de Mortie—quite a success—Nettie came & bought liberally—back by a country road—bed at 11.

WEDNESDAY, JUNE 7. Another very hot day— Mrs Gaines called with Mr. Henderson[29]—says she gave mortgage to Judge White[30] for 30.000 & 2000 note for 650! that he never told her my opinion that she cd. come safely through the lines— Mr. Conway, Superintendent of Freedmen & now appd. Commr. for La. came & I promised to visit schools with him tomorrow[31]— Gen Canby & Staff called—rather stiff—visited photographic gallery—postponed visit to Court[32] / visited by a number of Creoles intd by Mr. Durant [at] SubTreasury & 1st Natl. Bank[33]—never more surprised—about fifteen gentlemen, of refined manners & more than ordinary intelligence & to all appearance as white as any equal number of confessed whites in the city—I was amazed to find that they belonged to the disfranchised class—at 4 went to dine with Mr. Durant—guests Gen Canby, Judge Whittaker, Mr. & Mrs Waples &c[34]—

26. James Graham (b. 1819), notary, commissioner of deeds, secretary of the New Orleans Freedmen's Aid Association. *New Orleans Dir. (1866)*, 203; Tunnell, *Crucible of Reconstuction*, 225; *New Orleans Tribune*, June 4, 1865.
27. Pierre Soulé (1801–70), lawyer and politician, resided in New Orleans, 1828–62. His former residence was the temporary site of the Orphan's Industrial and Educational Home for the Children of Freedmen. *DAB*, 17:405–7.
28. Mary Theodosia Palmer Banks (d. ca. 1901) married Nathaniel P. Banks in 1847. She established herself in elegant surroundings while in New Orleans. Harrington, *Fighting Politician*, 5–6, 212; S. Frederick Starr, *Southern Comfort: The Garden District of New Orleans, 1800–1900* (Cambridge, Mass., 1989), 220–21.
29. Possibly either John Henderson, Jr., attorney and master in chancery, or William Henderson, partner with John G. Gaines in a crockery and glass business. Myra Clark Gaines (1805–85), illegitimate child of a New Orleans merchant and real estate speculator, gained national notoriety through more than fifty years of litigation in municipal, state, and federal courts over her claims on the property of her deceased father. *New Orleans Times*, June 3, 1865; *New Orleans Dir. (1866)*, 188, 218; James et al., *Notable American Women*, 2:6–7.
30. Possibly C. F. White, Fifth District Court. *New Orleans Dir. (1866)*, 466.
31. Former army chaplain Thomas William Conway (1840–87), an advocate of rights and education for freedmen, supervised the Bureau of Negro Labor in Louisiana. Johnson, *Twentieth Century Biographical Dictionary*, v. 2; Graf et al., *Papers of Andrew Johnson*, 8:447; Ripley, *Slaves and Freedmen*, 61–66, 83–86, 127–28, 183–87, 201–4.
32. From *visited* through *Court* is an interlineation in pencil. The body of the entry is in ink.
33. From *[at]* through *Bank* is an interlineation in pencil.
34. Rufus Waples (1825–1902), New Orleans lawyer, U.S. attorney for the eastern district of Louisiana since 1863, and a Radical Republican aligned with the Thomas J. Durant faction, married Margaret J. Alsworth in 1858. *Who Was Who*, 1:1296; Harrington, *Fighting Politician*, 101; Tunnell, *Crucible of Reconstruction*, 228.

Mr. May, Mr. Reid & Nettie with me—dinner too long protracted to suit me—returning to drawing room had some talk with Mr. D—— on political situation—home & to bed—

THURSDAY, JUNE 8. Mr. Conway came as he promised—went with him to schools—a "school of Medicine" converted into a "school of liberty"—several schools assembled in one room—more than half nearly white—a number wholly white but said to have a "taint"—had made respectable progress—urged to speak to children & did taking as texts Andrew Johnson & the war & exhorting to diligen[t] perseverance & to courageous battle agst. ignorance & debasement under their directors & teachers [as generals] &c[35]— Mr. Wheelock took me to Court & Custom House—met Mr. Duffield[36]—to top of C. House—returned to Mr. Mays—Denison & Tucker in carriage—went to Mr. Roselius to dinner—he has a charming place some 5 or 6 miles from Tivoli Circle[37]—met Mr. Morphy—Mr. Capella, Mr. R——'s son in law & several other gentlemen—took Mad. Capella to table found her very agreeable / Judge Durell on my right—my health—to wh. ansd. sitting[38]— Back to town & bed

FRIDAY, JUNE 9. Mr. Conway called again, & went again to schools—no notice of coming given—two schools taught by whites not very well qualified apparently but scholars tolerably proficient—female teachers best qualified—Dr. Randolph's school

35. Federal officials seized the School of Medicine of the University of Louisiana in New Orleans early in 1863 and operated an elementary school for "colored children" until 1866. The teachers and children prepared a special program for Chase and afterwards "with the greatest enthusiasm" listened to his address on "the war and the inestimable benefits to the colored race derived therefrom." Howard A. White, *The Freedmen's Bureau in Louisiana* (Baton Rouge, 1970), 51–53; *New Orleans Times,* June 9, 1865.
36. Likely Charles Duffield, meat provisioner, who began curing hams at Cincinnati in 1837. Edwin Miller Wheelock (d. 1901), a Unitarian minister who arrived in New Orleans as chaplain of a New Hampshire regiment, held official positions related to the education and labor of freedmen in the Department of the Gulf. *New Orleans Times,* June 9, 1865; Charles Kassel, "Edwin Miller Wheelock," *Open Court* 34 (1920): 564–69; Ripley, *Slaves and Freedmen,* 130–37, 141–42.
37. Tivoli Circle was "an unornamented public ground" until renamed Lee Circle upon dedication of a monument to Gen. Robert E. Lee in 1884. Starr, *Southern Comfort,* 249; Jewell, *Crescent City Illustrated.*
38. Paul Charles Morphy (1837–84), New Orleans lawyer and chess player of international renown; possibly Bernard Capella, who ran a coffee house and whose wife may have been named Lizzie Capella; and Edward Henry Durell (1810–87), a Unionist appointed U.S. judge of the eastern district of Louisiana in 1863. *DAB,* 5:545–46, 13:193–95; Reid, *After the War,* 261; *New Orleans Dir. (1866),* 113; ibid. (1877), 178.

best[39]—another gathered from [streets] by white &c colored teachers—old man—over sixty—brass spectacles—trying to learn to read—whole impression a glorious beginning though in the midst of difficulties— Mr. Reid accompanied me—returned to Mr. Mays— wrote reply to Creole Committee[40]— Mr. Reid took it to Mr. Roudanez, Tribune office— Mr. R—— Mr. May & myself to dinner at Judge Whitakers—beautiful grounds with oranges, lemons, crape myrtles—house small but comfortable—mansion burnt [at] begg. of war—new now being built—young Whitaker of Times[41] & wife, Mr. Denison, Mr. Tucker & others guests—from Judge W——s to Mr. Higgins,[42] where a very handsome party—Mrs H—— & her sister Mrs Morris daughters of C. J. Wright—intd. to several prominent planters & business men Messrs Allen of St Mary & Mr Shackleford, Prest. R.R. Co[43]—home—to bed—

SATURDAY, JUNE 10. No engagement out today—having declined two invitations to dinner at Lake—called on Capt. Green naval commr.[44] & on Gen Canby who busy with expedition to Texas—near 60.000 men to be concentrated cui bono? intended speaking to Capt Green about boat up river but yielded to May & Reid who thougt it *infra dig.*[45]— May went out to arrange / returned

39. Paschal Beverley Randolph (1825–74), a Northern black physician, spiritualist, and author, was in New Orleans, 1864–65. S. Austin Allibone, *A Critical Dictionary of English Literature and British and American Authors*, 3 vols. (Philadelphia, 1891), 2:1738; Wallace, *North American Authors*, 371; White, *Freedmen's Bureau*, 18–19.

40. Chase declined an invitation to speak before "the loyal colored Americans of New Orleans," but stated, as he had at Charleston, that blacks were entitled to all rights of citizens, including suffrage, and best gained support for the exercise of those rights through personal economy, industry, sobriety, and "constant practice of Christian virtues." Chase to J. B. Roudanez, L. Golis, and L. Banks, June 6, 1865, in *New Orleans Tribune*, June 10, 1865; Reid diary, June 6, 8–10, 1865 (Reid Family Papers, L.C.).

41. Likely William R. Whitaker, who lived near John S. Whitaker and shared his Radical Republican sentiments. *New Orleans Dir. (1866)*, 466; Harrington, *Fighting Politician*, 101.

42. Possibly William H. Higgins, former U.S. assessor of internal revenue in Louisiana. *New Orleans Times*, June 17, 1865.

43. Possibly R. M. Allen, a Louisiana planter who later participated in a labor assistance program offered through the Freedmen's Bureau; and Charles C. Shackleford (b. 1815) of Canton, Miss., president of the New Orleans, Jackson and Great Northern R.R., 1865–66, who sought funds and material to rebuild the road. White, *Freedmen's Bureau*, 126–27; Graf et al., *Papers of Andrew Johnson*, 8:447; *New Orleans Times*, June 13, 1865; John F. Stover, *The Railroads of the South, 1865–1900: A Study in Finance and Control* (Chapel Hill, 1955), 156–59;

44. In 1865, Capt. Charles Green (1814–87), a naval officer placed on the retired list three years earlier, was lighthouse inspector for the district extending from the Mississippi River to the Rio Grande. *Appletons'*, 2:742; *Register of Officers (1865)*, 72.

45. Whitelaw Reid wrote on June 9: "Called at Chandler's, to break the arrangement for little steamer tonight"; and on June 10: "Had prevented Mr. C. from seeing abt. boat. May & I now looked after Mellen & went into the business." Reid diary (Reid Family Papers, L.C.).

announcing Banks cd. not be had but that Fashion was siezed & placed at disposal[46]— Mr. Mellen came & I expressed my regrets & asked him to see Capt of boat & Qr. Master & say I wd. not interfere with her trip—all I wanted was stateroom & wd. go tonight rather than occasion any inconvenience—rode out to Mr. Roselius—stopped by way at Judge Whitakers whom we bro't home—bid good bye to Mrs W—adieux to Mr. R & Mrs Capella—back to dinner—Nettie at Mrs Hunt's—Denison & Tucker dined with us—hot—hot—after dinner callers

SUNDAY, JUNE 11. Mr. Hunt at breakfast [wants] good lawyer [for Fed] Judge / Mr. Conway called & Judge W—— who & I were taken by [Mr.] C—— to Colored Church metht. A Mr. Dove preached & preached well[47]—congregation of all colors from jettiest black to fairest white, but *all* negroes! very respectable however men dressed much like a summer congregation of N.E. farmers—some women with more city fashion—but many with turbans & very plain but neat—the preacher invited me to pulpit & to be introduced to congn. wh I declined— P.M. Mr. Reid & I accompanied Mr. Conway to Sunday School—several schools collected & abt 700 present—almost all slaves before the war & contd. in slavery by the exception in Mr. Lincoln's proclamation—now all so happy & so grateful to him—glad to learn on return to Mays that Fashion was actually gone & that arranged we shd. go as passengers on Carter[48]—determined to visit plantations on river with Wayanda—several gent to accompany

MONDAY, JUNE 12. Mr. Barker called remonstrating agst appt. of Judge Durell[49]—surprised when I sd. I did not expect to be consulted— Capt. Merryman with whom arranged to be on board abt. 8 P.M.— Nettie went to make calls & on return Mr May & Mr. Reid accd. me to call on Gen Sheridan who commands Texas Army &

46. The steamer *General Banks* or *Nathaniel P. Banks* was a captured blockade runner used as an army transport. The *Fashion*, a "new and splendid Saturday evening steamer" commanded by Capt. A. J. May, was scheduled to depart on its regular run up the Mississippi at 5 P.M. on June 10. *New Orleans Times*, June 10, 1865; *Daily Picayune*, June 8, 11, 1865; Lytle, *Merchant Vessels*, 64, 70; *OR*, ser. 1, v. 49, pt. 1:567–68; *ORN*, ser. 1, v. 22:220.

47. St. James, the largest African Methodist Episcopal congregation in New Orleans, Rev. W. A. Dove, pastor. *New Orleans Tribune*, June 11, 1865; Blassingame, *Black New Orleans*, 149.

48. Gen. Canby commandeered the *W. R. Carter*, a "fine passenger steamer" operated by the Atlantic and Mississippi Steamship Co., for Chase's party. Reid, *After the War*, 274; *New Orleans Times*, June 11, 1865.

49. Jacob Barker and Edward H. Durell belonged to opposing Unionist factions in New Orleans. Barker's faction maintained Southern sympathies. Durrell's faction cooperated with Gen. Benjamin Butler during occupation of the city. Harrington, *Fighting Politician*, 100–101.

Department—in good spirits—called at Mr. Durant's office—did not find him—purchased glasses at Duhamel's where saw abusive anti-admn. paper La Renaissance[50]—returned to house—dinner— Mr. Durant with us—says Judges Howell & Le Beauvre have declared in favor of negro suffrage[51] / Gen Banks called—says [he] wd. have authd. n. suffrage & then subd. amendt. to be voted on by all after year confident it wd. have prevailed— Reid asks Shall I lunch with Plumley—advised against it[52]—abt. ½ p 8 started for Wayanda—had to pass thro negro regiment—found launch at wharf & went on board—our party consists of Judge Whitaker, Col Starring,[53] Messrs May, Denison, Flanders, Tucker, [Stiles][54] & our set—Nettie & I [returned] early—rest on deck & merry

TUESDAY, JUNE 13. Up before day light & on deck before 5— beautiful morng—coffee—off to Rost Plantation[55]—partly used as depot for infirm & sick negros & partly cultivated by old hands under govt. Agent—who seems good man but system bad—wages unpaid & negroes discontented—two miles above—other side— river—Dick Taylor's plantation[56]—cultivated last year by lessee who

50. Clement Duhamel, optician; *La Renaissance Louisianaise* had begun publication in May 1861. *New Orleans Dir. (1866)*, 164.

51. Rufus K. Howell, a "consistent Unionist," and Zenon Labauve, associate justices of the Louisiana Supreme Court. *New Orleans Times*, June 8, 1865; John Kendall Smith, *History of New Orleans*, 3 vols. (Chicago, 1922), 1:293; *New Orleans Dir. (1866)*, 217, 515.

52. Chase and B. Rush Plumly became estranged in 1864 after Chase gave credence to rumors that Plumly had used his official connections for personal gain. Plumly was also distressed by the esteem in which Chase held Benjamin F. Flanders. Chase and Plumly never repaired the breach in their relations. Whitelaw Reid turned down Plumly's lunch invitation. Chase to Plumly, July 25, [1863], Feb. 26, 1864 (Chase Papers, Hist. Soc. of Pa.); Plumly to Chase, Apr. 30, June 12, 1864, Chase to Rebecca Plumly, Apr. 3, 1867 (Chase Papers, L.C.); Reid diary, June 10, 12, 1865 (Reid Family Papers, L.C.).

53. Frederick Augustus Starring (1834–1904), engineer, lawyer, and colonel of the 72nd Illinois, held commands in the Department of the Gulf after being breveted brigadier general of volunteers. Heitman, *Historical Register*, 1:917; *Who Was Who*, 1:1173.

54. H. Stiles, a Creole, operated the California planing mills and was a director of the New Orleans Freedmen's Aid Association. *New Orleans Tribune*, May 2, 1865; *New Orleans Dir. (1866)*, 426; Ripley, *Slaves and Freedmen*, 79.

55. The Bureau of Free Labor operated Rost Plantation in St. Charles Parish, formerly the property of Judge Pierre A. Rost, as one of its four "home colonies" to accommodate destitute and disabled freedmen and promote the transition from slavery to independent support. Various problems and criticisms led to the closing of the home colonies by 1867. Ripley, *Slaves and Freedmen*, 54–55; John C. Engelsman, "The Freedmen's Bureau in Louisiana," *Louisiana Historical Quarterly* 32 (1949): 206–12; Thomas W. Conway, *The Freemen of Louisiana: Final Report of the Bureau of Free Labor, Department of the Gulf*... (New Orleans, 1865), 3–5.

56. Richard Taylor (1826–79), only son of Zachary Taylor, served as a Confederate general. Union forces overran his more than 1,700-acre sugar plantation in

employed but only partly paid—this year by negroes themselves associated—children going to school—Thompson short, smart, thickset French negro noml. lessee—[Sorvile] preacher—Richardson an overseer—Sanford Thomas most forward & intelligent—constitution bad English but good sense—crops excellent—much garden stuff—melons, tomatoes, peas, sweet potatoes &c—very industrious—tasks & extra work—on right bank 15 miles further up May's Plantation Bonnet Carré—rode over it with him—tasks—patches beside—wages punctually paid—8 to 15 per month, food & privileges—cotton, cane & corn excellent—supper— Carter came abt 8—went aboard—good bye to friends—intd to Miss Hollcroft & Mrs Carroll[57]—recd. Times with Art. on me & Cutlers advt. & acct. of Red River catastrophe[58]—bed—

WEDNESDAY, JUNE 14. Passed Baton Rouge abt. half past 5—lively landing—State House most conspicuous object said to be ruined from effects of fire during war[59]—boat lying there which changed her name after rebellion to Jeff Thompson but has now painted Pauline Carroll over that of the rebel leader[60]—the town looks well—passed Port Hudson abt. 8: very handsome bluffs—Mellen does not like McCulloch's letter to Cutler giving him absolute disposal of cotton[61]—have heard compts that his favored men chge excessively for sampling, repacking, drayage &c in one instance near 25% of whole value—very hot but pleasant breeze passed Gunboat Choctaw[62]—near Bayou Sarah—passed tinclad—rain &

St. Charles Parish, La., styled "Fashion," in 1862. *DAB*, 18:340–41; Richard Taylor, *Destruction and Reconstruction: Personal Experiences of the Late War*, ed. Richard B. Harwell (1879; reprint, New York, 1955), xvii.

57. Possibly relatives of W. R. Hollcroft, master of the *W. R. Carter*, and J. W. Carroll, another captain with the Atlantic and Mississippi Steamship Co. *New Orleans Times*, June 11, 1865; *Daily Picayune*, June 8, 1865.

58. The *New Orleans Times* noted Chase's departure from the city and refuted insinuations that his tour had been undertaken "to engineer for any politicians or party." The newspaper also included a notice from U.S. Purchasing Agent O. N. Cutler, who advertised that he was prepared to buy cotton, and an account of a ruinous drop in cotton prices accelerated by heavy receipts from the Red River district, where rapidly falling water forced premature shipments to market. *New Orleans Times*, June 13, 1865.

59. The Tudor-Gothic Louisiana State Capitol, completed in 1850 on a bluff overlooking the Mississippi River, suffered fire damage during the Civil War. Writers' Program, Louisiana, *Louisiana: A Guide to the State* (New York, 1941), 256.

60. The Atlantic and Mississippi Steamship Co. operated the passenger steamer *Pauline Carroll*. Evidently the vessel had borne the name of Confederate Brig. Gen. Merriwether Jeff Thompson (1826–76) of Missouri, known for his leadership of partisan forces. New Orleans *Daily Picayune*, June 8, 1865; *Appletons'*, 6:94.

61. Treasury regulations gave Cutler "exclusive control of all cotton from insurrectionary districts" arriving at New Orleans. *New Orleans Times*, June 13, 1865.

62. USS *Choctaw*, ironclad sidewheel steamer, had been ordered to New Orleans. *ORN*, ser. 1, v. 27:253, 261–62, ser. 2, v. 1:57.

windstorm abt 10—approaching bend—fury increased as we turned it—driving mist darkened trees—storm brief as violent—great crevasse at Morganza & soldiers removed below—overflow swift & vast— Abt. 1 passed Mouth of Red Rr.—Tennessee lying in front[63]— sent for papers—all gunboats did so—dinner—another storm— thunder this time & lightning—reached Natchez [abt] 8—but only stopped to land & receive too dark to see anything—

THURSDAY, JUNE 15. Abt. 7 30 at Davis Bend— Capt came & went for ambulances—which arrived in abt. an hour—took seat in one with Col. Donaldson,[64] Mr. Mellen & Nettie—Reid afterwards joined—rode thro Jo Davis Plantation[65]—met little girl—belonged to Mass Jeff dont know whar he is—plantation now cultivated by small companies in partn. & mainly in cotton—tho' much in corn— crops in excellent condition & labor[er]s hopeful & cheerful—visited Jeff Davis Place, given him by Jo—house 8 rooms on ground 2 ea. wing & 4 main bdg—single story—garden still lovely—house used for officers—school on place—two yg. ladies teachers from north[66]—rode through Woods Place—visited Gin House, now occupied by soldiers—near by cold. regt. in line—said few words to them[67]—rode thence along Levee between Cypress Swamp on one side & woods next river on other to Bank Place—one of Quitman's places—this said to be best of the four on Bend[68]— Here the boat lay having come round the Bend— German Commy. very friendly—

63. USS *Tennessee*, an ironclad steamer captured from the Confederates at Mobile Bay in Aug. 1864 and commissioned as a Federal vessel. Ibid., ser. 2, v. 1:221.
64. James Lowry Donaldson (1814–85), a career officer who spent the Civil War in the quartermaster department. He began duty in the military district of Tennessee in June 1865. *Appletons'*, 2:198; *Nat. Cyc.*, 11:518; Heitman, *Historical Register*, 1:378.
65. In 1827, Joseph Emory Davis (1784–1870), Vicksburg lawyer and brother of Jefferson Davis, established a large plantation, named "Hurricane," on progressive social principles. The locale along the Mississippi became known as Davis Bend. *Appletons'*, 2:102; Janet Sharp Hermann, *The Pursuit of a Dream* (New York, 1981), 4–15, 38–41, 143–44.
66. Joseph Davis gave his brother a 1,000-acre plantation in 1835. Reid described Jefferson Davis's "white frame house" as "by no means palatial." Reid noted a couple of "Yankee school-mistresses" who taught "the boys and girls of Mr. Davis' slaves" as well as runaways from other plantations. Reid, *After the War*, 279–83; Hermann, *Pursuit of a Dream*, 13.
67. Robert Y. Wood was the absentee owner of a plantation at Davis Bend. The cotton gin on the Jefferson Davis plantation held military supplies. In his diary, Whitelaw Reid noted Chase's brief address to the black soldiers: "Reg't. paraded. Little spch. by Chf. J. & cheer after cheer." Hermann, *Pursuit of a Dream*, 25–26, 137–38; Reid, *After the War*, 283–84; Reid diary, June 15, 1865 (Reid Family Papers, L.C.).
68. John Anthony Quitman (1798–1858), lawyer, soldier, and politican, had operated an "interlocking system" of plantations in the vicinity of Davis Bend. *DAB*, 15:315–16; Robert E. May, *John A. Quitman: Old South Crusader* (Baton Rouge and London, 1985), 130–37.

June 1865 { 573 }

Col. D. & Capt. to Vicksburgh arrivd. abt 2.30— Gen Smith with us to Fortifications—rain—upset[69]—back to boat—Yeatman—Collins agt Hoyt, Sprague & Co—several others—left Vick abt 8, waited for W S M[70]

FRIDAY, JUNE 16. At Skipwiths Landing abt 7.30—wooded—met Bissell a character[71] / this one of chief depots for Porters fleet—Lake Washn. people leave boat here—Wade Hamptons bro. did[72]— Mrs Duncan's plantation here[73]—finest planting region from V———, including Millikens bend, Lake Providence, Goodrichs Landing & Skipwith extending back to Lake Washn. Missi & Bayou Macon La. It is now more ruined than any other part—after leaving Sk. Lg went with Mellen to Pilot House where remained till ½ past 12— wide views on either hand—ruined Ginhouse & dwellings—passed what were Greenville right bank & Columbia left bank—narrow crossing of long bend—guerillas wd. fire on passing boat & then pass to other side & renew fire—towns destroyed in consequence— Abt. 7 in evg. stopped to wood—steep bank—mate urged hands— some soldier attempted to steal a gun—it was taken from him & his companions came to his help—& there was likelihood of violence— but quiet restored—talked to rebel soldier who agst negroes in wh Union soldier joined—showers of sparks from tall chimneys[74]—

69. Reid also noted the sudden rainstorm and "the capsize," evidently of a carriage. Brig. Gen. Morgan Lewis Smith (1821–74) commanded the Vicksburg district, Sept. 1864–July 1865. Reid diary, June 15, 1865 (Reid Family Papers, L.C.); Reid, *After the War*, 289; *DAB*, 17:323–24; Heitman, *Historical Register*, 1:902.

70. William S. Mellen. The Sprague and Hoyt family concerns were operating a plantation in the Vicksburg area, and Collins, otherwise unidentified, was their agent. Chase to Kate Chase Sprague, June 19, 1865 (Chase Papers, Hist. Soc. of Pa.).

71. Possibly Josiah Wolcott Bissell (b. 1818), a military engineer who worked along the Mississippi River during the Civil War. *Appletons'*, 1:271; *OR*, ser. 1, v. 24, pt. 1:123–24.

72. Christopher Hampton, only surviving brother of South Carolina politician and Confederate soldier Wade Hampton (1818–1902), oversaw family plantations during the Civil War. He had discussed the question of black suffrage with Whitelaw Reid. Manly Wade Wellman, *Giant in Gray: A Biography of Wade Hampton of South Carolina* (New York, 1949), 40, 42, 53, 357; *DAB*, 8:213–15; Reid, *After the War*, 288–89.

73. Almost certainly property owned by the widow of Natchez banker and politician Dr. Stephen Duncan, considered the largest cotton planter and slaveholder in the U.S. during the 1850s. Charles S. Sydnor, *A Gentleman of the Old Natchez Region: Benjamin L. C. Wailes* (Durham, N.C., 1938), 46; D. Clayton James, *Antebellum Natchez* (Baton Rouge, 1968), 150–53; Dunbar Rowland, *History of Mississippi: The Heart of the South* (Chicago, 1925), 1:554, 561, 566.

74. Whitelaw Reid noted: "Scene with vagabond soldier trying to steal rifle. Talk of rebel soldier agst. negro suffrage. Glorious night on upper deck. Serpentine shower of sparks." Reid also indicated that the black woodchoppers at the wooding site were "being swindled" and "made little beyond their food." Reid diary, June 16, 1865 (Reid Family Papers, L.C.).

JOURNAL XVII

JUNE   SAT. [L]ate at breakfast—some 20 miles below Helena—passed Yazoo Pass where Porter went in to Coldwater—seemed impossible to get in—this about ½ past [8]—talk with —— Hawley Lieut Cold. troops[75]

JOURNAL XV

SATURDAY, JUNE 17. Passed Helena abt. 8 A.M. Mr. J. M. Walden & Mr. Thorne left us here[76]— Mr. W—— is an able & earnest man, deeply interested in the freedom of the negro & in suffrage as its best protection—at Helena first high land on right bank fr. gulf & it immediately recedes & does not appear again till 40 miles above mo. of Ohio—just below Helena is Yazoo Pass hardly visible from river— Thro this Porter took his fleet to Coldwater & came near getting in rear of Vicksburgh—abt. 7 PM. reached Memphis— W. S. M with Treasury Officer for letters—bro't me letter fr Katie which most welcome[77]—scene on Landing of great activity Liberty just leaving for Louisville—Commonwealth came in & went out ahead of us[78]— Mr. Norris, Cashr. 1st Exch. Bank—Capt. Lewis whom I met last fall at Mr. Hosea's & others came on board[79]— Papers recd. here contain Prests declaration agst Negro suffrage by his Missi. procln. & appl. of Sharkey[80]—wooded at 8 P.M—pictur-

---

75. Chase referred to the efforts of the Mississippi Squadron in 1863, under the command of David Porter, to circumvent the Confederate fortifications at Vicksburg by moving into the Yazoo River system. At June 18 (below), Chase identified the lieutenant as Zalmon Hawley of Indiana.

76. John Morgan Walden (1831–1914) of Cincinnati, corresponding secretary of the Western Freedmen's Aid Commission and the Methodist Freedmen's Aid Society; and possibly the Rev. J. A. Thorne of the American Missionary Association. They likely visited the mission school begun in 1864 at Helena, Ark. *DAB*, 19:330–31; Christine Bolt, *The Anti-Slavery Movement and Reconstruction: A Study in Anglo-American Co-operation, 1833–77* (London, 1969), 136; Augustus Field Beard, *A Crusade of Brotherhood: A History of the American Missionary Association* (Boston, 1909), 128–29.

77. Chase had been "very anxious" about his pregnant daughter Kate, and perhaps had telegraphed her asking for news. Just below Vicksburg he received a telegram from her advising him to expect a letter at Memphis. There William S. Mellen "& an officer of the Treasury . . . hunted up the Postmaster who was at the Theatre & brought me your letter. . . . I was delighted to hear that you were well." Chase to Kate Chase Sprague, June 19, 1865 (Chase Papers, Hist. Soc. of Pa.).

78. Probably *Liberty No. 2* or *Liberty No. 4*, steamers launched from Wheeling in 1863; and the *Commonwealth*, a steamer built in 1864 and based first at St. Louis. Lytle, *Merchant Vessels*, 39, 112.

79. Likely Capt. Lewis M. Hosea (see Nov. 27, 1864, above).

80. President Johnson's "Mississippi Proclamation" authorized a convention to reinstitute civil government in that state. Participation in the election of delegates was to be limited to persons who had taken and subscribed the oath of amnesty set forth in May 1865 and were qualified under the constitution and laws of Mississippi

esque scene—stout black man—slender white man on log—blazing torch on bank & boat—drunken man put ashore—cool evg.

SUNDAY, JUNE 18. Rose early—very pleasant / passed Fort Randolph while dressing—breakfasted—passengers all very quiet—passed Fort Pillow abt. 9 where the horrible massacre took place—Passenger remarked "Forrest is on his farm plowing."[81]— Gained on Commonwealth which went ahead at Memphis & passed her but while wooding she again went ahead— Another wooding from just before sunset till past dark—heavy gangway frame out—bank dug down—plank to shore—deck hands out on plank—load at woodpile—back on gangway—mate on bank urging the work—iron frame on support about 10 feet high filled with pine dipped in tar or turpentine for torch—through & off abt 8.30 / talk with Zalmon Hawley, Lt. Cold. Troops, resigned on his way home in North Hogan, Ripley Co, Ia / intelligent & earnest for cold. suffrage— At woodyard [wh] some 20 miles below new Madrid Capt[82] warned me to go inside lest some rebel might shoot—did not go—talk with Mr. Edwards[,] plant[ing] near Vicks[burg]

MONDAY, JUNE 19. Passed Columbus before rising—reached Cairo abt 8—walked through town wh. much impd. / [noticed one fine bank] &c / returned to boat—agent Ill. Cen. called & tendered President's car[83]—preferred to go up river in order to see Ham Smith & Louise[84]—boat cut & sunk passing round monitor—several lying at Cairo & other boats—Commonwealth in ahead of us—left abt. 9—passed fleet at Mound city—Lexn. & Tylor[85]—other gunboats 2 of the six built at St Louis—tinclads—a dozen being untinned & going to Red River / read papers obtd. at Cairo—

---

before secession. William Lewis Sharkey (1798–1873), Mississippi lawyer and antisecessionist, was appointed provisional governor under the Proclamation. *Chicago Tribune*, June 14, 1865; James D. Richardson, ed., *A Compilation of The Messages and Papers of the Presidents* (New York, 1897), 8:3512–14; *DAB*, 17:21–22.

81. Nathan Bedford Forrest (1821–77), Confederate general and cavalry commander, led forces that captured Fort Pillow, Tenn., on Apr. 12, 1864, and allegedly massacred black and white Union soldiers after surrender of the garrison. Forrest, a cotton planter in Mississippi and Arkansas before his military service, returned to his plantations in May 1865. *DAB*, 6:532–3; Long, *Civil War Day by Day*, 484.

82. W. R. Hollcroft.

83. Atlantic and Mississippi Steamship Co. vessels connected with the Illinois Central Railroad at Cairo. *New Orleans Times*, June 11, 1865.

84. Hamilton Smith's second wife, originally Louise Rudd of Springfield, Ky. They married in 1846. Chapman, *Sketches of the Alumni*, 250; Hamilton Smith to Chase, May 5, 1846 (Chase Papers, L.C.).

85. USS *Lexington* and USS *Tyler*, wooden sidewheel steamers transporting military stores from Mound City to other points. *ORN*, ser. 1, v. 27:252–53, ser. 2, v. 1:126–27, 227–28.

Senators Sherman & Wilson—Boutwell—Chic. Tribune strong for univ. suff[86]—evident that people will not yield—will Prest.? Call for great colored meeting in Nashville[87]—all the way up the river the country exceeding beautiful—passed Paducah & Smithfield before noon—towards eveng Cave-in-Rock—rebel soldiers & ladies came into cabin singing confed. songs—at request—all willing eno. now to submit—struck reef—crashing sound—alarm—one of [*illeg.* danced][88]—after singing bed—a beautiful day—

TUESDAY, JUNE 20. A lovely morning—cool & pleasant—hated to get up but did abt. 6—bkft at 7—passed mo. of Green river opening a vista between Green banks, abt 9—nice farms—pleasant fields & trees—comfortable homes on Ill. side—same but less on Ky side / passed Evansville abt 10—a flourishing town—talk with paroled prisoner fr. Dick Taylors Army a Tennesseean—talk with Captain who fears war b. black & white if blk alld. vote— At 11.40 passed a beautiful farm (farmer Spark) Ia side highly cultivated & a little above, Ky side, a fine farm, gone to decay. "Came to him by his wife—sold it—went to L—drank up the price—is sot—further up abt. 1 passed Rockport, Gen Veatch's place[89] pretty cottage brick [ored.] by David T. Laird—so on up river to Hawesville & Cannelton—Lincoln's [Vines] Story[90]—saw Mrs Louise, & daughter May & Ham & Mr Huntington—L & dr. & Ham to new mine[91]— where left them & took H. Smith—talk with him—he admits mistakes—to bed abt 10 30

---

86. The *Chicago Tribune* had recently printed extracts from a speech by John Sherman in favor of suffrage for blacks, as well as several other items relating to the subject. *Chicago Tribune*, June 13, 14, 15, 17, 1865.
87. Tennessee's blacks called for a mass convention to be held at Nashville on the first Monday in August. The meeting was in response to a bill pending in the state legislature, which according to the *Chicago Tribune* would have allowed "color ... to remain the badge of servitude and brand of permanent inferiority." Ibid., June 17, 1865.
88. According to Whitelaw Reid, Ann Sevier Churchill, the wife of Confederate Maj. Gen. Thomas James Churchill (1824–1905), led the singing. There was "general alarm over striking a sand-bank," followed by a renewal of the rebels' "sauciness." Reid diary, June 19, 1865 (Reid Family Papers, L.C.); *DAB*, 4:105–6.
89. James Clifford Veatch (1819–95), an Indiana attorney commissioned a brigadier general of volunteers in Apr. 1862. *Appletons'*, 6:271; Heitman, *Historical Register*, 1:986.
90. Abraham Lincoln once observed, after seeing a thriving vine wrapped around a tree, that such a "vine is like certain habits of men; it decorates the ruin that it makes." Noah Brooks, *Washington In Lincoln's Time* (New York, 1895), 302.
91. May was likely one of the younger of Hamilton and Louise Smith's several children. Their son "Ham," probably named Hamilton after his father, became superintendent of a California silver mine. The Huntingtons were evidently friends of the Smiths. Hamilton Smith to Chase, Jan. 9, 1871 (Chase Papers, L.C.).

WEDNESDAY, JUNE 21. On rising found we were approaching Portland—arrived before dressed—bkfted on boat after waiting long for Nettie—left boat & took carriage / Nettie had lost glasses—went to St. U. States—didnt like rooms & went to Anderson to leave at 4 P.M.[92] Meantime to Louisville Hotel[93]—Judge Ballard, Maj. Sidell, & Mr. Guthrie called[94]—old Cinti fd. Steele one of Hotel Lessees[95]— Mr. Guthrie says slavery dead in Ky—was for emancipation by consent of masters—dined at Hotel with H Smith—Mr. Belknap, Judge Ballard, Mr Newcomb & Geo. Alfd Caldwell guests[96]—went to boat at 3.30—met Dr. Bell / Mr. Needham, Gallagher, Dr Warriner, Mr. Calvert Tevis accompanied me to Jeffersonville where took leave[97]—want Ballard Sup. Judge—after tea went to pilot house, where at first hot then very pleasant—

THURSDAY, JUNE 22. Still more than 20 miles below Cincinnati when left my stateroom at 6.30 this morning—passed Aurora where I made speech last fall[98]—saw Mr Cobbs' mansion on the hill[99]—

92. The passenger steamers *United States* and *Major Anderson*, which had been employed during the war as an army transport, operated between Louisville and Cincinnati. *Cincinnati Daily Gazette*, June 21, 1865; Lytle, *Merchant Vessels*, 119, 193; *OR*, ser. 1, v. 22:296, v. 32, pt. 3:299, v. 47, pt. 2:257, 264.

93. Built in 1832 of native limestone. Federal Writers' Project, *Kentucky: A Guide to the Bluegrass State* (New York, 1939), 181.

94. Bland Ballard (1819–79) was judge of the U.S. District Court for Kentucky, 1861–79. West Point graduate and engineer William Henry Sidell (1810–73) served in various capacities at Louisville, 1863–65. Kentucky railroad financier and Democratic politician James Guthrie (1792–1869) had supported the Union during the Civil War. *New York Times*, July 30, 1879; *Louisville Dir. (1865–66)*, 30, 116, 531; *DAB*, 8:60–62, 17:151–52.

95. Thomas Steele, apparently an old acquaintance from Cincinnati, operated the Louisville Hotel with two other partners. *Louisville Dir. (1865–66)*, 257.

96. Hardware merchant, bank president, and Louisville civic promoter William B. Belknap; Warren Newcomb (c. 1815–66) or his brother H. D. Newcomb, commission merchants; and George Alfred Caldwell (1814–66), Louisville lawyer, politician, and Democratic congressman, 1843–45, 1849–51. Johnston, *Memorial History*, 1:357, 2:292, 325, 345; *Louisville Dir. (1865–66)*, 36, 56, 200; James et al., *Notable American Women*, 2:618–19; *DAB*, 13:451–52; *Bio. Dir. U.S. Cong.*, 727–28.

97. Louisville physician, Unionist, and civic benefactor Theodore S. Bell (1807–84); Edgar Needham; William D. Gallagher; U.S. Sanitary Commission inspector Henry Augustus Warriner (1824–71), who held a medical degree and taught at Antioch College in Ohio before the war; probably J. W. Calvert, a proprietor of the Louisville *Union Press;* and probably Joshua Tevis, a Louisville lawyer and U.S. district attorney, 1863–66. *Nat. Cyc.*, 6:385–86; *Louisville Dir. (1865–66)*, 36, 56, 104, 199, 237; Charles Capen McLaughlin, ed., *The Papers of Frederick Law Olmsted, Vol. 4, Defending the Union: The Civil War and the U.S. Sanitary Commission, 1861–63* (Baltimore and London, 1986), 348; Johnston, *Memorial History*, 2:33.

98. Chase had made a campaign appearance at Aurora, Ind., in "a pouring rain." Chase to John Sherman, Oct. 2, 1864 (J. Sherman Papers, L.C.).

99. During the Civil War, Oliver Perry Cobb (1817–91), a businessman of Aurora, Ind., acted as a U.S. government agent for hay and grain contracts. *History of Cincinnati and Hamilton County*, 602–3; *History of Dearborn, Ohio, and Switzerland Counties, Indiana . . .* (Chicago, 1885), 666.

passed the old familiar places on river—reach 5th St—our party broke up—Mellen & Son to their home—Nettie & I, Reid, & the servants to Burnet House[1]—Lowell, to his detective work— My host Miller gave me excellent rooms & the house was greatly improved[2]— Carson Ball, Judge Leavitt & others called[3]—Mrs Pugh on Nettie[4]—rode out with Nettie to Abingdon—Mrs Hunt just arrived Charlotte & Josie Jones gone to Cambridge where Lud graduates this year[5]—only Kate Whiteman & Josie Ludlow at home[6]— Josie just getting better of lung hemorrhage—met Bishop & Mrs McIlvaine on road[7]—Bp begs me to pass tomorrow night under his roof—back to town—callers—nothing important—called at Carson's (whose carriage & horses I had) as came back

FRIDAY, JUNE 23. Mr. Pendleton Larz Anderson, Ricd. Smith & Sam. Reed of Gazette & many others called[8]— Col. Collins lately returned from Rocky Mts called & insisted on Nettie's going with

---

1. The servants accompanying Chase and his daughter were probably the enigmatic "Marshall" and William Joice (for whom see July 6 below). Janet Chase was not accompanied by a maid. Janet Chase Hoyt, "Sherman and Chase," *New York Daily Tribune*, Feb. 22, 1891.
2. Silas F. Miller operated the Burnet House, 1864–69. *Cinc. Dir. (1865)*, 79; John W. Leonard, *The Centennial Review of Cincinnati* . . . (Cincinnati, 1888), 145.
3. Enoch T. Carson, Flamen Ball, Humphrey Howe Leavitt.
4. Possibly Theresa Chalfant Pugh (d. 1868), wife of George E. Pugh. *DAB*, 15:258; *Cinc. Dir. (1865)*, 320.
5. Abingdon: the Ludlow family homestead, at a place known as Cummingsville or Cumminsville, north of Cincinnati not far from Clifton. Mrs. Hunt: Ruhamah Ludlow Hunt. Lud: future Cincinnati attorney Ludlow Ap-Jones (b. 1844), the son of Charles A. Jones and Charlotte Chambers Ludlow Jones; he received an A.M. degree from Harvard in 1865. C. C. Clopper to Chase, June 30, 1852, Charlotte L. Jones to Chase, Feb. 8, June 30, 1863, Benjamin C. Ludlow to Chase, Feb. 19, 1865 (Chase Papers, L.C.); Robson, *Biographical Encyclopædia*, 629; *Quinquennial Catalogue*, 235.
6. Josephine Ludlow (1838–66), a daughter of James Chambers Ludlow and Josephine Dunlop Ludlow, and the sister of Chase's third wife, Sarah Bella Dunlop Ludlow Chase. Unpublished guide to Ludlow-Dunlop-Chambers Collec., Univ. of Wyoming.
7. Emily Coxe McIlvaine assisted her father with pomological research in Burlington, N.J., before she married Charles Pettit McIlvaine on Oct. 8, 1822. The couple, who remained married more than fifty years, resided on fourteen forested acres in Clifton. *DAB*, 4:489, 12:64; *Nat. Cyc.*, 7:2; Sidney D. Maxwell, *The Suburbs of Cincinnati* . . . (Cincinnati, 1870), 44.
8. Elliott Hunt Pendleton (1828–92), Cincinnati merchant and banker active with the Cincinnati Sanitary Commission, or his brother, George Hunt Pendleton; Larz Anderson (1803–78) of Cincinnati, brother of Robert Anderson and son-in-law of Nicholas Longworth; and Richard Smith (1823–98) and Samuel Rockwell Reed (c. 1820–89), Ohio journalists who maintained long associations with the Republican *Cincinnati Gazette*. *Biographical Cyclopædia*, 5:1260–61, 6:1336–37; *Appletons'*, 1:71, 5:584; Goss, *Cincinnati*, 4:27–78.

him to Hillsboro[9]—agreed if wd. return Monday evg & so arrangd / Nettie went accordingly— Mr. Mellen called—all well at home— telegram from Gov. Sprague in reply to mine yesterday—"We are all well— Brief pencil letter from Katie dated 20th—baby bright, black haired & handsome[10]— Hosea called—& again at 5 when he took me to Clifton— Called on Mrs Hosea & young ladies Hattie & *Lucy?*—went on to Bishop McIlvaines—nice tea—daughter, most agreeable & intelligent—evg very-very hot—*no* air—not a leaf stirred—some musketoes or other biting insects—sat out doors talking till between 10 & 11—retired after prayers— How delightful this family is— How blessed is Christian peace / they much interested about the freedmen

SATURDAY, JUNE 24. The Bishop goes to commt. at Gambier & leaves today[11]—took me to town & left me at Burnet— Many callers—LHommedieu who busier than ever abt. R.R. matters[12]—wants me to meet him at Meadville Monday week & go with him to New York—promises Presidents car / Judge Matthews[13] wishes his bro in law Veser made Dis. J. in Tennessee— Dinner at 6 at Carson's— Mellens there—Mrs M. looking very well. Mellen says Hooper here some days ago & Pendleton's guest—on wh. account some Republicans wd. not call on him—he approved this—Carson & I contra— returned to Hotel about 9— Burnside in the House—called yesterday—is on railroad business from wh. he expects something handsome[14]—I hope he will realize his anticipations—some officers speak slightingly of him as a military man—but he is certainly generous & modest— Hooker called today.

SUNDAY, JUNE 25. LHommedieu came & we went to Christ Church together—met S. Wyllys Pomeroy at St Pauls— Stranger preached at Christ's—walked from church with Judge Este,[15] who wishes suffrage alike for whites & blacks but restricted to readers & writers—rainstorm—did not go to meeting of Cold. Sunday Schools as I had thought of doing—dined with Sam Reed—met

9. William Oliver Collins.
10. William Sprague (1865–90), son of Kate Chase Sprague and Gov. William Sprague, led an unsettled life and worked at several jobs before committing suicide. Thomas Graham Belden and Marva Robins Belden, *So Fell the Angels* (Boston and Toronto, 1956), 338–40.
11. Kenyon College at Gambier, Ohio.
12. Stephen S. L'Hommedieu.
13. Stanley Matthews.
14. In 1865, Ambrose E. Burnside was elected president of the Cincinnati & Martinsville R.R. Co. Ben. Perley Poore, *The Life and Public Services of Ambrose E. Burnside* . . . (Providence, R.I., 1882), 265.
15. David Kirkpatrick Este.

young Captain Brown of Cold. Troops— He strong for universal suffrages & indignant abt disparagement of officers of Col. regiments— What an opportunity of great good & solid glory Mr. Johnson has put away from him!

Walked to Cor. 4th & Vine with Reid & bid him goodbye—to hotel & bed.

Dickson called before church—explained course of things at Columbus Convention—wd. have withdrawn fr. Convn. with fds but for fear of jeoparding constl. amendt.[16]

MONDAY, JUNE 26. Marshal Sands came & went with him to Dis Court & took seat with Judge Leavitt who sentenced two counterfeiters to 6 years each—tho't sentence too light—went to Superior Court with Mr Lincoln; to the Rooms of Judges Storer, Fox & Hoadly[17]— H—— absent from his—then to Rooms of Com. Pleas Judges Headington, Oliver & Murdock[18]—then to Library—wh much impd / met several brother lawyers of long time—Worthington, Taft, Henderson Stallo & others[19] / after noon rode to Clifton with Ball—tea—then to Probasco's—whose house is beautiful[20]— then to Mr. Ellis' where several gentlemen had been invited to meet me—Buchanan Hosea, Emanl. Miller, Probasco, Ellis, Judge Leavitt, Schoenberger and others[21]—pleasant talk—pleasant collation— then back to Ball— Nettie had come but gone to Mrs Deland's for the night[22]—so to bed in the same room as last fall

16. William M. Dickson reported on the Union Party Convention that met on June 21 in Columbus. This gathering elected candidates for Ohio state offices and adopted resolutions related to Reconstruction. *Daily Ohio State Journal*, June 21, 22, 23, 1865.

17. Timothy Daniel Lincoln, Bellamy Storer, Charles Fox, and George Hoadly.

18. Nicholas Headington, Melancthon Wade Oliver (1825–1900), and Charles Cone Murdock (b. 1828) sat as judges of the Hamilton County Court of Common Pleas. *Cinc. Dir. (1865)*, 189; *History of Cincinnati and Hamilton County*, 518–19; *Biographical Cyclopædia*, 3:760–61; Gilkey, *Ohio Hundred Year Book*, 550; *General Catalogue of the Graduates and Former Students of Miami University . . . 1809–1909* (Oxford, Ohio, 1909), 54.

19. Vachel Worthington, Alfonso Taft, Thomas J. Henderson, and Johann Bernhard Stallo (1823–1900), a German-born scholar, all practiced law in Cincinnati in the decades prior to the Civil War. *Cinc. Dir. (1840)*, 216; ibid. (1865), 193; *DAB*, 17:496–97.

20. In 1865, Cincinnati merchant and civic benefactor Henry Probasco (1820–1902) completed a limestone and sandstone mansion known as "Oakwood." *Biographical Cyclopædia*, 2:521; *Who Was Who*, 1:998.

21. John W. Ellis, whose property adjoined Henry Probasco's; Robert Buchanan; Robert Hosea; and George K. Shoenberger (1808–92), Cincinnati iron manufacturer. All resided in Clifton. Emanuel Miller may have been a Cincinnati cabinet maker. Maxwell, *Suburbs of Cincinnati*, 33–38, 42–44; *Biographical Cyclopædia*, 6:1457–58; *Cinc. Dir. (1865)*, 291.

22. Helen Cecelia Ball Deland (b. 1839), a daughter of Flamen Ball, married Clifton resident and Cincinnati dry goods dealer Charles W. Deland. Landy, *Cincinnati Past and Present*, 151; Maxwell, *Suburbs of Cincinnati*, 36; *Cinc. Dir. (1865)*, 111.

TUESDAY, JUNE 27. Took Nettie & to town with Mr. Ball, leaving regretfully his sweet daughters[23]— A. F. Perry came to dine with me—talked abt. freedmen & suffrage / Reid & Collins at table— Met Freedmen's Aid Commn at 3.30—gave brief account of what I had seen & of my conclusions—found them much of same opinion— Levi Coffin there just returned from England—says my note very useful to him—young Mr. Simpson also present—is from Manchester & is collecting infn. on Emancipation & Freedmen[24]— Nettie went to Abingdon with Kate Whiteman—left card for me saying Mrs Anderson desired me to meet some friends at her house—went— found a bevy of pretty young girls with quan. suff. of young officers—a few young married women & Gen Hooker & Mr Flagg.[25] These two & Mr & Mrs Anderson the only seniors & they not much so—returned to hotel abt 11

WEDNESDAY, JUNE 28. At home most of morning preparing for departure tomorrow—wrote Katie, will leave N.Y. Wedy. evening for Providence & be at Narra Beach next day D.V.[26]— Col Key came to dinner—favors univ. suffrage—thinks shirking of it a blunder— fears it is out of question now—praises McClellan's—says he is really brave—has seen him under hot fire perfectly cool & collected— thinks Stanton a hypocrite—says he wrote McClellan at Harrison's Landing proposing alliance offensive & defensive— Is this possible— Key says he wrote while McClellan dictated answer— K—— thinks strong force should be sent to Kentucky—and yet that Johnson shd. renounce military commissions— Going out to buy penknife met R. G. Corwin who came in eveng—seemed desirous to know my preference as b. Sherman & Schenck—himself for latter— Philip Hinkle called—talk abt. ready made houses wh he makes

23. At least four of Flamen Ball's twelve children by his first wife were female: Eva Candler (b. 1831); Helen Cecelia; Laura Amelia (b. 1844); and Susan Louisa Bowler (b. 1847). Landy, *Cincinnati Past and Present*, 151.
24. The Freedman's Aid Commission maintained an office in Cincinnati. Chase had provided a note of introduction when Coffin went to Europe the year before to work for the Western Freedmen's Aid Commission. Joseph Simpson, a Quaker, was a member of the National Freedmen's Aid Union of Great Britain and Ireland. His visit to the United States in 1865 lasted four months. *Cinc. Dir. (1865)*, 151; Coffin to Chase, May 2, 1864 (Chase Papers, L.C.); Chase to Coffin, May 5, 1864 (Chase Papers, Hist. Soc. of Pa.); Bolt, *Anti-Slavery Movement and Reconstruction*, 73, 95, 124–25, 135–36.
25. Catherine Longworth Anderson's brother-in-law William Joseph Flagg (1818–98), formerly a Cincinnati lawyer, was an agriculturist with a particular interest in grape culture. *New York Times*, Apr. 16, 1898; Nelson W. Evans, *A History of Scioto County, Ohio . . .* (Portsmouth, Ohio, 1903), 387–88.
26. Deo volente, "God willing." In a letter which Chase wrote to his daughter Kate four days earlier, he outlined his intended travel schedule. Chase to Kate Chase Sprague, June 24, 1865 (Chase Papers, L.C.).

THURSDAY, JUNE 29. Up about 4 & made ready for departure / Nettie punctual—bkft at 5—left depot at 6— Maj. Bannister, Maj. McDowell & Col. Lathrop on train[27]—arrived in Columbus 10.30—crops looking well—wheat better than corn— Deshler & Geiger came in— G—— remained after D—— gone—explained efforts for Swayne, of wh. I knew nothing & could not blame if I had[28]—expressed warm thanks for my kindness & readiness to serve me— Gen. Wright called with others—want me to welcome returning soldiers at Park—agreed & at 5 went with Gen W., Young of Piqua, Harrison of Springfield & another[29] / talked a little—Galloway talked more & delighted the boys—a fine collation though somewhat damaged by rain[30]—at George M Parsons to tea—some few gentlemen came in to see me—Gen Mitchell,[31] Galloway, Noble,[32] Gen. Wright, and some ladies to see Nettie—a pleasant eveng—back to Neil House at 11.

FRIDAY, JUNE 30. Gen. Mitchell called—advised him to go to New Orleans / inclines to Memphis—offered letters—Harrison for Co. presents accident Insurance—Dr. Coulter calls—wife very ill—Paymr. W. H. Johnston[33]—left for depot—difficulty of getting

27. Malcolm McDowell (c. 1828–1903), an army paymaster, 1861–65, was the youngest brother of Gen. Irvin McDowell. Lt. Col. Solon H. Lathrop (d. 1867), an assistant inspector general, had been a member of the judicial commission which tried Richard T. Semmes and others for conspiracy. *New York Times*, Dec. 27, 1903; Heitman, *Historical Register*, 1:617, 664; *OR*, ser. 1, v. 12, pt. 1:122–23, ser. 2, v. 8:645; *Message from the President . . . relative to the Case of George St. Leger Grenfel*, 3.

28. When the chief justiceship became vacant in 1864, some Ohio judges and lawyers, as well as a majority of the justices on the U.S. Supreme Court, had favored Noah Swayne for the position instead of Chase. Fairman, *Reconstruction and Reunion*, 11–12, 18–20.

29. George Bohan Wright (1815–1903), Ohio railroad attorney and manager, served in Columbus through the Civil War as quartermaster general of Ohio, commissary general, and military storekeeper. John H. Young (1813–95), son of a Piqua lawyer, served before the Civil War as a state militia general and supported the Union as a War Democrat. Raised in Springfield, Ohio, Richard Almgill Harrison (1824–1904) supported Chase while a member of the state assembly, 1858–61, and served in Congress as a Unionist, 1861–63. *Biographical Cyclopædia*, 1:207–9, 4:889, 5:1100–1102; *Who Was Who*, 1:527, 1384; Reed, *Bench and Bar of Ohio*, 1:462–64; *Bio. Dir. U.S. Cong.*, 1143.

30. The people of Columbus gave an open-air reception to three regiments of Ohio Volunteer Infantry just arrived from Washington. *Daily Ohio State Journal*, June 29, 30, 1865.

31. John Grant Mitchell (1838–94), an officer of Ohio infantry and brevet major general of volunteers. James Grant Wilson, ed., *Appletons' Cyclopædia of American Biography: Volume Seven, Supplement* (New York, 1901), 197; Heitman, *Historical Register*, 1:717.

32. Hotel keeper John Noble (1789–1871) became active after 1850 in Columbus politics and civic concerns. *Biographical Cyclopædia*, 5:1240.

33. Paymaster William Hartshorne Johnston (d. 1896), a native Ohioan, became a career soldier. Heitman, *Historical Register*, 1:579.

July 1865   { 583 }

sent—met Bundy & daughters[34]—off for Cleveland—cars crowded—many standing—at Delaware Prof. Donaldson—says Bishop Thomson was at commt.[35] reached Cleveland abt. 3—met Parsons who took me to Soldiers Home—met Mrs Rouse, Miss Brayton & Miss Terry—wonderful energy & zeal[36]—large provision— Wisconsin regt— Parsons carriage waiting & in it to his house on Prospect Street— Kind welcome from Mrs P—called on Gov. Brough who has been in much danger from a neglected bruise foot & hand—seems much better now— Acting Mayor Jones[37] called to ask me to welcome returning regt tomorrow—consented— Judge Starkweather & some others called[38]—rode with P & Mrs P & Nettie

SATURDAY, JULY 1. Went to Miss Ransom's studio with P—nothing done to my picture since last summer—don't impress me so favorably as then[39]— (1) to Judge Wilson's Court[40]—sat with him few minutes—Ranney arguing Patent case—Root came up & spoke to me.[41] after return fr. Miss Ransoms went to Judge W——s room—& waited till soldiers came— Wilson, Marshal Bill,[42] & Root

---

34. Hezekiah Sanford Bundy had four daughters who survived infancy: Sarah A., who married Benjamin F. Stearns; Lucy J., who married J. C. H. Cobb; Julia A., who married Joseph B. Foraker; and Ellen. *Biographical Cyclopædia*, 5:1151–52.

35. Edward Thomson addressed a gathering on June 27 during the anniversary exercises of Delaware College (Ohio Wesleyan). *Daily Ohio State Journal*, June 20, 24, 30, 1865.

36. Women of the Soldiers' Aid Society of Northern Ohio superintended construction of a new Soldiers' Home in Cleveland in late 1863 and operated this facility for traveling soldiers until it closed on June 1, 1866. Rebecca Cromwell Rouse (1799–1887), a leading social and benevolent worker; Mary Clark Brayton (1833–78); and Ellen F. Terry, daughter of a medical professor, served respectively as the first president, secretary, and treasurer of the Soldiers' Aid Society of Northern Ohio. Mrs. W. A. Ingham, *Women of Cleveland and Their Work* . . . (Cleveland, 1893), 124–33; Van Tassel and Grabowski, *Encyclopedia of Cleveland*, 845, 909–10.

37. Thomas Jones, Jr., Cleveland city council president, 1864–65. Orth, *History of Cleveland*, 1:794; *Cleveland Plain Dealer*, July 5, 1865.

38. Parsons's father-in-law Samuel Starkweather (1799–1876), Cleveland lawyer, Democratic politician, and judge of the court of common pleas, 1852–57. Holli and Jones, *Biographical Dictionary of American Mayors*, 341–42.

39. Portrait and landscape painter Caroline L. Ormes Ransom (1838–1910) eventually settled in Washington, D.C. Groce and Wallace, *Dictionary of Artists*, 524.

40. The *(1)*, which Chase inserted above the line, matches another *(1)* at the top of the day's entry. These notations indicate that in the day's sequence of events the visit to Hiram V. Willson's court came first, then the visit to Ransom's studio, then the return to Willson's chambers.

41. Rufus P. Ranney was in all likelihood acting as counsel for the defendants in a patent infringement suit by Elias Howe, Jr., against several venders of sewing machines. Joseph Mosley Root (1807–79) had been a Whig and Free-Soil member of Congress from Ohio, 1845–51, and became U.S. attorney for the northern district of Ohio in 1861. *Cleveland Plain Dealer*, June 30, 1865; *Bio. Dir. U.S. Cong.*, 1742.

42. Earl Bill, U.S. marshal for the northern district of Ohio. *OR*, ser. 2, v. 2:1042; *Daily Ohio State Journal*, June 21, 1865.

each in room for minute only— when soldiers came went & addressed them[43]—very well received—back to house— Benedict came to dinner[44]—not appointed Postmaster yet—ought to be—rained quite hard—Senter invited did not come— Judge & Mrs Starkweather passed evening at Parsons[45]—left in rain, h[or]se car not coming—called at Gov. Broughs before sunset—saw Mrs B.[46]— "Gov. quite exhausted but wd. see us a moment—tho't it best not to disturb him & did not

SUNDAY, JULY 2. To Presbyn. Church—P & wife remd. to comn. / wished to but did not— Mr. Goodrich's sermon good but too ornate & level[47]—referred, happily, to coming 4th—read, & wrote out substance of soldiers-speech—made it, I thought, better than as delivered—telegraphed LHommedieu will "be at Meadville as promised"— Col. Stager, Mr Handy, Judge Spalding, Mr. Bradburn, Mr. Hulburt, cashr. & Mr H—— his uncle called[48]—talk about journey south— Col. S—— promd to telegraph NY. I will be at St Nicholas Thursday—said had recd. Friday telegram to be forwarded to Foster, Pres. p.t. of Senate, requesting him to return & come to Washn.—F. is with Congl. Com. on Plains visiting Indian Tribes, & at three or four days journey from westernmost tel. station where telm. had been recd. & forwarded immediately by couriers—Stager thought Presidents illness might be serious[49]— Gov B——'s

43. Chase addressed the 118th Ohio Regt. after its arrival in Cleveland at half past noon. Such formal addresses were part of the welcome accorded all returning regiments arriving in Cleveland. *Cleveland Plain Dealer,* July 1, 1865; Mary Clark Brayton and Ellen F. Terry, *Our Acre and Its Harvest* (Cleveland, 1869), 350–51, 382–83.
    44. George A. Benedict (1812–76), lawyer, editor of the Republican *Cleveland Herald,* 1857–76, and Cleveland postmaster, 1865–69. Van Tassel and Grabowski, *Encyclopedia of Cleveland,* 90–91.
    45. Julia Judd Starkweather (1810–94) was active in Sunday school and temperance work. Ingham, *Women of Cleveland,* 52–53; Van Tassel and Grabowski, *Encyclopedia of Cleveland,* 342.
    46. Caroline A. Nelson (d. ca. 1890) of Columbus, Ohio, married the widowed John Brough in 1843. *DAB,* 3:95; *Biographical Cyclopædia,* 1:298.
    47. Chase meant he did not remain for communion. William Henry Goodrich (1825–74) became associated with the First Presbyterian Church of Cleveland in 1858. *Appletons',* 2:682; *Biographical Cyclopædia,* 3:672.
    48. Truman P. Handy (1807–98), banker, financier, civic and educational promoter; possibly Charles Bradburn (1808–79), a wholesale grocer and longtime member of Cleveland's school board; and probably Hinman Barrett Hulburt or Hurlbut (1819–84), Cleveland lawyer and banker, with a nephew. Van Tassel and Grabowski, *Encyclopedia of Cleveland,* 485; Orth, *History of Cleveland,* 1:524, 645; Kennedy, *History of Cleveland,* 283, 286, 306; *Nat. Cyc.,* 2:185.
    49. Andrew Johnson was ill during late June and early July. As president pro tempore of the Senate, Lafayette S. Foster stood next in line of succession to the presidency. Foster was in Santa Fe, N.M., early in July as part of a special joint congressional committee examining the condition of Indian tribes in the western

condition has been considered critical all day—Dr. Barr hopeful not sanguine[50]

MONDAY, JULY 3. Left friends at 8.30—Parsons with us to Depot—before leaving sent to enquire concerning Gov. B—— ansr. comfortable but some pain in arm— Hickcox[51] & Senter joined me—Stager failed to come & Parsons cd. not go—off at 9.25—talk with H—— abt old freesoil '48 when he lent me valise but voted for Taylor—with Senter abt '60 bad managet.—Cartter, Wade &c[52]—reached Meadville, 2 P.M—met Grow Dick old M.C. & others[53]—much urged to stay but L'H wanted to go on—dined hastily—goodbye to Senter & others—off—delayed by heat[ing] & burning of journal packing[54]—this happened often—supper on car—feared we shd. be obliged to abandon it—doctored again abt 8 P.M & again abt 10 improved so much by Hornell'sville that kept on to N.Y.—I lay down about 10.30 or 11—nice wide bed but did not undress fearing accident— Nettie in opposite State room.

TUESDAY, JULY 4. up & washed abt. 6—all right with engine—but delays had put us behind time—put out our flags—paper only & printed on but one side but better than none[55]—Mr. Church, formerly Judge & now Solr. of the Road, a pleasing gent. with us—also Charles Sherman & his son John[56]— S—— tells me his bro. the

---

states. Graf et al., *Papers of Andrew Johnson*, 8:220, 245, 529–30; *Bio. Dir. U.S. Cong.*, 1020; *Condition of the Indian Tribes: Report of the Joint Special Committee, Appointed Under Joint Resolution of March 3, 1865* . . . (Washington, 1867), esp. 323; Santa Fe *New Mexican*, July 7, 1865.

    50. Ohio Surgeon General Robert N. Barr, Gov. Brough's personal friend, telegraphed from Cleveland on July 3 that Brough "was some better, but was still in a critical condition." *Daily Ohio State Journal*, July 4, 6, 1865; Reid, *Ohio in the War*, 1:247.

    51. Charles Hickox.

    52. It is unclear whether Chase actually met David K. Cartter and Benjamin F. Wade or discussed them with Senter. Cartter spoke at Cleveland on July 4. *Cleveland Plain Dealer*, July 5, 1865.

    53. Galusha Aaron Grow (1822–1907) of Pennsylvania was speaker of the U.S. House of Representatives, 1861–63; John Dick (1794–1872) of Meadville was in the House, 1853–59. *DAB*, 8:30–31; *Bio. Dir. U.S. Cong.*, 905.

    54. Journal packing: "Waste cotton or wool saturated with oil or grease and filled into an axle-box to lubricate the axle." Edward H. Knight, *Knight's New Mechanical Dictionary* (Boston, 1884), 516.

    55. Independence Day decorations for the train.

    56. The railroad solicitor likely was John W. Church, an Ohio common pleas judge, 1859–64. Charles Taylor Sherman (1811–79), elder brother of Gen. William Tecumseh Sherman and Sen. John Sherman, was a Mansfield attorney before the Civil War, a railroad corporation director, and federal district judge at Cleveland, 1867–72. John Edward Sherman was his son. Gilkey, *Ohio Hundred Year Book*, 565; *Biographical Cyclopædia*, 4:1032–33.

General much gratified by my letter urging justice to him[57]—breakfasted & lunched on car—near 4 when we reached New York Ferry—found comfortable quarters at St. Nicholas—after dinner Joshua Hanna called—says his gold mining adventure promises great success—if stock *good* I shall have some[58]—rode with him in omnibus to call on Jno. A. Stevens—out of town—so back—more talk & parted—noise in Streets—illuminations—rockets—firecrackers—crowds—in short 4th of July.

WEDNESDAY, JULY 5. late bkf't—Nettie *rather* later than usual—Herald[59] full of 4th—Stager must have forgot to telegraph for no announcement of my coming— Sent cards to Haight, Howe, T. Brown, Tilton & one or two more[60]— Haight & Howe called Brown not fd—Tilton out of town— L'Hommedieu & Mellen called—sent by Haight card to O. Johnson & message to Vail.[61] Haight says all banks but 7 (Manhattan, America & five more) have become National— My system now sure of universal adoption[62]—told them, the other day, they wd. have done much better to come in 2 years ago when I asked them— Mellen has concluded to take contract for old claims collections with Treasy Dept—sent to Neptune S.S. Line & engaged State room for Providence—lost trunk came $1 to Porter 1 to house messenger— Howe talked over N.O. matters—expressed great confidence in Banks— O. Johnston called—late of A. [Slvy] Standard now of Indt.—dinner—J. Hanna with me to Steamer Oceanus for Prov.[63]

THURSDAY, JULY 6. Were approaching Providence when I left my stateroom—breakfast $1.50—horse car to Kingston depot 30c. for 3—baggage $1.50—train to Kingston arrd. 8.14—no car-

---

57. Probably Chase to W. G. Deshler, Apr. 29, 1865, printed in *Daily Ohio State Journal*, May 4, 1865. See Apr. 29, 1865 (above).

58. Chase did invest in Hanna's Pittsburgh and Idaho Gold Mining Co. A year later Chase regretted his involvement with the venture. Hanna to Chase, Aug. 31, Sept. 4, Oct. 14, 1865 (Chase Papers, L.C.); Chase to Hanna, Sept. 6, 1865 (Chase Papers, Hist. Soc. of Pa.); Chase to Jay Cooke, Sept. 14, 1866 (Cooke Papers, Hist. Soc. of Pa.).

59. *New York Herald*.

60. Edward Haight, Frank E. Howe, Thomas Brown, Theodore Tilton.

61. Antislavery editor Oliver Johnson (1809–89) was, as Chase noted later in this entry, associate editor of the *National Anti-Slavery Standard*, 1853–65, and of the *Independent*, 1865–70. *DAB*, 10:112.

62. The national banking system begun under the banking act (National Currency Act) of Feb. 1863.

63. The *Oceanus*, launched in 1865 and advertised as "unsurpassed in . . . arrangements for the comfort and safety of passengers," left New York for Providence at 5 P.M. as part of the regular service of the Neptune Steamship Co. *New York Daily Tribune*, July 4, 1865; Lytle, *Merchant Vessels*, 142.

riage—met Dr. Hazards brother[64]—says Dr. thinks Kate's baby a nonsuch— put Nettie in stage & Willie on box[65]—carriage came— exchanged / reached Sprague Farm—alias Melluna—alias Canonchet [D'Lande][66]—joyful meeting—baby all that had been told—excellent old nurse Mrs Morgan fr Phila, Katie quite well—in better health & handsomer than for years—found large packages of letters—most intg. from Mr. Bigelow at Paris & Mr. Pike at the Hague & Gen Gillmore at Hilton[67]—looked through the whole and also the newspapers—rode in the evening the Beach & to Wakefield with Katie & Nettie—pleasant—air cool enough for overcoat— passed several vehicles of visiters at the Pier who seem more numerous than ever before.

FRIDAY, JULY 7. The mail brings a number of letters—one fr Mr. Seward acknowledging mine of condolence[68]—his writing more unintelligible than ever whole sentences I cannot make out—one from Mr. Patterson offering home at Dartmouth commencement[69]—abt 3 recd. Prov. paper containing order for execution of conspirators— Payne, alias Powell, Atzerott, Harold & Mrs Surratt—today b. 9. &

64. William Henry Hazard (b. 1808) practiced medicine at Wakefield, R.I., and earned a reputation as "a most hospitable man." Edward Hull Hazard (b. 1812) was his only surviving brother as of 1865. Caroline E. Robinson, *The Hazard Family of Rhode Island, 1635–1894* (Boston, 1895), 102, 167–68.

65. William Joice worked as Chase's attendant and driver, c. 1865–73, apparently in the official capacity of a messenger for the Supreme Court. *Wash. Dir. (1870)*, 211; Chase to Joice, July 15, 22, 1872, Joice to J. W. Schuckers, Aug. 18, 30, 1873 (Chase Papers, Hist. Soc. of Pa.); Schuckers, *Chase*, 623–24.

66. Sprague Farm embraced 350 acres bordering the Atlantic Ocean in Narragansett, R.I. Gov. William Sprague purchased the estate, favorite camping ground of Canonchet, a seventeenth-century Narragansett Indian chief, during the early 1860s. A 68-room mansard mansion was built on the property following the Civil War. *Narragansett Times*, Oct. 15, 1909; *Providence Journal*, Oct. 12, 1909; Belden and Belden, *So Fell the Angels*, 218–20.

67. Author and editor John Bigelow (1817–1911) was U.S. minister to France. See July 14 below for Chase's reply to Bigelow's letter. James S. Pike (1811–82), also an author, editor, and Chase's friend, had been minister to The Hague since 1861. His letter of Apr. 19 tried to soothe feelings apparently hurt by his criticism of Chase's measures as secretary of the Treasury. Quincy Adams Gillmore had written on June 18, commenting on the formation of new military departments. *DAB*, 2:258–59, 14:595–96; Pike to Chase, Apr. 19, 1865 (Chase Papers, Hist. Soc. of Pa.); Gillmore to Chase, June 18, 1865 (William P. Palmer Collec., Western Reserve Hist. Soc.).

68. Seward replied to Chase's condolences after the death of Seward's wife. Chase to Seward, June 25, 1865 (Chase Papers, Hist. Soc. of Pa.).

69. James Willis Patterson (1823–93) taught mathematics, astronomy, and meteorology at Dartmouth College, 1852–65. He was also a Republican congressman, 1863–67, and U.S. senator, 1867–73. Patterson invited Chase to Hanover, N.H., for Dartmouth's commencement. *DAB*, 14:303–4; Patterson to Chase, June 30, 1865 (Chase Papers, L.C.).

2—all over then now[70]— Note from Sumner who much disturbed about prospect of reorganization[71]—wrote many letters—one to Pike, abt. his note to Seward just before resignation—abt. condition of labor south & wishes of blacks[72] / to Seward, enclosing one to me from Powers—to Dennison, enclosing one fr —McCulloch one from Coulter abt. Moore L.H. Keeper Racine[73]—rode to Kingston Station to meet Gov[74] who did not come—Mr Hazard, Mrs H. & Mrs H. Jr. & Miss Potter called[75]—dinner— Gov. arrd. on horse back fr Providence—talk & bed—

SATURDAY, JULY 8. delightful day—cool bracing air—late bkft— read Les Abimes de Paris—wrote letters to Col Howe & E. L. Pierce "Will be at Hanover & hope to meet Classmates say so in Newspapers"[76]—to Punchard & Blodgett, "be present"—to Waters asking him to tell Gannett to be there—enclg. $20 for expenses &

70. The *Providence Daily Journal,* July 7, 1865, reported the delivery of death warrants on July 6 to Lewis Thornton Powell (1845–65), also known by aliases Lewis Paine (or Payne) or Wood; George A. Atzerodt (1835–65); David Edgar Herold (1846–65); and Mary Eugenia Surratt (1820 or 1823–65), all convicted by a military court as conspirators in Lincoln's assassination. The sentences called for immediate execution, and the conspirators were hanged on July 7, 1865. Chase followed the newspaper account in rendering Atzerodt as Atzerott. Mark E. Neely, Jr., *The Abraham Lincoln Encyclopedia* (New York, 1982), 13–14, 148, 244–45, 298–99.

71. Sumner expressed unhappiness over Andrew Johnson's Reconstruction policies. Charles Sumner to Chase, July 1, 1865 (Chase Papers, Hist. Soc. of Pa.), printed in Palmer, *Selected Letters of Charles Sumner,* 2:312–13.

72. Chase's letter to James S. Pike, which he actually dated July 8, was in reply to Pike's of Apr. 19 (see preceding entry). Chase clarified his reaction to a note from Pike to William Seward, critical of Chase's administration of the Treasury, written shortly before Chase left the Treasury Department. Chase also described the situation of blacks in the South. Chase to Pike, July 8, 1865 (Pike Papers, Univ. of Maine).

73. Chase's brief letter to Seward covered one from Hiram Powers to Chase, written in Florence on Apr. 18, concerning diplomatic appointments in Italy. Powers (1805–73), a sculptor, had begun his career in Cincinnati. Chase evidently wrote also to William Dennison, U.S. postmaster general at the time, and to Secretary of the Treasury Hugh McCulloch. The letter to McCulloch apparently enclosed one from James H. Coulter concerning Milton Moore, keeper of the lighthouse at Racine, Wis. Chase to Seward, July 7, 1865 (Seward Papers, Univ. of Rochester Lib.); *DAB,* 15:158–60; *Register of Officers (1865),* 82.

74. William Sprague.

75. Rowland Gibson Hazard (1801–88), Rhode Island manufacturer, Free-Soil and Republican politician, and author, wrote a series of financial articles during the Civil War. He married Caroline Newbold, a native of Bucks County, Pa., in 1828. Their son Rowland Hazard (1829–98) managed the family textile factories, invested in other enterprises, and engaged in state politics. His wife was Margaret Rood Hazard (d. 1895), daughter of a Philadelphia minister. These Hazards, members of a particularly influential branch of the family, resided in Peacedale. Miss Potter was likely Mary Elizabeth Potter (1820–1901), sister of Elisha Reynolds Potter and James Brown Mason Potter of Kingston. Robinson, *Hazard Family,* 122–23, 198–99; *DAB,* 8:471–72; *Nat. Cyc.,* 12:221–22; J. R. Cole, *History of Washington and Kent Counties, Rhode Island . . .* (New York, 1889), 494–507; *Representative Men,* 1:53.

76. Chase to Edward L. Pierce, July 8, 1865 (Houghton Lib., Harvard Univ.).

enquiring abt. Mrs E & Mrs R[77]—to Susan Walker to learn whereabouts—to Prof. Patterson, accepting offd. hospitality[78]—rode with Gov. to Wakefd. & Peacedale—put letters in P.O—got papers with account of denial of hab. corpus & of execution—doubt if suspension of writ at this time justifiable though probably not unwarranted[79]— Gov. condemns mily. commissions—I don't see how cd. be dispensed with in war, but shd. be avoided when possible—matter necessarily of executive discretion— Gov., K. & N. rode to Hazard Castle[80]—Dr. & Mrs H[81] called also Miss Auferman & Hodgkin abt. corn paper—walked to beach by myslf—moon light & ocean—home—more [cornpaper]—to bed

SUNDAY, JULY 9. To church at Wakefield—Mr. Winkley preached against doctrine of absolute Equality[82]—attacked what nobody affirms & asserted what nobody denies—back to house—read not very improvingly—walk to Beach eveng—Mr. Winkley & his two find boys with me, Kate Nettie & Gov had gone in advance. long line of rays from shore to darkness under the moon—a life crowded with good & bright acts reaching through the dark of death to supernal glory—back reading & to bed.

MONDAY, JULY 10. Gov. to Providence this morning—I doing nothing special—reading a little & writing some letters—

TUESDAY, JULY 11. Agreed to go Providence tomorrow— Nothing particularly done—a call or two

77. George W. Punchard and Constantine Blodgett (1802–79), a Congregational minister in Pawtucket, R.I., were classmates of Chase at Dartmouth. Richard P. Waters, a friend of Charlotte Eastman and Jane Rantoul, evidently also had contact with Allen Gannett (1805–81), a minister and teacher who had been a member of Chase's class at Dartmouth. *Nat. Cyc.,* 9:456; Emerson, *General Catalogue,* 238.

78. Chase's filing note on James Willis Patterson's letter of June 30 acknowledged that he answered it July 8, "will come & hope to be in Han. 17th." Patterson to Chase, June 30, 1865 (Chase Papers, L.C.).

79. Andrew Johnson had suspended the writ of habeas corpus with reference to an application submitted on behalf of Mary Surratt the previous day. Attorney General James Speed supported the president's decision by distinguishing between civil and military jurisdictions. *Providence Daily Journal,* July 8, 1865.

80. Overlooking the sea at Narragansett Pier, "Hazard Castle," begun in 1846 and constructed entirely of granite masonry with towers at each end of the building, served as both a summer residence and a memorial to Hazard ancestors. Cole, *Washington and Kent Counties,* 574–75.

81. Louisa Arnold Hazard (b. 1820), daughter of a Rhode Island governor, married William Henry Hazard in 1840. Robinson, *Hazard Family,* 168; *Nat. Cyc.,* 9:395.

82. J. F. Winkley, rector, Church of the Ascension, c. 1864–67. Cole, *Washington and Kent Counties,* 589–91.

WEDNESDAY, JULY 12. Went to Providence with Sprague—street cars to Mrs S——'s—to Cranston with Gov. in buggy—lunch at Amasa Spragues[83]—visit to print works—prints 26c p. yd.—9c. before war—Canadians employed—get $2 per mo in Canada 3 per week here—visit to Amasa S—— stables—some horses valued $5000 each—went on to Arctic destroyed by fire last spring—rebuilding—returned soldiers employed—Supt. estimates of iron[—]taken from ruins—a little rain—farms connected with mills—nice houses for the workpeople—progressive increase of comforts for masses[84]—returned to Providence & Mrs Spragues—Mrs Nichols & Ida—Miss Almira[85]—and Miss Fisher a young lady friend of Ida—quite agreeable—bed—

THURSDAY, JULY 13. Breakfast—to office of A. & W. S.[86] with Gov—visited Medallion Gallery of Miller & Co / some of medallions seem to me really excellent greater number middling—mine of this class—tolerable[87]—called at Bookstore—bot some thin paper & envelopes—also new Edition of Tennyson[88] / returned to Farm afternoon— Mr. Stevens came yesterday & returned in rainstorm—to Newport[89]—

FRIDAY, JULY 14. Gov. Katie & I called at Dr. Hazards—drunken brother[90]—called at Mr. R. G. Hazards who absent—saw Mrs H— took Gov to cars—returning called at Mr. Potters[91] / Wrote Pike &

---

83. Gov. William Sprague's mother, Fanny Morgan Sprague (b. ca. 1805), daughter of a Connecticut shoemaker, resided in Providence. She was widowed upon the murder of her husband Amasa Sprague in 1843. Gov. William Sprague's brother and business partner, also named Amasa Sprague (1828–1902), resided in Cranston. *Providence Dir. (1865)*, 148; Sprague, *Sprague Families*, 299; *Representative Men*, 1:415, 417.
84. Chase visited the Sprague textile factory known as the "great print works at Cranston" and another Sprague installation in the village of Arctic destroyed by fire on Mar. 17, 1865. Oliver Payson Fuller, *The History of Warwick, Rhode Island* . . . (Providence, 1875), 204–5, 254.
85. Almira Sprague.
86. Amasa & William Sprague, manufacturers. This family company controlled textile works and manufacturing resources thoughout New England. *Providence Dir. (1865)*, 148, 149; Bicknell, *History of the State of Rhode Island* . . . *Biograhical*, 492–94; Fuller, *History of Warwick*, 202–5, 249–59.
87. The firm of William Miller & Co., sculptors and metallists, had cast Franklin Simmons's portrait medallion of Chase (see Mar. 17, 1865, above). Whiteman, *Paintings and Sculpture*, 116; *Providence Dir. (1865)*, 114.
88. "The Holy Grail," a poem included in Alfred Tennyson, *Idylls of the King*, was among books which Chase apparently owned. *Catalogue of a Most Superb Collection*, 83.
89. Probably John A. Stevens, Sr.
90. Edward Hull Hazard.
91. Elisha Reynolds Potter (1811–82), a prominent attorney and politician of South Kingston, R.I.; later an associate justice of the state's supreme court. *DAB*, 15:126–27.

Bigelow.[92] Gov. goes to Providence to organize Corporation to manage business & assume responsibilities of A. & W. Sprague & Co

SATURDAY, JULY 15. Rode to station in 45 m.—took cars to Prov. 8.40. AM. at Prov, saw Gov. a moment, also Col Viall who much interested in new linen factory[93]—on to Boston—met Hooper & Fessenden at Revere House— Prof. Parsons & Maj. Stearns left cards[94] / Sumner, Hooper, Gannett, Punchard & Capt Jones[95] called—left at 5.30 for Concord

TUESDAY, JULY 18. Mr. onslow Stearns of Northern N.H.R. called— Shortly after his Son Charles—a Soph! at Harvard abt. to be Jr.[96]—to take me to depot—met Mr. Stearns there who introduced me to Mr Holbrook of N.Y. his bro in law who spent some 10 years in Mexico,[97] also to some R.R gent en route to Mts—took cars—met Mr. John Aikens[98] Mr. Alpheus Crosby & Mr. Robinson— telegram fr Prof Patterson at Danbury— Met, accordingly, at Lebanon by Mr. Chase with buggy[99]—an hour to Hanover & Prof. P――s—family self, wife & child—to Prof. Browns (a little party) in the evening[1]—having, P.M. attended class speaking.

WEDNESDAY, JULY 19. Commencement day—exerc[2]

---

92. Chase's letter to John Bigelow discussed Reconstruction and U.S. relations with England and France. Bigelow printed it in his *Retrospections of an Active Life*, 5 vols. (New York, 1909), 3:116–17. Chase to Bigelow, July 14, 1865 (Schaffer Lib., Union College).
93. Nelson Viall (1827–1903), Mexican War veteran and manufacturer, was colonel of the 11th U.S. Cavalry Artillery. *Biographical Cyclopedia . . . of Rhode Island*, 2:494–95; Heitman, *Historical Register*, 1:987.
94. George L. Stearns and Theophilus Parsons (1797–1882), a Harvard Law School professor and advocate of black suffrage and other forceful Reconstruction measures. *DAB*, 14:273–74.
95. Capt. John M. Jones of the Revenue Cutter Service. List of addresses, end of Journal XIX; Jones to Chase, Oct. 20, 1863 (Chase Papers, L.C.); *Register of Officers (1863)*, 46.
96. Onslow Stearns (1810–78), president of the Northern New Hampshire R.R., and his son Charles Onslow Stearns (d. 1911), Harvard class of 1867. *Nat. Cyc.*, 3:14, 11:134; *Quinquennial Catalogue*, 240.
97. Evidently a son of Adin Holbrook of Lowell, Mass., who was Onslow Stearns's father-in-law. *Nat. Cyc.*, 3:14.
98. Massachusetts lawyer and manufacturer John Aiken (1797–1867), a Dartmouth graduate and former trustee. Emerson, *General Catalogue*, 129; *Nat. Cyc.*, 6:56.
99. Frederick Chase (1840–90) of Hanover, N.H., a Dartmouth College graduate who became an attorney, judge, and treasurer of the college. Emerson, *General Catalogue*, 138, 163; S. P. Chase to F. Chase, Jan. 23, 1861 (Dartmouth College Lib.).
1. Samuel Gilman Brown (1813–85), at this time Dartmouth's professor of intellectual philosophy and political economy. *DAB*, 3:153; Emerson, *General Catalogue*, 143.
2. Chase spoke briefly following these "protracted" Dartmouth commencement exercises. *Vermont Chronicle*, July 22, 29, 1865.

SATURDAY, AUGUST 5. Mr. Stearns came shortly after breakfast & took me to Lowell depot—found R. W. Emerson & his bro. fr. N. York & Prof. Parsons[3]—cars to Tufts College Station, near which Stearns house— College Universalist richly endowed over $400.000 already & more in prospect—talk with Emerson & Parsons—Stearns down on Stanton—Parsons anecdotical / Emerson generalizing— lunch—more talk after—hastened to Station but cars passed without stopping—returned to House—took carriage, with the three to Boston— I to Hoopers—with him to old-Colony Road[4]—coach car—very pleasant—rain—Newport—Mr. Bancroft met us at station[5]—rode to his beautiful place met Mr. Davis, son of late Senator & Mrs Davis daughter of Mr. King[6]—abt. 8.30 / chatted an hour or two & then to bed after a very pleasant & instructive day

SUNDAY, AUGUST 6. At church—old Trinity—where Bishop Berkeley preached & where is the organ which he gave— A Rev. Mr. White from Canada preached—a fair sermon on the lessons of the story of Naaman[7]—communion before which I left with Mr. Bancroft and Mrs Davis—met, coming out, Mr. Sidney Brooks & Mr. Nat Thayer[8]— Mr. Thayer came to dinner—much talk abt. Agassiz the expenses of whose expedition Mr. Thayer defrays except what transportation & supplies may be furnished by our own or the Brazilian governt.[9] / a generous act—some talk also of Dr. Eliot of St Louis & Washington College of Dr. Smith & Dartmouth College[10]— walk on Cliff—met Yznaga & Mr Finney— Barréda house unoc-

3. William Emerson (1801–68), Ralph Waldo Emerson's oldest and only surviving brother, practiced law in New York and pursued real estate ventures on Staten Island. Gay Wilson Allen, *Ralph Waldo Emerson: A Biography* (New York, 1981), 9, 96, 252, 293, 639.
4. A railroad which connected Boston and Newport, R.I. King, *King's Hand-Book*, 34–36.
5. George Bancroft.
6. John Chandler Bancroft Davis and Federica Gore King Davis.
7. 2 Kgs 5. Isaac P. White was rector of Trinity Episcopal Church. George Berkeley (1685–1753), bishop of Cloyne, lived in Newport, 1729–31. *Newport Dir. (1867)*, 250; Richard M. Bayles, ed., *History of Newport County, Rhode Island . . .* (New York, 1888), 454; *DNB*, 2:348–56; *Appletons'*, 1:245–46.
8. Sidney Brooks resided in Newport and may have been the person of that name who was an agent for sculptor Hiram Powers in his dealings with the U.S. government. Nathaniel Thayer (1808–83) was a Massachusetts financier and philanthropist. *Newport Dir. (1865)*, 123; Chase to Brooks, Sept. 22, 1863 (Misc. Letters Sent, Gen. Recs. Treasury Dept., Nat. Arch.); *DAB*, 18:409–10.
9. In the spring of 1865 Louis Agassiz embarked on a nineteen-month scientific expedition to Brazil. Agassiz dedicated the published report of the expedition to Nathaniel Thayer in gratitude for his sponsorship. *DAB*, 1:121; Louis Agassiz and Elizabeth Cabot Cary Agassiz, *A Journey in Brazil* (Boston, 1868).
10. William Greenleaf Eliot and Asa Dodge Smith (1804–77), president of Dartmouth College since 1863. *DAB*, 17:239.

cupied moonlit night. Mr. Hy & Mr. Robt. Sturgis came in[11]—R. S. crude abt. Equal Suffrage

SUNDAY, SEPTEMBER 17. Went to hear Dr. Boynton who preached an able sermon on the Church of the Future in America[12]— After the sermon an exposition of the principles on wh. the new Congl. Society in Washn. is to be formed was read by Mr. Morris—sent note to Susan Walker that I will go to New York tomorrow and will take charge of her if she desires—having received telegram from Gov. Sprague that Katie is at 5th Avenue[13]— She came—says she cannot well go before evening[,] and told her that if detained wd. let her know—

MONDAY, SEPTEMBER 18. Found in the morng that I cd. not get through in time to go by morning train / wrote note to Mr. Broom to look after consultation room—to Mr. Stanton about Marcel? no somebody else[14]—attended to divers matters—sent Willie to tell Miss W[15] / packed—sent carriage for Miss W—took 7.30 train— Engaged section in sleeping car for myself—Miss W—— preferred sitting car—sat with her to Baltimore—then betook myself to my section & tried to sleep—as comfortable as possible but cd. not sleep—tried to think.

TUESDAY, SEPTEMBER 19. At two this morning the cars came to a standstill—heard talk outside & learned that we were at Phil or near it, with a train ahead whose engine was off the track / it was five hours before it was got out of the way & I got a little sleep—after daylight got up—went to see Miss W—found her pretty tired—several gents of my acquaintance on cars—Gens Andrews & Webster—

11. Antonio Yznaga del Valle, a New York City merchant, had a residence in Newport. Beaulieu, the Newport mansion of F. L. Barreda, was constructed between 1856 and 1859. Henry P. Sturgis of Boston and Robert S. Sturgis of Philadelphia evidently summered at Newport. *New York Dir. (1864)*, 952; *Newport Dir. (1863)*, 201; ibid. (1865), 207, 224; *Phila. Dir. (1865)*, 658; Downing and Scully, *Architectural Heritage of Newport*, 138–39.
12. In the interval since the preceding entry, Chase returned to Washington, D.C. Charles B. Boynton preached at the Unitarian Church. Washington *Evening Star*, Sept. 16, 1865.
13. Chase both wrote and telegraphed his daughter Kate on the 16th in an effort to arrange a rendezvous in New York. Chase to Kate Chase Sprague, Sept. 16, 1865 (Chase Papers, Hist. Soc. of Pa.).
14. This letter concerned a cousin worried about losing his place as a hospital chaplain. Three days later Chase wrote Stanton about Maj. Marcellus Bailey ("Marcel"). Chase to E. M. Stanton, Sept. 18, 21, 1865 (Stanton Papers, L.C.).
15. Chase sent William Joice with a message for Susan Walker.

Mr. Arnold, Ill. Mr. Jenckes, R.I. & some others[16]—reached Fifth Avenue Hotel, Miss W, Gen A & myself going up together, about 12—ordered a little bkft for myself in my room— Katie out but came in about 3—baby in fine condition—Katie invited Miss W—— to use her rooms—dined at 6—met Mr. McAlester, Phil,[17] Mr. Probasco, & others—a number of gent called—Gov Andrew, Maj. Stearns, N.Y. Herald Reporter whom I turned over to Col Howe[18] / arranged for Miss W—— to go at 8 to Boston & she went— (bot watch & chain at Tiffanys with Katie, for Nettie[19]—called at furniture store)

WEDNESDAY, SEPTEMBER 20. A good many callers today & various talk but nothing important—went with Katie & Gen. McCook down town[20]—Mr. Hoyts store, Neptune Wharf, two drug stores, Optical instrument makers[21]—wrote letters to Cooke & Sprague for Maj. Stearns[22]— Busteed, Wilkes & Andrew called[23] / A—— said they had something important to say & wd. come again when callers had gone—after all gone waited for them till half past 11, but they did not return—went to bed— Gen. Sickles called, but of course did not see him.[24]

16. Christoper Columbus Andrews; possibly former Chicago engineer Joseph Dana Webster (1811–76), a brigadier general of volunteers who served as chief of staff for Generals Grant and Sherman; Isaac Newton Arnold (1815–84), Chicago lawyer, Republican congressman, 1861–65, sixth auditor of the U.S. Treasury, 1865–66; and Thomas Allen Jenckes (1818–75), Rhode Island patent lawyer and Republican congressman, 1863–71. *DAB*, 1:368–69, 10:41–42, 19:593–94; Heitman, *Historical Register*, 1:1013; *Bio. Dir. U.S. Cong.*, 546–47, 1258.

17. Probably Philadelphia financier Charles Macalester (1798–1873). *DAB*, 11:543–44.

18. John A. Andrew, George L. Stearns, Frank E. Howe. An article about Chase's visit to New York appeared in the *New York Herald* on Sept. 20.

19. Charles Lewis Tiffany (1812–1902), jeweler, then operated his store at 550 Broadway. *DAB*, 18:533; *New York Times*, Feb. 19, 1902.

20. Several members of the McCook families of Ohio held the rank of general. *Nat. Cyc.*, 4:130–31.

21. Edwin Hoyt (1804–74) was the senior partner of Hoyt, Spragues & Co., a dry goods firm at 56 Park Place. The Neptune Steamship Co. operated from Pier No. 27 on the North River at the foot of Robinson Street. *New York Times*, May 16, 1874; *New York Dir. (1864)*, 418; *New York Tribune*, Sept. 20, 1865.

22. Chase asked Sprague to assist George L. Stearns in his work on behalf of black suffrage. Chase to William Sprague, Sept. 20, 1865 (American Antiquarian Soc.).

23. Later in the year, Irish-born attorney Richard Busteed (1822–98) of New York City began a controversial tenure as U.S. district judge for Alabama, 1865–74. His companions were probably George Wilkes and John A. Andrew. *Appletons'*, 1:476; *Nat. Cyc.*, 4:531; Fairman, *Reconstruction and Reunion*, 828–32.

24. In a speech given the previous week in New York, Gen. Daniel E. Sickles alluded unfavorably to Chase's conduct as secretary of the Treasury. This address was printed in the *New York Times*, Sept. 13, 1865.

September 1865 { 595 }

Among callers today Cisco, Stuart Field Barney Joshua Hanna[25]

THURSDAY, SEPTEMBER 21. Mr. Stevens, & his son J. A. S. Jr, Mr. Neff & Col Howe called[26]— Col. H—— excused himself from going with me on a/c of gent. from West on business— Mr. Stevens thinks McC——[27] delays resumption too long—and depreciates currency too much—seems quite anxious abt. financial future— Younger Stevens went with me to Astor Library & to American Institute[28]—where he left me with some expectation that he wd. go with me to Buffalo—visit to Library was very interesting & instructive—that to American Institute, where Gen. Hall[29] & his son in law Dr. Ha[rries] took me in charge, equally so—met Dr. Warden there—returned to Hotel & arranged for departure at 6—K & I dined at same table with Mad & Miss LeVert[30]— Mr Leary came in—goes to West Point tonight & on same cars with me—off at 6— talk with Leary about Steamboats[31]— Mr. L. P. Noble came in[32]— L—— left abt 8—talk with Noble—had section arranged—slept—

FRIDAY, SEPTEMBER 22. Found myself near Syracuse when I waked—preferred to depend on lunch basket to going out to breakfast—talked with Louise Skinner & children[33]— Louise says Ralston

---

25. John J. Cisco; New York banker John Aikman Stewart (1822–1926), who had succeeded Cisco briefly as assistant treasurer at New York, 1864–65; probably Maunsell B. Field; Hiram Barney; and Joshua Hanna. *DAB*, 18:10–11; Chase to Stewart, June 25, 1864, Chase to Field, Sept. 6, 1865 (Chase Papers, Hist. Soc. of Pa.); Field to Chase, Sept. 4, 1865 (Chase Papers, L.C.).
26. John Austin Stevens, Sr. and Jr.; Peter Rudolph Neff (1832–1912), a brother of George W. and William Neff, who became the senior member of the family's Cincinnati hardware business and made annual business trips to New York; and Frank Howe. *Nat. Cyc.*, 25:274.
27. Hugh McCulloch.
28. The Astor Library, sponsored by the Astor family, was completed in 1853. The American Institute had opened its 36th anniversary fair, a "grand exhibition" of art, inventions, and agricultural products, on Sept. 12. *New York Times*, Sept. 11, 13, 19, 1865; *Appletons'*, 1:112, 113.
29. Former New York militia general William Hall (1796–1874), musical publisher, instrument maker, and president of the American Institute, 1860–65. *Nat. Cyc.*, 13:425–26; *New York Herald*, May 4, 1874.
30. Octavia Celeste Walton Le Vert and either Octavia Walton Le Vert or Celeste Annette Le Vert.
31. Arthur Leary (1831–93) of New York, owner of a line of merchant ships. *New York Times*, Feb. 24, 1893; Leary to Chase, Feb. 13, 1862 (5th Agency, Port Royal Corres., Recs. of Civil War Special Agencies, Nat. Arch.).
32. Chase had known Linneaus P. Noble since the 1840s, when Noble was active in the Liberty party in New York State. Noble to Chase, Sept. 1, 1842 (Chase Papers, L.C.); W. H. Seward to W. T. Carroll, Mar. 10, 1847, in *Jones v. Van Zandt* case file (Recs. of Supreme Court, Nat. Arch.).
33. The only known children of James Ralston Skinner and Eunice Louisa Wiggins Skinner were a little girl, name unknown, and a boy called Sammy. James Ralston Skinner to Chase, June 7, 1860, Apr. 16, 1861 (Chase Papers, L.C.).

much improved—hopes for his recovery—poor child! my heart aches more for her than for him—interesting talk with Mr. Nye of Chillicothe on his way home from Virginia[34]—gives an unpromising picture of things—reached Buffalo abt. 2—saw Louise to Cleveland cars & to dining saloon—found Mr. Wright waiting for me[35]— accompanied him to his house—kind welcome & nice lunch—Miss W showed me stereos[co]pic views of Yosemite Valley in California— went to see Jenny Jewett found her and children well—returned to Mr. Wrights—Jack Jewett & Mr. Spalding came in evening[36]— find everybody in favor of universal suffrage—from complaisance or conviction?

TUESDAY, OCTOBER 31. Up very early—and at Erie R. Road

THURSDAY, NOVEMBER 9. Telegram from Mrs Febiger—at home will be glad to see Judge Chase[37]—several gentlemen called— among whom Mr Horace Binney a very interesting gentleman author of resolutions tabled by Episcopal Convention[38]—
Telegram from Katie— Will go to hotel—please secure rooms.

MONDAY, NOVEMBER 13. Recd. tel from Mr. Garrett—will arrange car for Wednesday or Thursday as preferred[39]— Long ride with Col   & Mr.   stopped at Mr. Robinson beautiful house

---

34. Probably Arius Spencer Nye (d. 1884), Chillicothe bank cashier. His mother came from Virginia. Reed, *Bench and Bar of Ohio*, 1:210–12.

35. George Washington Wright had invited Chase to Buffalo for a trial voyage of a new revenue cutter, the *Commodore Perry*, on Sept. 20. Wright had built the *Perry*, which was powered by a new "Locomotive" process. *Who Was Who*, H:598; Wright to Chase, Sept. 16, 1865 (Chase Papers, L.C.); U.S. Department of Transportation, *Record of Movements*, 254.

36. J. J. L. C. Jewett was the husband of Chase's niece, Janette (Jenny) Skinner Jewett. Buffalo politician and banker Elbridge Gerry Spaulding (1809–97) had been in Congress as a Whig, 1849–51, and a Republican, 1859–63. He played an important role in passage of financial legislation in 1862 and 1863. *DAB*, 17:436–37; Jenny Jewett to Chase, May 18, 1859, June 22, 1863, Chase to Jenny Jewett, Mar. 28, 1867, Chase to J. J. L. C. Jewett, Aug. 24, 1868 (Chase Papers, L.C.).

37. Mrs. H. Febiger Jones had invited Chase to visit when he came to Wilmington, Del., on court business. Chase to Jones, Oct. 16, 1865 (Free Library of Philadelphia).

38. Horace Binney, Jr. (1809–70), lawyer and founder of the Philadelphia Union League, was a devout Episcopalian. *Nat. Cyc.*, 10:445; *Proceedings of the American Philosophical Society* 11 (May 6, 1870): 376–77.

39. John W. Garrett of the B. & O. R.R. On Nov. 12, Chase wrote to his daughter Kate arranging to meet her, her infant son William, and Janet Chase at Philadelphia: "I presume you will want to go to Washington on Wednesday: and if you desire it please telegraph me & I will telegraph Mr. Garrett for his Car." Chase to Kate Chase Sprague, Nov. 12, 1865 (Chase Papers, Hist. Soc. of Pa.).

December 1865   { 597 }

on the Delaware, at Mr. Shipleys & visited Gen Dupont at Powder Works[40] / Mr. ―― seemed quite to agree with me on universal suffrage—pleasant dinner at Mrs Febigers—walk to C.H. with Mr.   & Judge Hall[41]—found room pretty good—but improvable—several gentlemen called eveng.

SATURDAY, DECEMBER 2.   Did very little today— Reid called went over "Southern Tour after the War" with him[42]— Judge Miller called also— Colfax to breakfast—will be reelected Speaker without opposition—thinks feasible plan as to rebel states is to keep out Reps & Sens. except perhaps Tenn—thinks Congress unprepared for universal suffrage—is rather against it himself— Senator Wilson called—tells of visit of Scofield & M B Lowry of Erie to President last Oct[43]— P talked at 1st agst radicals & disavowed Wilson— finding them radicals changed his tone— I promd to write act suffrage for District & he will come for it tomorrow morning[44]—with

---

40. Possibly Thomas Robinson, register of the court of chancery and clerk of the orphan's court, 1861–66. The Robinson house dated from the eighteenth century. Joseph Shipley (1795–1867), a merchant and banker known for his hospitality, resided on a property called "Rockwood." Henry DuPont (1812–89), West Point graduate and explosives manufacturer, was appointed major general of Delaware forces in 1861. Henry C. Conrad, *History of the State of Delaware* . . . , 3 vols. (Wilmington, Del., 1908), 1:164; 2:691; Federal Writers' Project, *Delaware: A Guide to the First State* (New York, 1938), 320–21; J. Thomas Scharf, ed., *History of Delaware, 1609–1888*, 2 vols. (Philadelphia, 1888), 2:633, 733–34; *DAB*, 5:528.
41. Willard Hall (1780–1875), judge of the U.S. district court for Delaware, 1823–71. *DAB*, 8:146.
42. Whitelaw Reid's *After the War*.
43. Glenni William Scofield (1817–91), Republican congressman, 1863–75, from the district that included Erie, Pa. M. B. Lowry represented Erie and Crawford Counties in the state senate, c. 1865. *Bio. Dir. U.S. Cong.*, 1779; Lee F. Crippen, *Simon Cameron: Ante-Bellum Years* (Oxford, Ohio, 1942), 201–2; *OR*, ser. 1, v. 46, pt. 3:905.
44. *Promd* means *promised*. Chase prepared a draft "bill prescribing the qualifications of electors in the District of Columbia," to extend both the franchise and an acknowledgement of U.S. citizenship to black male adults. The first section of Senate Bill No. 1, introduced by Benjamin F. Wade on Dec. 4, resembled Chase's draft in some respects, but not in a way that demonstrates a clear linkage between the two. Henry Wilson was not a member, but Wade was, of the committee on the District of Columbia, the committee most concerned with the bill. Judging from the handwriting on a copy of the bill in the National Archives, Chase was the author of a minor amendment introduced by Lot M. Morrill, chairman of the committee on the District, on Jan. 16, 1866. An act allowing blacks to vote in D.C. was not passed until the second session of the 39th Congress, over Andrew Johnson's veto. Chase's draft, Oct. 1865–Feb. 1867 letterpress copies (Chase Papers, Hist. Soc. of Pa.), p. 28, transcription in *Chase Papers: Microfilm Edition*, 42:0910; *Cong. Globe*, 39th Cong., 1st sess., 1866, 1, 11, 89, 162, 245; copy of bill S. 1 (39th Cong., Senate Bills Acted Upon, Recs. of U.S. Senate, Nat. Arch.); Trefousse, *Benjamin Franklin Wade*, 263, 285, 295, 364–65.

Reid to Capitol—met Judge Field[45] who came home with me— agrees as to States under martial law— Spofford to talk abt. uniting Libraries Congress & Smithsonian—to depot at 6 for Katie who didn't come—

JOURNAL XVI

DECR. 10. SUN. Wilson called and talked some time on aspects of affairs— Mr Conness called very cordial— Comte de Chambrun, much infn. about photographs recd from Paris[46]

MON. DEC. 11— Thaddeus Stevens & Charles Sumner to dinner—both accidentally. Much talk about restoration— I could not adopt Stevens views about holding States as Territories with view to constitutional amendments but very willing he should bring them forward, thinking the right ground might perhaps be easiest found when extreme views most fully before the Country. Lawrence & Shellabarger & Dr. Elder called.[47]

TUES. DECR. 12. Gen. Gillmore, now reduced to Major, & in Engineer Dept under Delafield, called.[48] Chafes a little—counselled patience & assiduous devotion to duties. Mr. Mott of New Orleans desires to have his application to be allowed to practice without taking New Oath considered with that in behalf of Mr. Garland—cd. see no objection to it.[49]

---

45. Stephen J. Field.
46. Although Chase wrote *Comte*, he surely meant the Marquis de Chambrun, Charles Adolphe de Pineton (1831–91), a French writer and political observer who arrived in the United States early in 1865. Some of his letters were translated by his son as *Impressions of Lincoln and the Civil War: A Foreigner's Account* (New York, 1952). Marquis de Chambrun, "Personal Recollections of Mr. Lincoln," *Scribner's Magazine* 13 (Jan. 1893): 26; *La Grande Encyclopédie: Inventaire Raisonné des Sciences, des Lettres et des Arts* (Paris, 1886–1902), 10:396.
47. William Lawrence.
48. Richard Delafield (1798–1873), former superintendent of West Point, commanded the Corps of Engineers, Apr. 1864–Aug. 1866. *DAB*, 5:210.
49. Arkansas lawyer and politician Augustus Hill Garland (1832–99) challenged the oath that was required of attorneys practicing in federal courts (see Apr. 3, 1865, above). Chase (and the *Cincinnati Daily Gazette*) apparently confused Robert Mott, a New Orleans attorney, for Robert H. Marr, another lawyer from New Orleans whose petition the court agreed to consider along with Garland's. In Jan. 1867 *Ex parte Garland* was decided in the petitioners' favor (Chase being among the dissenters). 4 Wall. 333 (1867); *DAB*, 7:150–51; Minutes, Dec. 12, 1865 (Recs. of Supreme Court, Nat. Arch.); *New Orleans Dir. (1866)*, 303, 328; New Orleans *Daily Picayune*, Sept. 7, 1873; *Cincinnati Daily Gazette*, Dec. 13, 1865.

DECR. 18—[50] Not yet free from my cold—earnest in prayer for God's direction through day—wrote Mary Goldsborough[51]—prepared package Dr. Baileys letters to be sent with note written yesterday to Mrs Bailey[52] / handed Mrs C⎯⎯[53] for Katie all the money I had 5.75—walked to Capitol with John Sherman, who spoke of attack on him in Gazette—advised him to write Reed & state facts & leave matter to his own sense of justice wh he seemed to approve[54]—to S.C. Reception Room[55]—all Judges there but Wayne— A couple of Motions for admission when Dickinson concluded argument for def. in Binghamton Bridge Case. Mygatt replied briefly[56]— Then took up Puig & Co vs Ship Guthrie—Tracy opened—adjd. before he concluded[57]— Coming home overtaken by Wilson & went to his room—he gave me probable names of Senate Committee on Reorganization—Fessenden, Grimes & others—said Sumner cd. not be made Chairman[58]—spoke of interviews with President who will concede, he thinks, all that is substantial—said

---

50. In the original, this entry for Dec. 18 precedes those for Dec. 10–12. The Dec. 18 entry occupies its own page, however, so Chase did not necessarily write it first. He may have skipped that page by accident or for some other reason, written the Dec. 10–12 entries, and returned to the blank page later to write the Dec. 18 entry.
51. Mary Catherine Goldsborough (1827–99) of Frederick, Md., the elder sister of Edward Yerbury Goldsborough. Williams and McKinsey, *History of Frederick County*, 2:1241; M. C. Goldsborough to Chase, Feb. 7, 1873 (Chase Papers, L.C.).
52. Margaret L. Bailey.
53. A Mrs. Crawford was evidently a member of Chase's household staff in this period. Chase to Kate Chase Sprague, Sept. 18, 1866, Chase to Janet Chase, Oct. 1, 1866 (Chase Papers, L.C.).
54. John Sherman, standing for reelection, had delivered an address at Springfield, Ohio, in which he defended his record on a variety of issues. Sherman was upset over editor Samuel Rockwell Reed's commentary on the speech in the *Cincinnati Gazette*. *Cincinnati Daily Gazette*, Nov. 24, Dec. 7, 1865; Rachel Sherman Thorndike, ed., *The Sherman Letters: Correspondence Between General and Senator Sherman from 1837 to 1891* (New York, 1894), 258–59; John Sherman, *Recollections of Forty Years in the House, Senate and Cabinet*, 2 vols. (Chicago, 1895), 1:358.
55. The Supreme Court's reception room in the Capitol.
56. The motions were for the admission to the bar of attorneys Joseph H. Choate and William E. Chandler. The *Binghamton Bridge* case involved charters. Daniel Stevens Dickinson (1800–1866) was an attorney and politican of New York State. Henry R. Mygatt argued the case for the Chenango Bridge Co. 3 Wall. 51 (1866); *DAB*, 5:294–95; Minutes, Dec. 18, 1865 (Recs. of Supreme Court, Nat. Arch.).
57. *Magin Puig et al. v. The Ship James Guthrie*, with opening arguments by New York attorney Charles Tracy (1810–85). Minutes, Dec. 18–19, 1865, Jan. 8, 1866 (Recs. of Supreme Court, Nat. Arch.); *Appletons'*, 6:151–52.
58. Passage of a resolution to create a "Joint Committee on Reconstruction" mandated the appointment of six senators. The appointments made on Dec. 21, 1865, named William Pitt Fessenden and James Wilson Grimes, but not Charles Sumner, to the committee. *Cong. Globe*, 39th Cong., 1st sess., pt. 1:6–7, 24–30, 46–47, 57, 78, 106.

Stevens was making great speech in House[59] / wanted me to see Bingham, who inclined to impracticable views.[60] Sent to Binghams room. He was not in. Came home—lunched—recd. note from Wetmore that Corwin died this afternoon at 2.35[61]— Gen Garfield came in & remained till after dinner—long talk—explained my theory of reorganization, based on universal suffrage as a logical consequence of the facts which have already taken place. He accepts it & thinks of making a Speech based on these views. Matchett called to talk abt. reestablishing the old National Era[62]—declined to advise or have any thing to do with it—he wants Conway (T. W.) to join him— says Hahn will go in & Banks will support[63]—says Mrs Swisshelm has got out a new paper called the "Reconstructionist"[64]— Mr. Hazard & Mr. Day called—they dont think much of Mr McHenry Sir Morton Peto & the English Capitalists[65]—Mr. H—— says they have made a loan of 6 millions pounds ($30.000.000) on the Road— Note from Sherman say that a Meeting of Ohio men will be held tomorrow to arrange for Corwins funeral.[66]

---

59. Thaddeus Stevens, "Reconstruction," ibid., 72–75. Stevens argued that the Confederate states required congressional action to complete their restoration to the union and that no restoration should occur without a guarantee of equal privileges for blacks.
60. John Armor Bingham.
61. Thomas Corwin had been stricken with "an attack of paralysis" on the evening of Dec. 15 while attending a social gathering of Ohioans, including Chase, at the residence of James C. Wetmore. *Daily National Intelligencer*, Dec. 16, 1865; Chase to Elizabeth Ellicott Pike, Dec. 23, 1865 (James Shepherd Pike Papers, Univ. of Maine).
62. Probably William B. Matchett, a shadowy figure who claimed to have been an army chaplain and seems to have busied himself as a liaison for people seeking government positions. Nothing evidently became of his plan to reestablish the *National Era*. *Wash. Dir. (1865)*, 268; Robert F. Horowitz, *The Great Impeacher: A Political Biography of James M. Ashley* (New York, 1979), 135–36.
63. Nathaniel P. Banks and Georg Michael Decker Hahn (1830–86), Louisiana lawyer and politician. Hahn began a Republican newspaper at New Orleans in 1864; served as a U.S. representative, 1863–64, 1885–86; and as governor of Louisiana, 1864–65. *DAB*, 8:87–88.
64. The Washington, D.C., newspaper established by reform-minded author and editor Jane Grey Cannon Swisshelm (1815–84) took issue with Andrew Johnson's policies. Chase subscribed to the paper early in 1866. *DAB*, 18:253–54; receipt, Feb. 22, 1866 (Chase Papers, L.C.).
65. James McHenry (1817–91), a Liverpool merchant and financier who began his business career in Philadelphia, and Sir Samuel Morton Peto (1809–89), English railway contractor and politician, led a group of English capitalists who toured the U.S. to investigate prospects for railroad investments, Sept. 5–Oct. 31, 1865. Chase attended a farewell banquet for this party in New York City on Oct. 30 and gave a toast on similarities between English and American law and culture. Mr. Hazard was probably Rowland G. Hazard, who was involved in transcontinental railroad projects. *Appletons'*, 4:121–22; *DNB*, 12:552, 15:972–74; *New York Times*, Sept. 7, Oct. 31, 1865, and many issues between those dates.
66. Chase was appointed chairman of a meeting of senators, representatives, and friends of Corwin held the next afternoon in the retiring room of the Senate chamber. He made brief eulogistic remarks. The funeral took place on Dec. 20. *Daily National Intelligencer*, Dec. 20, 21, 1865.

1866

JANY 7. The past week though marked by nothing of great significance in my personal history has been deeply interesting and, in one event particularly, of great moment to friends & a cause in which I am deeply interested.

Last Sunday was the last day of 1865. As I took up a paper, on going into the sitting room, my eye fell upon an article announcing the death of Henry Winter Davis.[67] I could hardly believe it possible. So lately so well & so much engaged in the work of completing the enfranchisement so auspiciously begun; but it was too true.

The next day, Monday, I went with my daughter Mrs Sprague & Laura Cook,[68] a young daughter, only 16, in the Judicial Party to call on the President. All the Judges were present except Davis, who had gone to Baltimore to attend the funeral of his cousin.[69] Nettie came with Senator Sprague. The different legations were present in costume, and several members of the Cabinet & many others. We paid our respects to the President, & his daughters Mrs Stover & Mrs Patterson & exchanged salutations with such of our acquaintances as we met & soon came away.[70] As we left the Mansion the Military & Naval Officers were coming in making quite a grand show in full uniform. Returning home we received many calls—mostly from gentlemen of our general acquantance, officers of the Treasury Department, & members of the foreign legations—among the latter Sir Frederick Bruce seems most inclined to make himself agreeable & to have most capacity for it[71] / I only called myself, on my friend Mrs Eastman, just arrived from Massachusetts, on Mrs Swayne & Mrs Miller & Miss Walker at Mr. Forces where I saw the Christmas tree relighted and a serpent crawl out of one of Pharaohs Eggs[72]—the last curious enough as a scientific experiment, but rather disagreeable otherwise. A telegram came in the evening from

---

67. Davis had died on Dec. 30, 1865. For an account of the funeral, see *Baltimore Sun*, Jan. 3, 1866.
68. Laura Elmina Cooke (1849–1918), the daughter of Jay Cooke. She later married New York stock broker Charles D. Barney. *New York Times*, Oct. 25, 1945; Oberholtzer, *Jay Cooke*, 2:464.
69. David Davis (1815–86) joined the Supreme Court in 1862. *DAB*, 5:110–12.
70. Mary Johnson Stover (1832–83) was the widow of Carter County, Tenn., farmer Daniel Stover (d. 1862). Martha Johnson Patterson (b. 1828) had married David Trotter Patterson (1818–91), a Democrat and U.S. senator from Tennessee, 1865–69. Trefousse, *Andrew Johnson*, 30, 80, 101; *Appletons'*, 3:440; *Bio. Dir. U.S. Cong.*, 1617.
71. Frederick William Adolphus Bruce (1814–67), Britain's representative to the U.S. He had previously served in China. *DNB*, 3:97.
72. Sarah Ann Wager Swayne and Elizabeth Winter Reeves Miller, wives of Justices Noah Haynes Swayne and Samuel Freeman Miller; Susan Walker; and probably Peter Force (1790–1868), archivist, historian, and editor of the *American Archives*;

Judge Davis & Mr. Blow asking me to attend the Funeral of Winter Davis tomorrow. I replied that I would come & wrote a note to Judge Nelson asking him to inform the Judges tomorrow morning of the reason of my absence. Gov. Sprague said he would go with me.

Tuesday morning Sprague & I left for Baltimore on the 7.30 train: and on arriving took rooms at Barnums. Judge Davis & Mr. Blow soon came in & shortly after Judge Bond, Mr. Cresswell, Mr. Worthington, late of Nevada, & Gen. Green Clay Smith.[73] We went together to Mr. Davis house. He was lying in his coffin in the front room. His face was pale—very pale but it was difficult to think of him as dead: so much of the old living expression remained. Senator Sprague & I returned to the hotel & awaited the hour of the funeral, when in company with two or three gentlemen we returned to the house. A continuous stream of people of all classes & colored as well as white were passing up, taking their last look, & returning down the stairway. Some of the relations of Mrs D——[74] who did not sympathize with the liberal & reforming spirit of Davis had objected,—but Mrs Davis had said "Let every one who loved Winter Davis & wishes to look on him for the last time be gratified." Then came the funeral. I was one of the pall bearers. Three of the others in the same carriage with me were Mr. Foster, President of the Senate, Secretary Stanton & Gen. Hancock.[75] A Minister of the Episcopal Church conducted the religious services.[76] Mrs Davis accompanied her husband to his grave. She seemed petrified with grief. Not a tear, nor a sob, but anguish that seemed hardly to comprehend itself.

When all was over we went back to the house & then to the hotel. Senator Sprague remained there intending to go on to Providence. Secretary Stanton & I came back to Washington, calling on Mr. Garrett at the Washn. Depot, where Mrs Stanton joined us.[77] Coming back we had a good deal of talk in the car. Stanton remarked

---

Consisting of a Collection of Authentick Records, State Papers, Debates, and Letters and other Notices of Publick Affairs . . . , 9 vols. (Washington, D.C., 1837–53). *DAB*, 6:512–13, 12:638, 18:239; *Wash. Dir. (1865)*, 197.

73. Hugh Lennox Bond; John Angel James Creswell (1828–91), Maryland politician and U.S. postmaster general, 1869–74; Henry Gaither Worthington (1828–1909), U.S. congressman from Nevada, 1864–65, politician, diplomat, and judge. Smith (1826–95), a brevet major general of volunteers and an Unconditional Unionist congressman from Kentucky, 1863–66, would soon preside as governor of Montana Territory, 1866–69. *DAB*, 4:541–42; *Bio. Dir. U.S. Cong.*, 1829, 2088.

74. Nancy Morris Davis.

75. Lafayette Sabine Foster, Edwin M. Stanton, and Winfield Scott Hancock.

76. Evidently Protestant Episcopal clergyman John Henry Hobart (1817–89). *Appletons'*, 3:222; *Baltimore Sun*, Jan. 3, 1866.

77. John Work Garrett; Ellen Hutchison Stanton.

on the disproportioned estimates of military service—thought Hancock not valued as he should be in which I fully agreed—laughed a little at Hoopers zeal to furnish a Library to Grant[78]—spoke of McCulloch and his assumption that he had done all the financial work of the war—to which I replied that I had all the credit I cared to have & that he certainly had his full measure; and that we need not trouble ourselves if some had more than they deserved— He expressed himself warmly & decididly in favor of universal suffrage—without qualification of property or education—in the district—in the states he did not think it so important to ensure suffrage to the colored people as to ensure them lands. I agreed as to the District; but as to the states thought it easier to reach farms through suffrage than suffrage through farms— Mrs S―― who is one of the best women as well as one of the loveliest, I know expressed great horror of having negroes at her table! though anxious that they should have their *rights*.

On getting home found that Fessenden & his son the General[79] had come in to dine, according to a promise made yesterday, but, not finding me had just gone away again. I immediately sent Marshall[80] to their lodgings to tell them I had arrived & dinner was waiting. Returning he reported them gone out. I was vexed & mortified but there was no help for it & we took our dinner alone. Afterwards I went myself to Fessenden's lodgings, but they had not come back. I then wrote him a note of regret & explanation & then tried to study a little.

Not much of interest occurred on Wednesday. I was at the Court room as usual. Mr. Cushing concluded the argument of a cause begun yesterday.[81] He did not satisfy my opinion of his ability. After the adjournment I passed a couple of hours in the Consultation room studying & writing: and then went home at six to dinner. About half past nine we went over to Georgetown to a Fancy dress party of young people at H. D. Cooke's. Nettie was dressed very prettily but as I feared ran some risk of taking cold & is now quite unwell. Many of the dresses were handsome & some very odd. The young folks seemed to enjoy themselves much. There were two

---

78. In 1866, radicals attempted to use gifts to ingratiate themselves with Ulysses S. Grant. Samuel Hooper and others from the Boston area gave the general a library of books that cost $75,000. William B. Hesseltine, *Ulysses S. Grant: Politician* (New York, 1935), 61–63.

79. Maj. Gen. Francis Fessenden (1839–1906), U.S. Army. *DAB*, 6:345.

80. Chase's employee.

81. Attorney, politician, and diplomat Caleb Cushing (1800–1879) appeared for the Suffolk Manufacturing Co. in *Suffolk Manufacturing Co. v. Isaac Hayden*, a patent dispute over improvements in cotton cleaning equipment. 3 Wall. 315 (1866); *DAB*, 4:623–30; Minutes, Jan. 2–3, 1866 (Recs. of Supreme Court, Nat. Arch.).

ladies who excited a great deal of curiosity—one dressed in black velvet as Night & the other in plain costume as a quakeress. The lady in black when she came in declined to give her name but said to Mrs Cooke[82] when she enquired who she was "your best & dearest friend." She talked with young Jay Cooke[83] & asked if he knew her. He said he did not. Then she told him that they met at Niagara Falls last summer & he then professed to love her, & she was sorry he was so inconstant that he had forgotten it. At last supper came, and the lady unmasked. She was Mrs Jay Cooke & with Miss Bronaugh the Quakeress had come from Phila that day to surprise her friends, & had succeeded completely.[84]

I think it was this day that I received a call from Mr. Hornor of New Orleans & after Court had a long talk with him in the Consultation room about affairs in New Orleans[85] / He proposes to go home & take immediate measures for the organization of the Republican party on the basis of universal suffrage.

On Thursday our work went on as usual. We agreed to meet in consultation tomorrow immediately after hearing motions & any cause that ought not be concluded today. We adjourned after an unconcluded argt. by Browning in support of very familiar legal propositions.[86] In the evening Mr. Bowen, the Post Master, Mr. Brown & Mr. Gangewer called, and we had a very interesting talk about suffrage in the District.[87] Mr. Bowen had been in favor of qualified suffrage, but expressed him convinced that universal suffrage was better. Both the other gentlemen were of the same opinion, & they agreed to get action in the same sense from the Equal Suffrage Association[88] & to have committees see the members of Congress & urge them to make suffrage universal in the district.

---

82. Laura S. Humphreys Cooke, wife of Henry David Cooke. *Nat. Cyc.*, 10:510.

83. Jay Cooke, Jr. (b. 1845), later a leading Philadelphia financier. *Nat. Cyc.*, 1:253; Oberholtzer, *Jay Cooke*, 2:464.

84. Dorothea Elizabeth Allen Cooke (d. 1871) and probably Emily Bronaugh of Philadelphia. *DAB*, 4:384; *New York Times*, July 24, 1871; Oberholtzer, *Jay Cooke*, 2:483.

85. Charles W. Hornor (b. 1813), lawyer and corresponding secretary of the New Orleans Freedmen's Aid Association. Tunnell, *Crucible of Reconstruction*, 225; *New Orleans Tribune*, May 2, June 10, 1865.

86. Former Senator Orville H. Browning, arguing *Evans Rogers v. City of Burlington*, which concerned municipal bonds loaned to a railroad corporation. 3 Wall. 654 (1866); Minutes, Jan. 4, 1866 (Recs. of Supreme Court, Nat. Arch.); Fairman, *Reconstruction and Reunion*, 997–98.

87. Sayles Jenks Bowen (1813–96), commissioner of police, postmaster, and later mayor of the District of Columbia, promoted suffrage and public schools for blacks. Allen M. Gangewer and T. B. Brown, warden of the district jail, publicly supported Bowen. Chase to Gangewer, Jan. 2, [1866] (Chase Papers, Ohio Hist. Soc.); Johnson, *Twentieth Century Biographical Dictionary*, v. 1; Washington *Evening Star*, Dec. 28, 1865.

88. Apparently one of many organizations formed to promote universal enfranchisement for blacks in Washington, D.C. *Daily National Intelligencer*, Jan. 13, 14, 1865.

On Friday there was an elaborate argument on the petition of the United States for a Mandamus to the Circuit Court for the 10th District to allow an appeal from his decree confirming the Pueblo lands to the City of San Francisco.[89] Mr. Browning then concluded his arguments & was followed by Mr. Ewing, on the same side, in a brief argument which displayed all his old vigor & gratified us all very much.[90] We then went into consultation for an hour & disposed of one or two cases. Immediately afterwards I went home walking down with Swayne & Field.[91] Something led to the question of reorganization & I took the opportunity, as I now always do, to express myself in favor of universal suffrage. Field laughed at my zeal; but Swayne said he had been brought to the same conclusion; and then mentioned a difficulty between Gen Wager Swayne his son & the Alabama Legislature.[92] A bill passed the house by a large majority extremely unjust to the freedmen. He determined at once to disregard it if it should pass the Senate, but unwilling to have an unnecessary conflict with the Legislature, immediately called on leading members & protested against the bill. Fortunately the Legislature took a recess for ten days without action & so the difficulty was postponed & may be avoided. After dinner I was very busy preparing for the consultation tomorrow: but gave a few minutes to Clark of N.H. who called to talk of the Jury bill introduced by Doolittle.[93] I urged on him universal suffrage for the district. He expressed himself as rather favorable to qualification; but would vote for universality if it would help our friends in the District.

On Saturday morning Col. Gooding, our Crier, called with Col. Paschal from Texas who was Lt. Col. in Davis Regiment of loyal Texans.[94] He brought a letter from his father in New York who

---

89. *United States ex rel. Attorney General v. Judges of Circuit Court for District of California*, 3 Wall. 673 (1866).

90. Thomas Ewing, Sr. (1789–1871), former U.S. senator, cabinet officer, and Lancaster, Ohio, attorney, now practicing law in Washington with Orville H. Browning. *DAB*, 6:237–38; Fairman, *Reconstruction and Reunion*, 8–9.

91. Stephen J. Field.

92. At this time, Wager Swayne (1834–1902), a brigadier general of volunteers, served as an assistant commissioner for the Freedmen's Bureau in Alabama. *DAB*, 18:240–41.

93. Daniel Clark called in regard to the "bill in relation to the qualifications of jurors and to writs of error in certain cases," recently introduced by James Rood Doolittle. The proposal apparently never passed the Senate. U.S. Senate, *Journal*, 39th Cong., 1st sess., 1866, 330–31.

94. At this time David S. Gooding of Indiana served as marshal of both the District of Columbia and the U.S. Supreme Court. George W. Paschal, Jr., of the 2nd Texas Cavalry, had served under Edmund Jackson Davis. Fairman, *Reconstruction and Reunion*, 85; Heitman, *Historical Register*, 2:135; *OR*, ser. 1, v. 41, pt. 1:969, ser. 2, v. 4:890.

expects soon to be in Washington. He said that Hamilton[95] finds it difficult to get along in Reconstruction. I recommended universal suffrage & found him very willing to adopt it & quite convinced that it was safest & best for the thoroughly loyal men of Texas & especially those who had been in the Union army. It really seems to me that if men would say to Mr. Johnston[96] what they say to me he would join our side. Certainly if he were on our side there would be nobody, except those who have been on the side of rebellion during the whole war, who would be opposed to us.

Judge Busteed[97] & Mr. Andrews came in while we were at breakfast & waited till I came out. The Judge was a little indignant about the treatment he had received from the Military authorities in Alabama & especially that Stanton justified it. I laughed & told him it was all right—that laws must be silent amid arms—that the Military men must judge for themselves in a rebel state not yet fully restored & still under suspension of the Writ, whether a Habeas Corpus should be obeyed or not. He was very good-humored, but wanted to know whether I thought that a General ought to disregard the writ? I said "Certainly, if he thinks that his Military duty requires. A Habeas Corpus, why, what is it in a rebel state—why nothing more than a convenient way of certifying to the Military Commander the opinion of a respectable gentleman, which he may follow or not at discretion. Busteed was much amused by this definition. He and Andrews both concurred in saying that the President was much deceived if he supposed himself really popular in the South. They were getting what they could from him now; but as soon as they could dispense with him, wd. turn upon him. I doubted this opinion. We talked of universal suffrage. Busteed was quite earnest that I should, for prudential reasons, restrict myself to favor of qualified; but I thought that truest prudence was in boldest advocacy of fundamental justice.

This talk & that with Colonels Gooding & Paschal left me only time to reach the Consultation room a little in advance of the hour eleven. Some of the Judges were already there & the rest except Wayne soon came & we went to work; & continued till four disposing of many cases. Field intimated that Miller was dissatisfied with my assignment of cases & after we adjourned I took occasion to speak to M. frankly on the subject & found that there was no

---

95. Andrew Jackson Hamilton.
96. President Andrew Johnson.
97. Richard Busteed.

ground for the intimation. M. then spoke of Field's excitability & I learned What I had never suspected that it was due in part to the use of liquor occasionally. I must see if this is so & if so talk to him like a brother; for he is one of our best men & dear to me.

When I came home I found a number of persons at Mrs Sprague's reception among others Sir Frederick Bruce, with whom I had quite an interesting talk about Chinese matters. It made me wish for more time to read.

As soon as Sir F—— went away I rode up to Presidents Square to call on my dear friend Mrs Eastman & passed half an hour very pleasantly with her. I met Mr. Haven of Chicago there, who expressed regret that I was not still his Chief.[98]

Returning I found that Mr. Wright had called & left my Opera Glass, which I left on the Commodore Perry last Summer when I went up the Lake on her.[99]

Then came dinner—a young party Jay & Laura Cooke, Mrs H. D. Cooke, Will Moorhead,[1] Alice Porter, Miss Mills,[2] Col. Boyd & another, Nettie, Katie & I. It was quite pleasant. After dinner talk & work till bed time—then unusually sound sleep.

Today, Sunday, I woke feeling very well & very grateful. Coming down to breakfast found that Nettie felt too unwell to join us: and went up to see her, after the meal. She seemed to have considerable fever & headache; but not to be very ill. Soon after I went to Church & heard from Dr. Nadal a Sermon on Methodism, particularly its early history & objects. It was good but not very good for such a subject. The theme is one of the grandest which the History of Christ's Church affords.

Coming home visited Nettie again & found her somewhat better but still with a good deal of fever & sent for Dr. Hall.[3] He came while we were at dinner & saw Nettie. He does not seem to think that the sickness is serious, but says that he does not know & has

---

98. Luther Haven was collector of customs at Chicago. *Register of Officers (1865)*, 116.

99. George Washington Wright. For the *Commodore Perry* see Sept. 22, 1865, above.

1. Jay Cooke, Jr., Laura Elmina Cooke, Laura Humphreys Cooke, and probably William E. C. Moorhead.

2. Possibly relatives of Alex. M. Porter and William H. Mills, influential residents of Sandusky, Ohio, where Jay Cooke and his brothers were raised. See also June 25, 1870, below. Williams, *History of the Fire Lands*, 496; H. L. Peeke, *The Centennial History of Erie County, Ohio* (Sandusky, Ohio, 1925), 1:37, 44–46, 108, 111; Aldrich, *History of Erie County*, 414.

3. James C. Hall.

ordered some simple medicines. Since then I have been reading the Catholic Companion & the History of Methodism & writing part of what precedes.[4] It is now half past six.

MARCH 22. We had a very pleasant dinner today. Judges Nelson, Wayne, Swayne, Miller, Davis & Field, Senators Harris, Morgan, Foster, Representatives Garfield, Hooper, Generals Swayne & Custer, Messrs Carlisle, Wallace & Middleton.[5] Judges Grier & Clifford declined on a/c of death and sickness in their respective families & Speaker Colfax on a/c of engagements in House. All seemed to enjoy themselves very much.

APL. 3. Court adjourned about 3 P.M. and making hurried arrangements I started for N.Y. taking state room in sleeping car. Judge Clifford on train—talk with him abt. Admy. jurisdiction & found him of my mind, that commercial power no limn upon it. Passing through [arrd] Philadelphia aroused by sudden shock: on enquiry learned that engine had broken through bridge, & on going out learned that switch misplaced just before bridge across street & fifteen or twenty feet above it. The engine had therefore gone on planks & timbers which gave way letting engine plunge down. The fireman killed instantly lay [there] on the street. The engineer a pitiable object dreadfully mangled & scalded, had been carried away. The express car dragged after the engine, but not finding room in the narrow hole, was pointing downwards at an angle of abt. 45° the back part raised into the air. What was strange the second track across the bridge was uninjured; so that after the delay for getting a new engine, we went on.[6]

APL. 4. Reached New York abt. 7 AM. Went to Hoffman House & enquired for Katie & Nettie[7]—found they had left for

---

4. Possibly *School Recreations; the Catholic Teacher's Companion. Compiled for the use of Catholic Schools* (New York, [1866]), and Abel Stevens, *History of the Methodist Episcopal Church in the United States of America*, 4 vols. (New York, [1864]).

5. George Armstrong Custer (1839–76); Washington, D.C., lawyer James Mandeville Carlisle (1814–77); John William Wallace (1815–84), U.S. Supreme Court reporter, 1863–75; and Daniel Wesley Middleton (d. 1880), Supreme Court clerk. *DAB*, 3:494, 5:7–9, 19:374–75; *New York Times*, Apr. 29, 1880.

6. The engineer died some hours later. He and the fireman were the accident's only casualties. Philadelphia *Daily Evening Bulletin*, Apr. 4, 1866; Chase to Jane Auld, Apr. 14, 1866 (Chase Papers, Hist. Soc. of Pa.).

7. The Hoffman House hotel was at Broadway and 24th Street. *New York Dir. (1866)*, 70.

April 1866 { 609 }

steamer about half an hour before. hurried back to the Jersey City Ferry, with Mr Smith, who kindly accompanied me, crossed it & went on board the Australasian where I found the folks;[8] with Mr. & Mrs Orne & Mr. Geo. H Stuart[9] & his family & Mr. Roberts & others all off for Europe except Mrs O—— Not many minutes for final adieus for the boat was to leave (& did leave) her dock at 9. sad enough to let all my children go; but it seems best on the whole & I commit them to God's gracious keeping.

Back to Hotel & breakfast with Mr Smith—down town & went with Gov. Sprague to see Baron Eggloffstein's Helographic process: a wonderful work[10]—retd to Hotel & dined—several friends called.

APL. 6. After breadfast alone went down town with Barney talking of old times— Stopped at St Nicholas to see Mr Hanna & specimens of gold quartz from Idaho[11]— Mr. Hanna went with me to see Baron Eggloffsteins process—went to Jay Cooke & Co's office[12]—to Barney's—with Barney to see the process of Baron E— with him to lunch where met Wm Allen Butler & Mr. Stewart, late Asst. Treasr.[13]—then to Cars for Phila.—met J. C. Jr at Camden Ferry & rode out with him to Chelten Hills.[14]

---

8. The Cunard Line operated the *Australasian*, a 2,570-ton steamer. Charles R. Vernon Gibbs, *Passenger Liners of the Western Ocean: A Record of the North Atlantic Steam and Motor Passenger Vessels from 1838 to the Present Day* (London, 1952), 52.

9. Philadelphia merchant and philanthropist George Hay Stuart (1816–90) traveled to Europe to address the British and Foreign Bible Society. *Appletons'*, 5:728; Robert Ellis Thompson, ed., *The Life of George H. Stuart, Written by Himself* (Philadelphia, 1890), 188.

10. Frederick von Egloffstein had developed a process which used acid to make steel engravings from photographs. William Sprague invested in the venture with the intention of giving half his stock to Chase. *New York Dir. (1872)*, 333; S. M. Clark to Chase, Apr. 2, 1866, Chase to Janet Chase, Apr. 16, 1866 (Chase Papers, L.C.); Chase to J. Hannah, Apr. 12, May 17, 1866, Chase to S. Hooper, Nov. 8, 19, 1866 (Chase Papers, Hist. Soc. of Pa.); Von Eglofstein to Chase, Apr. 8, 1866, Chase to J. Cooke, Apr. 20, 1866 (Cooke Papers, Hist. Soc. of Pa.); Chase to W. Sprague, Aug. 7, 1867 (Sprague Collec., Rare Book and Manuscript Lib., Columbia Univ.).

11. The St. Nicholas Hotel, on Broadway. For Joshua Hanna's Idaho gold mining venture see July 4, 1865, above. *New York Dir. (1864)*, 752.

12. The office, on Third Street, had opened earlier in the year. Oberholtzer, *Jay Cooke*, 2:17, 422.

13. New York attorney and author William Allen Butler (1825–1902) and John Aikman Stewart. *DAB*, 3:369–71.

14. Chase's companion was Jay Cooke, Jr., whose father had recently completed "Ogontz," a new house at Chelten Hills north of Philadelphia. The mansion contained fifty-two rooms and about seventy servants. Oberholtzer, *Jay Cooke*, 1:153–54, 2:447–51.

MAY 10. Sir Fredk Bruce, Baron Gerolt,[15] Messrs Washburne Patterson,[16] & Hayes of the House Mr. McCulloch, Secy. of Treasy., Professor Henry, Gen. Brice,[17] Gen. Gillmore, Mr. Garrett & Mr. Alberts of Baltimore, Baron Eggloffstein & Col. Viall dined with me today. Gov. Swann accepted but sent an apology, engagements at Annapolis, several days ago; Mr. Blow accepted but was prevented from coming by the sickness of his brother;[18] Mr. Bingham, accepted but neither came nor sent an excuse / He made a great Speech in the afternoon & was probably revising the report.[19] The conversation was general & pleasant. Sir Fredk. in particular seemed to enjoy himself. Mr. McCulloch had called on Davis at Fortress Monroe: said he was well, but not very well.[20]

1866. JULY 2. Mr. Buckingham, called with accident policy from the Accident Insurance Company of Columbus, O, & a bill for $25 the premium. I declined to receive the policy or pay the bill; directing Mr. Buckingham to say to the Company that I did so because I never to the best of my recollection applied for insurance: and certainly never did so intentionally.

I note all the circumstances that have occurred connected with the Company in memoriam. About a year ago I was in Columbus & a gentleman connected with the Company called & handed me a paper which was, I think, something in the nature of an insurance ticket, saying that the Company desired my acceptance of it. I took the paper & put it in my pocket, thanking the gentleman but attaching no importance to the transaction. What has become of the paper I do not know. Some days ago Mr. Buckingham called with a memorandum with blanks similar to one filled up by Gov.

---

15. Friedrich Karl Joseph von Gerolt (c. 1798–1879), Prussian minister to the U.S., was interested in Egloffstein's photoengraving venture. *Wash. Dir. (1864)*, 81, 159; F. von Egloffstein to Chase, Apr. 8, 1866 (Cooke Papers, Hist. Soc. of Pa.); Chase to S. Hooper, Nov. 8, 1866 (Chase Papers, Hist. Soc. of Pa.); *National Union Catalog: Pre-1956 Imprints*, 156:505.

16. That is, Elihu Benjamin Washburne and James Willis Patterson.

17. Joseph Henry (1797–1878), U.S. physicist and first secretary and director of the Smithsonian Institution; and Maj. Gen. Benjamin W. Brice (1809–92), who spent his early years in Ohio and at this time presided over the army's pay department in Washington, D.C. *DAB*, 8:550–53; *Appletons'*, 1:372.

18. Peter Ethelred Taylor Blow (1814–66), mine operator and older brother of Henry Taylor Blow, died in July at St. Louis. John A. Bryan, "The Blow Family . . . ," *Bulletin of the Missouri Historical Society* 4 (July 1948): 224, 229; 5 (Oct. 1948): 26–27.

19. Earlier in the day, John Armor Bingham had presented a speech on the floor of the Senate which supported adoption of the Fourteenth Amendment. *Cong. Globe*, 39th Cong., 1st sess., 1866, 36, pt. 3:2541–44.

20. Jefferson Davis was held at Fortress Monroe from his capture in May 1865 to May 1867. *DAB*, 5:130.

July 1866 {611}

Dennison which he shewed me. The blanks to be filled up were statements of a personal character, such as age &c. I supposed that the Company had paid each of us a similar compliment to that of last year & filled mine as Governor Dennison had filled his. It was afterwards brought back with a request that I would fill a blank indicating to whom the Insurance Money should be paid in the event of liability & I inserted Netties name.

Unless this was an application, & I certainly did not think it was I have made none & have no notion of being made an involuntary or unconscious applicant for insurance which I dont want.[21]

JULY 13—FRI. Attended meeting of Military Asylum Board at Surgeon Generals Office. Generals Butler & Martindale, Secy. Stanton, Gov. Smyth, Messrs Walker of Wis & Gunckel of Ohio and myself were present[22]— Agreed to appoint Gen Hincks Governor of the Asylum, with pay &c of Colonel & made an appropriation of $45.000 for out door relief.[23]

After meeting made sundry small purchases—directed Frank to copy my letters—biographical—to Mr. Trowbridge & send them to me[24]— Gov. Sprague accompanied me to cars—had sleeping car stateroom—left at 6.30—Barney on train—also S. M. Clark each came in to talk[25]—half promised to visit Barney—weather extremely hot—vain attempts to sleep.

21. Despite lack of signature, Chase actually appears to have made a $5,000 insurance policy with the Accident Insurance Company of Columbus on June 30, 1865. Insurance policy, June 30, 1865 (Chase Papers, L.C.).
22. Benjamin F. Butler presided over the Board of Managers for the National Home for Disabled Volunteer Soldiers as president and treasurer. Also present: John Henry Martindale (1815–81), brevet major general of volunteers and attorney general of New York, 1866–68; Edwin M. Stanton; Frederick Smyth (1819–99), governor of New Hampshire, 1865–67; probably Isaac Pigeon Walker; and Lewis B. Gunckel (1826–1903), Dayton, Ohio, lawyer and Republican politician. Richard S. West, Jr., *Lincoln's Scapegoat General: A Life of Benjamin F. Butler, 1818–1893* (Boston, 1965), 316–18; *Appletons'*, 4:234–35; *Nat. Cyc.*, 11:133; *Bio. Dir. U.S. Cong.*, 1104.
23. Brig. Gen. Edward Winslow Hincks (1830–94) served as governor of the Soldiers' Home, 1866–67. *Appletons'*, 3:211; Johnson, *Twentieth Century Biographical Dictionary*, v. 1.
24. Frank Bronaugh, a young man approximately nineteen years of age at this time, copied letters and kept up Chase's scrapbooks. In 1864, author and editor John Townsend Trowbridge (1843–1923) wrote a biography of Chase aimed at young readers, *The Ferry-Boy and the Financier* (Boston, 1864). See p. xii above for Chase's autobiographical letters to Trowbridge, written Dec. 1863–Mar. 1864. Sept. 18, 1866, below; Chase memorandum, "Missing Papers," Sept. 18, 1866 (Chase Papers, L.C.); *DAB*, 18:655–56; Chase to Kate Chase Sprague, Sept. 6, 1865 (Chase Papers, Hist. Soc. of Pa.); Chase to R. C. Parsons, Dec. 15, 1870 (Chase Papers, L.C.).
25. Earlier, Spencer Morton Clark had given Chase a detailed analysis of Egloffstein's engraving process. Clark to Chase, Apr. 2, 1866 (Chase Papers, L.C.).

JULY 14. SAT.   Reached New York at 5.30—left my light grey overcoat in cars at Jersey City—took carriage for 5th Av. Hotel[26]— asked for bath & breakfast & shave—shown to room No. 13 with bath—bathed laying diamond pin on table or dressing bureau— dressed without thinking of pin—breakfasted—back to room noticed woman near door who came in after me apparently to take some articles she had left there supposing occupant had gone—she left immediately—used closet in bath room—shaved—took New Haven cars at 8 having some difficulty to find seat— Andrews formerly Collr. in car[27]—thinks Johnsonism will do the Union Party in New York no harm—dinner at Springfield—took cars for Nashua at Worcester & for Concord at Nashua—left umbrella at Nashua— Mr. Onslow Stearns in car from Boston to Nashua invited me into another car where joined by Capt [Merrett][28] about to marry relative of Mr. Stearns—large man opposite me—Conductor asked me if that Chief Justice— Arrived at Concord at 8.30 welcomed by Prentice & Hannah at depot & by Eliza at the house[29]—all well & kind as always.

JULY 15. SUN.   Went to Episcopal Church—very-very hot—sermon indifferent— In the eveng several called—among them Judge B   of the Supreme Court & Mr. Odlin[30]—an assessor, I believe of Internal Revenue—a very good [one]—who wanted to talk Finance / I not that way inclined.

JULY 16. MON.   Mr. Stearns called & invite me to breakfast tomorrow morng with Sherman[31] who comes from Portsmouth—went down town with Tucker[32] & bo't glasses & gloves—called at Gov. Gillmore's who too ill to see me—saw Mrs G[33]—hopeful but ap-

26. Completed in 1859 at 190 Fifth Avenue, this hotel was a Republican gathering place. *New York Dir. (1864),* 283; Federal Writers' Project, *New York City Guide* (New York, 1939), 206.
27. Probably Rufus F. Andrews.
28. Possibly Edwin Atkins Merritt (1828–1916), civil engineer, politician, and former commissary of subsistence with the 16th New York Volunteers. Heitman, *Historical Register,* 1:706; *Nat. Cyc.,* 17:444.
29. Josiah Prentice Tucker; his wife and Chase's niece, Hannah Ralston Whipple Tucker, the daughter of Chase's sister Hannah Chase Whipple; and Eliza Chase Whipple. Hannah Whipple Tucker to Chase, Sept. 23, 1872, and "Family Memoranda" (Chase Papers, L.C.).
30. Henry Adams Bellows (1803–73), at this time an associate justice on the Supreme Court of New Hampshire, and Concord merchant Woodbridge Odlin (1810–98), assistant assessor of internal revenue, 1862–72. *Appletons',* 1:230; Lyford, *History of Concord,* 2:1031.
31. William Tecumseh Sherman.
32. Josiah Prentice Tucker.
33. Ann Page Whipple Gilmore.

prehensive also—started with Tucker, (Hannah & Eliza also) for Hopkinton to see Aunt Eliza now over 90—spring broke & obliged to turn back— Judge Fowler & Mr. Dana called[34]— Heard that Upham &   had gone to Washn., summoned by Blair in relation to vacant district judgeship & Post Office at Concord, which to be filled in interest of "my policy"— Fogg had gone after them[35]

JULY 17. TUES.   Breakfasted at Mr. Stearns with Gen Sherman & his party, Gen. T. K. Smith, Capt Audenreid[36] & some others— After bkft Gen Sn. & Admiral Bailey called with me at Mrs Tuckers[37]—left at 11 for Hanover in Special car provided for Gen Sherman—a very handsome one belonging to some Vt. Railroad I believe—Eliza Whipple with me & a crowd (especially of pretty young ladies who had come into the car to take last leave of the General & had been carried off by accident) with Gen Sherman. Of those in the car on purpose were Mr & Mrs Stearns, Gov. & Mrs Smyth, Gen. Nat. Head, of State Militia.[38] The party was a merry one—the young ladies left us at a waystation, each taking a kiss from Gen S—— at parting—and some of them one from me. Prest Smith of Dartmouth College was at depot waiting for Gen. S—— & Prof. Patterson, Senator Elect, for me, & Major Dewey for Eliza.[39] Moses Kimball called on me at Senator P——s to say that very few of our class, (to attend a meeting of which was my main object in visiting Hanover this year) were in town—asked him to invite such as he met to come in after Class Exercises—which I attended in part—

34. Asa Fowler (1811–85), a New Hampshire politician and former associate justice on the state's supreme court, and lawyer and police justice Sylvester Dana (1816–1910), a Dartmouth graduate who had held earnest antislavery convictions. *Nat. Cyc.*, 5:192–93; Lyford, *History of Concord*, 2:984, 1013; Chapman, *Sketches of the Alumni*, 302; Emerson, *General Catalogue*, 256.

35. New Hampshire Republican George Gilman Fogg (1813–81) served as U.S. minister to Switzerland, 1861–65. He was appointed to fill the U.S. Senate seat vacated on July 27 by the resignation of Daniel Clark. Nathaniel Gookin Upham (1801–69), a former justice of New Hampshire's Supreme Court and a member of the state legislature, 1865–66, had apparently gone to see Montgomery Blair. *Bio. Dir. U.S. Cong.*, 781, 1010–11; *DAB*, 6:485–86; *Appletons'*, 6:213.

36. Joseph Crain Audenried.

37. Gen. Sherman and Theodorus Bailey (1805–77), who commanded the Portsmouth Navy Yard, 1864–66. Mrs. Tucker evidently was Hannah Ralston Whipple Tucker. *DAB*, 1:501–2; *New York Tribune*, July 18, 1866; Lyford, *History of Concord*, 2:1081.

38. Onslow Stearns, Mary A. Holbrook Stearns, Frederick Smyth, and Emma Lane Smyth (d. 1884). Natt Head (1828–83) served as adjutant general of New Hampshire, 1864–70, and later as state senator and governor. Sobel and Raimo, *Biographical Directory of Governors*, 3:965; *Appletons'*, 3:152; *Nat. Cyc.*, 3:134, 9:136–37.

39. Asa Dodge Smith; James Willis Patterson; and Israel Otis Dewey (1824–88), a former merchant and postmaster at Hanover, N.H., and a paymaster in the U.S. Army, 1867–88. *Nat. Cyc.*, 4:165.

Some of the class came in afterwards—agreed to meet again tomorrow at Senior Recitation Room—gave up idea of dining together— Went to Church—(Anniversary of Theological Society) & heard excellent discourse to a small audience by Dr. Kirk— Met Dr. Vermilye at the Church[40]— There was a large reception to Gen Sherman this eveng at Drs. Crosby's[41]—did not go.

JULY 18. WED. Attended meeting of ΦBK. Kimball moved for Shedd's admission vouching for him[42] / I seconded saying that he was next to first third, I being the last— Kimball privately insisted he was last— After attending oration at Church eight of our class came together at Senior Recitation Room in College Building— George W. Punchard, Allen Gannett, Spofford D Jewett, William Clagett, Moses Kimball, Weeks, Wm Ward, Chase.[43] and we had a very pleasant talk, accounting our several experiences, reviving old memories, exchanging mutual goodwill— Weeks related an anecdote of Punchard & myself— Punchard for some alleged offence had been dismissed or suspended— Weeks, not knowing of it, being himself under suspension, came to town to ask for remission of his sentence—going to the President's he met Chase, full of wrath coming out. Is the President in?" Yes, I've just seen him and I'm going off." "What's the matter." Why haven't you heard George Punchard is dismissed for nothing. Somebody has told the Faculty that he tore down old Farrar's fence[44] & theyve dismissed him / There's no truth in it but they wont hear, & I've just been to the President & told him I wont stay under such a Government." Weeks went on & saw the President, whom he found very ready to grant his request, and was then asked "Have you seen Chase." "Yes I just met him, boiling

---

40. Possibly Edward Norris Kirk (1802–74), pastor of Boston's Mount Vernon Congregational Church, and Robert George Vermilye (1813–75), at this time a professor of theology at East Windsor Theological Institute. *Nat. Cyc.*, 6:194; *Appletons'*, 6:279–80.

41. Dixi Crosby (1800–1873) and his son Alpheus Benning Crosby (1832–77), both physicians, taught surgery at Dartmouth College. Dixi Crosby was the brother of Prof. Alpheus Crosby. *Appletons'*, 2:16–17; Emerson, *General Catalogue*, 285, 478, 490.

42. Charles Shedd (1802–85), Dartmouth class of 1826, was a minister and missionary. The move to admit him was successful. Emerson, *General Catalogue*, 239.

43. Ministers Spofford Dodge Jewett (1801–88) and William Clagett (1796–1870); lawyer and New Hampshire state politician William Pickering Weeks (1803–70); and teacher and minister James Wilson Ward (1803–73). Chase inserted the first names above the line, and apparently by mistake he placed the "Wm" with Ward instead of Weeks. Emerson, *General Catalogue*, 238–39; Chapman, *Sketches of the Alumni*, 233.

44. Attorney and legal scholar Timothy Farrar (1788–1874) was secretary, treasurer, and librarian of Dartmouth College, 1822–26. *DAB*, 6:293; Chapman, *Sketches of the Alumni*, 132.

over." "Well" said the President "you had better call on him & tell him not be hasty." The upshot was that the Faculty discovered they had been precipitate—Punchard's sentence was revoked. But he & I went off together for a [*two words illeg.*], feeling ourselves quite heroic.[45] On comparing notes we found that nine of our class had died during the forty years since our graduation—twenty seven were still living as nearly as we could get at the facts, scattered all over the Union & one, a Missionary in the Sandwich Islands— One blind, but full of the light of the Gospel & Divine Plan—happiest & most exalted of us all, for he is Christ's & Christ is his[46]—

Our talk went on & we did not attend the oration before the Literary Societies, & I was not sorry that being prolonged till after five it gave me an excuse for not attending the laying of the Corner Stone of the Gymnasium where I was expected to make an address. At last we separated shortly after five. At Senator Pattersons, one of the Professors came for me to go to the laying of the Corner Stone. I excused myself and persuaded the Senator to go in my place. In the evg went to Prof. Sanfords,[47] & then to ———— where our class met again. I did not go to the Presidents Party preferring our meeting.[48] We talked—resolved to meet at the Centennial in 1869 if living—prayed—parted.

JULY 19. THURS— A committee of Alumni called to announce that I had been elected President / Accompanied them to Hall— took seat & made short address[49]— Procession formed—Gen Sherman & I together—proceeded to Church—heard the Exercises which very Creditable—during one part went to Dr. Crosbys & partook of collation— Capt & Mrs Pike called on me at Senator P———'s & invited me to visit them in Cornish—agreed to do so if I could— In the eveng accompanied Mrs Patterson first to Prof Noyes and afterwards to the Levee at the Literary Societies Rooms—

---

45. At this point Chase put two small x or & marks along the line, perhaps to show a change of subject or for *etc. etc.*
46. Chase referred to his classmates John Smith Emerson (1800–1867), a missionary in the Hawaiian Islands, 1831–67, and Caleb Kimball (b. 1798), a blind evangelist and author of works on religion. Chapman, *Sketches of the Alumni*, 230, 231; *Appletons'*, 2:342–43.
47. Probably Edwin David Sanborn (1808–85), professor of oratory and belles-lettres. *DAB*, 16:325–26.
48. Above the word *meeting*, Chase made an insertion that looks like a numeral 2 preceded by something else, perhaps a # sign. He may have intended to make clear that this reference was to the second meeting with his classmates during the day.
49. Chase "alluded to the beautiful day and the cheerful dinner" and expressed hope for renewed national union "under the old stars and stripes." *New York Times*, July 23, 1866.

JULY 20. FRI. My friends procured a carriage for me & Major Dewey accompanying Monstrator vice[50] we (Eliza Whipple & I) went over the Hills, by a very picturesque & pleasant road to Royalton— I preferring this to the Railroad & changes— Saw woman with a little boy [by] roadside gathering raspberries—proposed to purchase her tin pail & its contents; but while trying to make change she withdrew her offer saying "She'd heard tin [had *illeg.*], & she guessed the pail was worth more". Found our cousins the Denisons— Dudley & his children,[51] Rachel, Mrs Jo Denison and her children, ready to welcome us— They were expecting George from New-Orleans.[52]

JULY 21. SAT. Nothing of special interest took place today— some talk of old times when I attended the Academy here in 1824 under Mr. Sprague[53]—some pleasant recollections & some painful— The old Pinnacle which I climbed with Lauretta still stands.[54] Dr.   who married Betsy Fox called & asked me to come see them—coming up the river I had in vain tried to fix the place where Gratia & Fanny Parkhurst lived[55]—where I sometimes went to boys & girls parties—where our boat once upset & I jumped into the water, luckily not very deep, to save Lauretta from a wetting. how

---

50. That is, acting as a guide or pointing out sights.
51. Dudley Chase Denison (1819–1905), U.S. district attorney for Vermont, 1865–69, later served in Congress. He was the son of Dr. Joseph A. Denison, Sr., and Chase's aunt, Rachel Chase Denison. Dudley had five children: Joseph D., Catharine Amanda, John H., Gertrude M., and Lucy D. Denison. *Bio. Dir. U.S. Cong.*, 895; Lewis Cass Aldrich and Frank E. Holmes, eds., *History of Windsor County, Vermont* (Syracuse, N.Y., 1891), 779–80.
52. Rachel was Chase's cousin, Rachel Denison. "Mrs Jo Denison" was probably the same as "Cousin Eliza" of the next journal entry. She was evidently the widow of Chase's cousin, Dr. Joseph Adam Denison, Jr. (d. 1848). They had several children, including George Stanton Denison; those with Eliza at the time of Chase's visit are named in the following entry. July 21 entry, below; Child, *Cornish*, 2:62; Padgett, "Some Letters of George Stanton Denison," 1132, 1165, 1191; *General Catalogue of the University of Vermont*, 49.
53. The Rev. Nathaniel Sprague was preceptor of Royalton Academy. Charles T. Morrissey, ed., "A New York Doctor Recalls Vermont: The Memoirs of Calvin Skinner," *Vermont History* 40 (Autumn 1972): 277–78; Zadock Thompson, *History of Vermont...*, 3 pts. in 1 vol. (Burlington, 1842), 3:143, 152.
54. Lauretta Hitchcock was one of Chase's schoolmates at Royalton Academy. He later recalled that she "quite won my young heart." The Pinnacle was a hill near the school. Hitchcock to Chase, Feb. 24, 1829, Chase to J. T. Trowbridge, Feb. 7, 1864 (Chase Papers, Hist. Soc. of Pa.).
55. Betsy, Gratia, and Fanny were among Chase's acquaintances when he attended the academy. Fanny and Gratia, who was a friend of Chase's sister Jane, were probably descendants of Royalton pioneers Benjamin and Sarah Shepard Parkhurst. Chase to J. A. Denison, Jr., Apr. 22, 29, July [17], 1824 (Chase Papers, L.C.); Chase to Trowbridge, Feb. 7, 1864 (Chase Papers, Hist. Soc. of Pa.); Aldrich and Holmes, *Windsor County*, 783.

heroic I thought myself how silly it seems. Thinking of it now I feel sad— Mem. Cousin Dudley's wife was Miss Dunbar of Hartland[56]—Cousin Jo's Children at home are John, Katie & Gertrude—Cousin Jims son, Jo, is a fine boy adopted by Cousin Rachel—George's son is also with Cousin Eliza Jo's widow[57]—her daughter Eliza married Jamison of Chicago[58]—

Rode to Bethel with Cousin Dudley—pointed out place on rising ground where a few months since a most remarkable fire— Wife of wealthy farmer absent from home—leaving husband, a manservant, two female servants or help—fire broke out—manservant roused—ran round under window & called the farmer—no answer—ran to stable & obtained ladder—entered room—stumbled over body—found it farmers—carried to window—some now arrived—got him out but dead—hurried round where girls slept—called no answer—all in flames—impossible to enter—hastened to barn which connected with house as common in New England—all on fire—could not get the horses or other animals out—all perished—wife next morning a widow & poor.

At Bethel saw Mrs Moulton, Mrs Flinn, & Mrs Wilson, wife of Wilson young lawyer & partner of Dudley & her sister Miss Lois daughters of Mrs Flinn—pleasant visit—returned to Royalton played croquet with cousins

JULY 22. SUN— Attended Church—Cousin Dudley read services—his & Cousin Eliza's families made pretty much the whole Congregation— After Church called at Dr   & saw his wife[59]—formerly so gay & pretty—now old, shrivelled with rheumatism, a confirmed invalid—but still living in the heart & glad to see me

JULY 23. MON— Rainy morng—left Royalton friends with Eliza for Windsor about 11 am, reached Windsor about 1 P.M.—found

56. Eunice Dunbar. Aldrich and Holmes, *Windsor County*, 780.
57. "Cousin Jim" was James Denison. George S. Denison had a son, William (1857–86), whose mother had died shortly after his birth. Padgett, "Some Letters of George Stanton Denison," 1133; *General Catalogue of the University of Vermont*, 144.
58. In 1855, Eliza Denison, daughter of Joseph A. Denison, Jr., married Chicago judge John Alexander Jameson (1824–90), a Vermont native. Chase crowded the last two lines of this paragraph in order to fit them in before the July 22 entry, which in the original journal follows this paragraph. Chase's note at this point says, "next page for more of Sat. 21st." The continuation of the entry on the next page of the journal (the two paragraphs beginning *Rode to Bethel*) originally had another date, possibly *July 22. Sun*. Chase may have written those two paragraphs as another day's entry, then at some point transformed them into a continuation of July 21. In any event, the present entry for July 22 was in the journal before Chase wrote at least the last lines of the first paragraph for July 21, and perhaps before what became the continuation of the July 21 entry. *DAB*, 9:601–2.
59. Betsy Fox (see July 21 above).

Capt. Pike & Mr. Evarts at depot— Capt. P—— took Eliza & Mr. Evarts me promising to bring me over tomorrow— Mr. Evarts char[ming] family—Mrs. E—— mother of 12 children including two pair twins[60]—still handsome & young looking—children pretty & some of them more than pretty & all well behaved—dined—rode afterwards over farm—Mr. Stoughton a New York lawyer called[61]— Mr. & Mrs Pritchard guests.[62]

JULY 24. TUES. Mr. Evarts with Mr. Pritchard & self to Capt. Pikes where they left me—after looking at & admiring Capt P——'s fine horses—found Eliza well—dined & drive after dinner— when starting near 5 met some people agreeing to come—drove through Plainfield by Academy returned about six— Soon many came in from Cornish, Claremont & Hartland on Vt. side of River— Several old men who knew my father with whom had very interesting talk—some members of Bishop Chase's family from Claremont— Some of the Jarvis family—two bands of music came also & every thing went very pleasantly—thanks to kind Capt. Pike & his excellent wife & the good people

JULY 25, WED. Rose pretty early—usual duties—took a look at old Ascutney—dear old friend—through Capt Pikes' glass—wrote Stanton (Secy) in behalf of young Nichols—pleasant drive Capt P—— & I in buggy & Mrs P—— with her pretty sister Miss Fay of Windsor & Eliza in another carriage—down river through Cornish, across Bridge in Claremont—up through Ascutneyville to Windsor where my kind friends left me at Mr. Evarts— In Cornish called on Cousin David H Chase, my friend & playmate when a boy[63]—not much older than I but now an old man—he has had a hard working life—managing though not owning the farm & caring for his mother & sister during their lives. He now owns the farm & expects to improve—called at Cousin Simeons at the next farm—a second cousin[64] / called at Judge Putnams—recalled, painfully, sleighride

---

60. Helen Minerva Wardner Evarts (c. 1819–1903), wife of William Maxwell Evarts, hailed from Windsor, Vt. *New York Times,* Dec. 28, 1903.
   61. Probably attorney Edwin Wallace Stoughton (1818–82) of New York, a native of Windsor County and future U.S. envoy to Russia, 1877–79. *DAB,* 18:112–13.
   62. Possibly Harvard graduate and New York City lawyer William Mackay Prichard (c. 1814–97) and his wife. *New York Tribune,* Oct. 18, 1897; *Quinquennial Catalogue,* 191; *New York Dir. (1863),* 703.
   63. David Hall Chase (1805–76), whose peculiar voice earned him the nickname of "Squeaking David," was a son of Jonathan Chase and Hannah Ralston Chase, the sister of Chase's mother. Child, *Cornish,* 2:65.
   64. The paternal grandfathers of Salmon P. Chase and Simeon March Chase (1811–92) were brothers. Child, *Cornish,* 2:59–63, 65–66.

with his sister Anne so many years ago[65]—was I then a boy at Dunhams, or at Royalton or at College—passed birth place & old yellow house of brains[66]—at Ascutneyville called on Moses Kimball—saw his wife & pleasant home & glad to find him so comfortable[67]—dined at Stoughton's Judge Nelson, Judge Smalley & his son, Judge Redfield & several more[68]—Mr. & Mrs Pritchard, Mr & Mrs Evarts, Eliza &c a pleasant party—grand sunset view of Ascutney from town—

JULY 26. THURS. Called at tavern to see Denisons who had come down to ascend Ascutney then took a long drive—in vicinity of Ascutney—Mr. Evarts, Mrs Pritchard, Eliza & I—returned for lunch—took 1 P.M. train for Keene—Pritchards to take late train for Concord Mass. Some talk with Evarts about approaching Phil. Conv. & political prospects[69]—he not hopeful—reached Keene about half past three—welcomed by Mr. Wheeler & taken to his house[70]—large gathering of friends to welcome me—Dr. Barstow & Mrs Barstow, Mr Prentiss, near 80 but very vigorous & active & intelligent & devotedly patriotic[71] / Gen & Mrs Griffin, formerly Miss Lamson; Mrs Chapin, wife of R.R. Supert. Mrs Kittredge[72]—

65. John Lyscom Putnam (1792–1834) served many years as a Sullivan County judge. His sister was Ann Elizabeth Putnam (1808–47). Ibid., 2:295.
66. Near the house in which Chase was born stood his father's birthplace, of which it was said that "more brains were born in that house than in any other in New England." Trowbridge, *Ferry-Boy and Financier*, 20.
67. Abby Osgood Bartlett Kimball, a daughter of Bailey Bartlett of Haverhill, Mass., married Moses Kimball in 1832. Chapman, *Sketches of the Alumni*, 231–32.
68. Samuel Nelson, on circuit; David A. Smalley (b. 1809), U.S. district judge for Vermont, 1857–75; Bradley Barlow Smalley (1835–1909), clerk of federal courts for the district of Vermont, 1861–85; and Windsor County native Isaac Fletcher Redfield (1804–76), associate and chief justice of the New Hampshire Supreme Court, 1835–60, and later a Boston legal author. Lanman, *Biographical Annals*, 457; *Who Was Who*, 1:1135; *DAB*, 15:439–40.
69. Chase probably refers to the Southern Loyalists' Convention, which assembled in Philadelphia on Sept. 3. The gathering actually included representatives from both North and South who endorsed the Fourteenth Amendment but agreed on little else except opposition to the Reconstruction policies of Andrew Johnson. Eric Foner, *Reconstruction: America's Unfinished Revolution, 1863–1877* (New York, 1988), 270; Sept. 3, below.
70. Keene attorney William P. Wheeler (1812–76). Griffin, *Keene*, 656–57.
71. John Prentiss actually turned eighty-eight in 1866. Zedekiah Smith Barstow (1790–1873), a Congregational pastor from Keene and a member of Dartmouth's board of trustees, 1834–71, had previously taught Chase the classics. Mrs. Barstow, whose first name is unknown, died in 1869 at the age of 77. *Appletons'*, 1:182; Griffin, *Keene*, 561–62, 725.
72. Margaret R. Lamson Griffin, originally of Keene, married Simon Goodell Griffin in 1863. Mrs. Chapin may have been Dorcas Chapin, wife of Springfield, Mass., entrepreneur Chester William Chapin (1798–1883), who was president of the Boston & Albany R.R. and other firms. Mrs. Kittredge was probably the wife of Thomas B. Kittredge. *DAB*, 4:14–15, 7:622; Griffin, *Keene*, 473.

a Seranade [&c urgency] for Speech—said brief words of reminiscence & thanks—nothing political—

JULY 27—FRI: Took two rides one through Streets & over the hill calling at Dr. Barstow's—one towards Westmoreland & through what I used to know as the Swamp. logs lay in the mill pond just as they did when I was a boy forty six or seven years ago—but the Mills had grown to great factories not of lumber only— Visited my fathers grave in the old cemetery—the stone at its head commemorates "Hon Ithr. Chase, died Aug 8, 1815 And Now Lord What is My Hope; truly My Hope is Even in Thee." Visited the handsome new Church

In the eveng a number of last eveng's guests came in again & also Mr. & Mrs Ward.

JULY 28. SAT. Left Eliza at Mr. Wheelers, & took train for Boston about nine—Master Faulkner, son of Mr. W——'s partner[73] & Miss Lucy Parsons a lively young girl from near Boston, at school in Keene, were my companions—promised each of them a photograph & autograph which I afterward sent— A zealous admirer learning I was on the train came to speak to me & when the cars stopped at Groton where he left them astonished me by crying out "Fellow Citizens; I have the pleasure of announcing that Ch Justice Salmon P Chase is in the train & I propose three Cheers." He gave them himself, nobody else taking any notice! Reached Boston about three & found Tucker[74] waiting at Depot. He took me to the E.R.R Station[75] where I took the 3 P.M. train for Beverly, arriving in a pouring shower at 3.50—found servant who said that Mrs E—— could not send her carriage on account of the storm but wished me to take the hack which I did & soon after was safe at the castle[76] receiving the kindly greetings of my dear friends Mrs Rantoul & Mrs Eastman. the rain ceased & the sunset was most glorious— Mrs R being an invalid retired early & I sat talking with Mrs E—— till past 10 when I also sought my room— I found there a note from Mr. R. S. Rantoul inviting me to visit him—

---

73. Three sons survived lawyer and local politician Francis Augustus Faulkner (1825–79). Griffin, *Keene*, 595–96; *Quinquennial Catalogue*, 204.
74. Josiah Prentice Tucker.
75. The Eastern Railroad Station. Poor, *History of Railroads*, 114–17.
76. Castle Rantoul.

JULY 29. SUN. At Church with Mrs E—— sat in Miss Rantoul's pew[77]—Mr. Kimball preached on Children as the Care of Christ reading a beautiful little poem written, Mrs E—— says by his wife[78]— Mr. Haven & his son Col. H called to invite me to their house[79]— Accepted to come sometime during week—read a little—talked with Mrs E & Mrs R—a pleasant but I fear not profitable day.

JULY 30. MON— A pleasant day with my friends at the castle—dinner at Mr. Lorings in the afternoon[80]—Judge, Curtis, Mr. Sidney Bartlett & Prof Gray with myself made the party[81]—agreeable talk—a beautiful day—& a charming place.

JULY 31. TUES. Another pleasant day & a dinner at Mr. Endicotts.[82] In the morning a drive to Salem with Mrs E & a visit to the Essex Institute— The Librarian, Dr. Wheatland, was very obliging & showed us every thing[83]—called at the Custom House & saw old Manifest of Cargo principally teas in the days of Salems glory— Here Hawthorn composed his Seven Gables & was Surveyor of the Port[.][84] It is by no means the somber place he depicts. Mr. Rantoul, Surveyor,[85] with us to Soda Shop; delicious soda water— Mrs E called to give some directions—I to buy hat. Mr. Endicotts dinner rather more formal than that at Mr. Loring's— Mrs

---

77. Likely Hannah Lovett Rantoul (b. 1821), the youngest sister of Robert Rantoul (1805–52). "Rantoul Genealogy," 147.
78. Possibly John Kimball, a deacon who resided in Ipswich. *Essex Co. Dir. (1870)*, 329.
79. Franklin Haven, Sr. (1804–93), president of the Merchants' Bank of Boston and father of Col. Franklin Haven, Jr., first bought property at West Beach, Beverly, in 1846. Wiltse et al., *Papers of Daniel Webster*, Corres., 5:72; Katharine Peabody Loring, "The Earliest Summer Residents of the North Shore and Their Houses," *Essex Institute Historical Collections* 68 (1932): 197–200.
80. Charles Greeley Loring owned property at Beverly since 1844. Loring, "Earliest Summer Residents," 197–200.
81. Massachusetts jurist and politician Benjamin Robbins Curtis (1809–74), associate justice of the U.S. Supreme Court, 1851–57, and counsel for the defense during the impeachment trial of Andrew Johnson in 1868; Sidney Bartlett (1799–1889), Boston attorney and former Massachusetts legislator; and probably Asa Gray (1810–88), noted Harvard botanist. *Appletons'*, 2:34; *DAB*, 4:609–11, 7:511–14; *Nat. Cyc.*, 11:406.
82. William Endicott.
83. Henry Wheatland, M.D. (1812–93), was an early secretary of the Essex Historical Society. Russell Lee Jackson, "Physicians of Essex County," *Essex Institute Historical Collections* 84 (1948): 341.
84. Nathaniel Hawthorne (1804–64) had written *The House of Seven Gables: A Romance* (Boston, 1851) while working as surveyor at the port of Salem, 1845–49. *DAB*, 8:426–27.
85. Robert Samuel Rantoul.

E——[86] a very clever & really handsome woman. Mr. & Mrs Loring[87] & Mrs E. & Mrs R——[88] among the guests— I with these two ladies sitting with Joseph the driver— After return took key—but L[89] took it from me—putting hands in my pockets & taking it out without my knowing it

AUG. 1. WED. Mrs E—— took me to Marblehead in her carriage—visited the Fort;[90] rode round the cemetery, passed house of Mr. Hoopers late father, old merchant of Marblehead[91]— observed nothing remarkable unless some quaint old buildings—no rudeness from boys such as some speak of—air was delightful— though cool enough for afghan—took glass soda coming thro Salem—& Mrs E—— bot a parasol which she paid for from my portmonnaie—home to dinner—no engagement out today—incident about [*illeg.*—libry]

AUG 3. THURS.[92] Afraid Mrs E—— unwell, but she came down to breakfast & we passed most of the time in the Library reading & talking till 3 when she took me in her carriage to Mr. Havens where I am to stay a few days— Mr. H—— has a very delightful place at West Beach, opposite Great & Little Misery—Baker Island on which the Light House is &c—dinner today—Mrs E. would not stay. Dr. Hooper (M.D. & Dr. Lothrop (D.D.) talked much of foreign parts.[93]

AUG 4 FRI—TO AUG. 7 TUESDAY—[94] Remained at Mr. Havens—having a very pleasant time—billiards croquet—very awk-

---

86. Annie Thorndike Endicott.

87. Cornelia Amory Goddard Loring became the third wife of Charles Greeley Loring in 1850. *Nat. Cyc.*, 22:284–85.

88. Charlotte Eastman and Jane Rantoul.

89. Charlotte (Lottie) Eastman. She is signified by *L*—— or *L* in other entries for Aug.–Sept. 1866 also. Footnotes clarify those instances in which her initial might be confused with someone else mentioned in the journal.

90. Fort Sewall, repaired and enlarged during the Civil War. Hurd, *Essex County*, 2:1115; Sidney Perley, "Marblehead in the Year 1700," *Essex Institute Historical Collections* 47 (1911): 152–53.

91. John Hooper, the father of Samuel Hooper, also was president of the Marblehead Bank. *DAB*, 9:203.

92. Chase mistook either the date or the day of the week, as Thursday was Aug. 2 and Friday was Aug. 3. Taking into account his unbroken sequence of daily records preceding this entry, along with the greater chance of his forgetting the date than the day, it is most likely that this entry describes Thursday, Aug. 2.

93. Samuel Kirkland Lothrop and Robert William Hooper (d. 1885), who held three degrees from Harvard University and was a trustee of the Boston Athenaeum. *Quinquennial Catalogue*, 187; Howe, *Later Years of the Saturday Club*, 17, 256.

94. As noted above, Friday was Aug. 3. Chase was correct in making Aug. 7 a Tuesday.

ward at first with bad eyes & little better at second—taking a sail to Gloucester in little Cutter with Mrs Haven,[95] Dr. Lothrop, youngest Miss Haven, & Col H⎯⎯[96] visiting Castle, Mr. Lorings & Mrs Endicotts &c &c &c

AUG. 7. TUES. Left my kind friends, the Havens—with many regrets & went to Mr. Robt Rantouls,[97] who is son of Mrs R⎯⎯ & occupies next house to Mr. Havens on the Beach. a pleasant place, but small & unpretending— Mr. Phillips (Willard [P].)[98] & Mrs Haven's brother at dinner— I did not feel very well & went up stairs early in the evening after dinner leaving family & Mr. P⎯⎯ who remained over night but intending to return—but I concluded not to go down again & went to bed. Had a sail in the morning; but wind was high & the water dashed into the boat, & we came back— Mrs R⎯⎯ & Mr. R⎯⎯ however after landing me tried it again. Mr. Ed. Ev. Hale[99] & Mr. Haven called imy after dinner.

AUG. 8. WED. We had a fishing party today. Dr. Lothrop, Col Haven, Gen. Oliver of Salem, Mr. Brown, Assessor or Collr., Mr. Rantoul & several others[1]—stood out to Cod fishing grounds & caught nothing; but bought two or three from a boat which in the night had been a little more fortunate—went in shore not far from Normans Cove. Caught plenty of small fish, pollacks, chiefly, with some perch & small cods—beautiful sight to see them flashing in the water—had a capital chowder—light & baffling winds & slow voyage back—small prospect of getting friends back to Salem—so all landed at Mr. Rantouls and were furnished with carriages by Mr. R & Col Haven to Beverly horses cars after tea at Mr R⎯⎯s

AUG. 9. THURS. This day had been assigned for ride to Gloucester, Rockport & round Cape Ann; but it rained—after brkft it cleared & we expected Mrs E. & Mrs R[2]—but they did not come and it rained again—staid indoors & amused with bagatelle.

---

95. Sarah Ann Curtis Haven, wife of Franklin Haven, Sr. Wiltse et al., *Papers of Daniel Webster,* Corres., 7:6.
96. Franklin Haven, Jr.
97. Robert Samuel Rantoul.
98. Willard Peele Phillips.
99. Edward Everett Hale (1822–1909), Massachusetts author and Unitarian minister. *DAB,* 8:99–100.
1. Henry Kemble Oliver (1800–1885) was a teacher, former adjutant general of the Massachusetts militia, founder of the commonwealth's bureau of statistics and labor, and mayor of Salem, 1877–80. "Brown" was J. Vincent Browne. *DAB,* 14:18–19.
2. Charlotte Eastman and Jane Rantoul.

AUG. 10. FRIDAY. The friends came this morning & rendezvoused at Mr. Havens—whither Mr. R   & I went & we started for the excursion which we failed to make yesterday— L & I in Mrs E's carriage & Mr. Rantoul Dr. Lothrop, with M[rs] Haven & Mrs Rantoul Senr in Mr. Havens carriage—stopped in Gloucester to allow M[rs] R to see old friend—on to Gen. Butler's Camp near Lanesville[3]—very pleasant greeting & lunch— Miss Blanche & some friends bathing but joined us soon[4]—never saw her looking more beautiful— Dr. Lothrop insisted on [pig story] at lunch—and barred the door of tent—I took Miss B——'s arm & went out of the other—

AUG. 11—SAT. Returned to castle— Mr. & Mrs R Jr taking me in their carriage[5]—found Mrs R & Mrs E none the worse for trip yesterday—read part of Websters Sp. in reply to Hayne to Mrs E— more to myself—some conversation—some napping—towards evg rode out to Cherry Hill & promised Waters[6] to come to Church in morning— Joseph played Jehu back—begged L—— not to [lock door]—no use—would—[raps] but no spirit.

AUG. 12. SUN— At Church morning—with E   at North Beverly— Waters has done a good work in refitting the old edifice very neatly & getting the scattered people together— Mr. Porter from Boston preached & preached very well—

AUG 13. MON. No visiting or riding today— L—— to room with me [*five? words illeg.*]— Knocking at door in the night but no one answered—read—

AUG. 14. TUES. Met L—— coldly—she cordial though guided by coldness—coldness could not withstand her gentle kindness. Called at Whiting's Mrs E lending her carriage[7]—at Mrs Endicott's at Mr. Rantouls—where dismissed carriage & waited some time—finally Mr. & Mrs R who had been at Salem returned / some talk—then walked towards Mr. Havens—saw Dr. Hooper & Mr. Sam Hooper with young ladies playing croquet—joined them—went with Mr. S.

---

3. The state legislature had elected Benjamin F. Butler major general of the Massachusetts militia a few months earlier. Trefousse, *Ben Butler*, 186.

4. Blanche Butler (c. 1847–1939) was Gen. Butler's daughter and the future wife of Adelbert Ames. *DAB*, 3:357–59; *New York Times*, Dec. 28, 1939.

5. Robert S. and Harriet Charlotte Neal Rantoul married in 1858. Little, "Salem Custom House," 268.

6. Richard Palmer Waters.

7. William Whiting (1813–73), lawyer and solictor of the U.S. War Department, 1863–65, maintained a residence at Beverly. *DAB*, Supp. 1, 703–4; Loring, "Earliest Summer Residents," 202.

August 1866 { 625 }

Hooper to dinner at Mr. Haven's—escorted Miss H—guests Gov Bullock, Mrs & Miss B——[8] Mr. & Mrs Dexter,[9] Mr. Lothrop & Mrs L—— (Miss Hooper that was)[10] Dr. Lothrop, Mr. Hooper, self & others—drove back to Castle—expected L[11] to join me at Mrs Endicotts, but she not there—tea—& tea talk—de me—de te—de nobis—de quibus [*illeg.* alias][12]—took key—L put up bar—pulled—yielded a little but [gave] up—[morning she came in]—bent over & kissed me, but wd. [not join me]—had prayed Heavenly Father for strength—asked for key—guest get [moving & up early], door locked—locked it—

AUG 15. WED. Met L in Library—sat down & talked—distant—but soon over that—talked very kindly—bkft—went up to pack—came up to see if cd. do anything to help   Said she [wanted] me & wd have yielded if I had come in—showed bar—[*illeg.*] put across door & tied [with her garter]—wd. have given way if pulled [*illeg.*]—sat down on box—lay down on her [couch]—followed—also in my room[—]side by side—grieving at parting—with me to depot—sat in carriage till train came— I to Boston—& Mr. Hoopers—Sumner & Dana S. T. to dinner[13] / sent word to Tucker & Pierce asking P. to come to breakfast[14]

AUG. 16. THURS. Tucker came in—Pierce did not—Tucker with me to Pub Library—fine institution / took up Gannett—went to see Punchard—left Gannett—went to Clothing store & bot overcoat to

---

8. Alexander Hamilton Bullock (1816–82), governor of Massachusetts, 1866–69, and his wife, Elvira Hazard Bullock. The Bullocks had two daughters: one ultimately married Nelson S. Bartlett of Boston; the other, Fanny Bullock (1859–1925), became the wife of William Hunter Workman and, with her husband, gained notoriety as an explorer and writer. *Appletons'*, 1:446; *DAB*, 20:533–34.

9. Likely either George Dexter and his wife Sarah Rogers Endicott Dexter (b. 1838), or F. Gordon Dexter, son of a prominent Boston lawyer and owner of a house within the Haven property. Hurd, *Essex County*, 1:liii; Loring, "Earliest Summer Residents," 201–3.

10. Thornton Kirkland Lothrop (1830–1913), assistant U.S. district attorney during the Civil War, recently had married Ann M. Hooper, the daughter of Samuel Hooper. *Nat. Cyc.*, 14:225–26; *Who Was Who*, 1:747.

11. Charlotte (Lottie) Eastman.

12. "About me—about you—about us—about whatever—[about other things?]—"

13. Charles Sumner and Samuel Turner Dana. Chase originally wrote *Judge Gray & Mr.   to dinner*, then altered it to show Sumner and Dana as the guests instead. Judge Gray and "Mr.   " were dinner guests at Hooper's on Aug. 16 (see next entry), so Chase's alteration could indicate that he did not write this Aug. 15 entry until sometime after dinner the next day.

14. J. Prentice Tucker and Edward L. Pierce. Chase asked Tucker to call on him at Samuel Hooper's house that evening or the next morning, and indicated that he would leave for Providence the afternoon of Aug. 16. Chase to Tucker, Aug. 15, 1866 (Chase Papers, New Hamp. Hist. Soc.).

Jeweller's shop & bot pencil for Rbt. & [broach] for [*illeg.*] & [ring] for [Maggie] Rantoul[15]— Called [on] Mr. [Haven][16] at Bank who kindly consented to take them—back to Hoopers—Judge Gray[17] & Mr   to dinner pleasant talk—left them at table—& off for Providence—arrd. abt. 6—found [*illeg.*] at Depot & Ed. with carriage & kind welcome at Mrs Spragues.[18]

AUG. 17 TO AUG. 24 INCLUSIVE.   At Providence visited Friday Linen factory—another day Sat. all the Cotton Factories of A. & W Sprague—another day Monday went to Connecticut where Gov Sprague thinks of more mills— Sunday at Baptist Church excellent Sermon—saw Prest Sears Prof. Caswall & others[19]— Monday evg. Party given me by Prof. Caswall— Gen Burnside, Mr. Brown,[20] Prest Sears, Senators Anthony & Sprague & others— *Tuesday* Gov. Sprague went to Maine—more mills—letter fr. L & ansd. will return if *required*—nothing further heard till Friday when letter urging to repeat visit—meanwhile had been writing & reading & looking for the letter which came on Friday. One eveng Wednesday I think a Séance with Medium, Mrs Sprague Miss Palmer, Col Viall, Miss Viall[21] & others—guitars & bells in air &c &c—curious but unconvincing.

AUG. 25.[22]   To Boston by 7.50 train—arrived abt half past nine & took hack to [Eastern] Railroad Depot— Obliged to wait there for 10.30 train—and that delayed in Starting till near 11. Met Mr. Kimball formerly partner of Mr. Webster in depot[23]—who very po-

15. Margaret Rantoul (d. 1938) was a child of Robert S. Rantoul. Little, "Salem Custom House," 268; Cynthia B. Wiggin, "History of the Salem Book Club," *Essex Institute Historical Collections* 105 (1969): 138.
 16. Franklin Haven, Sr.
 17. Horace Gray.
 18. The home of Fanny Morgan Sprague. Edward was a driver employed by the Spragues. Chase to William Sprague, Sept. 24, 1866, Chase to Kate Chase Sprague, Aug. 9, 1868 (Chase Papers, Hist. Soc. of Pa.); Chase to Janet Chase, Oct. 15, 1866 (Chase Papers, L.C.).
 19. Barnas Sears and Alexis Caswell (1799–1877), former professor of mathematics, natural philosophy, and astronomy, and future president of Brown University, 1868–72. *DAB*, 3:570–71.
 20. Likely John Carter Brown (1797–1874), book collector and Brown University benefactor. *DAB*, 3:136–37.
 21. No information has been found on female relatives of Nelson Viall, but William Sprague carried on an extended affair with a woman whose given name was Mary Eliza Viall. Alice Hunt Sokoloff, *Kate Chase for the Defense* (New York, 1971), 70–71, 158–59; Mary Merwin Phelps, *Kate Chase: Dominant Daughter* (New York, 1935), 300–304.
 22. Chase inserted an unidentified mark, possibly an *r*, above the line to the right of the date.
 23. Edmund Kimball (1793–1873) read law with Daniel Webster in 1816. Wiltse et al., *Papers of Daniel Webster*, Corres., 3:171.

August 1866   {627}

lite & kind— Very long train on a/c of Camp Meeting just breaking up at Wenham—reached Beverly after twelve instead of 11.22, when due—found Joseph & Carriage—drove to castle—met by L⸺ most cordially & with real gladness—a delightful welcome—proposed to go to Cherry Hill & make visit to Mr. Waters[24] & then return for two or three days—agreed to take me up after tea— pleasant afternoon in talk & mutual endearments—after tea to Cherry Hill—arranged with Waters to come up next day & go to church & remain some days—back to castle—very pleasant drive— retired about 10—

AUG. 26—SUN. Anxious about L⸺ but had hardly dressed when she knocked at my door & summoned me to breakfast—she was quite well & met me very kindly— After breakfast Joseph took me to Cherry Hill met Waters & Mr. Porter & Louise Wilson in Avenue—kind greeting— Waters with me to [harnesser] where left Leather sack—followed the others—took Louise in—drove to Church—Mr. Porter preached. Lunch at the house & in P.M. over to Danvers with W⸺[25] where young theol. student [from] Andover preached; by South Danvers & Old Endicott place[26] back to Cherry Hill—met at Danvers Mr. Goodell, of Essex Institute & his intended a Miss Putnam, Mr. Tapley & Mr. Putnam.[27]

AUG. 27. MON. To Beverly with Waters—pleasant call—L[28] gave calf a gentle reminder—calf seemed to like the understanding— back to Cherry Hill—read Butler's speech at Gloucester—right in spirit, but not exactly the argument which I think strongest[29]— After dinner rode to Lynn Capt. Waters, (R. P's nephew) taking his own carriage & horses & driving us—i.e. his son of 14 / R. P, & self.[30] Called at Alleys & went over his new house—handsome

24. Richard Palmer Waters.
25. Richard Palmer Waters.
26. The seventeenth-century homestead of John Endicott, an ancestor of William Crowninshield Endicott. Hurd, *Essex County*, 1:lii–liii.
27. Abner Cheney Goodell (1831–1914), Salem lawyer and antiquarian, married Martha Page Putnam of Danvers in Nov. 1866. "Mr. Putnam" was probably Frederic Ward Putnam (1839–1915), archaeologist and curator of the Essex Institute Museum, 1864–67, but may have been Alfred Putnam, the father of Martha Page Putnam Goodell. George G. Putnam, "Abner Cheney Goodell," *Essex Institute Historical Collections* 51 (1915): 201–9; *DAB*, 15:276–78.
28. Charlotte Eastman.
29. On Aug. 25, Benjamin Franklin Butler had delivered a speech in Gloucester which advocated restrictive federal policies in the defeated South and urged support for congressional Reconstruction. *New York Times*, Aug. 27, 1866.
30. Thomas S. Waters worked at machine sewing; his son, Thomas Franklin Waters (1851–1919), Harvard class of 1872, became a Congregational minister. *Essex Co. Dir.*, 1870, 647; Hurd, *Essex County*, 1:590; *Who Was Who*, 1:1306.

& handsome situation—Mrs A. showed me rooms & prospects very kindly—Mr. Alley showed where garden & stable are to be. invited me to Silver Wedding Fri. 14 Sep—promised to come if within a hundred miles—Alley said it had been & was the great wish of his heart to see me President,—not much prospect of its gratification I thought—returned to C.H.[31] a little tired after a very pleasant day.

AUG. 28. To Castle with Waters who took some Corn to ladies—letting them think he had raised it, though in fact I saw him buy it— He went on to Salem, leaving me at Castle—when I went in found nobody / Called L at foot of Liby Stairs; heard door shut above but no answer—sat down & read [Comparison a la Plutarch b. *illeg.*] & Ch. J. Marshall[32]— L came in—seemed surprised to find me—we sat together on sofa & talked—on [sofa & on sill]—talked about her propy. in Wis. & best investments[33]—and other like matters mine & hers—begged her to let me do any thing I could to promote her interests— Mrs R——[34] soon came in & then Mr. Briggs,[35] & soon afterwards Waters returned & I went away with him to C.H. W—— says Butler will be nominated[36]— After dinner Capt. Waters came again and in his Carriage he, Mr. Wheatland, an old lawyer of Salem much in politics [formerly] & ardent Jacksonian[37] & self, & in another Carriage R [P] W & Miss Wilson (pas Louise)[38] went to Chebacco Ponds, where there is charming scenery & may be beautiful & delightful residences, now only a boarding house or hotel[39]—

AUG 29. WED.[40] Last night a good deal troubled with frequent disposition to urinate—which has been more or less inconvenient for years—slept from 9.20 to 2—then urn. & afterwards about every

31. Cherry Hill.
32. Chase apparently read an essay modeled after the style of the Greek biographer Plutarch. John Marshall (1755–1835) sat as chief justice of the U.S. Supreme Court, 1801–35. *DAB*, 12:315–25.
33. Chase had been advising Charlotte Eastman about her share of her late husband's estate. Chase to Eastman, Mar. 7, 1866 (Chase Papers, Hist. Soc. of Pa.).
34. Jane Rantoul.
35. Probably the pastor of the First Church of Salem, 1852–67, George Ware Briggs (1810–95). *Historical Catalogue of Brown University, 1764–1914* (Providence, 1914), 112.
36. Later in the year, Gen. B. F. Butler was elected as a Radical Republican congressman from Massachusetts. He served until 1875. *DAB*, 3:358.
37. Possibly Salem attorney George Wheatland (1804–93), a local politician and Massachusetts legislator. "Portraits in Public Buildings in Salem," *Essex Institute Historical Collections* 75 (1939): 287.
38. That is, "not Louise"—some other Miss Wilson, along with Richard Palmer Waters.
39. Chebacco Pond in Essex Township covered 260 acres. Nason, *Gazetteer*, 295.
40. Chase inserted an unidentified mark, possibly an *r*, above the line between the date and the day of the week.

hour or hour & a half till rose at 7—some palpitation also—wrote Parsons at Cleveld advising him to be at Phila 3d Sep. & to Miss Walker at Washn.[41]—returned to Castle, Waters taking me in— Kindly greeting by L & Mrs R—told me what Miss Walker asked & her remark "are you not one— Mr. Rantoul called about 9 in the evng—Mrs R had retired—talked abt R——'s going to Phila—L & I talked sometime about affairs—retired about 10.

AUG. 30. THURS. Troubled last night as night before—urg.[42] abt. 11, 12, 4½, 6.40. Brkft at 7.30— Pleasant greeting before brkfast— at bkft talk about Mrs Endicott's dinner this afternoon— L. inclined not to go—Mrs R—— quite bent on going—spent morning with L—— in Library except when trying to get a nap— Afternoon all went to Mr. Endicotts to dinner at half past two— Guests, Lt Gov & Mrs Claflin, Mr. Pierce, Mr. & Mrs R. Rantoul, Mrs R., Mrs E. & I[43]—retd. to Castle—nap before dinner L told Mrs R—— she wd. also take nap—afterwards both came down to tea—talk after tea—I reclined on sofa L on cushions near it—retired early—

AUG. 31. Breakfasted at half past seven—L took me to the depot in her carriage—goodbyes—I off to Boston—met Pierce at the Depot—also Wendell Phillips[44] who said Well you will take back to Washington that strong backbone— I replied I hope it would be strong [again] for any emergency likely to occur— Pierce with me to Providence Depot—met Rev. Mr. Storrs of Brooklyn there who took same car to Providence[45]—very [firm] & unlike Beecher, though confident that B—— had seen his mistake & would set himself right very soon[46]—arrived at Providence a little after 12—went to office A. & W. S[47]—wrote E & W.D.G.[48]—to Mrs S——s & dinner

41. Richard C. Parsons and Susan Walker.
42. Urinating.
43. William Claflin (1818–1905), lieutenant governor, 1866–68, and governor, 1869–71, of Massachusetts; his wife, Mary Bucklin Davenport Claflin; Edward L. Pierce; Robert S. and Harriet Neal Rantoul; Jane Rantoul; and Charlotte (Lottie) Eastman, identified elsewhere in this section of the journal as "L." Chase commented upon the guests at William Endicott's dinner in a letter written the next day. Chase to Janet Chase, Aug. 31, 1866 (Chase Papers, L.C.); *DAB*, 4:110–11.
44. Edward Lillie Pierce and Massachusetts antislavery leader and reformer Wendell Phillips (1811–84). *DAB*, 14:546–47.
45. Richard Salter Storrs (1821–1900), Congregational pastor of the Church of the Pilgrims. *DAB*, 18:101–2.
46. Chase referred to the apparent support which Henry Ward Beecher gave at this time to the Reconstruction policies of Andrew Johnson. *DAB*, 2:132; Joshua Hanna to Chase, Sept. 10, 1866 (Chase Papers, L.C.).
47. A. & W. Sprague.
48. Probably William Endicott, Jr., and William D. Gallagher.

with Governor[49]—then to Cranston & saw Amasa[50]—& on to Mr. Hughes where Gov. wished to see about purchase[51]—back about half past 8.

SEP. 1. SAT. Amos D Smith & J. B. Moorhead called[52]— Mr. Smith invited me to visit him near Newport—sorry I could not—went to Pier with Govr.—on way cars between Prov. & Kingston saw Lt. Gov. Greene, my old Cincinnati friend, & had some talk with him[53]—returned from Pier—having dined & taken tea with Mr. Hazard[54] & showed him Shawl Katie sent me—to Kingston & took cars for Stonington, finding in our Section Gen. Burnside, Col Goddard[55] &, Mr. Hazard— At Stonington took Steamer for New York.

SEP. 2. Reached New York early in morning & drove to Fifth Avenue—met Train before & Fenton, Wilson, Grow & others at breakfast.[56] Among others P.M.G. Randall came up & spoke to me—found it difficult to be civil to him.[57] Mr. Fogg came to my room—regrets Clarks apparent subservience while looking for appointment as District Judge & so do I[58]— Fogg is sure of being appointed Senator for unexpired term of Clark—that is next session & short term— Called on Mr. Hanna[59]—took cars at 6—taking Wilson &

49. Fanny Morgan Sprague and William Sprague.
50. Amasa Sprague.
51. Possibly Michael Hughes, an Irish immigrant who owned three farms in Cranston. Bicknell, *History of Rhode Island . . . Biographical*, 477.
52. Amos Denison Smith (1835–1912), Brown University graduate, merchant, and cotton goods manufacturer; and likely Philadelphia businessman J. Barlow Moorhead, who was a brother of William G. and James Kennedy Moorhead and future father-in-law of Jay Cooke, Jr. *Historical Catalogue of Brown University*, 181; Oberholtzer, *Jay Cooke*, 1:99–100, 2:264; *Phila. Dir. (1870)*, 1116.
53. William Greene.
54. Either Rowland Gibson Hazard or Rowland Hazard.
55. Rhode Island politician and cotton manufacturer William Goddard (1825–1907), a brevet lieutenant colonel of volunteers. *Nat. Cyc.*, 20:273.
56. George Francis Train; Reuben Eaton Fenton (1819–85), Republican congressman, 1857–64, governor of New York, 1864–68, U.S. senator, 1869–75; Henry Wilson; and Galusha A. Grow. Wilson, Grow, and Chase all stayed at the 5th Avenue Hotel. *DAB*, 6:326–27; *New York Times*, Sept. 4, 1866.
57. Former Wisconsin governor Alexander Williams Randall (1819–72) ardently defended President Johnson while serving as postmaster general in his administration. *DAB*, 15:344–45.
58. George Gilman Fogg, discussing Daniel Clark. Clark failed to secure renomination to the U.S. Senate in 1866 and resigned his seat to accept an appointment as U.S. judge for the district of New Hampshire. *DAB*, 4:126.
59. Joshua Hanna.

September 1866 {631}

Billings of Cal[60] with us (Sprague & me) arrived in Philadelphia after ten—drove with Tilton & some of his friends to Contl. where left them & then drove to Mr. Orne where we found a kind welcome & refreshing supper about eleven.[61]

SEP. 3. This was the day of the Southern Loyalists Convention & there was an immense concourse of people at Philadelphia.[62] Of course I could not take a part, but I could not help feeling deep sympathy & interest. The President is on his tour—mortifying his best & sincerest friends & injuring himself I fear beyond remedy.[63] These loyalists have come together to sustain Congress, & say what further they think necessary to the real restoration of the lately rebel states & to the security of loyal men in them. In the afternoon I met at Mr. Orne's table a number of the most prominant Philadelphians & among them Mr. McMichael, the Mayor, Mr. Henry C. Carey & Mr. Boker[64]—also Mr. Bayard Taylor, Col Parsons Gen Garfield, Mr. McVeigh and others.[65]

SEP. 4. TUES. Several gentlemen called—read proceedings of yesterday with much interest—wrote L & others—took a walk over the Chest. St Bridge

SEP. 5. WED. Mr. Cattell of New Jersey,[66] Mr. Boker & Mr. Taylor, two old citizens whose names I cannot remember—Parsons, Schenck & Wetmore called. In the afternoon dined with O'Neill, M.C.[67]

60. Probably Frederick Billings (1823–90), former attorney general of California, at this time a resident of Woodstock, Vt., and a developer of the Northern Pacific Railway. *DAB*, 2:265–66.
61. Theodore Tilton and probably James H. Orne.
62. See July 26, 1866, above.
63. Johnson was engaged in his famous "swing around the circle," an attempt to acquire popular support for upcoming congressional elections during a speaking tour of major cities in the East and Middle West. *DAB*, 10:86.
64. Morton McMichael (1807–79), mayor of Philadelphia, 1866–68, and a founder of the city's Union League Club; economist Henry Charles Carey (1793–1879); and George Henry Boker (1823–90), Philadelphia playwright and poet, secretary of the city's Union League, 1862–71, and U.S. minister to Turkey, 1871–78. Holli and Jones, *Biographical Dictionary of American Mayors*, 237–38; *DAB*, 2:415–18, 3:487–89.
65. Bayard Taylor (1825–78), traveler, author, and former secretary of the U.S. legation in Russia under Simon Cameron; Richard C. Parsons; James Abram Garfield; and Isaac Wayne MacVeagh. *DAB*, 18:314–16.
66. Alexander Gilmore Cattell (1816–94), a banker and Republican politician with interests in New Jersey and Philadelphia, entered the U.S. Senate in Dec. 1866. *DAB*, 3:577–78.
67. Charles O'Neill (1821–93), Republican member of Congress from Pennsylvania, 1863–71. *Bio. Dir. U.S. Cong.*, 1592.

Among the guests were Gov. Hamilton of Texas, Gov Fletcher, of Missouri,[68] Mr. Durant, of La, Ex Atto Gen. Speed, Gov. Curtin of Pa, Mr. Myers M.C. Mr. Thayer M.C.[69] & a number more equally distinguished— Had a good deal of talk with Gov. Hamilton & Mr. Durant & recommended to them earnestly to make the Congl. Amendment the platform for the present Campaign, expressing my full belief that, though not all we desire or need, still it was a sufficient basis of reconstruction and a bridge over which we can pass to final & decisive victory.[70] Letter from Cooke before dinner urging me to come to Chelten [Hill] which obliged to decline.

After dinner went with Gov. Curtin to League House & up to roof of north wing from which saw the great meeting.[71] Gen Cameron, Gen Butler Gen Gregory, Gen. Eaton, Gov Pease of Texas & Gov. Brownlow of Tenn & Mr. Billings of Cala. were there with me.[72] The meeting was great & grand beyond description, I never saw anything like it, either in numbers or apparent fixedness of purpose. Vermont had spoken in thunder & Maine was soon to utter her voice[73]— And it being fit that the great meeting should come between.

SEP. 6. THURSDAY— Called on Gov Brownlow with Mr. Orne— found him quite feeble body & semi paralyzed—but strong in purpose & thoroughly resolved. Gen Eaton was with him & Fred Douglass had been breakfasting with them.[74] Douglass bears himself extremely [fit] & has done & is doing himself & his race much good by his presence here. I wish he could come to Congress from his District. Returned to Mr. Ornes—begged him to explain why I

68. Brig. Gen. Thomas Clement Fletcher (1827–99), governor of Missouri, 1865–69. *DAB*, 6:468.

69. Leonard Myers (1827–1905) and Martin Russell Thayer (1819–1906), Republican congressmen from Pennsylvania. *Bio. Dir. U.S. Cong.*, 1556–57, 1925.

70. The Fourteenth Amendment. See July 26, 1866, above.

71. The Union League of Philadelphia built its new League House on Broad Street in 1864–65. *Second Annual Report of the Board of Directors of the Union League of Philadelphia, Dec. 12th, 1864* (Philadelphia, 1864), 7.

72. Edgar M. Gregory (c. 1803–71), a colonel of the 91st Pennsylvania recently promoted to major general; Bvt. Brig. Gen. John Eaton (1829–1906), former assistant commissioner of the Freedmen's Bureau, editor of the *Memphis Post*, 1866–67, and U.S. commissioner of education, 1870–86; Elisha Marshall Pease (1812–83), governor of Texas, 1853–55, and provisional governor of the state, 1867–69; and Unionist editor William Gannaway Brownlow (1805–77), governor of Tennessee, 1865–69, and U.S. senator, 1869–75. Brownlow suffered from palsy at this time. *New York Times*, Nov. 8, 1871; Heitman, *Historical Register*, 1:477; *DAB*, 3:177–78, 5:608–9, 14:368–69.

73. Voters in Vermont early in Sept., and in Maine on Sept. 10, gave Republicans resounding majorities in gubernatorial and congressional elections. *The American Annual Cyclopædia and Register of Important Events of the Year 1866* (New York, 1867), 468, 763.

74. Black abolitionist Frederick Douglass (c. 1817–95). *DAB*, 5:407–7.

could not go to Mr Cookes office this morning as I intended—took a carriage & went to N.Y. & W. Junction Depot—found myself too early—then went to P.W. & R. Depot[75]—took the cars—found Geo Wood who sat by me to Wilmington.[76]—then joined by Mr. Harlan,[77] who spoke of necessity of having a statesman as our next candidate for President— Met Mr. Sauerwein of Baltimore[78] in car who says Gov Swann is by wrongful appointments of Registers promoting the enrollment of rebel voters, who do not scruple to take false oaths & will be sufficently numerous to jeopard the success of the loyal [tickets] at the approaching election. He thinks it possible that two of the five Congress men may be elected however & two out of five is all that the policy of Congress has now.

Arrived at Washn. about six & had a slender dinner at home.

SEP. 7, FRIDAY. Attended Meeting of the Board of the Mily Asylums—present Generals Butler & Martindale, Messrs Gunckel, Stanton, Walker & myself— Gov Smith[79] was present yesterday & it was agreed that it should be considered that a quorum was present. The Executive Committee consisting of Gen Butler, Mr. Gunckel & Gen Hincks, the Governor was authorized to complete purchase of tract at Augusta & near Milwaukee & to enquire & report as to site in Ohio, Westn. Penna, West Va & Northern Kentucky— Gen Butler dined with me & related circumstances showing injustice of Gen Grants attack on him—his report & his anxiety to make up by invitation to party— He declared his purpose now to support him if nominated for the Presy[80]—

SEP. 8. SAT. Nothing of importance occurred today.[81]

---

75. The Philadelphia, Wilmington, and Baltimore Railroad Company. Poor, *History of Railroads*, 487–89.
76. Possibly author and longtime U.S. Treasury official George Wood (1799–1870). *Appletons'*, 6:593.
77. Probably James Harlan.
78. P. G. Sauerwein, a member of Baltimore's city council during the Civil War. Sauerwein to Chase, Apr. 12, 1862 (Chase Papers, L.C.).
79. Frederick Smyth.
80. Hostility between the two men extended back to Jan. 1865, when Grant had removed Butler from command of the Army of the James and issued a negative report of Butler's actions during operations around Richmond. The relationship had worsened in Jan. 1866 after Butler received a belated invitation to one of Grant's receptions. In reply, Butler rejected the offer and indicated a desire to sever all personal contacts. Cordial relations were not reestablished until 1868. William D. Mallam, "The Grant Butler Relationship," *Mississippi Valley Historical Review* 41 (Sept. 1954): 259–76.
81. Chase continued with the words, *The President returned*, then struck through them.

SEP. 9. SUN. At Wesley Chapel. Mr. Ames preached[82]—full of fervor & most earnest in prayer.

SEP. 10. MON. Nothing of importance—intended to call on President but did not. received kind letter from L—— & wrote a brief ackt promising long letter when answer to last should come. Walk & on return cramp in calf of leg.

SEP 11. TUES. Went up to Capitol to see about improvements of Supreme Court Rooms—they will be very acceptable to the Judges I think[83]— This was last week not today

SEP 12—WED. During the last two days have not, been very well—some touch of influenza sore throat— Dr. Elder called Monday eveng to ask for letters of commendation in order to facilitate [engagement] on London Press—promised him one to Sir M. Peto & one to John Bright.[84] [Mr]. Wood called friendship[85]— Mr J. S. Brown of Cleveland now in Qr. Mrs. Dept about politics[86]—[Tuesday] had note from Miss Walker enquiring of my health[87]—Ansd. not better though good enough to work—today went up to Jay Cooke & Co's to enquire for lost pocket book, hoping that I might possibly have left it there—found nothing of it; but found that I had converted Netties 7–30s with price of land bought by Kate Whiteman into Union Pacif U.S. bonds & so nothing of hers is lost.[88]

82. Edward Raymond Ames (1806–79), Methodist bishop and army chaplain. *DAB*, 1:242–43.
83. Chase may refer to changes in the Capitol building which were made around this time to facilitate the installation of steam heating. Glenn Brown, *History of the United States Capitol* (Washington, D.C., 1902), 147–48; Federal Writers' Project, Works Progress Administration, *Washington: City and Capital* (Washington, D.C., 1937), 212.
84. English reform politician John Bright (1811–89). *DNB*, 22:273–91.
85. George Wood.
86. Brown was a clerk in the Quartermaster's Department. *Wash. Dir. (1866)*, 176.
87. Susan Walker.
88. Chase could not ascertain if the missing documents had been mislaid or stolen. The lost papers included stock certificates of three investments: Joshua Hanna's Pittsburgh and Idaho Gold Mining Co.; the "Russian Telegraph," a venture by the Western Union Telegraph Co. to link Europe and America by telegraph via the Bering Strait; and the Cleveland Iron Co. Also missing were notes of indebtedness of William H. Ewell endorsed by John Frazer and notes made out to Janet Chase by Catherine Ludlow Baker Whiteman and other members of the Ludlow family relating to Ludlow estate property matters. Sept. 18 entry, below; Chase to O. H. Palmer, May 21, 1864, to Whiteman, Sept. 13, 1866, to Flamen Ball, same date, to Hanna, Sept. 17, 1866, to Parsons, same date, to William Sprague, Sept. 20, 1866, to Charlotte Ludlow Jones, Nov. 6, 1866 (Chase Papers, Hist. Soc. of Pa.); Palmer to Chase, May 19, 1864, Ball to Chase, Sept. 19, 1866, Chase to Janet Chase, Oct. 1, 11, 1866, and Chase memorandum, "Missing Papers," Sept. 18, 1866 (Chase Papers, L.C.); Robert Luther Thompson, *Wiring A Continent: The History of the Telegraph Industry in the United States* (Princeton, N.J., 1947), 371–72, 398–99, 427–34.

September 1866 { 635 }

Mr. Cooke with Harry called to take me to ride about [four] & came back & dined with me.[89] In evening called at Major Smiths[90] & passed an hour or two agreeably— Wrote a long letter to Lottie journal fashion—with paper on which I had written down some [expressions] but had erased the greater part. Sent to State Dept. copy of Reids "After the War" to be forwarded to John Hay at Paris & wrote him—

SEPT. 13. Wrote Nettie—Orvis,[91] enclosing introductions [for] Mr. Vyse to Bigelow & Harrington[92]—Lockwood at Natchez,[93] enclosing intrdn to Judge Durell—Ticknor & Field, commending Marshalls Engraving of Lincoln.[94]

SEP. 14 FRI. Wrote a few letters Jay Cooke & others[—]read accounts of Presidents progress[95] / Examined question of allotment of Judges[96]— Called at Mr. Harlans in eveng—he thinks Kasson is recovering his position in Iowa—will go out soon & ascertain opinions abt. candidates—will write me.[97] Mr. Shea called to know my

---

89. Apparently Henry D. Cooke and his son, Henry D. Cooke, Jr. (d. 1914), who became a Washington, D.C., banker. *New York Times,* Oct. 10, 1914.
90. Thomas L. Smith.
91. Joseph Upham Orvis (1816–83), a New York banker. *New York Times,* Apr. 1, 1883; Chase to Orvis, Apr. 26, 1866 (Chase Papers, Hist. Soc. of Pa.).
92. Probably John Bigelow and George Harrington.
93. Possibly George C. Lockwood, a resident of Natchez who had previously requested a permit to trade cotton. Lockwood to ————, Dec. 12, 1863 (Chase Papers, L.C.).
94. Chase was thanking the Boston publishing house of James Thomas Fields (1817–81) and William Davis Ticknor (1810–64) for an engraving of President Lincoln by William Edgar Marshall (1837–1906). *Appletons',* 6:112; Chase to Ticknor, Fields and Co., Sept. 13, 1866 (Dept. of Rare Books, Cornell Univ. Lib.); *DAB,* 6:378–79, 12:331–32.
95. On his "swing around the circle" (see Sept. 3, 1866, above). Chase's letter to Jay Cooke concerned Chase's investments, Cooke's desire for a portrait of him, and an invitation, which Chase declined, to visit the Cookes at their summer home on Lake Erie. Chase to Jay Cooke, Sept. 14, 1866 (Cooke Papers, Hist. Soc. of Pa.); Cooke to Chase, Sept. 13, 1866 (Chase Papers, L.C.).
96. The Judiciary Act of July 23, 1866, reduced the maximum number of justices on the Supreme Court but failed to rearrange their circuits. Chase was having the court's clerk draw together information on the history of the assignment of circuits preparatory to a canvass of the other members of the court on the issue early in Oct. Chase to D. W. Middleton, Sept. 15, 1866 (Office of the Clerk, Recs. of Supreme Court, Nat. Arch.); Middleton to Chase, Sept. 10, 15, 1866, Chase to associate justices, Oct. 5, 1866, and letters to individual justices, Oct. 3–6 (Chase Papers, Hist. Soc. of Pa.); Chase to D. Davis, Oct. 3, 4, 1866 (Davis Papers, Ill. State Hist. Lib.); Fairman, *Reconstruction and Reunion,* 160–75.
97. Probably James Harlan, discussing Iowa Republican politician John Adam Kasson (1822–1910), who at this time was a representative in Congress. Kassen failed to regain nomination to Congress in 1866. *Bio. Dir. U.S. Cong.,* 1288; *DAB,* 10:260–61.

views as to Presidents last proclamation & whether I wd hold Court at Richmond in October—did not inform him—but mention difficulty about allotment.[98]

SEP. 15 SAT. Slept all night last night—not awakened by disposition to u—read some chapters before rising—thought of my dear friend at B[99]—disappd. recg. nothing from her this morning. J.C. & Co Washn. sent me Portfolio which received from J.C. & Co Phila—sent it back by bearer—will call on Monday & examine.[1] Miss Walker called asked her to stay for dinner; declined, but having occasion to return for [some books] staid— When going away asked when I should come out to see her—replied "when you are in your new quarters—'not mean again to come to the camp." She seemed much displeased, seeming to think my reply rude, which certainly I did not intend[2]

SEP. 16. SUN. Recd. angry note from Miss W—— about despising her work—disgusted with the poor home she was obliged to be content with in order to fulfil it &c— Did not read it through thinking it very [unreasonable]— Went to Church W. Chapel morng & eveng—felt it good to be there—

SEP. 17. MON. Read note of Miss Walker—found she asked me to come up yesterday— Wrote that would come today if wished though did not like camp between three & four— Started to make the call in the Afternoon. Mr. Cooke & Harry[3] overtook me & Mr. Cooke went with me to see Miss W—then we three, Cooke Harry

---

98. New York lawyer George Shea (1826–95) was associate counsel for Jefferson Davis, who faced potential prosecution for treason in U.S. circuit court at Richmond. Andrew Johnson's proclamation of Aug. 20 declared that all insurrection against federal authority had ceased and that "peace, order, tranquillity, and civil authority now exist in and throughout the whole of the United States of America." *Appletons'*, 5:488; *New York Times*, Jan. 19, 1895; Richardson, *Compilation of the Messages and Papers*, 8:3632–36.

99. Charlotte Eastman, at Beverly, Mass.

1. Concerned about the missing documents referred to at Sept. 12 above, Chase had requested Jay Cooke to send Chase's "Old Portfolio." When the documents arrived, Chase asked that they be kept in the vault in the Washington offices of Cooke's firm until he could examine them. Chase to Cooke, Sept. 12, 1866, Chase to Jay Cooke & Co., Sept. 15, 1866 (Cooke Papers, Hist. Soc. of Pa.).

2. At about this time Susan Walker, working under the auspices of the Freedmen's Bureau, ran a school on the grounds of a military hospital. She had to shift her location at least once in heavy rains and persisted in what Chase called "a sort of martyrdom" until, late in Oct., she accepted his invitation to stay at his house while new facilities were prepared for her at a barracks. Chase to Janet Chase, Oct. 29, 1866 (Chase Papers, L.C.); Chase to Walker, Dec. 30, 1869 (Walker Papers, Cinc. Hist. Soc.).

3. Henry D. Cooke, Sr. and Jr.

& I, took a ride—round by Columbia College &c to Georgetown—went over Cooke's new house & stable which very nice—told him cant finish before Mrs C—— returns & must come bringing her and stay with me—returned home.

SEP. 18. TUES. Went to J.C. & Co's to examine contents of Portfolio—found every thing there except Cirtifs Idaho, Cleveland Iron Mining Co, & Russian Telegraph & the notes of Ewell indorsed by [Frazer], of C W. Whiteman [*illeg.*] &c Nettie, & of Ludlow heirs to Nettie which are in lost pocket book[4]— Met Gen Grant at Banking House—

Lowell called & explained to him about lost [pin] & lost pocketbook / He thinks Frank may have taken latter & circumstances do look against [him]; but I can't believe it.[5] Called at Wetmore's— young soldier from Wood Co O—son of Recorder—talked with him & Clerk abt. State of things in Ohio—all right they think / Letter fr L—— & ansd.

SEP 19—WED.— Met Wetmore in car—asked him to come & take potluck with me & bring friend—came & brought Judge Johnston, recently appointed one of the Code Commissioners[6]—long talk after dinner about many thing politics, spiritualism, Methodism. Judge J. related singular incidents which he witnessed / correspondence with his own father in writing &c but disbelieves naturally what seems so incredible. Recd. letter from Jennie Cameron asking contribution to Fair.[7]

SEP. 20. THURS. Letter from Mrs Marthell asking me for letter from Prest. to Mr. Smythe in behalf of her husband[8]—nothing else worth noting—except Journalizing for L.[9]

 4. See Sept. 12 above for the missing documents.
 5. Frank Bronaugh. Apparently Chase consulted Russell R. Lowell about his missing case of papers and the diamond pin evidently stolen in New York (see July 14, 1866, above).
 6. Judge William Johnston.
 7. Virginia Rolette Cameron (d. 1920) was the daughter of Simon Cameron and Margaretta Brewer Cameron, and later the wife of Wayne MacVeagh. Warner B. Berthoff and David B. Green, "Henry Adams and Wayne MacVeagh," *Pennsylvania Magazine of History and Biography* 80 (Oct. 1956): 496; *Who Was Who*, 1:766.
 8. Maggie Marthell, whom Chase had met during his Southern journey the previous year, hoped that Chase's influence would help attain a better position for her husband in the New York Custom House. Henry A. Smythe (b. 1819), a merchant and banker, had become collector of customs at New York earlier in 1866. Chase to Andrew Johnson, Sept. 22, 1866 (Johnson Papers, L.C.); memorandum book, 1864–69 (Chase Papers, Hist. Soc. of Pa.), 207; *New York Times*, May 11, 1866.
 9. Chase apparently wrote an account of his activities for Charlotte (Lottie) Eastman; see the next entry also.

SEP. 21, FRI. Letters from Nettie, & Mary Goldsborough— Whittaker of N.O. called[10]—refd. to my opinions at N.O. of which time has proved correctness—says all men who friendly to Govt. must succumb—Mayor responsible for Massacre[11]—says George Denison was sick in New Orleans some time and he knew nothing even of his being in the City—first informn. of his illness was from announcment in paper of his death & burial at sea—poor George. . . Finished journal for L & sent it by morng mail

SEP. 22 SAT. Up a little before 7—read Psalm—pr.—thought of L as usual— Letters from Nettie, C. A. Dana & Milton Kennedy— ansd. D. & K. enclosed D's letter to Gov. Sprague suggesting subscription to stock of new paper[12]— Andrews, I. D. called[13]—long talk but unprofitable—read Lucy Arlyn[14]— W. Prest. behalf of Marthell[15]—called on Judge & Mrs Whittaker at Ebbitt House[16]—at dinner & left card—took a long walk—dined—in the eveng Fogg, Mellen, Judge Whittaker & Dr. Duperier of St Martins Parish La. called.[17] Fogg before W. & D. came in explained official titles in Switzerland such as avoyer & Landamman—and talked about the Govt. under constitution of 1848.[18] Mellen is here to make out report for Secy. of Treasy. on cotton collected & sold—he has still the contract for collecting old claims & disposing of propy. taken for

10. John S. Whitaker.
11. A clash between supporters and opponents of black suffrage on the afternoon of July 30 had left thirty-eight Louisianians dead. Earlier in the day, New Orleans Mayor John T. Monroe had issued a proclamation, supposedly intended to calm the populace, which actually heightened tensions. Dawson, *Army Generals and Reconstruction*, 36–40; Holli and Jones, *Biographical Dictionary of American Mayors*, 257–58.
12. Milton Kennedy was a Portsmouth, N.H., Republican. Chase declined to purchase stock in a newspaper which Charles A. Dana intended to establish in New York City, but encouraged William Sprague to invest. Kennedy to Chase, Nov. 13, 1860, May 21, 1868 (Chase Papers, L.C.); Chase to Dana, Sept. 22, 1866, and to Sprague, same date (Chase Papers, Hist. Soc. of Pa.); James Harrison Wilson, *The Life of Charles A. Dana* (New York, 1907), 376–78.
13. Israel DeWolf Andrews (d. 1871), consul and lobbyist active in antebellum U.S.-Canadian trade relations, later a political gadfly. *DAB*, supp. 1:29–30; Chase to Andrews, May 26, 1866 (Chase Papers, Hist. Soc. of Pa.).
14. John Townsend Trowbridge, *Lucy Arlyn* (Boston, 1866).
15. Chase asked Andrew Johnson to write the collector of customs at New York on Emil Marthell's behalf. Chase to Johnson, Sept. 22, 1866 (Johnson Papers, L.C.); Sept. 20 entry, above.
16. On F Street. *Wash. Dir. (1865)*, 425.
17. New Iberia, La., in St. Martin (later Iberia) Parish, was laid out in the 1830s by sugar planter Frederick H. Dupérier. Writers' Program, *Louisiana*, 313.
18. *Avoyer* and *Landammann* were titles given to chief magistrates of Swiss cantons. *La Grande Encyclopédie*, 4:957; John Martin Vincent, *Government in Switzerland* (New York, 1900), 59.

September 1866 { 639 }

debts—which clms & propy amt. he estimates to 15 millions[19] / Shewed Whittaker stalactites from cave of Bellamar. He & Duperier talked of sugar cultures—condition of freedmen, prospects of south— Cotton crop failure on Tèche where D's plantation / army worm has eaten it—no more cane grown than will be wanted for plant next year perhaps not so much— May[20] has 600 acres fine cane— Dr. D. thinks free labor better than slave—

SEP. 23. SUN. At Church morning & evg—impressive sermons— most earnest prayers—felt it good to be there—read Langes Comm[y] & Herberts Temple[21]—wrote some pages for Lottie & copied one of Herberts pieces.

SEP. 24. MON. Andrews called to borrow $50 which lent him— says he will return it next Thursday—very doubtful I think— worked hard all day writing letters to Schuckers, Gov Sprague, Dr. Smith, Columbus, Kate Whiteman, Mary C. Goldsborough[22]—L. L. Rice to whom enclosed Leary's letter[23]— Gen. Wright, of Cols., called[24]—talked of site for Mily. Asylum opposite Columbus—told him I had written Dr. Smith & explained position of things—talked abt. prospects in Ohio—he said all safe but Delano agst whom Gen. Morgan is candidate[25]—urged me to come out & vote—told him I

---

19. William P. Mellen evidently assisted with the preparation of *Captured and Forfeited Cotton. Message from the President of the United States* . . . , 39th Cong., 2nd sess., 1867, H. Ex. Doc. 97, which was based on a report made by Secretary of the Treasury Hugh McCulloch in Nov. 1866.

20. Thomas P. May.

21. Probably an early segment of Johann Peter Lange, *A Commentary on the Holy Scriptures* . . . , 98 vols. (New York, 1865–1906); and George Herbert, *The Temple. Sacred Poems and Private Ejaculations* (Cambridge, England, 1633).

22. To Jacob Schuckers, Chase discounted rumors of an impending marriage between himself and Charlotte Eastman, and explained his understanding of the legal foundations for proceedings against Jefferson Davis. Chase also briefly discussed the Davis proceedings in his letter to William Sprague, and relayed a variety of news about family members and friends. He wrote to his sister-in-law, Catherine Ludlow Baker Whiteman, about property in the Ludlow estate and the papers relating to that matter which were missing along with other documents (see Sept. 12 and 18 above). Dr. Smith was probably Samuel Mitchel Smith. Chase to Schuckers, to Sprague, and to Whiteman, all Sept. 24, 1866 (Chase Papers, Hist. Soc. of Pa.).

23. Rice had written to say that his son needed a sea voyage to restore his health. Apparently Arthur Leary, at Chase's suggestion, offered to assist. Rice to Chase, Sept. 2, 1866 (Chase Papers, L.C.); Chase to Rice, Sept. 24, 1866 (Chase Papers, Hist. Soc. of Pa.).

24. George Bohan Wright.

25. Columbus Delano (1809–96) was a Whig and Republican congressman from Ohio, 1845–47 and 1865–69, U.S. commissioner of internal revenue, 1869–70, and secretary of the interior, 1870–75. His opponent was George Washington Morgan. *DAB*, 5:217–18.

had quarter of mind to—dinner—sent to ask Chandler[26] & Mellen to come to breakfast—called on Judge & Mrs Whittaker at Ebbitt House—their daughter a lovely girl of 15. & son bright boy of 8 or 10— Saw Dr. Duperier & Mr. Boyce formerly M.C. from S.C.[27] we talked of reconstruction—spoke of misunderstandings & blunders of southern men—of the needs of the future— I argued that true policy for the south adoption of Constitutional Amendment— little dissent, Boyce only arguing that unjust to ask surrender of political power—talked of suffrage, all agreed that the Colored citizens must vote sometime— I [argued] why postpone what is inevitable? And with it postpone restoration & prosperity? An interesting conversation. Asked Whittaker to come & breakfast with me tomorrow morng & bring his family—promised—asked Boyce to call—sd he had been intending to do so.— Home—tea—finished journal for Lottie & sent it to Post Office—bed.

SEP. 25 TUES. Mellen came to breakfast—Chandler did not— long talk with Mellen abt. future—he says that the confidence & esteem of the people is with me; but at present most look to Military man though uncertain what will come of it— Mentioned to him what Butler said abt. invitation to Grant's party—

Letter by morning mail from Rockford, Ill—[warning] from a Mason, against Southern Masons—writer thinks many things made plain by masonic connexions, if considered, between Northern & Southern men.—

WEDNESDAY, NOV. 21. [Wg wh *illeg*. Cd]— Mr. French called— anxious for means to enable Gen. Scott to purchase lands St. Johns Island to be resold to Freedmen[28]—25,000 wanted—$10,000 now— promd. to see what can be done & let him know on his return from N.Y. next week—advised him to try & enlist friends in New York—he talked to me about my Church relations— Wg. that I cd. feel my heart right for them!

Mr. Short called gave him note to Mr. Middleton— Is to be Crier if Judges approve.[29]

---

26. Most likely William Eaton Chandler.
27. William Waters Boyce (1818–90), U.S. congressman from South Carolina, 1853–60, and member of the Confederate Congress, 1862–64. *Bio. Dir. U.S. Cong.*, 653.
28. Mansfield French referred to Bvt. Maj. Gen. Robert Kingston Scott (1826– 1900), formerly of Ohio, who was assistant commissioner of the South Carolina branch of the Freedmen's Bureau, 1865–68, and governor of South Carolina, 1868– 72. *DAB*, 16:498–99.
29. William A. Short became court crier. William A. Short to Chase, Dec. 13, 1866 (Chase Papers, L.C.).

February 1868 {641}

Capt. [A]. L. Wallar, Agent Equal Suff. Asso. with note from Mr. Barrett[30]—wants subscription—subd. $50 & paid. He says first time saw me was when I spoke in Zanesville, in Beard's Hall—perhaps 1848?

Judge Spalding & Mrs S—— decline drive[31]—note to Gov. Hamilton asking him to [ride] & dinner

Wrote *Mary Goldsborough* at Baltimore— *Greeley,* abt interviews with Prest—hope he may be Senator. Barney ☞ copy;[32]

1868

FEB. 26, 1868. WED. On adjournment of the Court today was informed that Senators Howard & Edmund desired to see me; and met them in the Reception Room.[33] They informed me that the Senate had appointed a Committee to take order concerning the impeachment of the President, & that the Committee was about to prepare some rules for the Government of the proceedings and would willingly receive any suggestions from me, and would be pleased to have me attend their meeting if I could. Some other conversation took place almost if not quite wholly in relation to what I supposed my right to vote, should be. I observed that I had nothing but impressions on the subject for I had not considered it; but supposed that I should be a member of the Court and as such have a right to vote; though perhaps inasmuch as my being required to preside was in consequence of the disqualification of the Vice President the right might be limited to a vote in case of a tie. I gathered from the observations of the Senators, one or both, that the right of the Chief Justice to vote in any case was doubted or denied by some members of the Committee.

30. Likely Capt. Avery L. Waller, from the Zanesville area, with a message from Ohio Republican and journalist Joseph Hartwell Barrett (1824–1907), U.S. commissioner of pensions, 1861–68. *History of Muskingum County,* 300; Reid, *Ohio in the War,* 2:449; *Nat. Cyc.,* 13:167; *Who Was Who,* 1:61.

31. S. N. Pierson Spalding of Windsor, Conn., married widower Rufus Paine Spalding in 1859. Robson, *Biographical Encyclopædia,* 320.

32. To Horace Greeley, and in a separate letter to Hiram Barney, Chase related the substance of discussions he had had with Andrew Johnson during the preceding weeks. The president refused to support either the Fourteenth Amendment as passed by Congress or a modification of it, favoring instead a quicker acceptance of Southern states' representation in Congress. Chase was pleased to learn that Greeley might be sent to the U.S. Senate from New York. Chase to Greeley, Nov. 21, 1866 (Greeley Papers, L.C.); Chase to Barney, same date (Barney Papers, Huntington Lib.).

33. Jacob Merritt Howard was a member, and Republican Sen. George Franklin Edmunds (1828–1919) of Vermont was chairman, of a select committee to arrange rules for the impeachment trial of Andrew Johnson. *Cong. Globe,* 40th Cong., 2nd sess., 1868, 1406; *DAB,* 6:24–27, 9:278–79.

As to the framing of rules I remarked that I was not certain of the propriety of my attending the meeting of the Committee; but would cheerfully give any aid I properly could in conversation with its members[34] & would look over the draft when it was before the committee & make any suggestions that occurred to me.

Mr. Edmunds mentioned that he had turned his attention somewhat to the subject & said, I think, that he had himself drawn up something

This was the substance of our conversation. It was very brief: taking not five minutes; it was about 3. a little after

FEB. 27, 1868, THURSDAY. After the talk with Senators H—— & E—— last eveng I looked at the Constitution and a little at the precedents, & became very doubtful of the propriety of any action by the Senate in relation to the Impeachment until organized as a High Court of Impeachment under the Constitution, beyond the simple receipt of a notice from the House of its purpose to impeach.

This impression was so strong upon my mind that before going to the Court I sat down & wrote the following brief note to Mr. Howard who was as I understood Chairman of the Committee.

"Thursday Feby. 27th 1868.

Dear Sir,

Since our conversation of yesterday, my thoughts have been somewhat turned to the subject of it; and it has occurred to me as well deserving consideration, whether the Senate, acting in its legislative capacity, can properly take action for the government of the proceedings of the Court for the Impeachment of a President.

The precedents of cases in which the President of the Senate may preside in the Court of Impeachment may not be entirely applicable.

Yours very respectfully
S P Chase

Hon J. M. Howard
  Chn.

---

34. Chase originally wrote, *any aid I properly could either in conversation with its members [or] otherwise*. He struck through *either* and *otherwise;* what may have been the word *or* has a smeared blot of ink over it.

Before going in to Court at 11 I requested Col. Parsons to copy this note immediately & deliver the original to Mr. Howard at the room of the Committee which I understood was then in Session.[35] The note was accordingly copied by Col P—— and delivered to Mr. Howard before 12.

August 1868

1. In Washington

2 At Church—telegram that no fast train to Parkersburg

M. 3 Took Herbert & went to Baltimore[36]— Staid at Barnums over night

T. 4 Cars to Ellicotts Mills—fearful devastation— Omnibus to Woodbine—[lonely destitution] crossing [stream]—cars to Grafton— where slept.[37]

W. 5 Breakfasted at Grafton—went on slow train—rebel soldier's brags—found Judge Jackson waiting at depot[38]—home to his house & good dinner & kind welcome.

Th 6 Attended Court with Judge J—— charged the Grand Jury & got along much better than I expected.

---

35. A copy of Chase's letter to Howard, evidently in the handwriting of Richard C. Parsons, marshal of the Supreme Court in 1868, is among Chase's papers. The wording of the copy agrees with Chase's transcription in his journal, except that the copy includes the word "any" before the word "action" in the first paragraph. Chase to Howard, Feb. 17, 1868 (Chase Papers, Hist. Soc. of Pa.).

36. Herbert, otherwise unidentified, accompanied Chase on this trip as an attendant. He received half pay as a Supreme Court messenger "at the request of the Judges whom he attended last winter." Chase to Kate Chase Sprague, Aug. 9, 1868 (Chase Papers, Hist. Soc. of Pa.).

37. On July 24, 1868, the Baltimore area suffered what newspapers at the time called the worst flood of the city's history. Damage was particularly severe in the vicinity of Ellicott City on the Patapsco River, where over forty people died, numerous buildings and bridges were destroyed, and portions of the B. & O. Railroad were flooded. *Baltimore Gazette, Baltimore Sun,* and Washington *Evening Star,* July 25, 27, 1868.

38. John Jay Jackson (1824–1907), judge of the U.S. district court for the western district of Virginia since 1861. *Nat. Cyc.,* 11:521.

SUN 9   At Episcopal Church morng—evg at African— Judge J—— make short address.³⁹

TH 13   Reversed decree of District Court in Collision case, dividing damages—rode with Gen. & Judge Jackson to Fort overlooking town⁴⁰

FR. 14—   Took cars   for Grafton—extra car for self & friends—reached Grafton 10 P.M. bed—

SAT 15   Off at 2 A.M. reached Frederick abt. 2 P.M. Mr. Schley met me at Junction⁴¹— Mary G. at tea⁴²—

SUN 16   At Church in morng with Mrs S—— called after Mrs G——'s⁴³— Mary came to dinner & remained till after tea—

OCT.

M. 19   J H Gilmer at dinner Rosecrans full of zeal for change before dinner—also Adml. & Mrs Dahlgren⁴⁴

TU. 20—   Gen. Hancock. What Nye said saw Cagger in N. York 2 [weeks] long before Con.⁴⁵—said wd. nominate Seymour⁴⁶— showed him Monitor & portrait

    39. Chase also attended the "Wesleyan Sabbath School," but declined to speak. Jackson assured "his colored fellow citizens ... of his sympathy for their progress and prosperity." Parkersburg *Daily Times,* Aug. 11, 1868.
    40. Judge Jackson's father, also named John Jay Jackson (1800–1877), was a West Point graduate and an attorney. *Nat. Cyc.,* 11:521.
    41. Frederick Schley, editor of the Frederick, Md., *Examiner,* collector of internal revenue during the Civil War, and candidate for the marshalship of the U.S. Supreme Court in 1872. Williams and McKinsey, *History of Frederick County,* 1:392, 251, 2:784; Chase to A. Lincoln, Aug. 27, 1862 (Lincoln Papers, L.C.); *Register of Officers (1863),* 39; entry for Dec. 14, 1872, below; Washington *Evening Star,* Oct. 25, Dec. 14, 1872.
    42. Mary C. Goldsborough.
    43. Margaret Schley Goldsborough, the mother of Edward Yerbury Goldsborough and Mary Catherine Goldsborough. Williams and McKinsey, *History of Frederick County,* 2:1241; M. C. Goldsborough to Chase, Feb. 7, 1873 (Chase Papers, L.C.).
    44. John Adolphus Dahlgren's second wife, Sarah Madeleine Vinton Dahlgren (1825–98), daughter of Ohio politician Samuel Finley Vinton, had a long career as an author. John H. Gilmer was a resident of Richmond, Va. William S. Rosecrans had recently been appointed U.S. minister to Mexico. *DAB,* 5:31–32; Chase to Gilmer, May 17, July 14, Dec. 22, 1868 (Chase Papers, L.C.); *OR,* ser. 2, v. 3:732–33, 741, v. 8:960–61; *New York Times,* Sept. 8, 1868.
    45. 2 *[weeks]* is an insertion above the line.
    46. Peter Cagger (1812–68) was a New York Democratic politician. The Democratic national convention, held in New York City in July 1868, nominated former New York governor Horatio Seymour (1810–86) for the presidency. Gen. Winfield Scott Hancock received a number of votes in the convention's search for a candidate. *Appletons',* 1:494; *DAB,* 17:6–9, 8:222.

1870

JOURNAL XVIII

SATURDAY, JANUARY 1. The New Year came in pleasantly & in private & in the family I felt myself resolved & strengthened in faith & purposes of obedience.

About ten the Judges came with the Clerk & Deputy Marshal[47]— all except Judge Swayne who was belated [&] we proceeded to the Presidents where Judge Swayne & his ladies joined us.[48] Nettie, Mrs Beck, & Alice Auld were with me. The order of reception varied somewhat from that of former years— Heretofore the Cabinet came first—then the Members of the Supreme Court—then the Diplomatic Corps—then the Congress, Senators first, Representatives following—then the Army & Navy—then the Citizens generally. Now the Diplomats as guests were received before the Chief Justice & his associates—the reception was soon over—the General & Mrs Grant made the best impression—took Mrs Beck home & wished Judge & Mrs Grier happy New Year— Went back to our own reception which unexpectedly attend [by] by near four hundred callers.[49]

MONDAY, JANUARY 3. Ordinary duties—tried to get on with opinion, but with poor success.

TUESDAY, JANUARY 4. This day as yesterday.

WEDNESDAY, JANUARY 5. Mr. Corcoran called & we had a very agreeable talk[50]—he says I must hold myself in reserve for dinner with Carlisle[51] & his new wife on the 12th

Called on Sumner & had long talk principally about Cuba— I thought that more might have been done for the liberals; but

---

47. Daniel W. Middleton and William H. Rearden, the Supreme Court's assistant marshal. *Wash. Dir. (1871)*, 281.
48. Probably Sarah Ann Wager Swayne and the Swaynes' only daughter, who later married Edwin Parsens of New York City. *New York Times*, Feb. 15, 1872.
49. Julia Dent Grant (1826–1902), a Missouri native, married Ulysses S. Grant in 1848. Isabella Rose Grier, wife of Robert Cooper Grier, was the daughter of Scottish immigrant John Rose. A newspaper report described Chase's reception as "one of the most pleasant and enjoyable of the day." Washington *Evening Star,* Jan. 1, 1870; James et al., *Notable American Women*, 2:72–73; *DAB*, 7:612–13.
50. William Wilson Corcoran.
51. James M. Carlisle.

declared myself satisfied generally with the Admn & especially with the action of Genl. Grant as to colored citizens.[52]

Finished my walk & went home

THURSDAY, JANUARY 6. Nothing unusal today—at Mrs Fish's in the evening.[53]

FRIDAY, JANUARY 7. Called at Pomeroy's & left note about Additional Register in Kansas from Judge Delahay & others[54]—then went to Agricultural Department—found Commissioner Capron at his post & a cordial reception— Stabler there showing a new patent broom— Went with commissioner over building—much pleased with economy shown in the edifice combined with beauty & utility—particulary with the entomology relating to horticulture & agriculture—the bureau must do great good.[55]

Coming out Gen. Brice, my old school mate drove by— Called him to stop & take me home which he did—& the drive in the fresh cool air was very agreeable

Netties Reception— I spent some time in the parlor very agreeably

SATURDAY, JANUARY 8. Wrote to Geo H. Hill, Representative from Hamilton County, in Ohio Legislature in favor of the 15th Amendment[56]—having been informed by friends that the result will probably be determined by his vote—

---

52. Rebellions against Spanish rule in Cuba continued throughout this period. Grant favored the broad idea of black equality, and, with some equivocation, supported the Fifteenth Amendment and operations of the Freedmen's Bureau. Washington *Evening Star*, Jan. 1, 6, 1870; Allan Nevins, *Hamilton Fish: The Inner History of the Grant Administration* (New York, 1936), ch. 9, 11, 15; William S. McFeely, *Grant: A Biography* (New York, 1982), 285–86, 358–59, 363–70.

53. Julia Kean Fish (c. 1817–87), wife of Hamilton Fish, was an esteemed hostess. Nevins, *Hamilton Fish*, 17–19, 578–79, 904.

54. The Bankruptcy Act of 1867, passed amid controversy, obliged the chief justice to nominate registers in bankruptcy throughout the federal court system. A former newspaper editor, Mark William Delahay (1817–79) became U.S. district judge for Kansas in 1863. Fairman, *Reconstruction and Reunion*, 355–65; John G. Clark, "Mark W. Delahay: Peripatetic Politician," *Kansas Historical Quarterly* 25 (Autumn 1959): 301–11.

55. Horace Capron (1804–85), U.S. commissioner of agriculture, 1867–71, showed Chase through the Agriculture Department's building (completed in 1868). James Pleasants Stabler (b. 1839) was an employee of the department, 1866–82, and an inventor. *DAB*, 3:484–85; *Who Was Who*, 4:893; *Report of the Commissioner of Agriculture for the Year 1868* (Washington, D.C., 1869), 15–16, 191–93.

56. George H. Hill served in the Ohio House, 1870–72. Chase to Hill, Jan. 7, 1870 (Chase Papers, L.C.); Gilkey, *Ohio Hundred Year Book*, 221.

January 1870 {647}

Took my walk calling on Garfield—found him very indignant about withdrawal of a worthy nominee, & sending in name of a man known to be unfit, under solicitations[57]—

Home Judge Field came & took lunch with us—read part of his opinion in Key West wharf case—suggested modifications—some talk also abt legal tender[58]

Evening received the Club—a pleasant reunion & supper; but only fourteen present—first meeting this winter[59]

Woodward called[60]—promised to come to Wesley Chapel tomorrow & give something

SUNDAY, JANUARY 9. At Wesley Chapel— Bishop Ames preached excellent Sermon[61]— Contribution to pay for repairs recently made—subscribed fifty dollars—walked to & from Church—at home read Articles in Church Review on Celibacy of Clergy and on Darwinianism—both interesting & instructive[62]—bed at 11.

MONDAY, JANUARY 10. Prof. Mot at breakfast—paid him $20 for 20 lessons to Nettie— Worked on opinion—took walk—called on M. Blair[63] & had interesting talk— Stopped at Gov. S——'s found that family not expected soon nor the Gov.[64]—house undergoing refitment / called at Cooke's—found coupons on P. & E. bonds credited on my note $18.000[65]—worked & read. Brent & Steele called

---

57. James A. Garfield may have been upset over the appointment of Horatio C. Burchard, an Illinois congressman friendly with President Grant, to the House Committee on Banking and Currency just before potentially damaging investigations began into operations of the New York gold market. Theodore Clarke Smith, *The Life and Letters of James Abram Garfield, Vol. 1, 1831–1877* (New Haven, 1925), 446–51; *Bio. Dir. U.S. Cong.*, 702; *Cong. Globe*, 41st Cong., 2nd sess., 35–36, 184; *Gold Panic Investigation*, 41st Cong., 2nd sess., H. Ex. Doc. 31.

58. On Jan. 24, Field delivered his opinion in *Emily J. Filor et al. v. U.S.*, a claim arising from the army's use of a wharf at Key West, Fla. For the legal tender issue currently before the court, see Mar. 26, 1870, below. 9 Wall. 45 (1870).

59. Possibly the Metropolitan Club, which Chase joined in 1866. The club was officially inactive between 1867 and 1872. Carl Charlick, *The Metropolitan Club of Washington* . . . (Washington, D.C., 1964), 23–31.

60. Possibly Washington attorney William R. Woodward. *Wash. Dir. (1870)*, 395; Chase to Woodward, May 30, 1863 (Misc. Letters Sent, Gen. Recs. Treasury Dept., Nat. Arch.).

61. Edward R. Ames elaborated on the text, "My house shall be called a house of prayer" (Matt. 21:13). Washington *Evening Star*, Jan. 10, 1870.

62. "Darwinianism" and "Clerical Celibacy," *American Quarterly Church Review, and Ecclesiastical Register* 21 (Jan. 1870): 524–49.

63. Montgomery Blair.

64. William Sprague.

65. Chase had investments in the Philadelphia and Erie Land Company, one of Jay Cooke's enterprises. Oberholtzer, *Jay Cooke*, 2:86; Chase to Cooke, Dec. 30, 1869 (Chase Papers, L.C.).

about case at Richmond[66]— Nettie proposes dining with Mrs Freeman & going to theatre afterwards & I assent reluctantly[67]— letter from Katie to Nettie—walk with Didier[68] / dinner—

After dinner Jay Cooke & H. D.[69] called and a long talk about North Pacific Railroad—bed ½ past 11.

TUESDAY, JANUARY 11. Nothing of much interest today—Nettie going to Mrs Bancroft Davis[70] to dinner

SATURDAY, JANUARY 22. Morning duties as usual—walked to Capitol & Conference— Most of time taken in reading & considering opinions—affd. C.C. N York in Collision case[71]—agreed to *call* no case after Wedy next but to hear motions on Friday as usual & devote time saved to Conference with a view to dispose of all important cases in which Judge Grier takes a particular interest before his retirement on Monday next—

Home—wrote till near six & then went to dine with the Attorney General at Wormley's[72]—found the President there with all his Cabinet—also Carlisle, Sumner Commo. Alden, Gen. Badeau Mr. Hoar of Mass & Judge Foster of same state[73] & perhaps one or two others—Gen Grant on right & I on left of Atto. Gen; Sec. Fish opposite with Sumner on his right &   on his left / pleasant dinner—the Atto. Genl witty & racy as usual—Carlisle on my left ditto— Before dinner asked Prest. what he thought his most important movement

---

66. Likely Robert J. Brent and Isaac Nevitt Steele (1809–91), prominent members of the Baltimore bar. Fairman, *Reconstruction and Reunion*, 371; *Nat. Cyc.*, 12:429; Scharf, *History of Baltimore*, 716–17; *Proceedings of the Bench and Bar of Baltimore, Upon the Occasion of the Death of Hon. Roger B. Taney* . . . (Baltimore, 1864), 7.

67. Chase's daughter probably saw the performance of *Leah*, a French play on a biblical theme, at the National Theatre. President Grant's family and Gen. Sherman and his family also attended. Washington *Evening Star*, Jan. 11, 1870.

68. Eugene Lemoine Didier (1838–1913), an author and editor, acted as Chase's clerk, 1869–70. *DAB*, 5:307; *Appletons'*, 2:176; Chase to W. H. Rearden, Oct. 26, 1870 (Chase Papers, L.C.).

69. Henry David Cooke.

70. Frederica Gore King Davis.

71. *Mott Bedell v. Steamship Potomac*, in which the Supreme Court affirmed a judgment on appeal from the U.S. Circuit Court for the southern district of New York. 8 Wall. 590 (1870).

72. Attorney General Ebenezer Rockwood Hoar. The dinner was at the establishment of black hotelkeeper James Wormley (1819–84). *DAB*, 20:534–35.

73. Career naval officer James Alden (1810–77); author, soldier, and diplomat Adam Badeau (1831–95); E. R. Hoar's brother, Massachusetts Republican politician George Frisbie Hoar (1826–1904); and Boston lawyer Dwight Foster (1828–84), Massachusetts Supreme Court justice, 1866–69. *DAB*, 1:145–46, 485, 9:87–88; George F. Hoar, *Autobiography of Seventy Years*, 2 vols. (New York, 1903), 2:414–16; D. Hamilton Hurd, ed., *History of Worcester County, Massachusetts* . . . , 2 vols. (Philadelphia, 1889), 1:li.

during War— He did not appear to have thought much about it; but mentioned Fort Donelson & Shiloh— I said it always appeared to me that the movement behind Vicksburgh was the most important & this led to a brief but interesting talk—home about half past nine & work.

SUNDAY, JANUARY 23. At Metropolitan Church—Dr Newman[74]— unusually good sermon on the use & worth of the Scriptures— Afternoon & evening obliged to work on opinion except time for walk & meals

MONDAY, JANUARY 24. Morning duties as usual—bkft worked awhile— On way to Court called to leave cards for Prince Arthur & Mr Thornton[75]— Invited to register my name which I did— At Court opinions read. Some objections made to one of Fields & that of Swayne which they consented to remove by modification[76]— Wife's house case argued in part[77]— After adjt walk & cars with Field took me to Col. Freyre's where I stopped[78]—& left personal cards—then called at Miss Kinney's reception—home—wrote till dinner—dined with Prince Arthur & suite, Sumner, Sherman (Gen) & cabinet at Mr. Thorntons—reception after dinner—where Mades Catacazy & Garcia particular stars[79]—very agreeable—then took Nettie to reception of Mrs Riggs[80]—which extremely brilliant— Made la Marquise   the brightest star—home shortly after 12— A cup of tea & bed half past 12

---

74. John Philip Newman (1826–99), pastor of the Metropolitan Church, 1869–72, and later a Methodist Episcopal bishop. *DAB*, 13:464–65.

75. Arthur William Patrick Albert (1850–1942), duke of Connaught and Strathearn, spent a week in Washington, D.C. Edward Thornton (1817–1906) served as British minister at Washington, 1867–81. *DNB*, 2nd supp., 518–19, 6th supp., 16–21; Washington *Evening Star*, Jan. 24, 1870.

76. Field delivered opinions in *Filor v. U.S.; Joseph C. Willard v. Benjamin O. Tayloe;* and *Michael Reese v. U.S.;* Swayne, in *James Hickman v. William G. Jones et al.; U.S. ex rel. Henry Amy v. City of Burlington;* and *U.S. ex rel. Edward H. Learned v. Burlington.* Minutes, Jan. 24, 1870 (Recs. of Supreme Court, Nat. Arch.).

77. *John E. Neale v. Benjamin I. Neale and Mary H. Neale,* a dispute which originated in a man's gift of a lot to his daughter-in-law provided that she pay to build a house on it. 9 Wall. 1 (1870); Minutes, Jan. 24–25, 1870 (Recs. of Supreme Court, Nat. Arch.).

78. Manuel Freyre (d. 1878), Peruvian minister to the United States. *New York Times,* June 11, 1878.

79. The wives of Constantin de Catacazy and Manuel Garcia, ministers from Russia and the Argentine Republic. For this reception and dinner, see Washington *Evening Star,* Jan. 25, 1870. *Wash. Dir. (1871),* lxxi, 58; ibid. (1872), 198.

80. Janet Madeleine Cecilia Shedden Riggs married Washington, D.C., merchant and banker George Washington Riggs (1813–81) in 1840. *DAB*, 15:603–4; Washington *Evening Star,* Jan. 25, 1870.

TUESDAY, JANUARY 25. Morning duties & breakft at half past eight feeling very well & with good appetite / cold. man called abt repairs &c Berry place: & Norris from District[81] / rainy but walked from house to Courts Room in Capitol in 40 minutes—something too fast— Argt. in case begun yesterday—

MONDAY, MARCH 14. At capitol—our new associate Judge Strong appeared—the test oath was administered in the Reception room by the Clerk in presence of all the Judges—the regular oath at the Clerks table after Court opened[82]—he going in with us & pausing there—he then took his seat extreme right.[83]

THURSDAY, MARCH 24. Today Mr. Bradley, confirmed lately as associate judge appeared[84]— The oaths were administered as in the case of Judge Strong & took his seat on extreme left.

SATURDAY, MARCH 26. At conference—all the judges present—called up Attorney Generals mo. to assign day for hearing Lathams v U.S. & Deming v. Same[85]—explained that order was made that

---

81. Possibly engineer Charles A. Norris. In Sept. 1869, Chase had purchased Edgewood, a house with forty acres of land located two and a quarter miles north of the Capitol, within the District of Columbia but outside the Washington city limits of the time. Washington Berry had built the Federal-style house, which Chase renovated, about 1830. Chase did not move to Edgewood until 1871. *Wash. Dir. (1870)*, 292; James M. Goode, *Capital Losses: A Cultural History of Washington's Destroyed Buildings* (Washington, D.C., 1979), 52; Phelps, *Kate Chase*, 230–31; Chase to F. Ball, Oct. 4, 1869 (Chase Papers, Cinc. Hist. Soc.).

82. William Strong (1808–95) had been a congressman, 1847–51, and a justice on Pennsylvania's supreme court, 1857–68. The first oath to which he subscribed was that required of all civil and military officers of the U.S. by the act of July 2, 1862. *Ex parte Garland* had relieved only attorneys practicing in federal courts from this requirement. Publicly, Strong took the judicial oath prescribed by the Judiciary Act of 1789. *DAB*, 18:153–55; Fairman, *Reconstruction and Reunion*, 58, 732.

83. Chase wrote the following text under Mar. 21, then lined through it: *At Court Judge Strong took h.* Apparently this was a beginning for the Mar. 14 entry, begun on the page for the wrong Monday. The following text was written under Mar. 22, then struck through with a single large X: *Up quite early & prayer & breakfast—some snow on the ground—walked towards the Capitol—took the cars near 10th Street— Stranger enquiring for Vice Presidents room—told Phillips in cars that Court w'd probably adjourn [in] May.* Phillips was probably attorney Philip Phillips (see Apr. 24, 1872, below).

84. The Senate had confirmed New Jersey lawyer Joseph P. Bradley (1813–92) as an associate justice on Mar. 21. *DAB*, 2:571–73; *New York Times*, Mar. 22, 1870.

85. The motion made by Attorney General Ebenezer Rockwood Hoar on Mar. 25 asked that arguments be scheduled in *O. B. Latham et al. v. U.S.* and *Israel Deming v. U.S.* The validity of legal tender for payment of the government's obligations was an issue in both cases, and Hoar's action was an attempt to reopen the legal tender question recently decided in *Hepburn v. Griswold*. After two postponements of the date for argument, both appeals were dismissed on Apr. 20, 1870, upon motion by Latham's and Deming's counsel. Fairman, *Reconstruction and Reunion*, 738–52; 9 Wall. 145, 146 (1870); Minutes, Mar. 25, 1870 (Recs. of Supreme Court, Nat. Arch.).

the legal tender questions, so far as involved in these cases, should be argued in Bronson v Rodes & Hepburn v. Griswold, & not in these which were passed on that account:[86] and that the effect of this order was that these cases as to these questions should abide the decision in those. To my surprise this statement though supported by Judges Nelson, Clifford & Field, was [con]troverted by Judges Swayne, Miller & Davis; and to my greater surprise the new Judges, undertook to decide the point against the majority of their brethren. There was a good deal of talk which manifested a determination on the part of the present majority of the Court to force the rehearing of the legal tender questions with a [fixed determination] as I fear to reverse the decision already made. An order was made against our remonstrance to assign the cases for hearing on Monday Apl 4.

MONDAY, MARCH 28. Before going into Court I mentioned Mr Carlisle's note to the Court,[87] & said, if there was no objection I would not announce the order made Saturday until conference after adj't. today— This was agreed though with some manifestations of dissatisfaction by the rehearers— After court opened received telegram from Judge Bradley that he was prevented from returning by storm / perhaps not important[88]— Asked Miller to write reply which he did thus "conference will be delayed until Tuesday 3 P.M. The order for argument in cases considered on Saturday suspended until then. I signed & sent it at noon.

THURSDAY, MARCH 31. Heard argt Atto. Gen pro—Carlisle con.—on Mo to assign a day for Latham v. U. States & Deming v. U. States— Atto Gen Hoar not in cases heretofore— Carlisle for Latham insisted that rediscussion of Legal Tender question

---

86. In *Frederick Bronson v. Peter Rodes*, decided in Feb. 1869, the Supreme Court held that a contract which specified payment in coin and was made prior to the Legal Tender Act of 1862 could not be satisfied by payment in legal tender notes. Chase wrote the majority opinion; Davis and Swayne concurred, but only on the basis of the provisions of the specific contract at issue; Miller dissented. *Susan P. Hepburn v. Henry A. Griswold*, decided Feb. 7, 1870, engaged the broader issue of the constitutionality of the legal tender acts. Chase wrote the opinion for the majority, which deemed the acts unconstitutional. Miller wrote a long dissenting opinion, in which Swayne and Davis concurred. 7 Wall. 229 (1869); 8 Wall. 603 (1870).

87. James M. Carlisle, leading counsel for Latham, did not want the legal tender issue reopened in his client's case. Fairman, *Reconstruction and Reunion*, 740.

88. Justice Bradley had been delayed at Newark, N.J.: "If Tuesday afternoon will do for conference I can attend perhaps not important." Bradley to Chase, Mar. 28, 1870 (Chase Papers, Hist. Soc. of Pa.).

precluded by former direction— Hoar said no argument to that effect made by him & none by former Atto. Gen as advised by Mr. Evarts then now present[89]

Some other cases argued & a patent case began.[90]

After adjournment went into conference on Mo of Atto. Genl.— I recited briefly the facts—stated the circumstances under which the Court refused to hear the legal tender question argued in these cases heretofore—that they were passed because it was doubted if that question really arose in them & expressly because it was [avoided] to be argued in Hepburn v Griswold & Bronson v. Rodes in which the decision would be conclusive on the same question in these. that Counsel in both of these cases were so informed when the order to pass was made—that no rehearing of a case could be had except on mo of one of majy.—that this was an attempt to do by indirection what cannot be done directly— In vain— Maj of Court [ordered] reargument

THURSDAY, JUNE 9. Gen Patterson called when at bkft[91]—hurried And went with him—Abercrombie & Col. P. son of Gen. with us in carriage[92]—crossed river and took special car to Atsion Col. Patterson's place[93]—cordial welcome—fine horse—fine Alderneys—mills—old house but very solid—former proprietors had some 400.000 Acres—Col. P—— 30.000 / went out to drive— Gen. P. Mr. McMichael, Gen. Abercrombie, Mr. Scudder Col. R. Patterson in open wagon, drawn by six mules—rest in two other carriages / rode some sixteen miles—saw many large thickets of laurel in splendid bloom—returning—washed—& then the Farmers' Club dinner / Elect 13 only 5 present—Gen & Col P McMi. Col Craig

89. The word *now* is above the line, as if Chase added it for clarity.
90. *The Steam Tug Quickstep et al. v. Christopher Byrne*, which arose from a collision; *Elizabeth S. Pierce v. Walter S. Cox, Trustee*, concerning dismissal of an appeal from the D.C. Supreme Court; and the patent case, *Diodate Clark et al. v. John Bousfield*. 9 Wall. 665, 786 (1870); 10 Wall. 133 (1870); Minutes, Mar. 31, 1870 (Recs. of Supreme Court, Nat. Arch.).
91. Chase was in Philadelphia on the morning of June 9.
92. Retired Brig. Gen. John Joseph Abercrombie (1802–77), a professional soldier who had been Gen. Robert Patterson's aide-de-camp during the war with Mexico, and Robert Emmet Patterson (1830–1906), son of Robert Patterson and colonel of Pennsylvania infantry during the Civil War. Chase began this entry in ink. Everything following *carriage* is in pencil, as is the entry for June 10. *Appletons'*, 1:8; Heitman, *Historical Register*, 1:775; Nicholas B. Wainwright, ed., *A Philadelphia Perspective: The Diary of Sidney George Fisher Covering the Years 1834–1871* (Philadelphia, 1967), 446.
93. William Chamberlain Patterson, Gen. Robert Patterson's brother, owned Atsion, which was located about thirty miles from Philadelphia and derived its name from an earlier form, At-sy-unk. Chase to Janet Chase, June 10, 1870 (Chase Papers, L.C.).

Biddle & another[94]— Gen. P made complimentary remarks at table of myself & Gen Wm B Thomas—dinner over returned to Phil— Mrs Wm C. P with us—a lovely woman—with health ruined by labors & exposures during war[95]—back to hotel & to room

FRIDAY, JUNE 10. To New York by 12.45 train—pouring rain when arrived— Evarts met me at foot of Courtlandt St— Took me to his house 231 Cor 14 & 2d Av. / kind reception by Mrs E— dinner—told Evarts I had come to consult physician—he named Dr. Clark of whose fame as physiol. I had heard—determined to consult him tomorrow.[96]

MONDAY, JUNE 13. Saw Dr. Clark—thought heart trouble not serious—but uneasy abt. diab.—proposed stay in N.Y. & treatment—vapor bath[97]—called Kinney & also Sherwood[98]—home u. ¾ pint 1. P.M. lunch & nap—u. 3. P.M. ¼ p.—read Mort d'Arthur[99]

THURSDAY, JUNE 23. Finished opinions—went to station at 3.— found train hour for West changed

SATURDAY, JUNE 25. Breakfast on boat crossing Ohio—dined at Zanesville—saw Applegate & had short talked—finding we must wait at Newark a couple of hours went to Preston House where N.[1] & I each bathed—cars for Sandusky 4.25—very hot—Jay Butler by Cooke's direction met us at Monroeville to say that tug wd take us at once to Gibraltar[2]—arrived Sandusky at 10—went at once on

---

94. Craig Biddle (1823–1910), a Pennsylvania legislator and jurist, had served on the staffs of Robert Patterson and Andrew Gregg Curtin during the Civil War. Johnson, *Twentieth Century Biographical Dictionary*, v. 1; *New York Times*, July 27, 1910.

95. William Chamberlain Patterson's wife had worked in military hospitals during the Civil War. Chase to Janet Chase, June 10, 1870 (Chase Papers, L.C.).

96. Alonzo Clark (1807–87) practiced in New York City and taught at the College of Physicians and Surgeons. *Nat. Cyc.*, 1:354.

97. *Diab.* evidently means "diabetes." For a vapor bath, Chase was to have hot water or bricks placed under his chair and wrap himself in blankets to induce perspiration. Memorandum, end of Journal XVIII.

98. New York lawyers Franklin S. Kinney (d. 1871) and John Sherwood (c. 1820–95). *New York Times*, July 14, 1871; *New York Tribune*, Feb. 12, 1895; Kinney to Chase, Sept. 24, 1863 (Chase Papers, L.C.); James et al., *Notable American Women*, 3:284–85; addresses, end of Journal XVIII.

99. Sir Thomas Malory's *Le Morte d'Arthur*, perhaps in an 1865 edition by Thomas Wright entitled *La Mort d'Arthure*.

1. Chase's daughter Nettie (Janet Ralston Chase).

2. An island at Put-in-Bay, Ohio, where Jay Cooke erected a summer home. John M. Butler worked for Cooke and married one of Cooke's daughters in 1871. Oberholtzer, *Jay Cooke*, 2:459–63; James E. Pollard, ed., *The Journal of Jay Cooke; or, The Gibraltar Records, 1865–1905* (Columbus, Ohio, 1935), 225–26, 242; Larson, *Jay Cooke*, 426; *Phila. Dir. (1871)*, 302, 1209.

board tug—supper on tug—arrived hot & tired at Gibraltar about midnight—family and guests received us at landing with kindest welcome. Jay Butler came over with us— Will Moorhead & Dora; Peet, (Phila) White Cooke's phonographer, Mrs Mills, Misses Sarah & Essie Master Frank, were guests[3]—family Cooke, Mrs Cooke, Sally & Harry & Emily[4]

After some talk all went to bed—

SUNDAY, JUNE 26. Morning prayers—& church— I had not rested well—being greatly fatigued by journey—night & this day very hot—with Mrs Mills to church & back in company with whole family—prayers read with great feeling & excellent Sermon by Mr. Weldon[5] / spoke to him with C⎯⎯[6] after service did not go in evening—read, not I hope, unprofitably—tried to sleep but very hot—never perspired so much in same time as at Church in morning

MONDAY, JUNE 27. Up soon after five—breakfast abt 6, & went with Cooke, Mr. Roff of Ga,[7] & Mr. Weldon to Canada shore fishing—very hot—success not great though Cooke & Mr. W⎯⎯ each caught a respectable number—I only 6 & Mr. Roff a few more— dinner on tug—back to tea—a pleasant yet fatiguing day

WEDNESDAY, JUNE 29. Cooke, Mrs C⎯⎯ Sally & Harry— Off this morning for Sandusky—thence on Friday for Philadelphia— went fishing with Gottlieb[8]—caught three small—he one small, & one respectable bass—bkft ½ with Cooke's 6. & ¾ with rest at 9— after breakfast took drive over Put-in-Bay— Vineyards in fine

---

3. William E. C. and Dora Moorhead; Emerson W. Peet of Philadelphia, secretary and actuary of the National Life Insurance Company, a Jay Cooke enterprise; Stephen W. White, Cooke's private secretary; and perhaps Caroline M. Mills of Sandusky, who had connections with the Moorheads and the Cookes, with members of her family. Pollard, *Journal of Jay Cooke*, 223–26; Oberholtzer, *Jay Cooke*, 2:90–93, 519; C. M. Mills to Chase, Feb. 2, 1863 (Chase Papers, L.C.).

4. Jay and Dorothea Elizabeth Allen Cooke; two of their children, Sarah Esther Cooke (b. 1852), future wife of John M. Butler, and Henry Eleutheros Cooke (b. 1857), who became a Protestant Episcopal clergyman; and Emily Bronaugh, who was traveling with the Cookes. Larson, *Jay Cooke*, 426; Oberholtzer, *Jay Cooke*, 2:464; Pollard, *Journal of Jay Cooke*, 218.

5. S. R. Weldon, rector (1868–72) of St. Paul's Church at Put-in-Bay, which Jay Cooke had founded. Pollard, *Journal of Jay Cooke*, 46, 50, 176–77, 250, 273.

6. Probably Jay Cooke.

7. Toledo hardware merchant William Roff (b. 1802) spent part of his career at Savannah, Ga. Waggoner, *Toledo*, 766–67; Pollard, *Journal of Jay Cooke*, 225–26.

8. Gottlieb Hearley, evidently a Cooke family employee. Pollard, *Journal of Jay Cooke*, 218, 221.

June 1870   { 655 }

condition—glass lemonade at Stacy's[9]—home—dinner 2—row afternoon—stopped at Island—went to Sweny & West House portico[10]—several came & spoke to me—Geo. Benham formerly Columbus, now of La, Clegg,[11] Gunckel Sweny & West, proprietors &c—back to house— Package from Gallagher two Discourses (1850) Progress N. West—mailed one to Cooke at Sand'y[12]—bed at 10— fatigued—weather hot & oppressive

THURSDAY, JUNE 30. night 29–30 unpleasant—p. considble[13]— u frequent—from 8 yesterday to 8 today fully five pints—hot[14]

Rose soon after 5—sent Wm[15] & John for pond lilies—walked round island slowly—tired me but otherwise pretty well—read several chaps—breakfast—in house all morning—dinner 2— evening croquet Dora M[16] & I v. Mrs McMeens & Sally Stem[17] / defeated— Craighead,[18] Clegg, & Gunckel, of Dayton & Sweny, came over from Sweny House—talk—Sweny described his gas making apparatus—walked with them about island—all out sailing but me—sat on bench and enjoyed the breeze—talked with Mrs McM of her hospital experience in the war—back to house / glass lemonade—prayer—bed—

9. A family residing at Put-in-Bay. *Sandusky Daily Register,* June 27, 1870.
10. In 1870, Sandusky businessman William T. West (1815–99) evidently entered an agreement with a Col. Sweeney to operate the Put-in-Bay House. Williams, *History of the Fire Lands,* 521; Peeke, *Centennial History of Erie County,* 1:318–20.
11. Probably Charles Bailey Clegg (d. 1918), a businessman whose family was prominent in Dayton. George C. Benham, confidential clerk in the Ohio state treasury during Chase's tenure as governor, had become a planter in Carroll Parish, La. John C. Hover et al., eds. *Memoirs of the Miami Valley,* 3 vols. (Chicago, 1919), 3:116–17; *General Catalogue of the Graduates and Former Students of Miami University . . .* (Oxford, Ohio, [1909]), 226; *Annual Report of Secretary of State,* 1856, 2:360; Tunnell, *Crucible of Reconstruction,* 141–42.
12. William D. Gallagher sent his *Facts and Conditions of Progress in the North-west: Being the annual discourse for 1850, before the Historical and Philosophical Society of Ohio . . .* (Cincinnati, 1850). Chase included in his mailing to Jay Cooke a letter with news about his stay at Gibraltar and Gallagher's desire to write a piece on the "New North West." Chase to Cooke, June 29, 1870 (Cooke Papers, Hist. Soc. of Pa.).
13. Evidently "pain considerable."
14. In this and the next three entries, Chase wrote an opening memorandum summarizing his physical condition, drew a short horizontal line near the left margin as a separator, and then wrote a paragraph describing the day's activities. From this June 30 entry through the remainder of 1870, Chase made frequent notations of the quantity and frequency of his urination (often abbreviated as "u").
15. William Joice.
16. Dora Moorhead.
17. Anna C. McMeens (c. 1820–93), widow of a Sandusky physician who died while enlisted as a surgeon in the Civil War, managed Gibraltar for Jay Cooke. Her niece, Sally Stem, was one of the estate's household employees. Pollard, *Journal of Jay Cooke,* 12, 24–25, 85, 115, 322–24, 345.
18. Likely Dayton lawyer Samuel Craighead (b. 1818). Reed, *Bench and Bar of Ohio,* 1:222–24; Craighead to Chase, Dec. 17, 1864 (Chase Papers, L.C.).

FRIDAY, JULY 1. Yesterday p. less—walked around island 2ce;[19] mod. eat & drink—s. 9.30;[20]—Sleep good; u. 9.30 y. to 9 this morn. 5 times or 6[;—]2⅓ pints.

Slept unusually well last night—cool—windy—& heavy rain— rose abt 11.30 to put down window—up twice—rose 7, feeling unusually well—bkft 8.50 rainy, cloudy, & wet all day— East wind filled bay [&] brought water for a little while over the dock—walked about island some for exercise under umbrella—so cool that after tea (6:30) put on overcoat—splendid sunset—laid down awhile morning & afternoon & slept a good deal—more u. than common & more frequent—to bed about half past ten

SATURDAY, JULY 2. 9. AM July 1 to July 2. 5 p. 9 AM. u. more freqt. than usual from breakfast to bedtime say 5 times— also during night—in all 5½ pints—not much palpitation—but tiresome & faintish to walk up hill—sleep not so good as previous night—night cool—windows closed except one—and quilt—food & drink mod.

Felt quite well on rising—read Luke & prayer—bkft 8.00—st. 9.30 difficult not painful—quanty usual—felt well till after bkft— then some faintness stomach & oppression— Jno G. Lowe[21]—Capt Newbold & wife[22]—Richd Anderson & wife—Miss Lowe—called— walked with Lowe—felt better—he very kind & sympathetic—lunch 1 P.M— All [p]acked & ready to go to Sand'y—Evening Star came in but returns to Toledo[23]—u, 1.30—went out with John to fish— caught 3 small ones—u. 3.20 / "Ferris" came in[24]—hastened to get on board—met Dickn Phillips at dock found several acquaintances on "Ferris"—Mr. & Mrs Craighead—Mr. Leggett, Rev Dr Thomas, Rev. Mr. Reid, Steubenville &c[25]—Dora & Will Moorhead of our

19. That is, "twice."
20. Stool.
21. Dayton lawyer and public figure John Gilbert Lowe (1817–92). He had several children. *General Catalogue ... of Miami University ... 1809–1909* (Oxford, Ohio, 1909), 29; *Chicago Tribune*, Aug. 1, 1892.
22. Presumably former captain in the Union Army and Iowa Republican politician Joshua G. Newbold (1830–1903), and his wife since 1850, Rachel Farquhar Newbold. Sobel and Raimo, *Biographical Directory of Governors*, 2:435–36.
23. The passenger steamer *Evening Star* assumed the Sandusky Islands run in 1866. Pollard, *Journal of Jay Cooke*, 143; Lytle, *Merchant Vessels*, 60.
24. The *B. F. Ferris*, described as an "elegant new steamer." *Sandusky Daily Register*, June, 23, July 4, 1870.
25. Jeanette A. Miller Craighead, daughter of Judge William Miller of Cincinnati and wife of Samuel Craighead; possibly Mortimer Dormer Leggett (1821–96), Ohio lawyer and Union soldier, who later married a woman from Sandusky; and Alexander M. Reid (b. 1827), a licensed Presbyterian preacher and director of the Female Seminary at Steubenville. Reed, *Bench and Bar of Ohio*, 1:223; *DAB*, 11:146–47; *Biographical Cyclopædia*, 2:481–82.

party— Lake rough—arrd. Sany. 7.30—Lake House clean rooms & good supper[26]—u. 8—unusually well today—u. freqt during night

SUNDAY, JULY 3. Sat AM to Sun AM. bkft 8.50—st 9.30 difficult—quantity usual—felt quite well bef & immy after bkft—then feeling of faintness stomach & oppression— Lowe & others abt. 11—walked with L & felt better— Lunch or dinner—catawba & much better—u. 1.30—u till this morning 9. 4⅓ pints—

Rose at 7—having slept pretty well except interrups for u.— morning duties—finding I had lost umbrella sent Wm[27] for it—bkft 8.15—church—Mr. Leunsbury—dined 1.30—Nettie at Mrs Cooke's[28]—read Luke—also Carleton's North West[29]—slept some— to Mrs Cooke's at tea[30]

MONDAY, JULY 4. To bed last night at 10.30—rose at 5 good sleep—3ce up for u. 2 p from bed to bkft[31]

JULY 4. At Fairgrounds refused to be announced[32]—met some friends—felt pretty well but soon tired—came to town with Dr. M[33]—stopped at Mrs Cookes—glass catawba / dined at hotel—tea at Mrs Cookes / young people—music & a little dancing—returned to hotel early & bed. abt. 4 p. u. bed to bed—

JULY 5. Left for Toledo about 7. changed at Clyde—arrived T 8.50 carriage to Oliver House—went to Belle Walbridge's— she & Carry with me to "Oliver" to see Nettie[34]—dinner—after

26. The New Lake House was located on the site of the first hotel in Sandusky. Aldrich, *History of Erie County*, 287–88, 438.
27. William Joice.
28. Jay Cooke's mother, Martha Carswell (or Caswell) Cooke. Oberholtzer, *Jay Cooke*, 1:3.
29. *The Seat of Empire* (Boston, 1870), an account of a trip through Minnesota which boomed Jay Cooke's Northern Pacific and other railroads. Its author was Charles Carleton Coffin (1823–96), a popular writer who used the pen name "Carleton." *DAB*, 4:265–66; Chase to Cooke, July 7, 1870 (Cooke Papers, Hist. Soc. of Pa.).
30. The second half of this paragraph—everything following *8.15*—is in a different color ink from the rest of the entry.
31. *3ce* means "thrice." *2 p* is an alteration in pencil; the rest of the entry is in ink. This entry appears under the diary's printed heading for July 4. The second entry for July 4, which follows, and the succeeding entries for July 5–8, were all written on a folded sheet now found at the back of the journal.
32. Sandusky's Fourth of July festival took place at the Erie County Agricultural Society Fairgrounds. *Sandusky Daily Register*, June 24, 25, 1870; Aldrich, *History of Erie County*, 88–89.
33. Likely George W. Malin, the Cooke family physician from Germantown, Pa. Pollard, *Journal of Jay Cooke*, 236; *Phila. Dir.* (*1870*), 1043.
34. Isabel Skinner Walbridge and Carrie Walbridge. The Oliver House hotel opened in 1859 at Broadway, Charles, and Ottawa Streets. Waggoner, *Toledo*, 819.

Mr. Mott[35] called & invited us to ride after tea— Mrs. Hall[36] also put her carriage at our service—but did not use it—tea— Mr. Mott called & we took quite a long ride both up & down the river— stopped at Rink—Orphans fair[37]—saw Miss Cannie Mott Mrs William, Mr. Jesup W Scott, [Mrs] Kraus & several other old friends[38] / returned to hotel Helen & Dick Sk. had called missed them[39]—bed about ten—not much palp—say 4 pts u from 9 last night to this morning

JULY 6— Off by cars at 8.50 for Chicago—section in palace Car quite comfortable[40]—arr. 4, [*illeg.*] raining— Nettie took [carriage] & went out to make purchases—tea abt 7.30. Judge Davis & Mr. Stoughton (N.Y) called[41] / felt pretty well—bed—u. 3 pints

JULY 7. Took cars after bkft for Ludlow—arrived 1.48 / Mr L—— met us at cars—cordial welcome by Mrs L—three nice children[42]—dinner—walk. prayers bed abt 9—u. abt 3.

---

35. Richard Mott.
36. Harriet O. Holmes Hall (d. 1887), wife of James C. Hall. Waggoner, *Toledo*, 682–83.
37. Toledo women founded the Protestant Orphans' Home in Jan. 1867. This organization sponsored fund-raising activities on July 4–5 at "The Rink" on St. Clair Street. Ibid., 832; *Daily Toledo Blade*, July 2, 1870.
38. Cannie Mott, one of the first managers of the Protestant Orphans' Home (and who may have been Anna C. Mott, a daughter of Richard Mott); likely Sarah R. Langdon Williams, a leading Toledo reformer and wife of former *Toledo Blade* proprietor Joseph R. Williams; lawyer, land agent, and former *Toledo Blade* editor Jessup Wakeman Scott (1799–1874); and probably Cincinnati native Minnie Lauer Kraus, who in 1850 married Toledo (later New York) textile merchant William Kraus (b. 1823). Waggoner, *Toledo*, 85, 89, 91, 96, 106–7, 346, 476, 498, 650–51, 832, 837; *Biographical Cyclopædia*, 3:701; *Nat. Cyc.*, 3:275.
39. Dick Skinner was evidently one of Helen Skinner's siblings and a son of Chase's sister, Janette Logan Chase Skinner. He and Edward R. Skinner may have been the same person. James Ralston Skinner to Chase, Jan. 12, 1841, Sept. 23, 1846, Sept. 1, 1847, and family memoranda (Chase Papers, L.C.).
40. Pullman's Palace Car Company made "hotel cars" that combined seats, sleeping berths, and a full kitchen. Joseph Husband, *The Story of the Pullman Car* (Chicago, 1917), 47–52.
41. David Davis, who was on circuit, and Edwin Wallace Stoughton. *Chicago Tribune*, July 3, 7, 1870.
42. In the 1850s, Chase's brother-in-law James Dunlop Ludlow became a land agent and surveyor in Champaign County, Ill. He married Susan Middlekauff (or Middlecoff) in 1862. Two of their children were a son, Sam (b. ca. 1863), and a daughter, Theresa (b. ca. 1867). J. D. Ludlow to Chase, Apr. 16, 26, 1862, Oct. 5, 1868 (Chase Papers, L.C.); J. S. Lothrop, *J. S. Lothrop's Champaign County Directory, 1870–1, with History of the Same* (Chicago, 1871), 392–93; unpublished guide to Ludlow-Dunlop-Chambers Collec., Univ. of Wyoming.

JULY 8— talk—ride N[43] & I with Mr & Mrs L—— & little Teresa to see Col & Mrs Dudley abt 3 miles across the Prairie[44]—very pleasant—Col D—— indisposed & in bed 81 year old—but clear & bright & very glad to see us / Mrs D—— invited us to stay to dinner but we came back after glass of lemonade—writing letters walking reading, napping the rest of the day—bed about 9.45. u. abt 4 p—felt rather weak when walking—& riding [not] without back some pain in small of back

JULY 8— frequent u last night—in all say 2 p—before bkft—up 5 t—stool 745 u. 9—u. 11—q'y small—walk with L—wrote Katie— felt good deal oppressed & faint—lay down—but got up again very soon—w. telegram to send Tremont House fr. Paxton[45]—read— introduced to workmen—

WEDNESDAY, JULY 20. Up at 530—morning duties—u fr 8 AM yy.[46] to 6 [A]M. today 3 p.—frequent at night / sleep pretty good— night hot till 1 AM, cool aftwds—brkft at 6.30— Stool scanty— Off for Forest Lake kindness of L.S. & M. R.R. Co[47]—party for me— Gov. Austin Gen & Mrs Gorman Ch-Jus Ripley[48]—Justice McMillan, Judge [Finch,] Judge Hall, Dr. Stewart, Mr. Jones of Mankato Miss [Steele,] Nettie & others[49] / fishing—I caught the largest a black

43. Nettie (Janet Ralston Chase).
44. Apparently this was the same Col. Dudley whom Chase knew in Cincinnati in the 1840s.
45. The Tremont Hotel in Chicago, considered the finest in the West. Paxton was a town on the rail line from Ludlow to Chicago. A. T. Andreas, *History of Chicago* . . . , 3 vols. (Chicago, 1884–86), 2:501–2.
46. Yesterday.
47. The Lake Superior and Mississippi Railroad, a Jay Cooke enterprise connecting St. Paul and Duluth, was formally opened in the summer of 1870. Chase owned some of the company's bonds. Oberholtzer, *Jay Cooke*, 2:98, 104–11, 130–33, 244; Chase to Cooke, Dec. 30, 1869 (Chase Papers, L.C.).
48. Horace Austin (1831–1905), Republican governor of Minnesota, 1870–74; Willis Arnold Gorman (1816–76), former congressman from Indiana, governor of Minnesota Territory, and officer of volunteers; Gorman's wife, Emily Newington Gorman; and Christopher Gore Ripley (1822–81), chief justice of the Minnesota Supreme Court, 1870–74. Sobel and Raimo, *Biographical Directory of Governors*, 2:777; *DAB*, 7:435–46; *Nat. Cyc.*, 12:43–44.
49. Samuel James Renwick McMillan (1826–97), Minnesota district and supreme court judge, 1858–74, later a U.S. senator; Ramsey County common pleas judge William Sprigg Hall (1832–75); Jacob Henry Stewart (1829–84), physician, Republican politician, and postmaster of St. Paul, 1865–70; possibly Judson Jones, a lawyer of Mankato, Minn.; and evidently a daughter or other relative of Franklin Steele (1813–80), a founder of Minneapolis. The Steele family had hosted Chase the previous day. *Nat. Cyc.*, 4:469; C. C. Andrews, ed., *History of St. Paul* (Syracuse, N.Y.,

bass—dinner—German landlord March[50] / [or *illeg.*]—nice milk—
returned about 6—tea. At lake walked about mile to & from hotel
without inconvenience. On cars, Gov. Marshall going to Duluth
who gave very interesting account of Minnesota, & probable change
route of N. Pacific to line by Crow Wing[51]—also young lawyer
from Duluth[52] who expects to walk 8 miles tomorrow morning
fr end of RR to Steamboat / no cars yet from Duluth—all passengers
take this walk or wagons 13 miles—from Thompson[53] to Fon du lac—
Evg Rev Dr Paterson grandson of Gov. P—— member of Cont
Con & U.S Sup Court with C A Mann & Hale called[54] / wrote Bright
at [Sup].[55]
day very pleasant—felt well—little oppress[ing,]

THURSDAY JULY 21. Rose at 7.30—dress & morning duties better
sleep than usual—cool night—u. fr. 8 AM y. to [8] AM today 3
p.—brkft at 8—stool regular—

TUESDAY, NOVEMBER 1.[56] duties—breakfast— Walk about ½

1890), 254; *Bio. Dir. U.S. Cong.*, 1875–76; *Mankato Record*, July 2, 1870; Isaac Atwater, ed., *History of the City of Minneapolis, Minnesota* (New York, 1893), 1:387–91; *St. Paul Pioneer*, July 20, 1870.

50. German immigrant Michael March (b. 1828) opened the first store at Forest Lake in 1868 and then began a hotel. Edward D. Neill, *History of Washington County and the St. Croix Valley* . . . (Minneapolis, 1881), 467–68.

51. William Rainey Marshall (1825–96) was a St. Paul entrepreneur, an officer of volunteers during the Civil War, and governor of Minnesota, 1865–69. Crow Wing, Minn., became a minor station along the Northern Pacific Railroad. *DAB*, 12:333; Henry J. Winser, *The Great Northwest: A Guide-Book* . . . (New York, 1883), 35, 44.

52. Possibly William Weldon Billson (1847–1923), who moved his legal practice in 1870 from Winona to Duluth. *Who Was Who*, 1:95; *Duluth Minnesotian*, Aug. 6, 1870.

53. There is an unidentified character or mark above the line after this word in the original.

54. Andrew B. Paterson (d. ca. 1877), evidently a grandson of New Jersey politician and jurist William Paterson (1745–1806), was rector of St. Paul's Episcopal Church. Charles A. Mann may have been related to H. E. Mann, a Minneapolis attorney appointed clerk of the federal court at St. Paul in 1862. Henry Hale (1814–90) was a St. Paul businessman and politician. *St. Paul Daily Dispatch*, July 9, 1870; Andrews, *History of St. Paul*, 502–3; *DAB*, 14:293–94; addresses, end of Journal XVIII; John H. Stevens, *Personal Recollections of Minnesota and Its People* . . . (Minneapolis, 1890), 380–81; *Nat. Cyc.*, 18:185.

55. Jesse D. Bright, once a political enemy, evidently intended to support Chase for the Democratic presidential nomination upon receiving guarantees of a cabinet post and control over federal patronage in Indiana. Ethelbert C. Hibben to Chase, July 1870 (Chase Papers, L.C.).

56. In Aug. 1870, as he returned east from Minnesota, Chase suffered a stroke which caused partial paralysis of the right side of his body. During the period covered by these final journal entries for 1870, he was at the Spragues' home at Narragansett Pier, R.I. His right foot still dragged when he was fatigued. His voice and writing hand were regaining their strength. Chase to R. C. Parsons, Sept. 26, 1870 (Chase Papers, Hist. Soc. of Pa.); Chase to J. G. Perry, Nov. 14, 1870 (Chase Papers, L.C.).

way from lane gate to farm gate rode around Tuckers[57]— Katie went to Providence / dinner—quail—

TUES. DEC. 13—[58]   Mon night woke at 11.30, 2, & 6—two first times lay awake an hour or so—last time did not sleep again[—]rose soon after 8—could lie but not sleep on left side—pain about heart —felt pretty well on rising—took Ergo[59]—breakfasted tea, toasted bread, bit of steak—egg & baked apple[—]tried stool—no evac— walked about hour on beach—dragged coming up hill & stairs—no fatigue after seated a minute—but pain as before & some wind in bowel / rode at 12.30—W'd & P [&c][60]—dined at 2.15—took no more walk [out]doors—tea 6.15—Katie returned from Wn. [7.50][61]—walked in house good deal bed 10—

TUESDAY, DECEMBER 13. Woke last night & urnd. at 11.30; 2 & 6 two first times lay awake an hour or so—last time did not sleep again—rose soon after 8. Could lie best but not sleep on left side— pain about heart—felt pretty well on rising—took Ergotine—bkfd tea, dry toast, bit of steak, egg soft boiled, & baked apple—tried stool—no evac—walked about an hour to, from & on beach— dragged coming up hill & upstairs—no fatigue after seated a minute—pain as before & some wind in bowels—rode at 12.30— dined at 2.15—took no more walk outdoors—tea 6.15
(from mem at time 13 May '71)[62]

57. A resort hotel at Narragansett Pier, known formally as the Atwood House, operated by Joshua C. Tucker and his son, J. A. Tucker. Cole, *Washington and Kent Counties*, 561–62.
58. This entry for Dec. 13 is from a loose sheet at the rear of the volume.
59. Ergotine, an extract of ergot, which is a fungus occurring naturally on rye. Physicians used ergot most commonly in obstetrics, but experimented with it in other cases as well. In Chase's case the intention may have been to affect his nervous system or blood vessels, or perhaps to stimulate contraction of smooth muscle tissue (such as the intestinal muscles). Robley Dunglison, *A Dictionary of Medical Science* (Philadelphia, 1874), 372–73; *Encyclopædia Brittanica*, 11th ed., 29 vols. (Cambridge, 1910–11), 9:737–38; Frank James Bove, *The Story of Ergot* (Basel, Switz., 1970), 271–78; Arthur Osol and Robertson Pratt, eds., *The United States Dispensatory*, 27th ed. (Philadelphia, 1973), 484; Chase letters to John G. Perry, Oct.–Dec. 1870 (Chase Papers, L.C.).
60. Very likely Wakefield and Peace Dale, nearby towns that may have been on the route of Chase's ride.
61. Kate Chase Sprague traveled between Washington and Narragansett during her father's convalescence. Chase to James A. Hamilton, Dec. 8, 1870 (Chase Papers, L.C.); Chase to Hiram Barney, Dec. 12, 1870 (Barney Papers, Huntington Lib.).
62. This second entry for Dec. 13 appears on the diary page with a printed heading for that date. As Chase's note indicates, he made this entry in May 1871, basing it on a memorandum made "at time"—apparently the first Dec. 13 entry, which he had written on a separate sheet now located at the back of the original journal.

WED. DEC 14—[63] pill— Waked three or four times but soon slept again—refreshing—woke in morning free from pain & feeling remarkably well—bath—Tarrants Aperient[64]—Ergot—not [*two words? illeg.*] 8.40—read Acts—walk about mile with unusual vigor—felt really better—passage—walk to end of lane—35 min—rode to P.O., [W——, &] P[65]—letters from Parsons, Riddle & Barney[66]—dinner same time with lunch—walk on [farm road] abt 3 [hour]—passage small—tea with family dinner—reading of [*two words illeg.*]—bed at 9.15

TH. DEC 15— Waked 11.30—1—2.30—4.30—u. each time and before rising after light—up & both about 8—Ergot—breakfast—bread tea, chop, apple—walk to gates in lane—cold & wind—no drive today Katie thinking it too cold—cold walk in before noon by myself—farther in [lane] to tel. post & round triangle— Cold in house at dinner time—had Nettie bring blanket shawl / felt [rheu]matic pains right arm & wrist—bad & felt bad—bed at 9

FRIDAY DEC 16 Better in morning as usual—tho' twice awake long & twice shorter & frequent u—cold wind & neither walked nor rode / K—— [*two words illeg.*] &c as usual—bed ½ past 9 on Shuckers return from Providence whither for medicines &c[67]—

SATURDAY— Slept almost entire night little u—only half a pint—commenced with Eaton R—— water[68]—tumbler before bkft & about [11]—walked & rode as usual / Felt pretty well until evening—when

---

63. Chase made the entries for Wednesday, Dec. 14, through Saturday, Dec. 17, on folded sheets now found at the end of the original volume.

64. Dr. Perry prescribed pills and Tarrant's Effervescing Seltzer Aperient as laxatives. Chase to Perry, Nov. 11, Dec. 4, 18, 22, 1870 (Chase Papers, L.C.); Dunglison, *Dictionary of Medical Science*, 125, 742, 939.

65. Possibly "Post Office, Wakefield, & Peace Dale."

66. Richard C. Parsons reported on his activities as Chase's business contact and personal liaison in Washington. Albert G. Riddle conveyed personal anecdotes and touched upon politics. Hiram Barney's letter probably dealt with his efforts to help Chase procure hotel accommodations in New York. Chase to Barney, Dec. 6, Barney to Chase, Dec. 9, Riddle to Chase, Dec. 11, Parsons to Chase, Dec. 12, 1870 (Chase Papers, L.C.); Chase to Barney, Dec. 12, 1870 (Barney Papers, Huntington Lib.).

67. Eugene L. Didier left his position as Chase's secretary at the end of Oct. 1870. Jacob Schuckers replaced him until early 1871. Chase to W. H. Rearden, Oct. 26, 1870, Chase to Schuckers, same date, Chase to R. C. Parsons, Jan. 23, 1871 (Chase Papers, L.C.).

68. Chase's friend Thomas H. Yeatman had sent a shipment of Eaton Rapids Magnetic Water, one of several mineral waters recently discovered in Michigan. Chase to Yeatman, Dec. 12, 1870, Chase to John G. Perry, Dec. 18, 1870 (Chase Papers, L.C.); Charles Richard Tuttle, comp., *General History of the State of Michigan . . .* (Detroit, 1873), 658–65.

sharp pain left shoulder & arm / 2 [guests (*illeg.* &c)] adjacent—bed soon after 9—before took new [pill, *illeg.*] / had no evacuation

SUNDAY DEC 18.[69] Slept well though twice long awake—u. about 12 & again about 5—pint in all—2 pints day & night—bkft— no evacuation by 9 & 2d pill—walk—[*illeg.* & was] two hours—no evacu—— by 2—took Tarrant—dinner—chicken broth—breast of bird—tomatoes—bread—& an orange—

SUNDAY, DECEMBER 18.[70] Slept well last night, though long awake twice—urnd. twice about 12 & again about 5—one pint—2 pints yesterday & yesternight—bkft—walked about two hours—no evac. before two—took Tarrant's Aperient—dinner—chicken broth—breast of bird—tomatoes—bread

1872

JOURNAL XIX

MONDAY, JANUARY 1. Slept not very well last night—awake over an hour—up at 7—dressed with Wm's help as usual[71]—began the New Year with family prayer—Carrie Moulton with us—Mr Lloyd and William constituting rest of family[72]— After breakfast Hardin came in[73]—proposed working W of Brook to which I assented— sent W. to town for Records, Water closet paper, figs &c &c farm horse & wagon— Walked up & down piazza with Carrie—read

---

69. This first entry for Dec. 18 is from a loose sheet at the end of the journal.

70. This second entry for Dec. 18 comes from the diary page with a printed heading for that date. Chase probably made this entry at a later date, basing it, as he did the second entry for Dec. 13 above, on the rough entry which he had written on a separate sheet.

71. The William performing miscellaneous tasks in the entries for Jan. 1, 3, 4, and 7, was William Joice.

72. Caroline C. Moulton, one of Chase's cousins from New England, worked at the Agriculture Department in Washington. David Demarest Lloyd (1851–89), at this time Chase's secretary, later was a newspaper correspondent in Albany and Washington, D.C. He took a position with the *New York Tribune* about Aug. 1872. Moulton to Chase, Nov. 25, 1867, Oct. 14, 1868, Dudley C. Chase to ——, Nov. 28, 1867 (Chase Papers, L.C.); *Wash. Dir. (1871)*, 242; Johnson, *Twentieth Century Biographical Dictionary*, v. 6; Chester McArthur Destler, *Henry Demarest Lloyd and the Empire of Reform* (Philadelphia, 1963), 42, 61–62, 71.

73. Mr. Harden (or Harding) supervised the farm hands at Edgewood from 1870 into early 1872. Wages, [Jan.] 1, 1872, end of Journal XIX; P. E. Jones to Chase, Sept. 30, 1870, Sept. 2, 1871, Chase to Jones, Sept. 26, 1870, Chase to Janet Chase Hoyt, Feb. 4, 1872 (Chase Papers, L.C.).

Woodward, Thompson & Strong opinions on legal tender[74]—dinner at 2 P.M.—to town with Carrie. left her in carriage—at cor. NY Av. & [N.E 2] St— She went to church— I walked to Judge Field's— A. St. E—Judge out—Mrs F receiving with her mother Mrs Swearingen[75] & the two Miss [*illeg.*]—Judge Clifford, Judge Poland, Mr. Brown ([S. P.]) Mr. [*illeg.*], Ex. Sen. Williams & others came in while I was there[76]— Wm came with carriage—I home with him— road very muddy—took forty minutes to get to Edgewood—tea— read & bed abt 10.

TUESDAY, JANUARY 2. Family prayer abt 8—beautiful morning & day—after brkfst to gas house— Mr. Aston said Cementers to come out at noon[77]— Carpenters at work putting up gas house nearly finished— Some talk with Mr. Aston on working of machine—walked with Mr Lloyd along railroad to Bladensburgh road, then with that road & Lincoln Avenue home—wrote opinion partly[78] / dined—resumed opinion—walked with L——: across [brook] in lot— Men clearing briars & burning them and other brush—home abt. 5—tea—resumed opinion—& reading till bed time—retired

---

74. In 1865, in the case *Shollenberger v. Brinton*, the Pennsylvania Supreme Court upheld the validity of the federal legal tender acts. William Strong sided with the majority; George Washington Woodward (1809–75) and James Thompson (1806–74) dissented. Thompson served as a Democratic congressman from Pennsylvania, 1845–51; and as associate justice, 1857–66, and chief justice, 1866–72, of the state's supreme court. *Appletons'*, 6:91, 607; *Bio. Dir. U.S. Cong.*, 1932; Fairman, *Reconstruction and Reunion*, 698–99; *DAB*, 18:153.

75. Virginia Swearingen Field was the wife of Stephen Johnson Field. *DAB*, 6:375.

76. Luke Potter Poland (1815–87), chief justice of Vermont, 1850–65, U.S. senator (Republican), 1865–67, and member of the U.S. House of Representatives, 1867–75; probably Samuel Peters Brown (1816–98), merchant, real estate developer, and member of the District of Columbia Board of Public Works; George Henry Williams (1820–1910), U.S. senator from Oregon, 1865–71, member of the joint high commission negotiating claims against Great Britain in 1871, and, beginning Jan. 10, 1872, attorney general of the U.S. *DAB*, 15:33–34, 20:262–63; *Appletons'*, 6:522; *Nat. Cyc.*, 15:124; James H. Whyte, *The Uncivil War: Washington During the Reconstruction, 1865–1878* (New York, 1958), 106, 164.

77. Probably Albert Aston, first assistant engineer, U.S.N. The new "gas house" was to produce fuel for illumination by heating coal. Edgewood's apparatus may also have combined crude oil with the hot coals. The resulting gas was piped to a water-filled cistern. There it bubbled up into a storage tank, which rose in the cistern as it filled with gas. Leaks in the cistern at Edgewood required repeated cementing and other additional work in Jan. 1872. *Wash. Dir. (1872)*, 58; Chase to Janet Chase Hoyt, Jan. 23, 1872, and "Farm Notes," Mar. 9, 1872 and other dates (Chase Papers, L.C.); Knight, *New Mechanical Dictionary*, 379; Thomas Newbigging and W. T. Fewtrell, eds., *King's Treatise on the Science and Practice of the Manufacture and Distribution of Coal Gas*, 3 vols. (London, 1878–82), 1:25–26, 31–32.

78. For the legal tender cases *Knox v. Lee* and *Parker v. Davis* (see Jan. 15 below).

WEDNESDAY, JANUARY 3. Snowing & ground & trees slightly covered when I rose—usual morning duties—wakeful night—frequent urination say three times—unpleasant dreams—breakfast—beef steak, eggs—hominy—oat meal porridge with [cream]—dry toast—used egg boiler given me by Hoyt for first time[79]—went to gas house—cementers at work—said using   cement—best kind—attributed failure before to frost—talked with machinist about working of machine—said all ready but cement & water—cement should stay one day after put before cistern filled—two days required to fill it—so no gas this week—speak to Mr. Clark abt. wall in gas house[80]— Clark, messenger, called[81]— William went to town on sundry errands— Hubbard & other messengers came out to do sundry work about house[82]—dinner— Prof Henry & Alice Walbridge came[83]— Prof wanted my signature to authority to [ex]change regd. Va Bonds for coupons—[P.] proposed sale fearing repudiation—advised against sacrifice— Walked across brook with Mr L'd[84] to where men at work clearing—talked with them—home abt. 5.15—read papers—tea—settled with Harden & hands for last month—signed checks to pay sundry bills—wrote diary—till 9.30—

THURSDAY, JANUARY 4. Morning as usual—night much as preceding— After bkft William went to town to make purchases— walked with Lloyd reversing day before yesterday's walk— dinner—afternoon walked across brook—men busy clearing away briars &c—wrote on return—tea—read papers / not much

---

79. William Sprague Hoyt (1847–1905), a New York City merchant, married Chase's daughter Janet (Nettie) in Mar. 1871. Hoyt was a second cousin of Kate Chase's husband, William Sprague. *New York Times,* Mar. 24, 1871, Apr. 29, 1905; *Representative Men and Old Families of Rhode Island,* 1:416; Belden and Belden, *So Fell The Angels,* 168–69, 243.

80. Edward Clark (1822–1902), architect of the U.S. Capitol since 1865, designed the gas house and other projects at Edgewood. *Who Was Who,* 1:222; Chase to Clark, Aug. 26, 1871, Aug. 4, 1872, Clark to Chase, Sept. 7, 1871, Aug. 8, 1872 (Chase Papers, L.C.).

81. Henry Clarke served as Chase's messenger and also reported on work at Edgewood during Chase's absences from Washington. Chase to Clarke, Mar. 22, 1871, Clarke to Chase, June–Sept., 1872 (Chase Papers, L.C.).

82. Possibly either Edward Hubbard, a laborer at the U.S. Treasury, or George R. Hubbard or Ozro Hubbard, local messengers. *Wash. Dir. (1872),* 248.

83. Alice Walbridge was a daughter of Helen Chase Walbridge (Chase's sister) and Henry B. Walbridge. Helen Walbridge to Chase, Jan. 26, 1864, H. B. Walbridge to Chase, Dec. 4, 1867 (Chase Papers, L.C.).

84. David Demarest Lloyd.

done today—letter from Jay Cookes have cut off Jany coupons L. Sup. & Miss Bonds & *Feby?* coupons W. & Franklin Bonds[85]—

FRIDAY, JANUARY 5. Morning as usual— After bkfast Clark came[86]—gave him check for $1000—putting house in order much exceeds my expectation but have added many things to original design such as Gas House, more plumbing &c—spoke to him of wall & partition in gas house—walked around place with Lloyd—took an hour—wrote on opinion—dinner—went into town—tried to find Mr. Lewis went on 19th & G St[87]—in vain—altering grade of G so as to make it almost impassable— Went to Cookes—saw Simkins & Gill[88]— Cut off coupons from Telegraph Bonds & Pitts & Cleveland Bond $350 in all—amt of over draft surprised me—where *does* the money go? Called on Adml Porter—told me of Dr. Baxter & his wonderful success in treating his (Adml's) case & Mrs Lenthalls[89]—called Sir Ed Thornton's—not at home— Burchell, for crackers / Ballantynes got "P[ray]ers" & Thermometer[90]— Gov Spragues family not returned—home at 5.40—tea—wrote till 10—bed.

SATURDAY, JANUARY 6. Slept pretty well last night—a pleasant bright cool morning—felt pretty well but not a good walker yet— drank tumbler of Bethesda[91] / duties & brkft as usual / gave Wm

---

85. The Lake Superior and Mississippi Railroad and the Warren and Franklin, a Cooke-controlled railroad in Pennsylvania. These were coupon bonds, on which interest was paid semiannually in exchange for coupons clipped from the bond. Jay Cooke to Chase, Jan. 4, 11, 1872 (Chase Papers, L.C.); Oberholtzer, *Jay Cooke*, 2:72, 93.

This entry, written in ink, is followed by eight lines of very faint writing by Chase in pencil. The passage, a note concerning his time at Royalton Academy as a youth, is only partially legible. Its location in this journal seems to be coincidental, and the passage has not been reproduced here.

86. Edward Clark.

87. Possibly Thomas Lewis, an asphalt contractor. *Wash. Dir. (1872)*, 296.

88. Possibly Fisher A. Simkins and Henry C. Gill, clerks in the U.S. Treasury. *Register of Officers (1865)*, 36, 46; ibid. (1873), 66; *Wash. Dir. (1872)*, 203, 420.

89. Probably the wife of John Lenthall, chief of the Navy Department's bureau of construction and repairs. Lt. Col. Jedediah Hyde Baxter (1837–90) became surgeon general of the U.S. Army in 1890. *Wash. Dir. (1871)*, 202; ibid. (1872), 68; *Nat. Cyc.*, 4:180.

90. N. W. Burchell, a "Dealer in Choice Groceries"; and bookseller and stationer William Ballantyne. Chase's purchase at Ballantyne's was perhaps Christian Karl Josias Bunsen, *Prayers: from the Collection of the Late Baron Bunsen* (London, 1871). Burchell catalog and account, in household account books (Chase Papers, L.C.); *Wash. Dir. (1872)*, 62.

91. Therapeutic water from Bethesda Springs, Waukesha, Wis. Chase had visited these springs the previous summer. Dunglison, *Dictionary of Medical Science*, 1123; Schuckers, *Chase*, 621–22.

January 1872 {667}

$10—Mrs Harden to town with him[92]—bo't Card of her—wrote Cooke abt coupons[93]—walked over hills with L⎯⎯ towards Brentwood—determined to go there & call on Mrs Patterson[94]—very pleasant call—Mrs P⎯⎯ gave account of Mrs Barton Cora Livingston that was[95] & of Dr. Baxter who has treated Adml. Porter's case so well; returned by shorter way making about three miles in all—dined—shortly after Alice Walbridge & Fanny Sprague came out—walked with them over place—men burning brush heaps—back to house / tea—wrote & read on legal tender till near 11—bed.

SUNDAY, JANUARY 7. Morning as usual— Family prayer all present—except the two farm hands[96] / bkft— Capt ⎯⎯ called wishing to borrow a little money—had been burnt out at Chicago &c[97]— Seemed all right tho' a total stranger—lent or rather gave him $5—thought of going to Rock Creek Church—on enquiry of Mr. Harden learned that roads nearly impassable—gave it up & went in town to Dr. Newman. Dr. McCauley preached excellent sermon—now abideth Faith, Hope, Charity &c[98]—Communion—I approached the table for first time in any Church but the Episcopal [&] for first time in many years in any—began the new by renewing open confession of Christ before men—not that I feared to do so before but felt myself such a sinner—now I resolved to go & thank

---

92. The wife of Edgewood's foreman also worked at the estate, 1870–72. She and her husband left Chase's employ by early Feb. 1872. Wages, [Jan.] 1, 1872, Journal XIX; P. E. Jones to Chase, Sept. 30, 1870, Feb. 7, 1871, Chase to Janet Chase Hoyt, Feb. 4, 1872 (Chase Papers, L.C.).

93. Evidently Chase was confused about the Warren and Franklin Railroad bonds. Interest on the bonds' coupons was not payable until Feb. 1, but Cooke & Co. had already credited Chase's account. Cooke to Chase, Jan. 4, 11, 1872 (Chase Papers, L.C.).

94. Elizabeth Pearson Patterson (b. 1810 or after) was the widow of naval officer Daniel Tod Patterson (1786–1839). She resided on property given to her parents by her grandfather Robert Brent, once the mayor of Washington. Myra L. Spaulding, "Dueling in the District of Columbia," *Records of the Columbia Historical Society* 29–30 (1928): 126; Goode, *Capital Losses*, 34–35; *Appletons'*, 4:671.

95. Coralie Livingston Barton. Ruhamah Ludlow Hunt to Chase, Nov. 2, 1871 (Chase Papers, L.C.).

96. William Waters, who worked at Edgewood through Mar. 1872, and Robert Warren, who was discharged in April. Other members of the Edgewood staff in Jan. 1872 were Mr. and Mrs. Harden; Catherine Vaudry; an unidentified cook; and "Fanny," who was likely a chambermaid and may have been related to the Hardens, for she left Edgewood when they did. Wages, [Jan.] 1, 1872, end of Journal XIX; "Farm Notes," Mar.–Apr. 1872, and Chase to Janet Chase Hoyt, Feb. 4, 1872 (Chase Papers, L.C.).

97. The Chicago fire of Oct. 8–9, 1871, killed more than two hundred people and left thousands homeless and destitute. Federal Writers' Project, *Illinois: A Descriptive and Historical Guide* (Chicago, 1939), 37, 200.

98. Possibly William McCauley, who was apparently a theologian at Howard University. The sermon was from 1 Cor. 13:13. *Wash. Dir. (1873)*, 311.

God for the resolution / Went from Church to Governors—Katie & the children had come back yesterday P.M[99] / Home with Mr. Lloyd in carriage—dinner— Katie & children came out with Carrie Moulton— When they had gone, William on box with driver, Miss Fanny Sprague & Alice proposed to walk to town / Mr. Lloyd & I accompanied them to Boundary St[1]—back at 6 about two miles—tea

SUNDAY, JANUARY 14. Walked in town to Church—went first to Katie's—Eliza Whipple met me / arrived last night, well & joyous— heard Dr. Newman—Katie's at Lunch with Eliza Carrie Moulton & Children—

Telegram came to Katie just after I left & also one for me which I did not receive till next morning announcing birth of

Netties baby!

Well—10 lbs—& mother—doing well / Thanks to our Heavenly Father for this mercy—

This is a copy of Hoyts telegram.

New York Jany 14:

Nettie has a big girl born this morning— Both mother & large daughter doing well— Nettie says she looks like you.[2]

W. S. Hoyt

MONDAY, JANUARY 15. Morning as usual—after bkft went to Capitol— Judge Strong read the opinion of majority (five) & I the opinion of the minority (four) on the constitutionality of the legal tender clause in the currency act of 62. Bradley read a separate opinion for & Clifford & Field separate opinions against constitutionality.[3] The opinion of the majority reverses Hepburn v.

---

99. In addition to her son William, Kate Chase Sprague now had a daughter, Ethel Chase Sprague (1869–1936), who became an actress and married Dr. Frank Donaldson of Baltimore. Belden and Belden, *So Fell the Angels*, 241, 351; *New York Times*, Dec. 20, 1936.

1. At the time, Boundary Street (present Florida Avenue) marked the Washington city limits. Keim, *Washington and Its Environs*, 31.

2. William Hoyt's telegram actually had a question mark after the word *you*. The Hoyts named their daughter Janet. Hoyt to Chase, Jan. 14, 1872, Chase to Janet Chase Hoyt, Jan. 23, May 20, 1872 (Chase Papers, L.C.).

3. Despite Chase's desire to leave the question as settled by *Hepburn v. Griswold*, the Supreme Court again took up the legal tender issue in two cases which the court decided together, *William B. Knox v. Phoebe G. Lee and Hugh Lee* and *Thomas H. Parker v. George Davis*. In a decision announced May 1, 1871, the majority overturned the *Hepburn* decision and declared the greenback laws to be constitutional. Chase, Nelson, Clifford, and Field dissented. The court postponed the actual delivery of opinions until

January 1872 { 669 }

Griswold [5] to 3. It is I think a sad day for the contray[4] & for the cause of constitutional government. The consequences of the sanction this day given to irredeemable paper currency may not soon manifest themselves but are sure to come. The only thing I regret in connexion with my administration of the Finances is that I ever expressed even a qualified opinion that the making the United States notes a legal tender was necessary. It was a sad mistake into which I was drawn by my anxiety for the passage of the bill then pending / I regard this as the one blot upon my financial system.[5]

The reading of the opinions took five hours and a half—Field had not concluded when I left the Capitol at half past four. It was past five when I arrived at Edgewood.

[Te]legram from Will— N[etti]e has a girl![6]

TUESDAY, JANUARY 16. Prayer & family prayer as usual— Mrs Parker a poor suitor in the Court of Claims came out to get my *influence* to obtain Government employment for her while waiting the termination of her suit[7]— Could not persuade her that knowing nothing of her qualifications I could not recommend her & that what I would say would not avail her. Finally I promised that Mr. Lloyd should see Mr. Crookshank her attorney[8] & enquire into her case & its prospects & gave her little girls two dollars— Was too impatient with her—

Walked into town—fifty five minutes from my Library to Conference room in Capitol at 2¼ miles. Did not perform my part well in Conference, not having mastered the cases in consequence of time being occupied in preparing opinion in legal tender & property of pardoned persons in Treasury.[9]

Jan. 15, 1872, when the reading of the lengthy opinions in *Knox v. Lee* and *Parker v. Davis* occupied the court's entire day. 12 Wall. 457 (1871); Minutes, Jan. 15, 1872 (Recs. of Supreme Court, Nat. Arch.); Fairman, *Reconstruction and Reunion*, 745–46, 752–63.

4. Chase evidently wrote *contrary*, then altered it without clearly forming *country*.

5. In his opinion in *Hepburn v. Griswold* in 1870, Chase noted that some people who had favored legal tender as a wartime measure had, "since the return of peace, and under the influence of the calmer time, reconsidered their conclusions." 8 Wall. 625 (1870).

6. Refers to the telegram which Chase copied at Jan. 14, above.

7. Possibly Mrs. C. M. Parker, who apparently received an appointment as clerk in the U.S. Treasury. *Wash. Dir. (1872)*, 363.

8. John Cruikshank. Ibid. (1871), 82.

9. *U.S. v. John A. Klein, adm. of Victor F. Wilson* concerned the effects of proclamations of pardon on claims against captured and abandoned property sold by Treasury agents during the Civil War. 13 Wall. 128 (1872); Fairman, *Reconstruction and Reunion*, 843–46.

Called at Mrs Spragues— Letter from Mrs Jones saying Nettie & baby doing well[10]—rode home—walked over brook to see workmen clearing field—slow progress—but probably as good as could be expected—no gas yet—Capt King said this morning that they would *tin* cistern to prevent leak.[11]

Wrote nearly whole of above before I noticed that I was writing under head of Thursday instead of Tuesday[12]

WEDNESDAY, JANUARY 17. Walked into the City—50 minutes from my library to reception room—found Reverdy Johnson there returned from South Carolina— Heard two cases[13]—one involving validity of trial of Stout for murder in Utah—after Court adjourned Porter came up & mentioned conversations with Blaine & Morrill who condemned decision in legal tender case[14]—walked to Katie's— just going out Eliza[15] & she with children / home in carriage—Mr Lloyd with me—grateful letter from Jane Auld—declined Frelinghuysen's invitation to dinner next Friday because of previous engagement with Bristow[16]—letters to McLean,[17] Hamlin & Aspinwall—& by direction of court to Chairman of Judiciary Committee withdrawing consent to opening of library at night to law students[18]—read Taney's opinion in U.S. v. Gordon & in U.S. v Ferreira with note on Yale Todds case—exposition of limits of legislative and judicial power.[19]

---

10. Charlotte Ludlow Jones, Chase's sister-in-law, was visiting Janet Chase Hoyt at this time. Chase to Janet Chase Hoyt, Jan. 23, 1872 (Chase Papers, L.C.).

11. See the description of the Edgewood gas house at Jan. 2, above. James Wilson King (1822–1905) was chief of the navy's bureau of steam engineering, 1869–73. *Nat. Cyc.*, 13:186; *Wash. Dir. (1872)*, 279.

12. Chase wrote this entry on the page intended for Thursday, Jan. 18, and altered the page's printed heading. He changed the heading of the page meant for Jan. 16 as if he intended to write an entry there for Jan. 18, but instead made only a brief note, "See forward." The entry for Jan. 17 is on the correct diary page.

13. *County of Pendleton v. Henry Amy*, concerning coupon bonds issued by a Kentucky county, and *Hosea Stout v. Territory of Utah*. 13 Wall. 297 (1872); 20 L. Ed. 512 (1872).

14. Charles Howell Porter (1833–97), lawyer and Republican congressman from Virginia, 1870–73; James Gillespie Blaine (1830–93), at this time Speaker of the U.S. House of Representatives, later U.S. senator and secretary of state; and probably Lot M. Morrill. *Bio. Dir. U.S. Cong.*, 1662; *DAB*, 2:322–29.

15. Eliza Whipple.

16. At this time, attorney and politician Frederick Theodore Frelinghuysen (1817–85) was a U.S. senator from New Jersey. Benjamin Helm Bristow (1832–96) of Kentucky served as solicitor general of the U.S. from 1870 until Nov. 1872. *DAB*, 3:55–56.

17. Probably Washington McLean.

18. Chase actually wrote to the chairman of the Senate's Library Committee, Lot M. Morrill. Chase to Morrill, Jan. 17, 1872 (Morrill Papers, Maine Hist. Soc.).

19. *Ex parte Gordon* (1862) was an appeal by Nathaniel Gordon, who had been convicted of piracy for transporting slaves. The Supreme Court held that it could not review a circuit court's actions in a criminal case unless the circuit court judges sub-

March 1872

TUESDAY, JANUARY 23. Dinner at Attorney General Williams at 7 o'clock

TUESDAY, JANUARY 30. Dinner at Attorney General Williams'— at 7 P.M.—

SUNDAY, FEBRUARY 11. at church this morning—heard Dr. Newman on the Divine nature of Christ—very good—
lunched at Katie's— She & baby very well[20]—
Met Carrie Moulton, Alice Walbridge; Mr. Lloyd & Lily Walbridge came in with me.[21]
Home at 4—

MONDAY, FEBRUARY 12. at Court 11 [P].M.—leaving met Halstead— Who promised, if he remained, to go out with me on Wednesday—walking down the Avenue encountered Prof Ordronaux & had interesting talk with him[22]— Kate & her children well—& Governor—Lily & Lloyd home with me—
Read & made notes of two cases—read Bryants Iliad 2d Book[23]— bed at 10.
A beautiful day

SUNDAY, MARCH 3. A very inclement day—remained at Edgewood—wrote most of day on matters for court which must be read tomorrow—read Churchman, Methodist & Bible.[24] Exercised only in walking on portico

---

mitted the matter on a certificate of division. The opinion by Chief Justice Roger B. Taney also noted that with the circuit court's transmittal to a marshal of a valid warrant for execution, Gordon's fate had moved outside the judiciary's sphere of action. In *U.S. v. Francis P. Ferreira* (1851), the Supreme Court held that it could not hear an appeal of a ruling made by a federal district judge acting as a claims commissioner. Taney wrote the opinion and appended a long note on *U.S. v. Yale Todd*, decided in 1794, which also involved U.S. judges acting as claims commissioners. 1 Black 503 (1862); *U.S. v. Gordon*, Fed. Case No. 15,231; 13 How. 40 (1851).

20. In Feb. 1872 and Nov. 1873, Kate Chase Sprague bore daughters, her third and fourth children, named Portia Chase Sprague and Katherine (Kitty) Sprague. Alice Hunt Sokoloff cited evidence that Kitty was the girl born on Feb. 2, 1872, although earlier biographers of Kate Chase named Portia as the child born in 1872. Chase to Janet Chase Hoyt, Feb. 4, 1872 (Chase Papers, L.C.); Sokoloff, *Kate Chase*, 200, 304; Belden and Belden, *So Fell the Angels*, 262; Phelps, *Kate Chase*, 237.

21. Lillie Walbridge was a daughter of Chase's sister Helen Chase Walbridge. Helen Walbridge to Chase, Jan. 26, 1864, H. B. Walbridge to Chase, Dec. 4, 1867 (Chase Papers, L.C.).

22. John Ordronaux, M.D. (1830–1908) taught physiology and medical jurisprudence at Columbia College. *DAB*, 14:50–51; *Wash. Dir. (1872)*, 543.

23. *The Iliad of Homer. Translated into English Blank Verse by William Cullen Bryant*, 2 vols. (Boston, 1870).

24. The *Churchman* and the *Methodist* were Protestant Episcopal and Methodist Episcopal periodicals published in Hartford, Conn., and New York City, respectively. Mott, *American Magazines*, 2:67, 69–70.

MONDAY, MARCH 4. Went to Capitol—read dissent in barley case to Clifford & Field who approved & concurred[25]—dissented alone in habeas corpus case[26]—came home immediately after seeing Dr. Baxter at Mrs Spragues— Dr. said & I felt much better during last week—pricked shoulder[27]—ordered continuance of prescription till next Monday when he will call again—

Brought Shuckers & Baugh to Edgd[28]—

TUESDAY, MARCH 5. Schuckers walked in with Lloyd—I rode in with Alice W—— & Mr Baugh—

TUESDAY, APRIL 16. Walked to New York[29]—muddy having rained hard last night

Court— Afterward K. V. Whaley, Wirt &c. called[30]—gave favorable accts of prospects of Parkersburgh conference[31]— J. M. Gitchell from San F.—— came out to pass night[32]—

---

25. *The Vaughan and Telegraph* case involved a cargo of barley lost in a steamship collision. Chase, Clifford, and Field dissented because the circuit court's decree had specified the value of the lost cargo in legal tender notes at the time of the loss in 1864. The dissenters argued that the appreciation in value of legal tender notes relative to gold since 1864 "gives the libelants almost double indemnity." 14 Wall. 258 (1872).

26. The majority opinion in *Tarble's Case*, written by Stephen J. Field, held that a Wisconsin court commissioner could not use a writ of habeas corpus to free a young man from the custody of federal recruiting officers. In his dissent, Chase declared that the Supreme Court's restrictions would "deny the right to protect the citizen by habeas corpus against arbitrary imprisonment in a large class of cases." Chase explained later that his state of health prevented him from writing as full an opinion as he would have liked. 13 Wall. 397, 413 (1872); Fairman, *Reconstruction and Reunion*, 1421–26; Warden, *Chase*, 799.

27. Acupuncture was known in the United States at the time as a treatment "in obstinate rheumatic affections." See Apr. 17 below also. Dunglison, *Dictionary of Medical Science*, 18.

28. That is, "Edgewood." Charles C. Baugh was a clerk in the first auditor's office of the U.S. Treasury. *Wash. Dir. (1872)*, 67.

29. New York Avenue.

30. Kellian Van Rensalear Whaley (1821–76), a former congressman from West Virginia, and William C. Wirt. *Bio. Dir. U.S. Cong.*, 2031.

31. "At a conference of leading liberal republicans and liberal democrats held in Parkersburg, West Virginia . . . it was resolved that the liberal republicans of West Virginia who may attend the Cincinnati liberal republican convention, be requested to use all honorable means to secure the nomination of Chief Justice Chase to the Presidency." Washington *Evening Star*, Apr. 19, 1872.

32. Chase's friend James M. Gitchell moved from Cincinnati to San Francisco in 1860 and pursued both government positions and business interests. Gitchell to Chase, Nov. 20, 1860, May 25, 1861, Mar. 31, 1864 (Chase Papers, L.C.); *Register of Officers (1865)*, 119.

April 1872 { 673 }

Henderson & Mrs H—— called—Mr. Stanbery also[33]—
Wrote opinion in O'Dowd vs Russell[34] / Letters to Long, Church & Thomas[35]

WEDNESDAY, APRIL 17. Walked to N St with Gitchell, who withdrew application for Register not being resident of the District—in Court heard close of argument in preemption Case   v Joy[36]— Huntington's death suggested in Texas case & postponed till tomorrow morning[37]—letters from Nettie & Bannister enclosing $90 rent—walked from Court with Amasa Walker[38]—home alone from Katies where Dr. Baxter applied needles—found Wm Wirt & W. W. Wilson waiting for me, Mr. Jones & Mr   also[39]—Mr. B to put in drive well[40]—dinner—wrote short opinion in Germain v   & read some cases[41]—bed at 10

33. Cincinnati attorney Henry Stanbery (1803–81), former attorney general of the U.S., 1866–68, and chief counsel for Andrew Johnson during the latter's impeachment trial; and possibly John Brooks Henderson and his wife Mary Newton Foote Henderson (d. 1931). Mary Henderson was later an imposing figure in Washington society. *DAB*, 17:498–99; Goode, *Capital Losses*, 106–8.

34. *Michael O'Dowd v. Henry F. Russell*. Chase's opinion primarily concerned legal points relating to the case's writ of error. 14 Wall. 402 (1872).

35. To Alexander Long, Chase commented on his decision in *Clinton v. Englebrecht* (see Apr. 20 below) and discussed personal matters and the pending presidential nominations. M. C. C. Church, evidently a lawyer from Parkersburg, W.V., wanted Chase as the presidential nominee of the Liberal Republican party. William B. Thomas distrusted moves to ally liberal Democrats and Republicans. As 1872 wore on, Chase referred to Thomas as one of his "few friends . . . who have never wavered." Chase to Long, Apr. 15, 1872 (Long Papers, Cinc. Hist. Soc.); Church to Chase, Jan. 19, 1872, Chase to Church, Mar. 20, May 10, 1872, Thomas to Chase, Apr. 12, 1872, Chase to J. W. Schuckers, June 24, 1872 (Chase Papers, L.C.); Washington *Evening Star*, May 4, 1872.

36. *Peter F. Holden v. James F. Joy* and *William H. Warner v. Joy* involved disputed land claims relating to treaties with the Cherokee Indians. 17 Wall. 211, 253 (1872).

37. *William S. Huntington's Exrs. and First National Bank of Washington v. Texas; Texas v. Huntington's Exrs. and First National Bank;* and *First National Bank and Huntington's Admrs. et al. v. Texas*. These related cases all involved Texas indemnity bonds. Huntington had been cashier of the First National Bank. On Apr. 18, the administrators of his estate were substituted for him in the suits and the cases were argued. 16 Wall. 402 (1873); 20 Wall. 72 (1874); Minutes, Apr. 18, 1872 (Recs. of Supreme Court, Nat. Arch.); Fairman, *Reconstruction and Reunion*, 650–59.

38. Walker (1799–1875), a Boston merchant, politician, and economist, represented Massachusetts in the U.S. House, 1861–63. *DAB*, 19:338–39.

39. William W. Wilson was a clerk in the U.S. Treasury. Pierepont E. Jones, a clerk in the third auditor's office originally from Essex County, N.Y., helped oversee affairs at Edgewood. *Wash. Dir. (1870)*, 212; ibid. (1871), 381; Jones to Chase, Sept. 23, 30, 1870, and other Chase-Jones correspondence, 1870–72 (Chase Papers, L.C.).

40. Washington contractor A. O. Brummel sank a new well at Edgewood and proposed to build a horse-powered pumping apparatus for it. *Wash. Dir. (1872)*, 99; price list, Apr. 15, 1872, proposal, May 14, 1872 (Chase Papers, L.C.).

41. Chase's opinion dismissed *G. Jules Germain v. James Mason et al.* because the improper official certified the writ of error from the supreme court of Montana Territory. 13 Wall. 654 (1872).

THURSDAY, APRIL 18. Walked with Lloyd—William overtook us at D Street[42]—heard Argument in Texas cases—Casserly began in tax case, Houghton who opened having finished[43]—letter from Lottie[44]—picture, sent in Feby also came / very beautiful, one of Fra Angelico angels[45]—home alone—gave bill for picture—freight [&c]—to William to collect half from Dr. Parker[46] *16.80* = 8.40— Williams[47] took 52 advanced to him from check 90 & returned bal 38 / Advanced to Wm Chase[48] 2—wrote decisions & read law—bed at 10

SATURDAY, APRIL 20. Col Brooks came kindly to give me the benefit of his experience in tree-planting—& directed William[49]—to court—all the time spent in reading opinions only motions & one case disposed— Agreed to pass an hour in conference after adjournment Monday—to Katies at half past three— All well—wrote to Halstead about article in Commercial representing me as unable to attend to duty & sent him opinion in Utah case[50]—home—Lily W. with me—men dug 45 holes for dwarf pears—while at dinner Mullett & Gitchell came[51]— G—— may by sickness of child be compelled to go to S. Fr without going to Cin— M—— promised to

---

42. David Demarest Lloyd and William Joice.

43. *Ira G. French v. Thomas Edwards et al.* stemmed from the sale of a parcel of land in California for unpaid taxes. Both attorneys were from California: Eugene Casserly (1820–83), at this time a Democrat in the U.S. Senate; and Sherman Otis Houghton (1828–1914), a Republican in the House of Representatives. 13 Wall. 506 (1872); Minutes, Apr. 18, 1872; *Appletons'*, 1:553; *Bio. Dir. U.S. Cong.*, 755, 1214.

44. Charlotte Eastman.

45. Guido di Pietri (1387–1455), also known by his monastic name, Giovanni da Fiesole, was an Italian painter whose angelic figures earned him the name of Fra Angelico. Thorne, *Chambers's Biographical Dictionary*, 38.

46. Peter Parker (1804–88) moved to Washington in 1857 after completing a long term of service as a Presbyterian medical missionary and U.S. official in China. He was an active member of the Smithsonian Institution. *DAB*, 14:234–35.

47. Henry Williams did farm work at Edgewood. He had more responsibility than other farm hands and also operated the machinery used to generate illuminating gas. Cash accounts, Journal XIX; "Farm Notes," 1872 (Chase Papers, L.C.).

48. William Chase, no apparent kin to his employer, worked as a farm hand at Edgewood during the spring, and at least through the summer, of 1872. Cash accounts, Journal XIX; "Farm Notes" (Chase Papers, L.C.).

49. William Chase. "Farm Notes," Apr. 20, 1872 (Chase Papers, L.C.).

50. The article in Murat Halstead's *Cincinnati Commercial* had suggested that Chase was "no longer fit for the position of Chief Justice on account of his broken health." On Apr. 15, Chase had delivered the Supreme Court's unanimous opinion in *Jeter Clinton et al. v. Paul Englebrecht et al.* Selection of juries in Utah Territory was at issue in the case. *Cincinnati Commercial*, Apr. 18, 1872; 13 Wall. 434 (1872); Washington *Evening Star*, Apr. 16, 1872.

51. Alfred Bult Mullett (1834–93), supervising architect of the Treasury Department since 1866, had been an assistant to architect Isaiah Rogers of Cincinnati. *Nat. Cyc.*, 27:452; *Register of Officers* (1863), 42.

bring roads before board & to press them—suggested letter about them to him wh. was written— Sundry little matters till bed-time

Pretty well all day—lameness of left arm about the same as usual—evacuation [free]—no med except tonic at lunch—

SUNDAY, APRIL 21. Daily reading of Scriptures & prayer as usual at 7.30— Lily & I went to Metro. Church—Dr Eddy preached excellent sermon on the captivity of the thoughts to the obedience of Christ[52]— Alice & Mr. Lloyd went to Rock Creek Church— After service *we* went to Katie's—saw Carrie Moulton & Susan Walker there—C. M. came out with us— In the afternoon Col. Parsons & Mr. Townsend of Cleveland called[53]—corrected opinion & read account of Wesley[54]—bed at half past ten

Beautiful Spring day—about usual [*illeg.*] & symptoms—

MONDAY, APRIL 22. A bright morning— Sent Alice, Carrie, & Lloyd to city in carriage— Walked in myself, overtook Young Mr. Brooks—interesting talk with him— Opinions read & Casserly concluded his argument[55]—went into conference for an hour—decided Caperton & Texas cases[56]—to Mrs Spragues— William[57] went to Baltimore for her this morning & is not yet returned— So Mr. Lloyd drove Lily & [me] out— Col. Brooks kindly superintending tree planting—beds in garden worked over by Wm Chase— Col B—— dined with us—after dinner Clerk Middleton & Reporter Wallace called[58]—read cases & bed at 11.

Fair day—cool towards evening—felt very well—all seems right except fluttering about heart

TUESDAY, APRIL 23. Walked to town—Wm overtook me near Catholic Church[59]—heard arguments in California Ejectment &

---

52. Thomas Mears Eddy (1823–74) became pastor of the Metropolitan Church, a Methodist Episcopal church on C Street, N.W., in 1872. *Nat. Cyc.*, 11:23–24; Keim, *Washington and Its Environs*, xiv.

53. Perhaps Cleveland merchant and councilman Amos Townsend (1821–95). Van Tassel and Grabowski, *Encyclopedia of Cleveland*, 973.

54. Possibly Luke Tyerman, *The Life and Times of the Rev. John Wesley, M.A., Founder of the Methodists*, 3 vols., (London, 1870).

55. In *French v. Edwards*.

56. *Allen T. Caperton v. William A. Ballard, Admr.*, in which the court decided no "Federal question" was presented; and *Susan A. White et al. v. Francis A. Burnley et al.*, remanded to the U.S. circuit court for the eastern district of Texas for further proceedings. The court did not decide the Texas cases involving Huntington and the First National Bank until 1873. 14 Wall. 238 (1872); Minutes, May 6, 1872 (Recs. of Supreme Court, Nat. Arch.).

57. William Joice.

58. Daniel W. Middleton and John William Wallace.

59. Probably St. Aloysius Roman Catholic Church, I and North Capitol Streets, N.W. William Joice often drove for Chase. Keim, *Washington and Its Environs*, xiii.

20% Ct of Claims cases[60]—home at 3—brought Mr Robinson to Central Avenue— Men had staked grape vines, Wms & W. C.— J. P. plowed[61]— Lloyd went to N. York— Bed after 10 wind SW, Cool—

WEDNESDAY, APRIL 24. Slept well last night—urination moderate rather frequent this morning—slightly costive & palpitation—walked to cemetery gate—rode rest of way—heard Bradley A. C & Phillips in Ins. case[62] & [Gorh]am case, Blake, Gifford & Keller in part[63]—Lincoln, obliged to return to Cin., declined coming out with me[64]— Went to Katie's— Met Hamlin / Showed him letters from Long, Worster, & Halstead[65]—will go to Cincinnati—advised him to see Tisdel[66] / Came home— Saw our men planting trees— [Saul] & his men at work on flower bed &c[67]—dinner / Parsons called—also R. S. Hale & son & brother Matthew,[68] with A. C. Bradley—after they had gone spent some time on Texas case then evening devotions & bed

South wind this morning. Col Brooks came over & advised about planting trees.

60. The court had heard arguments in the California case, *French v. Edwards*, on Apr. 18 and 22 (above). The *Twenty per cent Cases* were suits by the U.S. against George H. Miller and nine other individuals, all on appeal from the Court of Claims. The cases stemmed from an 1867 joint resolution by Congress which granted 20 percent additional pay to certain federal workers in the District of Columbia. 13 Wall. 568 (1872).

61. Henry Williams, William Chase, and John Pendleton, who began work as a farm hand at Edgewood earlier in April. "Farm Notes," Apr. 9, 23, 1872 (Chase Papers, L.C.); cash accounts, end of Journal XIX.

62. *Phoenix Insurance Co. v. Vincent Hamilton et al.* concerned a policy to insure a quantity of stored grain. Philip Phillips (1807–84) of Washington, who had been an Alabama attorney and politician during the 1840s and early 1850s, and Alvin C. Bradley appeared as counsel for opposing sides in the case. 14 Wall. 504 (1872); *Bio. Dir. U.S. Cong.*, 1644.

63. *Gorham Manufacturing Co. v. George C. White* was a patent infringement case. Charles Frederic Blake (1834–81), a specialist in patent law; George Gifford (1842–1924); and Blake's partner Charles M. Keller (d. 1874) were among the attorneys involved with the case. 14 Wall. 511 (1872); *Nat. Cyc.*, 8:40–41; *Who Was Who*, 1:452.

64. Possibly Timothy Danielson Lincoln.

65. Both Alexander Long and J. Rutherford Worster, who was evidently a physician, desired Chase's nomination as the Liberal Republican presidential candidate. Long to Chase, Apr. 22, 1872 (Chase Papers, Hist. Soc. of Pa.); Worster to Chase, Apr. 7, Aug. 11, 1872 (Chase Papers, L.C.); Basler, *Collected Works*, 7:416.

66. Willard Parker Tisdel, an acquaintance of Richard C. Parsons, later superintended various steamship companies and in 1884 was appointed U.S. agent to the Congo. *New York Times*, Nov. 4, 1872, Aug. 23, 1884; *Biographical History of Northeastern Ohio* . . . (Chicago, 1893), 490.

67. John Saul operated a nursery in Washington. *Wash. Dir. (1872)*, 405; receipts, Apr. 27, 1870, Apr. 26, 1872 (Chase Papers, L.C.).

68. Albany, N.Y., attorney Robert Safford Hale (1822–81) was agent and counsel of the U.S. before the American-British Mixed Claims Commission, 1871–73. Matthew Hale (1829–97) was an attorney and former New York state legislator. *DAB*, 8:110–11; Johnson, *Twentieth Century Biographical Dictionary*, v. 5.

THURSDAY, APRIL 25. At Capitol—heard Admiralty—stopped Benedict[69]—home to dinner—went to Katies party—saw many acquaintances & some friends— Katie & the Governor looked extremely well & very happy— Katie seemed object of general admiration—took Mrs Schurz in to supper[70]— Goldsborough came home with me[71]—bed about half past twelve

FRIDAY, APRIL 26. Goldsborough & Gen T. K. Smith at breakfast— They went to town together at 9— Went to Capitol—heard unimportant motion, & for Mandamus to Court of Claims[72]— Went into Conference about 12— Disposed of all questions except in three cases & two motions— Adjourned to Monday—letter from Lloyd— Inconvenient for Barney to go to Cin but will if you wish[73]— Telegraphed ans yes— Telegram from Hoyt "Nettie will go to Washn on Monday"— Ansd "Will be joyfully welcomed &c". Came out about 3.25— Col. B―― here superintending planting in quincunx—gave me 3 flowering peach trees which I planted—sold me 30 peachtrees at 20 c per living peach

SATURDAY, APRIL 27. [In] country all day— Col Brooks called & assisted in planting trees purchased of him and Bartlett pears of Saul—walked home with him—note from Tisdel enclosing one from Wiegel asking money—ansd Tisdel Dont care for money but wont depart from principle cant seek must be sought

SUNDAY, APRIL 28. At Metropolitan heard Dr. ―― witnessed baptism of Kodama, Japanese law student under Judge Fisher[74]— home—Parsons & Judge & Mrs Miller called[75]—

69. Admiralty law expert Erastus Cornelius Benedict (1800–1880), appearing in *Steamtug R. L. Mabey v. Joshua Atkins and Ship Helen R. Cooper.* 14 Wall. 204 (1872); *DAB*, 2:176–77.
70. Margarethe Meyer Schurz (c. 1833–76), daughter of a Hamburg merchant, married Carl Schurz in 1852. Hans L. Trefousse, *Carl Schurz: A Biography* (Knoxville, 1982), 39–42, 227.
71. Probably Edward Y. Goldsborough.
72. *Ex parte in the matter of the United States,* 16 Wall. 699 (1872).
73. Hiram Barney believed that the Liberal Republican convention at Cincinnati would nominate Chase for president if satisfied with the state of his health. M. C. C. Church to Chase, Apr. 4, 1872 (Chase Papers, L.C.).
74. Ohio native Stephen Mason Merrill, D.D. (1825–1905), elected a Methodist bishop in 1872, delivered the sermon at Washington's Metropolitan Church. Kodama studied under George Purnell Fisher (1817–99), Unionist congressman from Delaware, 1861–63; justice on the supreme court of Washington, D.C., 1863–70; and U.S. attorney for D.C., 1870–75. After baptism, Kodama assumed the Christian name of John Phillip. *Bio. Dir. U.S. Cong.,* 999; *DAB*, 6:408–9, 12:565–66; Washington *Evening Star,* Apr. 29, 1872.
75. Samuel Freeman Miller and Elizabeth Winter Reeves Miller.

MONDAY, APRIL 29. At Conference—disposed of one case—passed to Adjourned term enforcement law case & Carskadon case[76]—home—to town to meet Nettie who with Hoyt & baby & nurses came 5. 5 PM—dined at Katie's— Sent letter to Mr. Church at Cin by Col Pearce of S.C.[77]—home abt 9.

TUESDAY, APRIL 30. In country all day— Nettie &c came about noon— Katie & children also—all lunched together—pleasant reunion— Katie brot telegrams from Ashley & Lloyd[78]—declined adding any thing to what had been already said to Church— Howard called having also received tel from A[79]— Told him to [refer] Ashley to Church— Hoyt left after dinner—

WEDNESDAY, MAY 1. Went in town with Nettie—called at Judge Swayne's—he starts for Europe tonight—had a pleasant call—saw him & Mrs S―― & bade him a cordial goodbye— Called on Mrs Barton & the Misses Hunt[80]— Mrs B―― said Randall Hunt to be Gov. of La—hope it may be so—went to Katies / brot Willie & little misses, & Albert to Edgewood & all, save I, went a maying[81]— Katie came back early quite unwell & went home—others came later—dinner—

Digging drive well— Wms & Pendleton hauling manure— Chase working garden[82]—

---

76. In *John T. Pierce et al. v. James Carskadon*, the court considered whether a wartime act of the state of West Virginia constituted a bill of attainder that deprived persons affiliated with the Confederacy of due process and equal protection under the law. 16 Wall. 234 (1873).

77. Likely S. A. Pierce, who was chosen on May 3 to represent South Carolina on the national executive committee of the Liberal Republican party. M. C. C. Church was the representative from West Virginia. Washington *Evening Star*, May 4, 1872.

78. James M. Ashley promoted the Liberal Republican party during the spring of 1872. Horowitz, *Great Impeacher*, 164–65.

79. Probably Republican partisan James Quay Howard (1837–1912), a lawyer who edited the *Ohio State Journal*, 1867–71, and held various newspaper and government positions. *Who Was Who*, 1:593; *New York Times*, Nov. 17, 1912; Chase to Howard, Aug. 11, 1867 (Chase Papers, L.C.).

80. Coralie Livingston Barton was visiting Washington with Louise and Julia Hunt, nieces of Randall Hunt and Ruhamah Ludlow Hunt. Ruhamah Ludlow Hunt to Chase, Nov. 2, 1871 (Chase Papers, L.C.).

81. Kate Chase Sprague's children and W. Albert Wells (b. ca. 1849), who was in Chase's employ from at least 1866. Chase note, Sept. 15, 1866, Wells receipt, Apr. 2, 1869, Chase-Wells account, Apr. 2, 1869 (Chase Papers, L.C.); memorandum book, 1864–69 (Chase Papers, Hist. Soc. of Pa.), 179.

82. William Chase, the farm hand. Henry Williams and John Pendleton took six barrels of "Petroleum"—probably oily by-product from the Edgewood gas house—to Georgetown for sale, and returned with "one load of manure from the Capitol."

May 1872   { 679 }

FRIDAY, MAY 3. Went to town—found Katie much better—Nettie & Lily[83] went with me—lunched at Governors—news of Greeley's nomination at Cincinnati—Amasa S—— & Mr. Harris at lunch[84]—home—wells in progress— Col. Brooks came & Mr. Jones[85]—looked at well, vineyard, garden & orchard—Chase who went for family this morning not returned— Col. B—— staid to dinner— [*illeg.*] killed by Dash—who whipped & tied—

SATURDAY, MAY 4. To Katies with Lillie after writing congratulations to Greeley—found them at breakfast / Hoyt had come—with Nettie, Lily & husband to Talla[poosa][86]—Admrl & Mrs Goldsborough—excursion party to Mt Vernon

SUNDAY, MAY 5. To church walked with Lily & Alice[87]—Rock Creek—woodland carpeted with beautiful flowers—communion—Nettie, her husband, Lily, Alice & I kneeling at the same table—oh what a precious Savior—went to Katies— After dinner she had a chill—came out to Edgewood—Nettie, Will, baby & nurses soon followed—& with little Willie passed the night with me[88]

MONDAY, MAY 6. To Capitol— Judges read opinions—Clifford very long[89]—I nothing but unimportant—lunched at Katies—home—Carpenter & Mrs C—— Judge & Mrs McArthur[90]—called—

Edgewood's fertilizer came from stables at the Capitol building. "Farm Notes," May 1, 1872 (Chase Papers, L.C.); P. E. Jones to Chase, Feb. 7, 1871, H. Clarke to Chase, Aug. 29, 1872 (Chase Papers, L.C.).
   83. Lillie Walbridge.
   84. Amasa Sprague and, likely, Edward Harris. The Liberal Republican party nominated Horace Greeley for president on May 3. Chase placed a distant third in the deciding ballot. James Parton, *The Life of Horace Greeley, Editor of "The New-York Tribune," from his Birth to the Present Time* (Boston, 1872), 539–48.
   85. Pierepont E. Jones
   86. Apparently the USS *Tallapoosa*, a sidewheel steamer. "Husband" refers to William S. Hoyt. *ORN*, ser. 2, v. 1:220.
   87. Lillie and Alice Walbridge.
   88. "Will" means William S. Hoyt; "little Willie" was Kate Chase Sprague's son, William.
   89. Nathan Clifford delivered opinions in fourteen cases, including the ten *Twenty per cent Cases*. Minutes, May 6, 1872 (Recs. of Supreme Court, Nat. Arch.).
   90. Attorney Matthew Hale Carpenter (1824–81), U.S. senator from Wisconsin, 1869–75, married Caroline Dillingham in 1855. Arthur McArthur (1815–96), as-

Evening rode to town with Lily to see & bid good bye to Will & Nettie who return to New York in morning—home 10.30 & bed Col Brooks kindly attended to trees today

TUESDAY, MAY 7. Called with Lily at Mrs Woods—saw the two young ladies—at Mr. Robinson's—saw him & Mrs R—walked through wood to Soldiers Home—saw Mrs Pitcher & General[91] / [home]—going to Mrs Wood overtaken by Dr. Wines[92] and Mrs Barton who promised to call at Edgewood tomorrow & bring Misses Hunt—

SATURDAY, MAY 11. My old friend Plumley came just as we were going to breakfast & stayed till after dinner[93]—walked with me over place—across brook where Cook digging up stumps[94]—nearly finished— Noticed growths—peaches about the size of large peas—gooseberries do—at dinner now for several days have had peas & asparagus from Norfolk—took Plumley to town called on Mrs Gen Sherman & young ladies[95]—left cards with Judge Bartley & Sen. Sherman / called at Katies saw nobody but Gov. & baby. home—after tea went to Middletons—saw ladies & son—learned that contracts for road wd be given out tomorrow & central avenue adopted as public road & to be improved—home about 9.
Very dry weather—ploughed under rye in orchard—watered plants

SUNDAY, MAY 12. To Rock Creek Church—Mr. Buck preached[96]—Col Parsons called in afternoon / read Churchman

---

sociate justice of the supreme court of Washington, D.C., 1870–87, was married twice, first to Aurelia Belcher and second to the widow of Benjamin Hopkins. *DAB*, 3:512–13; *Appletons'*, 4:72; *Nat. Cyc.*, 13:477.

91. Brig. Gen. Thomas Gamble Pitcher (1824–95), governor of the Soldiers' Home, 1871–77, and his wife. *Nat. Cyc.*, 13:420–21.

92. Educator and prison reformer Enoch Cobb Wines (1806–79). *DAB*, 20:385–86.

93. Alexander R. Plumley.

94. Cook evidently was a temporary laborer employed when extra work was needed around the estate. Cash accounts, Mar., Apr., June 1872, memorandum, May 24, 1872, Journal XIX; Henry Clarke to Chase, Aug. 29, 1872 (Chase Papers, L.C.).

95. Ellen Ewing Sherman (1824–88), daughter of Ohio politician Thomas Ewing, had married her childhood friend William Tecumseh Sherman in 1850. The family, which resided in Washington at this time, included four daughters: Maria Ewing (1851–1913), Mary Elizabeth (1852–1925), Ellen Ewing (1859–1915), and Rachel Ewing (1861–1919). McAllister, *Ellen Ewing*, ix, 8, 62–63, 324, 335, 367–68.

96. The Rev. J. A. Buck was rector of the Rock Creek Protestant Episcopal Church. *Wash. Dir. (1872)*, 542.

TUESDAY, MAY 14. Urine—sp. gr. 10—[b.l.] clear Ct. clear; recent sp. gr. 12 + 2 = 14—bl. clear—Ct. clear

WEDNESDAY, MAY 15. Morning gave directions about fig planting—96 slips recd from Gen. Worthington— Mr Saunders sent out 4 roots[97]—planted north of dining room—also 20 rosebushes in pots— After dinner went to town— Called on Judge Field—explained invitation thro P. Office—asked him to see Senators to which he agreed—went to Katie's & saw them all—what a sweet little creature Ethel is[98]—called at Gov. Swann's & asked him to dinner[99]—he accepted—also at Mrs Mitchells who had sent acceptance[1]—home & tea—sent note to Mr. Robinson who accepted— Note from Judge Magrath [ask]ing invn for Gen Simonton which I sent[2]—bed abt ten

THURSDAY, MAY 16. Wrote to Mrs Barton & Dr. Wines—began introduction to Livingston[3]—played croquet. Lloyd got life of Livingston *pour rien*[4] / lunch—prepared to dinner—guests, Judge Magrath & Col. Simonton S.C.; Senators Thurman, Ransom, Stevenson[5] & Sprague; Reps. Swann & Mitchell;[6] Judge Field; Messrs Robinson & Bright & Phillips[7]—Katie, Lily, Lloyd & I—pleasant dinner—bed at half past ten—

---

97. William Saunders (1822–1900), superintendent of the experimental gardens at the Department of Agriculture. *DAB*, 16:383–84.
98. Ethel Chase Sprague.
99. Thomas Swann, called "Rep." Swann in the entry which follows.
1. Martha Reed Mitchell married Wisconsin businessman and politician Alexander Mitchell in 1841. *DAB*, 13:40.
2. Actually Col. Charles Henry Simonton (1829–1904), a South Carolina politician and former officer of Confederate volunteers. Andrew Gordon Magrath (1813–93), also of South Carolina, had been a U.S. district judge, 1856–60, a Confederate district court judge, 1861–64, and governor of his native state, 1864–65. After the war Magrath lived in Charleston and practiced law. *DAB*, 12:203–4, 17:174–75.
3. Chase requested information for an introduction he was writing for a new edition of Edward Livingston's *A Code of Reform and Prison Discipline: To which is Prefixed an Introductory Report to the Same* (New York, 1872). The National Prison Association sponsored this edition in preparation for a conference to be held in London during the summer of 1872 (see May 18 below). Edward Livingston was Coralie Livingston Barton's father. Enoch C. Wines to C. Barton, May 20, 1872 (Chase Papers, Hist. Soc. of Pa.).
4. "For nothing." The book was Charles Havens Hunt, *Life of Edward Livingston* (New York, 1864).
5. Matt Whitaker Ransom (1826–1904) of North Carolina, a former brigadier general in the Confederate service and recently elected U.S. senator; and John White Stevenson. *DAB*, 15:379.
6. Alexander Mitchell (1817–87), financier and Democratic congressman from Wisconsin, 1871–75. *DAB*, 13:39–40.
7. Probably Jesse David Bright and Philip Phillips.

FRIDAY, MAY 17. Cleaning out Cistern—William went down into it[8]— Evening went to Anniversary of Y.M.C. Asso.—presided— Chapin of Beloit College & Gough spoke—latter wonderful[9]—

SATURDAY, MAY 18. At home all day— Col. Brooks came in morning and looked at trees & gave direction about mulching, cupping and harrowing ground between— Dr Wines at breakfast talking about conference at London / solicitous for my attendance.[10] looked into writings about Napoleon 1st—mixture of great & small, good & evil— Clark[11] sent men to put valve in cistern— Williams[12] bot corn 5 bbls / dinner—Lloyd, Lily and Alice[13]—read Hunts Livingston—bed about 11.
Cloudy, cool, & at night rain—fire in parlor

SUNDAY, MAY 19. Rose at 6 as usual—prayer at 7:30 breakfast at 8—to town at 10 20—at 15th St. Presbyterian Church—Colored— Mr Reves the pastor preached instead of Dr. Garnet, who by injury to arm prevented from coming[14]—good sermon God for us—God with us—God in us—wonderful progress of colored people[—]beautiful church—well dressed congregation—devout & decorous behavior—a representative in Congress from S.C.[15]
Called after service at Gov. Sprague's / All well—home to dinner—nap— Gov. Cooke & Col Magruder called[16]—promised road at once—tea—went to chapel at Soldiers Home—congregation just

---

8. Perhaps William Chase, but more likely Henry Williams, who on other occasions operated the gas-making machinery of which the cistern was a part. "Farm Notes," spring 1872 (Chase Papers, L.C.).
9. The Young Men's Christian Association celebrated its nineteenth anniversary with exercises in the Congregational church at the corner of 10th and G Streets. Congregational clergyman Aaron Lucius Chapin (1817–92), president of Beloit College, and John Bartholomew Gough (1817–86), temperance advocate and orator, addressed the meeting. Washington *Evening Star*, May 18, 1872; *DAB*, 4:12–13, 7:445–46.
10. Enoch Cobb Wines was one of the planners of an international congress which met in London in July 1872 to discuss reforms in correctional institutions. *DAB*, 20:385; *New York Times*, July 22, 1872.
11. Edward Clark.
12. Henry Williams.
13. Again, these were David Demarest Lloyd, Lillie Walbridge, and Alice Walbridge.
14. The Rev. J. B. Reeves was the congregation's pastor. Henry Highland Garnet (1815–82), a clergyman and antislavery leader who escaped from slavery in 1824, had been affiliated with Washington's Fifteenth Street Presbyterian Church since 1864. *Wash. Dir. (1873)*, 333; *DAB*, 7:154–55.
15. Probably Joseph Hayne Rainey (1832–87), a Republican from South Carolina and the nation's first black congressman, 1870–79. *DAB*, 15:327–28.
16. Henry David Cooke and James A. Magruder, treasurer of the board of public works for the District of Columbia. *Wash. Dir. (1872)*, 317.

dispersing as arrived—walked through paths to Mrs Woods—thence rode home—reading & bed

Rain last night & a little in morning cleared after 11—moonlight at night

MONDAY, MAY 20. Carrie and Alice to town with William / wrote letters Nettie, Mrs Eastman—Halstead &c[17]— Col Brooks came in—

WEDNESDAY, MAY 22. Most refreshing though violent & windy rain—beautiful sunset—double rainbow—splendid sky colors—loveliness unsurpassed. Lily & Lloyd & I observed from portico with delight—

THURSDAY, MAY 23. Clarkson Potter called this morning & talked of political situation[18]— Goldsborough, mother & sister came[19]—

SATURDAY, MAY 25. Judge & Mrs Field's note declining invitation to dinner—rode in town—invited Cooke who accepted for self & wife[20]—ordered boots of Richards[21]—rode to Columbian College & invited Welling who declined[22]—[home]—note to Katie authorizing her to bring Tucker[23]—lunch—guest at dinner President & Mrs Grant, Adm'l & Mrs Goldsborough—Iwakura, Kido, Yamagutsi, Yoshida, Mori, Gov. & Mrs Cooke, Mr & Miss & Mrs Goldsborough, Mr. Tucker & Mr Lloyd and Mrs Sprague[24]—[went]

17. Chase informed his daughter that he hoped to attend the London conference on prisons which Enoch C. Wines and others were organizing. To Murat Halstead, Chase wondered how appealing the Democrats would find Horace Greeley as a presidential nominee. Chase to Janet Chase Hoyt, May 20, 1872, Chase to Halstead, May 20, 1872 (Chase Papers, L.C.).

18. Clarkson Nott Potter (1825–82), a son of Episcopal Bishop Alonzo Potter, was a Democratic congressman and attorney from New York. *Appletons'*, 5:86.

19. Edward Y. Goldsborough, Margaret Schley Goldsborough, and Mary C. Goldsborough. They were also the "Mr & Miss & Mrs" Goldsborough of the next entry (May 25), where Chase identified Louis and Elizabeth Wirt Goldsborough as "Adm'l & Mrs." Mary and Margaret Goldsborough stayed at Edgewood for a few days and appear in the entries for May 26–31 as Miss and Mrs. G——. M. C. Goldsborough to Chase, Feb. 7, 1873 (Chase Papers, L.C.).

20. H. D. Cooke and Laura Humphreys Cooke.

21. John H. D. Richards operated a shoe store on Pennsylvania Avenue. *Wash. Dir.* (*1872*), 389.

22. James Clarke Welling (1825–94) was the president of Columbian College, incorporated in 1821, which became George Washington University in 1904. *DAB*, 19:633–34; Federal Writers' Project, *Washington: City and Capital* (Washington, D.C., 1937), 509–13.

23. J. Prentice Tucker.

24. The Iwakura embassy was a large delegation of Japanese officials who visited nations with which Japan had treaties. Members of the group dining at Chase's were: Tomomi Iwakura (b. 1825), vice prime minister and chief of the delegation; Takayossi Kido (c. 1830–77), member of the imperial board of councillors; and Massouka

off very pleasantly—two hours—7.30 to 9.30—guest left by 10.30—bed at 11.

Strawberries & peas from garden—slight rains about 2—cloudy all day—well finished say diggers—told Brummell that I feared water would prove insufficient & not satisfied—new saws came

SUNDAY, MAY 26. To Rock Creek Church with Mrs & Miss G—— after dinner [walk across] brook with Miss G—— Katie [came with] Mr Tucker & took children [home]—walk on portico with Miss [G—— bed] about ten—

Fair weather—no rain—[cherries] ripe—crows & birds plundered greater part—gathered some for Willie & Ethel[25]—

MONDAY, MAY 27. Devoted the whole working time of the day to the completion of the Introduction to the new Edition of the Codes & Introductory Reports of Livingston—

Played croquet against Lloyd & Mary G—— Mrs H. A. Goldsborough[26] & Mrs Ray called—also, later, Mr. Goodloe & Mr Mason from Raleigh—& Mr. Jones[27]

Rains copious but brief—

TUESDAY, MAY 28. Went in town to Bd. of Pub. Works—sprinkles of rain—met Gen Morgan[28]— Clerk said Board met at 4 PM—went to Tophams[29]—looked at carriage dusters & saddles—to Katies & home— Mary G—— with me. found Yoshida & others of his commission waiting to see me—talked with him on resources of Japan—promised letter to Jay Cooke— After dinner Mr. Bristow S.G. with Gen Wilson & Messrs Goldsmidt bankers

---

Yamagutsi (b. ca. 1838), assistant minister of foreign affairs. They were accompanied by Kiyonari Yoshida (b. 1845), assistant minister of finance, and Arinori Mori (b. 1846), chargé d'affaires at Washington. Mori to Hamilton Fish, Feb. 18, 1872 (Notes from Foreign Missions, Gen. Recs. State Dept., Nat. Arch.); Charles Lanman, ed., *The Japanese in America* (New York, 1872), 5–54; Charles Lanman, *Leading Men of Japan: With an Historical Summary of the Empire* (Boston, 1883), 104–7, 115–20, 135–37, 246–50.

25. Chase's grandchildren, William and Ethel Sprague.
26. Apparently the wife of Hugh A. Goldsborough.
27. Daniel Reaves Goodloe; likely William S. Mason (b. ca. 1829), a lawyer and former Unionist who held positions in the Reconstruction government of North Carolina; and probably Pierepont E. Jones. Graf et al., *Papers of Andrew Johnson*, 8:314–15, 463.
28. Probably George Washington Morgan.
29. James S. Topham and Company, sellers of saddles and harnesses. *Wash. Dir.* (*1872*), 465.

from Frankfort [Germany] called[30]—went to town—none of Bd present—saw Carpenter Supt.—advised me to address letter to Board[31]—bot carriage duster at Lutz[32] / home— Hy Goldsboro came[33]—dictated letters to Jay Cooke for Yoshida—& to Bd Pub. Works as advised by Carpenter—reading, talk & bed

Clear after morning sprinkle—garden and trees look well— Mailed copies of Introduction to Dr. Wines & Mrs Barton with notes—

WEDNESDAY, MAY 29. Remained at home morning—read to sleep by Mary G—walked in garden with her & Mrs G—dinner— went to town bid goodbye to Katie & children— Adml. Goldboroughs—Mrs G―― & Mary G―― with me—home / croquet—tea— Gov. Randolph called & talked politics[34]—has conversed with Schurz, Casserly & others— Thinks Greeley cannot be elected—that I can be—has plan for united vote on electoral ticket—thinks I should be nominated at Baltimore by democrats[35]—read—walked on portico with M. G―― bed at 10.

Fair day—

THURSDAY, MAY 30. Went thro' orchard with Mary G―― & cut off dry wood—wrote Nettie & Schuckers / nap & reading—dinner— to town thro Soldiers Home with M. G—saw Gov Sprague—called

---

30. Railroad manager James Harrison Wilson (1837–1925) was a Civil War cavalry commander and a friend of Solicitor General Benjamin Helm Bristow. Marcus Goldschmidt, a financial agent evidently associated with the Frankfurt House of Goldschmidt, may have been one of Chase's German visitors. *DAB*, 20:334–36; McFeely, *Grant*, 408; Oberholtzer, *Jay Cooke*, 2:194–95; Fritz Stern, *Gold and Iron: Bismarck, Bleichroder, and the Building of the German Empire* (New York, 1977), 98.

31. A much criticized five-member governing body directed the Board of Public Works of the District of Columbia and decided on all public improvement projects. Engineer and surveyor Benjamin D. Carpenter was a public works official. Constance McLaughlin Green, *Washington: Village and Capital, 1800–1878* (Princeton, N.J., 1962), 336–46; *Report of the Board of Public Works of the District of Columbia, from its Organization until November 1, 1872*, 42nd Cong., 3rd sess., 1872, H. Ex. Doc. 1, part 6.

32. F. A. Lutz Jr. & Bro., a leather goods establishment on Pennsylvania Avenue. Washington *Evening Star*, May 28, 1872.

33. Evidently Henry H. Goldsborough.

34. Theodore Frelinghuysen Randolph (1816–83), governor of New Jersey since 1868. *Appletons'*, 5:173.

35. The Democrats, with some reluctance, followed the Liberal Republicans and nominated Horace Greeley for president at their convention in Baltimore on July 9. Glyndon G. Van Deusen, *Horace Greeley: Nineteenth-Century Crusader* (Philadelphia, 1953), 409–10.

to enquire for Cox who ill[36]—home—tea—reading—unprofitable tho pleasant day
 Clear & cool weather—gas made[37]—

FRIDAY, MAY 31. Wrote Nettie & Will enclosing check for dividend collected & retained in Feb 598.50 / to Gov. Randolph & Mr Schuckers[38]— Potter came out—thinks Dems will probably take Greeley—Lloyd thinks they wont[39]— Early dinner—went in town with Mrs & Mary G—— who left for home—went to J. C. & Co—deposited refunded income tax, & int on Tel & P. & C. bonds[40]—talked about road— Called on Corcoran & had pleasant interview—just returned from France[41]— Called to enquire for Cox—saw Mori—br'o't Mellen home with me—talk about politics— Alice & Carrie came to tea & Sunday[42]— Mellen went to Cars— reading & talk—retired before ten

SUNDAY, JUNE 2.[43] To Rock Creek Church—Mr Buck— communion—Miss Moulton & Alice W—— with me— Afternoon read Tyerman's Life of Wesley— Wonderful man wonderfully prepared for his great work— Ev'g to Metro. Church— Stranger preached on Faith exemplified by diseased woman who touched hem of Saviors garment[44]—home & bed—
 Parsons about Field, Stockton & others.[45]

---

36. Probably politician and diplomat Samuel Sullivan Cox (1824–89), Democratic congressman from Ohio, 1857–65, and from New York, 1869–73 and later. *Bio. Dir. U.S. Cong.*, 836–37; *DAB*, 4:482–83.

37. See Jan. 2, 1872 (above) for gas production at Edgewood.

38. Chase reported on his travels and expressed his concern over the ill health of Schuckers's wife. Chase to Jacob W. Schuckers, May 31, 1872 (Chase Papers, L.C.).

39. Clarkson Potter and David Demarest Lloyd.

40. Telegraph corporation and "Pittsburgh & Cleveland" (probably Cleveland & Pittsburgh Railroad) bonds. Chase visited the Washington offices of Jay Cooke & Co.

41. William Wilson Corcoran resided in France during the Civil War and took several trips to Europe afterward. Cohen, *Business and Politics*, 207–12.

42. Alice Walbridge and Caroline Moulton.

43. Chase wrote this entry on the page intended for Tuesday, June 4, and changed the page's printed heading. The entry for Monday, June 3, is on the page meant for Sunday, June 2, again with Chase's alteration of the printed heading. He changed the heading of the page originally meant for Monday as if he intended to write an entry for Tuesday there, but the page is blank.

44. The incident is related in Matt. 9:20–22; Mark 5:25–34; Luke 8:43–48.

45. Possibly David Dudley Field, who observed the Liberal Republican convention at Cincinnati after being excluded from the official New York delegation, and John Potter Stockton (1826–1900), a controversial New Jersey Democratic politician and U.S. senator, 1869–75. James G. Blaine, *Twenty Years of Congress* . . . (Norwich, Conn., 1886), 2:521; *DAB*, 18:44–45.

clear day rainless—something costive—walked before tea—met Stevens[46]—

MONDAY, JUNE 3. Remained at home morning—Alice & Mr Lloyd went to town— Col. Brooks called—went through orchard—found plums all dead—most other trees living—employed Cook to spread hay[47]—began mowing— Sumner & Hooper[48] called—talked about political situation—doubtingly—dinner—read a little—long nap—went through fields & garden—read papers &c bed at 11.

Cloudy but no rain—cool— Prob "rain" / Evac. free—weak in morng—stronger toward evening—

Col Brooks—planted Bartletts in stiff clay soil—dug holes 3½ feet in diameter 22–24 in deep—reserved first 10 good soil—took next 12 clay away—filled about 16 inches leaf mould—put bucket water—put in surface mould—planted [trees] 4 or 5 inches below surface—filled with good earth—mulched & watered.

THURSDAY, JUNE 6. To N.Y.—saw Mrs Fish on cars—& talked with her—Col Freyre also who did not recognize me—$2 for carriage to Gramercy Park Hotel[49]—found Katie & children well thanks to God— Mr Field called in evening[50]—thanked for aid in Introduction to Livington which came too late—fatigued & not very well—retired at 9.30

FRIDAY, JUNE 7. Woke feeling better— Gov Randolph & Mr. Lloyd called—say that unwillingness of democrats to take Greeley increases— L—— asked me for names but did not send for any— Gov. R—— promised to call again but did not—

Went with Katie to Hutters—after dinner or lunch went to Linthicums & ordered dress coat[51]—

Rainy & chilly—regular in all respects except frequency in urination—ate perhaps too freely

SATURDAY, JUNE 8. Breakfasted heartily—beef, bread & butter, tea—strawberries—read papers felt chilly & soon had regular

---

46. Possibly B. F. Steven or Stevens, an attorney from Ohio staying in Washington, D.C. List of addresses, Journal XIX.
47. See May 11 above for Cook.
48. Samuel Hooper.
49. The Gramercy Park House, East 20th Street at Gramercy Park. *New York Dir.* (1872), 442.
50. Perhaps Maunsell B. Field.
51. Hutter Brothers, a jewelry store, and William O. Linthicum, a tailor on Broadway. *New York Dir.* (1872), 558, 681.

chills—tried to walk them off—walked 12 squares to 5th. Av. & back by 22 St but with some difficulty—assisted up stairs—vomited strawberries—fever—had sent card to Dr Perry before going out[52]— Mrs Judson came in—landlady[53]—gave me aconite— Katie returned & gave Dr Popes powder—vomited before & in parlor—servant having brot basin—this about 1 P.M. lay down on bed Katies rooms—relief gradually but fever— Mr Barney came about 3—got up & came into parlor— Dr. Perry came— Advised not to go to Pelham as intended at 4.30— Will came[54] but determined not to go— Katie & I exchanged rooms for the night

Clearing but somewhat cloudy weather no rain—

SUNDAY, JUNE 9. Much better this morning—indeed as well as usual except weaker

Dr. Perry came about 12—spoke very encouragingly of my general improvement since under his care a year ago

Missed going to church thro' mistake of time—sent card to Mrs Walters hoping to find & see Gerrit Smith[55]— Soon after he with Mrs W—— & her deafmute daughter, Gertrude came, and after a very pleasant conversation insisted that I should return to Mrs W—— with them & take part of their family dinner & see Mrs Smith[56]

MONDAY, JUNE 10. Barney, A T Stewart, Hoyt called[57] / chills came on as they left and after more severely about 1½ hours & then fever near three hours pretty severe— Dr. Perry called & prescribed—advised not to go to Pelham this P.M.—Katie went with baby

TUESDAY, JUNE 11. Letter from Katie advising to go to Narragansett— Dr. P—— coming in concurred— Wrote notes to Lloyd about [Handy Attny],[58] to Mrs. Barton, declining invitation / to

---

52. John Gardner Perry (c. 1839–1926) graduated from Harvard Medical School in 1863. Chase had been a patient of his since at least 1870. *New York Times*, Dec. 3, 1926; Chase letters to Perry, 1870 (Chase Papers, L.C.).

53. Curtis Judson operated the Gramercy Park House. *New York Dir. (1872)*, 586.

54. William S. Hoyt maintained a residence at Pelham, N.Y. J. Thomas Scharf, *History of Westchester County, New York* . . . (Philadelphia, 1886), 1:708.

55. Ellen Walter, Gerrit Smith's niece and widow of William H. Walter, resided at 60 Clinton Place. *New York Times*, Dec. 29, 1874; *New York Dir. (1872)*, 1194.

56. Ann Carroll Fitzhugh Smith. *DAB*, 17:270.

57. Hiram Barney, William S. Hoyt, and Alexander Turney Stewart (1803–76), a wealthy New York merchant and philanthropist originally from Northern Ireland. *DAB*, 18:3–5.

58. David D. Lloyd, possibly with reference to Mississippi lawyer and former secessionist Alexander Hamilton Handy (1809–83). *DAB*, 8:225.

Wallace about Slave Contract dissent & left for N—— at 12.15.[59]— met Mr Tuck on train[60]—lunch—arrived about 7:30 / rather lonely but beautiful

WEDNESDAY, JUNE 12. Chills & fever came on—chills at 7 30 lasting near two hours then fever about seven hours not quite so severe as last time—telegraphed to Dr. Perry who answered continue drapes[61]—didn't rise all day—

THURSDAY, JUNE 13. Pretty well again but weaker—Katie & children arrived—rose had bathed & dressed & shaved—breakfasted— After lunch walked to beach & by Life Boat House home—counted 19 sail at sea— Towards evening pains in breast bones & spine—

FRIDAY, JUNE 14. Chills came on at 7—lasted an hour and a half—fever till 11.30—weakness & restlessness all day, but good sleep at night—telegraphed Dr. P——

SATURDAY, JUNE 15. Woke feeling pretty well—rose dressed &c as usual—cup of beef tea before rising— Nettie & baby with Will came. breakfast—a little beef steak & rice & cream / cup of tea—felt weaker than heretofore / lay down on lounge—tel. from Dr. P—— advised 2 grains quinine with drops—read & napped—dinner— walked on balcony about 300 feet—felt weak & fatigued / took drops at 5—light pains (wind probably, last night & today, in left bowels. lounge & read OConnells Ireland till 8.15.[62] tea & crackers—

Two passages slight—usual [illeg.] not much appetite but more than gratified—dinner 4 table spoons of soup, a morsel of [illeg.] with spoonful of peas; a spoonful of beer & same of whipped cream; & a cup of tea—

---

59. Before his departure for Narragansett Pier, Chase evidently wrote to Supreme Court reporter John William Wallace about Chase's solitary dissent in *Henry T. Osborn v. Young A. G. Nicholson et al.* and *William White, Sr. v. John R. Hart and William D. Davis.* Both cases, decided Apr. 22, 1872, involved pre–Civil War contracts for the sale of slaves. Chase contended that the Thirteenth and Fourteenth Amendments made such contracts unenforceable under the 1868 constitutions of Arkansas and Georgia. Apparently he did not deliver a detailed opinion; Wallace's printed report of *Osborn v. Nicholson* simply lists five grounds for Chase's dissent. 13 Wall. 646, 654 (1872).

60. At this time, Amos Tuck (1810–79), a former antislavery congressman from New Hampshire, was involved in the development of western railroads. *DAB,* 19:27–28.

61. Perhaps similar to the vapor bath mentioned at June 13, 1870 (above).

62. Possibly either *Ireland and O'Connell. A Historical Sketch of the Condition of the Irish People, before the Commencement of O'Connell's Public Career* . . . , 5 parts, (Edinburgh, 1835); or Daniel O'Connell, *A Memoir on Ireland Native and Saxon.* Vol. 1. *1172– 1660* (Dublin, 1843).

SUNDAY, JUNE 16. Slight chill at 6, lasted about an hour fever till noon, & disquiet & feebleness all day— Nettie & Hoyt & Katie came in occasionally—but little relief

MONDAY, JUNE 17. [*illeg.*] day—wrote a couple of letters, Mayor of Boston[63]—Hotel / took quinine 2 grs every two hours very light diet— Nettie & husband & baby returned to Pelham—evening boat— very weak—no walk

Jubilee at Boston today—I left Washington to attend it as guest of the city intending to take Katie & Nettie with me & Nettie came on fr. Pelham with like intention—really disappointed to be obliged to decline[64]—

TUESDAY, JUNE 18. Thankful so thankful to escape chill & fever today, but very weak—did not rise till late afternoon—bath & dressed—continued quinine—till noon—rode with Katie & Willie through village and over Tower Hill[65]—returned feeling faint & dizzy

WEDNESDAY, JUNE 19. Katie with children went to Boston at seven—rose about noon—no bath—dressed did not shave—rode to Peacedale & left cards with Mr Hazard & for Mr. Lambard—home thro Wakefield—still very feeble—but slight improvement—

THURSDAY, JUNE 20. Rose at 8—took bath—dressed & was shaved—breakfast slight—chewed beef steak & ate a little toast— telegram from Katie urging me to come over—replied not this week tho' free from chill—told her old Buck sick—nothing heard from Governor—walked about ½ mile & then sat on rustic seat observing beautiful scenery & birds & man—went in house a good deal fatigued about 5—slight supper at 7—couple spoonfuls oat meal & cream & half cup of tea—felt a little better but all alone

FRIDAY, JUNE 21. Rose at 10—slept ordinarily well last night— After light breakfast walked to bridge & returned—read till dinner at 2.30—afterwards walked over brook—returned—walked 20 min

---

63. William Gaston (1820–94), Roxbury attorney, Massachusetts politician, mayor of Boston, 1871–72.

64. The World's Peace Jubilee was a musical extravaganza featuring thousands of performers en masse. Chase attended on June 29 (see below). *New York Herald*, June 18, 1872.

65. Tower Hill in South Kingstown, R.I., was both a hamlet and an eminence with a view of seascapes and landscapes. Cole, *Washington and Kent Counties*, 549–53.

very feeble but accomplished [more] than yesterday—read Boswell's Johnson[66] & French Testament—bed at 10
  Slight passage

SATURDAY, JUNE 22. Rose at 8—felt pretty well—weak but not so weak as yesterday—bathed & dressed—breakfasted a little blue fish & an egg—walked to beach & bathing house & home—sitting on rock, bench & rustic seat—out near two hours—read N.Y. Post— failure of conference—good platform drawn by Godwin & naming Adams & Groesbeck—no vote taken on it[67]—letter from Barney covering one from Dr. Perry—Greeley will be endorsed at Baltimore—this best I think—light dinner—walked down lane to [cows]—returned & sat in rustic seats, watching the dogs, the birds, the waves, the landscape till Katie & the children came out 6.30— light tea at 7.30.

SUNDAY, JUNE 23. Pretty well today—read Testament— Governor at home

MONDAY, JUNE 24. Walked on beach to Narrow River & back, an hour & twenty five minutes—a good deal fatigued—rather stronger however—
  read & wrote a little—Mr. Hazard called—going to Newport by new line connecting there with Providence[68]—
  Quite regular except frequent urination

TUESDAY, JUNE 25. Wrote Mrs Barton, D & H. D. Lloyd & Clark[69] / started to walk but turned back by rain

---

66. James Boswell, *The Life of Samuel Johnson, LL.D.* . . . , 2 vols. (London, 1791).

67. Liberal Republicans dissatisfied with the results of the convention that nominated Horace Greeley met in New York on June 20 to consider a new platform and alternative candidates. The "anti-Greeley" elements at this conference, among them Parke Godwin (1816–1904) of the New York *Evening Post*, desired a ticket of diplomat Charles Francis Adams for president and Ohio lawyer William Slocum Groesbeck (1815–97) for vice president. The proposed platform suggested a policy of lenient Reconstruction, respect for individual and states' rights, and a fiscal policy based on hard money, a balanced budget, and "an intelligent and permanent system of taxation." Destler, *Henry Demarest Lloyd*, 60–64; New York *Evening Post*, June 21, 1872; *DAB*, 1:48, 7:351–52, 8:13–14.

68. The Newport-Wickford Railroad, comprised of a branch rail line to Wickford Harbor and a ferry between Wickford and Newport, opened in 1871. Bayles, *History of Newport*, 536; Marion I. Wright and Robert J. Sullivan, *The Rhode Island Atlas*, (Providence, 1982), 204.

69. Probably Henry Clarke. David Demarest Lloyd's elder brother, Henry Demarest Lloyd (1847–1903), gained fame as a muckraking author in the 1880s. Both Lloyds played important roles in the June 20 Liberal Republican conference in New York. *DAB*, 11:331–33; Destler, *Henry Demarest Lloyd*, 60–64.

Tillinghast & Ida[70] came to dinner & Governor got back from Providence—talked of going to Boston, to Mr Wilson's,[71] & to Block Island—

After dinner wrote to Jay Cooke & Co Phila & Wash about collg div & salary & paying int & 1000 on principal of debt.[72] Also to P. E. Jones for news of Edgewood[.]

Gave Albert[73] $5—

Regular except &c

WEDNESDAY, JUNE 26. Gov & Willie to Providence by boat at 6.30 / Rose late at 8—read N.T.[74] & usual prayers / breakfast at 9.15—wrote Mr Barney—

THURSDAY, JUNE 27. Governor & Willie returned afternoon from Providence—rode morning beyond Wakefield—walked before dinner to brook & back—dined about 3—took nap walked down lane & along road to farm house & thence by farm road home—tea—letters from Miss Hunt, Sister Kate, & others[75]—tea—reading & bed— On Katies advice concluded to go to Jubilee at Boston (Governor kindly offering to accompany me) tomorrow—fair today & fog from sea about 6

Ida went to Prov. about 2 P.M.

FRIDAY, JUNE 28. Rose at 5.30—bathed shaved & dressed by 6.45—breakfast in a hurry—left for Kingston about 7—train moving off as arrived—failed to get on board—took freight train to Providence where arrived at ten—to Boston at 12.30 with Gov S—dined at Commonwealth Hotel[76]—nice room—went with Gov Sprague escorted by Mr Richardson, of the Council to Jubilee at 3—Gen & Mrs McCook of Colo. also with us[77]—audience 45.000—

---

70. Probably Ida Nichols.
71. Probably Henry Wilson, of Massachusetts.
72. A few months earlier, the Washington branch of Jay Cooke & Co. had asked Chase for a note of indebtedness of $15,000 to cover a deficit in his account. Jay Cooke & Co. to Chase, Mar. 6, 1872 (Chase Papers, L.C.).
73. Albert Wells.
74. Probably *Nouveau Testament*, since Chase mentioned "French Testament" at June 21 (above).
75. Catherine Ludlow Baker Whiteman and probably Louise or Julia Hunt.
76. At 1697 Washington Street in Boston. King, *King's Hand-Book,* 48.
77. Ohio native Bvt. Maj. Gen. Edward Moody McCook (1833–1909), territorial governor of Colorado, 1869–75, was married first to Mary Thompson McCook of Peoria, Ill., and then to Mary McKenna McCook of Colorado. Johnson, *Twentieth Century Biographical Dictionary,* v. 7.

July 1872 {693}

grand—architecture covering 4 acres—beautiful music, said to be superb— Met Gen & Mrs McDowell[78] & Col & Miss Haven, & engaged to go to Beverly Farms tomorrow[79]—
Returned to Hotel— Gov. to Providence after tea—

SATURDAY, JUNE 29. To Jubliee with Mayor Gaston & one of City Council—Hannah Tucker with me—met Gen McDowell Col Haven & others—missed hearing Anvil chorus to catch cars for Beverly Farms[80]—kind welcome from Mr. Haven[81]—

SUNDAY, JUNE 30. At Mr. Havens all day—evg Mr. Rantoul and Mr. Bartlett called[82]

MONDAY, JULY 1. Gen McDowell & family[83] left for Halifax early in morning & soon after Col. Haven & his father for the City— I went to Cherry Hill—cordial welcome from my old friend Waters & his neice Louise Wilson / offered to send me an Aldeney Cow in fall which I gladly accepted—returned to Mr. Haven's— Mr. Greene of the Post[84] & Mr. Bartlett came to dinner—Mr. G—— accepts Greeley—Mr. B—— is opposed—Mr H—— non committal but I think favors him

Mr Hooper & his brother the Doctor whose daughter Henry Adams married a few days ago called[85]— Hooper seemed uncertain as to Sumner's course & did not express his own opinion— Seemed pretty well over his recent illness

TUESDAY, JULY 2. To Boston at 10 A.M. with Mr Haven / rooms at Commonweath House as before

78. Irvin and Helen McDowell.
79. Summer residents had purchased former farm lands adjacent to the sea in Beverly. Loring, "Earliest Summer Residents," 193.
80. "The Star-Spangled Banner" and Richard Wagner's "Anvil Chorus," accompanied by "plenty of harmonious noise," were among the highlights of the World's Peace Jubilee. *New York Herald*, June 18, 1872.
81. Franklin Haven, Sr.
82. Robert Samuel Rantoul and likely Sidney Bartlett.
83. Irvin and Helen McDowell had three children: Helen E., Eliza, and Henry Burden McDowell. *Nat. Cyc.*, 4:50.
84. Charles Gordon Greene (1804–86) had founded the *Boston Morning Post* in 1831. *Appletons'*, 2:754.
85. The daughter of Robert and Ellen Sturgis Hooper, Marian ("Clover") Hooper (1843–85) belonged to a circle of New England intellectuals and became a photographer. She married historian and author Henry Brooks Adams (1838–1918) on June 27, 1872. At the time, Adams taught at Harvard and edited the *North American Review*. James et al., *Notable American Women*, 1:15–16; *DAB*, 1:61–67.

WEDNESDAY, JULY 3. To Newport by Old Colony Road at 8.30 / Gov Lawrence met me at Depot[86]—lunch with him—found that he had invited some friends to dine with me

FRIDAY, JULY 12. Better this morning—brkfast at 8—took 1 gr quinine every 2 hours—wrote Barney Parsons & Lloyd with Big letters to L[87]—read Memoirs of Brougham[88]—dined at 2.15—pd barber George Thompson $2 for 2 visits & 3 for work to come—last quinine pill at 9.
Cit. of Mag. operated in night about one freely[89]—

SATURDAY, JULY 13. Rose after disturbed sleep—bathed & put on underclothes & lay down again about 8 having taken [pair] goblets of Bethesda water—dressed at ten & was shaved—read papers & letters—walked on portico—cool—dined small steak, toast dry & oatmeal—quinine at 12 & 2—

TUESDAY, JULY 23. Talk weak & feeble—made no entries

THURSDAY, JULY 25. Stebbins & Tucker came from Boston by Newport boat[90]

FRIDAY, JULY 26. Tucker, & his two children & Eliza[91] left by Evening Stage for Kingston & Boston
Eliza has been a comfort to me & I am to follow to Northwood if suff'ly recovered—but not well enough to go to Saratoga &c with Katie & Governor—

---

86. In the early 1850s, William Beach Lawrence (1800–1881) of Newport, an authority on international law, had been lieutenant governor and acting governor of Rhode Island. *DAB*, 11:53.
87. To Hiram Barney, Chase reviewed his health, exhorted Barney to visit Narragansett, and stated that Horace Greeley "will make an excellent President." In his letter to Richard C. Parsons, Chase discussed politics and announced: "I shall vote for Greeley." Chase to Barney, July 12, 1872, and to Parsons, same date (Chase Papers, Hist. Soc. of Pa.).
88. Henry Lord Brougham, *Memoirs of the Public Life of Lord Brougham* (London, 1840).
89. Citrate of magnesium (magnesium salts used as a laxative).
90. Josiah Prentice Tucker and Henry Stebbins of Boston, who had married Chase's niece Alice Nora Skinner Stebbins, a daughter of Chase's sister Janette Logan Chase Skinner and Josiah K. Skinner. Alice Stebbins to Chase, May 6, 1873 (Chase Papers, L.C.); Schuckers, *Chase*, 623; James Ralston Skinner to Chase, Sept. 1, 1847, and "Family Memoranda" (Chase Papers, L.C.).
91. Eliza Chase Whipple. Josiah Prentice and Hannah Tucker apparently had two daughters, Alice and Winifred. Aug. 26, 1872, below; Hannah Tucker to Chase, Sept. 23, 1872 (Chase Papers, L.C.).

July 1872 {695}

MONDAY, JULY 29. Last night or this morning singular dream which I related to Doctor[92] / Lincoln—Davis—last battle—D—— beaten & prisoner—L resigned—D—— [fine] President—Congress met & [only 11] members of Conf. Cong—Constitution amended & slavery abolished—Suffrage made universal—Davis resigned—Lincoln elected / Universal Amnesty—Members of Congress elected in all [the] insurgent states—general harmony & reconciliation—finis—

Nash (Job M.) formerly of Zanesville, then of Cincinatti, now of New York, called[93]—goes strong for Greeley—

Pierce of Boston called[94]—talk of things old & recent—for Grant—but not strong / passed night[95]

TUESDAY, JULY 30. No passage yesterday—slept pretty well—night urine pint & ½

Bath—half dressed—returned to bed after Bethesda water & broth—Doctor advised Citrate

WEDNESDAY, JULY 31. Full dressed after bath—Bethesda & bkfast—before bkfast Dr P—— came—advd Aperient—took it—

Pierce left.

Dinner—Steak & beef tea— Grapes & Pear.

Katie had Clam bake in bowling Alley[96]— Ate piece of Watermelon—very good—just tasted Indian Pudding

K—— invited Japanese by telegram & letter to Mr. Mori.

Governor came bringing Mr. Lambard & Sumner's Letter to Colored People advising them to vote for Greeley[97]—read it—strong—must have great influence— Gov. expects Greeley here—

Walk before dinner in lane to opposite gates—after dinner to Boston neck road—before tea ride with Stebbins round by Tucker's old place—beautiful drive

Tea—broth—

Bed at nine

92. John G. Perry, who had visited Chase at Narragansett on at least one other occasion. July 31, below; Chase to Perry, Nov. 29, 1870 (Chase Papers, L.C.).

93. Job M. Nash, a wholesale liquor merchant, worked out of Cincinnati for about a decade. *Cinc. Dir. (1857)*, 207; ibid. (1860), 135, 232; ibid. (1867), 366.

94. Edward Lillie Pierce.

95. At the beginning of this entry Chase wrote, then struck through, text very similar to what he wrote as his entry for July 30. If the canceled text at July 29 is the false start of an entry intended for July 30, Chase wrote his entry for July 29, including the account of his "singular dream," no earlier than July 30.

96. This bowling alley evidently was on the grounds of the Sprague home at Narragansett. Janet Chase to Chase, Aug. 26, 1865 (Chase Papers, L.C.).

97. A copy of Sumner's letter, dated July 29, 1872, appears in *Charles Sumner: His Complete Works*, 20 vols. (Boston, 1900), 20:173–95.

Tarrant's operated an hour after taken in morning—felt decidedly better during day but still weak very

THURSDAY, AUGUST 1. Full dressed—after bath—Bethesda two goblets as usual for last six or eight days—bkfast—beef steak—dry toast & broth— Dr. came—advised Citrate in [hour] / talk about diet, made notes[98]—took citrate

FRIDAY, AUGUST 2. Same as yesterday but Doctor did not come

MONDAY, AUGUST 5. Went down to breakfast for first time for two weeks & more—took a little blue fish, dry toast & chicken broth— Mr Greeley at breakfast[99]— Mr Hazard came in to invite G & us to dinner which of course declined— Hoyt took photos—one of G & me & single one of me— G & Gov S went off by 9.30 boat— Ralston Skinner & I walked—farm road to public road & through lane home—took citrate—regulation dinner—read Sir Hy Holland[1]— Nettie & her husband & baby went home by P.M. train & boat—walk to beach & bath house—broth & tea—newspaper & bed between 9 & 10

Two passages—walked more & on the whole felt better than any day yet tho' far from well—Dr. P says continue diet &c for the present

Gov. Lawrence & Judge Potter & sister[2] called

SUNDAY, AUGUST 18. Walked a mile to Church Congl— Mr Wiggin preached an excellent conversational sermon[3]—rode home— read Testament—

WEDNESDAY, AUGUST 21. A violent rainstorm & high wind— Chimney blown down over my room—pane of glass broken—

---

98. Chase made notes concerning his health and diet, one of them dated Aug. 1, 1872, on memorandum pages at the end of the journal.
99. Horace Greeley had just begun a campaign speaking tour. William Harlan Hale, *Horace Greeley: Voice of the People* (New York, 1950), 341–44.
1. Henry Holland, *Recollections of Past Life* . . . (London, 1872); or perhaps a review of the book which appeared in the *Edinburgh Review* 276 (Apr. 1872): 163–76.
2. Mary Elizabeth Potter.
3. Chase visited J. Prentice Tucker and his family in a small cottage near Northwood, N.H., from Aug. 10 to the beginning of Sept. Henry Batchelder Wiggin (1813–90) preached and taught in Kentucky before he returned to his native Northwood. Chase to Richard C. Parsons, Aug. 13, 1872 (Chase Papers, Hist. Soc. of Pa.); Chapman, *Sketches of the Alumni*, 299; Emerson, *General Catalogue*, 255.

August 1872 {697}

read Life of Greeley during day[4]—rain ceased toward night & walked thro pines 1½ miles

Telegram from Katie—going home with Governor—send William with Willie to Boston[5] to come to Narragansett on Saturday with Mr Stebbins

THURSDAY, AUGUST 22.[6] Rose as usual—duties as usual rode with Eliza short ride—ate peach pear & figs—towards evening walked with Hannah to Durgin Place & back, 2 miles & a little more[7]—

read Parton's Greeley

Pleasant day—fair weather

FRIDAY, AUGUST 23. Took Willie to depot at Epsom / left William with him to go to Boston—Eliza went with me—took near three hours—distance 16 miles—hearty dinner—fruit grapes pears & figs and peach during morning—Rockbridge Alum water after each meal[8]

read Greeley

William returned about 9 P.M. having left Willie with Mr. Tucker[9]

Two evacuations 1st slight 2d after dinner & copious

Weather clear & pleasant

SATURDAY, AUGUST 24. Short walk before bkft— After long walk, round by school house, pond, mills, home—never walked that way—scenery beautiful—unexpectedly long—over 3 miles—took 2 hours / Evening rode with Hannah to Epsom for Prentice—home at 8.

Evacuation slight morng / do before bed[10]—

Pleasant & fair—but clouded towards evening

---

4. Parton, *Life of Horace Greeley.*
5. William Joice, escorting Chase's grandson, the younger William Sprague. See Aug. 23 below.
6. Chase wrote the entry for Aug. 22 on the page intended for Aug. 23, and the Aug. 23 entry on the Aug. 22 page, without altering the printed headings. To note the transposition of entries, he made cross-reference notes on both pages. The two entries appear here in correct chronological order, each under its true date heading, as if Chase had written them on the proper pages.
7. Chase's companions were his nieces, Eliza Chase Whipple and Hannah Whipple Tucker. The "Durgin Place" was evidently a property that the Tuckers wished to purchase. Hannah Tucker to Chase, Sept. 23, 1872 (Chase Papers, L.C.).
8. Therapeutic water from Rockbridge Alum Springs, located west of Lexington, Va. Dunglison, *Dictionary of Medical Science,* 1106.
9. Josiah Prentice Tucker.
10. That is, "ditto before bed."

SUNDAY, AUGUST 25. Walked to Church & half a mile on return—Mr. Coggswell preached—unfailing well of Water of Life[11]—
Read Bible Chiefly Deuteronomy
   Bowels regular— Ate too much—must restrain appetite
   Fair & pleasant but warm— Aurora b. 8 & 9 P.M

MONDAY, AUGUST 26. Walked a mile before breakfast—two miles more before dinner—read Parton's Greeley
   Tucker at home
   His father & mother came up in evening
   Rode with T. & Hannah, Alice & Winifred in afternoon.[12]
   All seems right except heart—no apparent change there—
   Fair pleasant & warm

THURSDAY, AUGUST 29. Walked before breakfast same as yesterday—three figs & pear after breakfast—somewhat acid at stomach—wrote Waters (R. P.) Hy Clark & Schellentrager about Greeley[13]—read Parton's Greeley—took nap
   Rode afternoon with Hannah around Jenness Pond—about 10 miles
   Letters evening from Katie, Barclay [*illeg.*]— Secy Col Scott, Capt Jones, Plumley & Didier[14]
   last night 2 pints—bad sleep but felt well this morning & walked more vigorously than heretofore—mile in 24 min
   Cloudy—after breakfast foggy & slight rain—

---

11. Elliott Colby Cogswell (1814–87), pastor of the Congregational Church and principal of Coe's Northwood Academy, preached on John 4:6–15. Emerson, *General Catalogue*, 254; D. Hamilton Hurd, ed., *History of Rockingham and Strafford Counties, New Hampshire* . . . (Philadelphia, 1882), 428–29.
   12. Hannah and Josiah Prentice Tucker, and their children.
   13. Richard P. Waters wrote earlier, in reply to an invitation to visit Narragansett, that he had injured himself in a fall and would be confined to his home "for some time." To E. A. Schellentrager, Chase expressed his political views and his support for Horace Greeley's presidential candidacy. Chase apparently wrote to Henry Clarke about affairs at Edgewood. Waters to Chase, July 22, 1872, Clarke to Chase, Sept. 3, 1872 (Chase Papers, L.C.); Chase to Schellentrager, Aug. 28, 1872 (W. P. Palmer Collec., Western Reserve Hist. Soc.).
   14. Capt. Jones was likely John M. Jones. Either Alexander R. Plumley or his son Gardner Spring Plumley (1827–94) wrote Chase, probably in regard to an intended visit by Chase to Metuchen, N.J. (see Oct. 3, 1872, below). G. S. Plumley was pastor of the Presbyterian Church of Metuchen, 1858–75. Eugene L. Didier apprised Chase of his search for a stenographic position with a "regular salary." Didier to Chase, Aug. 26, 1872, G. S. Plumley to Chase, Sept. 6, 1872, May 5, 1873 (Chase Papers, L.C.); *Alumni Catalogue of the Union Theological Seminary in the City of New York, 1836–1926* (New York, 1926), 82; W. Woodford Clayton, *History of Union and Middlesex Counties, New Jersey* . . . (Philadelphia, 1882), 846–47.

FRIDAY, AUGUST 30. Slept pretty well for first time under blanket—quite cool weather—north east wind & rain—wrote Katie, Plumley, Barclay, & Capt Jones

WEDNESDAY, SEPTEMBER 4. Left Boston at 8.30: Waters joined me—crossed from Newport to Narragansett on Ferry steamer Florence[15]—met Perry M.C. from Cincinnati on boat with his wife and daughter[16]—found all well—Jenny Jewett and Alice Stebbins / Carrie Moulton who had been at Newport returned in afternoon

THURSDAY, SEPTEMBER 12. Walked after bkft to foot of Narragansett Av & back—rode with Gov. Lawrence to make calls[17] *Not in* Stenerson & [*illeg.*] & Adml. Polo:[18] *in* de Noailles, McCurdy, Judge Curtis[19]—rode after dinner with Mr. & Miss Leary & Mrs[20]

FRIDAY, SEPTEMBER 13. Breakfast wth Mr & Miss Leary & Katie / after walked to Mr Russells[21]—then to Gov. Lawrence's— Rode with him to call on Mr. Cyrus Field[22]—then to Club[23]—Gov L⎯⎯ left me / met Mr. Paul Forbes—J. G. Bennett—Mr. Ledyard / Mr. Belmont—Mr Sanford[24]— Walking towards Hotel encountered Dr Lindsly of Washington— Newport democrats seem rather discouraged about Greeleys prospects— Gen Hunt commanding Fort

---

15. Built in 1866. Lytle, *Merchant Vessels*, 65.
16. Aaron Fyfe Perry, serving in Congress at this time, and his wife Elizabeth Williams Perry had three daughters. Edith Strong Perry, evidently the youngest, probably accompanied her parents. Reed, *Bench and Bar of Ohio*, 2:384.
17. In Newport, R.I.
18. José Polo de Bernabé.
19. Emmanuel Henri Victurnien, marquis of Noailles (1830–1909), France's minister to the U.S., 1872–73; New York merchant and banker Robert H. McCurdy (1800–1880); and Benjamin R. Curtis, who owned a house in Newport. Augé, *Larousse du XXe Siècle*, 5:92; *New York Times*, Apr. 6, 1880; *Newport Dir. (1873–74)*, 98, 100.
20. Annie Leary, sister of Arthur Leary, was his "constant companion" and household manager. Leary was unmarried, so Chase evidently omitted a name after the "Mrs." *New York Times*, Mar. 9, 1893.
21. Charles Handy Russell.
22. New York merchant Cyrus West Field (1819–92), brother of Stephen Johnson Field and David Dudley Field, successfuly promoted the first Atlantic telegraph cable. *DAB*, 6:357–59.
23. Presumably the Newport Reading Room, chartered in 1854. *Newport Dir. (1869–70)*, 78; Bayles, *History of Newport County*, 560–61.
24. Paul Sieman Forbes, a cousin of prominent merchant John Murray Forbes; *New York Herald* managing editor James Gordon Bennett, Jr. (1841–1918); diplomat and Michigan politician Henry Ledyard (1812–80); and Newport resident Milton H. Sanford. Hughes, *John Murray Forbes*, 1:294–95; *DAB*, 2:199–202; *Nat. Cyc.*, 22:27–28; *Newport Dir. (1871–72)*, 185; Downing and Scully, *Architectural Heritage of Newport*, 146, plate 176.

Adams called[25]— Went with Mr & Miss Leary to lunch with Mrs Moore at the Fort—met there Miss Edes who talked of Mr Evarts & other prominent Americans she had met abroad—Miss Greenhow[26]—Mrs Col [Baker]—Mrs Van Reed who talked of Adml. Foote &c[27]— Stenerson was there & Mr Holland Minister—home at 4— At 8 went to tea at Sanfords [& not]

MONDAY, SEPTEMBER 16. Gov. went to Prov by early Train—rainy morng—wrote R Patterson—Trear F. Co, Hy Clark,[28] enclosed $40 to Ocean House & $13 to O. Judd & Co—wrote Jones[29]—

walked before dinner on beach—Albert[30] & Arthur went to Washn

Read Corinthians—also [Dr Kilgallen]

Rainy or cloudy all day

No bad symptoms—except irregular heart action— Weak in walking

MONDAY, SEPTEMBER 30. Made farewell calls—at Clarkson Potters saw Miss P—— & Mrs McIlvaine[31] / Mr. [Richd] Emmets—saw Mrs Emmet[32]—Mr Prime saw him & Mrs Prime[33]—returned with Nettie to lunch after which I went alone to Mr. Morris—[all] out & left cards—to Rectory—sent Irvin home with carriage—went

---

25. Artillery officer Henry Jackson Hunt (1819–89) commanded various forts after the Civil War. *DAB*, 9:386–87; *Appletons'*, 3:316–17.

26. Possibly a daughter of artist Richard Saltonstall Greenough. William Maxwell Evarts was in Geneva representing the U.S. in negotiations with Great Britain over the *Alabama* claims. *DAB*, 7:589; Chester L. Barrows, *William M. Evarts: Lawyer, Diplomat, Statesman* (Chapel Hill, 1941), 196–213.

27. Career naval officer Andrew Hull Foote (1806–63). A "Mrs. Col. Baker" boarded at Newport and resided in Washington, D.C. *DAB*, 6:499–500; *Newport Dir. (1873–74)*, 77.

28. Henry Clarke. Chase sent a $20 deposit to Robert Patterson, Jr., a clerk with the Fidelity Insurance, Trust and Safe Deposit Company in Philadelphia. Cash accounts, end of Journal XIX; *Phila. Dir. (1872)*, 498.

29. Probably Pierepont E. Jones. The Ocean House, second Newport hotel with this name, opened in 1845. Orange Judd & Co., publishers, specialized in agricultural and scientific books. Downing and Scully, *Architectural Heritage of Newport*, 118, 131–32; *New York Dir. (1872)*, 586; *Appletons'*, 3:482.

30. Albert Wells.

31. Emily Coxe McIlvaine. Chase made these calls in New Rochelle, N.Y., where Clarkson Potter, who had three daughters, maintained a residence. *New York Times*, Jan. 24, 1882.

32. Attorney Richard Stockton Emmet (1821–1902) and his wife, Catherine Temple Emmet (d. 1895), resided in New Rochelle after 1867. Ibid., Nov. 24, 1902.

33. Probably New York banker and merchant Rufus Prime (1805–85) and his wife. *Appletons'*, 5:123.

with Mrs Higbee to call on Judge Emmet[34]—paralyzed in body but clear in brain—said he was near 81 & Judge Nelson a year older—walked home— Nettie who had gone for Will soon returned with him[35]

Pleasant day but turned cloudy towards night

TUESDAY, OCTOBER 1. Wet & disagreeable day—fished a little

WEDNESDAY, OCTOBER 2. Fished about an hour near rocks caught eleven—about ½ past 10 went to Stamford by rail with Nettie & Will and Mr & Mrs Higbee—thence all by carrige to Strong's Island which walked over & picknicked lunch—about 5 returned to Pelham

Beautiful day

THURSDAY, OCTOBER 3. Frightfull dreams from lunch / Up at 6—bid Nettie goodbye & take care of self & baby—to New Rochelle in carriage & New York by rail with Will—he took charge of urine for Dr. Perry—bid him good bye—rode to foot of Desbrosses Street—crossed to Jersey City took 10 oclock train for Metuchen— arrd soon after 11—taken to Rev Mr Plumleys by Mr   in buggy—old Mr P—— absent[36] / Rev Mr P—— misled by my telegram, had gone to New York to meet me—rode around town with Mr   lunched at Mrs Plumley[37]—to depot—found train did not leave New York till 2 instead of 1—introduced to several persons— Mr Campbell, Mr Patterson railsroad man with Mr. Packer[38]—took train shortly after 3 for Phila.—introduced to Mr. Robinson who talked extension of Lehigh Valley R R to Perth Amboy[39]—found Mr Wallace waiting for me at Camden—did not recognize me at first on a/c of whiskers—took me to his house—presented me to Mrs

---

34. Robert Emmet (1792–1873), a former justice of the New York state superior court. Evidently Chase's companion on this call was the wife of Charles Higbee, rector of Christ Church (Episcopal) in Pelham. *Appletons'*, 2:350; Scharf, *History of Westchester County*, 1:707.

35. William S. Hoyt.

36. Chase visited Gardner S. Plumley and Alexander R. Plumley.

37. Gardner S. Plumley's wife. G. S. Plumley to Chase, May 5, 1873 (Chase Papers, L.C.).

38. Probably Morris Patterson (1809–1878), Pennsylvania coal merchant and railroad financier, and Asa Packer (1805–79), president of the Lehigh Valley Railroad and a Democratic congressman from Pennsylvania, 1852–57. *DAB*, 14:131–32, 305; *Bio. Dir. U.S. Cong.*, 1603.

39. Likely Philadelphia investor Moncure Robinson (1802–91), a retired railroad engineer. *DAB*, 16:48–49.

W—— & Miss W[40]—charming & cultivated persons / Chief Justice Thompson at dinner[41] / retired abt 10—rare books in house[42]—bed about 11—
Pleasant day

FRIDAY, OCTOBER 4. Went with Mr. Wallace to Historical & Philosophical Room— Library large / Society easy not to say rich— Building on grounds of Pa Hospital—walked through Building & grounds of Hospital an ancient Institution[43]—visited Senate Chamber & Hall of Representatives of Congress before removal to Washington—S.E. corner 6th & Chesnut—[*illeg.*[44] have] been used for Court rooms I believe but Mr W—— told me are to be restored for Centennial[45]—passed Old State House on way to Independence Hall now occupied by Mayor & city Govt—S.W. corner 5th & Chesnut— Saw Mayor—& Plan of new City Hall to be occupied when present buildings—restored are vacated[46]— Visited Carpenters Hall where Congress of 1774 sat—now & then very impressive
After lunch called on Mr. Binney now in his 93d year[47]—found

---

40. John William Wallace married Dorothea Francis Willing in 1853. They had one daughter, Rebecca Blackwell Willing Wallace (c. 1855–1939), the future wife of Philadelphia attorney John Thompson Spencer. Henry Flanders, "A Commemorative Address Delivered at the Hall of the Historical Society of Pennsylvania, November 10, 1884, on John William Wallace, LLD," *Pennsylvania Magazine of History and Biography* 8 (1884): xxxi; *Nat. Cyc.*, 45:274; *New York Times*, Nov. 27, 1939.

41. James Thompson.

42. At this time Wallace was president of the Historical Society of Pennsylvania and was known for his "cultivated taste, and . . . great love of the arts, painting, sculpture, and architecture." He had written or edited a number of legal compilations and other works. Flanders, "Commemorative Address," xxxi, xxxvii.

43. The Historical Society of Pennsylvania then occupied a two-story building on Spruce Street leased from the Pennsylvania Hospital, which had been founded in 1751. Hampton L. Carson, *History of the Historical Society of Pennsylvania*, 2 vols. (Philadelphia, 1940), 1:355–56; Philip S. Klein and Ari Hoogenboom, *A History of Pennsylvania*, 2nd ed. (University Park, Pa., 1980), 253.

44. Possibly a canceled word.

45. Congress Hall at the southeast corner of Sixth and Chestnut Streets was in use from Dec. 1789 until the federal government moved to Washington, D.C. The International Exposition in honor of the centennial anniversary of American independence opened in Philadelphia on May 10, 1876. William H. Egle, *An Illustrated History of the Commonwealth of Pennsylvania* . . . (Harrisburg, 1877), 1033–34, 1044.

46. Philadelphia's mayor at this time was William Sturmburg Stokley (1823–1902). The French Renaissance style city hall was completed in 1881 and at the time was the largest office building in the world. Holli and Jones, *Biographical Dictionary of American Mayors*, 347–48; Klein and Hoogenboom, *History of Pennsylvania*, 397.

47. Philadelphia attorney, legal authority, and author Horace Binney, Sr. (1780–1875). *DAB*, 2:280–82.

him well & Cheerful just returned from drive in Park—had been reading Millers opinion in Church case which he praised[48]—various talk—he will outlive me

H. C. Carey & Dr. Elder at dinner

SATURDAY, OCTOBER 5. Mr. Joseph Patterson called—talked about finance[49] / Schuckers called—walked with me to Chesnut St bridge—down Chesnut calling at Baileys where saw beautiful pictures especially one of Niagara, & bronzes—& clocks & silver ware) & so home[50]— After lunch rode with Mr. & Miss Wallace to Park[51]—

After dinner looked after matters for Nettie[52]—

Fair day but cool towards evening

Long walk about 3 miles— Ch J Thompson lunched with us— took a little whiskey experimentally—

Bowels regular

SUNDAY, OCTOBER 13. Sent to Metropolitan Church to know if fire was lighted—finding that it was not & not being well did not go[53]

THURSDAY, OCTOBER 31. Call on Schleiden at Wormley's at 4.30[54]

WEDNESDAY, NOVEMBER 13. Schuckers at prayers & bkfast— looked at dfts Keely engine—could not understand[55]— Walked to Capitol E. 2d. East Cap—heard several cases argued—able to give good attention—home with Clifford—dinner—walked about

---

48. *John Watson et al. v. William A. Jones et al.*, decided by the U.S. Supreme Court in Apr. 1872, concerned a split in the Presbyterian church brought about by the Civil War and the slavery issue. Absent when the case was argued in Mar. 1871, Chase did not participate in the decision. 13 Wall. 679 (1872); Fairman, *Reconstruction and Reunion*, 899–917.

49. Patterson (1808–87), a Philadelphia banker and entrepreneur, had advised Chase on financial matters since the beginning of the Civil War. *Appletons'*, 4:672.

50. Bailey & Co., jewelers. *Phila. Dir. (1872)*, 166.

51. John William Wallace and Rebecca Blackwell Willing Wallace.

52. Probably relating to Ludlow family property. Chase to F. Ball, Oct. 17, 1872 (Chase Papers, Cinc. Hist. Soc.).

53. Chase was now back in Washington, D.C.

54. Rudolph Schleiden, formerly the Hanseatic Republic's minister in Washington, was traveling in the U.S. at this time. He and Chase knew each other from the 1860s, and Schleiden had extended courtesies to Chase's daughters when they visited Europe. Chase to Janet Chase Hoyt, Nov. 4, 1872 (Chase Papers, L.C.); Chase to Schleiden, Feb. 5, 1863 (Chase Papers, Hist. Soc. of Pa.); *Wash. Dir. (1865)*, 107.

55. Enigmatic Philadelphia inventor John Ernst Worrell Keely (1827–98) was working on an experimental engine. *DAB*, 10:280–81.

2 miles—called at Judge Swayne's—left card—home—Judge Bartley called at night / bed ½ past 11— William sick did not see him all day.[56]

THURSDAY, NOVEMBER 14. Pain on rising on bowels—pear & figs— Prayers quarter past eight—bkft half past— Schuckers came to (late) bkft—had overslept—to Court—walked with S—— who was to leave at 3—told me that royalties on his mower & reaper were $1800 last year endg in October—some Court of Claims case—Leary v US argued—then one from N York Miller v Rochester begun[57]—felt very tired—walked down with Clifford—weak—dined—wrote short opinion[58]—read &c till 10—timed how many words read by each in minute—Alice 171—Amy 170—Carrie 150[59] / I, 100—
Bowels open

FRIDAY, NOVEMBER 15. Slept well as usual, though waked by calls to urinate more frequently than usual of late, till about 5—then awake till after 6—then a little sleep till 7—up & dressed & bath— Fletcher helped me[60]—William has been absent, sick, for three days—weak—good deal of palpitation—voice weak—bkft as usual

WEDNESDAY, NOVEMBER 20. Morning duties as usual—figs, & pear from Mrs Schley—began letter to Katie & wrote to Mrs Barton enclosing letter for M. Lucas thanking him for Writings of Livingston, with Preface by him &c[61]—to Edgewood with Mr. Cobb,

---

56. Chase's helper, William Joice; see Nov. 15 also.
57. *Arthur Leary et al. v. U.S.*, an appeal from the Court of Claims involving charter of a vessel, and *Charles G. Miller et al. v. The People of the State of New York*, concerning the directorship of the Rochester & Genesee Valley R.R. and the power of a state to amend an act of incorporation. 14 Wall. 607 (1872); 15 Wall. 478 (1873).
58. Probably in the case *U.S. v. Henry J. Hunt*, which arose from a petition for military commutation pay and hinged on the difference between brevet and regular rank. Chase delivered his opinion on Nov. 18. 14 Wall. 550 (1872).
59. Alice Auld, Amy Auld, and Carrie Moulton. Chase to Amy Auld, Oct. 19, 25, 1872 (Chase Papers, L.C.); Warden, *Chase*, 805.
60. Fletcher, otherwise unidentified, worked at least part of the time at Edgewood as a farm hand. Cash accounts, Journal XIX; Henry Clarke to Chase, Sept. 26, 1872 (Chase Papers, L.C.).
61. French prison reformer and death penalty opponent Charles Jean-Marie Lucas (1808–89) wrote the preface to an edition of Edward Livingston's work on the criminal law of Louisiana, published in Paris in 1872 as *Exposé d'un Système de Législation Criminelle pour l'État de la Louisiane et pour les États-Unis d'Amérique*. Chase's letter acknowledged receipt of the Livingston work and of pamphlets written by Lucas. Chase declared that although he had taken no public stand on the issue, he favored limitations on, or abolition of, capital punishment. Lucas to Chase, Oct. 8, 1872, Chase to Lucas, Nov. 19, 1872 (Chase Papers, L.C.); *La Grande Encyclopédie*, 22:727.

November 1872

Engineer,[62] & Amy— Agreed with Mr. Cobb & Col Brooks on route of private road approach to house—looked at stable & vineyard[63]— walked back to town in consideration for horse just recovering from disease[64]—Mr. Cobb with me—finished letter to Katie & wrote & dictated several to Parsons, Mrs Jewett, Prentice Tucker, Mr. Mott & others.[65] Prof Henry and Mr. Carey[66] called in evening / talk about winds, fog signals &c with Prof & with Carey about railroads in West &c

THURSDAY, NOVEMBER 21. Rose about 7—feeling pretty well after sleep less disturbed than usual—usual morning duties—pear [from] Mrs Schley & dates—walked around square in 6 minutes before breakfast—letter from Wm Richards about Hy Dennison[67]— somewhat costive—

FRIDAY, NOVEMBER 22. Much the same as yesterday / walk 7 min round square— At Capitol a few of course motions— Carpenter finished & Sloan & Bennet replied— Carpenter on our walk to Capitol promised to have clerk continued[68]—

Walk with Lloyd[69] about a mile after dinner—

---

62. Probably Frederick Cobb. *Wash. Dir. (1872),* 129.
63. Edward Clark had designed a new building to serve as barn and stable at Edgewood. Chase to E. Clark, Aug. 4, 1872, Clark to Chase, Aug. 8, 1872, Henry Clarke to Chase, Sept. 12, 1872 (Chase Papers, L.C.).
64. During Nov. 1872, Washington was affected by an epizootic which had already killed or made ill a large number of horses in New York and other cities. Early in the month, Washington's street cars stopped running and livery stables were unable to provide horses to substitute for those, such as Chase's, which were ill. Chase to Janet Chase Hoyt, Nov. 4, 1872 (Chase Papers, L.C.); *New York Times,* Oct. 22, Nov. 1, 14, 1872.
65. Richard C. Parsons; probably Janette Skinner Jewett; Josiah Prentice Tucker; and possibly Richard Mott.
66. Henry Charles Carey.
67. Chase's old friend and political correspondent William Richards was a merchant in Columbus, Ohio, before becoming business editor of the Keokuk, Iowa, *Gate City,* 1854–60. Richards to Chase, Dec. 30, 1846, Feb. 24, 1860 (Chase Papers, L.C.); *Col. Dir. (1845–46),* 387; F. I. Herriott, "Iowa and the First Nomination of Abraham Lincoln," *Annals of Iowa,* 3rd ser., 9 (1909–11): 209–12.
68. At one time, Chase was provided with a clerk under the Bankruptcy Act. The chief justice's role in the nomination of registers of bankruptcy was reduced, and Chase sought means by which he could continue to have the use of a clerk. Matthew Hale Carpenter was chairman of the Senate's Committee to Audit and Control the Contingent Expense. In court, Carpenter argued *Horatio J. Olcott v. Supervisors of Fond du Lac County* against attorneys J. C. Sloan and J. R. Bennett. At issue was the use of public funds to support construction of a railroad in Wisconsin. 16 Wall. 678 (1873); Chase to W. H. Rearden, Oct. 26, 1870, Chase to R. C. Parsons, Jan. 9, Feb. 2, 1871 (Chase Papers, L.C.); *Bio. Dir. U.S. Cong.,* 746.
69. David D. Lloyd.

SATURDAY, NOVEMBER 23. Morning duties & walk as usual—Conference at Capitol—Judge Bradley sick with cold & not present—
After dinner called at Judge B——s—did not see him—at Judge Strongs—saw him & daughter[70]—agreeable talk—Mr. Fish's—saw Mrs F—afterwards Mr. Fish came in—gave me pamphlet about Indirect Claims & talked of treaty about immigrants providing for mixed commission—very good object—protection of emigrants[71] home—wrote several letters & dictated more—
Bed near 11
Pretty well today—a little costive but passage—slept well

SUNDAY, NOVEMBER 24. Morning duties & walk around City Hall—Metropolitan [Dr.] Tiffany[72]—*[two words? illeg.]* of Holy Spirit—Truth; Progress / Read "Praise" in Eadie— Life of Robt Hall[73]— What suffering—what patience—what elasticity of spirit / also Corea in Ed. Review[74]— Admired self sacrifice of missionaries
Pretty good day—a little costive however—slept pretty well last night—urinated three times—

FRIDAY, NOVEMBER 29. Read newspapers—Greeley dangerously ill—went out to make calls—walked to Dr. Perry's—saw him and Mrs P——[75] / found walking very slippery—snow & ice on steps & side walks—went home & lunched with Nettie—recd letter from Lloyd enclosing one from Katie— Took Clarence (1.50 per hour) & started on Calling Expedition—first at D D Field's saw Mrs F——[76] & Mrs Judge Field[77] & Mr Hastings from Engd—next

---

70. Strong had four daughters: Emily Elizabeth, Amelia Mallery, Mary Willson, and Julia Darling. *Nat. Cyc.,* 21:5.

71. Secretary of State Fish wanted Chase's opinion on a draft treaty "intended for the 'Better protection of Steerage Passengers.'" The pamphlet "about Indirect Claims" evidently related to the controversy over damage claims arising from assistance given in Great Britain to Confederate commerce raiders during the Civil War. Fish to Chase, Nov. 26, 1872 (Chase Papers, L.C.); Chase to Fish, Dec. 10, 1872 (Misc. Letters, Gen. Recs. State Dept., Nat. Arch.); Adrian Cook, *The Alabama Claims: American Politics and Anglo-American Relations, 1865–1872* (Ithaca, 1975), 207–40.

72. Likely the Rev. Dr. O. H. Tiffany, chaplain of the Senate. Schuckers, *Chase,* 625; *New York Times,* June 11, 1879.

73. John Eadie (1810–76), minister of Lansdowne Presbyterian Church outside Glasgow, Scotland, was well known for religious writings which appealed to popular and scholarly audiences. The English Baptist divine Robert Hall (1764–1831) was the subject of a memoir published as volume six of *The Works of Robert Hall . . .* , 6 vols. (London, 1832). *DNB,* 6:307–9, 8:969–71.

74. A review of several books about Korea appeared in the *Edinburgh Review* 278 (Oct. 1872): 155–72.

75. Martha Derby Perry later compiled her husband John G. Perry's *Letters from a Surgeon of the Civil War* (Boston, 1906).

76. Mary E. Carr Field. *DAB,* 6:360.

77. Virginia Swearingen Field.

Evarts—saw Mrs E—— and two daughters[78]—talked Geneva—looked at photos of arbitrators, counsel & attaches—next Mrs Walters saw her & Gertrude[79]—talked of political matters & G. Smith / left cards at Brevoort for Gen Hooker, at respective houses for Col. Van Buren, Mr Ward, Judge & Mrs Pierrepont, Mr & Mrs Stoughton, & then home[80]—very cold—dinner at 7— Mr Barney came in & we had pleasant talk—note from Gen McDowell fixing 12.30 for start tomorrow on visit to Govt. works at Hell Gate[81]— Bed a little after 10 having taken cup of tea & buttered roll.

Pretty well today—urine 1 pint—only a few squares walk in open air—good sleep last night

SATURDAY, NOVEMBER 30. "Death of Horace Greeley"— Such was the announcement which met my eyes when I opened the Herald this morning to look for tidings concerning the health of the great journalist—my personal friend. He closed his busy and eventful life last evening at 10 before 7. The night came & death came with the night. His last intelligible utterance was "I know that my Redeemer liveth

Wrote note to Reid asking if I could do any to manifest my respect & esteem & received reply thanking me & saying that note would be read at meeting of Tribune Association this evening[82]

Nettie gave a little dinner / Mr & Mrs Stoughton, Gen & Mrs McDowell & a few more—Mrs S—— did not recognize me in my beard

---

78. William and Helen Evarts had twelve children, five of them daughters. *Nat. Cyc.*, 27:26.

79. Ellen Walter and her daughter.

80. John Dash Van Buren (1811–85) was an attorney, a Democratic politician, and, at this time, the private secretary of Gov. John Thompson Hoffman of New York. During the Civil War, Van Buren had served as paymaster general of New York and advised Chase on national finances. Chase evidently called also at the homes of George Cabot Ward, Edwards Pierrepont and Margaretta Willoughby Pierrepont, and Edwin Wallace Stoughton and his wife, Mary Fiske Stoughton. Hotel Brevoort at Fifth Avenue and Eighth Street was built in 1854. Chase to Van Buren, Feb. 10, 1871 (Chase Papers, L.C.); *Nat. Cyc.*, 10:236; *DAB*, 14:587; *Who Was Who*, H:511; Federal Writers' Project, *New York City Guide*, 135.

81. The U.S. Army Corps of Engineers was drilling tunnels and blasting reefs to improve navigation. At this time Irvin McDowell was in command of the army's Department of the East and lived in New York. "Report of the Secretary of War," 42nd Cong., 3rd sess., H. Ex. Doc. 1, pt. 2, 79–80; *DAB*, 12:29; *New York Dir. (1872)*, 721.

82. Chase's note related his "astonishing shock" upon seeing the announcement of Greeley's death. Chase to Whitelaw Reid, Nov. 30, 1872 (Reid Family Papers, L.C.).

SUNDAY, DECEMBER 1. Church at Dr. Montgomery's[83]—
Dinner at Mr. A. T. Stewarts to meet Mr Froude[84]—but found a small company Gen. McDowell, Judges Hilton & James Mrs Smith of Smithton et al[85]— Saw fine pictures Church, Mlle Rosa Bonheur[86]—house magnificent but not completely furnished yet.
Tea at Hoyts—Mr. Leary, Mr. Stockwell & Miss Yznaga[87]
Mr. & Mrs Evarts called—also Mr Reid asking me to be pallbearer at Mr. Greeleys funeral—consented[88]
Advised with me about article counselling Greeley Electors to vote for Grant which I warmly approved[89]

MONDAY, DECEMBER 2. Telegraphed Mr Fish that engagement as pallbearer must excuse my absence from his dinner tomorrow— Will President attend funeral? Read Tribune Article
Received reply "President will attend unless prevented by offl duties"[90]
After dinner Mr Orton called & in morning Mr Cisco

---

83. Henry Eglinton Montgomery (1820–74) presided at New York City's Church of the Incarnation. *Appletons'*, 4:369.
84. English historian James Anthony Froude (1818–94) lectured in the U.S. between Oct. and Dec. 1872. *DNB*, 22:679–87; *New York Times*, Oct. 11, Dec. 28, 1872.
85. Henry Hilton (1824–99), former judge of the New York Court of Common Pleas and confidante of Alexander T. Stewart; and, probably, New York Supreme Court justice Amaziah Bailey James (1812–83). Descendants of founder Richard Smith comprised much of the population of Smithtown, Long Island, for generations. *New York Times*, Aug. 25, 1899; *Bio. Dir. U.S. Cong.*, 1253; Richard M. Bayles, *Historical and Descriptive Sketches of Suffolk County . . .* (Port Jefferson, N.Y., 1874), 183–95; Peter Ross, *A History of Long Island . . .* , 3 vols. (New York, 1905), 1:982.
86. Stewart's extensive art collection included "Niagara Falls, from American Side" (1867) by American painter Frederick E. Church, and "The Horse Fair" (1853) by French artist Rosa Bonheur. *Catalogue of the A. T. Stewart Collection of Paintings, Sculptures, and Other Objects of Art* (New York, 1887), 7, 10, 64, 106; Dore Ashton, *Rosa Bonheur: A Life and a Legend* (New York, 1981), 95.
87. Probably Arthur Leary; either Alden B. Stockwell (c. 1829–1905), stockbroker and president of the Pacific Mail Steamship Company, or Charles Blair Stockwell (1832–92), a jeweler associated with Tiffany & Co.; and one of Antonio Yznaga's three known daughters: Consuelo (d. 1909), Emily, or Nautica. The gathering was at the home of William and Janet Chase Hoyt. *New York Dir. (1872)*, 1111; *New York Times*, Aug. 4, 1891, Nov. 20, 1892, May 3, 1905, Jan. 25, 1908, Nov. 2, 1944; G[eorge] E[dward] C[okayne], *The Complete Peerage of England, Scotland, Ireland, Great Britain and the United Kingdom, Extant, Extinct, or Dormant*, rev. ed. by Vicary Gibbs et al. (London, 1910–59), 8:378; Chase to William T. Sherman, Nov. 26, 1872 (W. T. Sherman Papers, L.C.).
88. Chase also received a written request to serve as pallbearer. Whitelaw Reid to Chase, Dec. 2, 1872 (Reid Family Papers, L.C.).
89. Whitelaw Reid stated in "The Electoral Problem" that Greeley desired such an action and a unanimous electoral vote would make Grant "more emphatically the President of the whole people." After the article's appearance on Dec. 2, Chase notified Reid: "Your article this morning was just right." *New York Tribune*, Dec. 2, 1872; Chase to Reid, Dec. 2, 1872 (Reid Family Papers, L.C.).
90. Grant attended Greeley's funeral. *New York Tribune*, Dec. 5, 1872.

TUESDAY, DECEMBER 3. Made farewell calls

WEDNESDAY, DECEMBER 4. Attended Mr Greeleys funeral—impressive addresses at Mr Chapins Church by pastor & H W Beecher[91]—immense throng on streets—estimated by Senators Trumbull & Fenton[92] & Ex Atto Gen Evarts in carriage with at 300,000 between Church & Ferry— Interment at sundown in Greenwood— How sad to see Coffin committed to vault so recently opened to receive his wife[93]

THURSDAY, DECEMBER 5. Up early for train to Washington / met Gov Banks & Mr Spofford—talked with latter about Fisheries as appd by treaty of Washington[94] / Arrived soon after five—welcomed by Carrie & Amy.[95]

FRIDAY, DECEMBER 6. At Capitol & Court

SATURDAY, DECEMBER 14. At conference first business election of Marshal—voted alone for Mr Schley[96] / no one else seemed willing to vote for him—next voted with Judges Davis & Strong for Mr Nicolay who finally chosen[97]

SUNDAY, DECEMBER 15. At church—Dr Pennington preached

MONDAY, DECEMBER 16. At court—Marshal Parsons last day

THURSDAY, DECEMBER 19. Nicolay sworn as Marshal by me and assumed his duties

---

91. Edwin Hubbell Chapin (1814–80) was pastor of New York City's Fourth Universalist Society (the Church of the Divine Paternity) at Fifth Avenue and West 45th St., where the funeral services took place. *DAB*, 4:15; *New York Tribune*, Dec. 4, 5, 1872; *New York Dir. (1872)*, 18.

92. Reuben Eaton Fenton (1819–85) of New York, Democratic congressman, 1853–55, 1857–64; governor, 1865–68; Republican U.S. senator, 1869–75. *Bio. Dir. U.S. Cong.*, 989; *DAB*, 6:326–27.

93. Greenwood Cemetery was located on Gowanus Heights in Brooklyn. Greeley's wife, Mary Youngs Cheney Greeley, had died on Oct. 30. *DAB*, 7:528, 533; *New York Dir. (1872)*, 448.

94. Officials from the U.S., Great Britain, and Canada had negotiated the Treaty of Washington in 1871. The agreement included several provisions related to commercial fishing off the U.S. and Canadian coasts. Nevins, *Hamilton Fish*, 475–79.

95. Caroline Moulton and Amy Auld.

96. Frederick Schley. Washington *Evening Star*, Dec. 14, 1872.

97. The successful candidate for the position of marshal of the Supreme Court was John George Nicolay (1832–1901), who with John Hay had been Abraham Lincoln's secretary and became the late president's biographer. Nicolay was marshal until 1887. *DAB*, 13:510–11.

TUESDAY, DECEMBER 24. Called on Hooper, [Corwine] & Sumner / found all at home

WEDNESDAY, DECEMBER 25. Church—Amy & I. Dr P—— preached—after service introduced to him & his father daughter & sister

Gifts to servants— Recd from Katie Nettie & Carrie. Guests at Xmas dinner Gov & Mr Lawrence, Mr. & Miss Welling, Mr & Mrs Bridge Mr & Mrs Hoyt. Also Carrie Amy & self[98]— Miss Walker invited but absent because of the snow storm which set in towards evening.[99]

FRIDAY, DECEMBER 27. Called on Windom[1] & Edmunds at home—on Carpenter & Schurz out of town

SATURDAY, DECEMBER 28. Rode out to Edgewood with Nettie heavy snow every where & [not] melted— Stable not yet finished— but nearly / Culvert & road work wholly suspended by cold—

Sundry callers among them Conway formerly of Kansas[2] & Schley, also Dr. Pennington with whom interesting talk on genealogy of Christ, Methodism &c

SUNDAY, DECEMBER 29. Church with Nettie—Dr. Pennington preached

---

98. William Beach Lawrence and, evidently, his son Albert Gallatin Lawrence (1834–87), lawyer, soldier, and diplomat; James Clarke Welling and a daughter; Horatio and Charlotte Marshall Bridge; William S. and Janet Chase Hoyt; Caroline Moulton; Amy Auld. *Appletons'*, 3:642; Chase to Janet Chase Hoyt, Dec. 15, 1872 (Chase Papers, L.C.).
99. Susan Walker.
1. William Windom (1827–91), at this time a Republican U.S. senator from Minnesota; later secretary of the U.S. Treasury. *Bio. Dir. U.S. Cong.*, 2073; *DAB*, 20:383–84.
2. Martin Franklin Conway (1827–82), a leading free-state politician, had served as the state's first congressman, 1861–63. Recently, he had returned from a term as U.S. consul at Marseilles, France. *DAB*, 4:363–64.

Bibliography

SOURCES CITED BY ABBREVIATED TITLES

Reference Works

Appletons'
James Grant Wilson and John Fiske, eds. *Appletons' Cyclopedia of American Biography.* 6 vols. New York, 1887–89.

Bio. Dir. U.S. Cong.
Biographical Directory of the United States Congress 1774–1989 . . . Bicentennial Edition. Washington, D.C., 1989.

DAB
American Council of Learned Societies. *Dictionary of American Biography.* 20 vols. New York, 1928–36.

DNB
Leslie Stephen and Sidney Lee, eds. *The Dictionary of National Biography.* Reprint ed., 21 vols. London, 1973.

Nat. Cyc.
The National Cyclopaedia of American Biography. 63 vols. New York, 1891–1984.

OR
The War of the Rebellion: A Compilation of the Official Records of the Union and Confederate Armies. 128 vols. Washington, D.C., 1880–1901.

ORN
Official Records of the Union and Confederate Navies in the War of the Rebellion. 30 vols. Washington, D.C., 1894–1922.

Bibliography

Register of Officers (1861)	Register of Officers and Agents, Civil, Military, and Naval, in the Service of the United States, on the Thirtieth September, 1861. Washington, D.C., 1862.
Register of Officers (1863)	Register of Officers and Agents, Civil, Military, and Naval, in the Service of the United States, on the Thirtieth September, 1863. Washington, D.C., 1864.
Register of Officers (1865)	Register of Officers and Agents, Civil, Military, and Naval, in the Service of the United States, on the Thirtieth September, 1865. Washington, D.C., 1866.
Register of Officers (1873)	Register of Officers and Agents, Civil, Military, and Naval, in the Service of the United States, on the Thirtieth September, 1873. Washington, D.C., 1874.

City Directories

Baltimore Dir. (1842)	Matchett's Baltimore Directory, or Register of Householders. . . . Baltimore, 1842.
Boston Dir. (1836)	Stimpson's Boston Directory. Boston, 1836.
Boston Dir. (1840)	Stimpson's Boston Directory. Boston, 1840.
Boston Dir. (1850)	The Directory of the City of Boston. Boston, 1850.
Boston Dir. (1864)	The Boston Directory. Boston, 1864.
Chicago Dir. (1839)	[Chicago Business Directory, 1839]. Reprinted 1876 as No. 2 in *Fergus Historical Series*.
Cinc. Dir. (1831)	The Cincinnati Directory, for the Year 1831. Cincinnati, 1831.
Cinc. Dir. (1834)	The Cincinnati Directory, for the Year 1834. Cincinnati, 1834.
Cinc. Dir. (1836–37)	The Cincinnati Directory, for the Years 1836–37. Cincinnati, 1836.

Bibliography

Cinc. Dir. (1840)   David Henry Shaffer. *The Cincinnati, Covington, Newport and Fulton Directory, for 1840.* Cincinnati, 1839.

Cinc. Dir. (1842)   Charles Cist, comp. *The Cincinnati Directory, for 1842.* Cincinnati, [1842].

Cinc. Dir. (1843)   Charles Cist, comp., *The Cincinnati Directory, for the Year 1843.* Cincinnati, 1843.

Cinc. Dir. (1846)   *Robinson & Jones' Cincinnati Directory, for 1846.* Cincinnati, 1846.

Cinc. Dir. (1849–50)   *Williams' Cincinnati Directory and Business Advertiser, for 1849–50.* Cincinnati, [1849].

Cinc. Dir. (1850–51)   *Williams' Cincinnati Directory and Business Advertiser, for 1850–51.* Cincinnati, [1850].

Cinc. Dir. (1851–52)   *Williams' Cincinnati Directory and Business Advertiser, for 1851–52.* Cincinnati, [1851].

Cinc. Dir. (1853)   *Williams' Cincinnati Directory, City Guide, and Business Mirror.* Cincinnati, [1853].

Cinc. Dir. (1855)   *Williams' Cincinnati Directory, City Guide, and Business Mirror.* Cincinnati, [1855].

Cinc. Dir. (1857)   *Williams' Cincinnati Directory, City Guide, and Business Mirror; for 1857.* Cincinnati, [1857].

Cinc. Dir. (1859)   *Williams' Cincinnati Directory, City Guide and Business Mirror, for the Year 1859.* Cincinnati, [1859].

Cinc. Dir. (1860)   *Williams' Cincinnati Directory, City Guide and Business Mirror, for 1860.* Cincinnati, [1860].

Cinc. Dir. (1861)   *Williams' Cincinnati Directory, City Guide and Business Mirror . . . for 1861.* Cincinnati, [1861].

Cinc. Dir. (1862)   *Williams' Cincinnati Directory, City Guide and Business Mirror, for the Year Commencing June 1, 1862.* Cincinnati, [1862].

Bibliography

Cinc. Dir. (1864) — *Williams' Cincinnati Directory . . . June 1864.* Cincinnati, [1864].

Cinc. Dir. (1865) — *Williams' Cincinnati Directory . . . June 1865.* Cincinnati, [1865].

Cleve. Dir. (1848) — William Stephenson, comp. *Smead & Cowles' General Business Directory for the City of Cleveland, for 1848–49.* Cleveland, 1848.

Col. Dir. (1845–46) — *Kinney's Directory of Columbus, for 1845–6.* Columbus, 1845.

Col. Dir. (1848) — *Directory of the City of Columbus, for the Year 1848.* Columbus, 1848.

Col. Dir. (1850–51) — *Directory of the City of Columbus, for the Years 1850–'51.* Columbus, 1850.

Col. Dir. (1855) — *Columbus Business Directory, for the Year 1855.* Columbus, 1855.

Col. Dir. (1856–57) — C. S. Williams, comp. *Williams' Columbus Directory, City Guide, and Business Mirror. Volume 1. 1856–'57.* Columbus, 1856.

Essex Co. Dir. (1870) — *Essex County History and Directory.* Boston, 1870.

Hartford Dir. (1828) — *Hartford City Directory, for 1828.* Hartford, [1828].

Louisville Dir. (1832) — *The Louisville Directory, for 1832.* Louisville, 1832.

Louisville Dir. (1841) — G. Collins. *The Louisville Directory, for the Year 1841.* Louisville, 1841.

Louisville Dir. (1848) — *Gabriel Collins' Louisville and New Albany Directory, and Annual Advertiser, for 1848.* Louisville, [1848].

Louisville Dir. (1848–49) — John B. Jegli. *John B. Jegli's Louisville Directory, for 1848–1849, on the First Day of August, 1848.* Louisville, 1848.

Bibliography {715}

Louisville Dir. (1865–66)	Williamson's Annual Directory of the City of Louisville. 1865 & 1866. [Louisville], 1865.
New Bedford Dir. (1839)	Henry H. Crapo. *The New-Bedford Directory.* New Bedford, 1839.
New Orleans Dir. (1866)	Charles Gardner, comp. *Gardner's New Orleans Directory for 1866* . . . New Orleans, 1865.
New York Dir. (1833)	*Longworth's American Almanac, New-York Register, and City Directory.* New York, 1833.
New York Dir. (1841–42)	*The New York Business Directory, for 1841 and 1842. Second Edition.* New York, 1841.
New York Dir. (1850)	*The Great Metropolis: or New-York Almanac for 1850.* New York, 1849.
New York Dir. (1851–52)	*The New York City Directory, for 1851–1852.* New York, [1851].
New York Dir. (1852–53)	*The New York City Directory, for 1852–1853.* New York, 1852.
New York Dir. (1853–54)	*The New York City Directory for 1853–1854. Twelfth Publication.* New York, [1853].
New York Dir. (1863)	H. Wilson, comp. *Trow's New York City Directory.* New York, 1863.
New York Dir. (1864)	H. Wilson, comp. *Trow's New York City Directory.* New York, 1864.
New York Dir. (1866)	*The Great Metropolis: Phelps New York City Guide.* New York, 1866.
New York Dir. (1872)	H. Wilson, comp. *Trow's New York City Directory.* New York, 1872.
Newport Dir. (1863)	Andrew Boyd, comp. *Boyd's Newport City Directory.* Newport, R.I., 1863.
Newport Dir. (1865)	Andrew Boyd, comp. *Boyd's Newport City Directory.* Newport, R.I., 1865.

Bibliography

Newport Dir. (1867)	Andrew Boyd, comp. *Boyd's Newport City Directory.* Newport, R.I., 1867.
Newport Dir. (1869–70)	Andrew Boyd, comp. *Boyd's Newport Directory, for 1869–70.* Newport, R.I., 1869.
Newport Dir. (1871–72)	Andrew Boyd, comp. *Boyd's Newport City Directory, for 1871–72.* Newport, R.I., 1871.
Newport Dir. (1873–74)	Andrew Boyd, comp. *Boyd's Newport City Directory, for 1873–4.* Newport, R.I., 1873.
Phila. Dir. (1829)	*Desilver's Philadelphia Directory and Stranger's Guide, 1829.* Philadelphia, 1829.
Phila. Dir. (1835)	*Desilver's Philadelphia Directory and Stranger's Guide for 1835 & 1836.* Philadelphia, 1835.
Phila. Dir. (1843)	*McElroy's Philadelphia Directory for 1843.* Philadelphia, 1843.
Phila. Dir. (1859)	*McElroy's Philadelphia Directory for 1859.* Philadelphia, 1859.
Phila. Dir. (1864)	Salem *McElroy's Philadelphia City Directory for 1864.* Philadelphia, 1864.
Phila. Dir. (1865)	*McElroy's Philadelphia City Directory for 1865.* Philadelphia, 1865.
Phila. Dir. (1870)	Isaac Costa, comp. *Gopsill's Philadelphia City Directory for 1870.* Philadelphia, 1870.
Phila. Dir. (1871)	Isaac Costa, comp. *Gopsill's Philadelphia City Directory for 1871.* Philadelphia, 1871.
Phila. Dir. (1872)	Isaac Costa, comp. *Gopsill's Philadelphia City Directory for 1872.* Philadelphia, 1872.
Pittsburgh Dir. (1847)	Isaac Harris. *Harris's General Business Directory of the Cities of Pittsburgh and Allegheny, with the Environ.* Pittsburgh, 1847.
Providence Dir. (1865)	*The Providence Directory, for the Year 1865.* Providence, R.I., 1865.

Bibliography   { 717 }

Sandusky Dir. (1858–59)	M. T. McKelvey and Charles V. Old, comps. *Directory of Sandusky, Ohio, for 1858–9.* Sandusky, 1858.
St. Louis Dir. (1842)	*St. Louis Directory, for 1842.* St. Louis, 1842.
St. Louis Dir. (1854–55)	*The St. Louis Directory, for 1854–55.* St. Louis, 1854.
Wash. Dir. (1830)	*The Washington Directory.* Washington, D.C., 1830.
Wash. Dir. (1853)	Alfred Hunter, comp. *The Washington and Georgetown Directory, Strangers' Guide-Book for Washington, and Congressional and Clerks' Register.* Washington, D.C., 1853.
Wash. Dir. (1862)	Thomas Hutchinson, comp. *Boyd's Washington Directory.* Washington, D.C., 1862.
Wash. Dir. (1863)	*Hutchinson's Washington and Georgetown Directory.* Washington, D.C., 1863.
Wash. Dir. (1864)	Andrew Boyd, comp. *Boyd's Washington Directory. Containing Also a Business Directory of Washington, Georgetown and Alexandria.* Washington, D.C., 1864.
Wash. Dir. (1865)	Andrew Boyd, comp. *Boyd's Washington & Georgetown Directory.* Washington, D.C., 1865.
Wash. Dir. (1866)	Andrew Boyd, comp. *Boyd's Washington and Georgetown Directory.* Washington, D.C., 1866.
Wash. Dir. (1867)	William H. Boyd, comp. *Boyd's Directory of Washington & Georgetown.* Washington, D.C., 1867.
Wash. Dir. (1870)	William H. Boyd, comp. *Boyd's Directory of Washington, Georgetown, and Alexandria, together with a Compendium of their Governments, Institutions and Trades.* Washington, D.C., 1870.
Wash. Dir. (1871)	William H. Boyd, comp. *Boyd's Directory of Washington, Georgetown, and Alexandria,*

{ 718 } Bibliography

together with a Compendium of their Governments, Institutions and Trades. Washington, D.C., 1871.

Wash. Dir. (1872) William H. Boyd, comp. *Boyd's Directory of the District of Columbia.* Washington, D.C., 1872.

Wash. Dir. (1873) William H. Boyd, comp. *Boyd's Directory of the District of Columbia.* Washington, D.C., 1873.

OTHER SOURCES CITED

The Address and Reply on the Presentation of a Testimonial to S. P. Chase, by the Colored People of Cincinnati. Cincinnati, 1845.
Aldrich, Lewis Cass, and Frank E. Holmes, eds. *History of Windsor County, Vermont.* Syracuse, N.Y., 1891.
Aldrich, Lewis Cass, ed. *History of Erie County, Ohio.* . . . Syracuse, N.Y., 1889.
Andrews, C. C., ed. *History of St. Paul.* Syracuse, N.Y., 1890.
Arthur, Stanley Clisby. *Old Families of Louisiana.* New Orleans, 1931.
Ashworth, Henry. *A Tour in the United States, Cuba, and Canada.* London, 1861.
Augé, Paul, ed. *Larousse du XXe Siècle en Six Volumes.* 6 vols. Paris, 1928–33.
Avery, Elroy McKendree. *A History of Cleveland.* . . . 3 vols. Chicago, 1918.
Baker, George E., ed. *The Works of William H. Seward.* New York, 1884.
Baker, L. C. *History of the United States Secret Service.* Philadelphia, 1868.
Ballou, Maturin M. *History of Cuba; or, Notes of a Traveller in the Tropics.* Boston, 1854.
Basler, Roy P., ed. *The Collected Works of Abraham Lincoln.* 9 vols. New Brunswick, N.J., 1953–55.
Bayles, Richard M., ed. *History of Newport County, Rhode Island.* . . . New York, 1888.
Beale, Howard K., ed. *Diary of Gideon Welles: Secretary of the Navy Under Lincoln and Johnson.* 3 vols. New York, 1960.
Belden, Thomas Graham, and Marva Robins Belden. *So Fell the Angels.* Boston, 1956.
Berlin, Ira, ed. *Freedom: A Documentary History of Emancipation 1861–67. Series II, The Black Military Experience.* Cambridge, Mass., 1982.
Berryman, John R., ed. *History of the Bench and Bar of Wisconsin.* Chicago, 1898.
Bicknell, Thomas W. *The History of the State of Rhode Island and Providence Plantations: Biographical.* New York, 1920.
Bigger, David Dwight. *Ohio's Silver-Tongued Orator: Life and Speeches of General William H. Gibson.* Dayton, Ohio, 1901.
The Biographical Cyclopædia and Portrait Gallery with an Historical Sketch of the State of Ohio. 6 vols. Cincinnati, 1883–95.
The Biographical Cyclopedia of Representative Men of Rhode Island. 2 vols. Providence, 1881.

The Biographical Encyclopedia of Representative Men of Maryland and District of Columbia. Baltimore, 1879.
Blassingame, John W. *Black New Orleans, 1860–1880.* Chicago, 1973.
Blue, Frederick [J.]. "Kate's Paper Chase: The Race to Publish the First Biography of Salmon P. Chase." *The Old Northwest* 8 (1982–83): 353–63.
———. *Salmon P. Chase: A Life in Politics.* Kent, Ohio, 1987.
Bolt, Christine. *The Anti-Slavery Movement and Reconstruction: A Study in Anglo-American Co-operation, 1833–77.* London, 1969.
Botume, Elizabeth Hyde. *First Days Amongst the Contrabands.* Boston, 1893.
Bradburn, Francis H., comp. *A Memorial of George Bradburn.* Boston, 1883.
Bradburn, George. *A Statement, by George Bradburn, of his Connection with the "True Democrat," and John C. Vaughan.* Cleveland, 1853.
Bragg, Jefferson Davis. *Louisiana in the Confederacy.* Baton Rouge, 1941.
Brown, Albert J. *History of Clinton County, Ohio.* Indianapolis, 1915.
Browne, Jefferson B. *Key West: The Old and The New.* St. Augustine, 1912; reprint, Gainesville, Fla., 1973.
Calcagno, Francisco. *Diccionario Biográfico Cubano.* New York, 1878.
Campbell, Stanley W. *The Slave Catchers: Enforcement of the Fugitive Slave Law, 1850–1860.* Chapel Hill, 1968.
Carter, Alfred George Washington. *The Old Court House: Reminiscences and Anecdotes of the Courts and Bar of Cincinnati.* Cincinnati, 1880.
Catalogue of a Most Superb Collection of Extremely Rare and Elaborate Furniture . . . Formed by the Late Hon. Salmon Portland Chase. [New York, 1900].
Catalogue of the Officers and Graduates of Yale University in New Haven, Connecticut, 1701–1924. New Haven, 1924.
Celebration of the One Hundredth Anniversary of the Founding of Brown University, September 6th, 1864. Providence, 1865.
A Centennial Biographical History of Seneca County, Ohio. . . . Chicago, 1902.
Circular and Catalogue of the Law School of the University of Albany, for the Year 1864–5. Albany, N.Y., 1865.
Chapman, George Thomas. *Sketches of the Alumni of Dartmouth College. . . .* Cambridge, Mass., 1867.
Child, William H. *History of the Town of Cornish New Hampshire with Genealogical Record 1763–1910.* 2 vols. Concord, N.H., [1911?].
Cist, Charles. *Cincinnati in 1841: Its Early Annals and Future Prospects.* Cincinnati, 1841.
———. *Sketches and Statistics of Cincinnati in 1851.* Cincinnati, 1851.
Clarke, Adam. *The Holy Bible . . . with a Commentary and Critical Notes. . . .* 8 vols. London, 1810–25.
Clayton, W. Woodford. *History of Davidson County, Tennessee. . . .* Philadelphia, 1880.
Cleaves, Freeman. *Old Tippecanoe: William Henry Harrison and His Time.* New York, 1939.
Coates, William R., et al. *A History of Cuyahoga County and the City of Cleveland.* 3 vols. Chicago, 1924.
Coggeshall, William Turner. *The Poets and Poetry of the West: With Biographical and Critical Notices.* Columbus, 1861.

Cohen, Henry. *Business and Politics in America from the Age of Jackson to the Civil War: The Career Biography of W. W. Corcoran.* Westport, Conn., 1971.

Cole, J. R. *History of Washington and Kent Counties, Rhode Island.* . . . New York, 1889.

Cone, Stephen D. *Biographical and Historical Sketches: A Narrative of Hamilton and Its Residents from 1792 to 1896.* Hamilton, Ohio, 1896.

Conover, Frank, ed. *Centennial Portrait and Biographical Record of the City of Dayton and Montgomery County, Ohio.* . . . Logansport, Ind., 1897.

Cooper, Arthur E. "Col. Cornelius Ludlow." *Proceedings of the New Jersey Historical Society,* ser. 3, 3 (1898): 42–50.

Corner, George W. *Doctor Kane of the Arctic Seas.* Philadelphia, 1972.

Coyle, William, ed. *Ohio Authors and Their Books; Biographical Data and Selective Biographies for Ohio Authors, Native and Resident, 1796–1950.* Cleveland, 1962.

Cullum, George Washington. *Biographical Register of the Officers and Graduates of the U.S. Military Academy.* . . . 3 vols., 3rd ed. Boston, 1891.

Dana, Richard Henry. *To Cuba and Back. A Vacation Voyage.* Boston, 1859.

Dawson, Joseph G., III. *Army Generals and Reconstruction: Louisiana, 1862–1877.* Baton Rouge, 1982.

deChambrun, Clara Longworth. *The Making of Nicholas Longworth.* . . . New York, 1933.

des Cognets, Anna Russell. *Governor Garrard, of Kentucky, His Descendants and Relatives.* Lexington, Ky., 1898.

Destler, Chester McArthur. *Henry Demarest Lloyd and the Empire of Reform.* Philadelphia, 1963.

Dexter, Franklin Bowditch. *Biographical Sketches of the Graduates of Yale College with Annals of the College History.* 6 vols. New York, 1885–1912.

Donald, David, ed. *Inside Lincoln's Cabinet: The Civil War Diaries of Salmon P. Chase.* New York, 1954.

Downing, Antoinette F., and Vincent J. Scully, Jr. *The Architectural Heritage of Newport, Rhode Island, 1640–1915.* 2nd ed., rev. New York, 1967.

Drury, A. W. *History of the City of Dayton and Montgomery County, Ohio.* . . . Chicago, 1909.

Duff, William A. *History of North Central Ohio.* . . . 3 vols. Topeka, Kans., 1931.

Dunglison, Robley. *A Dictionary of Medical Science.* Philadelphia, 1874.

The Electric Telegraph. Substance of the Argument of S. P. Chase before the Supreme Court of the United States, . . . in the case of H. O'Reilly, and Others, vs. S. F. B. Morse, and Others. . . . New York, 1853.

Emerson, Charles Franklin, ed. *General Catalogue of Dartmouth College.* . . . Hanover, N.H., 1910–11.

Enciclopedia Universal Ilustrada Europeo-Americana. Barcelona, 1907–30.

Evans, W. McKee. *Ballots and Fence Rails.* . . . Chapel Hill, 1966.

Fairman, Charles. *Reconstruction and Reunion: 1864–88, Part One.* Vol. 6 of Paul A. Freund, gen. ed., *The Oliver Wendell Holmes Devise History of the Supreme Court of the United States.* New York, 1971.

Federal Writers' Project. *New Hampshire: A Guide to the Granite State.* Boston, 1938.

———. *New York City Guide*. New York, 1939.
Flanders, Henry. "A Commemorative Address Delivered at the Hall of the Historical Society of Pennsylvania, November 10, 1884, on John William Wallace, LLD." *Pennsylvania Magazine of History and Biography* 8 (1884): v–xliv.
Ford, Henry A., and Kate B. Ford. *History of Cincinnati, Ohio, with Illustrations and Biographical Sketches*. Cleveland, 1881.
Fuller, Oliver Payson. *The History of Warwick, Rhode Island*. . . . Providence, 1875.
General Catalogue of Bowdoin College . . . 1794–1950. Brunswick, Maine, 1950.
General Catalogue of the University of Vermont and State Agricultural College, Burlington, Vermont, 1791–1900. Burlington, Vt., 1901.
Gienapp, William E. *The Origins of the Republican Party, 1852–1856*. New York, 1987.
Gilkey, Elliot Howard. *The Ohio Hundred Year Book: A Hand-Book of the Public Men and Public Institutions of Ohio*. . . . Columbus, 1901.
Gilliland, Thaddeus S., ed. *History of Van Wert County, Ohio*. . . . Chicago, 1906.
Goode, James M. *Capital Losses: A Cultural History of Washington's Destroyed Buildings*. Washington, D.C., 1979.
Goss, Charles Frederic. *Cincinnati, the Queen City*. 4 vols. Chicago, 1912.
Graf, Leroy P., et al., eds. *The Papers of Andrew Johnson*. 10 vols. to date. Knoxville, 1967–.
La Grande Encyclopédie: Inventaire Raisonné des Sciences, des Lettres et des Arts. 31 vols. Paris, 1886–1902.
Greve, Charles Theodore. *Centennial History of Cincinnati and Representative Citizens*. Chicago, 1904.
Griffin, Simon Goodell. *A History of the Town of Keene*. . . . Keene, N.H., 1904.
Groce, George C., and David H. Wallace. *The New-York Historical Society's Dictionary of Artists in America, 1564–1860*. New Haven, 1957.
Gutgesell, Stephen, ed. *Guide to Ohio Newspapers, 1793–1973: Union Bibliography of Ohio Newspapers Available in Ohio Libraries*. Columbus, 1974.
Hammond, Bray. *Sovereignty and an Empty Purse, Banks and Politics in the Civil War*. Princeton, 1970.
Hammond, John Martin. *Colonial Mansions of Maryland and Delaware*. Philadelphia, 1914.
Harrington, Fred Harvey. *Fighting Politician: Major General N. P. Banks*. Philadelphia, 1948.
Harrold, Stanley. *Gamaliel Bailey and Antislavery Union*. Kent, Ohio, 1986.
Hart, Albert Bushnell. *Salmon Portland Chase*. Boston, 1899; reprint, New York, 1980.
Hazard, Samuel. *Cuba with Pen and Pencil*. Hartford, 1871.
Heitman, Francis Bernard. *Historical Register and Dictionary of the United States Army*. . . . 2 vols. Washington, D.C., 1903.
Hermann, Janet Sharp. *The Pursuit of a Dream*. New York, 1981.
Hilen, Andrew, ed. *The Letters of Henry Wadsworth Longfellow*. 6 vols. Cambridge, Mass., 1966–82.
Historical Catalogue of Brown University, 1764–1914. Providence, 1914.

A History and Biographical Cyclopædia of Butler County, Ohio. . . . Cincinnati, 1882.
History of Ashtabula County, Ohio. . . . Philadelphia, 1878.
The History of Brown County, Ohio. . . . Chicago, 1883.
History of Cincinnati and Hamilton County, Ohio: Their Past and Present. . . . Cincinnati, 1894.
History of Defiance County, Ohio. . . . Chicago, 1883.
History of Franklin and Pickaway Counties, Ohio. . . . Cleveland, 1880.
History of Logan County and Ohio. . . . Chicago, 1880.
The History of Montgomery County, Ohio. . . . Chicago, 1882.
History of Muskingum County, Ohio. . . . Columbus, 1882.
History of Ross and Highland Counties, Ohio. . . . Cleveland, 1880.
History of Seneca County, Ohio. . . . Chicago, 1886.
History of Trumbull and Mahoning Counties with Illustrations and Biographical Sketches. Cleveland, 1882.
The History of Tuscarawas County, Ohio. . . . Chicago, 1884.
History of Washington County, Ohio . . . 1788–1881. Cleveland, 1881.
Hitchcock, Walter Theodore. "Timothy Walker: Antebellum Lawyer." Ph.D. diss., University of Mississippi, 1980.
Holli, Melvin G., and Peter d'A. Jones, eds. *Biographical Dictionary of American Mayors, 1820–1980: Big City Mayors.* Westport, Conn., 1981.
Horowitz, Robert F. *The Great Impeacher: A Political Biography of James M. Ashley.* New York, 1979.
Howe, M. A. DeWolfe, ed. *Later Years of the Saturday Club, 1870–1920.* Boston, 1927.
Hughes, Sarah Forbes, ed. *Letters and Recollections of John Murray Forbes.* 2 vols. Boston, 1900.
Hugo, Victor Marie. *Notre-Dame de Paris.* Paris, 1836.
Hungerford, Edward. *The Story of the Baltimore & Ohio Railroad, 1827–1929.* . . . New York, 1928.
Hurd, Duane Hamilton, ed. *History of Essex County, Massachusetts.* . . . Philadelphia, 1888.
―――, ed. *History of Merrimack and Belknap Counties, New Hampshire.* Philadelphia, 1885.
Ingham, Mrs. W. A. *Women of Cleveland and Their Work.* . . . Cleveland, 1893.
James, Edward T., et al., eds. *Notable American Women, 1607–1950.* . . . Cambridge, 1971.
Jennings, H. C. *The Methodist Book Concern: A Romance of History.* New York, 1924.
Jewell, Edwin L. *Jewell's Crescent City Illustrated.* New Orleans, 1873.
Jewett, Isaac Appleton. "'Cincinnati is a Delightful Place': Letters of a Law Clerk, 1831–34." Edited by James Taylor Dunn. *Bulletin of the Historical and Philosophical Society of Ohio* 10 (Oct. 1952): 257–77.
Johnson, Guion Griffis. *Ante-Bellum North Carolina.* . . . Chapel Hill, 1937.
Johnson, Rossiter, ed. *The Twentieth Century Biographical Dictionary of Notable Americans.* . . . 10 vols. Boston, 1904; reprint, Detroit, 1968.
Johnston, J. Stoddard, ed. *Memorial History of Louisville from Its Settlement to the Year 1896.* Chicago, n.d.

Juettner, Otto. *1785–1909. Daniel Drake and His Followers: Historical and Biographical Sketches*. Cincinnati, 1909.
Keim, DeB. Randolph. *Keim's Illustrated Hand-Book: Washington and Its Environs*. . . . 4th ed. Washington, D.C., 1874.
Kennedy, James Harrison. *A History of Cleveland: Its Settlement, Rise and Progress. 1876–1896*. Cleveland, 1896.
Kennedy, John P. *Memoirs of the Life of William Wirt, Attorney General of the United States*. 2 vols. Philadelphia, 1849.
Kennedy, Robert P. *The Historical Review of Logan County*. Chicago, 1903.
King, Moses. *King's Hand-Book of Boston*. Cambridge, Mass., 1878.
Klein, Philip S., and Ari Hoogenboom. *A History of Pennsylvania*. 2nd ed. University Park, Pa., 1980.
Klement, Frank L. *Dark Lanterns: Secret Political Societies and Treason Trials in the Civil War*. Baton Rouge, 1984.
Klise, J. W. *The County of Highland: A History of Highland County, Ohio*. . . . Madison, Wis., 1902.
Knight, Edward H. *Knight's New Mechanical Dictionary*. Boston, 1884.
Landy, James. *Cincinnati Past and Present: Or its Industrial History, as Exhibited in the Life-Labors of its Leading Men*. Cincinnati, 1872.
Lane, Samuel A. *Fifty Years and Over of Akron and Summit County*. Akron, 1892.
Lang, William. *History of Seneca County*. . . . Springfield, Ohio, 1880.
Lanman, Charles. *Biographical Annals of the Civil Government of the United States*. . . . Washington, D.C., 1876.
Larson, Henrietta M. *Jay Cooke: Private Banker*. Cambridge, Mass., 1936.
Lee, Alfred Emory. *History of the City of Columbus, Capital of Ohio*. 2 vols. New York, 1892.
Letter of the Secretary of the Treasury, Transmitting . . . A List of the Special Agents of the Treasury Department and their Assistants. 38th Cong., 1st sess., 1864, S. Ex. Doc. 31.
Letter from the Secretary of the Treasury, Transmitting a List of Clerks and other Persons Employed in the Treasury Department for the Year 1863. 38th Cong., 1st sess., 1864, H. Ex. Doc. 62.
Letter from the Secretary of the Treasury, Transmitting List of Clerks Employed in the Treasury Department during the Year ending December 31, 1862. 37th Cong., 3rd sess., 1863, H. Ex. Doc. 70.
Little, David Mason. "Documentary History of the Salem Custom House." *Essex Institute Historical Collections* 67 (1931): 265–80.
Long, E. B. *The Civil War Day by Day: An Almanac, 1861–1865*. Garden City, N.Y., 1971.
Loring, Katharine Peabody. "The Earliest Summer Residents of the North Shore and Their Houses." *Essex Institute Historical Collections* 68 (1932): 193–208.
Lucid, Robert F., ed. *The Journal of Richard Henry Dana, Jr*. Cambridge, Mass., 1968.
Lyford, James O., ed. *History of Concord, New Hampshire, from the Original Grant in Seventeen Hundred and Twenty-Five to the Opening of the Twentieth Century*. 2 vols. Concord, N.H., 1903.

Lytle, William. *Merchant Vessels of the United States, 1807–1868.* Mystic, Conn., 1952.
McAllister, Anna [Shannon]. *Ellen Ewing: Wife of General Sherman.* New York, 1936.
———. *In Winter We Flourish: Life and Letters of Sarah Worthington King Peter, 1800–1877.* New York, 1939.
McClure, A. K. *Abraham Lincoln and Men of War-Times....* Philadelphia, 1892.
McFeely, William S. *Grant: A Biography.* New York, 1982.
Maizlish, Stephen E. *The Triumph of Sectionalism: The Transformation of Ohio Politics, 1844–1856.* Kent, Ohio, 1983.
Marten, James. *Texas Divided: Loyalty and Dissent in the Lone Star State, 1856–1874.* Lexington, Ky., 1990.
Martin, William T. *History of Franklin County: A Collection of Reminiscences of the Early Settlement of the County....* Columbus, 1858.
Martyn, Charles. *The William Ward Genealogy....* New York, 1925.
Maxwell, Sidney D. *The Suburbs of Cincinnati....* Cincinnati, 1870.
Message from the President . . . Transmitting Papers relative to the Case of George St. Leger Grenfel. 39th Cong., 2nd sess., 1867, H. Ex. Doc. 50.
Miers, Earl Schenck, ed. *Lincoln Day by Day: A Chronology, 1809–1865.* 3 vols. Washington, D.C., 1960.
Morse, Jedediah, and Richard C. Morse, *A New Universal Gazetteer, or Geographical Dictionary.* 4th ed. New Haven, 1823.
Mott, Frank L. *A History of American Magazines 1841–1850.* New York, 1930.
Nason, Elias. *A Gazetteer of the State of Massachusetts.* Boston, 1890.
*The National Union Catalog: Pre-*1956 *Imprints.* 754 vols. London, 1968–81.
Nevins, Allan. *Hamilton Fish: The Inner History of the Grant Administration.* New York, 1936.
Nouvelle Biographie Générale depuis les Temps les Plus Reculés jusqu'a Nos Jours.... 46 vols. Paris, 1853–66.
Oberholtzer, Ellis Paxson. *Jay Cooke: Financier of the Civil War.* Philadelphia, 1907.
Orth, Samuel P. *A History of Cleveland Ohio....* Chicago and Cleveland, 1910.
Owen, Thomas McAdory. *History of Alabama and Dictionary of Alabama Biography.* Chicago, 1921.
Padgett, James H., ed. "Some Letters of George Stanton Denison, 1854–1866: Observations of a Yankee on Conditions in Louisiana and Texas." *Louisiana Historical Quarterly* 23 (1940): 1132–1240.
Palmer, Beverly Wilson, ed. *The Selected Letters of Charles Sumner.* 2 vols. Boston, 1990.
Parks, Marian. "A Man For His Season: Victor Smith, 1826–1865." M.A. thesis, Claremont Graduate School, 1981.
Parton, James. *The Life of Horace Greeley, Editor of "The New-York Tribune," from his Birth to the Present Time.* Boston, 1872.
Pearson, Henry Greenleaf. *The Life of John A. Andrew: Governor of Massachusetts, 1861–1865.* 2 vols. Boston, 1904.
Peeke, H[ewson] L. *The Centennial History of Erie County, Ohio.* 2 vols. Sandusky, Ohio, 1925.

———. *A Standard History of Erie County, Ohio.* . . . 2 vols. Chicago and New York, 1916.
Perrin, William Henry. *History of Summit County.* . . . Chicago, 1881.
Phelps, Mary Merwin. *Kate Chase: Dominant Daughter.* New York, 1935.
Pierce, Edward L. *Memoir and Letters of Charles Sumner, 1845–1860.* 4 vols., 2nd ed. Boston, 1894.
Pinney, Norman. *The First Book in French; or, a Practical Introduction to Reading, Writing, and Speaking the French Language.* New York, [c. 1848].
Pollard, James E., ed. *The Journal of Jay Cooke; or, The Gibraltar Records, 1865–1905.* Columbus, Ohio, 1935.
Pool, William, ed. *Landmarks of Niagara County.* Syracuse, N.Y., 1897.
Poor, Henry V. *History of the Railroads and Canals of the United States of America.* . . . New York, 1860.
Portrait and Biographical Record of the City of Toledo and Lucas and Wood Counties, Ohio. . . . Chicago, 1895.
Quinquennial Catalogue of the Officers and Graduates of Harvard University, 1636–1915. Cambridge, Mass., 1915.
"Rantoul Genealogy, &c." *Essex Institute Historical Collections* 5 (1863): 145–52.
Reed, George Irving, ed. *Bench and Bar of Ohio: A Compendium of History and Biography.* 2 vols. Chicago, 1897.
Reid, Whitelaw. *After the War: A Southern Tour. May 1, 1865, to May 1, 1866.* New York, 1866.
———. *Ohio in the War: Her Statesman, Her Generals, and Soldiers.* Cincinnati, 1868.
Report of the Secretary of the Treasury, on the State of Finances, for the Year ending June 30, 1863. 38th Cong., 1st sess., 1863, H. Ex. Doc. 3.
"Report on Pardons, Governor Salmon P. Chase to the General Assembly." Ohio General Assembly, House of Representatives. *Journal.* 52nd Assem., 2nd sess., 1857.
Representative Men and Old Families of Rhode Island. . . . 3 vols. Chicago, 1908.
Richardson, Harold Edward. *Cassius Marcellus Clay: Firebrand of Freedom.* Lexington, Ky., 1976.
Richardson, James D., ed. *A Compilation of The Messages and Papers of the Presidents.* New York, 1897.
Riddle, A. G. "Recollections of the Forty-Seventh General Assembly of Ohio, 1847–48." *Magazine of Western History* 6 (Aug. 1887): 341–51.
Rightor, Henry, ed. *Standard History of New Orleans.* . . . Chicago, 1900.
Ripley, C. Peter. *Slaves and Freedmen in Civil War Louisiana.* Baton Rouge, 1976.
Robertson, Charles. *History of Morgan County, Ohio.* . . . Chicago, 1886.
Robinson, Caroline E. *The Hazard Family of Rhode Island, 1635–1894.* Boston, 1895.
Robson, Charles, ed. *The Biographical Encyclopædia of Ohio of the Nineteenth Century.* Cincinnati, 1876.
Rockel, William M., ed. and comp. *20th Century History of Springfield, and Clark County, Ohio and Representative Citizens.* Chicago, 1908.

Rose, William Ganson. *Cleveland: The Making of a City.* Cleveland, 1950; reprint, Kent, Ohio, 1990.
Rose, Willie Lee. *Rehearsal for Reconstruction: The Port Royal Experiment.* New York, 1964; reprint, New York, 1976.
Roseboom, Eugene H. *The Civil War Era, 1850–1873,* v. 4 of Carl Wittke, ed. *The History of the State of Ohio.* Columbus, 1944.
Russell, William Howard. *Pictures of Southern Life: Social, Political, and Military.* New York, 1861.
Scharf, J. Thomas. *History of Baltimore City and County.* . . . Philadelphia, 1881.
―――. *History of Westchester County, New York.* . . . 2 vols. Philadelphia, 1886.
Scheiber, Harry N. *Ohio Canal Era: A Case Study of Government and the Economy, 1820–1861.* Athens, Ohio, 1969.
Schuckers, Jacob W. *The Life and Public Services of Salmon Portland Chase.* New York, 1874.
Scribner, Harvey, ed. *Memoirs of Lucas County and the City of Toledo.* . . . Madison, Wis., 1910.
Sherman, William Tecumseh. *Memoirs of General W. T. Sherman.* New York, 1990.
Shinn, William Henry. *The County of Williams: A History of Williams County, Ohio.* . . . Madison, Wis., 1905.
Simon, John Y., et al., eds. *The Papers of Ulysses S. Grant.* 18 vols. to date. Carbondale, Ill., 1967–.
Simpson, Brooks D., et al., eds. *Advice After Appomattox: Letters to Andrew Johnson, 1865–1866: Special Volume No. 1 of the Papers of Andrew Johnson.* Knoxville, 1987.
Smith, Margaret Bayard. *The First Forty Years of Washington Society.* . . . New York, 1906.
Smith, Susan Sutton, and Harrison Hayford, eds. *The Journals and Miscellaneous Notebooks of Ralph Waldo Emerson.* Vol. 14, *1854–1861.* Cambridge, Mass., 1978.
Smith, William Prescott. *The Book of the Great Railway Celebrations of 1857.* . . . 2 parts in 1 vol. New York, 1858.
Sobel, Robert, and John Raimo, eds. *Biographical Directory of the Governors of the United States, 1789–1978.* 4 vols. Westport, Conn., 1978.
Sokoloff, Alice Hunt. *Kate Chase for the Defense.* New York, 1971.
Sprague, Warren Vincent. *Sprague Families in America.* Rutland, Vt., 1913.
Starbuck, Alexander. *The History of Nantucket, County, Island and Town.* . . . Boston, 1924.
Starr, S. Frederick. *Southern Comfort: The Garden District of New Orleans, 1800–1900.* Cambridge, Mass., 1989.
Stearns, Ezra S., comp. *Genealogical and Family History of the State of New Hampshire.* New York, 1908.
Sullivant, Joseph. *A Genealogy and Family Memorial.* Columbus, 1874.
Swisher, Carl B. *The Taney Period, 1836–64.* Vol. 5 of Paul A. Freund, gen. ed., *The Oliver Wendell Holmes Devise History of the Supreme Court of the United States.* New York, 1974.

Taylor, James Wickes. *"A Choice Nook of Memory": The Diary of a Cincinnati Law Clerk 1842–44*. Ed. by James Taylor Dunn. Columbus, 1950.
Taylor, William A. *Centennial History of Columbus and Franklin County, Ohio*. Chicago, 1909.
Taylor, William Alexander. *Ohio Statesman and Hundred Year Book, from 1788 to 1892, Inclusive*. Columbus, 1892.
Tebeau, Charlton W. *A History of Florida*. Coral Gables, Fla., 1971.
Thomas, Benjamin P., and Harold M. Hyman. *Stanton: The Life and Times of Lincoln's Secretary of War*. New York, 1962.
Thompson, James H. *The History of the County of Highland*. . . . Hillsboro, Ohio, 1878.
Thornbrough, Gayle, et al., eds. *The Diary of Calvin Fletcher*. 9 vols. Indianapolis, 1972–83.
Thorne, J. O., ed. *Chambers's Biographical Dictionary*. Rev. ed. New York, 1969.
Titus' Atlas of Hamilton County, Ohio. . . . Philadelphia, 1869.
Trefousse, Hans L. *Andrew Johnson: A Biography*. New York, 1989.
———. *Ben Butler: The South Called Him Beast!* New York, 1957.
———. *Benjamin Franklin Wade: Radical Republican from Ohio*. New York, 1963.
Trowbridge, John Townsend. *The Desolate South 1865–1866*. . . . Ed. Gordon Carroll. Boston, 1956.
[———]. *The Ferry-Boy and the Financier*. Boston, 1864.
Tunnell, Ted. *Crucible of Reconstuction: War, Radicalism and Race in Louisiana, 1862–1877*. Baton Rouge, 1984.
U.S. Adjutant-General's Office. *Official Army Register of the Volunteer Force of the United States*. 8 vols. Washington, D.C., 1865–67.
Van Tassel, David D., and John J. Grabowski, eds. *The Encyclopedia of Cleveland History*. Bloomington, 1987.
Vapereau, Gustave, ed. *Dictionnaire Universel des Contemporains: Contenant Toutes les Personnes Notables de la France et des Pays Étrangers*. 5th ed. Paris, 1880.
Venable, William Henry. *A Centennial History of Christ Church, Cincinnati 1817–1917*. Cincinnati, 1918.
Waggoner, Clark. *History of the City of Toledo and Lucas County, Ohio*. . . . New York, 1888.
Wakelyn, John L., ed. *Biographical Dictionary of the Confederacy*. Westport, Conn., 1977.
Wallace, W. Stewart, comp. *A Dictionary of North American Authors Deceased before 1950*. Toronto, 1951.
Warden, Robert Bruce. *An Account of the Private Life and Public Services of Salmon Portland Chase*. . . . Cincinnati, 1874.
Warren, Gordon H. *Fountain of Discontent: The Trent Affair and Freedom of the Seas*. Boston, 1980.
Webb, Walter Prescott, et al. *The Handbook of Texas*. Austin, 1952.
Weisenburger, Francis Phelps. *The Life of John McLean: A Politician on the United States Supreme Court*. Columbus, 1937; reprint, New York, 1971.

White, Howard A. *The Freedmen's Bureau in Louisiana.* Baton Rouge, 1970.
White, Ruth Young, ed. *We Too Built Columbus.* . . . Columbus, Ohio, 1936.
Whiteman, Maxwell. *Paintings and Sculpture at the Union League of Philadelphia.* Philadelphia, 1978.
Williams, Harrison. *Legends of Loudoun: An Account of the History and Homes of a Border County.* Richmond, 1938.
Williams, T. J. C., and Folger McKinsey. *History of Frederick County, Maryland.* . . . 2 vols. [Frederick, Md.], 1910; reprint, Baltimore, 1979.
Williams, W. W. *History of the Fire Lands, Comprising Huron and Erie Counties, Ohio.* . . . [Cleveland], 1879.
Wiltse, Charles M., et al., eds. *The Papers of Daniel Webster.* 14 vols. Hanover, N.H., 1974–86.
Winter, Nevin O. *A History of Northwest Ohio.* . . . Chicago, 1917.
Writers' Program, Louisiana. *Louisiana: A Guide to the State.* New York, 1941.

Index

Page references for footnotes that identify individuals are in bold type.

Abbott, Mrs. (wife of Joseph Carter Abbott), 544
Abbott, Joseph Carter, **544**
Abdy, Edward Strutt, *Journal of a Residence and Tour,* 109
Abercrombie, John Joseph, **652**
Abingdon (Ludlow homestead), 578
Able, Barton, 433
Abraham, Joseph, **206**
Ada Hancock (ship), 460
Adair, James A., **250**
Adams, 217, 218
Adams, Charles Francis, 225, **226**, 231, 377, 691; letter to, from Seward, 377
Adams, Green, **352**, 382, 383
Adams, Henry Brooks, **693**
Adams, Henry Joseph, **250**, 264; letter to, 250
Adams, John, 36, 329; as described by Benjamin Franklin, 36
Adams, John Quincy, xvi, **3**, 9, 11, 33, 50; receptions of, 3, 7
Adams, Marian ("Clover") Hooper, **693**
Adams, Nehemiah, **549**; *South-Side View of Slavery,* 549
Addison, article, 225
Addison and Steele, *Spectator,* xvi
Advocate of Freedom (Brunswick, Maine), 213
Advocate of Peace, 168
African-Americans: call for Nashville Convention, 1865, 576; Chase visits churches, 569, 644, 682; citizenship, 387; delegations, 542–44, 547–48, 550; fair visited, New Orleans, 1865, 566; first black admitted to Supreme Court bar, 519, 521; freed slaves' land and communities, 479, 538, 548, 549–50, 570, 571, 640; Freedmen's Aid Commission meeting,
Cincinnati, 581; Gen. Banks on arming blacks, 428; schools, 536, 550, 567–68; situation in South, described, 588; suffrage, 570, 574, 597, 603, 604, 605; Sumner advises on 1872 election, 695; troops reviewed, 563; woman calls on Chase for aid, 206, 208. *See also* Slavery; Emancipation Proclamation
African Methodist Episcopal Zion Church, 226
Agassiz, Jean Louis Rodolphe, 484, **485**, 490; Brazilian expedition, 592
"Agate." *See* Reid, Whitelaw
Agüero, Joaquin de, **235**
Aiken, John, **591**
Akenside, Mark, *The Pleasures of Imagination,* 56, 57
Alabama, politics, 605–6
Alabama (ship), 478, 479
Albany Atlas, 213
Albany Manual Labor University, 250
Albert, Arthur William Patrick, **649**
Albert, William Julian, **520**, 527, 610
Albrecht, Claire, 499, 501
Alden, ———, 195
Alden, James, **648**
Alden, Joseph W., **171**
Alden v. Alden, 195
Alder, Thomas, **276**
Ale, ———, 206
Alexander, J. H., 433
Alexander, Joseph, **83**
Alice Maud Mary, Princess, **362**
All Saints Episcopal Chapel (Newport, R.I.), 482
Allen, Diarca Howe, **186**
Allen, Ebenezer, **234**
Allen, George D., **560**
Allen, R. M., **568**
Allen, William S., **560**

{ 729 }

Alley, Mrs. (wife of John Bassett Alley), 484, 628
Alley, John Bassett, **483**, 484, 627, 628
Allston, Washington, 30
Allyn, John, 445
Almy, John Jay, **548**
Almy's hotel (Havana, Cuba), 556
Alpha Kappa Society, Marietta College, 156
Alston, Montgomery P., 280
Alton case, 127
Ambassador (steamboat), 153, 154
American Hotel (Columbus), 202, 253, 271, 273
American House (Van Wert, Ohio), 303
American Institute (New York), 595
American Institute of Homeopathy, 211
American Medical Association, 182
American Peace Society, 168
American Revolution, 71
American Sunday School Union, 106, 113, 115, 167, 212
American Temperance Society, 161; *Permanent Temperance Documents*, 159
Ames, Adelbert, 624
Ames, Edward Raymond, **634**, 647
Ames, G. W., **565**
Ames, Oakes, **503**
Anderson, Mrs., 103
Anderson, ———, 206
Anderson, Mrs. (wife of Richard Anderson), 656
Anderson, Alfred, 270
Anderson, Catherine Longworth. *See* Longworth, Catherine
Anderson, Charles, **275**
Anderson, Larz, 57, **578**, 581
Anderson, Paul, 262
Anderson, Richard, 656
Anderson, Robert, **544**
Andover Theological Seminary, 21
Andrew, John Albion, **403**, 404, 441, 490, 493, 503, 518, 594; letters to, 475, 531
Andrews, Mr., 606
Andrews, Christopher Columbus, **563**, 593, 594
Andrews, Ebenezer Baldwin, **372**, 375, 403, 404
Andrews, Israel DeWolf, **638**, 639
Andrews, Israel Ward, **283**
Andrews, John, **247**
Andrews, John W., **243**
Andrews, Joseph, 265, 271
Andrews, Mrs. O. M., **265**
Andrews, Rufus F., **328**, 612

Andromeda (ship), 519
Andrus, C., **565**
Angelico, Fra. *See* Pietri, Guido di
Angier House (Cleveland), 268
Antarctica, discovery of, 136
Anthony, Anna J., **257**, 266, 269, 273, 279, 292, 293, 297, 308, 311
Anthony, Charles, **117**, 257, 276
Anthony, Henry Bowen, **332**, 499, 626
Antietam, battle of, 404, 415, 417; and Emancipation Proclamation, xxxiv
Antimasons, 66
Antislavery organizations: American and Foreign Anti-Slavery Society, 186; American Anti-Slavery Society, 168; Ohio State Anti-Slavery Society, 165
Ap-Jones, Ludlow, **578**
"Appeal of the Independent Democrats": Chase's role in preparation, xxvii–xxviii
Applegate, Daniel, **304**, 653
Appleton, Jesse, **55**
Appleton, William, **55**, 55–56
Appomattox, Va., celebration of surrender at, 528
Aquinas, Thomas, 39
Arago (ship), 551
Archbold, Edward, **203**, 225, 227
Arendell, Michael F., **538**, 540
Aristotle, 39; *Works*, 54
Arkansas, politics, 527
Arletta (ship), 538
Armstead, Rosetta. *See* Rosetta case
Armstrong, James Smith, **82**, 131
Armstrong, William, **306**
Armstrong, William George, **557**
Armstrong, William Wallace, **306**
Army of the Potomac, 322, 331
Arnold, Isaac Newton, **594**
Artesian wells (Bryan, Ohio), 240
Ashley, ——— (preacher), 237
Ashley, James Mitchell, **241**, 302, 315, 316, 479, 514, 515, 518, 531, 678
Ashton, Joseph Hubley, **515**
Asper, Joel Funk, **225**
Aspinwall, William Henry, **317**, 416, 417, 419, 420, 421, 670; on McClellan, 416, 418
Aston, Albert, **664**
Astor, John Jacob, 369, **370**
Astor House (New York), 481
Astor Library (New York), 595
Atkinson, Robert J., **467**
Atsion (Patterson estate), 652–53
Atzerodt, George A., 587, **588**
Aubery, Jean, **267**
Aubrey, Mrs., 190

Index   { 731 }

Aubrey, John F., 190, **191**
Aubrey, W., 190, **191**
Audenried, Joseph Crain, **539**, 613
Auferman, Miss, 589
Augur, Christopher Columbus, **480**
Auld, Alice, **302**, 645, 704
Auld, Amy, **302**, 704, 705, 709, 710
Auld, Jane (Jenny), **302**, 515
Auld, Jane Chase (niece), **163**, 166, 302, 488, 515, 528, 670
Auld, Robert, 163
Austen, David, Jr., 151, **237**
Austin, Horace, **659**
Australasian (ship), 609
Avery, Edward, **212**
Avery, John L., **118**
Aydelott, Benjamin Parkham, **166**, 168, 214, 215; lecture and sermons, 195, 212, 216, 223
Azalea (ship), 485, 486

Babcock, James F., **363**
Backus, Abner L., **296**
Badeau, Adam, **648**
Badger, ———, 289
Badger, George Edmund, **209**, 236
Bailey, Ezra, **119**
Bailey, Gamaliel, **134**, 148, 166, 169, 174, 208, 233, 235, 255, 514, 599; Chase corresponds with, 204, 225, 227; Chase's acquaintance with, xx; "The Crisis—The Duty," 134; and Liberty party, xxii
Bailey, George W., **559**
Bailey, Marcellus, **513**, 514, 593
Bailey, Margaret Lucy Shands, **255**, 514, 599
Bailey, Theodorus, **613**
Bailey & Co., **703**
Bain, Alexander, 215, 222
Bainbridge, E. T., **88**
Baker, Mr., 223
Baker, Mrs. (wife of Col. Baker), 700
Baker, James Heaton, **247**, 253
Baker, John A., **542**, 543
Baker, John G., **481**
Baker, Nathan F., **190**
Baker, S. A., **239**
Balch, Francis Vergnies, **521**
Balcom, Ransom, **445**, 446
Baldwin, Hiram, **295**
Baldwin, John P., **555**
Baldwin, Major, 499, 500
Balestier, Joseph N., 118, **132**; letter to, 132
Ball, Eva Chandler, **581**
Ball, Evelina Chandler, **135**, 142, 163, 179, 189, 262

Ball, Flamen, **124**, 127, 131, 150, 167, 170, 177, 195, 206, 228, 236, 258, 261, 263, 266, 511, 581; death of child, 179; letters to, 228, 233; social relations with Chase, 130, 135, 136, 145, 156, 163, 169, 211, 214, 232, 258, 262, 264, 270
Ball, Helen Cecelia, **581**
Ball, Laura Amelia, **581**
Ball, Susan Louisa Bowler, **581**
Ballantyne, William, **666**
Ballard, Bland, **577**
Balloch, James, **541**
Baltimore, flood damage (1868), 643
Baltimore (ship), 340, 343, 344, 481
Baltimore American, 527
Baltimore and Ohio Railroad, 8, 32–33, 294, 324, 392, 454
Baltzell, Lewis, 291, **292**
Bancroft, George, **426**, 499, 592
Bank meeting, 313
Bank of the United States, 73, 75, 80, 150; Cincinnati Agency, xviii; Jackson's war against, xxxvii. *See also* under Chase—law practice
Bank of United States v. Longworth, 99
Bank of United States v. Matthews, 150
Bank of United States v. Prendergast et al., 150
Bank Tax Case, 513, 514
Bank v. Borden, Ferguson, et al., 114
Bank v. Martin et al., 141
Bank v. Wheeler et al., 114
Bankhead, John Pine, **390**
Bankruptcy Act (1867), 646
Banks, Mary Theodosia Palmer, **566**
Banks, Nathaniel Prentiss, **321**, 334, 345, 346, 347, 348, 402, 427, 436, 448, 565, 566, 586, 600, 709; on arming blacks, 428; on black suffrage, 570; letter to Lincoln, 428; relieves Benjamin Franklin Butler in New Orleans, 425–26
Bannister, Dwight, **379**, 390, 391, 393, 413, 414, 418, 419, 582; correspondence, 492, 673
Baptists, 333
Barber, Miss, 150
Barber, Levi, **403**
Barbour, James, **49**
Barclay, ———, 698, 699
Barker, Jacob, **565**, 569
Barlow, Francis Channing, **485**, 523
Barnard, Henry, **501**
Barnes, ———, 557
Barnes, C. P., 119
Barnes, Joseph K., **504**
Barnes, Mary T. Fauntleroy, **504**

Barney, Charles D., **601**
Barney, Hiram, **237**, 328, 372, 373, 382, 398, 410, 424, 426, 459, 460, 468, 502, 515, 595, 609, 611, 677, 688, 707; Custom House patronage, xxxviii; correspondence, 259, 395, 465, 641, 662, 691, 692, 694; and New York Labor Contract, 371, 373; removed from collectorship, xlii
Barnitz, David G., **433**
Barnum, David, 18
Barnum's City Hotel (Baltimore), 18, 602, 643
Barr, Robert N., **286**, 585
Barreda, Federico L., **482**, 592, 593
Barrell, Catherine Maria Ward, **20**
Barrell, Samuel Brown, 17, **18**, 20
Barrett, Joseph Hartwell, **641**
Barstow, Mrs. (wife of Zedekiah S. Barstow), 619
Barstow, Simon Forrester, **321**
Barstow, Zedekiah Smith, **619**, 620
Bartlet, John F., 289
Bartlett, Jonathan, **185**, 186
Bartlett, Nelson S., **625**
Bartlett, Sidney, **621**, 693
Bartlett ads Winans, 196
Bartley, Thomas Welles, **253**, 260, 680, 704
Barton, Coralie Livingston, **44**, 667, 678, 680; letters to, noted, 681, 685, 688, 691, 704
Barton, Thomas Pennant, 44
Bascom, William T., **277**, 279, 296, 301, 304
Bassett, Edward P., **258**, 312
Bates, Edward, **313**, 315, 352, 353, 360, 361, 366, 367, 368, 372, 373, 398, 436, 442; on citizenship for blacks, 387; on Mississippi River trade, 436; on recognizing Confederacy, 313
Bates, Elizabeth Dwight Hoadly, **263**
Bates, George H., 185
Bates, James Lawrence, **225**, 311; letter to, 225
Bates, John (Cincinnati), **112**
Bates, John (Wood County), **295**
Bates, Joshua Hall, **219**, 263
Bates, Wilson, **185**, 196
Bates v. Kellogg et al., 141
Baton Rouge, La., described, 571
Baugh, Charles C., **672**
Baxter, Jedediah Hyde, **666**, 667, 672, 673
Baxter, Richard, *The Saint's Everlasting Rest*, 111
Bayard, James Asheton, **332**

Bayley, L. S.: letter from, 502
Beach, Mrs. C., 132
Beach, Gilbert, 228, 239
Beach, Mrs. M., 133
Beard, James Henry, **216**
Beatty, John, **251**
Beatty, William M., **299**
Beaufort, N.C., old court records, 539, 540
Beauregard, Pierre Gustave Toutant, **407**, 409, 544
Beaver, John F., **207**
Beck, Mrs., 645
Beckett, William, **248**
Beckford, William, xiv
Beckwith, S. C., **241**
Bedell v. Steamship Potomac, 648
Beebe, Horace Y., **356**
Beecher, Henry Ward, **354**, 520, 629, 709; sermon in *Independent*, 354
Beecher, Lyman, **70**, 72, 79, 186, 190, 488; *Autobiography*, 488, 489; sermons, 70–71, 74, 75, 80
Beekman, ———, 276
Belden, Thomas, **76**
Belden, Thomas Graham, and Marva Robins Belden: and Chase's journals, lvii
Belknap, George Eugene, **548**
Belknap, William B., **577**
Bell, ———, 151, 173
Bell, Enoch, 539
Bell, James M., **195**
Bell, Theodore S., **577**
Bellamar, Cueva de (Cuba), 559
Bellows, Henry Adams, **612**
Belmont, August, **482**, 699
Benedict, ———, 390
Benedict, Erastus Cornelius, **677**
Benedict, George A., **584**
Benham, George C., **655**
Benham, Joseph S., **48**, 109, 114; death of, 137–38; description of, 138
Benjamin, Judah Philip, **458**
Benjamin Franklin (ship), 21
Bennet, ———, 276
Bennett, Elisha, 165
Bennett, J. R., **705**
Bennett, James Gordon, Jr., **699**
Bennett, James Gordon, Sr., **423**
Benton, Thomas Hart, 58, **59**, 172, 209, 230, 231, 276; letter to, 227; speeches of, 213, 246
Benton, William Plummer, **563**
Beresford, Mrs.: death of, 223
Berkeley, George, **592**
Bermuda case, 561

Bernabé, José Polo de. *See* Polo de Bernabé, José
Berry, Nathaniel Springer, **403**
Berry, Washington, 650
Berryman, James, **180**
Bethel, Vt., fire, 617
Bethel African Methodist Church (Cincinnati), 167
Bethel Chapel (Cincinnati), 167
Bethel Sunday School Library (Cincinnati), 167
Betts, Father, 239
Bibb (ship), 554
Bickham, William Denison, **261**, 333, 382
Bickley, George Washington Leigh, 374
Biddle, Craig, **653**
Biddle, Richard, **65**
Bierce, Lucius Verus, **308**
Bierce, William W., **263**, 269
Bigelow, Mrs., 99
Bigelow, H. G., 99
Bigelow, John, **587**, 591, 635
Bigelow, Mrs. John (Cincinnati, 1835), **99**
Bigelow, John P., xiii
Bill, Earl, **583**
Billings, Frederick, **631**, 632
Billings, James J. S., **194**
Billson, William Weldon, **660**
Bingham, John Armor, **276**, 431, 600, 610; speech of, 256
Bingham, Kinsley S., **227**, 228
Binghamton Bridge Case, 599
Binney, Horace, Jr., **596**
Binney, Horace, Sr., **702**
Biot, Jean Baptiste, *Life of Sir Isaac Newton*, 27
Birkem, ———, 206
Birney, Camp (Baltimore), 456
Birney, David Bell, **378**, 386, 389, 390
Birney, James, **378**
Birney, James Gillespie, xx, 119, 378; Liberty party presidential candidate, xxi, xxii, xxiii, xxiv
Birney, William, **230**, 456
Bissell, George P., **490**
Bissell, Israel M., **150**
Bissell, Josiah Wolcott, **573**
"Black Laws" (Ohio), 197, 202; repeal of, xxvi–xxvii, 201, 204, 207
Blackford, Isaac Newton, 81
Blackstone, William, *Commentaries*, 128
Blackwell, Henry Browne, **253**
Blaine, James Gillespie, **670**
Blaique, Mme., 120
Blair, ———, 131

Blair, Austin, **365**, 403
Blair, Francis Preston, Jr., **239**, 355, 376, 405, 406, 440, 465, 475; political attack on Chase in 1864, xxxix, 465; speech on colonization, 355
Blair, Francis Preston, Sr., 233, 313, 481, 530; and formation of Republican party, xxix
Blair, Mary Elizabeth Woodbury, 481
Blair, Montgomery, **313**, 314, 325, 349, 352, 355, 360, 368, 369, 377, 388, 442, 508, 530, 613, 647; and cabinet politics, xxxiv, xxxix, xli; on Emancipation Proclamation, 395
Blake, Charles Frederic, **676**
Blakeslee, Schuyler E., **240**, 259
Blanchard, Jonathan, **146**
Blatchford, Richard Milford, **464**, 466
Blickensderfer, Jacob, **298**
Bliss, George, **373**, 403, 404
Bliss, Philemon, **420**, 431
Blodgett, Constantine, 588, **589**
Bloodgood, Simeon DeWitt, **497**
Blow, Henry Taylor, **510**, 518, 602, 610
Blow, Peter Ethelred Taylor, **610**
Blue, Frederick J.: biography of Chase, xi
Board of Trade: Boston, 326; New York, 326; Philadelphia, 327
Bodisco, Waldemar de, **230**
Boker, George Henry, **631**
Bolton, Thomas, **218**, 220, 222
Bonaparte, Jerome Napoleon, **527**, 532
Bonaventure Cemetery (Savannah), 550
Bond, Hugh Lennox, 437, **438**, 456, 520, 527, 528, 602
Bond, William Key, **193**
Bonds. *See* Civil War finances
Bonds, Texas: recognition of, discussed, 390–91
Bonfils, St. Sauveur François, **77**; school, 120
Bonheur, Rosa, "The Horse Fair," 708
Bonney, Charles Carroll, **228**
Booth, John Wilkes, **529**
Booth, Sherman M., 269
Borden, James U., **213**
Borden, Samuel, **114**
Borland, Solon, 208, **209**
Bossuet, Jacques-Bénigne, *Oraisons Funèbres*, 278, 281, 293
Boston, Mass., 20, 21, 22, 122
Bostwick, Samuel W., **251**
Boswell, James, *Life of Johnson*, 691
Botume, Elizabeth Hyde, **549**
Boucher, Joshua, **221**

{ 734 } Index

Boutwell, George Sewall, **362**, 364, 378, 390, 518, 576
Bowden, Lemuel Jackson, **430**
Bowdoin College, 55
Bowen, Ozias, **278**
Bowen, Sayles Jenks, **604**
Bowler, Nodiah Potter, **268**
Boyce, William Waters, **640**
Boyce & Henry v. Timothy Edwards, 135
Boyd, Col., 607
Boyd, Henry, **229**
Boyd, John, 283
Boynton, Charles Brandon, **246**, 593; sermon of, 246
Boynton, Thomas Jefferson, **560**
Brackenridge, George W., **521**
Brackett, Edward Augustus, **125**
Bradburn, Charles, **584**
Bradburn, George, **238**, 268
Bradbury, ———, 180
Bradbury, Cornelius S., **181**
Bradbury, John, **181**
Bradbury, W. E., **181**
Bradford, Alexander Warfield, **513**
Bradford, Augustus Williamson, **403**
Bradford, Joseph M., **545**, 547, 548
Bradley, Alvin C., **676**
Bradley, Joseph P., **650**, 651, 668, 706
Brady, James Topham, **513**
Brady, William N., *The Kedge-Anchor*, 561
Bragg, Braxton, **418**, 419, 427
Brand, Joseph C., Jr., **440**, 506
Brand, Joseph Carter, **506**
Brand, Louis, **440**
Brannan, John Milton, **382**
Brasee, John Trafford, **250**
Brayton, ———, 237
Brayton, Isaac, **251**, 254, 255, 276, 308
Brayton, Mary Clark, **583**
Breckinridge, John Cabell, **374**, 375, 479
Breckinridge, Robert Jefferson, **508**
Breckinridge, Samuel Miller, **433**, 434
Breese, Mrs., 237
Breese, ———, 237
Breese, William G., **133**
Brent, Daniel, **59**
Brent, Robert, 667
Brent, Robert J., 647, **648**
Brentwood (District of Columbia), 667
Breslin, John G., **200**, 221, 285–90 passim, 296, 300; Chase letter to, on Democratic politics, 223; Ohio treasury defalcation, xxx
Brevoort Hotel (New York), 707
Brewster, George, **243**
Brewster, Randall, 202

Breyfogle, Charles, **286**
Brice, Benjamin W., **610**, 646
Bridge, Charlotte Marshall, **320**, 710
Bridge, Horatio, 320, **515**, 710
Briggs, George Ware, **628**
Briggs, James A., **198**, 238, 268
Briggs, Robert M., **250**, 307, 308, 309
Bright, Jesse David, 230, **231**, 239, 323, 660, 681
Bright, John, **634**
Brimmer, Martin, **490**
Brinkerhoff, Jacob, **172**, 224, 245; speech on Texas annexation, 172
Brisbane, William Henry, **174**, 225
Bristow, Benjamin Helm, **670**, 684
Broadway Exchange (Columbus), 273
Broadway Hotel (Cincinnati), 62, 82
Broadwell, C., 62, **63**, 127
Broadwell, Jacob, 62, **63**, 127
Brock, Isaac, 101
Broderick, David Colbreth, **514**
Bronaugh, Emily, **604**, 654
Bronaugh, Frank, **611**, 637
Bronson v. Rodes, 651, 652
Brooke, John T., **98**, 101, 107, 111, 112, 113, 155, 167; address of, 101; sermon of, 98, 105
Brooks, Col., 675, 676, 677, 679, 680, 682, 683, 687, 705
Brooks, Mr., 675
Brooks, Chauncey, **294**
Brooks, James, **122**
Brooks, Samuel Reeves, **325**
Brooks, Sidney, **592**, 674
Broom, Mr., 593
Brough, Mrs. (widow of Charles Henry Brough), 211
Brough, Caroline A. Nelson, **584**
Brough, Charles Henry, **188**, 204; death of, 210–11
Brough, John, **188**, 211, 261, 275, 531, 532, 583–85
Brougham, Henry Lord, *Memoirs*, 694
Brown, Mr., 47
Brown, Alfred, **303**
Brown, Augustus I., 185, 186, **211**
Brown, B. Peyton, **386**, 474
Brown, Benjamin Gratz, **510**
Brown, Benjamin N., **386**
Brown, Captain, 580
Brown, Frank, **303**
Brown, Helen, **303**
Brown, J. S., **634**
Brown, James Monroe, **275**
Brown, James Muncastor, 461, **462**
Brown, John Carter, **626**
Brown, Mary, **303**
Brown, Samuel, 193, 194

Brown, Samuel Gilman, **591**
Brown, Samuel Peters, **664**
Brown, T. B., **604**
Brown, Thomas (1819–67), **197**, 238, 366, 495, 517, 586
Brown, Thomas (fl. 1830), **46**
Brown, Wesley, 194
Brown, William A., 302, **303**
Brown University: centennial and commencement (1864), 499–500
Browne, Albert Gallatin, Jr., **484**, 492
Browne, Albert Gallatin, Sr., **492**, 545, 546
Browne, Charles Farrar, **393**; *Artemus Ward His Book*, 404
Browne, J. Vincent, **484**, 623
Browne, Sir Thomas, **49**
Browning, Orville Hickman, **332**, 604, 605
Brownlow, William Gannaway, **632**
Bruce, Frederick William Adolphus, **601**, 607, 610
Brummel, A. O., **673**, 684
Brunot, H., 99, 100
Brutus, Marcus Junius, 387
Bryant, William Cullen, *Iliad of Homer*, 671
Buchanan, James, 272, **273**, 296, 325, 374; presidential administration, 262
Buchanan, Robert, **155**, 169, 580
Buchanan v. Goodins, 169
Buck, J. A., **680**, 686
Buckingham, Mr., 610
Buckingham, ——— (deputy sheriff), 198
Buckland, Ralph Pomeroy, **301**
Buckler, Thomas Hepburn, **525**
Buckley, George S., **182**, 183, 184, 185, 194
Buckner, Simon Boliver, **316**
Buehler, William, **167**
Buell, Don Carlos, **355**, 358, 359, 360, 363, 364, 398, 401, 413; criticized for leniency toward Confederates, 406–9; evaluated as commander, 355, 412, 413; telegram to Lincoln, 418, 419
Bull Run, first battle of, xxxvi, 317
Bull Run, second battle of, xxxiv
Bullitt, Mr., 84
Bullitt, Cuthbert, **354**, 364, 366
Bullitt, John C., **211**
Bullock, Alexander Hamilton, **625**
Bullock, Elvira Hazard, **625**
Bullock, Fanny, **625**
Bulow, Col., 393

Bulwer-Lytton, Edward George Earle Lytton: *Devereaux. A Tale.*, 24; *England and the English*, 79
Bundy, Ellen, 583
Bundy, Hezekiah Sanford, **507**, 583
Bundy, Julia A., **583**
Bundy, Lucy J., **583**
Bundy, Sarah A., **583**
Bunsen, Christian Karl Josias, *Prayers*, 666
Burchard, Horatio C., 647
Burchell, N. W., **666**
Burdick, William, **248**
Burgoyne, John, **195**
Burke, Mrs., 218
Burkhead, Liryum Skidmore, **543**
Burnet, Edmund, **251**
Burnet, Isaac G., **226**
Burnet, Jacob, **41**, 42, 117, 153, 159, 160, 190, 192, 218; advises Chase about Cincinnati, xviii
Burnet, Robert, **217**
Burnet House (Cincinnati), 204, 205, 208, 216, 246, 247, 261, 262, 284, 287, 299, **510**, 578, 579
Burnett, B. L., 224
Burnham, Alfred Avery, **363**
Burnham, Curtis Field, 382, **383**
Burnside, Ambrose Everett, 317, 335, **340**, 363, 364, 367, 369, 373, 384, 404, 416, 418, 423, 451–54 passim, 538, 579, 626, 630; resigns command, 439; speaks at Brown University centennial, 500; telegram from, 366
Burr, Aaron, 48
Burr, Mrs. O. K., 150, 158, 159
Burrows, Mrs. (wife of John A. Burrows), 229
Burrows, John A., **210**
Burton, Gideon, 263
Bushnell, Asa B., **187**; sermons of, 187, 190
Busteed, Richard, **594**, 606
Butler, ——— (of Columbus), 334
Butler, ——— (of Society of Friends), 390
Butler, Andrew Pickens, 208, **209**
Butler, Benjamin Franklin (of Mass.; d. 1893), 325, **355**, 358, 376, 418, 513, 514, 518, 532, 541, 611, 624, 632; antagonism with Ulysses S. Grant, 633, 640; order on New Orleans trade, 407–8, 409, 410; pending nomination for Congress, 628; on Reconstruction, 627; replaced by Banks at New Orleans, 425–26

Butler, Benjamin Franklin (of N.Y.; d. 1858), **209**, 222
Butler, Blanche, **624**
Butler, Clement Moore, **165**, 194, 232, 246, 263; *St. Paul in Rome*, 554
Butler, Elizur, **169**
Butler, John M., 653, 654
Butler, Samuel, poem, **84**
Butler, William Allen, **609**
Butterfield, Daniel, **379**, 381, 454
Buttles, Albert B., 287
Buttles, Lucian, **296**
Byerley, Thomas, *The Percy Anecdotes*, 84
Byron, George Gordon, Lord, "Maid of Athens, Ere We Part," 19

C———, Charley, 512
Cabell, Elizabeth, **7**, 8; description of, 13
Cabell, Joseph Carrington, **6**
Cabell, William H., **7**
Cable, Fielding S., **279**
Cable, Jonathan, **212**
Cable, Joseph, **279**
Cadwalader, John, **442**, 443
Cadwell, Darius, 260, **266**
Cady, Philander Kinney, **168**
Caesar, engraving of, 23–24
Cagger, Peter, **644**
Caldwell, Mrs., 497, 498
Caldwell, George Alfred, **577**
Caldwell, John D., **282**
Caldwell, William B., **165**, 212, 213, 222, 223; on Free Democracy, 214
Calhoun, John C., xii, **49**, 49–50, 242, 387, 545; speech of, 196
California: oil production, 516; politics, 437
Calvert, J. W., **577**
Cameron, Simon, **324**, 325, 423, 426, 440, 509, 632; proposed as minister to Russia, 325; requests leave from Russia, 382; resignation from cabinet, 325, 326
Cameron, Virginia Rolette, **637**
Camp, Benjamin F., **459**
Camp Wild Cat, battle of, 316
Campbell, Mr., 701
Campbell, Alexander, **422**
Campbell, James, **236**
Campbell, John Nicholson, 4, 22, 23
Campbell, Lewis Davis, **532**
Canal Bank of Cleveland, 220
Canby, Edward Richard Sprigg, **564**, 565, 566, 568, 569
Canfield, Herman, **264**
Canonchet (Sprague estate), 587

Cape Carnaveral, Fla., 554
Cape Hatteras, N.C., 537
Capella, Bernard, **567**
Capella, Lizzie, **567**, 569
Caperton v. Ballard, 675
Capron, Horace, **646**
Carey, Henry Charles, **631**, 703, 705
Carey, John, **300**
Carleton, John L., **459**
Carlile, John Snyder, **332**, 348
Carlisle, Mrs. (wife of James M. Carlisle), 645
Carlisle, George, **270**
Carlisle, James Mandeville, **608**, 645, 648, 651
Carlton, Mr., 82
Carlton, Mrs., 82
Carlton (Carleton), Miss, 65, 82
Carlyle, Thomas, 149; *The French Revolution*, 153
Carmen (ship), 556
Carneal, Thomas D., **137**, 138, 175
Caroline (ship): diplomatic incident, 151
Carpenter, Benjamin D., **685**
Carpenter, Caroline Dillingham, **679**
Carpenter, Matthew Hale, **679**, 705, 710
Carpenters Hall (Philadelphia), 702
Carrington, Henry Beebee, **255**, 292, 294, 298, 304, 309, 364
Carroll, William Thomas, **376**
Carruth, Miss, 501
Carskadon case. *See Pierce v. Carskadon*
Carson, Enoch Terry, **485**, 510, 511, 578, 579
Carter, Alfred George Washington, **185**
Carter, Francis, **309**
Carter (ship), 569, 571
Cartter, David Kellogg, **235**, 459, 585
Carus, Titus Lucretius, *De Natura Rerum*, 54
Cary, Samuel Fenton, **173**, 254
Caryl, James B., **541**
Case, Miss, 273
Case, Mr., 273
Case, Charles, **307**
Case, Eliphalet, **313**, 382, 383, 388, 422; on politics and spiritualism, 386–87
Case v. Brown, 517
Casey, Samuel Lewis, **349**
Cass, Lewis, **195**, 239, 283, 284; 1848 Democratic nominee, xxv
Casserly, Eugene, **674**, 675, 685
Cassidy, Peter, **194**
Cassilly, Mary, 73, 81

Cassilly, Michael P., **62**, 64, 73, 81
Caswell, Alexis, **626**
Caswell, Daniel J., **47**, 51, 52, 67, 73, 80, 85
Catacazy, Constantin de, **649**
Catacazy, Madame de (wife of Constantin de Catacazy), 649
Cattell, Alexander Gilmore, **631**
Cattell, J. D., **251**, 259
Cavendish, Edward, **401–2**
Cavendish, Spencer Compton, **401–2**
Centre Hall Resolution, 228
Cervantes Saavedra, Miguel de, *Don Quixote de la Mancha*, 44
Chaffin, J. W., **239**
Chambers, Francis T., **255**, 271
Chambersburg, Pa., captured by Confederates, 419, 421
Chambrun, Charles Adolphe de Pineton, Marquis de, **598**
Chandler, Ann Caroline Gilmore, **496**
Chandler, Lucius H., **430**
Chandler, Theophilus P., **430**
Chandler, William Eaton, **496**, 497, 599, 640
Chandler, Zachariah, **321**, 322, 332, 335, 365, 424; discusses Army command, 321
Channing, William Ellery: *Emancipation*, 147; *Remarks on Character of Napoleon Bonaparte*, 10
Chapin, Aaron Lucius, **682**
Chapin, Chester William, **619**
Chapin, Dorcas, **619**
Chapin, Edwin Hubbell, **709**
Chapin, Josiah, **499**
Chapman, Anne Greene, **517**
Chapman, Bird Beers, 225, **226**
Chapman, John Lee, **528**
Chapman, Maria Weston, 517
Charleston, S.C., 384, 417, 427, 432, 544–46; capture planned, 382, 383–84, 390, 404, 405, 406, 415, 416, 417, 439, 440
Charley Bowen (ship), 282
Chase, Mrs. (wife of S. H. Chase), 221
Chase, Abigail Corbet. *See* Colby, Abigail Corbet Chase
Chase, Alexander Ralston (brother), **140**, 146, 150, 163, 229, 230; illness and death of, xxxii, 184, 186–87; steamboat paddle patent, 150, 151, 153
Chase, Alice Jones (sister), **19**, 174, 175, 177, 178, 179, 230, 302; assists in Chase's household, xxxii; death of, xxxii, lxii, 310–11
Chase, Baruch (uncle), xii, 496

Chase, Catharine Jane (first daughter Kate, 1835–40), xix, lviii, **85**, 89, 97, 108, 114, 118, 139–40; birth and naming of, 85, 86, 87; death of, xxiii, 120, 146, 148; description of, 105, 142; as infant, 100, 113; vaccination of, 107, 111
Chase, Catharine Jane (Kitty) Garniss (first wife), xix, **72**, 79, 139, 237; Chase mourns and remembers, 95–116; Chase's memoir of, lvi, lvii–lx, 81–94; dreams of Chase, 79; illness and death of, xxxii, 86–94, 104
Chase, Catharine Jane (second daughter Kate, 1840–99), **142**; birth of, 142; Chase disciplines, 170, 193, 255, 263–64; children of, 671, 678, 684, 685, 687, 689, 691; in Columbus, 1857, 247, 248, 249, 252–57 passim, 259–66 passim, 269, 271, 273, 274, 277, 279, 289, 290–94 passim, 297, 306, 308, 309; departs for Europe, 608–9; disapproval of Warden's biography, liv, lix; education, 174–77 passim, 180, 181, 226, 227, 257; gathers her father's papers, liv, lv; health of, 143, 145, 153, 154, 163, 167, 168, 176, 179, 256, 257, 278, 307; letters to and from noted, 227, 364, 385, 488, 494, 551, 553, 555, 574, 579, 581, 593, 648, 659, 683, 688, 695, 698, 699, 704, 705, 706; telegrams to and from noted, 593, 596, 668, 690, 695, 697; as young child, 161, 166, 171, 173–74; mentioned, xxiii, xxxii–xxxiii, 172, 177, 178, 187, 189, 206, 207, 237, 310–24 passim, 354, 357, 392–400 passim, 412–24 passim, 482, 499–506 passim, 512–28 passim, 534, 535, 587–99 passim, 601, 607, 630, 661–83 passim, 690–94 passim, 699, 710
Chase, Corbett (uncle), xii
Chase, David Hall, **618**
Chase, Dudley (cousin), 151
Chase, Dudley (uncle), xii, xv–xvi, xvii
Chase, Dudley Heber (brother), **230**
Chase, Edward Ithamar (brother), **132**, 141, 144, 163, 210, 229, 230, 237, 356; letters to, 55, 155, 187, 222, 230, 311
Chase, Eliza Ann (Lizzie) Smith (second wife), **120**, 121–23, 126, 130, 131, 133, 135–36, 138–40, 142–44, 146, 153–57, 161, 164, 172–75, 189, 192, 247; death of, xxiii, 173; gives birth to daughter, 164; health of,

{ 738 } Index

131, 140, 145, 146, 148, 161, 163, 164, 165, 167, 168, 172, 173; letters to, noted, 155, 156, 157; marries Chase, xxiii, 140; piety of, 161; pregnancy of, 141, 142; travels to New Orleans, 151, 153
Chase, Ellen Wiggin, **496**
Chase, Frederick, **591**
Chase, Hannah Ralston. *See* Whipple, Hannah Ralston Chase
Chase, Heber (uncle), xii
Chase, Helen Maria. *See* Walbridge, Helen Maria Chase
Chase, Ithamar (father), xii, **230**, 496; grave visited, 620
Chase, James E., **268**
Chase, Janet (Nettie) Ralston (daughter), **223**; accompanies father on Southern tour (1865), xliii, 535–81; attends play, 648; in Columbus, 1857, 247–67 passim, 269, 271, 274, 279, 282, 289, 294, 297, 306, 307, 309; departs for Europe, 608–9; health, 324; lessons, 244, 257, 258, 259; letters from, 110–11, 638, 673; letters to, xxxiii, 336–44, 385, 494, 635, 648, 683, 685, 686; marriage, 665; notation on journal flyleaf, lxvii; mentioned, xxxii–xxxiii, 129, 244, 320, 324, 354–57 passim, 424, 482, 499, 501, 506, 512–17 passim, 522, 528, 533, 535, 582–611 passim, 634, 637, 645–62 passim, 668, 669, 670, 677–80 passim, 689, 690, 696, 700–710 passim
Chase, Janette Logan. *See* Skinner, Janette Logan Chase
Chase, Jannette Ralston (mother), xii–xiii, xiv, **19**, 20, 21, 66, 111, 230; grave visited, 496
Chase, Josephine Ludlow (Zoe; daughter), **215**, 224
Chase, Kate. *See* Chase, Catharine Jane (first and second daughters Kate)
Chase, Lizzie (first daughter Lizzie), 164
Chase, Lizzie (second daughter Lizzie), **164**, 165, 167, 168
Chase, Mary Eliza (sister-in-law), 132, **210**
Chase, Mary Gillespie (sister-in-law), 66, **230**
Chase, Philander (uncle), xii, xv, xviii, 9, **16**, 162, 524, 618; description of, xiii; influence on S. P. Chase, xiii–xiv; *Reminiscences*, 162, 212
Chase, S. H., **221**

Chase, Salmon (uncle), xii
Chase, Salmon Portland: charity, 130, 132, 181, 215, 216, 220, 269, 517, 641, 647, 667, 669; teaching career, xiv, xv–xvi, 4, 9
—antislavery activities: addressed citizens' meeting, 1841, 147–48; antislavery views, xi, xxi; Brown, Samuel, case of, 193–95; convention call, will not sign, 138; helps blacks, 163, 196, 206; Matilda case, 119; Nashville black man, 184; organizes Free Territory convention (1848), 196; Parish case, 181; Reed kidnapping case, 182–84, 185; Rosetta case, 244–46; Smothers case, 184; State Free Democracy Committee meeting, 197; Townes, Mary, 162; Van Zandt case, 166, 168, 169, 171, 174, 175, 176, 184–85, 186; Watson, Samuel, case of, 172; mentioned, 166, 186, 195, 196, 261, 269
—chief justice: administration of oath to Andrew Johnson (1865), xliii, 530; admits first black to Supreme Court bar, 519, 521; appointment as, xli–xlii, 511, 582; attitudes toward position, xlv–xlvi; circuit court business, 523–24, 525, 527, 635–36, 644; *Ex parte Milligan* opinion, lxvii; health and fitness for office, 674; Johnson impeachment trial, xlviii–xlix, 641–43; judicial appointments, 630, 646; New Years calls on president, 601, 645; opinions of chief justiceship, 518; views improvements to Supreme Court chambers, 634
—described: biographical sketch of, xi–xlix; biographies of, xi; character, xxii, xxiii, xxxii; as public speaker, xxv
—education: at Dartmouth College, xiv–xv; Dartmouth class reunion (1866), 614–15; French lessons, 257–81 passim, 287; on infant schools, 15–16; intellectual life, 261–62; and progress, 15–16; in the law, 4, 30, 53
—family and domestic life: assistance to family, 66, 72, 76, 146, 151; birthday (forty-ninth), 253–54; boarding house anecdote, 25; boards in Cincinnati, 1853, 242; Chase as a parent, xxxii–xxxiii; children, xxiii; concerned over daughters' health, 534, 574, 607–8; condolences upon death of second wife, 174; conflict with in-laws, 107–8, 111; counsels Nettie, 522; disciplines and troubles

Index

with Kate, 170, 193, 255, 260, 263–64; guardian for Edmund and Caroline Smith, 189, 222; marriages, xix, xxii, xxiii, 72; memoir of and mourns first wife, 81–94, 95–116; memories of and mourns first daughter, 120, 139–40, 146, 148; New Years celebration, 1857, 247; occupies house in Columbus, 309; opinion of marriage, 3; rents Clifton house, 229; mentioned, 132, 138, 171, 172, 175, 181, 198, 203, 207, 210, 216, 223–24, 249–66 passim, 271, 289, 301–2, 309
—finances: accident insurance, 610–11; authorizes purchase of Florida island, 553; Clifton farm, 158; debts, 177, 180; Edgewood (estate in D.C.), 650, 665, 666; "Farm Notes" (Edgewood estate), lxix; Hardscrabble Hall (house outside Cincinnati), 171, 175, 176, 177; instructs sale of property, 492; and Jay Cooke on investments, 491, 503; invests in iron, 522; loses pocket book, 634, 636, 637, 639; misplaces portfolio and bonds, 481; pays for language lessons, 647; personal, 53, 66, 67, 81, 114–20 passim, 140–43 passim, 157, 176, 185–88 passim, 205, 206, 211, 215, 221, 223, 254–61 passim, 269, 280, 288–90, 291, 309–10, 528, 532, 586, 634, 647, 665–67 passim, 673, 674, 686, 692, 694, 700, 703; urged to invest in petroleum, 517
—governor of Ohio: advises on legislation, 275–76; annual message, 1857, 247–51, 254; appointments, 275, 276, 292, 294–95, 305, 306; attends funeral of Elisha Kent Kane, 274; Baltimore & Ohio railroad celebration, 281, 282, 283, 292, 294–95; on bank charter, 257; fugitive slave case, 284, 287, 288, 289, 291; Grand levee, 1857, 271; Hamlin controversy, 255, 256, 258; message to General Assembly, 254; New State House festival, 249; Ohio Wesleyan University commencement, 285; pardons, 254–55, 260, 261, 264, 265, 267, 271, 275, 276, 281; prepares 1857 proclamation, 258; renominated, 1857, 297; reviews militia, 304; treasury defalcation, xxx–xxxi, 285–94, 297
—handwriting: clerk's difficulty in reading, lxi; comments on his own, lxxiii

—health: acid stomach, 698; acupuncture, 672, 673; bowels, 656–63 passim, 675, 687, 688, 689, 691, 695–98 passim, 703, 704, 706; buys glasses, 1862, 387; chest and heart, 629, 656, 658, 675, 676, 689, 698, 700, 704; chills, 687–88, 689, 690; cramped leg, 634; decline of (1870–73), xlix; diabetes suspected, 653; faintness, 656, 657, 659, 660; feels well, 650, 658, 662; fever, 455, 688, 689, 690; fitness for office as chief justice, 674; headache, suffers from, 125; illnesses, 67–68, 155, 176–77, 188, 218, 219, 221, 393, 402, 518, 520, 598, 634, 678, 687, 688; lame in left arm, 675; medications, 661, 662, 663, 675, 688, 689, 690, 694, 695, 696; mineral waters taken, 662, 666, 694, 695, 696, 697; pain, 454, 655, 656, 657, 659, 661, 663; physician consulted, 248, 653, 688, 689, 695, 696; rheumatism, 248, 519, 520, 662; sleepiness, suffers from, 123; sleeps badly, 129, 131, 145, 177, 661, 662, 665; sprains wrist, 1841, 148; urination, 519, 628–29, 636, 653–65 passim, 676, 681, 687, 691, 695, 698, 704–7 passim; weakness, 687, 689, 690–91, 704; mentioned, xix, 169, 208, 258, 268, 281, 301
—law practice: admitted to bar, Ohio, 53; admitted to bar, Washington, D.C., lxiii, 30; Bank of the United States, solicitor, xviii, 150; begins practice in Cincinnati, 53–54; fugitive slave cases, xx–xxi; Lafayette Bank, solicitor and director, xviii, 80–81, 100, 103–4, 112, 117, 127, 131, 132, 145, 156, 158, 197; partnerships, xxi, 64, 67, 80–81, 101, 120, 177, 195, 228; mentioned, xviii, 53, 65–78 passim, 87, 94–96, 99–101, 103, 106, 108–24 passim, 126–32 passim, 135–41 passim, 145, 147, 148, 150–53, 156–58, 160–61, 164–81 passim, 185–89 passim, 192–208 passim, 211–14, 216, 222, 235, 259, 266, 267
—personal reflections and habits: achievement, envy and praise of, 57–58; on beauty, 43; on being an artist, 30–31; daily schedules, 126–43; on death of young Union soldier, 493; on discipline and personal progress, 45; effects of alcohol on talent, 11–12; on free thinking, 13; general,

276, 280; on good actions, 589; on hydropathy, 219–20; on intellectual accomplishments, 27; late to rise, 204, 205, 206, 210, 212, 214; mourns absent friends, 14; need for diligence and concentration, 178; recalls youthful life in New England, 616–17, 619, 620; reflects on year 1840, 146; on resigning as Treasury secretary, 471–73, 476, 479; self-assessment, 34–35, 74, 102, 124, 126, 146, 212; on time, 6, 27, 141, 178, 281; twenty-first birthday, thoughts on, 6; on women, 39
—political activities, xxi–xxii, xxiii–xxvii, xxxi, 213, 214, 238–42, 243; addresses Free Democrats of Lucas County, Ohio, 216; Cincinnati City Council, 121–22, 124, 133, 138, 147, 148, 150, 151–52, 155–56, 157, 159; Cincinnati flood relief committee, 64; Clinton County election, 1849, 208; considered for Congress, 1865, 505; contemplates gubernatorial candidacy (1857), 288; debate with John B. Weller, 238; defends William Henry Harrison, 125; denies partisanship, 571; desire for Chief Justiceship, 1863, xlii, 429; early political affiliations, xx; encouraged to run for Congress, 1864, 479, 485; family and political life, 207; Free-Soil and Democratic politics, 222, 223, 224–25; Free-Soil convention, expelled from, 227–28; and Free-Soil Whigs, 210; gubernatorial nomination, 1855, 245; interest rates, to limit, 207; and Joshua Reed Giddings, 210; Liberty party nominee for Congress, 1846, 181–82; on Morse and Townshend, 207; Ohio Democratic State Convention, 1857, 296; Ohio legislative session, 1848–49, 200, 201; Ohio Senate, 110; organizes convention, 1854, 243; patronage, 152; possibilities for U.S. Senate seat, 197–98, 202; presidential aspirations, xlix, 429–30, 433, 459, 460, 558, 628, 676, 685; presidential election of 1864, 488, 491, 494, 497, 498, 502–10 passim; presidential election of 1868, xlix, 633, 640, 644; presidential election of 1872, 672–73, 677, 679, 683, 686, 687, 691–99 passim; recommendations to William Henry Harrison, 149; recording vote at polls, 1841, 149; subscribes to Equal Suffrage Association, 641; supports Democratic party, 1851, 225; temperance reform, 158; votes, 1864, 508, 510; mentioned, 266, 267, 295
—political opinions and observations: advice to Andrew Johnson on Reconstruction, xliii, xliv, 534–35; on annexation of Texas, 172; on Apportionment Bill, Ohio, 1848, 207; on Benjamin Watkins Leigh and equal rights, 28; on capital punishment, 704; on deposits in national banks, 525; discusses politics, 1866, 619, 634, 637; on emigration, 706; on Kansas, 272–73; on licensing taverns, 152; on Ohio testimony law, 173; opinions, 66, 67, 202, 276, 278; on Pugh and Pierce, 207; Reconstruction, xlii–xliii, xlv, xlvi, 533–34, 541, 544, 552, 553, 555, 568, 591, 598, 603, 695; on secession and the Confederacy, 474–75, 544; on Senate seat, 1849, 208; support for Morse and Townshend, 208; on universal suffrage, 518, 521, 525–29 passim, 533–38 passim, 576, 580, 581, 594, 597, 600, 605, 606, 640
—portraits: medallion, 522, 590; photograph taken, 696; photographed as secretary of Treasury, 321; portrait of, 583; sits for Eaton portrait, 260, 263, 264, 266
—religion: Arianism, 234; assesses Christian purity, 106; attends African-American Presbyterian Church, 682; attends Baptist church, 626; attends Methodist churches, 39–41, 386, 474, 512, 526, 531, 541, 569, 607, 634, 636, 644, 647, 649, 668, 671, 675, 677, 706; attends Presbyterian church, 584; attends Unitarian church, 593; attentiveness in church, 162; camp meeting in Massachusetts, 1864, 491; Christmas observances, 31, 144–45; and communion, 324, 592, 667–68, 679, 686; dreams of sin, 118; memorizes Psalms and scripture, 122, 124, 125–26, 127, 128, 129, 131, 134, 136, 137, 138, 140, 141, 143, 210, 211, 219; New Years services, 103; piety, thoughts on, 111–12, 121, 125, 178, 210; piety of his wives, 97–98, 161; prayer meetings, 101, 111; questions church on slavery, 178; religious introspection, 69, 70, 101, 179, 187, 212, 512, 513, 521, 562, 598, 645; religious views, xv; rhetoric, ideal, 4;

seeks confirmation of belief, 48; self-criticism and assessment, 68, 120–21, 130, 141, 143, 148, 161–62, 167, 169–70, 178, 190, 212, 214; sermon, critical of, 143; Sunday School, 106, 113, 115, 129, 130, 134, 139, 143, 147, 148, 149, 155–67 passim, 212; temperance, 161; thoughts on order and peace, 465–66; vestry meetings, 108, 165; Wilberforce, example of, 210, 212; Young Men's Bible Society, 144, 146
—speeches: Adrian, Mich., 1864, 510; after Emancipation Proclamation, 1862, 400; antislavery, 1841, 147; at Brown University centennial, 1864, 500; Aurora, Ind., 1864, 577; Baltimore, 1865, 520; Baltimore railroad speech, 294–95; Chicago, 1864, 510; Chillicothe, Ohio, 1864, 507; Cincinnati, 128, 298, 507; Cleveland, 509, 584; Covington, Ky., 1864, 508; "Dangers of American Liberty," 1829, 16; Dartmouth College, 16, 17, 21, 591, 615; Davis Bend, Miss., 1865, 572; Detroit, 1864, 509; election campaign, 1857, 298–305; Fourth of July, 1829, 16; on Galileo, 1857, 264, 265, 266, 267, 268; Groveport, Ohio, 1857, 296; gubernatorial nomination, 1857, 298; Hamilton, Ohio, 1864, 507; Hartford, Conn., 1864, 489; Holly, Mich., 1864, 509; Irish Repeal Meeting, 1844, 170; Jackson, Ohio, 1864, 507; July 1848, 197; Keene, N.H., 1866, 620; Lexington, Ky., 1864, 508; Louisville, Ky., 1864, 507; Matilda case, 1838, 119; McArthur, Ohio, 1864, 508; New London, Ohio, 1857, 296–97; New Orleans, 1865, 567; Ohio election campaign, 1859, 312; Ohio State House dedication, 1857, 249; on public appointments, 1840, 127; railroad address, 1857, 282, 283, 284; Sea Islands, S.C., 1865, 549; on slave power, 1853, 242; *Speech at Toledo, May 30, 1851*, 227; St. Louis, 1864, 507, 510; to blacks, Charleston, S.C., 1865, 547; *Union and Freedom, Without Compromise*, xxvii, 227; Washington, 1864, 504, 506; West Chester, Pa., 1864, 509
—travels: Baltimore, 17–19, 22, 25–26, 30–33, 44–45, 455–56, 520–21, 522–28, 532, 602; Beaufort, N.C., 538, 539, 540, 541; between Meadville, Pa., and New York, 585–86; Buffalo, N.Y., 173; by boat, description of, 19–20; by coach, describes, 17, 38; Cairo, Ill., 575; Canada, 654; Cannelton, Ind., 576; Charleston, S.C., 544–48; Chicago, 144; Cincinnati, 46–47, 117, 277, 289, 577–81; Cleveland, 217–21 passim, 237–38, 268, 583–85; Columbus, Ohio, 116, 263, 582–83; Connecticut, 488–90, 626, 630; Cuba, 556–60; Delaware, Ohio, 583; Florida, 552–53; Fort Pulaski, Ga., 550; Hampton and Norfolk, Va., 536–37; Illinois, 510, 658–59; Indiana, 507; Jacksonville, Fla., 551–52; Kentucky, 507, 508; Key West, Fla., 555, 560; Lockport, N.Y., 144, 237; Louisiana, 570–71, 572; Louisville, Ky., 153–55, 577; Loveland, Ohio, 307; Marietta, Ohio, 282; Maryland, 644; Massachusetts, 483–88, 490–95, 498, 591–92, 620–29, 693; Meadville, Pa., 585; Memphis, Tenn., 574–75; Michigan, 509–10; Minnesota, 659–60; on Mississippi River, 571–75; Missouri, 510; Mobile, Ala., 562–63; Morehead City, N.C., 538–40; "Morven Park" (Leesburg, Va.), 38–39; Mt. Vernon, Virginia, 679; New Bern, N.C., 538; New England, xli, 20–22, 119; New Hampshire, 495–98, 591, 612–15, 618–20, 696–99; New Orleans, 564–70; New York, xli, 20, 223–24, 236–37, 317, 481–82, 483, 502, 586, 593–96, 608–9, 611–12, 630, 653, 688–89, 700–701, 706–9; North Bend, Ohio, 123; Ohio, 506–11, 653–58; on Ohio River, 575–77; Pennsylvania, 509; Philadelphia, 19–20, 88–89, 93, 480–81, 596, 609, 630–33, 652–53, 701–3; returns home from Columbus, 203; Rhode Island, 498–502, 586–93, 626, 629–30, 661–63, 689–92, 694–96, 699–700; Richmond, 119; St. Louis, 507; Savannah, Ga., 550–51; Sea Islands, S.C., 548–49, 551; ship fire, description of, 20; Southern tour (1865), xliii–xlv, 535–81; Springfield, Ohio, 117; Syracuse, N.Y., 237; Vermont, 616–19; Vicksburg, Miss., 573; Virginia, xxxiii–xxxiv; Virginia tavern, observes jury at, 43–44; West Virginia, 643–44; Wilberforce University, 269–70; Wilmington, Del., 596–97; Wilmington, N.C., 542–44

—Treasury secretary: administers expenditures, 398, 400, 460, 461; administers tax law, 377–78; on arming blacks, 428–29, 351; and bonds, 416, 417, 419, 421; in cabinet meetings, 313–15, 321–22, 348–49, 351–52, 357–60, 362, 366, 368–71, 391–95, 399, 402, 409, 415–19, 425, 436, 441–44, 449, 457; on Cameron, 325–26, 382; considers Reconstruction, 315–16, 331, 333, 437; and counterfeiting, 420, 421; criticism of his policies as, xxxv; and currency, 384, 427–28, 432, 444, 448, 460, 466; and emancipation, 329–31, 351, 355, 357–58, 362, 394–95; on federal expenses, 370, 381, 391, 432, 461, 464–67; and Federal lightships, 460; and finance, 354, 422; on franchise for slaves, 344; gives advice after resignation, 495, 503, 505, 506, 517–18, 532; gives military advice, 315, 322, 324, 405–6; on habeas corpus, 443–44; and judicial appointments, 431; and loans, 312–13, 315, 317, 322–23, 324, 326–28, 366, 373, 384–85, 399, 430, 440–42, 463, 466; loses official papers, 381; meets with various delegations, 328, 349, 433; and military affairs, 334–35, 345–48, 352–57 passim, 361, 363–67, 370, 371–73, 379–80, 383–91 passim, 401, 403–5, 418, 419, 423, 427, 434, 440, 445, 447, 448–54, 457, 467; and military appointments, 353, 354, 372–73, 375–76, 378, 382, 386, 388, 389–90, 393, 398, 399, 402, 404, 413, 414, 423, 437, 447, 450, 457; New York Custom House, 371–72, 373, 376, 387; opinions of Lincoln's policies, xxxiv–xxxv; patronage, xxxvii–xxxviii, 313, 334, 335, 354, 356, 361–69 passim, 376–402 passim, 420, 421, 428, 431–48 passim, 459–69 passim; personnel and department matters, 328, 335, 340, 460; on postage currency, 365, 411, 418, 419; proposes federal land bill, 462–63; resignation, xl, 468, 470; suspected espionage cases, 458; taxation, 430–31, 463–72; on the Gold Act, 461–62, 470; trade regulations, 316, 410, 418, 419, 429, 430, 431–34, 436–37, 439, 440, 442, 459, 460, 461, 465, 466; on trading cotton, 316, 317, 377, 383, 384, 388, 407, 408, 409–10, 425, 444, 445, 465, 475; on trading tobacco, 388; on trading with rebellious states, 391, 407–11; on *Trent* Affair, 318–20, 323–24
—U.S. Senator: appointments, 231; calls on officials, 230; Clayton-Bulwer treaty, 234; and Compromise of 1850, 227; congressional politics, 236; public land bill, 230–31; resolution on rules, 230–31; role, xxvii; sworn in, 208–10
—writings: "Address before the Agricultural Society," 77; "Address to the People of the United States," 533; "Appeal of the Independent Democrats," xxvii–xxviii; article on habeas corpus, 172; autobiographical letters, xii, xiii; *Cincinnati American*, xx, 55; on Constitution and slavery, 186; on convention, 1848, 198; description of Cincinnati, *Cincinnati American*, 47; "Effects of Machinery," *North American Review*, 57; *Illinois Monthly Magazine*, 66; introduction to Livingston, *Code of Reform*, 681, 684, 685, 687; journal, 28, 55, 56, 116–17, 120, 144, 210; letter to *Cinncinati Gazette*, 147; Library Address, 212; literary efforts, 52, 64–65; "Men Change Often—Principles Never!," 280; *Norwalk Experiment* letter in, 228–29; poetry, 5, 12, 13, 42–43, 56, 60–61, 83–84; *Statutes of Ohio*, xviii–xix; *Statutes of Ohio and Northwestern Territory*, 68, 71, 73, 74, 76, 102; temperance, memoranda on, lxix; on the army and Indians, 246; Toledo letter, 225, 227, 229; Yankee phraseology, 58

Chase, Sarah Bella (Belle) Dunlop Ludlow (third wife), 123, **179**, 187, 188, 189, 193, 194, 195, 197, 198, 203, 207, 209, 210, 214, 219, 223, 224, 229, 244, 251; at Morristown, N.J. (1850), 224; birth of daughter Josephine, 215; health, 186, 213, 227; hires black nurse, 216; marriage to Chase, xxxii, 179; vacation, 1851, 229

Chase, Simeon March, **618**

Chase, Stella King (sister-in-law), **140**, 163

Chase, William (employee), **674**, 675, 676, 679, 682

Chase, William Frederick (brother), **66**, 157, 163, 230; correspondence, 66, 76, 187, 222; death of, 229, 230

Chattanooga, Tenn.: plan for relief of Union troops at, 450–54, 456–57

Index   { 743 }

Cheever, Mrs. (wife of George Barrell Cheever), 491, 492
Cheever, George Barrell, **491**, 492, 495; *Lectures on the Pilgrim's Progress*, 177–78
Cheney, Charles, **171**, 172, 176, 179
Cherokee Indians, 169–70; relations with United States discussed, 399; treaty with Confederacy discussed, 357, 399
Cherry Hill (Waters home), 624, 627, 628, 693
Chesapeake Bay, 18, 19, 336
Chickamagua, Ga., battle of, 448–49
Chittenden, Lucius Eugene, **360**
Choate, Joseph H., 599
Chocorua (ship), 498
Choctaw (ship), 571
Cholera epidemic (Ohio, 1849), 210, 215, 220, 222
Choquet, Gustave, French grammars, 278, 280, 281
Christ Church (Cincinnati), 101, 155, 163, 165, 167
"Christian Missions" (article), 139
Chrysostom, St. John, 133
Church, Frederick E., "Niagara Falls," 708
Church, John W., **585**
Church, M. C. C., **673**, 678
Churchill, Ann Sevier, **576**
Churchill, Thomas James, **576**
Cincinnati, Ohio, 45, 84, 101, 176; attitudes about slavery, xx, 169–70, 173; Chase's decision to locate there and arrival, xvii–xviii, 42, 47; cholera epidemic, 66, 76, 77; firemen's parade, 1851, 228, 229; fires, 75, 97; Ohio River flood, 1832, 61–64; plans to improve city, 127; Temperance Hall construction, 1845, 173; society, xviii, 47–48, 50–51, 57, 70–74 passim, 79–80, 118, 120, 122, 129, 133, 136–37, 145, 146, 164, 166, 169, 171, 175–80 passim, 185–89 passim, 192, 194, 262–63; weather, 169, 176, 177, 178, 179, 579
Cincinnati American, xx, 55
Cincinnati and Whitewater Canal, 123, 138, 149, 150
Cincinnati Chamber of Commerce: consults Chase, 328
Cincinnati Chronicle, 128, 135, 141, 151, 205
Cincinnati City Council, 121–22, 124, 133, 138, 147, 148, 150, 151, 155–56, 158, 159; and internal improvements, 1841, 150; licensing of taverns, 150, 151–52, 155–56, 157; ordinances, 124, 147
Cincinnati College, xiv, 133, 215
Cincinnati Commercial, 205; suggests Chase unfit for Supreme Court, 674
Cincinnati courthouse, 158, 210; burns down (1849), 216–17
Cincinnati Daily Republican, 148
Cincinnati Enquirer, 188, 213, 227
Cincinnati Gazette, 128, 136, 137, 147, 148, 172, 196, 288, 599
Cincinnati Globe, 205, 206, 207, 213, 214, 238
Cincinnati Herald, lxi, 170, 182
Cincinnati Hotel, 62, 82
Cincinnati Literary Club, 262
Cincinnati Lyceum, 57
Cincinnati Theatre, 64
Cincinnati Water Works, 133, 138
Cincinnati Western Episcopal Observer, 149
Cincinnati Young Men's Catholic Literary Institute, 266
Circassian case, 512, 514, 518
Cisco, John Jay, xl, **312**, 328, 373, 399, 464, 466, 467, 468, 476, 481, 595, 708; correspondence, 399, 419, 420, 421, 430; telegrams, 312, 366, 467, 468
Cist, Charles, **176**, 212; on Cincinnati, 176
Cist, Charles E., **212**
Cist, Francis J., **212**
Cist, Lewis Jacob, **212**
Civil War, 142; draft discussed, 352, 405–6, 469; military leaders evaluated, 321–22, 366, 370–71, 379; military policy and strategy considered, 314–15, 324–25, 348, 349, 352, 358, 359, 360, 366; military recruitment, 360; Native Americans as Union soldiers, 314
—Union Army: black troops, 428–29, 440, 476; loyalty in, 413–14; pardon for deserters, discussed, 446. *See also* Prisoners of war
Civil War finances, 312–13, 315, 317, 327, 350, 381, 448, 475, 478, 481–82, 490, 495, 502; bonds, xxxvi–xxxvii, 312, 350, 416, 417, 419, 421, 433, 444, 478, 502; captured and forfeited cotton, 638–39; Internal Revenue Act (July 1862), 383; Internal Revenue Bill (1864), 462, 464, 466; internal revenue estimates, memorandum in Chase journal, lx; loans, 312, 322–23, 327; notes, xxxvi, 312, 315, 327; postage cur-

rency, 364; trade bill (1864), 466, 469, 471, 474; U.S. debt, xxxvii. *See also* Chase, Treasury secretary; Gold; Legal Tender; National Banking System; U.S. Treasury
Claflin, Mary Bucklin Davenport, 629
Claflin, William, **629**
Clagget, William, **614**
Claims of Japan and Malaysia upon Christendom, 149
Clapp, Theodore, 301
Clark, Mrs., 183–84
Clark, Alonzo, **653**
Clark, Daniel, **332**, 605, 630
Clark, Edward, **665**, 666, 682, 705
Clark, Israel D., **303**
Clark, James, **306**
Clark, Samuel, **254**; mother of, 254
Clark, Spencer Morton, **384**, 427, 432, 460, 480, 481, 505, 506, 611
Clark, Thomas March, **500**
Clark, William, **79**, 79–80
Clark, William F., **400**
Clark County rescue case, 284, 287, 288, 289, 291
Clarke, Adam, *Holy Bible with Commentary*, 252, 267, 269, 293
Clarke, Freeman, **464**
Clarke, Henry, **665**, 691, 698, 700
Clarke, Melvin, **403**
Clarkson, Charles S., 149, 150, 156, 160
Clarkson, Charlotte Dunlop, **229**
Clarkson case, 192
Clarkson v. Wagoner, 152
Clavin, Patrick, **263**, 264
Clay, Dr., 237
Clay, Mrs., 237
Clay, Cassius Marcellus, **193**, 195, 226, 376, 400; agrees on military command, 373; comments on *A Whig*, 168; correspondence, 193, 224, 225, 226, 228; Mexican War, service in, 193; *True American*, 195
Clay, Henry, xii, xvii, **9**, 14, 21, 23, 138, 227, 565; political supporters, 66; son attends Chase's school, 9
Clay, Lucretia Hart, **9**
Clayton-Bulwer Treaty, 234
Clegg, Charles Bailey, **655**
Clement, William Henry, **270**
"Clerical Celibacy" (article), 647
Cleveland, Charles Dexter, **54**, 55
Cleveland, John P., **169**
Cleveland (steamship), 144
Cleveland and Pittsburgh Railroad, 491
Cleveland Herald, 251

Cleveland Library Association, 269
Cleveland Plain Dealer, 219, 220
Cleveland True Democrat, 196, 197, 206, 207, 226, 238, 238, 243
Cliffburne Hospital (Washington), 357
Clifford, John Henry, **500**
Clifford, Nathan, **517**, 608, 651, 664, 668, 672, 679, 703, 704
Clinch, Duncan Lamont, **550**
Clinton v. Englebrecht, 673, 674
Cobb, Amasa, **506**
Cobb, Frederick, 704, 705
Cobb, Howell, **374**
Cobb, J. C. H., 583
Cobb, Jedediah, **154**, 217
Cobb, Oliver Perry, **577**
Cobbett, William, *Cobbett's Paper against Gold*, 144
Cochrane, John, **414**, 417, 419, 421, 423; discusses McClellan, 415–16
Cockerill, Daniel, **204**
Codman, Charles Russell, **486**, 487
Coe, George Simmons, **315**, 323, 327
Coffin, Miss, 487
Coffin, Charles Carleton, *Seat of Empire*, 657
Coffin, Charles Dustin, 165, **166**, 179, 185, 186, 187, 195
Coffin, Harriet Eliza Wooster, **187**
Coffin, Levi, **258**, 581
Coffin, Tristam, **487**
Coggeshall, William Turner, **247**, 249, 276, 282, 289, 296
Cogswell, Elliott Colby, **698**
Coit (ship), 550, 551, 552, 553
Colby, Abigail Corbet Chase (sister), **19**, 68, 74, 91, 104, 107, 230
Colby, Isaac (brother-in-law), xix, xx, 19, **68**, 71, 76, 80, 83, 86, 87, 91–96 passim, 104, 107, 116, 118; letter to, 235
Colby, Isaac (Cincinnati tailor), **186**
Colby, Samuel, **186**
Cold Harbor, battle of, xli
Coleman, Abraham B., **204**, 205, 208, 216
Coleman, John H., **205**
Coleman, Robert B., **499**, 506
Colfax, Schuyler, **412**, 413, 597, 608
Collamer, Jacob, **332**, 426, 521
Collins, Mr., 141
Collins, ———, 573
Collins, Bryan, 265
Collins, Catharine Wever, **244**, 251
Collins, Edward Knight, **236**
Collins, Helen K., **265**
Collins, S., **25**, 26, 532
Collins, William, *The Passions*, 25

Index { 745 }

Collins, William Oliver, **251**, 306, 307, 308, 578, 579, 581
Collins Line (ship company), 236
Colonel Osborn's Hotel (Leesburg, Va.), 38
Colton, Alexander M. F., **303**
Colton, Chauncey, **159**
Columbian College (D.C.), 19, 405, 406
Columbus, Ohio, 116, 195, 278; Bible Panorama display, 295, 296; social life, 247, 250, 255, 258, 259, 260, 265–66, 269, 271, 273, 274, 287, 290, 291, 293, 294, 295, 297; weather, 258
Columbus & Xenia Railroad, 308
Columbus Atheneum, 257
Columbus Daily Standard, 207
Columbus Fencibles, 269
Columbus High School Literary Society, 265
Columbus University Church, 274
Columbus Vedettes, 287
Colvin, James W., **460**
Comly, James M., **299**, 300
Commodore Perry (ship), 596, 607
Commonwealth (ship), 574, 575
Commonwealth and Emancipator (Boston), 225
Commonwealth Hotel (Boston), 692, 693
Compromise of 1850, 227, 234; Chase's role in debates, xxvii
Conahan, Charles, **126**, 127
Concord, N.H., 21
Condict case, 177
Confederacy, 318; claims from commerce raiders, 706; conspiracy to free prisoners of war, 533; Henry Stuart Foote's peace efforts, 516; number of troops estimated, 382, 385; recognition as belligerents considered, 313–15; treaty with Cherokees discussed, 357, 399
Confiscation Act (July 1862), 351, 408
"Congos," 304, 306
Congress (ship), 337
Conklin, Jacob S., 299, **300**
Conklin v. Bissell et al., 150
Conkling, Edgar, **505**
Connecticut politics, 489
Conness, John, 462, **463**, 598
Conover, Mrs. (wife of James F. Conover), **115**
Conover, James F., 51, **52**
Constitutional Convention of 1787, 69, 242
Continental Congress, 59, 60

Conventions: Democratic, 196, 224, 234, 295–96, 644; Free Democratic, 197, 218–19, 225, 226, 227, 235–36; Free Territory, 1848, 196; Free-Soil, xxiv–xxv, 197, 219, 222, 227–28, 231, 245; Friends of Freedom, 1851, 225, 226; "fusion," 243; Know-Nothing, 245; Liberty (Ohio), 174, 196; Ohio antislavery, 165, 166–67; Republican, xxix, 245, 254, 298, 304; Temperance Convention, Ohio, 254; Union party, 580; Whig, 196
Convers, Charles, C., **223**
Conversion clauses, 478
Conway, Martin Franklin, **710**
Conway, Moncure Daniel, **262**, 273; sermons, 256, 262, 274
Conway, Thomas William, **566**, 567, 569, 600
Cook, ———, **680**, 687
Cook, Asher, **276**
Cooke, Dorothea Elizabeth Allen, **604**, 654
Cooke, Henry David, Jr., **635**, 636
Cooke, Henry David, Sr., **532**, 603, 604, 635, 636, 637, 648, 682, 683
Cooke, Henry Eleutheros, **654**
Cooke, Jay, xxxvii, **323**, 324, 383, 386, 433, 444, 445, 481, 491, 503, 504, 528, 633, 647, 648, 653, 654, 684; correspondence, 384, 491, 506, 532, 594, 632, 635, 636, 655, 666, 667, 685; on loan negotiations, 373
Cooke, Jay, Jr., **604**, 607, 609
Cooke, Jay, and Co., 458, 609, 634, 636, 637, 686, 692
Cooke, Laura Elmina, **601**, 607
Cooke, Laura S. Humphreys, **604**, 607, 637, 683
Cooke, Martha Carswell, **657**
Cooke, Pitt, **383**, 384
Cooke, Sarah (Sally) Esther, **654**
Coolidge, Charles Austin, **450**
Cooper, James, **420**
Cooper, James Fenimore, *The Pathfinder*, 122
Cooper, Mary, 257
Cope, Mrs. (wife of Herman Cope), 92, 233
Cope, Herman, **69**, 74, 92, 150, 233
Corby, John, 222
Corcoran, Michael, **313**, 314, 365
Corcoran, William Wilson, **232**, 236, 645, 686
Corey, A. W., **68**, 77, 132
Corey & Fairbank, 73, 77
Corey v. Hall, 132
Corning, Erastus, **323**

Cornish, Sandy, **555**, 560
Cornwall and Brother, 222
Corry, William M., **175**, 272, 276
Corwin, Eliza Bruen, **304**
Corwin, Ichabod, **291**
Corwin, Robert G., **304**, 365, 581
Corwin, Thomas, **208**, 209, 235, 291, 494, 499, 504; death of, 600
Corwine, Richard M., **266**, 267, 273, 308, 710
Cottman, Thomas, **364**, 366
Cotton, Eliza, 175
Coulter, Mrs. (wife of James H. Coulter), 582
Coulter, James H., **248**, 257, 269, 271, 582, 588
Courrier des États-Unis, 277
Court, Lucian, 263
Covode, John, **322**, 429
Cowan, Edgar, **332**, 418, 419
Cowles, Laman, **363**
Cowper, William, poetry, 121, 124, 126, 127, 128, 132
Cox, Jacob Dolson, 403, **404**
Cox, Samuel Sullivan, **686**
Coxe, Brinton, lv
Craighead, Jeanette A. Miller, **656**
Craighead, Samuel, **655**, 656
Cram, Thomas Jefferson, **340**, 341, 342
Cranch, William, xvii
Crane, William Montgomery, **41**
Crawford, Mrs. (employee), **599**
Crawford House (New Hampshire), 497
Creed, Mr., 73
Creswell, John Angel James, **602**
Cromwell, Oliver, 71, 348
Crook, Mrs., 300
Crook, ———, 300
Crook, George, **372**, 375
Crosby, Alpheus, **484**, 591
Crosby, Alpheus Benning, **614**, 615
Crosby, Dixi, **614**, 615
Crosson, John, 278, **279**
Crowell, David A., **224**
Crowell, Margaret, 224
Crowley, F. C., **294**
Cruikshank, John, **669**
Cuba: described, 1865, 556–60; revolution, 646; slavery, 235, 557
Cudworth, Ralph, *True Intellectual System of the Universe*, 187
Cullum, George Washington, **384**
Culver, Charles Vernon, **305**
Culver, Lucius H., **305**
Cumberland (ship), 337
Cummings, Alexander, **383**, 424

Cummins, ——— (son of Joseph Cummins), 299
Cummins, Joseph, 299, **300**
Cunard Line, 236
Cunningham, James, **303**
Curtin, Andrew Gregg, 379, **380**, 385, 429, 430, 632
Curtis, Benjamin Robbins, **621**, 699
Curtis, George William, **500**
Curtis, Samuel Ryan, **352**, 358, 359, 361, 363
Cushing, Benjamin Tupper, **195**
Cushing, Caleb, **603**
Custer, George Armstrong, **608**
Cutler, O. N., **571**
Cutts, Mrs. (wife of James M. Cutts), 393
Cutts, James Madison, **365**, 378, 389

Dacotah (ship), 339
Dahlgren, John Adolphus Bernard, **545**, 546, 547, 644
Dahlgren, Sarah Madeleine Vinton, **644**
Dainese, Francis, **494**
Daisley v. Dennison, 138
Dale (ship), 555
Daley, ———, 515
Dall, ———, 176
Dana, Angela Henrietta Channing, **485**
Dana, Charles Anderson, **448**, 449, 453, 513, 514, 517, 638
Dana, Elizabeth Ellery, **485**
Dana, Eunice MacDaniel, **517**
Dana, Mary Rosamund, **485**
Dana, Richard Henry, Jr., **483**, 484, 485, 498
Dana, Ruth Charlotte, **485**
Dana, Samuel Turner, **488**, 625
Dana, Sarah Watson (b. 1814), **483**, 485
Dana, Sarah Watson (b. 1842), **485**
Dana, Sylvester, **613**
Dane, Nathan, 58–60, **59**; *A General Abridgment and Digest of American Law*, 58–60
Darling, William Augustus, **505**
D'Arnaud, Charles, **458**
Dartmouth College, xiv–xv, 16, 17, 21, 26, 54, 122, 234; commencements, 591, 613–15
"Darwinianism" (article), 647
D'Aubigné, Jean Henri Merle, *Réformation*, 162, 163
Daveiss, Joseph Hamilton, **48**
Davies, Henry Ebenezer, **313**, 446
Davies, Henry Eugene, **446**, 447

Davies, Samuel Watts, **131**, 148
Davis, Miss, 541
Davis, Mr., 541
Davis, David, **601**, 602, 608, 651, 658, 709
Davis, Edmund Jackson, **521**, 605
Davis, Frederica Gore King, **501**, 592, 648
Davis, Garrett, **332**, 467
Davis, Henry Winter, **435**, 527; death and funeral of, 601–2; dissatisfaction with Lincoln in 1864, xl
Davis, J. Amory, **490**
Davis, Jefferson, **374**, 414, 539, 572; Chase declines to see, 550; Chase has dream about, 695; potential prosecution of, 639; in prison, 610
Davis, Jefferson C., 406
Davis, Jesse L., **361**
Davis, John Chandler Bancroft, 500, **501**, 592
Davis, Joseph Emory, **572**; plantation described, 572
Davis, Lewis, 468
Davis, Nancy Morris, **527**, 602
Davis, Oliver Wilson, **386**
Davis, William H., **361**
Dawson, Moses, **95**, 121, 128
Dawson, William Crosby, 208, **209**
Day, Mr., 536, 600
Day, ———, 469
Day, Mrs. (wife of Israel Day), 224
Day, Calvin, **488**
Day, Israel, 224
Day, Timothy Crane, **232**
Day, William Howard, 225, **226**
Dayton, Lewis Mulford, **539**
Dayton and Michigan Railroad, 312
De Ahna, Henry C., **458**
De Witt, Alexander: and "Appeal of the Independent Democrats," xxvii
Dean, Mr., 218
Declaration of Independence, 60, 242
Delafield, John, **229**, 230
Delafield, Richard, **598**
Delahay, Mark William, **646**
Deland, Charles W., **580**
Deland, Helen Cecelia Ball, **580**
Delano, Columbus, **639**
Delany, Martin Robinson, **547**
Deming, Israel, 650
Deming v. U.S., 650, 651
Democratic Club (West Liberty, Ohio), 204
Democratic party: Independent Democracy, 238, 241; Locofocos, 307; policies, 1848, xxv; and Reconstruction, xliv–xlv. *See also* Free Democrats; Conventions
Democratic party, New York, xxiv, 222
Democratic party, Ohio, xxvi–xxvii, 198, 199, 200, 201, 202, 204, 205, 207, 224, 225; hard money Democrats, 202; Lorain County, 223; Ohio and Baltimore platforms compared, 1853, 241; Ohio Free Democracy, 197, 202; reputed coalition with Know-Nothings, 305; resolutions, 1851, 226
Democratic Republican party proposed, 423
Denison, Catharine Amanda, **616**
Denison, Dudley Chase, **616**, 617
Denison, Eliza, **616**, 617
Denison, George Stanton, **376**, 435, 494, 564, 567, 568, 569, 570, 616, 617, 638; criticized, 532; death of, 638; removed as Treasury agent, 533
Denison, Gertrude, 617
Denison, Gertrude M., **616**
Denison, James (cousin), **98**, 617
Denison, John, 617
Denison, John H., **616**
Denison, Joseph Adam, Jr. (cousin), 376, **616**, 617
Denison, Joseph Adam, Sr. (husband of aunt Rachel), 98, 203
Denison, Joseph D., **616**
Denison, Katie, 617
Denison, Lucy D., **616**
Denison, Rachel (cousin), **203**, 616, 617
Denison, Rachel Chase (aunt), 98, 203, 616
Denison, William, **617**
Denman, Edward H., 185
Dennison, Mrs., 292
Dennison, Anne Eliza Neil, **264**, 292, 294
Dennison, Henry, 705
Dennison, Henry M., **246**
Dennison, William, **254**, 256, 264, 266, 274, 276, 278, 285, 286, 287, 293, 294, 299, 304, 312, 334, 588, 611
Denny, William H. P., **304**
Dent, Alfred W., **276**
Derringer, Col., 255
Deshler, William Green, **269**, 280, 289, 290, 534, 582, 586
Desilver, John Ford, **185**
Develin, John Edward, **513**
Dewees, William Potts: *A Compendious System of Midwifery*, 99, 100; *A Treatise on the Diseases of Females*, 100

Dewey, Israel Otis, **613**, 616
Dewey, Lauren, **487**
Dexter, ———, 282
Dexter, Edmund, **83**; daughter of, 83
Dexter, F. Gordon, **625**
Dexter, George, **625**
Dexter, Sarah Rogers Endicott (wife of George Dexter), **625**
Dexter, T. C. A., **562**
Dialogues (French), 278
Dicey, Edward, 517
Dick, Franklin A., **398**
Dick, John, **585**
Dick, Thomas, *Works*, 89
Dickey, Miss, 255
Dickey, Alfred S., **307**
Dickey, Milton C., **272**
Dickinson, Daniel Stevens, **599**
Dicks, Harrison, **252**
Dickson, Anna Maria Parker, **245**
Dickson, William Martin, **244**, 245, 580
Didier, Eugene Lemoine, **648**, 662, 698
Dimmock, Asa G., **223**
Disney, David Tiernan, **198**, 200
Disney, William, **198**, 200
Dix, John Adams, **347**
Dixon, Archibald, **231**
Dixon, James, **332**, 363
Doane, Charles, **216**, 222
Doddridge, ———, 307
Dodge, Charles Cleveland, 342, **343**, 374
Dodge, George S., 541, **542**, 543, 544
Doesticks, Q. K. Philander. *See* Thompson, Mortimer Neal
Dolan, ———, 131
Dole, Mr., 470
Dom Pedro (steamship), 93
Dominick, Mrs. (wife of George Dominick), 262
Dominick, George, **262**
Donald, David Herbert, ed., *Inside Lincoln's Cabinet*, lxii, lxiv, lxv, lxvi, lxvii, lxviii
Donaldson, Alexander, **246**
Donaldson, Andrew, **246**
Donaldson, Frank, **668**
Donaldson, James Lowry, **572**, 573
Donaldson, Luther, **334**
Donaldson, Prof., 583
Donaldson, William, **180**
Donogh, Joseph B., **186**
Donogh, Robert P., **186**
Doolittle, James Rood, **332**, 605
Doren, John G., **307**
Dorsey, G., **166**
Dorsey case, 179

Douglas, Adèle Cutts, **284**, 365, 378, 389, 393; Chase visits, 381, 386, 393
Douglas, Stephen A., xii, **209**, 272, 273, 284, 296, 421, 422
Douglass, Frederick, **632**
Dove, W. A., **569**
Dowes, William, **276**
Downes and Haven, 156, 157, 172
Downing, Andrew Jackson, *Landscape Gardening*, 175
Downs, Solomon Weathersbee, **236**
Doyle, Thomas Arthur, 501
Drake, ———, 194
Drake, Charles Daniel, **457**
Drake, Colonel, 209
Drake, Daniel, 76, 84, **91**, 92, 93, 96, 107, 111, 154
Drake, Elias Franklin, **270**
Draper, Simeon, xlii
Dred Scott decision, xxx
Driskell, Peter, **181**
Driskell v. Parish, 181, 197
Drury v. Foster, 519
Dryden & Hunt, 67
Dudley, Colonel, 189, 659
Dudley, Mrs. (wife of Elias Dudley), 659
Dudley, Ambrose, **144**
Dudley, Elias, **144**, 156, 659
Duer, Denning, **463**, 502
Duffield, Charles, **567**
Duggan, James, **498**
Duhamel, Clement, **570**
Dulce y Garay, Domingo, **557**
Dummer, Charles, **506**
Dumont v. Gilbert, 196
Dunbar, Elijah, 83
Dunbar, Eunice, **617**
Dunbar, Mary Ralston, 83
Dunbar, William E., **83**
Duncan, Mrs. (wife of Stephen Duncan): plantation of, 573
Duncan, Green B., 137
Duncan, Samuel Augustus, **456**
Duncan, Stephen, **573**
Duncan, William Henry, **495**
Dunham, Cyrus Livingston, **238**
Dunlap v. Craig et al., 131
Dunn, William McKee, **334**
Dunning, George Freeman, 481, **482**
Duns Scotus, John, 39
Dupérier, Frederick H., 638, 639, 640
DuPont, Henry, **597**
DuPont, Samuel Francis, **548**
Durant, Thomas Jefferson, **354**, 477, 565, 566, 567, 570, 632
Durbin, John Price, **57**
Durell, Edward Henry, **567**, 569, 635

Durgin, Samuel, **240**
Dustin, M., **270**
Dutton, Henry, **489**
Duval, Jonathan, 304
Duval, Thomas H., **521**
Duvall, ———, 304, 305
Dwight, Henry, *Travels in the North of Germany*, 27
Dwight, William, **398**
Dymond, Jonathan, *Essays on Principles of Morality*, 159

E. P. (young woman), 50–51
Eadie, John, **706**
Eagle [Talon] (Buffalo, N.Y.), 173
Eagle Tavern (Van Wert, Ohio), 303
Early, Jubal Anderson, **479**; captured, 506
Eastman, Ben C., **273**
Eastman, Charlotte (Lottie) Sewall, **273**, 353, 361, 362, 483, 484, 491, 492, 494, 495, 589, 601, 607, 620, 621, 622, 636, 638; affectionate encounters with Chase, 624–29; correspondence with Chase, 273, 309, 353, 355, 361, 505, 532, 626, 631, 634, 635, 637, 638, 640, 674, 683; rumors of impending marriage to Chase, 639
Eastman, Zebina, **243**
Eaton, Emma Jane Goodman, **260**
Eaton, John, **632**
Eaton, John Henry, 22–23
Eaton, Joseph Oriel, **260**, 263, 264, 266, 273, 274; and family, 266
Eaton, Margaret (Peggy) O'Neale Timberlake, 22–23
Eaton, Mary, **83**
Eaton affair, 22–23
Ebbitt House (Washington), 390, 638, 640
Ebenezer Methodist Church (Washington), 39
Eberle, John, **86**, 92, 108; *Diseases of Children*, 100, 142
Eddy, Thomas Mears, **675**
Edes, Miss, 700
Edgar, Quinet, *Idées Sur la Philosophie*, 71
Edgeforest, 120
Edgerton, Alfred Peck, **240**
Edgewood (Chase estate in D.C.), lxix, 669, 671, 672, 678, 692, 704; Chase purchases, 650; construction work, 664–86 passim, 705, 710; cultivation, 677, 680–87 passim; gas production, 664, 670, 679

Edinburgh Review, 57, 227
Edmands, Horace S., **72**, 73
Edmonds, John Worth, **440**
Edmunds, George Franklin, **641**, 642, 710
Edmunds, James Madison, 462, **463**
Edson, Charles P., **250**
Edson, Tracy Robinson, **321**
Edward Shippen (steamship), 154
Edwards, Mr., 575
Edwards, John Miller, **203**
Edwards, Thomas McKey, **426**
Eells, Samuel, xxi, **101**, 117, 120, 122, 149; Chase recommends for consulship, 153
Egloffstein, Frederick von, **609**, 610, 611
Elder, William, **463**, 598, 634, 703
Electra (ship), 502
Elgar, Mrs. (wife of Joseph Elgar), **24**, 27
Elgar, Eliza, 26
Elgar, Joseph, **24**; family of, 26
Elgar, Margarette, **24**, 26
Elijah, 149
Eliot, Mrs. (mother of Thomas Dawes Eliot), 19
Eliot, Thomas Dawes, **19**, 20, 281, 387, 388, 389, 485, 501
Eliot, William Greenleaf, **239**, 592
Ellicott, Elizabeth. *See* Pike, Elizabeth Ellicott
Elliott, Miss, 73
Elliott, James, **248**, 250
Ellis, John W., **580**
Ellis, Roland, 171
Ells, George W., **179**
Ellsworth, Henry Leavitt, **218**
Ely, Alfred, **366**
Ely, Ezra Stiles, **22**, 23
Emancipation Proclamation, 351, 395, 396, 400, 404, 413, 428, 431, 432, 438, 534, 569; cabinet accounts of discussion on, xxxiv; exemptions, 429, 447, 527; Lincoln decides to issue, 393–95
Emerson, Mrs. (wife of Henry Emerson), 90
Emerson, Henry, 81, 90, 171, 171
Emerson, John Smith, **615**
Emerson, Ralph Waldo, **257**, 490, 592; lecture on Beauty, 262
Emerson, William, **592**
Emmet, Catherine Temple, **700**
Emmet, Richard Stockton, **700**
Emmet, Robert, **701**
Emmons, George Foster, **562**, 563

Endicott, Annie Thorndike, **483**, 621, 622, 623, 624, 625, 629
Endicott, John, 627
Endicott, William, **483**, 491, 621, 629
Endicott, William, Jr., 629
Endicott, William Crowninshield, 627
Enrollment Act, 1864, 469
Ensign, Deacon, 302
Ensign, William O., **240**, 302, 307
Epanthean Society, Woodward College, 179
Episcopal Church, 134, 310; committee on Sunday school, 113; and slavery, 134, 166
Equal Suffrage Association, 604, 641
Ericsson, John, 338
Ernst, Sarah A. Butler, 250
Ernst, William, **250**
Espinasse, Isaac, *Actions at Nisi Prius*, 30
Espy, Josiah Murdoch, 116
Espy, Lovinia, **116**
Essex Institute (Salem, Mass.), 621
Este, ——— (daughter of David Este, Sr.), **150**
Este, David Kirkpatrick, Jr., **396**
Este, David Kirkpatrick, Sr., **150**, 171, 579
Este, George Peabody, **513**
Este, Louisa, **150**
Este, Louisa Miller, **150**
Este, Lucy Ann Harrison, **150**
Este, Ursula C., **150**
Este, William Miller, **396**, 524, 525
Eulong, Miss, 565
Eutaw House (Baltimore), 506, 522
Evans, Allen, 543
Evans, Daniel P., **258**
Evarts, Helen Minerva Wardner, **618**, 619, 653, 707, 708
Evarts, William Maxwell, **519**, 618, 619, 652, 653, 700, 707, 708, 709; daughters of, 707
Evening Star (ship), 656
Evens, Platt, **168**
Everett, Edward, **230**, 235, 402; *Works of Daniel Webster*, 423, 424
Everett, Homer, **301**
Ewell, Richard Stoddert, **379**
Ewell, William H., 637
Ewing, Mr., 169
Ewing, James H., **213**
Ewing, Thomas, Sr., **605**
Ewing v. Borden, 213, 214
Ex parte Garland, 524
Ex parte in the matter of the United States, 677

Ex parte McCardle, xlvii
Ex parte Milligan, xlvi–xlvii; Chase's draft opinion, lxvii
Ex parte Milwaukee & Minnesota R.R. Co., 521

Fairbank, Daniel, **68**, 77
Fales, Stephen, 55
Farington, Betsey, **145**
Farley, John, **23**, 24
Farnham, John Hay, **59**, 59–60
Farnsworth, John Franklin, 510
Farragut, David Glasgow, **335**, 440, 516, 527
Farrar, Benjamin, **398**
Farrar, Timothy, **614**
Farwell, Moors, **221**
Farwell, W. B., 437
Fashion (ship), 569
Faulkner, ——— (son of Francis Augustus Faulkner), 620
Faulkner, Charles James, **375**
Faulkner, Francis Augustus, **620**
Faver, Joseph, 129
Faver, Sarah R. Bond, **129**
Fay, Miss, 618
Febiger, George L., **289**
Felton, Cornelius Conway, **186**
Felton, Samuel Morse, **454**
Fenton, ———, 180
Fenton, Joseph B., **178**
Fenton, Reuben Eaton, **630**, 709
Ferguson, Edward Alexander, **294**
Ferguson, Thomas Barker, 524
Feron, Mme., 7, **8**
Ferris, ———, 169
Ferris (ship), 656
Ferry, Orris Sanford, **374**
Fessenden, Francis, **603**
Fessenden, William Pitt, **322**, 326, 469–81 passim, 490, 503, 505, 506, 518, 591, 599; corresponds with Chase, 468, 487, 494, 495, 498, 511, 603; discusses U.S. finances with Chase, 478; as Treasury secretary, 472, 473–74, 476–77, 477
Ficklin, Orlando Bell, **196**
Field, Cyrus West, **699**
Field, David Dudley, **367**, 372, 373, 686, 706
Field, Mary E. Carr, 706
Field, Maunsell B., **440**, 442, 444, 449, 463, 464, 466, 467, 468, 595, 687; becomes assistant secretary of Treasury, 457, 458; printing of extract from Chase journal, lxiv–lxv; proposed as assistant treasurer at New York, 463

Index { 751 }

Field, Stephen Johnson, **513**, 514, 515, 598, 605, 606, 607, 608, 647, 649, 651, 664, 668, 669, 672, 681; letter from, 683
Field, Virginia Swearingen, **664**, 683, 706
Field, William, **254**
Field, William M., 152
Fields, James Thomas, **635**
Fifteenth Amendment, 646
Fifth Avenue Hotel (New York), 594, 595, 612, 630
Fillmore, Mary Abigail, **236**
Fillmore, Millard, **209**, 232, 236, 530; precedent of succession to the presidency, xliii
Filor v. U.S., 647, 649
Finch, Judge, 659
Findlay, James, **101**
Findley, Mrs., 122–23
Finney, Jerry, **180**
First National Bank and Huntington's Admrs. v. Texas, 673
Fish, Hamilton, **313**, 648, 706, 708
Fish, Julia Kean, **646**, 687, 706
Fishback, ———, 245
Fisher, Miss, 590
Fisher, George, 223
Fisher, George Purnell, **677**
Fisher, Isaac, 230
Fisher, S. R., 243
Fisher, S. W., 243
Fisher, William Alexander, 150
Fitch, John, **505**
Flagg, William Joseph, **581**
Flagler, Henry M., **396**
Flanders, Benjamin Franklin, **505**, 532–33, 564, 570
Fletcher, Thomas Clement, **632**
Flinn, Mrs., 617
Flinn, Lois, 617
Flora's Dictionary. *See* Wirt, Elizabeth Washington Gamble
Florence (ship), 699
Florentine v. Barton, 519
Florer, Mr., 172
Florida: capture considered, 1863, 438; coast described, 1865, 551, 554; politics, 1863, 446. *See also* Chase—travels
Florida (ship), 427
Flowers, Franklin L., **260**
Floyd, John Buchanan, **374**
Fogg, George Gilman, **613**, 630, 638
Foley, ———, 138
Foley, Bushrod W.: legal case, 334
Folger, Mr., 187
Folger, Mrs., 187

Follet, Oran, **250**, 278, 387
Follett, Jonathan S., 132
Foot, Solomon, **332**
Foote, Andrew Hull, **700**
Foote, Elizabeth Betts, **71**, 73
Foote, Henry Stuart, **516**
Foote, Jane Warner, **71**
Foote, John A., **254**, 275
Foote, John Parsons, **71**, 171
Foote, Rachel D. Smiley, **516**
Foote, Samuel Edmund, **71**, 119, 171
Foraker, Joseph B., 583
Forbes, John Murray, **485**, 486, 491, 503, 516
Forbes, Paul Sieman, **699**
Forbes, Sarah Swain Hathaway, **486**
Force, Peter, **601**
Ford, Mrs., 270
Ford, Gordon Lester, **491**
Ford, Seabury, **202**, 211
Ford, Thomas H., **270**, 292, 296
Ford's Theater (Washington), 529
Forney, John Wien, **503**, 505
Forrest, Nathan Bedford, **575**
Forsha, Samuel W., **393**, 397
Forsyth, William, **198**
Fort Caswell, N.C., 541
Fort Darling, Va., 346
Fort Donelson (ship), 548
Fort Fisher, N.C., 513, 518, 541
Fort Macon, N.C., 335, 538
Fort Monroe, Va., 536, 537; visited by Chase, 336, 338, 341, 342, 343, 344, 345, 346, 347
Fort Moultrie, S.C., 439
Fort Pulaski, Ga., 336, 550
Fort Sewall, Mass., 622
Fort Sumter, S.C., 330
Forward, Walker, **77**
Forward, William, **192**, 206
Foster, Dwight, **648**
Foster, Harriet Morton Perkins, **496**
Foster, James, *Christian Revelation*, 112
Foster, John Gray, 413, 414, 528
Foster, Lafayette Sabine, **332**, 584, 602, 608
Foster, Stephen Symonds, **174**
Foster, William Lawrence, **496**
Foster and Whitney, 229
Fostoria, Ohio, Methodist Episcopal Church, 301
Fourteenth Amendment, xlvii, 610, 619, 632, 640, 641
Fouts, Jonas, 280–82
Fouts, Phillip, 280–82
Fowler, Asa, **613**
Fowler, Austin, **396**
Fox, Betsy, **616**

Fox, Charles, **108**, 114, 160, 184, 196, 207, 580
Fox, Gustavus Vasa, **383**, 431, 439
Fox, Jabez, **239**
Fox v. Johnson et al., 168
Frank, Francis, **271**
Franklin, ——— (son of Nelson Franklin), 263
Franklin, Benjamin, 36, 329
Franklin, M. J., **387**
Franklin, Nelson, **263**
Franklin, William Buel, **325**, 367, 370, 372, 389, 390, 481
Franklin Bank (Cincinnati), 165, 197
Franklin County Court of Common Pleas, Grand Jury, 290
Franklin House (Cincinnati), 151
Franklin House (Columbus), 106
Fransworth, John Franklin, **510**
Frazer, John, 637
Frazier, Garrison, **521**
Frederick of Prussia, 52
Frederick William Louis, Prince, 362
Fredericksburg, Va., military operations around, 345, 347
Free Democrats, 202, 214; convention, Cleveland, 218; Lucas County, letter to, 216; meet with Chase, 231; union with old line Democracy in Vermont, 218–19
Free Enquirer, 13
Free-Soil newspaper, West Liberty, 204
Free-Soil party, xxiv–xxv, 206, 225, 245. *See also* Free Democrats; Conventions
Free-Soil party, Ohio, xxvi–xxvii, 198, 199, 201, 205, 207, 208, 209, 222, 224, 225, 228; Ohio Free Territory party, 196; Senate candidate, 1849, 206–7
Free-Soil party platform, 1848, 197
Free-Soilers, 200, 202
Free State party, 261
Freedley, Edwin Troxell, **205**
Freedmen's Bureau, xlvi–xlvii
Freedmen's Bureau Bill, 467
Freeman, Mrs., 648
Freeman, William, **184**
Freis, Mr., 183
Frelinghuysen, Frederick Theodore, **670**
Frémont, John Charles, **249**, 259, 302, 304, 305, 345, 346, 347, 348, 355, 356, 379, 387, 433, 458, 491; *Geographical Memoir upon Upper California*, 213; as presidential candidate, xxix, xl
French, Mr., 436

French, John R., **356**
French, Mansfield, **268**, 269, 270, 333, 334, 501, 548, 549, 640
French, Maynard, 174, 175
French Princes, 369
"French Rhetoric." *See* Choquet, Gustave
French v. Edwards, 674, 675, 676
Freyre, Manuel, **649**, 687
Friday, John, **175**, 176
Fries, George, **310**
Frink, Charlotte Wallace, **192**, 237
Frink, John, 192
Front Royal, Va., battle of, 345, 346
Froude, James Anthony, **708**
Fry, James Barnet, **480**
Fugate, Jeremiah (anecdote), 52
Fugitive Slave Act of 1793, 166
Fugitive Slave Act of 1850, xxx, xxxi, 236, 244, 284, 296
Fuller, Charlotte Bull Stuart, **525**
Fuller, Richard, **331**, 532, 535, 536, 538, 540, 541, 548, 549, 551; on emancipation, 331, 525, 526
Fulton, Robert, 20
Fulton, W. H., **295**
Fulton (steamship), 20
Fulweiler, Abraham, **141**
Fulweiler, Michael H., **141**

Gage, James L., **301**
Gaines, Myra Clark, **566**
Gaines, Richard, **225**
Galena (ship), 338
Gales, Joseph, 365
Galileo, 264
Gallagher, John M., 119, 173
Gallagher, William Davis, **120**, 147, 148, 160, 162, 168, 194, 408, 409, 577, 629, 655; *Facts and Conditions of Progress in the North-west*, 655
Gallatin, James, **313**, 315
Galloway, Mary, 295
Galloway, Samuel Buchanan, **248**, 252, 253, 256, 260, 290
Galloway, Samuel G., **247**, 248, 253, 257, 259, 292, 295, 296, 299, 306, 438, 582
Galt House (Louisville), 155
Gamble, Hamilton Rowan, **398**, 400, 405
Gangewer, Allen M., **233**, 310, 311, 459, 604
Gannett, Allen, 588, **589**, 591, 614, 625
Gano, W. G. W., **87**, 100, 131, 206
Gantt, Thomas Tasker, 369, **370**

Index

{ 753 }

Garcia, Madame (wife of Manuel Garcia), 649
Garcia, Manuel, **649**
Garfield, James Abram, **353**, 354, 398, 400–408 passim, 413–24 passim, 449, 469, 477, 600, 608, 631; telegrams, 450, 453; upset over House committee appointee, 647
Garland, Augustus Hill, **598**
Garnet, Henry Highland, **682**
Garniss, Amelia (mother of first wife), 72, **79**, 83–119 passim, 144, 146, 151, 155, 157, 158, 163, 164, 166, 172, 224; letter to, 120
Garniss, Catharine Jane. *See* Chase, Catharine Jane Garniss
Garniss, John P. (father of first wife), **70**, 72, 73, 74, 79–114 passim, 122, 124, 129, 133, 139, 145, 149, 151, 153, 155, 168, 180, 224, 227; family of, xix, 82, 83, 85, 96, 99, 108; letter to, 233
Garrard, Israel Ludlow, 196, **207**, 218, 225, 226
Garrard, Jeptha D., Jr., **413**, 414
Garrard, Jeptha Dudley, **110**, 179, 188, 207
Garrard, Kenner, **188**
Garrard, Sarah Bella Ludlow. *See* McLean, Sarah Bella Ludlow Garrard
Garrett, John Work, **294**, 295, 392, 448, 454, 455, 456, 596, 602, 610; communications with, 321, 454; visited, 455, 456
Garrison, William Lloyd: Chase's coolness toward, xxiv
Gassaway, Mr., 121, 123, 130
Gassaway, Henry, 121
Gaston, William, **690**, 693
Gates, Beman, **282**, 283
Geary, John White, **272**, 346
Gedney, Charles F., **95**, 99, 108, 114
Gee, Nathaniel, **491**
Geiger, Joseph H., **290**, 420, 582
General Banks (ship), 569
General Taylor (ship), 564
George, Nicholas, **482**
Gerard, John H., **294**
Gerard, S. C., **294**
Germain v. Mason, 673
Gerolt, Friedrich Karl Joseph von, **610**
Gest, Joseph G., **361**, 365
Getty, Archibald, **547**
Gettysburg, battle of, 426
Geyer, Henry Sheffie, **239**
Gholson, William Yates, **197**, 261

Gibbon, Edward, *Decline and Fall of the Roman Empire*, 306, 307, 309
Gibbs, Jonathan C., **542**, 543
Gibraltar (Cooke retreat), 654–56
Gibson, ———, 241
Gibson, Charles, **398**
Gibson, William H., **249**, 253; Ohio treasury defalcation, xxx, 285–97
Giddings, Grotius Reed, **445**
Giddings, Joshua Reed, 206, **207**, 208, 210, 219, 228, 238, 249, 269; and "Appeal of the Independent Democrats," xxvii; Chase corresponds with, 210, 222, 224, 228, 250; and Free-Soil party, xxvii, 224
Giddings, Laura, **269**
Giddings, Lura Maria, **269**
Gifford, George, **676**
Gilbert, Alfred West, 172, **173**
Gilbert, land patent, 230
Giles, Catharine Donaldson, **524**
Giles, Sarah Wilson, **524**
Giles, William Fell, **522**, 523, 524, 526, 531
Gill, Henry C., **666**
Gill, John Loriman, **271**
Gillespie, George de Normandie, **172**, 187; sermons, 172, 193
Gillespie, Joseph, 442, **443**
Gillmore, John Quincy: letter from, 587
Gillmore, Quincy Adams, **427**, 438, 439, 480, 547, 548, 550, 552, 553, 587, 598, 610; orders on Reconstruction, 551
Gilmer, John H., **644**
Gilmor, Harry, **481**
Gilmor House (Baltimore), 294
Gilmore, Ann Page Whipple, **496**, 612
Gilmore, Clarence D., **495**
Gilmore, Hiram S., **171**, 173, 174
Gilmore, J. R., 495
Gilmore, James, **495**
Gilmore, Joseph Albree, **496**, 497, 612
Gilmore, Virgil G., **495**
Gilpin, Henry Dilworth, **209**
Giorgi, Count. *See* George, Nicholas
Gitchell, James M., **672**, 673, 674
Glass, William, **275**
Gleason's Pictorial Drawing-Room Companion, 232
Glenn, Alexander Ewing, **274**
Goddard, Miss, 559
Goddard, Charles Backus, **305**
Goddard, William, **630**
Godwin, Parke, **691**
Goicouria, Domingo, **235**, 424
Gold Act, 1864, xli, 461, 465, 470

Golden, Michael, **176**, 177, 180
Goldsborough, Mrs. (wife of Hugh A. Goldsborough), 684
Goldsborough, Edward Yerbury, 302, 437, **438**, 599, 677, 683
Goldsborough, Elizabeth Gamble Wirt, **4**, 5, 7, **12**, 14, 18, 19, 22, 24, 25, 294, 337, 506, 679, 683; letter to, 256
Goldsborough, Henry H., 437, **438**, 685
Goldsborough, Hugh A., **445**
Goldsborough, Louis Malesherbes, 4, **337**, 338, 339, 343, 344, 679, 683, 685
Goldsborough, Margaret Schley, **644**, 683, 684, 685, 686
Goldsborough, Mary Catherine, **599**, 644, 683, 684, 685, 686; corresponds with Chase, 638, 639, 641
Goldschmidt, Marcus, 684, **685**
Good, John Mason, *The Study of Medicine,* 99
Goode, James S., **284**
Goodell, Abner Cheney, **627**
Goodell, Martha Page Putnam, **627**
Goodin, James, 169
Goodin, S. H., 169
Gooding, David S., **605**, 606
Goodloe, Daniel Reaves, **504**, 505, 684
Goodrich, William Henry, **584**
Goodwin, Oliver, **99**
Gordon, George Henry, 536, **537**
Gordon, John Brown, **479**
Gordon, Nathaniel, **670**
Gordon, William J., **244**
Gordon v. United States, 513
Gorham Manufacturing Co. v. George C. White, 676
Gorman, ———, 303
Gorman, Emily Newington, **659**
Gorman, Willis Arnold, **659**
Gough, John Bartholomew, **682**
Governors' Conference, Altoona, Pa., 1862, 402–3
Gow, Niel, *Law of Partnership,* 132
Graham, A. C., **488**
Graham, James, 565, **566**
Gramercy Park House (New York), 687
Granger, Gordon, **449**, 562, 563
Grant, Asahel, **158**; article in *Missionary Herald,* 158
Grant, Julia Dent, **645**, 683
Grant, Ulysses Simpson, **355**, 359, 363, 407–10 passim, 425, 427, 436, 461, 471, 478, 515, 523, 524, 531, 532, 539, 603, 683, 695; antagonism with Benjamin F. Butler, 633, 640; assessed as general, 355; and election of 1868, xlix; letter from, to Lincoln, 428; letter from William T. Sherman, 540; meets Chase, 637; military campaign against Lee, 1864, xl, xli; New Years reception, 645; policy toward blacks, 428, 645–46; recalls wartime accomplishments, 648–49; support from Greeley electors, 1872, 708; telegram from, 364
Grant v. Lafayette Bank, 264
Grauert, E. F., 505
Grauert, Professor, 505
Gray, Asa, **621**
Gray, Horace, **490**, 625, 626
Gray, John, **441**
Gray, John Chipman, **550**
Gray, Joseph William, **219**, 220
Great War Meeting (Aug. 1862), 360–61
Greaves, Mr., **377**
Greeley, Horace, **387**, 388, 459, 479, 505, 683, 685, 686, 687, 691, 693, 696, 698, 699; criticizes Chase's opportunism, xxviii–xxix; illness, death, and funeral, 706–9; letters to, 505, 641, 679; presidential candidate (1872), 679, 685, 695, 708; visits Chase, 696
Greeley, Mary Youngs Cheney, **709**
Green, Mr., 445
Green, Charles, **568**
Green, Duff, **33**
Green, John K., **508**
Green, John L., **250**
Greene, Mr., 88
Greene, Abby Lyman, **217**
Greene, Annie Jean, **217**
Greene, Catharine Ray, 217
Greene, Charles Gordon, **693**
Greene, Jacob J., **241**
Greene, William, **51–52**, 134, 180, 181, 630; critical of Chase's Senate election, 217
Greenhow (Greenough?), Miss, 700
Greenough, Richard Saltonstall, 700
Gregg v. Forsyth, 519
Gregory, Mr., 545, 546
Gregory, Dudley Sanford, 463, **464**, 466
Gregory, E. M., 196
Gregory, Edgar M., **632**
Greiner, John, **251**
Grier, Isabella Rose, **645**
Grier, Robert Cooper, **233**, 519, 608, 645, 648
Griffen, Simon Goodell, **370**

Index   { 755 }

Griffin, Charles, **376**
Griffin, Margaret R. Lamson, **619**
Griffin, Simon Goodell, 619
Grimes, James Wilson, 261, **332**, 599
Grimké, Frederick, **51**
Grindrod, Ralph Barnes, *Bacchus,* 161
Griswold, Alexander Viets, 113
Griswold, Samuel Goodrich, *Peter Parley's Common School History,* 290
Groesbeck, John H., 171, 198
Groesbeck, William Slocum, 691
Grow, Galusha Aaron, **585**, 630
Grow, George W., 179
Grundy, Felix, 125
Guild, Edward Chipman, **498**
Guilford, Nathan, **76**, 196
Gunckel, Lewis B., **611**, 633, 655
Gurley, John Addison, **261**, 308, 309
Gurney, William, **546**, 547
Gurowski, Adam, **348**, 372
Guthrie, James, **577**
Gwin, Mary Bell, **232**
Gwin, William McKendree, 232
Gwynn, Stuart, **432**
Gwynne, Baldwin, 255
Gwynne, Louise Jones, **255**

Habeas corpus, xlvi–xlvii; applications, 531, 672; defined by Chase, 606; suspension, 441–44, 446, 447
Habeas corpus act, Ohio, 172
Hadley, Amos, **496**
Hagerstown, Md., 46
Hahn, Georg Michael Decker, **600**
Haight, Benjamin I., **103**, 107, 113; sermons, 111, 115
Haight, Edward, **313**, 586
Haines, Mrs. (wife of E. S. Haines), 287
Haines, E. H., 221
Haines, E. S., **270**, 284, 287
Haines, Henrietta B., **225**, 227; Chase corresponds with, 225, 228, 233, 235
Haines, Seth S., **261**
Hale, Captain, 550
Hale, Edward Everett, **623**
Hale, George Silsbee, **486**, 490
Hale, Henry, **660**
Hale, John Parker, 208, **209**, 231, 233, 234, 235, 256, 332, 530
Hale, Lucy Lambert, 233, 236
Hale, Matthew, **676**
Hale, Robert Safford, **676**; son of, 676
Hall, Mrs. (wife of Henry Cook Hall), 559
Hall, Frank, **273**
Hall, Harriet O. Holmes, **658**

Hall, Harvey, **187**
Hall, Henry Cook, **559**, 560
Hall, James, **66**, 67, 132, 528
Hall, James C., **519**, 607
Hall, Lyman W., **226**, 228
Hall, Nathan Kelsey, **227**
Hall, Robert: *Excellency of Christian Dispensation,* 80; *Works,* 706
Hall, Willard, **597**
Hall, William, **595**
Hall, William Sprigg, **659**
Halleck, Henry Wager, **350**, 351–73 passim, 379, 382, 384, 386, 389, 391, 400–406 passim, 416, 417, 423, 426, 439, 440, 449–54 passim, 480, 539; on Army morale, 380; Chase assesses views of, 360; criticized for poor judgment, 392; evaluated as commander, 420, 421; evaluates McClernand, 405, 406; requests McClellan's help, 392
Halpine, Charles Graham, **418**, 419, 424; on Halleck, Lincoln, Stanton, and Douglas, 420–22
Halsey, George Armstrong, **499**
Halstead, Murat, 254, **255**, 307, 671, 674, 676, 683
Hamilton, Mr. (Cincinnati, 1830s), 79, 81
Hamilton, Alexander, 34, 137
Hamilton, Andrew Jackson, **412**, 413, 414, 415, 418, 419, 446, 448, 521, 606, 632, 641
Hamilton, Cornelius Springer, **249**, 256, 264
Hamilton, Eliza, **242**
Hamilton, James Alexander, **34**, 378, 379, 393, 398; criticizes Seward and Blair, 377
Hamilton County Agricultural Society, 70
Hamlin, Edward Stowe, **196**, 202, 203, 205, 208, 218, 239, 251, 255, 256, 261, 676; and Chase's papers, liv; corresponds with Chase, 204, 205, 207, 223, 670
Hammond, ———, 214
Hammond, Henry, **363**
Hammond (pseudonym), 147
Hampton, Christopher, **573**
Hampton, Wade, **573**
Hampton Roads, Va., naval battle described, 337–39
Hancock, Winfield Scott, **523**, 602, 644; evaluated, 603
Handy, Alexander Hamilton, **688**
Handy, Robert, **555**
Handy, Truman P., **584**

Handy's Boarding House (Washington), 25
Hankes, Master, 8
Hanks, Mr., 302
Hanna, Joshua, **261**, 282, 586, 595, 609, 630, 634
Hanna, W., 307
Hardee, William Joseph, **358**, 359
Harden (Harding), Mr., 663, 665, 667
Harden (Harding), Mrs., 667
Harding, Christopher, **175**, 176
Hardscrabble Hall. *See* Chase—finances
Harkness, Anthony, **213**
Harkness, D. M., **396**
Harkness, Julia Follett, **301**
Harkness, Lamon G., **301**, 396, 398
Harkness, William, **213**
Harlan, James, **259**, 332, 633, 635
Harney, William Selby, **405**, 406
Harper, William, **242**
Harpers Ferry, Va.: attack and surender of, 385, 386, 389, 390, 391
Harries, Dr., 595
Harrington, Eben, **206**, 207
Harrington, George, **320**, 353, 364, 367, 373, 389, 390, 391, 393, 398, 426, 449, 469, 490, 503, 506, 635; letters to and from, 480, 481, 488, 490; travels, 411, 449
Harris, Edward, **502**, 679
Harris, Ira, **332**, 364, 608
Harris, Jeremiah George, **555**
Harris, John, **206**
Harris, Sullivan D., **274**, 292
Harris, Susan, **474**
Harris, Thomas Alexander, **555**, 560
Harrison, Ebenezer, **96**
Harrison, John Scott, **157**, 158
Harrison, Richard Almgill, **582**
Harrison, William Henry, 42, 122, **123**, 125, 129, 134, 135, 137, 138, 160; Chase votes for, 1840, xxi; criticized by Gamaliel Bailey, 133–34; death of, xxi, 159–60; letter to, noted, 149
Harrisonburg, Va., military operations near, 345
Hart, Albert Bushnell: biography of Chase, and Chase's papers, xi, liv–lv, lvii
Hart, James Harvey, **180**
Hart, Ralph S., **180**
Hartwell, George H., **156**
Harvard College, 186
Harvey, Matthew, **496**
Harvey, Peter, **490**
Hassaurek, Friedrich, **515**

Hastings, Mr., 706
Hastings, Samuel Dexter, Jr., **534**
Hatch, John Porter, **545**, 546, 547
Hatch, William S., **495**
Hathaway, Henry, **197**, 214
Hathaway case, 197, 198, 213, 214
Hathorn v. Calef, 515, 517
Haven, Miss, 623, 625, 693
Haven, Miss (daughter of Franklin Haven, Sr.), 497, 498
Haven, Mrs. (wife of Franklin Haven, Sr.), 484
Haven, Charles H., **174**, 226, 239
Haven, Franklin, Jr., **371**, 621, 623, 693
Haven, Franklin, Sr., **483**, 484, 490, 491, 621, 622, 623, 624, 625, 626, 693
Haven, Luther, **607**
Haven, Sarah Ann Curtis, **623**, 624
Hawes, James Morrison, 247, **249**, 263
Hawkins, John Parker, **563**
Hawley, Joseph Roswell, 541, **542**, 543, 544
Hawley, Zalmon, **574**, 575
Hawthorne, Nathaniel, *House of Seven Gables*, 621
Hay, John Milton, **552–53**, 635
Hayden, Alfred H., **63**
Hayes, Edwin L., **542**
Hayes, Rutherford Birchard, 244, **396**, 610
Hayne, Robert Young, **58**; debate with Daniel Webster, 624
Haynes, Daniel A., **276**
Hayward, Jonathan Zane, 225, 227
Hayward, Joseph H., **51**
Hazard, Caroline Newbold, **588**, 590
Hazard, Edward Hull, **587**, 590
Hazard, Louisa Arnold, **589**
Hazard, Margaret Rood, **588**
Hazard, Rowland, **588**, 630
Hazard, Rowland Gibson, **588**, 590, 600, 630, 690, 691, 696; *Essay on Language*, 251
Hazard, William Henry, **587**, 589, 590
"Hazard Castle" (Narragansett, R.I.), 589
Head, Natt, **613**
Headington, Nicholas, **580**
Headry, Mr., 167
Hearley, Gottlieb, **654**
Heath, James Ewell, **227**, 230
Heaton, Daniel, 219; family of, 217
Heaton, David, **308**, 309, 438, 442, 538; letter to, 309
Heaton, Rachael, 218
Heaton House (Cincinnati), 217

Index   { 757 }

Hedrick, Benjamin Sherwood, **437**
Hendee, Charles J., **131**
Henderson, Gustavus A., **505**
Henderson, John, Jr., **566**
Henderson, John Brooks, **332**, 430, 673
Henderson, Mary Newton Foote, **673**
Henderson, Thomas J., **580**
Henderson, William, **566**
Henrie House (Cincinnati), 159, 215
Henrietta Maria (widow of Charles I), 293
Henry, Anson G., **445**
Henry, Joseph, **610**, 665, 705
Hentz, Caroline Lee Whiting, **72**
Hentz, N. M., 72
Hepburn v. Griswold, xlvii–xlviii, 650, 651, 652, 668, 669
Herald of Progress, 445
Herbert, George, *The Temple*, 639
Herold, David Edgar, 587, **588**
Hewes, Thomas H., **193**, 194
Hewit, Nathaniel, **28**
Hewson, Miss, 157
Hewson, Mrs. (wife of Bethuel W. Hewson), 153, 157
Hewson, Bethuel W., **153**, 154, 157; family of, 154
Hey, James, 95, 121, 129
Heyl, Christian, **286**
Heyl, Lewis, **286**
Hibbard, Freeborn Garrettson, **308**
Hibben, Samuel E., **307**
Hibben, Thomas, **205**, 208, 225, 238
Hickman, John, **426**
Hickman v. Jones, 649
Hickox, Charles, **306**, 585
Higbee, Mrs. (wife of Charles Higbee), 701
Higbee, Charles, **701**
Higgins, Mrs. (wife of William H. Higgins), 568
Higgins, William H., **568**
Higlin and Schaeffer, 172, 176
Hill, Miss, 525
Hill, Mr., 562
Hill, Daniel Harvey, **386**
Hill, George H., **646**
Hill, Isaac H., 224
Hilliard, Gray and Company, 113
Hills, William, **76**
Hillsboro Female College, 307
Hilton, Henry, **708**
Hilton Head, S.C., 551
Hinckle, Philip, 581
Hincks, Edward Winslow, **611**, 633
Hindelbath and Company, 181
Hinkle, Anthony H., **165**

Hinkle, Philip, **165**
Hinkson, Benjamin, **239**
Hinsdale, Elizabeth, **158**, 159
Hitchcock, Lauretta, **616**
Hitchcock, Peter, **171**, 220
Hitchcock, Phineas Warrener, **514**
Hitchcock, Reuben, **220**
Hoadley, Mrs. (wife of George Hoadley, Sr.), 220
Hoadley, George, Sr., **218**, 219, 220
Hoadly, George, Jr., **195**, 206, 207, 218, 221, 225, 254, 263, 287, 306, 391, 508, 580
Hoar, Ebenezer Rockwood, **490**, 648, 650, 651, 652
Hoar, George Frisbie, **648**
Hobart, John Henry, **602**
Hodge, Adam, **172**
Hodgkin, ——, 589
Hoffcroft, W. R., 575
Hoffman, Benjamin F., **210**; correspondence, 209, 224, 227
Hoffman, Charles Burrall, 461, **462**
Hoffman, George, 39
Hoffman, Henry W., **520**
Hoffman, John, 39
Hoffman, Ogden, Jr., **387**
Hoffman, Peter, 39
Hoffman, Samuel, 39
Hoffman House (New York), 608
Hogan, Christopher V., **458**
Hogan, John, **510**
Hogan and Thompson, 131
Hoge, James, **249**
Hogeboom, John T., **468**
Hoit, Albert Gallatin, **122**, 123; portrait of William Henry Harrison, 122, 125
Holbrook, Mr., 591
Holbrook, Adin, **591**
Holden, Mrs., death of, 223
Holden v. Joy, 673
Holladays v. Pugh and Duffield, 150
Holland, Mr., 700
Holland, Henry, *Recollections*, 696
Hollcroft, Miss, 571
Hollcroft, W. R., 575
Hollister, David F., **363**, 489
Holloway, Mr., 349
Holmes, Isaac Edward, **547**
Holmes, Samuel, **303**
Holmes, Sylvester, **155**, 156, 157
Holmes, William, 151, **152**
Holt, Addie Smith, **255**
Holt, Joseph, **325**
Holway, Rose Mathews, **502**
Homans, Isaac Smith, **356**

Homeopathic Hospital College, Cleveland, 219, 220
Homer, Charles C., **423**
Homer, Henry, **423**
Homes, Frederick B., **239**
Homesteads, Chase's opinions on, 181–82
Hooe, Peter H., **504**
Hooe, Robert A., **504**
Hooker, Joseph, 263, 361, **369**, 373, 379, 389, 393, 396, 401, 403, 404, 415, 451, 452, 454, 579, 581, 707; criticizes McClellan, 397, 400–401, 411, 412–13; evaluated as general by Chase, 397
Hooker, Olivia Groesbeck, **263**
Hooper, Alice Mason, **486**, 487
Hooper, Ellen Sturgis, 693
Hooper, John, 622
Hooper, Robert William, **622**, 624, 693
Hooper, Samuel, **316**, 323, 327, 425, 465, 466, 471, 484–91 passim, 498, 516, 517, 518, 579, 591, 592, 608, 622–26 passim, 687, 693, 710; approves Treasury report, 316; correspondence with Chase, 466, 475; gives library to U. S. Grant, 603; urges Lincoln to appoint Chase chief justice, xlii
Hopkins, Johns, **454**, 455, 523
Hopper, J. C., **361**
Hornor, Charles W., **604**
Hornton, Valentine Baxter, **69**
Horrel, Thomas, **98**; address of, 101; sermon of, 98
Horton, Mrs. (wife of William Horton), 183
Horton, John, 182, 183, 184
Horton, Valentine Baxter, 69, 323, 327, 349, 385
Horton, William, 183
Hosea, Miss, 273
Hosea, Harriet Newell Moore, **273**, 579
Hosea, Hattie, 579
Hosea, Lewis Montgomery, **511**, 574
Hosea, Lucy, 579
Hosea, Robert, **267**, 268, 273, 308, 511, 528, 579, 580
Hosmer, Elbridge, **226**
Hosmer, Hezekiah Lord, **479**
Hosmer, William, **308**
Hotel de Ville, 290
Houghton, Sherman Otis, **674**
Houghton (ship), 548
Houston, Samuel, **209**, 228
How, David, and Company, 131
How, John, **239**

Howard, Jacob Merritt, **332**, 641, 642, 643
Howard, James Quay, **678**
Howard, Mark, **268**, 363, 488, 489
Howard, William Alanson, **509**
Howe, Alfred, 542, 543
Howe, Charles, **560**
Howe, Elias, Jr., 583
Howe, Frank E., **482**, 483, 498, 505, 586, 594, 595; letter to, 588
Howe, John W., **231**
Howe, Mr., letter to, 225
Howe, Thomas Marshall, **473**
Howe, Timothy Otis, **322**, 332, 503
Howell, David, **59**
Howell, Rufus K., **570**
Howells, William Cooper, **248**, 249
Hoyt, Edwin, **594**
Hoyt, Janet (granddaughter), **668**, 669, 678, 689, 690, 696, 701
Hoyt, Janet Ralston Chase. *See* Chase, Janet (Nettie) Ralston
Hoyt, Sprague and Co., 573
Hoyt, William Sprague (son-in-law), 223, **665**, 678, 679, 680, 688, 689, 690, 696, 701, 708, 710; letters and telegrams, 668, 669, 677, 686
Hubbard, Edward, **665**
Hubbard, Edwin S., **230**
Hubbard, George R., **665**
Hubbard, John Henry, **489**
Hubbard, Ozro, **665**
Hubbard, Thomas R., **118**
Hubbard, William Blackstone, **271**
Hudson, T. B., 167
Hudson River Railroad, 237
Huffman, William, 183
Huger, Benjamin, **314**, 343
Hughes, ———, 127, 128
Hughes, Michael, **630**
Hughes Trustees, 188
Hugo, Victor: *Les Misérables*, 362; *Notre-Dame de Paris*, 280, 281, 286, 290, 291, 292
Hulburt (Hurlbut), Hinman Barrett, **584**; nephew of, 584
Hull, William, **101**
Humphrey, Edward Porter, **154**
Humphrey, Mrs. (wife of Edward Porter Humphrey), 154
Humphreys, Joseph Bloomfield, **308**
Hunt, ———, 67
Hunt, Charles Havens, *Life of Edward Livingston*, 681, 682
Hunt, Henry Jackson, 699, **700**
Hunt, Julia, **678**, 680, 692
Hunt, Louise, **678**, 680, 692
Hunt, Randall, **564**, 565, 569, 678

Index

Hunt, Ruhamah Ludlow (sister-in-law), **564**, 569, 578
Hunt, William Henry, **565**
Hunter, David, **314**, 358, 383, 385, 418, 419, 420, 421, 422, 478; musters Indians, 314; policy toward blacks, 344, 349, 391
Hunter, John, **276**
Hunter, William, **240**
Huntington, Elisha Mills, 137
Huntington (friend of Hamilton Smith), 576
Huntington ("of Waterford"), 282
Huntington, William S., **512**, 673, 675
Huntington's Exrs. and First National Bank v. Texas, 673
Huntt, Anna Maria Ringgold, 29
Huntt, Henry, **29**
Hurlburt, Hinman Barrett. *See* Hulburt
Hurley, Mr., 257
Hurst, Thomas, **185**
Huston, Alexander Botkin, **262**
Hutcheson, Joseph, **257**
Hutchings, Eusebius, 217
Hutchings and Company, 222
Hutchins, John, **252**
Hutchins, Rhoda M. Andrews, **252**
Hutter Brothers, 687
Hutton, Benjamin H., **502**
Huyek, Sanders M., **240**
Hyatt, Abram, **376**
Hypes, Henry, **270**

Ide, William E., **258**
Ilges, Guido, **445**
Illinois Monthly Magazine, 66
Illinois State Bulletin, 228
Independence (steamship), 153, 155
Independence Hall, Philadelphia, 702
Indiana: politics, 412, 413, 414; Supreme Court, 81
Indiana Bank, 206
Indians, Chase article on army and, 246
Infant School (Washington), 15
Ingham, Deborah Kay Hall, **44**
Ingham, Samuel Delucenna, **37**, 44
Inglis v. Trustees of Sailors Snug Harbor, 11
Internal revenue. *See* Civil War finances
Iowa politics, 635
Ireland and O'Connell, 689
Irvin, Eilen, **216**
Irving House (New York), 224
Irwin, James F., **133**
Irwin, Samuel W., **175**

Israelites, 78–79
Iwakura, Tomomi, **683**
Iwakura Embassy, 683–84

Jackson, Andrew, xvii, **10**, 13, 22, 23, 33, 35, 36, 37, 50, 138, 564, 565; and Bank of the United States, xxxvii; inauguration, 10–11; new administration of, 14; removal policy, 34
Jackson, James Strashley, 359
Jackson, John Jay, Jr., **643**, 644
Jackson, John Jay, Sr., **644**
Jackson, Thomas Jonathan (Stonewall), **335**, 345, 346, 355, 356, 379
Jacksonville, Fla., 552
James, Amaziah Bailey, **708**
James, Charles Tillinghast, **236**, 500
James, Garth Wilkinson, **550**
James, J. J., 154
James, Mr., of Urbana, 73
James, William Levis, **536**
James Christopher (ship), 544
James Island, S.C., and plans to take Charleston, 417
Jameson, Eliza Denison, **617**
Jameson, John Alexander, **617**
Janissaries, 41
Janney, John Jay, **536**
Janney, Mrs. R. A. S., 275
Japan: Iwakura delegation, 683–84
Jaquess, James Frazier, **477**
Jarvis, Kent, **522**
Jarvis, W. B., **211**
Jay, John (d. 1829), 137, 237
Jay, John (d. 1894), **420**, 421, 426
Jay, William, **237**; *View of the Action of the Federal Government*, 147
Jeff Thompson (ship), 571
Jefferson, Thomas, 29, **35**, 36, 58, 59, 60, 329; anecdote of, 35–36; *Manual of Parliamentary Practice*, 128, 129
Jenckes, ———— (son of William Scott Jenckes), **559**
Jenckes, Thomas Allen, **594**
Jenckes, William Scott, **559**
Jenkins, Josiah H., **254**
Jenks, Mr., 74
Jenner, William H., **506**
Jesup, Thomas Sidney, **232**
Jewett, Hugh Judge, **283**
Jewett, Isaac Appleton, **155**, 194
Jewett, J. J. L. C. (Jack), 120, 238, **596**
Jewett, Janette (Jenny) Skinner (niece), 120, 237–38, 311, 512, 596, 699, 705
Jewett, Jedediah, **427**
Jewett, Mendall, **260**, 271, 276
Jewett, Spofford Dodge, **614**

Jewett, Thomas Lightfoot, **456**
John and Nancy Haskell (schooner), 20
Johns, Henry Van Dyke, **16**, 130, 133, 147, 155, 172; sermons of, 31, 134, 144, 149, 156, 157, 159, 160, 161
Johnson, ———, 152
Johnson, Mr. (slave trader), 193–94
Johnson, Andrew, **316**, 322, 332, 464, 510, 518, 530, 531, 535, 552, 567, 576, 580, 581, 588, 597, 599, 601, 634, 636, 637, 641; and 1864 election, xl, xli; administration of oath to (1865), xliii, 530–31; authorizes Chase's Southern tour, 536; Chase advises on Reconstruction xliii, xliv, 533–34, 541, 542, 544, 551, 555; discusses Civil War in Kentucky, 316; illness, 1865, 584, 585; impeachment trial, xlviii–xlix, 641–43; letter to, from Lincoln, 439; letters from, noted, 534, 536; letters to, noted, 533, 537, 541, 544, 551, 553, 555, 638; Mississippi Proclamation, 574; New Years reception, 601; popularity assessed, 606; proclamation on insurrection, 1866, 636; Reconstruction policies, xliv, xlv, 619, 641; suspends habeas corpus for Mary Surratt, 589; takes "swing around the circle," 631, 635
Johnson, Charles J., **510**
Johnson, Charles L., 291, **292**
Johnson, Major, 362
Johnson, Oliver, **586**
Johnson, Peter W., **541**
Johnson, Reverdy, **232**, 364, 365, 366, 391, 670
Johnson, Samuel, **271**
Johnsoniana, 171
Johnston, Joseph Eggleston, **317**, 356, 533, 534; opposing Sherman in 1864, xl; surrender, 531, 539, 540, 541
Johnston, Mr., letter to, 142–43
Johnston, R. Rhodes, 291, **292**
Johnston, Samuel, **48**
Johnston, William (1804–91), **176**, 515, 637
Johnston, William (1819–66), **494**
Johnston, William Hartshorne, **582**
Johnston, William S., **132**, 151
Joice, William, 578, **587**, 593, 655, 657, 663, 664, 665, 666, 668, 674, 675, 683, 697, 704
Joiner and Brummel, 99
Joint Committee on the Conduct of the War: recommends appointment of McDowell, 321

Jonas, Joseph, **189**
Jones, Mr., 79
Jones, Alanson, **207**, 208
Jones, Charles, **464**
Jones, Charles A., **166**, 172
Jones, Charlotte Chambers Ludlow (sister-in-law), **166**, 262, 449, 578; corresponds with Chase, 514, 528, 670
Jones, G. G., 169
Jones, George T., **277**
Jones, George W., **79**, 94, 98
Jones, Mrs. H. Febiger, **289**, 596, 597
Jones, I. G., 255, **274**
Jones, John D., 274, **275**
Jones, John M., **591**, 698, 699
Jones, Josephine, **262**, 499, 501, 578
Jones, Judson, **659**
Jones, Louise, **255**, 274
Jones, Pierepont E., **673**, 679, 684, 692, 700
Jones, Roger, **227**
Jones, Thomas, Jr., **583**
Jones, Thomas Dow, **311**, 354; sculpts bust of Chase, 311
Jones, Wharton, 166
Jones v. Van Zandt. *See* Van Zandt case
Juárez, Benito Pablo, **375**
Judiciary Act, 1866, 635
Judson, Mrs. (wife of Curtis Judson), 688
Judson, Curtis, **688**
Julian, George Washington, 269, **412**, 413, 463
Justice, Jesse, **135**, 156
Justice v. Plough, 156

Kane, Elisha Kent, **274**; funeral, 275
Kane, John Kintzing, Jr., **274**
Kane, Robert Patterson, **274**
Kane, Thomas Leiper, **274**, 378, 383
Kansas: Lecompton government, 261; as political issue, xxxi
Kansas-Nebraska Act: Chase's opposition, xxvii–xxviii, 243
Kasson, John Adam, **635**
Kauffman, S. H., **282**
Kayser, Alexander, **239**
Kearny, Philip, **378**, 386
Kearsarge (ship), 478–79
Kebler, John, **275**
Keely, John Ernst Worrell, **703**
Keith, Alexander, writings on prophecy, 156
Keller, Charles M., **676**
Kelley, Abigail, **174**
Kelley, Alfred, **153**, 247, 249, 251, 265, 274, 285, 306

Kelley, Benjamin Franklin, **317**
Kelley, John A., **292**
Kellogg, Francis William, **562**
Kellogg, William Pitt, **564**
Kelly, Patrick, **228**, 229
Kelsey, William, **247**, 271, 273
Kelsey's house, possible rental, 310
Kemp, ———, 294
Kemper v. Trustees of Lane Seminary, 186, 199, 201, 202
Kemper's lessee v. Cincinnati, Columbus and Wooster Turnpike Co., 160
Kendall, Amos, 137
Kendrick, John, **282**
Kenly, John Reese, **345**
Kennedy, Anthony, **332**
Kennedy, John Gordon, **402**
Kennedy, John Pendleton, 235–36, **236**, 526; *Memoirs of William Wirt*, 525; *Swallow Barn*, 525
Kennedy, Joseph Camp Griffith, **236**
Kennedy, Milton, **638**
Kenner, Philip Minor, **565**
Kenner, William Butler, **83**, 132
Kenner and Brown, 174
Kenney, Mr., 553
Kent, Mrs., 164, 165
Kent, Edward, **483**
Kent, James: praise for Chase's *Statutes of Ohio*, xix
Kenyon College, 162, 181
Keokuk (ship), 544, 545
Kerr, Miss, 307
Kerr, James, **307**
Kerr, S. F., **307**
Kessler, Henry, **508**
Ketchum, Morris, **315**
Key, Thomas Marshall, **196**, 198, 211, 246, 324, 331, 368, 415, 417, 533; assessments of McClellan and Stanton, 581; on black suffrage, 581; on emancipation in Washington, D.C., 317; writes to Lincoln, 350
Key West, Fla., 555, 560; grounding near, described, 560–61
Keyes, Erasmus Darwin, **374**, 413, 414
Kido, Takayossi, **683**
Kilgallen, Dr., 700
Kimball, Abby Osgood Bartlett, **619**
Kimball, Caleb, **615**
Kimball, Edmund, **626**
Kimball, John, **621**
Kimball, Moses, **234**, 235, 613, 614, 619
King, Austin Augustus, **515**
King, Charles Bird, **30**, 30–31, 33
King, Edward, **64**, 65, 67, 69; death of, 112–13

King, Elizabeth Jane Neil, **291**, 294
King, Gen. Rufus, division of, 346–47
King, George W., **258**
King, James H., **292**
King, James Wilson, **670**
King, John W., **292**
King, Leicester, **164**, 167, 170, 205; as Liberty candidate, xxii–xxiii
King, Matthew, 52
King, Preston, **228**, 332
King, Rufus, 59
King, Thomas Worthington, **291**
Kinney, Miss, 649
Kinney, Franklin S., **653**
Kirby, Moses H., **300**
Kirby, Timothy, **145**
Kirk, Edward Norris, **614**
Kirkwood, Alfred W., **403**
Kirkwood, John H., 403
Kirkwood, Samuel Jordan, **402**, 403
Kirkwood House (Washington), xliii, 403, 531
Kittredge, Mrs. (wife of Thomas B. Kittredge), 619
Kittredge, Thomas B., 619
Klein, Herman H., **176**
Klinck, John G., **295**
Knights of the Golden Circle, 374–75
Know-Nothing party, 245, 305; Cleveland council meeting, 245
Knox, Samuel, **510**
Knox v. Lee, 664, 668, 669
Kodama, 677, **678**
Korea, article on, 706
Kraus, Minnie Lauer, **658**
Kraus, William, **658**
Krauth, John B., **213**, 227
Krummacher, Friedrich Adolf, *Cornelius the Centurion*, 187

"L." *See* Eastman, Charlotte Sewall
Labauve, Zenon, **570**
Lackawanna (ship), 562
Ladd, James D., **254**, 275
Ladd, William H., **254**
Lady Le Marchant (ship), 336
Lafayette Bank (Cincinnati), 80, 81, 87, 100, 104, 112–19 passim, 126, 127, 130–38 passim, 141, 197; board of directors and exchange committee, 117, 127, 133, 135, 136, 138, 150, 151, 156, 158; quarterly committee, 145
Lafayette Bank v. Jones, 172
Lafayette Bank v. Young et al., 150
Laird, David T., **576**
Lake Shore Railroad, 237
Lambard, Mr., 690, 695

Land reform, Ohio resolutions on, 231
Lander, Mrs., 483
Lander, Frederick West, **321**, 324
Lane, Ebenezer, **73**, 74, 75, 221, 335
Lane, Henry Smith, **332**
Lane, James Henry, **261**, 332, 507
Lane Seminary, 186
Lane Seminary case. *See Kemper v. Trustees of Lane Seminary*
Langarl, Mr., 257
Lange, Johann Peter, *Commentary on Holy Scriptures*, 639
Langford, Fanny S., **549**
Langston, John Mercer, **543**
Lanman, James Henry, *History of Michigan*, 144
Lannam, John, **302**
Lannam, William, **302**
Lansing, John, Jr., *Secret Proceedings and Debates*, 69
Lardner, James Lawrence, **339**
Larimer, William, Jr., **209**
Laskey, George, **312**
Latham, Milton Slocum, **332**
Latham, O. B., 650, 651
Latham v. U.S., 650, 651
Lathrop, Charles C., **335**
Lathrop, Solon H., **582**
Latrobe, Charles Joseph, *Rambler in North America*, 109
Latrobe, Ferdinand C., 294
Latrobe, Louise Swann, **524**
Latty, Alexander Sankey, **256**, 302
Laugel, Antoine Auguste, **517**, 518
Laugel, Elizabeth Bates Chapman, **517**, 518
Lavater, Jean-Gaspard, **36**
Law, William, **551**
Law Reporter, 135
Lawler, Mrs. (wife of Davis B. Lawler), 85
Lawler, Davis B., **82**, 171
Lawrence, Albert Gallatin, **710**
Lawrence, Amos Adams, 484, **485**
Lawrence, Francis E., **496**
Lawrence, Josiah, **87**, 100, 112, 114, 138, 152
Lawrence, William, **431**, 598
Lawrence, William Beach, **694**, 696, 699, 710
Layard, Austen Henry, 376, **377**
Le Vert, Celeste Annette, **563**, 595
Le Vert, Octavia Celeste Walton, 562, **563**, 595
Le Vert, Octavia Walton, **563**, 595
Leach, L. D., and Company, 193, 194
Leach, Reverend, 229
Leary, Annie, **699**, 700

Leary, Arthur, **595**, 639, 699, 700, 708
Leary v. U.S., 704
Leatherman, D. M., **444**, 445
Leavitt, Humphrey Howe, **287**, 578, 580
Leavitt, Joshua, xxiv, 130, 171 **209**, 283
Lebanon House (Lebanon, Ohio), 304
Ledyard, Henry, **699**
Lee, Mr., 217
Lee, Mrs., 217
Lee, Collins, 77
Lee, Isaac, **203**
Lee, John Fitzgerald, **316**
Lee, Robert E., xl, **386**, 389, 426, 450, 454, 523, 539, 567
Lee, Thomas, **222**
Lee, Zadoc Collins, 294, **295**
Leete, Ralph, **233**
Legal tender, xxxvi, xli, xlvii–xlviii, 445–46, 460
Legal Tender Act, 1862, xlvii, 462, 478
Legal Tender cases, 647, 650–52, 664, 667, 668–69, 670
Leggett, Mortimer Dormer, **656**
Leigh, Benjamin Watkins, **28**
Leland, Erastus H., **241**
Lenox, Lucy, 4
Lenox, Peter, **4**, 5
Lenthall, Mrs. (wife of John Lenthall), 666
Lenthall, John, **666**
El Leon de Oro (Matanzas, Cuba), 558–59
Leonidas (steamship), 93
Leslie, Colonel, 401, **402**
Leslie, Andrew, **108**
Leslie, Charles Robert, 30
Leslie, James, **108**
Letters Written by the Late Earl of Chatham, 74
Leunsbury, Mr., 657
Leverrier, Urbain Jean Joseph, **265**
Lewis, ———, 214
Lewis, Albert, 180, 185, **188**
Lewis, Daniel, **291**
Lewis, Henry, **152**, 174, 185, 188
Lewis, Joseph Jackson, **325**
Lewis, Samuel, **164**, 167, 174, 175, 177, 179, 188, 238, 241, 242
Lewis, Samuel Henry, 177
Lewis, Solomon, **254**
Lewis, Thomas, **666**
Lewis, Vina, **179**
Lewis, William Berkeley, **23**
Lewis, William David, **400**
Lewis, William G. W., **179**, 272; *Biography of Samuel Lewis*, 264, 272

Lewis & Wilkes, 289
Lewis case, 196, 198
Lexington (ship), **575**
L'Hommedieu, Richard F., **153**, 176, 215
L'Hommedieu, Stephen S., **153**, 215, 246, 507, 520, 528, 535, 579, 584, 585, 586
Libby Prison (Richmond, Va.), 493
Liberal Republican party: and Greeley nomination, 685, 691
Liberty No. 2 (ship), 574
Liberty No. 4 (ship), 574
Liberty party, xxi, xxii–xxv, 163, 167, 170, 174, 175, 181, 196, 228. *See also* Conventions
Library of Congress, li, liv–lv
Liggett, John, **193**, 194
Linck, Francis, **295**
Lincoln, Abraham, **313**, 336, 363, 373, 388, 391, 409, 412, 413, 414, 416, 423, 430–33, 439, 450–51, 453–54, 457, 458, 460, 464, 472, 493, 494, 497, 503, 504, 513, 515, 539; administration, xxxiii–xliii; and Amnesty Proclamation, 475; annual message, 1861, 329; and arming of slaves, 349, 351–52, 456; assassination, xliii, 528, 529–30, 532, 588; in cabinet meetings, 313–15, 324–25, 348, 355, 359, 370, 376, 382, 436–37; cabinet politics, xxxiv, xxxv, xl, 325, 352–53; Chase dreams about, 695; Chase letters to, 344, 467, 469, 527, 528; correspondence and telegrams, 350, 354, 361, 362, 366, 371, 392, 399, 418, 419, 428, 434, 439, 447, 452, 466, 467, 468, 469, 470, 512, 536; criticized, xxxviii, 335, 364, 366, 381, 382, 387, 389, 420, 421–22, 470–71, 476, 477, 488; defends Seward, 378; describes battle of Antietam, 415, 417; on deserters, 375, 446; on draft and enlistments, 352, 405–7, 440; election of 1864, xl–xli, 497, 505, 510; and emancipation, xxxiv, 328, 329, 351, 352, 358, 393, 400, 569; engraving of, 635; and Internal Revenue bill, 465; to James River military operations, 336–44; on Kentucky politics, 357; and McClellan, 322, 350, 368, 369, 370, 411; on McClernand, 403, 404; military affairs, 336–44, 345, 346–47, 348, 352, 353, 379–80, 386, 426, 449; nomination in 1860, xxxi; and patronage, 362, 367; petitioned by Quakers, 390; praised as leader, 344, 502; relations with Chase, xxxix, xlii, xlix, 470–71; social events, 333, 424–25, 516; speech, August 1862, 360; suspension of habeas corpus, xlvi, 441–43; tells humorous stories, 425, 452, 576; urges colonization, 362; and Reconstruction, xliii, 475, 527, 530

Lincoln, Mary Todd, 245, 386, 424, 515–16, **516**
Lincoln, Timothy Danielson, **203**, 209, 580, 676
Lindsley, Mrs. (wife of William Dell Lindsley), 236
Lindsley, William Dell, **236**
Lindsly, Emeline Colby Webster, **236**, 515
Lindsly, Harvey, **65**, 236, 515, 699
Linn, Mr., 117
Linthicum, William O., **687**
Little, Henry, **154**
Little Miami Railroad, 138, 308
Livermore, Abiel Abbot, **268**, 270
Livermore, Elizabeth Dorcas Abbot, **270**
Livingston, Coralie. *See* Barton, Coralie Livingston
Livingston, Edward, **25**, 44; *Code of Reform*, 681, 684, 685, 687; *Exposé d'un Système de Législation*, 704
Lloyd, David Demarest, **663**; as Chase's secretary (1872), 664–72, 674–75, 677–78, 681–84, 686, 687–88, 691, 694, 705, 706
Lloyd, Henry Demarest, **691**
Lloyd, William R., **388**
Lockhart, John Gibson, *Valerius, a Roman Story*, 216
Lockwood, George C., **635**
London Quarterly Review, 109
Long, Alexander, **201**, 673, 676
Longfellow, Henry Wadsworth, 293, 490; *Hyperion*, 253; *The Song of Hiawatha*, 290
Longstreet, Augustus Baldwin, *Georgia Scenes*, 138
Longstreet, James, **390**
Longworth, Catherine, 56, **57**, 60, 72, 73, 581
Longworth, Eliza, **57**, 72, 73
Longworth, Joseph, **65**, 70, 71, 72, 73, 74, 79, 140, 141
Longworth, Nicholas, **50**, 53, 57, 65, 117, 118, 140, 141, 292
Longworth, Susan Howell Connor, 292
Loomis, Mrs. (wife of M. D. W. Loomis), **402**
Loomis, B. J., **261**

Loomis, M. D. W., **402**
Lopez, Narciso, **424**
Lord, Daniel, **513**
Lord, Henry C., **263**
Lord, Nathan, **16**
Loring, Mr., 131
Loring, Charles Greeley, **490**, 621, 622, 623
Loring, Cornelia Amory Goddard, **622**
Lothrop, Ann M. Hooper, **625**
Lothrop, Samuel Kirkland, **484**, 622, 623, 624, 625
Lothrop, Thornton Kirkland, **625**
Lottie. *See* Eastman, Charlotte Sewall
Louis XVI, 141
Louisiana, 376, 434–35, 447, 448, 477, 527, 567, 569, 571, 604; University of, 567
Louisville Democrat, 357
Louisville Hotel, 577
Lounsbury, Edward, **163**
Low, Frederick Ferdinand, **437**
Lowber v. Bangs, 514, 517
Lowe, Miss, 656
Lowe, John Gilbert, **656**, 657
Lowe, Peter Perlee, **265**
Lowell, Francis, 487
Lowell, James Russell, **490**; Chase quotes *Biglow Papers,* 241
Lowell, Russell R., **535**, 550, 554, 557, 558, 559, 578, 637
Lowry, M. B., **597**
Lucas, Charles Jean-Marie, **704**
Ludlow, Adela, **195**, 511
Ludlow, Benjamin Chambers (brother-in-law), **188**, 514, 518
Ludlow, Catherine. *See* Whiteman, Catherine Ludlow Baker
Ludlow, Charlotte Chambers. *See* Jones, Charlotte Chambers Ludlow
Ludlow, George, **511**, 512
Ludlow, Helen A., 166
Ludlow, Israel (brother-in-law), 449, **513**
Ludlow, Israel (grandfather of Chase's third wife), 161, 179
Ludlow, Israel L., 166
Ludlow, James C. (father of third wife), 83, **132**, 158, 166, 167, 179, 187, 188, 223
Ludlow, James Dunlop (brother-in-law), **187**, 188, 224, 512, 514, 658, 659
Ludlow, Josephine, **578**
Ludlow, Josephine Dunlop (mother of third wife), **166**, 179, 187, 188, 223
Ludlow, Sam, **658**

Ludlow, Sarah Bella. *See* McLean, Sarah Bella Ludlow Garrard
Ludlow, Sarah Bella Dunlop. *See* Chase, Sarah Bella Dunlop Ludlow
Ludlow, Susan Middlekauff, **658**, 659
Ludlow, Theresa, **658**, 659
Ludlow family estate and property, 161, 167–68, 171, 186, 192, 195, 206
Ludlow's heirs' lessee v. William Barr, 161
Luther, Martin, 163
Lutheran Church (Columbus), 269
Lutz, F. A., Jr., 685
Lyman, Jos., 225
Lynah, James, **547**
Lynd, Samuel W., **79**, 99
Lynn, Mass., shoe factories, 483
Lyons, Richard Bickerton Pemell, **320**
Lytle, Edward H., **99**, 100, 114
Lytle, Robert Todd, **67**, 88
Lytle, William Haines, 292, **295**, 296, 298

Macalester, Charles, **594**
McAllister, Richard, **272**
McArthur, Mrs. (wife of Arthur McArthur), 679
McArthur, Arthur, **679–80**
McArthur, Aurelia Belcher, **680**
Macaulay, Thomas Babington, *Warren Hastings,* 561
McBain, Daniel, **258**
Macbeth, Charles, **547**
McBratney, Robert, **280**
McBride & Co., 77
McCall, Gen. George Archibald, division of, 346–47
McCandless, Mrs. (wife of James McCandless), **90**, 103
McCandless, James, 90, 93
McCandless, Wilson, **442**, 443
McCauley, William, **667**
McClellan, George Brinton, 196, **314**, 315, 325, 354, 355, 356, 359, 363, 364, 372, 374, 377, 379, 390, 396–97; assessed by Thomas M. Key, 413–14, 581; and cabinet intrigue, 366–69; Chase advises, 324; Chase comments on McClellan's command, 350–51, 354, 358, 360, 368, 369, 381, 420, 421; on Confederate maneuvers, 317; criticism of, 350, 366, 367, 397, 400, 403, 404, 413, 420, 421, 423, 449; delays, 335; dispatches, 321, 361, 386; on emancipation, 350; evaluated, 322, 353, 358, 415–18; meets with Lincoln, 368, 382, 411; as presidential candidate, xl, 497, 498; proposes coopera-

tion with Chase, 419, 421; railroad career evaluated, 335; regains command, 369–70; and reinforcements, 340, 345–47, 349, 405–6; relieved of command, xxxiv, 422; rift with Stanton denied, 361; on slavery, 417; telegrams, 376, 389, 392; visits Chase, 317
McClernand, John Alexander, **402**, 403–4, 405, 406, 416, 417, 418, 419
McCook, Alexander McDowell, **418**, 419
McCook, Edward Moody, **692**
McCook, General, 594
McCook, Mary McKenna, **692**
McCook, Mary Thompson, **692**
McCormick, Charles, 4, **209**
McCormick, Cyrus, 303
McCormicks (Groveport, Ohio), 299
McCoy, James Culbertson, **539**
McCub, Mr., 542
McCue, John, **308**
McCulloch, Hugh, xliii, **428**, 503, 506, 511, 518, 530, 531, 532, 533, 535, 571, 588, 595, 603, 610
McCulloh, R. S., **555**, 560
McCullough, M. S., **512**
McCurdy, Robert H., **699**
Macdaniel, Osborne, **459**
McDonald, Catharine, 223
McDonald, Ranald, **212**
McDonough Institute (colonization proposal), 166
McDougal, Joseph, **189**, 195
McDougall, James Alexander, **323**, 332
McDowell, Eliza, **693**
McDowell, Helen Burden, **320**, 398, 402, 693, 707
McDowell, Helen E., **693**
McDowell, Henry Burden, **693**
McDowell, Irvin, 320, **321**, 334–35, 345–48, 371, 373, 375, 383, 398, 402; appointment as major general, 322, 332; briefs Chase, 324; demands inquiry, 370–71; telegrams, 355–56, 379
McDowell, Joseph Jefferson, **308**
McDowell, Malcolm, **582**
McDowell, Sarah A. McCue, **308**
Mace, Daniel, **238**
McGee, ———, 221
McGilvra, John Jay, **488**
McGrew, Alexander, 87
McGuffey, William Holmes, **169**
McGuffey readers, 205
McGuire, Isaac, **95**, 96, 108
McGuire, William, 99
McHenry, James, **600**

Machiavelli, Niccolò, quoted, 331
McIlvaine, Charles Pettit, **77**, 166, 210, 268, 287, 390, 579; *The Evidences of Christianity*, 71
McIlvaine, Emily Coxe, **578**, 700
McIntyre, Archibald, **430**
McJilton, John F., **435**
McKean, S. M., **334**
McKee, William, **239**, 436
Mackenzie, James, 225, **226**
McKim, James Miller, **445**
McKinley, D. M., 225
McKinstry, Alexander, **563**
McKinstry, Louise Dade, **563**
McKinstry, Mary Ingersoll, **563**
McKinstry, Virginia Dade, **563**
McLain, Miss (daughter of William McLain), 556
McLain, William, **556**
Mcleady, ———, 128
McLean, Caroline Thew Burnet, 217, **218**
McLean, John, xviii, 51, **106**, 179, 193, 198, 209, 217, 218, 234, 237, 262
McLean, Nathaniel, 218
McLean, Nathaniel Collins, **217**
McLean, Rebecca Edwards, **106**, 217
McLean, Sarah Ann, **51**, 234
McLean, Sarah Bella Ludlow Garrard, **179**, 188, 207, 209, 217, 218
McLean, Washington, **213**, 214, 670
McMahon, James, **290**, 291
McMeens, Anna C., **655**
McMichael, Morton, **631**, 652
McMillan, Archibald, **172**
McMillan, Samuel James Renwick, **659**
McMillan judgement, 172
McMillen, William Linn, **293**, 294
McMullen, Fayette, **283**
MacVeagh, Isaac Wayne, **509**, 631, 637
Macy, Obed, *History of Nantucket*, 486
Macy, William Henry, **486**
Madison, James, **6**; *Two Letters to Joseph Cabell*, 6
Magrath, Andrew Gordon, **681**
Magruder, James A., **682**
Magruder, Samuel C., 504, **505**
Mahard case, 197
Mahmud II, **41**
Mahoning Index, 203
Maine, politics, 632
Major Anderson (ship), 577
Malin, George W., **657**
Mallory, C. W., **302**
Mallory, Stephen Russell, **236**
Malory, Thomas, *Le Morte d'Arthur*, 653
Manassas, battles of. *See* Bull Run
Manassas, Va., 331, 333, 356

Mann, Charles A., **660**
Mann, H. E., **660**
Mansfield, Edward Deering, **152**, 162, 169, 276, 279, 528
Mansfield, Joseph King Fenno, **342**, 343, 374–75
Mansfield, Ohio, 251
March, Michael, **660**
Marietta Cemetery, 283
Marietta College, 156
Marietta Congregational Church, 282
Marietta First Unitarian Society, 283
Marine Bank v. Fulton Co. Bank, 519
Markbreit, Leopold, **515**
Marko, James, 539, 540
Markoe, Francis, **230**
Markoe, Mary Galloway Maxcy. *See* Maxcy, Mary Galloway
Marley, Joseph K., **307**
Marr, Robert H., **598**
Marshall, Mrs. (wife of Edward Colston), 236
Marshall, Edward Colston, **236**
Marshall (employee), **503**, 535, 557, 578, 603
Marshall, Humphrey, **401**
Marshall, John, **628**
Marshall, John G., **258**
Marshall, Vincent, **91**
Marshall, William Edgar, **635**
Marshall, William Rainey, **660**
Marthell, Emil, **547**, 638
Marthell, Maggie, **545**, 547, 637
Martindale, John Henry, **611**, 633
Martineau, Harriet, *The Hour and the Man*, 155
Martinez, Mr., 559
Marvin, William, **431**
Mary Bangs (ship), 514
Maryland, politics, 435–36, 633
Maryland Institute, 294
Mason, James Murray, **318**, 320, 324, 375
Mason, John Sanford, **388**, 392
Mason, John W., 152
Mason, Rodney, 284, 388, 392
Mason, Samson, **388**
Mason, Stevens Thomson, 39
Mason, William S., **684**
Masonic Order suspected, 640
Massachusetts Historical Society, liv
Matchett, William B., **600**
Mathers, John H., 299, **300**
Matherson, Rufus S., **363**
Matheson, James. *See* Reed, Andrew
Matilda case, xx–xxi, 119, 172
Matlack, Bowen, **212**
Matthews, Addie, **522**

Matthews, Elizabeth, 203
Matthews, Joseph McDowell, 307
Matthews, Stanley, **194**, 198, 200, 203, 208, 209, 251, 263, 267, 579; letters noted, 204, 205, 207, 208, 209, 210
Matthias I, **52**
Mattoon, Calvin S., **247**, 275
Mattoon, Willis, **247**, 275
Maumee, Battle of, 129
Maxcy, Elizabeth Galloway, 77
Maxcy, Mary Galloway, **37**, 38, 42, 43, 44, 230
Maxcy, Virgil, **37**
Maxwell, Hugh, **418**, 419
May, Mrs. (wife of Samuel Joseph May), 237
May, A. J., **569**
May, Samuel Joseph, **237**
May, Thomas P., **564**, 565, 567, 568, 569, 570, 571, 639
Maynard, Horace, **323**
Mayo, Amory Dwight, **511**
Meade, George Gordon, **426**, 427, 450, 451, 452, 454
Mechanics' and Traders' Branch Bank (Cincinnati), 211, 223, 228
Mechanics Institute (Cincinnati), 70
Medill, Joseph, 245, **246**
Meigs, Montgomery Cunningham, **316**, 317, 325
Meline, T. M., 364, **365**
Mellen, Mrs. (wife of William P. Mellen), 579
Mellen, William P., **316**, 365, 408, 429, 430, 529, 532, 579, 586, 638, 639, 640, 686; corresponds with Chase, 408, 409, 485; with Chase on Southern tour (1865), xliii–xliv, 535, 536, 538, 551, 554, 558, 559, 560, 561, 569, 571, 572, 573, 578
Mellen, William S., **535**, 537, 558, 559, 573, 574, 578
Melodeon (Cincinnati), 192
Melodeon Hall (Cleveland), 268
Melville, Herman, *Typee*, 220
Mendenhall, Cyrus, **255**, 271
Mendenhall, George, **182**, 183
Mendenhall, Moses, **255**
Meng, A. P., 278, **279**
Mercer, Alexander G., **482**
Mercer, John Francis, **33**, 34
Merchant, Ahaz, **220**
Meredith, John F., **435**
Meredith, John R., **262**
Meridian Hill (Washington), 11
Meriweather (Merreweather), 185, 206
Meriweather, J. H., **185**
Meriweather, William, **185**

Merriam v. Hass, 519
Merrick, Frederick, **270**, 285
Merrill, Stephen Mason, **677**
Merrimac (ship), 337–40, 343–45
Merritt, Edwin Atkins, **612**
Merriweather, F., **185**
Merriweather, W., Jr., **185**
Merryman, James H., **427**, 540, 557, 559, 562, 569
Mersereau case, 171
Metropolitan Club (Washington), 647
Mexico, 211
M'Fingal (fictional character), 44
Miami (revenue steamer), xxxiii, 336, 337, 340, 341, 342, 411
Michael, Aaron, **176**, 177, 180
Michigan, election returns, 1862, 424
Michigan Territory, 101
Middleton, Daniel Wesley, **608**, 640, 645, 675, 680
Miles, ———, 151, 158
Miles, Dixon Stansbury, **386**, 389, 390, 391
Militia Act, 1862, 352
Miller, Mrs., 497
Miller, Alexander P., **295**
Miller, Captain, 497
Miller, Charles R., **225**; Chase's letter to ("Toledo letter"), 225–28
Miller, E., 73
Miller, Elizabeth Winter Reeves, **601**, 677
Miller, Emanuel, **580**
Miller, George C., **516**
Miller, George H., 676
Miller, Samuel Freeman, **519**, 520, 597, 601, 606, 607, 608, 651, 677, 703
Miller, Silas F., **578**
Miller, William, and Co., 590
Miller v. New York, 704
Millikin, Minor, **334**, 501, 504
Mills, ———, 501
Mills, Miss, 607
Mills, Caroline M., **654**
Mills, Elisha, 78
Mills, Essie, 654
Mills, Frank, 654
Mills, John, **283**
Mills, Jonathan, **254**, 307
Mills, Sarah, 654
Mills, William H., 607
Mills, William S. (Michigan), **365**
Mills, William S. (Sandusky), **221**
Milman, Henry Hart: *History of the Jews*, 79; *The Martyr of Antioch*, 216; notes to Gibbon, *Decline and Fall*, 306

Milne, George, 185
Milroy, Robert Huston, **434**
Milton, John: *Paradise Lost*, 75; *The Tenure of Kings and Magistrates*, 178
Milwaukee & Minnesota R.R. Co. v. Soutter, 521
Milwaukee Free Democrat, 269
Miner, John L., **117**, 157, 258, 261
Miner, William, **180**
Minnesota (ship), 337, 338
Minor, Charles S., **440**
Minor, John D., **157**
Minor, Thomas H., **157**
Minor, William Thomas, **556**, 557
Minturn, Robert Browne, **317**
Missionary Herald, 130, 156, 157, 179
Mississippi Delta, 564
Mississippi Proclamation, 574
Mississippi River, 358–59, 360, 416, 564, 571–75; opening planned, 416, 417, 418, 419
Missouri, 405, 406, 510
Missouri State Mutual Insurance Co., 239
"Mistakes in Education," 121
"Mistakes of Westminster Review on American Jurisprudence," 69
Mitchel, Michael, **176**, 177, 180
Mitchel, Ormsby MacKnight, **121**, 352, 353, 354, 358, 383, 384, 404, 405, 416, 417, 548
Mitchell, Mr., 170, 209
Mitchell, Mrs., 151
Mitchell, Alexander, **681**
Mitchell, John C., **559**
Mitchell, John Grant, **582**
Mitchell, Martha Reed, **681**
Mitchell, Thomas G., **186**, 195
Mitchell v. Schnetz, 171
Mix, John B., **363**
Mix, Simon H., **413**, 414
Mobile, Ala., 562–63
Molière: *Le Malade Imaginaire*, 75; *Le Misanthrope*, 501
Molitor, Adolph, **263**
Molitor, Stephen, **250**, 263, 356
Monfort, Luther, **201**
Monitor (ship), 337–39, 343–44
Monroe, James, **402**
Monroe, John T., **335**, 638
Montgomery, Mr., 393, 412, 413
Montgomery, Henry Eglinton, **708**
Montgomery (steamship), 165
Moore, Mr., family of, 88
Moore, Mrs., 700
Moore, Bartholomew Figures, **542**, 543
Moore, Florence Greenhow, 255

Moore, Frank, **502**; *Rebellion Record,* 502
Moore, Milton, **588**
Moore, Philip D., **444**, 445
Moore, Thomas (b. Canada), **258**
Moore, Thomas (Highland County), **299**
Moorhead, Dora, **495**, 654, 655, 656
Moorhead, J. Barlow, **630**
Moorhead, James Kennedy, **426**, 472
Moorhead, Sarah E. Cooke, **495**
Moorhead, William E. C., **495**, 607, 654, 656
Moorhead, William G., **481**
Morgan, Mrs., 587
Morgan, Edwin Denison, **390**, 461, 463, 466, 468, 476, 481, 516, 608
Morgan, Ephraim, **119**, 174
Morgan, George Washington, **353**, 354, 639, 684
Morgan, William D., **296**
Morher, La Fayette, **168**, 169
Mori, Arinori, 683, **684**, 686
Morphy, Paul Charles, **567**
Morrill, Justin Smith, 322, **323**, 470; *Report on Commerce and Navigation, 1863,* 460
Morrill, Lot Myrick, **332**, 466, 670
Morris, Mr., 593
Morris, Mrs. (daughter of Crafts J. Wright), 568
Morris, Benjamin Franklin, *Life of Thomas Morris,* 256, 259
Morris, Calvary, **114**
Morris, Charles (attorney), **180**
Morris, Charles (naval officer), **232**
Morris, Henry W., **232**
Morris, James Remley, **252**, 296
Morris, Joseph S., **263**
Morris, Matties Burton, **263**
Morris, Thomas, **156**, 166, 167
Morris, William Walton, **527**
Morrison, T. S. C., **240**
Morristown, N.J., 224
Morse, Mr., 511
Morse, Isaiah, **238**
Morse, John Flavel, xxvi–xxvii, **200**, 203, 205, 206, 207, 208, 222, 488
Morse, Samuel Finley Breese, **214**, 215, 235, 259
Morse telegraph, 217
Mortie, Louise de, **565**, 566
Morton, Edmund, **277**
Morton, George R., **277**
Morton, J. N., **277**
Morton, Oliver Hazard Perry Throck, **412**, 413, 414
Morton, T. P., **257**

Morton, William, **274**
"Morven Park" (Swann family estate), 38–39
Moses, 78
Moses, John, **402**
Mot, Adolphus, **257**, 259, 260, 263, 264, 265, 266, 267, 269, 270, 271, 272, 273, 277, 278, 279, 281, 287, 553, 647
Motley, Elizabeth Cabot, **517**
Mott, Anna C., **658**
Mott, Cannie, **658**
Mott, Richard, **289**, 302, 658, 705
Mott, Robert, **598**
Mott, Samuel R., **204**
Moulton, Mrs., 617
Moulton, Caroline C., **663**, 668, 671, 675, 683, 686, 699, 704, 709, 710
Mozart, Wolfgang Amadeus, 8
Mt. Vernon, 679
Mudge, Charles F., **491**
Mullett, Alfred Bult, **674**, 675
Munn, Lewis C., **230**
Munsell, Leander, **174**
Murdock, Charles Cone, **580**
Murphy, Mary, 195
Muse, R. W. P., **236**
Mussey, Francis Brown, **191**, 192
Mussey, Reuben Delavan, **532**, 535
Mussey, Reuben Dimond, **164**, 188, 191
Mussey, William Heberdon, **188**, 189, 191, 192
Mutterfeldt, ———, 557
Myer, Mrs., 512
Myer, John, **206**
Myers, James, **227**, 228, 229, 258
Myers, Leonard, **632**
Myers and Ale, 206
Mygatt, Henry R., **599**

Naaman, 592
Nadal, Bernard Harrison, **504**, 512, 515, 519, 526, 531, 607
Nahant (ship), 425
Nantucket, Mass., Athenæum, 486
Napoleon I, 10, 682
Nash, Job M., 695
Nashville Daily Orthopolitan, 194
Nast, William, **146**
National Anti-Slavery Standard, 586
National Archives, Chase's papers at, li
National Banking System, xxxvi–xxxvii, xlviii, 423, 425, 426, 428, 473, 478, 586
National Era, 213, 233, 600
National Home for Disabled Volunteer Soldiers, 611, 633

Index   { 769 }

National Hotel: Springfield, Ohio, 217; Washington, 403
National Intelligencer, 168, 474
National Reform Association, 181
National Republican party, xx
Naugatuck (ship), 337
Naval hospital (Cleveland), 220
Naylor, John M., **291**
Neale v. Neale, 649
Nebuchadnezzar, 109
Needham, Edgar, **420**, 421, 577
Needham, Erasmus, **271**
Neereamer, John F., **278**, 280
Neff, George W., **110**, 112, 113, 114, 121, 129, 131, 595
Neff, Peter Rudolph, **595**
Neff, William R., **114**, 125, 595
Neil, Mrs. (wife of John G. Neil), **264**
Neil, Jane Marshall Sullivant, **264**, 288, 291, 293, 294
Neil, Robert, **260**
Neil, Robert Elkin, **260**, 264
Neil, William, **143**, 264
Neil House (Columbus), 251, 253, 260, 263, 274, 276, 582
Nelson, ——— (son of J. M. Nelson), 244
Nelson, J. M., 244
Nelson, Samuel, **515**, 517, 519, 602, 608, 619, 651, 668, 701
Nelson, William, **406**, 408
Nemaha (ship), 548
Neptune Steamship Co., 594
Nesmith, James Willis, **332**
Neutrality, principle of, xlvi
Nevins, Richard, **247**, 255, 260, 264, 274, 291, 297
New Bedford, Mass., lightships seized at, 460
New Garden Chronicle (Ind.), 196
New Hampshire, politics, 496–97
New Hampshire Historical Society, lvi
New Ironsides (ship), 383, 384, 390
New Lake House (Sandusky, Ohio), 657
New Orleans, 564, 565, 567, 638
New Orleans Times, 571
New York, 103, 481–82, 612
New York Bank Cases. *See* Bank Tax Case
New York City, 20, 22, 60, 100
New York Custom House, xxxviii, xlii, 371–72, 373, 376, 387
New-York Evangelist, 130, 139, 157
New York Evening Post, 691
New York Express, 122
New York Herald, 403, 423, 545, 586, 594

New York Hotel, 237
New York Independent, 437, 586
New York Supreme Court, 184
New York Times, 424
New York Tribune, 387
Newbold, Joshua G., **656**
Newbold, Rachel Farquhar, **656**
Newcomb, H. D., **577**
Newcomb, Warren, **577**
Newell, William Augustus, **446**
Newman, John Philip, **649**, 667, 668, 671
Newport, R.I., Reading Room, 699
Newport Manufacturing Company (Ky.), 175
Newport-Wickford Railroad, 691
Newton, Isaac, **528**
Newton, John, **555**
Nicholas, John Spear, **295**
Nichols, ———, 618
Nichols, ——— (son of Matthias H. Nichols), 303
Nichols, Mrs. (wife of Matthias H. Nichols), 303
Nichols, Charles Henry, 396, 397
Nichols, Eli, 204, 233
Nichols, Ellen G. Maury, **396**
Nichols, Ida, **499**, 501, 512, 515, 590, 692
Nichols, Mary Ann Sprague, **501**, 590
Nichols, Matthias H., **303**
Nichols, O. E., 222
Nichols, Smith W., **548**
Nicholson, William Rufus, **287**
Nicolay, John George, **709**
Niles, Hezekiah, **32**
Ninth Street Baptist Church (Cincinnati), 169
Nixon, John Thompson, **426**
Noailles, Emmanuel Henri Victurnien, marquis of, **699**
Noble, John, **582**
Noble, Linneaus P., **595**
Noell, Mrs. (wife of John William Noell), 426
Noell, John William, **426**
Nolan v. Urmston, 214
Norfolk, Va., xxxiii–xxxiv, 341–44, 537
Norris, ———, 547
Norris, Mr., 574, 700
Norris, Charles A., **650**
North American Review, 57
North Bend, Ohio, 123
North Carolina, 437, 438, 537, 541, 542, 543
Northampton County, Va., taxes, 431, 432
Northcott, Mr., 379

Northerner (ship), 535
Northrop, Henry A., 179, **180**
Northrop, W. W., 179, **180**
Northwest Ordinance: 1784, 58; 1787, xix, 58, 59, 166, 218
Northwest Territory, 73
Norton, George Hatley, **311**
Norton, Jesse Olds, **477**
Norwalk Experiment, 228
Noyes, Emily Caroline, **488**, 489
Noyes, Julia F. Tallmadge, **488**, 489
Noyes, William Curtis, **488**, 489, 491, 615
Nullification, 59, 66
Nye, ———, 215, 644
Nye, Mr., and son, 174
Nye, Mrs., 187
Nye, Arius Spencer, **596**

Oakley, Thomas Jackson, **103**
O'Brien, Edward, *The Lawyer*, 168, 170
Ocean House (Newport, R.I.), 700
Oceanus (ship), 586
O'Connell, ———, 176
O'Connell, Daniel, **168**; *Memoir on Ireland*, 689
Odell, Moses Fowler, **322**
Odlin, Woodbridge, **612**
O'Dowd v. Russell, 673
Offley, David, **41**
Oglethorpe, James Edward, **552**
Ogontz (Cooke residence), 609
O'Gorman, Richard, **313**
O'Harra, George F., **383**, 384
Ohio, xxvi–xxvii, xxx–xxxi, lxii, 317
Ohio Bank Charter, 305
Ohio Belle (steamship), 156
Ohio Board of Public Works, 218, 251, 258, 296, 298
Ohio College of Dental Surgery, 191
Ohio commissioner of statistics, 276
Ohio Constitution, 262, 305
Ohio Court of Common Pleas, Hamilton County, 135, 147, 165, 167, 179
Ohio ex rel. Noah L. Wilson and others v. Salmon P. Chase, 257
Ohio Farmer, 223
Ohio General Assembly, 110, 114, 124, 260, 278; House of Representatives, 68, 173, 199, 200, 202, 203, 205, 253; Senate, 68, 110, 173, 180, 249, 257, 275
—1848–49 legislative session: Apportionment Bill, 206–7; Black Laws, repeal of, 204, 207; Chase's bills, 201, 203; Clinton County election, 201, 204, 205, 208; Democratic and Free-Soil coalition, 198–202, 207; election of governor, 202–3; Free-Soilers in, 199; Hamilton County, disputed seats, 199–201, 205–8; Swift's bill for separate schools, 204, 205
Ohio Land Seller, 201
Ohio Life Insurance and Trust Co., 114, 171, 177, 206, 297
Ohio Political Register, 119
Ohio politics, 199, 245–56, 297, 305–7, 310, 436, 438, 532, 637, 639–40
Ohio Press, 218
Ohio public institutions, 195, 252, 258, 276, 286, 306
Ohio Republican, 135
Ohio Standard, 196, 209, 218
Ohio Star (Ravenna), 226
Ohio State Anti-Slavery Society, 165
Ohio State Fair (Cincinnati), 299
Ohio State House, 248, 249, 250, 256, 260, 298
Ohio State Journal, 218, 248, 252, 269, 281, 311
Ohio State Teacher's Association, 290
Ohio Statesman, 227, 235
Ohio Supreme Court, 121, 122, 126, 130, 131, 132, 147, 158, 159, 160, 179, 201, 202, 203, 211, 212, 253, 271, 281
Ohio Surgeon General, 292
Ohio Wesleyan University, 285
Olcott, Thomas Worth, **426**
Olcott v. Supervisors of Fond du Lac County, 705
Olds, Edson B., **298**
Oliver, Henry Kemble, **623**
Oliver, Melancthon Wade, **580**
Oliver, William, **153**, 175
Oliver and Wood, 80
Oliver House (Toledo), 657, 658
Olmstead, Aaron B., **489**
O'Neale, Rhoda (mother of Peggy Eaton), 23
O'Neill, Charles, **631**
O'Neill, Patrick, **260**, 261
Opdyke, George, **328**, 459, 491
Orange Judd & Co., 700
Ord, Gen. Edward Otho Cresap, division of, 346–47
Ordronaux, John, **671**
O'Reilly, Henry, **214**, 215, 216, 222, 259
O'Reilly, Miles. *See* Halpine, Charles Graham
O'Reilly et al. v. Morse et al., 214, 235
Orléans, François Ferdinand Philippe Louis Marie d', 369, **370**

Index

Orléans, Louis Philippe Albert d', 369, **370**, 517
Orléans, Robert Philippe Louis Eugène Ferdinand d', 369, **370**
Orne, Mrs. (wife of James H. Orne), 609
Orne, James H., **509**, 609, 631, 632
Orton, William, **462**, 464, 466, 468, 469, 470, 502, 708
Orvis, Joseph Upham, **635**
Osborn v. Nicholson, 689
Otis, Harrison Gray, **59**
Otis, William C., **482**
Ottawa, Ohio, Agricultural Exhibition, 312
Otterbein College, faculty visits Chase, 468
Ottoman Empire, 137
Ouseley, Maria Van Ness, **25**
Ouseley, Sir William Gore, 25
Overdier, David, **290**
Owen, Mr., 134, 154
Owen, Allison O., 62, **63**
Owen, Robert Dale, **13**, 392
Owens, John, **119**
Owens, Owen, **119**

Pachet, A., & Co., 243
Pacific Mail Steamship Co. v. Joliffe, 514
Packard, William Alfred, **502**, 505
Packer, Asa, **701**
Paddock, T. S., **480**
Pain Quotidien, 279–81
Paine, Henry, **66**
Paine, Robert F., **238**
Palfrey, John Gorham, 213, **484**
Palladius, *De Vita S. Johannis Chrysostomi Dialogus*, 133, 135, 143, 167
Palmer, Miss, 626
Palmer, Cook, and Co., 387
Palmer, Innis Newton, **538**
Palmer, John M., **273**
Panic of 1836, xxiii
Papyrotomia, 8
Paragon (ship), 47
Pardee, Aaron, **225**
Parish, Francis Drake, **181**, 197, 221, 228
Parker, Mrs. (wife of C. M. Parker), 669
Parker, C. M., **669**
Parker, Elijah, **66**
Parker, J. W., **436**
Parker, James, **261**
Parker, James, Jr., **261**
Parker, John Cortlandt, **487**
Parker, John Todd, 245
Parker, Peter, **674**

Parker v. Davis, 664, 668, 669
Parkersburg, W.Va., 478
Parkersburg Conference (1872), 672
Parkeville Institute (N.J.), 224
Parkhurst, Fanny, **616**
Parkhurst, Gratia, **616**
Parmalee, ———, 239
Parmley, Reverend, 489
Parsens, Edwin, 645
Parsons, George M., **247**, 281, 304, 582, 583, 584, 585
Parsons, Jane Swan, **281**, 290
Parsons, Julia, **509**
Parsons, Lizzie, 424
Parsons, Lucy, 620
Parsons, Richard Chappel, Jr., **509**, 709
Parsons, Richard Chappel, Sr., **268**, 281, 364, 365, 509, 516, 517, 629, 631, 643, 675, 676, 677, 680, 686; correspondence noted, 522, 662, 694, 705
Parsons, Sarah Starkweather, **509**, 583
Parsons, Theophilus, **591**, 592
Parton, James, *Horace Greeley*, 697, 698
Paschal, George W., Jr., **605**, 606
Passaic (ship), 383, 384, 390, 545
Patapsco (ship), 544, 545
Patapsco River, 19
Patent Report, 244
Paterson, Andrew B., **660**
Paterson, William, **660**
Patmore, Coventry Kersey Dighton, *Angel in the House*, 252
Patterson, Mrs., 18
Patterson, Mrs. (wife of William C. Patterson), **653**
Patterson, Alexander, **555**
Patterson, Andrew, **152**
Patterson, Daniel Tod, **667**
Patterson, David Trotter, **601**
Patterson, Elizabeth Pearson, 50, **667**
Patterson, J. M., **291**
Patterson, James Willis, **587**, 589, 591, 610, 613, 615
Patterson, John S., **181**, 222
Patterson, Joseph, **703**
Patterson, Martha Johnson, **601**
Patterson, Morris, **701**
Patterson, Robert, **356**, 379, 652, 653
Patterson, Robert, Jr., **700**
Patterson, Robert Emmet, **652**
Patterson, Sarah Parker Wilder, 615
Patterson, William, **18**
Patterson, William Chamberlain, **308**, 652
Paul, Mrs. (wife of John Paul), 240

Paul, John, **233**, 240, 241, 250, 251, 253, 255, 259, 261, 269, 302, 303, 305; correspondence noted, 233, 245
Paul, John, Jr., **241**
Paulding, Ohio, election results (1857), 302
Pauline Carroll (ship), 571
Pawnee (ship), 545
Payne, Daniel Alexander, **270**
Payne, Henry B., xxxi, **296**, 298, 305, 306, 307, 310
Peabody, Ephraim, **70**
Pearce, James Alfred, **322**, 332
Pearl Street House (Cincinnati), xix, 83, 84, 85
Pearman, Mrs. (wife of William Pearman), 7–8
Pearman, William, 7–8, **8**
Pearton, Mr., 156
Pease, Calvin, **73**, 240
Pease, Elisha Marshall, **632**
Pease, J. J. R., **398**
Pease, John Usher, **302**
Peck, John James, **374**
Peerless (ship), 563
Peet, Emerson W., **654**
Pendery, John L., 244, 246
Pendleton, Edmund, 223
Pendleton, Elliott Hunt, **578**, 579
Pendleton, George Hunt, **479**, 498, 578
Pendleton, John, **676**, 678
Pendleton, Nathaniel Greene, 55, **67**
Pendleton County v. Amy, 670
Pennington, Dr., 709, 710
Pennington, J. L., **542**, 543
Pennington, Robert Gill, **257**, 291
Pennsylvania, 379–80, 429–30
Pennsylvania, Historical Society of, li, liv, lv, 702
Pennsylvania Central Railroad, 454
Perkins, David, 362
Perkins, Hamilton E., **496**
Perkins, James Handasayd, **79**, 126, 127
Perkins, Thomas H., 484, **485**
Perley, Ira, **496**
Perley, Mary S. Nelson, **496**
Perry, ———, 182, 185
Perry, Aaron Fyfe, **286**, 581, 699
Perry, Edith Strong, **699**
Perry, Elizabeth Williams, **699**
Perry, John Gardner, 662, **688**, 689, 695, 696, 701; *Letters*, 706
Perry, Martha Derby, **706**
Peter, Sarah Anne Worthington King, **69**, 271
Peter, William, 69

Peters, Hugh, **53**, 57
Peters, Judge, 233
Peters, Richard, **73**
Petit Dunning and Co. v. Wade, 150
Peto, Samuel Morton, **600**, 634
Pfau, John M., 151, **152**
Phelps, ———, 138
Phelps, Amos A., *Letters to Professor Stowe and Dr. Bacon*, 194
Phelps, John Smith, 232, **323**
Phelps, Mary Whitney, **232**
Phelps, Royal, **482**
Phelps, Samuel Shethar, 208, **209**, 236
Phelps, Timothy Guy, **387**
Philadelphia (ship), 545
Philadelphia (steamship), 88, 89
Philadelphia and Baltimore Railroad, 454
Philadelphia City Hall, 702
Philadelphia Evening Bulletin, 383
Philanthropist, xx, 119, 134, 135, 151
Philip, Robert, *George Whitefield*, 124, 125, 354
Phillip, John. See Kodama
Phillips, D., 656
Phillips, Horatio Gates, **265**
Phillips, John, **547**
Phillips, Philip, 650, 676, 681
Phillips, Wendell, xxiv, xl, **629**
Phillips, Willard Peele, 494, 623
Phillips House (Dayton, Ohio), 299
"Philopena," 84
Phoenix Insurance Co. v. Hamilton, 676
Piatt, Donn, **198**, 204, 396
Piatt, John James, **460**
Pickens, Francis Wilkinson, **242**, 544
Pickering, Charles Whipple, **548**
Picket, Miss C., 133
Picket, Delia, **151**
Pierce, Alexander N., 199, 200, 202, 204, 205, 206, 207, 208
Pierce, Edward Lillie, **238**, 265, 266, 277, 278, 295, 331, 445, 483, 485, 490, 495, 496, 497, 498, 500, 625, 629, 695; correspondence with Chase, 295, 488, 495, 588; *A Treatise on American Railroad Law*, 277
Pierce, Franklin, 272, **273**, 414
Pierce, S. A., **678**
Pierce v. Carskadon, 678
Pierce v. Cox, 652
Pierpont, Mr., 237
Pierpont, Francis Harrison, **403**, 434, 447, 537
Pierrepont, Edwards, **210**, 235, 395, 519, 707
Pierrepont, Margaretta Willoughby, **707**

Index { 773 }

Pietri, Guido di (Fra Angelico), **674**
Pike, Captain, 615, 618
Pike, Mrs. (wife of Captain Pike), 615, 618
Pike, Elizabeth Ellicott, **236**
Pike, James Shepherd, 236, **587**, 588, 590
Pike (steamship), 154, 155
Pillow, Jerome, **406**, 407, 408, 409
Pillsbury, Mrs. (wife of John H. Pillsbury), 547
Pillsbury, John H., **546**, 547
Pinney, A. H., **309**
Pinney, Norman, *First Book in French*, 266, 271
Pirtle, Henry, **215**, 507
Pitcher, Mrs. (wife of Thomas Gamble Pitcher), 680
Pitcher, Thomas Gamble, **680**
Pitkin, Timothy, *History of the United States*, 54
Pitt, William, 545
Pittsburgh, Cincinnati, and Louisville Telegraph Co., 259, 282, 307
Pittsburgh Bank, 172
Plants, Tobias Avery, 308
Plantz, Mrs. (wife of Homer G. Plantz), 555, 560
Plantz, Homer G., **308**, 309, 312, 317, 340, 381, 407, 414, 433, 529, 555, 560; copyist for Chase journals, xxxiii, lxiv, lxv, lxvi
Plantz, Sybel, 560
Platt, Orville Hitchcock, **363**
Platt, William Augustus, **278**, 292, 396, 398
Pleasonton, Mary Hopkins, **7**
Pleasonton, Matilda, 26
Pleasonton, Stephen, 7, **26**
Plumb, Ralph, **420**
Plumley, Mrs. (wife of Gardner Spring Plumley), 701
Plumley, Alexander R., xvi, **459**, 680, 698, 699, 701
Plumley, Gardner Spring, **698**, 699, 701
Plumly, Benjamin Rush, **435**, 447, 448, 459, 570
Plutarch, 628
Poe, William, **152**
Poland, Luke Potter, **664**
Polk, James K., xxiv, 177
Pollio, Symphorianus, 252, 253, 254, 257, 259
Polo de Bernabé, José, **557**, 699
Pomeroy, S. Wyllys, **171**, 579
Pomeroy, Samuel Clarke, xxxviii–xxxix, **332**, 425, 477, 478, 497, 498, 646

Pomeroy Circular, xxxix
Pond, Francis Bates, **280**
Pope, John, xxxiv, **348**, 349, 350, 353, 363, 367, 370, 373, 379, 392, 401; criticism after Second Bull Run, 372, 385, 388; letters and telegrams, 355, 362, 364, 366
Popular sovereignty, xxv, 195
Porch, Henry, **300**
Porrig, Jude (or Jim), 539, 540
Port Royal, S.C., 331–33, 336, 382, 383, 384, 404, 405, 548. *See also* Sea Islands, S.C.
Portage Railway, 88
Porter, Mr., 624, 627
Porter, Alex M., 607
Porter, Alice, 607
Porter, Charles Howell, **670**
Porter, David, 11
Porter, David Dixon, **481**, 513, 574, 666, 667
Porter, Fitz John, **367**, 370, 372, 416, 418
Porter, James D., legal case, 334
Porter, Letitia Breckenridge, **3**, 9
Porter, Peter Buell, **3**, 14
Porter et al. v. Foley, 334
Post, ———, 492
Post, Miss, 135, 151
Potter, Miss, 700
Potter, Clarkson Nott, **683**, 686, 700
Potter, Colonel, 560
Potter, Elisha Reynolds, **590**, 696
Potter, Eliza Palmer, **499**
Potter, James Brown Mason, **499**
Potter, John Fox, **426**
Potter, Joseph F., **191**, 192
Potter, L. F., 547
Potter, M. D., **287**
Potter, Mary Elizabeth, **588**, 696
Powell, Edward Payson, 494, **495**
Powell, Lazarus Whitehead, **332**
Powell, Lewis Thornton, 587, **588**
Powell, Thomas Watkins, **268**
Powell, William Henry, *Perry's Victory*, 500
Powers, Hiram, **588**
Pratt, William, **142**, 143
Prentice, George Dennison, **507**
Prentiss, Cyrus, 254, 255
Prentiss, John, **131**, 619
Presbyterian Church, 74
Preston, H. L., 225
Preston, Margaret Howard Wickliffe, **236**, 244
Preston, William (Columbus), **116**
Preston, William (Ky.), **236**
Preston House (Newark, Ohio), 653

Price, Josiah F., **292**
Price, Sterling, **358**, 359
Price, William (Cincinnati), **128**
Price, William (Md.), **522**, 523, 524, 526
Prichard, Mrs. (wife of William Mackay Prichard), 618, 619
Prichard, William Mackay, **618**, 619
Prime, Mrs. (wife of Rufus Prime), 700
Prime, Edward Dorr Griffin, **279**
Prime, Rufus, **700**
Prime, Samuel Irenæus, **279**
Prince, Frederick W., **541**
Prisoners of war, 313–14, 364, 365, 533
Proal, Pierre Alexis, **165**, 166
Probasco, Henry, **580**, 594
Proclamation of Neutrality, 318
Profile House (N.H.), 497
Prospect Hill Cocoonery, 128
Protestant Orphans' Home (Toledo), 658
Providence Bank, 236
Providence Daily Journal, 588
Pruden, A. J., **263**, 294
Puerto Príncipe (Camagüey), Cuba, 235
Pugh, George Ellis, xxvii, **199**, 200, 202, 204, 205, 206, 207, 208, 223, 298
Pugh, Jordan A., 165, 166
Pugh, Theresa Chalfant, **578**
Pugh and Pendleton, 199
Puig v. Ship James Guthrie, 599
Pulaski House (Savannah), 550
Pulte, Joseph Hippolyt, **211**
Punchard, George W., **21**, 588, 589, 591, 614, 615
Purcell, Edward, **356**
Purcell, John Baptist, **160**, 220
Purdy, John H., **201**
Putnam, Alfred, **627**
Putnam, Alfred Porter, **492**
Putnam, Ann Elizabeth, **619**
Putnam, David, 282, **283**
Putnam, David, Jr., **222**, 225, 228
Putnam, Douglas, **283**
Putnam, Eliza Tucker, **283**
Putnam, Frederick Ward, **627**
Putnam, Israel, **492**, 506
Putnam, J. W., **492**
Putnam, John Lyscom, 618, **619**
Putnam, Lewis, 282
Putnam, Maria Phelps, **493**
Putnam, Robert W., **493**
Pyne, Smith, **404**, 405

Quinet, Edgar, *Idées Sur la Philosophie,* 71
Quitman, John Anthony, **572**

Rabé, William, 352, **353**, 387
Radcliffe, Anne, xiv
Railroad accidents, 510, 608
Railroad celebration (1857), 281–84, 292, 294–95
Rainey, Joseph Hayne, **682**
Rakestraw, B. M., **240**
Ralston, Mrs. (wife of George Ralston), 20
Ralston, George, **20**, 22
Ralstram, Mr., 250
Ralstram, Mrs., 250
Ramsey, Alexander, **235**
Rand, C. W., **387**
Randall, Alexander Williams, **630**
Randall, Brewster, **202**
Randolph, John, lxiii
Randolph, Martha Jefferson, **29**, 36
Randolph, Paschal Beverley, 567, **568**
Randolph, Theodore Frelinghuysen, **685**, 686, 687
Randolph, Thomas Mann, 29
Randolph, William B., **460**
Ranney, Rufus Percival, **296**, 583
Ransom, Caroline L. Ormes, **583**
Ransom, Matt Whitaker, **681**
Rantoul, Mrs. (wife of Charles W. Rantoul), 484
Rantoul, Charles William, **484**
Rantoul, Hannah Lovett, **621**
Rantoul, Harriet Charlotte Neal, **624**, 629
Rantoul, Jane Elizabeth Woodbury, **273**, 483, 484, 491, 492, 494, 495, 589, 620, 621, 622, 623, 624, 628, 629
Rantoul, Margaret, 626
Rantoul, Robert, **273**, 621
Rantoul, Robert Samuel, **484**, 493, 620, 621, 623, 624, 626, 629, 693
Rantoul "castle" (Beverly, Mass.), 493, 620, 621, 623, 624, 625, 627, 628, 629
"Raspberry Plain," 39
Ray, Mrs., 684
Raymond, Charles A., **536**
Raymond, Henry Jarvis, **424**
Raymond, Robert Raikes, **142**, 237, 489
Raymond, Rossiter Worthington, **489**
Reab, Regyle, **563**
Read, Charles William, **427**
Read, Daniel, **361**
Read, Nathaniel C., **95**, 96, 147, 172, 198, 202, 214
Read, Theodore, **361**
Reamey, J. O., 289
Rearden, William H., **645**

Index { 775 }

Reconstruction, xxxix, xliii–xlix; black suffrage, xliv, xlvii, 536, 537, 549–50, 543, 553, 570, 574, 575–76, 579, 580, 581, 593, 594, 596, 597, 603–6; Chase considers, 331, 333–34, 475, 695; discussed, 315–17, 354, 437, 524, 527, 541, 543–44, 545, 547, 551, 552, 563, 587–88, 597–99, 600, 606, 610, 619, 627, 629, 639–40, 641, 645–46; Wade-Davis Bill, 475, 477. *See also* Fourteenth Amendment; Thirteenth Amendment
Reconstructionist, 600
Redfield, Isaac Fletcher, **619**
Reed, ———, 492
Reed, Andrew, and James Matheson, *Visit to the American Churches*, 109
Reed, David, **182**, 183, 185
Reed, John A., 224
Reed, Samuel Rockwell, **578**, 579, 599
Reemelin, Charles Gustav, **254**, 275, 289, 310
Rees, John E., **116**
Reese, ———, 440
Reese v. U.S., 649
Reeves, J. B., **682**
Reformation, 71
Reichenback, ———, 236
Reid, Mr., 132
Reid, Alexander M., **656**
Reid, Whitelaw, **479**, 494, 532, 536, 707, 708; *After the War*, 536, 597, 635; with Chase on Southern tour (1865), xliv, 536, 537, 548, 549, 553, 554, 557, 558, 559, 560, 561, 564, 565, 567, 568, 569, 570, 572, 578, 580, 581
Reinhard, Jacob, **296**
Ren (Wren), Luke, **185**, 186, 228
Renaissance Louisianaise, 570
Renick, Seymour G., **263**, 273, 295
Reno, Jesse Lee, **373**, 403, 404
Renouard, Augustin-Charles, "Theory of the Rights of Authors," 126
Republican party, xxviii–xxix, xl, 248–49, 604; in Ohio, 254, 255, 256, 257, 297–99, 301, 303–5, 312. *See also* Conventions
Revere House (Boston), 483, 495, 498, 591
Reynolds, Charles, **252**, 256, 259, 265, 267, 277, 306
Reynolds, Joseph, 150
Reynolds, L. D., **506**
Reynolds, Wiley, **163**
Rhodes, James Ford, liv

Rice, Mrs. (wife of Lewis Lippett Rice), 269
Rice, Henry Mower, **332**
Rice, Lewis Lippett, **248**, 265, 269, 274, 275, 280, 307, 639
Richards, Mr., 133
Richards, John H. D., **683**
Richards, William, 705
Richards, Wolcott, **91**, 92
Richardson, ———, 571
Richardson, Mr., 692
Richmond, Va., 119, 335, 345, 365; falls to Union Army, 524, 525
Richmond Enquirer, 28
Riddle, Adam N., **153**
Riddle, Albert Gallatin, **200**, 201, 203, 208, 209, 662; corresponds with Chase, 203, 204, 207, 209, 210
Ridgely, Andrew Sterett, **526**
Ridgely, James Lot, **438**, 446, 527
Riggs, George Washington, **649**
Riggs, Janet Madeleine Cecilia Shedden, **649**
Ringgold, Anna Maria, **29**
Ringgold, Tench, **26**, 29
Ripley, Christopher Gore, **659**
Riske, Ruhamah, **83**
Risley, Hanson A., **429**, 434, 460, 469, 503
Ritchie, Andrew, *Life and Writings of Rev. Samuel Crothers*, 299
Ritchie, Thomas, **110**
Ritter, Anthony, **186**, 189
Rives, Caroline, **397**
Rives, John Cook, **397**
Rives, Landon C., **142**, 143, 164, 165
Rives, Lucy, **397**
Roberts, Mr., 609
Roberts, John, 237
Roberts, Marshall Owen, **503**
Robertson, Joseph Clinton, *The Percy Anecdotes*, 84
Robertson et al. v. Ludlow, 188
Robinson, Mrs. (Columbus), 106
Robinson, Mr. (N.H.), 591
Robinson, Mr. (Washington), 676, 680, 681
Robinson, Mrs. (Washington), 680
Robinson, A. L., 225, **226**
Robinson, Abraham Hazen, **496**
Robinson, Jesse H., **398**, 400
Robinson, Moncure, **701**
Robinson, Thomas, 596, **597**
Robinson, J., and Son, 106
Robison, John Peter, **277**
Rochester, ———, 500
Rock, John Swett, **519**, 521
Rock Creek Church (D.C.), 16–17, 679

Rockhill House (Fort Wayne), 303
Rockwell, Julius, **230**
"Rockwood" (Moorhead estate), 481
Rocky Mountains, 79
Rodman, Gilbert, **326**
Rœdter, Henry, **203**, 204
Roff, William, **654**
Rogers, Andrew Denny, 265
Rogers, Annie, **307**
Rogers, Isaiah, **376**, 674
Rogers, Nathaniel Peabody, 307
Rogers, William Allen, **225**
Rogers v. Burlington, 604
Rollins, Edward A., **466**, 469
Rollins, Edward Henry, **497**
Rollins, James Sidney, **515**
Roman Empire, 71
Romilly, Sir Samuel, article on, 177–78
Rooks, Mr., 539
Roosevelt & Son, 277
Root, David, **74**
Root, Erastus, **103**
Root, Joseph Mosley, **583**
Rosecrans, William Starke, **427**, 432, 439, 450, 451, 452, 454, 457, 532, 644; telegrams from, 448, 449, 453
Roselius, Christian, **364**, 366, 503, 565, 567, 569
Rosetta case, 244–46
Ross, John, **399**
Ross County Bank v. Henry S. Lewis, 253
Rossini, Gioacchino Antonio, 8
Rost, Pierre A., **570**
Rothrock, James Harvey, **307**, 308
Roudanez, Joseph B., **565**, 568
Rouse, Rebecca Cromwell, **583**
Routh, James W., 174
Rumley, James, **538**, 540
Rumley, Reverend, 540, 541
Runyan, George W., **199**, 200
Rush, Nelson, **250**, 298
Rush, Richard, **9**
Russell, Charles Handy, **323**, 482, 699
Russell, Daniel L., **543**
Russell, Henry Sturgis, **485**
Russell, John B. F., **118**
Russell, Mary Hathaway Forbes, 485
Russell, William Howard, *Pictures of Southern Life*, 544, 562
Russia (ship), 538, 539, 540, 541
Russum, George M., **448**
Ryan, John S., **547**
Ryland, William, 39

"S. W." *See* Walker, Susan
Saffin, James, **198**
Safford, William Harrison, *Blennerhassett Papers*, 511

Sage, Francis P., **151**
St. Aloysius Catholic Church (Washington), 675
St. Augustine, Fla., 552–53
St. Charles Hotel (New Orleans), 565
St. Clair, Arthur, **81**
St. John's Church (Georgetown), 165
St. John's Episcopal Church (Washington), 404
St. John's Protestant Episcopal Church (Cincinnati), 287
St. Lawrence (ship), 337
St. Louis committee, letter to Lincoln, 433, 434
St. Luke's Protestant Episcopal Church (Marietta, Ohio), 282–83
St. Nicholas Hotel (New York), 609
St. Paul's Episcopal Church (Cincinnati), 98, 155, 157, 165, 172, 203, 210
St. Paul's Episcopal Church (Concord, N.H.), 496
Saintine, Joseph Xavier Boniface, *Picciola*, 257, 258, 266, 268, 271
Saisset, Émile, "Recherches Nouvelles," 386
Salade, Andrew M., 505
Salomon, Edward, **402**, 403
Sampson, Mr., 189
Sampson, Henry D., **542**, 543
Sampson, John, 77
Sams, C. C., **244**, 299
Sams, Marianna Stuart, **307**
San Jacinto (ship), 318, 339
San Pedro, Ca., explosion of steamer at, 460–61
Sanborn, Edwin David, **615**
Sanchez, Mr., 559
Sands, Alexander C., **505**, 580
Sandusky, Ohio, July Fourth celebration, 657
Sandusky Democratic Mirror, 221
Sanford, Edward Sewall, **440**
Sanford, Frederick C., **486**
Sanford, Milton H., **699**, 700
Santo, Dr., **559**
Saratoga (steamship), 221
Sargent, ———, 217, 218
Sargent, Nathan, **461**
Sartiges, Mme. (wife of Eugène de Sartiges), 232
Sartiges, Le comte Eugène de, **232**, 283
Saturday Morning Visitor (Baltimore), 197
Sauerwein, P. G., **633**
Saul, John, **676**, 677
Saulsbury, Willard, **332**, 521

Index

{ 777 }

Saunders, William, **681**
Savage, James W., **313**
Savage, Thomas, **556**, 557, 558, 559
Savage, William Montgomery, **278**, 279–80
Saxton, Rufus, **333**, 334, 346, 382, 438, 546, 548, 549, 553
Say, Jean Baptiste, *Traité d'Économie Politique*, 57
Scarborough, William W., **306**, 308
Schellentrager, E. A., 698
Schenck, Miss (daughter of Robert Cumming Schenck), 398
Schenck, Robert Cumming, **385**, 390, 398, 418, 434, 469, 477, 581, 631
Schillinger, Colonel, 180
Schleiden, Rudolph, **703**
Schley, Mrs. (wife of Frederick Schley), 644, 704, 705
Schley, Frederick, **644**, 709, 710
Schley, William, 526–27, **527**
Schmidt, Charles F., **361**, 391, 396, 432, 488, 494, 498
Schnetz, Martin, 171
Schofield, John McAllister, **507**, 541
School Recreations; the Catholic Teacher's Companion, 608
Schooley's Mountain, N.J., 224
Schouler, William, **247**, 248, 252, 279, 280, 281, 282, 483
Schroeder, Mr., 45
Schroeder, Miss S., 45
Schuckers, Jacob William, **501**, 534, 662, 672, 686, 703, 704; biography of Chase, xi, liv, lvi, lxiv; and Chase papers and journals, xxxiii, liv, lv, lxvii; letters to, 534, 639, 685, 686
Schurz, Carl, **391**, 448, 449, 685, 710
Schurz, Margarethe Meyer, **677**
Scioto and Hocking Valley Railroad, 279
Scofield, Glenni William, **597**
Scott, ———, 228
Scott, Miss, 257
Scott, Colonel, 698
Scott, Jessup Wakeman, **658**
Scott, Maurice A., **289**
Scott, Robert Kingston, **640**
Scott, Thomas Alexander, **454**, 516
Scott, Sir Walter, xiv
Scott, Winfield, **317**, 375, 392
"Scotty." *See* Gray, John
Scovill, Harris, **172**
Scoville & Co., 172
Scudder, Mr., 437, 652
Sea Islands, S.C., 548–49. *See also* Port Royal, S.C.
Sears, Barnas, **500**, 501, 626

Seaton, William Winston, **365**, 366, 522
Second Presbyterian Church (Cincinnati), 70, 169
Sedgwick, Charles Baldwin, **237**
Sedgwick, Theodore, **186**
See, George, **296**
Seelye, Thomas T., **219**
Segar, Joseph Eggleston, **430**
Selden, Charles, **356**
Selman, Mrs. (wife of Carberry Selman), **116**
Selman, Carberry, 116
Seminole (ship), 339
Semmes, Richard T., **533**
Seneca Advertiser, 200
Seneca County Bank, 288, 289, 291
Senter, George B., **494**, 584, 585
Septuagint Bible, 136, 248, 257, 258, 259, 264, 267, 269
Serle, Ambrose, *Horæ Solitariæ*, 119
Severance, Theodoric Cordenio, **220**, 548
Seward, B. J., **113**
Seward, Frederick William, **368**, 402, 529
Seward, Olive Risley, **429**
Seward, William Henry, **184**, 281, 346, 349, 359, 362, 368, 371, 375, 382, 383, 391, 401, 407–8, 415, 417–19, 425, 450, 452, 453, 454, 457, 516, 529–31; antislavery position, xxxi, 389; attempted assassination of, xliii, 529; and cabinet politics, xxxiv, xxxv, 325, 378; correspondence, 256, 377, 402, 407, 409, 410, 587, 588; and foreign relations, 348, 399, 409; on draft and enlistment, 352, 440–42; on emancipation, 358, 394–95; political patronage, xl, xlii, 209, 365; on recognizing Confederacy, 313–14; on *Trent* Affair, 320, 324; in Van Zandt case, xxi, 166
Seyffarth, Gustavus, *Recent Discoveries in Biblical Chronology*, 256, 259, 265
Seymour, Horatio, **644**
Seymour, Origen Storrs, **489**
Seymour, Robert W., **547**
Shackleford, Charles C., **568**
Shakespeare, William: *Hamlet*, 43; *Macbeth*, 6, 56
Shanks, John Peter Cleaver, **412**, 413
Sharkey, William Lewis, 574, **575**
Sharp, Ebenezer, **245**
Sharp, Eliza Lake, **245**
Sharp, William H., **387**
Shaw, Emily, **487**
Shaw, John, **250**

Shea, George, 635, **636**
Shedd, Charles, **614**
Sheffield, William Paine, **426**, 482
Sheldon, George, **199**
Shelford, Leonard, *Treatise on Law Concerning Lunatics*, 198
Shellabarger, Samuel, **426**, 431, 598
Shelman, ———, 243
Shenandoah Valley, 478
Sherer, Samuel B., **117**
Sheridan, Philip Henry, 506, **565**, 569
Sherman, Charles Taylor, **585**
Sherman, Ellen Ewing, **680**
Sherman, John, xxxvi, xxxviii–xxxix, 22, 253, **257**, 322, 332, 387, 518, 576, 599, 600, 680
Sherman, John Edward, 585
Sherman, Maria Ewing, **680**
Sherman, Mary Elizabeth, **680**
Sherman, Rachel Ewing, **680**
Sherman, William Tecumseh, xl, 253, **316**, 407, 409, 451, 452, 453, 461, 478, 521, 531, 532, 534, 581, 586, 612, 613, 614, 615, 649; meets Chase in North Carolina, 538–39, 540; and surrender of Joseph E. Johnston, 531, 539, 540, 541
Sherrill, Charles, 459
Sherwood, John, **653**
Shields, James, **209**, 213, 234, 345, 346, 347, 355, 356, 357, 374, 379
Shields, James W., **196**
Shipley, Joseph, **597**
Shoemaker, Joseph, 221
Shoenberger, George K., **580**
Shollenberger v. Brinton, 664
Short, William A., **640**
Shreve, Thomas H., **194**
Sickles, Daniel Edgar, **459**, 594
Sidell, William Henry, **577**
Sigel, Franz, **391**, 402, 478
El Siglo (Havana, Cuba), 558
Silliman, Benjamin Douglas, **513**
Sills, Elijah, **467**
Simkins, F. A. B., **311**
Simkins, Fisher A., **666**
Simmons, Franklin, **522**, 590
Simmons, James Fowler, **322**, 332
Simonton, Charles Henry, **681**
Simpson, Joseph, **581**
Simpson, Matthew, **424**, 531
Sinclair, James, **543**
Sioux Indians, 235
Sisco, Amelia M., **252**
Sisco, James, **252**
Sixth Presbyterian Church (Cincinnati), 164
Skerritt, William H., **193**, 194

Skinner, Alice (niece), **302**
Skinner, Alice Nora. *See* Stebbins, Alice Nora Skinner
Skinner, Dick (nephew), **658**
Skinner, Edward R. (nephew), **302**, 512, 658
Skinner, Eunice Louisa Wiggins, **512**, 595–96
Skinner, Helen (niece), **311**, 658
Skinner, Isabel (Belle). *See* Walbridge, Isabel R. D. Skinner
Skinner, James Ralston (nephew), liv, **155**, 207, 208, 223, 233, 246, 258, 261, 280, 377, 383, 511, 513, 595–96, 696; Chase correspondence with, 155, 230, 233, 257, 258, 309, 512, 514
Skinner, Janette (Jane) Logan Chase (sister), **19**, 120, 144, 222, 230, 233, 237, 302, 658
Skinner, Janette (Jenny) Logan. *See* Jewett, Janette Logan Skinner
Skinner, Josiah K. (brother-in-law), 19, 53, 120, **222**, 233, 237
Skinner, Sammy, 595
Slade, William, Jr., **288**
Slaughter House cases, xlvii
Slavery, 180, 182, 218, 234, 235, 242, 244–45, 333, 344, 348–49, 351, 358, 387–88, 546, 555, 557, 639; colonization schemes, 166, 399, 402; emancipation, 317, 328, 329–31, 351, 352, 355, 357–58, 362, 392, 438, 521, 525, 526, 577
Slidell, John, **318**, 320, 324, 407, 409
Sloan, J. C., **705**
Slough, John P., **253**, 260, 264, 266, 267
Slough, R. H., **563**
Smalley, Bradley Barlow, **619**
Smalley, David A., **619**
Smart, Hugh, **199**
Smedes, ———, 172
Smith, ———, 131, 207
Smith, Dr., 310
Smith, Mr., 609
Smith, Mrs., 708
Smith, Mrs. (New York), 495
Smith, Mrs. (wife of George G. Smith), 177
Smith, A. M., 538
Smith, Abram D., **378**
Smith, Adam, *Wealth of Nations*, 57
Smith, Amelia Wallace, **237**
Smith, Amos Denison, **630**
Smith, Mr. and Mrs. (Hickman Co., Ky.), 164
Smith, Ann Carroll Fitzhugh, **688**

Index   { 779 }

Smith, Asa Dodge, **592**, 613
Smith, Benjamin Bosworth, **500**
Smith, Benjamin E., **289**
Smith, Caleb, 367, 368
Smith, Caroline A. (sister-in-law), 153, **189**, 192, 206, 222, 289
Smith, Charles Ferguson, **315**
Smith, Delano T., **396**, 428
Smith, Edmund Curtis, Jr. (brother-in-law), xxxii, **136**, 181, 188, 189, 190, 192–93
Smith, Edmund Curtis, Sr. (father of second wife), 120, 132, **151**
Smith, Eliza Ann. *See* Chase, Eliza Ann Smith
Smith, Frances (Frank) Mary (sister-in-law), **132**, 136, 153
Smith, George G., **177**
Smith, George R., **127**, 129
Smith, Gerrit, xxiv, xxvii, **225**, 235, 688, 707
Smith, Goldwin, **500**
Smith, Green Clay, **602**
Smith, Gustavus Woodson, **335**
Smith, Ham, **576**
Smith, Hamilton, **26**, 53, 77, 80, 131, 138, 141, 155, 181, 195, 211, 222, 226, 288, 289, 575, 576, 577; "Indiana—Her Resources and Prospects," 214; letters to and from noted, 55, 67, 76, 78, 81, 181, 222, 226, 227
Smith, James Haddock, **227**, 273, 295
Smith, Jesse, **76**
Smith, John, **549**
Smith, John M., **295**
Smith, Joseph Vial (Victor), **205**, 207, 254, 307, 445, 518
Smith, Josiah D., **292**, 292–93
Smith, Louise Rudd, **575**, 576
Smith, Margaret Bayard, **29**, 36; *What is Gentility?*, 35; *A Winter in Washington*, 35
Smith, Mary (Henry Emerson's niece), 81
Smith, Mary (Victor Smith's sister), 307
Smith, Mary Colton (mother of second wife), 120, **132**, 142, 145, 150, 173, 188, 189, 192
Smith, May, **576**
Smith, Morgan Lewis, **573**
Smith, Richard, **578**
Smith, Samuel B., **264**
Smith, Samuel Harrison, 29, **35**
Smith, Samuel Mitchel, 257, **279**, 280, 282, 293, 297, 639
Smith, Susan H. Anthony, **257**

Smith, Thomas Church Haskell, **217**, 221, 334, 373
Smith, Thomas J. S., **264**
Smith, Thomas Kilby, **187**, 562, 613, 677
Smith, Thomas L., **364**, 396, 445, 635, 635
Smith, Victor. *See* Smith, Joseph Vial
Smith, Virginia, 393
Smith, William, **314**
Smith, William Ballard, **211**
Smith, William Prescott, **454**, 455, 456
Smith, Winthrop B., **205**, 206, 207
Smithsonian Institution fire, 520
Smothers, Mrs., 184
Smothers, John, 184
Smyth, Emma Lane, **613**
Smyth, Frederick, **611**, 613, 633
Smythe, Henry A., **637**
Snodgrass, Joseph Evans, **197**
Snowden, Mrs. (wife of P. T. Snowden), 247
Snowden, P. T., **247**, 252, 264, 275, 305, 307, 435, 504
Snydam, J. A., **334**
Snyder, John, **172**
Soldier's Home (Washington), 504
Sorvile, ———, 571
Soulé, Pierre, **566**
South Carolina, 358, 544, 550–51
Southern Loyalists' Convention (1866), 619, 631, 632
Southey, Robert, *Pilgrim's Progress, With a Life of John Bunyan*, 71, 146
Southgate, James, **135**, 168, 247
Southgate, Jane Smith (sister-in-law), **135**, 247
Southgate, Maria J., **247**, 249, 262, 263
Southworth, Mortimer M., **230**
Spalding, Rufus Paine, **213**, 218, 219, 224, 237, 474, 584, 641
Spalding, S. N. Pierson, **641**
Sparhawk, Thomas, xv, **21**
Sparrow, Thomas, **293**, 297
Spaulding, Elbridge Gerry, 322, **323**, 327, 596
Spear, Samuel A., **301**
Speed, James, xliii, **507**, 516, 530, 533, 632
Speed, John Jay, **349**
Speed, Joshua Fry, **316**
Spencer, Henry Evans, **150**, 151, 182, 184
Spencer, John Thompson, 702
Spencer, Oliver M., **180**, 199, 200, 261
Spenser, Edmund: *Faerie Queene*, lxiii, 277, 278, 279, 280, 309, 504; *Political Works*, 504

Spiece, Adam, **299**
Spinner, Francis Elias, **528**
Spirit of Missions, 166
Spiritualism, 626, 637
Spofford, Ainsworth Rand, **528**, 598, 709
Spooner, Thomas, **258**, 264
Spotsylvania, battle of, xli
Sprague, A. W., and Co., 591
Sprague, Almira, **501**, 522, 590
Sprague, Amasa, **590**, 626, 629, 630, 679
Sprague, Ethel Chase (granddaughter), **668**, 680, 681, 684
Sprague, Fanny, 667, 668
Sprague, Fanny Morgan, 499, 500, 501, **590**, 626, 629–30
Sprague, Kate Chase. *See* Chase, Catharine Jane (second daughter Kate)
Sprague, Katherine (granddaughter), **671**
Sprague, Nathaniel, **616**
Sprague, Portia Chase (granddaughter), **671**
Sprague, William (grandson), 579, 587, 594, 668, 671, 678, 679, 684, 690, 692, 697
Sprague, William (son-in-law), 142, **317**, 403, 473, 498, 503, 515, 518, 520, 522, 531, 535, 601–2, 609, 611, 626, 629–31, 638, 647, 666, 668, 671, 677, 679–82, 685, 690–97, 700; answers charges of Francis P. Blair, Jr., 465, 475; Chase visits Sprague factories, 588–91; corresponds with Chase, 317, 494, 506, 534, 579, 593, 594, 639
Sprague baby (Katherine or Portia), 680, 688
Spring, Mrs. R. B., 487
Springfield Estate (near Baltimore), 18
Squatter Sovereign (Atchison, Kans.), 280
Stabler, James Pleasants, **646**
Stacy, ———, 655
Stacy's Hotel (Zanesville, Ohio), 305
Stager, Anson, **418**, 419, 584, 585, 586
Stallo, Johann Bernhard, **580**
Stambaugh, D. W., **252**
Stanbery, Henry, **673**
Stanbery, William, **258**
Stanley, Mr., 500
Stanley, Luther, **365**
Stanley, Marcus Cicero, **459**
Stansbury, Arthur J., *Report of the Trial of James H. Peck*, 117
Stanton, Benjamin (Ind.), **196**

Stanton, Benjamin (Ohio), **300**
Stanton, Bessie, **504**
Stanton, Edwin Lamson, **504**
Stanton, Edwin McMasters, **212**, 213, 293, 324, 328, 346, 349, 353, 360, 362, 363, 368–93 passim, 398–425 passim, 431–43 passim, 449–58 passim, 469, 478, 479, 480, 497, 503–7 passim, 513–15 passim, 530–33 passim, 539, 553, 602, 606, 611, 633; appointed secretary of war, 325, 326, 328; assessed by Thomas M. Key, 581; authorizes clothes for freed slaves, 334; and cabinet politics, xxxiv, xxxix; Chase writes from South in 1865, xliv; criticized, 420, 422, 540, 592; criticizes Lincoln, 366; on draft, 352; interviews blacks in Savannah, 1865, 520–21; letter to Halleck, 366; letters noted, 212, 222, 225, 228, 437, 457, 553, 593, 618; military advisor to Lincoln, xxxii; on Reconstruction, 603; relates story, 447; relations with McClellan, 361, 366–67; sister of, 253; supports Chase's Southern tour in 1865, xliii; visits Army, 345; visits Chase, 326; with Chase and Lincoln to Norfolk, 336–44
Stanton, Eleanor Adams, **504**
Stanton, Ellen M. Hutchison, 480, **504**, 602, 603
Stanton, Frederick Perry, **334**
Stanton, Henry Brewster, xxiv, **209**, 213
Stanton, Lewis Hutchison, **504**
Stanton, William, **487**
Stapp, W. W., 227
Stark, Benjamin, **332**
Starkie, Thomas, *Treatise on Law of Evidence*, 54
Starkweather, Julia Judd, **584**
Starkweather, Samuel, **583**, 584
Starr, Henry, **124**, 185, 186, 196
Starring, Frederick Augustus, **570**
State v. Hoppess. See Watson, Samuel
States rights, 242
Statutes of Ohio. See under Chase—writings
Staughton, James M., **76**, 99, 174
Staughton v. Brisbane, 201, 202
Steam boiler explosions, Senate report, 213, 214
Steam Tug Quickstep v. Byrne, 652
Steamtug Mabey v. Atkins, 677
Stearns, Benjamin F., **583**
Stearns, Charles Onslow, **591**
Stearns, George Luther, **541**, 591, 594
Stearns, Mary A. Holbrook, 613

Stearns, Onslow, **591**, 592, 612, 613
Stebbins, Alice Nora Skinner (niece), **694**, 699
Stebbins, Henry, **694**, 695, 697
Steedman, James Blair, **241**, 305
Steele, Miss, 659
Steele, Franklin, **659**
Steele, Isaac Nevitt, 647, **648**
Steele, John Benedict, **365**
Steele, Thomas, **577**
Steele, William Gaston, **365**
Stem, Sally, **655**
Stenerson, ———, 699, 700
Stephen, Alfred, 442, **443**
Stephen, Henry John, *Principles of Pleading in Civil Actions*, 30
Stephen, Leslie, **442–43**
Stetson, Charles, **155**
Stettinius, John, **117**
Stettinius, Mary Longworth, **117**
Steven, B. F., 687
Stevens, Abel, *History of Methodist Episcopal Church*, 608
Stevens, Albert G., **498**
Stevens, Edwin Augustus, **338**, 339
Stevens, Isaac, Sr., **121**
Stevens, John Austin, Jr., **412**, 413, 502, 595
Stevens, John Austin, Sr., **312**, 328, 482, 498, 502, 586, 590, 595
Stevens, Stephen C., 212, **213**, 239
Stevens, Thaddeus, xxxvi, xxxviii, 322, **323**, 327, 468, 474, 600
Stevens Battery (ship), 337, 338, 339, 343, 344
Stevens v. Dawson, 122
Stevenson, Miss, 407, 408
Stevenson, John White, **186**, 681
Stewart, Alexander Turney, **688**, 708
Stewart, Jacob Henry, **659**
Stewart, John Aikman, **595**, 609
Stewart, Joseph J., **438**, 518
Stickney, Lyman D., **438**, 551, 553, 557, 560; "History of Florida," 554
Stiles, H., **570**
Stirling, Archibald, Jr., **520**, 527, 528
Stockbridge, Henry Smith, **527**, 528
Stockton, John Potter, **686**
Stockwell, Alden B., **708**
Stockwell, Charles Blair, **708**
Stoeckl, Édouard de, **320**
Stokely, Samuel, **145**
Stokley, William Sturmburg, **702**
Stone, Mrs., 266
Stone, Alfred Parish, **282**, 286, 288, 291, 310
Stone, Dwight, **259**, 266
Stone, Ethan, **176**

Stone, Walter F., **221**
Stoneman, George, **389**
Stonewall (ship), 557
Storer, Bellamy, **124**, 136, 225, 261, 271, 580
Storrs, Richard Salter, **629**
Storrs Township, 171, 176, 198
Story, Joseph, xix, **126**; *Commentaries on Conflict of Laws*, 126, 127, 128, 130, 131, 132, 133, 135, 137, 138, 140, 141, 142; *Commentaries on Equity Jurisprudence*, 113
Story, William W., *Reports of Cases in the Circuit Court*, 178
Stoughton, Edwin Wallace, **618**, 619, 658, 707
Stoughton, Mary Fiske, **707**
Stout, Hosea, 670
Stout v. Utah, 670
Stover, Mr., 498
Stover, Mrs., 498
Stover, Daniel, **601**
Stover, Mary Johnson, **601**
Stowe, Calvin Ellis, 186, **489**
Stowe, Harriet Beecher, *Uncle Tom's Cabin*, 166, 233, 245
Strasburg, Va., military operations near, 345
Stratton, John Leake Newbold, **323**
Straughn, L. E., **448**
Strech, Mr., 540
Stribling, Cornelius Kinchiloe, **560**
Strong, Mr., 497
Strong, Amelia Mallery, **706**
Strong, Emily Elizabeth, **706**
Strong, Julia Darling, **706**
Strong, Mary Wilson, **706**
Strong, William, **650**, 664, 668, 706, 709
Stuart, George Hay, **609**
Stuart, James Ewell Brown, **419**, 421
Stuart, William, 376, **377**, 401, 407, 408, 409, 410
Stubbs, Lorenzo, **163**
Stubbs, Robert, **163**
Sturgis, Henry P., **593**
Sturgis, Robert S., **593**
Sturgis, Russell, **487**
Sturgis, William, **487**
Suffolk Manufacturing Co. v. Isaac Hayden, 603
Sugar cultivation, 639
Sullivan, Algernon Sydney, **266**
Sullivan, John H., **317**, 324
Sullivant, Eliza G., **265**
Sullivant, Joseph, 261
Sullivant, Lucy Jane, **264**, 265
Sullivant, Mary Eliza Brashear, 261

Sullivant, Michael Lucas, 260, 264, **265**
Sullivant, Pamela B., **260**
Sullivant, Sarah Lapsley McDowell, 260, 266
Sullivant, Sarah McDowell, **260**, 264, 265
Sullivant, William Starling, 264, 265
Summons, James, **267**, 271, 273, 275
Sumner, Charles, xxvii, xliv, **194**, 227, 230, 234, 238, 246, 271, 332, 365, 475, 481, 484, 490, 517, 524, 591, 598–99, 625, 645, 648–49, 687, 693, 710; and Chase, xxxviii, 321; letters, 212, 213, 227, 276, 588; and presidential elections, 498, 695; on Reconstruction, 588; and Supreme Court, xlii, 521; on *Trent* Affair, 323
Sumner, Edwin Vose, **367**, 369, 373
Sunium, 65
Surratt, Mary Eugenia, 587, **588**
Susquehanna (ship), 339, 343, 344
Sutliff, Milton, 212, **213**
Suydam, Ferdinand, **151**
Suydam, Sage & Co., 151
Swain, ———, 186
Swallow (steamship), 153
Swan, Gustavus, **73**
Swan, Joseph Rockwell, **73**, 243, 255
Swann, Elizabeth Gilmor Sherlock, **294**
Swann, Jane Byrd, **524**
Swann, Louise, **294**
Swann, Mary Scott, **33**
Swann, Thomas, Jr., 8, 30, 38–39, 65, 77, 82, 283–84, 292, 294–95, 435, 456, 524, 525, 526, 527, 610, 633, 681
Swann, Thomas, Sr., 8, 33–34
Swan's Elevator (Columbus), 235
Swayne, ——— (daughter of Noah Haynes Swayne), 645
Swayne, Noah Haynes, **225**, 247, 272, 275, 287, 292, 293, 517, 582, 601, 605, 608, 645, 649, 651, 678, 704
Swayne, Sarah Ann Wager, **601**, 678
Swayne, Wager, **605**, 608
Swearingen, Mrs. (mother of Virginia S. Field), 664
Sweden, 136
Sweeney, Colonel, 655
Sweet, Emma Johnson, **560**
Sweet, George J., **560**
Swift, Colonel, 218
Swift, Jonathan, *Gulliver's Travels*, 231
Swift, Lucien, **201**, 204
Swisshelm, Jane Grey Cannon, **600**
Switzerland, canton government in, 638
Swormstedt, Leroy, 81

Symmes, Peyton Short, **138**
Symmons, C., *Prose Works of John Milton*, 179

Tabor, Isaac C., **388**, 389
Tacony (ship), 427
Taft, Alfonso, **172**, 175, 255, 436, 580
Talbott, Smith, **303**
Talcott, Edward N. Kirk, **550**
Talcott, Samuel Austin, **11–12**
Tallapoosa (ship), 679
Tallmadge, Benjamin, **489**
Tallmadge House (Lancaster, Ohio), 299
Taney, Roger Brooke, xli–xlii, **527**, 671; *Ex parte Gordon*, 670
Tannehill, Wilkins, 66, **67**
Tapley, Mr., 627
Tappan, Benjamin, **203**, 219, 233
Tappan, Eli Todd, 218
Tappan, Lewis, **186**
Tappin v. Magee, 151
Tarble's Case, 672
Tariffs, xxxvi, 6, 50, 66
Tarton, Mr., 555
Tassara, Gabriel García y, **348**
Tayler, Robert Walker, **480**, 512
Taylor, Miss, 175
Taylor, Miss (daughter of James H. Taylor), 541
Taylor, Bayard, **631**
Taylor, Benjamin, **241**
Taylor, Chloe Sweeting Langford, **175**
Taylor, David (major), **241**, 378–79, 383, 393, 418, 419, 432, 506, 521
Taylor, David (Treasury clerk), **361**
Taylor, Eveline Aurilla McLean, **209**
Taylor, Isaac, *Saturday Evening*, 104
Taylor, J. Rice, **269**
Taylor, James (b. 1769), **51**, 137
Taylor, James (b. 1821), **241**
Taylor, James H., **539**, 540, 541
Taylor, James Wickes, **172**, 174, 175, 195, 198, 204, 205, 206, 207, 221, 223, 225, 228, 462, 463, 479
Taylor, Jeremy: *Contemplations of the State of Man*, 124; *Works*, 159
Taylor, John (Ohio), **241**
Taylor, John (S.C.), **50**
Taylor, Joseph Pannel, **209**
Taylor, Lester, **259**
Taylor, Richard, **570–71**
Taylor, Robert Walker, 480
Taylor, William, **241**
Taylor, Zachary, xxv, **192**, 196, 209, 213, 570, 585
Temperance, lxix, 121, 157, 158, 159, 161, 254

Index { 783 }

Temperance Hall (Cincinnati), 173
Ten Eyck, John Conover, **332**
Tennessee, 439–40
Tennessee (ship), 572
Tennyson, Alfred, *Idylls of the King*, 590
Terry, Ellen F., **583**
Test Oath (1862), 650
Test oath cases, xlvii
Tevis, Joshua, **577**
Texas, 172, 177, 234, 412, 413, 521, 605–6
Texas v. Huntington's Exrs. and First National Bank, 673
Texas v. White, xlvii
Thacker, Captain, 175
Thal, Mr., 77
Thayer, Eli, **398**, 399, 498
Thayer, Martin Russell, **632**
Thayer, Nathaniel, **592**
Thayer, William Sydney, **308**
Therry, R., *Speeches of Canning*, 128
Thiers, Adolphe, *History of the French Revolution*, 136, 137, 138, 140, 141, 143, 144, 145, 146
Thirteenth Amendment, xlii, xliii, 514, 515, 518, 520
Thomas, ———, 225
Thomas, Benjamin Franklin, **426**, 500
Thomas, D. L., 32
Thomas, George Henry, **355**, 398, 449
Thomas, Henry L., **381**
Thomas, Nicholas W., **284**
Thomas, Rev. Dr., 656
Thomas, Sanford, 571
Thomas, W. R., 180
Thomas, William B., **507**, 653, 673
Thomas's subdivision (Cincinnati), 114
Thompson, ———, 129, 190, 571
Thompson, David, **131**
Thompson, E. A., **214**
Thompson, George, **213**, 694
Thompson, James (Cincinnati carpenter), **131**
Thompson, James (Pennsylvania jurist), **664**, 702, 703
Thompson, John, **131**
Thompson, Merriwether Jeff, **571**
Thompson, Mortimer Neal, **551**
Thompson, Patrick, **252**
Thompson, Waddy, *Recollections of Mexico*, 198
Thomson, Charles, 35, **36**
Thomson, Edward, **285**, 308, 583
Thomson, John Renshaw, 332, **333**
Thorn, J., **240**
Thorne, J. A., **574**
Thornton, Edward, **649**, 666
Thorp, Andrew, **97**, 103

Thorp, Angeline F., **179**
Thorp, David Whitcombe, **97**, 98, 99, 100, 104, 105, 112, 115, 116, 179
Thorp, John F., **97**
Thorp, Truman B., **97**, 119, 145
Thorp, William A., 274, **275**
Thrall, William Barlow, **291**
Thurber, Charles, **500**
Thurman, Allen Granberry, **265**, 286, 681
Ticknor, William Davis, **635**
Tiffany, Charles Lewis, **594**
Tiffany, Joel, **220**
Tiffany, O. H., **706**
Tiger (ship), 480, 481
Tilghman, Benjamin Chew, **552**
Tillinghast, ———, 692
Tillinghast, Joseph G., **208**
Tillinghast, W. T., 225
Tillotson, George M., **301**
Tilton, Theodore, **437**, 536, 586, 631
Timberlake, John B., 23
Tippecanoe, battle of, 48
Tipton, John, **47**
Tisdale, Samuel T., 77
Tisdel, Willard Parker, **676**, 677
Tivoli Circle (New Orleans), 567
Tobey v. Leonards, 514
Tocqueville, Alexis de, *De la Démocratie en Amerique*, 144, 148
Tod, David, **295**, 362, 403, 404, 472, 473, 474
Todd, Mrs., 172
Todd, Alexander, **212**
Todd, Charles Scott, **131**
Todd, John, *The Student's Manual*, 125, 126, 127, 128, 131, 132, 133, 137
Todd, Yale, 670
Toledo Republican, 227
Tolford, David Wilson, **390**
Tomeny, J. M., **494**
Tomlinson, Charles, 20
Tompkins, Cydnor Bailey, **277**
Tompkins, James, **174**
Topham, James S., **684**
Torrey, John, **482**
Townes, Mary, **162**
Townley, Miss, 215, 216
Townley, Asa, 215
Townsend, Miss, 84
Townsend, Mrs., 70
Townsend, Amos, **675**
Townshend, George: *The New Testament Arranged*, 234; *The Old Testament Arranged*, 234
Townshend, Margaret A. Bailey, **253**

Townshend, Norton Strange, xxvi–xxvii, **199**, 200, 203, 205, 206, 207, 208, 218, 219, 222, 223, 233, 253, 260, 276
Townshend House (Sandusky, Ohio), 218, 221
Tracy, Charles, **599**
Train, George Francis, **502**, 630
Treaty of Washington, 709
Tremain, Lyman, **509**
Trent affair, 318–20, 323–24
Trimble, Mrs. (wife of Carey Allen Trimble), 528
Trimble, Carey Allen, **299**, 307, 508
Trinity Church (Pittsburgh), 165
Trinity Episcopal Church (Columbus), 116, 269, 274, 309, 311
Trinity Episcopal Church (Utica, N.Y.), 165
Trinity Episcopal Church (Washington), 321
Trinity Protestant Episcopal Church (Cincinnati), 212, 223
Triplett, Robert, 185
Trist, Nicholas Philip, **12**, 13
Trowbridge, John Townsend, xii, xxxviii, **611**; *Ferry-Boy and Financier*, 611; *Lucy Arlyn*, 638
Trowbridge, Rowland Ebenezer, **365**
True American, 193, 195
True Democrat. See *Cleveland True Democrat*
Truman, E. D., 174
Trumbull, John, *M'Fingal*, 44
Trumbull, Lyman, **272**, 332, 709
Tuck, Amos, **689**
Tucker, Alice, **694**, 698
Tucker, Charles L., 433
Tucker, Hannah Ralston Whipple (niece), 495, **612**, 613, 693, 694, 697, 698
Tucker, J. A., **661**
Tucker, Joshua C., **661**
Tucker, Josiah Prentice, **495**, 564, 567, 568, 569, 570, 612, 613, 620, 625, 683, 684, 694, 695, 705; Chase visits family, 696–99
Tucker, Winifred, **694**, 698
Turks, 41–42
Turnbull, Mrs. (wife of Alexander Turnbull), **520**
Turner, George, 71, **72**
Turner, Henry McNeal, **437**
Turner, Lewis, **435**
Turner, Robert, **435**
Tutt, Charles Pendleton, **39**
Twenty per cent Cases, 676, 679
Twiggs, David Emanuel, **374**

Tyerman, Luke, *Life of John Wesley*, 675, 686
Tyler, John, xxi, xliii, 160, 530
Tyler (ship), 575

Ulke, Henry, **321**, 323
Underwood, Adin Ballou, **500**
Underwood, Joseph Rogers, **231**
Union Club (Boston), 490
Union Hall (Toledo), 302
Union League of Philadelphia, 632
Union party (1864). See Republican party
Unitarians, 145, 146, 333
United States (ship), 577
United States Mail Steamship Company, 236
Universalist and Ladies' Repository, 156
Universalist Church, 211
Upfold, George, **165**, 166
Upham, Nathaniel Gookin, **613**
Upham, William, 208, **209**, 236
Urmston, Samuel, 214
U.S. Agriculture Department, 646
U.S. Circuit Court: Cincinnati, 166; Columbus, 106, 170, 181, 197; Indiana, 122; Washington, 30
U.S. Congress, 67; committees, 227, 322, 324; House of Representatives, 333; Senate, 58, 196, 209
U.S. Constitution, 166
U.S. ex rel. Amy v. City of Burlington, 649
U.S. ex rel. Attorney General v. Circuit Court, 605
U.S. ex rel. Learned v. Burlington, 649
U.S. Supreme Court, xxi, xlvi–xlviii, 10, 11–12, 96, 99, 100, 106, 166, 209, 214, 235, 236, 634
U.S. Treasury, 279, 313, 315, 317, 334, 461. *See also* Civil War finances
U.S. v. Ferreira, 671
U.S. v. Hunt, 704
U.S. v. Klein, 669
U.S. v. Sutter, 521
U.S. v. Todd, 671
Usher, John Palmer, **357**, 358, 360, 361, 364, 402, 442, 518

Vail, Henry F., **312**, 482, 502, 586
Van Buren, John, xxv, **209**, 210, 218–19, 227
Van Buren, John Dash, **707**
Van Buren, Martin, xxv, **29**, 33–34, 196, 197, 352
Van Camp, Mrs. (wife of Aaron Van Camp), 458
Van Camp, Aaron, **458**
Van Doren, Isaac, **200**, 203

Index

{ 785 }

Van Reed, Mrs., 700
Van Rensselaer, Henry Bell, **376**
Van Rensselaer, Soloman, 131
Van Sant, Joshua, **456**
Van Slyke, Lewis G., **253**, 305
Van Trump, Philadelph, xxxi, **305**
Van Zandt, John, xxi, **166**
Van Zandt case, xxi, 166, 168, 169, 171, 174, 175, 176, 184–85, 186, 213, 223, 227
Vance, Joseph, **49**
Vanderbilt, Cornelius, 337
Vanderbilt (ship), 337, 338
Varnum, Joseph Bradley, Jr., **364**, 387
Vaudry, Catherine, **503**, 520, 667
Vaughan, John Champion, **127**, 128, 135, 187, 194, 195, 196, 197, 203, 204, 206, 207, 218, 220, 238, 245, 246, 266; corresponds with Chase, 225, 237, 265
Vaughan and Cranch, 127
Vaughan and Telegraph case, 672
Veatch, James Clifford, **576**
Veazie Bank v. Fenno, xlviii
Veazie v. Williams, 209
Venice case, 515, 521
Vermilye, Robert George, **614**
Vermilye, Washington R., **323**
Vermilye, William G., **323**
Vermont, politics, 632
Vernon, Mr., 184
Veser, ———, 579
Viall, Miss, 626
Viall, Mary Eliza, **626**
Viall, Nelson, **591**, 610, 626
Vicksburg, Miss., 358–59, 425, 427
Victoria (Cuban plantation), 559
Victoria, Queen, 318, **362**
Victurnien, Emmanuel Henri. *See* Noailles, marquis of
Viele, Egbert Ludovicus, **336**, 337, 342, 343, 550
Vinton, Samuel Finley, **209**
Virgil, xiv; *Aeneid*, 248
Virginia, lx, 28, 434, 447, 537
Virginia, CSS. See *Merrimac*
Vogdes, Israel, 551, **552**
Voorhees v. Jackson, 96, 99, 106
Vyse, Mr., 635

Wade, Benjamin Franklin, xxxviii, xlix, **167**, 189, 243, 259, 272, 298, 315, 316, 322, 332, 508, 585, 597
Wade, David, **152**
Wade, David E., **152**
Wade, Edward, xxvii, **189**, 220, 238, 272
Wade, Melancthon S., **152**
Wade, Stephen J., **152**
Wadsworth, James Samuel, **372**, 374, 375, 376, 395, 396, 400, 414, 415, 423
Wagner, Richard, "Anvil Chorus," 693
Waite, ———, 491
Walbridge, Alice (niece), **665**, 667, 668, 671, 672, 675, 679, 682, 683, 686, 687
Walbridge, Carrie, 302, 657
Walbridge, George, 233, **302**, 312
Walbridge, Helen Maria Chase (sister), **19**, 22, 66, 71, 72, 76, 98, 108, 116, 118, 119, 120, 125, 230, 311, 424, 508, 512
Walbridge, Henry B. (brother-in-law), 19, **125**, 239, 302, 311
Walbridge, Hiram, **352**
Walbridge, Isabel (Belle) R. D. Skinner (niece), **233**, 237, 302, 311, 512, 657
Walbridge, Jenny, 302
Walbridge, Lillie (niece), **671**, 675, 679, 680, 681, 682, 683
Walden, John Morgan, **574**
Waldo, F. Augustus, **119**
Walker, ———, 213, 281
Walker, Amasa, **673**
Walker, Charles Manning, **529**
Walker, Isaac Pigeon, **231**, 611, 633
Walker, James (Ohio), **288**, 289, 290
Walker, James (R.I.), **277**
Walker, James Bryant, **457**
Walker, Robert John, **334**
Walker, Susan, **118**, 232, 247, 248, 273, 275, 276, 278, 290, 320, 457, 511, 593, 594, 601, 629, 634, 636, 675, 710; letters from, noted, 230, 247, 259, 260, 273, 279, 290, 457, 634, 636; letters to, noted, 247, 248, 252, 277, 278, 279, 290, 311, 457, 522, 589, 593, 629, 634, 636
Walker, Timothy, **64**, 65, 66, 67, 118, 124, 135, 136, 205, 206, 214, 230, 244
Wallace, Dorothea Francis Willing, **702**
Wallace, John William, **608**, 675, 689, 701, 702, 703
Wallace, Rebecca Blackwell Willing, **702**, 703
Wallace, S. D., **542**
Waller, Avery L., **641**
Walley, Henshaw Bates, **398**, 399
Walley, Samuel Hurd, **327**, 328, 398, 399
Walter, Ellen, **688**, 707
Walter, Gertrude, 688, 707
Waples, Margaret J. Alsworth, **566**
Waples, Rufus, **566**

{ 786 } Index

Warburton, William, *Alliance between Church and State*, 194
Ward, Mr., 620
Ward, Mrs., 620
Ward, Artemas, **21**
Ward, Artemus (pseudonym). *See* Browne, Charles Farrar
Ward, George Cabot, 461, **462**, 707
Ward, James Wilson, **21**, 614
Ward, Nahum, **283**
Ward, Samuel G., **487**, 491
Warden, Dr., 595
Warden, Robert Bruce, xi, xx, 55, **295**, 298; and Chase's journals, liv, lvi, lvii–lx, lxiv–lxv, lxvi, 81–94, 145
Warder, Jeremiah, **141**
Ware, Mr., 184
Ware, Ashur, "Assignment by an Insolvent Debtor," 69
Warfield, Joshua, **83**
Warner v. Joy, 673
Warren, ———, 484
Warren, Robert, **667**
Warren Guards (Lebanon, Ohio), 304
Warriner, Henry Augustus, **577**
Washburn, Israel, **494**
Washburne, Elihu Benjamin, **425**, 466, 469, 610
Washington, D.C., 4, 19, 33, 35, 45, 53, 147, 151, 208, 218, 368, 454, 683, 705; Board of Public Works, 684, 685; construction in, 666, 680, 682, 686; suffrage, 597, 603, 604, 605; vulnerability to Confederates, 479–80; social life, 3, 4–5, 7–9, 12–13, 24, 26, 27, 29, 35–37, 44, 232–36, 424–25, 515–18, 601, 603–4, 607, 608, 610, 645–49, 683–84
Washington, George, 59, 137, 329, 387
Washington Asylum, 411, 412
Washington Capital, 198
Washington Chronicle, 474
Washington Ferry Company, 503
Washington Monument (Baltimore), 18
Washington National Republican, 421, 422
Waters, Richard Palmer, **484**, 491, 492, 493, 494, 495, 588, 589, 624, 627, 628, 629, 693, 698, 699
Waters, Thomas Franklin, **627**
Waters, Thomas S., **627**
Waters, William, **667**
Watson, Cooper Kinderdine, **291**, 292, 293
Watson, Griffin, **152**, 156
Watson, James, **262**

Watson, Peter H., **353**, 354, 367, 376, 386, 422
Watson, Samuel, **172**
Watson v. Jones, 703
Watt, Daniel, 201
Watt, David, **201**
Watts, Arthur, **255**
Watts, Ellen Worthington, **255**
Watts, W. H., **556**
Watts, William, **556**
Way, George Brevitt, **505**
Wayanda (ship), xliii, 537, 538, 539, 540, 541, 542, 544, 548, 553, 559, 562, 563, 564, 569, 570
Wayland, Francis, **500**
Wayne, Anthony, 129
Wayne, James Moore, **424**, 476, 517, 518, 599, 606, 608
Weasner, Thomas H., 274, **275**
Weber, Max, **342**, 343
Webster, Daniel, xii, **9**, 10, 11, 58, 152, 209, 232, 423, 490, 624, 626
Webster, Edwin Hanson, **446**
Webster, Joseph Dana, 593, **594**
Weddell House (Cleveland), 218
Weed, Thurlow, xxix, xl, xlii, **365**, 366, 385, 389, 390, 391, 395, 423
Weehawken (ship), 425, 544, 545
Weeks, ———, 181
Weeks, William Pickering, **614**
Welch, Benjamin, **353**, 362
Weld, Theodore Dwight, *Power of Congress Over District of Columbia*, 147
Weldon, S. R., **654**
Welker, Martin, **298**
Weller, John B., **163**, 238
Welles, Gideon, xxxiv, **361**, 363, 367, 368, 383, 390, 398, 402, 416, 417, 431, 439, 447, 536
Welles, Woolsey, **233**
Welling, Miss, 710
Welling, James Clarke, **683**, 710
Wells, W. Albert, **678**, 692, 700
Wesley Chapel (Washington), 474
West, Miss, 497
West, Mrs. (wife of William C. West), 538, 539
West, William C., **538**, 539, 540
West, William H., **300**
West, William T., **655**
West River, Md., 19
Western Episcopal Observer, 149
Western Law Journal, 186
Western Literary Journal and Monthly Review, 66
Western Literary Magazine, 243
Western Monthly Magazine, 66
Western Quarterly Review, 65, 66, 67

Index   { 787 }

Western Reserve College (Cleveland), 170
Western Virginia, 315. *See also* Virginia
Westminster Presbyterian Church (Columbus), 292
Wetmore, James Carnahan, **388**, 477, 479, 503, 532, 600, 631, 637
Wever, Caspar W., **209**
Whaley, Kellian Van Rensalear, **672**
Whately, Richard, *The Kingdom of Christ*, 168, 170
Wheatland, George, **628**
Wheatland, Henry, **621**
Wheaton, G. S., **396**
Wheaton, Horace, **237**
Wheeler, I. D., **185**, 196, 206, 207
Wheeler, Walter R., **163**
Wheeler, William P., **619**, 620
Wheeler v. Meriweather, 196
Wheeling glass factory, 46
Wheelock, Edwin Miller, **567**
Whig party, xx, xxi, xxvi–xxvii, 137, 201, 205; in Ohio, 200. *See also* Conventions
Whipple, Abraham, **283**
Whipple, Eliza Chase (niece), **119**, 120, 123, 230, 311, 496, 612, 613, 616, 617, 618, 619, 620, 668, 670, 694, 697
Whipple, Hannah Ralston. *See* Tucker, Hannah Ralston Whipple
Whipple, Hannah Ralston Chase (sister), **19**, 119, 187, 230
Whipple, John, **19**, 119
Whitaker, Mrs. (wife of John S. Whitaker), 569, 638, 640
Whitaker, Mrs. (wife of William R. Whitaker), 568
Whitaker, John S., **434**, 564, 566, 568, 569, 570, 638, 639, 640
Whitaker, William R., **568**
Whitaker v. Read, 518
White, Mr., 489
White, C. F., **566**
White, Isaac P., **592**
White, Julius, **386**
White, Oscar, **239**, 240
White, Stephen W., **654**
White, William, *Memoirs of the Protestant Episcopal Church*, 157
White House, 320
White Sulphur Springs, W.Va., 82
White v. Burnley, 675
White v. Hart, 689
Whitehurst, Jesse H., **232**
Whitehurst's Gallery (Washington), 232
Whiteley, M. C., **302**

Whiteman, Catherine Ludlow Baker (sister-in-law), 123, **223**, 224, 511, 578, 581, 634, 637, 639, 692
Whiteman, Lewis, **123**, 133, 223
Whiting, Augustus, **482**
Whiting, William, **624**
Whiting, William Henry Chase, **544**
Whitney, Captain, 491
Whitney, Luther, **175**
Whittier, John Greenleaf, **493**
Whittlesey, Elisha, **418**, 419
Whittlesey, William Augustus, **282**, 283
Wicker, Lawrence S., 174
Wickes, Thomas, 282
Wiegel, ———, 677
Wigfall, Louis Trezevant, **544**
Wiggin, Henry Batchelder, **696**
Wiggins, Adeline, **133**
Wiggins, Cornelia, 171
Wiggins, Laura, **177**
Wiggins, Samuel, **94**, 95, 96, 118, 131, 132, 133, 177, 180
Wilberforce, Robert Isaac, *Life of William Wilberforce*, 122, 131, 172, 210, 211, 212
Wilberforce University, trustees' meeting (1857), 269, 270
Wilder, F. J., lvi
Wildes v. Savage, 135
Wiley, Arthur, **280**
Wilkes, Charles, 136, **318**, 319, 320
Wilkes, George, **421**, 422, 423, 424, 459, 594
Wilkes' Spirit of the Times, 421
Wilkins, ———, 460
Wilkinson, Mrs., 300
Wilkinson, Judge, 300
Wilkinson, Morton Smith, **332**
Wilkinson v. Leland et al., 10
Willard v. Tayloe, 649
Willard's Hotel (Washington), 209, 325, 352, 365, 385, 390, 402, 403, 531, 532
Willcox, Orlando Bolivar, **365**
Willets, Miss, 273
Willets, Mrs., 273
Willey, Austin, **213**
Willey, Waitman Thomas, **332**
William P. Clyde (ship), 548
Williams, Mrs. (wife of Benjamin Williams), 300
Williams, Benjamin, 300
Williams, Charles D., **219**, 220, 221
Williams, Clark, **174**, 176, 177, 185, 186
Williams, Elisha, **103**
Williams, Elizabeth, **23**
Williams, Eunice, **167**

Williams, George Henry, **664**, 671
Williams, George Walton, **547**
Williams, Harrison A., **420**, 421
Williams, Henry, **674**, 676, 678, 682
Williams, J. Insco, 295
Williams, John E., **315**
Williams, Joseph R., **658**
Williams, M. C., **163**
Williams, Robert, 284
Williams, Samuel T., **397**
Williams, Sarah R. Langdon, **658**
Williams, Thomas (Cincinnati), **188**
Williams, Thomas (Pa.), **472**
Williams estate, 95
Williams v. Thacker, 175
Willis, Nathaniel Parker, *Pencillings by the Way,* 109
Willson, Hiram V., **220**, 238, 583
Wilmot, David, **228**, 332, 333, 334
Wilmot Proviso, xxiv
Wilson, ———, letter from, 225
Wilson, Miss, 628
Wilson, Mr., 617
Wilson, Mrs., 617
Wilson, Alexander C., **427**
Wilson, B., 494
Wilson, E. M., **295**
Wilson, Henry, **256**, 279, 281, 283, 332, 576, 597, 598, 599, 630, 692
Wilson, J. S., **268**
Wilson, James Harrison, 684, **685**
Wilson, John, **243**, 335, 512
Wilson, Louise, 627, 693
Wilson, Mary Ann, 203
Wilson, Noah L., 257, **283**
Wilson, Richard, 295
Wilson, Robert, 332, **333**
Wilson, William Martin, **306**
Wilson, William W., **673**
Wilstach, C. F., **99**
Winans, James January, **291**
Winans, Ross, **32**
Winchester (steamship), 155
Windom, William, **710**
Wines, Enoch Cobb, **680**, 681, 682, 685
Wing, Isaiah, **96**
Winkley, J. F., **589**
Winslow, A. S., 174, 175
Winter, ———, 129
Winthrop, Annie Neilson, **499**, 501
Winthrop, Edward B., **162**, 163, 167
Wirt, Agnes C., **4**, 18
Wirt, Catharine G., **4**, 6, 18, 19, 23, 25, 27
Wirt, Dabney Carr, **4**
Wirt, Elizabeth Gamble. *See* Goldsborough, Elizabeth Gamble Wirt

Wirt, Elizabeth Washington Gamble, xvi, **5**, 12, 14, 18, 22, 44–45, 50, 113
Wirt, Ellen Tazewell, **4**, 18, 209
Wirt, Henry G., **4**
Wirt, Rosa E., **4**, 18
Wirt, William, xvi, **4**, 5, 7, 8, 9, 12, 13, 14, 23, 31, 47, 49, 169, 170, 295, 506; family, xvi, xvii, 4–6, 8, 9, 12, 13–14, 18–19, 22, 25, 31, 44, 66, 77, 84
Wirt, William C., **4**, 672, 673
Wiseman, John A., **96**
Wiseman, Nicholas Patrick Stephen, *Lectures,* 234
Wiswell, William, **277**
Wolcott, Christopher Parsons, **253**, 285, 286, 287, 288, 290, 291, 292, 293, 299
Wolcott, Pamphilia Stanton, **293**
Wolfe, James, 493
Wood, Mrs., 82, 113
Wood, David L., **292**, 305, 306
Wood, Frederick W., **280**
Wood, George, **633**, 634
Wood, Robert Y., **572**
Wood, William, **270**
Wood, William W., **304**
Wood and Oliver, 80
Woodall, William, **131**
Woodbury, Mr., 221
Woodruff, George Catlin, **489**
Woodruff, George M., **489**
Woodruff, Lewis Bartholomew, **489**
Woods, Mrs., 680, 683
Woodside, William S., **480**
Woodson, John, **182**, 183, 185
Woodward, George Washington, **664**
Woodward, William R., **647**
Woodward College: Epanthean Society, 179; literary society, 169; trustees' meeting and commencement, 166, 168
Wool, John Ellis, **314**, 337, 340, 342, 343, 344, 345, 346, 347, 375, 390
Woolsey, Mrs. (wife of John M. Woolsey), 220
Woolsey, John M., **220**
Worcester, David F., 189, **191**, 192
Worcester, Noah, xxxii, **170**, 177, 184, 185, 186; illness and death of, xxxii, 188–92
Worcester, Samuel Austin, **169**
Worden, Mr., 117
Workman, William Hunter, **625**
World's Peace Jubilee (1872), 690, 692–93
Wormley, James, **648**
Worster, J. Rutherford, **676**

Worthington, Benjamin J., 175
Worthington, Henry Gaither, **602**
Worthington, James Taylor, **250**, 251, 371, 528, 681
Worthington, John G., 175
Worthington, Martha Piatt Read, 251, **371**
Worthington, Vachel, **175**, 196, 580
Wren, Luke. *See* Ren
Wright, Mr., 131, 189
Wright, Mrs., 311
Wright, Mrs. (wife of George Washington Wright), 596
Wright, Crafts James, **124**, 154, 504, 568
Wright, Frances, **13**
Wright, Francis Mastin, **247**, 285, 286, 287, 288, 289
Wright, George Bohan, **582**, 639
Wright, George Washington, **432**, 596, 607
Wright, I., 209
Wright, James, 277
Wright, John A., 379, **380**
Wright, John B., **363**
Wright, John C., **73**, 113, 124, 127, 159, 176, 177, 197, 205
Wright, John Flavel, **81**, 270
Wright, Joseph Albert, **238**, 332, 333
Wright, Marmaduke Burr, **215**
Wright and Swormstaedt, 81, 118
Wyndham, Percy, **458**

Yale University, 65
Yamagutsi, Massouka, 683, **684**
Yates, Richard, **402**, 403
Yeaman, George Helm, **515**
Yeatman, Elizabeth Hartzell, **190**
Yeatman, Thomas H., **190–91**, 445, 460, 528, 573, 662
Yellow Springs, Ohio, 116
York, B. H., **396**
Yorke, Mrs. (wife of Joshua Yorke), 106
Yorke, Joshua, 106
Yoshida, Kiyonari, 683, **684**, 685
Young, Edward, *The Complaint*, 94, 132, 137, 138
Young, George Murray, **299**
Young, John, **57**, 70, 71, 81
Young, John H., **582**
Young Ladies' Institute of Cleveland (Hosmer School), 225, 226
Young Men's Christian Association, 682
Youth's Temperance Advocate, 161
Yulee, David Levy, **552**
Yznaga, Consuelo, **708**
Yznaga, Emily, **708**
Yznaga, Nautica, **708**
Yznaga del Valle, Antonio, **592**, **593**

Zanesville, Ohio, 282
Zanesville Aurora, 236

The Salmon P. Chase Papers, Volume 1
was composed in 10/12 ITC New Baskerville
on a Xyvision system with Linotronic output
by BookMasters, Inc.,
with display type set in Bulmer Italic
by Dix Type, Inc.;
printed by sheet-fed offset
on 60-pound Glatfelter Writers Offset B-16 acid-free stock
with halftones printed on 70-pound enamel gloss stock,
Smyth sewn and bound over 98′ binder's boards
in Holliston Roxite B grade cloth
by BookCrafters, Inc.,
designed by Will Underwood;
and published by
The Kent State University Press
KENT, OHIO 44242

GETTYSBURG COLLEGE

3326800 0269401 0